Genealogical Society Serving Austin Family Researchers

Austins of America

Volume 1

PAGES 1 TO 310

EDITED BY

Michael Edward Austin, Sc.D.

THE AUSTIN PRINT

CONCORD, MASSACHUSETTS

1995

First Edition - October 1995

International Standard Book Number 0-9648804-0-7

Library of Congress Catalog Card Number 95-80763

23 Allen Farm Lane
Concord MA 01742

PREFACE

This book is an indexed compilation of the newsletters published by the *Austins of America* Genealogical Society during its first ten years, during which time its membership expanded to make it the largest group of Austin family researchers in the United States. This is the first in a series of such volumes preserving Austin lines and heritage for posterity. It is gratefully dedicated to the authors appearing herein, and to all those members who by contributing their own research to the *Austins of America* library have made the articles herein more complete and accurate.

We are indebted to Pauline Lucille Austin of Cedar Rapids, Iowa, to Sally Austin Day of Livonia, Michigan, and to the other Associate Editors listed herein for sharing their decades of basic Austin research with others. Special thanks to my beloved wife Patricia Biebuyck Austin, who has been instrumental in organizing raw research notes and correspondence into coherent articles, for without her years of devotion and companionship this volume would not have been possible.

— *Michael Edward Austin*

INTRODUCTION

This newsletter is intended to serve present and future genealogists in researching Austin family lineages. Over the years many persons have devoted a great deal of time and effort in researching their Austin lines. Unfortunately, the greater fraction of this valuable research has gone unpublished, hence others pursuing the same or parallel lines often conduct their research without benefiting from the labors of their predecessors. Thus, one purpose of *Austins of America* is to provide a place for such previously unpublished research.

Since local histories and newspaper articles often have limited regional circulation, *Austins of America* will also reprint articles previously published, whenever the original publication is of genealogical or historical interest to Austin lineages and the original is not generally accessible throughout the United States. An example is the article on Captain Artell Austin in this issue.

For those actively pursuing Austin lines, the best guidance often results from making contact with others who have searched or are searching similar lines, and we hope to publish lists of those doing research on lines in various states, so that resources may be pooled and problems shared with others looking in the same places or searching for the same ancestors.

If you are active in researching Austin lines, please let us know what lines and in what geographic areas you are searching. We also plan to publish queries, which may be sent to either Editor:

> Dr. Michael E. Austin
> 23 Allen Farm Lane
> Concord, Massachusetts 01742
>
> Carol A. Hull
> 15 Maple Avenue
> Sudbury, Massachusetts 01776

Please ask for information regarding only one family group in each query and make it as specific as possible. The queries in this issue may be used as examples when writing your queries. Also, if your own research might prove of interest to others, you are invited to submit your work for publication. Finally, if you know of published magazine or newspaper articles which would be suitable for *Austins of America* please send them along to one of the Editors.

The following article on Captain Artell Austin originally appeared in *THE LINCOLN COUNTY NEWS* in Damariscotta, Maine. It is reprinted with the permission of its author, Dr. George F. Dow of Nobleboro, Maine.

CAPTAIN ARTELL AUSTIN

by George F. Dow

A most exquisite statue, hand carved from the finest Italian marble, reposes in the Lincoln Cemetery in Newcastle, Maine. The statue is in memory of Georgia H. Austin and was made in her likeness from a daguerreotype picture provided by her father. The life-like appearance of the statue, kneeling in prayer, shows her beautiful features and well-sculped dress and curls. Her death in 1861 at six years of age was a tragic loss to her parents, but the marble statue is a fitting tribute to a father's devoted love for his daughter.

Georgia's father was Capt. Artell Austin, who was an excellent sea captain. Artell had learned the art of sailing from his father, Capt. Samuel Austin, who "could bring his ship through any storm." However, Capt. Artell Austin's life was interspersed with much sorrow. In 1847, he married Hannah Leighton, who accompanied him to sea. Their first daughter, Mary Weild, was born in 1851 while in Bermuda. But little Mary died off Cape Horn, at the tip of South America, and the captain was inconsolate. Arrangements were made to have her remains brought back, preserved in salt or rum, for burial in the family lot in Lincoln Cemetery. Her headstone has the following sentimental verse inscribed thereon:

> *"Little Mary thou wast lovely*
> *In thy sweet and spotless bloom,*
> *E'er the hand of death removed thee,*
> *From our presence to the tomb.*
> *Little darling we would never*
> *Call thee from thy new home down.*
> *T'were unrighteous thus to sever,*
> *Glory from the Saviour's Crown.*
> *Nor will we sweet child deplore thee,*
> *Now that all thy troubles o'er,*
> *But the hearts from whome death tore thee,*
> *Weep that thou art here no more."*

To the captain's eventual joy, a second daughter was born in August 1853, also named Mary Weild. Then, while the family continued at sea, a third daughter, Georgia Homans, was born in May 1855. But again the father became greatly shocked in August 1855, by the death of his second daughter. She also was buried in the Lincoln Cemetery, beside her sister. The headstone has a beautiful carving of three angels surrounding little Mary, with this inscribed verse:

> *"Angels watched thy spirit's flight*
> *From sorrow's world unto the light."*

Little Georgia, however, seemed especially robust and was her father's pride and joy, upon whom he bestowed even more affection than before. Then tragedy struck again. Georgia became ill, grew worse, and died in September 1861. She was buried beside her sisters, while her father was reportedly absent at sea. The captain was heartbroken. Upon his return he grieved prostrate at her grave all one night until Mrs. Austin induced him to come back into the house. There they had a daguerreotype of little Georgia, taken in France showing her standing, holding her doll. With this cherished picture, the captain made arrangements for an expert sculptor to use the daguerreotype as a guide in his carving. On the side of Georgia's monument is found this verse:

> *"Gentle Jesus meek and mild*
> *Look upon a little child*
> *Pity my simplicity*
> *Suffer me to come to thee*
> *Fain I would to thee be brought*
> *Gracious Lord forbid me not*
> *In the kingdom of thy grace*
> *Suffer me to have a place."*

In the meantime, Capt. Artell Austin continued his sea-going voyages, and two additional children were born, George Herbert in 1861 and Florence Leighton in 1864. Then Civil War erupted, and Capt. Austin found it desirable to sail under a French flag. While entering the English Channel in 1865, he collided with an English ship, was accused of negligence, and sued for damages. Lacking adequate funds, he was committed to an English prison. While awaiting the slow process of international law to obtain his release, he became greatly depressed. In the meantime, his wife died in 1869, and he had no interest in living longer. He requested his shipmate, Frank Smithwick of Newcastle, Maine, to do him the final favor of arranging to bring back his remains (he died in 1870) to be buried beside his beloved daughter, Georgia. This commitment was completed, and the statue stands now adjoining his grave.

This Austin burial lot is surrounded by an attractive iron fence, at the top of the rise, in this beautiful cemetery overlooking Damariscotta River. This well-cared-for cemetery is located on a knoll at the rear of the old Benjamin Lincoln homestead, a short distance from Damariscotta Mills when proceeding northwesterly on Route 215.

The Austin and Lincoln families are closely related and shared in various business ventures involving their sailing vessels. Martha Austin, sister to Capt. Artell, married Colonel Joshua Lincoln. This Joshua, with his brother Edward, operated father Benjamin Lincoln's shipyard in Nobleboro, Maine, on Great Salt Bay, just east of the alewive stream, adjoining the town landing.

Capt. Artell's brother, John Austin, was lost at sea in one of Capt. Edward Lincoln's vessels. Subsequently, Capt. Edward Lincoln also was lost at sea, with his wife and young daughter, during a severe storm off the coast of Maryland. Such were the all too frequent tragedies among these early sea-faring men who sought their fortunes in sailing ships built on Great Salt Bay, carrying cargoes of lumber sawed at Damariscotta Mills to be exchanged for goods in distant markets. The Lincoln Cemetery bears testimony to their leadership and courage, and also to their love of family and home. There could be no more lovely or fitting memorial than that for Georgia Austin to tell of a father's affection for his daughter.

QUERIES

2-1. **Oliver Austin** born 1760 died Berkshire, Vermont 10 March 1813, married before 1788 Sarah Powell born 1764 died Berkshire, Vermont 12 March 1818. Need ancestry, birth and marriage dates of Sarah and Oliver.

2-2. **Benjamin Austin** born Rhode Island circa 1794 died Berkshire, Vermont 20 February 1869, married Ruth (—) born Conn. 5 November 1784 died 29 August 1867. Need marriage date and ancestry of Benjamin and Ruth.

2-3. Milla Larabee born Springfield, Vermont circa 1794 died in Berkshire, Vermont on 14 December 1860 daughter of William and Amy (Ria) married **Oliver Austin** born Berkshire, Vermont May 1788 died there 21 May 1864. Need marriage date and ancestry of Milla.

2-4. **Jonah Austin** born 12 September 1782 or 1784 died Parkman, Maine 28 January 1859, married before 1813 Hannah Lombard of the greater Skowhegan, Maine area. Need ancestry of Jonah and Hannah.

2-5. **Daniel Austin** born 16 May 1788 married Nancy Reed 10 March 1811 in Greene, Maine. Nancy born 23 June 1787. Children recorded in Parkman, Maine. Need ancestry of Daniel and Nancy.

2-6. **Charles Henry Austin** resided in Farmington, Maine in 1798, thought perhaps to be part Abnaki Indian. One son Charles A. Austin resided in Phillips and later in Peru, Maine. Another son, Henry, 'half-brother' to Charles A., resided in Dixfield, Maine. Need the ancestry and wives of Charles Henry.

2-7. **Capt. William Austin** born probably circa 1757-62, fisherman sailed from ports in New London, Connecticut district. Resided Point Judith, Rhode Island area 1785-1788, resided New London 1790, owned land in Stonington, Connecticut 1796-1804. Arrived in Vermilion, Ohio in 1809, built ship *The Friendship* in 1816, was Captain on Lake Erie until his death in 1833 in Vermilion. Need William's ancestry and wife.

EDITH AUSTIN MOORE

1882-1979

Edith Austin Moore, who devoted much of her long life to researching Austin Family lines, passed away quietly on the evening of November 21, 1979 at the age of 97 years, 7 months and 2 days. She had been living in Rockville, Maryland, having moved there last year from St. Petersburg, Florida. Born on April 19, 1882 to Daniel Henry and Minnie Amelia (Chesebro) Austin, Edith May Austin graduated in 1901 from the Mexico Academy and High School in Mexico, New York. Four years later she married Wesley H. Moore on June 28, 1905. Edith was a member of O.E.S., D.A.R., and N.S. of New England Women. Her husband Wesley died in 1949 in St. Petersburg, Florida.

After her father's death in 1912, Edith became interested in searching for her ancestors who had served their country during the Revolutionary War. She later extended her research back to her first ancestor in this country. Finding little published on the Austin Family, and not being able to trace her own line, Edith began gathering Austin Family records in 1922, hoping in that way to find her line, either through her own research or through correspondence with others. In order to help further her family research, in 1942 together with her brother Henry Warner Austin, Edith founded the *Austin Family Association*, later renamed the *Austin Families Association of America, Inc.* This organization has grown through the years, currently having about 450 family memberships from all sections of the country.

Edith traveled extensively, visiting libraries in Westerly and Providence, R.I.; Boston; Hartford, Conn.; Montpelier, Vt.; New York, Brooklyn, Albany, Syracuse, Utica, and Buffalo, N.Y.; Chicago; Los Angeles; and Washinton, D.C. She wrote many letters and sent out several thousand blank forms.

The 1850 U.S. Census indicated that Edith's great grandfather, Edward Austin, was born in Rhode Island. Thus it was that she concentrated in gathering data on the Austin families of Rhode Island. Her first book, *A Genealogy of The Descendants of Robert Austin of Kingstown, Rhode Island*, was published in 1951. While gathering data for this impressive 738-page book, Edith copied down every Austin record she could find. This gave her data on eight different Austin Families who settled in the New England states during the 17th century. As correspondents kept writing to her for help in solving their own genealogical problems, she gradually accummulated and assembled all her records into two books and seven manuscripts:

ROBERT AUSTIN of Kingstown, R.I.
RICHARD AUSTIN of Charlestown, Mass.
THOMAS AUSTIN of Andover, Mass.
JOSEPH AUSTIN of Dover, N.H.
MATTHEW AUSTIN of York, Maine
JOHN AUSTIN of East Haven, Conn.
JOHN AUSTIN of Stamford, Conn.
JONAH AUSTIN of Taunton, Mass.
UNPLACED AUSTIN RECORDS

In addition to her *Robert* and *Richard* books, Edith donated a copy of each of her manuscripts to the D.A.R. Library in Washington, D.C. Copies of her *Thomas*, *Joseph*, and *Matthew* manuscripts were donated to the New England Historic Genealogical Society Library in Boston, while the *John of East Haven* manuscript was given to the Connecticut State Library at Hartford, Connecticut. A copy of the *John of Stamford* manuscript was given to the New York City Public Library. The *Unplaced Austins* manuscript was donated to the Fort Wayne, Indiana, City library. Two additional manuscripts of her unplaced records were typed up and also placed in Fort Wayne by Lorena Austin, Secretary of the *Austin Families Association.*

Those interested in pursuing Austin family lines owe a great debt to Edith Austin Moore for her lifetime of labors and fruitful research, for gathering and organizing volumes of records, many of which might otherwise have been lost forever. Edith will never be forgotten, for she left us all with a monumental legacy of genealogical research for which she will be remembered with admiration and gratitude, not only by the present generation, but by many generations yet unborn.

Austins of America is intended to serve present and future genealogists researching Austin family lines. Readers are encouraged to submit Queries, Responses, genealogical & historical articles to either Editor:

> Dr. Michael E. Austin
> 23 Allen Farm Lane
> Concord, Massachusetts 01742

> Carol A. Hull
> 15 Maple Avenue
> Sudbury, Massachusetts 01776

For those tracing Austin lines, the best guidance often results from making contact with others who have searched or are searching similar lines, and we hope to publish lists of those doing research on lines in various states. Please let us know what lines and geographic areas you are presently searching.

THE AUSTINS OF NOBLEBORO

by George F. Dow

An earlier article told of the beautiful statue in New-castle, Maine, of Georgia Austin, daughter of sea captain Artell Austin [see page 1]. His home as a boy was in Nobleboro, Maine, where his great-grandfather, Ichabod Austin, Sr. had settled near the center of the town. Ichabod Sr. was born about 1712, came to Nobleboro from York, Maine, about 1760, and lived to about 100 years of age. He was an expert blacksmith and iron worker. He had a son, Ichabod Jr., who was born in York in 1750 before his father moved to Nobleboro. He served as a Sergeant in the Revolutionary War and in 1779 participated in the expedition against the peninsula of Major-Bagaduce [named after a Frenchman, Major Biguyduce, now the town of Castine, Maine]. In the 1790 U. S. Census for Bristol, Maine, the Austin family was listed under the name of 'Ichabod Awstin,' with a large family of ten that probably included both father and son. The census count included four males 16 years or more of age, four males under 16 years of age, and two females. Obviously the Austin family had a good supply of manpower for shoeing oxen and horses and doing other blacksmithing. These men, however, may not all have been Austins because of the common practice in those days for a skilled craftsman to have an extra boy or two as apprentices from another family to learn the trade.

In later years, the Austin homestead was occupied by Samuel and John, two sons of Ichabod Jr. Samuel Austin was not a farmer or blacksmith but was a sea captain, and his 26 acres of land in Nobleboro (as shown on the 1813 town map) was adequate for his home. This Capt. Samuel was the father of Capt. Artell Austin who memorialized his deceased daughter with the marble statue [page 1].

John Austin was not a seafaring man but lived at home on his 103-acre farm, adjoining Samuel's land. John's land extended westward from Pemaquid Pond to a point on the southern tip of the "Great Heath," not far from the present railroad tracks crossing on East Neck Road. John lived from 1769 to 1854, and his home location is shown on the 1857 county map as that of "heirs of J. Austin." The house is no longer standing, but the old cellar is reported to be not far from the present residence of Barbara and Roland Bragg. An excellent spring, found by the Braggs nearby, presumably provided drinking water for the Austin family or their livestock.

John Austin's first wife was Hannah, a daughter of early settler James Hall, but she died at age 33. John next married Hannah's sister, Deborah, who cared for Han-nah's four children and also raised six of her own. Deborah died in 1849 aged 62, and John married a third time, to [—] Genthner.

The burial plot for John Austin and his two wives is located at a distance in back of the Bragg home and can be seen from new Route 1 on the north side of the highway. The plot is surrounded by well-placed tall granite posts, with connecting iron rods worthy of a blacksmith-iron worker family. We like to think of John in peaceful rest in this family cemetery, with his headstone displaying this verse:

"Go home my friends, dry up your tears,
I must lie here till Christ appears,
Then burst Death's bonds with saved surprise,
And in my Savior's image rise."

One of John's sons, Algernon Austin, was born in Nobleboro in 1811 and became a famous shipbuilder. He first learned the blacksmith trade at home; then in 1840 built a house in Newcastle, Maine; had a store across the road; and began shipbuilding in 1846. His shipyard was where the Congregational Church now stands. Within eight years, by 1854, he had built and sold ships worth $590,500, including the brig "Victory." He served Newcastle as a selectman, was a representative to the State Legislative, a director of The Maine Bank of Damaris-cotta, and became the first president of the Newcastle National Bank. One of his descendants, Dr. Charles B. Cheney of New Haven, Conn., has recently corresponded with the us concerning the Austin geneaogy, for which we have twelve pages of notes.

Alden Austin, another son of John, took to the sea, but lived only to age 28. He was an officer of the brig "Neptune" and died in port Aux Cayes in 1828, very likely having succumbed to yellow fever. However, Alden had a son, Addison Austin, born in Nobleboro, who became a sea captain at the age of 24 and made many long foreign voyages. Addison had a daughter, Minnie, who married Johnathan H. Chase, who was born at sea on the brig "Onward." Their grandson, also named Jonathan H. Chase, now lives in Damariscotta on the Bristol Road but is a "land-lubber." His talents include being an expert pianist and organ player whose services are much appreciated at the regular meetings of the Nobleboro Grange.

Capt. Addison's family also accompanied him on various voyages, and how the women folk must have yearned at times for the quiet peace of home, on shore! One of his daughters, Clara, died in Calcutta at the age of two years.

Another son of John Austin was Nathaniel, but he was a ship carpenter, stayed on dry land, and had a family of

13 children. One of his daughters married Capt. Frank Smithwick, who was a mate with Capt. Artell Austin and arranged to bring Austin's body back from England to be buried beside his beloved daughter, Georgia.

John Austin also had a daughter, Hannah, who married Deacon Zenas Hall of Nobleboro. Their son, Austin Hall, became a prominent citizen of Newcastle and the deacon in the Damariscotta Baptist Church. In 1889 he donated the bell that rings forth on Sunday in the First Baptist Church of Nobleboro, where he attended as a boy. The bell is inscribed with his name and the appropriate biblical verse: *"Let all the people praise thee, oh God. Let all the people praise thee."*

Mary Austin, an older daughter of John, married Josiah Winslow, a drummer in the War of 1812. A great-grandson of theirs is Hudson Vannah, one of the few remaining farmers in Nobleboro who operates an excellent livestock farm on Butter & Egg (Vannah) Road.

Willard 'Bill' Pinkham, former mail carrier of Noble-boro, who resides at the former Hussey Tavern, also is a John Austin descendant. Bill's grandfather was George Nelson Bartow, a Nobleboro blacksmith, who lived near the Tavern. He was a grandson of John Austin, following in the footsteps of his blacksmithing ancestors. Nelson Hancock also has George N. Barstow as an ancestor, and thus carries good rich Austin blood in his veins! Mr. Hancock is respected as an 'elder statesman' of Noble-boro, having served for many years as first selectman, lumberman, and supervisor of alewives.

We could cite numerous other Austin descendants (most all Nobleboro natives are related!), but we will close with Luella Genthner. She married William F. Morang, Nobleboro millionaire. She was a great granddaughter of John Austin. They lived in the home now owned by Albert and Gentelisca Bouffard. Mr. Morang constructed the ornate white picket fences across the road; beautified with hydrangeas and other flowering shrubs. This home was where our millionaire 'hung his hat' whenever he was not away in his Florida involved in major real estate developments in Fort Lauderdale and nearby areas.

Nobleboro folks can take justifiable pride in the accomplishments of her early settlers and their descendants! They built the ships, they sailed the seven seas, they were good farmers and blacksmiths, bankers, real estate promotors, lumbermen, mailcarriers, catchers of ale-wives, and devoted family people.

* * * * * *

The preceding article originally appeared in *THE LINCOLN COUNTY NEWS* in Damariscotta, Maine. It is reprinted here with the permission of its author, Dr. George F. Dow of Nobleboro, Maine.

JOHN & JERUSHA AUSTIN
OF FARMINGTON, MAINE
by Francis Gould Butler

John Austin was a native of England, and came from Brunswick to the township of Farmington, Maine. He was a soldier under General Wolfe, and shared the fortunes of that victorious general in the battle fought on the plains of Abraham, near Quebec, September 13, 1759. He was also in the Continental Army during the Revolutionary War. Mr. Austin was the first sexton in town, and served in that capacity many years. His settlement was on river-lot No. 46, west side, opposite the Center Village. Mrs. Austin, familiarly known among the early settlers as "Granny Asten," was a native of Cape Ann, and one of those rare women full of energy and capable of great endurance. As a doctress she rendered efficient service to the inhabitants for many years, and was largely employed in midwifery, a branch of medical practice in which she excelled. Few children were born in the township for the first fifteen years after its settlement, at whose birth she did not preside. Her field of visitation was mostly confined to the settlements on the river, occasionally, however, extending to what are now the towns of Stark and New Sharon, and also to Strong and Avon. When visiting her patients at a distance, she frequently went and came by boat; while at other times she would travel miles on foot, braving the merciless storms of midnight, and allowing no obstacles to prevent the accomplishment of her purpose. The town records state that "Jerusha Asten died in Jesse Gould's house, October y^c 6, A.D. 1804."

* * * * * *

The above article is drawn from Mr. Butler's book, *THE HISTORY OF FARMINGTON*, published by Knowlton, McCleary & Company, Farmington, 1885. The Gould house in which Jerusha Austin died is now occupied by Nelson and Betty Austin, who brought this article to our attention.

AUSTIN GOT THE GALLOWS

In February 1974 John Austin purchased the old steel Hangman's Gallows from the recently demolished Citrus County Jail, Florida, along with four large volumes of sheriff's records. You can imagine his surprise when his wife discovered his name in one of the volumes, dated April 1888! This led John to an interest in his family name, and after about a year of research, he traced his line through Edith Austin Moore's *JONAH AUSTIN* manuscript, and he contributed several colorful pages to that manuscript. Persons interested in the gallows or in John's unusual writeup of his branch of the Austins may send a SASE along with their questions to John Northam Austin, 6356 Sundown Drive, Jacksonville, FL 32210.

QUERIES

6-1. **Amos Austin** born 22 February 1758 Whitehall, New York, married Sally Skinner on 29 June 1793 in Westchester County, N.Y. (she was born 15 January 1751). Their daughter Maria was born 5 January 1795, married Jacob Nelson who died 3 March 1834. Maria died 6 January 1864. Need ancestry of Amos.

6-2. **Thomas Austin** born 1655 married Hannah Foster 15 September 1690, died Andover, Massachusetts on 23 March 1711-2. Seek ancestry of Thomas.

6-3. **Nathan Austin** married Hannah Farnum 25 January 1725 in Methuen, Mass. Hannah was born 19 January 1722 and died 5 May 1804 Andover, Mass. She was the daughter of Nathaniel and Hannah (Preston) Farnum. Seek both sets of Hannah (Farnum) Austin's grandparents.

6-4. **Deborah Austin** born St. Albans, Vermont circa 1780, resided Westford, Vermont, married Sylvester Crandell of Milton, Vermont, in 1806 (he was born in 1775 in Newfane, Vermont, the son of Mary Reeves, and he died in 1876 in Dunham, Quebec). Need Deborah's ancestry and Mary Reeves parents.

6-5. **Elijah Austin** born circa 1774 in North Carolina, died after 1840 in Burke County, N.C. census. Married first Mary Teague and second Temperance Payne. Absalom Chrisfield Austin was a son from the second marriage. Need dates and ancestry of Elijah and Temperance.

6-6. **Henry M.? Austin** born 1809 possibly Jefferson County, N.Y., married 2 January 1835 in Saratoga County, N.Y. to Lucy G. Hall. Their children: Helen S., Leonard Demick, Edwin Zenas, Rachel C., Martha C., Monroe. Need parents of Henry Austin, his mother was Susan M. (—).

6-7. Do the names Monroe, Munroe, and Demick enter into any of your Austin family records? Desire correspondence with Cattaraugus County, N.Y. Austin descendants and anyone with Austin ancestors in Fowler, Michigan, between 1855 and 1860.

6-8. **Moses G. Austin** born Delaware County, N.Y. around 18 June 1811. First wife was Sofhronce Bradly, second wife Elizabeth Gordon, daughter of John Gordon. Need ancestry of Moses, also his firm birthdate, marriage dates, date and place of his death.

6-9. **Elias Austin** born Rhode Island 28 February 1780, died 16 December 1867 in Milford, Michigan. He married in 1798 to Temperance Handy. She was born 1 September 1779 died Milford, Michigan, 3 September 1841. Need birthplaces of Elias and Temperance, their marriage place, and ancestry of Temperance.

6-10. **Joseph Austin** married Jenny Alford 3 June 1800 in Amherst County, Virginia. Need birth data and ancestry of Joseph.

6-11. **Jonathan Austin** born 29 June 1747 died 1800, son of Pasco and Margaret (Sunderland) Austin. Need data on Jonathan, his wife and parents.

6-12. **Merwin Austin** born 1 August 1814 son of Daniel, married 27 October 1851 Almira Haywood. Need parents of Daniel and of Almira.

6-13. **John Austin** born 29 February 1648, died New Haven, Connecticut, September 1690. Married there 5 November 1667 Mercy Atwater. Need ancestry of John.

6-14. **Lottie I. Austin** born Norton, Mass. 25 May 1888, daughter of Edward H. and Cora B. (Leonard) Austin. Need all data on parents of Lottie.

LITERATURE

ROCHESTER, VERMONT - Its History 1780-1975, by the Rochester Town History Committee. Published by Queen City Printers, Burlington, Vt. 1975, 219 pages.

In 1793 John Austin of Methuen, Mass. bought a farm in Rochester, Vt. This early settler and his wife Martha had eight children. He died in 1838 aged 83 years, while Martha died in 1829 aged 71. Other Austins - possibly related - came to the town shortly thereafter from New Hampshire. Phineas Austin's was one of many Rochester families who made an exodus to Potsdam, N.Y. in 1816. This excellent, well-indexed town history includes a reprint of an earlier work, *History of Rochester, Vt.* originally published by Wendell W. Williams in 1869. The book has 33 references to 20 different Austins. It is available from the Town Clerk of Rochester for $13.

THE AUSTINS OF SYRACUSE, by Maynard H. Mires, M.D. Published by The Village Press, Concord, N.H. 1979, 24 pages.

This well researched and written booklet traces Ezekiel Austin, born 18 November 1774 in Vermont, who migrated with his brothers to Onondaga Valley, N.Y. about 1810 and to Syracuse, N.Y. in 1819. Ezekiel and his wife Ann had ten children who are mentioned. One of these children was David Austin, born in 1811, and the remainder of the booklet traces some of his descendants. The booklet may be purchased from the author for $2.50. His address is R#1 Hopkinton Village, Concord, NH 03301.

SOME DESCENDANTS OF JOHN AUSTIN
OF WORTHINGTON, MASSACHUSETTS

by Charles Maxwell Austin

J. JOHN[1] AUSTIN was born in England in 1740, and died 25 May 1820 at Worthington, Massachusetts, in his 81st year. He came to this country as a young man, and assisted in establishing American Independence while acting in the capacity of private in Capt. Ebenezer Webster's Company of Worthington. John marched on 20 April 1775 to Cambridge, Massachusetts in response to the alarm of 19 April 1775. He served one month and five days.

John Austin married Rachel (Smith) Lawrence, born 4 March 1744 at Easton, Massachusetts, the daughter of Benjamin and Mary (—) Smith. Rachel had married first at Brockton, Mass. to Jonathan Lawrence on 22 May 1765. She died on 30 August 1827 at Worthington, Mass. John and Rachel had two children:

> J1. TIMOTHY, *b. 17 April 1780* +
>
> J2. JOHN, *b. 17 October 1783* +

References: *Massachusetts Soldiers in the American Revolutionary War, Vol. 1*; Becket, Mass. Vital Records; National No. 31185; Mr. Franklin Austin, Franklin, Nebraska (1929); Mrs. Charles Channing Allen of 419 Ward Parkway, Kansas City, Missouri.

SECOND GENERATION

J1. TIMOTHY[2] AUSTIN (*John[1]*) was born on 17 April 1780. He married Rebecca Harris at Becket, Mass. on 22 October 1801. Rebecca was born on 2 December 1785, the daughter of James and Martha (Parke) Harris. They removed to Ripley Twp., Huron County, Ohio, where Rebecca died on 30 August 1855 and Timothy died on 15 December 1859. They had fifteen children:

> J11. TIMOTHY JAMES, *b. 1802, d. 6 November 1806 age 4 at Worthington*
>
> J12. HORACE S., *b. —*
>
> J13. DEXTER, *b. —*
>
> J14. ALFRED B., *b. in 1809, d. 12 May 1816 at Worthington*
>
> J15. LYDIA MINERVA, *b. —, m. 10 January 1827 at Worthington to Samuel Cowing of Chesterfield, Massachusetts.*
>
> J16. HOMER JOHN, *b. 1813, d. 1889 in Kansas, m. 22 June 1843 at Fairfield, Ohio to Adaline Cherry, b. 1822, d. 1909 in Kansas.*
>
> J17. ADDISON A., *b. —, went to Wisconsin.*
>
> J18. EDWARD [EDWIN?] L., *b. —*
>
> J19. SIDNEY P., *b. 1818, d. on 25 October 1820 at Worthington in his 3rd year.*

> J1A. MARTHA PARKE, *b. 5 November 1821, d. 30 August 1908, m. 4 May 1843 to William Hoy, m. 2nd 19 October 1852 Norman Stanley, b. 1819 d. 1889.*
>
> J1B. MARY E. (or C.), *b. —, m. 26 October 1842 Phile R. Hoy at Ripley Twp., Ohio.*
>
> J1C. SARAH A., *b. —*
>
> J1D. ELIZA B., *age 22 in 1850 Ohio Census, m. — Eaton.*
>
> J1E. FRANCES A., *age 16 in 1850 Ohio Census*
>
> J1F. BENJAMIN DWIGHT, *Minor at the time his father made his Will on 17 June 1848.*

J2. JOHN[2] AUSTIN (*John[1]*) was born 17 October 1783 at Worthington, Massachusetts. Baptized on admission to church on 5 May 1822. He died 25 August 1827 at Becket, Massachusetts, and is buried in the Church Yard in Becket Center. John married on 4 September 1806 at Worthington to Lodemia Herrick Daniels. She was the daughter of Dan and Zeruiah (Herrick) Daniels, born 6 February 1785 at Worthington, admitted to the church 3 November 1816, and died 1 April 1869 at Oberlin, Ohio. She is buried in the Rugby Cemetery, Vermillion Township, Ohio. John and Lodemia had ten children, the first five were born at Chester, Massachusetts, the others at Becket:

> J21. EMELINE, *b. 29 April 1807, m. 15 January 1828 to Jesse Johnson at Becket.*
>
> J22. MARIAH, *b. 4 February 1809, m. 12 December 1827 Dr. Chester Freeland at Becket.*
>
> J23. CHARLES EDWARD, *b. 5 October 1810, m. 24 May 1842 Amanda Harris at Becket.*
>
> J24. MARY ANN, *b. 2 July 1813, m. — May 1840 to Edward Morse.*
>
> J25. WILLIAM ELBRIDGE, *b. 23 June 1815, m. 2 December 1845 Emeline Clark at Becket, m. 2nd 6 November 1867 Fannie Elvira Lester at Gilman, Iowa.*
>
> J26. CAROLINE, *b. 21 August 1817, m. 31 December 1846 Frederick Clarke at Becket.*
>
> J27. FRANKLIN DEXTER, *b. 3 October 1819, m. on 13 January 1853 to Caroline Florella Sprague at Worcester, Mass., m. 2nd 1 May 1865 Julia Maria Goddard at Worcester.*
>
> J28. HENRY ALLEN, *b. 23 November 1821, m. on 28 September 1851 to Mary Wright Johnson at Becket, m. 2nd on 30 November 1871 to Caroline Maxim at Pleasanton, Michigan.*
>
> J29. ELIZA JANE, *b. 5 April 1824, d. 12 August 1827 at Becket, buried Becket Center.*
>
> J2A. SAMUEL JOHN, *b. 22 November 1826, m. 31 March 1858 Jennie S. Clarke at Lancaster, Mass., m. 2nd 8 December 1863 Susan Maria Miller at Royalston, Massachusetts.*

THE DESCENDANTS OF SAMUEL AUSTIN
OF BOSTON, MASSACHUSETTS

by Michael Edward Austin
and Patricia Biebuyck Austin

S. SAMUEL[1] AUSTIN was probably an immigrant, although his origins have not yet been found. Indeed, little is known of Samuel except that he was in Boston by the time of his son's birth in 1669. His wife's first name was Hopestill, sometimes shortened to 'Hope'. Where Samuel and Hope resided before or after the births listed below has not been learned. Two of their children were born in Boston:

    S1. SAMUEL, *b. 8 October 1669* +
    S2. THOMAS, *b. 12 September 1671* +

SECOND GENERATION

S1. SAMUEL[2] AUSTIN (*Samuel[1]*) was born in Boston on 8 October 1669. He first appears on the list of taxpayers in Andover, Mass. on the Tax List dated 20 September 1690, along with his brother Thomas. Samuel married Lucy Poor in Andover on 11 October 1691, and they settled in the North End of the Towne. Lucy, the daughter of Daniel Poor and Mary Farnum, was born 28 September 1670 in Andover. Daniel, the Town Constable in 1689-90, was a close neighbor of Samuel's, for on 7 March 1697-8 the land records have: 'Sold to Samuell Asten that peece of land which Sargt Samuel Frie changed with ye Astine, which Leith on ye East Side of Daniel Poors land.' Also, in 1698 Samuel bought 13 acres from the Town (land formerly that of Samuel Frye's), lying to the east of Daniel Poor's land. Samuel appears several times more in the Andover land records, as he continued to add to his land holdings. On 14 July 1721, Samuel Austin sold to Samuel Smith four acres in Andover, 'lying Eastward of a brook called Boston or Beacher Brook'. Samuel died on 28 September 1753 in Andover aged 'about 84' years, while his widow Lucy died there 25 June 1759 aged 88 years. Their children were born in Andover:

    S11. SARAH, *b. 28 March 1692* +
    S12. SAMUEL, *b. 27 August 1694* +
    S13. JOHN, *b. 13 July 1697* +
    S14. MARY, *b. 28 February 1700-1* +
    S15. LUCY, *b. 3 April 1706* +
    S16. DANIEL, *b. —— 1711* +

S2. THOMAS[2] AUSTIN (*Samuel[1]*) was born in Boston on 12 September 1671. On 15 September 1690 in Andover, Mass., Thomas married Hannah Foster, daughter of Andrew Foster, Jr. and Mary Russ. Hannah was born 16 July 1668. Thomas first appears on the Andover Tax List dated 20 September 1690, along with his brother Samuel,

in the North End of the town. He was last taxed in the North End on 26 January 1690-1, and first appears on the Tax List for the South End of town on 29 June 1691. Like his brother, Thomas continued to add to his Andover land holdings, and on 26 November 1698 the town records have: 'Laid out to Thomas Austin halfe an acre of land that he bought of ye Towne, Lyeing on ye North Side of his other land & Lyeing on ye East side of Nathaniel Abbotts Land. . . '. He is last found on the Tax Lists in Andover in December 1709, the Minister's Rate tax, and must have removed from Andover shortly thereafter.

Thomas, along with Lt. Stephen Barker and John Gutterson, purchased of the widow Lydia Griffin land on the North side of the Merrimack River in the Township of Haverhill. . . eight score and eighteen acres which they divided into nine lots, three lots to each purchaser. This part of Haverhill was later to become the town of Methuen, and later still Salem, New Hampshire.

At the Haverhill Town Meeting of 1712, Thomas Austin and his neighbors applied for an abatement of their taxes for the ministry and the school, on account of the great distance they lived from the Town, and the difficulty they met with in coming. The town voted to abate one half of their ministry rate. Perhaps because of this great distance, it appears Thomas still attended church back in Andover, for Andover town records state that 'Joshuah Stevens & Thomas Austin were both drowned in Merrimake River going home from Meeting on the Sabbath Day being the 23 of March 1711-12'.

Thomas died intestate, his widow was granted administration of his estate on 10 May 1714. The inventory of his estate listed 150 acres of land, books, iron pots and wares, bedding, chairs and tables, cow-plow-husbandry tackling, three pigs, three cows, four oxen, two pair of steers, four heifers, a broad ax, and a young calfe, plus a few other illegible items. The widow received 'the house lott with the pasture land thereto adjoining for her third,' the other two thirds being divided into seven shares. The eldest son Thomas received two shares, while the other children each received one share.

The widow Hannah married again on 2 October 1722 to Jotham Hendrick in Haverhill, and a third time on 17 April 1729 at Haverhill to Henry Bradley of Newbury, Mass. It is of interest to note that Hannah's grandmother, Ann Foster, was accused, tried and condemned as a witch, as described in great detail in the *Foster Genealogy*. The children of Thomas and Hannah were born in Andover:

    S21. THOMAS, *b. 23 January 1691-2* +
    S22. BENJAMIN, *b. 16 June 1694* +
    S23. DANIEL, *b. 7 August 1698* +
    S24. ZEBADIAH, *b. 17 July 1701* +
    S25. ABIEL, *b. — 1703* +
    S26. HANNAH, *b. 7 April 1706* +

THIRD GENERATION

S11. SARAH³ AUSTIN (*Samuel*²,¹) was born 28 March 1692 in Andover, Mass. She married James Bodwell of Methuen on 28 November 1739 in Methuen. James, the son of Henry and Bethiah (—) Bodwell, was born 10 January 1690-1 in Andover. Sarah died in Andover on 18 September 1769.

S12. SAMUEL³ AUSTIN (*Samuel*²,¹) was born 27 August 1694 in Andover, Mass. He married Mehitable Frye of Andover on 2 February 1737. Mehitable, the daughter of Ebenezer Frye and Elizabeth Farnum. Samuel died in Andover 31 December 1764 aged 70, intestate. His widow Mehitable posted bond on 27 April 1765 and took an inventory of the estate in May 1765. She herself died 26 August 1778 in Andover. Samuel and Mehitable were apparently childless, for no children are recorded in Andover, nor is any mention of their offspring made in John Austin's will (below).

S13. JOHN³ AUSTIN (*Samuel*²,¹) was born 13 July 1697 in Andover, Mass. He lived unmarried in Andover, and died there on 13 March 1764 'aged 68' years, leaving a will:

*In the Name of God Amen I John Austin of Andover in the County of Essex and Province of the Massachusetts Bay in New England yeoman calling to mind the mortallity of my body Do make this my last Will & First I commend my Soul into the hands of God my Creator believing through his mercy and the merritt of my Saviour Jesus Christ I shall Inherit Eternal Life my Body I Committ to the Earth to be Decently Buried att the Discretion of my Executor hereafter mentioned and Touching Such Worldly Estate with which it hath Pleased God to Bless me in this Life I give and Dispose of the Same as followethe— Imprimis I Will that all my Just Debts and funeral Charges be Paid by my Executor in Conveiniant Time after my Dec*ˢ*:— Item I give to my sister Mary Austin forty pounds Lawfull money to be Paid to her by my Exec*ʳ* within two years after my Decease— Item I give to my sister Sarah Bodwell Wid*ᵒ* of James Bodwell Dec*ᵈ* Twenty pounds Lawfull money to be paid to her by my Executor within two years after my Dec*ˢ*:— Item I give to my syster Lucy Swan Wife of Asie Swan of Methuen thirteen pounds six shillings and Eight pence Lawfull money to be paid to her by my Executor within two years after my Decease— Item I give to my House keeper Ruth Stephens the Use and Improvment of my East and Lower room in my Dwelling house and so much Priviledge in the Sellar as Shee Shall have Occation for also one good Cow out of my Stock of Cattle to be kept for her Use Summer and Winter all which to be used and improv*ᵈ* by her during her Natural Life— Also I give to the s*ᵈ*: Ruth two good Bed Blanketts to be att her Disposal also I give to the s*ᵈ*: Ruth the Use and improv*ᵗ*: of so much of my household goods as she shall have occation for so long as she shall be pleased to Continue her Habitation in my house— Item I give to my three sisters aforenamed all my household goods to be Equally Divided Amongst them after the Decease or Removal of the s*ᵈ*: Ruth Stephens— the foregoing Bequests to my three sisters is in full of what is my Pleasure they should have out of my Estate— Item I give to my Brother Daniel Austin my Mare & Colt— Item I give to my two Brethren Namely Samuel Austin & Daniel Austin all my money and the Contents of my bonds notes and other Debts that are Due or that may become Due to my Estate att my Dec*ˢ*: also my Husbandry Tackler Stock of Cattle horses sheep and swine also all my Provision of every sort all my corn meat and Hay and all other my*

*Personal Estate of Every Denomination to be Equally Divided between them after the payment of my Debts Legacies funeral charges and the cost of the Settlement of my Estate is Deducted out of my personal Estate afores*ᵈ*:— Item I give to my s*ᵈ*: Brethren Namely Samuel Austin and Daniel Austin all my buildings and lands in Andover to be Occupied Used and Improved by them in Equal Shares during their Natural Lives and in case their Wives or either of them should survive their husbands my Will is that my Real Estate shall be improved by them in Like manner During their Natural Lives and after the Decease of my afore named Brethren and their Wives my Will is that all my Real Estate Building and Lands shall be the Property in fee simple the first male heirs of the Body of my Brother Daniel Afores*ᵈ*: that shall survive the Term of twenty one years and in case of Default in Male Issue of my Brother Daniel Afores*ᵈ*: my Will is that my Real Estate afores*ᵈ*: shall be the Property of the feemale heirs of the body of my Brother Daniel afores*ᵈ*: in fee simple and in Equal Shares Lastly I do herby Constitute and appoint my Brother Samuel Austin afores*ᵈ*: the only Sole Executor of this my Will and I do herby Revoke all other Wills heretofore by me made and do make and declare this to be my Last Will and Testament— In Witness whereof I have here unto sett my hand and Seal the Twenty Eighth day of february Anno Domini one thousand seven hundred and sixty four and in the fourth year of his Majesties Reign— Signed Sealed Published and declared by the s*ᵈ* John Austin to be his Last Will and Testament in presence of us the Subscribers—   John Austin his mark Seal*

It is clear from John's Will that he was unmarried and without children of his own. Since John's brother Samuel died shortly after John, and was unable to carry out his role as Executor, it was undoubtedly Samuel's wife who was the 'Mehitable Austin' who gave bond in administering John's estate, which is confirmed by the fact that she also gave bond for her husband's estate on the same date, 27 April 1765. Thus Mehitable was John's sister-in-law, and not his widow as has been erroneously published.

S14. MARY³ AUSTIN (*Samuel*²,¹) was born 28 February 1700-1 in Andover, Mass. She never married, and died in Andover on 27 December 1774 in her 74th year.

S15. LUCY³ AUSTIN (*Samuel*²,¹) was born 3 April 1706 in Andover, Mass. She married Asa Swan of Methuen, Mass. on 6 February 1734-5 at Methuen. Asa, the son of Robert Swan, Jr. and Elizabeth Storie, was born 27 November 1687 in Haverhill, Mass. He died 14 January 1766 in his 78th year, having 'served the Town of Methuen 28 or 9 years in the office of Town Clerk.' Lucy died 10 June 1764 in her 56th year. SWAN CHILDREN: SUSANNA 1735, LUCY 1737, DANIEL 1740, JOHN 1742, MARY 1746, MARY 1747.

S16. DANIEL³ AUSTIN (*Samuel*²,¹) was born between 22 April and 1 July 1711. He lived in Andover, where he married Eunice Kimball on 25 February 1762. She was the daughter of Ephraim and Mary (—) Kimball and was born 3 July 1724 in Boxford, Mass. Daniel died on 14 September 1776 aged 65 years, while his widow Eunice died 27 December 1819 in Andover. The children of this couple who married so late in life were all born in Andover, and saved the S1. Samuel Austin line from extinction.

The second child John was undoubtedly named for Daniel's older brother John (S13) who died but a few months before his namesake's birth and who was so generous to Daniel's offspring in his Will (above). Children:

    S161. LUCY, *b. 18 December 1762, d. 17 May 1764*
    S162. JOHN, *b. 1 July 1764* +
    S163. SAMUEL, *b. 20 November 1765* +
    S164. SARAH, *b. 13 August 1767* +
    S165. LUCY, *b. 23 April 1769* +
    S166. MARY, *b. 15 August 1771* +
    S167. BETTY, *b. 8 June 1773*

[CONTINUED ON PAGE 14]

NOTE: The preceding article was abstracted from a book of the same title currently in preparation by the authors, who would welcome additional information on Samuel Austin and his descendants for inclusion in the book.

LITERATURE

1979 AUSTIN REUNION BOOKLET, by Janet Austin Curtis, Genealogist for the Austin Families Association. Prepared for the Western Regional Reunion in Albuquerque, New Mexico 1979, 36 pages.

This booklet discusses 12 different Austin Coats-of-Arms, 120 Austin Immigrants, and contains a bibliography of 40 books and manuscripts relating to Austin families genealogies. The immigrants were found by searching the 1880 Soundex Census schedules, and the author has covered about half the states. Since this booklet was published, Mrs. Curtis has continued her searching for Austin immigrants (see her article on page 12 of this Newsletter). Copies of the booklet may be obtained from the author for $3.50 postpaid. Her address is 3329 Santa Clara, S.E., Albuquerque, N.M. 87106.

AUSTINS IN THE EARLY NEW HAMPSHIRE TOWN RECORDS, by Patricia Biebuyck Austin. Published by The Austin Print, Concord, Mass. 1980, 20 pages.

Copies of early New Hampshire town records are in the State Library in Concord, N.H., where they are also available on microfilm. The author has copied over 2900 references to Austins from the comprehensive Card Index to those records. Pages on which marriage and family records occur are so noted. Over 700 individuals are indexed by name and have also been cross-referenced in an alphabetized index by towns. While containing no dates, these indices do permit one to determine spouses, family groupings, and geographic distributions, and thus prove a useful aide in researching N.H. Austins. Copies may be obtained from the author for $1.75 postpaid. Her address is 23 Allen Farm Lane, Concord, Mass. 01742.

QUERIES

10-1. **Joseph Austin** married Jenny Alford 3 June 1800 in Amherst County, Virginia. Her father was William Alford, and Benjamin Austin and Thomas Alford were witnesses. Joseph Austin came to Macon County, Illinois, about 1830 from Rutherford or Davidson Counties, Tennessee. He apparently died in Macon County about 1832. Need birth data and ancestry of Joseph.

10-2. **Moses G. Austin** born Delaware County, N.Y. after 18 June 1811. First wife was Sofronce Bradly, second wife Elizabeth Gordon, daughter of John Gordon. Moses lived in Delaware County, N.Y.; Bolivar, Allegany County, N.Y.; Cranberry Twp., Venango County, Penn.; Forest Twp., Richland County, Wisconsin, and Center Twp., Dade County, Missouri. Need ancestry of Moses, also his firm birthdate, marriage dates, date and place of his death.

10-3. **Randall Austin** born 1778-9 N.Y. (probably Pittstown, Rensselaer County) married Elvira Marsh born 1789 in Mass. Randall and Elvira named a son Holstead Austin, possibly after Elvira's mother. Randall and his brothers Perrigo, Peter, and Joseph went to Onondaga County, N.Y. Randall also resided in Wheeling, W. Virginia, and Belmont County, Ohio. Seek ancestry of Elvira and record of her marriage to Randall.

10-4. Have Revolutionary War document of ancestor of **Harold Washburn Austin** of Taunton, Mass.: a commission of Edward Martin as 1st Lt. in first regiment of Militia of Bristol Co., Mass. commanded by Capt. Noah Allen. Signed by Mass. Governor John Hancock, dated 1 July 1781. Seek advice as to best method of preservation and disposition of this document for future generations.

10-5. **Nathaniel Austin, Sr.** born circa 1720 (England?), married Agnes Richardson circa 1740 (England?). Left Lunenburg County, Virginia 1765 for South Carolina. Lived Laurens, Newberry, and Greenville Counties. Revolutionary War soldier. Indents 1779-1786. Acquired 'Gilder' 14 February 1797 Simpsonville, S.C. on Gilder's Creek. Died after 1800 Greenville County, S.C. Family tradition states Nathaniel had brothers Moses and Jeremiah. Need ancestry of Nathaniel and Agnes, also their birth and marriage dates.

10-6. **Nathaniel Austin, Jr.** born circa 1744-5 in England. Left Lunenburg County, Virginia for North Carolina. Participated Revolutionary War with South Carolina Militia. Res. Pendleton, S.C. 1790, Granger County, Tennessee 1799. Died in Gwinnett County, Georgia after 1832 land lottery. Children from bible records: Mary, Franky, Walter, John, Nathaniel, Henrietta, William Anderson, Sarah, Thomas Henry, and Anne. Seek wife's name, ancestry, birth and marriage dates.

11-1. **Robert Aiston** married Sarah Malvina Leete in Batavia, N.Y. 16 November 1844 coming from Canada. Sarah remarried George Allen and is buried in Azalia, Michigan. Need ancestry of Robert.

11-2. **Bill Austin**, 'famous Indian Scout', had a boy William captured by Indians. William allegedly married a daughter of Wamsutta, son of Massasoit and brother of King Philip. William's sons, Benoni and John, went to Wales, Maine from New Meadows (part of Brunswick, Maine). Seek ancestry and wife of Bill Austin.

11-3. **James Austin** born 1770 near Harpers Ferry, Virginia, moved to Washington County, Kentucky in 1790. Married Ann Howard of Virginia. Known children: Ambrose, Benedict, John, Thomas Aquinas, Catherine, Sally, Theresa, and Rose. Seek ancestry of James.

11-4. **George Austin** born circa 1761 Rhode Island, enlisted in the Rhode Island Regimentals and after the war went to live in Vermont. There he married Louisa Nichols and they named their first son Jonathan, born 5 August 1796 in Townshend, Vermont. Seek George's ancestry.

11-5. **William H. Austin** was born circa 1817 and died in Greeneville Center, ???? on 20 June 1890. His death certificate lists parents as Samuel Austin and Easter (Esther?) James. After William's death, a telegram was sent to New Canaan, Connecticut, to a Jonathan Austin and a James I. Samson. William was married to Harriet Stevens, possibly the daughter of Spencer Stevens whose family also came from New Canaan. They had two sons, Gould and George. Seek William's birth and ancestry.

11-6. **Zephaniah Austin, Jr.** born 12 March 1764 in Sheffield, Massachusetts, son of Zephaniah and Sarah (Egglestone) Austin. He married Miss — Comstock. Seek marriage data and Miss Comstock's ancestry.

11-7. **Truman D. Austin** was born 10 February 1788 in New York, married Susan B. Guyant in 1825 in Orleans Co., New York. Susan born 3 August 1803 in New London, Conn. Need all data on Truman & Susan.

11-8. **Stephen Austin** of New Haven, Conn. married on 19 April 1732 to Martha Thompson, born February 1709-10 to William and Martha Thompson in New Haven. Need all data on Martha's parents.

11-9. **William Austin** born 6 May 1769 probably Washington County, New York, married 10 November 1791 to Elizabeth Stevenson, daughter of Andrew Stevenson, born 23 October 1772, died 30 October 1845. William died 10 May 1858. Children born in Westfield, NY and Canada: Margaret 1792, Maurice 1794, Elizabeth 1796, Susanna 1798, William 1800, Gilbert Stevenson 1802, Mary 1804, James 1806, Robert Moffet 1811, Charles Gordon 1814. Seeking William's ancestry.

11-10. **John Austin** born 1755 married in 1777 to Ann Baden (Beeden?) in Anne Arundel County, Maryland. They lived in Virginia by 1782. Need John's ancestry, siblings, birthplace, deathplace, and deathdate. Also, where did John reside in Virginia, and did he remove to Kentucky as did his children circa 1804?

11-11. **Mary Austin** daughter of Jonah of Hingham and Taunton, Mass. married Thomas Lincoln, Jr., also of Hingham and Taunton, circa 1651. Their six child, Hannah Lincoln, was born 15 March 1663. Edith Austin Moore's *Jonah Austin of Taunton, Mass.* manuscript states that Hannah married Daniel Owen, and indeed the Taunton vital records have 'Hannah Lincolne and Daniel Oen' married on 23 December 1689. In *Lincolns of New England* by Waldo Lincoln (1926), it states that Hannah Lincoln (daughter of Thomas) married Peter Branch about 1684, and that the Hannah who married Daniel Owen was born 24 March 1666 in Taunton, the daughter of Samuel Lincoln. Seek proof to resolve this conflict.

11-12. **John Austin** born circa 1739 married Charity Kendrick? Their son Zachariah born 1763 Prince Georges Parish, Frederick County, Maryland. Other issue: James, Amelia, John K., Hezekiah, Amos, and Jonas. John's will 1823 Montgomery County, Maryland. Charity could have been married first to John's brother Thomas Austin, and was perhaps daughter of Thomas and Ann Kendrick of Frederick County. Need ancestry of John and Charity.

11-13. **Elizabeth Austen** born 4 September 1788 in Peekskill, N.Y., married Stephen Berrien and resided in Yonkers, N.Y. Elizabeth died 13 April 1880. Seeking the ancestry of Elizabeth.

Correction to Query 6-6 on page 6: Change Lucy G. Hull to Lucy G. Hall.

Austins of America is intended to serve present and future genealogists researching Austin family lines. Readers are encouraged to submit Queries, Responses, genealogical & historical articles to either Editor:

Dr. Michael E. Austin
23 Allen Farm Lane
Concord, Massachusetts 01742

Carol L. Hull
15 Maple Avenue
Sudbury, Massachusetts 01776

For those tracing Austin lines, the best guidance often results from making contact with others who have searched or are searching similar lines, and we hope to publish lists of those doing research on lines in various states. Please let us know what lines and geographic areas you are presently searching.

AUSTIN IMMIGRANTS FOUND

IN THE 1880 OHIO CENSUS

by Janet Austin Curtis

The immigrants listed here are found in the 1880 Soundex Index of the Ohio Census, and are additions to the Austin immigrants published in the 1979 Reunion Booklet by the author (see *Literature*, page 10). The Soundex was made for Social Security purposes, and only includes those families with children 10 years of age or younger, so it is quite possible that not all immigrants have been found. Unless otherwise indicated, persons were born in the United States:

B. Austing age 44 b. Oldenburg; wife Anna b. Prussia. Ch: Kate 9, Anna 6, Agnes 4, Lina 2, and Joseph 2/12. Res. Cincinnati, Hamilton County.   30-180 / 56-24

Bernard Austing age 26 b. Oldenburg; wife Theresa 24 b. Oldenburg, Frank 2, Bernard 5/12. Res. Cincinnati, Hamilton County.   31-183 / 23-29

Charles E. Austin age 41 b. England; wife Ruth 36, Edwin 18, Ernest H. 16, Frank W. 7, Charles M. 5. Res. Cleveland, Cuyahoga County.   14-32 / 35-18

Cyrus Austin age 35 b. England; wife Mabel 21, Alice 3/12. Res. Cleveland, Cuyahoga County.   14-30 / 70-29

Daniel Austin age 51 b. England; wife Susan 51 b. England, Lannie 20, Minnie 17, Edward 14, Stanley 10. Res. Cleveland, Cuyahoga County.   13-19 / 61-44

David Austin age 35 b. England; wife Jane 35 b. England, Humphorus H. F. 5, Ethel 3. Res. Cleveland, Cuyahoga County.   15-50 / 22-8

Erwin Austin age 46 b. England; wife Kate 33 b. Canada, Frank 6, Gilbert 4, Earnest G. 2, Eva P. 1. Resided Cleveland, Cuyahoga County.   15-54 / 7-39

Frank Austing age 48 b. Oldenburg; wife Catherine 44 b. Oldenburg, John 22, Joseph 21, Alvinins 19, Mary 12, August 9, William 5. Resided in Cincinnati, Hamilton County.   29-151 / 46-4

Frank Austing age 24 b. Prussia; wife Mary 23, Mary 4, Fresen 2. Res. Cincinnati, Hamilton County.   28-134 / 20-32

Gilbert Aston age 35 b. England; wife Mary 30 b. England, William 9, Hulbert 7, Emanuel 5, Lois 2, George 1/12. Resided in Corning, Monroe Township, Perry County.   51-215 / 34-1

James Austin age 45 b. England; wife Dinah 40 b. England, Bessie 18 b. England, Emily 16, Anna 11, George 8. Res. Cleveland, Cuyahoga County.   13-17 / 47-1

James Austin age 31 b. England; wife Catherine 26 b. Bavaria, Louisa 9/12. Res. Avondale, Mill Creek Twp., Hamilton County.   26-96 / 38-13

John Austin age 47 b. England; wife Mary H. A. 41 b. England, Florence 4, Albert B. 2, Jessie 4/12. Res. Dover Township, Cuyahoga County.   16-60 / 37-17

John Austin age 35 b. England; wife Elizabeth 33, Blanche 5, Bertha 3, Lottie 4/12. Resided Mt. Vernon, Clinton Township, Knox County.   37-163 / 13-26

John Austin age 31 b. England; wife Margaret 27 b. England, Henry J. 4, Margie E. 2. Res. Geneva, Geneva Township, Ashtabula County.   2-10 / 28-29

John Austin age 33 b. Wales; wife Anna, Thomas 6, William S. 3. Res. in Youngstown Township, Mahoning County.   43-105 / 48-45

Joseph Austen age 78 b. England; wife Catherine 47, Lucy D. 6. Res. Mohican Twp., Ashland Co.   2-86 / 25-42

Margaret Aston age 38 b. Wales; John 21 b. Wales, Sarah 15 b. Wales, Margaret 13 b. Wales, Richard 12 b. Wales, William 9, Mary 6, Anna 6, Emma 4, Eliza 2. Resided Lawrence Township, Stark County.   60-142 / 82-2

Mary Austin age 41 b. Ireland; Michael 18 b. Ireland, John 16 b. Ireland, Timothy 13, Thomas 12, Mary 9, Katie 7, Nora 4. Resided in McArthur, Elk Township, Vinton County.   65-185 / 10-19

Michael Austen age 30 b. Ireland; William 2. Resided Zaleski, Madison Township, Vinton County.   65-189 / 23-25

Samuel Austin age 29 b. England; Sarah J. 28 b. England, Ida Martha 5, Wilber John 3. Res. Cleveland, Cuyahoga County.   15-44 / 1-37

Samuel Austin age 49 b. England; wife Georgine 45, Thomas 25, James 22, Harriet 19, John 17, Alexander 14, David L. 10, Mary A. C. 7, Elizabeth 5, Richard 2, *all* b. England. Resided in Massillon, Perry Township, Stark County.   60-148 / 13-8

Samuel Austin age 49 b. Scotland; wife Sarah 44, Edward 16, Sarah 11 and Julia 8. Resided in Cleveland, Cuyahoga County.   12-16 / 59-46

Thomas Austin age 10 b. England; a nephew of John Murphin. Resided in Saybrook Township, Ashtabula County.   2-24 / 13-17

William Austin age 61 b. England; wife Sarah 45 b. England, Ellen 18 b. England, Alice 16 b. England, Jane 14 b. England, Sadie 10, Mary 7. Res. in Cincinnati, Hamilton County.   29-15 / 27-4

THE AUSTIN DUELS

by Edward Rowe Snow

Paul Revere, who was a man of many pursuits, actually was court-martialed because of his participation in the Revolutionary Penobscot Bay campaign. The court-martial resulted in the complete vindication of Revere. Later, however, politically he is believed to have favored one of the duelists in an encounter which occurred fairly close to the Old State House.

It is rare that one family participates in two duels in a single year, but such is the case with the Austin family of New England.

The duel between William Austin and James Henderson Elliot was fought March 31, 1806, less than two years after the memorable Hamilton-Burr duel of July 11, 1804. It is hard to realize that the period between the beginning of the century and the ending of the War of 1812 was one of extreme political beliefs, passions, and prejudices. In the Austin-Elliot duel Austin was hit in the thigh and Elliot was not hit at all. The wounded Austin lived to be 65, while Elliot lived barely two years after the encounter.

The second duel of the same year in which members of the Austin family participated came about because of an incident on the Fourth of July. The Republican Party of Boston had arranged a procession for July 4, 1806, with a banquet to be held afterward in a tent at Copp's Hill in the North End of Boston. All went well during the parade, but when it became known that the ambassador from Tunis would be attending the banquet in the tent, scores of people without tickets stormed the tent, and in the confusion the ticket taker was overwhelmed. Upward of one hundred persons without tickets 'crashed the gate.'

Two particular items for which the caterer had not been paid I shall never forget. They were, according to the Jefferson Tavern landlord who had supplied the feast, "seven roast pigs and ten bushels of green peas." When the payments were in, he found that he was far short of making expenses and put the bill in the hands of Boston attorney Thomas Oliver Selfridge. The attempts of Selfridge to collect the shortage by suit against the committee as individuals ultimately failed.

When the head of the committee, Benjamin Austin, was being questioned one day about the suit he answered that it was instigated by the Federalist lawyer Selfridge. The latter, who had an office in the Old State House, at the head of State Street, stated that Austin was mistaken. When it was proved to Austin that Selfridge had not been responsible for the suit action but had merely served as the lawyer in the matter, Austin retracted, but not with the sufficient enthusiasm needed to pacify Selfridge.

Thomas Selfridge now wrote a letter to the Boston Gazette in which he called Austin a "coward, a liar, and a scoundrel." Austin followed with a counter statement, and matters reached a crisis.

The details of this unusual duel are buried in the realm of obscurity. On August 6, 1806, in the middle of the day, Thomas Selfridge put his affairs in order. He then took a pistol from a drawer in his desk, left his room in what is now the Old State House, and started walking down the middle of State Street. He reached a point no less than ten feet from the location where the 1770 Boston Massacre had occurred. There he had expected to confront Benjamin Austin, but it was Austin's son who was awaiting him.

Eighteen years of age, Charles Austin was a student at Harvard College. Having chosen to act for his father, Charles had armed himself with a rattan cane. The two slowly approached each other. Then, before Austin was actually able to strike his opponent, Selfridge cocked his gun and fired, mortally wounding the Harvard youth. The lad managed to get in a few feeble blows with the cane before he collapsed, after which he was carried inside Mr. Townsend's shop nearby. Descendants of those who lived in Boston at the time still argue as to whether Selfridge, a relatively feeble man, shot Austin before Austin had a chance to strike him with the rattan cane. In any case, after being treated by Dr. Thomas Danforth, Austin died.

Selfridge was accused of the murder, as there had been many who had watched the encounter. The trial began before Judge Isaac Parker on November 25, 1806. Testimony of two important witnesses of the encounter follows, the first being that of Edward Howe.

"At a quarter past one o'clock on the 4th of August, I set off from Mr. Townsend's shop in State Street, with an intention of going home to dinner. Crossing the east end of the Old State House, met Mr. Selfridge, at the distance of about two rods from Townsend's shop. He passed me about three feet off on my right hand. I took particular notice of him, having seen the publication in the Chronicle that morning. He had on a frock coat, and his hands were behind him, but I am not able to say whether they were outside of his coat or not.

"I passed on six or eight steps when I heard a very loud talking behind me. I turned immediately round, and the first thing I saw was Mr. Selfridge's hand with a pistol in it, and immediately the pistol was discharged. The instant afterwards, I saw the person, who had been shot, step forward from the side walk, and strike Mr. Selfridge several heavy blows on the head. These blows were struck with so much force, that I think, if Mr. Selfridge had not had on a very thick hat, they must have fractured his skull. He stood about three or four feet from the brick pavement

[CONTINUED ON PAGE 15]

THE DESCENDANTS OF SAMUEL AUSTIN
OF BOSTON, MASSACHUSETTS

by Michael Edward Austin
and Patricia Biebuyck Austin

THIRD GENERATION [CONTINUED FROM PAGE 10]

S21. THOMAS[3] AUSTIN (*Thomas,*[2] *Samuel*[1]) was born 23 January 1691-2 in Andover, Mass. He went with his father to that part of Haverhill later set off as Methuen. He married Sarah Lovejoy of Andover on 26 October 1714. Sarah, the daughter of Christopher Lovejoy and Sarah Russ, was born on 9 March 1689-90 in Andover, and was a second cousin to Thomas Austin through their common great-grand father John Russ who was born in England about 1612 and died in Andover in 1692. Their children were born in Methuen:

    S211. THOMAS, *b. 26 February 1716*
    S212. SARAH, *b. 8 December 1717, d. 1739-40*
    S213. HEZEKIAH, *b. 7 April 1719* +
    S214. HANNAH, *b. 8 April 1722* +
    S215. ISAAC, *b. 8 November 1723* +
    S216. NATHAN, *b. 25 January 1725* +
    S217. ELIZABETH, *b. 4 November 1726* +
    S218. JOHN, *b. 23 August 1728* +
    S219. PETER, *b. 12 May 1730* +

S22. BENJAMIN[3] AUSTIN (*Thomas,*[2] *Samuel*[1]) was born 16 June 1694 in Andover, Mass. He was a yeoman and lived in Andover, where he married Mary Stevens of Andover on 17 July 1718. Mary was born 23 August 1695 in Andover, the daughter of John and Ruth (Poor) Stevens. Benjamin and Mary were still living in Andover in 1749, but later removed to Hollis, NH. Their children are recorded in Andover:

    S221. MARY, *b. 7 April 1719* +
    S222. RUTH, *bp. 16 July 1721, d. 4 Dec. 1739*
    S223. BENJAMIN, *b. 12 February 1722-3, died 16 December 1739*
    S224. MARTHA, *b. 1 June 1725*
    S225. THOMAS, *b. 24 April 1727* +
    S226. [daughter], *b. and d. 9 December 1729*
    S227. JOHN, *b. 25 January 1729-30* +
    S228. SARAH, *b. 13 Dec. 1731, d. 16 May 1732*
    S229. TIMOTHY, *b. 16 March 1732-3* +
    S22A. SARAH, *b. 21 May 1735* +
    S22B. PHINEHAS, *b. 3 Nov. 1737, d. 10 Dec. 1739*
    S22C. BENJAMIN, *b. 11 January 1740-1* +

S23. DANIEL[3] AUSTIN (*Thomas,*[2] *Samuel*[1]) was born 7 August 1698 in Andover, Mass. He was a cordwainer, and married Priscilla Stevens of Andover on 26 June 1722 in Andover. She was born 12 August 1699 in Andover, the daughter of John and Ruth (Poor) Stevens. Daniel and Priscilla lived in Andover until about 1726 when they removed to South Town or Turkey Hills, now the town of Lunenburg, Mass., occupying the house where Calvin Eaton had lately lived. Daniel was chosen constable 11 March 1729-30, and later served as tythingman, selectman, assessor, surveyor of the highways and other offices. In 1745 a road was laid out "Begining at the Road that comes from Hezekiah Wetherbes and Runs upon M[r] Benj[a] Bellows and Daniel Astins Land and Between the said Austin and John Fisks Land and across some common Land and across the ministreal Land. . ." On 30 September 1751, a Town Committee reported selling a pew on the Lower floor of the New Meeting house: "Sold the third pew Ground on the Left hand Going in at the front Dore adjoining to Daniel Austens: to Docter John Dunsmoor. . ."

Daniel died 29 May 1773, while Priscilla died 10 May 1782. Both are buried in the South Cemetery in Lunenburg. Their first two children are recorded in Andover, while the others appear in the Lunenburg town and church records. The repetition of the first two children's names is somewhat troublesome since neither town has a record of their deaths. Judging by the marriage date, the Andover birthdates for the first two children seem reasonable. The Lunenburg records show only one Priscilla born in Andover and one Daniel born in Lunenburg. The dates differ distinctly from the Andover dates, and fill up very well what would otherwise be an uncharacteristically long gap between children. For these reasons we have chosen to believe both towns' records, and assume that the first two children died young:

    S231. PRISCILLA, *b. 26 July 1723, d. young*
    S232. DANIEL, *b. 1 October 1724, d. young*
    S233. PRISCILLA, *b. 11 February 1725-6* +
    S234. DANIEL, *b. 13 April 1727* +
    S235. LYDIA, *b. 3 June 1729*
    S236. TIMOTHY, *b. 2 March 1731*
    S237. RUTH, *b. 1 April 1733*
    S238. HANNAH, *b. 1 February 1734-5*
    S239. PHEBE, *b. 24 October 1736*
    S23A. PETER, *bp. 17 September 1738*
    S23B. JOSHUA, *bp. 13 July 1740*
    S23C. MARTHA, *bp. 4 April 1742*
    S23D. JOHN, *bp. 3 April 1743*

S24. ZEBEDIAH[3] AUSTIN (*Thomas,*[2] *Samuel*[1]) was born 17 July 1701 in Andover, Massachusetts. He lived in Methuen, where he was a husbandman. He married Sarah Gutterson of Methuen on 18 April 1729 in Haverhill. Their children are recorded in Methuen:

S241. PHEBE, *b. 20 April 1730*
S242. SUSANNAH, *b. 19 September 1732*
S243. RUBEN, *b. 3 February 1734-5*
S244. DEBORAH, *b. 14 June 1737*
S245. DAVID, *b. 4 February 1739-40*
S246. JONATHAN, *b. 10 June 1742*
S247. JOHN, *b. 27 September 1744*
S248. CALEB, *b. 19 March 1746-7*

S25. ABIEL[3] AUSTIN (*Thomas,[2] Samuel[1]*) was born —
1703 in Andover, Mass. He was a cooper and yeoman,
and lived in Methuen. Abiel enlisted from Haverhill in the
fourth Indian War, begun in 1722, commonly referred to
as the *Three Years'* or *Lovewell's War.* He was engaged in
the fight, but was not wounded. He married Sarah
Moulton of Haverhill on 24 May 1727 in Haverhill. Sarah
was the daughter of Nathan Molton, and was born in
Haverhill and baptised 19 May 1706. Abiel, aged 86, was
reported living in Salem, N.H. in 1790.

Although Abiel and Sarah continued to occupy the homestead which once belonged to his father, town and even
provincial boundary adjustments continued to change his
town of residence: his part of Haverhill was set off as the
town of Methuen, and still later became Salem, N.H. Thus
their first child is found in the Haverhill records, the next
four children in the Methuen records, the last five in the
Salem, N.H. records:

S251. HANNAH, *b. 1 May 1728*
S252. ABIGAIL, *b. 15 February 1729-30*
S253. NATHAN, *b. 23 March 1732*
S254. MARY, *b. 22 February 1734-5*
S255. SARAH, *b. 24 October 1737*
S256. DOLLY, *b. 29 May 1740*
S257. ABIEL, *b. 8 September 1743*
S258. RACHEL, *b. 27 August 1746*
S259. LYDIA, *b. 20 August 1749*
S25A. JOHN, *b. 25 August 1751*

S26. HANNAH[3] AUSTIN (*Thomas,[2] Samuel[1]*) was born 7
April 1706 in Andover, Mass. She resided in Haverhill,
and was married there on 16 July 1722 to Hezekiah
Lovejoy, also of Haverhill. The Lovejoys had ten children
whose births or baptisms appear in the Haverhill or
Andover records. They lived in Haverhill until their
removal to Amherst, New Hampshire, where Hannah died
on 1 December 1805, 'aged 101'. LOVEJOY CHILDREN: *Hezekiah
1721-2, (stillborn) 1723, Hannah 1724, Phebe 1727, Hezekiah 1729,
Abiel 1731, Francis 1734, Phebe 1737, John 1739, John 1743.*

FOURTH GENERATION [TO BE CONTINUED]

Note: The preceding article was abstracted from a book of the same title
currently in preparation by the authors, who would welcome additional
information on Samuel Austin's descendants for inclusion in the book.

THE AUSTIN DUELS
[CONTINUED FROM PAGE 13]

or sidewalk, in front of Mr. Townsend's shop, and was
facing up the street. I saw the Defendant throw his pistol at
the deceased, but I cannot say whether it hit him or not. I
saw it roll on the pavement towards Mr. Russell's door."

Another witness, Ephraim French, testified: "About one
o'clock I was in Mr. Townsend's shop and seeing old Mr.
Austin go down, expected a squabble. I saw two young
gentlemen go down street, and presently return. Mr.
Bailey said one of them was young Mr. Austin. I saw Mr.
Selfridge coming from the corner of the State House; he
walked very deliberately, and looked sober. Young Austin
went from near where I was standing, towards Mr.
Selfridge. As he advanced I saw the pistol go off, and Austin struck several severe blows, and then fell near my feet.

"I should say that the pistol, according to my observation, was one or two seconds before the first blow was
struck. I did not see any cane raised before the pistol went
off. I looked particularly at Mr. Selfridge from the time he
came in sight. After he had discharged the pistol, he threw
up his arms to defend his head from the blows, and afterwards threw his pistol. No person stood between me and
the parties, so that I saw them very distinctly, having gone
out of the shop and stood on the sidewalk by Mr.
Townsend's shop before they met."

The actual charge was that Selfridge "in his right hand,
then and there held, to, against and upon the said Charles
Austin, then and there, feloniously, willfully, and of the
fury of his mind, did shoot and discharge; and that he the
said Thomas Oliver Selfridge, with the leaden bullet aforesaid, out of the pistol. . . did kill and slay, against the peace
of the Commonwealth aforesaid, and the law in such case
made and provided."

The illustrious Paul Revere was foreman of the jury,
which brought a verdict of 'Not Guilty,' but whether or not
the jury had been influenced as was claimed by 'political
predelictions of the jurors' will never be known. Christopher Gore, Samuel Dexter, Harrison Gray Otis, and
Charles Jackson defended Thomas Oliver Selfridge, and
without question did their best for 'their fellow-laborer in
the Federalist vineyard.'

* * * * * *

The preceding article originally appeared in *THE QUINCY PATRIOT
LEDGER* in Quincy, Massachusetts. It is reprinted here with the per-
mission of its author, Edward Rowe Snow of Marshfield, Mass. Mr.
Snow, a well-known lecturer and historian, has authored 96 books
relating to New England history and legends. One of these books,
Fantastic Folklore and Fact, references several other Austins.

Austins of America

SOME DESCENDANTS OF OLIVER AUSTIN
OF BERKSHIRE, VERMONT

by Carol Leighton Hull

O. OLIVER[1] AUSTIN was born 18 January 1761, died 10 March 1813 at Berkshire, VT. He married Sarah Powell, born 14 March 1764, died 12 March 1818. Oliver appears in the 1800 and 1810 census for Berkshire. He served frequently as a town officer from highway surveyor to selectman. He was serving as town treasurer at the time of his death in 1813. The fact of his death and the subsequent audit of his accounts are in the town books. He died leaving three minor children whose guardianship papers are at St. Albans: Raymond's guardian was Penuel Leavins, Powell's was Caleb Stevens, and Mary's was John Stone. Oliver and Sarah had five children born in Berkshire:

O1. SALLY, *m. Caleb Stevens*

O2. OLIVER, *b. 10 April 1788 +*

O3. RAYMOND, *b. 7 May 1794 +*

O4. POWELL, *b. 25 May 1800, m. Alzada Haynes on 9 January 1825 in Berkshire.*

O5. MARY, *m. Thomas Sinders on 22 August 1813 in Berkshire.*

SECOND GENERATION

O2. OLIVER[2] AUSTIN (*Oliver[1]*) was born 10 April 1788 in Berkshire and died there 21 May 1864. On 1 December 1811 in Berkshire he married Milla Larabee, daughter of William and Amy Royce/Rice, born 7 October 1791 in Springfield, VT, died 14 December 1860 in Berkshire. Oliver is listed in the census records for Berkshire from 1820 to 1860. Their children were born in Berkshire:

O21. SOPHRONIA, *b. 19 February 1812, d. 24 July 1868, m. Stephen Stevens.*

O22. SARAH E., *b. 13 March 1814, d. 20 December 1903 in Berkshire, m. Watson Richard Willis.*

O23. MALVINA, *b. 25 January 1816, d. 30 April 1906 Enosburgh, m. Stephen Gates.*

O24. HARRIET N., *b. 13 January 1818, d. 27 January 1892 Enosburgh, m. in 1837 to Dolphus Paul, Jr.*

O25. MALINDA, *.b 11 January 1821, d. 16 August 1912 Enosburgh, m. on 23 February 1842 to Ethan Hull.*

O26. ARVILLA, *b. 2 May 1823, d. 8 June 1908, m. — Andrus.*

O27. OLIVER ELHANON, *b. 13 February 1826 +*

O3. RAYMOND[2] AUSTIN (*Oliver[1]*) was born on 7 May 1794, died 3 July 1862 in Berkshire, Vermont. He married Abigail Ladd, born 5 February 1799, died 12 December 1887 in Berkshire. Raymond is listed in the Berkshire census from 1820 to 1860. He was an ordained Baptist elder as certified in the town book. Their children were born in Berkshire:

O31. HORATIO NELSON, *b. 5 November 1818 +*

O32. HAZARD PERRY, *b. 24 September 1820*

O33. EZRA MERRILL, *b. 14 July 1824*

O34. ALPHEUS M., *b. 30 July 1828, d. 11 May 1848 in Berkshire.*

O35. ABIGAIL CELIA, *born 25 July 1838, died 21 November 1903.*

THIRD GENERATION

O27. OLIVER ELHANON[3] AUSTIN (*Oliver,[2] Oliver[1]*) was born 16 February 1826 in Berkshire, and died there 29 June 1894. He married Charlotte R. Moore, who was born 19 July 1829 and died 22 November 1891. Their children were born in Berkshire:

O271. OLIVER EZRA ABIJAH, *b. 25 November 1851, d. 1 March 1864 of spotted fever.*

O272. IRVING POWELL, *b. 28 September 1853 +*

O273. MARY H., *b. August 1856, d. 17 September 1857*

O274. ELLA H., *b. 16 February 1861, m. Miland N. Coffin on 6 November 1884.*

O275. WILLIAM J., *b. 24 October 1863*

O276. IDA MILLA, *b. 9 July 1872*

O31. HORATIO NELSON[3] AUSTIN (*Raymond,[2] Oliver[1]*) was born 5 November 1818 in Berkshire, died 27 November 1889 in Berkshire. He married on 6 April 1840 in Berkshire Caroline R. Comings, born 12 January 1821 in Cornish, New Hampshire. Their first four children were born in Berkshire, the fifth in Swazey, New Hampshire:

O311. ELLA ANNETTE, *b. 8 October 1841, m. Henry W. Kellog on 15 December 1864 in Berkshire.*

O312. CAROLINE ROSALIND, *b. 20 February 1844, m. Charles P. Whitford 1 January 1870 Berkshire.*

O313. RUTH ARABELLE, *b. 14 July 1847, m. to Moses Kellog on 24 February 1874.*

O314. EZRA, *b. 10 May 1849 +*

O315. JULIA V., *born 1855 Swazey, NH, m. to James H. Kenison on 21 February 1875.*

O32. HAZARD PERRY[3] AUSTIN (*Raymond,[2] Oliver[1]*) was born 24 September 1820 in Berkshire, Vermont, and died there 24 May 1887. He married Mary Ann Wheeler, who was born 13 April 1824 and died on 22 December 1888.

FOURTH GENERATION

O272. IRVING POWELL[4] AUSTIN (*Oliver Elhanon,*[3] *Oliver,*[2] *Oliver*[1]) was born 28 September 1853 in Berkshire, and died there in 1915. He married on 19 February 1894 in Berkshire to Pearl M. Chausett, who died 27 Nov. 1945.

O314. EZRA[4] AUSTIN (*Horatio Nelson,*[3] *Raymond,*[2] *Oliver*[1]) was born 10 May 1849 in Berkshire, and died 5 December 1920. He married Anna C. Hall, who was born 1852 and died 1933. The children were born in Berkshire:

    O314-1. MERRITT LEON, *b. 14 October 1870, d. 20 April 1888 Berkshire of diabetes*
    O314-2. CHARLES L., *b. 24 April 1872*

LITERATURE

DESCENDANTS OF BENJAMIN AND ANNA AUSTIN 1778-1978, by Charles Arthur Wright and Lorraine Austin Wright. Published Columbus, Wisconsin 1978, approximately 551 pages, Accopress[322] binding.

The authors' family bible recorded the birth of Samuel McConnell Austin on 6 January 1794 in Grafton County, New Hampshire, to Benjamin and Ann Austin. Becoming thereby interested in genealogy, the authors have engaged in extensive correspondence since the late 1950's with Samuel's descendants, and have compiled an impressive work encompassing descendants of all surnames.

Samuel Austin married in Grafton County, and his first wife died there. He then moved West to Ohio, living there for about ten years before moving on to Wisconsin. This book traces the descendants of Samuel down to the time of publication in 1978, and has records covering the states from the East to West Coast and from the Gulf of Mexico up into Canada and Alaska.

The Benjamin appearing in the title of this book is a descendant of Samuel Austin of Boston, having a sequence number of S227-6 in the Samuel Austin genealogy (see pages 8ff and 14f of this *Austins of America* newsletter). Found in the book are a number of interesting photo>graphs, including even one thought to be that of Benjamin himself. The book contains colorful descriptions of families, their travels, weddings, etc., in addition to the expected wealth of genealogical data. Indeed, perhaps the only deficiency of this book is its lack of a comprehensive index, making it difficult to quickly locate persons in the book. Each section of the book, however, does contain a partial index to the persons in that section. Copies of this fine book may be obtained from the authors for $30.00 plus $2.50 shipping. Their address is 424 North Lewis Street, Columbus, Wisconsin 53925.

QUERIES

17-1. **Almon A. Austin** born N.Y. 1830, married Emily (—). His brother, **Merritt F. Austin**, was born in N.Y. in 1826 and married Phebe (—). All were living 1850 in Freedom, LaSalle County, Illinois. Need ancestry of Almon and Merritt.

17-2. **Thomas Austin** and family from N.Y. state were residing in Knox County, Ohio, circa 1833-1842. Where did they move to, and what are the names and birthdates of the children?

17-3. **Francis Austin** and Mary Barton his wife were Quakers living in Burlington, N.J. Is anyone searching this line?

17-4. **Lucina Austin** born probably E. Hartford, Conn. 17 February 1784, married there 10 April 1804 Elijah Burnham. Need parents of Lucina and Elijah.

17-5. **Thankful Austin** born 22 August 1785 died 15 September 1814, married 17 February 1791 to Abraham Crabs, born 9 March 1767 died 5 February 1836. Need all data and ancestry of Abraham and Thankful.

17-6. **Caroline Austin** died 20 June 1879 in Fond Du Lac, Wisconsin. She married circa 1840 in Onon County, N.Y. Charles Mitchell, born 1 March 1819 perhaps Middletown, Connecticut, son of Samuel and Lucinda (Cook). He died 13 April 1906 in Fond Du Lac. Need ancestry and data on Caroline and ancestry of Charles.

17-7. **James Austin** born Suffield, Connecticut 6 February 1776, son of Seth and Mary (Seymour). Need wife and death of James.

17-8. **James Austin** of Charlestown, R.I., married on 16 February 1812 in Hopkinton, R.I. to Wealthy Witter, born there 17 February 1776. Need parents of James.

17-9. **Frances E. Austin** was born on 18 May 1842 in Dixfield, Maine, daughter of Peter A. and Fanny Park (Newton) Austin. Frances married on 5 August 1891 to M— Dow, she was of Livermore, Maine, he of Jay, Maine. Seek ancestry of M— Dow.

17-10. **Moses Astin** of Berwick, Maine, was born 1742, married Elizabeth Clark 6 August 1767 in Berwick. He died 22 March 1820 aged 78. Seek ancestry of Moses.

17-11. **Nahum Austin** was born on 30 October 1789, married Jane Farnham 28 November in Belgrade, Maine. He d. 13 March 1881. Need parents of Nahum and Jane.

17-12. **Truman Dudley Austin** (see Query 10-13) came to Illinois in 1840 via Battle Creek, Michigan. Have collected genealogical data on some 230 of his descendants, and would be pleased to answer inquiries.

WILLIAM AUSTIN:

THE CREATOR OF PETER RUGG

by Walter Austin

Editor's Note: The following article was extracted by Carol A. Hull from the book *William Austin: the Creator of Peter Rugg, being a biographical sketch of William Austin, together with the best of his short stories*, published in Boston in 1925 by his grandson Walter Austin. Known errors have been noted and placed in brackets.

The earliest recorded notice of the Austin name in the Charlestown, Massachusetts, records is that of Richard Austin, who was admitted a freeman in 1651, probably when he became twenty-one years of age. From this Richard descended Benjamin Austin, commonly known as 'Honestus'; Jonathan Loring Austin, secretary to Dr. Franklin in Paris and afterward Secretary of State and Treasurer of Massachusetts; and the late Attorney-General, James Trecothick Austin. . . there is a tradition that two boys, brothers, came to Charlestown in 1638 - one of whom was Richard. . . and the other named Anthony, who first went to Rowley, Massachusetts, and thence to Suffield, Connecticut. . . These two boys were probably the 'two children' accompanying that Richard Austin of Bishopstoke, England, enumerated by John Hotten in his *Original Lists of Persons of Quality 1600-1700* as embarking from Southampton [Southton], bound for New England, in the ship *Bevis* in May 1638.

William Austin was born in Lunenburg, Massachusetts 2 March 1778, the third [fourth] child of Nathaniel and Margaret [Damon] (Rand) Austin. His family left Charlestown when the British torched the town during the battle of Bunker Hill; their home was destroyed and they remained in Lunenburg until it was rebuilt in 1778.

Austin was a member of the class of 1798 at Harvard. After graduating he was appointed schoolmaster and chaplain in the Navy. He sailed with Commodores Nicholson and Talbot in the frigate *Constitution*. During the cruise of the *Constitution* in 1799 under Commodore Talbot's command a ship was captured from the French; in 1800 the court decreed that the captors were entitled to one-sixth of the value for salvage. Commodore Talbot had expected more and sent Mr. Austin to engage Alexander Hamilton to handle the case. According to tradition, Hamilton sent Austin, who was planning to study law, to examine the case as he had an interest in the salvage. Austin's portion of the salvage, about $200, enabled him to study the law at Lincoln's Inn in London. The chaplaincy ended, Austin began his legal training with the commendation of Hamilton.

During the time he was in London he shared the company of such former neighbors and Harvard friends as Washington Allston, John Blake White, Edmund Towbridge Dana and Arthur Maynard Walter. As well as studying he sent home letters which were published in the newspapers and later, in book form as *Letters from London*. The letters were about men, morals, politics, and literature; they expressed his Republican politics very strongly. He returned to this country and began to practice law in 1803 in Charlestown; he carried on this practice until shortly before his death in 1841. He represented Charlestown in the General Court in 1811, 1812, 1816, 1827 and 1834; he was elected to the Senate in 1821, 1822, and 1823.

In the early years of the Republic party feelings were very strong. Mr. Austin was a prominent Republican whose views were often in print. He was challenged to a duel for sentiments expressed in a newspaper article in March 1806 by James Elliott, a Federalist. The duel, though against the law, was fought 31 March 1806 in Cold Spring, Rhode Island (now a part of Providence). Austin was wounded, but not seriously, and Elliott was uninjured. Later in his life Austin deeply regretted his part in the duel.

Austin's publications ranged from a rebellious essay written while a student at Harvard to a group of short stories which influenced major New England writers such as Hawthorne and Melville.

Publications: *Strictures on Harvard University* By a Senior, Boston 1798; *Oration Before the Artillery Company, Charlestown, June 17, 1801* Charlestown, 1801; *Letters from London* Boston 1804; *Essay on the Human Character of Jesus Christ* Boston 1807; 'Peter Rugg, the Missing Man' *New England Galaxy*, 10 September 1824 continued 1 September 1826 and 19 January 1827; 'The Sufferings of a Country Schoolmaster' *New England Galaxy* 8 July 1825; 'The Late Joseph Natterstrom' *New England Magazine* July 1831; 'The Origin of Chemistry, a Manuscript Recently Found in an Old Trunk' *New England Magazine* January 1834; 'The Man with the Cloaks: a Vermont Legend' *American Monthly Magazine* January 1836; 'Martha Gardner; or Moral Reaction' *American Monthly Magazine* December 1837.

Austins of America is intended to serve present and future genealogists researching Austin family lines. Readers are encouraged to submit Queries, genealogical & historical articles for publication. Previously published books or pamphlets containing Austin genealogical data are also sought for review.

EDITOR: DR. MICHAEL E. AUSTIN   CONCORD, MASS.

ASSOCIATE EDITOR: CAROL A. HULL   SUDBURY, MASS.

Austins of America is published each February and August by The Austin Print, 23 Allen Farm Lane, Concord, Massachusetts 01742. All correspondence, including subscriptions and responses to queries, should be sent to this address. Subscriptions are included in the membership fee of the Austin Families Association. The annual subscription rate for non-members is $1.25.

AUSTINBURG, OHIO

by Mrs. Arnold Burton

"And they shall dwell safely in the Wilderness and sleep in the woods." God's promise to ancient Israel must have been in the mind of Eliphalet Austin when, in the spring of 1799 he led a small band of men, women and children from their comfortable homes in Connecticut into the trackless Western Reserve. Here, in this place called "Austin's Camp," but known for thirteen years as Richfield, on the banks of Coffee Creek, Eliphalet Austin began his cabin on June 5th, 1799. Built as a bulletproof blockhouse, it served as a community center for some time.

The people who came here with Mr. Austin were Mr. and Mrs. Roswell Stevens, Mr. and Mrs. George Beckwith and two children, and three young men hired by Mr. Austin, Anson Colt, David Allen and Samuel Fobes. The Beckwith family built a cabin near the present site of Grand River Academy. Mr. Austin's cabin was located on the east side of Route 45 where the brick house owned by Don Armstrong now stands. That summer the pioneers cleared the land, planted and harvested the first wheat.

Satisfied with these meager beginnings, Mr. Austin returned that fall to Connecticut to find colonizers for his camp. Early in the spring of 1800 Deacon Sterling Mills arrived with his family and built the third cabin in the southern part of the township. Other arrivals, either with or because of Mr. Austin, were Deacon Noah Cowles, Captain Joseph Case and his son, afterwards Deacon Joseph M. Case, Adna Cowles, Joseph B. Cowles, Roger Nettleton, Dr. Orestes K. Hawley, John Wright, Jr., Jonah Moses, Daniel C. Phelps, Isaac Butterfield, Ephraim Rice, Calvin Stone, and David Allen. It was not until the spring of 1801 that these men, including Judge Austin, brought their families.

During the first season, 1800, there were but three families here, yet they met regularly every Sunday for worship at Eliphalet Austin's. With the arrival of the other families, in the spring of 1801, meetings were held either at Austin's house, or his barn, when the population had increased, and also at Deacon Sterling Mills. The first regular sermon was preached here in August 1801, by Rev. Joseph Badger, the first Congregational Missionary on the Western Reserve. The first church on the Reserve was organized here by Rev. Badger on Thursday, October 24, 1801. The first members were Mr. and Mrs. Joseph Case, Mr. and Mrs. Joseph M. Case, Mr. & Mrs. Stephen Brown, Deacon and Mrs. Noah Cowles, Mr. and Mrs. Roger Nettleton, Roswell Austin, Clarissa Cowles, Mrs. Chloe Henderson, Deacon Sterling Mills, Mrs. Sibbell Austin and Mrs. Lois Cowles.

The first school was opened in 1801 by Miss Betsy Austin in her father's barn. The first school house was built just west of the Academy, on the north side of College Street, in 1802. It was of notched plank with a mud and stick chimney.

The first saw mill in the county was set up by Eliphalet Austin in 1801. Mr. Austin then built his frame house, the first frame house on the Western Reserve, believed by some historians to be the first frame house in Ohio. It is located on the old Girdled Road, now known as College Street, on the west bank of Coffee Creek. In that same year Ambrose Humphrey built a grist mill near Austin's saw mill. Both were located on Grand River at Mechanicsville.

In 1803 Eliphalet Austin contracted for the first mail route along the Lake Shore. Thus the first post office was established here in 1803 with Mr. Austin as postmaster.

In 1804 the first meeting house was built. It was of log and was located on the west side of Route 45, opposite the present cemetery. It was replaced by a second one in 1810. The first resident minister arrived here from Connecticut in 1811. This was Rev. Giles Hooker Cowles, his wife and eight children. For a time they lived in the meeting house, while their own cabin was being built.

The War of 1812 delayed the development of the settlements, and the blockade established by the British, together with their foraging expeditions, increased the hardships of the pioneers and delayed building. Perry's victory in September 1812, which because of his youth came as a great surprise to the county residents who had seen him in Erie, relieved transportation and the people began the first frame church on the Reserve in 1814. This church was also the first in Ohio to have a steeple, and the ringing of the 500 lb. bell is said to have frightened away the wolves forever. This church was used for meetings from 1815 on, and although there was no way of heating it, it was filled winter and summer.

In 1815 Rev. Cowles built the house now occupied by his great-great-granddaughter, Mrs. Robert Ticknor (Margaret Cowles) and family. It stood at the rear of the log church, across from the cemetery south of the village. The parsonage study has, at the request of Miss Betsey Cowles, been kept intact since 1833. The same furniture, wallpaper and bright woven carpet are still there. Rev. Giles Hooker Cowles' walking stick rests against the communion table from the first church. The huge stone fireplace with the Dutch Oven is still in use.

Also in 1815 Eliphalet Austin was building the beautiful brick home at the northwest corner of the intersection of the present Route 45 and College Street. Known as Syca-

[CONTINUED ON PAGE 22]

THE DESCENDANTS OF
JAMES AND ANN HOWARD AUSTIN

by Katherine Fleming Wright

J. JAMES[1] AUSTIN was born in 1770 near Harper's Ferry, Virginia. He was married to Ann Howard, who was born in Virginia. James came to Cartwright's Creek, Washington County, Kentucky, in 1790. His wife Ann died in that county around 1830, and there is pretty good proof that she was buried at St. Rose's Priory cemetery near Springfield, Kentucky. Two years later James moved to Union County, Kentucky, where he died on 23 July 1850 and was buried in the Sacred Heart Cemetery in St. Vincent, Kentucky. The children of James and Ann were born in Washington County:

J1.   BENEDICT, *born in 1792* +
J2.   JOHN, *born circa 1794*
J3.   CATHERINE, *born circa 1797, single*
J4.   THERESA, *born circa 1800, died in Illinois, m. Benedict Smith in Union County*
J5.   AMBROSE, *born 1804* +
J6.   SARAH, *born circa 1806, single*
J7.   ROSE ANN, *b. October 1807, d. 6 November 1859 in Union County, m. Edward Yates 4 October 1853*
J8.   THOMAS AQUINAS, *born 15 October 1810* +

SECOND GENERATION

J1. BENEDICT[2] AUSTIN (*James[1]*) was born in 1792 in Washington County, Kentucky. He was married in Washington County on 21 August 1825 to Margaret Yates. Margaret, the daughter of John and Henrietta (Cambren) Yates, was born circa 1804. Benedict died in July 1849 in Paducah, McCracken County, Kentucky, while Margaret died on 10 January 1855 in Union County, Kentucky. Benedict and Margaret may have had children prior to Edward, but if so they are unknown, as the St. Rose Church registers did not begin until 1830. Their children that were recorded in Kentucky included:

J11.   EDWARD, *born circa 1832 in Washington County*
J12.   MAHALA ANN, *born 17 September 1834 in Union County, m. John T. Bowles*
J13.   TERESA JANE, *born 1 December 1836 in Union County, m. Samuel Elliot 19 November 1856*
J14.   SARAH ELLEN, *born 28 May 1839 Union County, married a Willett or Pierceall*
J15.   ISABELLA, *born on 12 October 1841 in Union County, d. 3 November 1868, m. Philip Greenwell 29 October 1861*
J16.   SOPHRONIA CATHERINE, *b. 9 January 1847 in Graves County, m. Joseph A. Melton 14 June 1870*
J17.   MARGARET EDELIA, *born 10 February 1850 Graves County, married a Bolds or Ballou*

J5. AMBROSE[2] AUSTIN (*James[1]*) was born in 1804 in Washington County, Kentucky. He was married in Washington County on 31 January 1827 to Mary Ann Herbert. Mary, the daughter of Jeremiah and Mary (Hill) Herbert, was born on 28 December 1807 in Washington County, and died circa 1880 in Graves County. Ambrose also died in Graves County. Children recorded in Kentucky:

J51.   FRANCIS ROSEMOND, *born circa 1828 in Washington County, reportedly died in the Civil War*
J52.   MARY ANN, *born 1 July 1829 Union County, d. as an infant*
J53.   MARTHA ELLEN, *b. 4 May 1830 Union County, m. Charles Purcealle (Pierceall) on September 1856 in Graves County*
J54.   RICHARD LOGAN, *born 31 May 1834 in Union County, reportedly died in Texas*
J55.   TERESA ANN MELISSA, *b. in February 1835 in Union County, m. Henry Ryan*
J56.   ELIZABETH PAULINE, *born 20 February 1838 in Union County, m. John Riley*
J57.   MARGARET JANE, *born 10 January 1840 Union County, d. circa 1908 Carlisle County, m. Jeremiah M. Riley circa 1854 in Graves Co.*
J58.   JOHN ALFORD, *born 26 January 1842 in Union County, died as an infant*
J59.   JAMES, *born circa 1843 in Graves County, m.(1) Kate Anderson on 4 October 1888, m.(2) Elizabeth Nest on 24 February 1894.*
J5A.   JOHN AMBROSE, *born 4 August 1844 in Graves County, died 22 July 1894 in Carlisle County, single*
J5B.   SARAH FRANCES, *born 4 August 1844 in Graves County, m. Alfred 'Puss' Hargiss*
J5C.   ANN MODESTA, *b. circa 1849 in Graves County, died in Paris, Tennessee, m. James Carroll*
J5D.   SUSANNA JOSEPHINE, *born on 24 March 1852 in Graves County*
J5E.   THOMAS GULIELMAN, *born on 12 August 1854 in Graves County*

J8. THOMAS AQUINAS[2] AUSTIN (*James[1]*) was born on 15 October 1810 in Washington County, Kentucky. He was married in Union County, Kentucky on 26 July 1836 to Mary Ann Railey. Mary, the daughter of Basil and Elizabeth (Spaulding) Railey, was born on 2 March 1812 in Marion County, Kentucky. Mary died 29 November 1856 in Union County, while Thomas died there 12 March 1864. Their children were born in Union County, except perhaps the last, who was born in Kentucky:

J81.   JAMES BASIL, *born 1 September 1837*+
J82.   MARY ANN ELIZABETH, *b. 20 January 1839*+
J83.   JANE VICTORIA, *born 20 August 1840*+
J84.   FRANCIS XAVIER, *born 26 February 1842*+
J85.   MARGARET ANN, *born 13 December 1843*+
J86.   THOMAS AQUINAS, JR., *born 7 March 1846*+
J87.   JOHN HOWARD, *born 5 December 1847*+
J88.   BENEDICT JOSEPH, *born 7 October 1849*+

THIRD GENERATION

J81. JAMES BASIL³ AUSTIN (*Thomas Aquinas,² James¹*) was born 1 September 1837 in Union County, Kentucky. He was married in Union County on 31 May 1864 to Mary Ellen Yates. Mary, the daughter of William and Maria (Montgomery) Yates, was born circa 1839 and died on 14 October 1921 in Union County. James died 29 July 1924, also in Union County. Children:

> J811. GEORGE EDWARD, *born 7 August 1866, died on 14 August 1866*
>
> J812. MARY GERALDINE, *b. 8 January 1868, d. 23 June 1918 m. — Greenwell*
>
> J813. CHARLES MARTIN, *born on 25 December 1869, died on 7 November 1934 m. Nettie V. Johnson on 31 October 1894 (five children)*
>
> J814. JAMES HERMAN, *born on 25 April 1871, m. Sue Emma Cruz 11 January 1898, had a large family*
>
> J815. ROBERT AARON, *b. 25 April 1873, d. 1 August 1948, single*
>
> J816. ANNIE CARRIE, *b. 5 December 1876, died single*
>
> J817. WILLIAM JOSEPH, *born in April 1881, died on 13 August 1881*

J82. MARY ANN ELIZABETH³ AUSTIN (*Thomas Aquinas,² James¹*) was born 20 January 1839 in Union County, Kentucky, and was married to — Mills. She died 29 November 1856. MILLS CHILDREN: BEN, WILLIAM, JOSEPH.

J83. JANE VICTORIA³ AUSTIN (*Thomas Aquinas,² James¹*) was born 20 August 1840 in Union County, Kentucky. She was married first on 7 June 1863 to Lafayette Martin, and second to — Hite. Her children were all by her first husband. Jane died on 7 November 1890. MARTIN CHILDREN: LAFAYETTE, LAVELLE, JAMES THOMAS 1865.

J84. FRANCIS XAVIER³ AUSTIN (*Thomas Aquinas,² James¹*) was born 26 February 1842 in Union County, Kentucky. He was married on 19 January 1874 to Mary Emma Hardin. Francis died in Mississippi or Arkansas. Francis and Mary are known to have had two sons.

J85. MARGARET ANN³ AUSTIN (*Thomas Aquinas,² James¹*) was born 13 December 1843 in Union County, Kentucky. She was married on 14 April 1874 to William Kendrick Yates. William was born on 6 April 1846, and died 29 November 1917. Margaret died 17 October 1921. The YATES CHILDREN: ANNIE LAVAILLE 1875, JOHN KENDRICK 1877, MARY MABEL CLARE 1879, THOMAS EDWARD 1881, GEORGE SYLVESTER 1883, MARY MAGDALEN 1886, AND MARTHA AGNES 1889.

J86. THOMAS AQUINAS³ AUSTIN (*Thomas Aquinas,² James¹*) was born 7 March 1846 in Union County, Kentucky. He was married on 11 November 1874 to Frances Elizabeth Casey. Frances, an orphan living at St. Vincent Academy in St. Vincent, Kentucky, at the time of her marriage, was born on 17 January 1852 in Daviess County, Kentucky. Thomas and Frances both died circa 1925 in Union County. Children:

> J861. LEE T., *b. 8 February 1887, d. 13 July 1964, m. Johanna Minton (two children)*
>
> J862. GEORGE EARL, *b. circa 1891, d. circa 1962, m. Mary Emma Wathen (six children)*
>
> J863. HAROLD, *d. single*
>
> J864. BENEDICT THOMAS, *m. Lucy Earl Sandefur, early widow of John Raymond Austin (five children)*
>
> J865. REGINA, *b. circa 1894, d. circa 1975, single*
>
> J866. ETHEL *m. Henry Greenwell (two children)*
>
> J867. WALTER *m. Gertrude Clark (six children)*
>
> J868. FLORENCE GENEVIEVE, *m. William Yancy Compton (eight children)*
>
> J869. HELEN MAY, *born 8 April 1889*
>
> J86A. JOSEPH JOHNSON, *born 29 November 1880*

J87. JOHN HOWARD³ AUSTIN (*Thomas Aquinas,² James¹*) was born 5 December 1847 in Union County, Kentucky. He was married on 2 January 1871 to Martha L. Brown, the daughter of John and Susan Brown. John died in Henderson County, Kentucky. Children:

> J871. JOSEPH EDWARD, *b. 22 December 1874 Union County, d. 30 August 1919 Lincoln, Nebraska. m.(1) Mabel — circa 1905, m.(2) Cora Alice Tate circa 1907 (two children)*
>
> J872. CLAUDE, *born 10 August 1877 (twin), died on 2 November —, single*
>
> J873. HERBERT WILLIAM, *b. 10 August 1877 (twin), d. 17 April 1928 Evansville, Indiana, m. Claudia Morton Ely 11 July 1904 Evansville (five children)*
>
> J874. MARY MAGDELINE, *b. 20 October 1878 Uniontown, Kentucky, d. on 2 November 1932 in Beloit, Kansas. She married Charles Lawrence Peak on 1 February 1904 (eight children)*
>
> J875. JOHN RAYMOND, *b. 10 march 1882, d. 30 December 1905 (was thrown from a horse), m. Lucy Earl Sandefur 10 June 1903 (one child)*

J88. BENEDICT JOSEPH³ AUSTIN (*Thomas Aquinas,² James¹*) was born 7 October 1849. He was married first to Mary E. Leonard, an orphan living at St. Vincent's Academy, St. Vincent, Kentucky. Her father was born in Kentucky, her mother was born in France, according to the 1880 census. Mary was born circa 1848, and died circa 1887. Benedict was married second Catherine Clare Manning. Catherine was born on 8 April 1863, and died on 1 March 1946. Benedict died 14 February 1924. His first five children were by Mary, the others by Catherine:

J881. WALTER T., *b. circa 1871, d. circa 1883 drowned (thought to have been murdered)*

J882. ROSE ANNA, *b. January 1873, d. 17 October 1953, m. George M. Elder (eight ch.)*

J883. BENEDICT, *b. circa 1876, d. circa 1876*

J884. VICTORIA EMMA, *b. 4 June 1877, d. 30 October 1942, m. James Ladd (six children)*

J885. MARY JOSEPH, *b. 2 November 1883, d. November 1970*

J886. EMMA LEWIS, *b. 24 May 1891, living in 1981, m. James Francis Fleming 4 June 1913 (five children)*

J887. ROBERTA CATHERINE, *b. 13 October 1892, d. living in 1981, m. James Martine Pearce 15 September 1939 (no children)*

J888. EDNA CHRISTINE, *b. 3 July 1895?, d. 23 January 1973, m. Bayard McIntosh Starnes 30 November 1916 (two children)*

J889. EVA CLARE, *b. 18 March 1898, d. 13 December 1948, entered convent 18 January 1923 - Sister Clare Benedict*

J88A. MARGUERITE MARY, *b. 2 November 1899, d. 8 May 1900*

J88B. WILLIAM JOSEPH, *b. 19 August 1901, d. 20 February 1930, m. Mary Thomas 9 June 1926 (one child)*

J88C. CORNELIA JANE, *b. 29 December 1902, d. 2 June 1960, entered convent 18 January 1923 - Sister Catherine Joseph*

The preceding article was abstracted from a book currently in preparation by the author. Parts of the information were furnished by Mrs. Francine Halter of Baldwin, MD, Mrs. Lucile Austin Dinnin of Oceanside, CA, and Mrs. Bernadine Yates LaRee of Evansville, IN. Any additional information on the descendants of James and Ann would be welcomed by the author for inclusion in the book.

LITERATURE

NICHOLAS AUSTIN THE QUAKER AND THE TOWNSHIP OF BOLTON, by Harry B. Shufelt. Published by The Brome County Historical Society, Knowlton, Quebec, Canada 1971, 230 pages.

Nicholas Austin was brought up as a Quaker in New Hampshire, but married out of that sect and was consequently 'disowned' from being a member of the Quaker Society. He continued, however, to follow Quaker customs and "retrieved his standing and was forgiven." Nicholas was a resident of Middleton, NH in 1774 when he acted as an agent to employ carpenters to build Quarters for General Gage's troops in Boston. Publicly repenting of this action, Nicholas nontheless warned New Hampshire Governor Wentworth in 1775 of a plan to seize him. A few years after the Revolutionary War, loyalist Nicholas turned his attention to ungranted lands in Canada.

AUSTINBURG, OHIO [CONTINUED FROM PAGE 19]

more Hall, because of the towering Sycamore tree beside it, this house was for many years a refuge for runaway slaves on the Underground Railway. The traditions established by the Austin family which made the great house a community gathering place have been carried on by the present owner, Austin Ellsworth.

In 1820 the Ashtabula-Warren Turnpike was completed and Austinburg was on the stage coach line. Thus both water and overland transportation aided in the growth of Austinburg. The first county fair was held here in 1823, with Mrs. Eliphalet Austin winning a prize for the best woolen flannel, and her husband a prize for the best bull. A total of $40 was awarded. Joab Austin built a fine brick store here in 1826. It was the best in this part of the country. Merchants from Cleveland came to buy from him. In 1841 he tore it town and rebuilt it on the northwest corner of Route 45 and Route 307. It is now owned and operated by Pelton and Throop.

A beautiful brick church was completed in 1877. It was designed by Rev. J. K. Nutting, pastor here at the time, after one he had built in Iowa which was noted as the inspiration for the song "Little Brown Church in the Vale." It was erected at a cost of $17,000 on land given by Capt. L. B. Austin. Miss Betsy Cowles, one of the truly great women of her day, was an active member of the building committee. One of the first gatherings in the church was for her funeral, as she died just as it was completed.

The preceding article originally appeared in the *Souvenir Program, Austinburg Sesqui-Centennial* in 1950.

After unsuccessful attempts to be granted two other Quebec province townships along the border with the U.S., Nicholas eventually was granted the township of Bolton in 1797, having been one of its pioneer settlers in 1793 or 1794.

This book makes for very interesting reading, filled as it is with numerous stories of Nicholas and his contemporaries. It is profusely illustrated with photographs and maps, tracing the history of the Eastern Townships of Quebec province. Although it contains some of the most comprehensively-referenced genealogical research ever to appear in print, this book is not an exhaustive study of Nicholas' descendants. Rather it is a fascinating collection of romantic reflections and recollections concerning the remarkable pioneer, Nicholas Austin, and the historic times in which he lived. Copies of this excellent and unique book are available for $12.85 postpaid from The Brome County Historical Society, Box 690, Knowlton, Quebec, Canada J0E 1V0.

HOPESTILL AUSTIN OF SHELBURNE, NH

by Benjamin G. Willey

The following article was taken from *Incidents in White Mountain History*, published by the author in 1856.

The history of Shelburne is strikingly diversified with scenes of toil and hardships endured by its early settlers. Mr. Hope Austin with his family, consisting of a wife and three children, moved into this town April 1st, 1781. At that time there was five feet of snow on the ground. All the way from Bethel (Maine) they waded through this depth of snow, occasionally going on the ice of the Androscoggin river, along which their path lay. The furniture was drawn by Mr. Austin and two hired men, on hand-sleds. Mrs. Austin went on foot, carrying her youngest child, nine months old, in her arms, with Judith the eldest girl, six years of age, and little James, then four years, trudging by her side. They went, in this way, at least twelve miles to their place of residence.

When they arrived at their new home, they found simply the walls of a cabin without floor or roof. To make a shelter from the rains and snows, they cut poles and laid them across the walls to serve as the support of a roof. On these they laid rough shingles covering a space large enough for a bed. With no more covering on its roof, and with only some shingles nailed together and put into one of the sides for a door, they lived till the next June. Then they covered all its walls, and gave it an entire roof. For something to shelter their cow, they dug a large square hole in the snow, down to the ground, and covered it over with poles and boughs. This served as a house till the snow went off, and then the poor cow needed no shelter but the open heavens. Thus they lived quietly and happily, if not very comfortably, till August, the time of the Indian massacre.

An account of this has been given, in part, in the narrative of the captivity of Nathaniel Segar. What was omitted by him, not coming under his observation, we shall here give. Segar tells us that a party of Indians from the woods, painted and armed with tomahawks, came upon him and some others while in a field in Bethel, bound them, and after plundering the house and making a rude assault upon the wife of one of the prisoners, started them off, saying they were prisoners and must go to Canada. The first halt they made was at Gilead, where they killed and scalped Mr. James Pettengill. After this they crossed the Androscoggin with these prisoners, and went to the house of Hope Austin of Shelburne.

Here they searched for plunder. Mr. Austin being away from home, they told his wife to remain in the house, and she should not be hurt. Hurrying on, they went to the house of Capt. Rindge, further up the river. Here they killed and scalped Peter Poor, and took Plato, the colored man, prisoner. So far Segar, in his narrative, has traced their course, though much more minutely in its various details. Now, leaving him to pass on his way to Canada with the Indians, we shall take up those parts of the sad scene which he did not witness. Hope Austin, who was at Capt. Rindge's at the time the Indians and their prisoners went into his own house, when they approached Capt. Rindge's, after seeing Poor killed, and Plato taken prisoner, fled immediately across the Androscoggin. Following down this river a mile or two, he came to the house of Mr. Daniel Ingalls. Here he found his three children. His wife had been here, brought over the river in a boat by Mr. Ingalls, but had just gone back to her house on an important errand. The children came, one with a Mrs. Wentworth, who waded the river with it in her arms, and the other two in the boat with their mother. Mrs. Austin had just gone back to her house just before her husband came, in company with Mrs. Wentworth, to get some meal and bring it to Ingalls', she having more of that article than any other one in the vicinity. Very soon after Austin arrived at Mr. Ingalls', most of the neighbors came hurrying in, excited by the news of the sad affair that had just taken place near Rindge's house.

Mrs. Austin and Mrs. Wentworth not returning so soon as they were expected, the whole company crossed the river and went to Mr. Austin's house. Here they found them making all haste to gather the meal and return to Mr. Ingalls'. But after consulting awhile, and reflecting that there might be danger in all the houses, they concluded to take the meal and some maple sugar, and go to the top of a mountain near by, and spend the night. They did this, and after ascending its precipitous side, spent the night on the summit, in full hearing of the whoopings and shoutings of the Indians. From this circumstance the mountain has since been called "Hark Hill."

Finding, on their return from this mountain the following morning, that there were signs of Indians still in the neighborhood, they fled to Fryeburg (Maine), all the way through the forest, fifty-nine miles from Shelburne. Here they remained till the danger was passed. Then again they sought their home in the wilderness. The season being unpropitious, the return company, numbering about twelve persons, old and young, made their way back through many hardships and sufferings. It was March, and a large quantity of snow was on the ground. Their journey about half accomplished, they encountered a terrible storm of rain. The men were compelled to stand out in the open air, and buffet its force through one whole night, while the women and children were protected from it only by ticks of beds drawn over poles. These exposures they endured with noble courage and at length reached the end of their journey.

AUSTINS IN THE MASSACHUSETTS
TAX VALUATION LIST OF 1771

The following data was abstracted from *The Massachusetts Tax Valuation List of 1771*, edited by Bettye Hobbs Pruitt, published in 1978 by G. K. Hall & Company, Boston. Maine was a district of Massachusetts until 1820, thus Austins living in Maine also appear here.

Andrew Asten	Berwick, Maine	1 house
Anthony Austin	Sheffield, Mass.	Note 6
Anthony Austin, Jr.	Sheffield, Mass.	1 house
Baby Austin	Sheffield, Mass.	Note 5
Benjª Asten	Berwick, Maine	1 house
Benjª Austin	Boston, Mass.	1 house
Benoni Astin	Brunswick, Maine	0 house
Caleb Asten	Methuen, Mass.	Note 1
David Asten	Dracut, Mass.	1 house
David Auston	Norton, Mass.	1/4 house
Ebenezer Austin	Charlestown, Mass.	Note 7
Gad Austin	Sheffield, Mass.	Note 6
Hannah Asten	Methuen, Mass.	Note 2
Ichabod Austn	York, Maine	Note 8
Isaac Asten	Methuen, Mass.	Note 3
Jacob Austin	Taunton, Mass.	0 house
James Austin	Charlestown, Mass.	0 house
James Auston	Norton, Mass.	1/4 house
Joab Austin	Sheffield, Mass.	1 house
John Austin, Jr.	Charlestown, Mass.	1 house
John Austin II	Charlestown, Mass.	house
John Austin	Charlestown, Mass.	Note 7
John Asten	Dracut, Mass.	
John Asten	Methuen, Mass.	1 house
John Asten, Jr.	Methuen, Mass.	Note 1
John Auston	Norton, Mass.	1 house
John Austin	Sheffield, Mass.	1 house
John Austin	Stockbridge, Mass.	0 house
Jonathan Austen	Dighton, Mass.	1 house
Joseph Austin	Charlestown, Mass.	1/2 house
Joseph Astens	Dartmouth, Mass.	1/3 house
Joseph Austin	Springfield, Mass.	0 house
Joseph Austin, Jr.	York, Maine	0 house
Joseph Austin	York, Maine	Note 8
Joshua Austen	Dartmouth, Mass.	1 house
Joshua Auston	Norton, Mass.	1/4 house
Josiah Austin	Charlestown, Mass.	1/4 house
Josiah Austin, Jr.	Charlestown, Mass.	1/2 house
Josiah Auston	Norton, Mass.	1/4 house
Judah Austin	Egremont, Mass.	1 house
Lemˡ Austin	Sheffield, Mass.	Note 9
Mary Austin	Charlestown, Mass.	1 house
Matthew Austin	York, Maine	Note 8
Moses Asten	Berwick, Maine	0 house
Nathˡˡ Austen	Dighton, Mass.	Note 4
Nathˡ Austin	Charlestown, Mass.	1/2 house
Nathan Asten	Methuen, Mass.	Note 2
Nathanˡˡ Austin	Sheffield, Mass.	1 house
Nathanael II	Charlestown, Mass.	1/2 house
Peter Asten	Methuen, Mass.	Note 2
Reuben Asten	Methuen, Mass.	Note 1
Richard Austin	Springfield, Mass.	1 house
Ruth Austin	Charlestown, Mass.	1/2 house
Samˡˡ Austin	Sheffield, Mass.	1 house
Samuel Austin	Boston, Mass.	1 house
Samuel Austin	Charlestown, Mass.	0 house
Stephan Austin	Taunton, Mass.	0 house
Stephen Auston	non-resident	Note 10
Thomas Austin	Charlestown, Mass.	1 house
Thomas Asten	Methuen, Mass.	Note 3
Timothy Austin	Charlestown, Mass.	1/2 house
William Auston	Taunton, Mass.	1 house
Zachariah Austen	Dighton, Mass.	Note 4
Zephⁿ Austin	Sheffield, Mass.	1 house

NOTE 1: Caleb and John, Jr. each owned half a house, Reuben listed with them.

NOTE 2: Nathan and Hannah each owned half a house, Peter listed with them.

NOTE 3: Thomas and Isaac each owned half a house.

NOTE 4: Zachariah had one house, apparently adjacent to another house owned by Nathaniel.

NOTE 5: 'Baby' owned no house, but did own land & grain.

NOTE 6: Anthony owned a house, Gad listed with him.

NOTE 7: John owned a house, Ebenezer listed with him.

NOTE 8: Joseph and Matthew each owned half a house, Ichabod and Joseph, Jr. listed with them.

NOTE 9: Lemuel was listed with Samuel Slate.

NOTE 10: Stephen was listed with Joshua, John, James, David and Josiah, all in Norton, Mass.

Austins of America is intended to serve present and future genealogists researching Austin family lines. Readers are encouraged to submit Queries, genealogical & historical articles for publication. Previously published books or pamphlets containing Austin genealogical data are also sought for review.

EDITOR: DR. MICHAEL E. AUSTIN CONCORD, MASS.

ASSOC. EDITOR: CAROL LEIGHTON HULL SUDBURY, MASS.

Austins of America is published each February and August by The Austin Print, 23 Allen Farm Lane, Concord, Massachusetts 01742. All correspondence, including subscriptions and responses to queries, should be sent to this address. Subscriptions are included in the membership fee of the Austin Families Association. The annual subscription rate for non-members is $1.25. The membership fee of the Austin Families Association is $3.00, payable directly to the Secretary of the Association, Lorena Austin, R-1 Box 233, Claude, Texas 79019.

DAVID AUSTIN LETTER OF 1820

The following letter was written by David Austin of Bloomfield, Ohio, to his brother Isaiah Austin in Tunbridge, Vermont. A reproduction of the handwritten orginal appears on pages 496a,b of Edith Austin Moore's book on *Richard Austin of Charlestown, Massachusetts.*

Bloomfield Township Febuary 13ᵗʰ 1820

*Dear brother I take this oppertunity of writing a few lines for your perrusal informing you that we are all well at present likewise all the rest of your brothers & sisters in this plase we all want to se you vrry mutch but as we hav all got families except Hannah it is unlikly that we shoud except you come and se us, we hav all enjoyed good health since we hav ben here except Mary lost one child that was about nine Months old as you wished to know how and what was the price of land, it can be bought for two*ᴰ *in cash per acre and from that to 3- 4 5- and 6 dollars according to the quality and you can buy land to vrry good advantage with good likely horses or perhaps waggons or other good property it is a vrry healthy country and I own sevnty acres of land that I would not giv for the best farm in that country if I had got to spend my days there on as it respect Crops the land here producees extremely well bottom land will produce from 40 to 75 bushels per acre and wheat produces well and also wry - Father Higgins and family are all well and send there respects to you we have not heard any thing from you since we left that Country untill we recievd your letter. I would wish you to write to me again as quick as posible and write whether you calculate to come to this this country or not and when, and I want you should write concerning our relations in that place.*

I have a good deal of anxiety about my relation for they are scattered about considerably howevr we are all in the hands of a wise God who knows all things and will reward evry one according to the deeds done in the boddy whether that they be good or evil therefore I think I feel the importance of being prepaired to meet him who is in the hiest degree worthey of our praise and adoration.

I would inform you that Olives husband is ded and she is married again your brothers and sister have all seen your letter and all likewise Send there best to you. I have no more to write at pressent but remain your loving Brother

David Austin

Isaiah Austin

NB you will pleas to direct your letters to Bloomfield Township Knox County State of Ohio

AUSTINS OF KNOX COUNTY, OHIO

*by Pauline Lucille Austin
and George William Austin*

The information we have gathered so far on the Austin family of Knox County, Ohio, mostly concerns the two brothers David and Benjamin Austin. David Austin of Bloomfield Township wrote a letter (reproduced at left) to his brother Isaiah Austin in 1820 in response to an earlier letter from Isaiah. Isaiah Austin had been left behind with relatives Stephen and Comfort (Wallis) Smith in Tunbridge, Vermont, when his parents and older brothers and sisters left for the west circa 1804.

In his letter, David refers to sisters Hannah who was still unmarried, Mary who had lost a child, and Olive who was remarrying. He mentions also a "Father Higgins," referring to Joseph Higgins who married widow Hannah Austin in 1804, according to the Higgens bible. According to the bible record, Hannah died in 1814, and the letter from Isaiah may have resulted from a previous letter written to Isaiah concerning the death of his mother Hannah. The only brother we have proven in Knox County is Benjamin Austin, who was born in Vermont in 1792. Benjamin married Ruth Hardesty of Knox County, and raised a family there, later removing to Lima County, Ohio. Land records in Knox County include one in which Clarina Backus bequeathed a tract of land to David Austin, Benjamin Austin and Myrick Higgens for their kind acts bestowed upon her sister Lucy Woodbridge during her illness. Other records are 1812 military records, and the Will of Joseph Higgens.

David Austin was married to Mary (Thompson?). They raised a large family and removed to Shelby County, Illinois in 1838. Isaiah remained in Vermont, and married Olive Hall of Tunbridge, Vermont. It is our belief that this family descends from the Ebenezer or Nathaniel Austin families found in the 1790 Putney, Vermont census, and we would welcome any information on these families.

★★★★★★★★★★★★★★★★★★★★★★★★★★★

Many researchers are needed to author sections by state and county of a volume entitled:

Austins in the Federal Census of 1850

Thirty states were admitted to the Union prior to the 1850 Federal Census. If you are interested in helping to compile Austins from this 1850 census, please write to *Austins of America*, 23 Allen Farm Lane, Concord, Massachusetts 01742 for details on this valuable genealogical project.

★★★★★★★★★★★★★★★★★★★★★★★★★★★

QUERIES

26-1. Jeremiah Austin was born 29 November 1792 in Vermont, died 15 December 1879 in Morley, St. Lawrence County, New York. Married Elizabeth Howard (born in New Hampshire) on 28 February 1819. Children and birthyears: Albert 1821, William 1823, Mahalia 1825, Joseph 1827, Minerva 1829, George 1832, John 1835, Pauline 1838, James 1840, Mary 1842, Samuel 1844. Need ancestry of Jeremiah.

26-2. Freeman Austin was born on 25 March 1770 (in Rhode Island according to 1850 Illinois census). From R.I. to New York 1784. Married Catherine Von Wagenen 18 April 1799. To Delaware, Seneca, and Niagara Counties (all N.Y.), then to LaSalle County, Illinois. At least four of his thirteen children were born in Delaware County, six in Seneca County. Freeman died 24 April 1856 LaSalle County. Seek birthplace and ancestry of Freeman.

26-3. Thomas Austin had at least two sons, Freeman and ??. Freeman was born in Massachusetts or Rhode Island 1770, married Catherine Van Wagenen a New Jersey Holland Dutch girl in 1799 state of New York. Freeman, Jr. married Niagara County, New York, Phebe Adair born in Canada. Seek ancestry of both Thomas and Phebe.

26-4. Oren Austin (Orin/Orinn) was born about 1809 in Rhode Island or New York, married Helena De LaMotte, daughter of Andrew DeMotte, in Yates County, New York. Need ancestry of Oren and information on Andrew.

26-5. Grant Lincoln Austin was born in Nebraska in 1853. He was an employee of the National Print Shop in Washington, D.C. He had an older brother Oscar Phelps Austin (who appears prominently in the early 1900's edition of *Who's Who*), and a sister Louella Austin born in Nebraska in 1859 who married Albert A. Post, lived in Rogers, Arkansas in early 1900's. Need parents of Oscar, Grant and Louella.

26-6. Joseph Austin married Jenny Alford 3 June 1800. Her father William Alford, consent, Benjamin Austin, surety *Marriage Register 1753-1852 Amherst County, Virginia*). Joseph came to Macon County, Illinois circa 1830 via Rutherford County, Tennessee, with three sons Benjamin Robert, William Alford, and Joseph. A half-brother of these three, Jesse, also came a little later. Need parents of Joseph.

26-7. William Green Austin was born in 1806 in North Carolina and was in Dickson County, Tennessee in 1820. He married Mary Cathey, had a son John F. Austin born circa 1838 in Dickson County. Would like ancestry of William and any descendants of John.

26-8. John Austin was born circa 1796 in Jacksonville, Alabama. He married Frankie King, born circa 1800 in Alabama. Their children were born in Alabama, the last four in Jackson: William K. ca. 1826, Emily ca. 1828, Eliza ca. 1830, Daniel Wesley 20 May 1832, James Madison ca. 1834, Mary ca. 1836, Delia ca. 1838. Seek ancestry of John Austin.

26-9. James Austin was born in 1838 in New York, died 1869, probably in Wisconsin. He married Mary Elizabeth Wright 1 April 1849. They had at least one child Mattie who married Frank Lemuel Waterman. Need ancestry, complete vitals for James and children.

26-10. Lyman Austin was born in 1824 in Cambridge, Vermont, married Selina Spaulding in Fletcher, Vermont. Sons were Zachary Taylor, Curtis, and Alfred Lyman. Need parents of Lyman.

26-11. Sylvester Atwood Austin was born 19 March 1832 in Michigan, died 4 March 1898 in Jasper County, Michigan, buried Wheatfield Cemetery. Came to Porter County, Indiana, in 1835 with parents. Searching for his brother Joseph P. Austin who also lived in Kankakee River area.

26-12. John Austin, son of John and Tamson (Mead), married Lucy French 5 August 1805, probably in Dorset, Vermont. They had eight children born in Hamburg, Erie County, New York. Seek all information on John and Tamson.

26-12a. Mehitable Austin was born on 14 January 1772, married Eli Grover born 1763 died 2 September 1837, son of Dea. James and Sarah (Wellman). Need ancestry of Mehitable and Sarah.

26-13. Merwin Austin was born on 1 August 1814 married Almira Haywood on 27 October 1851, probably in Rochester, New York. Need the birthplace and parents of Almira.

26-14. Edward H. Austin born in Norton, Mass. on 18 February 1856 died Taunton, Mass. 4 September 1927. He married Cora B. Leonard b. Norton December 1862, died Taunton 20 March 1940. Seek ancestry of Cora.

26-15. Middy Austin born circa 1856 in Quebec Province, Canada, son of Abram and Harriet. He m(1) in 1880 to Alice Ramo of Wilmot, NH, m(2) in 1882 to Mary Minar or Mary Rowe, m(3) Sophronia Laborse. Middy was a farmer, resided at Wilmot & Danbury, NH. Seek ancestry of Middy's wives and parents.

26-16. Benoni Austin married Abigail Lane in Swanzey, NH on 28 November 1805, both residents of Swanzey. They had at least two children: Mary b. 1817, Sylvester b. 1822. Seek ancestry of both Benoni & Abigail.

JEFFERSON C. AUSTIN

The following is based on a 1921 obituary submitted by Linda Austin Finster of Newbury Park, California. The accompanying photograph of Jefferson C. Austin was made available courtesy of Lee Watkins of Sedgwick, Kansas.

Jefferson C. Austin was born in Wisconsin on 28 March 1830. He died at the home of his son Alex near Dunlap, Oklahoma on 21 January 1921. Of sturdy German and English pioneer stock, Jefferson grew to manhood on his father's farm. When 16 years old he moved with his father to Illinois, where he met and a few years later married Miss Evelyn Echols. They settled in Knoxville, Knox County, Illinois. Happiness there, however was short-lived, for a few years later Evelyn died, leaving Jefferson with an infant daughter, the only child of their union. This daughter is still living, now Mrs. Henry Bohard of Dunlap. Jefferson soon after moved to Lewiston in Jefferson County (sic) where he met and later married Miss Katheryn Childress.

The Civil War came on, and in 1862 Jefferson enlisted in an Illinois regiment and served his country until the close of the war. After the war he made his home for a few years in Lewiston, but his pioneer blood called him westward, and in 1871 he moved his family by covered wagon to Macon County, Missouri. Here he lived for eight years, but the west was still calling and again the covered wagons were brought into use as he moved to Greenwood County, Kansas. Jefferson and Katheryn purchased a farm near Madison which became the family home for more than twenty years. Here their younger children grew to manhood and womanhood, and here in September 1902 Katheryn died and was buried in the family burying ground.

Mr. Austin was not satisfied after the death of his wife, and selling his farm to one of his sons, he came to Oklahoma in 1904 with five of his children and filed on land a few miles north of Dunlap, forming the settlement still known as Austin Valley.

Grandfather Austin, as Jefferson was now familiarly called, became an active booster for northwest Oklahoma, and by his influence many of his relatives and friends came to the area. He was an active farmer himself, and encouraged others, both by his words and actions. He was loved by everybody and for years his birthday has been celebrated by his relatives and friends for miles around.

Several years ago, his last daughter married, grandfather Jefferson found himself without a housekeeper and he closed up his home and went to live with his son Alex where he lived the last few years. He was strong and active, and raised his truck and potato patches each summer where he worked with more vigor than most men years younger than himself.

Soon after the first of the year, Grandfather had an attack of gall stones which at his extreme age was very severe. He suffered intensely for several days and the children, of whom there are 17 living, were notified and soon began to arrive. On Tuesday the 18th there were 15 of his children at his bedside. He was conscious and knew them and called each by name. He lingered on until Friday evening when he passed away.

Grandfather was the father of a remarkable family of 22 children, 21 of whom are full brothers and sisters. His oldest child is 64 and his youngest 35 years of age. There are 84 living grandchildren and 76 great-grandchildren.

The body was prepared for burial by Mr. Callaway, and on Sunday a beautiful funeral talk was given by Rev. McClain, after which the body was taken to Fargo and shipped to Madison, Kansas, where it was interred by the side of his loving wife and life companion.

Grandfather Jefferson is survived by two half-brothers, one of whom is Mr. Jerry (Jeremiah) Austin of Harmon, Oklahoma, and two half-sisters living in Missouri. His surviving children are: Mrs. Almira Bohard of Dunlap; Mrs. Pauline Jobson of Mission, Texas; Alison Austin of Woodward; Charles Austin of Doby Springs; Mrs. Amanda Tatman of Hartford, Kansas; Thomas Austin of Dunlap; Alex Austin of Dunlap; William Austin of Dunlap; Nathaniel Austin of Madison, Kansas; Mrs. Emma Weidrich of Doby Springs; Mrs. Rachel Baker of Oklahoma City; Fred Austin of Hamilton, Kansas; Mrs. Evelyn Mahaffey of Burlington, Kansas; Mrs. Wills of Dunlap; Mrs. Belle Blank of Madison, Kansas; Mrs. Lillie Stead of Woodward; John Austin of Madison, Kansas. Three granddaughters with families in Harper County are: Mrs. Ida Lipsic of Buffalo; Mrs. Margaret Simpson of May; Mrs. Katheryn Nixon of Laverne.

AUSTIN IMMIGRANTS FOUND
IN THE 1880 CENSUS OF
MINNESOTA AND WISCONSIN

by Janet Austin Curtis

The following list of Immigrants has been compiled from microfilm of the 1880 Soundex index cards prepared by the U. S. Government for Social Security purposes, which cards were copied from original census records. Errors of interpretation have quite possibly occurred. Check originals to be sure of facts. Bear in mind that Soundex only includes those families with children under ten years of age. Newly married with no children will not be listed, nor families in which all of the children are over ten. This list does not include immigrants from Canada, who will be covered at a later date. Unless otherwise indicated, persons were born in the United States:

August Austin age 33 b. Saxony; wife Maria 38 b. Baden, Charles 4, Frank 3. Res. Cannon Falls, Goodhue County, MN 5-152/37-15.

Gilbert T. Austin age 23 b. Norway; wife Georgie 21 b. Norway, Bertha A. 7/12. Res. Harmony, Fillmore County, MN 4-76/9-23.

John Austin age 27 b. Scotland; wife Edith 25 b. Canada, George 2, Elizabeth 6/12. Res. Dundas, Rice County, MN 13-134/32/27.

John W. Austin age 39 b. England; wife Elizabeth 32, George 15, Joseph 13, Esther 7, William 1. Res. Butternut Valley, Blue Earth County, MN 1-16/8-49.

Langamire Austin age 28 b. Norway; wife Bessie 24 b. Sweden, Ida 5. Res. Excelsior, Hennepin County, MN 7-219/16-47.

Olison Austin age 42 b. Norway; wife Valborg 33 b. Norway, Anna 13, Olena 10, Ernest 8, Inga 6, Aretta 4, Theodore 2. Res. Money Creek, Houston County, MN 7-115/14-11.

Robert Austin age 29 b. Scotland; wife Martha 25, Maggie 2, Babe 5/30, Margaret 60 b. Scotland. Res. Walcott, Rice County, MN 13-143/4-31.

David Austin age 66 b. Wales; wife Mary A. 45 b. England, David 20, Joseph 9, Frank 7, Byron 4, Alice 18. Res. Eldorado, Fond du Lac County, WI 9-36/27-41.

Elizabeth Austin age 70 b. England. Res. Deerfield, Waushara County, WI 31-187/6-8.

Ellen Austin age 40 b. Ireland; Belle 18, Charles 15, Lizzy 13, William 11, Nellie 6, John 3. Res. (town not legible), Dunn County, WI 8-150/23-8.

German Austin age 35 b. Norway; wife Margaret 33, Adoph K. 4, Annie H. 6/12. Res. Lowville, Columbia County, WI 4-28/2-10.

Harry Austin age 27 b. England; Elizabeth 23, Parker 3, Martha Peely 11. Res. Spring Green, Sauk County, WI 26-261/8-10.

Henry Austin age 58 b. England; wife Mary 38 b. England, Elisa 27 b. England, Walter 19, Reuben 15, Alice 13, Edwin 10, Maple 3. Res. Lancaster, Grant County, WI 10-111/27-46.

Holiver Austin age 55 b. Norway; wife Betsy 49 b. Norway, Austin 18, Thomas 16, Lewis 13, Isibelle 11, Betsy 9, Christian 7. Res. Burnside, Trempealeau County, WI 28-62/35-1.

James B. Auston age 37 b. England; wife Minnie 36, James 10, Arthur 8, Albert 6, William 4, Joseph 11/12. Res. Hazel Green, Grant County, WI 10-108/7-46.

Jessie Austin female age 35 b. Scotland; John 13. Res. Racine, Racine County, WI 23-162/3-33.

John Austin age 41 b. England; wife Sarah M. 39, Mary 14, Nellie 12, Amy 10, Wm. H. 5. Res. Arena, Iowa County, WI 12-148/23-50.

John S. Austin age 40 b. England; wife Annie 35, Frank B. 3, Walter J. 2, Hannah 80 b. England. Res. Racine, Racine County, WI 23-166/58-14.

Lisabeth Austen age 69 b. Norway; Grinder 24, Marion 32, A. Olaves 1, Flora 10. Res. Waupaca County, WI 31-178/16-13.

Nelson Austin age 53 b. Norway; wife Gurnell 47 b. Norway, Thomas 20, Edward 18, Ameliaa 14, George 10, Willie 6, Emma 1. Res. Winchester, Winnebago County, WI 32-217/5-38.

Thomas Aston age 27 b. England; wife Mary 32 b. England, James 4, Betsy 2. Res. Milwaukee, WI 18-126/27-47.

William Austin age 50 b. England; wife Mary 47, John 22, Alenda 13, Elnora 10, Luther 12. Res. Cadiz, Green County, WI 11-134/23-37.

William Austin age 30 b. Prussia; wife Elizabeth 30, Carrie May 4, Edwin 1½. Res. Fond du Lac, Fond du Lac County, WI 9-42/3-18.

JOHN AUSTIN HOUSE
by Michael Edward Austin

The following article was based upon notes in the possession of the North Andover Historical Society, copies of which were provided to *Austins of America* courtesy of Mrs. Mary Flinn of the Society. The photograph of the house was taken by the author during a 1981 field trip.

John Austin, S13 in the Samuel line (see page 9), built his home in that part of Andover, Mass. which later became the town of North Andover. Perhaps the oldest existing Austin home in the country, John's home was certainly built sometime before 1743, for on July 5th of that year his father Samuel deeded "to my beloved son [John] all my land and meadow where he now dwells."

In his Will (page 9) John left the property to "the first male heirs of the Body of my Brother Daniel." This turned out to be John Austin S162, who was born in 1764, the same year his uncle John S13 died.

In 1831 John Austin S162, his wife Dorcas (Carlton) and his two sons John Austin, Jr. S162-4 of Methuen and Daniel Austin S162-8 of Haverhill sold the home on 29 acres 120 rods of land to Ezra Clark of Waltham. According to notes by Phila Slade of North Andover, who searched through the registry of deeds, the house title passed in 1880 to Charles O. Hemenway, in 1881 to Eveline H. Clark, in 1884 to George S. Chadwick, in 1888 to Horatio B. Ellis, in 1902 to Gustav A. Yunggebauer, in 1915 to Anthony Rogers, in 1927 to Thomas A. Tattersall, in 1930 to Margaret A. Rogers, and in 1966 to Margaret A. and Anthony Rogers.

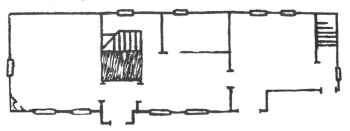

Although much of the interior detail is gone, John Austin's farmhouse remains a cogent reminder of North Andover's early farmsteads. It is still standing today at 307 Clark Street, at the corner of Holt Road. In 1975 Marshall Rogers conducted inspection visits by Steve J. Roper, N. J. Stack, and Frank Demers. Their sketch of the first floor is shown above. Some of their observations:

☐ *West room downstairs has Georgian panelled wainscot, chair rail, corner cupboard in southwest corner. Posts project and cased in flat boards, no flare. Greek mantelpiece. Summer not visible behind lath and plaster. East room downstairs was remodeled in mid-20th century. Marshall Rogers says his father removed summer, was rough-hewn and had no chamfering. [Editor's Note: a 'summer' is a heavy horizontal timber which serves as a support beam for the floor above].*

☐ *Staircase - remodeling both sides of staircase. Lined with mid-Georgian panelling at second floor level, of long and narrow variety (see sketch), was not used as doors, but must have been wall panelling.*

☐ *Second floor East - summer, posts, girts exposed, very rough hewn, no sign of any decorative treatment whatsoever. Posts very strongly flared. Second floor West - remodeled mid-20th century. Greek Rev. mantelpiece. No flared posts were visible.*

☐ *Attic - Purlin roof system on heavy principals, top back purlin acts as ridge stud wall construction, did not notice any discontinuity in roof to indicate two periods of house construction - reached conclusion that house is one build, chimney stack rebuilt. Frame probably intended to be cased, though cast chamber may never have been finished. Probable date 1720-30's.*

☐ *Cellar - under whole house. Chimney stack rests on large brick barrel vault running out from front wall. A peculiar timber at springing of vault projects into East end to carry hearth of fireplace in East end of house not into West.*

WARREN SYLVANUS AUSTIN

by Mark Austin Fountain

The following article is based in part upon an unpublished 1979 manuscript by the author entitled *The History of Our Portion of the Austin Clan*. The manuscript provides colorful details in the lives of some of the Austins of Hollis and Brookline, New Hampshire. Other details are found in the notes circa 1966 of Aleada Helen (Hammond) Austin, wife of Frank A. Austin. These notes are currently in the possession of Ellsworth Allan Austin and his wife Elizabeth Catherine (Jensen) of Brookline, NH.

Warren Sylvanus Austin was the second of five children of Warren Eldridge Austin and Dorothy Ann Bean, and was born in 1844 in Hollis, NH, later moving to Brookline, NH. Like his father, he was a cooper all his life, but being an adventurous sort his life was a little more exciting than that of his father, who stayed around Brookline all his life.

Warren went on several whaling voyages, where coopers are always needed, and are highly valued among the ship's personnel, being on an even rank with the 2nd mate.

A cooper was a well-paying craft even on land. The going price was 1½ cents a shook (all the parts of a barrel or box unassembled). A good cooper could make $2.50 to $3.00 a day, equivalent now to about $50 a day.

In the summer of 1871 Warren was looking for coopering work in New Bedford, Massachusetts, the Whaling Capital where many casks of whale oil were produced every year. It was on August 20th that Warren, always an eager man with the brew, got drunk, possibly with some help along the way. At any rate, when the dawn of August 21st came, he woke up to find himself at sea - shanghaied!

Warren learned he was on the New Bedford three-masted bark *Hercules*, a whaler headed for the Indian Ocean! He was told that as long as he was cooperative he would be all right. The Captain, Warren later recalled, was a very rough individual, and as the Captain was the only law in sight, it behooved Warren to bide his time, which he wisely did. It was a busy time onboard the *Hercules*. He served as a cooper, making the barrels to hold the oil from the dead whales. He often spoke of doughnuts fried in the fat from the whales. Once Warren came close to being killed, when he saw a whale sounding just under the hull of their whale boat. He yelled to the others and jumped. It was lucky for him that he had seen the whale coming, for it broke the boat in half, just where his knees had been!

Time passed, until finally they came to the rich whale-hunting grounds of the Indian Ocean. They came so close to the shore of Australia that Warren jumped ship, and in this way escaped. They tried to capture him, but were unsuccessful, and they were left without their cooper. He got ashore, and came eventually to a sheep farm where he found work and saved money. On this farm with over 1000 sheep, his job was to cart supplies to the shepherds.

He thus worked his way across the Australian continent, finally reaching Sidney where he set sail for America.

Warren had been away for two or three years. He came up to the house where his sister Jennie was living on Canal Street. He had changed somewhat in appearance, for he was wearing a full beard and wore sailor's clothing . . . his own sister didn't even recognize him at first!

That was not the only voyage that Warren went on, but it is the only one of which we have any great deal of knowledge. Warren later settled down, marrying Nellie F. Cleveland of Brookline on 9 December 1880 in Mason, NH. He was 36, she 22, and it was the first marriage for both. They had three children: Frank Allen Austin born 19 November 1881 in Wilton, NH, died 19 February 1956; Rolan Austin born 14 September 1883 in Brookline, NH, died 1 August 1953 buried in Brookline; and Jennie Etta Austin born 17 March 1889 and died 19 July of that same year. Warren died in 1913 and is buried in Brookline.

★★★★★★★★★★★★★★★★★★★★★★★★★★★★★★

Researchers are needed to author sections by state and county of a volume entitled:

Austins in the Federal Census of 1850

Thirty states were admitted to the Union prior to the 1850 Federal Census. If you are interested in helping to compile Austins from this 1850 census, please write to *Austins of America*, 23 Allen Farm Lane, Concord, Massachusetts 01742. Details on this valuable genealogical project will be mailed to volunteer researchers in the near future.

★★★★★★★★★★★★★★★★★★★★★★★★★★★★★★

Austins of America is intended to serve present and future genealogists researching Austin family lines. Readers are encouraged to submit Queries, genealogical & historical articles for publication. Previously published books or pamphlets containing Austin genealogical data are also sought for review.

EDITOR

DR. MICHAEL E. AUSTIN   CONCORD, MASS.

ASSOCIATE EDITORS

PATRICIA BIEBUYCK AUSTIN   CONCORD, MASS.

JANET AUSTIN CURTIS   ALBUQUERQUE, N.M.

CAROL LEIGHTON HULL   SUDBURY, MASS.

Austins of America is published each February and August by The Austin Print, 23 Allen Farm Lane, Concord, Massachusetts 01742. All correspondence, including subscriptions and responses to queries, should be sent to this address. Subscrip tions are included in the membership fee of the Austin Families Association. The annual subscription rate for non-members is $1.75. The membership fee of the Austin Families Association is $3.00, payable directly to the Secretary of the Association, Lorena Austin, R-1 Box 233, Claude, Texas 79019.

WILLIAM AND MILLY AUSTIN
OF ANDERSON COUNTY, TENNESSEE

by Janet Austin Curtis

The following article was submitted in response to Query 26-8 which appeared in the August 1981 issue of *Austins of America*.

William Austin first showed up about fifteen years ago, when the late Bess Machtley, at my suggestion, stopped at the Court House in Anderson County, Tennessee. In the *Index to Court Orders 1801-1809* she found listed, all on page 38, the following Austins: William, John, Hezekiah, Robert, Elizabeth, Zachariah, Daniel, and Nancy.

Unfortunately, the Order Book itself was *not* available in the Court House. The above information, however, implied an estate settlement, and so it has turned out to be.

About 1801, William Austin and his wife Milly were residents of Anderson County. Both died circa 1802. Milly apparently died first, and William was ordered to bring the above children into Court, but before he could do so, William died, and a Hannah and Nathaniel Austin settled his estate. Some of their children were bound out. The children included the John Austin of Query 26-8:

Zachariah Austin born circa 1784 in Virginia, was living in 1850 in Coffee County, Tennessee. He married 26 August 1807 in Grainger County, Tennessee to Martha 'Patsey' Thomson.

Robert Austin born 1785 in Virginia, living in 1850 in Fayette County, Alabama. Married, probably in Grainger County, Elizabeth Webster, daughter of Reuben Webster. When Reuben died they were residents of Marion County, Tennessee.

Elizabeth Austin, probably born circa 1786 or before.

Hezekiah Austin born 17 February 1787, died after 1844 probably in DeKalb County, Alabama. He married Nancy Jane Blevins, born in 1795 and living in 1860. The Stephen Blevins Austin discussed below at White's Chapel was the son of Hezekiah and Nancy.

John Austin born 26 October 1789 in Virginia, as was learned by Charles Edwin Austin from a microfilm of *Anderson County Tennessee Court Orders 1802-1815*. John died in April 1850 aged 59, a resident of Dade County, Georgia. The 1850 Census of that County, District 21, was taken in October 1850 and included John's family: Mary Austin 53 born in Tennessee, and children William 24, Daniel 18, Delila 12, and Mary 8, all born in Alabama. Note that Mary is John's second wife, not the Franky King mentioned in Query 26-8. Probably the daughter Mary is by this second wife. His daughter Emily born circa 1824/5 by his first marriage, married 18 September 1839 in DeKalb County, Alabama, to William J. Bean. She married second circa 1844 to John R. Vance, and they were living in 1850 in Carroll County, Arkansas.

Daniel Austin born 16 October 1793 in Kentucky, died after 1873 in Vernon County, Missouri. He married on 17 November 1817 to Nancy Edwards in Anderson County.

Nancy Austin is perhaps the Ann Austin who married 27 December 1808 in Roane Co., Tenn., to Robert White.

In addition to the above children, William and Milly apparently had an older son Joseph born circa 1780 and a daughter Phoebe born circa 1795 who perhaps died between 1840 and 1850 who was listed in the 1840 Census of Fayette County, Alabama, as Phoebe Osten. She was not found in the 1850 Census, however her brother(?) Robert Austin was there in both the 1840 & 1850 Census.

At White's Chapel, near Grapevine, Texas, there is a marker which reads:

FOUNDED BY SETTLERS WHO CAME BY WAGON TRAIN FROM DADE COUNTY, GA. 1871. EARLY SERVICES WERE IN HOME OF S. B. AUSTIN, THE LEADER. AUSTIN GAVE LAND FOR A CEMETERY AND CHURCH. A LOG MEETING HOUSE WAS BUILT AND IN USE IN FEB. 1872. THIS WAS THE FIRST METHODIST CHURCH IN THIS VICINITY. CIRCUIT RIDER PREACHERS DREW CROWDS HERE FROM AS FAR AWAY AS 20 MILES. AT FIRST CALLED "OAK HILL" FOR HOME CHURCH IN GEORGIA, THIS WAS SOON RENAMED FOR A PERMANENT PASTOR, THE REV. MR. WHITE. THE COMMUNITY SCHOOL WAS HELD IN SUCCESSIVE CHURCH BUILDINGS UNTIL 1916. MANY SETTLERS REST IN NEARBY CEMETERY.

The S. B. Austin referred to here is Stephen Blevins Austin, son of Hezekiah and Nancy (see above). The following inscriptions were copied by the author and by Mark A. Curtis in 1976 from the cemetery mentioned, where asterisks indicate broken stones:

S. B. Austin	4 Oct 1817 - 26 Mar 1894
Susan C. Ashburn*	2 Jul 1859 - 25 Jul 1886
Mrs. M. A. Austin	15 Nov 1819 - 8 Jun 1899
Sarah Naoma, d. H.H. & S.E. Austin	1 Nov 1889 - 10 Oct 1894
Ann E., wife J. B. Austin	5 Oct 1855 - 26 Aug 1880
John Brady Austin	1852 - 1933
Sarah Ellen Austin	1872 - 1952
Ruth, wife J. B. Austin*	25 Nov 1864 - 15 Sep 1886
John Brady Austin, Jr.	27 Mar 1901 - 21 Nov 1954
William Jefferson Austin	29 Sep 1873 - 1 Dec 1954
Sallie Bracken, wife W.J. Austin	6 Feb 1877 - 3 Sep 1964
Jennie Lou Austin	14 Oct 1888 - (no death date)
Charley Albert Austin	29 Aug 1886 - 24 Nov 1963
Permelia Austin	28 Feb 1879 - 2 Apr 1879
Nancy (Austin?)	9 Aug 1875 - 22 Mar 1876
Hezekiah H. Austin	6 Aug 1843 - 15 Nov 1913
Sarah Frances Austin	28 Dec 1853 - 23 Jan 1942
Blev. Austin	24 Oct 1869 - 12 Sep 1932
Mattie Lue Austin	26 Jul 1907
J. S. Austin	29 Aug 1832 - 5 Mar 1908
Elizabeth, wife of J. S. Austin	25 May 1832 - 7 Jul 1904
J. F., son of J. S. & E. Austin*	1852 - 13 Feb 1884
William Rhodes Austin	17 Dec 1846 - 20 Oct 1930
Elizabeth Tatum, wife W. R. Austin	1 Dec 1842 - 9 Mar 1911
S. Shelton, son W.R. & E.T. Austin	25 Oct 1875 - 7 Jan 1879
M. A. Austin, son J. S. & E.	(no dates)
M. M. Austin	17 Sep 1849 - 12 Jan 1931
Margaret, wife M. M. Austin	26 Nov 1846 - 10 Feb 1916

AUSTINS IN THE OLD BURYING GROUND
IN NORTH ANDOVER, MASSACHUSETTS

by Patricia Biebuyck Austin

Searching for ancestors can sometimes be exciting, even in cemeteries. Last summer our children lead my husband and me through dozens of cemeteries in search of their ancestor Thomas Austin (S2 in the Samuel Austin line, see page 8). The children were perhaps motivated less by genealogical interest than by money, as a bounty had been offered for each Austin gravestone found! Since Thomas had moved circa 1710 across the Merrimack River into Haverhill, settling in that part of the town later to become Methuen and later still the City of Lawrence, we painstakingly searched the oldest of those towns' cemeteries without success, although we did find and record the monuments of a number of other Austins. Recalling that Thomas had drowned coming back from 'Meeting on the Sabbath Day' in Andover (now North Andover), we located the oldest cemetery in the North Parish where he and his brother Samuel S1 had first settled.

The Old Burying Ground on Academy Road in North Andover was the first cemetery in Andover. From Ref. 1 we learn that men from Newbury and Ipswich began a settlement at Andover as early as 1641 or 1642, organizing a church in 1645. Their first Meeting House probably stood within the limits of the Old Burying Ground (Ref. 2). This cemetery served the North Parish of Andover until 1817, when the town voted to purchase an acre and a quarter of land from Jonathan Stevens for a new burying ground, also located on Academy Road, but closer to the present-day church. In his introduction to Ref. 3, Walter Muir Whitehill attempts to explain why few early settlers are found commemorated by gravestones in the old burying ground:

"Although it has always been believed that the first settlers of the town were buried here, it is to be noted that the inscriptions are almost entirely of the eighteenth and early nineteenth centuries. Apparently stone carvers were not generally employed in Andover in the first half century of the town's existence. The inscription commemorating John Stevens, who died on 11 April 1662, is the only one whose date goes back to the second decade of the settlement of Andover, and it is without contemporary companions. No stone commemorates the Reverend Francis Dane, who died on 17 February 1697 after 48 years service to the church, nor is there any indication of the resting place of Anne Bradstreet, the first American poetess . . . Dr. Marius Barbeau of the National Museum of Canada, while staying with me in the spring of 1952, at once observed that the John Stevens stone so closely

resembled others of the first third of the eighteenth century that it seemed likely to have been erected many decades after the death of the man it commemorates, and this suggestion was confirmed by John Howard Benson of Newport, Rhode Island, whose skill in carving stone inscriptions gives unique weight to his views upon the technique of the craft. When the John Stevens stone is recognized as of the eighteenth century rather than 1662, one need no longer speculate about the absence of stones for seventeenth century founders and patriarchs."

Not yet having read and been discouraged by the article just quoted, we optimistically and carefully went through the cemetery, overlooking no stone in search of Austins and their relatives, naively hoping to stumble upon the early graves of the brothers Samuel and Thomas Austin. Thomas S2 drowned in 1712, too early perhaps for other than a wooden marker. Even Samuel S1, who died decades later in 1753 had no stone monument to mark his final resting place. We were all elated, however, to discover the gravestones of two of Samuel's sons (see photographs and transcriptions on next page) - those of Samuel Austin S12 and John Austin S13, both of whom died in 1764.

Right across the road from the burying ground, a Dr. Thomas Kittredge built his house in 1784. He had two granddaughters, Miss Mary Hodges Kittredge and Miss Sarah Kittredge, who never married. They took an interest in the Old Burying Ground, and in the 1860's raised money to build the stone wall which now encloses it, and for many years they saw to its mowing. According to Reference 2, "Mowing once a year by scythe was considered sufficient, with an occasional pulling of ivy."

In October 1869, the Misses Kittredge and Messrs. Isaac Osgood and Frank Appleton copied down the inscriptions in the Old Burying Ground, which are available in Ref. 3. Their indexed compilation included only the same two Austin gravestones we ourselves had found, so it appears no Austin graves were 'lost' in the intervening 112 years. For subsequent Austin generations, one must search further down Academy Road at the second Burying Ground - a good excuse for yet another field trip!

REFERENCES

1. Sarah Loring Bailey, *Historical Sketches of Andover, Massachusetts*, Houghton, Mifflin and Company, Boston 1880.

2. Kate Hastings Stevens, "The Old Burying Ground on Academy Road, North Andover," article published in Vol. XLI, pp. 13-15 of *Old Time New England, the Bulletin of the Society for the Preservation of New England Antiquities*, 1950.

3. Mary Kittredge, Sarah Kittredge, Isaac Osgood and Frank Appleton, *Inscriptions on Tomb-Stones in the Old Burying Ground at North Andover, Massachusetts*. Original manuscript made in October 1869, published in *The Essex Institute Historical Collections*, Vol. LXXXIX pp. 57ff, Salem, Mass. 1953.

Here lyes Buried

the Body of M.^r

SAMUEL AUSTIN

Who departed this life

Decem^r y^e 3I^{ft} 1765 in y^e

7I^{ft} Year of His Age

Here lyes Buried

the Body of

Mr JOHN AUSTEN

Who departed this life

March y^e 13th 1764 in y^e

68th Year of His Age

Slate gravestones of the brothers
Samuel Austin and John Austin can still be seen in the
Old Burying Ground in North Andover, Massachusetts. They were sons of
Samuel Austin S1 of the Samuel Austin of Boston line. The death year on Samuel's stone is not
correct, as the town and probate court records indicate he died in 1764, and his wife took an inventory of his estate
in May 1765. John Austin's original house, built circa 1720-30, still stands as a private residence today (see page 29).

THE DESCENDANTS OF
JOHN AND CHARITY KENDRICK AUSTIN
OF FREDERICK COUNTY, MARYLAND

by Jeane Austin King Galau

J. JOHN[1] AUSTIN was born circa 1739, place of birth and parents unknown at this writing. He wrote his will in Montgomery County, Maryland in 1818, which was probated 12 November 1823.

John married circa 1761/62, apparently in Frederick County, Maryland, as his first child was born there in 1763. His wife was Charity, born circa 1732 by the 1776 census. The record of this marriage cannot be found, however all evidence points to the fact that she was Charity Kendrick, the daughter of Thomas and Ann Kendrick of Frederick County. It is also believed that Charity was first married to John's brother, Thomas Austin. A birth is recorded in Prince George's Parish, Frederick County, a son born to Thomas and Charity Austin in 1760. This son Thomas is found living with John and Charity in the 1776 census, along with Alexander and Kesiah, believed to be children of Thomas and Charity. In the same census, a Mary Austin age 80, is also found in John's household, and no doubt is the mother of our John Austin. They are shown living in the Lower Potomack Hundred, land which was taken from Frederick County in 1776 and made into Montgomery County.

John and Charity were members of Prince George's Parish (Protestant Episcopal Church), then Frederick County, now Montgomery County. This parish covered a very large area, all records being kept in the same book. Today our Austin records are found recorded at St. Paul's Episcopal Church in Washington, D.C. and at Christ Church, Rockville, Maryland. We cannot know with any certainty just to which of these two churches John and Charity belonged. Although the listing of graves in Montgomery County is fairly complete, the burial place of John and Charity has not been located. Neither can the grave be found for John's mother. However, time and the farmer's plow have destroyed many of these old sand stones.

In 1778 John Auston (sic) took the 'Oath of Fidelity and Support' during the revolution before the Worshipfull Samuel W. Magruder. No other records can be found of John's contribution to the rebellion.

John's plantation, as it was called in those days, consisted of 246 acres which was named 'Conclusion.' We have been unable to pinpoint this land exactly, but it appears it was in the area of the present day Bethesda, Maryland.

The children of John and Charity were born in Frederick County (now Montgomery County), Maryland.

CHILDREN:
J1. ZACHARIAH, *b. 20 January 1763, d. between 1830-34*
J2. JAMES, *b. 1765, married Ann (Nancy) Howard.*
J3. AMELIA, *b. circa 1768 (from census)*
J4. JOHN KENDRICK, *b. 2 May 1770, d. 14 March 1857*
J5. HEZEKIAH, *b. circa 1772*
J6. AMOS, *b. 1775*
J7. JONAS, *b. between 1777 and 1779*
J8. [son], *b. after 1774 (under 16 in 1800)*
J9. [son], *b. after 1774 (under 16 in 1800)*

SECOND GENERATION

J1. ZACHARIAH[2] AUSTIN (*John*[1]) was born 20 January 1763 in Prince George's Parish, Frederick County. He was married to Margaret (Offutt) Odle of Frederick County. Margaret, the daughter of William Offutt 3rd and Elizabeth Magruder, was born on 22 July 1760 in Frederick County. She died 1820-24 in Ohio County, Kentucky. Zachariah died 1830-34 in Ohio County, Kentucky. Their children were born in Montgomery County.

CHILDREN:
J11. BARUCH, *b. 1792*
J12. BROOKS, *b. 1794*
J13. WILLIAM, *b. 1796*
J14. ZACHARIAH OFFUTT, *b. 30 November 1797, d. before 1855*
J15. ENOCH, *b. 18 November 1799, d. circa 1820*
J16. SAMUEL, *b. 18 November 1801, d. 1 December 1884*
J17. JOHN MAGRUDER, *b. 14 December 1803, d. 1 July 1852*

Zachariah, Enoch, Samuel, and John were baptized at Rock Creek Chapel, Prince George's Parish.

J4. JOHN KENDRICK[2] AUSTIN (*John*[1]) the son of John and Charity Austin, was born in Frederick County 2 May 1770, and died in Ohio County, Kentucky, 14 March 1857. He was married on 13 February 1799 by Rev. Thomas Reed of Rock Creek Chapel to Cassandra Odle, who was born 29 February 1780 in Montgomery County, and died 17 January 1832 in Ohio County, the daughter of Baruch Odle and Margaret Offutt.

John and Cassandra's first eight children were baptized at Rock Creek Chapel where they were married. It is believed John and his family attended the Church in Rockville.

It is thought that John and his family removed from Montgomery County, Maryland, to Ohio County circa 1814, and the Church records seem to bear this out, as their ninth son William was born 26 November 1814, and he is not listed in the Church Registry.

Some feel that the family came via the Cumberland Gap driving oxen, which was the land route usually taken from Maryland. Along with John and Cassandra and their eight children, was John's brother Zachariah and his family, who also settled in Ohio County, and another brother Hezekiah with his family, who first stopped in Ohio County before going on into Christian County, Kentucky.

Indeed these must have been hardy men, to pull up roots, all with large families, and venture into the then-wild country of Kentucky. John would have been about 44 at the time. Without checking deeds, it is not known just where in Ohio County that John settled, but when his will was made in 1855, he mentions a tract of 300 acres he then lives on. On the 1840 census he owned four slaves.

I feel that John lived in the vicinity of south Beaver Dam, as he is buried in an Old Austin Cemetery, along with his wife Cassandra and several of his children, just outside of Beaver Dam, on the old Taylor Mines Road. I visited this cemetery in the summer of 1977 and found it badly overgrown. Both John's and Cassandra's stones were broken and hers was buried about four inches deep, and was only found with the help of a tire iron. We dug up several other stones, and feel many more lay just beneath the surface, and plan to return this year and dig some more, looking for Zachariah Austin and his wife Margaret (Offutt) Odle. A good project for the descendants of John, and there are hundreds of us, would be to restore this very old cemetery. Cassandra was buried there in 1832.

After the death of Cassandra, John married Polly Redman on 9 October 1832, and on 25 October 1837 he married for the third time to Polly's sister, Anna Redman. There were no children from either of these marriages. The first eight children of John and Cassandra were born in Montgomery County, the last five in Ohio County.

CHILDREN: J41. BARUCH ODLE, *b. 17 November 1799, d. 10 April 1800*

J42. HELEN, *b. 26 Feb. 1801, d. 29 August 1844*

J43. JOHN, *b. 24 August 1802, d. young*

J44. ROBERT, *b. 19 July 1804, d. 18 January 1866*

J45. THOMAS ODLE, *b. 6 August 1806, d. 21 February 1875*

J46. ELIZABETH, *b. 27 November 1807*

J47. KITTY ANN, *b. 23 September 1809, d. 17 November 1872*

J48. MARGARET, *b. 28 Mar. 1812, d. 23 Oct. 1873*

J49. WILLIAM, *b. 26 Nov. 1814, d. 8 June 1883*

J4A. ANDREW JACKSON, *b. 7 March 1816, d. 26 June 1886*

J4B. HENRY, *b. circa 1818*

J4C. ZACHARIAH, *b. 18 October 1819, d. 10 March 1862*

J4D. GEORGE W., *b. circa 1823, Will dated 5 January 1867*

J5. HEZEKIAH[2] AUSTIN (*John*[1]) was born circa 1772 in Frederick County, Maryland. He was married in Rock Creek Chapel, Prince George's Parish, Montgomery County on 15 December 1796 to Elizabeth Odle. Elizabeth, the daughter of Baruch and Margaret (Offutt) Odle. Elizabeth died in Kentucky. Hezekiah also died in Kentucky, probably in Christian County. Their children were born in Montgomery County, Maryland.

CHILDREN: J51. ELIZA, *d. circa 1839*

J52. MARY ANN

J53. MARGARET, *b. 17 November 1799*

J54. JANE

J55. SARAH ODLE, *b. 25 December 1802*

J56. BARUCH ODLE, *b. 27 April 1807*

THIRD GENERATION

[continued on page 40]

The information in the above article was abstracted from a 1978 manuscript by the author entitled: *The Austin Family of Montgomery County, Maryland, and Ohio County, Kentucky, and Related Lines*. The author would like to express her appreciation to Mrs. Martha Pate Heavrin of Grand Prairie, Texas, who died in June of 1979, and to Mr. Arthur Clemet Austin of New York City, who descends from Zachariah Austin J1, for their generosity in sharing their genealogical material.

EDITOR'S NOTE: Volume 1 of the three-volume manuscript deals principally with the John Kendrick Austin lines. It contains a wealth of references, detailed copies of church records, deeds, wills, probate records, etc. Unfortunately this superbly-documented volume is not available for sale. However, copies have been placed in the following libraries:

Austins of America Library, Concord, Mass.
Kentucky Historical Society, Frankfort, Kentucky
W. Central Kentucky Fam. Research Assoc., Owensboro
Butler County Genealogy Society, Morgantown, KY
Wisconsin Historical Society, Madison, Wisconsin
Morman Library, Salt Lake City, Utah

Some additional Prince George's Parish Records:

Violinda Austin, dau. Thos. & Martha	b. 19 Jan. 1753
Thos. Auston, son Thos. & Charity	b. 30 Sep. 1760
Charity Auston, dau. Jas. & Sarah	b. 7 Jun. 1761
James Austin, son James & Nancy	b. 10 Feb. 1792
Warren Burgess Austin, son Thos. & Eliz.	b. 7 Mar. 1800
Cassandra West Austin, dau. James & Ann	b. 20 Feb. 1802

These records are on file at St. Paul's Episcopal Church, Washington, D.C., Montgomery County Library, Rockville, Maryland, the Hall of Records, Annapolis, and Christ Church, Rockville, Maryland. —*J.A.K.G.*

QUERIES

36-1. **Thomas Austin** of Stamford and Fairfield, Conn. sold land in 1708 in Bedford, Westchester County, New York, to John Copp of Norwalk, Conn. His daughter Abigail marrried Samuel Canfield of Norwalk. She died 11 June 1710 in Norwalk. Need ancestry, wife, and other children of Thomas.

36-2. **Lydia Astens** of Dracut, Mass. married 26 December 1789 Jeremiah Stevens, probably born Methuen, Mass. 12 June 1755 son of Benjamin and Rebecca (Hunt). Resided Methuen and later Maine. Need deaths of both Jeremiah and Lydia, and ancestry of Lydia.

36-3. **Steven Austin** married Mary Briggs, daughter of George and Lydia (Warren) Briggs. Mary was born about 1785 in N.Y. She probably married Steven between 1806 and 1814, in Sherburne?, Chenango County, N.Y. They lived in Harbor Creek, Erie County, Penn. Steven died between 1830 and 1840, while Mary died between 1860 and 1870 in West Springfield, Erie County, Penn. They had daughter Huldah (Diadama) Austin who married Rila (Riley) Potter of West Springfield. Was Steven the son of Gad and Susanna (Callender) Austin of Sheffield, Berkshire County, Mass.? Did Steven marry first Betty Clark? Did Steven have son Nathaniel of Harbor Creek?

36-4. **Joan Austin** was the second wife of Gideon Rathbone, who was born 1736 and died 1810, the son of John and Patience of Exeter, RI. Need exact dates and ancestry of Joan.

36-5. **Arvilla M. Austin** was born 2 May 1823 in Berkshire, Vermont, the daughter of Oliver and Milla (Larabee) Austin (see page 16). She married —— Andrus, died 8 June 1908, and is buried in Berkshire. Need marriage date and given name of husband.

36-6. **Barbara Austin** born 3 June 1729 married 29 September 1752 to Daniel Butler who was born 20 March 1735. They had son Allen born Monson, Mass. 14 May 1770. Also had Samuel, William, Benjamin, Nathaniel, Joseph, Daniel, Anna, and Hannah. Need parents and residence before 1770 of Barbara.

36-7. **Jeremiah Austin** born 29 November 1792 in Vermont, died 15 December 1879 in Morley, St. Lawrence County, New York. Married Elizabeth Howard (born in New Hampshire) on 28 February 1819. Children and birthyears: Albert 1821, William 1823, Mahalia 1825, Joseph 1827, Minerva 1829, George 1832, John 1835, Pauline 1838, James 1840, Mary 1842, Samuel 1844. Need ancestry of Jeremiah.

36-8. **Isaac S. Austin** was born 1805, probably in Vermont. Married Irma or Louisa (——). Removed to N.Y. where Philtus was born and removed to Blissfield, Lenawee County, Michigan, in late 1830's or early 1840's. Seek ancestry of Isaac.

36-9. **Bletcher Austin** or Bledsoe Austin was born in 1807 in Virginia, married 4 December 1828 in Grayson County, Virginia, to Nancy Moore, daughter of Isaac and Sally. The family had nine children in the 1850 census. Nancy died 9 March 1853 in Grayson County. Seek ancestry of Bletcher or Bledsoe Austin.

36-10. **Austin Sisters** married Charles Roberts of South China, Kennebec County, Maine. Circa 1830 Charles had three children by (——) Austin: George, Ellen, and Emma. When his first wife died, Charles married her sister (——) Austin and by whom he had two other children: Minnie, and Charles born 1856. Seek names and ancestry of the Austin sisters.

36-11. **Truman Austin** born 1787 in Mancester, Vermont, the son of John and Tamson (Mead), married first Hannah Williams 26 November 1809 at Danby, Vermont. Had nine children. Seek information on ancestors and descendants of Truman and Hannah.

36-12. **Susan Austin** married Andrew Foshay. Their daughter? Susan Foshay born 1835 in New York City, married John Joseph Knox, a carpenter and joiner born in Glasgow, Scotland (he immigrated via Ireland). Their orphaned daughter Margaret (Mae) B. Knox born 18 February 1869/73 N.Y.C., shipped to Illinois in 1888/89 as a teenager. Seek information on Susan and Andrew's children, and on Susan and John's marriage.

36-13. **William Austin** married 23 August 1771 in Barkhamsted, Conn. to Sarah Fish, born in Voluntown, Conn., possibly the daughter of Samuel and Ruth. Seek parents of Sarah.

36-14. **Roderick Ransom Austin** born 18 February 1797 in New York, resided Muskingum County, Ohio; Pontiac, Illinois in 1876; Fairfield, Nebraska in 1878. Roderick married Nancy Wear/Weir who died in 1879. He died ca. 1880, and they are both buried in a country cemetery near Fairfield, Clay County, Nebraska. Need parents and ancestry of Roderick and Nancy.

36-15. **William Austin** died 1834 in Clay, Michigan. He had son William who resided in Ohio, Indiana, and Wisconsin. Need wife and children of William, Sr.

36-16. **James Austin** born 6 February 1776 at Suffield, Conn. son of Seth and Mary (Seymour). Need all information on his wife, children, residences, death.

PRUIT ALIAS AUSTIN

by Janet Austin Curtis

J. JOSEPH AUSTIN was probably born circa 1730-35 in what is now Pittsylvania County, Virginia, and died circa 1810 in that same county. He married first circa 1760 perhaps a Terry, this surmise is based on the fact that he named a son Champness. She apparently died right after the birth of son David in 1775-76. Joseph married second on 26 November 1777 in Pittsylvania County to Welthy Prewett, Wm. Goggin was surety. Welthy died after 1818 in Pittsylvania County, when she was last taxed on her personal property. She is also listed in the 1820 census for that county. Children by first wife:

J1. JOHN AUSTIN, *b. 1760-65, d. 1827 Union District, S.C. m. 11 September 1788 Polly (Molly) Bennett in Pittsylvania County. He was a Revolutionary War soldier.*

J2. WILLIAM AUSTIN, *b. before 1766 (over 21 in 1787 Tax Roll) died prior to 1830 Census in Pittsylvania County. He m. 24 August 1809 Mary Smith Hankins, daughter of William and Elizabeth Hankins of Pittsylvania County.*

J3. CHAMPNESS AUSTIN, *b. 1769, died between 1850 and 1860 in Rockingham County, N.C. He married first 27 July 1796 in Pittsylvania County to widow Aincy Morton Dear, daughter of John Morton. He married second 31 October 1826 in Pittsylvania County to Elizabeth 'Betsy' Gover, who was b. 1796.*

J4. STEPHEN AUSTIN, *b. 1769-71, d. after 1850 probably in Rutherford County, Tennessee. He m. 23 April 1800 Rebecca Hankins, daughter of Wm. & Elizabeth Hankins, who was b. Pittsylvania County 1780 and was living in 1850.*

J5. DAVID AUSTIN, *b. 1775-76, died after 1850 probably in Drew County, Arkansas. He m. 8 January 1797 in Pittsylvania County to Elizabeth Oliver, b. 1778, living in 1850.*

The above children are all Joseph's children by his first wife, and probably his only children by her, for in John Austin's Revolutionary War pension application he states that he is the eldest of *five* brothers, and makes no mention of any sisters.

Welthy Prewett (Pruit) had at least two children when she married Joseph Austin:

P1. ARCHIBALD PRUIT, *b. 1767, d. 1866 Tunnel Hill, Georgia. He m. 22 February 1790 in Pittsylvania County to Rebecca Blankenship, Charles Kendrick surety. He was known as Archibald Pruit Austin on Tax Rolls and in deeds. He left Pittsylvania County in the fall of 1795 and by 1800 paid one tithe in Capt. McDonald's Company, Jefferson County, Tennessee (East Tennessee Society Publication 1953-6, p.157).*

P2. FRANCES 'FANNY' PRUIT, *m. first on 3 October 1777 Edward Covington and signed her own consent. Knorr in Pittsylvania Marriages gives James Austin as the surety, however in looking at the microfilm of the original it is written as Jas. or Jos. and I believe that Joseph Austin was surety for*

this marriage just a few weeks before he married her mother, Welthy. Frances m. second as Frances Covington on 7 October 1817 to Obediah Minter in Pittsylvania County, with William Austin as the surety.

Children by second wife, *perhaps*:

J6. LUCY AUSTIN, *married Thomas Kendrick. They were in Rutherford County, Tennessee by 1810 and he died there in 1833. No marriage record per se has been found, either under the Pruit or Austin name, but deeds settling the estates of Joseph and Welthy name Lucy, wife of Thomas Kendrick.*

J7. MARY AUSTIN, *m. 12 January 1796 to William Hankins, Jr. in Pittsylvania County, son of William and Elizabeth Hankins. David Austin surety.*

J8. PATSY AUSTIN, *m. 21 September 1801 to Abraham Johns in Pittsylvania County, surety Joseph Johns.*

These three sets of children lead to some confusion, and this compiler believes at this time (1982) that these are all the children of Joseph Austin, but proof is not likely to crop up. A diligent effort was made to find a widow Welthy Pruit, but none was forthcoming, that is not to say that it cannot be found, but that to date it has not.

In May 1755 John Austin, Sr. and John Austin, Jr., father and brother of Joseph Austin, witnessed the will of Daniel Pruit of Halifax County, Virginia. Among the heirs was a daughter Welthy Pruit (Will Book O, pages 71-72). This data shows that the Austin and Pruit families had close ties, and it also provides us with a Welthy Pruit of about the right age to have married in 1777 Joseph Austin and to have had at least two children prior to that time. There is no proof at this time that the Welthy Pruit who married Joseph Austin is indeed the daughter of Daniel Pruit, but it seems quite likely. If this is the case, we have a Welthy Pruit, unmarried with two children fathered by someone, and this compiler believes that Joseph Austin was the man. To lend support to this contention is the fact that in the settlement of Joseph Austin's estate there was no differentiation between the three sets of children. In a lawsuit in Pittsylvania County in 1813 to settle the estate of Joseph Austin, it states John Austin, Archibald Austin, David Austin, and Lucy Austin Kendrick and husband Thomas were not then residents of the Commonwealth of Virginia.

It will be noted that Archibald is referred to as Archibald Austin at this time and yet when he was married in 1790 his marriage record is recorded under the name Pruit. In 1793 Archibald Pruit Austin purchased property in Pittsylvania County from John Alsop (Deed Book 9, page 372) and in September 1795 he sold this same property as Archibald Pruit Austin to John Carter (Deed Book 10, page 225).

All of this proves nothing, but it does indicate that the man Archibald P. or Pruit Austin regarded himself as an Austin, perhaps because he had grown up in Joseph Austin's household. However, Joseph's eldest son made a differentiation when he stated in his Pension application

that he was the eldest of five brothers. Since he was perhaps sixteen when his father married Welthy Prewett (Pruit) he may have had some animosity, and this point of view could be substantiated by the fact that he left home and saw service in the Revolutionary War and when he came back was not around many years before he married and went to South Carolina.

Interestingly, Maud Carter Clement in her *History of Pittsylvania County, Virginia* does not mention the Austin family, and yet they were in the area at an early date and are found successively in Brunswick, Lunenburg, Halifax, and Pittsylvania County Court records. John Austin, father of Joseph, held around two thousand acres of land which is hardly to be sneezed at, and he left each son about 400 acres in his will probated in 1760 in Lunenburg County, Virginia. By 1765 all the sons except Joseph had left and gone to other Colonies. Joseph remained in Pittsylvania and had a sizeable family, and while many of these migrated, there are still numerous Austins in the Pittsylvania County area.

For further information on this family, see "Southside Virginia Austins" by Janet A. Curtis in *The Virginia Genealogist*, December 1961, Edited by John Frederick Dorman. The article above corrects some of the data published in the 1961 article. – J.A.C.

★★★★★★★★★★★★★★★★★★★★★★★★★★★★★★

Austins of America is intended to serve present and future genealogists researching Austin family lines. Readers are encouraged to submit Queries, genealogical and historical articles for publication. Previously published books, pamphlets or articles containing Austin genealogical data are also sought for reprinting or review.

EDITOR

DR. MICHAEL E. AUSTIN   CONCORD, MASS.

ASSOCIATE EDITORS

PATRICIA BIEBUYCK AUSTIN   CONCORD, MASS.

JANET AUSTIN CURTIS   ALBUQUERQUE, N.M.

CAROL LEIGHTON HULL   SUDBURY, MASS.

Austins of America is published each February and August by The Austin Print, 23 Allen Farm Lane, Concord, Massachusetts 01742. Subscriptions are $2.00 per year postpaid. All correspondence, including subscriptions and responses to queries, should be sent so the above address. Subscriptions are also included in the $5 membership fee of the Austin Families Association, payable to the Secretary, Lorena Austin, R-1 Box 233, Claude, Texas 79019.

★★★★★★★★★★★★★★★★★★★★★★★★★★★★★★

QUERIES

38-1. Uriah Austin, R227 in the Richard Austin of Charlestown line (pg. 29 in Edith Austin Moore's book) d. 28 December 1799, in Suffield, Connecticut. Need his burial place, occupation or Service Record; also need his wife Abigail Case's ancestry.

38-2. Uriah Austin, R227-4 in Richard Austin of Charlestown line (pg. 68 in E.A.M. book), d. 1 March 1820 at Suffield, Conn. Need his burial place, occupation or Service Record; need information on his second wife Rachel Hale. We are searching line of his grandson, blacksmith R227-414 Mark Anthony Austin, who settled in Logan County, and later in Union County, Ohio.

38-3. John Austin was b. ca. 1817 in Tennessee. In 1837 he was in Jackson County, Illinois; married Lucinda Polk 19 February 1845. Children all b. Illinois: Mary J. ca. 1840, Thomas ca. 1843, Elizabeth 1846, Minerva 1847, Oliver 1848, Henry 1850, Matilda 1852, Mahala 1853, Sarah 1854, George 1855, Jane 1858. John Austin d. 1872, age 55. Seek his birth and ancestry.

38-4. Owen Ed Austin b. ca. 1803 in Pittsylvania Co., Virginia, d. ca. 1850's. He married Telitha or Tabitha Jane Covington in Rutherford County, Tennessee in November 1829. Children: Levinia Margaret, John Covington, James, Mary, Lafayette, Eliza, Tabitha J. Seek missing link between Owen Ed Austin and J4. Stephen Austin of Pittsylvania County (see page 37).

38-5. John Delos Austin b. 1807 in New York, married Anna Maria Yolman (Yoeman?), b. 1813, also in New York. Removed to Oakland County, Michigan, where son Charles was b. 1844 and son Abner Delos was b. 1846. John & Anna both d. 1851 in Detroit. Need their ancestry.

38-6. Robert Austin was in Calaveros County, California in 1850. Seeking his descendants, and those of: James Aston whose wife Ellen d. 26 October 1853, age 23, buried Mission Dolores, CA. Also, Hiram Austin whose brother William went to Gold Rush circa 1849.

38-7. George Austin b. Port Hope, Canada in 1855, went to El Reno, Oklahoma, was the son of Hiram Austin. Hiram was b. 1823 in Ferrisburg, Vermont, and d. in 1896 in Wichita, Kansas. He was first child of Nicholas Austin who had seven other children all b. Canada. Seek the descendants of George Austin.

38-8. Henry Austin came from Virginia and settled in Pendleton or Harrison County, Kentucky. The Falmouth, Kentucky, library has an incomplete list of his children: James, Richard, Clay and Mary. I could not find his wife's name. Henry fought in the Civil War. I have the James Austin line, seek Henry's ancestry, wife and children.

ALFRED AUSTIN OF MEIGS COUNTY, OHIO
AND MASON COUNTY, WEST VIRGINIA

by Marjorie Austin Smith

C1. ALFRED ANDREW[2] AUSTIN (*Caleb*[1]) was the son of Caleb and Lydia (—) Austin. Caleb and Lydia were born in Canada, and moved their family to Meigs County, Ohio, from New York when Alfred was twelve years old. Caleb Austin was first enumerated in the 1820 Meigs County census in Salisbury Township. Apparently Caleb and Lydia's other children were Elijah R. Austin, buried in Miles Cemetery at Rutland, Ohio; John P. Austin, Sheriff of Meigs County in 1845, later moving to Athens County, Ohio, then to Minnesota; and Abel J. Austin.

Alfred married first to Sally Grant, by whom he had two sons. He married second in Meigs County, Ohio, on 11 August 1842 to Ann McGee, born in 1813 in Virginia. They moved to West Virginia about 1865. Ann died in December 1865 at West Columbia, West Virginia, where she is buried. Alfred married third in Mason County, West Virginia on 31 July 1871 to Maria Hoit, widow. A legal separation between A. A. and Mariah Austin dated 21 July 1877 is recorded in Mason County. In 1880 Alfred was living with his son, Horton, in Clendenin District, Mason County. No record of Alfred's death exists, but his gravestone in the Austin Cemetery in Mason County states he died 12 May 1882.

CHILDREN: C11. LAFAYETTE MARCUS

C12. ALONZO D., *m. Alice Gaston 4 Sept. 1865*

C13. HORTON ROLANDO, *b. 4 October 1844*

C14. JOHN PARK, *b. 1848, m. Annie Frances Brown 12 Sept. 1869 in Mason Co., d. 1916*

C15. CASSIUS COLUMBUS, *b. 1850, m. Lydia Ellen (Gillespie) Jeffers, sister of Dora Elizabeth, on 5 November 1880 in Gallia County, Ohio, he died 1925*

C16. EVA ANN, *b. 1852, m. Lemuel Shiflet 26 July 1871 in Mason County, she d. 1937*

C17. JANE O., *b. 1855, m.(1) Mr. Werner, m.(2) Harrison Clagg, she died 1931*

C13. HORTON ROLANDO[3] AUSTIN (*Alfred,*[2] *Caleb*[1]) was born 4 October 1844 in Pomeroy, Meigs County, Ohio. He moved with his parents to West Virginia about 1865. He was married in Mason County, West Virginia on 2 May 1875 to Dora Elizabeth Gillespie, sister to Cassius' wife Lydia. Their children are recorded in Mason County:

CHILDREN: C131. ARTHUR PARK, *b. 1876, m. Maude Ann Rhoades 11 Feb. 1900 in Mason Co., d. 1928*

C132. KATHRYN L., *b. 1877, m. George Robert Mayes 12 May 1909 in Mason County, d. 1958*

Horton Rolando Austin

C133. GERTRUDE A., *b. 1879, m. Ernest F. Day, she died 1960*

C134. ARCH, *b. 1882, married Edna Barker 19 December 1909 in Mason County, d. 1932*

C135. ODEN CASSIUS, *b. 1884, m. Helen Hope, he died 1966*

C136. HARRY O., *b. 1886, m.(1) Eva Stockoff, m.(2) Lena (Crow) Pancake, he d. 1961*

C137. ALICIA ALICE, *b. 1888, m. Russell E. Vaughan 19 March 1913 in Mason County, she died 1967*

C138. PEARL M., *b. 1890, m. Gilbert Francis Rogers 14 November 1908 in Mason County, she died 1967*

Horton Austin was a farmer. His obituary in a Mason County newspaper reads in part as follows:

"At his home on last Friday, October 9, 1903, Mr. Horton Austin, who is well known by a legion of the county's citizens, answered his Maker's call, after suffering for some time from a complication of diseases. The deceased was 59 years and four days at the time of his death, and his remains were laid to rest in the family burying ground at Redmond. Mr. Austin was one of Mason County's best citizens, and was a man held in the highest estimation of all who knew him."

Austins of America

THE DESCENDANTS OF
JOHN AND CHARITY KENDRICK AUSTIN
OF FREDERICK COUNTY, MARYLAND

by Jeane Austin King Galau

[Continued from page 35]

THIRD GENERATION

J11. BARUCH[3] AUSTIN (*Zachariah,*[2] *John*[1]) was born 1792 (58 in 1850 Census Ohio County, KY) in Montgomery County, Maryland. He married in Ohio County, Kentucky, on 10 August 1818 to Polly Render, the daughter of George and Sarah (Rowe) Render.

CHILDREN: J111. JAMES F., *b. 21 May 1821, Ohio County, where he m. 9 November 1843 to Corinna Thomas, b. 5 August 1825 dau. of William and Sarah (Jackson) Thomas. Corinna died 4 December 1893, while Rev. Bishop James F. Austin, a prominent Baptist Minister, died 4 October 1883*

J112. ELIZABETH, *m. Solomon Chapman*

J113. MARTHA J., *b. 1829, d. 1852 married John Benton*

J114. JULY ANN, *m. Nathaniel Shultz*

J115. SALLY, *m. James Lee*

J116. JOHN T., *m. Eliza Mason*

J117. QUINT C. S., *m. Elly Ann Lee*

J118. J. BROOKS (ENOOKS), *m. Mary Sanderfur*

J12. BROOKS[3] AUSTIN (*Zachariah,*[2] *John*[1]) was born 1794 (56 in 1850 Census Ohio County, KY). He was married to Rachel Benton.

CHILDREN: J121. URIUS, *m. 1838 Minerva Stevens who was b. 1819 daughter of Daniel*

J122. SARAH EMILY, *m. 1839 James Axley Stevens 1817-1833, son of Henry*

J123. MARGARET, *m. 1839 Tobert Leach*

J124. LUCINDA, *never married*

J125. HARRIS, *never married*

J126. GANETTA, *never married*

J127. RACHEL, *m. — Durham*

J128. WILLIAM, *m. Cintha Martin*

J129. MARY, *m. a preacher*

J12A. JOHN THOMAS

J12B. JEMIMA B., *d. 1853, age 25*

J13. WILLIAM[3] AUSTIN (*Zachariah,*[2] *John*[1]) was born 1796 (54 in 1850 Census Ohio County, KY). He was married in 1826 to Henrietta Ritty Laundrum.

CHILDREN: J131. JOSEPHINE, *b. 1832, m.(1) Col. Benjamin Field, m.(2) Rev. James Coleman*

J132. EMILY, *m. Henry Field*

J133. MOLLY, *m. Jim Skillens*

J134. HENRY

J14. ZACHARIAH OFFUTT[3] AUSTIN (*Zachariah,*[2] *John*[1]) was born 30 November 1797 Prince George's Parish, Montgomery County, Maryland, died prior to 1855 when estate settled Ohio County, Kentucky. No issue.

J15. ENOCH[3] AUSTIN (*Zachariah,*[2] *John*[1]) was born 18 November 1799 in Prince George s Parish, Montgomery County, Maryland. He was apparently unmarried.

Judge Samuel Austin

J16. SAMUEL[3] AUSTIN (*Zachariah,*[2] *John*[1]) was born 18 November 1801 in Montgomery County, Maryland. He was married in Butler County, Kentucky on 9 August 1831 to Nancy (Annie) Wand James. Nancy, the daughter of Foster and Elizabeth (Wand) James, was born on 3 October 1811. Samuel was the first elected judge of Butler County, Kentucky, elected in 1850 and serving two terms. The accompanying photographs of Judge Samuel Austin (above) and of his son Richard and Richard's wife Aurilla (next page) were kindly furnished by Arthur Clement Austin. Nancy died 23 December 1871. Samuel died on 1 December 1884, and is buried in the Old Salem Church Yard (Baptist) in Logansport, Kentucky.

CHILDREN: J161. RICHARD ELLIOTT, *b. 16 April 1833, m. 1856 Aurilla Janet Reid (see photo next page)*

J162. HENRIETTA, *b. 3 June 1839, m. Ike Goodall*

J161. **Richard Elliott Austin and his wife Aurilla Janet Reid.** They married on 10 July 1856, and had eight children: Thomas Newell b. 11 May 1858, m. 21 November 1883, d. 8 January 1934; Infant daughter b. & d. 25 February 1860; Mary Louella (Lulu) b. 28 February 1862, m. January 1881, d. 12 March 1890; Nancy Elizabeth b. 27 April 1864, m. 18 January 1884, d. 4 May 1906; Amanda A. b. 12 December 1866, m. 28 August 1890, d. February 1906; Samuel Elvis b. 4 September 1869, d. 25 December 1950; Clement Reid b. 10 December 1871; John Robert b. 7 May 1875, unmarried, d. 1 July 1894. Richard died 26 August 1895 in Marlow, Oklahoma.

J163. WILLIAM HENRY, *b. 2 March 1841, m. Mary E. Hill daughter of Samuel E. Hill*

J164. JOSEPH GARLAND, *b. 24 January 1843, m. Martha Hill (sister of Mary), Union Army*

J165. SAMUEL HAMILTON, *b. 2 July 1845, m. Helen Porter, daughter of Clark N. Porter*

J166. ZERELDA, *b. 7 March 1847, m.(1) John Taylor, m.(2) John Brown*

J167. JOHN MAITLAND, *b. 11 April 1849, m. — Barnes*

J17. JOHN[3] AUSTIN (*Zachariah,[2] John[1]*) was born 14 December 1803 in Montgomery County, Maryland. He was married in Butler County, Kentucky on 17 December 1827 to Zerelda James. Zerelda, the daughter of Foster and Elizabeth (Wand) James, was born on 1 December 1813. She died 22 July 1839, while John died 1 July 1852.

CHILDREN: J171. AMANDA, *m. John C. Howard*

J172. ADDISON, *never married*

J173. ROSILENA, *m. John McKenown (Mary R. Austin)*

J174. COLUMBUS, *d. age 8*

J175. FOSTER TUCK, *m. (—) Herreld*

J42. HELEN[3] AUSTIN (*John Kendrick,[2] John[1]*) was born 26 February 1801 in Montgomery County, Maryland. She was married in Ohio County, Kentucky, on 10 November 1818 to Joseph E. Miller. Joseph, the son of David A. and Dorcas (Holliday) Miller, was born on 3 November 1776 in Maryland. Joseph died 24 July 1875. Helen died 29 August 1844, and is buried in Austin Cemetery. MILLER CHILDREN: *J. Hamilton, David Austin 1826, Amelie, Thomas, Mary, John, Elizabeth, Dorcas, Cerilda, Martha, Joseph.*

J44. ROBERT[3] AUSTIN (*John Kendrick,[2] John[1]*) was born 19 July 1804 in Montgomery County, Maryland. He was married in Ohio County, Kentucky, on 17 March 1829 to Mary (Polly) Render. Mary, the daughter of Robert Jr. and Charlotte (Barnes) Render, was born on 14 August 1809 in Ohio County. Mary died 19 July 1851. Robert married second on 4 October 1853 to Sallie (Porter) Chapman, no issue from this marriage. Robert died on 18 January 1866 in Ohio County, Kentucky.

CHILDREN: J441. ELIZA, *b. 20 March 1830, m. William Render*

J442. JOHN ROBERT, *b. 2 June 1831 m.(1) Susan Ann Steven, m.(2) Lizzie Arbuckle*

J443. JOSHUA LOUIS, *b. 9 April 1833, m.(1) Frances Robertson, m.(2) Betty Maples, m.(3) (—) Hillard*

J444. WILLIAM NEWTON, *b. 20 January 1837, m. Rena Hillard*

J445. JOSEPH PENDLETON, *b. 19 May 1840, m. Ann Richard Wade, d. 7 March 1914*

J446. MARGARET ELLEN, *b. 26 April 1835, m. Clark Thomas Porter*

J447. CHARLOTTE ANN, *b. 7 September 1842, m. Robert Forsythe*

J448. MARY CASSANDRA, *b. 5 January 1845, m. Nick Daniels*

J449. THOMAS BERRY, *b. 30 October 1847, m. Lacke Gordon*

J44A. ADDISON M., *b. 19 Nov. 1850, died young*

J44B. ALFRED KELLY, *b. 1 Jan. 1839, d. young*

J45. THOMAS ODLE[3] AUSTIN (*John Kendrick,[2] John[1]*) was born 6 April 1806 in Montgomery County, Maryland,. He was married in Ohio County, Kentucky on 6 September 1830 to Amelia Barnes. Amelia, the daughter of Weaver and Elizabeth (Miller) Barnes, was born on 11 November 1810 in Ohio County. Thomas was a merchant in Beaver Dam, Kentucky. Amelia died 19 March 1891, while Thomas died 21 February 1875 in Ohio County. Both are buried at Goshen Cemetery just outside of Beaver Dam.

CHILDREN: J451. ELIZABETH MELVINA, *b. circa 1831, m. William T. Miller*

J452. WEAVER HENRY, *b. 25 December 1832, m.(1) Katherine Arnold, m.(2) Lucinda Henry*

J453. JOHN THOMAS, *b. 2 June 1834, d. ?9 January 1864, marker in Austin Cemetery*

J454. DAVID HAMILTON, *d. in infancy*

J455. SALLIE MARY, *b. 17 October 1843, d. 7 July 1852 of flux*

J456. DORCAS CAROLINA, *b. 1 January 1838, m. 25 February 1858 James F. Carson 1835-1908, d. 9 December 1891*

J457. WILLIAM ANDERSON, *b. circa 1840, m.(1) Judith Chick, m.(2) Mary T. Martin*

J458. CASSANDRA, *b. 10 May 1844, m. David Gentry 1837-1899, d. 14 November 1920*

J459. ANN ELIZABETH, *b. circa 1848, m. 10 June 1867 J. Warren Baker b. 1846, son of Isaac Harvey and Charlotte (Render) Baker*

J45A. ELLA V., *b. 31 January 1850, m. 20 May 1866 John P. Morton 1841-1901, son of Jessie and Sally (Paxton) Morton of Virginia and Kentucky, d. 26 February 1944 age 94 years*

J45B. ELVIS, *m. Nanny Rhoads*

J45C. FLAVIUS ODLE, *b. 30 November 1851, m. Laura Ann Baker 1850-1920, daughter of Isaac Harvey and Charlotte (Render) Baker, d. 10 May 1907*

J46. ELIZABETH[3] AUSTIN (*John Kendrick,[2] John[1]*) was born 27 November 1807. She was married on 10 January 1828 to Harbor Blackstone Taylor, who was born on 28 December 1806. Harbor died 25 April 1870, while Elizabeth died 26 July 1888 and is buried in Liberty. TAYLOR CHILDREN: *Clarissa Ann 1829, Susan Mahulda 1830, Horace 1832, Darcus Emeline 1835, William Harrison 1837, John Richard 1839, Samuel Payton 1842, Cassandra Odle 1845, Elizabeth Helen (Betty) 1847, Cordelia 1850.*

[Continued on page 51]

MOSES G. AUSTIN & FAMILY

by Russell A. Williams

Our Moses G. Austin in 1880 told the census taker of the Township of Center, Dade Co., Missouri, that his parents were from Massachusetts but that he was born in New York. Family tradition that Moses was born in Delaware County, New York, has not been proven.

We first find a record of M. Austin in the 1840 Census in Friendship, Allegheny Co., NY. His family is listed as one male under 5, two between 5 and 10, and one between 20 and 30; two females under 5, one between 30 and 40. No other record has been located in that area.

Moses probably married Sophronia Bradley about 1830 in New York. Although her parents are unknown, we do find Charity, David, Peter and Stephen Bradley appearing in the 1810 Census of Delaware Co., NY, all having daughters in the correct age bracket. The best possibility is David, since Moses and Sophronia named a son David. This Delaware Co. data gives some faint credence to the tradition that Moses was born and raised in Delaware Co.

Moses' daughter Caroline, one of my great-grand-mothers, said she was born in Bolivar, NY, which was set off from Friendship in 1825. After her birth, the scene shifts to Cranberry Twp., Venango Co., Penn. There the 1841 tax roll has Franklin Austin with two horses, two cows, 200 acres and Moses Austin, occupant. Township records dated 20 October 1842 list Silas Austin, although no connection has been found. Franklin and Silas do not appear in the following year's records. Moses and Sophronia named their first son Franklin W., but for whom?

In 1843 tax records Moses has a cow, two oxen, and 175 acres of land. He was taxed until 1854, although only 75 acres were taxed to him then. There is always an entry to Allison and Shannon for the David Poorman heirs of 200 acres entered next to Moses' assessment, which may be of some significance.

It is interesting to note that *another* Moses Austin settled in the nearby Twp. of Irvin, Venango Co., at an early date. He left a Will dated 4 July 1806, naming his wife Sarah, daughter Mary Davison, son Aaron and Aaron's wife Hannah, and daughters Hiley Leonard and Charlotte Austin. While I have not found a family connection, it is very possible that one exists, and could have been one reason for Moses G. Austin to move to Venango Co.

Sophronia died in Cranberry Twp. In 1977 my wife Alice and I visited the Brandon Cemetery located just north of Cranberry. Her tombstone was in excellent shape after 130 years, bearing the inscription "Sophronia, wife of M. G. Austin, died Feb. 19, 1847, age 38 years 9 mo. 26 da." This indicates a birthdate of 23 April 1808.

Correlating the 1840 and 1850 Friendship census records, we find that in 1840 Moses would have been 30, Sophronia 32, Franklin 8, Collins 6, Maryan 4, and Caroline 2. Wallace must be included to make everything match (the 1850 Census has him born in Penn.), but that lack of correlation isn't critical, since his mother had died and the 1850 census might have been in error.

John Gordon was a neighbor with a daughter Elizabeth, aged 17 in the 1850 census. While the local census records show several girls named Elizabeth, only Elizabeth Gordon's age corresponds with Moses's second wife's age from census records, 22 or 23 years younger than Moses.

The Cranberry Twp. 1855 tax roll has no Moses Austin. Where the family went is unknown. A great grand-daughter (my mother, Freda May Ambrose Williams, alive and well at 87) always heard the family came to Wisconsin from Missouri, but this is not proven. A Sophronia C. Austin m. 8 November 1853 James Spain in Greene Co., Missouri, but we've found no connection.

Moses G. and Elizabeth appear on an indenture dated 18 September 1858 for the N.E. section 21 Tn 12 N, R2 W, of Forest, Richland Co., Wisconsin. On 5 December 1858 daughter Caroline married Hiram William Ambrose. Son David married 23 December 1870 Mary Jane Bender. Son Marshall married 9 February 1868 Caroline A. Wiltrout. These three couples spent the rest of their lives in Wisconsin. Eldest son Franklin W. wed Myrtle Dell Kintz of Richland County, and they moved to Missouri.

About 1872 Moses and Elizabeth went to Missouri with those children still at home. The 1880 Census finds them in Center, Dade Co. Moses is now 69, Elizabeth 47. Collins is shown as 26 but this is incorrect. Collins was listed as "idiotic" and had long been a care to the family (born circa 1834). Lawrence 21, Laura 15, and Ida 4 were the other children still at home.

Dade Co. Land Records show Moses and Elizabeth purchasing several parcels of property in 1885 in the Green-field, Mo. The home was registered in Elizabeth's name. It seems likely that Moses died that year or shortly after-wards, though no record of his death has been located. The local newspaper recorded Elizabeth's death in December 1899, evidently a widow for a number of years, and her burial in the Greenfield Cemetery. Alice and I searched plot records and the cemetery. The only Austin stone car-ries the legend "Edward Austin, son of Lawrence and Nancy Austin." Moses and Elizabeth might be buried in this same plot with their grandson Edward.

We have followed much of Moses' long life, covering many hundreds of miles, yet we do not known when his life began or ended. Our record pages are still open, however, and we will be most grateful to anyone who can provide additional information on the Moses G. Austin family.

JOHN AND ELIZABETH AUSTIN
OF PLAINFIELD, NEW HAMPSHIRE

by Michael Edward Austin

Genealogist-historian Vernon Hood spent many years gathering records on Plainfield, NH, families. Pauline L. Austin of Marion, Iowa, provided *Austins of America* a copy of a 1967 letter Hood sent her, referring to John Austin's ''account book'' containing the births of John's children. Since none of the births appear in town records, we sought to locate and publish these unique vital records.

Plainfield Librarian Nancy Norwalk informed us that Mr. Hood died circa 1971, leaving his manuscripts and papers to the Special Collection Room of the Baker Library on the Dartmouth College campus in Hanover, NH. With the help of Ethel Mayo Warren of Shrewsbury, Mass., we sorted through several boxes of Hood's papers. The Account Book itself was not there, but according to Hood's notes, had been in the possession of Floyd H. Rogers of Plainfield as late as 1954. Mr. Rogers' son lives in Plainfield today, but he had no knowledge of what became of the Account Book after his father's death.

Unless and until John Austin's original Account Book can be found, all we have are the rather extensive notes extracted from the book by Vernon Hood. Hood's notes are *exactly* reproduced in their entirety on the next three pages, providing many colorful insights into the lives of an industrious, hard-working Austin family. Elijah Austin wrote his own accounts in Vol. II of his father's Account Book, but they are not reproduced here. The dates in Hood's notes are completely scrambled, whether by John Austin or Hood himself we do not know. Hood added some parenthetical comments, and in a few places he notes abridging portions of the accounts. The term 'Dr' stands for 'debtor' in these notes, while the frequent 'to' probably stands for 'ditto'. The name Muodey was so written, with the 'o' crossed out. It was probably written as 'Mudey' (for 'Moody') in John's original book.

The labors of John Austin's sons Joseph and John are recorded in the Account Book, along with a pair of shoes for his daughter 'Betty,' a nickname for Elizabeth. In Vernon Hood's small book entitled 'Notes from John Austin's Account Book' was no list of births. However, we did find births included in another set of Hood's notes, and annotated: ''Birth records taken from John Austin's account book.'' From these notes Hood compiled the list of children shown below. Some facts concerning John Austin eluded Hood, however, and he reports: ''No record of the date of his b. or d. have been found. No record of the name or date of b. or d. of his wife has been located.''

Determining the ancestry and wife of John Austin was a triumph of sorts for modern technology. Correlating the children's names against its extensive files, the *Austins of America* computer enabled us to locate a farmer Isaac Austin who had died in Lowell, Massachusetts from ''chronic disease of brain'' on 3 June 1845 age 52y 5m 1d, born in Plainfield, Vt. (sic), son of John and Elizabeth. The computer further found only one John Austin of Methuen marrying an Elizabeth in that time frame – the seventh child of S24 Zebediah and Sarah (Gutterson) Austin of the Samuel Austin of Boston line (see *Austins of America* pages 14-15). John and Elizabeth's first child was undoubtedly named after her father. These discoveries, coupled with additional research, enabled us to complete Vernon Hood's picture of John Austin's family:

S247. JOHN[4] AUSTIN (*Zebediah,*[3] *Thomas,*[2] *Samuel*[1]) was born 27 September 1744 in Methuen, Massachusetts, son of Zebediah and Sarah (Gutterson) Austin. his marriage to Elizabeth Pettengill on 13 July 1769 is also recorded in Methuen. Elizabeth, the daughter of Joseph and Elizabeth (Lancaster) Pettengill, was born 14 October 1749 in Methuen. After living a few years in Methuen, John and Elizabeth moved circa 1774 to Dracut, Mass. Circa 1777 they moved to Dunbarton, New Hampshire, where on 10 March 1778 John was chosen Surveyor of Highways. They finally settled circa 1784 in Plainfield, New Hampshire, in the Black Hill section of that town. John died after 1811. All this while, John, a carpenter by trade, recorded their children's births only in his personal Account Book:

CHILDREN:
S247-1. JOSEPH, *b. 15 October 1769 in Methuen, taxed 1798 Plainfield, but not in 1799.*

S247-2. JOHN, *b. 25 January 1772 in Methuen*

S247-3. ELIZABETH, *b. 6 Sept. 1773 in Methuen, m. 5 January 1792 Thomas Cady in P.*

S247-4. JOSIAH, *b. 15 October 1775 in Dracut, d. 25 July 1797 in Plainfield*

S247-5. ELIJAH, *b. 25 August 1777 in Dracut, m. Levina Williams 8 January 1818, d. 5 July 1853 ae 75y in Plainfield*

S247-6. DARKIS, *b. 14 April 1779 in Dunbarton, d. 23 July 1797 in Plainfield*

S247-7. SARAH, *b. 19 June 1781 in Dunbarton*

S247-8. DANIEL, *b. 22 May 1783 in Dunbarton, m. Electa Lyman 5 or 15 April 1812*

S247-9. WEALTHY, *b. 5 April 1785 in Plainfield*

S247-A. MARY, *b. 4 July 1787 in Plainfield, m. 14 October 1823 James Kenyon*

S247-B. ISAAC, *b. 3 January 1789 in Plainfield, m. Sarah (—), d. 3 June 1845 in Lowell, Mass.*

S247-C. —, *b. 7 March 1791 in Plainfield, d. young.*

S247-D. BENJAMIN, *b. 16 July 1792 in Plainfield*

S247-E. LYMAN, *b. 15 March 1796 in Plainfield, m. Hannah Silloway 4 or 24 Dec. 1828, d. 20 June 1870 ae 73y*

VERNON HOOD'S NOTES FROM
JOHN AUSTIN'S ACCOUNT BOOK

Plainfield May th 17 1788
Daniel Coal Dr to me for
Seven Days work   1/10/0
to Six Days work   1/6/0
to on hankechife   0/1/0
May the 9 1789
to framing his Barkhouse   1/10/0
to three chares frames   0/8/0
to half a Day of Joseph   0/2/0
to four coutered chairs   1/0/0

Cred to Mr Daniel Coal for
Lather for one Pare of Shoes
and for two Days work choping
to Shuger
to two Pounds of tow
to ox work two days

Leu Joseph Kinyon Dr to me
the sum of   0/3/0
Credit to Mr Kinyon for work
a halling wood five Days
hinself and oxen and Brought
Rufus Gilbord one Day to chop

Plainfield May th 17 1788
Cred to Mr Coal for two
Boshels and a half of whet
to weeving 36 yards of
cloth   0/18/0
to one Boshel of whet—
to weving 30 yards of cloth   0/15/0
to 24 yards of cloth 6 Pur yard   0/12/0
to two yards and a half
of cloths   0/8/0
to weeving nine hankechifs   0/9/0

Plainfield May th 28 1785
Daniel Coal Dr to me
for two Days work   0/9/0
to making of a Pare
of   0/1/0
to making of a Pare of
Pulle Bloks   0/1/0
September to four Days work   0/18/0
October th 28 to three
Days and a half work   0/15/0
to Sashes   0/4/6

Plainfield March 10 1786
Mr Abram Carpender Dr
to me for one Day going
to Cornish with Slay
and horse   0/5/0
May 9 to two Days work   0/9/0

Plainfield 1801 May the 9
Magar Joseph Smith Dr
to me for Sawing 1048
feet of Plank   1/15/0
to 332 feet of Boards   0/8/0

Plainfield 1796
Majar Jospeh Smith Dr
to me for sawing 11522

feet of Pine Boards   6/18/6
1801 June the 1
to Sawing 1370 feet
of Pine Boards   0/17/0
to Six Days work   1/16/0

Plainfield Majar Joseph Smith
Dr to me for Sawing 8864
feet of Pine Boards   5/6/0
to Sawing Sletwork   0/8/0
to Sawing Plank 1342 feet   1/12/2

Plainfield June 2 1787 Moses Chase
Dr to me for Six Days and
a half   1/10/0
to Seven Days and a half
August 24 1790   1/14/9
to 9 Days and a half   2/0/0

Plainfield April 26 1787
Joseph Chase Dr to me for
four Days work   0/18/0

Plainfield febuary 24 1786
Nethniel alen Dr to me
for work on his house five Days
and a half of Joseph   0/11/0
and John work half one Day   0/1/0
to two Days work a
framing his Barn   0/8/0
to two Days of Joseph   0/5/0
to two Days of John   0/4/0
to John Six Days   0/9/0
to John one Day haing   0/2/6
to making a Plow   0/7/0
to one Day and a half   0/6/0
of Joseph   0/5/0
   1/19/6
to half a Day of Joseph
to John two Days a haing   1/6/3
   0/13/3

Plainfield Januar th 18 1788
than Reckned with Nathniel
Allen and Setiled all acompts
and found Due me   0/13/3
february the 20
to five Days of Joseph   0/17/6
to half a Day work   0/1/6
to making of a cofen   0/2/6
to making of coffin   0/2/3
   1/17/0

Plainfield february th 20
1786 John Mcneal Dr to
me for macking of a chest
the Sum of   0/7/6

Plainfield January 3 1787
Mr Benjamin Kimal
Deptor to me for Six
Days work   1/7?/0
July the 19 to making of
a Pare of Cart wheals   1/10/0
to Seven Days work framing
his mill   2/2/0
to four Days work   0/16/0

Plainfield December the 18 1789
than Recknd with Mr Bejaman

Kimbel and found Due to me   0/3/0
Received of Mr Kimbel in
the year 1786 two pare of
shoes the Sum of   0/10/0
March 2 1787
one Sheep Skin   0/4/0
Received two Pare of
mens Shoes   0/18/0
one Boshel of whet   0/6/-
to three Pare of shoes   1/15/0

Plainfield January th 19 1786
This Day Reckned with Cap.
Joseph Smith and found Due to
me the sum of   0/12/8
to one Day a framing his
hog Peen   0/4/6
to four chairs   0/16/0
January th 9 1789
to three Days work   0/13/6
to a Bedstead   0/10/0

Plainfield June 6 1790
James Cate Dr to me for framing
his Barn Six Days of my Self   1/7/0
to five Days of Joseph   1/0/0
Plainfield August 21 1795
than Reckned with James Cate
and Setled all acompts and
found Due to me   0/18/0
for three Days work

Plainfield february the 22 1791
than Recknd with Mr Nathnial
Alen and Setled all Book accompts
and found Due to me   0/4/3

Plainfield April 12 1785
Nathniel Dean Dr to me
for half a Days work   0/2/3
May the 18
to two Days work   0/8/6
May 21 to one Day and
a half work   0/6/9
August 22 Dr to me five
days and a half work upon
his mill   1/4/9
to half a Days work upon his mill   2

Plainfield August 12 1784
Asa Gallop Dr to me for
nine Days work a framing
his Barn   2/5/0

Plainfield April 2 1787
Let Able Stone Dr to me for
eleven Days work n half   2/11/9
to eight Days of Joseph   1/4/0

Plainfield April th 2 1789
Let Able Stone Dr to me
for making of flyars   0/1/6
to one Day huen timber   0/4/0
to me for five Days of
Joseph huen timber   1/0/0
to framing his house
four Days of my Self   0/18/0
to Joseph three Days   0/12/0

Let Able Stone Dr to me   2/15/6

to making of fliers   0/1/6
to one Bed Poast   0/1/3
July th 10 1790
to Joseph and John five
Days a framing your Barn   1/17/6

Plainfield April 28 1784
Cap. Bengaman Captman
Dr to one Days work   0/4/6
to 19 Days work upon his Barn   4/5/6
to making of a tabel   0/9/0
May the 13 1785
to Seven Days work   1/16/0
December 1785 to two Days   0/9/0
March 30 1786
to five Days work   1/2/6
to one Day work   0/3/8
to one Days work   0/4/6
April 27 1787
to six chares   1/10/0
June 28 1792
to making cart whels   1/10/0

Plainfield January the 12 1797
Joseph Chapman Dr to me for
five Days work the Sum of   0/115/0
1797 to making his
Brak the Sum of   0/12/0
June th 15 1797
for framing his Barn Six Days
of my Self and five Days and
a half of Joseph   2/12/3

Plainfield 1784
James Cate Dr to work huing
and framing his house and Barn
20 Days and a half   4/12/6
Febuary 23 1787
to five Days work upon
his house the Sum of   1:2:6
to two chares   0/8/0
Plainfield June th 5 1788
James Cate Dr to me for
framing Mr huggins
Barn five Days   2/0/0
Cr to Mr Cate for one boshel
of corn and half a Boshel of
rye to two Boshels of corn
and one Boshel and half of whet
and half a Boshel of rye
January to one Boshel of corn.

Plainfield th 22 1785
Than Recknd with the wido
Atwood williams found Due
to hur the sum of   0/15/0
Plainfield December 1799
Cap Benjamin Chapman
Dr to me for two Days   0/8/0
1801 April 21 Dr to two Days
and half - Two Dolers and fifty cents

Plainfield July th 27 1785
Docter Ebenezer Wright Dr
to me for work Sixteen
Days upon his house   3/12/0
(and 21 more days of work
July 12 - Nov. 12) V.H.

Plainfield December 22 1785
than movd to Ebenezer
thomas house

Plainfield August 29 1785
Simon Blancher Dr to me
to six teen Boshels and a
half of ashes   0/11/0
to six chares   1/4/0
to to great chares   0/16/0

Plainfield December 18 1787
than Reckned with Robord
Dunlap — due me   1/5/0

Cred to Robord Dunlap for teen
hundred of hay   1/0/0
two Boshels of chaff   0/2/0
four Boshels of Purtaters   —

Plainfield April 24 1788
Atwood Williams Dr to me
for 24 Square of Sishes   0/8/0
to six Days of Joseph huen   1/1/0

Plainfield March 16 1787
Mary Williams Dr to me
for one Chest the sum of   1/4/0
to mending of a wheal   0/5/0
to a Set of Spools   0/4/0
to a Suger Box   0/3/0

Plainfield April 2 1786
frances Smith Eq Dr to me
for one Days work   0/6/0
to a Bread troff   0/4/6
to thurteen Days work
upon his mill   2/18/6
to six chairs   1/4/0
to making ox yoke   0/2/0
to making a Beed Steed
and finding of Posts   0/8/0
1789 April 6
Bottoming chairs   0/8/1

Plainfield June 1787
John Whitton Dr to me
for five Days work   1/2/6

Plainfield March 16 1787
Younis Spaldon Dr to
me for five chares   0/15/0
to one wheal   0/10/0
By the hand of hur
Brother Phines

Plainfield June th 13 1786
Jesse Carpender Dr to me
for work a framing his Barn
six Days of my Self and five
Days and a half of Joseph   1/18/3

Plainfield June 28
1787 David Read Dr to me for
fourteen Days and a half a
framing the meeting house   3/8/6
Cre to mr Read four Boshels
of whet and to half a Boshel
of inding corn

Plainfield November 14 1786
(a long list of credits to Ebenezer

Thomas, reeping, haying, plowing,
"harring" etc. inc.)
to Laying the Chamber flower   0/6/0
to seven Days upon his house   —

Plainfield November 10 1787
thomas Willson Dr to me
thirty nine Days work
upon his house the sum of   8/15/6
1788 Sishes
(also more work on house in 1788,
and seventy "sishes.")

Plainfield January 1 1788 Cred to
Jesse Carpender for two
Boshels of Chaff
to one Boshel of Purtaters
Nov th 7 1789 Jesse Carpender
Dr to me for one great chair   0/7/6

Plainfield 1790
Simon Blancher Dr to me
for Eleven Boshils and
a half of ashes   0/1/8
March the 18
to making of coffin   0/2/0

Plainfield Marth th 11 1789
Abraham Carpender Dr for
one chest   0/8/0
to one tabel   0/9/0
to three chairs   0/18/0
April 8 1789
to a Shugar tob   0/4/0
to half a goose   0/2/0

Plainfield June th 21 1788
Steven Cleavland Dr to me
for Cobs 39 Boshels
to making wheals   0/17/0
to Bottoming chairs   0/7/6

Plainfield July th 28 1790
Mr Robart Miller Dr to me for
framing your Sons Barn 7 Days
and half my self   1/13/9

Plainfield June th 27 1788
David Davis Dr to me
for work   1/16/0
Cr to Mr Davis for
fifteen Pound and a half
of Chees 7 Pence Pur Pound   0/8/9
to 22 Pound of Poark   0/14/8

Plainfield 1791 Joshua Willson
Dr to me
to framing your Barn five Days
my Self and Joseph   2/2/6

Plainfield May th 26 1788
Mr Rusel Dr to making
of a coffen   0/4/0

Plainfield Decembe 31 1788
Crd to Mr Coal for
Seventy three Pound and half
of Poark 4 Pence Pur Pound
to half Boshel of Peas   0/2/6

Plainfield December 11 1789
thomas Gallop Dr to me

five Days of my self and
Joseph a making the water
wheal the sum   2/2/6

Plainfield 1791
frances Smithe Dr to me
for three Days and half
a sawing   0/14/0
1799 to making his Sider
Mill nine Days and half   2/7/6

Plainfield May th 18 1791
Mr Timothy Cory Dr to me
for Cart wheels   2/2/0
to axeltree and Spire(?)   0/5/0
to making Sishes   0/4/6

Plainfield May th 9 1801
Majer Joseph Smith Dr for
sawing 1048 feet of Plank   1/15/0
to 332 feet of Boards   0/8/0
to six Days work   1/16/0
to Claboard 5 hund feet   0/18/0
to Sawing Slitwork   0/12/0

Plainfield Daniel Coal Dr to me
1791 to Spinnig nine Run and
half   0/9/6
1792 to Spinning Seven Run   0/7/0
1800 to nine Days a framing
his house   2/14/0

Plainfield 1793
John Muadey Dr to me for one
Day work upon your house
to making Sashes   0/4/6
to Sashes   0/2/6

February 22, 1791
Cred to Jesse Carpender
to making one Pare of Shoes for Betty
to making three Pare of Shoes
to mending two Pare of Shoes

1798 Jesse Carpenter Dr to me
for four Pounds and eleven ounces
of So Lather one doller and
18 cents
to Lather 8 Shilings

Plainfield Janury 11th 1793
then we Reckoned and Settled all
Book acounts from the Beginning
of the World to this Day
found Due to me one Pound nine
Shilling and Elevon pence Lawfull
mony as witness our hands

         Joseph Smith
         John Austin

Plainfield Lemuel Smith Dr to me
1798 for Setting your hitchell   0/11/0
to making a yoak   0/3/0
1800 making harro and fering
Cart tong   0/6/6

Plainfield May th 25 1795
Reckned with Walter Smith
and found Due to me the sum of   0/18/0

Plainfield April 1794
Credeate to Bejamam Cutler

for six Boshels of whet
to teen Pounds of Poark

Plainfield Leu Joseph Kinyon Dr to
me for tember to one Pare
cider mill Screws and Boaring
the Beams   2/2/0

Plainfield March the 15 1798
Doctor Parkhurt Dr to me
for one Sheep   0/12/0
to one ox halve   0/01/6
to making Plow   0/10/0
1799 to one mule   5/14/0

Plainfield 1796
(account of labor etc. with Peter Bogby)

Plainfield March th 20 1798
Mr. James Ward Dr
making Cobard   0/9/0
1801 to Sawmill Saw which
wade 21 Pound and half   0/12/6

Plainfield September 1799
Lynard Pulcpher Dr to me for
six Days framing   1/16/0
to 1275 fet Claboards

1792 Cred to Daniel Rusel
to two Pare of mens shoes
to half Pound of indego   0/16/0
to one quarter of tea   0/6/0
to two quarts of molases   0/3/0
to half Pint of Rum
Sweetned with melases
to one comb   0/0/8
to one Paper of Peens   0/0/8
to six nedels   —

VOL. II JOHN AUSTIN'S ACCOUNTS

Plainfield June th 9 1801
Amos Stafford Dr to me   2/3/0
for sawing 3593 feet of Pine Board
to making a coffing for his child   0/3/0
to making a coffing for your father   0/6/0
to making a coffing for your mame   0/6/0
Plainfield Silas Levemore Dr to me for
August   one Day work   0/6/0
1802 December to six Days work
upon the chool house   1/4/0

Plainfield July th 7 1806
Lynard Pulcefer Cre to one
galon of Rum   0/1/0
to one Pen nife   0/1

Plainfield Cady and Kingsbury Dr to me for
framing ten Days and finding my self
two meals a Day and finding   4/0/0
Dog two meals a Day nine Days   0/18/0
(1801? see Prop. records: first
Tues of Jan. 1802 proprietors of
Plainfield met at house of ''Kings-
bury & Cady'' now Baptist Parsonage)

Plainfield May the 11 1803
Samuel harroon Dr to me
for twenty nine nots of Shoe
thread   0/1/10
to one Run of Shoue thread

and a half   0/1/10
Jonathan herrone Dr to me
for one Sheep   0/9/0

Plainfield   hesekiah french Dr
September   to me for three Days
the 6 1801   upon his Sider mill   0/18/0

July the 6   John Colburn Dr to me
1805   for mending his whels   0/4/0
September to four Days and half
making your Sider Mill   1/4/0
and Boaring the Beam   0/3/0
to mending your Slay   0/1/6
to making tee Pot handel   0/1/0

Plainfield March the 17 1808
Levi Bloss Dr to me for
half Day work on the mill   0/3/0
to Putting in your Crank
to your Sawmill   0/1/6
to twenty lits of Sheses   0/3/0

Plainfield April 30 1808
Peter Abot Dr to me for one
Yard of tow Cloth
to twenty three nots of
Sone thread

Plainfield 1805 Mr Porter Dr
to me for weven twenty one
yards of two cloth at Six Pence
per yard   0/10/6
to one harrow crock   0/4/0

1805 Daniel Kingsbury had
65 yard of Cloth (Tow
in mostly small lots.)

1807 Joesph Swan Dr to me for
four days work   1/4/0

Plainfield July the 30 1810
Sylas Reed marchant Dr to
me for thurty one Pound and
one forth of Rags   0/7/6
Cred to Sylas Reed marchant
for one Pound of tobacker   0/1/6
to one Small Puden Pan   0/0/8
to one Pare of taps   0/1/6
to one Set of Cops and Saursers   0/4/3

July the 8 1809
Barney Tisdel Dr to me
for one Day work

Plainfield June 24 1809
Benjimin Cutler Dr to me
for work a framing   0/18/0

Plainfield July the 25 1810
Cyrel Drown Dr to me
for work   0/5/0

1800 Recieved one Log that made
600 feet of Claboards of
Ebenezer.

Plainsfield May 1798 Amos Farnum Dr
to me for sawing five thousand
feet of Pine Boards the sum
of teen Dolers.

END OF VERNON HOOD'S NOTES

KENDALL AND EMILY AUSTIN
OF ALSTEAD, NEW HAMPSHIRE

by Ethel Mayo Warren
and Floyd Ellison Warren

S225-36B. KENDALL FREDERICK[7] AUSTIN (*Thomas,*[6,5,4] *Benjamin,*[3] *Thomas,*[2] *Samuel*[1]) was born 15 June 1837 in Surry, NH, the 11th child of Thomas and Lucy (Kendrick) Austin of the Samuel Austin of Boston line (Reference 1). As a young man he moved to a small farm in Alstead, NH, where he lived the rest of his life. He married on 2 July 1856 to Emily Roxanna Nash, daughter of David and Abigail (Howard) Nash of nearby Sullivan, NH. Emily was born 16 January 1838 in Marlow, NH, and she died on 2/3 March 1897 in Alstead. After Emily's death Mrs. Ella Putney was Kendall's housekeeper for over twenty years.

Kendall Austin was a Civil War soldier, serving in the "Fighting Fifth" regiment of the New Hampshire volunteers. He was mustered in 30 September 1863 as a private; missing 25 August 1864 at Ream's Station, Virginia; returned; mustered out 28 June 1865.

Some colorful insight into Kendall's war service is provided by Dr. William Child, a major and surgeon with the "Fighting Fifth," who later wrote of the 1864 Ream's Station conflict in Reference 2:

> August 24. No rebels in sight. We are destroying the railroad below Reams's Station. At 7 p. m., we are laying at Ream's Station, expecting to remain for the night.

> August 25. We were in the breastworks during the forenoon. About noon the enemy came down on us in heavy force, drove in our pickets and attacked our left flank, but were repulsed. Now they attack our center closed *en masse*; again they were repulsed with terrible slaughter. Again and again they attack, but each time are repulsed, our artillery mowing them down by hundreds. The fifth time they assaulted our right center, and succeeded in breaking our line, capturing several of our guns. The Second Corps, under General Hancock, leave the works and retreat past the church, down the hill, through the woods, leaving sixteen cannon in the hands of the enemy. At about 6 p. m., Major Larkin of the Fifth, with some choice men from his regiment, returned to the works, now between the two lines, and brought away several of the captured cannon. Other officers and another regiment are mentioned as having done this. The writer of this can testify to this action, and remembers the anxiety with which he witnessed the operation from a comparatively safe position in the edge of the woods. The writer also remembers how earnestly General Hancock attempted, with his staff, to arrest the retreat of his men. With sword in one hand and hat in the other, he faced his retreating regiments coming from the center, and exclaimed "For God's sake do not run!" But they did run. They ingloriously retreated. The writer also remembers how two mule teams, loaded with intrenching tools, also ingloriously retreated, tools flying,

> mules galloping, wagons jumping and rocking from side to side. The corps in this disastrous conflict lost 3,500 men, seven colors and five guns. The Fifth lost twenty-three in killed and wounded. Among the killed was Lieutenant Robert H. Chase, lately promoted from sergeant.

> August 26. We found ourselves, at about 3 p. m., on the extreme left of our lines, where we had destroyed breastworks on the 12th and 13th of July, having fallen back from Ream's Station last night. We are encamped near the Williams house.

> August 27. We remained near the Williams house until 10 a. m., and then returned to our old camp-ground in front of Petersburg. Sutler arrived to-day.

> Sunday, August 28. To-day all are busy cleaning camp. Had an inspection. All quiet along the lines. There was heavy firing last night.

> August 29. Pleasant; heavy cannonading during afternoon, continuing until 11 p. m.

> August 30. An occasional shot from our guns. Pay-rolls for six months made out.

> August 31. To-day all mustered for six months' pay. Weather very hot during middle of the day; cool at night and morning. Quiet along the lines.

> Thursday, September 1. No firing; last night cool, to-day hot. Still in camp near Ninth Corps. At 7 p. m. we have order to pack and be ready to move at a moment's notice. Same countermanded and we remain in camp.

> September 2. This morning a deserter was shot in the presence of the division. He deserted from a picket post, became mired in a marsh, was discovered, brought in, tried, found guilty and was shot sitting on his burial box.

> September 3. Nothing of importance has transpired to our regiment, brigade, division or corps. A man was hung in the Tenth Corps to-day for murder—shot a comrade. News of the capture of Atlanta, Ga., was received with cheers.

Kendall clearly saw action, and his eyesight was much impaired by a slight wound he received in the service. Back in Alstead, he was an active member of the W. S. Hancock Post N.9, G.A.R., and is pictured here in 1910 with other Alstead veterans in a photograph being preserved by the Alstead Historical Society.

In 1918 Kendall sold his farm where he had lived for over fifty years to Ernest Burroughs, with whom Kendall lived until his death on 9 March 1919 in East Alstead. The parents, siblings, and children of Kendall Austin and Emily are well documented in Reference 3. They had five children, the first born in Keene, the others in Alstead:

CHILDREN: S225-36B1. FRED MERRILL, *b. 23 August 1858, d. 31 December 1883 Alstead*

S225-36B2. JULIA EMMA, *b. 10 April 1861*

S225-36B3. CELIA MELISSA, *b. 4 May 1867*

S225-36B4. ARTHUR MORRIS, *b. 23 April 1870, d. 17 July 1879 from kick of a horse*

S225-36B5. PROCTOR ALLEN, *b. 2 Feb. 1874*

Civil War Veterans, Alstead, NH 1910. Back Row: Wilson Colburn, Kendall Austin, Jonathan Rawson, Manley Gasset, — Webster; Front Row: Julius Porter, Solomon Davis, James Nash, Dr. George Belt, Edward Kingsbury, (unidentified)

S225-36B5. PROCTOR ALLEN[8] AUSTIN (*Kendall Frederick,*[7] *Thomas,*[6,5,4] *Benjamin,*[3] *Thomas,*[2] *Samuel*[1]) was born on 2 February 1874 in Alstead. He married (1) in September 1897 to Marcia Baine, daughter of Edward R. and Lilla Ann (Spooner) Baine. They divorced, and Proctor married (2) Mrs. Eva Belle (Dupies) Ellis, born 4 January 1875 in Alstead, the daughter of Joseph Feansant and Laura Jane (Howard) Dupies. Proctor, shown in the photograph on page 50, was a well-known horse trader in his time. He had a few problems with the Cheshire County Humane Society, as recorded in the 1912 New Hampshire newspaper article reprinted on page 50. Apparently *caveat emptor* – let the buyer beware – was not a very popular concept in those times! Whether because of his horse-trading activities or not, we do not know, but in any event using the alias "John Bolio" Proctor moved to New York where he again married Eva Austin. Eva Bolio died 11 September 1949, John Bolio died soon after in April 1950, and both are buried in Graceland Cemetery, Delaware Avenue, Albany, New York, in the same plot with their sons Fred Marshall and Walter.

CHILDREN:

S225-36B5-1. LAWRENCE A., *b. 9 Dec. 1898, d. 1913*

S225-36B5-2. FRED MARSHALL, *b. 28 November 1899, m. Florence B. Moore 10 December 1919 Southbridge, Mass., d. October 1963*

S225-36B5-3. LOUISA JANE, *b. 22 June 1901, m. 29 April 1919 Louis Joseph Mayo, Jr., d. age 72 yrs.*

S225-36B5-4. WALTER ALLEN, *b. 28 April 1908, m(1) Grace Greene, div., m(2) Julia Abdellia, d. 7 June 1942*

S225-36B5-5. ARTHUR JAMES, *b. 9 September 1910, d. 14 November 1953*

REFERENCES

1. Michael E. & Patricia B. Austin, *The Descendants of Samuel Austin of Boston, Massachusetts*, to be published by The Austin Print, Concord, Massachusetts.

2. William Child, *A History of The Fifth Regiment New Hampshire Volunteers, in the American Civil War, 1861-1865*, published by R. W. Musgrove, Bristol, NH, 1893.

3. Frank B. Kingsbury, *History of Surry, New Hampshire, 1769-1922*, published by the Town of Surry, New Hampshire, 1925.

Well Known Horse Trader Brought Into Court in Troy by Agent Jennie B. Powers

Through the efforts of Agent Jennie B. Powers of the Cheshire County Humane society, A. P. Austin of Troy, known as "Proc" Austin, a horse jockey who has done business in this county for several years, has been sent to the house of correction at Westmoreland for selling a horse unfit for labor.

Austin was arrested Tuesday by Agent Powers for selling a horse Sunday, July 22, to William Harding of Troy, the animal getting down within three days and being so weak it could not get up. Four witnesses testified to the condition of the horse, which was found in "fearful" shape, according to their testimony. Agent Powers shot it. Harding had paid $8 for it.

When Austin was brought to Troy he refused to enter the court room and it was necessary to call Deputy Sheriff Stanley and Constable Nelson, who took him before Judge Platts. Constable Nelson and Mr. Dustin accompanied Agent Powers when she took Austin to Westmoreland. Besides the three month's sentence he was fined $25 and costs of $15.28.

For years Austin has traded and sold horses in the county among the poor people, many of whom have had to kill the animals soon after, or the horses have died. Agent Powers has been called in numerous cases, but until the present one has not been able to get sufficient evidence to bring Austin into court. Austin was in a mixup in this city a year ago, having traded horses with a North end resident.

QUERIES

50-1. Nathaniel Austin born 1775 in Rhode Island, m. Betsey Dodge, b. 1781 NY. Need Ancestry of Nathaniel.

50-2. Stephen Decatur Austin b. 1 December 1819 in Maine, m. circa 1856 Lucy Barnard in Wisconsin, d. 18 April 1888, Langlade Township, Langlade County, WI. Need Stephen's parents, and was he a brother of John Bailey Austin?

50-3. Charles William Austin b. 7 December 1884 Newport, Arkansas, m. 1 April 1910 Cedenia Elvira Pierson. He d. 30 January 1960 Stevinson, California. On his army record Mrs. Elsie Frazier, 1411 East 10th St., Sedalia, Missouri, was listed as next of kin in 1906. Need ancestry of Charles, also any data on Mrs. Frazier.

50-4. Mary Austine m. 28 October 1852 in York County, Penn., to William Neal b. in Perry County, Ohio, 15 October 1828. Seek descendents of William and Mary.

50-5. Molly Austin b. 5 November 1750, dau. of Samuel and Mary. She m. Jesse Rice/Roys/Royce, who was b. 10 September 1742 in Wallingford, Conn., d. after 1832 in Aurelius, Cayuga County, New York. He was the son of Josiah and Eunice (Alling/Allen) who lifed in Sheffield, Berkshire County, Mass. (1790 Census) and Aurelius, New York (1810-20-30 Census). Jesse was a Revolutionary War soldier. Need children of Jesse and Molly.

50-6. Abigail Austin daughter of Thomas of Stanford, Conn., d. 11 June 1710. She m. 1 August 1709 in Fairfield, Conn., to Samuel Canfield, who was b. 1679 and d. 1712. One son, Samuel Canfield, Jr., was b. 4 June 1710. Samuel, Sr. m. Abigail Dean in 1711, he d. in 1712. Need birthdate of Abigail and all data on Thomas Austin.

50-7. John Austin b. 1787 in New York, d. 1859 in Fulton County, Illinois. He m. Rachel (—), b. 1795 in New York and d. 1876 in Fulton County. Children: Hiram 1810, Alison 1812, Russell 1814, Peter 1815, Alvina 1817, Justin 1819, James 1820, Syntha Jane 1822, Jesse 1824, Elizabeth 1825, Cyrus 1827, Hariett 1828, Almyra 1834, Wm. Jasper 1836. Need data on John and Rachel, and their descendants.

★★★★★★★★★★★★★★★★★★★★★★★★★★★★★★

Researchers are needed to author sections by state and county of a volume entitled:

Austins in the Federal Census of 1850

Thirty states were admitted to the Union prior to the 1850 Federal Census. If you are interested in helping to compile Austins from this 1850 census, please write to *Austins of America*, 23 Allen Farm Lane, Concord, Mass. 01742.

★★★★★★★★★★★★★★★★★★★★★★★★★★★★★★

THE DESCENDANTS OF
JOHN AND CHARITY KENDRICK AUSTIN
OF FREDERICK COUNTY, MARYLAND

by Jeane Austin King Galau

THIRD GENERATION [Continued from page 42]

J47. KITTYE ANN[3] AUSTIN (*John Kendrick,*[2] *John*[1]) was born 23 September 1809 in Montgomery County, Maryland. She married on 15 February 1830 to George M. Borah, the son of George E. and Mary (Treaster) Borah, born on 30 March 1801. George died 16 September 1853, Kittye died 17 November 1872. Both are buried in Whalen Cemetery, Butler County, Kentucky. BORAH CHILDREN: *Valentine 1832, Margaret 1834, William Posey 1836, John H. 1841, George 1843, Caroline 1848, Calvin 1848.*

J48. MARGARET[3] AUSTIN (*John Kendrick,*[2] *John*[1]) was born 28 March 1812 in Montgomery County, Maryland. She was married on 18 February 1830 to Willis Borah, the son of George E. and Mary (Treaster) Borah, born 3 December 1805 in Near Borah's Ferry. Willis died 3 May 1859, and is buried in Mt. Ida Cemetery in Grant County, Wisconsin. Margaret died 23 October 1873 in Butler County, Kentucky and is buried in Taylor Cemetery. BORAH CHILDREN: *Sarah ca1831, Elizabeth 1833, Sally 1834, George 1838, Amanda 1841, Eliza 1845, Martha 1846, John J. 1847.*

J49. WILLIAM[3] AUSTIN (*John Kendrick,*[2] *John*[1]) was born 26 November 1814. He was married on 31 October 1836 to Sarah Ann Taylor, the daughter of Harrison and Philina (Pigman) Taylor, born 30 October 1818. William died 8 June 1883, while Sarah died 25 December 1913. Both are buried at the Austin Cemetery.

CHILDREN: J491. SUSAN ANN, *b. 3 August 1837, d. 31 October 1860, buried Austin Cemetery*

J492. HARRISON, *b. 4 April 1839, m. Josephine Brown, d. 1 November 1927*

J493. JOHN, *b. 3 January 1842, m. Mary Frances Cooper, he died 20 June 1877*

J494. HANNIBAL, *b. 12 March 1844, d. 7 February 1872, buried Austin Cemetery*

J495. BETTY, *m. Daniel Tichnor, no issue*

J496. CATHERINE, *b. 25 March 1849, d. 20 August 1870, unmarried, buried Austin Cemetery*

J497. HELEN, *b. 21 February 1852, d. 16 May 1883 bur. Austin Cemetery, m. John Hocker*

J4A. ANDREW JACKSON[3] AUSTIN (*John Kendrick,*[2] *John*[1]) was born 7 March 1816 in Ohio County, Kentucky. He married in that county on 31 August 1840 to Dorothy Chinn. Andrew died 26 June 1886 and is buried in Old Austin Cemetery, Beaver Dam, Kentucky. Their children were born in Ohio County, Kentucky:

CHILDREN: J4A1. BURGESS, *m. Calidonia Chick*

J4A2. LUCY ANN, *b. near Slaty Creek, Ohio County m. 13 October 1864, d. to Archie L. Chick, son of Ambler & Eleanor (Sanders) Chick*

J4A3. LOUETTE, *m. William Blankenship in 1884, no issue.*

J4A4. ALICE, *m. I. Barnard*

J4A5. MARILDA, *m. — Shaklefore, moved to Texas.*

J4A6. BETTY, *m. Adam Nave*

J4A7. EUGENE, *b. 28 February 1860, d. 13 March 1862, buried Austin Cemetery.*

J4B. HENRY[3] AUSTIN (*John Kendrick,*[2] *John*[1]) was born circa 1818 in Ohio County, Kentucky. He was married in that county on 6 November 1838 to Marelda Stevens. Their children are recorded in Ohio County, Kentucky:

CHILDREN: J4B1. ADA, *m. Jefferson Patton*

J4B2. LENA, *m. Jefferson French*

J4C. ZACHARIAH[3] AUSTIN (*John Kendrick,*[2] *John*[1]) was born 18 October 1819 in Ohio County, Kentucky. He was married to Caroline Taylor. Caroline was still living in 1866. Zachariah's Will was dated 7 October 1866 in Ohio County, Kentucky. Their children are recorded in Ohio County, Kentucky:

CHILDREN: J4C1. DALLAS, *m. — Hines*

J4C2. BETTY, *m. Robert Oglesby*

J4C3. OLA, *m. Fred Humphrey*

J4D. GEORGE W.[3] AUSTIN (*John Kendrick,*[2] *John*[1]) was born circa 1823 in Ohio County, Kentucky. He was married in that county on 2 May 1844 to Amanda Thomas. Amanda, the daughter of William and Sallie (Jackson) Thomas, was born on 14 June 1827 in Ohio County. Amanda died 8 January 1899 in Ohio County, and is buried in Beaver Dam Baptist Church Cemetery. George's Will dated 5 January 1867 in Ohio County. Their children are recorded in Ohio County:

CHILDREN: J4D1. MELISSA, *b. 20 June 1845, d. 30 May 1870; m. James Clinton Davis, son of Alexander H. and Sarah (Liles) Davis*

J4D2. HENRY, *m.(1) Liza Barnes, m.(2) Lizze Herring*

J4D3. MARCELLA, *b. 1849, m. Edward Cooper*

J4D4. SARAH, *m. William Stewart*

J4D5. JOHN, *b. circa 1853 from census, m. Time Walker*

J4D6. CHRISTOPHER (KIT), *b. 1854, m. Laura Ashford*

J4D7. MARY (MOLLY), *b. 1858, m. — Simpson*

J4D8. BYRON, *b. 3 April 1869, d. 11 June 1933; m. Frances French 1869-1954.*

THE COOPER–FROST–AUSTIN HOUSE OF CAMBRIDGE, MASSACHUSETTS

by Bainbridge Bunting
and Robert H. Nylander

The Cambridge Historical Commission permitted the reprinting of this article from their book *Survey Of Architectural History In Cambridge, Report Four: Old Cambridge*, M.I.T. Press, Cambridge, 1973. Photographs by the Society for the Preservation of New England Antiquities, courtesy of the Cambridge Historical Commission.

Cambridge is almost unique in terms of domestic architecture. Although many communities have larger, more elaborate dwellings dating from a particular period, few have so wide a range with examples of every period from the 17th century to the present. Within the few square miles of this survey district, one finds an extraordinarily complete review of three centuries of American houses.

In 1635 five years after the founding of Cambridge, a register made for the town fathers listed 74 houses; in 1642 the number was 104; in 1647 only 90. A great proportion of these buildings was within the limits of the original town close to Harvard Square and has therefore disappeared. Further from the square, however, two important dwellings survive which retain aspects of their 17th-century character although remodeled in the 18th century. Fortunately both buildings are owned by historical societies that keep them in excellent repair and open to the public.

The Cooper-Frost-Austin house, 21 Linnaean Street, was begun about 1691 by Samuel Cooper, at a time when the Cambridge Common extended as far north as Linnaean Street. Originally only half its present size, the house was enlarged about 1720 by Walter Cooper, who added the left half, with further changes made about 1810 and 1830 by Thomas Austin. In 1912, after the Society for the Preservation of New England Antiquities purchased the property from the Austin heirs, the house was carefully restored by Joseph Chandler.

Rising to its present height, the original house contained only the entry and rooms on the right. Fenestration also has been altered, once in the first half of the 18th century and again in the early 19th; but traces of the original scheme survive in the framing. It is probable that the facade had banks of triple casements filled with diamond-shaped panes which might have resembled those in the restored Abraham Browne house of about 1695 in Watertown. A 17th-century origin is also announced by the steep roof where the framing of the rafters indicates there was originally a front gable. Such cross gables were not uncommon, as one knows from the House of Seven Gables in Salem. Still other Medieval aspects are the overhanging end gable and the rear lean-to roof with its long sweeping lines. Indeed, the rear view of the house is the most

convincing: set in a thicket of trees it presents a picture of an early Cambridge dwelling.

One more typical 17th-century feature is the large central chimney whose exterior surface is decorated with brick pilasters. Despite its unified appearance, the chimney-stack was built at three different times. Because of the way the flue for the hearth of the lean-to is joined to the masonry, it is clear that it has been added; likewise, another pair of flues must have been fused to the center chimney when the left half of the house was added about 1720. This means that originally the main downstairs room served for cooking as well as for living, a true "hall" in the Medieval sense, but when the fireplace was added in the lean-to, kitchen activities were removed there. As in so many other old houses "modernized" in the 18th and 19th centuries, the huge 17th-century hearths were reduced in size by the simple expedient of building a new, smaller, and more efficient fireplace within the older one. When the house was restored in 1912, the fireplaces were reopened to their original size.

The Cooper-Frost-Austin "hall" and parlor give an accurate impression of 17th and early 18th-century interiors. The ceiling of the old "hall" (now used for dining; see upper photograph) was originally unplastered, so that the wooden framing and flooring of the chamber above were exposed. Most notable is the enormous 12-by 11-inch summer beam that extends between the outside and fireplace walls, a clear expression of the hierarchy of support as the floor load above is transferred to joists, to summer beam, to chimney and end girts, to vertical posts. The notching and fitting of the joists is skillful and the chamfer of the summer beam complex. This open ceiling was later plastered over but was uncovered during the 1912 restoration. The somewhat later parlor (see middle photograph) also has a summer beam (which had to be shored up by an interior post when the house was restored) but, in keeping with the 1720 date, the ceiling here has always been plastered in order to hide the joists and thus to obtain a smoother, flatter, more formal appearance. Still the transition was not yet complete, because hewn girts and summer

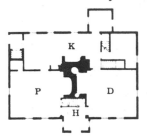

beam project below the plaster surfaces; now, however, their corners are finished with a bead molding instead of a chamfer. Furthermore, a fireplace of such large scale as that in the parlor was decidely old-fashioned for the 1720's; (the present rough-hewn lintel is an accurate restoration of 1912).

Both second-floor rooms contain fairly elaborate paneling, because it appears that, until the end of the first half of the 18th century, upstairs chambers were often considered the best rooms and were used for entertaining as well as for sleeping, undoubtedly a reflection of the European *piano nobile*. In both instances, paneling on the fireplace wall is supported by wooden framing members independent of the brick chimneystack, so that the paneling projects slightly in front of the fireplaces. The fireplace wall in the older hall chamber is composed of vertical, shadow-molded sheathing that has a linear look recalling Tudor linenfold work, while the rear wall of the same room is sealed with horizontal boards (see lower photograph). The raised paneling in the parlor chamber has a tentative Early Georgian look, its fireplace opening and mantel shelf enlivened by complex moldings that do not yet conform to standard Classical profiles.

Since almost no house remains untouched generation after generation, so the Cooper-Frost-Austin house was again modified in the 19th century. The out-building now serving as an open porch with graceful elliptical arches dates from about 1810, while the entrance hall was enlarged about 1830. Uncomfortably dark and narrow in its original form, the hall enlargement took the form of a projecting vestibule with windows on the sides. At the same time, the stairs were rebuilt and their direction reversed, a relatively simple change entailing no modifications of major structural members; there was, however, insufficient room to make them straighter or less steep. The details of the new stairs are typical of Old Cambridge usage between 1800-30: the newel is gracefully turned, and the rectangular balustrades have thin, light proportions.

AUSTINS OF GENESEE COUNTY, NEW YORK

by Jean C. Denison

The following material was copied from *The Salisbury Collection* found in the Holland Land Office in Batavia, New York. Evidently circa 1904 a group of individuals who were interested in genealogy started collecting information on many of the Genesee County families. The information is gathered together in approximately ten notebooks, arranged alphabetically by surname.

John Austin married Eliza Huyck and lived in Buffalo, NY. Their daughter **Elizabeth Austin** was born in 1848, and married Edwin J. Niles of LeRoy NY on 29 August 1867. Edwin was the son of Ebenezer and Eliza (Sprague) Niles. Elizabeth Austin Niles died in 1913, and is buried in Me Peleh Cemetery in Le Roy.

Mabel Austin of Connecticut m. Jedediah Crosby of Connecticut and settled in Bergen NY in 1805.

Jennie Austin m. Elias O. Albee, son of Isaac and Sophia (Lincoln) Albee of Vermont. Elias was born 7 June 1841 in Norfolk, St. Lawrence County NY, removed to Buffalo and then to Le Roy in 1880.

Elizabeth Austin 1822-1864 buried in Me Peleh Cemetery in Le Roy.

Ira Austin was born 13 February 1816 in Darion, married **Adeline Austin** and lived in Cowlesville, Wyoming County, NY. Adeline was born in Le Roy on 12 May 1836. Their daughter **Iola Austin** was born 12 May 1861 in Cowlesville, married on 28 February 1888 to John W. Mullen of Stafford, son of William and Elizabeth (Ford) Mullen. John was b. 17 September 1854 in Stafford.

Maria Austin was first wife of F. S. Wright, son of Samuel & Hannah (Judd) Wright, resided in Oakfield NY.

Robert Austin married Martha Searles. Their daughter **Jane Austin** married Albert Wesley Ward, son of Daniel and Catherine (Phelps) Ward.

James Austin came to Bergen NY between 1801 & 1810.

Joseph Austin came to Le Roy NY at an early date, died 25 August 1813, buried in Myrtle Street Cem. in Le Roy.

James Austin came to Le Roy NY in 1803.

Eliza Austin died in Le Roy 25 December 1864, aged 42.

Pheobe Austin Butler 1855-1919, buried in Hillside Cemetery in the town of Pembroke.

Bertha E. Austin 1878-1924, buried in Byron Cemetery.

Albert Austin 1812-1902, buried in Elba Village Cemetery, with his wife Charlotte B. 1817-1871.

Cordelia E. Austin 1840-1902, buried at Elba.

Hattie J. Austin 1856-1892, buried at Elba.

Richard Austin died 26 February 1873 aged 89, buried in Hunn Cemetery in town of Alexander, with his wife Laura who died 20 September 1878 aged 92.

Lucy Austin 1831-1920, buried in Hunn Cemetery in Alexander.

Maria A. Austin 1813-1906, wife of Alden Higgins, buried in Hunn Cemetery in Alexander.

Abel Austin's wife Hannah died 20 April 1830 aged 84, buried in Temperance Hill Cemetery in Batavia NY.

Elizabeth Austin married Edwin Niles and lived in Stafford in 1874.

Ruth I. Austin on 12 December 1912 became the first wife of William Nelson Wellman, son of Albert and Laura (Smith) Wellman.

BIOGRAPHICAL SKETCH OF
HENRY AUSTIN OF KINCAID TOWNSHIP
IN JACKSON COUNTY, ILLINOIS

The following article was extracted by Anthony Kent Austin from *The Portrait and Biographical Record of Randolph, Jackson, Perry and Monroe Counties, Illinois*, Biographical Publishing Company, Chicago 1894, pp. 556–557.

Henry Austin, one of the enterprising and successful farmers of Kincaid Township, Jackson County, residing on section 2, has the honor of being a native of this locality, for his birth occurred in Bradley Township, on the 24th of December 1850. His father, John Austin, was a native of Tennessee, and when a young man came to Illinois, settling in Bradley Township. Throughout life he followed farming, and was very successful in his undertakings. His death occurred in 1872, at the age of fifty-five. His wife, who bore the maiden name of Lucinda Polk, passed away during the early childhood of our subject. Their children were: Thomas, deceased; Mary, deceased wife of Elias Glenn; Ann, wife of Frank McBride; Minerva, deceased wife of William Stanton; Oliver, deceased; Matilda, wife of Willis H. Bilderback; Mahala, widow of Benjamin Bilderback; Sarah, who died in childhood; John, Caroline and George, all deceased; and Jane, widow of Alfred Wiggins. After the death of his first wife, Mr. Austin wedded Susan Creath, and they became the parents of three children, but all died in early life. Mr. Austin was a popular and prominent citizen of this county, and took an active part in politics, supporting the Democracy. Socially, he was connected with the Masonic order.

Henry Austin passed his boyhood quietly upon his father's farm, and early became familiar with all the duties of agricultural life. When he had attained man's estate, he began farming for himself on the place where he now lives. It was then a tract of wild land, but with characteristic energy he began its improvement. The farm comprises one hundred and forty-seven acres, much of which is highly cultivated. The fine residence, good barns and other necessary buildings all stand as monuments to his thrift and enterprise. He also purchased the old home farm of three hundred and twenty acres in the same township, of which one hundred and sixty acres are under the plow. Much of the remainder is pasture land. This place is also improved with good building and a large orchard.

On 21 September 1871, Mr. Austin was united in marriage with Miss Sophronia J. Talbott, daughter of William E. Talbott. Ten children were born to them. Horace G., born 22 September 1872, was married 31 July 1892 to Lavanda Jarrett, and they have one child, Grace.

The other children are: Albert, born 14 September 1874; Emma born 8 December 1876; Harry born 27 September 1878 and died 29 Septmeber 1880; Charlie E. born 10 August 1880; Lydia born 1 October 1882 and died 30 August 1889; Freddie H. born 20 April 1885; George Morris born 19 September 1887; Minnie Beatrice born 11 December 1889; and John Conner born 11 November 1893.

Mr. Austin is a member of the Masonic fraternity of Ava and the Knights of Honor. He has always been a faithful Democrat and is prominent in local politics. He has served as Highway Commissioner, was elected Justice of the Peace, but refused to qualify, and is now holding the office of Collector for the fourth term, discharging his duties with a promptness and fidelity which win him high commendation. Pleasant and genial in manner, he has many friends throughout the community, and the high regard in which he is held is justly merited.

QUERIES

55-1. **Seth Austin** married — Smith. Their daughter, Sarah/Sally Austin, was b. 2 August 1793 in Salisbury, Connecticut, or Tunbridge, Vermont. She married William Kelsey. Need Sarah's ancestry. *See Page 57!*

55-2. **Philo Austin** b. Vermont circa 1824, listed in several census records for Moriah, Essex County, New York, with mother Susannah Austin, b. Rhode Island circa 1790. Both are buried in the Sherman Burying Ground in W. Moriah VT, next to Densy/Prudence (Austin) Shaw, wife of Richard Shaw b. Vermont circa 1820. Was she also a daughter of Susannah? Need ancestry of Philo.

55-3. **Lyman Austin** was born circa 1800 in Oneida County, New York, died in 1863 in Palermo, Owsego County, NY. He married circa 1825 Pauline Reed, born 2 June 1799 in Lee, Mass., the daughter of John & Elizabeth (Crocker) Reed. Need ancestry & children of Lyman.

55-4. **Richard Austin** was born in England circa 1598, died in Charlestown, Massachusetts. He married in England. Need death of Richard and wife.

55-5. **Nancy Austin** was probably born in New York in 1801, died Altmar, Oswego County, New York on 7 January 1887. She married, probably in NY circa 1819, Asa P. Parkhurst born Whitesboro NY, 1796, died 15 October 1872 Dugway, NY. He was the son of Josiah and Hannah (Tyler) Parkhurst. Need ancestry of Nancy.

55-6. **Abigail Austin** married Samuel Hale, born 26 October 1741 died circa 1809, an Ensign from Connecticut in Revolutionary War. Need all data on their children.

MARY AUSTIN CAPTURED BY ABENAKI
INDIANS AT YORK, MAINE IN 1692

by Kenneth Roberts
and Emma Lewis Coleman

The following excerpts were taken from Kenneth Roberts' 1933 book *Trending into Maine,* and Emma Lewis Coleman's 1925 book *New England Captives Carried to Canada between 1677 and 1760 During the French and Indian Wars*, Southworth Press, Portland.

On Sunday, 24 January 1692, one hundred and fifty Abenakis from the Kennebec, under the chief Madocko-wando, came to the foot of Mt. Agamenticus on snow-shoes, and sent scouts forward to examine York Village. They were hungry Indians after their long journey, and they had no time to waste; so although snow was falling heavily, they decided to attack the settlement early the next morning.

So numerous were the Indians, and so sudden the appearance of those hideously painted red men when they attacked, that the inhabitants made no resistance. One of the first to be slaughtered was Mr. Dummer, the minister, who was preparing to mount his horse to pay a visit to a parishioner. He was shot down, his clothing torn off, and his body mutilated in the manner approved by Indians in the early days, and more recently by Ethiopian warriors.

In two hours all important houses in York and its neighborhood had been burned, all the women and children captured, nearly all the men killed and horribly mangled, all horses, cattle, sheep and pigs killed or burned, and all the corn and fodder destroyed. Three hours after the attack the Indians, loaded with loot, were on their way back to the Kennebec, driving their prisoners before them through the thick woods.

Seventy-three captives, mostly women and children, made that long trip to Canada through the snow and the dark forests. Some were young – incredibly young to make such a journey. Mary Austin, for example, was five years old. How difficult it would be, lacking the records, to believe that little Mary Austin, sometimes carried by red men and sometimes by white, and sometimes stumping along on her own small legs, traveled four hundred miles, beneath dark pines, over mountains, across frozen rivers, and at last came safely to Montreal! Yet the record exists. She was sold as a servant to a French family, brought up as a Roman Catholic, and entered on the French records as Mary "Haustein."

In 1695 Mary "Astin" remained in Canada, and in 1710/11 Mary "Osten" is still there. In the summer of 1708 Lieut. Josiah Littlefield wrote from Montreal that "Mary Austin of York is well."

On 7 January 1710, Etienne Gibau, twenty-three years old, son of Gabriel Gibau of the parish of La Valterre, and of Suzanne Duvand, living now in this parish, married Marie Elizabeth Haustein, daughter of Mathiew Haustein and of Marie Littlefield his wife, of the town of York in New England, in the presence of Etienne's brother; Jaques la Selle, his brother-in-law; the Sieur de Senneville and of several other relatives and friends.

Etienne could not write his name but Mary could. Among the witnesses was Marie Francoise (Freedom) French of Deerfield. Etienne was a carpenter.

On the Notre-Dame register are baptismal records of nine children: 1711, M. Elizabeth, whose godmother was Marie-Joseph Sayer, the only name of a N.E. friend appearing as a sponsor; 1712 Etienne; 1714 Jean-Baptiste; 1716 Genevieve; 1718 Marie-Therese - the mother's name given as Hasting; 1720 Jacques-Joseph; 1722 Jean-Francois; 1724 Charlotte; 1725 Antoine.

On 4 October 1755, Marie Elizabeth Hastin, wife of Etienne Gibau, joiner, was buried in the cemetery near the church (Notre-Dame of Montreal) having died the preceding day about 8 o'clock A.M. and about 68 years old. Present were priests Amplement and Durumer.

★★★★★★★★★★★★★★★★★★★★★★★★★★★★★

Austins of America is intended to serve present and future genealogists researching Austin family lines. Readers are encouraged to submit Queries, genealogical and historical articles for publication. Previously published books, pamphlets or articles containing Austin genealogical data are also sought for reprinting or review.

EDITOR

DR. MICHAEL EDWARD AUSTIN   CONCORD, MA

ASSOCIATE EDITORS

ANTHONY KENT AUSTIN	PROSPECT, KY
PATRICIA BIEBUYCK AUSTIN	CONCORD, MA
PAULINE L. AUSTIN	MARION, IA
JANET AUSTIN CURTIS	ALBUQUERQUE, NM
CAROL LEIGHTON HULL	SUDBURY, MA

Austins of America is published each February and August by The Austin Print, 23 Allen Farm Lane, Concord, Massachusetts 01742. All correspondence, including subscriptions, articles and responses to queries, should be sent to this address. Subscriptions are $2.50 per year postpaid.

★★★★★★★★★★★★★★★★★★★★★★★★★★★★★

SETH AND HANNAH SMITH AUSTIN
OF TUNBRIDGE, VERMONT

by Pauline L. Austin

This response to Query 55-1 is based upon the author's own research, and a 1966 letter from Mrs. Louise Austin of Ocean Park, Washington.

Seth Austin was the sixth of eleven children of R242 Thomas and Hannah (Hale) Austin, of the Richard Austin line (see pp. 35,88,89 of *The Descendants of Richard Austin of Charlestown, Massachusetts*, by Edith Austin Moore and William Allen Day). He was born 13 September 1748 in Salisbury, Connecticut, married Hannah Smith on 26 April 1770, died in Tunbridge, Vermont on 23 July 1819. Seth sold land to an older brother Samuel b. 3 May 1746 (deed reproduced below), and after whom he probably named his son Samuel Austin whose birth is recorded in Vol. II of the Salisbury records, along with Seth and Hannah's marriage.

Seth Austin served in the Revolutionary War as a Sergeant (pension record), Lieutenant (State of Connecticut Records Vol. IV, page 184), and as a Captain (State of Connecticut Records Vol. V, page 212). Many years after his death, widow Hannah petitioned for a pension:

Declaration   *State of Vermont At Tunbridge*

On this 24 day of August at 1844 personally appeared Hannah Austin of Tunbridge in the County of Orange and State of Vermont aged ninety years who being first duly sworn according to law douth on her oath make the following declaration in order to obtain the benefit of the provisions made by the act of Congress passed July 4th, 1836 that she is the widow of Seth Austin who during the Revolution resided in Sulsberry in Connecticutt. She supposed he was a sargent and served in the War of the Revolution several campains. the first service he was gone from home in said war was the alarm at Lexington or Bunker Hill but did not reach place until the battle was over and returned in a few days. The next year he went into the service early in the spring or summer and was at the Battle or about where the Battle of Long Island was fought and the abandoning of New York and White Plains Battle. I heard him talk of these Battles and early in the spring 1777 he went in the service as she supposed was at the burning of Danburry and Sarus? and he was out at the Battle of Bennington and Still Water or near them. I well recollect this year on one of the alarms my husband hired Deacon Hesekiah Camp's mare to go to see Col. Burnell and his horse was shot and he brought his saddle home on his back but got orders to go in the service from Col. Burnell and went of the following morning. He had to pay 18 lbs. for the horse. On one of these alarms he helped make horse shoes in the night to be ready for an early start, and he went to guard Poughkeepsie the same season. She thinks he was out that year about 8 months and it may have been more and he was afterwards out to gard New Haven and was gone some months but don't know how long. Her husband spent most of his time engaged in said war through the whole of the war. He had authority to enlist soldiers and take up cowboys and was always ready at his country's call. She supposed that he filled different posts of office during said war, some times as Captain or Commander. At one time by reason of sore eyes hired Daniel Stanand to take his place 2 months in the winter but Stanand was taken prisoner as she understood and escaped by hiding in a brush heap and the enemy suspecting him there pounced on the heap gouging him and said damn him if he is under here he is dead enough now and left him. He stayed some time in the cold until it was dark and he escaped. This is as he told me.

She further declares that she was married to the said Seth Austin April 1770 by minister Lee and prior to that time her name was Hannah Smith and her husband the aforesaid Seth Austin died on the 23rd day of July, 1819, aged 71 and she has remained his widow ever since. As will more fully appear by the proof here unto anexed and by reason of age and loss of memory I cannot recollect any facts more particular.

         (signed) Hannah Austin

Witness
  Samuel Austin
  Wm. Hebard

Sworn to and subscribed the Day and year first above written
         Wm. Hebard Judge of the Supreme Court

Hannah's claim was suspended awaiting specific statements as to the amount of service and names of officers under whom Seth served in each enlistment (and which was never furnished).

SETH AUSTIN DEED TO SAMUEL AUSTIN

To all People to whom these presents shall come greeting. Know ye that I Seth Austin of Tunbridge in the County of Orange and State of Vermont for the considera tion of thirty pounds L.Mo. receivd to my full satisfaction of Samuel Austin of Tunbridge in the County & State afors^d Do give grant bargain Sell and Confirm unto the said Samuel Austin his Heirs and assigns to their own propper use benefit, and behoof forever a certain tract or parcel of Land lying and being in Tunbridge it being the one half of Lots No. 65 & 80 belonging to the original Rights of George Palmer and William Whitney it being the Easterly Half of Each Lot. Containing in the Whole one Hundred Acres more or less as may be Seen by the Plan and Records of s^d Town.

To have and to Hold the above granted and bargained premises with the Appurtenences thereof unto him the said Samuel Austin his Heirs and Assigns forever to them and their own proper use and behoof and also I the Said Seth Austin do for my Self my Heirs Executors and administrators Covenant with the said Samuel Austin his Heirs and assigns that at and untill Enseiling these presents I am well seized of the premises as a good indefensible Estate in fea simple and have good Right to Bargain and Sell the Same in Manner and form as above written and that the Same is free of all Incumbrance whatsoever and further more I the said Seth Austin do by these Presents bind my Self and my Heirs forever to warrant and defend the above granted and bargained Premises to him the said Samuel Austin his Heirs and Assigns against all Claims and Demands Whatsoever claiming by from or and me or the original grantee.

In Witness whereof I have hereunto Set my Hand and Seal this 1st Day of October Anno Domini 1773

         Seth Austin (seal)

Signed Sealed and Delivered
in Presence of
Abiel Austin
Eli Austin

State of Vermont Orange County Personally appeared Seth Austin the Signer and Sealer of the above written Instrument and acknowledged the same to be his free act and Deed before me this 11 Day of July Anno Domini 1797 Alexander Hadman, Justice of Peace

Tunbridge August 5th 1797 Receiv^d the above Deed for Record Attest Hezekiah Hutchinson Town Clerk

HEZEKIAH AND NANCY AUSTIN
OF ANDERSON COUNTY, TENNESSEE

by Charles Edwin Austin

Editor's Note: The following article concerns the same family discussed in Janet Austin Curtis' article on *William and Milly Austin of Anderson County, Tennessee* published on page 31 of *Austins of America*. The present article questions whether William was the father of the children attributed to him by Mrs. Curtis, including the subject, Hezekiah Austin.

The first recorded history of Hezekiah Austin is found in the transcription of the *Minutes of the Pleas and Quarterly Court of Anderson County, Tennessee*. The *Minutes* for the third session, September 1802, include:

p.16: *Ordered that William Austin bring the orphan children herein named, which were presented by the Grand Jury (viz): Joseph Austin, Elizabeth Austin, Zachariah Austin, Hezekiah Austin, John Austin, Daniel Austin, Pobe [Phoebe] Austin, and Nancy Austin to the next Court to be held for the county of Anderson on the second Monday of December next, to be disposed of as the Court may think proper.*

Few conclusions are possible from this entry alone. However, based upon the assumption that the children are listed in the order of their birth (such is the case with Hezekiah, John, and Daniel), it would appear that there is an excellent possibility that there were additional adult children. The following transcripts from the December session of the Court establish some important facts about the family. They do not, however, indicate who was the father of the children. At first glance it may appear that William Austin was the father, but this is not confirmed by the available Court transcripts:

p.19: *Ordered by the Court that Hannah Austin and Nathaniel Austin have the Administration of all and singular the goods and chattels and credits of William Austin deceased. They having entered into Bond in the sum of One Hundred Dollars and give Arthur Crozier and John Howard - Securities - they were qualified accordingly.*

p.19: *Ordered by the Court that Arthur Crozier have Hezekiah Austin, a boy born Feby 17th 1787 Bound to him until he attains the age of twenty one years. That John Howard have John Austin, a boy born 26 Oct., 1789 until he attains to the age of Twenty one and that Stephen Heard have Daniel Austin, a boy born 16 October, 1793 until he shall attain to the age of twenty one years.*

p.19: *Ordered by the Court that Hannah Austin be allowed the sum of ten dollars for keeping the children of Milley Austin (viz): John Austin, Daniel Austin, Nancy Austin, and Pheobe Austin, from September 1802 to December.*

p.86: *John Howard brought into court an orphan boy named John Austin who had been formerly bound to him by this Court and was discharged from the obligation of his indenture. Said Howard being about to release.*

p.87: *Ordered by the Court that an orphan boy named John Austin be bound as apprentice until William Underwood Esquire until he shall attain to the age of twenty one years who entered into indentures as the law requires.*

Additional information is available on one Betsy Austain on pages 86 and 152 of the above Court records.

As mentioned above, the possibility of additional, older children, does exist if the first list of the children is in the order of their birth. Thus, the children were probably of the following ages in 1802: Joseph ca.20, Elizabeth ca.19, Zachariah ca.17, Hezekiah 15, John 13, Pheobe ca.11, Daniel 9, and Nancy ca.7. As can be seen in the above records, Pheobe and Nancy may be in reverse order. If there are any adult children, there is an *unproven possibility* that William Austin, of neighboring Grainger County, may have been one of the adult children of this family. It is *presumed* that the William Austin who was directed to bring Milley Austin's *orphan* children to the December Court term is the same William Austin who married Rebecker Moses 22 March 1798 in Grainger County, Tennessee. Note that Anderson County was formed from Grainger and Knox County lands, and William may well have been living in what was later to become Anderson County.

A deed to William Austine dated 16 March 1801 in Knox County, was recorded in Anderson County on 8 June 1802. (Anderson County was formed in 1802.) The same land was sold on 27 November 1802, and was proven in Court on 30 May 1803. The later deed was witnessed by Valentine Austin with his name being stricken, with Nathaniel being added in place of Valentine. Thus the deed was accepted in court with Nathl Austin and Ruben Ragland as witnesses. For the deed to have been proven in court at least five months after the death of William seems unlikely, therefore, it would appear that there were two William Austins, perhaps father and son. Additional Anderson County and Grainger County court records reflect other Austins in the immediate area in that time period, including a Stephen Austin. There is little doubt that Valentine, Stephen, and Clisbe Austin were of the

John Austin family of Halifax and Pittsylvania Counties, Virginia. The last known record of William Austin, circa 1750-60, of the said John Austin family is in Surry County, North Carolina in 1777. Even though there is a possibility that Hezekiah Austin was a descendant of this John Austin, there is no positive proof that this is the case.

The next record of Hezekiah Austin is found in the Tennessee Governor's appointment book, when Hezekiah was appointed to the rank of Lieutenant in the 31st Regiment of the Tennessee State Militia for Bledsoe County on 16 April 1811. It would appear that Hezekiah stayed in Bledsoe County at least until 1815, when he, Daniel and John signed a Land Law Petition there. That being the case, Hezekiah met and married Nancy Jane Blevins circa 1812, in Bledsoe County. They were blessed with their first child, John H. Austin, in 1813. The 1830 Census for Bond County, Illinois, lists a female child 10 to 15 years of age who is unknown to the Hezekiah Austin family researchers. This child was apparently born to Hezekiah and Jane while they lived in Bledsoe County, if indeed she was their child.

Shortly after the formation of Marion County, partially from Bledsoe County lands, Hezekiah apparently bought his first tract of land. This is a very broad statement, since Hezekiah never recorded a deed of conveyance to him. Fortunately Hezekiah bought three tracts of land in Marion County that were original purchases, therefore these required government surveys which were recorded in the county. The first two of these tracts were surveyed 29 June 1825, the third on 3 October 1826. Of these three tracts, there is only one deed of conveyance from Hezekiah of record in Marion County. Hezekiah's failure to record deeds was perhaps because in those days a man's word was his bond, and the southern pioneer was a very independent and individualistic person, not wanting anyone to know his business unless it was necessary.

As noted above, Hezekiah was bound out to Arthur Crozier at age 15 for his food, shelter, clothing, and presumably his education. The brother of merchant John Crozier, Arthur was an attorney, and served six years as Chief Justice of the Anderson County Pleas and Quarterly Court. It appears that Hezekiah remained in touch with Arthur Crozier until Mr. Crozier's death, perhaps in 1838. Hezekiah is indexed as being on the same page and paragraph as was a hearing to determine Mr. Crozier's death date at a session of the Bledsoe County Civil Court. Since the resource document was a very poor transcription of the original document, neither Hezekiah's name nor Mr. Crozier's death date were found therein.

Hezekiah and Nancy Jane (Blevins) Austin were further blessed with the following children while they lived in Marion County, and apparently in neighboring Jackson County, Alabama: Steven Blevins 1817, Malinda Belle 1821, Jonathan Asbury 1823. In addition, the Bond County Census lists another male child under five years old. In some instances the U.S. Census indicates the above children were born in Tennessee, while in other cases they are listed as born in Alabama.

Sometime in 1828, Hezekiah and (Nancy) Jane moved, along with their Marion County neighbor Stephen A. Blevins, to Bond County, Illinois. While there, they completed their family with William Hezekiah Austin 1829, and James S(cruggs) Austin 1832. At that time they returned to Jackson County, Alabama. They remained in Jackson and DeKalb Counties, Alabama, for the remainder of their lives.

Hezekiah and his brother John were both Lay Deacons in the Methodist Church. Family tradition relates that they preached the first Methodist sermon to the white pioneers of Dekalb County, Alabama, and Dade County, Georgia. Hezekiah lived south of Sulpher Springs, Alabama, in DeKalb County, John lived north of Sulphur Springs just inside the Georgia State line. Hezekiah, John, and possibly Zachariah, moved to the old Cherokee Nation immediately after the infamous "Trail of Tears" of the Cherokee people in 1838. The Hezekiah and John Austin families were close neighbors in the pioneer days with some ties remaining between the two families down to modern times. This unusually strong bond exists partially due to a double relationship created by the descendants of Hezekiah and John marrying descendants of Daniel Brunson Burkhalter. A total of five marriages came of this relationship. Additionally, John Austin's family migrated along the same paths as did two of Hezekiah's sons, as well as portions of other Hezekiah families.

The descendants of Hezekiah Austin are extremely proud of their heritage, and prouder still that five of the six known families remain in active contact with each other one hundred ninety-six years after the birth of our progenitor, the Rev. Hezekiah Austin. We are also proud of the Christian heritage of our forefathers, with some member of every generation having served as ministers in various Christian churches.

Acknowledgments

The author would like to thank the following persons who contributed greatly to the research on the Hezekiah Austin line: Irene Austin House of the Jonathan Asbury Austin line; Jack Dalton Reynolds, James Russell Wilkinson, and Sherry Cotton Reynolds of the Steven Blevins Austin line; Harold Roy Blevins, Swaney Ethel Cagle Price, and Bill DeWayne Blevins of the Malinda Belle Austin Cagle line; Myra Elizabeth Austin Cunningham of the William Hezekiah Austin line; & AFA Genealogist Janet Austin Curtis.

HOLLANDS CREEK CHURCH CEMETERY
OF HARDIN COUNTY, TENNESSEE

by Janet Austin Curtis

This cemetery was copied about 1970 by the author. It is located in what was the old 8th Civil District, now the 5th Civil District, on Hollands Creek in Hardin County, Tennessee. This is an old Methodist Church Cemetery, and the early graves were marked with only fieldstones, if at all. Nearly everyone in this cemetery is related in some way to the Austin and Qualls families. Maiden names have been included in parentheses where they are known.

Marked Graves

Stephen Austin (see photograph next page)	1755-1850
Fredye George Austin	1933-1935
Grover C. Austin	1887-1938
Amy Q(ualls) Austin	1892-1939
Louisa E. Qualls, wife of J.W.	17 Jul 1876 - 28 Feb 1939
J. W. Qualls	31 May 1867 - 11 Jul 1938
Kennie C. Austin	26 Dec 1888 - 24 Dec 1967
Martha (Benson) Austin, wife K.C.	23 Jan 1894 - (no death date)
Mack Austin	1 Oct 1885 - 1 Jan 1950
Ethel (Scott) Austin, wife of Mack	13 Apr 1895 - 30 Jul 1936
Otis Lee Austin, WWII Pfc 793 Field Art.B	24 Jun 1924 - 14 Jul 1967
Allie M. (Austin) Freeman	18 Sep 1901 - 15 Dec 1938
Robbie Marie (Benson) Austin, wf. Albert	16 Mar 1921 - 24 Jul 1944
Mattie Lee (Fox) Tidwell	27 Feb 1905 - (no death date)
S. Lon Tidwell, husband of M.L.	23 Oct 1906 - 10 Oct 1956
Mollie Franks	22 Dec 1891 - 15 Aug 1951
James A. Austin	24 Jan 1862 - 12 Jan 1935
Nancy E. Austin	13 Sep 1868 - 24 Feb 1941
Retha Austin	5 Jul 1902 - 2 Jul 1948
Martha T. Austin	20 Aug 1897 - 15 Apr 1949
William Stan Austin	14 Nov 1889 - 20 Aug 1956
Hilda (Austin) Tune	6 Nov 1906 - 5 Dec 1960
D. Hamilton Tune, hus. of Hilda	15 Aug 1902 - (no death date)
Mattie Benson	1881 - 19—
Jeff Benson	1882 - 1963
Marlin Lloyd McDaniel	15 May 1920 - 9 Jun 1921
William L. Nolen	31 Jul 1838 - 28 May 1919
Rosy Etta (Austin) Nolen	18 Jul 1875 - 18 Apr 1907
W. M. Seaton	10 Sep 1873 - 18 Aug 1919
Vicey Fox	1877 - 1949
Mintie Ida (Johnson) Sheppard, wf. Elijah	12 Mar 1876 - 24 Sep 1914
Ada Lee Seaton	14 Mar 1910 - 22 Dec 1932
John Wm. Seaton, son Wm. & Vicey	15 Feb 1903 - 24 Jan 1904
James H. Atkinson	1890 - (no death date)
Osha (Austin) Atkinson, wife of J.H.	1889 - (no death date)
Lizzie (Austin) Smith	29 May 1882 - 19 Dec 1949
John Quincy Smith (obit. in Courier)	d. 21 Mar 1971 ae 87y
Louisa (Sharp) Seaton, wife of L.N.	6 Mar 1835 - 30 Dec 1915
Levi H. Seaton	3 — 1832 - 25 Mar 1904 ae 72y 7m 22d
Betty (Austin) Pickens, wf. of Avery	11 Nov 1869 - 22 May 1947
James A. Lard	Mar 1859 - (no death date)
Judia (Austin) Lard	11 Oct 1858 - 26 Dec 1926
Richard Lard, Co.H 5th Tenn. Cav. CSA	1823 - 1900
James Lard	circa 1836 - 27 Oct 1890
Hiram Haynes	1835 - 1896

Sarah (Lamb) Haynes	1834 - 22 Nov 1905
Archie D. Benson	15 Nov 1908 - 2 Nov 1961
Lue (Austin) Benson	4 Jul 1912 - (no death date)
Arch Qualls	9 Sep 1831 - 19 Jun 1887
Calvin H. Benson	1872 - 1945
Mary E. (Lard) Benson	1876 - 19—
H. R. 'Bob' Benson	12 Sep 1868 - 17 Jun 1944
Mattie (Qualls) Benson	18 Jun 1871 - 4 Feb 1940
Sally (Milligan) Banks	15 Apr 1864 - 18 May 1953
Samuel H. Banks	15 Feb 1856 - 25 Oct 1915
Manus Milligan	1869 - 1947
Erasmus D. Lambert	1854 - 1928
George W. Qualls	W.W.I
Hubert L. Alexander WWII Pfc TN 4 Div 22 Inf Co B	18 Dec 1921 - 19 Nov 1963
James D. Alexander	5 May 1879 - 23 Mar 1935
Mary E. Wood	1920 - 1953
Benj. Newton Barrier	20 Jul 1876 - 3 May 1949
Laura (Haynes) Barrier, wife of B.N.	13 Mar 1877 - 15 Nov 1955
William T. Barrier	1883 - 1939
Rose Ann (Atkinson) Barrier, wife of W.T.	1889 - 1939
John M. Qualls	9 Oct 1861 - 30 Apr 1943
Betty (Tune) Qualls	8 Mar 1862 - 20 Nov 1928
Claton Beam	d. 1963
Louise Beam	(no dates)
Henry E. Pollard	19 Sep 1885 - 31 Oct 1971
Myrtle J. (Benson) Pollard	27 Aug 1897 - 23 Jan 1959
Geo. Washington Martin	1877 - 1960
Mary Ellen Jones Martin	1886 - 1965
T. D. Fox	14 Apr 1873 - 10 Jan 1960
Ida Fox	8 Feb 1876 - 23 Aug 1923
Wilson Fox	d. 1962
Mary E. Fox	d. 1917
John Wesley Johnson	1836 - 1910
Mary A. F. Johnson, wife of J.W.	1830 - 1916
Nancy (Moore) Austin, wife of David	1813 - 31 Dec 1886
Artie Tidwell	1910 - 19—
Sudie Bell Tidwell	1877 - 1913
Wife of E. L. Fox	d. 1918
Frank G. Ward	d. 16 Sep 1972 ae 77y
Julia Stricklin Ward	(1st wife, pre-deceased F. G. Ward)
Allie Seaton Ward	(2nd wife, pre-deceased F. G. Ward)
Mandy Martin	1859 - 1929
Osker Martin	1885 - (no death date)
Albert Steeley	1883 - 1918
Mattie (Barrier) Steeley	1885 - 1960
Ezra Lee Fox	1887 - 1967
John T. Fox	1882 - 1948
Anna E. (Barrier) Fox, wife of J.T.	1880 - 22 Jun 1970
Elmer E. Fox	1948 - 1951
Junior Ray Johnson	1932 - 1961
Turner D. Benson	1925 - 1953
John D. Austin	28 Feb 1844 - 18 Dec 1918
Sarah A. (Armstrong) Austin, wf. of J.D.	13 Jul 1850 - 9 Apr 1912
A. G. Austin	14 Sep 1847 - 21 Feb 1912
Mrs. Emma Scott	1887 - 1911
John Carroll Qualls	1886 - 1951
Frederick M. Lard	21 Jul 1950 - 27 Jul 1950
Wallace G. Lard	28 Jan 1925 - 21 Feb 1965
Eller Haynes	1903 - 1904
Mary Elizabeth Conway	1881 - 1898
Mrs. Johnnie McDaniel	d. ae 62y (no dates)
J. C. Johnson	27 Mar 1840 - 9 Aug 1920
Mattie (Austin) Johnson, wf. of Coss	20 May 1871 - 21 Nov 1936
Henry Seaton	1905 - 1916
Jim Barrier	d. 1918

Jewell Barrier	d. 1918
Clarence Barrier	1900 - 1938
W. Enoch Qualls	2 Feb 1884 - 11 Jul 1956
Annie L. (Sharp) Qualls, wf. of Enoch	23 May 1884 - 21 Aug 1922
Milton Abner, son of Orval	b. & d. 9 Jan 1928
Infant son of Tim Austin	b. & d. 2 Jul 1945
Joyce Faye Austin	b. & d. 13 Jul 1937
Levin Benson	28 Jul 1895 - (no death date)
Bessie J. (White) Benson, wife of L.	12 Nov 1902 - 3 Apr 1967
Josie Qualls	1890 - 1921
William Elmer Qualls	26 Jun 1892 - 15 Feb 1962
Rosa Qualls, wife of Elmer	1895 - 1937
Rachel (Austin) Qualls, wife of Arch	29 Dec 1830 - 9 Feb 1928
S. Artemus Austin	1920 - 1922
E. A. 'Buddy' Swinford	27 Aug 1916 - Sep 1954
Elsie M. Swinford	21 Apr 1922 - (no death date)
Rosie Lee Swinford, dau. I.H. & Bell	19 Jul 1908 - 19 Mar 1933
Isaac H. Swinford	12 Sep 1877 - (no death date)
Belle (Barrier) Swinford, wife of I.H.	18 Jun 1877 - 8 Mar 1959
Willie A. Lee, son of J.W. & N.J.	1878 - 1889
John V. Stansell	1889 - 1939
Amy (Milligan) Stansell, wife of J.V.	1894 - (no death date)
Harrison White, WWI Pvt 42 Co 165 Depot Brig.	18 Sep 1888 - 23 Oct 1961
Lottie (Smith) White, wife of H.	1908 - (no death date)
Willie D. Smith	1940 - 1965
Bed. B. Qualls	1896 - 1949
James T. Qualls	1865 - 1949
Mary A. (Austin) Qualls	1866 - 1942
Betty J. Qualls, dau. Arch & Gert	1935 - 1935
Dave D. White	1875 - 1961
Louizy E. (Pollard) White, wife of D.D.	1878 - 19—
Ben Milligan	d. 29 Jun 1970 ae 69y 9m 10d
Carmon Robert Steeley	15 Feb - 9 Dec 1917
Linia Estell Steeley	13 Jan 1910 - 12 Jun 1911
Baby Boy Steeley	d. 6 Jul 1970 ae 10hrs 45min
Gustie Austin	d. 24 Aug 1969 ae 61y 9m 27d
Henry Lamb	1843-1929
Tommie Johnson, son of Coss & Mattie	d. 6 Nov 1902 ae 7m 10d
Jesse M. Austin	8 May 1872 - 26 Jan 1948
Nancy (Lard) Austin, wife of J.M.	20 Apr 1877 - 11 Nov 1960
Cassie Lola Austin, dau. of Z.T. & M.J.	12 Sep 1884 - 25 Nov 1918
Ola Ethel Austin	14 May 1903 - 16 Jul 1903
Beulah A. Austin, dau. T.F. & Selina	14 Jan 1888 - 5 Aug 1892
Thomas Frank Austin	23 Apr 1863 - 9 Aug 1938
Zuba Austin, dau. T.F. & M.	15 Jul 1909 - 14 Nov 1926
Roe Austin	28 Sep 1877 - 1 May 1954
Tennie (Qualls) Austin, wife of Roe	3 Nov 1889 - (no death date)
Tilda A. Austin	16 Mar 1886 - 21 Apr 1886
Noah Austin	1875 - 1953
Nancy (Hopper) Austin, wife of Noah	1873 - (no death date)
Robert N. Johnson	3 Apr 1875 - 20 Mar 1956
William Owen Austin	15 Feb 1867 - 8 Aug 1936
Millard Austin, son of W.O.	4 Dec 1907 - 9 Jan 1932
Rubie E. Austin, son	12 May 1902 - 20 Sep 1904
Tennessee Qualls	d. 19 May 1948
Thomas B. Austin	5 Oct 1862 - 9 Oct 1910
Lina (Tune) Austin, wife of Thos.	1 Dec 1863 - 14 Dec 1935
George Earlin Austin	27 Feb 1911 - 20 Apr 1932
Marvin Austin	1879 - 1948
Lillie E. (Lard) Austin	1886 - 1953
Katie A. Austin	24 Jul 1884 - 8 Mar 1958
John Austin	8 Jun 1816 - 2 Nov 1896
Isabell V. (Qualls) Austin, wife of John	2 Apr 1851 - 2 Jul 1924
Jane (Lamb) Austin, 1st wife John, m. 31 May 1835	1819 - 1880
Zachary T. Austin	7 Sep 1848 - 1 Feb 1892

Nancy E. (Qualls) Austin, wf. of John	12 Jul 1863 - 13 Feb 1934
Martha J. (Qualls) Austin, wf. of Z.T.	1 Apr 1848 - 7 Mar 1929
Johnny W. Austin, hus. Nancy	28 May 1864 - 2 Jan 1898
Ralph N. Austin	11 Sep 1877 - 14 Dec 1938
Ina Gustelle Milligan, wife of Waymon	d. 21 Feb 1873 ae 43y

STEPHEN AUSTIN

ARMSTRONG'S
N.C. CO.
WASHINGTON
DRAGOONS
REV. WAR

B. 1755
D. 1850

Stephen Austin was born November 1755 Pittsylvania County, Virginia. He died 1850 per marker, but his last Revolutionary War pension payment was in 1844, which is probably a more accurate death year.

Unmarked Graves

In addition to the marked graves listed above, the following individuals are probably also buried here, but there is little to prove it.

Dorcas Austin, wf. of Stephen, d. 13 Apr 1836 (Bible record). **Sanders Austin**, son of Stephen & Dorcas, b. 1782 Virginia and d. between 1856 (made a deed) and 1860 (census). **Nancy Qualls Austin**, wife of Sanders, b. 1791 Virginia (census) d. 186– (1860-70 census). **David Austin**, b. 1816/7 Tennessee (1850 census), d. between February 1850 (census) and August 1850 (His estate in Court) as result of a knife fight with a man named McDougal. **Stephen Austin**, b. ca. 1810 (1850 census), d. ca. 1872 per Court records. **Ann Lamb Austin**, wife of Stephen, b. ca. 1815/6 (per census), living in 1880. **William Austin** b. ca. 1820 (census), living in 1880. **Sarah Qualls Austin**, wife of William, b. ca. 1826 (per census) living in 1880. John Qualls, brother of Nancy Qualls Austin, b. 1798 (census), d. 186– (1860-70 census). Mary (Polly) Qualls, b. 1805 Tennessee (1850 census), d. bef. 1878 (court record). Henry Qualls, son of John, b. 1824 (census), living in 1880. **Angeline Austin Qualls**, wife of Henry, b. 1825 Tennessee (census), living in 1880. Henry Lamb, b. 1776 Va. (1850 census), d. after 1854 (deed).

PHINEHAS AND LODICA AUSTIN
OF ROCHESTER, VERMONT
AND POTSDAM, NEW YORK

by Fanny R. Andrews

The following material was obtained from many sources. Early information from Edith Austin Moore, and more recent contributions by AFA Midwest Historian Pauline L. Austin and the *Austins of America* Editor, Dr. Michael E. Austin, are gratefully acknowledged. The single most important resource for the present article, however, was the collection of many letters and photographs which belonged to my husband's grandmother, Adelaide Hannah Austin Andrews, who was a granddaughter of Phinehas and Lodica.

Phinehas Austin was born circa 1774, the son of S216-1 Nathan and Phebe (Barker) Austin of the Samuel Austin of Boston, Massachusetts line (Reference 1). Phinehas is believed to have been their fourth child. Mrs. Moore (Reference 2) has his birthplace as Antrim, NH, but it is not found recorded there. Dr. Austin points out that Nathan and Phebe's third child Daniel was born 16 January 1773 in Methuen, Massachusetts, and that they probably were not even in Antrim, New Hampshire, until after 22 March 1775 for on that date Nathan and his brother S216-3 Abijah Austin were warned out of Pelham, New Hampshire. Thus, it seems more likely that Phinehas was born in Methuen, or even in Pelham, rather than in Antrim.

Phinehas moved with his parents from Antrim, New Hampshire, to Rochester, Vermont. There he met and married Lodica Washburn on 18 December 1800. Lodica (sometimes her name is found spelled 'Lodice,' and she was variously nick named 'Dicey,' 'Dicy,' or 'Disa') was born 7 August 1786 in Connecticut, the daughter of Ezra Washburn, Jr. and Lucy Fuller. It is interesting to note that Phinehas' younger sister, S216-16 Hannah Austin, married Lodica's older brother, Ezra Washburn III.

In Reference 3 we find that in March 1802 in Rochester, Vermont, Ebenezer Sparhawk surveyed the 20 acres of land that Phinehas Austin sold to Jared Hall. Reference 4 has a sheep mark recorded for 'Phinehas Austen' on 6 April 1904, and later that same year records:

> *"be it remembered that I the subscriber decent from the major Part of this Town in Religious opinion"* - Rochester July ye 3rd 1804
> (signed) Phinehas Austen.

From page 65 of Reference 3 we learn "In February (1816) the exodus of Rochester families to Potsdam, N.Y., begun the year before by Elkanah Shaw, grew in numbers, taking the families of Willard Jefferson, Phineas Austin, Forrest Morgan, J. B. McCollom and Simeon Parker." Phinehas Austin died in Potsdam, St. Lawrence

County, New York, on 15 April 1863, while his wife Lodica died 20 August 1865 aged 80. The portrait above is believed to be that of Phinehas and Lodica. Their children were born in Rochester, except for the youngest, who was probably born in Potsdam, New York.

CHILDREN:
S216-141. OLIVER, son of 'Phinehas and Disa' b. 23 December 1801, d. 14 August 1808

S216-142. OLIVE, b. 1 September 1803, d. 5 September 1812, bur. Rochester

S216-143. LUCY, b. circa 1805, m. William Sealy

S216-144. PHINEAS, b. 18 March 1807, d. 25 March 1896 (see below)

S216-145. OLIVER, b. 22 July 1809, d. 22 March 1893 (see next page)

S216-146. LODICA, 'Disa' d. 26 September 1812 age 5 months.

S216-147. MELISSA, b. circa 1815, m. -- Brown

S216-148. JOESPH B., b. 1817, m. Rhoda A.

S216-144. PHINEAS[7]AUSTIN (*Phineas*[6]*, Nathan*[5,4]*, Thomas*[3,2]*, Samuel*[1]) was born 18 March 1807 in Rochester, Vermont. He was married in Rochester, Vermont, first to Harriet Abbott, and second to Harriette M. Powers. Harriette, the daughter of Ai Powers, was born on 26 September 1816 in Potsdam, New York. Phineas and Harriette were in Sterling, Illinois (where he was working 22 September 1870) and La Crosse, Wisconsin. They eventually migrated to Garnet, Kansas, with at least one of their children, Adelaide Hannah. Harriette died 4 May 1891 in Garnet, and Phineas died in there also on 25 March 1896. Both buried in Garnet. The first three children are by Phineas' first wife. All the children were born in Potsdam, New York.

**Phineas Austin
1807-1896**

CHILDREN:

S216-1441. EDGAR A., *b. 1834, d. age 84, San Diego, California*

S216-1442. BETSY JANE, 'Jennie' *b. 1836, d. 12 April 1907 Sandwich, Illinois*

S216-1443. JULIA, *b. 1838, m. Ezra Carter Palmer on 12 October 1856. Ezra was b. 28 February 1832 in North Troy, Vermont, died 1 January 1899 in Sandwich, Illinois. He was a 2nd Lieutenant in the Civil War, built a church at Poplar Grove, Virginia, 25 February 1865 with 50th Reg. U.S. New York Volunteer Engineers.*

S216-1444. ADELAIDE HANNAH, *b. 6 July 1851 m. John Whiteside Andrews, resided Topeka, Kansas, m. 26 March 1874 Sterling, Illinois, d. 28 April 1946 Glendale, California. See page 64.*

S216-1445. EDWARD AI, *b. 9 June 1853, m. Carrie Snow in April 1883, d. 18 January 1911, Demoines, Iowa*

S216-1446. ELLA BERTHA, *b. 24 June 1857, m. Ellery D. Parks*

**Harriette Powers
1816-1891**

The obituary of S216-145 Oliver Austin appeared in a newspaper at the time of his death:

Oliver Austin

Mr. Oliver Austin died at his home in Potsdam, March 22, 1893, at the age of 84 years. The funeral services were conducted at the house by his pastor, Rev. A. C. Loucks, assisted by Rev. A. Bramley.

Fourteen years ago Mr. Austin suffered from paralysis. Since that time his health has been quite delicate. During the present winter he has seemed usually well, but the death of his wife, which occurred so recently, seemed to rob him of all power to resist the encroachments of disease, and so, suddenly, and almost as peacefully as the going to sleep of a child, he passed away.

Mr. Austin was the son of Mr. and Mrs. Phineas Austin. He was born in Rochester, Vt., in 1809. At the age of six years his father removed with his large family to Potsdam, N.Y. The country was at that time so much of a wilderness that the older members of the family were obliged to use the ax in clearing a road to their place of settlement, while Oliver drove the ox team. One brother, Phineas Austin, of Kansas, aged 86; and two sisters, Mrs. Wm. Sealy and Mrs. Melissa Brown, of Potsdam, survive him.

At the age of 22 years Mr. Austin went to Canada, where he remained two years. While here he became acquainted with Harriet Sarah Sealy, to whom he was married Aug. 1, 1833. At the time of his marriage he gave up his position as stage driver in Canada and settled on a small farm two miles east of Potsdam. This he enlarged from time to time until it reached its present proportions. His work for many years in this, then, comparatively new country was largely pioneer work. The land had to be cleared. To bring the fields to their present state of cultivation required and amount of toil and effort that can hardly be appreciated by the present generation. To this task Mr. Austin brought an energy of character and strength of physique that enabled him to cope successfully with the difficulties that confronted him. The cultivation of his land and the care of his large family so taxed his time and energies that he had little time to cultivate the social or aesthetic side of his character, and yet he read and took a lively interest in all questions pertaining to the church and to the public good. His sympathies and efforts were always on the side of virtue and sobriety.

REFERENCES

1. Michael E. & Patricia B. Austin, *The Descendants of Samuel Austin of Boston, Massachusetts*, to be published by the Austin Print, Concord, Massachusetts.

2. Edith A. Moore, *Some Descendants of Thomas Austin of Methuen, Mass. and New Hampshire*, unpublished manuscript, copies in D.A.R. Library in Washington, D.C. and New England Historic Genealogical Society Library in Boston, Mass.

3. *Rochester, Vermont - Its History 1780-1795*, by Rochester Town History Committee. Published by Queen City Printers, Burlington, Vermont, 1975. See review of this book under **Literature** on page 6 of *Austins of America*.

Above: Adelaide Hannah Austin with her husband John Whiteside Andrews and two of their children, Herbert & Gertrude. Below: Phineas Austin's daughters (left to right): Ella Bertha b.1857, Julia b.1838, Adelaide Hannah b.1851, Betsy Jane b.1836.

ZACHARIAH AUSTIN
OF PRINCE GEORGE'S PARISH
FREDERICK COUNTY, MARYLAND

by Arthur Clement Austin

The Zachariah Austin discussed in the following article is the son of John and Charity Kendrick Austin (see *Austins of America*, page 34).

When General Burgoyne surrendered his Army at Saratoga, N.Y. on 17 October 1777, Zachariah was 14 years old in Montgomery County, Maryland. The troops numbered some five thousand men, half British and half Hessian, and posed a serious problem for the Continental Congress. It was agreed by the *Convention Treaty* that the prisoners would be shipped back to England via Boston. The Congress feared they would be diverted if shipped to a Tory port like New York, and returned to the fighting. Much confusion and charges of perfidy on both sides followed while the troops were held in the North. Finally they were marched through Connecticut, New Jersey, Pennsylvania (where it was hoped some of the Hessians would escape into the German-speaking farms, and a few did), Maryland and finally Charlottesville, Virginia.

The Baroness Riedesel who with her three daughters under age five had accompanied her husband, a surrendered Hessian General, wrote an account of her experience in Charlottesville. Violinist Thomas Jefferson at nearby Monticello had the officers and their wives frequently as guests for dinner and musicales. The Baroness sang for these affairs.

In 1780 came Cornwallis & Tarleton and the savaging of the South. It was correctly thought that an attempt would be made to free these *Convention Treaty* prisoners so they were moved to Frederick, Maryland. Zachariah Austin was now seventeen years old, and enrolled in the Second Company, Class (Squad) One, of the Lower Battalion of Montgomery County. Col. John Murdock commanding, July 15, of that year. Clan Gregor records it as the 29th Battalion. In Class Seven was Baruck Odle (Odel), recently married to Margaret Offutt, granddaughter of patriot and Judge, Samuel Magruder the Third. Thirteen other men named Offutt were in the Battalion. In the middle Battalion, Fourth Company Class 40, was John Austin, who may have been Zachariah's father.

The directives from the Maryland Council to Colonel Murdock and others in 1781, as found in the Archives of Maryland, Vol. XLV, Maryland Historical Society:

February 3 - Full Company of militia to Frederick to guard the Convention troops. **March 20** - Convention troops ordered to Lancaster, Pennsylvania . . . "March Them There." **April 9** - Troops (county) cannot be ordered out of the county until they are "cloathed . . .

move them to the border." **June 6** - "You will deliver the recruits and Draughts . . . to Col. Adams . . . their cloathing will be delivered to them as soon as they get here and their unwillingness to march must not be regarded." **June 29** - (Letter to General Washington) Two battalions of militia . . . 1340 effective men and officers will be raised. **July 2** - Release selected militia for harvest time. **August 4** - Warning of invasion of Baltimore from Cape Henry "40 Sail of Vessels, 12 barges rumored." **October 19** - Cornwallis gives up Yorktown and the War. **November 5** - "We are informed there are a number of Militia Draughts and substitutes in and about Georgetown who are useless and an expense to the State. We therefore request you to give them a discharge and send them off to their respective homes." The POW's were moved to Lancaster and most got back to England.

Some months before Yorktown, Margaret Offutt Odle presented her husband with Cassandra, the first of six daughters she would bear in the next eight years. Baruck's will dated late 1788 and probated 9 June 1789 has: " . . .to my beloved wife, Margaret, and my six children (not named) my plantation Grubby Thicket." When the enumerator for the first federal census arrived at Grubby Thicket in June 1790 he listed as head of household Zachariah Austine (sic), three males under sixteen, and seven free white females (the term "free" was still used as a holdover from the days of indentured servants) and three slaves. As Zachariah's wife, Margaret delivered seven sons by mid-1803 (see *Austins of America* page 34). Two of Zachariah's younger brothers would marry two of Margaret's daughters, thus his step-daughters would become his sisters-in-law. No blood lines crossed here. All thirteen children reached adulthood, and most made the trip to Kentucky. Plantation owner Zachariah sat on the Grand Jury of Montgomery County Court in November 1791.

Not a fire bell in the night, but a good-sized alarm and shakeup was the Whiskey Rebellion in Western Pennsylvania occasioned by Alexander Hamilton's tax on whiskey. The farmers out on that frontier found it more profitable to distill their grain crops into liquid than to try to transport it via land and water to distant markets. Troops were called up, primarily from Virginia, Maryland, and Pennsylvania. Washington was to command some 15,000 troops, more than he ever had during the so-recent war. Under Militia Appointments for the 18th Regiment is found: June 18, 1794 - Zachariah Austin, Ensign; September 6, 1794 - Zachariah Austin, Lieutenant; October 22, 1795 - Zachariah Austin, Captain and resigned.

No shots were fired in anger or otherwise, and this might well be called the Whiskey Whimper. In nearby Federal City, soon to be known more familiarly as Washington, D.C., Thomas Jefferson had been elected President by one vote in the Electoral College. The census of 1800 lists the household of Zachariah Austin thus: three males under 10 years of age, one male 10-16, two females 10-16, one female 16-26, one female 26-45, ten slaves. When the census of 1810 was taken, land deeds were still recorded in British pounds or American dollars, and President James

Madison was about to have an upcoming war named, by its opponents, as "Mr. Madison's War." Later historians called it "The Second War with Britain." Of this "War of 1812" Zachariah's sixth son, Judge Samuel Austin of Butler County, Kentucky, in his later years would tell his grandchildren how he had watched the Capital City in flames in the year 1814. By late 1815, Zachariah, having bought from Margaret's daughters and their husbands their two-thirds rights to Grubby Thicket, sold the entire plantation to George Bohrer of Georgetown for $2960.

If all the Austins-Offutts-Odles who settled in Kentucky at this time moved in a group by ox-cart and mules, they formed a formidable caravan, and probably travelled the recently-completed Cumberland Road across the top of Maryland and Pennsylvania, then along the Ohio River into the mid-heart of the state. Here in 1816 Zachariah bought for $1,589 on Rough Creek some 800 acres of land where the tax records of Ohio County for 1821 list by name Zachariah, Zachariah Jr., John, Brok, William O., Francis, and Barrock, plus thirteen slaves and five horses. In the census the preceding year only one female was listed as "over 45 years" . . . Margaret would have been age 60. This is likely the last record found of this remarkable woman, for on 5 June 1824 Zachariah, "For and in consideration of the natural love and affection he bears toward his said son, (name of son), and the further consideration of one dollar . . ." distributed his land to four sons by separate deeds. Since Margaret did not sign away her dower rights, it can be presumed that she had died.

In 1830 President Andrew Jackson opened up the White House in Washington City to any citizen who wanted to walk in and look around. That same year the Ohio County, Kentucky, census revealed the household of Zachariah

Austin was truly diminished by earlier standards: one male 15-20, one male 60-70, nine slaves.

A legal settlement among two sons and a third party over land and slaves bears the laconic line "a gift of Zachariah Austin deceased." This was dated 18 October 1834. Zachariah left no will. His son Baruk filed a final paper in 1837 accounting for notes due him and small payments for funeral expenses. Neither the exact date of death nor the location of the graves for Margaret or Zachariah has been discovered. The most likely site is the Austin Cemetery on Taylor Mines Road, noted by Jeane Galau (page 35). A Bare Bones Obituary might read:

> *Zachariah Austin was born at the close of the French and Indian War, enrolled as a Private in the American Revolutionary War, served as a Captain in the Militia of Maryland in the Whiskey Rebellion. He witnessed the construction and destruction of the national capital in the War of 1812. (see photo next page)*
>
> *He transported his multi-complex family to a land formerly known as the dark and bloody ground, where ten years earlier the county was paying 8 shillings bounty for wolf pelts and where the land survey used such terms as "35 degrees north from a white oak tree . . . to a sour gum tree . . . 23 poles west."*
>
> *Zachariah lived under the presidencies of Washington, Adams, Jefferson, Madison, Monroe, Adams, and Jackson. From his mother's birth circa 1732 to his own death circa 1832, a century was spanned. In truth and in sum it was the time of the birth and establishment of this new nation.*

QUERIES

66-1. **Jeff Austin** b.1844 in So. Carolina? d. 1 July 1897 in Anderson County, Texas. Married Mary Jane (Jennie) Wilson b. 14 January 1843 in Alabama, probably Talladega County. William Austin, a brother, visited in Texas. Need ancestry of Jeff Austin.

66-2. **Hannah Austin** was born 23 March 1820 in Westchester County, New York. She died 25 April 1909 in Portis, Osborne County, Kansas. She married Walter W. Hoyt 15 March 1840. Her parents were Samuel Austin and Esther James. Need ancestry of Samuel and Esther.

66-3. **James C. Austin** was born 19 September 1790, purchased land in Brewer, Maine, in 1816, married there in 1818 Sarah Bradley. Seek parents of James and Sarah.

66-4. **Margaret Ann Austin** was born 17 September 1837 in Auburn, Cayuga County, New York. Supposedly orphaned (with two siblings, gender unknown), married 12

November 1851 to John Quincy Adams Doan/Doane, son of Eleazor and Margery (Catell) Doane, Quakers I believe. John died in 1861, and by November 1862 Margaret Ann remarried in Morris, Grundy County, Illinois. She also married a third time there, later came to Nodaway County, Missouri, until her death 18 April 1919. Seek her parents.

66-5. **Lydia Austin** born 25 July 1838 in Addison County, Vermont. She married first William Ramsdale, circa 1854, where? He died circa 1858. They had a son, William born circa 1856. Lydia then married second Alonzo L. Percival in 1860 in Kendall County, Illinois. Alonzo was born in Washington County, New York. They lived in Nebraska, Kansas, and Oklahoma. Their children were: Edgar, Ruby, Merley, Georgia, and Viola. Lydia died in 1921 in Meeker, Oklahoma. Seek parents or the brothers and sisters of Lydia.

George Town and Federal City, or City of Washington. Engraving published June 1st 1801. Reprinted with permission, from I.N. Phelps Stokes Collection, The New York Public Library Astor, Lenox and Tilden Collections. This might well have been the view Zachariah had from his homestead, from which he witnessed the construction & later the burning of our nation's capital.

QUERIES

67-1. Lyman L. Austin was born 1799 in Connecticut, m. Oswego County, New York, Pauline Reed (1799-1845); lived Green Lake County, Wisconsin. Need parents of Lyman and descendants of children: Angeline Crouch, Lyman, Amanda Martin, Minerva Peckham, Theron, Andrew J., Melinda Baker, Elizabeth Ames, Matilda Phillips, and William H. *See Query 55-3!*

67-2. Ambrose Austin was born 19 June 1757 in England, married Susannah Beard on 18 November 1779. She was born 3 December 1759. They lived in Jeromesville, Wayne County, Ohio, in 1816. Seeking parents of Ambrose or their prior residence.

67-3. Daniel Austin married Hamden, Connecticut, circa 1800 Adah Dorman, had a son Henry Austin. Need the parents of Daniel.

67-4. Phoebe Austin, born about 1760, married Benja-min Carter in 1795. Living in Washington County, New York in 1800. Need place of birth, parents, and any other data on Phoebe.

67-5. Orson David Austin was born in New York in 1818, moved to Michigan by 1846, and on to Wisconsin about 1863. His wife was buried in 1889 in Dunn County, Wisconsin. Orson moved back to Michigan by 1897 and died and was buried there in 1908. Obituary states he died after an illness in the home of Mrs. Edwards, and the funeral was also held in her home. What relation was Mrs. Edwards to Orson, if any? Seek all information on Orson.

67-6. Moses Austin married Berwick, Maine, 6 August 1767 to Elizabeth Clark. Elizabeth died 27 February 1793, and Moses m.(2) Esther Garland of Lebanon on 19 February 1794. Moses died in Berwick on 22 March 1820, age 78. Seek all data on Moses, Elizabeth, and Esther.

EDITOR'S CORNER

Contemplating the current issue of *Austins of America*, I was struck by how our newsletter has grown in just a few years. This current issue boasts the largest printing ever, and both the number of articles and photographs have set new records. Even our Staff continues to grow, as we welcome historian Anthony Kent Austin of Prospect, Kentucky, and genealogist Pauline Lucille Austin of Marion, Iowa, as Associate Editors.

While *Austins of America*'s physical growth is gratifying, even more rewarding is the ever-growing number of queries, responses and articles received from our readers. Readers have both learned much from, and added a great deal of information to the *Austins of America* computerized files. They have contributed dozens of articles concerning their Austin branches, information which otherwise might have gone unpublished, or even lost. I recall the stories of how my great-grandfather Amos Sprague spent a lifetime researching the Sprague Family, only to have his wife toss out all his work after he died - perhaps she felt he had spent *too* much time on genealogy! If only Amos had published while he had the chance!

Austins of America is *your* publication. Its continued success depends upon the research and contributions of those like yourself who are interested in their Austin lines. Don't be like poor Amos - *don't let your lifetime of research become lost!* We are anxious to obtain photocopies of any and all your research on your Austin lines. Also any Austin manuscripts, books, or articles you may come across will be a welcome addition to our *Austins of America* reference library, and will be used to help others trace their Austin family roots. Don't worry if your notes are in rough form . . . our staff delights in turning them into polished articles, with you credited as the author since it is your research!

In submitting your materials for publication, please don't forget those old photographs of Grandpa & Grandma Austin you have tucked away in ye olde family album, or in that cardboard box in the attic. *Austins of America* can publish those precious pictures along with your article, and return the photographs to you unharmed. We will gladly reimburse you for any photocopying or postage expenses incurred. Please send all correspondence and materials to our

      NEW ADDRESS: *Dr. Michael E. Austin*
                      Box 73   MIT/LL
                      Lexington, MA 02173

This new address should also be used for all Queries, Responses, Subscriptions, Address Changes, etc. Any change of your address should be reported to us at once, as we mail the newsletter using Bulk Mail, which the Post Office will not forward. This keeps the subscription price as low as possible, and permits nearly every penny of it to go into publishing the newsletter itself, rather than into postage costs.

A number of readers have inquired as to how they might approach computerizing their genealogical research, and how the *Austins of America* files are organized and used to answer queries by those searching their Austin family roots. This is clearly an area of growing interest to genealogists, and will be discussed in our next issue.

Remember the Austin Families Association Reunions! A regional reunion June 25-26 at the *Best Western Campus Inn*, Beaver Dam, Wisconsin, telephone (414) 887-7171 for reservations. The National Reunion August 5-6 at the *Dayton Mall Holiday Inn Holidome*, 7999 Prestige Plaza Drive, Miamisburg, Ohio (Exit 44 off I-75), telephone (513) 434-8030 for reservations. This year's National should prove even better than last year's . . . a meeting room is reserved from 9 to 5 on August 6th . . . plan to bring along your genealogical notes and join in the fun!

                                          Michael E. Austin
                                          Editor

THE REVOLUTIONARY ADVENTURES
OF JOHN AUSTIN OF VIRGINIA

by Anthony Kent Austin

John Austin of Fauquier County, Virginia, was among the first to respond to the crisis at Boston. He enlisted in the summer of 1775 for three years; however, he served seven, receiving his final discharge in 1782. His military adventures took him as far north as Canada and as far south as Georgia. He was a participant in several battles, the most notable, Quebec, Saratoga and the Cowpens.

In his pension declaration, Austin says, "He marched from Winchester, Virgina, to Quebec, then to New Jersey, then to Connecticut, then to Pennsylvania, then through Virginia and North Carolina to South Carolina and Georgia, and on his return was at the seige of York." Also, "he was in the battle of Stillwater, Monmouth Courthouse, White Plains (sic) and the Cowpens." He served under Daniel Morgan, Colonel (Richard) Butler, Major Benjamin Morris, Captain Charles Porterville (sic), Captain Gabriel Long, and others he couldn't recollect [1].

John Austin was 96 years of age when he made the above declaration on 20 August 1832, at the Courthouse in LaGrange, Oldham County, Kentucky. It had been fifty years since he had received his discharge in Frederick County, Virginia, from General Morgan. There was a great deal he couldn't recollect; time and old age had dulled his memory.

Using John Austin's pension declaration as a guide, the following text traces John's military activities during our glorious revolution. John was illiterate and did not leave a diary or a journal of his saga, so most of the information on his activities has come from the military historians of the units in which he served. When he originally enlisted in 1775, John joined Daniel Morgan's rifle company. Later he was in Morgan's Rifle Regiment, and still later in the Eleventh and Seventh Virginia Regiments, Continental Line. In pinpointing John's participation and specific duties, we have had to examine the pension applications, diaries and journals of veterans who at one time or another stood at John's side during a particular battle, shared his mess, or accompanied him on any of the number of long grueling marches that the defense of liberty from imperial tyranny required.

John Austin was born in 1736 and lived an incredible one hundred and nine years, passing on in 1845. Little is known of his early history. Family tradition has him born in England or Virginia, and possibly on the ocean-sea while his parents were enroute to the Old Dominion [2]. There is some unsupported material that suggests that he

took part in the Colonial Indian Wars and that he had been married to a Miss Grigsby [3]. However, documentation on his parents, his childhood, early manhood and marriages (if any) have yet to be uncovered. In a future article we will look into his family life after the revolution, that is, his marriage on 3 November 1788 to Elizabeth (Lindsey) Browning, their children, grandchildren, and great-grand-children [4].

On 14 June 1775, the Second Continental Congress resolved to raise ten companies of "expert riflemen" – six from Pennsylvania, two from Maryland, and two from Virginia, to aid in the siege of Boston. On that day the American Army was born. The next day, 15 June, George Washington was chosen to be commander-in-chief.

At the time congress was making its resolves, John Austin was a resident of Fauquier County, Virginia. He was thirty-nine years old, living in Leed's Parish, where he was a farmer and possibly a widower with grown children.

In neighboring Frederick County, the Committee of Safety appointed Daniel Morgan to captain one of the two Virginia companies mentioned in the congressional resolve. Drummers were sent into the countryside and into the neighboring counties to recruit the rank and file. In Leed's Parish, Austin must have heard the beat of one of Morgan's drummers.

There is no telling why Austin decided on joining Morgan. However, it is known that Virginia was up in arms over the inflammatory tales of Lexington and Concord, and Englishmen were worried about their rights under an unsympathetic Parliament. One of the Virginia patriotic songs of this critical period called upon men of valor to defend their liberty. It was called "American Hearts of Oak," and was written in 1775 by J. W. Hewlings of Nansemond, Virginia:

Come rouse up my lads, and join this great Cause,
in defence of your liberty, your property, and laws!
'Tis to honor we call you, stand up for your right,
And ne'er let our foes say, we are put to flight.

For so just is our cause, and so valiant our men,
We always are ready, steady boys, steady;
We'll fight for our freedom again and again.

The valient Bostonians have enter'd the field,
And declare they will fall there before they yield;
A noble example! In them we'll confide,
We'll march to their town, stand or fall by their side.

The last few lines seem to have been most appealing to John Austin, or again, maybe it was the need for adventure. Whatever, sometime in late June, he put together a few personal belongings, secured his tomahawk and hunting knife to his belt, picked up his rifle-gun, and

crossed the Blue Ridge into Frederick County, and there made his way to Winchester.

In Winchester, Austin found that he was not the only one to hear the drummer: the town was crowded with potential recruits. He was by far the oldest, but he didn't feel out of place. Most of the recruits were in their early twenties, but like John they were tall, rangy men, with close-cropped hair, wearing hunting shirts and leggins, or loose-fitting trousers; some wore felt hats, others coonskin caps. But all had come equipped with their rifles, tomahawks and scalpin' knives [5].

More than likely, Morgan's recruiting station was in the Golden Buck, Phil Bush's popular tavern. Here John would have made his way, in order to make his presence known to Captain Morgan. Looking about for familiar faces, John would have seen William Heth, Peter Bryan Bruin, and John Brown, all young men from Fauquier County who had come to enlist. There were several from Frederick that he knew, but there were also many strangers. One stranger he would get to know well was Charles Porterfield, a gentlemen volunteer; they would serve together over the next couple of years.

Morgan's company was supposed to have sixty-eight men, but so many "crowded to the standard" that only the most promising could be accepted. Possibly Morgan, like several other rifle captains, held a contest to see which men would accompany him north to Boston. "One commander, according to an eyewitness, took a board, a foot square, and drew a moderate nose in the center, and propping the board against a tree one hundred and fifty yards distant, announced that he would accept those whose bullets came closest to the target." [6] Whatever Morgan's criteria for acceptance, John Austin was one of the accepted marksmen.

On 14 July, one month from the day Congress passed its resolve, Morgan with an oversubscribed company of ninety-six men set out for Boston. The men paraded out of town mounted on horses secured from their own or nearby farms. Austin was one of the few in this parade to make it back to Virginia.

The company travelled north by the Great Wagon Road, crossed the Potomac at Harper's Ferry and through Pennsylvania by way of York, Lancaster and Bethlehem. Then they rode through northern New Jersey, crossing the Hudson at Peekskill, and continued to Boston by way of Hartford [7].

Enroute, the troop attracted a great deal of attention from the "city folk." Their dress was the most noticeable thing about them. They cut a unique figure in their brown hunting shirts, buckskin leggings, swinging powder horns, ugly tomahawks and dangerous looking hunting knives; it

was all so reminiscent of earlier frontier war parties. Noting the affect of their apparel, some riflemen wore warpaint; and their savage, warlike appearance provoked terror among the parochial coastal denizens. Silas Deane, a member of congress from Connecticut, was describing John Austin's attire, when he wrote his wife:

> *"They take a piece of Ticklenburgh, or tow cloth that is stout, and put it in a tan-vat until it has the shade of a dry or fading leaf; they they make a kind of frock of it, reaching down below the knee, open before, with a large cape. They wrap it around them tight, on a march, and tie it with their belt, in which hangs their tomahawk."* [8]

The hunting shirt was so distinctive it earned the riflemen the nickname "shirtmen." In his *The Winning of the West*, Theodore Roosevelt was to call the riflemen's frock "the most picturesque and distinctive dress ever worn in America." [9]

Morgan's company arrived in Cambridge on August 6th; the company had covered the six-hundred mile trek, Winchester to Boston, in twenty-one days. The New Englanders were highly impressed with the response and speed of these men from Virginia. Washington, hearing of their arrival, broke his busy schedule and took time to meet his fellow Virginians. It has been reported that Washington was so moved by the performance of Captain Daniel Morgan's 96 Virginians in travelling 600 miles in three weeks without a loss (of a man) that he went along the company front shaking hands with each man . . . (as) tears streamed down his cheeks [10]. Thus did John Austin meet the commander-in-chief.

Austin and the other riflemen were billeted in Roxbury, and the besieging provincials made it a point to visit their camp. Word was out that the frontiersmen were giants, that "they were remarkably stout and hardy men; many of them exceeding six feet in height." This in a day when the average man stood only around 5 feet 4 inches tall [11].

The visitors also wanted to examine John's rifle-gun; they wanted to see this "peculiar kind of musket with its circular . . . groves within the barrel, (that shot) a ball with great exactness to great distances." [12] Most of the New Englanders were unfamiliar with the rifle; their weapon was the smooth-bore musket. Called the Queen's Arm, the smooth-bore musket had a barrel some 3½ feet long, weighed about 10 pounds, and had no rear sight. A good musket was capable of hitting a man-sized target quite consistently at 50 or even 60 yards, but beyond that distance it would largely depend on luck. The musket didn't have a rear sight since soldiers and militia of the period were taught little or nothing about marksmanship. Recruits were usually told to look in the direction in which they were to fire, point the musket straight ahead, and fire on command. In the formal warfare of this period the enemy line normally presented a continuous linear formation that could hardly be missed.

John's rifle, on the other hand, was a highly personalized weapon. It would have been about 5 feet in length, and between 8 and 11 pounds in weight, and it had a rear sight. It looked ill-balanced, but was accurate at 250 yards. It is a good bet that Austin's weapon would have been made by a quality craftsman. John would have seen the maker personally and discussed the characteristics he wanted the rifle to have. The weapon was small-bored, but groves had been 'sawed' inside the barrel so that the bullet would rotate in its flight, giving the possessor greater range and accuracy. The straight-grained maple stock had a brass patch box in the butt, the box and stock could have been etched – there might have been a bit of carving, or a simple inlay or two which were occasionally sparsely engraved. As an individualized piece, the rifle would be Austin's most prized possession.

With his rifle in hand, Austin would stock his supper table with meat, defend his life and property, and as a sharpshooter in local matches, he would gain prestige. He was a proficient marksman.

At some time or another, Austin had been trained in field service. From all appearances, he was a veteran hunter and Indian fighter; somewhere, he had learned the hit-and-run tactics of the Indians; he made each ball count, and he knew how to hit a moving target. Above all, if conditions were right, wind and range, he expected to hit a target, no bigger than an orange, at 200 yards [13].

We know the riflemen were asked to demonstrate their remarkable proficiency with their long-barrelled rifles at Boston. In the first three months of the seige the long range weapon had not been used, and the British outposts had been safe enough, though close to the American lines. But now, Austin and the other "shirtmen terrorized the British by picking off sentries and stragglers and sending dignified officers scurrying for cover." [14]

Based on reported facts, we can take a hypothetical look at John Austin's marksmanship. Asked to demonstrate his shooting ability, John would finger from his bullet pouch one of the half-ounce lead balls, and wrapping the ball in a greased patch, he would push the ball and patch down the inside of the barrel with his ramrod, until it reached the breech section and came to rest on top of the powder charge. Removing the ramrod, and replacing it beneath the barrel, he tapped some fine-grained powder into the pan, and brought the piece to cock. Looking about at the inquisitive provincials, he asked, "What's the mark?" All too often, the mark was a British sentry. If the target was 200 or more yards distant, he would assume the prone position, and rest the long barrel of the rifle on some support, then, he proceeded to show the locals real marksmanship. "The redcoats found to their cost that they were risking death by exposing their heads within 200 yards of one of Morgan's riflemen." [15]

So frequently did there show on the daily reports of the British, the loss of officers, pickets and artillerymen shot at long range, that Edmund Burke exclaimed in Parliament, "Your officers are swept off by the rifles if they but show their noses." [16]

The rifle was deadly in the hands of an expert, and Austin was an expert; undoubtedly his accuracy contributed to the losses the British sustained during the seige at Boston.

Some of the riflement reputedly could hit an object at 250 yards while marching at the quickstep. "One Boston historian had added marvellously to their fame by ascribing a similar feat to each member of the company at the double-quick." [17] Obviously the riflemen were amazing shots, for "in the hand of its owner the long rifle

was probably more deadly than any other combination of man and weapon in existence at that time.'' [18] However, the amazing feat of hitting a target at 250 yards at the double-quick has to be an exaggeration of fanciful imagination.

It didn't take the British very long to figure out they had better keep their heads down. In an effort to remain inconspicuous, the redcoat officers and non-commissioned officers found it necessary to lay aside their halberds and spontons, their most obvious badges of rank. And the sentries and pickets, in an effort to remain alive, hunkered down so ''that nothing was to be seen from their breastworks but a hat.'' [19]. The British countermeasure of staying concealed was a rather simple but effective deterrent to the aim of the riflemen. ''There was not a random shot of a riflemen done any execution lately, worth mentioning,'' stated a letter published in the *Gaines Mercury* on August 21st [20].

Austin and the others hadn't marched 600 miles just to stand around and wait for a redcoat to stick his head up, and the inactivity of camp life began to chafe at their self-restraint. Bored with the British in hiding and with nothing to snipe at, the Virginians began to get into trouble. They began to carouse and flirt with the local women, and, of course, got into fights with the local men.

Things came to a head when the riflemen got into a big brawl with John Glover and his Marblehead fishermen – who were also encamped at Cambridge. George Washington himself had to break up the free-for-all.

> **Fortunately, Morgan's men did not have their rifles, only their brawny fists. But these flew, and the Virginians and the Massachusetts men tore into each other with a mighty vengeance. The free-for-all resulted in a riot which blazed up like fire in tinder, and a small 'civil-war' followed** [21].

Washington, when he heard about the ruckus, sprang into his saddle and galloped to the scene. Once on the field he waded into the fight and separated the two angry contingents. He gave the men 'what-for' in no uncertain terms, and awed, the men fell back, and what could have been a serious outbreak ended [22].

Early in September, the outlook for John Austin and the others in Morgan's company brightened. Congress, in an effort to curtail any attacks from Canada, planned on sending an army to seize Montreal. Washington, when he learned of a route through the wilderness, decided ''to penetrate into Canada by way of the Kennebec, and so to Quebec.'' He added an expeditionary force to strike in a pincer movement, and planned on sending three rifle companies with the expedition.

All of the rifle commanders wanted their companies to participate, if only to get the restless men out of Cambridge. For it was about this time that the shirtmen decided to liberate some of their comrades from the guardhouse. Because only three companies were going, and all wanted to take part, the rifle commanders cast lots to see who would go. As fortune would have it, Daniel Morgan drew one of the lucky numbers.

Following his lucky cast, Morgan called his men together and told them the news. However, he told them he was going to have to cut the company back from 96 men to 81, since all companies were to have a standard complement of 81 men: a captain, three lieutenants, four sergeants, four corporals, a drummer, and 68 privates.

Congress, when it passed the resolve for ten rifle companies, expected 840 men, at the most, to show up in Cambridge. However 1400 riflemen had arrived – Morgan was not the only captain with an over-subscribed company. The most exceptional marksmen would be kept, the rest would be sent home.

From the rosters of the different company commanders it appears that marksmanship overrode state representation, for while Morgan ended up with a company composed of mostly Virginians, men from Pennsylvania, Maryland, and even New Jersey also filled his rank and file [23].

On the evening of 13 September 1775, Morgan moved the company out of Roxbury and marched toward Newburyport on the coast. Austin and the other men had little idea of what was in store for them. However, there were great expectations. Rifleman Jesse Lukins accompanied the departing men on foot as far as Lynn, 9 miles away. ''Here I took my leave of them with a wet eye,'' he wrote a friend. ''The drums beat and away they go . . . to scale the walls of Quebec and spend the winter in joy and festivity with the sweet nuns.'' [24]

On Saturday, September 16th, Arnold's army reached Newburyport on the Coast. On the 18th, the troops embarked on sloops and schooners for Ft. Weston, on the Kennebec. They were headed for a great adventure, it would be a test of nerve and endurance on the part of the American soldier, which until modern times has scarcely been equalled.

The march to Quebec was to be the ''tragic-romance'' of the American Revolution. In his declaration, John Austin said, ''He marched to Quebec,'' four words covering one of the most grueling marches ever performed since the time of Alexander the Great. Benedict Arnold, the hero of Ticonderoga and later our most infamous traitor, was to command the expedition. In a letter to Congress, Arnold wrote, ''From the mouth of the Kennebec River to Quebec, on a straight line, is 210 miles [25]. He anticipated it

would take his little army twenty days to force their way through the wilderness to Canada. On a map, the route did not appear too difficult. But how those early maps could deceive! The distance was more like 360 miles, and it took them two months, not twenty days, to reach the St. Lawrence. It was a wonder they made it through.

Arnold's little army was made up of thirteen companies, three rifle and ten infantry. Arnold placed Captain Morgan in overall command of the rifle companies. Morgan and the two Pennsylvania captains, William Hendricks and Matthew Smith, were to head the column, their men were to act as pioneers and break the trail for the infantry companies. The ten companies of infantry – musketmen – were divided into two small battalions, one commanded by Lt. Colonel Roger Enos of Vermont, the other by Lt. Colonel Christopher Greene of Rhode Island.

Unknown to John Austin, but in Lt. Colonel Greene's battalion, in Captain John Topham's company, there marched another Austin, Pasco Austin of Rhode Island. Somewhere along the line of march, it is possible they could have met.

Arnold's army numbered eleven hundred men, and a few wives accompanying their men. John Austin was one of only 700 who made it through the wilderness to Quebec. In a later article, we will follow along with him as he forced his way up the Kennebec and across to the Dead River, the terrible portage across the Height of Land, to the swift and seething Chaudiere River, and the night crossing of the St. Lawrence. We will join him in the night attack on Quebec, see his capture and eventual release and his return to the colonies.

References

1. John Austin's Pension Application, R318.
2. *England:* Edward W. Skene and Eugene H. Sperry, Sons of the American Revolution, Applications 33997 and 34805; *Virginia:* S.A.R. Application 26591; *Enroute:* Quoted in *Americans of Gentle Birth* by Hannah D. Pittman, Genealogical Publishing Company, Baltimore 1970, pp.1-2.
3. Pittman, op. cit., p.1. See also J. Stoddard Johnson, *Memorial History of Louisville*, Volume I, American Publishing Company 1896, p.453
4. Marriage Bond, 23 October 1788; married on 3 November 1788.
5. Hamilton J. Eckenrode, *The Revolution in Virginia*, New York 1916, pp.49-52.
6. Frank Moore, Editor, *The Diary of the American Revolution*, New York 1875, p.111.
7. T. Triplett Russell and John K. Gott, *Fauquier County in the Revolution*, Warrenton 1977, pp.69-70.
8. Justin H. Smith, *Our Struggle for the Fourteenth Colony*, Vol. I, New York 1907, p.150
9. Theodore Roosevelt, *The Winning of the West*, Vol.I, New York 1905, p.149.
10. Mark M. Boatner III, Encyclopedia of the American Revolution, New York 1906, p.934
11. James Thacher, *Military Journal of the American Revolution*, Hartford 1862, p.131.
12. Charles F. Adams, Editor, *Familiar Letters of John Adams and his Wife Abigail During the Revolution*, Boston 1857, pp.65-66.
13. James C. Ballagh, Editor, *Letters of Richard Henry Lee*, Vol.I, New York 1913, pp.130-131.
14. Don Higginbotham, *Daniel Morgan " Revolutionary Rifleman*, North Carolina 1975, p.25.
15. North Callahan, *Daniel Morgan " Ranger of the Revolution*, New York 1973, p.53
16. Ibid., p.53.
17. Thacher, op. cit., p.31.
18. Joe Kindig, Jr., *Thoughts on the Kentucky Rifle in its Golden Age*, Pennsylvania 1970, p.3.
19. Moore, op. cit., p.183.
20. Ibid., p.129.
21. Peter Force, Editor, *American Archives*, Vol.III, New York 1972, p.457
22. Connecticut Historical Society Collections, Vol.II, p.292.
23. *Transcripts of the Colonial Office Records (1776)*, N.12, Quebec. Correspondence between Governor Carleton and Lord G. Germain, pp.159-169.
24. American Historical Record, Vol.I, p.548: Jesse Lukins to John Shaw, Jr. 16 September 1775.
25. John Codman II, *Arnold's Expedition to Quebec*, New York 1902, p.23.

QUERIES

73-1. Elizabeth Austin of Rhode Island - need proof she was wife of Robert West. Rhode Island records one of first purchasers 20 December 1637/8. On various Providence records. Inhabitant of Portsmouth 1659, sold Portsmouth land in 1663. Was among original purchasers Monmouth County, New Jersey. Died before 1681. Children: Joseph, Robert, John, Elizabeth, Mary and Ann. Seek others working this line.

73-2. Rufus Austin born 1792 in Pawlett, Vermont. Wife Eleanor Fittock born 1796 in Ticonderoga, New York. Rufus died in Gallipolis, Ohio, 1840. Eleanor died in Meadville, Pennsylvania. Looking for descendants of Rufus and Eleanor.

73-3. Andrew Austin perhaps born Castle Michael on the River Annan in Dunfrieshire, Scotland, had two brothers Alex and Robert. Married Mary Clarke McKee, daughter of Samuel and Jane (Clarke) McKee, born 1818 in Ballymacairn, Ireland. Andrew and Mary had three children: Margaret Rutherford McKee Austin who married Peter Miller (they had two girls); John Andrew Austin; Jennie Arabella Austin born 28 September 1846, married Gary H. Moulton in St. Johnsbury, Vermont. Jennie always said she was born in Brooklyn, New York, but her death certificate says she was born in Scotland. Jane Clarke McKee arrived in New York on the ship *Basque Statria* in 1838 with her children Jane aged 12 and Samuel aged 10. When did Mary Clarke McKee come to America? Was she then married to Andrew Austin? What happened to Andrew?

SOME DESCENDANTS OF
LUCIUS MONROE AUSTIN
AND ELIZA HOBART

by Clarence Edward Egan, Jr.

This article was drawn from Edwin L. Hobart's *Hobart History & Genealogy 1632-1912*, Denver 1912; Edith Austin Moore's *Thomas Austin* manuscript in the New England Historic Genealogical Society in Boston; contemporary sources; a 1968 visit to a cemetery about a mile east of Clarion, Iowa, where stones were found for Lucius, Eliza, and Winfield, in northeast part of second section from East and second section from the main road (Route 3).

S216-1115. LUCIUS MONROE[8] AUSTIN (*Francis Brown,*[7] *Nathan,*[6,5,4] *Thomas,*[3,2] *Samuel*[1]) was born 30 November 1826, probably in Vermont, the son of Francis Brown Austin and Eleanor L. Whitten. A descendant of Samuel and Hopestill Austin of Boston (see page 8), Lucius was married on 1 January 1852 to Eliza Hobart in Webster, Illinois. Eliza was the daughter of Jonas and Polly (Farr) Hobart, and was born on 20 June 1831 in Essex, Vermont. Lucius died 15 December 1889 age 63 years 25 days in Clarion, Iowa. Eliza died 24 December 1928 in Mullinville, Kansas, and is buried with Lucius and Winfield in Clarion, Iowa. Children:

S216-1115-1.　MARY ANN, *b. 16 March 1852, d. 16 January 1854*

S216-1115-2.　WINFIELD SCOTT, *b. 3 November 1853, d. 17 February 1886 age 33 buried Clarion, Iowa, m. 4 July 1879 Margaret Smith*

S216-1115-3.　NORMAN HOBART, *b. 16 January 1856 in Hancock County, Illinois, m.(1) 1884 Lona Long (2 children), m.(2) 1901 Mary Marshman (1 child)*

S216-1115-4.　ARIUS EDSALL, *b. 16 December 1857 in Bushnell, Illinois, d. 1 April 1926 Albion, Nebraska, m. 28 October 1891 Selma Sophia Lawson (see below)*

S216-1115-5.　LILLIAN, *b. 12 July 1859, d. 31 August 1911 buried Worthington, Minnesota, m. 11 August 1878 Joseph C. Williamson*

S216-1115-6.　ROSE CAROLINE, *b. 29 September 1861, d. 10 December 1956, m. 25 December 1884 George Hildyard (3 children)*

S216-1115-7.　PHOEBE ORILLA, *b. 3 September 1863, d. 11 November 1931 in Fowler, Kansas, m. 24 March 1889 Hiram Veeder (4 children)*

S216-1115-8.　HARRIET LINCOLN, *b. 14 July 1865, d. 7 May 1959 in Mullinville, Kansas, m. 19 April 1888 John Marriage (3 children)*

S216-1115-9.　LEVI BROWN, *b. August 1867, d. 1870*

S216-1115-A.　WILLIE, *b. 28 June 1869, d. 29 July 1870*

S216-1115-B.　JAMES NOBLE, *b. 27 June 1871, d. 5 October 1954, m.(1) 5 April 1898 Marion Pearl Dickey (3 children), m.(2) 27 April 1905 Minnie Pauley, m.(3) Della Wells*

S216-1115-4. ARIUS EDSALL[9] AUSTIN (*Lucius Monroe,*[8] *Francis Brown,*[7] *Nathan,*[6,5,4] *Thomas,*[3,2] *Samuel*[1]) was born 16 December 1857 in Bushnell, Illinois. He was married in Albion, Nebraska on 28 October 1891 to Selma Sophia Lawson (Nelson in Sweden). Selma was born on 15 January 1873 in Kalmar, Sweden. In October 1882 she came to New Jersey, and in 1883 she went to Nebraska with the John Hoffman family from Asbury, New Jersey. Arius died 1 April 1926 age 68 in Albion, Nebraska. Selma died 4 November 1943 ae 70y in Albany, Oregon, and is buried in Albion with Arius. Children:

S216-1115-41.　WILBURN NOBLE, *b. 2 August 1892 in Corwith, Iowa, d. 13 January 1972 Vancouver, Washington (cremated), m. 1 January 1941 Elizabeth Rasmus b. 20 January 1902 Carlstadt, New Jersey (no children)*

S216-1115-42.　BEULAH, *b. 22 April 1894 Loretto, Nebraska, m. James Homer Thomas b. Oct. 1891. Thomas ch. all b. Madera, California: Lylola 1925, Viola 1925, David James 1927, Thelma 1930*

S216-1115-43.　VERA RUTH, *b. 25 December 1899 Loretto, Nebraska, m. 12 June 1922 Clarence Edward Egan - Egan children: Clarence Edward, Jr. 1923, Merlin Austin 1926, James Francis 1928, Marion Elizabeth 1932, Richard Noble 1936, Robert Roland 1937*

★★★★★★★★★★★★★★★★★★★★★★★★★★★★★★

Austins of America is intended to serve present and future genealogists researching Austin family lines. Readers are encouraged to submit Queries, genealogical and historical articles for publication. Previously published books, pamphlets or articles containing Austin genealogical data are also sought for reprinting or review.

EDITOR

DR. MICHAEL EDWARD AUSTIN　　　CONCORD, MA

ASSOCIATE EDITORS

ANTHONY KENT AUSTIN　　　　　PROSPECT, KY

PATRICIA BIEBUYCK AUSTIN　　　CONCORD, MA

PAULINE LUCILLE AUSTIN　　　　　MARION, IA

JANET AUSTIN CURTIS　　　ALBUQUERQUE, NM

CAROL LEIGHTON HULL　　　　　SUDBURY, MA

Austins of America is published each February and August by The Austin Print, 23 Allen Farm Lane, Concord, Massachusetts 01742. All correspondence, including subscriptions, articles and responses to queries, should be sent to this address. Subscriptions are $2.50 per year postpaid.

The photograph shown above was received in December 1973 by the author from Dotty Veeder of Fowler, Kansas, a granddaughter of the Phoebe Orilla (Austin) Veeder appearing in the photograph. Front row (left to right): Norman Hobart Austin, Eliza (Hobart) Austin, James Noble Austin, Lucius Monroe Austin, and Lillian Austin. Back row (l to r): Phoebe Orilla Austin, Winfield Scott Austin, Rose Caroline Austin, Arius Edsall Austin, and Harriet Lincoln Austin. James Noble Austin is thought to have been around eight years old when the photograph was taken, dating it circa 1879.

QUERIES

75-1. Absalom Chrisfield Austin, Sr. was a judge. Need proof that he was son of Elijah Austin and Temperance Payne, daughter of Robert and Rachel Payne. Absalom was born in 1812 in North Carolina (probably Burke County), he removed to Greene County, Missouri, in 1840-1, died 1872 Dallas County, Missouri. Absalom married Nancy Presnell (1807-1852), and had children: Wesley 1834, Elijah 1835, Temperance 1836, Nathaniel 1838, Mary 1840, Daniel 1842, Martha 1844, Nancy J. 1846, Mildred J. 1850, and Selian 1852. Absalom m.(2) Nancy Gass (1829-1869). Children: Absalom C. 1863, Samuel P. 1864, William T. 1867. Want to share records.

75-2. Charles F. Austin was born circa 1848 in Fairfield County, Connecticut. He lived in Union Township, Montgomery County, Indiana. Enlisted in the Union Army 13 October 1864 at Indianapolis, Indiana. He died in Philadelphia, Pennsylvania, 25 June 1894. Seeking parents, birthdate, and any other information on Charles.

75-3. Abraham Austin married Mehitable Campbell. A son Benjamin Campbell Austin was born 23 July 1808, died 9 November 1880 in Barryville, New York. Benjamin married Mary Gardiner. Seeking all information on Abraham and Mehitable and their descendants.

AUSTIN HALL AT HARVARD UNIVERSITY
IN CAMBRIDGE, MASSACHUSETTS

*by Bainbridge Bunting
and Robert H. Nylander*

The Cambridge Historical Commission permitted the reprinting of this article from their book *Survey Of Architectural History In Cambridge, Report Four: Old Cambridge*, M.I.T. Press, Cambridge, 1973. The photograph below is from Plate 1 in *American Architect and Building News, Monographs of American Architecture*, Volume 1, Boston, Ticknor & Company 1886. Photographs provided by the Society for the Preservation of New England Antiquities, courtesy of the Cambridge Historical Commission.

A short distance away from Harvard's Hemenway Gymnasium stands Austin Hall, a building of great beauty but one whose peculiar emplacement still defies attempts by planners to bring some measure of order to this part of the North Yard. The commission to design a building for the Law School came to H. H. Richardson from the donor rather than from the administration. Edward Austin, a merchant who had made a fortune in the China trade and retired before he was fifty-five, seems to have been as autocratic in building his hall as had Nathaniel Thayer. The new building memorializes the invigoration the Law School was experiencing under Dean Langdell as it moved away from the old apprentice system of education established by Story. The enrollment began to rise in 1880, and in his Annual Report for that year President Eliot appealed for a new building for the school. Although the com-

mission came to the Richardson office in February 1881, the first reference to the building in the Corporation records is in April of the following year, by which time the complete design had been approved by Austin. There had, however, undoubtedly been prior consultation with the university as the program for the building was defined. Nevertheless, a note in the minutes for 24 April 1882 confirmed officially that "no modification of the outside of the building...to be made without Mr. Austin's consent." The administration also agreed that no building would ever be erected within 60 feet of Mr. Austin's hall. Given this kind of independence, there was no more possibility of architectural consistency on the campus than on a street of suburban mansions.

The present situation of Austin Hall, today facing nowhere in particular, is explained by reference to a former street called Holmes Place. This was an L-shaped passage bordering two sides of a small triangular park known as the Little Common, then owned by the city but once part of the Cambridge Common. The north arm of Holmes Place ran not quite parallel to Kirkland Street, hence the lack of alignment between Austin, which fronted Holmes Place, and Jefferson laboratories or Hemenway gymnasium (and later Littauer Center) which faced Kirkland Street. Like other early buildings in the North Yard, Austin simply faced the street that ran in front of it and took no notice of neighbors. Besides the university buildings just mentioned, there were two residences here: Gannett House (1838), which then faced south rather than east as today,

A contemporary view of Harvard's Austin Hall

and the very important early 18th-century Holmes House. When his hall was finished in 1884, Mr. Austin paid another $3000 to have the Holmes residence demolished, despite its historic and architectural importance, simply to improve the appearance of his building.

While Austin Hall turned its handsome facade toward an ambiguous front yard, it completely ignored what was to the north, a field then used for athletics but since transformed into one of the most interesting outdoor spaces at Harvard. So disdainful of this field were architect and donor that not even a back door provided access to the area, an oversight that has caused no little inconvenience to later generations of law students who must get from Langdell to Austin in inclement weather through an underground passageway. Only very recently has this backyard been reclaimed by the construction of the International Legal Studies Center and especially by Ben Thompson's two handsome office buildings for the law faculty.

The facade of Austin Hall is picturesquely asymmetrical without sacrificing order. Triple arches at the entrance center the composition, and wings of one story containing a lecture hall balance it. In the upper level variations in fenestration express differences of internal use – as for book stacks, faculty offices, and a lounge – but the constant width of window bays prevents these differences from creating disunity. The most striking quality of the building comes from its masonry, which combines pink granite and two shades of sandstone. The quarry-faced masonry generates a feeling of enormous strength, a sensation augmented by skillful contrasts with smooth surfaces and with carved decoration of small scale. Clear massing, consistency in fenestration, contrasting textures, and exquisite carving – a quality readily appreciated as a result of a recent cleaning – make this building a textbook example of Richardson Romanesque design. Yet one questions whether the polychromatic masonry, whose contrasts in color must have been garish when the building was new, did not then diminish the sense of the masonry's integrity? A little grime may be a good thing, and the university was well advised not to have cleaned the entire outside surface.

JOHN MORRIS AUSTIN, PIONEER DENTIST OF SAINT JOSEPH, MISSOURI

by Anna Martha Utterback Clendenning

From Maude Conrad Baker's 1928 book, *Genealogical Record of Robert Austin and his Lineal Descendants*, we find: "At the outbreak of the Civil War, John Morris Austin went to Washington, D.C. and joined the Construction Corps with headquarters at Alexandria, Virginia, where with his company he was engaged in keeping the Orange and Alexandria railroad and bridges in repair. He remained at his post until the Battle of the Wilderness, when, because of ill health, he was sent to the hospital and advised to go north.

"In the fall of 1864 he took up the study of dentistry at Ogdensburgh, New York. In 1867 Dr. Austin went to St. Joseph, Missouri, where he was a pioneer dentist. Dr. Austin had an enviable reputation among St. Joseph dentists. He was one of the original stockholders in the Kansas City Dental School and served as an instructor of demonstrative work in the school for several years.

"He was a member of the Kansas Dental Association. He organized and named Charity Lodge and served as Worshipful Master. He was a member of the Shrine and served as treasurer for many years in Moila Temple."

Being the granddaughter of Dr. Austin, I was privileged to know more details of his life. Always he was at the front of pioneering. St. Joseph, Missouri, was founded by a man named Roubidoux who had dreams of that city becoming a great metropolis. Situated at the northwest corner of the state, it did indeed become "the gateway to the West" with the establishment of the Pony Express. It was during the early planning that young Dr. Austin was welcomed as the necessary dentist.

John Austin found an acre of land situated on the main thoroughfare, Frederick Avenue, and he purchased it. There he built a two-story office building with the ground floor rented and his office occupying the large second floor. The city was built with slanting streets all joining Frederick Avenue at angles. This was to accomodate rails on which horse-drawn cars originally were operated; later the cars were converted to electricity.

John was the son of Daniel Austin, a prosperous farmer. Daniel had married Amanda Hurlburt, granddaughter of Captain Sweet of the War of 1812. With his background of farming, it was natural for young John to plant the acre of ground. For this purpose he built a barn and stable on his property, adjacent to an alley. In a natural way, the alley was made to turn sharply near the back entrance of the dental office. Because the ground sloped upward from Frederick Avenue, the alley was only a few steps down from the rear of the office.

As a convenience, what could be better than a blacksmith shop at the corner of the alley? The property was near the center of town and in the 19th century no business was more urgent than blacksmithing. Thus it came about that another building was constructed fronting on Frederick Avenue, next to Dr. Austin's office. The blacksmith was of German descent and named Bertram.

Dr. Austin made his home at the rear part of his office, but it was necessary to build a shelter to house his hired hands. This was placed near the barn in the middle of the acre lot. A well was dug and a cistern was constructed to catch rain water. The hired hands were blacks recently freed, who had come north. A cow was purchased, and chickens. Fruit trees and a vegetable garden were planted. Although near the center of a developing young city, this was a small farm, and not at all different from other residential neighborhoods.

Dr. Austin became one of the city fathers as a necessary cog in the wheel of development. He grew mature as a bachelor, nearing the age of 32 when he met Anna Elvira Nash, a young woman of 18. Immediately the farming

came to a stop and a house was erected in the center of the lot. At first it was four rooms, two stories in height. They were married on 22 April 1875. Anna Nash was a descendant of Richard Warren, a passenger on the *Mayflower*.

John and Anna Austin had eight children and adopted a ninth: Daniel Milton b. 25 February 1876, Bessie Ruby b. 1 August 1877, John H. b. 28 June 1879, Anna Edine b. 8 March 1881, Orrin Wilmer Nash b. 12 December 1884, Florence Picolla b. 7 July 1887, Deedie May b. 17 April 1889, Kate Douglas b. 13 December 1892, and Edward Nash b. 4 March 1897 (see Baker, op.cit., p.68). The four males left no offspring to further this branch of the Austins.

Orrin was an M.D. and served in World War I, was married briefly, and had a son who died in infancy.

Three of the five daughters married. Bessie, my mother, married Prof. William I. Utterback, who pioneered in Biology and discovered a fresh-water shellfish similar to an oyster. It was named for him, species Utterbacki. He also was the first President of the School of the Ozarks in Missouri. Some of the family pioneer spirit rubbed off on me. After marriage and four children, I worked in the field of Engineering from 1942 to 1974. When I applied for work with the Corps of Engineers, I was told that Congress had just passed a law allowing women to work in that capacity, so I must have been one of the first in that field. "Pioneers, Oh Pioneers" as poet Walt Whitman once wrote.

Anna Edine Austin, the second daughter, married but produced no offspring. The third daughter, Kate Douglas Austin, married Ralph Bradshaw and had two sons and a daughter.

I want to recount an actual experience with my grandfather. He wanted to examine my teeth when I was six years old. Naturally, I was afraid, so he told me to close my eyes, and imagine the most beautiful sight I could think of. I saw a mountain of ice cream . . . and I had a spoon. Later, when I was grown, a member of the family told me that that was his technique of self-hypnosis. He had stumbled upon this when working on a woman who had a severe problem. He had run out of "laughing gas," as it was then called, so he made a pretext of giving her that anesthetic. She promptly dozed off and felt no pain.

Dr. John Morris Austin died 20 October 1921 in St. Joseph, Missouri. The house he built there still stands at 1123 Frederick Avenue. Eight rooms had been added to the original four as the family grew. Although the dreams of Mr. Roubidoux to have his city become a great metropolis did not materialize, St. Joseph is still known as the "Gateway to the West" and the stables of the Pony Express still stand as a tourist attraction.

"We, today's procession heading, we the route for travel clearing, Pioneers! Oh Pioneers!"

QUERIES

79-1. David Austin was born in Connecticut, married Hannah Rathbun, and had a son Jehiel (Jehial) who was born 11 November 1814 in Delaware County, New York. Seek parents and any other information on David and Hannah.

79-2. Isaac Austin m. Ann Belden of Sheffield, Berkshire County, Mass., bought land in Canandaigua, Ontario County, New York 1794. In the 1810 Census he was listed in Geneva, Ontario County, New York. Had a son George Aison b. Upper Canada 20 December 1796, died 28 May 1860, buried Oak wood Cemetery, Warren Township, Trumbull County, Ohio. Wish correspondence with descendants.

79-3. Capt. James Austin was an early millwright in LeRoy, Genesee County, New York from 1801-1812. He was among settlers of Bergen, New York. A colony from E. Guilford, Connecticut came in 1808. His name is also listed with those who located in Alexander, New York. Need all data.

79-4. Capt. Anthony Austin was born in England circa 1636, died in Suffield, Connecticut, 29 August 1708. He married Esther Huggins who died Suffield 7 March 1697. Lived in Hadley, Mass. before 1660, moved to Suffield 1678. Need all data on this family.

79-5. Bede (Beede, Beide) Austin was born circa 1794, died 4 March 1846. She married 22 January 1815 to Enos Hayward, born 28 March 1790 in Norwich, Vermont, died 3 March 1863 in Chelsea, Vermont. Both buried Tunbridge, Vermont. Need birth, deathplace, marriage place, parents, and siblings of Beede.

79-6. Edward Austin died circa 1810. He married in 1902 to Agnes Tyckowski, born 1886 died 1935 in New Haven, Connecticut. Agnes was the daughter of Joseph & Kazimira (Gedroic) Tyckowski. Need all data on Edward.

79-7. Briant Austin came to North Carolina on a convict ship from London in October 1774. Is this the same Briant Austin who appears in the 1790 Montgomery County, North Carolina Census? Also need the names of his spouse and children.

79-8. Elizabeth Austin born circa 1762 in Washington County, Maryland, the daughter of James Austin. She married about 1779 Joseph James in that county. She died 21 March 1833 in Perryville, Missouri. Need all information on Elizabeth.

79-9. William Austin born 6 May 1752 in Methuen, Massachusetts, m. 15 June 1779 to Hannah Clark. William was son of Isaac and Mehitable (Harris) Austin. Need ancestry of Hannah and Mehitable.

THE DESCENDANTS OF
JORDAN WILSON AUSTIN
AND CHARLOTTE SOPHIA EWING

by Charlotte Felsted

The following is from the author's manuscript *Jordan Wilson and Charlotte Sophia (Ewing) Austin and Their Descendants 1818-1982*.

J. JORDAN WILSON[1] AUSTIN was born 4 April 1818 in Otsego County, New York. He was married on 23 May 1841 to Charlotte Sophia Ewing, daughter of Samuel H. and Hannah (Race) Ewing, born on 1 April 1822 in Orleans (of the North), on the banks of the Maumee River below Fort Meigs. In 1848 and 1849 Jordan was a Township Trustee for Middleton Township, Wood Co., Ohio. Around 1867 the family moved to northern Michigan to work in the pine forests. The family remained there for about two years, and then returned to Haskins, Ohio. Jordan died 27 May 1872 in Haskins, Ohio and is buried in Wakeman Cemetery, Waterville, Ohio. Charlotte died 20 June 1910 at the home of her daughter, Mrs. Noah (Rosa) Cox, in Miltonville, Ohio, and is also buried in Wakeman Cemetery. The children of Jordan and Charlotte were born in Miltonville, Ohio, except as noted:

CHILDREN: J1. MARY JANE (JENNIE), *b. 23 September 1842 in Haskins, Ohio*

J2. OLIVE EMILY (EMMA), *b. 4 June 1844*

J3. HARRIETT LUCINDA, *b. 7 August 1846*

J4. WILSON DAYTON, *b. 14 September 1848*

J5. MATILDA, *b. 1850, d. before 1860*

J6. JAMES MADISON, *b. 10 April 1852*

J7. MATHILDA ANN, *b. 31 December 1853*

J8. MINERVA, *b. circa 1857, d. before 1860*

J9. GEORGE, *b. after 1850, d. 23 July 1859, buried Miltonville Cemetery, Wood County, Ohio*

JA. FRANCES ROSALIA, *b. 6 July 1860*

JB. CORA BELLE, *b. 20 November 1861, in Haskins, Ohio*

JC. WILLIAM L., *b. circa 1866, d. before 1880*

JD. CHARLOTTE LODUSKA, *b. 8 April 1868 in Pentwater, Michigan*

SECOND GENERATION

J1. MARY JANE[2] AUSTIN (*Jordan Wilson[1]*) was born 23 September 1842 in Haskins, Ohio. She married on 24 February 1861 to Silas Genson (his second marriage), born on 4 August 1836 in Tioga County, Penn. Silas died 9 January 1907 in Haskins, Ohio, and is buried in Wakeman Cemetery, Waterville, Ohio. Mary died 29 January 1920 in Haskins, Ohio and is also buried in Wakeman Cemetery. GENSON CHILDREN: FRED L. 1861, SILAS WILSON (WILLIAM) 1866, SAMUEL WALLACE 1867, SPENCER WILLARD 1869, JENNIE MAE 1875, ELLA 1878, NELLIE 1878.

Jordan Wilson Austin 1818-1872

J2. OLIVE EMILY[2] AUSTIN (*Jordan Wilson[1]*) was born 4 June 1844 in Miltonville, Ohio. She was married in Perrysburg, Ohio on 10 February 1864 to William Barnes. William was born on 25 December 1839 in London, England. Olive died 25 August 1920 in Bowling Green, Ohio and is buried in Wakeman Cemetery, Waterville, Ohio. William died 8 April 1927 in Waterville, also buried in Wakeman Cemetery. BARNES CHILDREN: SOPHIA ELIZABETH 1871, OLIVE MAE 1874, JULIA MYRTLE 1881.

J3. HARRIET LUCINDA[2] AUSTIN (*Jordan Wilson[1]*) was born 7 August 1846 in Miltonville, Ohio. She was married in Bowling Green, Ohio on 24 October 1870 to William Morgan Montgomery. William was born on 6 March 1845 in Portage, Ohio. Harriet died 25 August 1889 and is buried in Wakeman Cemetery, Waterville, Ohio. William died 2 March 1926 in Toledo, Ohio, and is buried there in the Woodlawn Cemetery. MONTGOMERY CHILDREN: WILLIAM, JOHN 1871, TULLA ca.1874, WHITNEY 1876, IRA 1878, ROBERT SCOTT 1879, FANNY, HARRIETT 1882, WINONA ALICE 1883, FRANKIE 1888, MORGAN.

Charlotte Sophia Ewing 1822-1910

J4. WILSON DAYTON[2] AUSTIN (*Jordan Wilson*[1]) was born 14 September 1848 in Miltonville, Ohio. He was married in Toledo, Ohio on 10 December 1872 to Julia Ann Bowers. Julia was born on 7 April 1855 in Brooklyn, New York. Wilson died 29 February 1928 in Haskins, Ohio and is buried in Wakeman Cemetery, Waterville, Ohio. Julia died eight days after Wilson, on 8 March 1928, in Haskins, Ohio. She is buried with Wilson in Waterville. Their children were born in Haskins, Ohio:

CHILDREN: J41. JORDAN W., *b. 6 April 1874, d. 4 May 1874*
J42. FRANCES VIRGINIA, *b. 11 February 1876*
J43. PERCY LEROY, *b. 9 October 1878*
J44. CHARLOTTE EMMA, *b. 10 January 1882*
J45. CHESTER JAMES, *b. 20 January 1885*
J46. FRED ELIAS, *b. 24 July 1889*

J6. JAMES MADISON[2] AUSTIN (*Jordan Wilson*[1]) was born 10 April 1852 in Miltonville, Ohio. He was married in Bowling Green, Ohio on 3 October 1887 by William Ewing, J.P. to Elvira Eugenie (Ella) Birdsall. James died

25 March 1923 in Bowling Green, Ohio and is buried there in the Oak Grove Cemetery. Elvira died 17 February 1933 in Los Angeles and is buried there.

CHILDREN: J61. EDNA, *b. March 1887 Haskins, Ohio*
J62. CORRAH, *b. 1 November 1888 Perrysburg, Ohio*
J63. W. M., *d. 1890 Wakeman Cemetery*
J64. CLARENCE, *b. 1891*
J65. J. M., *d. 1892 Wakeman Cemetery*
J66. ERNIE D., *b. 2 March 1893, d. 12 January 1896 Wakeman Cemetery*
J67. JAMES D., *b. 12 January 1899 twin*
J68. J., *twin, b. & d. 12 January 1899 Wakeman Cemetery*
J69. WOERLIN

J7. MATHILDA ANN[2] AUSTIN (*Jordan Wilson*[1]) was born 31 December 1853 in Miltonville, Ohio. She was married to Abner Mason Clark, who was born on 13 March 1847. Abner died 21 December 1924 in Toledo, Ohio, and is buried in Woodlawn Cemetery, Toledo. Mathilda died 17 December 1943 in Toledo and is also buried in Woodlawn Cemetery. CLARK CHILDREN: AUSTIN RAY 1873, JESSE MABEL 1874, JAMES EARL, OLLIE MYRTLE 1879, FANNY IRENE 1882, LLOYD ca.1887, VERNA MARIE 1889, MASON McKINLEY 1891.

JA. FRANCES ROSALIA[2] AUSTIN (*Jordan Wilson*[1]) was born 6 July 1860 in Miltonville, Ohio. She was married first on 10 October 1877 to George Deselms, who was born on 14 February 1852 in Ottawa County, Ohio. They later divorced. George died 13 November 1928 in Bowling Green, Ohio, and is buried in Portage Cemetery, Portage, Ohio. Frances was married second to Noah Wilson Cox, who was born on 1839 in Ohio. Noah died 21 May 1910 in Miltonville, and is buried in Wakeman Cemetery, Waterville, Ohio. Frances died 8 March 1946 in Toledo, Ohio and is also buried in Wakeman Cemetery. DESELMS CHILDREN: ARCHIE 1880, EVA GERTRUDE 1882; COX CHILDREN: NOAH WILSON JR. 1897, DAYTON McKINLEY 1899.

JB. CORA BELLE[2] AUSTIN (*Jordan Wilson*[1]) was born 20 November 1861 in Haskins, Ohio. She was married on 10 March 1880 to Reuben Marks, who was born on 18 August 1859 in Findlay, Ohio. Reuben died 24 August 1924 in Mt. Pleasant, Iowa, and is buried in Conesville Cemetery, Conesville, Iowa. Cora died 19 April 1942 in Conesville and is also buried in Conesville Cemetery. MARKS CHILDREN: TWO SONS (died in infancy), FLORA 1895 (adopted).

JD. CHARLOTTE LODUSKA[2] AUSTIN (*Jordan Wilson*[1]) was born 8 April 1868 in Pentwater, Michigan. She was married first on 23 December 1890 to Frank Ryder, who was born on 17 October 1850 in Monroeville, Ohio. They later divorced. Frank died 3 November 1920 in Perrys-

burg, Ohio, and is buried in Fort Meigs Cemetery, Perrysburg. Charlotte was married second on 27 July 1895 to William Wallace Bernthisel, who was born on 3 March 1854 in Haskins, Ohio. William died 24 December 1944 in Haskins, and is buried in Union Hill Cemetery, Bowling Green, Ohio. Charlotte died 13 July 1920 in Haskins and is buried in Union Hill Cemetery. RYDER CHILD: RUBY BELLE 1891; BERNTHISEL CHILD: HELENE ANGENETTE 1896.

THIRD GENERATION

J42. FRANCES VIRGINIA³ AUSTIN (*Wilson Dayton,² Jordan Wilson¹*) was born 11 February 1876 in Haskins, Ohio. She was married in Haskins on 25 June 1894 to William Wilson, who was born in July 1867 in Volcano, West Virginia. William died August 1942 in Bartlesville, Oklahoma, and is buried in Oak Grove Cemetery, Bowling Green, Ohio. Frances died 19 February 1962 in Ellsworth, Kansas, and is buried in Great Bend, Kansas. WILSON CHILD: CHARLES DAYTON 1894.

J43. PERCY LEROY³ AUSTIN (*Wilson Dayton,² Jordan Wilson¹*) was born 9 October 1878 in Haskins, Ohio. He married first on 12 August 1908 to Clara Bell Meek, who was born on 19 March 1888 in Haskins. Clara died 21 March 1927 in Toledo, Ohio, and is buried in Wakeman Cemetery, Waterville, Ohio. Percy married second to Nellie McComb Stultz, who was born in March 1889. Nellie died 15 April 1942 in Bowling Green, Ohio, and is buried in Wakeman Cemetery. Percy died 27 May 1950 in McClure, Ohio and is also buried in Wakeman Cemetery.

CHILDREN: J431. ELSIE MAE, *b. 7 September 1906, Tontogany, Ohio (foster daughter), m. — Stickles*

J432. GEORGE LEROY, *b. 3 December 1911 Haskins, Ohio, d. 25 April 1973 Haskins, Union Hill Cemetery, Bowling Green, Ohio, m. 24 November 1939 Helen M. Kuntz b. 7 February 1920. Children: Ronald L. b. 11 August 1940 Haskins, Bonnie b. 8 February 1942*

J433. LEONA BELL, *b. 27 August 1915, d. 19 January 1921 Toledo, Ohio, buried Wakeman Cemetery*

J434. HAROLD DON (BUD), *b. 21 June 1917 Sand Pit, Michigan, d. 3 January 1977 Toledo, buried Union Hill Cemetery, Bowling Green; m.(1) 2 February 1937 Hazel Marie Amos b. 24 July 1921 Berkey, Ohio, div. 1944; m.(2) 26 August 1946 Bowling Green, Ohio, Virginia R. Allen b. 24 March 1923 Portage, Ohio. Children: Betty Jane b. 1 November 1938 m. 7 September 1957 Lowell Fitch in Whitehouse, Ohio; Harold Don Jr. b. 4 February 1944 Toledo, Ohio, m.(1) 11 January 1968 Carolyn Janet Scott b. 16 January 1947 Toledo, div. 1972, m.(2) 24 January 1975 in Lambertville, Michigan, Jean Marie Carey b. 28 June 1951 New York City; Tommie Lee b. 13 September 1953 Bowling Green, m. 20 October 1979 Perrysburg, Ohio, Marilyn Kay Henry b. 7*

April 1955 Toledo; David Don b. 21 July 1955 Bowling Green, m.(1) 12 June 1976 Huron, Ohio, Nettie May Smith b. 15 November 1955 Huron, div. 1977, m.(2) 12 September 1981 Vollmar's Park, Wood County, Ohio, Barbara Ann Henry b. 2 October 1959 Toledo; Susanna b. 2 March 1957 Bowling Green

J435. JULIA MAY, *b. 11 February 1927 Haskins, Ohio, m. 29 June 1946 Paul Amos b. 22 September 1923 Palmyra, Michigan.*

J44. CHARLOTTE EMMA³ AUSTIN (*Wilson Dayton,² Jordan Wilson¹*) was born 10 January 1882 in Haskins, Ohio. She was married in Haskins on 12 October 1899 to Reuben Mourdock, born on 20 September 1876 in Tontogany, Ohio. Charlotte died 21 April 1967 in Haskins and is buried in Union Hill Cemetery, Bowling Green, Ohio. Reuben died 6 February 1968 in Haskins and is also buried in Union Hill Cemetery. MOURDOCK CHILDREN: CURTIS WILLARD 1900, BEOLIA 1905, DONALD WILSON 1915

J45. CHESTER JAMES³ AUSTIN (*Wilson Dayton,² Jordan Wilson¹*) was born 20 January 1885 in Haskins, Ohio. He was married in Haskins on 5 May 1909 to Essie Cox, born on 6 May 1889 in Kansas, Ohio. Essie died 5 February 1962 in Bowling Green, Ohio, and is buried in Tontogany Cemetery, Tontogany, Ohio. Chester died 8 April 1962 in Toledo, Ohio and is also buried in Tontogany Cemetery.

CHILDREN: J451. HELEN, *b. 14 February 1911 Haskins, d. 19 April 1979 Toledo bur. Tontogany Cemetery, m. Harold W. DeShone b. 28 March 1918, d. 28 January 1982 Whitmore Lake, Michigan, bur. Woodlawn Cemetery, Toledo*

J452. CHARLES, *b. 21 April 1914 Haskins, m. 27 March 1937 Lois Adams b. 14 January 1914, Haviland, Ohio. Children: James Earl b. 13 August 1939, m. 26 February 1972 Catherine Waters, child: Allison b. 21 September 1964; Robert Glenn b. 11 May 1941; Joyce Faye b. 8 October 1943 m. 8 January 1966 Dennis M. McDaniel; Paul William b. 27 December 1944, m. 28 December 1968 Elsie Calevro, children: Toni Renee b. 20 February 1970, Tara Lynn b. 18 October 1971, Robert (stepson) b. 4 July 1964; Patty Jean b. 29 October 1946 child: Jacob Louis b. 22 June 1978*

J453. ROBERT WILSON, *b. Haskins, d. 9 July 1970 Toledo, m. 20 April 1934 Ruby Dauster b. 28 November 1908, Child: Rebecca June b. 17 June 1942 m. 9 October 1961 Ray A. Hofner*

J454. JESSLYN BEOLIA, *b. 9 October 1922, Maumee, Ohio, d. 29 January 1959 buried Tontogany Cemetery, m. 1 June 1940 Bowling Green to Paul Leo Swanson b. 13 September 1920 Bowling Green, d. 7 February 1971 Toledo*

J455. INFANT, *b. and d. 13 October 1927, buried Wakeman Cemetery, Waterville, Ohio*

J46. FRED ELIAS[3] AUSTIN (*Wilson Dayton,[2] Jordan Wilson[1]*) was born 24 July 1889. He was married to Margaret Fern Ferris. Fred died 8 December 1922 in Toledo, Ohio, while Margaret died on 8 December 1944.

CHILDREN: J461. MYRTLE, *b. 2 February 1913, m. 30 August 1930 John E. Moore b. 22 February 1902*

J462. EDWARD FERRIS, *b. 25 February 1917, m. 11 February 1938 Mirabelle Lavaun Greer, b. 8 February 1920 Cloverdale, Ohio, d. 2 April 1982 Toledo, bur. Weaver Cemetery, Bloomdale, Ohio, children: Mona Lee b. 19 September 1942, m. 23 August 1967 Menelio Santiago Gomez b. 25 July 1938; April Ann b. 14 April 1956, m. 25 April 1981 Donald Marion b. 9 November 1948*

J61. EDNA M.[3] AUSTIN (*James Madison,[2] Jordan Wilson[1]*) was born March 1887 in Haskins, Ohio. She was married to Arthur W. Blackburn. Arthur died 10 December 1937 in Toledo, Ohio. Edna died 28 May 1947, also in Toledo, and is buried in Toledo Memorial Park Cemetery, Sylvania, Ohio. BLACKBURN CHILDREN: DOUGLAS, VIRGINIA, JEANNE.

Acknowledgements — The author wishes to thank the many relatives who have cooperated in compiling this Austin genealogy. Special thanks are extended to Katie Macaro, and to Tom Felsted and Marilyn Wiley who helped with the tedious proof-reading, and to members of my family who helped assemble the book.

★★★★★★★★★★★★★★★★★★★★★★★★★

Austins in the Federal Census of 1850

Thirty states were admitted to the Union prior to the 1850 Federal Census. This was the first census to list all individuals by name . . . think of how valuable a comprehensively indexed book listing all the Austins living in 1850 might have been in your own research! Join now with other experienced genealogists to help future researchers to trace their Austin roots. If you can help to compile Austins from the 1850 census, either searching the microfilm census records of a particular state or sharing a state with other volunteer authors, please write:

Austins of America
23 Allen Farm Lane
Concord, Mass. 01742

★★★★★★★★★★★★★★★★★★★★★★★★★

SOLOMON AUSTIN
NORTH CAROLINA LOYALIST
by Robert Orley DeMond

The following was extracted from the author's book *The Loyalists in North Carolina During the Revolution*, Archon Books, Hamden, Connecticut 1964, p.198f.

As late as 1817 the sons and daughters of former Loyalists in North Carolina were moving to southern Ontario in Canada, and receiving grants of two hundred acres each. Governor Simcoe, who was made lieutenant governor of Ontario in 1791, and who during the war had commanded the Queen's Rangers in which many Loyalists of North Carolina were enrolled, was the attraction that called many people to Ontario during this period.

Solomon Austin, who had served in the Rangers and who greatly admired Simcoe, decided in 1794 to leave North Carolina and to move to Ontario to be near his old friend. Austin with his wife and nine children was well received by Simcoe and granted six hundred acres of choice land. He chose a site on Patterson Creek, now called river Lynn. In the War of 1812 he and his four sons fought under General Brock, two of the sons holding the rank of captain. Before 1886 the direct descendants of the original Solomon Austin numbered 734 (*Ontario Historical Society, Papers and Records, II, 112*).

One of the strange requests for lands in Canada was that made by the traitor Benedict Arnold. In 1797 he petitioned for a grant of 10,000 acres for himself and of 5000 acres for his wife and seven children. He was given 13,400 acres. In support of his petition he gave his loss in real and personal property as £16,000, and loss of half pay as an officer as £4050. Arnold also asked for the grant to be a general one in order that he might make his selection in any province where land might be available. In answering the request, General Simcoe told Arnold that there was no legal impediment to his and his children's having the land, provided that they had not already received a grant in the Province of New Brunswick. At the same time he informed Arnold that he was a character particularly obnoxious to the original Loyalists of America. The fact that Arnold did not intend to live in Canada removed in part the objection to his being granted the land (Canadian Archives (1891), Introduction, pp. xiv-xv).

In November 1789, Lord Dorchester requested the council at Quebec to put a mark of honor upon the families who had adhered to the unity of the Empire and joined the Royal Standard in America before the treaty of separation in the year 1783. The council convened, and thereafter all Loyalists were to be distinguished by the letters ''U.E.'' affixed to their names, alluding to their great principle — the Unity of Empire. The distinction of being a descendant of the U.E. Loyalists has continued to the present day.

SOME DESCENDANTS OF
LEONARD AUSTIN AND LYDIA GILBERT
OF JACKSON, SAC COUNTY, IOWA

by Pauline L. Austin

L. LEONARD[1] AUSTIN was born 17 April 1803 in Quebec, Canada East and had one known brother, Joseph H. Austin, a blacksmith born in 1802 in Vermont. The parents are unknown but presumably resided in both Vermont and Quebec. Leonard married Lydia Gilbert, who was born 15 June 1804 in Vermont. They married circa 1825-6, possibly in Quebec as three of their children were born there, giving them residency there until 1833-4. Next they are found in Harding County, Ohio, where their fourth child was born. In 1840 they are listed in the Bath Township, Allen County, Ohio census records with their four children. By 1844 the family had moved to Maine Township, Linn County, Iowa, where they are recorded as the first white settlers in Spring Grove Township, it not yet having been set apart as a civil township. Leonard's cabin was built of clapboards and had a spacious fireplace. The breaking plow was soon running and Austin and his sons had a good-sized field with as good a soil as a crow ever flew over. The Austin farm was along a good creek, as can be seen in the 1907 Linn County Atlas, page 167. In 1854 the family removed to the western part of Iowa, purchasing land in Jackson Township, Sac County, where the sons and their families took up farming as well. Soon after that, Leonard's brother Joseph joined them in Sac County, and is listed as a single man and a blacksmith. It is not known whether Joseph had ever married and had a family.

CHILDREN: L1. JOSEPH H., *b. 1827 in Quebec, Canada East*
L2. JOEL S., *b. 1829 in Quebec, Canada East*
L3. ELIZABETH, *b. 14 July 1832 Quebec*
L4. JOHN GILBERT, *b. 1835 in Hardin County, Ohio*
L5. JANE, *b. circa 1840 in Allen County, Ohio*
L6. LYDIA, *b. 1842 in Allen County, Ohio*

SECOND GENERATION

L1. JOSEPH H.[2] AUSTIN (*Leonard[1]*) was born 1827 in Quebec, Canada East. He was married in Linn County, Iowa on 9 February 1848 to Sarah Sutton, who was born in 1830 in Ohio. Joseph was a farmer in Jackson Township, Sac County, Iowa.

CHILDREN: L11. LEONARD S., *b. 1849*
L12. ELVIRA J., *b. 1851*
L13. ALMOND H., *b. 1853*
L14. MARGARET E., *b. 1855*
L15. WILLIAM M., *b. 1857*

L2. JOEL S.[2] AUSTIN (*Leonard[1]*) was born in 1829 in Quebec, Canada East. He was married on 2 April 1851 to Elizabeth Metcalf, who was born circa 1836 in Illinois. Joel was a farmer in Jackson Township, Sac County, Iowa.

CHILDREN: L21. LYDIA, *b. 1851*
L22. MARGARET, *b. 1853*
L23. JOSEPH G., *b. 1855*
L24. ROBERT, *b. 1860*

L3. ELIZABETH[2] AUSTIN (*Leonard[1]*) was born 14 July 1832 in Quebec, Canada. She was married in Linn County, Iowa, on 25 February 1850 to William V. Lagogrue. William was born on 15 October 1822 near Spanish Town, Jamaica (land surveyor and farmer). He died 10 October 1902 in Odell, Gage County, Nebraska, and is buried in Odell. Elizabeth died 14 March 1920 in Sac City, Iowa and is also buried in Odell Cemetery, Odell, Nebraska. LAGOGRUE CHILDREN: ALICE R. 1851, MARY MATILDA 1853, HORACE 1854, FRANK R. 1855; ISABELLE 1859, ELIZA JANE 1865-7, WILLIAM VICTOR 1869, MINNIE

L4. JOHN GILBERT[2] AUSTIN (*Leonard[1]*) was born 1835 in Hardin County, Ohio. He was married circa 1859 to Auerila Maria Tufts. Auerila was a native of Wisconsin, the daughter of Joseph Tufts, an early settler in Sac County. She came to Sac County with an uncle. John Gilbert Austin and Maria Tufts were married in Sac County and went to Nebraska, but they returned to Sac County in April 1863, living on a farm near Sac City until about 1896. John died 26 November 1901 in Sac County and is buried in Oakland Cemetery. At the time of his death he was city marshal of Sac City. Auerila died April 1907, also in Sac County.

CHILDREN: L41. ALMIRA, *b. 1860, m. – Fletcher, resided South Dakota*
L42. JAMES ELMER, *b. 22 January 1863*
L43. JOHN, *b. 1865, resided South Dakota*
L44. EDWARD, *b. 1872, was the Standard Oil Company's representative at Sac City*
L45. WILLIAM V. (or B.), *b. 1876, resided in Fonda, Iowa*

THIRD GENERATION

L42. JAMES ELMER[3] AUSTIN (*John Gilbert,[2] Leonard[1]*) was born on 22 January 1863 in Nebraska. He was reared on the parental farm near Sac City, Iowa, and followed the active life of a farmer until 1898. In 1886 he married Nellie M. Nichols, and they rented a farm in Jackson township where they lived for three years. Next they lived five years on James' father's farm of 160 acres, after which they bought a residence in Sac City and removed to town. For three years James was employed by the Chicago,

Milwaukee & St. Paul Railroad Company. In 1907 he became deputy sheriff of Sac county, serving in that capacity until 1910. He succeeded his father as city marshal of Sac City when his father died. Politically, James Elmer Austin was a Republican, and a member of the Woodmen of the World.

CHILDREN: L461. CLARENCE, *resided Lake View, Iowa*
L462. LEONARD
L463. EVELINE, *m. – Stutzman, resided Corning, Iowa*
L464. CHARLES
L465. LLOYD

References

Sac County History, published in 1914. Page 211 states that the first settler of Sac County was Ortho Williams, and those who soon followed included F. M. Cory, Leonard Austin, Joseph Austin, William Lagogure, William I. Wagoner, and Seymour W. Wagoner. Page 811 has a biographical sketch of James Elmer Austin. Lagogrue information was contributed by Carol Moritz of Hadley, Minnesota.

CORRECTIONS TO THE DESCENDANTS OF JOHN AND CHARITY KENDRICK AUSTIN OF FREDERICK COUNTY, MARYLAND

The following corrections and additions to the article appearing on page 51 of *Austins of America* were submitted by Associate Editor Janet Austin Curtis, who has not yet checked the earlier pages of this article.

In J47 and J48, the George Borah was from Lancaster, Penn. J495. Margaret Elizabeth "Betty" was born in 1846. (1850 & 1860 Census for Ohio County, Kentucky.) J4A. Dorothy B. Chinn, wife of Andrew Jackson Austin, was born in 1822 in Kentucky (1850, 1860, 1870 & 1880 Ohio County Census). Children: James Rolly b. 1842/3; Lucy A. b. 1845; Marilda b. 1847; Burgess b. 1851; Louetta b. 1854; Alice b. 1857; Wynne b. 1860 probably "Eugene"; Elizabeth b. 1865 "Betty".

J4B. Henry J. Austin was born in 1825 (1870 Ohio County Census). His wife Marelda was born in 1826 in Kentucky. Children: Ada b. 1850 m. circa 1868 George Patton b. 1840 Kentucky; Lena (Leona?) b. 1852. J4C. Zachariah Austin m. Nancy Caroline Taylor, b. 1828 Kentucky, living in 1870 (per 1850 and 1870 Ohio County Census). Children: Sally b. 1847; Dallas D. b. 1852; Ellan b. 1855/6; Zelda P. b. 1857; Elizabeth b. 1862 "Betty"; Viola b. 1866 "Ola".

J4D. George W. Austin & Amanda children (1860 & 1870 Ohio Co. Census): Malvina A. b.1846; Richard Henry b. 1847; Sarah C. b. 1848 ("Sallie"); Mariah b. 1849 (Marsella); Louisa b. 1851; John W. b. 1853; Christopher P. b. 1854/5; Martha C. b. 1856; Mary b. 1858; Eliza J. b. 1859. No Byron b. 1869 appears in the 1870 Census, and if George's Will was dated 1867, who is Byron? Amanda was a widow in 1870, living ae 53 in 1880.

QUERIES

85-1. **Absalom Chrisfield Austin**, 1812-1872, married circa 1833 Nancy Preston born 1807, died in March 1852 in Dallas County, Missouri. Children: Wesley, Elijah, Temperance, Nathaniel, and Mary A. were born in Burke County, North Carolina; Daniel was born in Greene County, Missouri; Martha C., Nancy Judy, Mildred Jane, and Selian were born in Dallas Co. Need Nancy's parents.

85-2. **Mary A. Austin** was born 10 March 1840 Burke County, North Carolina (see Query 85-1). She was the second wife of Rial (Ryall, Riley?) Barnett, who was born 1 November 1818, 25 miles upriver from Knoxville, Tennessee. His first wife was Elizabeth Case, by whom Rial had five children in Searcy County, Arkansas: Hartwell, Agnes, William M.C., George C., and Milton G. Rial and Mary settled near Redtop, Polk County, Missouri. Barnett children by Mary Austin: Absolom Chrisfield, James Spurlock, Perry Franklin, Wesley Harrison, Tempy A., Nancy C., Millie E., Edward Danield Gatewood, and Elijah 'Joe' Callaway. Rial died 12 December 1891 near Redtop, Missouri, and is buried in New Life Cemetery, Polk County. Seek his parents.

85-3. **Temperance Austin**, 1836-1895 (See Query 85-1) was married circa 1858 in Dallas County, Missouri, to John Case. John's sister was Elizabeth (see Query 85-2). Need parents of John and Elizabeth.

85-4. **John Austin** married widow Buelah (Viets) Cochran, the daughter of Henry and Buelah (Messenger) Viets, born 6 November 1775 in Becket, Mass. She had married on 6 October 1796 in Becket to Solomon Cochran. Solomon left Blandford, Mass., went to Ohio in 1805, and died between 1805 and 1812. Children of John and Buelah Austin born in Becket: John Harvey b. 12 February 1815 and James B. b. 17 September 1817. John and Buelah moved to Ohio in late 1817. She died 1 August 1827 in Aurora, Portage County, Ohio. Seek John's parents.

85-5. **Stephen Austin** was born 13 November 1819 in Parkman, Maine, the son of the Jonah Austin in Query 2-4. Need to know what became of Stephen & who he married.

85-6. **Henry Austin**, the son of Charles Henry Austin, resided in Dixfield, Maine (see Query 2-6). Does anyone know who this Henry's children were?

85-7 **Stephen Decatur Austin** born in Maine 1 December 1819, according to his gravestone. Seeking his parents.

85-8 **John Austin** 30010-20101 in 1800 Census, Washington Co., Maryland, believed to be: John Austin 35, wife Sarah 25, children Joseph 8, Hannah 6, Rebecca 4, Cornelius 3, William 1, and grandmother Christina Fraley 45. Need John's ancestry.

EDITOR'S CORNER by Michael Edward Austin

COMPUTERIZING GENEALOGICAL RESEARCH
PART 1

In the past few years, personal home computers have gained rapidly in popularity and have dropped considerably in cost. They have now reached a point where their application to the research needs of the individual historian or genealogist is reasonably affordable. The major drawback at present is the lack of a set of high-quality commercially-available computer programs which can be applied to all phases of genealogical research.

Genealogists' activities center around those historical and genealogical data records which form the basis for their subsequent research and publishing efforts. Those activities can be grouped into the four principal phases of research:

- Location of data sources
- Collection of raw data
- Storage of data records
- Retrieval of data records

This article considers the potential benefits personal computers have for the genealogist, in each of the above phases of his research. Factors entering into the selection of a particular brand of computer, and its desireable software features, are not addressed in the present article, but will be the topic of a future *Editor's Corner*.

LOCATION OF DATA SOURCES

Although not always apparent to the beginning researcher, locating sources of genealogical data is often the easiest of the genealogist's tasks! Numerous books are available which discuss sources where genealogical data may be located. Primary sources include family records, church records, town records, state records, federal records, etc. Secondary sources include published histories, genealogies, newsletters, etc. By joining various historical or genealogical organizations, or through submission of queries to magazines or family newsletters, today's genealogist may personally contact or correspond with others searching the same or related family lines.

Research Control

The personal computer can assist considerably during the "location of data sources" phase of research. The computer's chief contribution is in helping to keep the research systematically organized – *Research Control* is a good name for this function, which entails keeping track of

which sources have been studied and which remain to be studied. Without some form of research control, the genealogist may well find himself repeating research done in previous years. A few examples should serve to illustrate the value of computer's role in research control.

Suppose a researcher reads page 83 of this newsletter and is inspired to volunteer to locate all the Austins in the 1850 census for the State of New York. His computer can be used to keep track of which census volumes and microfilms are available, providing him with a checklist as he searches through the census. He can use it to maintain current listings of which counties and towns have been searched, which remain to be searched, and perhaps the number of Austins found in each town. Or perhaps our researcher is the athletic type and undertakes to trudge through all the cemeteries in his county or state. His computer might provide him with listings of all known cemeteries, and keep the list currently annotated as to which cemeteries have already been searched.

A less active researcher undertaking a systematic search through published genealogies or histories at his local library might ask his computer to provide him with a current listing of those books which he has searched to date, to avoid searching through the same books more than once. Or perhaps our ambitious researcher is planning a trip to the State Archives to search through a particular town's vital records on microfilm. It is easy enough for him to remember to look for Austins, but his computer might be asked to provide a list of other surnames of particular interest in that town, or in towns in the nearby area.

In each of the preceding examples, the computer is assisting in *research control*, arming the researcher with printed listings of those sources which are desireable for future research, plus a summary of past research to avoid duplication of effort. Admittedly, this research control

could all be done by hand, and it alone would not justify the expense of a personal computer. Given the availability of a computer, however, the genealogist can easily create and modify lists which are very useful in conducting his or her research.

COLLECTION OF RAW DATA

During the collection of data, it is always essential to include a full reference to the source from which the data was obtained. Accuracy is also of utmost important, of course, but with a good reference the genealogist himself or other researchers can verify the data at some future time. In practice raw data is collected in various ways. Some genealogists rely heavily on photocopying machines, others will carry cameras as they search through cemeteries. Most researchers simply collect data in the field by writing on index cards or forms. One approach to avoid is the "back of the envelope" technique of jotting down notes on whatever scraps of paper happen to be at hand. Another method – dictating material into an audio recorder – is also not recommended, for transcribing the data into a more useful form for storage and retrieval can be a tedious process, especially prone to spelling errors. The more recent invention of the portable video recorder is an improvement over the audio recorder (one can photograph gravestones along with the sound track), but this too involves a tedious transcription process. Taking photographs of gravestones is one of the better methods, since the photographic prints can be filed with written data as to the location of the cemetery, the plot, and adjacent graves.

None of these raw data collection methods involves the use of a computer. There are those computer enthusiasts who advocate taking your new portable microcomputer into the state archives or library and start typing away, filling the computer with the genealogical information found. While this seems efficient, and can indeed be used to avoid error-prone transcriptions, it does have serious drawbacks. Consider discovering in the book *The History of Bethel, Maine* a few pages relating to an indian attack on Peter Austin's camp. To go to the trouble of typing all that material into a computer would be a waste of valuable research time. It is far faster to photocopy those few pages, and do any desired typing later at home. When you have traveled to get to a valuable source location, typing into a computer can be inefficient. There are also situations where *only* a photocopy will do. For example, the deciphering of old handwriting can sometimes be extremely difficult and take a great deal of time. Attempting to do that at the library or state archives is not only a waste of valuable research time, but it is extremely error-prone. In general, then, attempting to collect raw data using the computer is inadvisable – there is little a computer can do to assist in the collection of raw data phase of genealogical research.

STORAGE OF DATA RECORDS

In storing data records one should attempt to minimize the amount of transcription of the raw data which is required. The fewer times data is copied, the fewer chances for errors. Ideally, storage would involve only the physical filing of those same index cards or sheets of paper (perhaps with photographs attached) which were used in collecting the raw data. The main difficulty in storage is deciding *where* to file the raw data. Should a raw family data sheet mentioning several persons be filed alphabetically under the name of the head of the family, or perhaps under the state, county, or town in which the record was found? Whatever method is chosen, how does the genealogist locate other persons recorded on the sheet some months or even years after filing it?

Austins of America Files

The difficult decision of where to file raw data sheets can be totally avoided through use of a computer. The *Austins of America* files provide an example of this. These files presently consist of many notebooks filled with data of all types. The filing mechanism is quite simple. First the raw data sheet (which may be *anything* – vital record, family sheet, photocopied book, correspondence, etc.) is assigned a six-digit number, which is stamped in the upper right hand corner of the sheet (see next page). The first three digits match the number of the notebook in which the sheet is to be filed, the last three digits correspond to the page number within that notebook. With up to 999 notebooks of nearly 200 sheets each, approximately 200,000 such raw data sheets may be filed. If it is necessary to go beyond that, notebooks will be labeled A01, A02, etc. With 26 alphabetic characters, there are another 520,000 raw data sheets one might file, surely enough combinations to satisfy even the most avid collector of genealogical data!

The next step – before actually filing the raw data sheet into its assigned notebook – is to abstract the data contained on the sheet, typing the abstract into the computer. The abstract consists of all the basic genealogical facts, including names of all persons, dates, and places. To minimize storage requirements, certain rules are followed when abstracting a raw data record:

• DATES – Days and months are ignored, only the year is included in abstracts. When appropriate, the year is immediately preceded by a letter and period indicating the type of information associated with the date: b.1656 for a birth record, m.1678 for a marriage record, r.1695 for a residency record, d.1813 for a death record, etc. As discussed below, these date conventions facilitate later retrieval of the abstract.

• PLACES – States are abstracted using the same two-letter designation used by the United States Postal Service – Massachusetts becomes MA, California becomes CA,

etc. Town and city names are spelled out in full. Each town or state only appears once in the abstract, regardless of how often it may appear in the original raw data record.

● REFERENCE – The source of the raw data sheet is not included in the abstract. While the reference is invaluable, it is of little help in the information retrieval process discussed below, and it can always be found on the raw data sheet itself once the sheet's abstract has been located.

The genealogist types the abstract into the computer. The computer stores it in its mass storage, along with a unique *primary key* number (assigned sequentially by the computer's database management program). This primary key permits the computer to index and later to locate the abstract. Besides storing the abstract, the computer checks all proper names against a large dictionary of individual and place names which the computer maintains. The computer warns the genealogist of a possible misspelling whenever an unrecognized name is typed in. If the genealogist informs the computer that the name is indeed spelled correctly, the computer adds the name to its dictionary. For each word in its dictionary, the computer maintains a list of those abstracts in which the word appears, identifying each abstract by its primary key.

The abstract input to the computer is not intended to replace the raw data sheet itself. For example, photocopies of pages from *The History of Bethel, Maine,* describing in detail an Indian attack on Peter Austin's camp in 1781, might be abstracted quite briefly:

#124116 Peter Austin r.1781 Bethel ME: Indian attack

Clearly the abstract does not pretend to convey the details of the original raw data sheet – *the abstract is simply the means by which the computer can help the genealogist locate the original raw data sheet.*

An example of a raw data sheet and its abstract is shown below. Note that the data sheet shows that both Joseph and Judith were born in Rochester, VT. These facts do not appear in the abstract, however, for Rochester, VT was previously mentioned in the abstract as Truman's birthplace. Similarly, Abram Hook's birthplace in New Hampshire does not appear since Clara's birthplace was previously mentioned in the abstract. As can be seen from this example and the rules given earlier, the abstract is intended to contain only sufficient information on all persons, dates, and places mentioned in the raw data sheet to permit the genealogist to later get back to the raw data sheet, as discussed in the next section.

RETRIEVAL OF DATA RECORDS

Data retrieval is perhaps the most rewarding phase of research, for in this phase the genealogist sorts out facts, and attempts to reconstruct a clear record or history of a person or family from the bits of raw data he has previously

---

Austins of America GENEALOGICAL NEWSLETTER SERVING AUSTIN FAMILY RESEARCHERS

018113

DATA CONCERNING YOU

NAME TRUMAN DANIEL AUSTIN	ADDRESS ROCHESTER, VT. DEATHS 1903-1923
BIRTH DATE 24 DECEMBER 1837 d. 16	OCTOBER 1921
BIRTH PLACE ROCHESTER, VERMONT	
FATHER'S NAME JOSEPH AUSTIN	MOTHER'S NAME JUDITH LYON
BIRTH DATE	BIRTH DATE
BIRTH PLACE ROCHESTER, VERMONT	BIRTH PLACE ROCHESTER, VERMONT

DATA CONCERNING YOUR FIRST SPOUSE

NAME CLARA HOOK	MARRIAGE DATE
BIRTH DATE 18 JULY 1843	MARRIAGE PLACE
BIRTH PLACE WASHINGTON, NH DEATH DATE 22 MAY 1905 ae 61y 10m 4d DEATH PLACE	
FATHER'S NAME ABRAM HOOK	MOTHER'S NAME LUCY PICKET
BIRTH DATE	BIRTH DATE
BIRTH PLACE NEW HAMPSHIRE	BIRTH PLACE

DATA CONCERNING YOUR SECOND SPOUSE

NAME	MARRIAGE DATE

Austins of America raw data sheets are stamped with a number, corresponding to the notebook and page in which they are to be filed. Before the above sheet is filed in notebook 018 as page 113, an abstract is typed into the computer:

#018113 Truman Daniel Austin b.1837 Rochester VT d.1921, s. Joseph & Judith (Lyon) Austin; m. Clara Hook b.1843 Washington NH d.1905, dau. Abram & Lucy (Picket) Hook

located, collected and stored. It is in this phase of research that the computer can be of greatest help. With appropriate information-retrieval software, and a mass storage device such as a floppy disk or a Winchester hard-disk drive, a computer can locate previously stored data sheet abstracts with great speed. The *Austins of America* system will serve as an example of how such a modern information retrieval system can be used.

Retrieval at the Reunion

Below and on the next page are shown some photographs, courtesy of Lewis and Dorothy Austin of Toledo, Ohio, of the Austin Families Association National Reunion held this summer on August 5th and 6th in Miamisburg, Ohio. Attendees were able to submit their own queries directly to the *Austins of America* computer (shown below), typing in their queries in English. Typical of the form of these queries are the following examples:

    Find Benjamin with Mary or Sarah in OH
    Find Thomas and Joseph and Judith
    Find Hook or Picket
    Find Rochester in VT
    Find Truman
    Find b.1837 in NH or VT or NY
    Find Joseph with Judith in VT or NH
    Find Frederick and b.180* or b.181*

The *Austins of America* computer first scans a query, and then looks up each proper name and date in its dictionary. The dictionary lists those raw data sheet abstracts in which each proper name and date occurs. By correlating the primary keys of these abstracts for each proper name and date in the query, the computer determines which abstracts (if any) satisfy all items in the query. Finally, the computer uses a *primary key index* file to physically locate those abstracts matching the query, and displays them on the computer's video monitor. If one or more abstracts are of interest, the querist may obtain more details by referring to the appropriate volume and page associated with the abstract. Unfortunately, only a small fraction – approximately 20 volumes – of the *Austins of America* files were available at the National Reunion this year. Hopefully next year we'll have the files on microfiche and a greater fraction of them will be available for detailed reference.

In checking for proper names in its dictionary, the *Austins of America* computer automatically allows for common nicknames and for alternative spellings. Thus, in the first query example, raw data sheet abstracts having a Benjamin with a Polly or a Sally in Ohio would also be located and presented to the querist. Towns such as Nobleborough would also be located even if typed in as Nobleboro, etc. In considering nicknames and alternative spellings, the computer often responds to what the querist means to request, rather than exactly what was requested.

In its *Research Mode* (the mode used at the Reunion), the *Austins of America* computer displays raw data sheet abstracts in response to queries typed in, and it also presents other "related" abstracts of potential interest to the querist. In its *Modification Mode*, the computer allows the querist to add new abstracts or to modify existing abstracts. It also allows the genealogist to "relate" two or more abstracts, so subsequent access of one abstract will cause the other "related" abstracts to be found as well.

As new data continues to be sent in by Austin family researchers, becomes stored in the *Austins of America* files, and gets abstracted into the computer, more and more queries – both past and future – will be quickly answerable by the *Austins of America* computer. Please help make this Austin database as complete as possible by sending copies of your own research notes, photocopied articles, etc. to the *Austins of America* Editor:

> Dr. Michael E. Austin
> Box 73   MIT/LL
> Lexington, MA 02173

See you at next year's Reunion . . . you can see for yourself how the *Austins of America* computer helps Austin family genealogists in their research . . . you might even learn more of your own Austin line, with the computer presenting you with new abstracts "related" to abstracts typed in from the Austin data you have contributed! □

AFA National Reunion in Miamisburg, Ohio
Viola Louise Austin of Beaver Dam, Wisconsin, retrieves data from the *Austins of America* computer (above) while others compare research notes (below).
Photographs courtesy of Lewis and Dorothy Austin.

EUNICE COAL WITCHCRAFT TRIAL
REVEALS THE BIRTHYEAR OF
HOPESTILL AUSTIN

by Glenn Matthew Austin

Editor's Note: The following article concerns Hopestill Austin, the wife of Samuel Austin of Boston (see *Austins of America* pages 8ff), and establishes her approximate birthyear as 1644, a date which was previously unknown to Austin family genealogists. Along with Hopestill's deposition which establishes her age, we also publish here the other papers of the trial, for they provide valuable insight into the period during which Samuel and Hopestill Austin were raising their small sons Samuel and Thomas Austin.

While brousing through old volumes in a bookshop, I discovered a June 1914 magazine *Colonial Wars*, published by the Society of Colonial Wars In the Commonwealth of Massachusetts, Boston, Mass. On page 171 of Volume I No. 3, an article entitled "Birth-Dates of Many Early Colonists as Given in the Court Files at Boston" included a most intriguing line:

Austin, Hopestill   29   1673

Having learned from page 8 of *Austins of America* that Samuel & Hopestill had sons Samuel and Thomas born in 1669 and 1671 in Boston, and that nothing further was known of what subsequently became of Samuel and Hopestill, I speculated that perhaps Hopestill had died in 1673 while bearing a third child, and that the 'Court Files' referred to were perhaps involved with settling her estate.

Searching through the records of the Massachusetts Superior Court and its predecessors (today preserved in the New Court House at Courthouse Plaza in Boston) for the years circa 1673, I soon learned that my speculation had been entirely wrong, and that Hopestill was still very much alive in 1673! She was giving her deposition in Case 1228 - a most interesting case of a woman named Eunice Coal (or Coale), who was on trial for Witchcraft.

The papers presented here have been carefully transcribed directly from excellent photocopies of the original court papers. 'Translated' might be a better description of the tedious process, for these papers were hand written in distinctively seventeenth-century script, which sometimes proved most difficult to interpret. Wherever the interpretation is dubious, I have placed question marks to indicate the uncertainty. My own additions and comments are included in square brackets. Because of its particular interest to Austin family researchers, the original deposition of Hopestill Austin is reproduced here. The papers are presented in the same order in which they appear in the Massachusetts Court records, and are not necessarily in chronological order.

First Paper

To William Salter Goale Keeper of Boston prison: You are herby requiered in his Maties name by order of ye County Court held att Salisbury ye 29th: Aprill 1673 by adjo^em^t: to take into yor Costody ye body of Eunice Cole & then safely to keepe her untill shee come to a legall tryall upon suspition of haveing familliarty wth ye devill, as apears by former & latter evidences & hereof you are not to faile att yor perrill: dat: ye 1st of May 1673 by ye Court   Tho: Bradbury rec[order].

Second Paper

Abraham Perkins Senr testifieth thatt when William Fifield now Constable 24 Nov on the night befor thatt he caried Unis Coule Down to boston this Deponent being one of ye Sehst? men was deliver to Coule a payr of Kniting pins to Unis Coule - and when I came thear I heard a disrouseing in her house and Harkening I hird the voyse of Unis Coule & a Greatt Hollow Voyse answer her & the s^d Unis seemed to lauff & to bee displeased with something finding falt & the s^d Hollow Voyse spake to her again & in a Avange & unworld manner butt I could nott understand any sentuns butt as if one had spoken outt of the Earth or in sid Hollow Vestile itt being an inslouishing? voyse thatt Answered her, & I being much Amased to hear the voyse: I wentt & called Abraham Drake & Allexsander Dunnum and wee three wentt to Her house and Harkned and heard the s^d Unis Cole speake & the s^d Strang voyse answer her divers times, and the s^d Unis Coule went up & down in the House & claterrd the Doors to & against? and spake as she wentt & the s^d voyse made her Answer in a Shr?ing manner as is above s^d and ther was the shimerring of a Kirs Culler in that chimney corner & upon thatt wee wentt & informed Mr Dalton of whatt wee had heard & seene & so wee went to her house again & Called & asked who it was that did talke to her & she s^d thatt there was no body there & wee Asked her if there had bin no body with her that night & she s^d no there had bin nobody thatt night & wee Asked her who itt was that she spake to & discussed with & she Answered thatt she did nott talke to any body. Abraham Perkins Sen & Alexsander Dunnum under oath to this as above written ye 7 [?] 1673 Before me

Sam^{ll} Dutton, Comiss^r

Sworn by Abraham Drake, Marshall before County Court held at Salisbury ye 29th day of Aprill 1673 by adjormt. Thos. Bradbury, Rec^d

They further witness on the reverse sid

[REVERSE SIDE OF SECOND PAPER]

The said Abraham Perkins & Alexander Dennum on their oath affirmed that the hol[low] voyse they mentioned w^{ch}

they heard was a distinct voyse from Unice Cole wᶜʰ they knew well & that the said Unice Cole was violent whene Jethero? Goms? ons eford? Voome nike another & often Comming to the chimney did having? yᵗ way speake something louder & somthing more mildly and though they cannot sweare to the word spoken by yᵉ hollow voyse yett are certaine weu?an Pecuular voyse & that the glimering in the corner seemed to them to be a substanse & further saith not. Yᵉ whole euvent were this ted?disa? sworne unto in open Court this 5ᵗʰ of September 1673. Yᵉ prisoner at the Barr. as Attest Edward Rawson, Secrey

The prisoner at the barr swore in Court once & Againe that there nor had Bin no body w[ith] her yᵗ night spoken of minzvdiet? Lin?.
 Attest Edw Lawson Secrety

Third Paper

The Deposition of Ephraim Winsley who sayth yᵗ att that time when Goodwife Cole was whipt at Salisbury in Capᵗ Wiggins time Rich Ormsby being Constable as he was taking of her clothes when she was naked about her breasts Rich Ormsby spake after this maner: yᵉ shere no good woman will come hither - she turning her about from yᵉ magistrates ward did take hold of something about her brest and with her fingers did wring of something and it did bled and drop blod I saw it when she was a whiping to bled there and her brest yeill collored as it had ben beatten black and bluish

Some yearres after in Capᵗ Wiggins time I saw her whipt att Hampton by John Huggin and I did take good notise of her breast and then it was not of that collor butt clear as yᵉ other or yᵉ rest of her body yᵗ was naked: farther when she puld yᵗ of her brest she sayd it was auold sorre.

Sworn before yᵉ Court held att Salisbury yᵉ 29ᵗʰ April 1673 2 Session: Tho Bradbury rec

Sworn in Court 3ᵈ Sept 73 Attest Edw Rawson Secret

Fourth Paper

The Deposition of John Mason aged about aboutt 20 years who saith thatt Coming upon the watch the last sumer on Sabath day att night Coming near the house of Unis Coule where she dwelleth, and hearing of her mutter in the House I went to the Door with James Bruse the sᵈ Unis Coule called mee Divill & said she would splitt out my Brains and the next day I felt sick & lay sick aboutt a fortnight after. Sworne yᵉ 7 : 2 mo 1673 befor mee

                    Samˡˡ Dutton Conistible

Fifth Paper

Elizabeth Person aged about therty n[ine years] Testifieth & sayth yᵗ: I Laying in of [the house of Widow] Iester Naneye my Neece come & to[torn]f me thereould goodwife

Cole of hampton desired to [torn] & yᵉ women yᵗ was In yᵉ Chamber was not w[torn] shee should come up. Sᵈ niece tould me yᵗ she gave this answer yᵗ I was not willing she should come up[.] That night or yᵉ next I fell into anague & fever & yᵉ child was tacken sick in an unusiall maner & at six weeks End Dyed & furder sayeth not.
Deposed in Court 5 September 1673 yᵉ prisoner at the Barr - as Attest Edward Rawson Secrety

Sixth Paper

Johanathan Thinge aged about 56 years testifieth that about 16 or 17 years agone I goinge in yᵉ street at hampton I saw one yᵗ did Judge was Unice Colle, about 20 rod: behind: or in a triangell sid ways of mee & in a short time sooner yⁿ aney man could posibly goe it I saw, her as I did Judge was she about 20 rods or more before mee upon yᵗ I went apece wondring at yᵉ thing & when I Come to her as I did Judge was shee I talked with her & found her to be Unice Coale Also about yᵗ time coming out of my gate I saw no body nor there was no body neare: as I could see & presently shee yᵉ sᵈ Unice Cole was before mee loking into yᵉ house amonge my cattell, I askeed her what shee did there she answered what is yᵗ to you, Jawsboxe, I hasted to come up to her & shee semed as it weare to swime away I could not catch her I yⁿ Goinge stronge & in health I followed her 20 or about 30 rod
 Sworne to in Court 5 Sept 1673 yᵉ prisonᵉʳ at yᵉ Barr

                                        Edw Rawson Secret

HOPESTILL AUSTIN DEPOSITION

Seventh Paper

The Deposition of Hopestill Austin Aged Twenty nine yeares or therein about saith that about Tenne years agoe: Liveing in the house of Mʳˢ Nanneye: defⁿᵗ Goody Coale at the said Mʳˢ Nanneye house: wheras the said Goody Coale heareing that Mʳˢ Pearson was lately brought to bed in the said house: had a desire to goe se the said Mʳˢ Pearson & her litle one, wheare upon Mʳˢ Pearsons Nurse replyed yᵗ her Mʳˢ was not Doeng well: & did not desire any more Company: But she the said Goody Coale presed to goe up the staires: but this Deponent pulled her downe againe sayinge that she should not goe up: wheare upon the said Goody Coale replyed that it had benne better she had Gonne up: said went away mutteringe; what she said this deponent cannot tell: but in a very Litle time both Mʳˢ Pearson and her Child was tacken very ill; and in a very sad manner: wheare ofe the Child Died: Goody Coale said is theire Gentle folks above: this deponent said, Gentle or Simple yᵉ shall not Goe up: wʳ upon she went a way muttering as above sd & further saith not. Deposed in Court 5 September 1673. yᵉ prisoner at the Barr:

                                    Edward Rawson Secrety

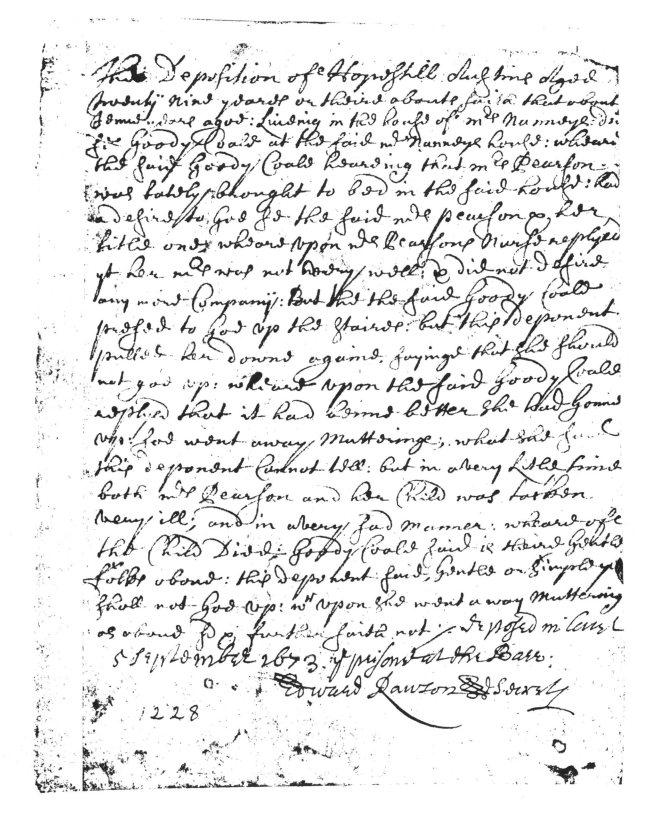

The deposition of Hopestill Austin, given 5 September 1673 during the witchcraft trial of Eunice Coal. This is the only known document which reveals the birthyear of Hopestill as being circa 1644. A recent transcription of the deposition appears on page 92.

Eighth Paper

The Deposityon of Abraham Perkins Sen aged 60. This Deponantt wittnesseth yᵗ divers cases first being att Salsbery Courtt when Unise Cole had her triall when goodman Ormsby was Constabell and sawe her breste plucked of as hee Sath and I myself saw yᵉ blud run downe whear yᵉ said Constaboll saw yᵉ teatt and caled others to see it and att yᵉ same time Unis Cole being whiped: yᵉ next nygt after as goodman ormsby was in bed as he saith somthing like a catt hoped opon his fase and very much scrached him yᵉ next morning coming to courtt Captin wigins asked him how his fase came to bee so scraced hee said somthing in yᵉ night came and scrated him and told yᵉ courtt all yᵉ story and they all wondred att itt and further saith yᵗ About nine or tenn yeares agon he had severall of his lambs lying dead- Unise Coale coming by & would hem & when she depart looking up said utder you #$%@#xe she would say it is so & shall be so doe what you will. Also about the same time he had 3 or 4 swine a fatting yᵗ at first they fed on the corne well but after whine would eate no corne meale pease or els but during wᶜʰ I Pild them & bring opeenig of them my self & wife D-ar-ly buried them notgnigbuty that during in Cifenupld year ??? Goody Unice Coale coming bye Quig a emily d it must be so Stshange so do wᵗ you will and further saith that his wife & family was present & heard the words of Henniget. Deposed in Court 5ᵗ Septr 3. Attest ERS

Ninth Paper

The Deposition of Elizabeth Shaw yᵉ wife of Joseph Shaw who saith thatt yᵉ latter end of yᵉ Last Sumer the secund Day thatt the wife of Joseph Dow was Brought to bed of her last child being the sabath Day & the same day in the afternoon this Deponantt being in the same seatt whear Unis Coule did sitt: and Mʳ Cotton being att prayer this Deponantt did hear a noyse like to the whining of pupies when they have a mind to sriek & this Deponantt sitting next to Unis Coule did to her Best discrning judg thatt the noyse of whineing was under the sᵈ Unis and the sᵈ Unis being sitting in yᵉ seatt this deponantt hearing such a noyse for some time to Gether did turne her head & looke on Unis Coule & then the sᵈ Unis did stir her selfe or nessell a little as she satt & I heard no more of the noyse of whining which I had heard Befor and this deponatt looked diligently aboutt in the seatt to see yᵗ there were any dog butt could see none nor any other creature yᵗ should make such a noise there being nobody in the seatt att thatt time butt Unise Coule & this deponantt & the wife of Jacob Perkins and after yᵗ this Deponant had turned her head from Unis Coule she turned to the wife of yᵉ sᵈ Jacob Perkins and she was stooping to looke towards Unis Coule & she smiled on this Deponent whereby I confirmed that she might also Heare the noyse as I did. Sworne yᵉ 28: 1 mo 1673 Befor

mee Samuell Dalton Constable. Mary Perkins yᵉ wife of Jacob Perkins doth testified thatt she did hear yᵉ same noise above mentioned when Unis Cole went by her into the seat and att yᵗ time when she smiled on Goody Shaw & could se no creature in or aboutt yᵉ seatt yᵗ could make such a noise: Sworne yᵉ 8: 2 mo 1673 upon oath in open Befor mee Samˡˡ Dalton Constabil 5 Septebr 73: yᵉ prisoner & Elizabeth Shaw only being present [at the] Barr　Edw. Rawson Secrety

Tenth Paper

This is to Certify all whom it may Conserne ordinary Peepel of yˢ Jurisdicton:　that the psons here under expressed have theire semple creditte on The Tresurer who is to sattisfy them theire semple expenses do yᵉ semple value here expressed as being yᵉ Remaynder of wh was allowed them for theire time expended in wittnessing agᵗ Eunise Cole on triall for witchcraft

as To Thomas Coleman & his wife _____	14 ˢ	00 ᵖ
To Goodwife Hobs _____	07	00
To widdow wedgewoode _____	15	08

By the Court　Edw. Rawson Secrety   *1 : 16　08*

★★★★★★★★★★★★★★★★★★★★★★★★★★★★★★★

Austins of America is intended to serve present and future genealogists researching Austin family lines. Readers are encouraged to submit Queries, genealogical and historical articles for publication. Previously published books, pamphlets or articles containing Austin genealogical data are also sought for reprinting or review.

EDITOR

DR. MICHAEL EDWARD AUSTIN　　CONCORD, MA

ASSOCIATE EDITORS

ANTHONY KENT AUSTIN	PROSPECT, KY
PATRICIA BIEBUYCK AUSTIN	CONCORD, MA
PAULINE LUCILLE AUSTIN	MARION, IA
JANET AUSTIN CURTIS	ALBUQUERQUE, NM
CAROL LEIGHTON HULL	SUDBURY, MA

Austins of America is published each February and August by The Austin Print, 23 Allen Farm Lane, Concord, Massachusetts 01742. All correspondence, including subscriptions, articles and responses to queries, should be sent to this address. Subscriptions are $2.50 per year postpaid.

★★★★★★★★★★★★★★★★★★★★★★★★★★★★★★★

ILLINOIS AUSTIN BIOGRAPHIES

The following biographies were submitted by Beverly Jean Kim of Champaign, Illinois. They were adapted from *The Biographical Record of Whiteside County, Illinois*; *The History of Coles County, Illinois*, Chicago, Wm. LeBaron Jr. & Co., 1879; *History of Coles County 1876-1976*, Charleston & Mattoon Bicentennial Commissions.

ISAAC AUSTIN

Isaac Austin, whose farm is conveniently located near Lyndon, owns and operates three hundred acres of rich land, lying in Lyndon and Mount Pleasant townships. This place is neat and thrifty in appearance, and indicates the careful supervision of the owner. The substantial residence and outbuildings are surrounded by well-tilled fields, cultivated by the latest improved machinery, and the owner of this desirable place is accounted one of the most progressive agriculturists of the community.

Mr. Austin was born 4 September 1833 in Tioga County, Pennsylvania, and is a son of Steward and Louisa (Reynolds) Austin, the former a native of Oneida County, New York, and the latter of Tioga County. Their marriage was celebrated in the Keystone State, and they became the parents of six children, two of whom died in infancy. Hiram married Laura Morse, and to them were born seven children – Etta, Lyman, Cora, Lester, Clara, Phoebe and Ray. The mother died in Illinois and Hiram Austin afterward removed to Kansas, where he has since married again. He is now living in Cowley County, Kansas. William was one of the early settlers of the Sunflower State, and is now living in Dickinson County. Isaac is the next of the family. Lenore is the widow of Charles L. Conyne, of Lyndon, and has five children – Ida, Martin, Stewart, John and Lola. In 1847 Steward Austin removed from Pennsylvania to Illinois, making an overland trip, and located on a farm owned by Lyman Reynolds, one of the early settlers of the county. He was a whole-souled man of kindly spirit and generous disposition, sheltering all who came to him in those pioneer days. After a time he purchased the farm on which he had settled, making his home there until his death. He was one of the leading farmers of the community and had many warm friends. His wife died before the removal to Illinois.

Isaac Austin attended school for a short time in Pennsylvania, but though his educational privileges were meager, reading, experience and observation have brought him a broad general knowledge. He remained with his father until eighteen years of age, and then purchased a half interest in the old homestead. His brother Hiram purchased the other half, and together they pre-empted eighty acres. At the age of eighteen, Isaac Austin went to California on a prospecting tour, making the journey overland with six yoke of oxen, one wagon and five men,

two being from Illinois and three from Comanche, Iowa. This was in the year 1852, and Mr. Austin remained on the Pacific slope until 1856, residing in Placer and Nevada Counties. He made some money during his sojourn in the west and upon his returned he resumed agricultural pursuits, adding to his property, at different times, tracts of seventy-five and one hundred and twenty acres of land. He therefore has at the present time a very valuable and desirable farm of three hundred acres, and in his farming operations he follows the most approved methods and has therefore met with creditable success.

In September 1859, he married Cornelia A. Smith, who was born in New York and during her early girlhood came with her parents to Illinois in 1840. Two children were born of this union, but one died in childhood. The other, Walter, is now a farmer of Lyndon township. He married Chloe Joyce, and they have four children – Rex, Harry, Mary, and Clarence. Mrs. Austin died in 1865, and on 2 March 1869 Mr. Austin was again married, his second union being with Lola Hanson, daughter of Jacob and Virginia (Benham) Hanson, who are now residents of Iowa. Mrs. Austin was born in Dutchess County, New York, in 1853, and by her marriage became the mother of seven children, but two died in infancy. Floyd was drowned in Rock River at the age of fourteen years. The others are Belle, wife of Warner Hurlbut, a butcher of Prophetstown, by whom she had two children, Winnie and Essie; Effie, wife of Fred Pratt, who operates a creamery in Bureau County, Illinois; Edna, a student in the Fulton Schools; and Winnie, who is attending school in Lyndon.

Mr. Austin cast his first vote for General Scott while in California, and since the organization of the Republican Party he has been one of its staunch supporters. Various offices have been offered him, but he has always refused to serve except as path master and school director, in which positions he has rendered effective and able service to his fellow townsmen. He is a Master Mason and he and his wife belong to the Order of the Eastern Star. Highly respected, they well deserve mention in this volume.

WILLIAM F. AUSTIN

William F. Austin, of the firm of Austin, Brown & Kimball, dealers in hardware, lumber, agricultural implements, furniture, etc.; is a native of Coles County, Illinois, being a son of John and Susan (Carter) Austin; his father was born 9 September 1809 near Nashville, Tennessee, and came with his father's family to the county in about 1828; his father, William Austin, took up a farm, comprising the site of the present village of Ashmore. Mr. Austin was married 15 October 1835 to Miss Susan Carter, a daughter of John and Mary Carter, both natives of East Tennessee; she was born in East Tennessee 24 September 1815; removed with her parents to Kentucky in early

childhood, and came to Coles County in 1830, landing April 10th in Ashmore, where her father took up a farm east of and adjoining the present village, and where Mrs. Austin still resides; Mrs. Austin's father, John Carter, was born in 1790 and died 19 July 1841; her mother Mary was born 24 December 1792 and died 11 November 1857.

Mr. Austin remained a substantial and highly-respected citizen until his death 9 September 1845; he left five children – James M. born 13 March 1837 and died 23 July 1866; Mary C., now Mrs. Thomas White of Ashmore, born 13 August 1838; William F. born 12 November 1840; Edith born 22 September 1842, married F. M. Waters of Ashmore, and died 4 January 1862; Thomas born 10 October 1844.

William F. Austin remained on the homestead until the age of 22, and then engaged in the manufacture of wagons and carriages, in company with A. J. Waters; this he continued two years, after which he followed carpentering until he entered upon his present business in 1872. Mr. Austin has been a member of the village Council for the past five or six years. He was married on 10 November 1864 to Miss Mary A. Sousley, who was born in Ashmore Township 5 August 1843; she is a daughter of David and Lucinda (Groves) Sousley, who were among the early settlers of the county; her father was born 1 September 1816, came to Coles County with is parents circa 1832 and died 26 November 1847. Mr. Austin has two sons, Alcephus L. and Thomas E. Austin.

Alcephus L. Austin, son of William F., was born 22 July 1867 in Ashmore, and died 25 September 1915. He married Minnie Leland Cox, born 9 March 1878 in Ashmore and died 9 March 1967. Their only child was Winifred L. Austin, born 17 August 1907 in Ashmore; she married Harry Joseph Shea on 15 November 1927 in Charleston, Illinois. Joseph was born 16 October 1903 in Mattoon, Illinois, and died 13 March 1956. They had one child, Thomas William Shea, born in 1931 in Mattoon.

Thomas Early Austin, the second son of William F. Austin, was born 24 July 1871 and died 17 February 1948. He married Anna Mable Hogue on 3 August 1899. Anna was born 19 January 1875 and died 11 December 1961. They had two children: Thomas Marion Austin, born 17 August 1906, and Edith Virginia Austin, born 25 August 1906 (sic) and died 31 January 1947. Thomas Marion married on 27 December 1933 to Kate Emily Smith. They had two daughters: Nancy May born 17 March 1937 and Sheila Kay born 3 January 1942. Nancy married Gerald D. Kastl, they had four daughters: Elaine Ann, Diane Marie, and twins Sharon Lee and Karen Sue. Edith Virginia Austin married on 7 September 1929 to Donald Sparks; they had two daughters: Rosalie Ann born in 1932, and Donna Jean born in 1935.

DENNIS AUSTIN

For over 45 years Dennis Austin has resided in Whiteside County, Illinois, and his name is inseparably connected with its agricultural and stock-raising interests. His thoroughly American spirit and great energy has enabled him to mount from a lowly position to one of affluence, and he is now living retired in Morrison.

Mr. Austin was born in Switzerland County, Indiana, 30 December 1825, a son of William and Margaret (Livings) Austin. The father was born in New York 9 November 1795, and when only seven years old lost his parents, Isaac and Deborah (Reynolds) Austin, who were born in the New England states, and had six children, namely: Isaac, Joel, Stewart, Seymour, Sarah and William. Mary Livings was born 2 April 1799 in New Jersey, a daughter of Daniel and Polly (Ellison) Livings. Her father was born in 1776 and died in 1863, while her mother was born in 1769 and died in 1852. William Austin, father of our subject, was a soldier in the war of 1812 at the age of 18 years. From his native state he went to Ohio, where he made his home for two years on a farm, and spent the following two years in Indiana where he owned large tracts of land. On selling his property there in 1854, he came to Whiteside County, Illinois, and in Mount Pleasant township purchased four hundred acres of land, on which he made his home until his death on 22 October 1859. He was one of the most successful farmers of the county and was highly respected by all who knew him. His wife survived him several years, dying on 3 October 1877.

To this worthy couple were born ten children: (1) Ezra died in infancy. (2) Maria born 27 January 1820 in New York, married Joseph Myers and died 3 October 1877. Their children were Indiana, Job, Florence, John, Joseph, and Victoria. (3) Miranda was born in March 1822, married 1840 Silas Richmond. They had one child, Silas. Widow Miranda remarried in 1847 to Henry Murphy. He died leaving four children: Charles, Clark, Almeda, and Julius are residents of Kansas. In 1858 she took a third husband, Thomas Rock, by whom she had twins Clarence and Clinton. (4) Daniel L. Austin, b. 22 October 1823 was m. 1846 Myra A. Gary, and they had six children: Myra J., wife of John McGregor of Winfield, Kansas; Celia A., wife of Noah Vest of Storm Lake, Iowa; George W., who married Eveline Hurd and lives in Storm Lake; Charles W.; Augustus E., who was married in July 1884 to Gertie Cobleigh; and John. After the death of his first wife Daniel L. married again and by the second union had one daughter, Sue. (5) Dennis, our subject, is next in the family. (6) Jonathan b. 1828, d. aged two years. (7) Silas R. b. 6 December 1830, is a retired farmer of Lyndon, Whiteside County. He was married in 1860 to Fanny McGee, and to them were born six children: Marion;

Lettie; Carrie, deceased; Annie, Norma, and Ermie. (8) Martin V., born 1833 married 1857 Hannah M. McGee, and had eight children: Olive M.; William G.; Nellie; Nettie; Bert; Harry; Edna; Vernie; and Silas, deceased. (9) Georgiana, born 1837 is the wife of Homer Olmstead of Ordway, Colorado, and they have five children: Alice, Minnie, Nellie, Charles and Marion. (10) William S. born 1841 is a resident of Unionville and is employed as a stock buyer by Baker Brother, of Morrison. He married 1867 Eliza Harris, who died in 1898. They had six children: Charles B. S.; Edith M.; Mary L.; Homer, deceased; Glen H.; and Marguerite E.

Dennis Austin was educated in the subcription schools of Indiana, which he was only able to attend through the winter months as his services were needed on the home farm in summer. He remained under the parental roof until he was married 17 September 1848 to Miss Harriet Gary, who was born 4 June 1831 in Allegany County, New York, a daughter of Charles and Eunice (Spalding) Gary, natives of Connecticut and Vermont respectively. From New York the Gary family removed to Indiana, where Mrs. Austin's parents both died.

Ten children were born to our subject and his wife: (1) Emory W. born 19 May 1848 was drowned in Rock Creek at the age of twelve. (2) Millard F. was born 27 October 1850 and is now a prosperous farmer of Kansas. He married 4 September 1873 to Alice Moss, and has six children: Ethel, now the wife of Marion Covey of Miltonvale, Kansas; Ray; Lela; Josephine; Mabel; and Hazel. (3) Frank P. born 20 March 1853 is a retired farmer of Clark, South Dakota. He was married 17 February 1874 and had six children: Emma; Emery who died in 1889; Arthur; Frank; Lillian; and Glen D. (4) Harrison C. born 9 April 1855 is a successful farmer living near Fillmore, Nebraska. He was married in 1878 to Emma R. Follansbee, and had one child, Jennie M. who was born in 1879 and died in 1896. (5) Esther W. born 20 April 1857, was married 27 December 1876 to S. A. Maxwell, who is a teacher in Fulton College and lives near Morrison. They have four children: Edith born 1878; Ralph born 1881; Vera born 1883; and Harold born 1889. (6) Olive B., born 17 September 1860, married 17 September 1880 to Frank Weimer, now of South Dakota, and they had six children: Roy; Austin, deceased; Eva; Grace; Ada; and Frank. (7) Lincoln A. born 11 January 1864 is a successful unmarried farmer of Clark County, South Dakota. (8) Hattie B. was born 22 December 1869, married 22 April 1891 to Mason P. Brewer who lives on his father's farm in Lyndon township, Whiteside County, and they have four children: Buell, Carl, Harriet and Nellie. (9) Clara E. was born 21 March 1870 and is employed as a stenographer in Chicago. (10) Clark D. was born 17 April 1873, is a gardener in Galt, Whiteside County. He was married in November

1894 to Alice Holcomb. Clark and Alice have two children: Fay E. and Dewey Austin.

After his marriage, Dennis Austin purchased fifty acres of his father's farm and erected thereon a log house and log stable with clapboard roof. He began to clear away the timber and break the land, and continued to reside there until 1854, when he sold his place and came to Whiteside County. His first purchase here consisted of 160 acres of wild land, and he again went though the arduous task of converting an unimproved tract into a well cultivated farm. In his new home he met with excellent success, and he added to his farm a tract of 60 acres, which he converted into one of the best places of its size in Lyndon township. He gave considerable attention to stock raising, making a specialty of horses and cattle, and he bought young stock to fatten for the market. In 1889 he met with a heavy loss, his house and its contents, valued at three thousand dollars, being completely destroyed by fire. It was one of the finest homes in the township. Nothing daunted, he immediately began the erection of another dwelling, though not so pretentious. In 1894 he left the farm and removed to Morrison, where he purchased a fine modern residence on East South street, and has since lived retired, having sold his farm. He well merits the success he has achieved in life as it has come to him through his own unaided efforts, industry and enterprise.

Politically Mr. Austin has always affiliated with the Republican Party, but has taken no active part in politics, preferring to give his undivided attention to his farming. However, he most efficiently served as school director in his district for a number of years. Although not a member of any religious denomination, he gives liberally toward the support of the Methodist Episcopal church of Morrison, of which his wife is an earnest member.

Austins in the Federal Census of 1850

PLEASE HELP . . . SEE DETAILS PAGE 83.

MISCELLANEOUS PENNSYLVANIA
AUSTIN RECORDS & BIOGRAPHIES

by Pauline Lucille Austin

The following records were copied while the author was working on a line in Erie County, Pennsylvania, and Chautauqua County, New York. There were several different unrelated Austin families who resided in these counties before moving on to Ohio, Illinois, Iowa, Kansas, and Nebraska. The author is interested in contacting others researching these or related Austin lines.

BIRTHS

George Erwin Austin born 12 July 1886 in Cooperstown, Venango County, son of George Hiram Austin and Ellen Eliza Collins.

Harry Glenlouie Austin born 25 August 1866 in Forest Lake, Susquehanna County, son of Judge William Austin and Elizabeth Reynolds.

Herbert Leroy Austin born 30 July 1884 in Cooperstown, Venango County, son of George Hiram Austin and Ellen Eliza Collins.

Herbert Leroy Austin born 30 July 1885 in Franklin, son of George Austin. *(Same as previous record?)*

Mary M. Austin born 4 June 1898 in Cooperstown, Venango County, daughter of George Hiram Austin and Ellen Eliza Collins.

Mary Teresa Austin born 6 August 1876, daughter of Joseph Henry Austin and Mary Teresa Loftus.

Rachel Matilda Austin born 5 May 1829, daughter of Zebulon and Elizabeth Austin.

Robert E. Austin born 2 April 1894 in Cooperstown, Venango County, son of George Hiram Austin and Ellen Eliza Collins.

MARRIAGES

A. B. Austin married Miss L. A. Duncan on 6 August 1874; both of Fairview Township, Erie County.

Calista Austin married Henry Lyman Spafford in August 1873 in Conneautville, Crawford County.

E. A. Austin married Miss R. A. Falkner on 26 December 1860; of Buffalo and Amity, Erie County.

E. D. Austin married Miss Bertha Dunn on 29 June 1892; both of Erie, Erie County.

Edward Austin married Elizabeth Boyer on 27 September 1737 in Philadelphia.

Edward Austin married Sarah Wetherby on 6 May 1748 in Philadelphia.

Ezra Austin married Anne Stouffer on 19 February 1861 in Chambersburg, Franklin County.

Frank Austin married Clara Mooney on 20 May 1873; of Erie and Fairview, Erie County.

Henry Austin married **Mildred Estella Austin** on 9 May 1897 in Russell City, Elk County.

Hester Austin married Nickdemus Steedman on 14 February 1824 in Philadelphia.

J. A. Austin married Isabella Williams 13 August 1861; of Erie, Erie County.

James Austin married Mary Fitzgerald on 29 [–] 1804 in Philadelphia.

Jane Austin married Daniel Vancourt on 21 May 1771 in Philadelphia.

John Austin married Martha Morgan in February 1748 in Philadelphia.

Lewis L. Austin married Elise Weaver on 2 December 1813 in Philadelphia.

Lyman Austin of Marquette, Wisconsin Terr. m. Miss L. Church of Springfield on 18 Sept. 1845 at Albion, Erie Co.

Lyman B. Austin of Nebraska married Dora Wakely of Greenfield, Erie Co., on 14 January 1885 in Greenfield.

Mildred Estella Austin m. **Henry Austin** *(see above)*.

Moses Austin married Mary Brown on 28 September 1785 in Philadelphia.

Nathan Austin married Marian Dockstader on 4 July 1842 in Charleston Township, Tioga County.

Sarah Austin married David Jones on 6 June 1786 in Caernarvon Township, Lancaster County.

Selah R. Austin married Hannah Rosetta Applebee on 10 March 1847 in Erie County; both of Venango.

Theodore P. Austin married Mary Catharine Frety on 8 September 1868 in Doylestown, Bucks County.

Thomas Austin married Mary Thomas on 5 January 1761 in Philadelphia.

Thomas Merrill Austin of Erie Co. m. Clarrisa M. Harris of Salisbury, Conn. on 14 September 1842 in Salisbury.

Judge **William Austin** married Elizabeth E. Reynolds on 5 October 1865 in Montrose, Susquehanna County.

William V. Austin married Frances Carpenter on 18 December 1876; of Edinboro and Erie, Erie County.

DEATHS

Alice Austin d. 7 June 1868 age 14 years in Erie, daughter of T. M. and Clara M. Austin.

Arthur Austin d. 18 January 1885 age 41 years in Erie.

Augustine Ashley Austin d. 18 Nov. 1896 age 86 in Erie.

Charles H. Austin d. 13 June 1901 age 77 years; of Erie.

Clara Austin d. 23 Nov. 1868 age 22 yrs in Erie, dau. of T. M. Austin.

Clarrisa H. Austin d. 22 February 1905 age 85 years; of Erie.

Mrs. Evaline Austin d. 12 May 1874 age 27, wife of **William V. Austin** of Edinboro.

Mrs. H. B. Austin d. 7 August 1857 age 29 years in West Springfield, wife of **John A. Austin**.

Maria L. Austin d. 6 August 1905 age 90 years in Erie.

Mrs. Mary Austin d. 2 December 1863 age 89 yrs; of West Springfield.

Sidney J. Austin d. 22 March 1904 age 18 years in Swansville.

Capt. T. M. Austin d. in December 1897 at Troy, N.Y. Resided at Erie, Erie County. Article published 14 December 1897 in Erie.

ERIE COUNTY PENNSYLVANIA
BIOGRAPHICAL HISTORY

PAGE 203: **Nathaniel C. Austin**, retired, Edinboro, b. 25 September 1811 in Chenango Co., N.Y., son of Seymour and Mary (Chapman) Austin, natives of Berkshire Co., Mass. & Washington Co., N.Y., and settled in Washington Twp. in 1833. Nathaniel came with his parents, and m. 12 February 1835 Nancy A. Lewis, dau. of Lot and Jemima (Garwood) Lewis of Meadville, Penn., by whom he had seven children: William V. who served in the Rebellion for three years; Emeline, wife of Robert R. Burchfield who enlisted in 1863 and died in prison at Florence, S.C. on 8 January 1865, leaving two daughters and a son; Charles S., now Justice of the Peace, elected in February 1881 when only 23 years old; Edgar H. who enlisted 14 August 1862 in Company B 145th P.V.I. and participated in the battles of Antietam, Fredericksburg, Spottsylvania, Chancellorsville, Wilderness, Cold Harbor, Petersburg, and Gettysburg - he received a very severe head wound at Deep Bottom, Virginia, was wounded in the thigh at Petersburg, and was honorably discharged 31 May 1865. He m. 13 February 1866 Rachel S. Everett, dau. of Jacob B. Everett of Welland Co., Canada; Sarah; Mary; and Teresa, are deceased. Mr. Austin began life as a carpenter, which occupation continued until 1881 when he retired. He has in all probability erected two-thirds of the principal buildings in Edinboro and vicinity. He filled various township offices and was Burgess of Edinboro for two terms.

PAGE 203: **Charles W. Austin**, farmer of Edinboro, was born in McKean Township on 27 May 1843, a son of William and Elizabeth (Osborne) Austin, natives of England who settled in McKean Township in 1843. He was married on 3 June 1863 to Marett Haggarty, daughter of Joseph and Phebe (Fish) Haggarty, by whom he had one child, Elanson B. Austin. Mrs. Austin departed this life 6 April 1879; Mr. Austin was in the late war, enlisting 30 August 1862. He participated in the battles of Chancellorsville, Fredericksburg, Wilderness, Gettysburg, Cold Harbor, and in other important engagements. Charles was wounded at Gettysburg and also at Grove church near Richmond. He was discharged on account of disability in July 1865.

PAGE 127 - IN MILLCREEK TOWNSHIP: Hiram H. Miller married, as his second wife, **Emily Austin** of Ohio, daughter of Moses Austin, a native of Ohio. Hiram and Emily had eight children.

PAGE 33: Joseph Lawrence, born in Dutchess Co., N.Y. on 25 December 1782, was married to **Jerusha Austin** on 1 January 1804. With his family and two yoke of oxen he moved here from the town of Berne, Albany Co., N.Y. Joseph had eight children by his first wife Jerusha Austin.

PAGE 221: Cornelius Haley, a farmer of Waterford Township, was born in 1830 in County Cork, Ireland. He emigrated to America in 1849, working on the railroad for four or five years to accumulate enough money to buy a farm of 95 acres, which he now owns in Waterford. He married in 1850 in St. Patrick's Church, Erie, Miss **Nora Austin**, a native of County Clare, Ireland. They had four children, two of whom died young. Those living are Daniel and a daughter Maria, residing with her parents.

PAGE 238: William B. Pier, lumberer and farmer of Cory, is the grandfather of Adah Peir who married **William H. Austin** and have two children, Clara Belle and Frank Guy.

PAGE 754: **John A. Austin** is listed among the earliest principals of West Springfield Academy in Erie Co.

PAGE 946: R. J. Saltsman was born in Erie Co. on 24 April 1842, the son of Jesse and Polly (Shadduck) Saltsman. R. J. married in Erie City on 25 April 1865 to **Anna A. Austin**, daughter of Thomas M. Austin.

PAGE 211: The Reeder, Taylor, McWilliams, Campbell, Twichell, Clark, Lewis, and **Austin** families are the principal founders of the Northwestern Normal School at Edinboro.

[CONTINUED ON PAGE 104]

THE DESCENDANTS OF
JEHIAL AUSTIN AND ANN RAPPLEYE
OF INTERLAKEN, NEW YORK

by Jean Ellis Grace

J. JEHIAL[1] AUSTIN was born on 11 November 1814 in Delaware County, New York, and he lived there during his early childhood. His father, David Austin, was born in Connecticut, and his mother was Hannah Rathbun, birthplace unknown. According to a newspaper clipping, he came in 1846 to Farmer (today known as Interlaken) in Seneca County, New York, living on a farm one mile west of town. However, since he married a local girl in 1838 and joined the Baptist Church on 14 March 1841, I believe that he must have come to Seneca County about 1836 rather than in 1846.

Jehial was married on 22 December 1838 to Ann R. Rappleye. Ann, the daughter of William and Barbara (Swick) Rappleye, was born on 5 May 1823. Her immigrant ancestor, Joris Jansen Rapalje, came to America in either 1623 or 1624 on the ship *Unity*. Jehial's granddaughter, my Aunt Clara Austin Close, at age 85 still remembers that as a very small child she was afraid of her grandfather, for he carried a cane and wore dark glasses. It seems he had cataracts, and the doctor came from Ithaca, about 20 miles away, to do surgery right at the house.

Ann Austin was frequently called upon to care for those in the community who were ill. She raised herbs, dried them, and steeped them to make medicinal teas. If the sick person she was called upon to treat had scarlet fever, her own children had to wear a red flannel cloth soaked in turpentine around their necks. This was supposed to prevent them from catching scarlet fever. Aunt Clara also remembers what good pumpkin pies her grandmother made in oblong black tins, not in round pie plates. She never used a recipe - just a pinch of this and a pinch of that, and the pies were almost black with spices. She always gave Clara a corner piece so she could have more crust.

Some information here is from an Austin Family bible owned by Fred Austin, and from death certificates. The children of Jehial and Ann were born in Seneca County:

CHILDREN: J1. SARAH B., *b. 19 September 1841, m. 23 October 1872 Aaron M. Kishpaugh, d. 16 February 1925. Resided in Auburn, New York; one child: Willis G. Kishpaugh b. 1876.*

           J2. HANNAH C., *b. 8 January 1844, unmarried, d. 29 September 1921 at her brother Winfield's home in Kelly's Corner, buried Lakeview Cemetery*

           J3. ANSEL PIETTE, *b. 26 July 1846*

           J4. FRANCES CORNELIA, *b. 7 February 1854*

           J5. WINFIELD SCOTT, *b. 13 March 1861*

Jehial Austin 1814-1901

Jehial Austin died on 11 May 1901 in Farmer, New York, and is buried there in the Lakeview Cemetery in Interlaken. On 16 July 1904, Ann died in Interlaken, where she is also buried at the Lakeview Cemetery.

SECOND GENERATION

J3. ANSEL PIETTE[2] AUSTIN (*Jehial[1]*) was born on 26 July 1846. At age of 18, on 12 December 1863 at Covert, New York, Ansel Piatt Austin enlisted as a private in Company E, Ninth Artillery. He was discharged on 15 May 1865. Ansel was married on 14 January 1875? to Mary S. Allen, and they resided in Tonowanda, New York. In Tonowanda he was a member of Scott Post G.A.R., and was commissioned as an aide-de-camp by Brigadier General Stanley on 9 August 1897, 8th Judicial Brigade, Department of New York Grand Army of the Republic. He represented Niagara County. My Aunt Clara remembers Ansel as being a jolly, portly man, and she always looked forward to his visits. He died on 26 August 1926.

CHILDREN: J31. FLORENCE M., *b. August 1883, m. Vernon W. Curtis*

            J32. MABEL MARCELENE, *b. 16 July 1892, m. Abraham Van Sice*

Ann Rappleye 1823-1904

J4. FRANCES CORNELIA[2] AUSTIN (*Jehial*[1]) was born 7 February 1854 in Seneca County, New York. She was married on 23 December 1874 to George Wheeler Bassett, the son of Jared Beardsley and Mary (Wheeler) Bassett, who was born on 1 October 1851 in Covert, Seneca County. George died 15 August 1889 in Ovid, Seneca County, and is buried in Lakeview Cemetery, Interlaken, New York. Frances died 19 December 1942 in Interlaken and is also buried in Lakeview Cemetery. BASSETT CHILDREN: ANNA 1879-1922 and MARY 1879 (twins), HOWARD WHEELER 1883-1936.

J5. WINFIELD SCOTT[2] AUSTIN (*Jehial*[1]) was born 13 March 1861 in Covert, Seneca County, New York. He was married on 3 October 1891 to Jesse Catherine Miller, the daughter of Elijah and Charity (Abbott) Miller, who was born on 25 July 1873. Elijah Miller owned the *Hotel Robinson* in Farmer, New York. Winfield tended bar there, and he met Jesse there. Their first child, Alice Austin, was born on Sunday 10 July 1892 in the hotel, and her name is the third one listed on the hotel register as if she were a guest that day. Jesse left Winfield about two years after Fred was born. She later lived with Fred Winters, but it was never certain whether or not they were ever married.

Jesse died 25 February 1957 in Lodi and is buried in Ovid Cemetery. Winfield was a retired farmer when he died on 9 December 1946 at the home of his daughter, Mrs. Edward Ellis, in Lodi. He is buried in the Interlaken Cemetery. Children:

J51. ALICE CHARITY, *b. 10 July 1892 in Farmer*

J52. CLARA E., *b. 16 September 1898 Interlaken*

J53. FRED WINFIELD, *b. 11 August 1912 Interlaken*

Winfield Scott Austin 1861-1946

THIRD GENERATION

J51. ALICE CHARITY[3] AUSTIN (*Winfield Scott,*[2] *Jehial*[1]) was born 10 July 1892 in Farmer (Interlaken), New York, in her grandfather's *Hotel Robinson*. Her birth appears in the hotel register as "Miss Austin - City" . . . a unique record of her birth! She m. in Ithaca, Tompkins Co., New York on 26 November 1924 to James Edward Ellis. Ed worked for the Lehigh Valley R. R. and later at the Willard State Hospital. Alice worked at the Seneca Ordinance Depot, and also took in foster children. She died 9 November 1974 in Lodi, and is buried in West Lodi Cem. ELLIS CHILDREN: MILDRED JEAN 1926, KEITH AUSTIN 1930.

J52. CLARA E.[3] AUSTIN (*Winfield Scott,*[2] *Jehial*[1]) was born 16 September 1898 in Interlaken. She was married in Interlaken on 17 February 1921 to Marion David Close. Clara worked at the Sampson Naval Base for a time. Marion ('Pete') owned the Gulf Station in Lodi, and later formed the Close Oil Company. CLOSE CHILD: ROBERT PAUL 1926.

J53. FRED WINFIELD[3] AUSTIN (*Winfield Scott,*[2] *Jehial*[1]) was born 11 August 1912 in Interlaken, Seneca County, New York. He was married in Lodi, New York, at the bride's home on 8 October 1935 to Dorothy May Pulver of Lodi. The flood of 1935 took out the big bridge to Pulver's house, so 'Dort' and Fred had to cross the gulley by foot to get to their car after the wedding. Fred was a truck driver, Dort a registered nurse. Children born in Ithaca, NY:

J531. ROGER LEE, *b. 27 July 1938, m. 19 August 1961 Barbara Terhune in West Milford, New Jersey. Children: Ronald Jay b. 30 July 1962 Largo, Florida, d. 27 June 1978 Florida; Robin Lee b. 16 March 1967 Fort Pierce, Florida; twins Christopher Mark and Amy Jean b. 31 October 1972 Norwich, Connecticut.*

J532. CAROL ELIZABETH, *b. 31 October 1941, m. 27 August 1960 Robert Morris Voorhees in Lodi. Children: Robert Morris 1962, Connie Elizabeth 1964, Scott Austin 1968, Peter William 1970.*

A PIONEER WHO LIVED IN THE
EXECUTIVE LOG MANSION -
THE SOLOMON AUSTIN FAMILY

by E. A. Owen

Editor's Note: The following article concerns the same Solomon Austin discussed on page 83. This article was adapted from the author's book, *Pioneer Sketches of Long Point Settlement or Norfolk's Foundation Builders and Their Family Genealogies*, published by William Briggs, Toronto, 1898. Long Point settlement was in Norfolk County, Ontario Province, Canada. The book was discovered by Associate Editor Anthony Kent Austin, and is now part of the growing *Austins of America* library of books containing Austin genealogical data.

As Charlotteville is the home of the McCalls, so is Woodhouse the home of the Austins; in fact, the bare mention of 'Woodhouse' suggests the name 'Austin.' There are names which are peculiarly Norfolk names - names which were planted in the virgin soil of the county and so firmly rooted to the foundation of our social fabric that each succeeding generation adds to their strength. Among these old elementary names are the Austins of Woodhouse.

Love of home is a leading characteristic with such families, and tends to good and desirable citizenship. When a family becomes numerous in the locality where the grand-ancestor built his pioneer cabin, it denotes on their part loyalty to country, fidelity to local interests and affection for each other.

Solomon Austin was one of our prominent old foundation builders. His family came to Upper Canada with a party of U.E. Loyalists, consisting of twelve families. They came from Maryland and North Carolina, and arrived on the Niagara frontier as early as 1793. The Austins came from Orange County, North Carolina, and previous to the war of the Revolution all had comfortable homes and kind neighbors; but the terrible result of that war made them homeless and despised aliens in the land that gave many of them birth.

It is said that shortly after the new province was organized these twelve families clubbed together and sent one of their number to the new country to learn what were the natural advantages of settlement, and the inducements offered settlers by way of land grants, etc. The name of this trusted emissary was John Davis, who subsequently settled in Windham, a little north of Simcoe; and later on his brother Robert came from North Carolina and settled near him.

Mr. Davis reported favorably, and in due time the party was en route for the new country. They came in canvas-covered wagons, bringing their household effects and a number of cows and other farm stock with them. Buffalo,

at this time, was a small village containing about a dozen houses. The party crossed the river at Old Niagara, and remained there a short time.

In common with most of their fellow-Loyalists, they came into the forests of Upper Canada with little or no means. Governor Simcoe offered his executive log mansion at Newark to Solomon Austin, as a temporary shelter for his family until he could locate his land. He was awarded 600 acres for himself and wife and 200 acres for each of his children, to be selected by themselves from any of the untaken lands, which at that time included pretty much the entire province.

But why did Governor Simcoe show Solomon Austin so much kindness? Sir John Graves Simcoe had fought England's battles in the war of the Revolution, and was a U.E. Loyalist himself. He had been an officer, and Mr. Austin had been a private in his command and had distinguished himself at some minor engagement, and his old General had not forgotten it; hence the extra favors shown him and his family when they arrived in the new country.

Mr. Austin was accompanied by his son, Solomon, when he made his tour of inspection in view of locating his lands. They had lived on high, leachy lands in North Carolina, and they made up their minds to locate their new lands in some pleasant valley where the droughts would not trouble them as of yore. Futhermore, they had resolved to build a mill, and this also made a choice of valley lands necessary in order to secure the required water-power privileges. They travelled through the forest on foot, and held a conference with Chief Brant at Brant's Ford (Brantford), and the chief pointed out a southerly course, toward the 'big lake.' They proceeded according to Brant's directions, and in due time, came to a stream, which they followed to the lake. This was Patterson's Creek, and the place where they came upon it was near the spot where the old home of Elder Steinhoff was located. When they reached the mouth of the creek they found a squatter living in a log cabin on the east bank. This man's name was Walker, and was, no doubt, the first settler in Port Dover. They were very much surprised when they reached the lake, and, after a conference with Walker, took a westerly course up the lake shore. When they reached the mouth of Big Creek, they wended their way up the cedar-entangled valley of that stream to a point some distance above the site of the present village of Delhi. Nothing they had seen pleased them as well as the little valley down which they had found their way to the lake, and so, taking a south-easterly course, they struck their old trail, and located their lands in what is now known as Lynn River Valley. They spent about three weeks in the forests of Norfolk, mostly, before they decided on a location. Unlike so many of our old Long Point pioneers, the Austins made a wise choice when they located their new homes. The natural surround-

ings of the old Austin homestead are picturesque and the soil is exceedingly fertile.

When Mr. Austin and his son returned to Newark, they found the family suffering with that pest of pioneer life, chill-fever. This detained them a whole season in the Niagara settlement, and it was some time in 1794 before they were settled in Lynn Valley. They suffered, of course, the hardships and privations which fell to the lot of all the old pioneers.

The war of 1812 broke in upon their work of home-building, and Solomon Austin and his four stalwart sons marched out of the little valley to fight for the Old Flag in the defence of their new homes. They were at the battle of Lundy's Lane, and before the war closed, it is said, each one of the sons had been promoted to the rank of captain. It is no wonder the Austins are noted for loyalty to country, fidelity to sound principles and love of home.

The grand-American ancestor of the family emigrated from the border of Wales about 175 years ago, and settled on a little bay in the Petapsco River, about twelve miles above its entrance into the Chesapeake Bay, in Baltimore County, in the colony of Maryland. Here, on the Austin estate, was founded the city of Baltimore, in 1729. When the colonies threw off their allegiance, the Austins were wealthy and influential - as, indeed, were all the leading Loyalists - but when the war was over they were reduced to poverty and subjected to persecution. The overthrow and expulsion of the Loyalist element proved an irreparable loss to the tone and moral worth of the colonies, but it proved a 'God-send' to the new British Province of Upper Canada. It is but little more than a century since these victorious colonies, which had been long established, confiscated the homes of their old colonial leaders because they fought to put down rebellion, and with kicks and curses sent them penniless into an unbroken wilderness; but in 1893 the new Ontario met these same thirteen old colonies at Chicago before the assembled world, and clearly established her superiority over every one of them in the degree of material development attained, and in the intellectual status of her people as measured by the standard of her educational institutions. What is the secret of this wonderful development in one short century? It lies in the superior qualities which these old U.E. Loyalist foundation builders possessed and which they transmitted to their children. Let us not forget this important fact while boasting of the intellectual and industrial achievements and the moral excellencies of our people.

Solomon Austin had four sons - Solomon, Jonathan, Philip and Moses; and five daughters - Mary, Amy, Esther, Elizabeth and Anna.

Solomon Austin, eldest son of Solomon, was twelve years old when the family came to Canada. He married Sarah Slaght, by whom he had six sons - Philip, John S., David, Jonathan, Abraham and Samuel; and four daughters - Susan, Julia Ann, Mary Ann and Elizabeth, who married respectively, Nathan Pegg, William Shand, Henry Paskins and Alfred Farnum. Philip, David and Samuel married and settled on farms in Woodhouse. John S. and Jonathan established a carriage manufactory and built up a trade and a reputation for square, honest dealing, that any business firm might envy. Abraham became a Baptist preacher, and thirty years ago there were few Baptist Sunday School scholars in the County of Norfolk who did not kow the familiar face of Elder Austin.

Jonathan Austin, second son of Solomon, married Hannah Potts. He had two sons - William and John; and six daughters - Charlotte, Mary, Joanna, Catherine, Elizabeth and Rebecca Ann. He and his younger son built the mills in Lynn Valley, known as 'Austin's Mills.' Four of his daughters - Charlotte, Joanna, Elizabeth and Rebecca Ann, married, respectively, John Wheeler, John Hinds, Thomas M. England and Robert Laning.

Philip Austin, third son of Solomon, was born in 1790. He married Mary Slaght and succeeded to the old homestead. On one occasion during their early married life, Mrs. Austin was nearly frightened to death by a band of armed Indians who came to the house during the husband's absence, and coolly ordered a meal of hot buckwheat pancakes. In their estimation this was a great delicacy, being far ahead of anything 'Ingin's squaw' ever made of pounded corn. They stacked their guns in front of the door, and Mrs. Austin proceeded at once to comply with their demands. She baked up all the 'pancake timber' she had, and the 'noble red men' swallowed the red-hot flapjacks as they came from the griddle. When the material was exhausted the half-satisfied warriors shouldered their guns and went on their way. It was in a time of peace, and they were, no doubt, a band of hunters; but at that early time to have such a band of armed Indians suddenly drop in upon a lone woman, was enough to nearly frighten her to death.

Mrs. Philip Austin was the mother of seventeen children, fourteen of whom grew up to man's and woman's estate. There were six sons - Aaron, Isaac, Philip B., Joshua, Joseph and Oliver; and eight daughters - Nancy, Elizabeth, Rebecca, Mary, Hannah , Esther Ann, Emily Jane and Priscilla. It is said our best people come out of large families, and no one of our old families is more in evidence as to the truthfulness of this old saying than the family of Philip Austin. Among them we find some of Norfolk's most distinguished citizens. Four of these sons - Isaac, Aaron, Joseph and Oliver - have added dignity, tone and moral worth to the solid yeomanry of Woodhouse, the first having served many years in the Township and County Councils as Reeve of Woodhouse, and the last is at present

serving in the same capacity. Oliver Austin is not only a leader in township and county affairs, but he displays the same progressive energy in the advancement of agriculture and the support of every movement tending to develop a stronger moral and religious sentiment among the people. Joshua, the fourth son, stands for the first half of that old familiar mercantile firm—name, 'Austin & Werrett,' that found its way into every household in the county years ago. Emily married her brother's business partner, George Werrett. Several members of this large family settled in the Western States, where they raised families and prospered. Philip Austin died in 1876, in his 83rd year, having survived his wife eleven years.

Moses Austin, youngest son of Solomon, married Mary Misner, and settled in Woodhouse. Subsequently, he built a sawmill in the vicinity of Tyrrel, Townsend. He had four sons - Lewis, Edward, Nathaniel and William; and four daughters - Margaret, Mary, Sarah and Julia. These sons and daughters married and settled, mostly in Woodhouse and Townsend.

Mary Austin, eldest daughter of Solomon, and first-born child, married Henry Walker and settled near her father's homestead. Her children are enumerated in the Walker genealogy.

Amy Austin, second daughter of Solomon, married Selah Styles, and settled in Woodhouse. She had two sons - Peter and Selah; and one daughter, Lavinia.

Esther Austin, third daughter of Solomon, married Raynard Potts, and settled just north of her father's homestead. Her children are enumerated in the Pott's family genealogy.

Elizabeth Austin, the fourth daughter married John Pegg. Her children are enumerated in the Pegg Genealogy.

Anna Austin, youngest daughter of Solomon married David Marr, of Marr's Hill. The names of her children are given in the Marr genealogy.

Solomon Austin and his pioneer wife both attained the age of eighty-two. None of their sons reached so great an age, except Philip, who reached his eighty-seventh year, being the last survivor of the family. Moses died comparatively young, being only about fifty-five, while Solomon reached his sixty-eighth year. For several years previous to Philip's death, the members of his large family held a reunion on the anniversary of his birth. At the last of these reunions there were present one hundred and thirty-seven descendants of Philip Austin, and the direct descendants of the original Solomon Austin numbered, at this time, over seven hundred. If this was the number twenty years ago, what a mighty host they must be today!

But according to a family tradition, the destiny that gave

Norfolk this vigorous and most excellent element, hung on a very slender thread at one time. It happened while Solomon Austin was fighting for British supremacy in America. As the story goes, he and six others were taken prisoners, and himself and another were condemned to death. Just before the time fixed for execution, Mr. Austin and another prisoner were permitted to go to a spring for a drink. They were accompanied by two guardsman, and when they arrived at the spring, one of the guards handed his gun to the other guard and lay down to take the first drink himself. While thus engaged the standing guard passed his comrade's gun over to Austin and gave him the wink to make good his escape. It was a narrow escape, but it proved successful. He knew the man who thus saved his life, and had always looked upon him as a bitter enemy; but he never saw him afterwards, and never knew what became of him.

The twelve families referred to in the first part of this sketch, all settled in the Niagara and other Eastern sections, except the Austin families. As before stated, John Davis moved up from Niagara subsequently. Accompanying the party were several young men with no family connections. Two of these - John Pegg and Henry Walker - settled in Norfolk. John Austin, a young man, son of a brother of the original Solomon Austin, came with the party, and was awarded land in the County of York, where he settled, married, and raised a family.

PENNSYLVANIA AUSTINS

[CONTINUED FROM PAGE 99]

PAGE 209: John Morrison, farmer of Edinboro, had a daughter Margaret who was married to **Henry Austin**.

PAGE 208: Marvin McLallen of McLallen's Corners was born 24 March 1834 in this township, son of William and Philena (Davis) McLallen. He married 31 October 1855 to Mary Austin, daughter of William and Elizabeth (Osborne) Austin, natives of Devonshire, England. To this union were born four children. Two survive: William N. and Ida B. McLallen.

PAGE 864: Frank A. Austin, Supervisor No. 1 of P&E R.R., Erie, was born in this city 11 November 1898, son of Augustin Austin, a native of Massachusetts, and a silversmith by occupation. Frank was reared in Erie and vicinity and at age twenty he began merchandising in the spring of 1872, he took up railroading as clerk in Superintendent's Office, and as such remained until May 1881, when he received his present appointment. Mr. Austin was united in marriage in 1873 with Clara A. Mooney, daughter of Jacob and Sophia Mooney. They are the parents of Herbert D. Austin and Edith P. Austin, and are members of the First Presbyterian Church.

BIOGRAPHIES & RESEARCH NOTES
ON THE AUSTIN FAMILIES OF
TIOGA COUNTY, PENNSYLVANIA

by Rhoda English Ladd

Editor's Note: The following material concerns descendants of S246-7 Caleb Austin, a son of Jonathan Austin of the Samuel Austin of Boston line (see *Austins of America*, page 15 for Jonathan's birth), as well as other Austin lines. The author is the Genealogical Records Chairman & Librarian for the Tioga County Historical Society. Following some published historical and biographical information on Tioga County Austins, we reproduce here the author's ''Austin Family Notebook'', a rich source of Austin genealogical data.

HISTORY OF TIOGA COUNTY, PENNSYLVANIA
R. C. Brown & Company, 1897

PAGE 137-8: In March 1866 County Commissioners were appointed to purchase real estate for a county farm. They purchased twenty-five acres of the old **Caleb Austin** farm just east of Wellsboro, on the south side of the State road, in Charleston township.

PAGE 361: The Pioneers... **Caleb Austin**, who came about 1806, located on what is now the county poor farm, near where the State road crosses the western line of the township, and enters Wellsboro.

PAGE 366: The cemeteries of Charleston... were originally family graveyards which later became public places of burial. Among the earliest of these... the old graveyard on the **Caleb Austin** place, now a part of the county farm...

PAGE 7o7: **Caleb Austin**, a native of New England, was one of the early settlers of Charleston, locating on the land now occupied by the poor farm, about the beginning of the present century. He married Clarissa Peterson, who bore him nine children: Caroline, deceased wife of James Kimball, of Wellsboro; Adeline, the deceased wife of Rudolph Christenot; Emily, who married Luman Fenton, of Cherry Flats; Charles, a farmer in Charleston; Nelson, deceased; Angeline, deceased wife of Col. Alanson E. Niles; Nathan, deceased; Ruth, wife of John Doumaux, and Benjamin, deceased. Mr. Austin and wife spent their declining years in Charleston, and died on the homestead.

Charles Austin, a son of Caleb, was born in Charleston on 15 August 1815. He attended the subscription schools of pioneer days, and worked on the homestead farm for his parents until he reached age 28. He then bought a farm in Charleston, on a part of which he now resides, and has devoted his entire attention to agriculture. He married Sarah Losinger, of Wellsboro, who bore him seven children, viz: Dwight, deceased; Hiram J., S.C. and C.N., all of whom are farmers in Charleston; Clarissa, wife of

Joshua Atherton; Mary Josephine, wife of George Wilkinson, & Sarah Angeline, deceased. Mrs. Austin died upon the homestead farm, where her husband now resides.

C. N. Austin, youngest son of Charles, was born on 25 December 1855 in Charleston. He attended the common schools of his native township, and assisted his parents on the farm until age 24. In 1881 he bought his present place of seventy-five acres, where he has since continued in agricultural pursuits. On 21 November 1879, Mr. Austin married Rosella Wilkinson, a daughter of William Wilkinson, of Charleston, and has two children: Blaine Dwight & Mary A. A Republican, he has filled several local offices, and is a member of the Patrons of Husbandry.

PAGE 1092: **Alvin B. Austin** was born in Chenango Co., New York, in 1800, and was a farmer and mason. In 1820 he came to Sullivan township, Tioga County, locating at what is now Mainesburg. On 8 January 1824 he married Sally D. Rumsey, a daughter of Noah Rumsey, Sr., a pioneer of Sullivan. They had seven children: Mrs. Ameda Shelton, deceased; Aaron, who resides in Nevada; Luther, a resident of Bradford County; Leander R., deceased; Daniel B., who lives in California; Joseph B., deceased, & Jesse W., a resident of Mainesburg. Mr. Austin and family were adherents of the Methodist Episcopal Church, and in politics, he was first a Whig and afterwards a Republican. Mrs. Austin died 11 March 1878, and her husband 21 December 1881.

Leander R. Austin, third son of Alvin, was born in Sullivan on the site of the Mainesburg church, 28 June 1831. Except for a short period that he clerked in a store for his uncle, L. D. Rumsey, he followed agriculture until 1876, when he embarked in merchandising at Mainesburg, in partnership with Baldwin Parkhurst. In 1880 they dissolved partnership, and in 1882 he purchased H. E. Bartlett's dry goods and grocery store, which he sold to R. W. Rose in 1884. On 26 June 1884 he bought the drug store of Dr. I. N. Wright, and converting it into a grocery and hardware store, he formed a partnership with Capt. Homer J. Ripley. In 1886 he sold his interest to Capt. Ripley, and in 1888 he went to work for the Keystone View Company as salesman, in which capacity he acted until 1890 when he became a partner in the business until his death, 9 October 1893. Mr. Austin was married first in 1857 to Rebecca Brown of Covington, who died in 1876. On 20 February 1878, he married Mittie E., a daughter of P. P. Smith, of Sullivan, who bore him one daughter, Ethel L., on 10 February 1892. L. Emory Austin, third son of Jesse W. Austin, became a member of the family of Leander & Mittie 10 April 1880, and 5 March 1890 he married Miss Minnie Rumsey. They have one daughter, Leah Graice, born 1 August 1895. Mr. Austin was a member of the Methodist Episcopal church and of Mainesburg Lodge, No.754, I.O.O.F.

Austins of America

NOTES FROM RHODA LADD'S AUSTIN FAMILY NOTEBOOK

AUSTIN CEMETERY - CHARLESTON TOWNSHIP
BY COUNTY FARM ON SHUMWAY HILL ROAD

Nathan Austin b. 6 Feb. 1820 d. 19 June 1890
Maria, wife of N. Austin, died 7 March 1868,
aged 44 yrs 1 mo 21 das

Benjamin Austin d. 4 Nov.1873 age 50 yrs 4 ds
Zena, wife of Benjamin Austin, d. 16 March
1860 aged 36 yrs 1 mo 16 das

Caleb Austin 1777-1853
Clarissa, his wife 1785-1853

Nelson Austin d. 19 March 1865
Lydia, wife of Nelson Austin, died (date
buried under ground)

DARTT SETTLEMENT CEMETERY - CHARLESTON TWP.

Leroy G. Austin 1876-1937
Alberta P. Austin Campbell 1878-1966
Lawrence L. Austin 1906-1931

Clara N., wife of James K. Austin, d. 30 April
1871 aged 23 yrs 5 mos 17 das

PHOENIX CEMETERY - GAINES TWP. ON ROUTE 6

Florence L., dau. of Edgar F. & Lovina A.
Austin, d. 18 June 1850 aged 4 mo 11 das
Josephine M., dau. of Edgar F. & Lovina A.
Austin, d. 18 April 1849 aged 6 mo 20 das

ACADEMY HILL CEMETERY - WELLSBORO ON PEARL ST.

George Dwight, son of Nelson and Lydia
Austin, d. 2 Aug. 1843 aged 3 mo 10 das

OGDENSBURG CEMETERY - UNION TOWNSHIP
CHURCH OF CHRIST CEMETERY

Simeon Austin d. 1870 age 62
Amy, wife of Simeon Austin, d. 1902 age 81

A. J. Austin d. 1909 age 70

Ira Austin d. 1878 age 88

Francis H. Austin 1841-1919
Wealtha wife of Francis H. Austin, 1841-1928

Caroline Austin 1837-1881 (Mother)

RUMSEY-DOUD CEM. - MAINESBURG, SULLIVAN TWP.

Luther Austin d. 1854 age 74, 2nd husband of
Susannah Rumsey
Hannah, wife of David Austin, d. 1828 age 72
(the parents of Lucy Ann Austin,
who married Lyman Rumsey)

Ruth A., dau. of Hobby & Diantha Austin,
died 1843 age 5

MAINESBURG CEMETERY - SULLIVAN TOWNSHIP
COPIED BY FRANCIS O. MORGAN, CARETAKER
ALSO COPIED BY HILDA CHANCE (PARENTHESES)

Aaron Austin (Co H 7th Pa Reg Cav)

Alvin B. Austin 1864-1932
Ida C. his wife 1865-1925

Ella H. Austin, dau. of L. C., d. 1 Nov. 1868

Freddie Austin 1891-1892

A. B. Austin d. 21 Dec. 1881 aged 81y 11m 8d
Sally D. (Rumsey), wife of A. B. Austin,
d. 11 March 1878 aged 77y 6m 10d

Hobbie Austin 1793-1883
Martha, wife (of Hobby Austin), 1800-1865

Jeremia Austin d. 24 Mar. 1896 aged 69 yrs
Sylvia Ann his wife d. 7 Feb. 1885 ae 54y 10m
Louisa his wife d. 14 Jan. 1896 aged 55 yrs

Jesse W. Austin 1840-1922
Hannah Austin 1843-1930
Willie J., son of J. W. & Hannah Austin,
d. 20 Aug. 1875 aged 2y 1m 20d

L. Emory Austin 1868-1940
Minnie E. (Rumsey, his wife) 1869-1948

Lloyd Emerson Austin 1901-
Margaret Hagar 1906-

Lois J. Austin 1931-1975

L(eander) R. Austin b. 28 June 1831,
d. 9 Oct. 1893
Rebecca his wife d. 16 Nov 1876 40y 10m 4d

(M. Emily Austin 1842-1905)

Luther B. Austin 1828-1903
Mary E. (Rumsey, his wife) 1828-1895
Charles R., son of L. B. & Mary E. Austin,
d. 3 June 1873 aged 10 mos

STATE ROAD CEMETERY - SULLIVAN TOWNSHIP

Enoch Austin 1856-1938
Rhoda, his wife 1857-1925

CATLIN HOLLOW CEMETERY - CHARLESTON TWP.

Charles Austin b. 15 Aug 1815 d. 12 Oct 1897
Sarah, wife of Charles Austin,
b. 8 July 1818, d. 30 July 1892
Sarah, dau. of Charles & Sarah A. Austin,
b. 30 May 1862, d. 14 Feb. 1881

Hiram J. Austin 1849-1929
Mary J., his wife 1849-1925

S. C. Austin 1852-1922 (Father)
Abbie Austin 1858-1922 (Mother)

Leon Austin 1886-1941
Rosilla, wife of Leon Austin, 1892-1947

Mary Austin 1846-1909

B. Dwight Austin b. 1886 -
Floye C., his wife b. 1889 -

SABINSVILLE CEMETERY - CLYMER TOWNSHIP

Homer D. Austin 1895-1956
Leanna G. Austin 1894-19

MIDDLEBURY UNION CEMETERY - KEENEYVILLE

Carrie Austin 1894-1948 (Mother)

CORY PRESBYTERIAN CEM. - WELLS, BRADFORD CO.

Austin, infant son d. 18 Dec. 1836 aged 1 day
Samuel A., d. 23 Feb. 1863 aged 6 mo 22 das,
sons of S. & H. Austin
Thomas C. Austin b. 22 Jan. 1848 d. 27 Jan.
1853, son of S. & H. Austin

Margaret R., wife of John Austin,
b. 19 April 1822 d. 12 July 1881

WELLSBORO CEMETERY - NICHOLS ST. IN WELLSBORO

Hezekiah Austin 1796-1871
Ercy Rogers Austin 1803-1870

Robert Riley Austin 1833-1908

Martha Gifford Austin 1848-1920

Baby Austin 1872-1873

Lucy Louise Austin 1883-1944

Frances Mabel, dau. Frank & Mabel Austin,
b. 19 Mar. 1898 d. 22 Oct. 1899

C. Nathan Niles 1855-1935
Rosella P. 1859-1938

Chauncey Austin d. 17 May 1862 aged 67 yrs
Lois, wife of Chauncey Austin,
d. 22 March 1860 aged 65 yrs
Caroline, dau. of Chauncey & Lois Austin,
d. 18 May 1871 aged 46 yrs

Louis Clifford Warren 1874-1966
Charlotte Austin Warren 1876-1952
Marie Elten Warren 1887-1967

B. Frank Austin 1870-1943
Mabel G. Austin 1877-1948

Franklin G. Austin WW2 Sgt Army Air Force,
26 June 1915 - 30 Jan. 1959

Dorna A. Austin 1867-1934
Attie B. Austin 1864-1924

Nellie Austin Bly 1865-1963

AUSTINBURG CEMETERY - BROOKFIELD TOWNSHIP
NAMED FOR WILLIAM AUSTIN, PIONEER SETTLER
FOUNDER 1835 - WOODHULL ROAD - RTE 58010

William Austin b. 2 April 1840 d. 25 May 1897
Co. H. 86th NY Vol
Emeline, wife of William Austin,
b. 18 December 1844 d. 22 January 1884
Harriet, wife of William Austin,
b. 7 November 1836 d. 22 April 1902
Vesta M., dau. of William & Emeline Austin,
b. 7 September 1880 d. 7 May 1883
(Emeline and Harriet - last name Seeley)

WILLS & ADMINISTRATIONS 1804-1880

Registers Docket A - p.229: Last Will & Testa-
ment of Israel Greenleaf 21 June 1847; wife
Mary; son David; daughters Sarah Austin &
Betsey Sligh; date of Will: 3 February 1846

Registers Docket B - p.251: Caleb Austin,
Charleston Twp. 2 February 1853 (b.1777
d.1853 buried Austin Cemetery, Charleston);
sons: Benjamin, Charles, Nathan, Nelson;
daus: Adeline Christenat, Emeline Fenton,
Angeline Niles, Ruth Dumaus; my wife's son
Hiram Brooks; executor: Clarissa Austin;
witnesses: B. B. Smith, Samuel R. Smith

Registers Docket B - p.435: Nelson Austin, no
town given,16 November 1868; Administra-
tors: Nathan Austin, Hiram Brooks

Registers Docket B - p.350: Susannah Austin,
Sullivan Twp., 16 March 1863; dau. Abigail
Rumsey; mentions Leander D. Rumsey; Exec:
Aaron Rumsey; Wit: E. A. Fish, Ellen Graudy

Registers Docket B - p.325: Chauncey Austin, Delmar Twp. 26 May 1862; son Edgar S. F. Austin; daughters Susan Emeline Walker, Caroline P. Austin, Sophia C. Alexander; Executor: Israel Stone; Witnesses: John O. Johnson, Daniel Monroe

Registers Docket C - p.133: Simeon Austin, Union Twp., 20 May 1871; Adm: Amy Austin, widow; Bail: A. A. Griswold, S. A. Randall

Registers Docket C - p.267: Benjamin Austin, Wellsboro, 7 November 1873; Adm: Walter Sherwood; Bond: Henry Sherwood

Registers Docket D - p.46: Emma N. Austin, 21 December 1879; minor child of Benjamin Austin, now Emma M. Hihl; Guardian: Thomas Allen

R. B. BAILEY FAMILY RECORD

Myron F. Bailey m. 8 September 1878 Miss Carrie Austin

BIRTHS, DEATHS & MARRIAGES 1852-53-54

Adeline Austin b. 8 April 1853 Charleston, dau. Nelson & Lydia (Thompson) Austin. Other living children: Lucretia Ann, Charles P., James R., Susan Clarissa

Caleb Austin, aged 75 years, d. 24 January 1853 Charleston, buried Niles Farm near Wellsboro, b. 16 November 1777 Mass., son of Jonathan Austin; wife - Clarissa Peterson; signed by Hiram Brooks

(buried Charleston Twp. this record says b. Ct no 25)

Broadacres records (County Farm): Nettie Austin age 16 Rutland PA d. 26 June 1887, buried County Farm Cemetery

1850 CENSUS TIOGA COUNTY PENNSYLVANIA

Charleston - No.191 farmer $400; Benjamin Austin 26 Pa; Zena 26 Pa; Lucenon C. (male) 2 mo. Pa; Caleb Fenton 14 Pa

No.192 farmer $9000; Caleb Austin 72 Ma; Clarissa 64 NY

No.194 farmer $2000; John Dumaux 35 France; Ruth 28 Pa; Mary 3 Pa

No.203 Nathan Austin 30 Pa; Maria 26 NY; George H. 5 Pa; Sarah A. 3 Pa; Oratio 1 Pa

No.213 farmer $1500; Nelson Austin 33 Pa; Lydia 26 Pa; Lucretia 10 Pa; Charles 6 Pa; James 4 Pa

No.264 farmer $1000; Charles Austin 35 Pa; Sarah 33 Pa; Clarissa 6 Pa; Mary J. 4 Pa; Hiram J. 8 mo. Pa

Delmar Twp. - No.114 Chauncey Austin 55 NY; Soniz 55 NY; Caroline 25 NY; Sophia 18 Pa; Leander Swope 17 NY

Jackson Twp. - No.130 farmer $500; George Austin 31 NY; Mary 29 NY; Abigail 10 NY; Samuel 8 NY; Adam 6 Pa; George 4 Pa

Sullivan Twp. - No.8 household of Wm. H. Montgomery: Joel Austin 21 b Pa, occupation Joiner

No.59 laborer; Daniel Austin 33 NY; Harriet 24 NY; Aaron 10 Pa; Louisa 9 Pa

No.60 farmer $250; Isaac Austin 63 NY; Ann 60 NY; Anna 21 Pa; Mary M. 8 Pa; A. (male) 16 Pa; Edmund 12 Pa

No.61 William Austin 24 Pa; Mary 17 NY

No.93 farmer; Luther Austin 68 CT; Susan 67 MA; Abigail Rumsey 49 VT

No.230 farmer $2800; Alvin B. Austin 49 Pa; Sally 49 Vt; Luther 21 Pa; Leander 18 Pa; Joseph 13 Pa; Jesse 11 Pa

No.236 Inn Keeper John B. Strong; Daniel Austin 15 Pa

No.250 farmer $1400; Hobba Austin 56 NY; Martha Austin 54 Ireland; Jane E. Austin 25 Pa; Mary Mack 7 Pa

Union Twp. - No.10 farmer $300; Simeon Austin 40 Vt; Amy 28 NY; Sophia 8 NY; Mary A. 5 NY

Wellsboro - No.71 Sarah Austin 63 NH; Henry Wells 18 NY

1860 CENSUS TIOGA COUNTY PENNSYLVANIA

Delmar Twp. - No.1920 Chauncey Austin 65 NY; Caroline 27 NY; Helen Smedley 17 NY; Daniel Coburn 22 NY

Sullivan Twp. - No.1395 A. B. Austin 59 Pa; Sally 59 Vt; Joseph 23 Pa; Jesse 20 Pa

No.1396 Leander Austin 29 Pa; Becca 23 Pa

No.1166 Hobby Austin 68 NY; Martha 62 Ireland

1870 CENSUS TIOGA COUNTY PENNSYLVANIA

Sullivan Twp. No.24 Alvin Austin 25 Pa; Sally 20 (ages should be 70) Abigail Rumsey 68

No.26 Joseph Austin 33 Pa; Emily 36 (should be 26); Aaron 6

No.46 Luther Austin 40; Mary 40; Florence 14; David 10; Ameda 6; Mary Shelton 75

No.48 Leander Austin 29; Rebakah 34

1880 CENSUS TIOGA COUNTY PENNSYLVANIA

Sullivan Twp. - No.160 Joel H. Austain 23; Rozetta wife 19; Justus P. son 1

No.325 Emily Austin 36; Alvin Austin 80 father; Aaron B. 15 son; Becky 10 dau.

No.334 L. B. Austain 45 Pa; Mary E. wife 42 Pa; Daniel B. 17 Pa; Melvina 12 Pa

THE TIOGA EAGLE NEWSPAPER FILE

13 November 1839 m. 5th inst. by B. B. Smith, Esq., Col. James Kimball to Miss Caroline, dau. of Caleb Austin, all of Tioga Co Pa

13 July 1842 m. 4th July by A. E. Niles, Esq., Mr. Nathan Austin to Miss Maria Dockstader, all of Charleston.

16 November 1842 m. 10th inst. in Charleston by the Rev. D. B. Lawton, Alanson E. Niles, Esq. to Miss Angeline, dau. of Mr. Caleb Austin, all of Charleston.

23 August 1843 m. at the residence of A. E. Niles, Esq., in Charleston, Tioga Co Pa on the 17th inst by Rev D. B. Lawton, Mr. Charles Austin to Miss Sarah Ann Lossinger of Wellsboro.

21 January 1846 m. in Charleston on the 4th ult by Rev Charels Breck, Mr. John Doumaux to Miss Ruth Austin, dau. of Mr. Caleb Austin of Charleston Tioga Co Pa

16 March 1847 m. in Delmar 11th inst. by Rev. J. F. Calkins, Mr. Archibald Walker of Charleston to Miss Emeline Austin of Delmar.

7 March 1849 m. at Covington on the 1st inst. by Benjamin Kress, Esq., Mr. Benjamin Austin to Miss Zena Culver, dau. of Joel Culver, Esq., all of Charleston.

THE TIOGA COUNTY AGITATOR NEWSPAPER FILE

8 July 1858 m. 1st July by Rev. J. F. Calkins in Delmar, John Alexander of Wellsboro & Miss Sophia Austin of Delmar.

22 March 1860 d. in Charleston 16th inst. Mrs. Zena Austin, wife of Benjamin Austin, aged 35 yrs.

29 March 1860 d. in Delmar 25th inst. Mrs. Lois, wife of Chauncey Austin, Esq., aged 65.

27 August 1862 d. in Sullivan 24 August 1862 Mrs. Susannah Austin, aged 83 yrs 4 mos. Her maiden name was Cudsworth, she came with her husband Noah Rumsey into Sullivan Twp. in 1809, formerly from Vermont. Migrated to northern New York, and thence to Tioga County, Pa. She had 14 children by her first husband, 8 living in Sullivan Twp., 1 in the far West, 5 children deceased. She had 53 grandchildren, 21 great-grandchildren; a few years ago m. Luther Austin, who survives. Member of the Baptist Church.

24 March 1869 m. in Charleston 18th March at the residence of Nathan Austin by Rev. A. G. Hammond, Mr. A. F. Herrington of Potter County, Pa. & Miss Susan C. Austin of Charleston, Pa.

8 June 1870 d. in Wellsboro 19th May Mrs. Ercy, wife of Hezekiah Austin aged 67 years.

19 April 1871 d. at Wellsville, NY 10th March 1871 Capt. E. F. Austin aged 48 yrs, son of the late Chauncey Austin.

19 April 1871 d. in Charleston, Pa 19th March, Miss Caroline P. Austin aged 44 yrs, sister of E. F. Austin & dau. of Chauncey Austin, Esq. of Delmar.

5 July 1871 m. 15 June 1871 by Rev. J. F. Calkins, Mr. James K. Austin to Miss Clara M. Dartt, both of Charleston.

6 September 1871 died in Wellsboro 3rd September Hezekiah Austin aged 75 yrs.

22 November 1871 m. in Mansfield 8th November 1871 by Rev J. A. Rossecel, Mr. Daniel D. Austin of Austin, Nevada, to Miss Sarah C. Rumsey of Mainesburg.

17 January 1872 m. in Charleston 31st December 1871 by Rev. G. S. Transue, Mr. George Wilkinson & Miss Mary J. Austin, both of Charleston.

THE WELLSBORO ADVERTISER NEWSPAPER FILE

28 January 1853 d. in Charleston on Monday last (24th) Mr. Caleb Austin in the 76th year of his age (aged 75, b. circa 1778).

12 August 1853 d. in this place on the 3rd inst. Mrs. Clara Austin, widow of the late Caleb Austin aged 68 years.

WELLSBORO WEEKLY DEMOCRAT NEWSPAPER FILE

March 1860 d. in Charleston on Friday 16th inst., Mrs. Zena Austin, wife of Benjamin Austin aged 35 years.

THE WELLSBORO AGITATOR NEWSPAPER FILE

7 August 1872 m. at the M. E. Parsonage in Charleston 28th July by Rev. G. S. Transue, Mr. H. J. Austin & Miss Mary J. Wilkinson, both of Charleston.

12 May 1874 d. Clara Austin wife of James K. Austin, aged 23. April 30th, of Charleston.

15 June 1875 m. James K. Austin & Miss Fannie E. Dartt of Charleston in Wellsboro June 10th by Rev. J. F. Calkins.

5 September 1876 Miss Amanda Austin aged 15 yrs 1 mo 15 das of Sullivan, d. 21 August of pneumonia.

28 November 1876 d. Rebecca Austin wife of L. R. Austin, November 15th at Mainesburg.

26 February 1878 m. L. R. Austin of Mainesburg and Miss Mittie Smith of Sullivan Township, at Mainesburg, February 20th by Rev. H. Lamkin.

23 April 1878 d. Mrs. A. B. Austin age 77 April 11th residence of Mr. R. G. Shelton, Mainesburg. Married twice, both husbands being among the first settlers. She leaves a husband and a family of children.

17 September 1878 m. Myron F. Bailey, Richmond Twp., & Miss Carrie B. Austin, Charleston, at the residence of Jeremiah Dockstader, Charleston, September 8th by Rev. J. V. Lowell.

1 October 1878 m. James L. Austin of Gillette, Pa. & Miss Emma Chapman of Cherry Flats, Pa, September 10th at Mansfield by Rev. George M. Richter.

7 January 1879 m. John C. Blair, Reading Center, New York, and Miss Florence E. Austin of Mainesburg, December 29th Mansfield by Rev. H. C. Moyer.

6 May 1879 d. Clarence E. Austin aged 15 days, son of H. J. Austin, April 9th at Charleston.

15 July 1879 m. Henry E. Dyke, Elk Run, and Miss Mary Austin in Mansfield June 21st at Arnot by D. T. Evans, Esq.

23 September 1879 Austin, Nevada, named for Aaron Austin, son of Alvin Austin of Mainesburg, the first settler to break ground in that region 30 years ago while prospecting for gold. He now lives in California.

2 December 1879 d. Anna L. Austin, only child of H. J. and M. J. Austin, aged 4 yr 9 mo 6 da. Died October 27th at Charleston of diptheria.

THE MANSFIELD ADVERTISER NEWSPAPER FILE

22 November 1876 d. Rebecca Austin November 15th, wife of L. R. Austin.

27 February 1878 m. L. R. Austin & Miss Nettie Smith of Mainesburg in Mainesburg February 20th by Rev. H. Lamkin.

1 May 1878 d. Mrs. A. B. Austin aged 77 years in Mainesburg.

24 November 1880 m. Robert G. Austin of Wellsboro and Miss Ada Coles, daughter of James of Wellsboro, at Wellsboro, last week Tuesday.

30 November 1881 m. J. B. Dyke of Richmond Twp. and Martha C. Austin at Mansfield November 27th by William Adams, Esq.

28 December 1881 died Alva Austin of Mainesburg, buried last Friday aged 82 years. Father of Leander Austin, he was an early settler.

16 February 1887 - Milo Austin and Miss Fanny Herrington, both of Ansonia, m. at Ansonia February 1st by Rev. G. Meigs.

20 July 1887 Alvin Austin of Mainesburg m. Miss Ida Robbins of Robbins Hollow at Covington July 14th by Rev. H. Lamkin.

9 November 1887 William Austin of Austinburg married Miss Hattie Seely of Knoxville at Troupsburg, New York, October 29th by Rev. J. Stevens.

10 April 1889 Mrs. H. N. Williams formerly of Wellsboro, d. Towanda last week of pneumonia, a sister of Robert G. Austin of Wellsboro.

2 July 1890 Nathan Austin d. Charleston Twp. a lifelong resident b. 6 February 1820.

25 October 1893 Leander R. Austin died October 9th at Allentown, Pa, aged 62 yrs 3 mo 11 das of typhoid. Former resident of Mainesburg - funeral & burial there. Leaves 1 child (not named), 4 brothers: Luther of Mainesburg, Jesse of Mainesburg, Daniel of California, Aaron of Colorado.

17 January 1894 James S. Coles d. Saturday at Wellsboro age 60, b. Chenango County, New York, leaves a daughter Mrs. R. G. Austin.

REVOLUTIONARY PENSION FILE ABSTRACT

David Austin - Revolutionary Pensioner S-39948 N.Y. In an old cemetery near Mainesburg is this tombstone - Hannah, wife of David Austin, died 2 March 1828 age 73 yrs 7 mo 20 das. Part of a query sent to Pension Office asking for data on David. Pension record states these children: Luther (son), Alvin (son), Lucy (dau.) m. Lyman Rumsey. David Austin received an Invalid Pension - he served as a Private in the Revolutionary War, enlisting 25 November 1776 in Dutchess County, N.Y., in Capt. Abraham Swartwort's Company, Colonel Peter Gansevoort's 3rd N.Y. Regiment until 25 November 1779. He was a resident of Sullivan Twp., Tioga Co. Pa. when he applied for a pension 17 February 1824. On 17 February 1824 he stated he was 70 years old (so born circa 1754). Date of death, name of wife or children not given, only as stated. Seth Rowley swears David Austin was a Revolutionary Soldier and served in Col. Peter Goursevoorte's Regiment in 1777 and 1778 at least two years in the 3rd N.Y. Regiments. They were together (1833) Otsego Co. N.Y. Jonathan Pinckney also swears he was in service with David Austin - 29 December 1823 Montgomery Co. N.Y. date & place of statement.

WELLSBORO COURT HOUSE RECORDS

47/44 William Austin d. 25 May 1897 aged 57 yrs 1 mo 23 d; retired merchant b. Carroll, Chataugua County, New York. Died Knoxville Penn., buried Austinburg.

53/19 Charles Austin d. 12 October 1897 aged 82 yrs 1 mo 27 das farmer b. Charleston, d. Charleston buried Welsh Settlement.

63/35 Sarah M. Austin d. 28 July 1899 aged 80 yrs 5 mos 8 das, died and buried in Ogdensburg.

65/17 Sarah Austin d. 30 November 1899 aged 82 yrs 5 mos 12 das; born, died and buried in Ogdensburg, Pa.

70/9 Francis M. Austin d. 20 October 1899 aged 1 yr 7 mo 3 das b. Delmar Twp., buried Wellsboro Cemetery; child of B. F. and Mabel Austin.

87/43 Nancy E. Austin died 24 February 1900 aged 64 years; born & died in Charleston, buried in Wellsboro.

90/2 Jeremiah Austin died 22 September 1901 aged 74 yrs 1 mo 7 das; born Benington County, Vermont; died Ogdensburg, buried Ogdensburg Cemetery.

104/29 Harriet Austin d. 22 April 1902 at Knoxville, Pa.; buried Austinburg.

105/24 Luther B. Austin died 23 February 1903, aged 73 yrs 10 mos 16 das; born in Mainesburg, died in Sullivan, buried Mainesburg Cemetery.

105/39 Amy Austin died 2 December 1902 aged 80 yrs 9 mos 7 das; born New York state, died and buried at Ogdensburg.

116/4 Edmund Austin died 17 January 1904 aged 68; born Richmond, died Richmond, buried Lawrence Corners Cemetery.

AUSTIN FAMILY ASSOCIATION BULLETIN 6 - JULY 1955
ABSTRACTS OF WELLSBORO COURTHOUSE WILLS
COMPILED BY JANET AUSTIN CURTIS

Bk.B p.73 Registered 2 February 1853 Caleb Austin Charleston Twp; Widow Clarissa; children: Benjamin Austin, Caroline Kimball, Adaline Christinat, Emeline Fenton, Angeline Niles, Ruth Domaux, Charles Austin, Nathan Austin, Nelson Austin, & Hiram Brooks son of Clarissa by her first marriage.

Bk.B p.325 Registered 26 May 1862 Chauncey Austin of Delmar Twp.; children: Edgar S. Y. Austin, Susan Emeline Walker, Caroline F. Austin, Sophia C. Alexander.

Bk.B p.345 Registered 29 April 1869 Nelson Austin; Adm: Nathan Austin, Hiram Brooks.

Bk.B p.350 Registered 16 March 1863 Susannah Austin widow of Luther of Sullivan Twp.; Executors: Leander D. Rumsey, Aaron Rumsey; Child: Abigail Rumsey. Note: Susannah Cudsworth m. 1st Noah Rumsey, m. 2nd Luther Austin.

Bk.D p.215 Registered 31 January 1882 Alvin B. Austin of Mainesburg; ch.: Amelia Shelton wife of Robert, Aaron, Luther, Leander, Daniel, Joseph, Jesse.

Bk.G p.413 Made 3 February 1896, recorded 30 March 1896: Jeremiah Austin of Mainesburg; ch.: Amos Austin of Chatauqua County, New York; Thomas Austin of Allegheny County, New York; nephew William Austin.

Bk.C p.121 Registered 24 May 1894 Leander R. Austin of Allentown, Lehigh County, Pennsylvania; Executor: Mittie E. Austin, wife; heirs: brother Jesse Austin of Mainesburg; nephew L. E., son of Jesse Austin.

Bk.H p.89 Registered 16 September 1896 William Austin, merchant of Knoxville, Pa.; Admin: Harriet Austin; heirs: Laura Cook of Troupsburg, Steuben County, New York, and Julia Miller. Relationships not given.

AUSTIN FAMILY ASSOCIATION BULLETIN 8 - FEB. 1956
RECORDS COMPILED BY EDITH AUSTIN MOORE

Jonathan Austin b. 10 June 1742 Methuen, Mass. (see Austins of America page 15), m. Hannah. He was a housewright. Children born at Methuen: Sarah b. 2 April 1767; Hannah b. 14 February 1768; Jonathan b. 25 February 1770; Daniel b. 9 August 1771;

Benjamin b. 25 March 1773; Olive b. 21 November 1774; Caleb b. 17 November 1777 m. Mrs. Clarissa (Peterson) Brooks; Dorcas b. 18 January 1779; Persis b. 29 January 1781; Alice b. 29 February 1783; Charlotte b. 19 September 1784. Ref: Essex Antiquarian; V.R. of Methuen, Mass.; abstracted by Mrs. Mary Kerrich of Wellsboro.

AUSTIN FAMILY ASSOCIATION BULLETIN - JULY 1957
MRS. MARCIA A. BEATON, WOODSVILLE, NH (1944)

Caleb Austin b. 17 November 1777 Methuen, Mass. d. 24 January 1862 Charleston, Tioga Co., Pa.; m. 28 January 1810 Chelsea, Vermont to Clarissa (Peterson) Brooks, a widow b. October 1785 d. 3 August 1853 Charleston Twp. She had a son Hiram Brooks by her first husband b. 1807 NH. He served as executor of his stepfather's Will. Children: Caroline b. 12 February 1811 d. 19 July 1851 m. James Kimball of Wellsboro, Pa.; Adaline b. 18 May 1812 m. 1804 (sic) Rudolph Christenat; Emily b. 30 November 1813 d. 5 August 1881 m. 27 October 1828 Luman Fenton b. 11 November 1811 d. 18 February 1886; Charles b. 11 February 1817 m. 1843 Sarah Ann Sosinger; Nelson b. 11 February 1817 m. 1840 Lydia Thompson; Angeline b. 26 August 1818 m. 10 November 1842 to Col. Alanson E. Niles - served in Civil War in Pa. Bucktail Regiment; Nathan b. 6 February 1820 m. 1st 1842 Maria Dockstader, m. 2nd Mrs. Nancy E. Gibson; Ruth b. 6 February 1822 d. 1901 Pa. m. 4 December 1845 to John Doumaux; Benjamin b. 1 November 1823 m. 1st Zena Culver m. 2nd Fannie (Wilson) Young.

Caleb Austin is listed in the 1810 Census of Tioga County, Pa. He was the first of the family who settled at Charleston Twp. near Wellsboro. He cleared a farm of 180 acres and lived there until his death. His heirs sold the property to the County. Parents and children were members of the M. E. Church at Wellsboro.

AUSTIN FAMILY ASSOCIATION BULLETIN - JULY 1958

Adaline Austin b. 18 May 1812 in Tioga Co., m. 13 March 1834 to Rudolph Christenut b. 15 March 1804 d. 23 April 1865 Pa. Children: Robert Gilbert 1835-1864; Sarah 1836-1886; George Washington 1838; Benjamin Rudolph 1843; James Albert 1840-1865; Nelson Austin 1847-1849; Samuel Willis 1852.

NEW YORK IN THE REVOLUTION

Robert Austin served as an enlisted man in Dutchess County Militia 6th & 7th Regiments.

HISTORY OF TIOGA COUNTY PENNSYLVANIA (1883)

p.114,116,140: Caleb Austin in Tioga Co. circa 1811, settled on farm where Tioga County Poor House is located. Listed in 1815 tax assessment Caleb Austin, a tax collector.

p.151 Chauncey Austin was one of the first elders of the Presbyterian Church of Wellsboro, organized 11 February 1843.

p.31 Appendix: Sullivan Township Jeremiah Austin's birth occurred in 1826 at Butternuts, Otsego County, New York. The town of Butternuts is now known as Gilbertsville, it does have a town historian. His father removed to Caton, Steuben County, New York, in 1837, where Jeremiah m. Miss Sylvia A. Wing. In 1868 he located at Chatham Twp., Pa. In 1870 he removed to Alleghany County, New York, and in 1881 returned to Mainesburg, Tioga Co., where he purchased a farm of 119 acres.

p.33 Appendix: Union Twp. Jeremiah Austin, son of Pardon & Hepsibah Austin, was b. in Arlington, Vermont 15 August 1827. In 1857 he m. Rhoda Ann, dau. of Dennis & Sarah McGuire of Granville, New York. Their children were: Frank B., Maggie L., Lawrence G., Addie M., Sarah J.

p.13 Appendix: Delmar Township Robert R. Austin was born in Broome County, New York 14 September 1833. His parents were natives of New England, coming to Tioga County circa 1854.

p.16 Andrew G. Sturrock is a carpenter, a joiner, a contractor and builder at Wellsboro. He was born in 1835 in Delmar and married Miss Charlotte C. Austin of Wellsboro.

EDITOR'S CORNER

*YOUR RESEARCH
NOTES CAN EVEN
OUTLAST CEMETERY
MONUMENTS AND
ORIGINAL TOWN
VITAL RECORDS*

Your genealogical research notes may be more valuable than you think. Old cemetery gravestones you have copied may not exist one day, perhaps sooner than you imagine. Gravestones erode away with time, become broken, or sink into the ground. I encountered fragments of several freshly-broken monuments heaped under a tree in one old cemetery . . . it seems vandalism must be added to the ways cemetery monuments can become damaged or lost.

A few years ago my wife and I returned to a Town Hall to recheck marriage records we had copied there just the previous year. The Town Clerk explained how that particular volume had been stolen!

Your research notes can contain unique information, if your original sources are ever lost or destroyed. Even if not unique, I would urge you to publish your notes, for your sources may be inaccessible to many others.

The notes submitted by Mrs. Rhoda Ladd and reproduced on pages 106-109 of this issue show the value of publishing your research. I would urge all readers to follow Mrs. Ladd's example, and to submit their raw research data for publication, by sending either their original or photocopied research notes to the *Austins of America* Editor:

> Dr. Michael E. Austin
> Box 73   MIT/LL
> Lexington, MA 02173

Austins of America will gladly reimburse any photo-copying or postage expenses, and will return any original field notes to you. As with Mrs. Ladd's material, your notes need not be in the form of an article . . . just send them as they are, thus making them readily available to hundreds of other Austin family researchers! These *Austins of America* newsletters will be published as a well-indexed book, with copies placed in state and other major libraries, thus your research notes might even outlast some of the original sources from which they were taken!

QUERIES

110-1. Catherine Austin dau. John & Sena/Sean Austin, b. 25/30 May 1831 poss. Elyria OH, m. David M. Dutcher of Hillsdale NY ca 1847, res. Alford MA 1853, Great Barrington 1860, Colebrook River CT 1872. Catherine d. Winsted CT 18 March 1897. Seek data on John & Sena.

110-2. Benjamin Austin born circa 1785 in MA or RI, m. circa 1804 to Ruth Burleson (1784-1867). He lived in Berkshire, VT from 1810 to his death in 1869. Need his birth place and date: was his father Pasco Austin of RI?

110-3. Barbara Austin b. 5 June 1729 d. 6 June 1790 m. 20 September 1752 Daniel Butler, son of Daniel & Hannah (Bennett) Butler b. 26 March 1735 Stonington, CT d. 20 March 1814. In 1767 they res. Monson, MA, in 1784 they res. Sandisfield, MA Butler ch: Samuel 1753, William 1755-1771, Anna 1758, Daniel 1760-1790, Hannah 1762, Nathaniel 1766, Benjamin 1769, Allen 1771, Joseph 1773, Sarah. Ch. moved into Tioga County, Penn. Need parents of Barbara Austin.

110-4. Mary Austin m. William Leighton in Somersworth, NH (or thereabouts) about 1795. Seek proof that Mary was the dau. of Moses & Phoebe (Hussey) Austin.

110-5. Hannah Austin born circa 1824 perhaps in Delaware County, NY, married John E. Canfield b. 6 February 1821 perhaps in Steuben County, NY, d. 24 July 1864 and buried in Scio, Allegany County, NY. Records indicate she may have married second Stephen Reynolds between 1868-1870, probably in Allegany County. Need parents and vital statistics on Hannah.

110-6. Joseph Austin res. French Creek. Ch. by wife Armina: Nelson, Angeline, Homer, Eli, Caroline, Elias G., Sophronia, Levi W. & Leonard. Was the William H. Austin who m. Angeline Austin related to her? Believe he was son of Ashley Austin. Who is the Palmer Austin there . . . a son of Joseph or Ashley? Information on these or other Austin families of Chautauqua Co. NY, and Erie County PA, areas will be appreciated.

110-7. Joseph Austin and spinster Jenny Alford m. 3 June 1800 Amherst Co. Virginia. Ch: Benjamin Robert b. 1804 m. Margaret Warnick d. Decatur IL, bur. Greenwood Cem.; William Alford b. 26 April 1806 d. 3 March 1892 bur. Macon Co. IL, m. 5 January 1832 Eleanor Warnick; Joseph Jr. owned land in Macon Co. ca 1828. All these (unless Jennie was deceased) moved to Macon Co. from Rutherford Co. TN, ca 1826 & lived there until their deaths. Seek parents of Joseph Austin.

110-8. Jeremiah Austin b. 29 November 1792 VT m. 28 February 1819 Betsy Howard b. NH; res. Morley, St. Lawrence Co. NY; had 11 children; died & buried in Morley. Seek parents of Jeremiah.

NOTES ON LYMAN AUSTIN
OF WEBSTER, NEW YORK
AND BURLINGTON, KANSAS

by Marjorie Hentzen Turrell

Editor's Note: These notes concern the Lyman Austin found on page 428 of Edith Austin Moore's 1969 book *The Descendants of Richard Austin of Charlestown, Massachusetts*. Mrs. Turrell was the major contributor to this line in the book. Besides the additional information on Lyman himself, these present notes provide the birthplace and approximate deathyear of his grandfather Morris, the birthdate and other information on his father Edward, and the names and birthyears of two of Lyman's previously unknown brothers.

Lyman's grandfather Morris Austin was born 22 January 1790 in Sheffield, Massachusetts, and died circa 1844. He married Jerusha Faskett, their four children are found in on page 245 of Edith Austin Moore's *Richard Austin* book. Their fourth child, Melissa Austin, had a middle name of Samantha.

Their second child, Edward E. Austin, was born 19 August 1816 in New York state. An 1872 map of Fairport, New York, showed he lived at the northeast corner of High Street and Watson (or Turk Hill Road). The 1850 Census listed Edward's occupation as "cooper." The 1869-70 Gazetteer of Monroe County listed his name with the following: "Lot 32, dealer in fruit trees and farmer of 6 acres." He married three times, as found on page 351 of EAM's book. His children were Mary b. 1838, James b.1842, Harriet b. 1844, David b. 1846, Lyman b. 1848, George b.1849. At the time of his death 2 June 1902, Edward and his third wife Elizabeth lived at 7409 Harvard Avenue in Chicago.

Lyman M. Austin was born 12 May 1848 in Webster, New York. His mother, Maria (Sutton), died when he was only two years old. When he was in his early 30's, Lyman moved to Burlington, Kansas, to be associated with his cousins in the Hopper-Peasley Insurance Company. His cousin Isaac Hopper was the son of Alice Alvira (Austin) Hooper, a sister to Lyman's father Edward. Albert Peasley was Alice's son-in-law. Lyman married 4 October 1882 to Marguerite Laura Hempy, and their family is found on page 428 of EAM's *Richard Austin* book. They had two children before they were divorced on 22 January 1889. Lyman moved back to Webster, New York, residing at 212 East Main Street. He died there 26 May 1900 at age 52 unmarried, and was buried in Fairport, New York. His only daughter, Edith Mae (Austin) Hentzen, lived in Kansas and Missouri most of her life. She taught in one-room schools in the Iola, Kansas, area. She died 28 April 1973 in Kansas City, Missouri. Lyman's only son, Clyde Edward Austin, had no children.

Lyman M. Austin 1848-1900

★★★★★★★★★★★★★★★★★★★★★★★★★★★★★★

Austins of America is intended to serve present and future genealogists researching Austin family lines. Readers are encouraged to submit Queries, genealogical and historical articles for publication. Previously published books, pamphlets or articles containing Austin genealogical data are also sought for reprinting or review.

EDITOR

DR. MICHAEL EDWARD AUSTIN   CONCORD, MA

ASSOCIATE EDITORS

ANTHONY KENT AUSTIN	PROSPECT, KY
BERT ADDIS AUSTIN	QUEEN CREEK, AZ
PATRICIA BIEBUYCK AUSTIN	CONCORD, MA
PAULINE LUCILLE AUSTIN	MARION, IA
JANET AUSTIN CURTIS	ALBUQUERQUE, NM
CAROL LEIGHTON HULL	SUDBURY, MA

Austins of America is published each February and August by The Austin Print, 23 Allen Farm Lane, Concord, Massachusetts 01742. All correspondence, including subscriptions, articles and responses to queries, should be sent to this address. Subscriptions are $2.50 per year postpaid.

RESTORING THE 1822 STONE HOUSE
BUILT BY GENERAL NATHANIEL AUSTIN
IN CHARLESTOWN, MASSACHUSETTS

by Marvin Pave

Editor's Note: The following article, submitted by Associate Editor Carol L. Hull, originally appeared in the 29 January 1984 *Boston Sunday Globe*, and is reprinted here with permission. Photographs were furnished by Amy Jordan of Historic Boston, Inc. The Nathaniel Austin herein is R126-52 in Edith Austin Moore's book *Richard Austin of Charlestown, Mass.* (page 38). He was born 19 March 1772, died 3 April 1861 in Cambridge, Mass. unmarried. Serving as Brig. General of the 3rd Div. Mass. Troops in 1817, General Austin was one of the best known men in Charlestown. He was a Federalist, and was elected to the Massachusetts General Court circa 1812, in opposition to his brother, the Hon. William Austin, an ardent Jeffersonian Republican. Nathaniel Austin was a strong advocate of free bridges.

Charlestown's architecturally unique three-story "house of stone" at the corner of Main and Harvard streets was built in 1822 by Middlesex County Sheriff Nathaniel Austin. By 1980, deserted for 20 years, it had become a house of cards on the verge of collapse because of the ravages of time and weather.

Enter Historic Boston, Inc., and its fund manager, Stanley Smith, who left no stone unturned in authentically restoring the structure. The ground floor facade of the house had been replaced by store fronts about 1900, Smith said, so a major priority was to restore that portion of the building.

"In poking through the old records, we discovered that Gen. Austin built his house with splitstone from a quarry on Outer Brewster Island in Boston Harbor. He had inherited the island from his father in 1799," said Smith, former development director of the Society for the Preservation of New England Antiquities.

The search for Austin's quarry began with a nautical chart and a Harbor Islands history book and with a permit from the state to search on what had become the property of the Department of Environmental Management. It ended at the island's northeast corner at a man-made inlet surrounded by walls of stone, created by the early 19th century quarry workers.

"What a find, it was like time stood still," said Smith. Getting to his quarry was the easy part. Finding a way to transport 12 tons of stone to Charlestown was another story.

"We tried to get the Army or the Air Force to take the stone by helicopter. That didn't work," Smith said. "We finally did it in two trips with a barge, six workmen and a stone mason."

The Stone House, on Charlestown's historic Austin block, was one of only two course rubble granite houses built in Boston by the early 19th Century. The other much smaller stone house is also located in Charlestown and is a private residence.

Austin eventually rented part of his house for law offices and a West India goods store. Its historical significance is enhanced because Charlestown's first regular newspaper, the Bunker Hill Aurora, was established in an upstairs office in 1827.

Historic Boston, Inc., which works in conjunction with the Boston Landmarks Commission, was able to get the Stone House project started with a grant of $5000 from the 200-member Charlestown Preservation Society. Smith said a developer is expected to buy the Stone House property within the next month and that the building should be ready for office rental by late spring.

"We put the buildings on line. The rest is up to potential developers," said Smith. "Our goal is not total restoration," he added. "What we do, through grants from the Massachusetts Historical Commission and private donations, is restore these sites as a first step to neighborhood and commercial revitalization."

Historic Boston, Inc., was founded in 1960 to purchase, preserve and restore Boston's Old Corner Bookstore, then in danger of being demolished to make room for a parking garage. Rental revenue from the bookstore property enabled the organization, in 1979, to begin to purchase other historic sites, or loan money to their owners.

"Right now, we've got a list of 35 potential structures in the city that are irreplaceable-culturally, economically and aesthetically," Smith said. "Most are in disrepair because of owners who either cannot afford to fix or restore them or who can't get development funds from traditional sources because of their location."

Restoration projects currently receiving or targeted for assistance by Historic Boston, Inc., include the 1790 Hurd House, located diagonally across the street from the Stone House. Total cost of restoring the Stone and Hurd Houses is projected at $400,000. The list also includes the Oak Square School in Brighton, the last standing wooden schoolhouse in Boston; two 18th Century buildings and a 19th Century row of marble front houses near John Eliot Square in Roxbury and the Trinity Neighborhood House in East Boston, built in the late 19th Century.

"The money we invest to restore these sites will translate into a bigger return to the city and its residents in commercial development and in taxes," said Smith. "At the same time, it's a way to keep Boston's cultural and historical heritage from literally crumbling away."

The Stone House in 1890, then a furniture warehouse.

BOSTON PUBLIC LIBRARY PHOTOGRAPH

The Stone House in 1980, before its restoration.

PHOTOGRAPH BY WILLIAM OWENS

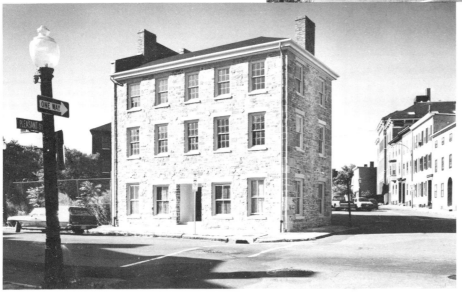

The Stone House in 1983, after its restoration.

PHOTOGRAPH BY JAMES HIGGINS

THE DESCENDANTS OF
JOHN AUSTIN AND ANN BADEN
OF ALBEMARLE COUNTY, VIRGINIA

by Bert Addis Austin

J. JOHN[1] AUSTIN was born 25 July 1755, and was married in Anne Arundel County, Maryland, on 11 May 1777 to Ann Baden. Ann was born on 21 November 1757. They lived in Albemarle County, Virginia by 1782. John Austin perhaps died on 3 December 1823.

CHILDREN: J1. REBECCA, *b. 17 February 1778 m. 25 July 1803 in Albemarle County, to Nelson Martin (wit. Jonas Austin)*

J2. CATHERINE, *b. 18 February 1780 m. 8 October 1802 in Albemarle County to Daniel Rodgers (wit. Jonas Austin)*

J3. JONAS R., *b. 10 December 1782*

J4. ELIZABETH, *born 12 March 1785, m. 1811 in Garrard County to Stephen Martin*

J5. JOHN BADEN, *b. 10 October 1787*

J6. ROBERT, *b. 14 October 1790*

J7. THOMAS, *b. 24 December 1792*

J8. NANCY, *b. 23 June 1795*

J9. MARY (POLLY), *b. 8 February 1798, m. 1820 in Garrard County to Shelton Smith*

JA. MARTHA (PATSY), *born 13 January 1801*

SECOND GENERATION

J3. JONAS R.[2] AUSTIN (*John[1]*) was born 10 December 1782 in Albemarle County, Virginia. He married first in Garrard County, Kentucky on 11 July 1804 to Mary (Polly) Loyd, born in August 1785. Family tradition has it that Mary and her family were attacked by Indians. The stories vary and contain known errors, but there must be some basis in fact, for the accounts come from different people, widely separated and unknown to one another:

> *"Our great great Grandmother, Margaret Austin, was scalped by Indians when a child. Her parents had a silver plate made to fit in the opening, and she wore it constantly. She died suddenly without having any illness in 1830 or 1831, a moment after her daughter, Elizabeth Ann (Austin) Parks and husband, Levi Parks, and their four children, William Thomas, Jonas Austin, Sarah Jane, and George Britton Parks arrived from Indiana for a visit. She went out to the gate to meet them, and in a moment, fell dead."* [Nettie Barnes to her cousin William A. Parks 1934]

> *"Our family history has it that the Loyd family had to flee for their lives during the Indian Wars and Mary was left in the wood pile for dead. When the family had returned the next day, Mary had crawled into the house under a mattress and was saved. This story is found in some English History."* [George B. Austin, Oklahoma City 1972]

> *"I will try to tell you a story grandmother (Malinda) often told me about running her fingers through her grandmother's hair feeling the scar left by an Indian tomahawk thrown at her as she ran, as a little girl. She, her brother and father escaped, but the mother was killed as she sat milking the cow. The children hid in a stake and rider fence. The father dove into the creek and swam under a ledge thereby getting away. The Indians destroyed everything. Leona Leonard sent me this as I had told her about the Silver Plate. She received it from a Townsend connection in Oregon. Melinda couldn't have felt the scar on her grandmother's head - the dates of Melinda's birth and Mary's death aren't right for it, but Betsey might have felt the scar and told Melinda about it."* [Miss Anna J. Foley of Greensburg, Indiana, 1976. Melinda the dau. of J32 Elizabeth (Austin) Parks.]

Jonas Austin was given a grant of 200 acres South of Green River on waters of Trace Fork & South Fork of Knoblick Creek, surveyed 1 January 1806. This grant is between Dunnville and Labascus, Casey County, Kentucky. Jonas was appointed surveyor and road superintendent at the first recorded meeting on 14 November 1806 to form Casey County from Lincoln County. He was granted another 110 acres on Knoblick Creek, surveyed 5 May 1814. Jonas and Polly sold 200 acres to his brother Thomas Austin on 1 January 1827. On 18 February 1828 Jonas was granted 50 acres on Short Creek, North Side of Green River, Casey County. The family had one slave in 1810 and again in the 1830 census for Casey County, but no slaves in the 1840 census. Mary died 15 November 1832, and Jonas remarried on 3 February 1834 to Mikey Gentry in Adair County, Kentucky; no issue. Jonas and Mikey sold 100 acres of land in Casey County in 1837. Jonas died on 14 October 1846, a sale bill dated 30 December 1846 has John, Benjamin and Jonas Jr. Austin buying shoe tools, a horse, and a rifle of Jonas Austin, deceased. Mikey died 10 December 1848. Children born in Casey County:

CHILDREN: J31. BENJAMIN W., *b. 14 June 1805*

J32. ELIZABETH P., *b. 29 April 1807*

J33. JOHN L., *born 6 March 1809*

J34. ISAAC B., *born 22 May 1810*

J35. MARIAH JANE, *b. 29 December 1812, d. 17 August 1860, m. [Robert W.]? Staton before 1830 census?*

J36. ROBERT J., *b. 23 December 1814*

J37. THOMAS W., *b. 22 Jan. 1817, d. 23 April 1818*

J38. JONAS, JR., *b. 2 January 1819*

J39. [daughter], *born and died in 1821*

J3A. POLLY S., *born 21 February 1822*

J3B. JOSEPH HARRISON, *b. 12 February 1824*

J3C. SHELTON SMITH, *b. 14 November 1826*

J3D. JAMES W., *born 7 May 1830, m. 27 September 1849 Martha Adeline Snow in Lincoln County, KY. They were not in the 1850 Kentucky Census.*

J3E. GEORGE WASHINGTON, *b. 23 June 1832*

J5. JOHN BADEN[2] AUSTIN (*John*[1]) was born 10 October 1787 in Albemarle County, Virginia. He was married on 13 April 1815 in Somerset, Pulaski County, Kentucky to Nancy VanHook. Nancy, the daughter of Revolutionary Soldier Samuel VanHook, was born on 28 June 1788 in Virginia. John was a school teacher in Kentucky, and was also a Baptist Minister. He brought his family to Crawfordsville, Indiana, from Pulaski County in 1827-28. He preached for many years in Indiana and held the office of County Auditor for several terms. John B. Austin is the first Austin listed in Deed Books of Garrard County, Kentucky, in 1819. He and Nancy sold land on Sugar Creek on 13 October 1820, land originally patented to Arabia J. Brown. Nancy died on 28 February 1852, while John died on 25 September 1868 in Montgomery County, Indiana.

CHILDREN: J51. MARTHA ANN, *b. 27 December 1815 Pulaski County, died 12 February 1888; m. Charles Shanklin*

J52. MARY B., *born 23 February 1817 Lincoln County, Kentucky, d. 27 August 1858; m. James McKinley*

J53. SAMUEL WILSON, *b. 21 November 1818*

J54. CATHERINE ANN, *born 28 August 1821 Harrison County, Kentucky, d. 28 July 1906, m. John B. Ashenhurst*

J55. JOHN MARTIN, *b. 12 August 1823 Harrison County, d. 21 July 1877, m. Sarah Jane Webb*

J56. NANCY, *b. 21 August 1825 Harrison County, d. 30 March 1901, m. John M. Nicholson*

J57. HARRIETT, *b. 11 July 1827 Harrison County, d. 12 February 1909, m. William Campbell*

J58. ABNER VANHOOK, *b. 29 November 1828 Montgomery County, d. 8 May 1896, m. Catherine Huffman*

J59. ARCHELAUS, *b. 21 October 1831 Montgomery County, d. 15 April 1835*

J6. ROBERT[2] AUSTIN (*John*[1]) was born 14 October 1790 in Albemarle County, Virginia. He was married in Garrard County, Kentucky, on 12 October 1818 to Prudence Bland, born circa 1800, one of thirteen children of Charles Bland, and sister of Milly Bland wife of J7 Thomas Austin. Robert resided in Casey County, Kentucky, when he sold land there to Thomas Blaine on 14 December 1825. Robert Austin and four sons appear in the 1830 Census for Garrard County. Robert died before the 1840 census, and widow Prudence Austin is listed as head of the household with five sons and a daughter. Prudence Austin sold her heir's interest in the Garrard County land of Charles Bland, deceased, to John Bland on 18 March 1853. She was residing in Ray County, Missouri, when she sold 73 acres on waters of Boon Creek and Dick's River in Garrard County to Eiley Ball on 2 May 1857. She was still in Ray County when she sold land she had received from the Charles Bland estate on 27 December 1882.

Of the children, only George age 22 appears with widow Prudence in the 1850 Garrard County Census. In the 1830 Census, Robert had one male under 5 (J64 George age 2), two males 5 and under 10 (J62 & J63), one male 10 and under 15 (J61). No females are listed with the family in 1830: Prudence was apparently visiting elsewhere with her youngest son J65. In the 1840 Census, widow Prudence had three males 10 and under 15 (J63, J64 George age 12, & J65), two males 15 and under 20 (J61 & J62), and one female 5 and under 10 (J66). To have been 10 or older in 1830 yet under 20 in 1840, J61 must have been born in 1820, his 10th birthday before the 1830 Census, and his 20th birthday after the 1840 Census. To have been 5 or older in 1830 yet under 15 in 1840, J63 must have been born in 1825, his 5th birthday before the 1830 Census, and his 15th birthday after the 1840 Census. The census was apparently taken earlier in 1840 than in 1830. J65 and his mother missed the 1830 Census, but he was 10 or more in 1840, so he must have been born in or before 1830 (and after J64 George b. circa 1828). Constrained by their sibling's birthyears, J62 was born between 1821 and 1824, J66 between 1830 and 1835. Thus one concludes:

CHILDREN: J61. [son], *b. 1820*

J62. [son], *b. circa 1823*

J63. [son], *b. 1825*

J64. GEORGE, *b. circa 1828*

J65. [son], *b. 1829-30*

J66. [daughter], *b. circa 1832*

If like their widowed mother Prudence Austin, these children are among the Austins in the 1850 Garrard County Census (see *Austins of America* page 127), most of their identities can be uniquely determined from their ages. J61 James is the only Austin male age 30 in the County, J63 John the only Austin male age 25. John is living with his brother J62 William Austin age 27, along with Joan Austin age 20 (probably William's wife since she was listed ahead of John, but possibly their sister J66). That leaves only Thomas Austin and Will Austin, both listed as age 21, as possibilities for J65. Will Austin is in the household listed immediately after Prudence Austin's, yet it seems unlikely to have two sons, one named 'William' and another 'Will', since Will is a common nickname for William. That leaves only Thomas Austin for J65. *THUS WE VENTURE TO SPECULATE:*

CHILDREN: J61. JAMES, *b. 1820 Kentucky, m. Eleanor (—) b. circa 1826 Kentucky*

J62. WILLIAM, *born circa 1823 Kentucky, m. Joan (—) b. circa 1830 Kentucky*

J63. JOHN, *b. 1825 Kentucky*

J64. GEORGE, *b. circa 1828 Kentucky*

J65. THOMAS, *b. circa 1829 Kentucky*

J66. [daughter], *b. circa 1832, perhaps married before the 1850 Census*

J7. THOMAS[2] AUSTIN (*John[1]*) was born 24 December 1792. He was married in Garrard County, Kentucky, on 2 January 1825 to Milly Bland, the daughter of Charles Bland. Thomas bought 200 acres of land in Casey County, Kentucky, on 1 January 1827 from his brother Jonas Austin. On 23 September 1831 he and Milly sold 200 acres to Isaac Austin. Thomas Austin heirs to the lands in Garrard County of Charles J. Bland, deceased. Said interest having descended to them from their mother, Milly Bland Austin, at her death; dated 7 October 1857. Heirs were: Kittura Austin Johnson, John Johnson, Micajah Murphy, Julia Ann Austin Murphy, Robert Austin, Benjamin Austin, all of Warren County, Missouri. From the evidence it appears that Thomas & Milly's grandson William M. Austin murdered Betsey Bland, Milly's sister, on 20 January 1882 using an axe. Betsey was within 10 days of her 80th year; she had never married. William was hanged on 13 October 1882, the last person to be hung in Garrard County.

CHILDREN: J71. KEZIAH (KITTURA), *b. circa 1826, m. John Johnson*

J72. ROBERT, *b. circa 1828, was still residing in Warren County, Missouri, when he gave a Power of Attorney to C. J. Bland to settle any and all business Robert may have in Kentucky, dated 12 March 1868.*

J73. JULIA ANN, *b. after 1830 census, m. Micajah Murphy*

J74. BENJAMIN

THIRD GENERATION

J31. BENJAMIN W.[3] AUSTIN (*Jonas R.,[2] John[1]*) was born 14 June 1805 in Casey County, Kentucky. He was married in Casey County on 13 August 1829 to Ann Sherwood by Thomas Wallace, Methodist Minister. Ann was born in 1805, perhaps a daughter of the Thomas Sherwood who was living in Casey County in 1810, and a sister of Daniel Sherwood. Benjamin's family appears in the 1830 Census for Casey County. They moved to Russell County, Kentucky, before Benjamin bought land on Goose Creek in that county in 1833 from Phillip Winfrey of Casey County. They were in Russell County in 1837 when they sold Ann's right of dower in 190 acres in Casey County. The family was still in Russell County at the time of the 1840 Census, but had moved before 1843 to Wayne County, Kentucky, for Benjamin was of Wayne County on 26 August 1843 when his assignee Jonas Austin, Jr. bought more land for Benjamin on Goose Creek, this time from William Moore of Russell County. Benjamin and his wife Ann returned to Casey County before 26 October 1846, the date they sold land on Goose Creek to Jonas Austin. In 1850 Benjamin and Ann and their four oldest children appear in the census for Casey County, with Benjamin listed as a farmer. Ann

died before the 1860 Census, and Benjamin Austin remarried on 1 September 1857 in Adair County, Kentucky, to Mary Ann Butt, who was born circa 1836 and was 24 in the 1860 Census for Casey County. A Ben Austin age 69 died in December 1870 of consumption in Casey County, although Benjamin Austin's personal property inventory was dated 4 December 1869.

CHILDREN: J311. MARY F., *b. circa 1837 m. John S. Sayer, res. Wayne Co.*

J312. ELIZABETH P., *b. circa 1842, m. 29 November 1865 John W. Coffey*

J313. THERESA E., *b. circa 1844; the Hassey E. Austin b. Casey County who d. 21 September 1858 at age 14 in Casey County of scarlet fever was the child of Benjamin Austin: probably she was this Theresa E. Austin.*

J314. JOHN B., *b. circa 1847*

J315. AMANDA Y., *b. circa 1858, m. Samuel B. Shelton, resided Russell County.*

J316. HENRIETTA, *b. circa 1860, m. Howard A. Murrell (or Murry), resided Adair County.*

J317. ALEXANDER H., *resided Winslow, Arizona Territory, in 1884.*

J318. GEORGE G., *resided Wayne County in 1884.*

J319. SOFA J., *resided Wayne County in 1884.*

J32. ELIZABETH P.[3] AUSTIN (*Jonas R.,[2] John[1]*) was born 29 April 1807 in Casey County, Kentucky. She was married in Casey County on 11 July 1824 to Levi Parks. Levi, the son of William and Agnes (Collier) Parks, was born on 28 December 1793 in Lincoln County, Kentucky. A 1934 letter from Nettie Barnes to her cousin William A. Parks states: "They had eleven children. They went to Indiana four or five years after they were married, locating in Decatur County, 4½ miles south of Greensburg, and lived there until they broke up and moved to Howard County in 1854." Levi died 29 August 1855 in Alto, Kokomo County, Indiana. Elizabeth died 14 March 1868 in Alto. First three children were born in Casey County, the others in Decatur County. PARKS CHILDREN: WILLIAM THOMAS 1825, JONAS AUSTIN 1826, SARAH JANE 1828, GEORGE BRITTON 1830, JOHN ALLEN 1832, MARIANNE 1834, MARTHA ANN 1836, MARGARET ELIZABETH 1838, MELINDA CATHERINE 1840, NATHANIEL JAMES MATISON LEVI 1842, EMILY (EMMA) JOSEPHINE 1844.

J33. JOHN L.[3] AUSTIN (*Jonas R.,[2] John[1]*) was born 6 March 1809 in Casey County, Kentucky. He was first married there on 12 March 1827 to Elizabeth Fletcher, a daughter of John and Elizabeth Fletcher, who was born on 13 August 1807 in Lincoln County, Kentucky. John Austin was listed as a farmer in the 1850 Census of Casey County. Elizabeth died on 18 April 1838, and John married second in Lincoln County on 18 January 1839 to Sarah Fletcher, a younger sister to Elizabeth. Sarah was born on 1 October

1813 in Casey County and died there on 25 April 1876 of a fever. John died 20 July 1884, also in Casey County. John had six children by his first wife and two children by his second wife. The children were born in Casey County:

CHILDREN: J331. WILLIAM GEORGE, *b. 3 March 1830, d. 17 August 1900; a farmer in 1850 Census*

J332. ISAAC BILL, *b. 26 October 1831*

J333. NICODEMUS (NICHOLAS), *b. 13 Dec. 1832*

J334. NAOMI J., *b. 8 May 1834, d. 6 July 1892, m. cousin J343 John William Austin (below)*

J335. SARAH, *b. 5 June 1835*

J336. NATHANIEL JAMES N., *b. 22 April 1837, d. 31 May 1838*

J337. ROSE ANN, *b. 27 August 1839, d. 21 May 1928, m. 25 July 1864 her cousin J349 Jonas W. Austin*

J338. ELIZABETH, *b. 25 Oct. 1841 d. 22 Sept. 1865*

J34. ISAAC B.[3] AUSTIN (*Jonas R.,*[2] *John*[1]) was born 23 November 1810 in Casey County, Kentucky. He was married on 7 August 1829 in Casey County to Nancy Fletcher, who was born on 1 October 1808 in Lincoln County, Kentucky, the daughter of John and Elizabeth Fletcher. Nancy was a sister to Elizabeth and Sarah Fletcher, the wives of J33 John L. Austin. Isaac Austin bought 200 acres of land in Casey County from Thomas and Milley Austin on 23 September 1831. Isaac Austin died on 20 September 1870. Perhaps Nancy was the Nancy J. Austin who married 15 May 1871 to Jacob W. Absher in Casey County.

CHILDREN: J341. MARTHA ANN, *b. 13 July 1830*

J342. MELISSA JANE, *b. 9 July 1831*

J343. JOHN WILLIAM, *b. 23 September 1832*

J344. GEORGE A. C. (E. C.?), *b. 2 October 1834; m. 24 September 1856 to Martha J. Vaught: both were single and age 22, Silus Vaught surety.*

J345. MARY E., *b. 6 December 1835, died before the 1840 Census in Lincoln County*

J346. SARAH CATHERINE, *b. 6 March 1837 Lincoln County, m.(1) 18 August 1857 George W. Jones, m.(2) 10 August 1863 Henry C. Moreland age 21 b. Clay County, Kentucky, a soldier serving in Co. G 1st Kentucky Cavalry.*

J347. LYDIA MARGARET, *b. 25 October 1838, m. 8 August 1854 Michael Ely*

J348. BENJAMIN F., *b. circa 1841, m. 12 October 1859 Miss Nancy E. Carter, with permission of his father Isaac Austin, witnessed by Jonas Austin and Robert W. Staton (probably his uncles, J38 and spouse of J35).*

J349. JONAS W., *b. 1 January 1842, d. 10 June 1919, m. 25 July 1864 his cousin J337 Rose Ann Austin*

J34A. NANCY E., *b. 14 October 1843 Lincoln County, m. 11 August 1863 John Wesley Thompson age 22 b. Fayette County, Kentucky,* a soldier serving in Company F 1st Kentucky Calvary; their son David H. Thompson b.1878

J34B. JAMES C., *b. 7 September 1845*

J34C. JOSEPH W., *b. 7 September 1845*

J34D. RUBEN TAYLOR, *b. 4 October 1847*

J36. ROBERT J.[3] AUSTIN (*Jonas R.,*[2] *John*[1]) was born 23 December 1814 in Casey County, Kentucky. He was married to Ann Frances Evans, born 15 August 1814. Robert and Ann Austin were of Casey County when they sold their interest in the estate of John W. Miller, deceased, to Johnston E. Miller of Casey County on 20 September 1847, and Ann relinquished her right of inheritance to the lands conveyed in the deed. and moved that same year to Albany, Missouri. Robert died 25 February 1871, Ann on 24 December 1871, both are buried in City Cemetery, in the southern part of Albany. Their children in my records are shown here, although it is possible they had more children in Missouri:

CHILDREN: J361. [daughter], *b. 1830-35: was age 5 and under 10 in 1840 Census for Casey Co.*

J362. JOHN H., *b. 18 January 1844*

J363. ROBERT, *b. circa 1865??*

J38. JONAS[3] AUSTIN (*Jonas R.,*[2] *John*[1]) was born 2 January 1819 in Casey County, Kentucky. He was married in Wayne County, Kentucky, on 9 October 1838 to Nancy E. Cooper, daughter of Henry Cooper, born in 1818 in Wayne County. Jonas and Nancy sold land in Wayne County to William A. Cooper on 15 August 1839, with Nancy the daughter and heir of Henry Cooper, deceased. On 26 August 1843 Jonas Austin, Jr., assignee of (J31) Benjamin Austin of Wayne County, bought land on Goose Creek in Russell County, Kentucky, from William Moore of Russell County. Three years later, on 26 October 1846, Jonas bought land on Goose Creek from Benjamin Austin and his wife Ann of Casey County. Jonas and wife Nancy E. Austin of Russell County sold to John Austin of Lincoln County, Kentucky, 1/12th part of five tracts of land located in Casey County on 8 January 1847. Jonas became Justice of the Peace in Russell County 4 October 1849, and he bought land on Goose Creek in that county from Jesse Spencer on 10 October 1849. Jonas and Nancy appear in the 1850 Census for Russell County with their four oldest children, two of whom were apparently twins (see Census on page 129). Jonas bought another six acres on Goose Creek from Elijha Sutherland on 9 November 1854, and 17 acres from the Liberty Academy on 7 May 1868. Jonas made out his Will on 15 June 1867, leaving his 112 acre home tract to infant son William D. Austin. He was listed as the bride's father when Mary wed in 1868, but when Thursday wed in 1869 her mother signed the permission. Nancy married "at Mrs. Austin's" in 1875, so Jonas certainly died before that date. Nancy E. Austin sold land

on Goose Creek to George W. Burton on 5 May 1879. Nancy died before 9 September 1879, on which date the property was appraised at $103.55 by administrator Henry C. Austin.

CHILDREN: J381. MARY PATIENCE, *born circa 1844, m. 3 February 1868 Josiah Cravens age 22, s. of Thomas Shaw Cravens and Zerelda Sweeney. Josiah served in Co. B 13th Kentucky Cavalry, Union Army. Mary is buried in Old Friendship Cemetery, Font Hill, Russell Co., Kentucky.*

J382. ELIZABETH F., *b. circa 1847*

J383. EXONA J., *b. circa 1847*

J384. THERESA J. (THURSEY), *b. circa 1848, m. 9 December 1869 William O. Cooper, son of Thomas J. Cooper*

J385. ELIZA E., *b. circa 1851*

J386. NANCY MONTGOMERY, *b. 16 March 1853 Russell County, Kentucky, m. 29 September 1875 Jeremiah Cravens farmer age 40 (his second marriage), b. Casey Co. son of Ira Russell Cravens and Sarah Shaw, brother to Thomas Shaw Cravens (see J382 Mary above).*

J387. HENRY C., *b. 9 May 1855 Russell County*

J388. WILLIAM D., *b. 12 April 1857 Russell County*

J3B. JOSEPH HARRISON[3] AUSTIN (*Jonas R.,*[2] *John*[1]) was born 21 February 1824 in Casey County, Kentucky. He was married on 13 September 1843 in Wayne County, Kentucky, to Louisa Jane Cooper. Louisa was born on 23 July 1826 in Wayne County, the daughter of Henry Cooper and Elizabeth Patience Back. Joseph lived in Clayton and Wayne Counties, Kentucky, but was a farmer living in Casey County in the 1850 Census. Louisa died in 1873 in Casey County, while Joseph died there in 1883. Their first six children were born in Wayne County.

CHILDREN: J3B1. SERELDA (ELLEN), *b. 1844*

J3B2. ELIZABETH ANN (BETSEY), *b. 1846*

J3B3. HENRY SHELTON, *b. 18 May 1848*

J3B4. JANE STATON, *b. 1850*

J3B5. EMERSON COOPER, *b. 19 August 1852*

J3B6. WILLIAM ROSE, *b. 15 January 1855*

J3B7. QUINTELLA SMITH, *b. 1859*

J3B8. LABAN STEWART, *b. 1860*

J3B9. NANCY PATIENCE, *b. 1863*

J3BA. JAMES JACKSON, *b. 1865*

J3C. SHELTON SMITH[3] AUSTIN (*Jonas R.,*[2] *John*[1]) was born 14 November 1826 in Casey County, Kentucky. He moved in 1847 to Albany, Missouri, with his brother J36 Robert J. Austin. In 1848 he moved to St. Joseph, Missouri, and in the spring of 1849 he went to California. There he engaged in mining until 1854, when he returned to Gentry County, Missouri, where he married on 5 November 1854 to Margaret Elizabeth Hill, the daughter of Harris Hill. Their ten children are recorded in the *History of Gentry County, Missouri.*

CHILDREN: J3C1. MARY ELIZABETH, *m. George Wiley, two children: Berty and Della Wiley*

J3C2. AMANDA JANE

J3C3. MARTHA PRETY, *m. Joseph Ballinger, two children: one died as an infant, and Jesse.*

J3C4. HARRIS SLACK, *m. —; their son Frank Austin m. Nellie McNeese*

J3C5. WILLIAM L.

J3C6. JOHN CALVIN, *m. — Darby, two children: Earl Austin m. Recca Runyon; Jennie Austin*

J3C7. McKINZIE BURTON

J3C8. RHODA ELLEN, *m. John Darby: six children*

J3C9. CORDELIA ANGELINE

J3CA. CORA ANN, *m. Jasper Barber*

J3E. GEORGE WASHINGTON[3] AUSTIN (*Jonas R.,*[2] *John*[1]) was born 23 June 1832 in Russell County, Kentucky. He married first on 1 October 1851 in Lincoln County, Kentucky to Nancy J. Richards, born in Lincoln County. Nancy died 23 April 1854, and George remarried on 27 December 1854 to Catherine Inyart (Inyard?), born 1 February 1823. George was a Civil War soldier, was captured by Confederates at Vicksburg, Mississippi, and sent to prison in Tyler, Texas. He made whiskey in Eubank, Kentucky. George died 1896 in New Salem Road, Lincoln County and is buried in Estes Cemetery (no stone). The first two children were by his first wife:

CHILDREN: J3E1. MARGARET A., *born 7 April 1853 Lincoln County, m. there 29 January 1874 to William J. A. Eason age 24, he and parents b. N. Carolina*

J3E2. NANCY J., *b. 1854 Lincoln County, at age 18 she m. 8 October 1873 William J. Montgomery age 28, he and his parents were born in Lincoln County*

J3E3. HENRY S., *b. 26 March 1856*

J3E4. JOHN R., *b. 29 March 1858, d. 10 September 1879 unmarried age 21y 5m 12d.*

J3E5. ARCHIBALD (BLACK ARCH), *b. 18 April 1860*

J3E6. GEORGE WASHINGTON, *b. 11 May 1862*

J53. SAMUEL WILSON[3] AUSTIN (*John Baden,*[2] *John*[1]) was born 18 November 1818 in Garrard County, Kentucky. He was married three times. He married Nancy Bener. He married the third time on 5 March 1870 to Matilda Swearingen, the daughter of John Swearingen of Crawfordsville. Samuel had five children by his first wife, two children by his second wife. One son Archelaus fought in the Civil War. Samuel died 26 November 1892. See p.215 of the *History of Montgomery County, Indiana,* published in 1881.

FOURTH GENERATION

[CONTINUED ON PAGE 131]

SOME DESCENDANTS OF
CORNELIUS & CATHERINE MORGAN AUSTIN
OF PORTLAND, OREGON

by Arline Austin Richards

Editor's Note: This article concerns the Cornelius found on page 124 of Edith Austin Moore's book *Robert Austin of Kingstown, Rhode Island*.

R123-199. CORNELIUS[7] AUSTIN (*David,*[6] *Gideon,*[5,4] *Pasco,*[3] *Jeremiah,*[2] *Robert*[1]) was born 12 February 1836 in New York state. At seven years of age, Cornelius and his family moved to McHenry County, Illinois. In 1847 his father David Austin drowned when the steamship *Phoenix* caught fire in Lake Michigan off Waukegon, Illinois. Cornelius sailed to Portland in 1859 via the Gulf of Mexico and the Isthmus of Panama, where he contracted a fever which left him hard of hearing for the rest of his life.

Cornelius' older brother, Russell Downing Austin, had arrived in Portland by ox train in 1852. During the Civil War the brothers edited the *Oregon Weekly Times* in Portland. Later they sold this newspaper to another, the *Oregonian*, which is still in print. On page 123 is reproduced an election ticket which was set up by Cornelius for the re-election of Abraham Lincoln in 1864.

Cornelius Austin was married in Portland on 16 May 1864 to Catherine Epha Morgan. Catherine, called "Effie," was the daughter of Rawley Morgan and Eliza Sayre, and was born on 11 January 1843 in Iowa. Her mother died in 1852 just before the family was ready to leave for Oregon, and her father and brother died of cholera on the Platte River that same year. Effie also came down with cholera on the way west, and was never very strong. For a time Cornelius owned and operated a drug store in Portland, and he was an agent for the Wells Fargo Company's "Pony Express" over an Indian trail, now the Columbia Highway. In later years he and his son Edmund built many large outstanding houses in Portland.

Catherine died 2 May 1892 in Portland, and Cornelius moved to Neharts for several years, and later to McMinnville and vicinity. He died 22 March 1924 in the Salem hospital, and is buried in the Lone Fir Cemetery, Portland, with his wife and his mother Olcha Downing Austin. He was survived by three sisters: Mrs. Angela Rose Canfield and Mrs. Harriet Adelia Spafford, of McMinnville, and Mrs. Helen Adelaide Hutchinson of Ouray, Colorado.

CHILDREN:
R123-1991. ANDREW MELLISON, *b. 7 March 1865*
R123-1992. EDMUND A., *b. 17 January 1868*
R123-1993. DAISY, *b. 18 July 1871, m. 14 October 1891 — Miller*
R123-1994. RUBY, *b. 11 December 1876, m. 14 December 1897 — Newman*

Cornelius Austin 1836-1924

Catherine Morgan Austin 1843-1892

SECOND GENERATION

R123-1991. ANDREW MELLISON[8] AUSTIN (*Cornelius,*[7] *David,*[6] *Gideon,*[5,4] *Pasco,*[3] *Jeremiah,*[2] *Robert*[1]) was born on 7 March 1865 in Portland, Oregon. He was married first to Ida Morgan, a second cousin. They moved in 1889 to Netarts, Oregon, a very small settlement about ten miles west of Tillamook. Their property overlooked Netarts Bay and the Pacific Ocean, which were divided by a sand spit. In 1892 when Andrew's mother Effie died, his father Cornelius told him to come and get anything that he wanted from his home, which Cornelius planned to sell. Andrew took his sailboat to Portland and brought many things back to his home on Netarts Bay. Cornelius got a timber claim, and it was not far from Andrew's, so he built a small cabin on Andrew's place and at times he would be there.

Soon after Effie died, Ida died leaving Andrew with a tiny girl. Andrew married second in Tillamook, Oregon on 9 December 1900 to Lillie Augusta Wells, a tiny sprightly little woman. Lillie, the daughter of Nathaniel Augustine and Amanda Ellen (Cook) Wells, was born 16 February 1876 in Ocquakah, Henderson County, Illinois. She came to Oregon as a small child with her parents in a covered wagon train, and her family lived for a while in La Grande before moving to Tillamook County. The family's first home on the Trask River utilized a hollow cedar tree as a kitchen and starting point for the building. As a child, Lillie attended the Trask river school, and later she worked at the famous Trask House.

When his sons were ready for school, my father Andrew moved the family to Tillamook, where he served for many years as county engineer and surveyor. My mother was an active member of the First Methodist Church, and for her many faithful years of service she was given a life membership in the Women's Society of Christian Service. She was also a member of the Pioneer Association, the Daughters of the American Revolution, and the Women's Christian Temperance Union.

We went to Netarts to spend the summers. I loved summers at our place on Netarts Bay. Effie's things I really enjoyed. I would go upstairs and watch ocean-going ships with binoculars, and they would usually be in a group of three. My father told me they were freighters. Before moving to Tillamook, my father raised small cocktail oysters, leasing the beds in Neharts Bay from the government. He imported the seed from Japan, the type of oyster that likes to fasten to objects. Soon he had oysters, but people would come and gather them, claiming that the bay was public property. When Prohibition came my father had to discontinue operating his successful saloon. He and my brothers liked to go to Netarts to fish and hunt during the winter months, and they would often discover that someone had stayed in our house, eaten our food, once

Andrew & Lillie Austin's Wedding Picture

even mixing the salt and sugar together before they left! The last time I was there about the only thing left was a very large dining table.

Roads there were very bad, made from big planks of wood. We had a steep hill and would walk up and down the other side, my brothers walking behind the wagon, carrying big rocks, so that the wagon could not roll backwards. Sometimes they would drive part way and take a boat the rest of the way. We had to ford a stream called "Whiskey Creek," so named when a road boss dumped his workmen's still into the stream one night. There is now a very good State highway along the coast there, and a State Park.

My father Andrew Mellison Austin died on 24 October 1937 in Tillamook, and my mother Lillie also died there, on 21 March 1958.

CHILDREN:	R123-1991-1. ELVA, *born 29 September 1891 Netarts, Oregon; d. 1968 unmarried*

R123-1991-2. BRUCE MELLISON, *b. 3 Dec. 1901*

R123-1991-3. ANDREW MILES, *b. 6 January 1904*

R123-1991-4. IRMA, *b. 20 February 1906*

R123-1991-5. ARLINE, *b. 18 February 1909*

R123-1991-6. HALLIE, *b. 3 August 1912*

R123-1992. EDMUND A.[8] AUSTIN (*Cornelius,*[7] *David,*[6] *Gideon,*[5,4] *Pasco,*[3] *Jeremiah,*[2] *Robert*[1]) was born 17 January 1868 in Portland, Oregon. He was married in

---

Photographs on page 121: Arline, Irma, Miles, Bruce and Lillie Austin at our place on Neharts Bay where we spent the summers when I was small, and portraits of Bruce, Miles, and Irma. Top photograph on page 122: Elva, Bruce, and Miles Austin; bottom photograph: Irma, Arline, and Hallie Austin.

Portland on 15 October 1889 to Virginia A. Wood, born on 23 January 1867 in Portland. Edmund died on 17 January 1916 in Portland. Their children were born in Portland:

CHILDREN:
R123-1992-1. GRACE, *b. 1890*
R123-1992-2. CHARLES S., *b. 1892*
R123-1992-3. RUTH A., *b. 1897*
R123-1992-4. MELVIN, *b. 1899*
R123-1992-5. MARIE, *b. 1899*
R123-1992-6. EDMUND, *b. 1901*
R123-1992-7. FRANK, *b. 1904*
R123-1992-8. ZELLA, *b. 1907*
R123-1992-9. IVAN, *b. 1911*
R123-1992-A. HELEN, *b. 1911*

THIRD GENERATION

R123-1991-2. BRUCE MELLISON⁹ AUSTIN (*Andrew Mellison,*⁸ *Cornelius,*⁷ *David,*⁶ *Gideon,*⁵,⁴ *Pasco,*³ *Jeremiah,*² *Robert¹*) was born 3 December 1901 in Tillamook, Ore. He was married to Jewell Ola Hensley, who was born on 7 December 1910 and died 19 April 1973 in Klamath Falls, Oregon. Bruce died 5 November 1981 in Klamath Falls. Their children were from Jewell's former marriage: JUNE HENSLEY, RALPH HENSLEY.

R123-1991-3. ANDREW MILES⁹ AUSTIN (*Andrew Mellison,*⁸ *Cornelius,*⁷ *David,*⁶ *Gideon,*⁵,⁴ *Pasco,*³ *Jeremiah,*² *Robert¹*) was born 6 January 1904 in Tillamook, Oregon. He was married to Esther Easton, who was born on 4 September 1904 and died 16 April 1973. Andrew is now living in Forest Grove, Oregon. Their children were from Esther's earlier marriage: RICHARD EASTON, DAVID EASTON.

R123-1991-4. IRMA⁹ AUSTIN (*Andrew Mellison,*⁸ *Cornelius,*⁷ *David,*⁶ *Gideon,*⁵,⁴ *Pasco,*³ *Jeremiah,*² *Robert¹*) was born 20 February 1906 in Netarts, Oregon, and she died in 1974. She was married to Hubert Mathews. Their son Eric was a medic in Korea, and was killed by a land mine explosion while he was attending to some wounded men. MATHEWS CHILDREN: ERIC LIONEL 1926, PHYLLIS 1929.

R123-1991-5. ARLINE⁹ AUSTIN (*Andrew Mellison,*⁸ *Cornelius,*⁷ *David,*⁶ *Gideon,*⁵,⁴ *Pasco,*³ *Jeremiah,*² *Robert¹*) was born 18 February 1909 in Tillamook, Oregon. She was married in Ontario, Oregon, on 17 March 1934 to Noah O. Richards, and she moved to Ontario at that time. Noah, the son of Robert O. and Abbie Coulson Richards, was born on 26 July 1907 in Blaine, Oregon. He was very active in Shrine work until he died 7 July 1971 in Ontario. Arline moved in 1977 to Carlsbad, California. RICHARDS CHILDREN (adopted): ROBERT AUSTIN 1945, CAROL ARLINE 1945.

R123-1991-6. HALLIE⁹ AUSTIN (*Andrew Mellison,*⁸ *Cornelius,*⁷ *David,*⁶ *Gideon,*⁵,⁴ *Pasco,*³ *Jeremiah,*² *Robert¹*) was born on 3 August 1912, and died in 1962 in Tillamook. She was married in Tillamook, Oregon to Samuel Hubbard. HUBBARD CHILD: SALLIE JANE.

Irma Austin Mathews with her children Eric & Phyllis

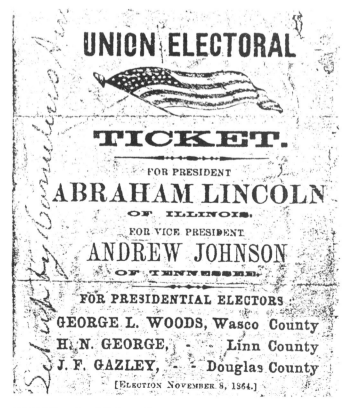

1864 Election Ticket Composed by Cornelius Austin

AUSTINS FOUND IN THE
POINSETT COUNTY, ARKANSAS
MARRIAGE REGISTERS 1876-1948

by Janet Austin Curtis

Editor's Note: The following records were transcribed by Associate Editor Janet A. Curtis at the County Court House in Harrisburg, Arkansas. A former Secretary and present Genealogist of the Austin Families Association, Mrs. Curtis has devoted many years to helping researchers discover their Austin family roots.

Bk.1 p.42 Samuel C. Astin age 40 and Mary Calerman m. 4 March 1876.

Bk.1 p.252 James W. Astin age 23 and Florence E. Hawkins age 16 m. 3 January 1883.

Bk.1 p.271 Samuel H. Astin age 24 m. to Dora Hawkins age 19 on 5? February 1884.

Bk.1 p.225 Mollie Astin age 25 m. to W. H. Adkins age 19 on 19 February 1881.

Bk.3 p.308 J. W. Aston age 41 and E. C. Molder age 22 m. 13 January 1901 by J. P. Jones, J.P.

Bk.4 (Bk.D) p.167 S. L. Astin age 26 and Nora Moulder age 18 m. 30 December 1903 by J. H. Harrison, J.P.

Bk.4 (Bk.D) p.472 Samuel Aston age 19 and Emma Bradsher age 19 m. 11 November 1906 by J. H. Hall, J.P.

Bk.E p.4 J. C. Aston age 22 & Annie Hill age 19 m. 23 December 1906 by J. C. Hall, J.P.

Bk.E p.5 Earl Aston age 28 and R. Bell age 18 m. 22 December 1906 by D. H. Hall, J.P.

Bk.E p.81 J. E. Aston age 20 and Jeanette Williams age 18 m. 18 August 1907 by J. D. Hall, J.P.

Bk.E p.158 Thos. Aston age 20 and Fannie Moulder age 18 m. 9 February 1908 by T. R. Shepherd.

Bk.F p.552 S. L. Aston age 27 and Emma Whitlock age 18 m. 10 February 1914 by J. D. Hall, J.P.

Bk.G p.532 Col. Jas. Austin of Marked Tree age 28 and Ella Wilson age 19 m. 28 February 1917 by Henry Nalley.

Bk.H p.215 Sam Aston age 31 and Mary Davis m. 2 June 1918 by Ollie Clampet, J.P.

Bk.I p.85 Charlie Austin age 20 and Mariah Griffin age 19 m. 21 December 1919 by Rev. W. M. Bonner

Bk.I p.209 Lincoln Austin age 28 and Mattie Lowe age 20 m. 8 May 1920 by C. M. Carter

Bk.I p.610 Walter Auston age 40 and Alice White age 40, both of Tyronza, m. 18 September 1921 by Wm. Jackson.

Bk.I p.611 Clarence E. Astin age 22 and Alma L. Hodges age 18, both of White Hall, m. 25 September 1921 by S. W. McKurney.

Bk.I p.198 Nettie Austin age 19 and Cad Garner age 19 m. 24 April 1920 by C. M. Carter.

Bk.I p.71 Easter Austin age 18 and Henry Sanders age 18 m. 17 January 1920 by J. A. Norton, J.P.

Bk.J p.137 George Austin of Marked Tree age 22 and Maybelle Harrison age 27 m. 24 January 1922 by Henry Nolley, J.P.

Bk.K - no Austins

Bk.L p.359 Phillip Austin age 28 and Rosa Hobbs age 28, both of Lepanto, m. 24 October 1925 by Henry Nolley, J.P.

Bk.N p.417 Murray Ausdon of Lepanto age 24 and Tommie Ashley age 18 m. 4 November 1928 by W. G. Thurman.

Bk.N p.304 Aetabe Aston age 17 and Odis Smith age 21 m. 19 August 1928 by W. M. Brecheen.

Bk.O p.310 Arthur Austin age 23 and Allie George age 22, both of Tyronza, m. 9 November 1929 by W. O. Parish.

Bk.O p.557 Bedford Austin age 22 and Alta White age 21, both of Tyronza, m. 29 March 1930 by E. E. Tatum.

Bk.O p.582 Gertrude Aston age 18 and Robt. Enderson age 21 m. 27 April 1930 by James H. Johnson.

Bk.O p.198 Bethel Austin of Whitten age 15 and Hundley Kelly of Tyronza age 22 m. 1 September 1929 by Don Holman.

Bk.O p.335 Johnnie Austin age 17 and Samuel Miles age 27, both of Tyronza, m. 24 November 1929 by Rev. L. Armstrong.

Bk.P - no Austins or Astins

Bk.Q p.191 Ollie Aston age 29 and Eunice Angle age 20, both of Harrisburg, m. 16 April 1932 by E. W. Huskey.

Bk.Q p.567 Herman Aston age 25 and Beatrice Finley, both of Bay Village, m. 22 February 1933 by S. A. Clements, J.P.

Bk.Q p.386 Hattie Austin age 19 and Herman Dawson age 20, both of Marked Tree, m. 15 October 1932 by C. P. Wigginton, J.P.

Bk.Q p.34 Mary Lou Austan age 18 and Elevie Henlay age 21 m. 12 December 1931 by C. E. Gray.

Bk.Q p.600 Etnea Aston of Bay Village age 18 and Ralph Hodges of Cherry Valley age 21 m. 12 April 1932 by Willie Harlan.

Bk.Q p.171 Lillie Austin age 19 and Clarence Sisk, both of Frys Mill, m. 28 March 1932 by E. E. Braskears.

Bk.Q p.439 Frances 'Fannie' Austin age 20 and Marion Steele age 21, both of Harrisburg, m. 5 November 1932 by J. E. DuBois.

Bk.R p.38 Theron Austin age 20 and Mammie Watkins age 18, both of Trumann, m. 3 July 1933 by C. H. Bumpers.

Bk.R p.145 Ruben Austin age 22 and Attie Begard age 18, both of Tyronza, m. 7 October 1933 by W. W. Woberton.

Bk.R p.337 Clifford Austin age 23 and Jewel Cannon b.1916 age 18, both of Tyronza, m. 21 January 1934 by Rev. Guy D. Magee.

Bk.R p.219 Nannie (Minnie?) Bell Austin of Deckerville age 25 and Pinkney Murray age 27 m. 13 November 1933 by S. G. Wilson.

Bk.S p.274 Edgar Austin age 31 and Dehlia Smith b.1916 age 19, both of Marked Tree, m. 27 April 1935 by Rev. Guy D. Magee.

Bk.S p.459 Irma Austin age 18 and Chas. Barnes age 21, both of Tyronza, m. 17 April 1935 by James Nelson.

Bk.T p.575 Almer Austin (female) of Harrisburg age 18 and R. L. Smith (male) m. 27 February 1937 by Rev. T. E. Ellzey.

Bk.U p.400 Ottie Auston age 21 and Beatrice Phillips age 18, both of Tyronza, m. 17 December 1937 by J. C. McCroy, J.P.

Bk.U p.111 Louise Austin of Tyronza age 19 and Thurman Combs age 18 m. 12 June 1937 by W. O. Parish, J.P.

Bk.U p.380 Altabe Aston of Harrisburg age 26 and Willie F. Davis age 27 m. 6 December 1937 by L. G. Minton, J.P.

Bk.U p.557 Docia Mae Austin age 18 and Wm. T. Dunn age 24, both of Cherry Valley, m. 4 April 1938 by J. O. Gilbert.

Bk.V p.110 Roy Aston age 16 and Mabel Williams age 14, both of Harrisburg, m. 7 September 1938 by Herman Jacobs, J.P.

Bk.V p.180 Herbert Austin age 20 and Lidle Roberts age 17, both of Bald Knob, m. 30 September 1938 by C. C. Wallace, J.P.

Bk.V p.345 Thos. Lee Austin age 24 and Cleo Edwards age 18, both of Lepanto, m. 14 January 1939 by W. C. Nowlin, J.P.

Bk.V p.367 Louis Austin of Cherry Valley age 29 and Mrs. Ruey Meredith of Harrisburg age 24 m. 18 February 1939 by Claud Haste, J.P.

Bk.V p.388 Leon Austin age 21 and Elsie Boyer age 19, both of Rivervale, m. 15 March 1939 by W. M. Wolverton.

Bk.V p.161 Gladys Austin of Harrisburg age 16 and Ira Leo Eads age 16 m. 24 September 1938 by Herman Jacobs.

Bk.V p.215 Marie Acton Austin age 18 and A. W. Hudenall age 55, both of Tyronza m. 21 October 1938 by J. C. McCroy, J.P.

Bk.W p.20 Emmie Austin age 18 and Thurman Evans age 26, both of Harris burg, m. 14 September 1939 by Rev. J. J. Decker, M. E. Church.

Bk.W p.356 Edith Aston age 16 and Orvil Thomas age 19, both of Harrisburg, m. 18 May 1940 by Herman Jacobs.

Bk.X p.549 Harry Lewis Aston age 23 and Winetta Robertson 19, both of Marked Tree, m. 30 January 1941 by J. C. McCroy, J.P.

Bk.X p.555 Charlie Aston age 21 and Louise Goodman age 18, both of Harrisburg, m. 6 September 1941 by Herman Jacobs, J.P.

Bk.X p.447 Lorine Austin age 21 and Opie Baker age 21, both of Trumann, m. 18 September 1941 by Geo. E. Patchell.

Bk.X p.130 Inez Austin of Harrisburg age 18 and Berley Sefers age 25 m. 28 December 1940 by Herman Jacobs, J.P.

Bk.Y p.572 Herschell Austin age 22 and Lusynthia Horton age 16, both of Tyronza, m. 23 September 1942 by N. J. Hazel, J.P.

Bk.Y p.571 Reeder C. Austin age 28 and Lillie Roberts Gann age 20, both of Tyronza, m. 23 September 1942 by N. J. Hazel, J.P.

Bk.Y p.632 Winston Aston age 26 and Juanita Highland age 18, both of Marked Tree, m. 13 October 1942 by N. J. Hazel, J.P.

Bk.Y p.127 Helen Austin of Walnut Ridge age 22 and Wilford Withem of Marked Tree age 21 m. 5 January 1941 by Herman Jacobs, J.P.

Bk.Z p.428 Columbus Austin age 20 and Hazel L. Decker age 18, both of Harrisburg, m. 14 June 1943 by R. W. Minton, J.P.

Bk.Z p.480 Mary Lee Austin of Judd Hill age 31 and Col. Howard Logan age 38 m. 19 July 1943 by Herman Jacobs, J.P.

Bk.1A p.70 Barney Austin age 19 and Christine Davis age 18, both of Harrisburg, m. 26 December 1943 by Herman Jacobs, J.P.

Bk.1A p.130 Ray Aston of Harrisburg age 21 and Garnett Qualls age 20 of Trumann m. 3 February 1944 by Herman Jacobs, J.P.

Bk.1A p.157 Arthur L. Austin of Harrisburg age 24 and Dorothy Jean Mitchusson of Trumann age 19 m. 26 February 1944 by Herman Jacobs, J.P.

Bk.1A p.195 Lee Austin age 21 and Leila Deloach age 19, both of Cherry Valley, m. 17 March 1944 by R. P. Doss, J.P.

Bk.1A p.561 Ruby Gene Austin of Blytheville age 18 and James D. Honeyput age 21 m. 10 September 1944 by E. M. Perry, J.P.

Bk.1B p.107 Dalton Willard Austin age 20 of Savannah, Tennessee, and Anie Gene Highland age 17 of Tyronza m. 19 November 1944 by J. J. Ensor, J.P.

Bk.1B p.308 Era Aston age 21 and Earline Whittingham age 18, both of Harrisburg, m. 3 February 1945 by Herman Jacobs, J.P.

Bk.1B p.503 Grundy Austin age 23 and Elnorra Gruff age 36 m. 28 June 1945 by Aaron C. Milton.

Bk.1B p.563 Glen Edbert Austin of Rivervale age 20 and Edith Pauline Smith of Monette age 21 m. 27 August 1945 by W. C. Nowlin, J.P.

Bk.1B p.330 Adell Austin age 25 and Sgt. Curtis Wade age 31, both of New Albany, Mississippi, m. 19 March 1945 by Rev. J. S. Onerman in Marion, Arkansas.

Bk.2B p.569 Verna Mae Austin age 29 and Ray Huskey of Rivervale age 40 m. 27 May 1946 by W. C. Nowlin, J.P.

Bk.3B p.102 Albert O. Austin age 26 and Bobbie Kate Gibbs age 19, both of Tyronza, m. 3 August 1946 by J. E. Hudgins, J.P.

Bk.3B p.443 George Earl Austin age 21 and Mary Lois Rodgers age 18, both of Heafer, m. 19 November 1946.

Bk.3B p.617 Grundy Austin of Tyronza age 24 and Annie Milton of Marked Tree age 26 m. 18 January 1947 by Rev. Lee Davis

Bk.3B p.556 Willie Joe Austin of Lepanto age 28 and Oliver Mangrum age 33 m. 21 December 1946 by W. C. Nowlin, J.P.

Bk.1C p.511 Wintford C. Austin age 21 and Helen Ruth Bennett age 18, both of Marked Tree, m. 12 March 1948 by Herman Jacobs.

Bk.1C p.536 Lee Austin age 21 and Katherine Merideth age 18, both of Cherry Valley, m. 30 March 1948 by S. V. Blake, J.P.

Bk.1C p.591 Pierce Austin age 39 and Maudie Kellett age 25, both of Marked Tree, m. 8 May 1948 by N. J. Hazel, J.P.

Next Book: 1D.

QUERIES

125-1. Hannah Austin b. 16 March 1782 (bible record), poss. in ME or NH. She m. Trustrum Hurd, b. 4 July 1779 (bible record) at Alton, NH. Trustrum was the son of Trustrum Heard, a Revolutioner. The elder Trustrum moved ca. 1796 to what is now Harmony, ME and the younger Trustrum followed shortly thereafter. He m. Hannah Austin in that area, although poss. they m. in Eddington, Maine, on the Penobscot River. They moved ca. 1824 to what is now Burlington, ME being the first settlers there. According to early store account books of Burlington-Lowell (dated 1828-1832), there also were Stephen Austin, John Austin, and James Austin (b. 19 September 1790 in New Hampshire, d. 13 May 1850 at Eddington, m. Sarah Bradley 31 May 1818) mentioned in the store account books, who might be brothers to Hannah. Seek data on the ancestry of Hannah and the other Austins.

125-2. Benjamin Austin was born 1765-68 in Pembroke, New Hampshire. His wife Ann McConnell was born 9 February 1765 in Pembroke, died 2 December 1849. Need Benjamin's death information and Ann's deathplace.

125-3. Richard Austin of Bishopstoke, England, and Charlestown, Massachusetts, arrived on the ship *Bevis* in 1638. He is the subject of a book published by Mrs. Edith Austin Moore in 1969. Has anyone been researching his ancestry? Does anyone know his parents?

125-4. Eliza Ann Austin married Benjamin D. Swett on 1 October 1842 in Farmington, Maine, and she died on 12 January 1895 in Beatrice, Nebraska. I believe her to be the daughter of Zadoc and Elizabeth (—) Austin, born 5 January 1825 in Salem, Maine. Need proof of Eliza's birthdate and information on her parents and ancestry.

Austins in the Federal Census of 1850

Kentucky

by Anthony Kent Austin

Name	County	Age	b.ca.	Sex	Bpl.	Pg.	Hse.	Fam.
Dory	Allen	25	1825	m	TN	174	1034	1044
Jane	"	20	1830	f	"	"	"	"
M. E.	"	4	1846	f	"	"	"	"
E. F.	"	1/12	1850	f	"	"	"	"
G.	Allen	61	1789	m	NC	127	379	387
E.	"	58	1792	f	KY	"	"	"
C.	"	22	1828	m	"	"	"	"
C.	"	17	1833	f	"	"	"	"
J. C.	"	13	1837	m	"	"	"	"
William	Allen	30	1820	m	KY	127	380	388
C.	"	25	1825	f	TN	"	"	"
W.	"	8	1842	m	KY	"	"	"
D.	"	6	1844	m	"	"	"	"
H.	"	4	1846	m	"	"	"	"
D. A.	"	1	1849	f	"	"	"	"
Williamson	Allen	43	1807	m	KY	128	395	403
Martha	"	39	1811	f	"	"	"	"
W. T.	"	14	1836	m	"	"	"	"
N. A.	"	12	1838	f	"	"	"	"
T. W.	"	9	1841	m	"	"	"	"
M. E.	"	6	1844	f	"	"	"	"
J. P.	"	3	1847	m	"	"	"	"
Willis	Allen	46	1804	m	TN	137	535	543
E. A.	"	42	1808	f	KY	"	"	"
M. E.	"	16	1834	f	"	"	"	"
W. M.	"	14	1836	m	"	"	"	"
W. R.	"	12	1838	m	"	"	"	"
J. B.	"	9	1841	m	"	"	"	"
N. J.	"	6	1844	f	"	"	"	"
W.	Ballard	11	1839	m	KY	259	116	116
R.	Ballard	19	1831	m	KY	265	201	201
L.	"	16	1834	f	"	"	"	"
M.	Ballard	45	1805	f	KY	269	265	265
R.	"	23	1827	m	"	"	"	"
W.	"	23	1827	m	"	"	"	"
M.	"	18	1832	f	"	"	"	"
I. J.	"	14	1836	f	"	"	"	"
S. E.	"	11	1839	f	"	"	"	"
J.	"	8	1842	f	"	"	"	"
F.	"	7	1843	f	"	"	"	"
C.	"	4	1846	f	"	"	"	"
M.	"	6/12	1850	f	"	"	"	"
Nancy	Ballard	20	1830	f	TN	273	321	321
Thomas	Ballard	9	1841	m	KY	280	413	413
Charles	Barren	53	1797	m	NC	380	1083	1108
Levisa	"	50	1800	f	KY	"	"	"
William F.	"	20	1830	m	"	"	"	"
Sarah J.	"	17	1833	f	"	"	"	"
Martha B.	"	14	1836	f	"	"	"	"
Adoline F.	"	10	1840	f	"	"	"	"
Charles H.	"	8	1842	m	"	"	"	"
Helen B.	"	5	1845	f	"	"	"	"
William H.	Bath	35	1815	m	KY	015	203	203
Mary	"	33	1817	f	"	"	"	"
Thomas	"	10	1840	m	"	"	"	"
Mary	"	7	1843	f	"	"	"	"
Martha	"	4	1846	f	"	"	"	"
Ashley	"	2	1848	m	"	"	"	"
Arch	Bourbon	36	1814	m	KY	291	367	374
China A.	"	20	1830	f	"	"	"	"
Mary	"	1	1849	f	"	"	"	"
Louisa	"	1/12	1850	f	"	"	"	"
William	Bourbon	30	1820	m	KY	254	431	431
Thomas	"	23	1827	m	"	"	"	"
Thomas	Breckenridge	16	1834	m	NY	095	008	009
John M.	Butler	46	1804	m	MD	252	532	532
Addison	"	20	1830	m	KY	"	"	"
Amanda	"	18	1832	f	"	"	"	"
Rosaline	"	14	1836	f	"	"	"	"
Foster	"	11	1839	m	"	"	"	"
Nancy	Butler	60	1790	f	Unk	269	755	755
Samuel	Butler	48	1802	m	MD	274	837	837
Nancy	"	37	1813	f	KY	"	"	"
Richard	"	17	1833	m	KY	"	"	"
Henrietta	"	12	1838	f	"	"	"	"
William	"	9	1841	m	"	"	"	"
Joseph	"	7	1843	m	"	"	"	"
Samuel	"	4	1846	m	"	"	"	"
Zirelda	"	3	1847	f	"	"	"	"
John	"	1	1849	m	"	"	"	"
B.	Calloway	55	1795	m	VA	458	175	175
M.	"	54	1796	f	NC	"	"	"
S. P.	"	17	1833	f	"	"	"	"
N. .	"	16	1834	f	KY	"	"	"
R. G.	"	11	1839	m	"	"	"	"
John	Casey	42	1808	m	KY	296	124	124
Sally	"	36	1814	f	"	"	"	"
William G.	"	20	1830	m	"	"	"	"
Isaac	"	18	1832	m	"	"	"	"
Peamy	"	17	1833	f	"	"	"	"
Nichodemus	"	16	1834	m	"	"	"	"
Sally	"	15	1835	f	"	"	"	"
Rose Ann	"	11	1839	f	"	"	"	"
Elizabeth	"	10	1840	f	"	"	"	"
Jonas H.	Casey	26	1824	m	KY	296	127	127
Louisa	"	24	1826	f	"	"	"	"
Elen	"	6	1844	f	"	"	"	"
Elizabeth	"	5	1845	f	"	"	"	"
Henry C.	"	2	1848	m	"	"	"	"
Ben	Casey	45	1805	m	KY	356	430	430
Ann	"	45	1805	f	"	"	"	"
Mary F.	"	13	1837	f	"	"	"	"
Elizabeth P.	"	8	1842	f	"	"	"	"
Theresa E.	"	6	1844	f	"	"	"	"
John B.	"	3	1847	m	"	"	"	"
S.	Cumberland	16	1834	f	KY	283	086	086
F. J.	Cumberland	18	1832	f	KY	287	127	127
Richard	Cumberland	28	1822	m	KY	339	857	857
R.	"	29	1821	f	"	"	"	"
P.	"	7	1843	m	"	"	"	"
S.	"	5	1845	f	"	"	"	"
R.	"	3	1847	f	"	"	"	"
S. F.	"	1	1849	m	"	"	"	"

Name	County	Age	Year	Sex	State			
James M.	Daviess	28	1822	m	KY	433	195	197
Eliza	"	21	1829	f	"	"	"	"
George H.	Daviess	10	1840	m	KY	433	197	199
Mary	Daviess	57	1793	f	VA	435	234	236
William H.	"	24	1826	m	KY	"	"	"
Martha	"	21	1829	f	"	"	"	"
Lucy	"	16	1834	f	"	"	"	"
Francis M.	"	13	1837	m	"	"	"	"
Lycidias	"	12	1838	m	"	"	"	"
R. P.	Fayette	25	1825	m	KY	115	020	022
Lucinda	"	21	1829	f	"	"	"	"
Mary A.	"	3	1847	f	"	"	"	"
William	Fayette	32	1818	m	MD	115	025	027
Mintha I.	"	30	1820	f	KY	"	"	"
Rosea Ann	"	12	1838	f	"	"	"	"
Mary M.	"	11	1839	f	"	"	"	"
Leonidas B.	"	8	1842	m	"	"	"	"
Francis O.	"	6	1844	f	"	"	"	"
Sidney E.	"	4	1846	m	"	"	"	"
Davidella	"	2	1848	f	"	"	"	"
Robert	Fayette	57	1793	bm	VA	137	357	362
Rosana	"	55	1795	bf	"	"	"	"
Ellen	"	13	1837	bf	"	"	"	"
Sasshia	"	75	1775	bf	"	"	"	"
Polly	Garrard	23	1827	f	KY	269	029	030
Arteminda	"	20	1830	f	"	"	"	"
Samuel	"	17	1833	m	"	"	"	"
Samuel	Garrard	50	1800	m	KY	271	052	053
Sylvia	"	37	1813	f	"	"	"	"
Louisa	"	11	1839	f	"	"	"	"
Thomas	"	9	1841	m	"	"	"	"
Aaron	"	8	1842	m	"	"	"	"
Marian	"	3	1847	f	"	"	"	"
James W.	"	11/12	1849	m	"	"	"	"
Jane	Garrard	75	1775	f	SC	271	053	054
Almira	"	14	1836	f	KY	"	"	"
Elizabeth J.	"	5	1845	f	"	"	"	"
Elizabeth	Garrard	52	1798	f	GA	272	077	079
Ann	Garrard	33	1817	f	KY	272	083	085
Mitchel	"	10	1840	m	"	"	"	"
Mary J.	"	8	1842	f	"	"	"	"
Sylvia	"	7	1843	f	"	"	"	"
Prudence	Garrard	50	1800	f	KY	211	106	106
George	"	22	1828	m	"	"	"	"
Will	Garrard	21	1829	m	KY	274	107	112
Walter	Garrard	40	1810	m	KY	216	178	180
Martha Jane	"	29	1821	f	"	"	"	"
Arthusa	"	11	1839	f	"	"	"	"
Thomas T.	"	9	1841	m	"	"	"	"
Mary	"	6	1844	f	"	"	"	"
Martha J.	"	4	1846	f	"	"	"	"
Samuel	"	1	1849	m	"	"	"	"
Thomas	Garrard	21	1829	m	KY	280	195	211
Mitchel	Garrard	38	1812	m	KY	280	197	213
Elizabeth	"	5	1845	f	"	"	"	"
James	Garrard	30	1820	m	KY	241	591	628
Elenor	"	24	1826	f	"	"	"	"
William	Garrard	27	1823	m	KY	245	672	709
Joan	"	20	1830	f	"	"	"	"
John	"	25	1825	m	"	"	"	"
Ambrose	Graves	48	1802	m	KY	366	043	043
Mary	"	42	1808	f	"	"	"	"
Francis R.	"	22	1828	m	"	"	"	"
Martha	"	17	1833	f	"	"	"	"
R. L.	"	15	1835	m	"	"	"	"
Paulina	"	12	1838	f	"	"	"	"
Margaret	"	10	1840	f	"	"	"	"
James	"	7	1843	m	"	"	"	"
John	"	5	1845	m	"	"	"	"
Frances	"	4	1846	f	"	"	"	"
Ann	"	1	1849	f	"	"	"	"
Phillip	Graves	52	1798	m	NC	370	089	089
Sally	"	41	1809	f	TN	"	"	"
Susan	"	20	1830	f	"	"	"	"
James	"	14	1836	m	KY	"	"	"
William	"	13	1837	m	"	"	"	"
Charles	"	11	1839	m	"	"	"	"
D. C.	"	10	1840	f	"	"	"	"
Elizabeth	"	8	1842	f	"	"	"	"
Lucian	"	6	1844	m	"	"	"	"
Sally T.	"	6	1844	f	"	"	"	"
Harriet	"	5	1845	f	"	"	"	"
Martha E.	"	4	1846	f	"	"	"	"
Philip	"	3	1847	m	"	"	"	"
Thomas	"	1	1849	m	"	"	"	"
Nicholas	Graves	21	1829	m	TN	370	091	091
Mary	"	21	1829	f	"	"	"	"
D. P.	"	1	1849	m	KY	"	"	"
James	"	2/12	1850	m	"	"	"	"
Mary	Graves	19	1831	f	TN	373	123	123
Jeremiah	Hardin	65	1785	m	MD	340	507	507
Elizabeth	"	60	1790	f	KY	"	"	"
Elizabeth	"	25	1825	f	"	"	"	"
Zarayda	"	20	1830	f	"	"	"	"
Alexander	"	18	1832	m	"	"	"	"
Louisa	"	5	1845	f	"	"	"	"
Minerva J.	"	3	1847	f	"	"	"	"
John H.	"	1	1849	m	"	"	"	"
Elizabeth	Hardin	38	1812	f	KY	340	508	508
Bayless F.	"	12	1838	m	"	"	"	"
Mary J.	"	10	1840	f	"	"	"	"
Sarah E.	"	7	1843	f	"	"	"	"
William E.	"	1	1849	m	"	"	"	"
Andrew J.	Harrison	24	1826	m	KY	057	091	091
Henry	Harrison	40	1810	m	VA	067	246	246
Louisa	"	40	1810	f	KY	"	"	"
Henry	"	5	1845	m	"	"	"	"
James	"	3	1847	m	"	"	"	"
Mary	"	2/12	1850	f	"	"	"	"
Presley	Jefferson	35	1815	m	VA	450	1023	1158
Candace	"	26	1824	f	IN	"	"	"
Oscar	"	5/12	1850	m	KY	"	"	"
Ann	Jefferson	70	1780	f	VA	450	1024	1159
Grafton	"	29	1821	m	KY	"	"	"
Fred	Jefferson	43	1807	m	Ger	126	1503	2066
Caroline	"	33	1817	f	"	"	"	"
William	Jefferson	65	1785	m	VA	276	532	606
John	Jefferson	40	1810	m	NY	428	680	777
Elizabeth	"	36	1814	f	"	"	"	"
Mary	"	18	1832	f	OH	"	"	"
John	"	11	1839	m	KY	"	"	"
Louisa	"	8	1842	f	"	"	"	"
Theresa	"	6	1844	f	MO	"	"	"
James	"	4	1846	m	KY	"	"	"
Elizabeth	Jefferson	44	1806	f	TN	435	781	887
Mary	Lawrence	50	1800	f	VA	103	707	713
Thomas	"	24	1826	m	KY	"	"	"
Francis	"	20	1830	m	"	"	"	"
John	"	18	1832	m	OH	"	"	"
Virginia	"	17	1833	f	VA	"	"	"

Name	County	Age	Year	Sex	State			
Elizabeth	"	15	1835	f	OH	"	"	"
A. L.	Lincoln	38	1812	m	KY	256	210	210
Elizabeth	"	36	1814	f	"	"	"	"
W. C.	"	11	1839	-	"	"	"	"
Abner	"	9	1841	m	"	"	"	"
Pamelia	"	7	1843	f	"	"	"	"
May	"	6	1844	f	"	"	"	"
James	"	5	1845	m	"	"	"	"
Samuel	"	4	1846	m	"	"	"	"
Matilda	"	6/12	1850	f	"	"	"	"
George	Lincoln	18	1832	m	KY	256	214	214
Isaac	Lincoln	20	1830	m	VA	258	233	233
Isaac	Lincoln	38	1812	m	KY	273	460	460
Nancy	"	41	1809	f	"	"	"	"
Jno.	"	17	1833	m	"	"	"	"
A. C.	"	15	1835	m	"	"	"	"
Sarah	"	13	1837	f	"			
Margaret	"	11	1839	f	"	"	"	"
Benj	"	8	1842	m	"	"	"	"
James	"	7	1843	m	"	"	"	"
Nancy	"	6	1844	f	"	"	"	"
Rubin	"	2	1848	m	"	"	"	"
James	Lincoln	32	1818	m	KY	274	486	486
Mary	"	30	1820	f	"	"	"	"
A. F.	"	9	1841	m	"	275	"	"
M. C.	Marshall	29	1821	m	SC	449	271	271
Sarah	"	18	1832	f	KY	"	"	"
James H.	"	9/12	1849	m	"	"	"	"
Edwin	Marshall	32	1818	m	TN	466	487	487
Lucinda J.	"	30	1820	f	"	"	"	"
Mary L.	"	5	1845	f	KY	"	"	"
Elener T.	"	2	1848	f	"	"	"	"
Charles C.	Marshall	37	1813	m	VA	469	534	535
Nancy	"	35	1815	f	KY	"	"	"
Sarah F.	"	8	1842	f	"	"	"	"
Martha L.	"	7	1843	f	"	"	"	"
William S.	"	6	1844	m	"	"	"	"
Ann E. O.	"	2	1848	f	"	"	"	"
Mahallen	"	4/12	1850	f	"	"	"	"
Margaret	Marshall	38	1812	f	KY	469	535	536
Martha A. E.	"	12	1838	f	"	"	"	"
Luisa D. J.	"	10	1840	f	"	"	"	"
Jacob	"	8	1842	m	"	"	"	"
William H.	"	6	1844	m	"	"	"	"
James C.	"	4	1846	m	"	"	"	"
Williams	Marshall	53	1797	m	SC	481	693	695
Eliza	"	47	1803	f	KY	"	"	"
Calvin	"	22	1828	m	"	"	"	"
Fountain P.	Mason	19	1831	m	TN	047	215	236
Nicholas	Mason	8	1842	m	OH	097	582	582
James P.	Mason	23	1827	m	TN	108	731	731
Nancy	"	24	1826	f	Ire	"	"	"
George W.	McCracken	38	1812	m	TN	181	282	283
Nancy	"	37	1813	f	VA	"	"	"
Lucinda	"	18	1832	f	TN	"	"	"
Sarah Ann	"	16	1834	f	"	"	"	"
Eliza J.	"	14	1836	f	"	"	"	"
Ewen	"	12	1838	m	"	182	"	"
Elizabeth	"	10	1840	f	"	"	"	"
Susanna C.	"	8	1842	f	"	"	"	"
George T.	"	6	1844	m	"	"	"	"
John B.	"	3	1847	m	"	"	"	"
Nancy C.	"	6/12	1850	f	KY	"	"	"
Thomas O.	Ohio	43	1807	m	MD	003	038	038
Amelia	"	39	1811	f	KY	"	"	"
Elizabeth M.	"	19	1831	f	"	"	"	"
Amelia H.	"	17	1833	f	"	"	"	"
John S.	"	15	1835	m	"	"	"	"
Dorcas C.	"	12	1838	f	"	"	"	"
William A.	"	10	1840	m	"	"	"	"
Sally M.	"	7	1843	f	"	"	"	"
Amelia C.	"	6	1844	f	"	"	"	"
Ann C.	"	2	1848	f	"	"	"	"
Alinisia	"	4/12	1850	f	"	"	"	"
Robert	Ohio	45	1805	m	MD	003	040	040
Mary	"	40	1810	f	KY	"	"	"
John R.	"	19	1831	m	"	"	"	"
Joshua L.	"	16	1834	m	"	"	"	"
Margaret	"	14	1836	f	"	"	"	"
William N.	"	12	1838	m	"	004	"	"
Jonas P.	"	10	1840	m	"	"	"	"
Charlotte	"	7	1843	f	"	"	"	"
Mary	"	5	1845	f	"	"	"	"
Thomas	"	3	1847	m	"	"	"	"
Jonas	Ohio	49	1801	m	VA	062	154	154
William	Ohio	36	1814	m	MD	012	158	158
Sarah	"	30	1820	f	KY	"	"	"
Susan	"	13	1837	f	"	"	"	"
Harrison	"	11	1839	m	"	"	"	"
John	"	9	1841	m	"	"	"	"
Hannibal	"	6	1844	m	"	"	"	"
Margaret	"	4	1846	f	"	"	"	"
Catherine	"	1	1849	f	"	"	"	"
John	Ohio	80	1770	m	MD	012	164	164
Anna	"	56	1794	f	"	"	"	"
George W.	"	27	1823	m	KY	"	"	"
Amanda	"	22	1828	f	"	"	"	"
Melissa	"	5	1845	f	"	"	"	"
Richard	"	3	1847	m	"	"	"	"
Sarah	"	2	1848	f	"	"	"	"
Marcella	"	1	1849	f	"	"	"	"
Zachariah	Ohio	52	1798	m	MD	013	177	177
William	"	24	1826	m	KY	"	"	"
Andrew	Ohio	34	1816	m	KY	017	243	243
Dorothea	"	28	1822	f	"	"	"	"
James	"	7	1843	m	"	"	"	"
Lucy	"	5	1845	f	"	"	"	"
Matilda	"	3	1847	f	"	"	"	"
Henry	Ohio	32	1818	m	KY	018	246	246
Marilda	"	23	1827	f	"	"	"	"
Baruch	Ohio	58	1792	m	MD	018	250	250
Mary	"	50	1800	f	KY	"	"	"
Elizabeth	"	23	1827	f	"	"	"	"
Sarah	"	17	1833	f	"	"	"	"
John	"	14	1836	m	"	"	"	"
Quintin	"	13	1837	m	"	"	"	"
Joshua	"	11	1839	m	"	"	"	"
James	Ohio	32	1818	m	KY	018	251	251
Corinna	"	23	1827	f	"	"	"	"
Sarah	"	6	1844	f	"	"	"	"
Josephine	"	6/12	1850	f	"	"	"	"
Zachariah	Ohio	29	1821	m	KY	026	377	377
Nancy	"	22	1828	f	"	"	"	"
Sally	"	2	1848	f	"	"	"	"
Brooks	Ohio	56	1794	m	MD	033	471	471
Rachel	"	54	1796	f	"	"	"	"
Horace	"	27	1823	m	KY	"	"	"
Samuel	"	20	1830	m	"	"	"	"
Janetta	"	18	1832	f	"	"	"	"
Enoch	"	16	1834	m	"	"	"	"

Name	Place	Age	Year	Sex	State			
Mary	"	14	1836	f	"	"	"	"
John	"	11	1839	m	"	"	"	"
Urias	Ohio	35	1815	m	MD	034	474	474
Minerva	"	34	1816	f	KY	"	"	"
Richard	"	9	1841	m	"	"	"	"
Daniel	"	8	1842	m	"	"	"	"
William	"	6	1844	m	"	"	"	"
James	"	4	1846	m	"	"	"	"
David	"	1	1849	m	"	"	"	"
William	Ohio	54	1796	m	MD	048	677	677
Henrietta	"	45	1805	f	VA	"	"	"
Henry	"	23	1827	m	KY	"	"	"
Emerilla	"	16	1834	f	"	"	"	"
Mary	"	12	1838	f	"	"	"	"
James	Oldham	60	1790	m	VA	156	457	469
Elizabeth	"	50	1800	f	KY	"	"	"
Jno. L.	"	25	1825	m	"	"	"	"
Daniel	"	23	1827	m	"	"	"	"
Frances	"	23	1827	f	"	"	"	"
Martha	"	18	1832	f	"	"	"	"
Daniel	Oldham	53	1797	m	KY	160	508	520
Eliza	"	37	1813	f	"	"	"	"
Alice	"	9/12	1849	f	"	"	"	"
Robert	Pike	38	1812	m	NC	456	325	325
Aly	"	23	1827	-	"	"	"	"
Lydia	"	11	1839	f	"	"	"	"
Nancy J.	"	9	1841	f	"	"	"	"
Prudence	"	7	1843	f	VA	"	"	"
Mary	"	6	1844	f	KY	"	"	"
Margaret	"	1	1849	f	"	"	"	"
Samuel W.	Pike	26	1824	m	NC	457	341	341
Christina	"	19	1831	f	VA	"	"	"
Nancy S.	"	3	1847	f	"	"	"	"
Jonas	Russell	32	1818	m	KY	218	093	093
Nancy E.	"	33	1817	f	"	"	"	"
Mary P.	"	6	1844	f	"	"	"	"
Elizabeth F.	"	3	1847	f	"	"	"	"
Exona J.	"	3	1847	f	"	"	"	"
Theresa J.	"	2	1848	f	"	"	"	"
Elizabeth	Simpson	62	1788	f	Unk	002	025	025
David P.	Trigg	27	1823	m	TN	377	745	745
Frances	"	17	1833	f	KY	"	"	"
Mary E.	"	11/12	1849	f	"	"	"	"
William	Trimble	23	1827	m	KY	395	242	242
Lanson	Trimble	40	1810	m	NY	397	278	278
Mary	"	30	1820	f	KY	398	"	"
Daniel	"	2	1848	m	"	"	"	"
Martha	"	3/12	1850	f	"	"	"	"
Saull C.	Union	45	1805	m	KY	449	143	143
Jefferson	"	40	1810	m	"	"	"	"
William T.	"	13	1837	m	"	"	"	"
Thomas	Union	39	1811	m	KY	496	500	500
M. A.	"	38	1812	f	"	"	"	"
J. B.	"	12	1838	m	"	"	"	"
M. E.	"	11	1839	f	"	"	"	"
V. J.	"	9	1841	f	"	"	"	"
Francis	"	8	1842	m	"	"	"	"
Margaret	"	7	1843	f	"	"	"	"
Thomas	"	4	1846	m	"	"	"	"
Jno.	"	3	1847	m	"	"	"	"
Ben	"	1	1849	m	"	"	"	"
Catherine	Union	53	1797	f	KY	499	538	538
Sarah	"	43	1807	f	"	"	"	"
J. E.	Union	20	1830	m	DE	513	751	751

QUERIES

129-1. **Paul Austin** received an English Crown grant in St. George Parish, SC, adjoining property of Davis Austin and his brother Drury (Drewry) Austin, who were granted their land on 5 July 1768. They were sons of Bartholemew and Elizabeth Austin, but Paul is not listed among Bartholemew's children. Need Paul Austin's ancestry.

129-2. **Hannah Austin** m. John King b.1764 Hampton, NH, son of James King b.1727 England & 2nd wife Delia Harriman. John & Hannah had seven children: John 1790, Polly 1791, Sally 1793, Betsey 1795, James 1796, Ebredge 1798, Guy 1800. Need Hannah's ancestry.

129-3. **Thomas Austin** m. Mary Sims in Tenterden, England, on 5 July 1793. Need data on their ancestry.

129-4. **Mary Austin** had her intention of marriage entered at Walpole, MA, on 28 July 1754. Her prospective husband, Abraham Burrell, was b. 1 April 1729, possibly in Lynn, Massachusetts. He died on 18 November 1798 at Sheffield, Massachusetts. Need proof of Abraham's birth.

129-5. **Samuel Austin** born 11 July 1703, possibly at Charlestown, MA, died 8 October 1792. He m. Mary (Bayley?), they had a daughter Mary Austin b. Walpole, MA in 1734. Need Samuel and Mary's ancestry.

129-6. **Stephen Austin** b. circa 1755 in Pittsylvania Co., VA, moved circa 1757 to Grayson Co., VA. He enlisted in Revolutionary War Army from Surry Co. NC, circa 1766, serving five years. After the war he returned to Grayson County, resided there about twenty years. He moved to Wayne Co., Tennessee, where he lived for about twelve years. He next lived several years in Alabama, and d. there in Hardin Co. in 1850. Is Stephen the father of Rebecca Austin, b. circa 1796 in Virginia who m. James Gray in either Wayne Co. or Lincoln Co., Tennessee?

129-7. **Phenix Austin** m. in 1783 at Sheffield, MA, to John Collins, b. 1730 in Enfield, CT. They settled at Burlington, VT, had nine children: Annis [White], Elijah, Hulda [Tubbs], Nathaniel, Surrene, Lucy [Stevens], Asa, Henry, Phenix. Seek information on their descendants.

129-8. **Seth Austin** m. 26 April 1770 in Salisbury, CT, to Hannah Smith b. 19 June 1753. Hannah d. 19 February 1848 in Tunbridge, VT. Who were Hannah's parents?

129-9. **Lester Moss Austin** born 14 February 1867 in Lynden, IL, m. 1894 in Logan Co., OK to Nannie Frances McClelland, b. 1878 Marion, Indiana. Lester d. 31 July 1945 at Corona, Riverside County CA. Need his parents.

129-10. **Mary Johnson Austin** b. 1820 in OH or MI, dau. of William & Deborah Austin. She m. 1850 in WI Stephen Wiseman, b. 1820, son of James Wiseman & Mary Ann Legge. Seek all available data on William & Deborah.

JOHN AND MARTHA AUSTIN
OF MISSISSIPPI AND
MOBILE COUNTY, ALABAMA

by Linda Thomas

John Austin was born in 1820 in New York state, possibly he died in Mobile, Alabama. He married Martha (—) born 1827 in Mississippi. I do not know when John and Martha died, but they are not found in census records after 1860. In the 1870 Census Eliza is shown living alone in what is now Bayou La Batre and Alabama Port, Alabama.

CHILDREN: J1. JOHN BAPTISTE, *born 10 February 1846 in Mississippi, d. 20 February 1900 in Biloxi, MS; buried Oddfellows Cemetery.*

J2. CHARLES, *b. 1849 in Mobile County, Alabama*

J3. ELIZA, *b. 1854 in Mobile County, Alabama*

J4. MARTHA A., *b. 1860 Mobile County, Alabama*

Their eldest son John married Ida Catherine Green, born in Barnwell County, South Carolina. They married on 26 January 1874 in the Catholic Church, but they got a marriage license on 15 May 1873. Perhaps they were first married by a J.P. and later decided to have their marriage blessed by the Church. Their children were all born on Dauphin Island, Mobile County, Alabama.

CHILDREN: J11. THERESA GENEVIEVE (LUCY), *b. 23 December 1873, d. 23 March 1900 in Biloxi; m. Elias Rhodes on 20 April 1891.*

J12. MARY, *b. 30 January 1875, d. 5 August 1878 buried Oddfellows Cemetery*

J13. ESTELLE (STELLA), *b. 1878, m. 18 Oct. 1892 in Biloxi to Walter M. Moore, removed to NY.*

J14. NORA CELESTE, *b. 19 July 1881, d. 15 April 1945 Biloxi, buried Biloxi Cemetery in White family plot; m. 24 November 1897 in Mobile, Alabama to Olliphant Todd Musslewhite (they sometimes shortened the name to M.White)*

J15. CATHERINE (CARRIE), *b. 30 October 1883, m. N. E. Skinner in Biloxi on 27 November 1901.*

J16. AGNES, *b. 10 February 1886, m. Percy Winchester in Biloxi on 25 January 1905. They lived in New Orleans, LA.*

J17. ANNA (ANNIE), *b. 28 February 1888, d. 15 September 1955 Biloxi, buried Old Biloxi Cemetery; m. Spurgeon 'Tom' Borden in Biloxi on 14 May 1905.*

J18. MANUEL ELIAS (MATT), *b. 27 July 1891, d. 12 October 1960; m. Julia Helena Elder in Biloxi on 26 January 1905, removed to Fort Worth, TX.*

J19. LAURA, *b. 15 March 1896, d. in Biloxi; m. Salvadorre Navarro on 20 June 1914.*

My great grandmother Nora (Austin) and Olliphant T. Musslewhite lived in Bayou La Batre until 1904, when they moved all of their possessions and family to Biloxi,

Mississippi, on a flat-bottom boat. There they opened a grocery store and cabinet-making shop on Pine Street. In 1910 they opened the Specialty Cabinet Shop, which later became the White Hardware store. They were among the first families to see the importance of the tourist trade on the Gulf Coast, and built summer cottages and apartment houses to accomodate tourists. I would like to correspond with others researching this John Austin line.

REFERENCES

Mobile County, Alabama, Census 1860; Daily Herald newspaper; Headstones in Oddfellows Cemetery, Biloxi, Mississippi; Dauphin Island Family Records; Mobile County Census 1880; Mobile Catholic Missions Books for Bayou La Batre & Dauphin Island.

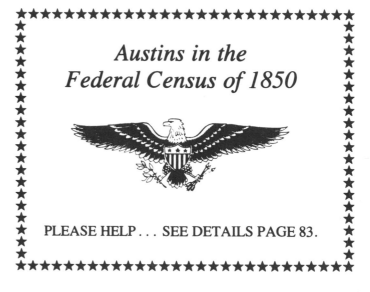

Austins in the Federal Census of 1850

PLEASE HELP . . . SEE DETAILS PAGE 83.

QUERIES

130-1. **Catherine Austin**, daughter of Homer and Seana Austin, was born 23 April 1829 and died 18 March 1897 (gravestone). Death cert. has b. Elyria, Ohio, aet 66y 10m 25d. Her son Ambrose Dutcher's death cert. has Mother's birthplace as Holland. Son David Morris Dutcher II said his grandparents came from Holland and his grandfather was a peddler. Need correct birth data on Catherine, and anything on her parents.

130-2. **William Austin**, son of Homer & Seana Austin, had a son Morris whose wife and four children died of scarlet fever. Morris remarried to Hattie Kilborn, b. 5 May 1873 d. 4 December 1942 Harwinton, Connecticut. Need birth data on William and Morris Austin, and name of William's wife (possibly Jewell).

130-3. **Alonzo Austin**, son of Homer & Seana Austin, had a daughter Alta who married — Cook, had a daughter Lois who possibly lived in Winsted, Connecticut ca. 1922. Need any and all data on these people.

THE DESCENDANTS OF
JOHN AUSTIN AND ANN BADEN
OF ALBEMARLE COUNTY, VIRGINIA
by Bert Addis Austin

[CONTINUED FROM PAGE 118]

CORRECTION TO THIRD GENERATION

J36. ROBERT J.[3] AUSTIN (*Jonas R.,*[2] *John*[1]) was born 23 December 1814 in Casey County, Kentucky. He was married to Ann Frances Evans, born 15 August 1814. Robert and Ann Austin were of Casey County when they sold their interest in the estate of John W. Miller, deceased, to Johnston E. Miller of Casey County on 20 September 1847, and Ann relinquished her right of inheritance to the lands conveyed in the deed. They apparently moved that same year to Albany, Missouri. In the November 1850 U.S. Census for Gentry County, Missouri, Robert J. Austin was a farmer with 250 acres. Both he and Ann Frances Austin were listed in 1850 as 36 years old, in the 1860 Census as 45 years old, and in the 1870 Census as 55 years old. Robert died 25 February 1871, Ann on 24 December 1871, both are buried in City Cemetery, in southern Albany. *THE FOLLOWING LISTING OF CHILDREN POSSIBLY CONTAINS ERRORS (see note below):*

CHILDREN: J361. [daughter], *b. 1830-35: was age 5 and under 10 in 1840 Census for Casey Co.*

J362. MARY J., *b. circa 1838 (12 in 1850)*

J363. JANE, *b. circa 1839*

J364. BETSY A., *b. circa 1840 (10 in 1850)*

J365. JOHN HENRY, *b. 18 January 1844 (6 in 1850)*

J366. SARAH F., *b. circa 1846 (4 in 1850)*

J367. ELLEN, *b. circa 1849 (1 in 1850)*

J368. NANCY, *b. circa 1851*

J369. ALMIRA, *b. circa 1854*

J36A. HESTER, *b. circa 1856*

J36B. ROBERT J., JR., *b. circa 1859*

Editor's Note: The preceding is a revision of the J36 Robert J. Austin family appearing on page 117. John W. Austin, a grandson of J365 John Henry Austin, wrote on 17 August 1976 that he had combined the 1850, 1860 and 1870 Census Reports for Gentry County, to determine the list of children shown above. Among other inconsistencies, however, Jane does not appear in the 1850 Census, so this family may still be inaccurate. Any corrections and additions would be most appreciated both by the author of this article and for our *Austins of America* files.

FOURTH GENERATION

J332. ISAAC BILL[4] AUSTIN (*John L.,*[3] *Jonas R.,*[2] *John*[1]) was born 26 October 1831 in Casey County, Kentucky. In the 1850 Census for that county Isaac was listed as a farmer and was living with his parents. He was married to Lucinda W. Thomas, born on 30 December 1833 in Casey County. If her gravestone was correct and accurately copied, Lucinda died 23 November 1879. There must have been an error, however, and Lucinda's deathyear was more likely 1877, for Issac remarried on 24 January 1878 to Nancy Jane Fox, and their first child was born in December 1878. Nancy was born 26 June 1856. Isaac, sometimes called "Ike," died on 13 February 1900 and is buried in the woods on the farm of J332-34 Forrest A. Austin in Dunnville, Casey County. According to Forrest and his sister Mossie in November 1971, buried with Isaac are his first wife Lucinda W. Austin, their daughter Isabella, their son Marcus and his daughter Dellie, the latter two without stones. Nancy died 18 August 1922, and is buried in Thomastown Cemetery in Dunnville. The first eight children were by Lucinda, the last four by Nancy:

J332-1. ISABELLA, *born 7 February 1858, died 4 October 1876 (gravestone) unmarried; Casey County Vital Statistics has "Isabetta" Austin died 20 December 1875 in Casey County age 18, born in Casey County, cause of death unknown, her parents Isaac and Lucy Austin were both born in Kentucky.*

J332-2. WILLIAM M., *b. 29 February 1860*

J332-3. GEORGE A., *b. 31 March 1863*

J332-4. MARCUS HENRY ("BARK"), *b. circa 1864*

J332-5. ELNORA S., *b. circa 1866, m. 16 June 1883 Squire W. McDonald*

J332-6. MATILDA E. ("MATTIE/MITTIE"), *b. 14 November 1869, d. 15 July 1966 as a widow "age 96" in Monmouth, Illinois; m. 31 August 1893 Andrew J. Brown, they resided in Dunnville, Kentucky. She was survived by three sons, a daughter, and several grandchildren.*

J332-7. ARCHIBALD WILLIS ("WILSE"), *b. 25 August 1870*

J332-8. JESSIE, *born circa 1874?, died young*

J332-9. JOHN FRANK, *born 26 December 1878 in Casey Co.*

J332-A. PATSY ISABELLA AUSTIN, *b. 18 January 1880 Casey County, m. 1905 Adam Marshall Thomas; children: Kirby, Odie Laforest, Iva Jo, J. C., and Hattie. "Addie" died in 1956, while Patsy died 24 November 1972 "age 93" in Danville, Kentucky, buried Thomastown Cemetery. She was survived by 25 grandchildren, 44 great grandchildren and 4 great-great grandchildren.*

J332-B. MARY MARTHA ("MOLLY"), *b. 1 May 1882 in Casey County*

J332-C. RHODA, *b. circa 1895?, m. 25 August 1907 to*

Welby Lay, at home of bride in presence of Al DeHart and James Lay.

J332-D. ADAM B. ("ADD"), *b. 13 January 1890 in Dunnville, m. 10 October 1912 to Minnie Breeding, in presence of George Austin and W. Thomas; Add Austin was in W.W.1, inducted 26 August 1918, Service No. 3905380.*

J333. NICODEMUS (NICHOLAS)[4] AUSTIN (*John L.,*[3] *Jonas R.,*[2] *John*[1]) was born 13 December 1832 in Casey County, Kentucky. He was married to Nancy Jane Staton, possibly in Lebanon, Marion County, Kentucky. The Lebanon Court House burned once during the Civil War and again later, and nearly all its records were destroyed. Nancy, the daughter of Reuben and Jane Staton, was born 11 September 1843 in Casey County. Nicholas Austin and his brother-in-law Joshua L. Bradshaw (husband of J335 Sarah Austin - see their photographs on page 132) owned a blacksmith shop in Lincoln County, Kentucky, before the Civil War. Nicholas joined as a Private in Company I, the 8th Kentucky Volunteer Cavalry, Union Army, while Joshua became a Confederate soldier. They never spoke to each other again. Nicholas served from 28 July 1862 to 17 September 1863. He was injured in the war, his hip and shoulder were displaced, his address was Mt. Salem. Nancy died on 18 January 1891 in Lincoln County, and was buried with her only daughter Sciota at the edge of Mt. Salem, Lincoln County, in a cemetery that can no longer be found.

When I visited the cemetery in 1971 the stones were piled in the center of a cow pasture. These stones were gone on my second visit in 1977. The church that this cemetery belonged to was moved many years ago, on wagon wheels, to another site about two miles away. It is now known as the New Salem Baptist Church. William Clarence (Bud) Austin helped to move this church. Kenneth Austin was the Church Secretary in 1979. According to his Pension Record 623711 in the National Archives, Washington D.C., Nicholas died on 19 April 1899 in Lincoln County, and is buried there in the McKinney Cemetery. The children of Nicholas and Nancy were born in Lincoln County, Kentucky:

CHILDREN: J333-1. ARCHIBALD B. (RED ARCH) *born 31 August 1861*

J333-2. GEORGE JEFFERSON, *b. 16 July 1864*

J333-3. WILLIAM CLARENCE, *b. 20 February 1866*

J333-4. SIDNEY CLARENCE, *b. 20 February 1866*

J333-5. SCIOTA, *b. 19 Nov. 1870, d. 9 July 1881*

J335. SARAH[4] AUSTIN (*John L.,*[3] *Jonas R.,*[2] *John*[1]) was born 5 June 1835 in Casey County. She was married in Casey County on 28 December 1856 to Joshua L. Bradshaw. Sarah died 27 February 1901. They had eleven

**Sarah Austin Bradshaw 1835-1901
and her husband Joshua L. Bradshaw**

daughters but no sons; Joshua and Sarah's brother Nicholas owned a blacksmith shop before the Civil War; Joshua served as a Confederate soldier (see the write-up on J333 Nicholas Austin). Their daughter Sarah married her first cousin, J333-2 George Jefferson Austin. Some of the BRADSHAW CHILDREN: ROSE ANN 1857, MARY ELIZABETH 1858, MARTHA E. 1860, BELLE 1863, SARAH C. 1869

J343. JOHN WILLIAM[4] AUSTIN (*Isaac,*[3] *Jonas R.,*[2] *John*[1]) was born 23 September 1832 in Casey County, Kentucky. He was married in Casey County on 23 December 1852 to his first cousin, J334 Naomi J. Austin, the daughter of John L. Austin and Elizabeth Fletcher, born 8 May 1832 in Casey County. Their farm lay on both sides of Rife Creek road and was part of the land left by Jonas R. Austin. The land on the east side of the road was sold by John's heirs, while John Laban Austin kept the part on the west side with the homestead. John enrolled 8 September 1863, and mustered as a Private in Company I, 13th Regiment of Kentucky Volunteer Cavalry, Union Army, on 23 December 1863. He died on 14 June 1864 in Casey County of measles contracted in the Service. His address was listed as Dunnville, Kentucky, and he is buried next to his home in Rife Creek. Naomi filed for a pension as John's widow on 23 July 1864, and again on 30 April 1867, pension application #85677 on file in the General Services Administration, and she gives the birthdates and ages of each of her children in those applications. While the dates differ slightly in the two applications, the second set of dates agrees with family bible records and are the dates shown below. Naomi died 6 July 1892 in Casey County. The children were born in Casey County:

J343-1. MARY ELIZABETH, *b. 27 March 1854, m. 11 December 1873 John W. Jones*

J343-2. NANCY JANE, *b. 4 January 1856, m.1 James Huston Vaught, m.2 his brother Isaac Newton Vaught; no issue from first marriage; James and Isaac were children of Silas Vaught and Melissa J. Austin. Melissa's ancestry is unknown at this time.*

J343-3. JOHN LABAN W., *b. 25 January 1858*

J343-4. ROSE ANN ("JOSIE"), *b. 21 September 1860, m. Logan Green Vaught (brother to James and Isaac), resided in 1896 in Pulaski County, Kentucky*

J343-5. SALLY DOUGLAS, *b. 1 February 1862, m. 26 March 1895 at John Austin's to George W. Hatfield, his 2nd marriage. All his children were by first wife. George was of the Eastern Kentucky Hatfields who fought the McCoys.*

J34A. NANCY ELLEN[4] AUSTIN (*Isaac B.,*[3] *Jonas R.,*[2] *John*[1]) was born 14 October 1843 in Lincoln County, Kentucky. She was married in Lincoln County on 11 August 1863 to John Wesley Thompson, the son of Thomas Thompson (b. Clark County, Kentucky) and Sarah Ann Kent (b. Fayette County, Kentucky). John was born 28 August 1841 in Fayette County. He was a Private in Company F, 1st Kentucky Volunteer First Cavalry, formed in Casey County, and mustered in at Camp Dick, Robinson, Kentucky, 28 October 1861. John Thompson died 30 March 1923 in Parksville, Boyle County, Kentucky, and is buried in Wilson Cemetery in Parksville. Nancy died circa 1883 or 1884 in Casey County, Kentucky. The THOMPSON CHILDREN: JOHN WILLIAM 1865, SARAH MARGARET 1866, REUBEN TAYLOR 1868, JONAS BEADEN 1869, ROSEY JANE 1871, AMBERS RASH 1872, BENJAMIN BOYD 1873, JAMES M. 1875, DAVID HAYS 1878, ROSEY LEE 1879, JEREMIAH 1880, GEORGE WASHINGTON 1883.

J365. JOHN H.[4] AUSTIN (*Robert J.,*[3] *Jonas R.,*[2] *John*[1]) was born 18 January 1844. He was married on 24 November 1867 to Hila Ireland, who was born on 25 February 1842. John died on 25 March 1912, and is buried in Lone Star, Missouri, with Hila who died on 22 January 1919.

J365-1. MYRTLE ANN, *b. 19 November 1870, d. 15 May 1966, m. 22 March 1896 John William Arnold b. 4 September 1868, d. 29 June 1947; their children: William Elvis b.1897, Elsie Myrtle b.1899. Myrtle and John are buried in Lone Star.*

J365-2. LILLIE FRANCIS, *b. 27 August 1874, d. 10 August 1930, m. Logan Campbell b. 29 July 1875, d. 18 April 1962; one son Orville b.1897; all are buried in Lone Star.*

J365-3. ROBERT THOMAS, *b. 20 May 1878*

J36B. ROBERT J. JR.[4] AUSTIN (*Robert J.,*[3] *Jonas R.,*[2] *John*[1]) was born circa 1859 in Albany, Missouri. He was married to Leona Stapleton. The following information is from a 4 September 1973 letter from J365-31 John Wesley Austin, a grand-nephew of Robert. Before he and Leona retired to California, Robert worked in the old Pension Bureau for the Federal Government in Washington. He spent his spare time collecting information on the Austin family. Robert talked with John quite a bit about his research when John went to Washington to work in 1927, for his own four boys were not interested in it:

J36B-1. BURL, *d. in infancy*

J36B-2. EDWIN, *had a son and a daughter, d. "several years ago in Dallas, Texas."*

J36B-3. GEORGE, *"I think he went to California"*

J36B-4. SHERWOOD, *"I think he went to California"*

J386. NANCY MONTGOMERY[4] AUSTIN (*Jonas,*[3] *Jonas R.,*[2] *John*[1]) was born 16 March 1853 in Russell County, Kentucky. She was married "at Mrs. Austin's" in Russell County on 29 September 1875 to Jeremiah Cravens of Casey County. Jeremiah was a farmer, born circa 1835 in Casey County. CRAVENS CHILDREN AND AGES IN 1880 CASEY COUNTY CENSUS: SARAH S. 19, THOMAS 17, POLLY J. 15, JOHN I. 13, NANCY C. 10, ROSETTA 8, HENRY 4, PINIA 2, [daughter] 6/12.

J387. HENRY C.[4] AUSTIN (*Jonas,*[3] *Jonas R.,*[2] *John*[1]) was born 9 May 1855 in Russell County, Kentucky. He was married in Russell County to Sarah Ellen Holt, who was born on 26 October 1859 in Russell County. Henry died 6 November 1881 and is buried in Faubush Cemetery, east of Russell Springs on Highway 80, Russell County. Sometime after Fred's marriage, Sarah remarried to — Cooper. She died 16 September 1955 and is buried with Henry in Faubush Cemetery, along with their children and their spouses. Children:

J387-1. FRED H. AUSTIN, *b. 17 February 1879 Russell County, d. 18 September 1919. He m. 18 November 1895 at age 16 at Sarah E. Austin's home to C. E. Cooper age 13 b. Pulaski County, Kentucky, daughter of W. C. & Mary A. Cooper who were both b. Pulaski County. Sharing Fred H. Austin's cemetery headstone there is an Ella Austin Roy, b. 12 October 1882 d. 25 July 1965, whose birthyear is the same as that of C. E. Cooper. We believe that C. E. Cooper was C. "Ella" Cooper and that after Fred's death "Ella" Austin married to — Roy.*

J387-2. HENRY C., *b. 16 April 1882, d. 10 October 1934, m. M. D. (—) b. 3 July 1885, d. 31 January 1937; their daughter Lillie M. b. 25 November 1914, d. 10 April 1918*

J3B3. HENRY SHELTON[4] AUSTIN (*Joseph Harrison,*[3] *Jonas R.,*[2] *John*[1]) was born on 18 May 1848 in Casey County, Kentucky. He was married on 1 June 1880 to Sylvia A. Jones, who was born on 5 August 1858 in Michigan, the daughter of Benjamin Jones and Eveline Cooper. Henry came home after the war to find everything gone, including the house roof. This was a sight he could not stand up to, so one day he saddled his horse and told the family that was left that he was going west. The younger brother, Emerson Cooper Austin, began to cry to go with him, so the family consented and took up a collection to give them eating money. They left, never to see their family again. They went to St. Louis, Missouri, where they worked to get more eating money. They left Missouri and went to Kansas, when Wichita was composed of just one lone cottonwood tree. They rode the range from the Mexican border to the shipping points at Kansas City and Newton, Kansas. They sometimes lived on raw buffalo meat. At night one stood watch to give alarm in case of Indians. Emerson stayed with cattle, and finally settled in Cross Plains, Texas, and raised a large family. He was a Methodist Preacher. Henry stayed in Kansas, helping settle the country, raising a family and helping to build the Santa Fe railroad from Newton, Kansas on west. He settled in what became Sylvia, Kansas, named after Henry's wife. (Editor's Note: For further details on Henry Shelton Austin see article in the February 1986 issue of *Austins of America*.) Henry died on 18 July 1935 in Oklahoma City, while Sylvia died in 1942. Both are buried in Memorial Park Cemetery, Oklahoma City, Oklahoma. Their children were born in Sylvia, Kansas:

J3B3-1. LOUISA EVELINE, *b. 11 January 1882, d. 19 August 1969; m. 23 May 1901 to Walter W. Wells. Both Louisa and Walter were Doctors of Medicine. They had two children who died as infants.*

J3B3-2. WALTER HENRY, *b. 1 May 1884, d. 23 August 1958 in Phoenix, Arizona; m. June 1920 to Myrtle Willis.*

J3B3-3. GRACE ELIZABETH *b. 9 Aug. 1886 m. 1 June 1920 Joseph Kinch, res. 1972 Oklahoma City*

J3B3-4. GEORGE BENJAMIN, *b. 4 January 1889*

J3B5. EMERSON COOPER[4] AUSTIN (*Joseph Harrison,*[3] *Jonas R.,*[2] *John*[1]) was born 19 August 1852 in Wayne County, Kentucky. He left Kentucky with his brother J3B3 Henry Shelton Austin (see Henry's write-up for details on Emerson's early life). He was married on 27 May 1875 to Lucinda Marcile Thomason, born 1 November 1856 in Lavaca County, Texas, daughter of George W. Thomason and Mary L. Bell. Emerson joined the M. E. Church South in August 1875, and in 1878 he was licensed to exhort, the latter part of 1878 he was licensed to preach. He served the church as Steward, District Steward, Recording Steward, Sunday School Superintendent, and in many other ways. As a minister he performed more marriage ceremonies, held more burial services than any one man in the county in which he lived. Brother Emerson Austin was a Master Mason in good standing. Emerson died on 11 March 1912 in Cross Plains, Callahan County, Texas and is buried there with Lucinda who died on Thanksgiving morning, 30 November 1933, at the home of her daughter, Mrs. Sam Swafford. Their children were born in Texas:

J3B5-1. HENRY J., *b. 3 April 1876, d. 11 November 1954, m. 1894 Nancy Morris. Resided 1933 O'Donnell, Texas.*

J3B5-2. MARY L., *b. 25 September 1877, d. 25 September 1878 somewhere between Lavaca & Callahan Counties, Texas*

J3B5-3. GEORGE RILEY, *b. 17 December 1879, alive in 1972, m. 1901 Vida McGee. Resided in Snyder, Texas in 1933.*

J3B5-4. JOSEPH E. (A.?), *b. 4 February 1882, d. May 1936, m. 1905 Ollie Swafford. Resided in Tye, Texas in 1933.*

J3B5-5. WILLIAM T., *b. 17 September 1884, d. August 1951, m. 1908 Rosa Smith. Resided in Anson, Texas in 1933.*

J3B5-6. SARAH ELIZABETH, *b. 19 March 1887 in Cross Plains, d. 19 January 1938, m. 1910 Sam L. Swafford. Resided in Cross Plains in 1933.*

J3B5-7. JAMES J., *b. 12 October 1889, d. September 1936, m. Vina Woods. Resided in Baird, Texas in 1933.*

[CONTINUED ON PAGE 167]

SOME DESCENDANTS OF
EDSON NORMAN AUSTIN
AND INEZ JENNY PARR OF
ST. LAWRENCE COUNTY, NEW YORK

by Helen Austin Popeck

Editor's Note: The following article concerns lines from Samuel Austin – see *The Descendants of Samuel Austin of Boston, Massachusetts* on page 8 of *Austins of America*. The progenitor of this particular branch was S216 Nathan Austin, who was born in Methuen, Massachusetts, in 1725 (see *Austins of America* page 14).

S216-1839. EDSON NORMAN[8] AUSTIN (*Norman,*[7] *Abijah,*[6] *Nathan,*[5,4] *Thomas,*[3,2] *Samuel*[1]) was born 13 March 1857 in Norwood, St. Lawrence County , New York. He was married in Potsdam, St. Lawrence County, on 24 April 1886 to Inez Jenny Parr. Inez was born on 19 November 1868 in Moira, St. Lawrence County. Edson died 2 January 1930 in Ogdensburg, St. Lawrence County, while Inez died on 2 October 1944 in Norwood. Their children were all born in Norwood:

S216-1839-1. ODA CLARA, *b. 19 October 1886*

S216-1839-2. TRUMAN HENRY, *b. 1 November 1887, m. 29 June 1911 Harriet Brownell, d. 6 July 1968 in Watertown, Jefferson County, New York. They had children Lyle and Harriette.*

S216-1839-3. WARNER EDSON, *b. 10 January 1889, m. 23 August 1914 Nora Durant in Watertown, d. 18 September 1952 in Brasher, St. Lawrence County, New York. They had children Margaret and Richard.*

S216-1839-4. ETHEL GRACE, *b. 26 September 1890, m. 25 November 1924 William N. Crouch, d. 5 June 1975 in Valhalla, Westchester County, New York. They had a daughter Helen.*

S216-1839-5. BLANCHE EMILY, *b. 21 August 1892, m.(1) 31 May 1912 Charles Willard, m.(2) June 1943 Claude N. Nichols, d. 1 December 1953*

S216-1839-6. NORMAN, *b. 10 August 1895, m. 6 October 1915 Abigail Bernetta Sullivan in Canton, St. Lawrence, New York; died on 22 March 1970 in Syracuse, Onondaga County, New York.*

Edson Norman Austin 1857-1930
Inez Jenny Parr 1868-1944

Truman Henry Austin with his wife Harriet Brownell and their children Lyle and Harriette are shown in the photograph to right. Truman was the eldest son of Edson and Inez Austin.

Oda Austin Carpenter with her husband Wilbur Carpenter and their children (left to right) Earl, Frank, Donald, and Genevieve.

S216-1839-1. ODA CLARA[9] AUSTIN (*Edson Norman,*[8] *Norman,*[7] *Abijah,*[6] *Nathan,*[5,4] *Thomas,*[3,2] *Samuel*[1]) was born 19 October 1886 in Norwood, St. Lawrence County, New York. She was married in 1910 to Wilbur Austin Carpenter. Wilbur was born on 10 April 1885. Wilbur died on 30 October 1955 in Plattsburgh, Clinton County, New York. Oda died 19 November 1957 in Plattsburgh. Except for their oldest child Grace, their children were born in Malone, Franklin County, New York. CARPENTER CHILDREN: GRACE ANNABELLE 1911, FRANK LYLE 1912, GENEVIEVE INEZ 1914, EARL JAMES 1915, DONALD AUSTIN 1919, NORMA HELEN 1923, WILBUR AUSTIN JR. 1925.

Warner Edson Austin 1889-1952

his wife Nora Durant Austin

and children Margaret Austin and Richard Austin

S216-1839-6. NORMAN[9] AUSTIN (*Edson Norman,*[8] *Norman,*[7] *Abijah,*[6] *Nathan* [5,4] *Thomas,*[3,2] *Samuel*[1]) was born on 10 August 1895 in Norwood, St. Lawrence County, New York. He was married in Canton, St. Lawrence County on 6 October 1915 to Abigail Bernetta Sullivan. Abigail was born on 27 April 1896 in Potsdam, New York. Norman died 22 March 1970 in Syracuse, Onondaga County, New York and is buried in Potsdam. (*See photograph p.138.*)

CHILDREN: S216-1839-61. HELEN MARJORIE, *b. 20 Nov. 1916 Potsdam*
           S216-1839-62. MERRILL SULLIVAN, *b. 9 January 1918 in Watertown, New York*
           S216-1839-63. PAUL REGINALD, *b. 12 Jan. 1920 in Norwood*
           S216-1839-64. ELIZABETH, *b. 27 March 1922, d. 31 July 1924 in Potsdam*
           S216-1839-65. JOHN WILLIAM, *b. 7 July 1927 in Canton*
           S216-1839-66. ROBERT EDSON, *b. 27 Feb. 1930 in Potsdam*

Ethel Grace Austin (1890-1975) is shown at left. Below is Blanche Emily Austin (1892-1953) with her husband Charles Willard and their children Ethel and Ruth (back row), Mabel (center), and Marjorie (front).

Family of Norman and Abigail Sullivan Austin - Back row: John William Austin and Helen Austin Popeck; Front row: Paul Reginald Austin, Norman, Abigail, Robert Edson Austin, and Merrill Sullivan Austin.

S216-1839-61. HELEN MARJORIE[10] AUSTIN (*Norman*,[9] *Edson Norman*,[8] *Norman*,[7] *Abijah*,[6] *Nathan*,[5,4] *Thomas*,[3,2] *Samuel*[1]) was born 20 November 1916 in Potsdam, New York. Her baptismal name was 'Katherine'. Helen Katherine was married in Potsdam on 22 October 1945 to Donald Paul Popeck (who preferred to transpose his first and middle names: Paul Donald Popeck.) Donald was born on 26 July 1916 in Canandaigua, New York, and died on 18 May 1971 in Newark, New York. He is buried in Phelps, New York. Their children were both born in Potsdam. POPECK CHILDREN: RICHARD MARK b.1947, GREGORY BRIAN b.1948.

S216-1839-62. MERRILL SULLIVAN[10] AUSTIN (*Norman*,[9] *Edson Norman*,[8] *Norman*,[7] *Abijah*,[6] *Nathan*,[5,4] *Thomas*,[3,2] *Samuel*[1]) was born 9 January 1913 in Watertown, New York. His baptismal name was 'Joseph'. Merrill Joseph Austin served in World War II, entering the service on 8 May 1941 at Albany, New York. He took basic training at Camp Blanding, Florida, then maneuvers in Louisiana and

North Carolina from July to December 1941. He was promoted to Corporal on 1 April 1942, and was sent to Officer Training School at Camp Lee, Virginia, the No. 4 Quartermaster Corps. Commissioned as a 2nd Lieutenant on 22 May 1942, served in Trinidad, British West Indies, from 25 September 1942 to 11 May 1943. Merrill was sent to the Pacific Theatre on 19 October 1944, where he took part in the liberation of the Phillipines from the Japanese occupation forces. Reaching a final rank of Captain, he returned to the states on 1 January 1946, and was separated at Fort Dix, New Jersey, on 14 January 1946. His final discharge was on 9 March 1946. Merrill was awarded the American Campaign, Asiatic-Pacific, Phillippine Liberation, and World War II Victory medals.

Merrill Austin was married in Ogdensburg, New York on 4 February 1950 to Katherine Tierney. Katherine was born on 16 April 1926 in Ogdensburg. Their children were born in Ogdensburg, except for Patricia who was born in Binghamton, New York:

S216-1839-621. DAVID PAUL, *b. 13 Oct. 1950, d. 10 June 1971 Whitesboro, NY, buried there.*

S216-1839-622. JOAN ELIZABETH, *b. 15 July 1953, m. 28 June 1975 Whitesboro NY to Terrance Andrew Ainslie*

S216-1839-623. MICHAEL JOHN, *b. 26 April 1957, m. 19 June 1982 Rochester NY to Faye Ann Smith Kirchner b. 20 February 1960 Buffalo NY. Their daughter Aprile Marie Austin b. 14 September 1983 Rochester.*

S216-1839-624. PATRICIA CATHERINE *b. 22 August 1965*

S216-1839-63. PAUL REGINALD[10] AUSTIN (*Norman,*[9] *Edson Norman,*[8] *Norman,*[7] *Abijah,*[6] *Nathan,*[5,4] *Thomas,*[3,2] *Samuel*[1]) was born 12 January 1920 in Norwood, New York. Paul served in World War II, entering the service at Fort Niagara on 22 March 1943. He was assigned B.T.U. #10 Greensboro, North Carolina; APO 403A A.A.B. Derider, Louisiana; Squadron N, Scott Field, Illinois. 3505 B.U. Corporal 1943, Sergeant 1945. He was a radio man and gunner, and was discharged at Fort Dix, New Jersey, on 31 January 1946. Paul was married in Watertown, New York on 16 August 1952 to Helen Veronica Fortune. Helen was born on 2 February 1920 in Watertown, and died there on 15 February 1971. Children:

S216-1839-631. MARGARET LYNN, *b. 31 July 1953 Watertown, m. on 27 October 1974 Watertown to Thomas Raymond Tallant. Tallant Children: Jennifer Kathryn 1975, Christopher Matthew 1978, Elizabeth Veronica 1980.*

S216-1839-632. JOHN MICHAEL, *b. 11 January 1956 in Massena, New York*

S216-1839-633. TIMOTHY GERARD, *b. 5 October 1957 in Massena, m. 3 January 1981 in Dallas, Texas to Donna Currier*

S216-1839-65. JOHN WILLIAM[10] AUSTIN (*Norman,*[9] *Edson Norman,*[8] *Norman,*[7] *Abijah,*[6] *Nathan,*[5,4] *Thomas,*[3,2] *Samuel*[1]) was born 7 July 1927 in Canton, New York. He enlisted in the Navy on 8 May 1945 in Albany, New York, and served on the U.S.S. L.C. 107 Huntington. John was discharged 17 July 1946. He was married in Potsdam, New York, on 29 January 1951 to Charlene Theresa Flynn. Charlene was born on 24 November 1930 in St. Albans, Vermont. Children:

S216-1839-651. WILLIAM ROBERT, *b. 27 February 1952 Potsdam, m. 1 May 1976 Potsdam to Elizabeth Alice Bullard b. 30 October 1951 Potsdam. Children: Emily Kathleen b. 2 December 1977 Utica, Oneida County, New York; Elliot Charles b. 26 April 1982 Oswego, Oswego Co., NY.*

S216-1839-652. THOMAS PATRICK, *b. 3 March 1953 Potsdam, m. 2 September 1973 Alexandria Bay, St. Lawrence Co., NY, to Sarah Jean Washburn. Divorced 1983.*

S216-1839-653. MARY KATHERINE, *b. 15 April 1954 Potsdam, m. 2 March 1974 Oswego, New York, to Richard Leon Durfey, son of Jack Sylvester and Dorothy Mable Manwaring Durfey, b. 1 June 1951 in Fulton, New York. Durfey Children born in Oswego: Sean William b.1974, Kimberly Rose b.1976, Allison June b.1978.*

S216-1839-654. JOSEPH JOHN, *b. 2 July 1955 Massena, New York, m. 13 September 1980 Morristown, St. Lawrence County, to Clara Catherine Simpson.*

S216-1839-655. ELIZABETH ANN, *b. 1 December 1956 Massena, m. 6 December 1974 Oswego to Richard Patrick Turner, son of Joseph Richard & Eleanor Ann McGinn Turner, b. 21 August 1956 in East Providence, Rhode Island. Turner Children born in Oswego: Kerrie Ann b.1975, Ryan Flynn b.1977, Adam Richard b.1981, Abbie Elizabeth b.1983.*

S216-1839-656. CAROL JOAN, *b. 23 September 1959 Massena, m. 15 September 1979 Oswego to Matthew Donald Grey. Their son Nathan Thomas Grey was b.1984.*

S216-1839-657. NORMAN PAUL, *b. 15 November 1960 Massena*

S216-1839-66. ROBERT EDSON[10] AUSTIN (*Norman,*[9] *Edson Norman,*[8] *Norman,*[7] *Abijah,*[6] *Nathan,*[5,4] *Thomas,*[3,2] *Samuel*[1]) was born 27 February 1930 in Potsdam, New York. He was married in Plattsburg, New York on 6 August 1956 to Ann Jennine Sumbler. Ann was born on 18 February 1932 in Plattsburg. As a young doctor, Robert was inducted into the U.S. Medical Corps on 9 August 1956. He took basic training in Texas and was sent to Germany with the rank of Captain in the Medical Corps. He served in the 5th General Hospital there. Robert was discharged on 30 June 1958 at Fort Hamilton, New York. Their children were born in Rochester, New York, except for Mark who was born in Stuttgart, Germany:

S216-1839-661. MARK PAUL, *born 4 October 1957*

S216-1839-662. STEPHEN GREGORY, *born 18 September 1958*

S216-1839-663. JAMES ANDREW, *b. 28 September 1959, m. 4 June 1983 Syracuse, New York, to Elizabeth Urbansky. Their son Patrick James Austin was b. 1 November 1983 in Pittsburgh, Allegheny County, Pennsylvania.*

S216-1839-664. ANN CELESTE, *b. 15 November 1960, m. 8 September 1979 Potsdam to Michael Sullivan. Sullivan Children born Utica, New York: John Michael 1980, Katherine Ann 1983.*

S216-1839-665. ROBERT BALDWIN, *born 7 February 1962*

S216-1839-666. AMY BRIDGET, *born 24 May 1963*

JAMES AUSTIN AND SARAH BRADLEY
OF BREWER & EDDINGTON, MAINE

by Winthrop Allison Haskell

J. JAMES[1] AUSTIN was born 19 September 1790 in NH (Reference 1). He was a cooper, and first appeared about 1816 in Brewer, Penobscot County, Maine, where on 28 October 1816 he purchased a "lot of land and shop" for $250 from Daniel Clapp of Brewer (Reference 2). He purchased an additional 3 acres in Brewer on 3 February 1818 for $175 from Thomas Cobb (Reference 3).

James Austin was married in Brewer on 31 May 1818 to Sarah Bradley. Sarah, the daughter of Bryant and Sarah (Neal) Bradley, was born on 1 August 1794 in Orrington, Maine. Her father was a mariner, and in 1791 at Mt. Hope, Maine, he built the 79-ton sloop *Polly*, probably the first vessel to be constructed on the Penobscot River (Reference 4).

James Austen (sic) appears in the 1820 Census for Brewer. He purchased a further 6 acres in Brewer from Mason Shaw for $300 on 7 February 1821 (Reference 5). On 19 March 1822 he began buying land in nearby Eddington, Maine, with a purchase of 25 acres from Joseph Little of Brewer (Reference 6). James Austin was still in Brewer in the 1830 Census and 1840 Census. James Austin had several other land dealings (Reference 7), including one which was a quitclaim deed of land in Brewer to his oldest son, James T. Austin, on 30 August 1836 (Reference 8). James Austin died 13 May 1850, aged 59 years 8 months, and is buried in the Meadowbrook Cemetery in Eddington.

Sarah Austin age 56 appeared as the head of the family in the 1850 Census taken on 7 August in Brewer, along with her children Eliza P. 24, John W. 19, Dorothy J. 18, Mary E. 16, Arthusa C. 13, and Victoria A. 11. An 1855 Tax List shows Mrs. James Austin owned 60½ acres of land in Eddington. On 1 November 1855 Sally Austin sold land in Eddington for $20 to Joel Thompson (Reference 9). In the 1860 Census Sarah age 65 resided in Eddington, along with two of her children.

Sarah Austin died in Eddington on 21 March 1870, aged 75 years and 7 months. She is buried in Meadowbrook Cemetery beside her husband. Their children James, Charlotte, Eliza, Dorothy, and Arathusa are buried in the same cemetery.

CHILDREN: J1. JAMES T., *b. 30 June 1819 in Brewer, d. 3 January 1850 in Eddington; unmarried.*

J2. LUCRETIA C., *b. 29 August 1820*

J3. CHARLOTTE S., *b. 19 June 1823 in Brewer, d. 24 November 1841 ae 18 yrs 5 mos unmarried.*

J4. ELIZA P., *b. 26 December 1825 Eddington, d. 2 May 1912 ae 87 Eddington; unmarried.*

J5. JOHN WILLIAMS BRADLEY, *b. 7 August 1830*

J6. DOROTHY JANE, *b. 1833*

J7. MARY ELIZABETH, *b. 5 October 1834*

J8. ARATHUSA C., *b. 1837*

J9. VICTORIA ADELAIDE, *b. 1839*

J2. LUCRETIA[2] C. AUSTIN (*James[1]*) was born 29 August 1820 in Brewer, Maine. She married Lewis Simpson, a millwright and master mechanic, who was born on 22 December 1817. Lewis died 9 October 1885, and is buried in the Milford, Maine, Town Cemetery. Lucretia died 27 January 1901 in Milford and is buried there with Lewis. SIMPSON CHILDREN: CHARLOTTE b.1847, LUCRETIA b.1850?, JULIA, SARAH, LEWIS b.1845, JENNIE b.1849.

J5. JOHN WILLIAMS BRADLEY[2] AUSTIN (*James[1]*) was born 7 August 1830 in Eddington or Brewer, Maine (Reference 10). John served twice in the Civil War. He first enlisted on 25 April 1861 in Company F, 2nd Maine Volunteer Infantry, as a musician, and was mustered in at Willets Point, New York. He was discharged for disability ("failing fast") on 9 August 1861 at Fort Cocoran, Virginia. His occupation was given as "farmer". John W. B. Austin re-enlisted on 27 November 1863 in Company D, 30th Maine Volunteer Infantry as a private, and was honorably discharged on 20 August 1865 at Savannah, Georgia. He was described as a cooper, with a florid complexion, grey eyes and black hair, born in Brewer, Maine. A Maine recruiting certificate describes John as 5 feet 6 inches in height, and blue eyes, dark hair, and a light complexion. Regretably his military record shows nothing except he was always present for duty, and we have not yet located the regimental history.

John W. B. Austin of Eddington was married in Bangor, Maine, on 2 December 1866 to Mary J. Bradley, a widow of Bangor. Mary was born circa 1843 in Scotland. Her daughter, Minnie Bradley, was later clawed to death by a lynx when investigating strange noises in the chicken house. The date and place of death and burial for John and Mary Austin have not been located (Reference 11). They seem to have had only one child:

CHILDREN: J51. JAMES, *b. circa 1868 (age 2 in the 1870 census)*

J6. DOROTHY JANE[2] AUSTIN (*James[1]*) was born circa 1832 (she was 18 in the 1850 Census for Brewer, Maine). In the 1900 Census Dorothy J. Austin age 67 was living next door to her sister Eliza P. Austin in rental property, while Eliza owned her property free and clear in the town of Eddington. Dorothy died unmarried on 18 April 1907 aged 74 years, and was interred in the family plot at Meadowbrook Cemetery in Eddington, Maine.

Mary Elizabeth Austin 1834-1875

J7. MARY ELIZABETH² AUSTIN (*James¹*) was born 5 October 1834 in Brewer, Maine. She appears twice in the 1850 Census, once on 7 August in Brewer with her mother, and again on 20 September 1850 in Milford, Maine, with her married sister Lucretia and Lewis Simpson, perhaps to help care for their young children. This apparently gave rise to the incorrect fact that Mary was "from Milford" – or even born there – that appears in several later records. Mary was married on 3 January 1854 to Capt. Stephen Babbidge Haskell, born 13 December 1828 at Deer Isle, Hancock County, Maine, son of Capt. David and Lucy (Saunders) Haskell. Stephen was Master of the brig *Financier* of Deer Isle, but not long after their marriage he gave up the sea and opened a sail lot at Deer Isle. Mary died 5 December 1875, Stephen died 20 April 1893, both are buried in Mount Adams Cemetery, Deer Isle. HASKELL CHILDREN: ALMA MARIA b. 1854, AUSTIN DAVID b.1858, LUCY JANE b.1860, JAMES LEWIS b.1867.

J7. ARATHUSA C.² AUSTIN (*James¹*) was born circa 1837 (she was 13 in the 1850 Census in Brewer, Maine). She was 23 years of age in the 1860 Census. In the 1880 Census she was 43 and living with her sister Dorothy J. Austin at Eddington, both being unmarried and their occupations being given as "tailoress". Arathusa died 8 August 1886 age 50 years and is buried in with her parents at Meadowbrook Cemetery, Eddington, Maine.

J8. VICTORIA ADELAIDE² AUSTIN (*James¹*) was born circa 1839 (she was 11 in the 1850 Census in Brewer, Maine). She apparently preferred her middle name over her first name, for in the 1860 Census she was living in the household of her older sister, Lucretia C. Simpson in Milford, listed as "Adalade B. Austin" age 21 tailoress. She married on 3 August 1861 to Joseph B. Pierce of Milford, Maine, using her correct name "Victoria A. Austin". In the 1870 Census in Milford, however, she was listed as "Addie V. Pierce". Two of their children are known, there may have been others. PIERCE CHILDREN: LETTIE b.1863, ANNIE b.1867.

The author would like to contact anyone researching this line, or anyone having information on the birthplace or ancestry of James Austin, or further information on his descendants.

References

1. — Thayer and Agnes Ames, *Brewer, Orrington, Holden, Eddington: History and Families*, p. vii, published 1962. Mrs. Ames confirmed James Austin's birthdate from town records.
2. Penobscot County Deeds Book, Volume 2, page 499.
3. Ibid., Volume 4, page 50.
4. Brewer Vital Records and *Sailing Days on the Penobscot*.
5. Penobscot County Deeds Book, Volume 7, page 10.
6. Ibid., Volume 8, page 35.
7. Ibid., Volume 10, page 524: James bought 100 acres in Brewer on 10 January 1821 from Abraham Hill, collector of taxes, for only $1.99. Volume 10, page 523: he sold same land to Timothy George of Wrentham, Norfolk County, Massachusetts for $6 on 3 September 1824. Volume 20 page 323: James bought land in Brewer from Jonathan W. Sibley of Eddington on 15 June 1829, mortgaging the property to the seller. Volume 67, page 184: James sold Brewer property to Jefferson Chamberlain on 18 August 1835. Volume 92, page 126: Chairmaker Dan Foster of Brewer quitclaimed a shop and privileges located in Brewer to James Austin on 13 July 1837. Volume 93, page 189: James Austin, cooper of Brewer, sold house lot in Brewer to Eldridge G. Thompson for $100, and Sarah relinquished her rights to the property, on 14 June 1836. Volume 84, page 216: James purchased land in Eddington for $300 from Mason Shaw on 30 August 1836 (probably the property still owned by his descendants). Volume 163, page 83: On 2 March 1839, Edward H. Burr of Brewer for $12 quitclaimed Brewer property "near the bend in the river" to James Austin, described as "an undivided half of a gore of land."
8. Ibid., Volume 182, page 344: Land in Brewer purchased from Mason Shaw (see Reference 5 above) was quitclaimed to James T. Austin for $500.
9. Ibid., Volume 262, page 209.
10. John W. B. Austin's 1861 military record has his birthplace as Eddington, Maine, but in 1863 his military record has his birthplace as Brewer, Maine.
11. Editor's Note: From the *Austins of America* files, we find there was a John Austin born in Maine who was age 50 in the U.S. 1880 Census for Leicester, Worcester County, Massachusetts. With him were his wife Rebecca age 45 born in Scotland, and son Harry age 1 born in Massachusetts. While it has not been proven this is J5. John Williams Bradley Austin, there is no likelier candidate in our files, which are estimated to be 95% complete for the State of Maine.

GLASS LAMP PAINTER

GEORGE AUSTIN OF MARION, IOWA

NEEDS STEADY HAND

by Thomas Fruehling

Editor's Note: The following article was reprinted with permission. It was originally published in the *Cedar Rapids Gazette* on 12 April 1981.

As hobbies go, George Austin's pastime requires a steadier hand than most, and infinitely more patience.

A carpenter by trade, Austin spends most winter nights and many weekends painting intricate, multiple-color scenes and designs on opal glass lamp globes. He has spent as much as 120 hours of tedious painting on one piece. And, in a true test of the man's mettle, he has experienced a few failures when all his work was wasted.

Glass painting, Austin explains, is similar (though trickier) to painting on china. A big difference is that glass, when put in a kiln for firing, will melt if the temperature is not exact. If that happens, George's labor goes for naught.

"I've had glass globes just fall apart," says Austin of 2895 23rd Avenue in Marion, Iowa. "And I've had some just go slump on me. That makes you sick after all the work. But it's one of the hazards of the profession."

Austin, 63, got into glass lamp painting about 10 years ago. A grandmother had given his wife, Pauline, and him a 90-year old heirloom lamp with painted glass base and globe.

When the globe broke, the Austins could find no matching replacement and no one in this area was able to make a match for them. Finally, Austin found a Mount Pleasant artist, Edith Lane, who performs the specialized work.

His interest was piqued, and he signed on to take lessons from her in Mount Pleasant twice a week over an entire winter. He has been at it since, making glass lamps and shades for himself and family members, and doing contract work for others.

"I've always been somewhat artistic," says Austin, a former home-builder now employed as a carpenter at Cornell College. "It goes back to winning a Killian's drawing contest back in the seventh grade. I won a gray belt for my drawing of an eagle."

The most common request Austin receives is to paint a new globe on an antique lamp to match the base. That's also the hardest thing to accomplish.

A paint brush, a dab of paint on a broken globe to check the color, and George W. Austin of Marion, Iowa, is ready for fine-line painting on milky-white lamp bases and shades.

He first draws the design on tracing paper and inks-in an outline on the rounded glass. That is followed by several coats of paint (which he mixes himself) and as many firings in the kiln to achieve the exact same color shade. Years of experimenting with paints have given him a range of 72 different shades.

"Most of the antique lamps have gold-based colors such as ruby or lavender. And they're the hardest to match, since in the kiln they're likely to discolor easily.

"I'm pretty persnickety. That's why it takes me so long. I try to paint a match exact in the smallest detail."

George Austin also makes glass globes with his own designs, and has copied pictures that customers have brought to him. One of his undertakings in the latter category involved transposing onto a hanging globe several scenes from old photographs: a school, a church, and farm buildings.

Although Austin says his work is "a hobby and not a business," he has sold enough of his work to pay off the initial $900 investment made several years ago, and he claims customers in several Midwest states.

"It's mostly word of mouth," he says. "We get referrals from antique stores. And Mrs. Lane is pretty well known, and she's told a lot of people I do the work."

While time-consuming and sometimes disappointing, George Austin says he enjoys the hobby. "It's a challenge. I plan to retire in a couple of years, but I'll have plenty to do to keep me busy. I don't plan to stay idle."

Austins in the Federal Census of 1850

Vermont

by Ruby Bruffee Austin

ADDISON COUNTY, VT

BRIDPORT 18

Austin, Holland	25	1825	m	VT
" , Jehiel	15	1835	m	"
Hemenway, Jonas	57	1793	m	"
" , Freelove	47	1803	f	"

Holland & Jehiel were Farmers

CORNWALL 103

Austin, Susan	16	1834	f	VT
Wooster, Abel	47	1803	m	"
" , Harriet	46	1804	f	"
Parker, Joseph	23	1827	m	

. . . . 153

Austin, Horace	26	1824	m	VT
" , Harriet	18	1832	f	"
" , Amorette	7/12	1849	f	"

Horace was a Laborer

FERRISBURGH 118

Austin, James W.	34	1816	m	VT
" , Lucia A.	28	1822	f	"
" , Olive	10	1840	f	"
" , Ira B.	8	1842	m	"
" , Amos E.	6	1844	m	"
" , Catherine A.	4	1846	f	"

James was a Wheelwright

GRANVILLE 49

Austin, Samuel	44	1806	m	VT
" , Martha	43	1807	f	"
" , Samuel	21	1829	m	"
" , Mary	19	1831	f	"
" , Daniel	17	1833	m	"
" , Edwin	15	1835	m	"
" , Henry	5	1845	m	"

HANCOCK 31

Austin, Thaddeus	64	1786	m	NH
" , Betsey	64	1786	f	MA
" , Julius	17	1833	m	VT

LEICESTER 115

Austin, Benjamin	40	1810	m	VT
" , Louisa	24	1826	f	"

Benjamin was a Blacksmith

. . . . 116

Austin, Buskley	78	1772	m	MA
" , Betsey	73	1777	f	NH

MONKTON 202

Austin, Andrew	50	1800	m	VT
" , Eliza	20	1830	f	"
" , John W.	4/12	1850	m	"
" , Orlando	14	1836	m	OH
Palmer, Elen	4	1846	f	VT
H(?)ollry, Anna	69	1781	f	NH

NEW HAVEN 1

Austin, Samuel D.	28	1822	m	VT
" , Olive	26	1824	f	"
" , Alma	6	1844	f	"
" , Alice	4	1846	f	"
" , Albert	2	1848	m	VT

. . . . 69

Austin, Nathaniel	61	1789	m	VT
" , Emily	56	1794	f	"
" , Eli	23	1827	m	"
" , Charlotte	20	1830	f	NY
" , Emily	4/12	1850	f	VT

ORWELL 81

Austin, Melinda	20	1830	f	VT
Griswold, Lester	64	1786	m	"
" , Lucinda	62	1788	f	"

. . . . 206

Austin, Gustavus	38	1812	m	VT
" , Emma	36	1814	f	"
" , Sarah	14	1836	f	"
" , Eliza	11	1839	f	"
" , Julia	8	1842	f	"
" , Kate	3	1847	f	VT
" , Sally	74	1776	f	"
Wilson, Martha	30	1820	f	NY
Bean, Franklin	25	1825	m	CAN
Blakely, Mehitabel	19	1831	f	"
Phelps, Mary	16	1834	f	"

SALISBURY 12

Austin, Levi	26?	1824	m	VT
Boardman, Alonzo	38	1812	m	"
" , Mary	37	1813	f	"

. . . . 166

Austin, Daniel	44	1806	m	VT
" , Mary	26	1824	f	"
" , Maria	16	1834	f	"
" , Alonzo	14	1836	m	"
" , Jane	12	1838	f	"
" , William	6	1844	m	"
Merritt, Thomas	21	1829	m	"

Thomas was a Laborer

. . . . 187

Austin, Josiah	50	1800	m	VT
" , Eliza	39	1811	f	"
" , Levi	19	1831	m	"
" , Clarinda	17	1833	f	"
" , Francis	14	1836	m	"
" , Juliette	8	1842	f	"
" , Phebe Ann	6	1844	f	VT
" , William	4	1846	m	"
" , Louisa	1	1849	f	"

SHOREHAM 103

Austin, Cordelia	20	1830	f	VT
Jones, Asa	60	1790	m	"
" , Electa	49	1801	f	"
" , Carlos	22	1828	m	"
" , William	17	1833	m	"
" , Susan	14	1836	f	"
" , Sarah	7	1843	f	"
Clare, Joseph	13	1837	m	"

SHOREHAM 118

Austin, Edward	72	1778	m	VT
" , Lydia	65	1785	f	NY
" , Anna	44	1806	f	VT

. . . . 310

Austin, David	62	1788	m	VT
" , Clarissa	48	1802	f	"
" , Holland	25	1825	m	"
" , Cordelia	19	1831	f	"
" , Susan	17	1833	f	"
" , Ge(hiel)	15	1835	m	"
" , Amanda	12	1838	f	"
" , Huldah	10	1840	f	"
" , Roxana	8	1842	f	"
" , William	6	1844	m	"

WHITING 9

Austin, Jane	10	1840	f	VT
Re(mele?), Nelson	33	1817	m	CAN
" , Jane	32	1818	f	VT
" , Adelaide	5	1845	f	"
" , Mary	2	1848	f	"
Padno, Zebulon	15	1835	m	CAN

Zebulon was a Laborer

BENNINGTON COUNTY, VT

ARLINGTON 706

Austin, Dyer	21	1829	m	VT
" , Cordelia	27	1823	f	"
" , Frances	5	1845	f	"
" , Caroline	2	1848	f	"
McC(ra)chen, Affa	54	1796	f	"

. . . . 714

Austin, George	30	1820	m	VT
" , Eliza	29	1821	f	"
" , Frances	11	1839	f	"
" , Ira	6	1844	m	"
" , George H.	4	1846	m	"

. . . . 728

Austin, Pardon	63	1787	m	VT
" , Hepsibeth	59(7)	1791	f	NY
" , Jeremiah	22	1828	m	VT
" , James	15	1835	m	"

. . . . 729

Austin, Elijah	25	1825	m	VT
" , Jane	25	1825	f	NY
Trippe, Sarah	11	1839	f	"

BENNINGTON 413

Austin, Lorenzo A.	45	1805	m	VT
" , (R)uly	43	1807	f	"
" , Charlotte	30	1820	f	"
" , Ruth Ann	19	1831	f	"
" , John M.	15	1835	m	"
" , Sarah (J?)	13	1837	f	"
" , Martha A.	10	1840	f	"
" , George H.	8	1842	m	"
" , Ruby E.	6	1844	f	"
" , Frederick L.	4	1846	m	"
" , Charles E.	8/12	1849	m	"

				525
Austin, James H.	7	1843	m	VT
Carpenter, Richard	61	1789	m	MA
", Betsey	50	1800	f	VT
", Daniel	13	1837	m	"
				566
Austin, Ruth	20	1830	f	VT
Walbreag, John L.	26	1824	m	"
", Polly M.	17	1833	f	"

POWNAL ... 168

Austin, Job	47	1803	m	NY
", Betsey	40	1810	f	VT
", Charles	13	1837	m	"
", Henry	10	1840	m	"
", James	3	1847	m	"
", Mary	8/12	1849	f	MA
W(hitten), Seth	63	1787	m	VT

SANDGATE ... 646

Austin, William	12	1838	m	NY
Quackenbush, Alex	46	1804	m	VT
", Mary	35	1815	f	"
", Sophia	39	1811	f	NY

SHAFTSBURY ... 65

Austin, Benonia	70	1780		CT
", Mary	70	1780	f	"
				181
Austin, Caleb	44	1806	m	VT
Gould, William	26	1824	m	"
", Sarah	22	1828	f	"
", Hiram	2/12	1850	m	"

Caleb was a Farmer

CHITTENDEN COUNTY, VT

BOLTON ... 93

Austin, David	58	1792	m	CT
", Pamelia	58	1792	f	VT
", Phebe	28	1822	f	"
", David Jr.	24	1826	m	"
", Warren E.	13	1837	m	"
Wright, Matilda	11	1839	f	"

BURLINGTON ... 835

Austin, Elnathan	50	1800	m	VT
", Amanda	39	1811	f	CT
", Ha(rv)ey E.	17	1833	m	VT
", Luanna	13	1837	f	NY
				1131
Austin, Eliza	32	1818	f	VT
", Joseph	12	1838	m	OH
", Hanry	6	1844	m	VT
Harrington, Catherine	20	1830	f	"

CHARLOTTE ... 44

Austin, Delia	16	1834	f	VT
McNeil, John	65	1785	m	"
", Fanny	61	1789	f	CT

COLCHESTER ... 129

Austin, Henry W.	34	1816	m	VT
", Sally J.	30	1820	f	NY
", Francis H.	8	1842	m	VT
", C.W.	6	1844	m	"
", Ella L.	4	1846	f	"
", Mary J.	1	1849	f	VT
				442
Austin, Dennis	30	1820	m	VT
", Harriet	30	1820	f	"
", Augusta	4	1846	f	"
", Charles L.	2	1848	m	"
", Lucy	69	1781	f	"
", Hannah	47	1803	f	"

				464
Austin, Nathaniel	46	1804	m	VT
", Elizabeth			f	NH
", Betsey	11	1839	f	VT
", Solo	9	1841	m	"
", Sally	7	1843	f	"
", William M.	3	1847	m	"
", Hiram	1	1849	m	"
", Sally	83	1767	f	NH

Latter Sally in same house

ESSEX ... 378

Austin, Alpha	30	1820	f	VT
", Abigail	25	1825	f	"
", Francis	5	1845	m	"
Gates, George	32	1818	m	"
", Rebecca	27	1823	f	"
", James	5	1845	m	"
", Ezra	6/12	1850	m	"
", Hannah	55	1795	f	"
", Caroline	25	1825	f	"

ESSEX ... 416

Austin, Elias	47	1803	m	VT
", Hannah	43	1807	f	ME
", Lucian	17	1833	m	VT
", Mercy	13	1837	f	"
", Lucy	12	1838	f	"
", Elizabeth	10	1840	f	"
", Riuben	9	1841	m	"
", Emerson	3	1847	m	"
", Albert	4	1846	m	"
", Martha	2	1848	f	"
", Electa	2/12	1850	f	"
				425
Tyler, Rodney	52	1798	m	VT
", Sabrina	44	1806	f	"
				426
Tyler, Lewis	20	1830	m	NJ
Austin, Nancy	66	1784	f	VT

Lewis was a Farmer

				433
Austin, Samuel	21	1829	m	VT
Joiner, Fletcher	79	1771	m	"

Samuel was a Farmer

				603
Austin, Manerva	53	1797	f	VT
", Sarah A.	28	1822	f	"
Bates, Thomas	42	1808	m	"
", Juliet	8	1842	f	"
", Emeret	5	1845	m	"

HINESBURGH ... 278

Austin, William	40	1810	m	VT
", Sarah	39	1811	f	MA
", William	9	1841	m	VT
", Laura	7	1843	f	"
", John	5	1845	m	"
", Lodema	3	1847	f	"
", Benjamin	1	1849	m	"
Wit, Saminda	8	1842	f	"
", Jane	5	1845	f	"
", Leander	3	1847	m	"

JERICHO ... 299

Austin, Leonard	40	1810	m	NH
", Laura A.	36	1814	f	VT
", John B.	12	1838	m	"
", Burnham	10	1840	m	"
", Henry H.	2	1848	m	"
Seeley, Ann	20	1830	f	"

Leonard was a Miller

MILTON ... 963

Austin, Adin	27	1823	m	VT
", Cordelia	24	1826	f	"
Evans, Mary	12	1838	f	"
", Ellen	16	1834	f	"
Austin, James	4	1846	m	"
Win(kle), —	17	1833	?	ENG
				983
Austin, Ethan	61	1789	m	VT
", Clarissa	58	1792	f	"
", Eliot	16	1834	m	"
Crunden, Buel	18	1832	m	NY
				986
Austin, Edgar	28	1822	m	VT
", Ruth	23	1827	f	"
", Mary	4	1846	f	"
", Augusta	3	1847	f	"
", Ellen L.			f	"
				988
Austin, Allen	24	1826	m	VT
", Matilda	20	1830	f	"
", Mary	1	1849	f	"
				992
Austin, Newman	53	1797	m	VT
", Joan	53	1797	f	"
", Moroni	16	1834	m	"
", Simeon	14	1836	m	"
", Samantha	12	1838	f	"
", John	17	1833	m	"
				1011
Austin, Elnathan	50	1800	m	VT
Woodruff, Sally			f	"

Elnathan was a Carpenter

				1041
Austin, Eleazer	64	1786	m	RI
", Eliza	56	1794	f	VT
", Jeanette	30	1820	f	"
", George	26	1824	m	"
", Abigail	18	1832	f	"
", Lenora	14	1836	f	"
				1307
Austin, Edmond	31	1819	m	VT
", Maryon	27	1823	f	"
", Henry	4	1846	m	"
", Catherine	2	1848	f	"
Sibley, Caroline	60	1790	f	"
				1348
Austin, Henry	60	1790	m	VT
", Polly	55	1795	f	"
", Cornelia	17	1833	f	"

UNDERHILL ... 45

Austin, Isaac N.	28	1822	m	VT
", Diadama	23	1827	f	"
", Allbrina	3	1847	f	"
Jubert, Charles	23	1827	m	"

Charles was a Farmer

WESTFORD ... 752

Austin, Elijah	60	1790	m	VT
", Maria	46	1804	f	"
", Franklin	26	1824	m	"
", Sarah	22	1828	f	"
", Julia	15	1835	f	"
", Andrew	12	1838	m	"
", Saphronia	10	1840	f	"
", Hanibel	7	1843	m	"
", Chancy	4	1846	m	"
", Cornelia	2	1848	f	"

WILLISTON 219

Austin, David	42	1808	m	VT
" , Sally	50	1800	f	"
" , Herman	17	1833	m	"
" , George	9	1841	m	"
" , Electa	7	1843	f	"
" , Gardner	70	1780	m	MA

. . . . 282

Austin, Harvey	19	1831	m	VT
Ballou, William M.	30	1820	m	"
" , Crestina	29	1821	f	"

Harvey was a Laborer

- -

ESSEX COUNTY, VT

BRUNSWICK 16

Austin, David S.	45	1805	m	VT
" , Betsey	44	1806	f	"
" , Lucind E.	19	1831	f	"
" , Louisa A.	17	1833	f	"
" , Stephen G.	16	1834	m	"
" , Mary A.	12	1838	f	"
" , David	4	1846	m	"
" , Allice	1	1849	f	"

Stephen was a Laborer

. . . .

FRANKLIN COUNTY, VT

BERKSHIRE 170

Austin, Hazzard P.	30	1820	m	VT
" , Mary Ann	26	1824	f	"
" , Rayman	55	1795	m	"
" , Abigil	50	1800	f	NH
" , Annette C.	12	1838	f	VT

. . . . 178

Austin, Nelson	32	1818	m	VT
" , Caroline	29	1821	f	"
" , Ella A.	9	1841	f	"
" , Rosalinda	7	1843	f	"
" , Arabel	3	1847	f	"
" , Ezra M.	1	1849	m	"

. . . . 238

Austin, Oliver	62	1788	m	VT
" , Milly	58	1792	f	"
" , Elhanan	25	1825	m	"

. . . . 315

Austin, Benjamin	67	1783	m	VT
" , Ruth	66	1784	f	MA
" , Norman	28	1822	m	VT

FAIRFAX 170

Austin, Julia	14	1836	f	VT
Maxfield, William	83	1767	m	NH
" , Mercy	48	1802	f	VT
" , Emily	16	1834	f	"

FRANKLIN 25

Austin, David B.	53	1797	m	NY
" , Rebecca	51	1799	f	CAN
" , Edward P.	20	1830	m	VT
" , Harriet	16	1834	f	"
" , Augusta	15	1835	f	"
" , Waldo	11	1839	m	"
" , Warren	9	1841	m	"

David was a Blacksmith

. . . . 27

Austin, Hiram	30	1820	m	
Olds, Lorenzo			m	VT

GEORGIA 192

Austin, Byrum B.	38	1812	m	VT
" , Almira	34	1816	f	"
" , Charles	12	1838	m	"
" , Mary	9	1841	f	"
" , Saphronia	7	1843	f	"
" , Allen	5	1845	m	"
" , Saloma	3	1847	f	"

. . . . 196

Austin, Elan	37	1813	m	VT
" , Abigail	32	1818	f	RI
" , Eleazor	10	1840	m	VT
" , Edward	8	1842	m	"
" , Mary	7	1843	f	"

. . . . 322

Austin, Albert	75	1775	m	VT
" , Chalista	20	1830	f	"
Waters, Terrissa	25	1825	f	"

Albert was a Wheelwright

HIGHGATE 301

Ostin, Michael	70	1780	m	VT
" , Thomas	24	1826	m	IRE
O'hine, Jr.	21	1829	m	"

. . . . 306

Austin, Timothy	68	1782	m	RI
" , Abigail	64	1786	f	MA

. . . . 386

Austin, Frederick	70	1780	m	VT
" , Polly	66	1784	f	RI

. . . . 387

Austin, Lucinda	17	1833	f	VT
Dunton, John	49	1801	m	"
" , Fila	51	1799	f	"

. . . . 427

Austin, Sylvester	35	1815	m	VT
" , Mariah (C)	32	1818	f	MA
" , Daniel	12	1838	m	VT
" , Abigail	10	1840	f	"
" , Abi	8	1842	f	"
" , George	5	1845	m	"
" , Malissa	3	1847	f	"
" , Diana	3/12	1850	f	"
" , Burt	21	1829	m	"
" , Truman	29	1821	m	"

Burt was a Blacksmith

. . . . 428

Austin, Charles	42	1808	m	VT
" , Lucy	49	1801	f	CAN
Cruford, Anetta	19	1831	f	VT
" , Elizabeth	17	1833	f	"
" , Lester	14	1836	m	"
" , Mary	13	1837	f	"
" , Jane	10	1840	f	"
" , Electa	5	1845	f	"
" , Fanny	3	1847	f	"

Anetta married within year

SHELDON 64

Austin, Emery	21	1829	m	VT
" , Sarah	19	1831	f	"

Married within year

. . . . 78

Austin, Rodney N.	38	1812	m	VT
" , Eliza A.	34	1816	f	"
" , Apollos	14	1836	m	"
" , Eliza J.	7	1843	f	CAN

. . . . 79

Austin, Horace	36	1814	m	VT
" , Sarah	37	1813	f	"
" , Ransom	9	1841	m	"
" , William W.	2	1848	m	"

. . . . 120

Austin, Seymour	35	1815	m	VT
" , Wealthy	23	1827	f	"
" , Samuel A.	5	1845	m	"
" , Rhuben	1	1849	m	"

. . . . 172

Austin, Eli	26	1824	m	CAN
" , Constance	20	1830	f	VT
" , Alice	2	1848	f	"
" , Constance	3/12	1850	f	"
" , Rosalett	58	1792	f	CAN
Vancour, Harriet	18	1832	f	"
Austin, Mary	15	1835	f	VT
" , Cordelia	12	1838	f	"
Phanuff, Peter	21	1829	m	CAN

Eli was a Blacksmith

. . . . 258

Austin, Alvin	40	1810	m	VT
" , Lucia	42	1808	f	"
" , Curtis	16	1834	m	"
" , Clark	10	1840	m	"
" , Charles	7	1843	m	"
" , Rodney	5	1845	m	"

Alvin was a Shoemaker

. . . . 259

Austin, Levi	39	1811	m	VT
" , Ira	36	1814	m	"
Little, Persis	68	1782	f	NH

Levi & Ira were both blind

ST. ALBANS 19

Austin, John	51	1799	m	VT
" , Bridget	45	1805	f	IRE
" , Mary Ann	17	1833	f	VT
" , Catherine	15	1835	f	"
" , James	13	1837	m	"
" , John Jr.	11	1839	m	"
" , Anna	9	1841	f	"

. . . . 391

Austin, Alonzo	25	1825	m	VT
Meach,			m	

Meach was an Innkeeper

. . . . 418

Austey, James	30	1820	m	VT
" , Helen	25	1825	f	ENG
" , George R.	3	1847	m	VT
" , Ann E.	1	1849	f	"

. . . . 548

Austin, Catherine	16	1834	f	VT
Davis, James	64	1786	m	RI

Lawyer and his family

SWANTON 20

Austin, Joseph	35	1815	m	VT
" , Adeline	32	1818	f	CAN
" , Franklin	9	1841	m	VT
" , John	7	1843	m	"
" , Eli	4	1846	m	"
" , Adeline	2	1848	f	"

. . . . 81

Austin, Jesse	56	1794	m	VT
" , Rebecca	54	1796	f	NH
" , George W.	19	1831	m	VT
" , Andrew	16	1834	m	"
" , Jane L.	13	1837	f	"
" , James	12	1838	m	"

				99
Austin, Delia	27	1823	f	VT
Faxon, Stiles			m	
Stiles was an Innkeeper				
				256
Austin, Esther	87	1763	f	CT
Burnell, Chester	37	1813	m	VT
" , Amanda	35	1815	f	"
				265
Austin, Erasmus	27	1823	m	VT
" , William	22	1828	m	"
Rich, Charles W.	32	1818	m	"
				271
Austin, Franklin	25	1825	m	VT
Green, Samuel S.	40	1810	m	"
" , Mary	33	1817	f	CAN
Franklin was a Blacksmith				

LAMOILLE COUNTY, VT

CAMBRIDGE 16

Austin, Joseph	79	1771	m	MA
" , Louisa C.	35	1815	f	VT
Bacon, Mary H.	33	1817	f	"
" , Mary D.	2	1848	f	"
Joseph was a Miller				
				38
Austin, Lyman	27	1823	m	VT
" , Saline T.	24	1826	f	"
" , Wealthy	63	1787	f	NH
Lyman was a Carpenter & Joiner				
				75
Austin, Almond	23	1827	m	VT
Farmer with Enoch Carlton				
				144
Austin, John			m	VT
" , Rhoda	48	1802	f	"
" , Emerson	18	1832	m	"
" , James	16	1834	m	"
" , Samuel	11	1839	m	"
" , Jerusha	5	1845	f	"
				155
Austin, Enoch	46	1804	m	MA
" , Nancy	45	1805	f	CAN
" , Harmon P.	20	1830	m	VT
" , Harriet M.	18	1832	f	"
" , Adelia A.	16	1834	f	"
" , Julia A.	12	1838	f	"
" , John	43	1807	m	NH

CAMBRIDGE 180

Austin, Emerson			m	
" , Charlotte	74	1776	f	NH
Thompson, Clark	31	1819	m	
Charlotte died in February				

EDEN 109

Austin, Orrin Jr.	29	1821	m	VT
" , Henrietta J.	26	1824	f	NH
" , Electa A.	3	1847	f	VT
Phillips, Allen	11	1839	m	"
				110
Austin, Orrin	68	1782	m	VT
" , Anna	69	1781	f	CT

WATERVILLE 72

Austin, Elliot	26	1824	m	VT
" , Olive	59	1791	f	"
Stanley, Lorinda	35	1815	f	"
Austin, Alfred	22	1828	m	"
" , Almon	22	1828	m	"
" , Mirenda	15	1835	f	"

ORANGE COUNTY, VT

BRADFORD 618

Austin, Seth	52	1798	m	VT
" , Manerva	37	1813	f	"
" , Helen E.	20	1830	f	"
" , Albert E.	15	1835	m	"
" , George	6	1844	m	"
" , John	3	1847	m	"
Seth was an Attorney				
				693
Austin, Hiram M.	26	1824	m	VT
" , Mahala C.	21	1829	f	"
" , George H.	1	1849	m	"
				694
Austin, (Banj?)	46	1804	m	VT
" , Ann	57	1793	f	"
" , Albert N.	18	1832	m	"
				758
Austin, George A.	12	1838	m	NH
Humphrey, Henry	35	1815	m	VT

BROOKFIELD 41

Austin, George	2	1848	m	VT
" , Mary	5/12	1850	f	"
" , Benjamin	71	1779	m	"
" , Mary	60	1790	f	"
Bagley, Benjamin C.	35	1815	m	"
" , Rosanah M.	26	1824	f	"
" , Azro L.	12	1838	m	"

FAIRLEE 21

Austin, John H.	28	1822	m	NH
" , Almira	28	1823	f	VT
" , Julianna	5/12	1850	f	"
John was a Shoemaker				
				26
Austin, Selena (K)	30	1820	f	VT
Joslyn, Josiah	74	1776	m	"
" , Sarah	68	1782	f	MA

NEWBURY 46

Austin, William R.	34	1816	m	CT
" , Hepzi E.	38	1812	f	VT
" , Sarah M.	8	1842	f	"
William was a Carpenter				

STRAFFORD 318

Austin, Martha	71	1779	f	MA
Wood, Albertus	36	1814	m	VT
" , Lydia	40	1810	f	NH
" , Albert L.	10	1840	m	VT
Albertus was Carpenter & Joiner				

THETFORD 362

Austin, Sarah	66	1784	f	NH
Snow, Isaac C.	32	1818	m	VT
" , Luthera	33	1817	f	"
" , Loretta	8	1842	f	"
" , Frances E.	4	1846	f	"
				367
Austin, Nathan	50	1800	m	VT
" , Sophia	48	1802	f	"
" , Azro O.	15	1835	m	"
" , David	14	1836	m	"
" , Mary Ann	20	1830	f	"
" , Orin S.	10	1840	m	"
" , Harvey M.	6	1844	m	"
				368
Austin, Thomas	36	1814	m	VT
" , Eliza A.	37	1813	f	"
" , William	14	1836	m	"
" , Alina A.	7	1843	f	"
" , Minerva	24	1826	f	"

TUNBRIDGE 71

Austin, Isaiah	52	1798	m	"
" , Olive	48	1802	f	VT
" , Nathaniel H.	21	1829	m	"
" , Isaiah W.	19	1831	m	"
Moody, Theresa	13	1837	f	"
				95
Austin, Eli	71	1779	m	VT
" , Sally	69	1781	f	CT
" , Amos E.	32	1818	m	VT
" , Mercy	25	1825	f	NH
" , Sarah	2	1848	f	VT
" , Clara	11/12	1849	f	"
Allen, Hannah	99	1750	f	CT
Cutler, Marilla	54	1796	f	VT
Dodge, Miles	15	1835	m	"
Eli was a Blacksmith				
Hannah was 99 & 7/12				
				100
Austin, John F.	55	1795	m	VT
John was living alone				
				193
Austin, Samuel	77	1773	m	CT
" , Electa	49	1801	f	VT
Dickinson, Henry R.	30	1820	m	"
" , Chloe E.	28	1822	f	"

ORLEANS COUNTY, VT

CRAFTSBURY 356

Austin, Daniel H.	29	1821	m	VT
" , Betsey	22	1828	f	"
" , Gideon H.	10	1840	m	"
" , Ellen H.	3	1847	f	"
" , Unice H.	7/12	1849	f	"
Daniel was a Teacher				
				450
Austin, Asa	62	1788	m	CT
" , Nancy	56	1794	f	VT
" , Chandler	18	1832	m	"
				537
Austin, Asa	30	1820	m	VT
" , Nancy	56	1794	f	"
" , Chandler	18	1832	m	"
" , Marian L.	15	1835	f	"
" , Orlo H.	12	1838	m	"
" , Lorenzo	8	1842	m	"
" , Daniel H.	29	1821	m	"
" , Betsey H.	22	1828	f	"
Henry, Edward A.	10	1840	m	"
" , Ellen B.			f	"
" , Unice H.	6/12	1850	f	"
Daniel was a Teacher				

GREENSBORO 1334

Austin, Elijah	56	1794	m	VT
" , Loviza	53	1797	f	"
" , Loviza Ann	29	1821	f	NH
Stanley, Mary	74	1776	f	MA
McGuire, Mathew	49	1801	m	IRE

RUTLAND COUNTY, VT

BENSON 15

Austin, Sylvester	56	1794	m	
" , Maria A.	56	1794	f	VT
" , Artilda	35	1815	f	"
" , Melinda M.	20	1830	f	"
" , Riley C.	18	1832	m	"
" , George E.	15	1835	m	"
" , Martha Jane	15	1835	f	"
" , Julius R.	13	1835	m	"
" , Benjamin F.	5	1845	m	"

BRANDON 1484

Austain, Armina	32	1818	f	VT
Hunt, H. A.	44	1806	m	"

Hunt was a Blacksmith

POULTNEY 1135

Austin, John W.	47	1803	m	VT
" , Olive	47	1803	f	"
" , Nathaniel	19	1831	m	"
" , Charlotte L.	18	1832	f	"
" , Lewis A.	16	1834	m	"
" , Judson W.	12	1838	m	"
" , Sidney F.	10	1840	m	"
" , Charles E.	8	1842	m	"
" , Sarah E.			f	"
" , Eliza P.	14	1836	f	"

Sarah & Eliza were at Seminary

RUTLAND 486

Austain, Paul	52	1798	m	CAN
" , Charlotte	38	1812	f	VT
" , Anthony	14	1836	f	"
" , Joseph	12	1838	m	"
" , George	10	1840	m	"
" , Julia	9	1841	f	"
" , Mary	5	1845	f	"
" , Henry	3	1847	m	"
" , Paul	2	1848	m	"
Durkee, Joseph	70	1780	m	"
" , Mary	75	1775	f	CAN

SHERBURNE 1958

Austain, Thomas I.	45	1805	m	CAN
" , Seviah	40	1810	f	VT

WASHINGTON COUNTY, VT

BERLIN 214

Austin, Ellwin	27	1823	m	VT
" , Lucretia	26	1824	f	"
Andrews, Aaron	37	1813	m	"
" , Betsey	41	1809	f	"

. . . . 217

Austin, Ezekiel	68	1782	m	RI
" , Nancy	64	1786	f	CT
" , Maria	31	1819	f	VT
" , Mary	33	1817	f	"

. . . . 225

Austin, Chester	24	1826	m	VT
Nye, Chester	64	1786	m	CT

Chester Austin was a Laborer

EAST MONTPELIER 537

Austin, Willard	20	1830	m	VT
McKnight, Putnam	47	1803	m	"
" , Lemuel	75	1775	m	MA

Willard was a Farmer

. . . . 612

Austin, Mary	18	1832	f	
Little, Walter	53	1797	m	

and others in Little family

MARSHFIELD 184

Austin, Friend M.	58	1792	m	VT
" , Clarrissa	48	1802	f	"
" , Samuel	22	1828	m	"
" , William	20	1830	m	"
" , Mehitabel	18	1832	f	"
" , Nathaniel	17	1833	m	"
" , Isaac	13	1837	m	"
" , Ruth	11	1839	f	"
" , Hester	9	1941	f	"

. . . . 189

Austin, Rhoda	39	1811	f	MA
" , Lydia	80	1770	f	VT
" , Mehitabel	46	1804	f	"

NORTHFIELD 300

Austin, Harvey	32	1818	m	VT
Buzzell, Eli	46	1804	m	"

Harvey was a Laborer

WATERBURY 1883

?ustin, Luke	47	1803	m	NH
" , Eliza	45	1805	f	VT
" , Mary E.	22	1828	f	"
" , Francis	20	1830	m	"
" , George	18	1832	m	"
" , Martha	14	1836	f	"
" , Betsey	12	1838	f	"
" , Adeline	10	1840	f	"
" , Edwin	5	1845	m	"

Luke was a Miller

. . . . 1899

Austin, Smith	54	1796	m	VT
" , Susannah	41	1809	f	"
" , William	11	1839	m	"

WINDHAM COUNTY, VT

ATHENS 25

Au()t lin,	48	1802	m	VT
" , Minerva	45	1815	f	"
" , John	21	1829	m	"
" , Lodatha	22	1828	f	"
Henry, William	11	1839	m	MA

family head was a Physician

BRATTLEBORO 48

Austin, Jonathan	52	1798	m	VT
" , Margaret	42	1808	f	"
" , Rosette	17	1833	f	"
" , Laurel	14	1836	f	"
Lock, Sargent	40	1810	m	"
" , Laura	40	1810	f	"

And children

. . . . 372

Austin, Oscar	23	1827	m	VT
Wheeler, Lucy F.	50	1800	f	"

Oscar was a Merchant

. . . . 564

Austin, James	50	1800	m	VT

at the insane asylum

. . . . 579

Austin, Mary	25	1825	f	IRE
" , Hannura	11	1839	f	"
Williston, Bathan B.			m	

and his family

DUMMERSTON 419

Austin, James	60	1790	m	IRE
" , Margaret	50	1800	f	"
" , Morris	20	1830	m	"
" , Martin	12	1838	m	"
" , James	7	1843	m	NH

STRATTON 33

Austin, Arnold	50	1800	m	VT
" , Martha	47	1803	f	"
" , Royal	24	1831	m	"
" , Merill	18	1832	m	"
" , Helen	16	1834	f	"
" , Addison	13	1837	m	"

" , Catherine	11	1839	f	"
" , Augusta	8	1842	f	"
" , Henry	6	1844	m	"

. . . . 251

Austin, Melvin	24	1826	m	NY
Follett, Eliza			f	

Melvin was a Farmer

. . . . 256

Austin, Keyes	18	1832	m	VT
Wiswall, Samuel			m	

Keyes was a Farmer

. . . . 258

Austin, Riley	25	1825	m	VT
" , Hannah	25	1825	f	"
" , Mary	2	1848	f	"
" , Mary	86	1764	f	MA
" , Rebecca	64	1786	f	VT

Riley was a Farmer

. . . . 259

Austin, Asa	61	1789	m	VT
" , Martha	53	1797	f	"
" , Granville	24	1826	m	"
" , Maria	22	1828	f	"
" , Martha	18	1832	f	"

WINDSOR COUNTY, VT

ANDOVER 23

Austin, Benjamin	48	1802	m	VT
" , Lucinda	45	1805	f	"
" , Horace B.	19	1831	m	"
" , Mary L.	15	1835	f	"
" , Henry	7	1843	f	"
" , Lorin L.	2	1848	m	"

. . . . 147

Austin, Franklin	37	1813	m	VT
" , Lydia	36	1814	f	"
" , Hannah	11	1839	f	"
" , John F.	7	1843	m	"
" , Rhoda I.	5	1845	f	"
Clark, Samuel	79	1771	m	MA
Lovejoy, Stephen	18	1832	m	VT

Farmers

BARNARD 160

Austin, Harriet	29	1821	f	VT
Chamberlain, Lot	55	1795	m	"
" , Hannah	56	1794	f	"
" , Henry	19	1831	m	"

BETHEL 161

Austin, Abial	76	1774	m	CT
" , Anna	66	1784	f	VT
" , Alice	28	1822	f	"
" , Harriet	25	1825	f	"

and two farmers

. . . . 162

Austin, Charles L.	43	1807	m	VT
" , Lavisa			f	"

CHESTER 130

Austin, Lydia	83	1767	f	VT
Edgell, Aaron	51	1799	m	"
" , Marinda	46	1804	f	"
" , Stephen	21	1829	m	"

POMFRET 81

Austin, Frederick (T)	15	1835	m	MA
Whitman, Charles R.	34	1816	m	VT
" , Thirza	69	1781	f	"

Frederick was a Farmer

READING			87
Austin, Dianna	27	1823	f	VT
Whittemore, Nelson	42	1808	m	"
", Lucy	44	1806	f	"
		and children	

			158
Austin, Henry	36	1814	m	VT
", Eliza	36	1814	f	"
", Mary	7	1843	f	"

ROCHESTER			35
Austin, Lyman	42	1808	m	VT
", Lucy	72	1778	f	NH
Root, Sybil M.	23	1827	f	VT

ROCHESTER			36
Austin, Isaac F.	36	1814	m	VT
", Clarissa M.	24	1826	f	"
", Sydney M.	4	1846	m	"
", Unity A.	2	1848	f	"
		same house as Lyman above	

			37
Austin, Robert	66	1784	m	NH
", Phebe	60	1790	f	CT
", Joseph L.	41	1809	m	VT
", Betsey	31	1819	f	"
", John H.	24	1826	m	"
", Mary	17	1833	f	"
", Phebe J.	16	1834	f	"
", Truman D.	12	1838	m	"
", Milo D.	9	1841	m	"

", George E.	5	1845	m	"
", Amelia R.	1	1849	f	"

ROCHESTER			46
Austin, Stillman	38	1812	m	VT
", Louisa	32	1818	f	"
", Esther A.	12	1838	f	"
", Erastus	10	1840	m	"
", Harriet	7	1843	f	"
", Moses T.	5	1845	m	"
", Lucy	1/12	1850	f	"

SPRINGFIELD			178
Austin, Minerva H.	17	1833	f	VT
Lewis, Isaac	42	1808	m	"
", Laura	46	1804	f	"
	Minerva b. Athens, Laura b. Jericho	

			425
Austin, Minerva	17	1833	f	VT
Jenkins, Nathaniel	45	1805	m	"
", Phebe	45	1805	f	"
", Samuel W.	26	1824	m	"
	Minerva & Phebe born in Townshend	

WESTON			36
Austin, Charles	45	1805	m	VT
", Lucy C.	41	1809	f	"
", Jefferson M.	14	1836	m	"
", Ransom L.	11	1839	m	"
", Lucy E.	7	1843	f	"
	Charles was a Shoemaker	

			61
Austin, Stephen	50	1800	m	VT
", Sarah	52	1798	f	"
", Betsey	23	1827	f	"
", Hannah	14	1836	f	"
", Dorcas	79	1771	f	NH

			67
Austin, Gilman	42	1808	m	VT
", Burnice	35	1815	f	"
", Lydia I.	13	1837	f	"
", James T.	11	1839	m	"
", Harvey K.	9	1841	m	"

WINDSOR			184
Austin, William H.	28	1822	m	VT
", Maria	30	1820	f	"
", Marion	1	1849	f	NH
	William was an Artisan	

			275
Austin, James	24	1826	m	VT
Bridge, James M.	33	1817	m	"
", Ann A.	32	1818	f	"
	James was an Artisan	

			356
Austin, Lebius H.	32	1818	m	NY
", Almira L.	32	1818	f	VT
", Susan A.	9	1841	f	"
	Lebius was a Farmer	

QUERIES

148-1. **Elizabeth Austin** and her first husband Amos Sheffield were both of Rhode Island. He was born circa 1764, probably in Newport. She was related to the Sweet family. She married second to a son of John and Amanda Merriss. Seek information on Elizabeth.

148-2. **Daniel Austin** was born circa 1773, married Mary (Polly) Brackett born circa 1780, moved in 1795 to Cumberland County, Maine, then in 1800 to Kennebec County, Maine. Three children were born in Maine, a girl (name not known), Daniel Brackett Austin born 1800, and Nathaniel C. Austin born circa 1806. Between 1806 and 1811 they moved to New York, where two girls (names unknown) and two boys were born, William Norris Austin born 1811 and Shadrach born circa 1813. Was Daniel originally from Massachusetts? Where did he marry? Seek parents and siblings of Daniel and Mary, and further information on their children.

148-3. **Daniel Webster Austin** was born 19 November 1844 in New York. Seek his ancestry.

148-4. **Agrippa Austin** had a daughter Angelina born 26 January 1822, who married Philip Cole of Jefferson County, New York, on 24 November 1840. An Agrippa Austin served in the War of 1812, his bounty land claim of February 1858 lists his residence as Montogue, Lewis County, New York, and his age as 72 years. A prior claim dated March 1855 lists his age as 66 years. Seek proof that this Agrippa is the father of Angelina.

148-5. **Elizabeth Austin** was born in 1848 in Russell County, Virginia, daughter of Thomas and Nancy Austin. She married on 14 March 1866 in Russell County to Samuel Worley Helton, born 1840 in Washington County, Virginia. Seek all information on this Austin line.

148-6. **Solomon Austin** born circa 1744 in Maryland. Lived around Baltimore. Moved to Orange County, North Carolina. Married Joanna Thomas in NC. He was a Loyalist, fled to Canada after the Revolutionary War. His parents may be Samuel Austin and Mary Green. Seek information on Soloman's ancestry. (see also *Austins of America*, pages 83 and 102-104).

148-7. **Elizabeth Austin** was born 22 February 1778, perhaps in Massachusetts or New York. She married circa 1795 to Israel Dodge, who was born in 1773 and died in 1854. Their ten children were born from 1796 to 1820, some at least in Rockland, Sullivan County, New York: Abigail, Austin, Elizabeth, Augustus, Israel, Harriett, Hannah, Cyrus, Lavina, and Julia. Seek birth and ancestry of Elizabeth Austin.

148-8. **Daniel Austin** b. 1782 in Massachusetts, m. Adah Dorman (1782-1815) from Hamden, Connecticut. They had children Francis, Adah Urana, Henry (1804-1891) and Merwin, the latter two being famous architects from New Haven CT and Rochester NY respectively, during the 19th century. Daniel married a second time, and moved to Canandaigua, New York, circa 1825 and was still there in 1850. His wife's name was Elizabeth, and his daughter by her was Esther. Need death and parents of Daniel.

COMPUTER

UPGRADE

DELAYS

1985 ISSUES

Austins of America files: one of two library carts holding notebooks forming the largest collection of Austin genealogical data available anywhere. The computer locates any desired information in the files in just seconds.

Dear *Austins of America* Reader:

I am writing to explain and apologize for the unusually long delay in your receiving the ''FEBRUARY 1985'' and ''AUGUST 1985'' issues of our *Austins of America* genealogical newsletter. We hope to have the August issue mailed out by the end of the year.

Publication of the two 1985 issues was delayed by a changeover in our *Austins of America* computerized typesetting system. Upgrading the computer was made necessary by the vast amount of Austin genealogical and historical data which has been contributed by our readers, which severely taxed the processing and storage capabilities of the old *Austins of America* computer shown on page 89 of the newsletter. The conversion this spring to an IBM PC/AT computer with 54 million bytes of disk storage will enable us to continue being responsive to reader Queries and to assist in the publication of articles sent in by Austin family researchers.

Cataloging and Retrieving Information

Information contributed by our readers is first filed in *Austins of America* notebooks, which now form the largest collection of Austin genealogical data available anywhere. As described on pages 87-90 of the newsletter, the information is then carefully abstracted into the *Austins of America* computer, so that everything filed in the notebooks can be located within seconds. You can perhaps appreciate the magnitude of the collection from the photograph here which shows our youngest daughter Melissa standing beside one of the two library carts used to hold the volumes of *Austins of America* information.

Sharing and Preserving Your Austin Data

In my correspondence and the *Austins of America* EDITOR'S CORNER I have often urged those who have transcribed Austin records or studied Austin lines to send us Queries and photocopies of their information so that their efforts will be shared with others and preserved through our newsletter. As is clear from each *Austins of America* issue, the response has been tremendous!

Each of our *Austins of America* issues is now donated to 54 state and territorial libraries. When complete sets of issues are comprehensively indexed and bound as hardcovered books, 54 copies will be reserved for the libraries to insure permanent preservation of this valuable Austin research data for future generations.

Austins of America and the AFA

There has been some confusion about the relationship between our *Austins of America* and the Austin Families Association (AFA). These separate organizations complement each other: *Austins of America* makes Austin data widely available by publishing and distributing it to Austin family researchers, while the AFA holds annual meetings around the country to encourage and guide newcomers searching for their Austin roots.

Operating independently, the two organizations share the common goal of helping Austin family researchers by trying to answer Queries, and by suggesting potential areas of research. The major difference between the organizations lies in the fact that *Austins of America* has a second very important goal – a goal not shared by the AFA. As was stated in the very first paragraph ever published on page 1 of our newsletter, *Austins of America* is intended ''to provide a place for previously unpublished research.''

Thus while *Austins of America* tries to help Austin family researchers either by answering Queries or by publishing them for a large readership at no cost, we also provide a unique opportunity for researchers to publish their data and Austin family lines and photographs without charge.

When Will My Material Be Published?

A few people have written wondering why their material has not yet appeared in *Austins of America*. We have a large number of articles in various stages of editing, and of course it is impossible to put everything into a single issue in any event. Unfortunately, a few people have mistakenly sent in their Queries and information to the AFA Secretary or Genealogist, expecting they would be published in the *Austins of America* newsletter. While the AFA Secretary and Genealogist do try to answer Queries whenever possible, they rarely forward the unanswered Queries to us for publication. Please send your Queries and other Austin information directly to:

Austins of America
23 Allen Farm Lane
Concord, MA 01742

Queries which cannot be answered directly from our computerized *Austins of America* files will be published, and hopefully someone among our wide readership will know something about your line. This often takes time . . . just recently we received a response to QUERY 26-11 which was published over four years ago! Genealogists will come across *Austins of America* back issues at their State Libraries, so do not become too discouraged if responses fail to come in immediately!

Unshared Correspondence and Lines

We have also received complaints that Austin lines previously sent to the AFA Secretary were not included in Austin articles we published. Here I must once again emphasize: any Austin materials you may have sent to the AFA in the past have *not* been shared with *Austins of America* readers. In fact, those older readers who may have written to Edith Austin Moore will be appalled to learn that their letters may no longer even exist - Edith's correspondence was mostly destroyed and thousands of letters irretrievably lost! To insure that your research efforts are not lost, please share your information with others and preserve it through its publication. Please send photocopies of your research directly to *Austins of America* at the address above.

Strong Ties With the AFA

Austins of America continues to enjoy strong ties with the AFA. A majority of those submitting articles to *Austins of America* have been AFA members, and a large fraction of *Austins of America* readers also belong to the AFA – 46% of our FEBRUARY 1984 and 48% of our AUGUST 1984 issues were mailed out to readers who were also active AFA members. I personally am a member of the AFA – as are all of the Associate Editors of our newsletter. All of us

have worked hard at promoting AFA membership though our correspondence and support of AFA meetings. My wife Patricia and I have attended six of the last seven AFA National Reunions by traveling to New York, Colorado, Tennessee, Ohio, Illinois and Indiana. We hosted the South Bend Reunion, placing a large notice in the local newspaper and personally telephoning every Austin family in the area. The turnout was rather disappointing, but we will still look forward to seeing you at next year's Reunion!

Reducing Subscriptions Confusion

Past confusion between *Austins of America* and the AFA occurred partly because a subscription to *Austins of America* has always been included in each AFA member's dues. Thus in recent years $2.50 of the AFA member's annual dues were spent to cover his or her *Austins of America* subscription. Due to AFA financial problems, at the 1985 National Reunion in South Bend it was first voted to raise the AFA dues to $7.50 per year. To further reduce the confusion between *Austins of America* and the AFA, it was then voted to separate out the *Austins of America* subscription cost by listing it apart from the AFA dues.

Thus, starting with their 1 August 1985 to 31 July 1986 dues, AFA members will be asked to pay $5.00 AFA dues plus $2.50 for their *Austins of America* subscription. They may elect to include the $2.50 subcription fee along with their $5.00 1985-86 AFA dues payment, and the AFA Secretary will forward their subscription fee to *Austins of America*. Alternatively, just as all non-AFA subscribers do, AFA members may now elect to send their $2.50 subscription fee directly to *Austins of America*. — *M.E.A.*

★★★★★★★★★★★★★★★★★★★★★★★★★★★★★

Austins of America is intended to serve present and future genealogists researching Austin family lines. Readers are encouraged to submit Queries, genealogical and historical articles for publication.

EDITOR

DR. MICHAEL EDWARD AUSTIN   CONCORD, MA

ASSOCIATE EDITORS

ANTHONY KENT AUSTIN	PROSPECT, KY
BERT ADDIS AUSTIN	QUEEN CREEK, AZ
PATRICIA BIEBUYCK AUSTIN	CONCORD, MA
PAULINE LUCILLE AUSTIN	MARION, IA
JANET AUSTIN CURTIS	ALBUQUERQUE, NM
CAROL LEIGHTON HULL	SUDBURY, MA

Austins of America is published each February and August by The Austin Print, 23 Allen Farm Lane, Concord, Massachusetts 01742. All correspondence, including subscriptions, articles and responses to queries, should be sent to this address. Subscriptions are $2.50 per year postpaid.   Copyright © 1985 by The Austin Print

★★★★★★★★★★★★★★★★★★★★★★★★★★★★★

AUSTIN VITAL RECORDS FROM THE
PROTESTANT CHURCHES OF
QUEBEC CITY AND NEARBY TOWNS

by Michael Edward Austin

Editor's Note: The following records were copied from microfilms of the original church records at the Centre d'archives de la Capitale, 1210 avenue du Seminaire, Sainte-Foy, Quebec, Canada. The facilities for research there are excellent, as fine as I have encountered anywhere. The records here were transcribed exactly as found, except that the years have sometimes been written numerically – for example, 'One Thousand Eight Hundred & Six' has been written as '1806.' Also, the phrase 'in the year of our Lord' has sometimes been abbreviated to 'A.D.' The records were generally well-indexed, although some errors were found, and a few Austin records discovered which were not indexed.

Alice Elizabeth daughter of Edward Aston Colour Serg^t First Battalion Rifle Brigade and of Elizabeth his wife by her maiden name Heazle Born on the twenty-eighth day of August 1869 and was baptized on the Fifth day of September in the same year by me, C. A. Wetherall, Chaplain H. M. Forces. The Sponsors were Elizabeth Aston and Margaret Hopkins. [Ref. 1]

Alfred John Austin, Bachelor, of the parish of Quebec, in the district of Quebec, was married after Banns duly published, to Anne McKenzie Vance, of the same place, Spinster, this twenty first day of October, in the year of our Lord 1841, By me, W. W. Wait, Minister of St. Paul's Chapel. Contracting Parties: Alfred John Austin X & Ann McKenzie Vance X Witness: Arthur Chaffey X [Ref. 12]

Alfred Knight Son of Henry Charles Austin of Quebec, Notary, and of Henrietta Maria (by her maiden name Knight) his wife, was born on the third of October one thousand eight hundred and fifty nine, and baptized on the eighteenth of January one thousand eight hundred and Sixty, By me, E. W. Worth, Incumbent of the Chapel of the Holy Trinity. Present: Henry Austin, Father; Henrietta Maria Austin, Mother; Wm Henry Knight, sponsor; Maria Ellen Austin, proxy for Lousia Jane Isilyam? [Ref. 3]

Moses Austin, Shoemaker & Sarah his wife had a Daughter born on the seventeenth of March last, and baptized this twenty-first day of May, One Thousand Eight Hundred & six, named Anne, by Alex^r Spark Min^r Present: Moses Austin, Father; Sally Austin, Mother; William Sharpe; Marg^t Fitzgibbon X [Ref. 10]

Anne Austin, daughter of Moses Austin, shoemaker, aged about four months, died on the nineteenth day of July inst. & was buried this Twentieth day of July, One Thousand Eight Hundred and Six. Alex^r Spark Min^r Present: Theophilis McGregor, Josiah Stiles [Ref. 10]

Ann, Daughter of Robert Austin private Soldier in his Majesty's ninety eighth Regiment & of Elizabeth his wife, died aged One Year on the fifth day of October in the Year of our Lord 1808 and was Buried the day following. By me, John Jackson, Evening Lecturer of English Church of Quebec. Present: Robt Austin, Father; The Mark of James McDoual X; The Mark of Laurence Kelly X [Ref. 2]

Moses Austin of Quebec Inn-Keeper and Sarah his wife had a Son born on the eleventh of November last, and baptised this Sixteenth day of January, One Thousand Eight Hundred & Ten, named Beman, by Alex^r Spark, Min^r Present: Moses Austin, Father; Sally Austin, Mother; Josiah Stiles; Elizur Miller [Ref. 10]

Charles Austin, private Soldier in His Majesty's thirteenth Regiment of Foot, aged about twenty five years, died November the seventh, and was buried November the eleventh in the year of our Lord 1813. By me, Father Jehosaphat Mountain, Officiating Minister of Quebec. [Ref. 2]

David son of John Austin and of his wife Sarah by her maiden name Bailey was born on the twelfth day of September and baptized on the twenty-eighth day of the same month eighteen hundred and sixty two, By me, Henry James Petry, B.A. Present: John Austin X [Ref. 9]

Edmund, son of Francis Austin Esqr of the City of Quebec, late Captain in the Army, and of Lucretia his wife, by her maiden name Hall, was born on the eleventh of June, A.D. 1835 and privately baptized on the fifteenth of February 1836, by me, J. Brown, Evening Lecturer. Present: Francis Austin, Father; Hammond? Gowan?; and J. W. Chear?. The above mentioned infant Edmund Austin died on the fourteenth and was buried on the eighteenth of March in the same year. By me, J. Brown, Evening Lecturer [Ref. 2]

Edmund Hale, son of Henry Charles Austin of the City of Quebec, Notary and of Henrietta Maria (by her maiden name Knight) his wife, was born on the twenty eighth day of July 1867 and privately baptized on the ninth day of February 1868. G. H. Phillip. Present: Henry C. Austin, Father; Henrietta M. Austin, Mother [Ref. 3]

Edward, son of Francis Austin, Esqr late Captain in the Army, and of Lucretia his wife by her maiden name Hall, was born on the eleventh of July and privately baptized on the twenty-fifth of September A.D. 1837, By me, J. Brown, Evening Lecturer. Present: F. Austin, Father; Lucretia Austin, Mother [Ref. 2]

Edward Aston, a Serjeant in the Rifle Brigade, Bachelor, and Elisabeth Hazel Spinster both of the City and parish of Quebec, were married by License on the First day of August 1867. Witnesses: Francis Lowe and Elisabeth Falconbridge [Ref. 1]

Eliza Jane, daughter of John Austin of Quebec, Rigger, & of Sarah his wife, by her maiden name Bailey, was born on the fifth day of May and was baptized on the twenty-first day of July eighteen hundred and fifty, By me, R. G. Plees. Parents: John Austin his X mark; Sarah Bailey her X mark. Sponsors: George O'Brien and Eliza Harris [Ref. 11]

George Forsyth of the City of Quebec Ship Carpenter aged about twenty two years, & Frances Austin of said City Spinster aged about nineteen years, were joined in marriage by License from His Excellency Sir James Henry Craig, at Quebec, this thirtieth day of November, One Thousand Eight Hundred & Seven by Alexr Spark Minr. Signed by George Forsyth, Frances Austin (her X mark), Thomas Forsyth, Colin Campbell [Ref. 10]. MEA Note: This couple had a daughter Mary born 22 October bp. 7 January 1810.

Francis Lewis Christian, son of Francis William Austin of Quebec, Advocate, and of Myrrha Harriet Bradshaw his wife, born the first day of December A.D. 1864 privately baptized the seventeenth of the same month in the same year, by Me, Henry Roe, B.A. Present: Myrrha Austin and Mary Ann Densser? [Ref. 7] MEA Note: This was recorded with the 1865 records.

Francis T. Austin, late Captain 76th Regt, died January Second, and was buried January Fifth, 1853, By me, Gilbert Percy [Ref. 9]

Francis Charles Gowen, Son of Henry Charles Austin, of the City of Quebec, Notary, and of Henrietta Maria (by her maiden name Knight) his wife, was born on the thirteenth of December one thousand eight hundred and sixty one, and baptized on the eightenth day of April in the year of our Lord one thousand eight hundred and Sixty two, By me, E. W. Worth. Present: Henry Austin, Father; Henrietta M. Austin, Mother; Sponsors: E. A. Beuchette; Hammond Gowen Jnr [Ref. 3]

Frances Frederika, daughter of Francis William Gowen Austin of Quebec, Advocate, and of Myrrha Harriet (by her maiden name Bradshaw) his wife, was born on the eighth of December one thousand eight hundred and fifty nine, and was privately baptised on the third of February one thousand eight hundred and Sixty, By me, E. W. Worth, Incumbent of the Chapel of the Holy Trinity. Present: Myrrha H. Austin, Mother, and Margaret McCowmien? [Ref. 3]

Francis William Gowen, son of Francis Austin Esqre Lieutenant in His Majesty's 76th Regiment of Foot & of Lucretia his wife, was born December the twenty-second A.D. 1818, and baptized February the seventeenth A.D. 1819. By me Joseph Langley Mills, Chaplain to H. M. Forces. Present: Francis Austin, Father; Lucretia Austin,

Mother; Wm Hall, godfather; Hy Cowan proxy for Willm C. Gowen godfather; Ellen Hall [Ref.1]

Francis William Gowen Austin of the City of Quebec, advocate, was married by license to Myrrha Harriet daughter of J. F. Bradshaw Esquire, spinster this twenty-fifth day of November A.D. 1856. Revt Cardin? Asst. Pastor The Holy Trinity. Contracting Parties: Francis W. G. Austin, Myrrha H. Bradshaw; W. Bradshaw, Father of the Bride; Maria? Motz?; Adila? Jashman?; Chas Phillips; Iduves? Bradshaw [Ref. 2]

Frederick St. Clair, son of Francis William Gowen Austin Esqr Advocate, and of Myrrha H. (by her maiden Name Bradshaw) his wife, was born in the eighth of October, and baptized on the tenth of November in the Year of our Lord One thousand eight hundred and Sixty one. By me, E. W. Worth. Present were F. W. G. Austin, Father; Myrrha H. Austin, Mother; Henry Austin proxy for George F. Austin; Mary Bradshaw proxy for Emily F. Austin [Ref. 3]

Gilbert Henry, son of Henry Austin, Brewer, of the City of Quebec, and of Elizabeth Barnard his Wife, was born September the sixteenth, and baptized October the seventh, in the year of our Lord One thousand eight hundred and four, By me, Father Jehosaphat Mountain, Officiating, Minister at Quebec. Present: Henry Austin, Father; Elizath B. Austin, Mother; Gilbert Austin, Godfather; Richd Qulliot?, Godfather; Hosmer Harpar her mark X, godmother [Ref. 4]

Gilbert Henry, son of Henry Austin, Brewer of the City of Quebec, and of Elizabeth Barnard his Wife, aged two months, died November the tenth, and was buried November the twelfth, in the year of our Lord 1804, By me, Father Jahosaphat Mountain, Officiating Minister at Quebec. Present: Henry Austin, Father; Heny Judah, Clerk at Brewery [Ref. 4]

Hamilton Austin, son of Thos Austin laborer, parish of Kilmoch Co of Artrian? Ireland and of Martha Jeffery, his wife, died on the 27th of May - a board the Ship Constitution, was lying in the quarantine station - and was buried on the same day of the said month A.D. 1847. G. M. Charles Frost, Chaplain Quar. Station. Present: Thomas Austin, Father; Andrew Shields [Ref. 5]

Henrietta Lucretia, daughter of Henry Austin of the Parish of Quebec Esqr Notary and Henrietta Maria (by her maiden name Knight) his wife, was born on the twenty first day of September and privately baptized on the twenty third day of November 1863. by me Charles M. Fox, A.B., Adjutant Minister of Holy Trinity. Present: Henry C. Austin, Father; Henrietta Maria Austin, Mother [Ref. 3]

Henry Austin of the City of Quebec, Foreman in McCallum's Brewery in St. Roch aged sixty years, died on the eighth and was buried on the tenth of March in the year

of our Lord 1826. By me J. Mountain D.D. Rector of Quebec. Present: Tho McCallum, John McCallum [Ref. 2]

Henry Charles, son of Francis Austin Esqr Lieutenant in H. M. 76th Regt and Lucretia his wife, was born in London June the Second A.D. 1820, and baptized May the twentieth A.D. 1821, By me, J. L. Mills, Chaplain to H. M. Forces. Present: Francis Austin, Father; Lucretia Austin, Mother; Henry Cowan, Godfather; Charles H.T.? Hall, godfather; Elinor Cowan, proxy for Margaret Gowen, godmother [Ref. 1]

Henry Charles Austin, Esquire of the City of Quebec, Notary, was Married by License to Henrietta Maria, eldest daughter of Captain Knight, Town Major, of the same place Spinster, this Tenth day of June AD 1856, By me D. Falloon, Off. Min. Contracting Parties: Henry Austin, Henrietta Maria Knight. Present: A. Knight, father to the Bride; F. W. G. Austin, Brother [Ref. 2]

Henry Goldie, son of Henry Charles Austin Esquire of the City of Quebec Notary and of Henrietta Maria his wife, by her maiden name Knight, was born on the thirtieth day of June and Baptized this twenty first day of August in the year of our Lord 1857, By me, R. A. Carden Asst. Mstr Ch Holy Trinity. Present: Henry Austin, Father; Henrietta M. Austin, Mother; Edmund St. C. Austin, Sponsor; Julia H. J. Knight; Henry C. Austin, proxy for Alfred F. A. Knight [Ref. 6]

Herbert Knight son of Henry Charles Austin of Quebec Notary and his wife Henrietta Maria, by her maiden name Knight, was born on the fifteenth of August 1869 and privately baptized this twenty fifth day of June 1870 By me, Charles Hamilton, M.A. Present: Henry C. Austin, Father; Henrietta M. Austin, Mother [Ref. 7]

Hugh Austin, mariner onboard the Bark Admiral Benbow, of Liverpool, Robert Dixon, Master, aged forty-eight years, died on the eighth and was buried on the ninth of June, in the year of our Lord, 1832, By me, J. Mountain, D.D. Rector of Quebec. Present: Robt Dixon, Master; Alenn Thomson [Ref. 2]

Ida Louisa, daughter of Henry Charles Austin of the City of Quebec, Notary and of Henrietta Maria (by her maiden name Knight) his wife, was born on the twenty third day of August 1865 and baptized on the twenty fourth day of June 1866, By me, E.W. Worth, M.A. Present: Henry C. Austin, Father; Henrietta M. Austin, Mother; A. F. A. Knight, Sponsor; H. Knight, Sponsor [Ref. 3]

James Hill Bradshaw, son of Francis William Gowen Austin of the City of Quebec, Esquire Barrister at Law, and of Myrrha Harriet his wife, by her maiden name Bradshaw, was born on the twenty first of February and

---

privately baptized on the Eleventh day of March A.D. 1858, by me, R. Casten, Asst Mstr. Present: F. W. G. Austin, Father; Myrrha H. Austin, Mother [Ref. 2]

John Austin of the parish of Quebec widower sail maker was married (By Banns) duly Published to Sarah Dinninton widow of the same place this twentieth day of July in the Year of Our Lord 1846, By me, John. By me, E. W. Worth? Incumbent of the Chapel of the Holy Trinity Quebec. Contracting Parties: John Austin his X mark; Sarah Dinninton her X mark; Present: Samuel Cutbarth; Martha McCarrol [Ref. 8]

John Joseph, son of John Austin of the city of Quebec, shiprigger, and of his wife Sarah by her maiden name Bailey, was born on the fifth day of June 1856 and baptized this twenty eighth day of August in the year of our Lord 1859, by me, Charles Hamilton, M.A. Present: John X Austin, Father; Sponsors: James Tilk, Elizabeth Tilk, Margaret Pearle, George X Pearle [Ref. 9]

Moses Austin of Quebec & Sarah his wife had a daughter born on the twelfth of November 1807 and baptised this twentieth day of April 1809, named Lucy by Alexr Spark. Present were: Moses Austin, Father; Sarah Austin, Mother; Josiah Stiles; Elizur Miller (male) [Ref. 10]

Lucy Austin, Daughter of Moses Austin of Quebec, aged about four years, died on the twenty fourth inst. & was buried on this twenty fifth day of December 1810. Alexr Spark, Minr. Present: Elizur Miller, George Stanley [Ref. 10]

Moses Austin of Quebec and Sarah his wife were baptized this twenty-fourth day of April, one Thousand Eight Hundred and nine. Alexr Spark Minr. Moses Austin born Decr 25 1778, Sarah Austin born August 9th 1779 [Ref. 10]

Myrrha Charlotte Austin, daughter of Francis William Gowen Austin of Quebec, Advocate, and of Myrrha Harriet Bradshaw his wife born the fourth of September was baptized the sixteenth of October A.D. 1864, By me, Henry Roe, B.A. Present were: F.W.G. Austin, father and proxy for J. L. Bradshaw, sponsor; Myrrha H. Austin, Mother; Charlotte Forsyth, Godmother; Ellen E. Arnold, sponsor [Ref. 7]

Richard, son of John Austin of the city of Quebec, and of his wife Sarah, by her maiden name Bailey, was born on the twenty fifth day of July 1854 and baptized this twenty eighth day of August 1854, By me, Charles Hamilton, M.A. Present: John X Austin, Father; Sponsors: James Tilk, Elizabeth Tilk, Margaret Pearle, George X Pearle [Ref. 9]

Sarah, daughter of John Austin of the city of Quebec Shiprigger and of his wife Sarah by her maiden name Baily (sic) was born on the twenty sixth day of March 1858 and

baptized this twentty eighth day of August in the year of our Lord 1859, by me, Charles Hamilton, M.A. Present: John X Austin, Father; Sponsors: James Tilk, Elizabeth Tilk, Margaret Pearle, George X Pearle [Ref. 9]

Sarah Lucy daughter of John Austin, Labourer Quebec and of his wife Sarah by her maiden name Bailey was born on the ninth day of August and baptized on the twenty sixth day of the same month in the year of our Lord one thousand eight hundred and sixty. By me, Henry James Petry, B. A. Present: John Austin X his mark, T. J. Tremain [Ref. 9]

Sophia Maude Lluellyn, daughter of Francis W.G. Austin Esq. of Quebec Barrister at Law and of Myrrha Harriet his wife by her maiden name Bradshaw was born on the nineteenth of December A.D. 1867, and baptized on the fifteenth of February in the year following. By me, George V. Goodman?, M.A., Rector of Quebec. Present: F. W. G. Austin, Father; Myrrha H. Austin, Mother; Eliza Rogers, Godmother; Lizzie Rogers, Godmother [Ref. 2]

William, Son of Robert Austin, private Soldier in His Majesty's ninety eighth Regiment of Foot, and of Elizabeth his Wife, was born July the twenty first and baptized July the thirtieth in the year of our Lord 1809, By me, John Jackson, evening Lecturer of the English Church at Quebec. Present: Robert Austin, Father; Elesabth Justin?, Mother; Denis Hozier?, Godfather; Jas Austin, Godfather; The Mark of Mary Munro, Godmother [Ref. 2]

William Austin, aged twenty five years, died on the third, and was buried on the fifth, day of September, in the year of our Lord 1847, By me, R. G. Plees [Ref. 11]

William Augustus, son of Francis Austin Esqr Captain on Half pay, unattached (residing now in Quebec) and of Lucretia his wife. Born on the 11th May 1829 and was privately Baptized on the eleventh day of June in the year of our Lord, One thousand Eight hundred and thirty two by me, R. R. Burrage, Minister of Aubigny Pointe Levi & the other Protestant Congregations in parts adjacent to Quebec. Present: Francis Austin, Father; Lucretia Austin, Mother. [Ref. 1]

William Charles, son of Thomas Austin a Private in the Fourth Battalion Sixtieth Rifles, and of Emily his Wife by her Maiden Name Rogers, Born on the fifteenth day of June 1862, was Baptized on the third day of August immediately following, by me, D. Robertson, Chaplain to H. M. Forces. The parents are Thos Austin & Emily Austin. The Sponsors are Henry Page, Color Sergeant, and William Dempster who have hereunder signed their names. [Ref. 1]

William David, son of John & Sarah Austin of Mark's, was born May fifteenth, and baptized June thirteenth, eighteen hundred and fifty-two, By me, Gilbert Percy. Parents:

John Austin, Sarah Austin; Sponsors: John Wills, Mary Jane Wills, John Austin [Ref. 9]

John Phimester of the royal artillery Bombardier aged about twenty six years, and Winifred Austin of Quebec, Spinster, aged about 22 years, were joined in marriage at Quebec, by Licence from the Honle Thomas Dunn Esquire President of the Province of Lower Canada, this sixteenth day of June, one Thousand Eight Hundred & six by Alexr Spark, Minr. Present: J. Phimester, Winifred Austen, Jno Gilmour, Seth? Carruthers? [Ref. 10]

John Auston, son of Geremiah Auston and Mary, bp. 15 September 1771. [Ref. 6]

Church References

[1] Military Congregation of the Garrison of Quebec; [2] Metropolitan Church; [3] Holy Trinity Church Quebec; [4] Anglican Cathereral, Quebec; [5] Dispersed Protestants; [6] English Cathedral; [7] St. Matthew's Chapel; [8] St. Paul's Church; [9] St. Peter's Chapel; [10] St. Andrew's Church, Quebec; [11] St. Peter's Anglican Church, Quebec; [12] St. Paul's Chapel (English Church Quebec).

QUERIES

154-1. Barbara Austin was born 5 January 1729, died 8 January 1790. She married 20 September 1752 at Stonington, Conn., to Daniel Butler born 26 March 1735 and died 20 March 1814 or 1819. Seek her ancestry.

154-2. Henrietta Virginia Austin was born circa 1842 in Ohio. Her father was born in New York, her mother in Kentucky. She married Ezra Thomas. Children were born in Missouri: Minnie 1861, Cora Bell 1862, Rosa 1863, Emma 1865. Children born in California: Lee 1868, Edward 1872, Charles 1875, Jennie 1877, Mattie 1881. Seek ancestry of Henrietta Austin.

154-3. Lockwood Austin was born 3 October 1797 in Greene County, New York. He was a veteran of the War of 1812, married 26 June 1830 Agitty Lewis. She was born August 1801 in Durham, New York. Both are buried in Orleans County, New York. Seek ancestry of both Lockwood and Agitty.

154-4. Sue Anna Austin was born 8 April 1874 in Henderson Co., North Carolina. She married in June 1889 to William Alonzo McEntire (1865-1925). She died 4 December 1956 at Hendersonville, Henderson Co. Their children were Rutledge 1890, Lloyd 1892, Bessie 1895, Glenn Lee 1897, Marry Lottie 1901, Paul 1903, Ralph Earl 1905, and Nina 1907, all born in Asheville, Buncombe Co., North Carolina. Seek others searching this Austin line.

QUERIES

155-1. Josephine Austin m. Theodore J. Slater. I believe her father was Gideon, but need this verified as well as the name of her mother. Also need Josephine's birth and death dates.

155-2. Francis Austin married Mary Borton in 1696 in Haddonfield, Burlington County, New Jersey. Their children were born and married there, including the direct descendant Hannah Austin who married William Sharp. Where did Francis come from?

155-3. Homer Austin appears in the 1830 Census in Charlestown, Portage County, Ohio: one male of twenty and under thirty, one male of thirty and under forty, three females under five, one female of twenty and under thirty. Need all data on Homer, his wife and children.

155-4. C. C., Amos and **Peacable Austin** appear in 1830 Census in Charlestown, Portage County, Ohio. Are these people connected with the Homer Austin of Query 155-3?

155-5. Theron Austin was born in Vermont on 3 December 1788. He bought 80 acres in Ripley County, Indiana. He married Philena Cunningham, born 7 October 1803, the daughter of William Cunningham. Seeking ancestry of Theron Austin.

155-6. Joseph Austin married Ailsey Curry. They had daughters Polly born 1818, Elizabeth born 1820, Rebecca born 16 December 1821, and Clary born 1823. Joseph died in 1823, Ailsey married in October 1824 to Josiah Bradway. Rebecca married Samuel Leonard on 13 March 1842 and they resided near Smithfield in Delaware County, Indiana. Seeking birth data and parents of Joseph.

155-7. Charles Austin had a daughter Pheriba born circa 1789. She married at age 21 in 1810 to Ambrose Manion, Jr. and had nine children probably born in Scottsville, Allen County, Kentucky. Seeking birth data on Pheriba, information on her mother, and ancestry of Charles.

155-8. Nathaniel Austin and Abigail (—) are buried in Westfield Flats Cemetery, Roscoe, New York. He died 28 February 1807, Abigail died 3 March 1803. Elizabeth Austin Dodge, who had ten children by Israel Dodge, died 11 December 1866 and is also buried there next to Nathaniel and Abigail. Seek proof that she is their daughter, Abigail's maiden name, and names of other children of Nathaniel and Abigail.

155-9. Ann E. Austin was of Tennessee, according to Sarah H. Steeves *Book of Remembrances of Marion County, Oregon, Pioneers 1840-1860*, pages 137-143. She married first to — Kurhler, second to Rev. John McKinney in Missouri. Seek Ann's ancestry.

155-10. Walter Austin was born 14 October 1801 and died 21-22 November 1866 in Washington, Washington Co., Iowa. He married 12 July 1827 in Portsmouth, Scioto Co., Ohio, to Sarah Nurse/Nourse, who was born 10 July 1809 in Chenango Co., New York, died 18 May 1885 in Iowa or Missouri, and buried in New Liberty Cemetery, Mound City, Holt Co., Missouri. Children born in Scioto County: Nelson b.1828 m. Mary Yonker; Samuel b.1830-2 m. Annie Kirkpatrick; Mary b.1833 m. — Sampson; Linis/Lewis b.1835; William Rile b.1837. Children prob. b. in Pike Co., Ohio: Isobel 1840 m. — Nash; Martha b.1843 m.1 L. C. Nourse m.2 Sam Curtis; Clemenza Josephine b.1845 m. James Tyler; Lyman Worth b. 3 January 1848 in Marion Twp. m. Mary Emeline Sitler; Sarah b.1850. Seek birthplace of Walter (KY, PA, NY, OH?) and parents and siblings of Walter and Sarah.

155-11. Ormal Austin born circa 1790, married Sally or Sarah Purple born circa 1801, they lived in Green County, New York, and Potter County, Pennsylvania. Seek Ormal Austin's birth data and ancestry.

155-12. Moses G. Austin thought born in Delaware County, New York, of parents who were natives of Massachusetts. He married Sophronia Bradley, probably born in Allegany County, New York. There may be a Collins family connection, as they named a son Collins and the name follows through to grandchildren. Also, their first-born son was Franklin W. Austin, which may provide a clue. Seek parents of Moses and Sophronia.

155-13. William Austin married Deborah (—), they had two children I know of: Joseph C. Austin born in May 1809 and Mary Johnson Austin born 17 February 1819. Mary married Stephen Wiseman on 4 December 1850, and she died in 1903 in Omro, Wisconsin. I have indications that the family came from Indiana to Wisconsin, and am seeking all information on William and Deborah.

155-14. Joseph Austin m. 3 June 1800 Jenny Alford, spinster, in Amherst County, Virginia, with Benjamin Austin, surety, and consent of her father Wm. Alford. They had at least two sons born in Amherst County: Benjamin Robert Austin b.1802 and William Alford Austin b.1806. Some time later the family moved to Tennessee and by 1828 had moved again to Macon County, Illinois. Seeking Joseph's ancestry.

155-15. James A. Austin was born 11 June 1829 in Meigs County, Ohio. He migrated with his family circa 1866 to southern Illinois. His son was George H. Austin who resided in Effingham County, Illinois. Possibly James descends from Anthony, via Ralph who lived 1804-13 in Franklin County, Ohio, and Joseph who perhaps married in Franklin County. Seeking ancestry of James Austin.

Austins in the Federal Census of 1850

Alabama

by Jennie Mae Austin Auld

BUTLER COUNTY, AL

. . . . B737
Austin, David	70	1780	m	AL
" , Lucinda	50	1800	f	GA

David was a Farmer

. . . . D101
Austin, George H.	29	1821	m	GA
" , Eliza	27	1823	f	SC
" , Washington	8	1842	m	AL
" , Mary Ann	6	1844	f	"
" , Thomas	4	1846	m	"
" , Rebecca	2	1848	f	"

George was a Wheelright

COASA COUNTY, AL

. . . . p.34-?
Austin, Tolliver L.	31	1819	m	SC
" , Elizabeth	22	1828	f	GA
" , Virginia	4	1846	f	"
" , William	2	1848	m	"

DALE COUNTY, AL

. . . . p.196-434
Austin, John A.	35	1815	m	GA
" , Louisa	30	1820	f	"
" , Albert	11	1839	m	AL
" , William	7	1843	m	"
" , John	2	1848	m	"
" , Jefferson	1	1849	m	"

. . . . p.196-433
Cooper, R.J.	32	1818	m	GA
" , Sarah	20	1830	f	AL
" , Frances	8	1842	f	"
" , Matthew	4	1846	m	"
" , Marion	3	1847	m	"
" , John	3/12	1850	m	"
Austin, Sarah	62	1788	f	NC

R. J. was a Farmer

DALLAS COUNTY, AL

. . . . p.281-?
Austin, John	49	1801	m	NC
" , Louiza	35	1815	f	"
" , Esther	23	1827	f	"
" , Catherine	19	1831	f	"
" , -	15	1835	m	"
" , Louiza	13	1837	f	"
" , John T.	12	1838	m	AL
" , Penelope	9	1841	f	"
" , William	7	1843	m	"
" , ?elmen	5	1845	m	"
" , Alphonza	3	1847	m	"

John was a Farmer

DEKALB COUNTY, AL

. . . . p.406-650
Auston, Jeremiah	29	1821	f	AL
" , John P.	3	1847	m	"

. . . . p.388-193
Rice, Joseph	50	1800	m	TN
" , Rhonda A.	25	1825	f	GA
Auston, William	6	1844	m	AL

FAYETTE COUNTY, AL

. . . . p.94-244
Austin, Robert	65	1785	m	VA
" , Elizabeth	65	1785	f	"

Robert was a Farmer

FRANKLIN COUNTY, AL

. . . . p.107-68
West, Peter	57	1793	m	TN
" , Elizabeth	45	1805	f	"
Austin, James (John)	3	1847	m	"

. . . . p.123-298
Austin, John	25	1825	m	SC
" , Nancy	25	1825	f	GA

. . . . p.167-69
Austin, Thos J.	43	1807	m	VA

Thomas was a Planter

HANCOCK COUNTY, AL

. . . . p.368-153
Austin, Jessey	22	1828	m	TN
" , Emeline	18	1832	f	AL

Jessey was a Farmer

JACKSON COUNTY, AL

. . . . p.32-619
Austin, A. C.	36	1814	m	TN
" , Elizabeth	24	1826	f	AL
" , William	3	1847	m	"
" , Robert H.	2	1848	m	"

A. C. was a Merchant

. . . . p.52-15
Austin, Allen	45	1805	m	TN
" , Anny	44	1806	f	"
" , William	23	1827	m	AL
" , John	21	1829	m	"
" , Henry	-	-	m	"
" , George	19?	1831	m	"
" , David	17	1833	m	"
" , Francis	12	1838	f	"
" , Mary	10	1840	f	"
" , Eliza	8	1842	f	"

Allen a Farmer, William a laborer

. . . . p.62-459
Austin, James	24	1826	m	AL
" , Elizabeth	21	1829	f	TN
" , Frances	8	1842	f	AL
" , Gerome	7	1843	m	"
" , Leroy	4	1846	m	"
" , John	1	1849	m	"

James was a Farmer

. . . . p.43-618
Austin, Jane	55	1795	f	KY
" , James	20	1830	m	AL

James was a Laborer

. . . . p.131-379
Austin, Martha	45	1805	f	NC
" , Charles	23	1827	m	TN
" , William	21	1829	m	AL
" , Eliza C.	17	1833	f	"
" , Julia H.	15	1835	f	"
" , David	11	1839	m	"
" , Therman	9	1841	m	TN

Charles was a Laborer

. . . . p.122-251
Austin, Mary	25	1825	f	TN

Household of James S. Thompson

. . . . p.124-294
Austin, Redda	46	1804	f	NC
" , Marida	25	1825	m	VA

. . . . p.32-466
Austin, Robert	62	1788	m	VA
" , Mary E.	38	1812	f	IN

. . . . p.121-250
Austin, Robert C.	35	1815	m	TN
" , Jane E.	25	1825	f	"
" , James H.	8	1842	m	-
" , Thomas A.?	7	1843	m	AL
" , Matilda P.	5	1845	f	"
" , David	3	1847	m	"
" , Margret ?	1	1849	f	"

Robert C. was a Farmer

. . . . p.124-288
Dubois, Elias	57	1793	m	NC
" , Rebecca	50	1800	f	TN
Austin, Sinda	19	1831	f	AL

. . . . p.43-619
Austin, William	21	1829	m	AL
" , Mallinda	21	1829	f	"

William was a Laborer

. . . . p.81-436
Austin, William A.	38	1812	m	TN
" , Elvine	23	1827	f	"
" , Robert	8	1842	m	AL
" , James C. G.	1	1849	m	"
Dulancy, Nancey	35	1815	f	TN

William was a Merchant

LAUDERDALE COUNTY, AL

. . . . p.233-44
Auston, Alexander	54	1796	m	SC
" , Sarah	44	1806	f	NC
" , Sinthia	65	1785	f	SC

. . . . p.246-231

Auston, Jessy Y.	31	1819	m	AL
" , Harriett	25	1825	f	"
" , Parilee	11	1839	f	"
" , Jane	9	1841	f	"
" , Robert	7	1843	m	"
" , John	8/12	1849	m	"

Jessy was a Farmer

. . . . p.246-230

Auston, John	61	1789	m	VA
" , Martha	57	1793	f	SC

John was a Farmer

. . . . p.246-218

Auston, Robert	30	1820	m	AL
" , Eliza	27	1823	f	"
" , Francis Marion	5	1845	m	"
" , Columbus	3	1847	m	"
" , Sarah	16	1834	f	"
" , Mary Elizabeth	14	1836	f	"

Robert was a Farmer

LAWRENCE COUNTY, AL

. . . . p.462-?

Austin, William	57	1793	m	TN
" , Mary	51	1799	f	KY
" , Tho. J.	31	1819	m	AL
" , Sarah A.	26	1824	f	"
" , Hugh J.	23	1827	m	"
" , Martha	18	1832	f	"
" , Albert G.	16	1834	m	"

LIMESTONE COUNTY, AL

. . . . p.86-623

Davis, Robert C.	52	1798	m	VA
" , Sarah	48	1802	f	NC
" , George F.	11	1839	m	AL
" , Catherine C.	8	1842	f	"
" , William	6	1844	m	"
Austin, James P.	14	1836	m	"

Robert C. Davis was a Postmaster

MARENGO COUNTY, AL

. . . . p.19-?

Bickley, Wm. A.	35	1815	m	SC
Austin, J.G.	30	1820	m	NC

Farmer

. . . . p.83-1239

Austin, William K.	23	1827	m	NC

Overseer res. Edward Curtis hsehld

MARSHALL COUNTY, AL

. . . . p.415-395

Austin, Isaac	32	1818	m	GA
" , Cynthia	27	1823	f	"
" , Clarsitta	7	1843	f	"
" , Rachael W.	2	1848	f	"
" , Mary L.	6/12	1850	f	"
" , John V. B.	7	1843	m	"

Isaac was a Farmer

. . . . p.201-326

Auston, James	21	1829	m	GA
" , Mary	35	1815	f	"
" , William	17	1833	m	AL
" , Charlotta	15	1835	f	"
	13	1837	m	"
" , Candis	8	1842	f	"
" , Jesse M.	6	1844	m	"

James was a Farmer

. . . . p.496-396

Miess, Jacob	36	1814	m	TN
" , Nancy	33	1817	f	NC
" , John W.	6	1844	m	AL
Austin, Mathew J.	5	1845	m	GA

MOBILE COUNTY, AL

. . . . p.310-?

Austin, H. B.	40	1810	m	CT
" , Mary Jo	28	1822	f	AL
" , George	9	1841	m	"
" , Anna	8	1842	f	"
" , Olivia	6	1844	f	"
" , Ellen	4	1846	f	"
" , Brig	2	1848	m	"
" , Virginia	2/12	1850	f	"
McNamara, Virginia	22	1828	f	"
Adams, Jasper	42	1808	m	DEN
" , Anna	6	1844	f	AL
" , Martin	3	1847	m	"

H. B. was a Merchant

. . . . p.352-1242

Austin, Henry	16	1834	m	AL

Clerk; household of Jane Springer

. . . . p.456-226

Austin, Albert	18	1832	m	AL

Laborer household of George Asberry

. . . . p.360-1225

Austin, D. W.	29	1821	m	CT
McClaskey, Joe	32	1818	m	NY
Myers, F.	25	1825	m	GER

D. W. was a Clerk in Mobile

. . . . p.393-274

Marshall, Wm. T.	32	1818	m	GA
" , Mary A.	25	1825	f	AL
" , Augusta	8	1842	f	"
" , Robert	6	1844	m	"
" , Edward	3	1847	m	"
Austin, Josephine	12	1838	f	"
" , —	10	1840	m	"

Wm. was a Merchant

. . . . p.393-1842

Austin, Sarah	50	1800	f	NH
" , Susan	21	1829	f	AL
Gelder, Simon	30	1820	m	"
" , Jane	20	1830	f	"
" , M.M.	3	1847	-	"

MONTGOMERY COUNTY, AL

. . . . p.163-173

Boyd, Margaret	61	1789	f	SC
Austin, Elizabeth	28	1822	f	"
Scippen, Edmond	21	1829	m	"
Austin, Louisa	11	1839	f	AL
" , Mary A. M.	8	1842	f	"
" , Margaret E.	6	1844	f	"
" , John W.	4	1846	m	"

. . . . p.130-981

Maloney, Wm.	38	1812	m	IRE
Austin, Jno. C.	35	1815	m	GA
" , Mary	28	1822	f	NC
" , Sarah E.	10	1840	f	GA

Wm. a Merchant, Jno. a Mechanic

MORGAN COUNTY, AL

. . . . p.234-574

Owens, Wm.	68	1782	m	SC
" , Elizabeth	65	1785	f	"
Austin, George	21	1829	m	AL
" , Mary A.	21	1829	f	"

Wm. & George were Farmers

. . . . p.203-104

Austin, Nancy	42	1808	f	NC
" , William F.	18	1832	m	"
" , Leanden M.	16	1834	m	"
" , Lawson	14	1836	m	"
" , Mary E. M.	10	1840	f	"
" , Elmira	5	1845	f	"

Austin males were Laborers

. . . . p.187-11

Matthews, John A.	24	1826	m	PA
Austin, John A.	27	1823	m	NC
" , Mary E.	28	1822	f	AL

John Austin was a Tailor

MADISON COUNTY, AL

. . . . p.466-508

Terrell, Wm.	32	1818	m	TN
" , Cornelia	21	1829	f	AL
" , William	5	1845	m	"
Austine, Amanuel	18	1832	m	MEX

Wm. was a Barber

. . . . p.448-279

Jacobs, Becka	43	1807	f	SC
" , Wm. H.	15	1835	m	AL
" , Martha	10	1840	f	"
" , Isaac	7	1843	m	"
" , Stanhope	1	1849	m	"
Austin, Mary E.	38	1812	f	"
" , James M.	21	1829	m	"
" , Prudence E.	18	1832	f	"
" , Cyntha N.	11	1839	f	"
" , Mary E.	11	1839	f	"

James was a Farmer

PIKE COUNTY, AL

. . . . p.268-1825

Austin, Jefferson W.	23	1827	m	GA
" , Thdorf?	21	1829	f	"
" , William	1	1849	m	AL

Jefferson was a Farmer

. . . . p.268-1826

Austin, John F. B.	22	1828	m	GA
" , Mary	19	1831	f	SC
" , John	2	1848	m	AL
" , Mary	4/12	1850	f	"

John was a Farmer

. . . . p.268-1828

Austin, Lubbonn	48	1802	m	AL
" , Lavislana	42	1808	f	"
" , Subron	16	1834	m	"
" , James	15	1835	m	"
" , Charity	12	1838	f	"
" , Andrew J.	11	1839	m	"
" , Martha Ann	8	1842	f	"
" , Pleasant	6	1844	m	"
" , Mahala	4	1846	f	"

Lubbonn was a Merchant

SOME AUSTIN SOLDIERS

IN THE WAR OF 1812

by Sally Austin Day

Author's Note: The following data was obtained from the National Archives Microfilm 602, Reel 7. Mostly southern states were copied: District of Columbia, Georgia, Indiana, Kentucky, Louisiana, Maryland, Mississippi, Missouri, North Carolina, Pennsylvania, South Carolina, Tennessee, and Virginia. The New England states were not copied, nor were Michigan, New Jersey, New York, or Ohio.

— Austin, Pvt.	Planche's Batt. LA Militia
— Austin, Servant	33rd Regt. VA Militia
Adley Austin, Cpl.	1st Regt. Means' SC Militia
Alexander Austin, Col.	3rd Regt. Dickson's VA Militia
Alexander Austin, Pvt.	1st Regt. Biddle's PA Militia
Amon Austin, Pvt.	Nash's Regt. SC Vol.
Archibald Aston, Pvt.	Youngblood's Regt. SC Militia
Archibald Austin, Pvt.	5th Regt. VA Militia
Archibald Austin, Surgeon	3rd Regt. Dickson VA Militia
Barruch Austin, Pvt.	32nd Regt. Hood's MD Militia, Capt. Wallace's Co.
Benjamin Austen, Pvt.	Montgomery's Regt. PA Militia
Benjamin Austin, Pvt.	1st Rifle Batt. Pinkney's MD Militia
Benjamin Austin, Pvt.	Extra Batt. MD Militia
Benjamin Austin, Pvt.	Watkin's Command MD Militia
Benjamin Auston, Ensign	Bunch's East TN Militia (1814)
Bennett Austin, Pvt.	8th Regt. Wall's VA Militia
Benson Austen, Pvt.	Kemper's VA Militia
Benson F. Austin, Pvt.	41st Regt. Bramham's VA Militia
Benson F. Austin, Pvt.	Kempers' Detachment VA Militia
Blalock Austin, Pvt.	1st Regt. McDonald's NC Militia
Brooke Austin, Pvt.	Extra Batt. MD Militia
Caleb Austin, Pvt.	Capt. Bordeaux's Co. NC Militia
Chapman Austen, Pvt.	41st Regt. Braham's VA Militia
Chapman Austin, Cpl.	11th Regt. Parker's VA Militia
Charles A. Austin, Sgt.	LA Mounted Riflemen Capt. Rankin's Co.
Charles Austin, Pvt.	1st Regt. Crutchfield's VA Militia
Charles Austin, Pvt.	4th Regt. Jones' GA Militia
Cliffe Austin, Pvt.	9th Regt. Boyd's VA Militia
Cornelius Austin, Pvt.	2nd Regt. Tisdale's NC Militia
Cornelius Auston, Pvt.	1st Regt. Flower's NC Militia
Daniel Austin, Pvt.	13th Regt. Gray's KY Militia
David Austen, Pvt.	49th Regt. Veazey's MD Militia
David Austin, Drummer	111th Regt. Parker's VA Militia
David Austin, Lt.	Mounted Gunmen TN Militia Russell's Separate Batt.
David Austin, Pvt.	41st Regt. Braham's VA Militia
David Austin, Pvt.	49th Regt. Veazey's MD Militia
David Austin, Pvt.	4th Regt. Mounted (Evans) IN Militia
David Austin, Pvt.	5th Regt. VA Militia
David Austin, Pvt.	7th Regt. Gray's VA Militia
David Austin, Pvt.	8th Regt. Wall's VA Militia
David Austin, Pvt.	Capt. Cowan's Co. Mounted TN Militia

David Austin, Pvt.	Capt. William Russell TN Vol. Mounted Spies
David S. Austin, Pvt.	5th Regt. VA Militia
David S. Austin, Pvt.	6th Regt. Coleman's VA Militia (Jan–May 1814)
Edward Austin, Sgt.	36th Renno's VA Militia
Evan Austin, Lt.	Maj. Smoot's Batt. MS Militia
Fleming Austen, Pvt.	7th Regt. Gray's VA Militia
Fleming Austin, Capt.	Batt. of Artillery (1813–14) VA Militia
Fleming Austin, Cpl.	4th Regt. VA Militia Lt. Cols. McDowell, Koontz & Chilton
Fleming Austin, Pvt.	4th Regt. Beatty's VA Militia
Fleming Austin, Pvt.	7th Regt. Gray's VA Militia
Francis Austin, Pvt.	19th Regt. Ambler's VA Militia
George Austin, Pvt.	1st Rifle Regt. Allen's KY Vol.
George W. Austin, Pvt.	4th Regt. VA Militia Lt. Cols. Huston & Wooding
Gideon Austin, Pvt.	1st Regt. Mean's SC Militia
Harmon Austin, Drummer	Gibb's NC Militia Middlecreek Co.
Isaac Austen, Pvt.	4th Regt. Booth's GA Militia
Isaac Austin, Lt.	4th Regt. Booth's GA Militia
Isiah Austin, Pvt.	52nd Regt. Christian's VA Militia (see Josiah Austin)
James Austeen, Pvt.	Newman's Command Georgia Vol.
James Asten, Pvt.	1st Regt. Metcalf's West TN Militia
James Austin, Pvt.	1st Regt. Truehart's VA Militia
James Austin, Pvt.	1st Regt. Wear's East TN Vol.
James Austin, Pvt.	33rd Regt. Major's VA Militia
James Austin, Pvt.	6th Regt. Coleman's VA Militia (Jan–May 1814)
James Austin, Pvt.	8th Regt. Wall's VA Militia
James Austin, Pvt.	Dubois' Batt. Mounted Spies KY Vol.
James Austin, Pvt.	SC Militia (Matross) Howard's Detachment
James Austin, Sgt.	13th Regt. Gray's KY Militia
James M. Austin, Pvt.	1st Regt. West TN Vol. Perkin's Mounted
Jean Austin, Pvt.	8th Regt. Meriam's LA Militia
Jeremiah Austin, Pvt.	Maj. Smoot's Batt. MS Militia
Jeremiah Osten, Pvt.	13th Regt. Gray's KY Militia
Jesse Austen, Pvt.	4th Regt. Jones' GA Militia
Jesse Austin, Pvt.	4th Regt. Jones' GA Militia
John Austin, Lt. & Adjutant	10th Regt. LA Militia
John Austin, Lt.	11th Regt. Caldwell's KY Militia (Hudspeth & Brown)
John Austin, Lt.	11th Regt. KY Militia Hudspeth & Brown's Regt.
John Austin, Lt.	14th Regt. Mitchisson's KY Militia
John Austin, Lt.	Lt. Gen. Thomas' Detachment KY Militia (see 14th Regt.)
John Austin, Pvt.	1st Regt. Dist. of Columbia Cols. Lynn & Daingerfield
John Austin, Pvt.	1st Regt. Perkin's Mounted West TN Vol.
John Austin, Pvt.	1st Regt. Truehart's VA Militia
John Austin, Pvt.	27th Regt. Long's MD Militia
John Austin, Pvt.	2nd Regt. Cocke's West TN Militia
John Austin, Pvt.	35th Regt. Brown's MD Militia

John Austin, Pvt.	4th Regt. VA Militia Lt. Cols. Wooding & Huston	Simeon Austin, Pvt.	53rd Regt. VA Mil. (Aug 1814 – Jan 1815)
John Austin, Pvt.	52nd Regt. Christian's VA Militia	Spotswood Austin, Pvt.	33rd Regt. VA Militia (Aug – Sept 1814)
John Austin, Pvt.	Bunch's Regt. East TN Vol.	Stephen F. Austin, Pvt.	Col. McNair's Mounted Regt. IL & MO Militia
John Austin, Pvt.	Chile's Batt. East TN Vol. Mounted Gunmen	Thomas Austin, Cpl.	68th Regt. VA Militia Cols. Walker & Bassett
John Austin, Pvt.	Craven's Regt. NC Militia	Thomas Austin, Pvt.	2nd Regt. Jenning's KY Vol.
John Austin, Pvt.	MS Militia Lt. Col. Neilson's Detachment	Thomas Austin, Pvt.	2nd Regt. Tisdale's NC Militia (see J. Worrell)
John Austin, Pvt.	Shanck's Detachment PA Militia	Thomas Austin, Pvt.	74th Regt. Truehart's VA Militia
John Austin, Quartermaster	Austin's Regt. SC Militia	Thomas Austin, Pvt.	Batt. of Artillery VA Militia (1813 – 14)
John Austin, Sgt.	15th Regt. Slaughter's KY Militia	Thomas Austin, Pvt.	Capt. Bourdeaux's NC Militia
John H. Austin, Pvt	52nd Regt. Christian's VA Militia	Thomas Austin, Pvt.	Capt. King's Co. Artillery VA Militia
John M. Austin, Pvt.	2nd Regt. Thomas' GA Militia	Thomas Austin, Pvt.	Craven's Regt. NC Militia
Jonas Austain, Pvt.	LA 1st Batt. U. S. Vol. Maj. Wm. Henry	Thomas Auston, Pvt.	4th Regt. Bayless' East TN Militia
Jonathan Auston, Pvt.	1st Regt. McDonald's NC Militia	Thomas C. Austin, Paymaster	Austin's Regt. SC Militia
Joseph Austin, Pvt.	2nd Regt. Lillard's East TN Vol.	William A. Austin, Cpl.	3rd Regt. Alston's SC Militia
Joseph Austin, Pvt.	Lt. Col. Dodge's Missouri Militia	William Austen, Pvt.	1st Regt. Means' SC Militia (see Wm. Aston)
Joseph Austin, Pvt.	Newman's Command GA Vol.	William Austin, Cpl.	1st Regt. Dyer's TN Vol. Mounted Gunmen
Joseph Auston, Pvt.	2nd Regt. Evan's VA Militia		
Joseph Auston, Pvt.	4th Regt. Bayless' East TN Vol.	William Austin, Cpl.	Maj. King's Detachment, D.C.
Josiah Austin, Pvt.	52nd Regt. Christian's VA Militia	William Austin, Lt.	57th Regt. VA Militia Lt. Cols. Mason & Minor
Lawless Austin, Pvt.	39th Regt. Fowler's MD Militia		
Levi Austin, Pvt.	2nd Regt. Williamson's TN Vol. Mounted Gunmen	William Austin, Lt. Col.	Austin's Regt. SC Militia
		William Austin, Pvt.	13th Regt. Gray's KY Militia
Lewis Austin, Pvt.	1st Regt. Riflemen Sutherland's PA Vol.	William Austin, Pvt.	1st Regt. Bradley's TN Vol.
Miles Austin, Pvt.	68th Regt. VA Militia Lt. Cols. Walker & Bassett	William Austin, Pvt.	1st Regt. Clark's VA Militia
		William Austin, Pvt.	1st Regt. Hall's TN Vol.
Morton Austin, Pvt.	19th Regt. Ambler's VA Militia	William Austin, Pvt.	1st Regt. Truehart's VA Militia
Moses Auston, Pvt.	1st Regt. Flower's NC Militia	William Austin, Pvt.	1st Regt. Wynne's West TN Vol.
Moton Austen, Cpl.	6th Regt. Coleman's VA Militia (Jan – May 1814)	William Austin, Pvt.	2nd Regt. Jenning's KY Vol.
		William Austin, Pvt.	2nd Regt. Sharp's VA Militia (see 1st Regt. Clark's VA)
Nathaniel Austen, Pvt.	4th Regt. South's Mounted KY Vol.		
Nathaniel Austin, Pvt.	5th Regt. South's Mounted KY Vol.	William Austin, Pvt.	33rd Regt. Mayo's VA Militia
Obadiah Austin, Pvt.	Randolph's VA Militia 1st Corps d'Elite	William Austin, Pvt.	49th Regt. Veazey's Maryland Militia
		William Austin, Pvt.	4th Regt. Greenhill's VA Militia
Orville Austin, Pvt.	111th Regt. Parker's VA Militia	William Austin, Pvt.	7th Regt. Gray's VA Militia
Orville Austin, Pvt.	4th Regt. VA Militia Lt. Cols. McDowell, Koontz & Chilton	William Austin, Pvt.	8th Regt. Wall's VA Militia (see Jacob Smith)
Ozias Austin, Lt.	Col. Claiborne's Regt. MS Militia	William Austin, Pvt.	Capt. Wm. Russell's Co. TN Mounted Spies
Ozias Austin, Sgt.	Hind's Cavalry Batt. MS Militia	William Austin, Pvt.	MS Militia Lt. Col. Neilson's Detachment
Patrick Austin, Pvt.	Maj. Woodford's Cavalry VA Militia		
Pekn Austin, Sgt.	Woodford's Squad VA Militia	William Austin, Pvt.	Lt. Col. Nixon's Regt. MS Militia
Peter Austin, Sgt.	6th Regt. Barbour's KY Militia	William Austin, Pvt.	Prisoner of War
Pleasant Austin, Pvt.	McCrory's Regt. West TN Militia	William Austin, Sgt.	2nd Regt. Brent's Dist. of Columbia
Ransom Austin, Pvt.	4th Regt. Greenhill's VA Militia	William Auston, Lt. Cmdr.	26th Regt. Auld's MD Militia
Ransom Austin, Pvt.	68th Regt. VA Militia Lt. Cols. Walker & Bassett	William J. Austin, Pvt.	4th Regt. MD Militia
		William N. Austin, Pvt.	5th Regt. VA Militia
Reuben Austin, Pvt.	1st Regt. Truehart's VA Militia	William W. Austin, 2nd Lt.	VA Militia Maj. Woodford's Cavalry
Richard L. Austin, Lt.	26th Regt. Auld's MD		
Robert S. Austin, Pvt.	4th Regt. VA Militia (Jul – Oct 1814)	Willis Auston, Pvt.	2nd Regt. Sharp's VA Militia
Samuel Austin, Pvt.	1st Regt. Pipkin's West TN	Wilson Astin, Pvt.	7th Regt. Saunder's VA Militia
Samuel Austin, Pvt.	35th Regt. Brown's MD Militia	Woodson Austin, Pvt.	4th Regt. Beatty's VA Militia
Samuel Auston, Pvt.	26th Regt. Auld's MD Militia	Woodson Auston, Pvt.	Artillery Batt. VA Militia (1813 – 14)
Samuel G. Austin, Pvt.	1st Regt. West TN Vol. Perkin's Mounted		

THOMAS AND MARY KNOX AUSTIN
YANKEES OF BENTONVILLE ARKANSAS
AND LEAVENWORTH KANSAS

by Maude L. Ashe

T. Thomas Austin, who called himself a Yankee, married Mary Crawford Knox in Onandaga County, New York, on 18 November 1827, according to family records. In later Census returns, Thomas gave his birthplace as New York, but neither the town nor county are known, and his parents are also unknown. His birthdate was probably 22 July 1804. His young wife was said to have been born in Massachusetts on 4 April 1811, but again there is no word of town, county, or parents. Since only the towns kept vital records in Massachusetts before 1850, genealogical research is rather difficult unless the name of the town is known. Onandaga County sources have not been helpful in yielding information. They are believed to have had nine children, although Charles does not appear in Census records:

CHILDREN: T1. SUSAN T., *b. 13 October 1828 New York, m. – Patton*

T2. WILLIAM H., *b. 20 May 1831 Ohio*

T3. WINFIELD, *b. circa 1835 Ohio*

T4. WESLEY, *b. 7 October 1837 prob. Izard Arkansas*

T5. JOHN N., *b. circa 1841 Arkansas*

T6. SARAH JANE, *b. 1843 Arkansas, m. circa 1862 – Keith*

T7. MARY MELISSA, *b. 24 October 1847 prob. Independence, Arkansas, m. 15 August 1867 W. D. Loudon, d. 18 July 1923*

T8. ROBERT LEWIS, *b. 11 June 1857 Arkansas*

T9. CHARLES, *portrait taken in Leavenworth, Kansas, shown on p.164*

Thomas Austin 1804-1879
Mary Knox Austin 1811-1878

Soon after the birth of their first child, Thomas and Mary left New York and moved the family westward, "to grow up with the country," he said. Mary was accustomed to add that "hunting and fishing were becoming played out in New York." They may have traveled by land, or taken passage on the new Erie Canal, which had been completed in 1827, the year of their marriage. They may have settled temporarily in Cleveland, Cuyahoga County, Ohio. A Thomas Austin, wife and small daughter, who fell within their age brackets, are listed there in the 1830 Census for Ohio. Properly researched, the old Cuyahoga County records might reveal more information, but those readily available do not tell of William's birth. According to the 1850 Census, taken in Arkansas, Winfield was also born in Ohio, probably in 1835. Five younger children are known to have been born in Arkansas, but no record is given for Charles, either in the family records or in the Census

The Bentonville, Arkansas, Austin home had become 'The Eagle House' fifty years later, as shown in this photograph brought to California by Mary Melissa (Austin) Loudon circa 1905.

returns. It was in Ohio that Thomas Austin acquired a small leather case for pill bottles. This may have been his introduction to the practice of country medicine, which he pursued along with his tailor's trade.

Family tradition had it that Thomas and Mary (Knox) Austin entered Arkansas Territory before it became a state in June 1836. If not, they were there soon after, for Wesley was born 7 April 1837 in Arkansas. Two years later, Thomas was elected Captain of the 2nd Battallion of the Arkansas Militia. His Commission, dated 5 October 1839, was issued by Gov. James S. Conroy. The Commission and the pill case are now in the possession of Thomas' great-great-grandson Richard Blaisdell. When the 1840 Census was taken, the family was located in the Black River District of Izard County, with four children, who would have been Susan, William, Winfield and Wesley. The (copied) family record gives John Austin's birthdate as 1839, but this may have been miscopied, for the 1850 Census taker wrote John's age as nine years, and in the 1860 Census he was said to be eighteen. The 1850 Census, taken in mid-October, gives the names of seven children living at home with Thomas and Mary. Susan is 22,

William 19, and Winfield 15, and both boys were listed as farmers born in Ohio. Younger children listed were Wesley 10, John 9, Sarah Jane 7, and Mary Melissa 3, all born in Arkansas. Their address was the Black River District of Independence County. It is possible that the family home was on the borderline between Izard and Independence Counties, and that they had not moved since the 1840 Census. Thomas is described as a "taylor" whose real property was valued at $250. His name is spelled Auston, but the given names of his wife and children confirm his identity. He was forty-five when the Census was taken, and was to move twice more, first to Bentonville, Arkansas, and later to Leavenworth, Kansas.

When the Austins left Independence County for Bentonville in the northwest corner of Arkansas is not clear, but it must have been soon after 1850. Mary Melissa always spoke of Bentonville as her childhood home, and some members of her family thought she was born there. It is likely that the family lived in Bentonville at least ten years before leaving in 1862. This was to be a prosperous decade for them. As the children grew up, Thomas continued his tailor's work, assisted in part by his wife.

Patton Family - Susan Austin Patton middle front, Elizabeth on her right, Sadie on her left.

Not only is he a "taylor" in the 1860 Census, but Mary is listed as a "tayloress." He acquired a comfortable home "with a fireplace in every room." When Mary Melissa visited Bentonville fifty years later, it was still standing and had become the Eagle House. The youngest child, Robert Lewis Austin, may have been born there in 1851. Susan married — Patton and began rearing her own family: the older sons were farmers, and the younger children attended school. A family story tells that some of the conservative neighbors predicted future trouble because Sarah Jane and Mary Melissa studied fractions along with the boys. "Uncle Charles," whose picture was taken in Leavenworth after the Civil War, is still not accounted for.

Thomas Austin bought land, which may have been farmed by his sons, for his real property holdings in the 1860 Census are valued at $900, and his personal property at $100. Thomas was a prosperous man for that time and place. He also became part owner of a country store, managed by his partner, John N. Curtis. The inventory is ennumerated in a claim filed after the Civil War. All during this time, political divisions which would lead to the Civil War were heating up in Arkansas, as elsewhere in the nation. Bentonville people were mainly southerners, and many among them favored the institution of slavery and supported the idea of secession to protect states' rights. Thomas Austin was opposed to both in principle, and was

not hesitant about voicing his opinions. He owned land, but never owned slaves. However, he did on occasion hire the services of slaves, paying their wages to their owners. This may have been begging the question, but it was a common practice. National divisions may be duplicated in small communities and even in families. Neighbors became progressively less friendly, and three of the six Austin sons were said to have declared for the Confederacy. Since there are no pictures of William, Wesley, and John in the album preserved by Mary Melissa's eldest daughter, these may have been the dissidents. In the Arkansas Confederate forces, there were soldiers by their names, but identification of enlisted men from the meager information on service cards is difficult.

In March 1862, the decisive "Battle of Pea Ridge" (or "Battle of Elkhorn Tavern" in the South) was fought in Benton County. When Union Gen. Sigel led his weary troops north to Fort Leavenworth, Bentonville citizens invited Thomas Austin to leave with the Army. After nearly thirty years in Arkansas, the Austins packed what possessions and supplies they could into two wagons and became refugees. Thomas drove one wagon, and Sarah Jane's husband, — Keith, drove the other: Mary Melissa, not yet fifteen, remembered riding a horse most of the way. By present day standards, the distance from Bentonville to Leavenworth (a little more than two hundred miles) is not great, and modern cars on modern

Winfield Austin Family ca. 1870

Sarah Austin Keith ca. 1870

roads can traverse it in a few hours. Horse-drawn wagons following unpaved trails in the wake of an army would take days for such a journey. When they reached Leavenworth, on the Missouri River, they faced making a new life, again dependent on the tailor's tools and skills.

Thomas Austin tried to salvage the Arkansas property. After the end of hostilities, he went back to Bentonville, according to family tradition, but found himself unwelcome. His former neighbors advised him to leave again, and believing them capable of violence, he returned empty handed. His real property (Census value $900) was sold for taxes.

Congress set up a commission to adjudicate claims for war damage to non-combatants. These claims came in by the hundreds. Thomas Austin and his partner, John Curtis, field a claim for losses when their Bentonville store was looted by Union soldiers. The partners presented an inventory which is interesting, for it shows the merchandise to be found in a country store of the period: horse collars, ladies shoes, hammers, lard, 2000 cigars, whiskey by the barrel, one buffalo robe ($7.00), gin and brandy by the gallon, sugar, salt, cloth by the bolt, wagon whips, etc.

Their itemized valuation totaled $4630, but the claim was disallowed by the commission with the following remarks:

"The claimants were partners in a country store at Bentonville, Arkansas in the Winter and Spring of 1862. General Sigel with a considerable force was in the vicinity, and on the 19th of February, 1862, had a severe battle with the rebel General Price at Sugar Creek, defeated him and drove him away. Immediately after the fight and on the same day a body of Union Cavalry dashed into Bentonville, took the men of the town prisoners, shut them up in the court house, and then proceeded to pillage the stores. The claimants were so arrested and shut up, and when the troops left the town they took the claimants with them a distance on the road and then let them go free. On their return home they found their store pillaged and stripped of almost everything. They say that the articles charged were then taken. Without going into any consideration of other questions, it is plain that the transaction was lawless pillage, done by soldiers, as it were, in the heat and excitement of battle, when it was almost impossible to restrain them and when the taking of property was not for the use of the Army, but for individual pleasure and gain.

Austins of America

Such lawless pillage does not come within the terms "stores or supplies taken for the use of the Army." However meritorious the claimants may be (of which we express no opinion) and however hard it may be to bear these losses, we are not authorized to allow compensation for them." [Claim #5776]

In 1868, six years after reaching Leavenworth, the Austin family lived at "Prospect between 5th and 2nd Ave" and remained there though 1871 or 1872. The 1873 directory lists them at "2nd Ave." between Fanny and Mary: that year Robert, the youngest son, still lived with is parents, but was given a separate listing as a brick mason. They continued to live at the same address until 1876, when Thomas is left out of the directory. He again appears in 1877, living and working as a tailor at 608 So. 5th. This move to a new home was made so that the aging Mary Austin could be closer to her youngest daughter, Mary Melissa, who had married William Davis Loudon in the summer of 1867.

Mary Melissa Austin Loudon ca. 1870

Mary (Knox) Austin died in Leavenworth 18 February 1878, age 66 years and 10 months, sincerely mourned by her husband and family. He called her his "French doll," but whether this was a term of endearment or indicated her ancestry is uncertain. Her grandaughter, Marguerite Loudon, who was ten when Mary Austin died, said she had a severe stroke which left some paralysis and mental weakness. She remembered her grandmother as having brown hair and eyes, and being a small woman who could stand erect under her husband's outstretched arm.

The same grandaughter remembered Thomas Austin as being "tall, slender, blue-eyed and almost blond." He seemed to have little left to live for, and did not survive his wife very long. He died eleven months after her death, on 11 January 1879, age 74 years and 6 months. Both Thomas and Mary were buried in Leavenworth, but so far we have not located the site of their graves.

Reference Sources

U.S. Census for 1830 Ohio, for 1840, 1850 and 1860 for Arkansas. Leavenworth City Directories. Artifacts saved by Mary (Austin) Loudon and her daughter Maude Loudon. Family traditions remembered by grandaughter Marguerite (Loudon) Ashe, who also copied family records, perhaps from a family Bible. Southern Claims Commission Records.

HENRY AUSTIN OF NEW YORK, MICHIGAN, IOWA & COLORADO

by Michael G. Law

My great-great-grandfather Henry Austin was born on 1 November 1829 in New York state, a date established from the 1870 & 1880 Federal Census and cemetery records. The 1880 Census states that his father was also born in New York and his mother in Connecticut, but I have not yet identified his parents. The 1850 Census for Oakland County, Michigan, does show a Lydia Austin age 47 with a family consisting of a Henry Austin age 20 and daughters Lucy age 16 and Phoebe age 12, all born in New York, but additional research is needed to establish that this is my Henry Austin. The 1860 Census shows a Francis Austin age 61 born in New York, and Lydia Austin age 58 born in New York, living in White Lake, Oakland County. I have not found Henry in the 1860 Census, and I do not know when he migrated to Michigan, or when he married Calista Kelley.

On 5 October 1855, Dennis Bradford Austin was born to Henry and Calista in Oakland County, Michigan. The significance of the child's name is not known, but perhaps Dennis Bradford was a friend or relative of Henry or Calista. Dennis B. Austin is mentioned in Stoner's *History of Colorado*, which states that his mother died during his early childhood, and that he was educated in Michigan schools until about age fourteen. I have not found any cemetery record for Calista, however, and the only other reference I have to Calista Kelley is in my baby book, completed by Dennis' daughter, Florence Lucille (Austin) Law.

On 18 March 1869 Henry remarried, this time to Sarah J. (Phillips) Nash in Commerce, Oakland County, Michigan. Sarah's first husband, Charles J. Nash, had died in the Andersonville Prison during the Civil War, leaving her with a son Charles J. Nash. Even though Charles Nash and Dennis Austin were only step-brothers, they would remain close all their lives, and they eventually owned adjacent farms in Colorado. The 1870 Census shows Henry, Sarah, Dennis, and Charrles living on a farm in Grant Township, Ringgold County, Iowa. In 1875 Sarah gave birth to William Henry Austin, who might have been named for Sarah's brother William.

In the late 1870's Dennis Austin worked as a teamster, and he drove wagons to Colorado. Apparently he liked this country, because he rented some land near Eaton and began farming it. In 1881 Henry moved his family to Colorado, and for the next few years he, Dennis, and Charles either farmed together or near each other. Henry

died of cancer on 27 November 1884, and is included in the mortality schedule of the 1885 Colorado Census. He is buried in Greely's Linn Grove Cemetery. His stone reads born 1 November 1859 - the '5' is an error. The Poudre Valley I.O.O.F. Lodge recognized Henry as a good father, citizen, husband, and friend, and sent a copy of their resolution to the Mt. Ayers Lodge in Iowa. The 1885 Colorado Census shows the four remaining family members living on a farm in Weld County, Colorado. On 12 April 1887, Henry's second son, William Henry Austin, died at age 12 and is also buried in Linn Grove Cemetery.

On 26 January 1887, Dennis B. Austin married Katherine Lee in Fort Collins, Colorado. The Lees were a strong Irish-Catholic family, which accounts for why many of Dennis and Katherine's descendants are Catholics. The photograph on the next page is believed to have been taken on or near their wedding date.

About 1890 both Charles Nash and Dennis Austin established 160-acre farms adjacent to each other just northeast of Windsor, Colorado. Sarah Austin continued to live with Charles' family, but was always welcome in either home. She passed away on 7 May 1924 and is buried in Linn Grove Cemetery with Henry. Charles Nash's first wife and child died during childbirth. He and his second wife Adella Kempton had seven children, of whom four are still alive, and one still works the original Nash farm.

Dennis and Katherine Austin had two children, Florence Lucille born on 28 November 1888 and William Henry born 25 September 1891. On 5 March 1900 Kate Austin died in their home of a ruptured appendix, before medical help could save her. Dennis had loved her dearly, and he never remarried. Several members of the Nash family pointed out the farmhouse where the Austins were living when Kate died. It has been remodeled from the old log cabin it once was, but it still stands on the paved road north and east out of Windsor.

A few years later, Dennis bought a farm about a half a mile east of the farm where Kate had died. The children were raised on this farm, and attended local schools until their high school years. Florence attended high school in Fort Collins, and then was a student at Colorado A&M (now Colorado State University) for a time. She took many photographs and wrote many letters. She saved poems, photographs, post cards, etc. that she enjoyed. The family still has many of these items that date to her elementary school days. They tell an interesting story of the person who collected and saved them.

On 19 February 1907 tragedy again struck the Austin family. Young Willie was attending high school in Fort Collins and Dennis had traveled there to visit his children

Dennis and Katherine (Lee) Austin ca. 1877

that weekend. After Sunday dinner, Dennis stayed in the house to visit and Willie went out to a shed where he and some of his friends had a rope trapeze. The next day someone went to the shed and found that Willie had tried to adjust the ropes, but had fallen and hung himself. The local newspapers carried several articles about this, and of how grieved everyone was for Dennis Austin.

Florence Austin was always very close to her mother's family, and spent a lot of time in Fort Collins, Boulder, and on her father's farm. She married Guy Law on 20 January 1914 in Boulder, Colorado. The Laws have a long and rich history in Weld County, Colorado. For a time Guy and Florence lived in Denver, but during World War I Guy worked the Austin farm under Dennis' direction, and this proved to be very profitable. After the war, farm prices softened, and Guy returned to the construction business in Fort Collins, and later in Denver.

Dennis Austin leased his farm, but continued to live on it until the 1930's when he came to live with his daughter's family in Denver. He passed away in Denver in 1936, but is buried in Fort Collins with his wife and son. The many people who knew Dennis Austin described him as a

completely devoted father, loving husband, successful farmer, and a very supportive citizen and neighbor. He was a quiet, private man. He often drove to Windsor to attend Town Meetings or school functions, but he rarely spoke at these meetings... always a supporter of the popular causes but not a leader. He was well loved and respected by everyone in this rural community. Some of the land he used to farm is now part of the Windsor Reservoir. The family no longer owns the farm, but the big barn that Dennis had built on it was a local landmark for years before it was torn down in the 1960's. The original house has been remodeled several times, but Dennis Austin's farm is still in production.

Our branch of the Austin surname ended with Dennis Austin's death, but Guy and Florence Austin Law had six children, and their four sons served proudly in World War II. One son passed away shortly after the war. The remaining five have raised good families. The author is only one of their seventeen grandchildren, and though my name is not Austin, I am still proud of my Austin heritage. If anyone desires more information about any of these people, or can help me to learn more about Henry Austin's parents, please contact me through *Austins of America*.

★★★★★★★★★★★★★★★★★★★★★★★★★★★★★★★★★★

Austins of America is intended to serve present and future genealogists researching Austin family lines. Readers are encouraged to submit Queries, genealogical and historical articles for publication. Previously published books, pamphlets or articles containing Austin genealogical data are also sought for reprinting or review.

EDITOR

DR. MICHAEL EDWARD AUSTIN   CONCORD, MA

ASSOCIATE EDITORS

ANTHONY KENT AUSTIN	PROSPECT, KY
BERT ADDIS AUSTIN	QUEEN CREEK, AZ
PATRICIA BIEBUYCK AUSTIN	CONCORD, MA
PAULINE LUCILLE AUSTIN	MARION, IA
JANET AUSTIN CURTIS	ALBUQUERQUE, NM
CAROL LEIGHTON HULL	SUDBURY, MA

Austins of America is published each February and August by The Austin Print, 23 Allen Farm Lane, Concord, Massachusetts 01742. All correspondence, including subscriptions, articles and responses to queries, should be sent to this address. Subscriptions are $2.50 per year postpaid.

★★★★★★★★★★★★★★★★★★★★★★★★★★★★★★★★★★

THE DESCENDANTS OF
JOHN AUSTIN AND ANN BADEN
OF ALBEMARLE COUNTY, VIRGINIA

by Bert Addis Austin

[CONTINUED FROM PAGE 134]

J3B5-8. CHARLES R., *b. 19 March 1892 in Floyd?, Texas; d. May 1932/37; m. Cleo Lawler. Resided in Lamasa, Texas in 1933.*

J3B5-9. LUCINDA M., *b. 1 September 1894, d. April 1896. She may have been born in Oklahoma and died on the trip back to Texas.*

J3B5-A. JOHN M., *b. 20 September 1897 in Cross Plains; d. 16 July 1971 in Lubbock, Texas; m. 14 December 1922 to Myrtle Wills. Resided in Fluvanna, Texas in 1933.*

J3B5-B. NANCY PATIENCE, *b. 21 September 1900 in Cross Plains; m. 14 December 1927 Claude Bagwell. Res. 1933 Bradshaw, Texas.*

J3B6. WILLIAM ROSE[4] AUSTIN (*Joseph Harrison,*[3] *Jonas R.,*[2] *John*[1]) was born 15 January 1855 in Kentucky. He was married to Rosa Leamed. Rosa, the daughter of William Leamed and Martha Lamping, was born in 1863 in Kansas. William perhaps died in Kansas. Their son was born in Sylvia, Kansas:

J3B6-1. ROBERT E., *b. 28 April 1884*

J3E3. HENRY S.[4] AUSTIN (*George Washington,*[3] *Jonas R.,*[2] *John*[1]) was born 26 March 1856 in Lincoln County, Kentucky. He was married in Lincoln County on 18 July 1878 to Mollie Collins age 18, she and her mother were born in Lincoln County, her father was born in Virginia. Their daughter Emma said Henry moved from Kentucky to Henry County, Missouri, where he lived for 15 years. He then moved to Comanche County, Oklahoma (now Cotton Co.). They lived in Walters, Oklahoma, and Henry is believed to have died there. Their children were all married in Walters, except for Farris who was married in Lawton, Oklahoma.

J3E3-1. ALONZO, *b. Kentucky, m. Grace Wernett*

J3E3-2. CARRIE, *b. Kentucky, m. Hugh Oliver*

J3E3-3. FARRIS, *m. Ola Carter*

J3E3-4. EMMA, *b. 4 January 1893 in Clinton, Missouri; m. 28 February 1911 to Roy Price; their son Kenneth Austin Price b. 1919 in Walters, OK.*

J3E3-5. FLOYD, *m. Bessie Smith*

J3E5. ARCHIBALD[4] AUSTIN (*George Washington,*[3] *Jonas R.,*[2] *John*[1]) was born 18 April 1860 in Casey County, Kentucky. He was married in Lincoln County, Kentucky on 25 December 1879 to Hannah J. Estes, at the home of

the bride's father, George W. Estes. Hannah was born on 20 September 1861, died 7 May 1901 in Lincoln County, and is buried in Estes Cemetery, New Salem Road, Lincoln County. Archibald married again in Lincoln County on 23 December 1907 to widow Bettie J. (Lenard) Estes of Lincoln County, both were age 47. Archibald died 12 February 1946 in Lincoln County and is buried in Estes Cemetery. His children, all by his first wife, were born in Lincoln County, except for William born in Casey County, Kentucky:

J3E5-1. BERTHA, *b. ca. 1882, at age 22 m. 2 March 1905 Joseph F. Fletcher at her Aunt Minnie Wall's home. Joseph, son of Archibald and Ann Elizabeth (Wilcher) Fletcher, was also 22, first marriage for both. Joseph and his parents b. Lincoln Co. Son Edsel J. Fletcher b.1914. They are buried in Estes Cemetery.*

J3E5-2. WILLIAM CLARENCE (BUD), *b. 13 June 1885 Casey Co.*

J3E5-3. HENRY JASON, *b. 2 November 1888*

J3E5-4. WILMOTH, *b. ca. 1888, at age 23 m. 22 December 1911 in Lincoln County to George L. Leeper age 27, first marriage both. George and his parents b. Lincoln Co. Leeper children: Juey b.1912 Indianapolis, Indiana; Ruby Mae b.1914 and Myrtle b.1918 in Lincoln Co.*

J3E5-5. PEARL, *b. ???? died young.*

J3E5-6. SELENA, *b. ca. 1895, age 19 m. 2 November 1914 Logan Johnson age 23, first marriage both. Logan and his parents b. Lincoln Co., he worked on Railroad.*

J3E5-7. THEODORE, *b. 1896, m.(1) Stella Griffin, m.(2) Alene Skidmore on 22 December 1923, he widower age 27 she single age 18, b. Lincoln Co. dau. Lenzey & Mae Skidmore.*

J3E5-8. EUGENE, *b. 20 March 1899*

J3E6. GEORGE WASHINGTON[4] AUSTIN (*George Washington,*[3] *Jonas R.,*[2] *John*[1] was born 11 May 1862. He was married first to Sarah Jane Ryan, who was born on 3 July 1865. Sarah died on 5 February 1891, and is buried in McKinney Cemetery, Lincoln County, Kentucky. He was married second to widow Ruth Ellen (Carman) Horton. Ruth, the daughter of Daniel and Sarah Jane (Bastin) Carman, was born on 15 February 1877 in Casey County, Kentucky. Ruth died 9 February 1933 in Grove Ridge, Casey County, and is buried in Campbell/Patterson Cemetery, Grove Ridge. George died 30 November 1934 in Grove Ridge and is buried with his second wife Ruth. His first two children were by Sarah, the others by Ruth. The order and birthdates of some of the children are not known, but all are believed born in Casey County:

J3E6-1. VIRGINIA ANN, *b. July 1883 according to 1900 Casey County Census where she was listed as a 'servant.' She m. 17 March 1901 at Geo. Austin's to James William Hatter. Their known*

children: Oren b.1906, Edith, Ruby, Carlos, Esker, Earl.

J3E6-2.   NORA L., *b. 23 September 1885 (1900 Census has her age 14 born 'Sept. 1885'), m. 1 September 1904 at Geo. Austin's to Kendrick R. Elliott, born 28 January 1880 son of Silas and Artie Priscilla (Douglas) Elliott. Like her sister, Nora was a 'servant' in 1900 Casey Co. Census. She d. 1 September 1939 Boyle Co., KY, buried Salyers Cemetery, Mt. Olive, Casey Co. Children: Fred Elden 1904, Ida Ethel 1905, Della Laurel 1907, Herman Reid 1909, William Finley 1911, Elmer Austin 1912, Roberta 1914, Della May 1920, Eula Maureen 1923, Calvin Coolidge 1925, Ervin Edsel 1928, Hazel 1931. Kendrick died 30 July 1974 and is buried with Nora.*

J3E6-3.   EUGENE, *b. unknown - 1898??*

J3E6-4.   PAULINE, *b. unknown - 1900??*

J3E6-5.   RAYMOND, *b. unknown - 1902??*

J3E6-6.   ANNA PEARL, *b. unknown - 1904??*

J3E6-7.   MARTIN, *b. circa 1906 - at age 24 he m. 10 June 1931 in Kings Mountain, Casey Co., to widow Jeanette Sword, dau. Butler & Polly Wall Sword. She was 34, both b. Casey Co. Martin, a farmer, was killed in a fight with an ax in 1940.*

J3E6-8.   EVERETT ("BIG PIG"), *b. ca. 1909 - at age 20 he m. 17 July 1929 in Liberty, Casey County, to Elsie Tabscott, dau. G. F. and Rosie Tabscott. He worked on the Railroad, she was 17. Both were b. Casey Co., first marriage for both.*

J3E6-9.   BARBARA, *b. unknown - 1911??*

J3E6-A.   NOVICE, *b. unknown - 1913??*

J3E6-B.   BENJAMIN, *b. unknown - 1915??*

J3E6-C.   EDWARD, *b. unknown - 1917??*

J3E6-D.   GEORGE, *b. ca. 1919 - at age 21 he m. 19 January 1940 in Casey County to Viola Napier, dau. Henry & Ida Napier. He was a farmer, she was 15. Both b. Casey Co., first marriage both.*

J3E6-E.   ELMER ("LITTLE PIG"), *b. 4 June 1921*

FIFTH GENERATION

J332-2.   WILLIAM M.[5] AUSTIN (*Isaac Bill,*[4] *John L.,*[3] *Jonas R.,*[2] *John*[1]) was born 29 February 1860 in Casey County, Kentucky. He was married to Julia Estes, who was born in 1870. Julia died in 1947, and is buried in Thomastown Cemetery south of Dunnville, Casey County. William died on 5 April 1926 and is also buried in Thomastown Cemetery. Their known children were:

J332-21.   STELLA, *b. 5 October 1888, d. 20 September 1904*

J332-22.   LUCIAN W., *b. ca. 1889, at age 42 m. 7 May 1932 to Nettie Thomas, dau. of Joseph and Mary Thomas, age 37. Both were born in Casey Co., were single, resided in Junction City, KY.*

J332-23.   LUCY, *b. 16 May 1890, d. 26 June 1966 age 76 years, 1 month, 10 days, apparently unmarried. She is buried with William, Julia and Stella, and was perhaps a twin to Lucian.*

J332-3.   GEORGE A.[5] AUSTIN (*Isaac Bill,*[4] *John L.,*[3] *Jonas R.,*[2] *John*[1]) was born 31 March 1863 in Casey County, Kentucky. He was married on 12 September 1887 in Casey County to Bersheba B. Thomas, daughter of J. M. and Martha Thomas, and perhaps related to the James H. Thomas who witnessed her wedding. Bersheba, born on 6 September 1870 in Casey County, was called 'Bersha,' (Birsha/Bursha). She died 12 January 1904, and is buried in Thomastown Cemetery, south of Dunnville, Casey County. George was married a second time in Dunnville on 14 January 1911 to Lucy Clementine Lay, the daughter of William and Louvena (Stephens) Lay, who was born 16 May 1890 in Casey County. George died 6 June 1932 in Casey County and is buried in Thomastown Cemetery with his first wife. His widow Lucy m.(2) at age 42 on 1 July 1933 in Dunnville to Silas Sallee age 39, son of James and Nora Salle, his first marriage. They divorced, and Lucy m.(3) on 14 September 1938 at age 48 to Christopher C. Baker age 48, the divorced son of George and Minerva (Warner) Baker. The first four children were by George's first wife Bersheba, all were born in Casey County:

J332-31.   THEODORE, *b. 19 June 1888*

J332-32.   DOLLIE, *b. circa 1890, m. Hershall McDonald*

J332-33.   WILL, *b. circa 1892, m. Verna Lee*

J332-34.   ERNEST K., *b. 2 September 1894, m. Ann Lou Tate who was b. 1 July 1891 in Texas, dau. of James W. and Patsy J. (Fox) Tate. She resided in Friendship Nursing Home in Danville in November 1976. Ernest was in the first World War. Ann was of Moreland when she died on 3 November 1976, survived by husband Ernest. Obituary mentions no children.*

J332-35.   MOSSIE, *b. 1 December 1912, m.(1) on 4 April 1931 in Liberty, Casey County, to Otha Vitatoe, son of George and Lizzie Vitatoe, born in Clinton County, Kentucky, and resident of Hamilton County, Ohio. She m.(2) on 26 November 1963 to Charles H. Reckner, a resident of Louisville, KY. Charles died 19 April 1979, age 64 buried Thomaston Cem. in Dunnsville. Mossie was still alive in 1979.*

J332-36.   FORREST EGBERT, *b. 30 January 1922*

J332-37.   HERMAN H., *b. 21 April 1924, m.(1) perhaps to Juanita Frederick, dau. of James Cephas Frederick & Julia Green Jones of Middleburg, Casey Co. Perhaps divorced, Juanita or "Mrs. Herman Austin," resided in Okeechobee FL in 1971, and still resided in Florida in 1979. Herman m.(2) on 7 May 1957 in Lebanon, Marion Co. KY to Jewell M. (Thomas) Brown, dau. of Clarence & Maud Thomas, b. 27 May 1923 in Casey Co. Herman d. 16 October 1976 at the V.A. Hospital in Lexington KY, having been "seriously ill for a long time." Jewell d. 15 January 1981 Casey Co., b. Thomastown Cemetery. According to his sister Mossie, Herman had a daughter Carolyn A. by his first wife, and the Carl & James Frederick obituaries imply they may have had other children.*

J332-4. MARCUS HENRY[5] AUSTIN (*Issac Bill,*[4] *John L.,*[3] *Jonas R.,*[2] *John*[1]) was born 1864 in Dunnville, Casey County, Kentucky. He was known as "Bark" Austin. He married in Casey County on 10 May 1886 to Florence P. Turner. Marcus and Florence are buried in the woods near J332 Isaac Bill Austin, no dates on stones. Their children:

J332-41. DELLIE, *b. unknown, perhaps d. young. She is buried beside father, with no dates on her stone.*

J332-42. ANDREW, *b. circa 1891, m. 1 June 1915 at Chilton, Casey County, to Mamie Vandyke, in presence of Rosa Vandyke.*

J332-43. LUCY, *b. circa 1893, m. 21 August 1910 at Dunnville to Jesse D. Thomas, born at Dunnville the son of James B. and Mollie Rubarts Thomas. He later remarried, d. 1972 age 82 in Belleville, Illinois. Thomas children: Howard, Woodrow, 'Miss' Otis, and Jesse D.*

J332-44. O. W. (WILLIE), *b. circa 1895 Casey County, m. 23 December 1917 in Slickford, Wayne County, Kentucky to Tressie Upchurch, born in Wayne County, the daughter of Moses and America Upchurch. O. W. Austin was 22, Tressie was 18 and resided at Slickford, they were both single. O. W. resided at Cooper, Kentucky.*

J332-45. W. T., *b. circa 1898 Casey County, m. on 9 October 1920 in Wayne County to Edna McGahan, born in Wayne County the daughter of H. S. and Sallie McGahan. W. T. Austin was 22, Edna was 20, both were single and both were residing at Kavito, Kentucky.*

J332-46. WALTER, *b. circa 1902 Casey County, m. 24 September 1924 in Casey County to Della B. Wilham. Both Walter and Della were 22, first marriage for both, both residents of Dunnville. Della was the daughter of Leonard and Nancy Fox Wilham, born 15 September 1901 in Dunnville. Walter resided with son Phillip in Lancaster, Garrard County, Kentucky, in the early 1970's. Della died 14 December 1983 at the Fort Logan Hospital in Stanford, Lincoln County, at age 82 years, and was buried in Thomastown Cemetery. She was survived by four sons and four daughters: Hugh Austin of Jamestown, Phillip Austin of Lancaster, Guenn and Royce Austin of Indiana, Evelyn Austin Rich of Bowling Green, Wilmeth Austin Hall of Indianapolis, Carolyn Austin Gier of Omaha, Nebraska, and Alice Austin Jeffries of Falls Church, Virginia, plus 26 grandchildren and 27 great-grandchildren. Evelyn was born in Casey County and m. on 18 February 1950 in Dunnville to Donald Rich, son of Hershel and Fannie Roy Rich born in Pulaski County, Kentucky. She was 25, he was 24, first marriage both, both resided in Liberty.*

J332-47. MARIE, *b. circa 1911 Casey County, m. 28 July 1928 in Liberty, Casey County, to Arkley Garrett, son of Roland and Fena Garrett, born in Metcalf County, Kentucky. Marie was 17, Arkley was a farmer age 18, first marriage both, both resided in Casey County.*

J332-7. ARCHIBALD WILLIS[5] AUSTIN (*Issac Bill,*[4] *John L.,*[3] *Jonas R.,*[2] *John*[1]) was born 25 August 1870 in Casey County, Kentucky. He called himself "Wilse," and was a farmer and a blacksmith. He was married in Casey County on 8 July 1894 to Patsey W. Stephens. Patsey was perhaps the daughter of 'Duck' Stephens, for they were married at his home. She was born on 9 May 1876, and died 6 July 1908. Wilse was 'age 48' when he married for the second time in Casey County on 24 September 1918 to widow Hannah Calhoon of Casey County. Hannah, whose parents were listed only as 'Calhoon', was age 42 born in Casey Co. Three years later Wilse was still 'age 48' when he married for the third time in Liberty, Kentucky on 16 June 1921 to widow Mary A. (Williams) Love of Casey Co. Mary, the daughter of Haden and Willie Ann Williams, was age 48 born in Casey Co. They divorced, and Wilse was only 'age 45' when he married for the fourth time in Casey Co. on 19 October 1935 to Margie Garrett of Casey Co. It was the first marriage for Margie, the daughter of J. R. & Venie Garrett, who was age 19 and born in Casey Co. Wilse is believed to have married a fifth time, in Tennessee. He died 30 May 1941, bur. Thomastown Cem., Dunnville. Known children:

J332-71. SAMMIE B., *b. 31 August 1901, d. 22 — 1907.*

J332-72. JOHNNIE AUSTIN, *d. 15 April 1907 at age 6 of Whooping Cough.*

J332-9. JOHN FRANK[5] AUSTIN (*Issac Bill,*[4] *John L.,*[3] *Jonas R.,*[2] *John*[1]) was born 26 December 1878 in Casey County. He was married in Casey County on 3 October 1897 to Hannah Calhoon. They divorced, and Hannah married John's older brother J332-7 'Wilse' Austin in 1918 (see above). John was a farmer 'age 50' when he married a second time in Dunnville, Casey County, on 10 February 1927 to widow Lizzie (Combest) Vitatoe 'age 42'. Lizzie, the daughter of John Combest, was born in Casey County. The known children are believed to have been by his first wife Hannah:

J332-91. ALBERT, *b. unknown, known as "D" Austin, he drowned at New Castle, Indiana*

J332-92. OSCAR, *b. unknown. I talked with him and his son Jerald Austin by phone in 1976, but have no further information on their line.*

J332-B. MARY MARTHA[5] AUSTIN (*Issac Bill,*[4] *John L.,*[3] *Jonas R.,*[2] *John*[1]) was born 1 May 1882 in Dunnville, Casey County, Kentucky. "Mollie" was married in Jamestown, Russell County, Kentucky on 30 November 1901 to Perry Owens, son of James and Melissa M. (Turner) Owens, who was in 1880 in Tennessee. According to their son Alvin Owens when I visited him at his home in Dunnville on 26 January 1972, Perry and his half-brother Fletcher Owens were in the Casey County Jail for

Sallie C. Bradshaw Austin, Robert L. Austin and J333-2 George Jefferson Austin in 1902 at Mt. Salem, Kentucky.

making whiskey. Perry broke out of jail and went to Tennessee. The family was notified of Perry Owen's death in a letter from the Sheriff of Columbus, Georgia, stating that Perry, his brothers Dillard Owens and John Allen Owens, and a woman were fighting, and that Dillard had shot and killed Perry during the fight using John's gun. Dillard was convicted and sent to prison for several years, after which he returned to Casey County. Dillard later told Alvin that he had not killed Perry, but that Perry was killed by a woman who had caused a fight. The family does not know the date of Perry's death, or where he is buried. Mary died 18 August 1973 in Liberty, Casey County and is buried in Thomastown Cemetery, Casey County. Born in Casey County were the OWENS CHILDREN: FANNIE BELLE 1903, ROSETTA 1905, BERNETTA 1907, ALVIN 1908, DEWEY, MELVIN, BESSIE WILLIAMS 1918, LEO 1922.

J333-1. ARCHIBALD B.[5] AUSTIN (*Nicodemus,*[4] *John L.,*[3] *Jonas R.,*[2] *John*[1]) was born 31 August 1861 in Lincoln County, Kentucky. He was married in South Fork, Lincoln County on 21 June 1883 to Betty B. Duncan of Lincoln County. Betty was age 22 and born in Washington County, Kentucky. The letterhead on the consent slip for their daughter's marriage has "A. B. Austin, dealer in Spokes, Shingles, and Crossties." The slip was dated 23 December 1908 at McKinney, Kentucky. Their only child known to me was born in Lincoln County:

J333-11.   MAUD L., *b. circa 1889, m. at age 18 on 24 December 1908 to George T. Rice, age 29. George and his parents were born in Casey County.*

J333-2. GEORGE JEFFERSON[5] AUSTIN (*Nicodemus,*[4] *John L.,*[3] *Jonas R.,*[2] *John*[1]) was born 16 July 1864 in Junction City, Kentucky. He was married in Mt. Salem, Lincoln County, Kentucky on 28 April 1901 to Sallie C. Bradshaw. Sallie, the daughter of Joshua L. Bradshaw and J335 Sarah Austin, was born on 24 September 1869 in Casey County, Kentucky. George eventually took over the blacksmith shop that had been operated by his father & father-in-law Joshua Bradshaw before the Civil War. He was a blacksmith and wheelwright, and he also ran a public gristmill. The family is pictured above in 1902 in Mt. Salem. George had one eye missing, due to a harness needle. He died on 19 February 1937 on the Casey & Lincoln County Line and is buried in McKinney Cemetery in Lincoln County. Sallie died on 4 September 1947 in San Francisco, California, and is also buried in McKinney Cemetery. George and Sallie were my grandparents, and I was present at both of their burials. Their two children were born in Mt. Salem:

J333-21.   ROBERT L., *b. 20 February 1902*
J333-22.   BERTMAN (BERT), *b. 23 March 1904*

[CONTINUED NEXT ISSUE]

THE DESCENDANTS OF
JOHN AUSTIN AND ANN BADEN
OF ALBEMARLE COUNTY, VIRGINIA

by Bert Addis Austin

[CONTINUED FROM PAGE 170]

J333-3. WILLIAM CLARENCE[5] AUSTIN (*Nichodemus,*[4] *John L.,*[3] *Jonas R.,*[2] *John*[1]) was born 20 February 1866 in Lincoln County, Kentucky. He was married in Stanford, Kentucky on 30 November 1888 to Permelia E. Brown. Permelia, also called 'Melia' or 'Mellie,' was born circa 1869 in Lincoln County, where her parents were also born. William died in 1941 in Lincoln County, Permelia died there in 1949, both are buried in McKinney Cemetery, Lincoln County. In the same cemetery are buried their son John ('Johny' on stone), J333 Nicholas Austin, J333-2 George Jefferson & Sallie C. Austin (these two have no stones), Eliza Austin wife of J333-4 Sidney Clarence Austin, J349 Jonas W. Austin & his wife J337 Rosen Ann Austin, and other related Austins as reported elsewhere in this article. The children of William and Permelia were born in Lincoln County:

> J333-31.   GEORGE JEFFERSON, *born in 1900, Jeff was single age 26 resident of Lincoln County when he m. on 3 July 1926 in Lincoln County to Annie Parks, widow age 34 resident of Cincinnati, Ohio. Annie was b. in Tennessee, the daughter of Robert & Sarah Frazier.*
>
> J333-32.   JOHN ('JOHNNIE'), *b. 4 June 1906, d. 13 March 1909*
>
> J333-33.   SIDNEY CLARENCE, *b. 27 November 1907, m.(1) Ellen Allen, m.(2) Lillie Hatter in North Vernon, Indiana, m.(3) Nannie — in Harlan County, Kentucky, m.(4) Rita Danforth in Jamaica Island, m.(5) (name of fifth wife not remembered by Martha Austin Coffman in August 1979), d. 8 December 1966.*
>
> J333-34.   MARY, *b. 22 December 1909* +
>
> J333-35.   MARTHA, *b. 4 July 1912* +

J333-4. SIDNEY CLARENCE[5] AUSTIN (*Nicodemas,*[4] *John L.,*[3] *Jonas R.,*[2] *John*[1]) was born 20 February 1866 in Lincoln County, Kentucky. He was married in Lincoln County on 22 December 1887 to Elizabeth Brown, sister to Permelia E. Brown who married Sidney's twin brother J333-3 William Clarence Austin. Elizabeth was born on 7 September 1860, died 25 April 1913 in Lincoln County, and is buried in McKinney Cemetery. Their children were reared in Campbell County, Kentucky, and are listed here as recalled by J333-35 Martha Austin Coffman on 29 September 1980. Although having little contact with this family, Martha believed the children were still living in the Campbell County and Cincinnati, Ohio area:

William Clarence Austin 1866-1941
Permelia E. Brown ca. 1869-1949

J333-41.   WILLIAM

J333-42.   NICHOLAS ('NICK')

J333-43.   IDA

J333-44.   JENNY, *possibly the Jenny Austin b. circa 1893, who m. at age 21 on 2 December 1914 in Lincoln County to Grover Miracle, also age 21, first marriage for both. Her parents were born in Lincoln County, but were not named in the marriage record.*

J333-45.   VERNA

J333-46.   NETTIE

J343-3. JOHN LABAN[5] AUSTIN (*John William,*[4] *Isaac,*[3] *Jonas R.,*[2] *John*[1]) was born 25 January 1858 in Casey County, Kentucky. He was married in Cumberland County, Kentucky on 22 December 1887 to Mary E. Pierce. Mary, the daughter of a blind minister Joseph Pierce, was born in 1867 in Pulaski County, Kentucky. John Laban Austin donated the land for the Rife Creek, Casey County, Church of Christ, a small building holding

about 30 people, which was still standing and being used in 1980. His father, J343 John William Austin, had donated the land for the Austin Cemetery. The east side of the land was still owned by the Pendleton family, with the cemetery being about 200 yards behind their house. Glen Pendelton took care of this cemetery for several years, and in 1970 told me: "A man died who had been a Confederate Soldier, and John Laban Austin would not let him be buried in the cemetery. As the land around the cemetery belonged to the Pendleton's, they let the man be buried outside the cemetery fence. After John Laban's death they moved the fence over 10 feet, and the man is now in the cemetery." John Laban Austin died in 1924 in Rife Creek, Mary died there in 1925, both are buried in Austin Cemetery in Rife Creek. Their children were born in Casey County:

J343-31. LUTHER C., *b. 13 November 1892* +

J343-32. VIRGIL, *m. Della —, worked with his brother Luther in the U.S. Post Office in Louisville until retiring in 1958.*

J343-33. ORPHIA LEARIE +

J365-3. ROBERT THOMAS[5] AUSTIN (*John H.,*[4] *Robert J.,*[3] *Jonas R.,*[2] *John*[1]) was born 20 May 1878. He was married on 10 October 1899 to Jennie Belle Walker, at her parent's home south of Darlington, Missouri. Jennie, the daughter of Wesley S. and Mary Walker, was born on 7 November 1877. Robert died 1 September 1962 and is buried in Albany, Missouri. They had seven children:

J365-31. JOHN WESLEY, *b. 1 May 1901, m. on 1 September 1934 in Washington, D.C., to Mildred Mabel Hanson, who was b. 18 December 1906.*

J365-32. BERYLE THOMAS, *b. 24 January 1903, m. 30 May 1931 in St. Joseph, Missouri, to Edith Allen Rand, who was b. 2 March 1900. They farmed south of Albany, and had one son: Allen Duane Austin b. 7 November 1933.*

J365-33. CARL WILLIAM, *b. 3 March 1905* +

J365-34. THELMA MAY, *b. 20 April 1907, m.(1) 15 May 1936 at her parent's home north of Albany, to Carl Oelrich, who was b. 17 May 1907. They divorced in March 1952, and she m.(2) on 17 July 1953 to Glenn Rensink, who was b. 19 November 1915.*

J365-35. FRED, *b. 8 September 1909, m. 13 October 1940 in Albany, to Mary Arlene Mercer, who was b. 26 February 1913. Fred d. 15 May 1963, is buried in a cemetery north of Albany.*

J365-36. RETHA FERN, *b. 25 August 1912, m. 3 December 1929 to Veryl Cleone McCall, who was b. 25 July 1912. They had seven children: Robert Max b.1931, Rex Cleon b.1933, Marilyn Glee b.1935, Charles Ray b.1937, Madeline Joy b.1939, Sharon Dale b.1943, Gary John b.1944 d.1945.*

J365-37. LELIA RUTH, *b. 26 January 1921, d. 18 December 1921, buried in Lone Star, Missouri.*

J3B3-2. WALTER HENRY[5] AUSTIN (*Henry Shelton,*[4] *Joseph Harrison,*[3] *Jonas R.,*[2] *John*[1]) was born 1 May 1884 in Sylvia, Kansas (see article on pages 187ff). He was married in June 1920 to Myrtle Willis of Fairview, Major County, Oklahoma. Walter died on 23 August 1958 in Phoenix, Arizona. They had two children:

J3B3-21. BLAIR AUSTIN, *died in his early thirties, unmarried.*

J3B3-22. HAZEL, *adopted. Lost contact with family of her cousin J3B3-41 George Nicolo Austin.*

J3B3-4. GEORGE BENJAMIN[5] AUSTIN (*Henry Shelton,*[4] *Joseph Harrison,*[3] *Jonas R.,*[2] *John*[1]) was born 4 January 1889 in Sylvia, Kansas. He was married in Fairview, Oklahoma, on 18 April 1915 to Julia Leah Shoemaker. Julia, the daughter of John B. and Ann (French) Shoemaker, was born on 6 May 1888 in Wichita, Kansas. This family is discussed at length in an article on Henry Shelton Austin on pages 187ff of this issue. George was a registered pharmacist and businessman, owning property in Blaine, Cleveland, Major, and Oklahoma Counties. George died on 8 January 1976 in Oklahoma City. He and Julia had two children, the first born in Canton, Oklahoma, the second in Longdale, Oklahoma:

J3B3-41. GEORGE NICOLO, *b. 2 June 1919* +

J3B3-42. BONNIE JEAN, *b. 30 December 1926 in Longdale, Oklahoma, m. 27 June 1948 to John Henry Coleman. They resided in Tulsa, Oklahoma in 1985, and had three children: John Henry Jr., Christine Marie, Susan Annette.*

J3B6-1. ROBERT EMMETT[5] AUSTIN (*William Rose,*[4] *Joseph Harrison,*[3] *Jonas R.,*[2] *John*[1]) was born 28 April 1884 in Sylvia, Kansas. He m.(1) in Wakita, Oklahoma, on 24 November 1904 to Eva Rhoda Loomis, who was born in 1887 in Kansas. Robert m.(2) on 10 September 1931 in Long Beach, California, to Marian F. Hoskins, born 1 November 1901 in Los Angeles (see 'Cousin Bob Austin' on page 194). He had two children by each wife:

J3B6-11. MARVIN EMMETT, *b. 2 September 1905, m. Edith Boyd*

J3B6-12. ESTER MARY, *b. 2 November 1907, m. Sidney M. Heyser*

J3B6-13. MARILYN ARLENE, *b. 11 October 1932*

J3B6-14. ROBERT EMMETT, JR., *b. 11 January 1934*

J3E5-2. WILLIAM CLARENCE[5] AUSTIN (*Archibald,*[4] *George Washington,*[3] *Jonas R.,*[2] *John*[1]) was born 13 June 1885 in Casey County, Kentucky. He was married in Lincoln County, Kentucky, on 7 August 1909 to Pina Belle Fletcher. Pina, the daughter of Archibald and Ann Elizabeth (Wilcher) Fletcher, was born in Lincoln County (as were her parents) on 27 August 1885. William, known

William Clarence (Bud) Austin, Bert Addis Austin, and Viola (Austin) Frederick in 1979.

as 'Bud,' was a blacksmith, having been taught the trade by J333-2 George Jefferson Austin. I talked with Bud, Pina, and their widowed daughter Viola on 7 June 1970. Bud and Pina stated they were born the same year about three months apart. They resided in Hustonville, Lincoln County. Bud's obituary has him born in 1884, Pina's obituary has her born in 1886, but I believe 1885 was correct for both. Pina died 2 November 1972 in Lincoln County, and is buried in Estes Cemetery, New Salem Road, Lincoln County. William died 10 January 1977 at the Fort Logan Hospital in Stanford, Lincoln County, and is also buried in Estes Cemetery. I attended both their burials. Their children were born in Lincoln County:

J3E5-21. VIOLA, *b. 29 May 1910 (twin), m. on 1 August 1925 to Alex Frederick, born in Casey County, the son of H. K. and Josephine Frederick. She was 16, he 25, first marriage for both. Viola was a 'widow' in 1970, and resided in Middleburg, Casey County, at the time of her father's death, and was still there in January 1985, living on the bank of Green River in the house owned and occupied by George Jefferson Austin prior to 1915. George had a blacksmith shop on the opposite bank of the river.*

J3E5-22. [son], *b. and d. 29 May 1910 (twin)*

J3E5-23. CECIL JOSEPH, *b. 1 August 1912* +

J3E5-24. GARLAND, *b. 1914, m. Irene Thompson, d. 7 August 1944 on the Island of Saipan during World War II, he is buried in Hawaii.*

J3E5-3. HENRY JASON[5] AUSTIN (*Archibald,*[4] *George Washington,*[3] *Jonas R.,*[2] *John*[1]) was born 2 November 1888 in Lincoln County, Kentucky. He was married in Lincoln County on 2 November 1912 to Elizabeth Pearl Wall who was 18 years of age. Elizabeth, the daughter of William and Sarah Jane (Sluder) Wall, was born in 1894 in Lincoln County, as were her parents. Jason, as he was known, worked as a 'railroader' for the Southern Railway System. Elizabeth died 26 August 1947 in Lincoln County, and is buried in Estes Cemetery, New Salem Road, Lincoln County. I last talked to Jason on Labor Day 1971. He died at the McDowell Hospital in Danville, Boyle County, Kentucky, on 12 August 1972 and is also buried in Estes Cemetery. Their children were born in Lincoln County:

J3E5-31. ALMA, *b. 27 June 1914* +

J3E5-32. ARNOLD, *b. 13 January 1916* +

J3E5-33. EUGENE, *b. circa 1918???*

J3E5-34. GLENN ROBERT, *b. 5 December 1920* +

J3E5-35. EDITH, *b. 11 September 1923* +

J3E5-36. ORVILLE, *b. 15 August 1925* +

J3E5-37. ARCHIBALD KENNETH, *b. 23 April 1931* +

J3E5-38. HENRY JASON, JR., *b. 12 January 1933* +

J3E5-39. DONALD, *b. 1935, d. 1936*

J3E5-3A. BETTY, *b. 24 March 1937, m. Randall Sims*

J3E5-3B. SHIRLEY, *b. 24 April 1939* +

J3E5-8. EUGENE[5] AUSTIN (*Archibald,*[4] *George Washington,*[3] *Jonas R.,*[2] *John*[1]) was born 30 March 1899 in Lincoln County, Kentucky. He was married in Indianapolis, Indiana, on 15 April 1921 to Madeline Pack. Madeline, the daughter of Judson Marcus and Josie (Fowler) Pack, was born on 23 May 1903 in Brandenburg, Kentucky. Eugene died 17 May 1971 in Indiana and is buried in Forest Lawn Cemetery, Stones Crossing, Indiana. Madeline was residing in Casey County, Kentucky, in September 1971. Their four children were born in Indiana:

J3E5-81. MARY JOSEPHINE, *b. 17 December 1923, m. William Emmett Bastin*

J3E5-82. WILMA JEAN, *b. 15 August 1925, m. Howard Dale Stickford*

J3E5-83. GLADYS JOAN, *b. 8 August 1930, m. John J. Stammer*

J3E5-84. BETTY ROSE, *b. 12 January 1934, m. John Herman Klemm*

J3E6-8. EVERETT[5] AUSTIN (*George Washington,*[4,3] *Jonas R.,*[2] *John*[1]) was born circa 1909 in Casey County, Kentucky. He was married to Elsie Tapscott. At least until 1983 they had a farm in Turnersville, which is a small town with one General Store and a very old church, about half way between Hustonville and Stanford in Lincoln County, Kentucky. Everett's life-long friend is a man of colour and

Everett Austin and wife Elsie Tapscott

where you see one the other will be close by. Their farms are side by side. Only one child is known to me:

> J3E6-81. ROBERT, *was a tobacco farmer in 1983, residing in Carroll County, Kentucky (see photograph in next column).*

J3E6-C. EDWARD[5] AUSTIN (*George Washington,*[4,3] *Jonas R.,*[2] *John*[1]) was born in Casey County, Kentucky, possibly around 1917. He was married, and two of his children (George and his twin sister Georgia) are buried in the Patterson & Falconberry Cemetery, located on the Chester Sims Farm, Highway 501, Grove Ridge, Casey County. I accompanied Edward's younger brother, J3E6-E Elmer Austin, to this cemetery in June 1976, and Elmer told me his brother 'Eddie' had another set of twins. Edward's known children thus include:

> J3E6-C1. GEORGE EDWARD ('EDDIE'), *born on 19 November 1940 (twin), d. 10 May 1941*
>
> J3E6-C2. GEORGIA EVELYN, *b. 19 November 1940 (twin), d. 14 May 1941*
>
> J3E6-C3. [twin], *still living in June 1976*
>
> J3E6-C4. [twin], *still living in June 1976*

J3E6-E. ELMER[5] AUSTIN (*George Washington,*[4,3] *Jonas R.,*[2] *John*) was born 4 June 1921 in Casey County, Kentucky. He was married in Lincoln County, Kentucky, on 8 May 1942 to Naomi Napier. Naomi, the daughter of Owen and Ethel (Martin) Napier, was born on 9 July

Everett Austin holding 37½-inch tobacco leaf grown on his son Robert Austin's farm in Carroll County, Kentucky.

1927 in Casey County. When I contacted Elmer & Naomi in 1976, he was retired from the Southern Railroad, and Renita Gail lived next door to them. Naomi, a member of the Grove Baptist Church in Casey County, died on 26 September 1983 in Lexington, Kentucky, and is buried in the K. P. Hall Cemetery in King's Mountain, Kentucky. Elmer and Naomi had three children:

> J3E6-E1. ROBERT OWEN, *born on 6 April 1943 in Greenwood, Indiana* +
>
> J3E6-E2. RENITA GAIL, *b. 15 October 1945 in Lincoln County* +
>
> J3E6-E3. ROY ARNOLD, *b. 10 March 1946 in Casey County. When a child, he was crippled in one leg as the result of a hit-and-run accident. Roy later married Donna G. Brown. In 1976 he worked for Arvin Industries and was still living in Greenwood, Indiana, in September 1983.*

SIXTH GENERATION

[CONTINUED ON PAGE 207]

QUERIES

175-1. **Abigail Austin** was perhaps born circa 1780, died in 1855 in Ohio. She married Stephen Wallace Doughty born circa 1774. Abigail died in 1855 in Morrow County, Ohio, and is buried in Ebenezer Cemetery. Seek ancestry of Abigail.

175-2. **Agnes Austin** was born 13 May 1839 Kentucky, and taken from Kentucky to Iowa as a child by her married sister, Mrs. Isaac Whitaker. Agnes m. 1856 Madison 'Mat' Baker in Iowa, six of their eight children were born there. They moved to Norton County, Kansas, where they helped settle the area and added the last two children. Madison died in Norton County; Agnes died 24 March 1914 at Long Island, Phillips County, Kansas. Her death certificate states her father was M. Austin, mother unknown. Need to know Agnes and Madison's parents.

175-3. **Annis Austin** was born on 1 February 1596 at Titchfield, England, married on 16 October 1614 to Edmund Littlefield at Titchfield, and died on 12 December 1677 at Wells, Maine. Her parents were Richard and Annis Agnes Austin, seek more information on their ancestry.

175-4. **John Austin**, by his first wife, had a son David who lived in Texas. John married a second time in New York to Sarah Jones. Their daughter Sarah Jones Austin married in 1811 to – Goodrich and lived in Ohio. Their son, John F. Austin, married first in New York. His wife died and John F. Austin moved in 1803 to Saint Francisville, Louisiana, and married Sarah Palmer. He had six children by his two wives. Need ancestry of the elder John Austin.

175-5. **Lockwood Austin** married Agitty Lewis. Their son Ambrose Austin married Jane 'Jennie' Fitzpatrick. Frances, daughter of Ambrose and Jane, married Allen J. Benedict. There was a Lockwood (known also as Locksed) Austin who served in the War of 1812, having enlisted at Hudson, Columbia County, New York. He moved to Carlton, Orleans County NY, and opened a cooper shop, early maps show the location. There is a Revolutionary War record of pay received by a Lockwood Austin, but nothing to prove that he was either the father or grandfather of the Lockwood in the War of 1812. Need information on ancestry of Lockwood.

175-6. **Samuel Austin** married Elizabeth Marshall, their son Henry was born 1740-43 in Calvert County, Maryland. Henry married Sarah Hardesty/Harrison, and their daughter Nancy Austin married on 25 January 1790 to Burdit Skinner in Albemarle County, Virginia. Would appreciate any information on this Samuel Austin line.

175-7. **Julius Austin** was married to Caroline Amelia Schoonover. She was born in Scotland. Children: Rachel, Amond, David, Emma, George, Franklin Julius, William, and Amelia. I need information on Julius' parents, who were born around Rochester, New York.

175-8. **Harrison Austin** married Dilla Pace, they were both born in North Carolina. Their daughter Sue Anna Austin was b.1874 NC and married ca. 1889 to Alanzo McEntire who was b.1865 NC d.1925 NC. McEntire children: Rutledge b.1890, Lloyd b.1892, Bessie b.1895, Glen Lee b.1897, Mary Lottie b.1901, Paul b.1903, Ralph Earl b.1905, and Nina b.1907 in Asheville, Buncombe County, NC. Need information on ancestry of Harrison.

175-9. **Anna Austin** married on 16 September 1731 in Rhode Island to Obediah Rathbun. Could she have been the daughter of Jeremiah and Elizabeth Austin who married about 1713 at Exeter, Rhode Island? Seek information on ancestry of Anna Austin.

175-10. **Sarah Austin** was born in New England, married in 1805 or 1806 to Benjamin Harham, who was probably born in Vermont. Is there a known record of this marriage? Sarah died on 23 May 1863 at age 82 yrs and 11 mos in Cass County, Illinois. Need information on her parents.

175-11. **James Austin** married ca. 1765-1770 to Sarah Walker. Among other children, they had a son James and a daughter Priscilla. Is this younger James the same person who married Ann Howard and moved to Washington County, Kentucky?

175-12. **Samuel W. Austin** ancestors were originally from England. According to family reports, his grandparents were Maryland planters, but Samuel chose a team of oxen, wagon and $500 instead of land there. Samuel's oldest daughter, Mary Elizabeth Austin, was born in 1835 (according to 1860 Census), in Virginia or Kentucky. Samuel's wife Mary died on 6 January 1849, and was buried in Hopewell Cemetery, Boone County, Indiana. They then moved to Rock Island, Illinois. I cannot find them in the 1850 Census. Mary Elizabeth m. on 5 August 1852 to Samuel Milton Adams in Rock Island County. Seek information on this family and Samuel's ancestry.

175-13. **Captain William Austin** of Hanover County, Virginia, married Hannah Glen(n). They resided in Bedford County, Virginia, and had at least two children: Ann born 10 March 1758 and James born 4 December 1760. Seeking descendants of William and Hannah.

175-14. **Bertha Edna Austin** was born 7 September 1886 in Amery, Wisconsin, she died on 1 January 1932 in Brainerd, Minnesota. Bertha Austin married on 31 August 1903 to Bertram Deforest Cooley at St. Paul Park, Minnesota. Seek parents and siblings of Bertha.

DIARY OF CONFEDERATE SOLDIER JOHN AUSTEN SHEDS LIGHT ON THE CIVIL WAR'S LONGEST SEIGE

by The Associated Press

Editor's Note: The following article appeared in the 29 April 1984 edition of the *Sunday Press* newspaper of Atlantic City, New Jersey, and was submitted by Maj. Lawrence Stratton, U.S.A. Retired, of Bridgeton, New Jersey.

Baton Rouge, La. – Even mule meat is tasty toward the end of a siege, according to a diary kept by the Confederate chief telegrapher at Port Hudson, the South's last Mississippi River stronghold in the Civil War.

"This day we had mule steak for dinner for the first time. I partook of it most heartily, and indeed found it good," John D. Austen wrote July 4, 1863–43 days into the siege and five days before the garrison surrendered.

Austen's diary spans all but the surrender in the 48-day siege – the longest in U.S. military history until the 77-day siege at Khe Sanh during the Vietnam War.

Port Hudson isn't as famous as Gettysburg or Bull Run. But some Louisiana historians say it would have been the most important fight of the Civil War if it hadn't been for Vicksburg, which surrendered five days earlier.

Port Hudson and Vicksburg, 110 miles upriver, were besieged in a two-pronged attack to complete one of the North's main objectives: controlling the Mississippi River to divide the Confederate army and cut off supplies.

Port Hudson was atop high bluffs overlooking a sharp bend in the river. After New Orleans fell, artillery batteries were set up on the bluff, backed by a network of natural ravines and earthworks.

Nathaniel Banks besieged the batteries at Port Hudson. 'He was one of the most inept Northern generals,' says Art Bergeron, curator at the State Commemorative Area here. 'It's easy for people to forget Banks.'

Bergeron notes that Banks had 30,000 troops. Only 6,800 defended Port Hudson, but two major assaults against the garrison failed.

"U.S. forces advancing from Baton Rouge," begins Austen's first entry, penned May 21. "Heavy skirmishing all day... Colonel Miles' Battalion of Infantry and Boone's company of artillery encountered Enemy at Plains Store. Heavy fight ensued in which both parties retired. Loss quite heavy on both sides."

May 23 – the day now considered the start of the siege because it was the day Union troops surrounded the fort – read only: "Our skirmishers on the left retired within breastworks. Sharpshooters continued firing all day." It is similar to several brief notations, which read only, "Sharpshooting all day." However, the first major assault – a May 27 attack all along the 4½-mile Confederate line – provoked a much longer entry.

"After fight concluded with fleet, fight by land continued with much vigor. It was indeed terrific," Austen said. "During the night, a new fight took place. During the whole day's fighting Enemy made 8 attempts to storm our works, but were repulsed with heavy loss each time."

June 14 brought the second major Union assault. "At 4 o'clock this morning a most desperate assault commenced

all along the line," Austen reported. "Enemy attacked our right, left and center. The fire of artillery was the most violent of the whole siege, it was indeed terrible."

Austen wrote that another attack was expected on or before July 4. But it did not come. "The 4th has arrived, and no attack yet! What can the enemy be doing? This morning was the most favorable for an attack that could have been devised by Enemy – Nature seemed to favor them," Austen wrote. "A heavy fog enveloped the Country, rendering the formation of Enemy's Columns within short distance of our lines an easy matter; yet – he did not take advantage of it. It can not be understood, unless indeed, he desires to await the moment when, being out of provisions, he thinks we will quietly surrender. Time will show."

The surrender came, Bergeron says, partly because word of Vicksburg's collapse had filtered through and Gen. Franklin Gardner was worried that Grant would lead his troops to Louisiana.

Few people outside Austen's family had seen the journal until Paula Brooks Stubbs, then married to Austen's great-great-grandson, showed it to her history teacher at Southeastern Louisiana University three years ago.

She says Dr. Bertrom Groene, a Civil War enthusiast, played a major part in persuading Julia Stubbs, Austen's great-granddaughter, and her brother and sister to donate the book to the state in January.

Austen's last sentences, written July 7, are, "At 12 m (meridien, or noon) U.S. fleet and land forces fired salute, and it is reported that Vicksburg is taken. Some regard this as a ruse of Enemy. We shall see."

Terms of surrender were worked out the next day, and the garrison gave up early July 9. Austen, however, apparently was among the numerous men who sneaked out of the garrison. He wasn't captured there but at Osyka, Mississippi.

Julia Stubbs says he was imprisoned in the cotton press building in New Orleans and, because he refused to take the 'Ironclad Oath,' kept there for several months after the war ended.

After its surrender, Port Hudson became the training ground for most of the Union's black troops in the area and was used as Union garrison until the end of the war.

The state plans to keep Austen's notebook in a museum to be built at the battlefield. So far, the museum is only lines on paper, and construction is at least 18 months away, says John Wiest of the Louisiana Office of State Parks.

★★★★★★★★★★★★★★★★★★★★★★★★★★★★

Austins in the Federal Census of 1850

All current volunteers are requested to send in their state's information as soon as possible. Some additional volunteers are still needed, please write *Austins of America* for details.

★★★★★★★★★★★★★★★★★★★★★★★★★★★★

QUERIES

177-1. **Horace Austin** was born ca.1787 in Connecticut (83 in 1870 census). He was listed as living with Robert E. McBride and wife Eliza J. in the 1850 Ogle County Illinois census and again with them in the 1870 census of Nodaway County, Missouri. Eliza J. was born 9 August 1816 in New Jersey. Was she a daughter of Horace? Need his ancestry, date of birth, death and place of burial.

177-2. **John Austin** married to Mary Kirksey. Their daughter Nancy was born 10 September 1821 (place unknown), married Milton Montgomery 19 January 1843 in Franklin County, Tennessee, and died 9 March 1887 in Franklin County. Seek all information on John and Mary.

177-3. **Mahala Austin** was born on 22 October 1827, married John D. Wooldridge 20 October 1847. These dates are the same as in Fort Knox Cemeteries, McDowell, but the LDS Archive record states that Mrs. Mahala Wooldridge was born in 1828 in Hardin County, Kentucky. A distant relative wrote that 'Uncle Bud (Wooldridge) said that John D. and Mahala came to Kentucky from Old Virginia.' Would like Mahala's birthplace and ancestry.

177-4. **Richard Austin** was born in 1598 in England, is buried in Watertown, Mass. Who was his wife and mother of children Richard b. ca. 1632 and Anthony b. ca. 1636?

177-5. **Nathaniel Austin** was born in 1781 in Virginia, died in 1867/69 in White County, Tennessee. His brothers and sisters were: Joseph, Elizabeth, Lucy, John born 1779 died 1858, David, Hannah and Robin. Need ancestry of Nathaniel.

177-6. **Austin Henry Morey** was born in 1846 in New York, son of Erastus Morey (b. 9 February 1812) and Electa Carr (b. 19 November 1818). They later moved to Iowa, where Erastus died in 1890 and is buried in Anamosa. Seek origin of the name 'Austin' . . . is there a connection to Nathaniel Austin?

177-7. **James M. Austin** was born ca. 1807, perhaps in Maryland. In 1836 he married to Martha A. (−), who was born ca. 1818 in Kentucky. They moved to Randolph County, Missouri by the 1850 Census. Children: Stephen F. b.1837 Kentucky; James H. b.1840 Kentucky; Samuel B. b.1842 Missouri; John (T. or P.) b.1845 Missouri; William (S. or T.) b.1849 Missouri; Henry C. b.1854 Randolph County, Missouri and married Sarah E. 1875. Need ancestry of James M. and Martha.

177-8. **John H. Austin** was married in 1838 in Dickson County, Tennessee, to Penelope Creach. He died in 1872 in Johnson County, Illinois. Seek information on John's parents and on Penelope's parents and birthplace.

THE DESCENDANTS OF
THOMAS AUSTIN AND REBECCA TURNER
OF AMHERST COUNTY, VIRGINIA

by Cornelia Bradshaw Austin

T. THOMAS[1] AUSTIN is believed to have been born before 1755, although his ancestry is unknown. He was likely married at least once prior to his marriage on 3 December 1798 to spinster Rebecca Turner. They were married in Amherst Parish, District of James Montgomery, in Amherst County, Virginia, with the consent of her father James Turner, and with James Turner, Jr. as Surety. Rebecca was born circa 1779 in Virginia. Thomas and Rebecca resided in Amherst Parish at the time the 1800 Tax List was made (see the *Virginia Genealogist*, Vol.5, No.2, p.80). On 16 July 1804 a Bond was recorded in the Amherst County Court (Wills & Inventories Book 4, p.387) in which Rebecca Austin, John Turner, and James Turner signed to make an Inventory of the Estate of Thomas Austin, deceased. On 1 March 1805 the Inventory was returned by Zach Roberts, John Mosby & William H. Mosby, showing a value of £80-7. Rebecca remarried on 12 July 1810 in Nelson County, Virginia, to John Jopling. She was living in Nelson County at the time of the 1850 Census, a widow aged 71. She wrote her Will (see next page) in February 1852 and it was presented in the Nelson County Court on 23 March 1852. Thomas' only known children are those named in Rebecca's Will, and all were born in Virginia:

CHILDREN: T1. LUCINDA, *b. ca. 1800, m. 3 November 1841 in Nelson County to Bluford Ball, their daughter Ann Maria was b. in 1845.*

T2. SARAH AUSTIN, *b. ca. 1801, m. 15 November 1816 in Nelson County to Nathaniel C. Townsend, who was b. 1786 in Virginia and d. 1863 in Nelson County, the son of the Nathaniel who d. 1822 in Nelson County. Sarah and Nathaniel had at least one child, Jesse Austin Townsend, probably a witness to his grandmother's Will. Sarah Austin Townsend d. 1868 in Nelson Co.*

T3. JESSE, *b. circa 1803* +

SECOND GENERATION

T3. JESSE[2] AUSTIN (*Thomas[1]*) was born circa 1803 in Virginia, probably in Amherst County. He was married on 2 November 1822 to Sally Jopling in Nelson County, Virginia, with her brother Benjamin Jopling, surety. Sally was born in Virginia, her father Ralph Jopling left her $1 in his Will. Jesse appears in the 1830 and 1840 Census for Burke County, North Carolina, and the land there on which Jesse and Sally resided once belonged to a Ralph Jopling. In 1841 Caldwell County was formed out of Burke and Wilkes Counties in North Carolina. Rebecca Turner Austin Jopling's Will was probated there as well as in Nelson County, leaving little doubt as to this Jesse's parents. Jesse was a wagoner working for James Harper who owned a store near where Lenoir, North Carolina, is today. His work can be imagined from page 95 of Nancy Alexander's book *Here Will I Dwell*, in the chapter covering 'The Story of Caldwell County':

> "James Harper later became the sole owner of the Burke store. His trade was done mostly through bartering. People brought in produce, dried herbs, brandy, furs, and apples, for which he traded articles in his store. These bartered products were then sent in great wagons to Columbia, Charleston, and other places to be sold or traded for such commodities as salt and other goods. Wagoners who made the long trips, which often required as long as a month's time, camping by the wayside, were Cannon Lowdermilk, Jesse Austin, James Adams, Perry Tomplin, Reddick Freeman, Hiram Clarke, David Hennessee, and Warren Allen.

> "Among the records is one which shows produce sent to Charleston for sale by William C. Lowdermilk, 2 December 1837: bear skins $34; snake root; 1220 pounds of butter at 12½ cents, $205; 25 bushels of apples $22; 40 pairs of shoes $60.00; 25 horse collars; 18 bushels of corn $5.40; cash to purchase cotton $100.00; cash to purchase groceries $200.00; cash for expenses $5.00."

Jesse's first wife Sally died, and by the 1850 census one finds their young daughter Susan living with her grandmother Rebecca Turner Austin Jopling in Nelson County. Jesse's farm was sold 15 November 1849 by the Sheriff in Caldwell Co. to Jesse's son Thomas (Deed Book 2, pp.131-134), who sold it in that same year to Benjamin Jopling.

From his mother's Will (see next page) we know that Jesse married a second time. It is likely that it was the same Jesse Austin who married circa 1850 in Statesville, Iredell County, North Carolina, to Lucinda Vaughn, who was born circa 1825 in Virginia and died in 1900. 'Austin' in Iredell County was sometimes spelled 'Ostun.' In 1852 Jesse inherited his mother's house and some of her land in Nelson County, plus two slaves: a boy Cleaton and a girl Betsy. Jesse and Lucinda had a son Jesse Lafayette Austin born circa 1853, and they are found in the 1860 Iredell County census. Frances Townsend Andrews states that T2 Sarah Austin Townsend wrote around 1857 to her son Jesse Austin Townsend in Ste. Genevieve, Missouri:

> "We had a letter from Bur(?) Monday not long since and he said your Uncle Jesse had spent all his money and had sold Betsy, but William wouldn't let the man take her, then gave him a bill of sale on Cleaton. He wrote to me to send him a copy of Mother's Will by the 2nd Monday in October and said if I did not, they would both be gone. I don't reckon it will do any good. There weren't any trustees left to the Will."

The Last Will and Testament of Rebecca Turner Austin Jopling

Note: The following was copied from a true copy of Will recorded in Will Book J, page 104, in office of Austin Embrey, Clerk, Circuit Court of Nelson County, Virginia. Cover reads: "Jopling Will. Rebecca dec'd 1852."

I, Rebecca Jopling, of Nelson County and State of Virginia, being infirm of body, but of sound mind, in view of the uncertainty of life, do make this my last will and Testament.

Item 1st. I wish my body decently buried, and after all the necessary expenses thereof are paid, I will and request the following disposition of my property:

Item 2nd. I give and bequeath to Bluford Ball and Lucinda, his wife, for the term of their lives, and at their death to descend to their daughter, Ann Maria Ball, a Negro woman named Violet and two boys named Sam and Jim, and in case of the said Ann Maria Ball dying unmarried, these slaves are to revert back to my other children and their heirs.

Item 3rd. I give and bequeath to Ann Maria Ball, the daughter of said Bluford Ball and Lucinda, his wife, the sum of Two Hundred Dollars, which sum is to be held in trust for said Ann Maria Ball's use, by Lewis Ball, until said Ann Maria Ball shall become of age, or shall be married.

Item 4th, I give and bequeath to Nathaniel Townsend and Sally, his wife, during their lifetime, and at their death to their children, the following slaves, Edmund, a boy, and a girl by the name of Nancy.

Item 5th, I give and bequeath to Nathaniel Townsend and Sally, his wife, a portion of my land adjoining the lands of said Nathaniel Townsend's tract, as follows. The line is to commence at the corner of said Nathaniel Townsend's fence, and running a straight line to Powell's line, said line touching the north corner of my new clearing, and all the land lying north of said line, is portion alloted to Nathaniel Townsend and Sally, his wife.

Item 6th, I give and bequeath to my son, Jesse Austin, the following slaves, Cleaton, a boy and Betsy, a girl, for the term of said Jesse Austin's life, and at his death to the children of his first wife.

Item 7th, I give and bequeath to my son, Jesse Austin, my dwelling house, and all my lands except those given as above to Nathaniel Townsend and Sally, his wife.

Item 8th, I give and bequeath to my Grand Daughter, Susan Austin, now living with me, the sum of Fifty Dollars, to be held in trust by my Grandson, William Austin, for the use of said Susan Austin, until her marriage, or until she shall become of age.

Item 9th, It is my desire that all the Slaves bequeathed above shall be fairly appraised, and to go as bequeathed at such appraised value.

Item 10th, I wish my household, kitchen furniture, stock of all kinds, crops of all kinds, and all other property not otherwise provided for to be sold at public sale, and that the proceeds thereof be applied so as to make Bluford Ball & Lucinda, his wife; Jesse Austin; and Nathaniel Townsend and Sally, his wife, equal as to their portions of slaves, after which the balance is to be equally divided among them.

Item 11th, It is my desire that William S. Murrill and Nathaniel Townsend shall be the executors of this my last Will and Testament, and that they carry out all its provisions.

In testimony whereof I hereunto set my hand and seal in the presence of Jesse Townsend and George M. Drumheller on this the ? day of February, One Thousand Eight Hundred and Fifty-Two.

her
Rebecca + Jopling
Mark

H. L. Blain
Wm. H. Bowman
Wm. S. Smith

At court held for Nelson County on the 23rd day of March 1852, this Instrument of writing purporting to be the last Will and Testament of Rebecca Jopling dec'd was produced in said court, and proved by the oaths of Wm. H. Bowman and Wm. S. Smith, two subscribing witnesses hereto, and ordered to be recorded, and on the motion of Wm. S. Murrill and Nathaniel Townsend, the Ex'ors in said will mentioned, who made oath and together with Alex. Fitzpatrick and Wm. H. Bowman, their securities, entered into and acknowledged a bond in the penalty of $1000 conditioned (?) according to law. Probate of said will is granted herein in form of law.

Test. Thomas J. Massie, Clerk

Thomas J. Austin (1825-1909) and his wife Margaret Jane Bean (1827-1907)

Several of Jesse's children's names and birthdates are unknown, but their sexes and approximate birthyears can be determined from the 1830 and 1840 Census records for Burke County, North Carolina, along with ages gleaned from later Census records for Caldwell County, North Carolina:

CHILDREN: T31. [daughter], *b. circa 1823-26*

T32. THOMAS J., *b. 8 February 1825* +

T33. CAROLINE, *b. circa 1823-28, m. Anson Deal. Children: William, Caroline, Thomas, Aaron, Boone, Mary. [Source: Walter B. Davis letter to author].*

T34. [daughter], *b. circa 1825-28*+

T35. ALFRED WEBB, *b. circa 1829* +

T36. WILLIAM THOMAS, *b. 1831* +

T37. SUSAN, *b. circa 1832-35, resided in 1850 with her grandmother Rebecca Jopling in Nelson County, and was still there in February 1852 when Rebecca willed $50 in trust for Susan until she "shall become of age."*

T38. [son], *b. circa 1832-35*

T39. SARAH ELIZA, *b. circa 1836* +

T3A. [son], *b. circa 1837-40*

T3B. JESSE LAFAYETTE, *b. circa 1853* +

THIRD GENERATION

T32. THOMAS J.[3] AUSTIN (*Jesse,[2] Thomas[1]*) was born 8 February 1825 in Virginia. He married in Caldwell County, North Carolina, on 7 February 1846 to Margaret Jane Bean of Baton (see portrait above). Margaret, the daughter of John Bean and Margaret Hayes, was born 18 August 1827 in North Carolina. They lived and farmed in Little Mulberry, and were in the Lenoir, North Carolina, 1860 Census. Their son Julius stated that he and a brother took care of the farming while their father was in the Confederate Army. By the 1870 Census they were in Patterson Township, Caldwell County, and Margaret Bean age 75 was living with them. In later life they lived in a log house (later weather-boarded) at the junction of Roby Martin & Coy Miller roads in Patterson. Margaret died 20 March 1907, and is buried behind the Harpers Chapel Methodist Church in Patterson. Thomas died 7 February 1909 and is buried with his wife. His *Lenoir News* death notice stated that he was in his 85th year, a member of the Presbyterian Church, having joined under the preaching of Rev. Jesse Rankin. They had ten children, eight were living in 1900:

CHILDREN: T321. JOHN P., *b. 1849* +

T322. JULIUS JEFFERSON, *b. 27 March 1850* +

T323. MARTHA, *b. 1852, m. 30 November 1871 to John W. Dula, b. circa 1832 the son of William Hulme Dula and Sarah Witterspoon. John had an earlier wife, his cousin Susan A. Dula, the daughter of Alfred and Elizabeth Carpenter Dula. Martha & John had children John F. b. 1875 and William b. 1880. Martha Austin Dula died sometime after the 1900 Census, and was buried in Caldwell County.*

T324. GEORGE THOMAS, *b. 10 February 1854* +

T325. MARY JANE, *b. 6 March 1855* +

T326. CHARLES DAVID, *b. 25 December 1856* +

T327. JOSEPH MILTON, *b. 21 October 1859* +

T328. MARGARET ELLA, *b. 24 May 1864* +

T329. RUFUS LENOIR, *b. September 1866* +

T32A. SARAH ETTA, *b. 26 June 1869, she married Robert A. Wood. She died on 22 January 1892, and was buried in Harpers Chapel. The young couple had no children.*

T35. ALFRED WEBB[3] AUSTIN (*Jesse,*[2] *Thomas*[1]) was born circa 1829 in North Carolina. He was married on 7 November 1848 to Julia Bean in Caldwell County, North Carolina. Julia was born circa 1830 in North Carolina, her father John Bean was born in Virginia, and her mother Margaret Hayes was born in North Carolina. It is likely that Alfred Webb Austin was the 'A. W. Austin' who served as a Confederate Sergeant, as reported by A. J. Dula in the *The Lenoir News* in 1908:

> "Company A, 22nd N. C. Regiment, was the first company organized in Caldwell County, and was mustered in for twelve months service. The enrollment for the Company began sometime about the middle of April 1861.

> "The election for officers took place in front of the jail about where the livery stable now stands. The officers were chosen by the men rallying around their respective candidates. W. F. Jones was elected Captain on account of his military record. Dr. T. D. Jones was elected 1st Lieutenant; J. M. Isbell, 2nd Lieutenant; J. B. Clarke, 3rd Lieutenant; with J. Wilburn Suddreth as orderly Sergeant; W. T. Suddreth, 2nd Sergeant; Gaston Hood, 3rd Sergeant; A. W. Austin, 4th Sergeant; I. H. Oxford, 5th Sergeant. Corporals: W. G. Allen, L. M. Dinbin, Elhanan Austin, and Monroe Lingle."

'A. W. Austin' was a farmer in the 1880 Census, residing with Julia and their family in Lenoir, Caldwell County.

CHILDREN: T351. GEORGE HARVEY, *b. circa 1849, m. 24 March 1867 in Caldwell Co. to Harriet A. Dula, daughter of James W. & Margaret Dula.*

T352. MARGARET CAROLINE, *b. circa 1851, m. John Warren Allen, twelve children.*

T353. JANE, *b. circa 1854, m. – Jenkins*

T354. WILLIAM, *b. circa 1856, m. – Townsend. He was of Hildebran, lived and died in High Point.*

T355. T. WALTER, *b. circa 1859* +

T356. ALFRED WEBB, JR., *b. circa 1860, he and his bride Mary Bradford were both 'age 19' when they married on 7 December 1879.*

T357. ALICE, *b. circa 1863, m. 2 November 1882 to Julius Justice, at the home of Minister D. C. Stimpson. Known children: Julia Jones Justice b. 1890.*

T358. EMMA, *b. circa 1866, m. Elijah Smith. They resided in Watauga County in 1899. Known child: Grace Hodges.*

T359. EDMUND JONES, *b. 22 June 1870* +

T36. WILLIAM THOMAS[3] AUSTIN (*Jesse,*[2] *Thomas*[1]) was born circa 1833 in Burke County, North Carolina. In his youth he worked as a tanner in Lenoir. He was married on 16 May 1855 to Sarah E. Fullwood of McDowell County, North Carolina. Sarah was born 18 September 1834. They lived on their farm on Paddy's Creek where they raised their family. Later they sold the farm for the establishment of Lake James. William was associated with William Howard, who had married his wife's aunt, they operated the Burke Tannery. William T. Austin also served as a squire and wrote the deed through which Joshua Gibbs gave the land for the Obeth Methodist Church Cemetery and church yard. William died on 16 January 1912, and was buried at Obeth at age 79. His wife died the following December and is buried beside him. William was a member of the Masonic Lodge and his tombstone bears that emblem. His obituary appeared in *The News Herald* in January 1912. The editor said he had been privileged to know him and that he left behind "a life well-spent." He also spoke of his pleasant disposition and friendly manner. Sarah's obituary in the same newspaper states that she died at her home in Linville Township, and "was a woman of rare traits of character. Her whole life was a beautiful Christian life."

CHILDREN: T361. HARPER G., *b. circa 1856* +

T362. ELLEN J., *b. circa 1858, m. William W. James before 1880. Ellen died in early adulthood, leaving five small children: Alice James, Minnie, Daisy, Grover, and Walter.*

T363. WILLIAM THOMAS, *b. circa 1864* +

T364. WALTER L., *b. circa 1866* +

T365. SAMUEL EDWARD, *b. circa 1869* +

T366. VANCE ZEBULON, *b. circa 1871* +

T367. JOHN FULLWOOD, *b. circa 1875* +

T39. SARAH ELIZA[3] AUSTIN (*Jesse,*[2] *Thomas*[1]) was born circa 1836 in North Carolina. She was married in October 1856 to Samuel B. Fullwood. They had three children before Samuel died of wounds in 1863 while serving as a Confederate Soldier in the Civil War. Widow Sarah married a second time on 6 May 1865 to William Fullwood. Samuel and William were brothers of the Sarah

[CONTINUED ON PAGE 197]

INDEX TO SOUTHERN AUSTIN PENSION APPLICATIONS FOR THE WAR OF 1812

by Sally Austin Day

Author's Note: This data is from the National Archives Microfilm 313, Reel 3. The notation s/o is for 'soldier', w/o is for 'widow'. Bounty warrant numbers are followed by the acreage, and by the year the law was enacted under which they were filing, either 1850 or 1855.

Alexander Austin s/o 28592 s/c 20403, Pennsylvania Militia; 1852-1872 living in Philidelphia, PA; Pvt. in Capt. John Mifflin's Company; death 1873-74; wife died 1816; Bounty Warrants 46240-80-50 and 20244-80-55.

Alexander Austin s/o 28824 s/c 20895, Lt. Col. in 3rd Virginia Militia; wife Elizabeth Burgess married 6 January 1812, Halifax Co. NC; 1852-55, 1873-74 living Campbell Co. VA; death 1874, New London, VA; wife died –; Bounty Warrants 78705-40-50 and 53933-120-55.

Bennett Austin s/o 19126 rejected, Pvt. in Capt. T. Estes Company Virginia Militia.

Brooks Austin s/o 13524, Pvt. in Capt. I. Gettings Company, Maryland Militia.

Charles Austin s/o 27885 s/c 19567, Pvt. in Capt. Henry Lane's Georgia Militia; 1853-55-72 living in Fayette Co. GA; wife Elizabeth Strawn, died 24 March 1816, Jackson Co. GA; Bounty Warrants 50399-80-50 and 26822-80-55.

Charles Austin, file 130, U.S. Marine Corps. Death of Disability.

Daniel Austin, s/o 29208 s/c 21121, Pvt. in Capt. McClellan's 7th U.S. Infantry; wife Nancy Edwards m. 17 November 1817 Anderson Co. TN; 1873 living Vernon Co. MO; Bounty Warrant 113577-160-55.

David Austin file 12177, Pvt. in Capt. Russell's Company Tennessee Militia; Widow Mary Austin.

Dickerson Austin s/o 4865, Pvt. in Capt. Hamilton's Tennessee; living 1850-55-71 Sumner Co. TN; 1st wife Sally Hall; 2nd wife Emily Anderson m. 26 March 1835; Dickerson d. 26 February 1876, Richland Station, Sumner Co. TN; Bounty Warrants 9949-80-50 and 26662-80-55.

James Austin s/o 16688 s/c 12595, Sgt. in Capt. Joseph Funks' Kentucky Militia; 1850-55-71 living in Goshen, Oldham Co. KY; wife Elizabeth Deal, died 14 December 1820, Jefferson Co. KY; Bounty Warrants 13601-80-50 and 29013-80-55.

James M. Austin w/o 4334 w/c 33838, married Sarah Ann Green 10 August 1814 in Winchester, Franklin Co. TN; James died 1836, Augusta, Richmond Co. GA; Sarah was living 1851-53 in Newton Co. GA, in 1858 in Henry Co. GA, in 1884 in Gordon Co. GA; Sarah died April 1885; Bounty Warrants 103920-40-50 and 95211-120-55.

John Austin w/o 6584, Mourning Austin widow; Pvt. in Capt. Steel's Company Virginia Militia.

John H. Austin w/o 27807 w/c 31026, Pvt. in Capt. John G. Colbertt's Company Georgia Militia; wife Rachael Anderson m. 14 December 1819 Green Co. GA; resided 1850-55-78 Newton Co. GA; John d. 21 December 1868 Newton Co. GA; Warrants 288-80-50 & 13344-80-55.

Joseph Austin s/o 2182 s/c 1298, Pvt. in Capt. Samuel G. Wilson's Virginia Militia; 1850-55-78 living in Morgantown, Monongalia Co. VA; wife Camilla Martin married December 1813, Monongalia Co. VA; death of Joseph 10 April 1888; Bounty Warrants 1554-80-50 and 670-80-55.

Peter Austin w/o 14415 w/c 8380, Cornet in Capt. James Leftwich's Company Virginia; married Sally Leftwich, 7 July 1819 Bedford Co. VA; Peter died 5 October 1835, Bedford Co. VA; Sally died 18 July 1882, Carrollton, MO; Bounty Warrants 67308-40-50 and 45073-120-55.

Samuel D. Austin s/o 6875 s/c 3735, Pvt. 1st Tenn. Regt. Mounted Gunman Capt. John Strothers; wife Mary Baker m. 2 March 1817, Dickson Co. TN; resided 1851-55 in Dickson Co. TN, in 1871 in Humphreys Co. TN, in 1876 in Walter Valley, Graves Co., KY; Bounty Warrants 31766-80-50 and 14851-80-55.

Thomas Austin w/o 14415 w/o 8380, Cprl. in Capt. Thomas Archer's Virginia Militia; wife Sarah Faucett m. 29 January 1825, Hanover Co. VA; Thomas d. December 1840-48 Henrico Co. VA; Sarah living in Henrico Co. VA. 1870-78; Bounty Warrant 109571-160-55.

Thomas Austin s/o 3843 s/c 7400, Pvt. in Capt. J. Neville's Company Virginia; wife Sallie Halbert m. 24 March 1826, Athens, OH; living 1850 Athens Co. OH, 1855 Meigs Co. OH, 1875 Monticello, IN; Thomas d. 1878-79; Bounty Warrants 1304-40-50 & 30679-120-55.

Thomas C. Austin s/o 24781 2/0 42741 w/c 33132, Lt. and Paymaster with Col. William Austin's Company South Carolina; wife Polly James m. 27 February 1823, Spartanburg, SC; living 1850-55; 1871-74 Greenville, SC; Thomas died 20 January 1883, Spartanburg, SC; Bounty Warrants 77072-40-50 and 47791-120-55.

William Austin s/c 14012 s/o 22809 w/c 14846 w/o 20228, Pvt. in Capt. Hamilton's 1st Regt. Tenn. & Capt. Hudson's Company (2 tours of duty); wife Dicey Horner m. 21 October 1819, Dickson Co. TN; William Austin b. Orange Co. NC; William died 9 October 1876 Dickson Co. TN; Dicey died 7 January 1884 Dickson Co. TN; Bounty Warrants 2535-80-50 and 52697-80-55.

William Austin w/o 14414 w/c 9439, Pvt. in Lt. Charles Thompson's Company Virginia Militia; 1st wife Susan Wade; 2nd wife Ann Quarles, widow of Edmond Quarles; married Ann 14 September 1837, Hanover Co. VA; William died June 1850 Richmond, VA; Ann Austin living in Hanover Co. 1853; 1878 living in Richmond, VA; Bounty Warrants 92108-40-50 and 344-120-55

William Austin 12176, Pvt. in Capt. Russell's Co., Col. Dyer's Regt., General Coffee's Div., Death of Disability.

AUSTINS PURCHASING LAND FROM THE
STATE OF ILLINOIS - 1817 TO 1889

by Anthony Kent Austin

Editor's Note: The following data is from the State of Illinois Archives Division Public Domain Sales Land Tract Record Listing. Records are listed here alphabetically by purchaser (including some possible misspellings of Austin), and are chronological for purchasers of the same name. The last two numbers in each record are the Volume and Page on which it is found in the Archives.

Aaron Austin - 320 acres in Hancock County on 3-18-1818 for Warrant   808-388

Albert R. Austin 240 acres in Edgar County on 8-20-1852 for Warrant   296-168

Alexander Austin - 40 acres in White County on 2-17-1849 for $50   819-67

Alexander Austin - 80 acres in White County on 11-29-1852 for $100   819-67

Alexander Austin - 80 acres in White County on 8- -1853 for $60   SWP-26

Alexander Austin - 80 acres in White County on 9- -1856 for $80   SWP-25

Alexander Austin - 80 acres in White County on 1-24-1857 for $80   SWP-25

Algernon Austin, Jr. - 80 acres in Iroquois County in 1871 for $1040   794-38

Algernon S. Austin, Jr. - 80 acres in Iroquois County on 4-30-1870 for $1120   793-223

Algernon S. Austin, Jr. - 80 acres in Iroquois County on 3-31-1871 for $800   793-359

Algernon S. Austin, Jr. - 120 acres in Iroquois County on 4-29-1871 for $960   793-361

Allin Austin of Fayette Co. - 41.64 acres in Fayette Co. on 10-10-1833 $52.05   145-37

Allen Austin of Fayette Co. - 42.40 acres in Fayette Co. on 2-28-1837 for $53   145-149

Allen Austin - 41.60 acres in Fayette County on 3-19-1853 for Warrant   155-182

Anthony Austin of Bond County - 40 acres in Bond Co. on 1-5-1837 for $50   339-145

Ardon Austin - 40 acres in Henry County on 6-30-1852 for Warrant   707-179

Ardon Austin - 80 acres in Henry County on 12-2-1852 for Warrant   708-7

Ardon Austin - 40 acres in Henry County on 8-10-1857 for $410   819-110

Augustus Austin - 40 acres in Ogle County on 3-24-1846 for $50   716-96

Barber Austin - 11.55 acres in Pike County on 5-5-1836 for $14.43   700-33

Bartholomew C. Austen - 80 acres in Kankakee Co. 5-4-1846 for $100   686-131

Benjamin Austin of Coles County - 80 acres in Coles Co. on 5-13-1833 for $100   145-34

Benjamin Austin of Coles Co. - 160 acres in Coles Co. on 12-20-1834 for $200   145-47

Benjamin Austin of White County - 40 acres in White Co. on 7-25-1837 for $50   110-108

Benjamin Austin of White Co. - 43.78 acres in White Co. on 4-7-1845 for $54.72   110-195

Benjamin Austin - 80 acres in LaSalle County on 2-17-1848 for $100   704-105

Benjamin Austin - 160 acres in LaSalle Co. on 2-17-1848 for Warrant   704-106

Benjamin Austin - 80 acres in LaSalle County on 7-18-1849 for Warrant   704-106

Benjamin Austin - 200 acres in White County on 8-20-1849 for Warrant   105-27

Benjamin Austin of White County - 40 acres in White Co. on 11-4-1850 for $50   110-256

Benjamin Austin - 85.44 acres in White Co. on 3-14-1853 for $85.44   SWP-25

Benjamin Austin - 40 acres in Coles County on 1-6-1854 for Warrant   296-269

Benjamin F. Austin - 40 acres in Christian County on 3-31-1870 for $320   793-200

Benjamin R. Austin of Macon Co. - 40 acres in Christian Co. 10-25-1834 for $50   145-45

Benjamin R. Austin of Macon Co. - 40 acres in Macon Co. on 6-28-1836 for $50   145-94

Burgess Austin - 40 acres in Dupage County on 7-15-1844 for $50   686-181

Catharine Austin - 41.99 acres in Ogle County on 11-18-1844 for $52.49   716-79

Charles Austin - 160 acres in Stark County on 2-19-1818 for Warrant   807-352

Christopher Austin - 160 acres in Bond Co. on 1-15-1853 for Warrant   155-58

Christopher B. Austin of Conn. - 160 acres in Pike Co. 12-2-1817 for Warrant   807-272

Cyrus Austin of Macoupin - 160 acres in Montgomery Co. 3-4-1837 $200   145-152

David Austin - .29 acres in Marshall County on 4-29-1834 for $.29   817-45

David Austin of Shelby County - 80 acres in Shelby Co. on 10-17-1839 for $100   146-90

David Austin of Shelby County - 40 acres in Shelby Co. on 10-30-1839 for $50   146-93

David P. Austin - 40 acres in Lake County on 4-27-1846 for $50   686-99

David W. Austin - 40 acres in McHenry Co. on 8-26-1846 for $50   684-105

Duley Austin - 51.38 acres in Mercer County on 3-1-1852 for $64.23   711-148

Eben H. Austin - 40 acres in Kane County on 10-4-1843 for $50   684-65

Edward Austin of Menard County - 40 acres in Menard Co. on 8-1-1851 for $50   070-153

Edward Austin - 80 acres in LaSalle County on 9-27-1852 for $280   819-180

Edward W. Austin - 160 acres in Kane County on 6-18-1840 for $200   685-102

Edward W. Austin - 160.13 acres in Kane Co. on 9-28-1840 for $200.16   685-102/3

Edward W. Austin - 160 acres in Kane County on 9-29-1840 for $200   685-102

Edward W. Austin - 69.70 acres in Winnebago County on 9-2-1842 for $87.13   716-130

Eleanor Austin of Macon County - 40 acres in Macon Co. on 1-25-1837 for $50   145-137

Eleanor Austin - 160 acres in Dekalb County on 5-19-1851 for Warrant   683-53

Eleazer Austin - 160 acres in Knox County on 5-1-1818 for Warrant   808-428

Eleazer Hazen Austin - 160 acres in Kane County on 6-6-1842 for $200   684-65

Eleazer H. Austin - 80 acres in Kane County on 6-7-1842 for $100   684-187

Eli Austin of Morgan County - 80 acres in Morgan Co. 3-6-1835 for $100   343-175

Eli Austin of Morgan County - 40 acres in Morgan Co. on 1-25-1836 for $50   343-271

Elijah Austin - 320 acres in Winnebago Co. on 10-26-1839 for $400   706-49

Elijah Austin - 160 acres in Winnebago Co. on 10-26-1839 for $200   706-49/50

Elisha Austin of Shelby County - 80 acres in Shelby Co. on 5-15-1834 for $100   145-43

Elisha Austin of Shelby Co. - 37.37 acres in Shelby Co. on 12-5-1836 $46.89   145-125

Elisha Austin of White County - 40 acres in White Co. on 7-25-1837 for $50   110-108

Elisha Austin of White County - 40 acres in White Co. on 8-15-1838 for $50   110-125

Elisha Austin - 160 acres in Shelby County on 1-14-1850 for Warrant   154-49

Elisha Austin of Shelby County - 40 acres in Shelby Co. on 8-20-1850 for $50   147-90

Elisha Austin - 80 acres in White County on 10-8-1852 for Warrant   105-70

Elisha Austin - 40 acres in White County on 1-11-1853 for Warrant   105-90

Elisha Austin of White Co. - 43.78 acres in White Co. on 8-28-1854 for $54.73 112-121

Elizabeth W. Austin of Alexander County - 40 acres Alexander Co. 2-24-1854 $50   32-207

Elizabeth W. Austin of Alexander County - 40 acres Alexander Co. 12-12-1854 $5   32-259

Ellike Austin of Fayette County - 40 acres in Fayette Co. on 10-19-1833 for $50   145-37

Freeman Austin - 160 acres in LaSalle County on 8-29-1848 for Warrant   704-106

George Austin of St. Clair County - 40 acres in St. Clair County on 8-1-1848 for $50   32-64

George Austin of St. Clair County - 40 acres in St. Clair County on 5-1-1849 for $50   32-80

George Austin - 40 acres in Williamson County on 3-11-1853 for Warrant   105-124

George Austin - 80 acres in Livingston County on 5-2-1864 for $68   819-109

George Austin - 40 acres in Shelby County on 2-29-1871 for $360   793-312

George Austen - 40 acres in Shelby County on 11-24-1876 for $320   794-244

George W. Austin of Union County - 40 acres in Union County on 11-9-1869 for $- CM1-8

Harriet Austin - 40 acres in Will County on 10-11-1852 for Warrant   687-30

Henry Austin - 40 acres in Peoria County on 5-3-1855 for $50   697-8

Henry Austin - 40 acres in Peoria County on 6-18-1855 for $50   697-68

Henry Austen of Fulton County - 65.76 acres in Fulton Co. 3-26-1856 for $49.32   70-231

Henry S. Austin - 40 acres in Winnebago County on 11-1-1845 for $50   705-60

Henry S. Austin - 40.44 acres in Fulton County on 1-7-1846 for $50.55   696-158

Henry S. Austin - 160 acres in Peoria County on 11-1-1851 for $200   697-15-17

Henry S. Austin - 80 acres in Peoria County on 11-1-1851 for $100   697-17-18

Henry S. Austin - 40 acres in Peoria County on 4-10-1855 for Warrant   697-121

Henry S. Austin - 40 acres in Peoria County on 5-3-1855 for $50   697-8

Henry S. Austin - 161.62 acres in Peoria County on 5-3-1855 for $202.03   697-57

Hiram Austin - 80 acres in Kendall County on 10-24-1846 for $100   685-49

Horace Austin -160 acres in Dekalb County on 4-26-1851 for Warrant   683-56

Hugh Austin - 82.29 acres in White County on 10-13-1840 for $102.86   110-171

Hugh Austin - 40 acres in White County on 7-1-1851 for Warrant   105-5

Hugh Austin - 80 acres in White County on 2-8-1853 for Warrant   105-108

Ira Austin - 80 acres in Will County on 11-18-1841 for $560   L5A-133

Ira Austin of Illinois - 80 acres in Will County on 11-18-1841 for $560   R13-11

Ira Austin - 80 acres in Will County on 6-9-1842 for $480   L5A-133

Ira Austin - 80 acres in Will County on 6-9-1842 for $480   R13-19

Ira Austin - 240 acres in Will County on 5-9-1854 for $1480   L7A-165

Ira Austin - 160 acres in Will County on 5-9-1854 for $960   L7A-166

Isaac S. Austin - 20 acres in Jo Daviess County on 6-14-1848 for $25   711-43

Isaac R. Austin - 40 acres in Jo Daviess County on 11-23-1849 for $50   711-39

James Austen of Edwards County - 61.88 acres in Edwards County on 12-14-1836 for $77.35   110-83

James Austin of Livingston Co. - 160 acres in Livingston Co. 11-7-1838 for $200   236-256

James Austin - 160 acres in Mason County on 8-7-1847 for Warrant   59-1

James Austin of Coles County - 20.90 acres in Coles County on 6-2-1849 for $26.13   291-75

James Austin - 41.75 acres in Cumberland County on 10-20-1850 for $133.60   819-71

James Austin of Cumberland Co. - 40 acres in Jasper County on 3-10-1854 for $50   148-139

James Austin of Cumberland Co. - 80 acres in Cumberland Co. 3-10-1854 $100   148-139

James Austin of Cumberland Co. - 40 acres in Cumberland Co. 11-2-1854 for $50   291-276

James B. Austin - 40 acres in Wayne County on 3-16-1852 for Warrant   105-25

James B. Austin - 36.03 acres in Wayne County on 8-28-1852 for Warrant   105-58

James B. Austin - 40 acres in Wayne County on 2-15-1853 for Warrant   105-111

James B. Austin - 160 acres in Will County on 5-9-1853/4 for $960   L7A-168

James B. Austin of Wayne County - 40 acres in Wayne County on 9-24-1853 for $50   112-20

James S. Austin - 80 acres in Wayne County on 8-14-1852 for Warrant   105-53

James S. Austin - 80 acres in Wayne County on 2-11-1853 for Warrant   105-109

James S. Austin of Wayne Co. - 29.20 acres in Wayne Co. on 10-11-1855 for $3.65 112-217

Jauvier J. Austin - 40 acres in Morgan County on 10-8-1853 for Warrant   351-139

Jeremiah C. Austin - 80 acres in McHenry County on 10-31-1849 for $100   684-239

Jeremiah C. Austin - 40 acres in McHenry County on 9-17-1851 for $50   684-238

Jesse Austin of White County - 40 acres in White County on 3-2-1838 for $50   110-119

Jesse Austin - 40 acres in Shelby County on 11-27-1865 for $320   791-292

Jesse W. Austin of St. Clair County - 80 acres in Perry Co. on 11-9-1853 for $100   32-183

Jesse W. Austin - 80 acres in Christian County on 12-31-1869 for $1040   793-199

Jesse W. Austin - 80 acres in Christian County on 1-15-1877 for $1400   794-244

John Austin of Bond County - 40 acres in Bond County on 6-15-1836 for $50   325-43

John Austin - 135.84 acres in Fulton County on 6-15-1836 for $169.80   696-149

John Austin of Coles County - 20.90 acres in Coles Co. on 10-19-1836 for $26.13 291-133

John Austin of Coles County - 40 acres in Coles County on 3-4-1837 for $50   291-154

John Austin - 82.19 acres in Ogle County on 1-24-1843 for $102.74   716-79

John Austin - 39.90 acres in Ogle County on 1-30-1843 for $49.88   716-79

John Austin - 123.32 acres in Winnebago County on 11-3-1843 for $154.15   705-60

John Austin - 40 acres in Ogle County on 12-22-1843 for $50   716-96

John Austin, Jr. - 40 acres in Ogle County on 11-18-1844 for $50   716-96

John Austin of Jackson County - 40 acres in Jackson Co. on 8-30-1852 for Warrant 16-84

John Austin of Jackson County - 80 acres in Jackson County on 12-6-1854 for $10 32-256

John Austin - 40 acres in Fayette County on 6-3-1886 for $124   795-20

John D. Austin of Marion County - 40 acres in Marion County on 4-8-1844 for $50   147-1

John H. Austin - 40.82 acres in Fayette County on 9-16-1889 for $126.54   795-57

John W. Osteen - 40 acres in Williamson County on 3-4-1853 for Warrant   105-120

Joiner Austin - 39.65 acres in Fulton County on 11-3-1838 for $49.56   696-75

Joseph Austin of Macon County - 80 acres in Macon County on 8-5-1830 for $100 145-14

Joseph Austin of Macon County - 80 acres in Macon County on 8-5-1830 for $100 677-170

Joseph Austin of Macon County - 40 acres in Macon County on 9-17-1835 for $50 145-52

Joseph Austin - 40 acres in Montgomery County on 2-27-1836 for $50   324-182

Joseph Austin of Macon County - 40 acres in Macon County on 6-28-1836 for $50 145-94

Joseph Austin of Alexander County - 40 acres in Alexander Co. 2-10-1838 for $50   31-116

Joseph Austin of Montgomery Co. - 40 acres Montgomery Co. on 3-7-1839 for $50 146-58

Joseph Austin - 5 acres in Winnebago County on 1-18-1844 for $51.88   818-110

Joseph Austin of Montgomery Co. - 40 acres Montgomery Co. 1-9-1854 for $50   148-126

Joseph B. Austin - 40 acres in Carroll County on 9-2-1845 for $50   714-50

Joseph B. Austin - 40 acres in Carroll County on 7-4-1848 for $50   714-50

Joseph B. Austin - ? acres in Champaign County on 4-30-1859 for $200   792-33

Joseph B. Austin - ? acres in Champaign County on 4-30-1859 for $200   796-186

Joshua Austin of Pope County - 80 acres in Pope County on 3-12-1836 for $100   110-44

Joshua Austin of Pope County - 40 acres in Pope County on 9-16-1839 for $50   110-156

Joshua Austin of Pope County - 40 acres in Pope County on 4-24-1844 for $50   110-188

Joshua D. Austin of Morgan County - 160 acres Morgan Co. 11-13-1823 for $200 68-4

Joshua D. Austin of Morgan County - 160.44 acres Morgan Co. 11-13-1823 $200.55 68-4

Joshua D. Austin of Morgan Co. - 80 acres in Morgan Co. on 7-13-1829 for $100 68-54

Joshua D. Austin of Morgan Co. - 80 acres in Morgan Co. on 8-29-1829 for $100 68-55

Joshua D. Austin of Morgan County - 160 acres Morgan Co. 8-3-1830 for $200   68-79

Joshua D. Austin of Morgan County - 80 acres in Morgan Co. on 5-5-1831 for $100   68-99

Joshua N. Austin - 476.67 acres in Kendall County on 11-22-1839 for $595.84   684-45

Joshua N. Austin - 160 acres in Iroquois County on 11-17-1871 for $2080   794-77

Josiah Austin of Bond County - 40 acres in Bond County on 7-25-1836 for $50   145-101

Josiah Austin of Bond County - 40 acres in Bond County on 2-21-1839 for $50   146-53

Josiah Austin - 160 acres in McHenry County on 9-11-1846 for $200   684-253

Josiah Austin - 40 acres in McHenry County on 12-18-1847 for $50   684-253

Kisiah Austin - 40 acres in Pope County on 3-31-1852 for Warrant   105-26

Laevetta Osteen of Franklin County - 40 acres Franklin Co. on 12-20-1841 for $50 110-178

Larkin R. Austin of Wayne County - 17.62 acres Wayne Co. 5-8-1855 $141.04 112-193

Lawless Austine of Baltimore, MD - 160 acres Fulton Co. 11-8-1817 for Warrant   807-106

Lewis Austin - 160 acres in Pike County on 10-6-1817 for Warrant   807-26

Lewis Austin - 80 acres in Stark County on 11-10-1843 for $100   714-203

Lewis Austin - 40 acres in Knox County on 1-25-1844 for $50   713-148

Lewis Austin - 1 acres in Stark County on 11-23-1847 for $18   819-49

Lucy Austin - 40 acres in Lake County on 2-17-1846 for $50   685-234

Margaret Austin of Macon County - 40 acres in Macon Co. on 1-25-1837 for $50 145-137

Morton Austin - 160 acres in Adams County on 11-29-1817 for Warrant   807-159

Nathan Austin of Coles County - 80 acres in Coles County on 12-20-1834 for $100 145-47

Nathan Austin of Coles County - 40 acres in Coles County on 12-27-1836 for $50 291-144

Nathan Austin - 31.31 acres in Clark County on 9-9-1851 for Warrant   296-116

Nathaniel Austin of Louisiana - 160 acres in Hancock Co. 7-8-1818 for Warrant 808-491

Nathaniel L. Asten - 160 acres in Fulton County on 10-6-1817 for Warrant   807-27

Nathaniel T. Austin - 160 acres in Kane County on 7-23-1841 for $200   684-189

Nathaniel T. Austin - 160 acres in Kane County on 7-23-1841 for $200   684-189-90

Nathaniel T. Austin - 186.89 acres in Kane County on 6-7-1842 for $233.61   684-190

Nathaniel T. Austin - 109.46 acres in Kane County on 5-6-1845 for $136.82   684-175

Nathaniel T. Austin - 40 acres in Kane County on 6-27-1845 for $50   684-189

Nathaniel T. Austin - 40 acres in Kane County on 12-26-1845 for $50   684-189

Peter Austin - 40 acres in McHenry County on 3-27-1843 for $50   685-137

Phineas Austin - 160 acres in LaSalle County on 9-3-1847 for Warrant   704-106

Phineas Austin - 54.48 acres in Stark County on 10-2-1851 for Warrant   709-65

Rachael Austin - ? acres in Marion County on 4-24-1868 for $200   792-131

Rachael Austin - ? acres in Marion County on 4-24-1868 for $200   796-252

Reuben Austin - 76.56 acres in DuPage County on 1-12-1843 for $95.70   685-188

Reuben Austin - 40 acres in DuPage County on 2-28-1844 for $50   685-204

Richard L. Austin - 160 acres in Knox County on 10-3-1818 for Warrant   808-558

Robert J. L. Austin - 160 acres in Adams County on 10-6-1817 for Warrant   807-66

Russell Austin - 64.32 acres in Fulton County on 6-15-1836 for $80.40   696-122

Samuel Austin of Fayette County - 40 acres in Fayette Co. on 2-28-1837 for $50   145-149

Samuel Austin of Fayette County - 40 acres in Fayette County on 3-22-1839 for $50 146-62

Samuel Austin of Alexander Co. - 48.12 acres Pulaski Co. 9-12-1839 for $60.15   110-155

Samuel Austin - 40 acres in Pulaski County on 5-12-1842 for $60   818-109

Samuel Austin - 180 acres in Fayette County on 7-19-1888 for $360   795-46

Samuel Austin - 60 acres in Fayette County on 7-19-1888 for $120   795-46

Simeon Austin - 160 acres in LaSalle County on 8-20-1848 for Warrant   704-108

Spencer Austin - 160 acres in LaSalle County on 4-11-1849 for Warrant   704-102

Stephen Austin of Maine - 160 acres in Knox County on 5-15-1818 for Warrant   807-268

Stephen Austin of Effingham Co. - 40 acres in Effingham Co. on 11-10-1838 for $50 146-32

Stephen Austin of Effingham Co. - 40 acres in Effingham Co. on 4-23-1840 for $50 146-108

Stephen Austin of Effingham Co. - 40 acres in Effingham Co. on 5-14-1851 for $50 147-115

Susan Austin - ? acres in Jackson County on 4-17-1867 for $125   792-114

Susan Austin - ? acres in Jackson County on 4-17-1867 for $125   796-37

Susan B. Austin - 40 acres in Kendall County on 8-11-1845 for $50   685-45

Sylvia Austin - 40 acres in Union County on 7-15-1867 for $432   791-351

Thadeus R. Austin - 160 acres in Peoria County on 2-9-1836 for $200   697-13

Theodore Austin - 125.26 acres in Ogle County on 11-18-1844 for $156.58 709-113

Theodore Austin - 40 acres in Ogle County on 12-3-1844 for $50   709-114

Theodore Austin - 40 acres in Ogle County on 2-14-1845 for $50   709-114

Theodore Austin - 40 acres in Ogle County on 8-11-1846 for $50   709-114

Theodore R. Austin - 120 acres in Peoria County on 7-22-1836 for $150   697-13

Thomas Austin of Pope County - 40 acres in Pope County on 3-12-1836 for $50   110-44

Thomas Austin of Sangamon County - 40 acres in Mason Co. 7-2-1836 for $50 69-130

Thomas Austin of Edwards Co. - 28.37 acres Edwards Co. 4-20-1837 for $35.46 110-102

Thomas Austin of Pope County - 40 acres in Pope County on 10-23-1840 for $50 110-171

Thomas Austin - 160 acres in LaSalle County on 8-29-1848 for Warrant   704-106

Thomas Austin of Pope County - 80 acres in Pope County on 3-28-1855 for $20   112-176

Thomas J. Austin of Pope County - 40 acres in Pope County on 7-26-1855 for $5   112-204

Ure Aston of Vermilion County - 42.70 acres in Vermillion Co. 7-5-1844 for $53.38 237-9

Ure Aston of Vermilion County - 40 acres in Vermillion Co. on 4-26-1845 for $50 237-12

Walter Austin - 160 acres in Knox County on 8-8-1818 for Warrant   808-516

Walter Astin of Johnson County - 40 acres in Franklin Co. on 4-6-1839 for $50   110-144

Walter Astin of Johnson County - 40 acres in Massac Co. on 4-11-1839 for $50   110-144

Wesley M. Austin - 40 acres in Montgomery County on 3-1-1853 for Warrant   155-159

William Austin of Clark County - 171.84 acres in Coles Co. 5-10-1830 for $214.80 291-37

William Austin of Coles County - 91.84 acres Coles Co. 7-4-1831 Coles $114.80   291-57

William Austin of Edwards Co. - 27.29 acres in Edwards Co. 8-22-1834 for $34.11 110-32

William Osteen of Franklin County - 80 acres in Franklin Co. 4-20-1837 for $100 110-102

William Austin of Coles County - 25.72 acres in Coles Co. on 6-2-1837 for $32.15 291-163

William Osteen of Franklin County - 80 acres in Franklin Co. 3-14-1838 for $100 110-119

William Austin - 80 acres in Henry County on 5-6-1839 for $100   707-119

William Osteen of Franklin County - 80 acres in Franklin Co. 1-6-1843 for $100   110-183

William Austin - 5 acres in Kane County on 7-1-1843 for $22.50   818-96

William Osteen of Franklin County - 80 acres in Franklin Co. 1-3-1849 for $100   110-228

William Austin - 160 acres in LaSalle County on 4-11-1849 for Warrant   704-102

William Osteen - 160 acres in Effingham County on 3-29-1850 for Warrant   154-56

William Austin of White County- 40 acres in White County on 12-1-1851 for $50   111-23

William Austin - 320 acres in Whiteside County on 10-22-1852 for Warrant 714-126

William Austin - 80 acres in Whiteside County on 4-18-1853 for Warrant   714-125

William Austin of White County - 40 acres in White County on 11-11-1853 for $50 112-36

William Osteen - 80 acres in Franklin County on 12-18-1853 for Warrant   105-113

William Osteen of Franklin County - 80 acres in Franklin Co. 10-9-1854 for $10   112-144

William Auston - Lot in Marion County on 10-8-1859 for $-   791-51

William Austen - ? acres in Marion County on 10-8-1859 for $-   796-15

William Osteen - 40 acres in Franklin County on 1-20-1863 for $240   791-112

William Austin - Lots in Marion County on 2-7-1866 for $345.50   796-24

William Austen - ? acres in Marion County on 2-7-1866 for $172.25   792-96

William Austin - 79.87 acres in Shelby County on 6-29-1872 for $551   794-85

William A. Austin of Macon County - 40 acres in Macon Co. on 9-17-1835 for $50   145-52

William A. Austin of Macon County - 40 acres in Macon Co. on 6-28-1836 for $50   145-94

William A. Austin - 40 acres in Franklin County on 8-31-1869 for $252   793-122

William D. Austin of Coles County - 40 acres in Coles Co. on 8-30-1837 for $50   291-170

William D. Austin - 160 acres in Coles County on 5-16-1859 for Warrant   296-58

William F. Austin - 160 acres in White County on 8-20-1849 for Warrant   105-27

William F. M. Austin - 40 acres in White County on 10-8-1852 for Warrant   105-70

William G. Austin - 160 acres in Cook County on 6-13-1835 for $200   687-67

William H. Austin - 40 acres in LaSalle County on 9-30-1869 for $640   793-163

William M. Austin - .50 acres in Kane County on 7-1-1843 for $2.25   818-96

William S. Austin - 160 acres in Franklin County on 2-6-1854 for Warrant   105-170

William S. Austin - 40 acres in Franklin County on 12-23-1865 for $360   791-287

QUERIES

186-1. **John Austin** of East Haven CT was b. 1647 d. 1690, married Mercy Atwater b. 1647 d. 1683. My branch moved to Wallingford CT where Phebe, the daughter of Abel Austin, was born on 28 July 1767. Seek information on the descendants of John Austin.

186-2. **Caleb Austin** was born 2 April 1779, married Hannah (–) and had 11 children: Jeremiah, Polly, Robert, Elmira Elsie who married Jesse Orvis, John R., George W. and Betsey B. (twins), William H., Merrilla S., Emeline A. and Louisa Jane. I am especially interested in information on the Elmira and Jesse Orvis branch.

186-3. **Ormal Austin** born circa 1790 and wife Sally or Sarah Purple born ca. 1801, lived in Green County NY and Potter County PA. Seek information on Ormal Austin.

186-4. **William S. Austin** possibly son of Samuel and Elizabeth (Williams) of Stonington CT married on 23 August 1771 to Sarah Fish, born 31 April 1757 in Voluntown CT, possibly the daughter of Samuel and Ruth. Seek all data and ancestry of William and Sarah.

186-5. **Daniel Austin** - Need proof or disproof that S246. Jonathan[4] Austin (*Zebediah,*[3] *Thomas,*[2] *Samuel*[1]) was the father of Daniel Austin born ca. 1772-3, who had sons Nathaniel b. 1806 ME and Shadrach b.1813 NY (see *Austins of America* page 15 and Query 148-2 on page 148).

186-6. **Levi Austin** born ca. 1782 in NC, married Anna (–) born ca. 1791 in KY. Levi died 1850-60 in Smith County TN. Their son Philip was b. ca. 1808 TN, m. Phoebe (–) b. ca. 1809 TN. Seek data on Levi and Phoebe.

186-7. **Thomas Austin** had son Freeman born 26 Mar/May 1770 on a small island not far from Martha's Vineyard who m. 18 April 1799 in NY or NJ to Catherine Van Wagenen, born 18 April 1780. Freeman Austin Jr. married 1835 Phoebe Adair, Niagara County NY; Freeman married 3rd cousin Louisa (Austin) Blake, who had divorced John Blake. Orin/Orrin Austin, nephew of Freeman and grandson of Thomas, born circa 1800, married Helena DeLaMotte/DeMotte; both buried LaSalle County Illinois. Seeking any information on Thomas's wife, Freeman's siblings, or Catherine's ancestry.

THE MEMOIRS AND FAMILY OF
HENRY SHELTON AUSTIN
OF KANSAS AND OKLAHOMA

by George Nicolo Austin

Author's Note: Henry Shelton Austin (1848-1935) descends from John Austin and Ann Baden of Albemarle County, Virginia, as described on pages 114-118 and 131-134 of *Austins of America*. In the early 1930's, Henry was urged by his children to write about his early years and adventures as a pioneer in the old west. Henry took a tablet and began writing in pencil, putting down different things as they came to mind.

The present author is a grandson of Henry. I first typed up Grandpa's memoirs at age 14 in 1933, two years before his death [see Footnote at the end of this article]. In most instances the notes have been transcribed verbatim. This has been done wherever possible to preserve Henry's manner of speaking and writing, to give an idea of his vocabulary, and to show the words and phrases that were in common usage during his lifetime. Minor editing has been done to avoid duplication and to improve sentence structure and punctuation. Since today it is impossible to determine whether the many spelling errors in my original typewritten notes were Grandpa's or mine, then in the interest of making the material easier to read, correct spelling has been used throughout.

Historical Recollections

"In the mid-eighteenth century (1740-1750), many families immigrated from Europe to America. For the most part, these people were seeking religious and personal freedom from the more or less continuous warfare and associated oppression that characterized the states of central Europe at that time. From the southern or upper Rhine river country, several German families named, Bach, Cooper, and Beck immigrated and settled in the colony of Virginia. They settled mainly in the interior, in the mountainous regions, away from the coast.

"Many of the adult men fought in the Army of Virginia during the Revolutionary War, some being absent from their homes for months or years at a time. When the war was over, they returned home with some papers called, 'Land Script'. This Land Script was in partial payment for their military service. They could buy land with it.

"While the men were off at war, the people that were left at home became interested in new opportunities farther to the west in what was then called the Northwest Territory of Virginia, but later became the state of Kentucky. For a variety of reasons, many of the Bachs, Coopers, Becks and others moved from western Virginia, taking the entire family, hired help and slaves, over the mountains, through the Cumberland Gap region and settled in the Cumberland River Region of southeastern Kentucky.

"They picked their land, had it surveyed and paid for it with their Land Script.

"About this same time (1780-1790-1800), people from other colonies immigrated into the country west of the Blue Ridge Mountains of Virginia. Among these were the Lloyds, the Austins, the Prathers and the Schmidts. They settled in the Green River country (central Kent County, Virginia). [Editor's Note: Green River was not in Virginia, but rather in Casey County, Kentucky: see page 114.] They lived in log cabins and cleared land for farming. Log forts were constructed at strategic locations to provide defense against the Indians who frequently carried out savage attacks on the settlers.

Indians Attack Grandmother

"One family who suffered from an Indian attack was the Lloyd family. Sometime in 1780 or 1790, a band of Indians attacked the Lloyd home, and killed the entire family except one three year old girl, and the father, who was away at the time. The baby was hit on the head and apparently left for dead, but she revived, and crept onto a bed where she was found early the next morning by her father, with her skirt wrapped around the wound and sticking fast to her hair. This little girl grew to womanhood and became the grandmother of the writer, Henry S. Austin.

Joseph Harrison Austin

"For the record, the above noted Lloyd girl (Mary Lloyd), married Jonas Austin. They had, among many other children, a son named Joseph Harrison Austin, who was born in 1822. This family lived, as noted, in western Virginia. As a young adult, Joseph Harrison Austin traveled from the Green River region of western Virginia, south, to the Cumberland River Valley of Kentucky, where he settled and married. [Editor's Note: Henry is in error here, for Jonas Austin was born in Virginia and married in Kentucky, while his son Joseph Harrison Austin was born in Casey County, Kentucky, location of the Green River. See page 114.] He married a girl named Louisa Jane Cooper, a daughter of a man named Frederick Cooper. The mother of Louisa Jane was named Patience Bach, before she married Henrich Cooper.

"With the union of J. H. Austin and Louisa Jane Cooper came the family negro slaves as the servants of Louisa Jane Cooper Austin. They were inherited by her from her parents who had brought a young man and woman named Nick and Dilla with them when they came from Virginia. This couple raised a large family of black slaves at the same time that the white father and mother were raising a large family of white children. The slaves grew up and were trained to be good, honest, servants, were taught morals and honesty, were taken by the Mrs. to church and were given a chance to join, which some of them did. They were all well fed and well clothed, so my first memory of being cared for was by blacks who stayed with the different members of the family two or three years after they were freed. In fact, many of them stayed until the dissolution of

Joseph Harrison Austin 1824-1883

the older families by natural causes. They were never mistreated in any way by the owners. I never saw but one grown one whipped, and that was for stealing a small article from a neighbor, and it never occurred again. These blacks, seventy years later have become a very important part of the population of the U.S., with more than their proportion of the wealth, many being well educated. But, they do most all of the unskilled labor all over the country, especially in the cities.''

Henry Shelton Austin himself was born 18 May 1848 in Casey County, Kentucky, and his family record appears on page 134 of *Austins of America*. In his memoirs he discusses his early schooling, how the Civil War adversely affected his family, of his heading west, and of his experiences before being married:

Early Education

''I attended the common three-months school until the War of the Rebellion (Civil War) destroyed the school. I then went south of the river into Russell County and got a year of schooling. At the close of the war, a professor of Latin and English opened a school in Albany, the county seat of Clinton County, Kentucky. Although all of the public buildings had been burned during the war, an old frame church remained standing and the school was held in this building. The professor offered high school grades. I went two terms, getting two years of Latin grammar and some higher mathematics, which gave me the best education of any young man in the county. I then taught school for a year (two terms). This year of teaching was very difficult. For want of funds, I taught for twenty dollars a month. Classes were held in an old sheep shed as there were no sheep left alive to need it.

Civil War Aftermath

''The entire country was caught up in a famine and depression. Disease was rampant, often aggrevated by lack of food and medical care. Food and Housing were bad. There were a few doctors, no surgeons and no hospitals. Some of the people ate parched corn and acorns. In the spring of 1866, some of them picked up corn cobs and boiled them with elm buds which they salted with salt recovered from the dirt out of the house where meat had been salted and the waste left on the ground. We raised a little grain, mostly rye. Hickory wood and corn cobs were burned on the hearth to get the ashes to use as soda to raise the unbolted meal or flour. We cut green corn off of the cob to dry so it could be ground on little home made mills. Some children got to eating clay.

''Be it noted that there was no Red Cross or any other charitable organization, and no provision by the state or federal government for relief. The Freedman's Bureau fed the freed slaves in some instances.

Migrations After Civil War

''After the close of the Civil War in 1865, many of the million men who were discharged were unable to quietly settle down to civilian life. The great plains country, stretching from Nebraska in the north to the Indian Territories in the south was reported to be good farm land. The Government promised every soldier a homestead of 180 acres, and so there started a stream of civilian soldiers west to settle on the public lands lying in western Kansas and Nebraska.

Leaving Home to Head West

''The situation at home at this time was nothing but melancholy, sadness and grief. I did not want to remain in such gloom, especially as there did not seem to be any way of relieving it in the near future. Most of the young men were leaving the country, for the same reasons, and going to the great west, exactly as our forefathers had done one hundred years earlier.

"So, not knowing where or what, I had a desperately sad mother pack my grip. Daddy, looking on with tears in his eyes, said to me; 'Henry, your brother Emerson (then only 17 years old), wants to go with you and says if he does not go now he will go next year, so I think he will be better off to go now, if you will look after him!' They got sixty dollars for him in currency and we bid good-bye to the most heart-broken parents that you ever saw, never to see them again.

"It was the climax from a happy home and family with plenty of the comforts of life before the war, to unbeliev-able sadness and despair after the war. The first sadness was the taking of all of the horses and rest of the stock (farm animals) for war purposes. Then the food went with most of bedding out of the house. By then, one of the family had died and another was sickly from want, and lack of medical care. There was burning of houses, mills, courthouses and even churches. The climax was, as I said, the two boys leaving home. Maybe it was wrong, but even Mother said I was the only one who could get out and that I had better save myself. Soon afterwards, she and two of the girls were relieved by death. Six years later, Daddy followed them to a well-earned rest. The youngest boy (Bill) came west with broken health, probably caused by conditions after the war, and soon died in Kansas.

To Missouri and Kansas

Family records indicate that Henry Shelton Austin and his brother Emerson Austin left Kentucky in 1868. How they traveled to Missouri is unknown. They may have ridden horses, but there were few if any available in those days. Railroad travel was possible, but Henry's narrative indicates they did not have enough money to travel very far on the railroad. Emerson stayed behind in Missouri while Henry went on to Kansas:

"Traveling west, we stopped in Missouri where we made many friends. In October 1868 I bought me a horse and a blanket to sleep under. I found two families that were going to Kansas in wagons and they gladly received me as company. So, on the 20th day of November 1868, I arrived at the place where Wichita now is. We talked to some men who were driving some stakes in the tall grass near the Arkansas river. They said they were starting a town. We drove on about twenty miles farther west to the last clump of small timber, on an island in the river. This seemed to be the last stand of timber until the Rocky Mountains. That is why they called this country the Great Plain. In those days you could see Pikes Peak 200 miles away. It would look like a painted cloud on the horizon. We camped near this island with the clump of trees, and found some Missouri boys there. The father of one of them had entrusted a hundred dollars to me to carry to him. They had sewed it into a small packet and I delivered it safely. It was a trust I have always remembered with pride.

Buffalo Hunting

"It was about this time that I killed my first buffalo. One day one of the Missouri boys and I went out from camp about ten miles and sighted some buffalo. The nearest to us was a large fine cow. Sam said that we must get this one for it was a fine one. So, we both agreed to aim about half-way up the body just behind the shoulder. Sam counted three and we both fired, our bullets going in about two inches apart and both coming out the same hole.

"On another day, we rode out west and north of camp and found a small bunch of buffalo which we stalked until in gunshot range and killed one or two. We were then close to the Flint Hills, the highest mountains for hundreds of miles around.

Bitter Cold Winter

"During the winter of 1868-69 we got a dugout built and a sod house ready for the families to winter in, and we started on a hunt to follow up the game (buffalo). We got as far west as Walnut Creek where it enters the Arkansas River. We camped in a grove of willows and box elders not far from the site of the old stone Fort Zaro on the great bend of the Arkansas River. That night there came up a very cold northerner with snow and wind which lasted three days and three nights. Luckily, the second day of the storm a buffalo cow and some calves straggled by our camp. We got the cow which gave us meat for a few days. In that camp of fourteen men, all but two had some part of their body frozen. There were so many with frozen fingers and ears that we decided to give up on the hunt and returned to camp.

"On arriving at the home camp we found the freeze breaking up in the Arkansas River. The husband of one family had gone to the other side of the river where he had a job of work, but the wife and children were out of bread, eating only beans. So, in the morning I went on foot across the frozen river to get flour at a little store. Carrying it on my shoulders, I found, when I returned to the river that the ice was melting. I had to wade when I got to the center of the stream where it was waist deep. Climbing onto the bank, my clothes began to freeze to me. I carried it three miles with my clothes stiff on my body, but the joy of the mother and kiddies was abundant reward.

"We stayed in camp till warmer days gave sign of spring. When the weather was warmer we started out for buffalo, but did not find them until we were about fifty miles west. Drifting back north, we killed a great many. I killed about twenty myself and everyone got hides and meat aplenty.

Emerson Rejoins Henry

"About this time the brother that I had left in Missouri came out to me. He arrived in Wichita, which was now settling up fast, but to him it looked desperately desolate.

No houses, only a few dugouts, not a tree, not even a hill. There was lots of grass though and with the grass came herds of Texas cattle being driven to northern markets. The Santa Fe Railroad was now built as far as Newton, Kansas, and most of the cattle were shipped out of Newton on this line.

Herding Cattle

"Emerson and I both got work, herding and driving cattle. He with a man that was selling off a large herd, and I got a job with a man who was herding 2000 head through to Montana to feed the men building the Northern Pacific Railroad. We had trouble all the way, keeping the buffalo away from our herd. The cattle were frightened at the big shaggy creatures. We saw not a settlement for 350 miles. We saw an occasional sod house and an occasional dugout, but no real settlements. I went across the plains with him to Wyoming where I turned back to my first settlement in Kansas, near Wichita. There I got work with a herd about 25 miles west of Wichita.

Emerson Heads for Texas

"In a few days, my brother came riding into our camp, and finding me alone, hurriedly told me that he was on his way to Texas with the man he had been working for, who had promised him steady employment, and a home, and that he was going immediately. We shook hands, and as he galloped away, never looking back, I felt that the earth had given away and had swallowed up everything worth living for. His going to Texas [in 1870] left me without a living relative within hundreds of miles. He married and raised a family in Texas, but I never saw him again. He died in 1913 in Callahan County, Texas.

"In the summer after my brother left, I traveled with a herd up the South Platte river into the mountains west of Cheyenne City, which was a small frontier town frequented by miners. We stopped at Fort Hays and while we were visiting the Indian camp near the Fort, we found two white men who were glad to see us. They introduced us to their squaws and gave each of us a small belt of buckskin and beads. We came back by Denver, a little mining town, and then on down the Arkansas river where settlers were fast claiming farms.

Protection from Renegades

"The next year, 1871, we went north across the Solomon and Republican rivers, stopping again at Fort Hays, which had a garrison of Cavalry Soldiers. With the exception of the soldiers at the Fort, there were no settlers on our route. We stayed at the Fort for three days as there was a band of renegade Indians from a reservation in South Dakota that had been making trouble on the trail west. This was the old Pikes Peak trail which we were following to the mountains.

For safety's sake the commander sent some soldiers with us as far as Lodge Pole.

"On this same trip we encountered a band of roving Cheyenne Indians who proved to be some of the last of the Southern Plains Indians that had refused to stay on the Reservatons in North Dakota. They were drifting towards Mexico where a considerable number of their tribe had already gone, but they were away from the game and were starving and had robbed some immigrant trains and cattlemen in the area. We visited their camp and they were very friendly, but had nothing to sell or trade.

"The next fall and winter we encountered a remnant of the same tribe in the extreme southwestern part of Kansas, where they were finally gathered up by soldiers and held at Camp Supply. Soon afterwards, they were given land in the Indian Territory. This tribe was probably the poorest and most backward tribe of all of the original inhabitants of the great plains. These once brave and liberty-loving people had many virtures worthy of admiration. They were more indulgent and patient with their children than any people I know. Every man and woman of the tribe claimed personally every child of the tribe. They were wholly unmixed with any other race, white or black, kindly to a friend and appreciative of kindnesses."

[CONTINUED NEXT ISSUE]

★★★★★★★★★★★★★★★★★★★★★★★★★★★★★

Austins of America is intended to serve present and future genealogists researching Austin family lines. Readers are encouraged to submit Queries, genealogical and historical articles for publication. Previously published books, pamphlets or articles containing Austin genealogical data are also sought for reprinting or review.

EDITOR

DR. MICHAEL EDWARD AUSTIN   CONCORD, MA

ASSOCIATE EDITORS

ANTHONY KENT AUSTIN   PROSPECT, KY

BERT ADDIS AUSTIN   QUEEN CREEK, AZ

PATRICIA BIEBUYCK AUSTIN   CONCORD, MA

PAULINE LUCILLE AUSTIN   MARION, IA

Austins of America is published each February and August by The Austin Print, 23 Allen Farm Lane, Concord, Massachusetts 01742. All correspondence, including subscriptions, articles and responses to queries, should be sent to this address. Subscriptions are $2.50 per year postpaid.

★★★★★★★★★★★★★★★★★★★★★★★★★★★★★

THE MEMOIRS AND FAMILY OF
HENRY SHELTON AUSTIN
OF KANSAS AND OKLAHOMA

by George Nicolo Austin

[CONTINUED FROM PAGE 190]

Providing Buffalo Meat

"Another time, we followed the Buffalo far to the southwest. We saw a herd some miles away and followed at a distance with a team and supply wagon. When we saw that they were quietly grazing, I left the supply wagon and went to stalk them. They were laying on some high ground. After laborously creeping toward them I found a draw or drain running up towards them, and by creeping I proceeded very close to some of them that lay in a half-moon shape around the head of the draw. When I peeped over the bank of my hiding place I saw a very large bull looking right down on me, not 20 feet away, with his large liquid eyes glaring at me. I kept very still untio he semed satisfied that I was harmless and turned to walk off. I got off one well-placed shot which caused him to make one frantic leap and fall bleeding. All were soon in commotion, bellowing and pawing up the earth, milling around. Watching for a broad-side I kept shooting and they kept falling and milling around till I had discharged some twenty shots. They then moved off out of range, and with one remaining shot, I thought it safe to raise up and signal the supply wagon to come down. The game, seeing me for the first time, took fright and ran away, leaving about a dozen or so dead, making this the most destructive day I ever had. We took back a load of meat to the settlement, which was cut and dried, making a good supply for many days.

Gun-Shy Horse

"In 1872-73 game was getting scarce and one of our last efforts to get sport and profit was a trip to the southwest, along the upper reaches of the Cimmaron river. Only a few straggling remanents of the great herds remained and they were so very wary they could not be successfully stalked, so we decided to give chase on horseback. Mounting up and dashing after a small herd of full grown males, we were soon along side, firing into their sides. Our best and fastest horse, a fine gray gelding could not stand the firing and his owner, Mr. Kimberly dismounted and shot a round or two while holding onto the horse's bridle. The horse broke loose and plunged off across the plains. We never saw him again. We got very few Buffalo, had to walk part of the way back to the settlement, and so had little reward for our chase.

Cheyennes Create Stampede

"On a trip about 50 miles west of where Wichita now is, we came in sight of a considerable number of Buffalo away to the west. Traveling after them, we were within a mile of the herd of several hundred, but we decided to bed down for the night, planning to keep quiet till morning, then crawl up on them and kill what we wanted before they were alarmed. We did not know it that night, but there was a camp of fifty or more Cheyennes with their squaws, camped on the other side of the sleeping herd. Had we known this, we would have attacked then. At dawn the Indians made an attack on the herd, riding their ponies and using bows and arrows. We later learned that they had five guns, but no ammunition. In a moment these great lumbering animals were thrown into great confusion and they came in a mad rush toward us, yet in camp. The red horsemen were right on their flanks, shooting steel tipped arrows into the side of the victims. One Buffalo cow ran thru our campfire, scattering it in all directions. She ran up against our wagon, nearly upsetting it. We did not shoot for fear of hitting an Indian. When the chase was over, the ground lay covered with dead and dying animals for a mile or more. The Indians were very friendly and proud of their Coup on us and told us to take all we wanted. Their squaws came up and ran all of the meat before it got cold. That was life in action.

Trading with Commanches and Kiowas

"Sometime during the winter of 1872-73, I went with a company of forty men and twelve teams to the Indian country under General Griffin. We had goods to trade to the Commanches and Kiowas who were off of the reservations, stealing and occasionally killing straggling settlers and hunters. We built a permanent camp on the upper Medicine River near the Indian Territory. We traded some, and killed a great number of buffalo, deer, and turkey. We sent the hides into Wichita to be traded for supplies. Wichita had become a shipping point by this time.

Indians Attack Camp

"In February, two bunches of the men loaded two wagons and started southwest to trade with the Indians, but as they left, they separated into two parts. The first night out, the camps were several miles apart. At one camp were six men and two teams of horses. Three of the men went out to hunt while the other three made camp and cooked supper. While they were cooking, about twenty Indians raided their camp and killed one, fatally wouned another and slightly wounded the third. The camp was rifled and robbed of everything valuable. We buried them at night, wrapping them in their blankets and laying them on the east side of Donkey Creek, near the mouth, in what is now Barber County, Kansas. I did not know their names for we all went under a nom de plume name.

Another Indian Victim

"Not long after that our Captain and manager decided he would go to Camp Supply where there was a company of soldiers to see if he could get help against the Indians. He determined to ride home alone on his little bay mare, Ribbon. The Indians were probably watching him, for they attacked him on the way back. They must have dragged him off to the river and buried him in the sand. All we ever found was his wooden leg, some empty shells and some horse bones.

Blizzard Costs Feet, Toes and Fingers

"In January of 1873, a very cold blizzard came up lasting several days. Many persons were badly frozen coming into the settlement of Wichita on the Santa Fe Railroad from Hutchinson. Notable Harry VanTrees, Representative from Barber County was on his way to Topeka and had both his feet frozen, losing all his toes. Will Jones, returning to Wichita from a hunt in the southern part of the state lost part of his feet. On one of these nights I was out camping on the high prairie, alone, with a light team. I pushed on until I reached the south bank of the Arkansas river. I tried to stop, but saw that I would freeze if I did, so I turned my team down the river, and walked and ran to keep warm. Early the next morning I came to a dugout with a family in it. I stopped and got a feed of half-cooked beans which made me very sick, so I stayed till the next day. Others came in and told about people who had stayed in their camps and had things frozen. Old Negro Price, the former body servant of General Price of Missouri came in. Most of his fingers were frozen, one very bad. I took the old Negro's finger off at the joint with a butcher knife and later got a surgeon to care for it properly. That was about the last hunt that I took part in.

Buffalo Traits and Habits

"While watching the buffalo on those hunting trips I learned their traits and habits, some of which were almost human. The old bulls always grazed, traveled and slept around the outside of the cows and young up to two years old. Gradually the young bulls would take the place of the old ones which would be gradually dropping off and left behind, sleeping on some sunny hillside, quietly waiting for some wolves or hunters to come and make a meal off of their carcass, leaving their bones for the button factory. Humans stand by each other in old age, but like Job's comforters do not make life's end any easier.

Wichita Farming and Grasshoppers

"In the spring of 1875, I decided to go back to the settlement near Wichita. I located on a piece of land and plowed ten acres to corn in the spring of 1875. I returned from a trip east [Author's note: perhaps a trip to Pleasant Grove, Missouri, near Kansas City to see old Missouri friends and/or Sylvia Jones] and found the whole country covered with grasshoppers. While I was on the train coming in to Wichita, they had to stop the train and put sand on the track for the train had run over so many grasshoppers and the track was so slippery that the wheels just spun around and the train would not move. This was on the third day of July.

"I could not walk in the fields for the swarms in my face. In a few days there was only the hard part of the corn stalk left standing, and this was eaten down to the ground. All young trees wre destroyed and even the soft parts of pine boards were eaten. Garments left out were ruined and many settlers were left almost destitute. A call went out to the east for help.

Opening Grocery Store

"About this time I opened a small stock of groceries to sell to the U.S. Pensioners as they were the only ones with a steady income. The Relief Committee made my store a depository for relief supplies sent from the east which came in carloads. But a great many people left their claims and went back east, never to return.

Land Sale Profit

"One day a young man came in and said he was going back home to Indiana. He was very much disgusted with the country and its grasshoppers, and he told me he had paid out 15 dollars for 160 acres of government land which he wanted to sell. I told him that he had no transferable title. He said his time was short and said just give him anything. As it was near noon, I gave him a can of sardines and a handful of crackers for his dinner. Later, I had his papers cancelled and made my own filing on the land, which proved to be a very fine section of farm land just 25 miles west of Wichita. One year later I sold it for 200 dollars.

Settling Down at Last

"I spent the winter of 1875-76 in the store with only enough to keep me in supplies. I sold the store and drifted back to the cattle range. I spent a year on the range in 1876. About that time I decided to settle down and located on a claim in Reno County in western Kansas. In 1877 I had some work done on the land and sowed ten acres to wheat, but stayed most of the time in Wichita. The wheat made a very good yield. That winter, I made up my mind to settle down permanently, and to do so required a companion, which I found in Miss Sylvia Jones of Missouri. After building a little three room house, we were married in Reno County, Kansas on the first day of June, 1880. Thus ended thirty-two years of my life which had been full of action, uncertainty, romance, rumors, loneliness and hardships, but always with a star of hope ahead that refused to quit me, which I attribute to a

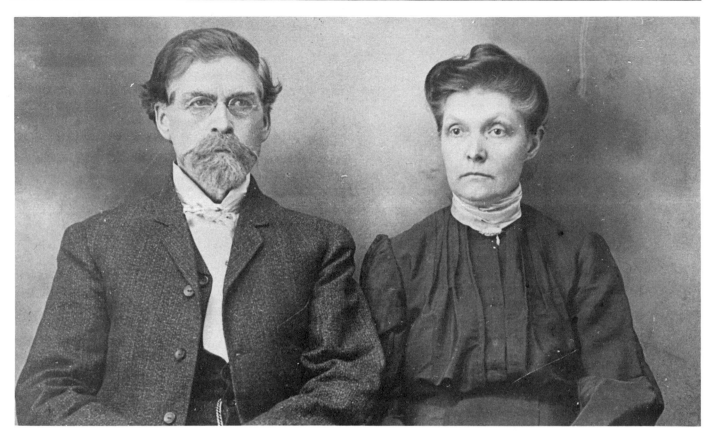

Henry Shelton Austin (1848-1935) and his wife Sylvia Almeda Jones (1858-1942)

Christian Mother's training and an all-wise, loving God who guides all for the best.''

Marriage to Sylvia Almeda Jones

Henry married Sylvia Almeda Jones on 1 June 1880 in Reno County, Kansas. Sylvia was born 3 August 1858 in Michigan, a daughter of Benjamin Jones. The Jones family had moved from Michigan to Missouri, where Benjamin farmed near Pleasant Grove, a short distance southeast of Kansas City, Missouri. Today it is included in the suburbs of Kansas City. The Jones family, believed to be of Welsh extraction, was large with many sons - all tall, skinny and long-legged. I have a vague recollection that Sylvia had come out to western Kansas to visit some relatives. She met Henry Austin, and a romance developed. This was at least 2-3 years before they were married. I recall further that Henry made one or more trips to Pleasant Grove to visit the Jones family.

The present author does not recall hearing that Sylvia did anything special, prior to her getting married. I do not recall, for example, that she taught school or attended any noteworthy schools. That she had an education consistent with the times is evidenced, however, by the fact that she ran the Post Office in Sylvia, Kansas, and she also managed the business and farm when Henry was away.

The homestead in Reno County, Kansas, must have been on the site that later became Sylvia, Kansas. In his memoirs Henry is strangely silent on the details of his courtship, engagement (if any), and marriage. When he wrote his memoirs in the early 1930's, he apparently took it for granted that all concerned knew these things, as they had been recounted frequently over the years for the benefit and interest of his children and grandchildren. So, they were never written down. Now everyone who knew about these things is dead, and the details with them. Henry S. wrote only briefly about his activities in Sylvia:

A Town Named for Sylvia

"Having a worthy and willing mate, I settled down to work and business of whatever kind seemed to offer the best return. As the business of farming seemed to be rather uncertain, I was drawn to Mercantile Business of a general nature, suited to the new country. I sold a vast array of all kinds of goods, including food, furniture, dry goods, hardware items, lumber, school supplies, clothes, shoes, undertaking goods and cradles. So, I was with the people from the cradle to the grave. Seeing the need for same, I dispensed justice and performed marriages, saying that the babies must be christened. We therefore needed a church house, and I certainly did my part at that. When the

need for a schoolhouse arose, I helped haul the lumber, 25 miles for that. Seeing the need for a railroad, I spent time and money to get the railroad where we wanted it.''

Raising a Family

Henry and Sylvia Austin spent about thirteen years in the Sylvia, Kansas location, and their four children - Louisa Eveline, Walter Henry, Grace Elizabeth, and George Benjamin - were all born there (see page 134 of Austins of America). Henry had red hair, while Sylvia had reddish-brown or auburn hair. I think her hair had a little natural curl. Three of their four children were definitely red-haired: Eva had brownish hair, Walter had auburn hair, and Grace and George had flaming red hair. The recessive gene came through in the next generation only in Walter's son, Blair Austin.

During the later years in Sylvia, Kansas, Henry became involved in a sheep ranching venture, and owned and operated a general store. Raising sheep was necessarily tied to the availability of a railroad, so Henry worked hard to get the railroad to come through his settlement. With the coming of the railroad, a new Post Office was established in Henry's general store, and he named the settlement after his wife Sylvia who served as Postmaster for several years.

Run for the Cherokee Strip

For reasons that are not completely clear, Henry's sheep ranching venture was a complete catastrophe. Either the sheep got sick and died, or the bottom dropped out of the sheep market, or there were some dry years on the range and the sheep starved for lack of pasture. In any case, Henry lost a lot of money in this venture, and probably for this and other reasons, he decided to make a move.

The first opening of the Indian Territory to white settlers was in 1889. The first 'Run' did not begin at the present Kansas-Oklahoma State border, but was much farther south. In 1893, the second 'Run' was held and this was known as 'The Run for the Cherokee Strip.' This Run started from what is now the Oklahoma-Kansas line and opened up a strip of land all across the northern part of what is now Oklahoma. Henry Shelton made this Run on 16 September 1893. He filed a claim on a section of land near Cleo Springs, in Major County, Oklahoma Territory. The family moved there in 1893. The children were still small. Henry began farming his own land, and other leased land at different times from 1893 until 1902.

Cousin Robert Austin

My recollection is that sometime while the Henry and Sylvia were living and farming in Cleo Springs, 'Cousin Bob' came to live with them. Unfortunately today those who could give any accurate information about Bob Austin are all deceased. His name was obviously Robert, but I do not know his middle name. He was a cousin of Eva, Walter, Grace and George. He was therefore a nephew of Henry S. Austin. He was about the age of Grace and George. His parents are unknown to me, but there must have been a family tragedy, that precipitated his coming to live with his Aunt and Uncle. [Editor's Note: Robert was the son of J3B6 William Rose Austin and Rosa Learned - see page 167.] Since he was about the same age as the other children, he fitted easily into the family and was received more as a brother than a cousin. Bob left the family after four or five years, but they kept track of him until he died. Robert Austin became a lawyer and lived and practiced in California all of his adult life. He visited the relatives in Oklahoma many times and was always received with much warmth and affection. Bob was popular and well-liked, a large man, well over six feet tall. He was an extrovert with an easy-going, expansive personality. He laughed a lot and made friends easily. He always had a joke to tell and was a great 'kidder.' Everyone liked Bob Austin. All of the Austins were very fond of Bob and enjoyed his letters at Christmas time and at other times during the year. I do not know who he married, or if he had any children. In his later years, he developed diabetes and became obese. His diabetes was severe and he subsequently underwent amputation of first one leg and then the other. He died sometime in the 1940's.

University of Oklahoma

In 1902 the family moved to Norman, Oklahoma, apparently so that the children could go to the University. The oldest daughter, Eva, had already married Walter W. Wells, a local Cleo Springs farm boy and they both decided to undertake the study of medicine. The Wells were prosperous farmers and the newly married couple were able to finance themselves to two years of medical school in Fort Worth, Texas. Their other three children attended the University of Oklahoma, where Walter and George took courses in Pharmacy.

Shortly after George received his License to practice Pharmacy, the family left Norman and moved back to northwestern Oklahoma, opening a drug store in Fairview, the county seat of Major County. Henry, Walter and George ran the drug store. They all waited on customers and Walter and George filled prescriptions. Leaving the family in Fairview, Henry and George spent some time in Castle, Oklahoma, where they took a flyer at a drug store in the Creek Nation in southeastern Oklahoma. The Castle drug store apparently did not work out, and they returned to Fairview.

Around 1910, Henry Shelton and George sold the store in Fairview, and bought or put in a drug store in Longdale, Blaine County, Oklahoma. The Austin Drug Company of Longdale provided a good living for Henry and George and

their families. Both Henry and George were experts at the 'hunt-and-peck' system of typing, which they used to type prescription labels and short letters.

The present author's first recollections of his grandparents Henry and Sylvia are when we lived in Longdale. In that town I recall Grandpa and Grandma had their own four-room home, where Grandma ran the house and prepared the meals. She was an excellent cook and could prepare a noon meal of fried chicken, mashed potatoes, gravy and biscuits in an astonishingly short time.

At that time I recall Grandpa's hair was completely white. He always had a white moustache and a short, white beard, in the style that has been called a Van Dyke beard. The sideburns were not long and he shaved every day along the cheeks and neck. He told me that in his youth, his hair and beard were red. His posture was erect with a very straight back, not stooped. He was about five foot ten and was not obese, although he developed a small paunch in his old age. He had a pleasant disposition, enjoyed a good joke and was never cross.

Grandma Sylvia Austin was left-handed. She had a congenital ankylosis, or fusion of the middle joint of the little fingers on both hands. She was of average height for women of her day, being about five foot five or six. In her very old age, she became slightly stooped. I never saw her in anything but a long dress that came to the ankles, to the wrists and buttoned up at the neck. Her hair was long, and she usuallly wore it up in a bun at the back of her head.

Grandma had a low-pitched voice for a woman, and would have sung alto, if she could have sung, but she was tone-deaf and could not sing at all. In her old age, she was a quiet person and rarely spoke unless spoken to. She could be assertive however, and get Grandpa's attention with a sharp 'Henry!' that would rattle the window shades. She had a wonderfully kind disposition and a good sense of humor.

Visits by Grandpa and Grandma

In the fall of 1927, George and Henry sold the Austin Drug Company in Longdale, and George moved his family to Norman, Cleveland County, Oklahoma. Henry and Sylvia stayed in Longdale for a year or so, but around 1929 they moved to Oklahoma City to live out the remainder of their lives with their son-in-law and daughter, Dr. Walter W. and Dr. Eva Wells. The Wells had no children of their own, but they purchased a new house at 730 N.E. 19th Street in Oklahoma City, especially to accomodate Henry and Sylvia. After that we saw them frequently, routinely having Christmas dinner in Oklahoma City, and often having Thanksgiving dinner there. In the summertime we would often visit overnight at Dr.'s lakeside cabin, which was located west of town.

Sometimes Grandpa or Grandma, or both, would spend a week visiting us in Norman. One time, Grandpa showed up in Norman, alone, with his grip, and announced that he had come for a visit. The next day, Grandma appeared with her suitcase, saying that she too had come for a visit. Apparently the old man had gone off on his own without offering to bring his wife along!

Except in the very hottest weather, Grandpa always wore a tie and coat. He wore detachable collars, cuff links and a stick pin or tie clasp in his tie. He preferred the mien of a retired businessman rather than a farmer, and rarely mentioned that he had ever been a farmer. As a boy in Norman, I sometimes wore overalls. Grandpa told my mother once that he did not like to see me wearing overalls, because it made me look like a farmer.

Grandpa smoked cigars, perhaps one or two a day. At times he would not smoke the cigar all the way, but would let it go out and then carry it in his mouth for an hour or so, chewing on the end. His teeth were unbelievable. They were very, very brown and black. He said that he had never been to a Dentist, and to my knowledge he had no dental complaints. He read a great deal. he read the morning and evening papers from front to back, from the headlines right through the want-ads. He also read various books that Dr. Eva brought home for all to read. He was very interested in politics and followed all elections with great interest. He was also continually interested in the economy, local, regional and national, and delighted in discussing trends in the business world with anyone who would listen.

The Final Years

Because he lived to be 87 years old, Henry S. outlived many of his contemporaries. He was often saddened by the news that one of his pioneer friends of bygone days had passed away. This information usually came by way of a newspaper article. Such was the case of 'Cottonwood Davis.' After reading the notice: 'Died, Dec., 26, 1933, C. W. Davis of Grant County, Oklahoma. A pioneer buffalo hunter. Born in 1854.' he wrote:

"Cottonwood Davis drops off the scene of action and passes into a quiet rest that he has so well earned. Yet, hardly a farewell thought appears in the local newspaper. Less than four lines. Cottonwood Davis, in the 70's was a well remembered, noble soul. He was one of many who took their lives in their own hands and cleared the plains west from where Wichita now is, to the foothills in the west. He worked with such men as Colonel Griffith, Amos Chapman, Heiserman, Mannameee, Austin, Brown and last but not least, old Negro Price. These, and a lot of others have long since gone to their reward. Yes, I knew Cottonwood very well. We used to write local news for the

[CONTINUED ON PAGE 215]

QUERIES

196-1. Hannah Austin m. Nathaniel Lincoln who was b. 6 July 1704. Their daughter Hannah Lincoln was born 19 June 1730 in Harwich, MA. Torrey, in his book *New England Marriages Prior to 1700*, has her parents as Robert Austin (1634?-1687) and his wife (1661-) of Kingston, RI. Seek to document and prove the parents of Hannah Austin.

196-2. Herman DeForest Austin was the son of the George Austin listed in the 1850 Census of Franklin County, Highgate, VT. Perhaps Sylvester Austin is George's father? Listed under Greensboro, Orleans County VT, is Elijah Austin age 56. Somehow Sen. Warren Austin, grandson of Elijah Sopher Austin, is all related to this. Senator Warren Austin is buried at Highgate Cemetery with my grandfather's sister Ida and many others. Senator Austin was the First Ambassador to the United Nations. I need to find out the ancestors of Herman.

196-3. Ann Austin m. Simeon Dunn who was b. 1752 in Scotland. Their son Simeon III was born in 1774. Ann was b. 1756 in New Brunswick, New Jersey. Need information on Ann's ancestry.

196-4. Jesse Austin b.circa 1838, married Emily Turner, daughter of Philander and Eliza (Young) Turner in Maple Grove Township, Barry Co. Michigan on 24 December 1859. When married, Jesse was age 21 and Emily was age 16 and was born in Michigan. I need descendants of Jesse and Emily and seek others of this Austin branch.

196-5. Jordan Wilson Austin was born 4 April 1818 in Oswego County, New York. He married 23 May 1841 to Charlotte Ewing in Wood Co., Ohio; died 27 May 1872 in Haskins, Ohio. Seek information on parents and family of Jordan Wilson Austin.

196-6. Archibald Pruit Austin born 1767 in Virginia; died 1866 Tunnel Hill, Georgia. Married Rebecca Blankenship 22 February 1790 in Pittsylvania Co., Virginia. Would like to correspond with anyone connected to Archibald.

196-7. Eliza Ann Austin married William Wilson Deering. They are buried in Covington, Tipton Co., TN. Is Eliza the daughter of Stephen and Rebecca Austin? Would like to correspond with anyone who has information on the parents of Eliza.

196-8. John Austin was born circa 1680/70; died 1759 in Lunenburg Co., VA. He married Hannah Love and had children John, Jr., Joseph, Valentine, Richard, Stephen, and David. Would like to correspond with John's descendants.

196-9. Lewis Austin married Margaret (—) from Pittsburgh, PA circa 1815. Lewis lived in Letcha County KY in 1920's and 1930's. Margaret had sons by the name of Leroy, Harry, George, and —, possibly from her 1st marrage. Need Lewis's ancestry.

196-10. Phineas Austin was born in 1790 in Vermont. He is my great-great-great-grandfather. Would like to exchange information with others in this same line.

196-11. Judge Abiathar Austin of Taunton, MA married Mary C. Bradley, had 10 or 12 children. Our line comes from their daughter Agnes Austin born 3 July 1813 in Canton, ME. The family had moved from Brookline, MA in the winter of 1800. Do you know when they moved from Taunton, MA?

196-12. John Gideon Austin was born circa 1801 in the Carolina's. I believe his father was James G. Austin. John married Sarah Elizabeth Jones and had children: James Gideon, Wills Grady, Drury Jane, Celia Angeline, Willa, John H., Cassie Catherine, and Sarah Melinda. This family lived in Hall, Forsyth and Polk Counties, GA, according to the census. Seek information on John's parents, siblings, wife and children.

196-13. William Norris Austin b. 1811 NY, d. 1873 Richfield, MI, m. Sarah Ann Newman b. 1816 NY. Many of their descendants attended Austin Family Reunions from 1920 thru 1925 in Flint, Detroit, Orian, and Orchard Lake, Michigan. Seek descendants of those attending.

196-14. Harvey H. Austin was born in October 1836 in Clarendon, Orleans County NY, the son of Shadrach S., son of Daniel Austin. He left NY with parents in 1853 for Bloomingdale, Van Buren Co., MI, where he stayed until at least 1900. m.(1) Sarah (—) b. 1837 MI, m.(2) Lydia Jennie (—) b. 1848 Canada. Children: Sylvous A., Emma, Andee, Hurbert, Mister, Siba? B., Clyde R., Bellva R., and Dee Clayton Austin. Seek descendants of Harvey.

196-15. Nathaniel C. Austin was born in March 1845 in Clarendon, Orleans County NY, the son of Shadrach S., son of Daniel Austin. He removed from NY to Bloomingdale, Van Buren Co., MI in 1853 with parents and resided there until circa 1906 when he removed to Buffalo, Harper County OK. He m.(1) Phoebe (—) b. 1851 WI, m.(2) Mary (—) b. 1860 IL. He and Phoebe had one son, Milan P. Austin b. 1872 Bloomingdale, MI, m. Belle Troup and had Olive and Clair (son). Seek descendants of Nathaniel.

196-16. Norris C. Austin was born in 1847 in Clarendon, Orleans County NY, the son of Nathaniel C. Austin, son of Daniel Austin. He removed to Warsay, Wyoming County NY and m. Elizabeth D. Filkins in 1870. Their first three children were: Charles b. 1871, Henry b. 1874, and Jennie born 1876. Seek descendants of Norris.

THE DESCENDANTS OF
THOMAS AUSTIN AND REBECCA TURNER
OF AMHERST COUNTY, VIRGINIA

by Cornelia Bradshaw Austin

[CONTINUED FROM PAGE 181]

E. Fullwood who married T36 William Thomas Austin. Sarah and William had two children born in Arkansas. Widow Sarah and her five children are found in the 1880 Census for Patterson Township, Caldwell County, North Carolina. Sarah married a third time to widower Joshua Gibbs, whose first wife Saphronia Conley had died. After the death of her third husband, Sarah's health declined and she went to live in Texas with a daughter. She is buried in Bonham, Texas. FULLWOOD CHILDREN: MARY ADA b.ca.1858, LELA EMMA b.ca.1860, MARTHA ELLA b.1862, SARAH ANN b.ca.1866 d. age 17, WILLIAM AUSTIN b.ca.1871.

T3B. JESSE LAFAYETTE[3] AUSTIN (*Jesse,*[2] *Thomas*[1]) was born circa 1853, probably in Iredell County, North Carolina. He was married on 18 March 1886 to Margaret Bellona Lundy, who was born in 1857. Jesse died in 1918, while Margaret died in 1932.

CHILDREN: T3B1. WILLIAM CLYDE, *b. 1886, m.(1) Della Pharr, m.(2) Texie Ford*

T3B2. CARL BAGBY, *b. 30 July 1888* +

T3B3. [daughter], *b. 1892, m. Marshall Creedmore*

T3B4. JETTIE DEAL, *b. 1895, m. Eugene Mitchell, still living in 1980*

T3B5. SADIE ETHEL, *b. 7 July 1897, m. 1 August 1915 to Lonnie Pinkney Payne (b. 13 May 1889, d. 25 April 1956). Sadie died 11 April 1975, and is buried at Rose Chapel Cemetery with Lonnie. Payne children: Mary Helen b.1916, Lonnie Pinkney Jr. b. 1919, Thomas Austin b. 1922, Margaret Gernell b. 1924, Nancy Violet b. 1927, Charles Herman b. 1936*

T3B6. ROY HOBSON, *born in 1899, married Nannie Chambers*

FOURTH GENERATION

T321. JOHN P.[4] AUSTIN (*Thomas J.,*[3] *Jesse,*[2] *Thomas*[1]) was born circa 1849, probably in Caldwell County, North Carolina. He was married on 1 November 1868 to Adeline M. Harris. Adeline was the daughter of Lewis and America (Gragg) Harris, and was also born circa 1849. John P. Austin died sometime before 1873, probably in Mulberry/Clark Town, Caldwell County, NC. His widow Adeline m.(2) Joseph F. Estes on 13 February 1873. John and Adeline had two children, who were living with their grandparents Thomas and Margaret Austin in the 1880 Census for Patterson Township, Caldwell County.

CHILDREN: T321-1. LEWIS THOMAS, *b. May 1870, m.(1) Anna Penley. She died on 27 June 1905 at age 31, and is buried in Globe Cemetery. Lewis m.(2) her sister Cora Penley.*

T321-2. JANE, *b. circa 1872 (8 in 1880 Census), m. John Wilson*

T322. JULIUS JEFFERSON[4] AUSTIN (*Thomas J.,*[3] *Jesse*[2] *Thomas*[1]) was born 27 March 1850 in Caldwell County, North Carolina. A poor farm boy, Julius eloped with Celia Isabell Harris, a rich planter's daughter. They were married in Mulberry, Caldwell County, on 24 June 1871 by Magistrate George Washington Moore. Celia was born on 22 May 1851 in Mulberry, the daughter of Lewis Harris and America Gragg. America's mother was Celia Boone, a niece of the well-known Daniel Boone. Celia Harris' sister Adeline married Julius' older brother John P. Austin.

Julius and Celia lived with his father Thomas Austin in Patterson, Caldwell County, where they farmed and raised their children. Julius helped enumerate the 1900 Census for Caldwell County, and served from 1906 to 1910 as Caldwell County Treasurer. In the 1910 Census the family lived on North Main Street in Lenoir, Caldwell County. They also lived 25 years on the former Dr. Houck farm across the Yadkin River near Clover Hill farm. In later years they bought the old Coles Farm in Happy Valley, Caldwell County. Julius also served as County Commissioner from 1928 to 1930, and was instrumental in building a new County Courthouse in 1928. An avid reader, a lifelong farmer who loved the land, he was a dyed-in-the-wool Republican. The photograph on the page 198 shows Julius and Celia Austin just prior to celebrating their 75th wedding anniversary in 1946, at which time they had 18 grandchildren and 41 great-grandchildren. Celia was blind by then, and in very poor health. She died two months later at age 95, on 16 August 1946, and is buried in Bellview Cemetery, Lenoir. Julius died six months later at age 96, on 6 March 1947, and is buried with Celia.

CHILDREN: T322-1. JOHN P., *born 11 September 1872, m. Elizabeth C. Julian. Their son Fred was b. circa 1893 in Charlotte, dau. June Julian was b. 9 June 1896. John d. 3 August 1897 at age 25, was buried at Harpers Chapel*

T322-2. WILLIAM JEFFERSON ('BUD'), *born 4 April 1874* +

T322-3. ELLA W., *b. 11 May 1876, m. 21 January 1896 to S. Findley Hartley. Ella d. 2 or 7 September 1897, buried in Harpers Chapel.*

T322-4. MARY JENNIE, *b. 11 May 1878, m. Alonzo McGinnis. She died 31 August 1970*

T322-5. GEORGE LEWIS, *b. 31 January 1880, m.*

Photograph on page 198 shows Julius Jefferson Austin (1850-1947) and his wife Celia Isabelle Harris (1851-1946) at the time of their 75th wedding anniversary in June 1946. Photograph to the right shows Julius Jefferson Austin with his two younger brothers: Rufus Lenoir Austin (1866-1936) in center, and George Thomas Austin (1854-1929) at the right.

Alice Austin. He died on 6 April 1965 at age 85, is buried in Bellview Cemetery.

T322-6. ROSA ANNA, *b. 30 May 1884, m.(1) Jesse Eller, m.(2) Bob Bean of/in? Kimberly, Idaho. Rosa died in 1977.*

T322-7. NELLIE BEULAH, *b. 24 January 1891, m.(1) — Clark (she was Nellie Clark, age 19 with child 0/12 in 1910 Census), m.(2) S. Findley Hartley. She died in 1978.*

T324. GEORGE THOMAS[4] AUSTIN *Thomas J.,[3] Jesse,[2] Thomas[1]*) was born 10 February 1854 in North Carolina. He was married on 11 May 1878 to Sarah Isabell Simmons. Sarah, the daughter of Hugh Simmons and Anna Gilbert, was born on 26 October 1854. They lived in the two-story home located near his father's homeplace at the junction of Mulberry and Esq. Miller roads in Patterson. This house was transferred to his son (George) Thomas Austin on 15 March 1921. On 14 December 1929 the property, consisting of 184 acres, was sold to C. Rudolph Morety & Epsic. In 1929 the Coy Miller Road was called old Austin Mill Road. George Thomas Austin's next home is said to have been Cedar Hill on the banks of the Yadkin, built by Col. William Hulme Dula Sr. in the 1830's, belonging to Dr. & Mrs. Gerald Bolick in 1983. In July 1984 his granddaughter Roxie Faw remembered her family assisting him in farming there. George later moved to a white house (no longer standing) on highway 268 where Early Greene later built. Then he built a home near Yadkin Baptist Church, where he also lived at the time of his death in 1929. His son Tom also lived in this house during his last years. George died on 12 March 1929 at age 75, and is buried in Harpers Chapel Church, Patterson. His widow Sarah died on 21 April 1937 at age 82, and is buried with her husband. Their children were probably born in Caldwell County, North Carolina:

T324-1. EDWARD, *b. 25 August 1879, d. 6 April 1916, was killed on railroad*

T324-2. GEORGE THOMAS JR., *b. 21 April 1881* +

T324-3. ESTELLA VIRGINIA, *b. 31 March 1883, d. 24 September 1959. She m. Jesse L. Coffey, b. 19 June 1883 and d. 6 Dec. 1942, son of William Coffey & Martha Sharp.*

T324-4. JAMES S., *b. in 1885, d. 10 April 1886, buried Harpers Chapel*

T324-5. HUGH HERNDON, *b. 17 March 1887, d. 25 May 1959. He m. Alma Setzer. Children: Hugh Jr., Kenneth, and Mae Alda Powell.*

T324-6. SUSAN, *b. in April 1889, m. Wiley Greene*

T324-7. ANN, *b. 19 May 1891, d. 20 March 1976 buried Yadkin Baptist Church, Patterson. She m. Fillmore Faw, b.1886? d. 20 September 1948. Faw children: D. Station b.1907, Mamie Bently b.1909, Roxie b.1912, Garson b.1914, Stella Ray b.1916, Vertie Lee b.1917, Elaine b.1919, Annie V. b.1920, Millard Fillmore b.1922, Elsie Pauline b.1924, Ada Mae b.1926, Mildred Ruth b.1928, Opal Jean b.1932*

T324-8. CORA LEE, *b. June 1894, m. Finn Adams. She d. 9 June 1979, buried Harpers Chapel.*

T325. MARY JANE[4] AUSTIN (*Thomas J.,*[3] *Jesse,*[2] *Thomas*[1]) was born 6 March 1856, probably in Caldwell County, North Carolina. At 'age 16' she was married in Caldwell County on 25 December 1873 to Julius Theodore Simmons 'age 26' by N. H. Gwyn, J.P. Julius, the son of Hugh Simmons and Anna Gilbert, was born on 6 February 1839. Julius died 26 March 1932, and is buried in Harpers Chapel in Patterson, Caldwell County. Mary, who was ill for over 50 years, died on 18 November 1947 at age 91, and is also buried in Harpers Chapel. Their children were probably born in Caldwell County, and have been remembered as being: THOMAS R., JAMES R., MATILDA, ANNA MARGARET, MINNIE b.1882

T326. CHARLES DAVID[4] AUSTIN (*Thomas J.,*[3] *Jesse,*[2] *Thomas*[1]) was born on 25 December 1856, probably in Caldwell County, North Carolina. He was married in Mountain City, Tennessee on 10 February 1877 to Rebecca Main of Shouns, Tennessee. Rebecca, the daughter of Sidney Main and Sarah Dunn, was born on 29 November 1856, probably in Lumplins Branch, Shouns, or Mountain City, Tennessee. Around 1900 the family followed their eldest son 'Will' to Nebraska. They remained there except for Joseph, who returned to Caldwell County, and Walter who later returned to Mountain City, Tennessee. Rebecca died on 27 May 1944 in Bayard, Morrill County, Nebraska (or nearby), and is buried in Bayard City Cemetery. Charles died on 1 December 1944 in Bayard, and is buried with his wife and their children William, Nettie, John, and Fred Hill Austin. Their first four and last two children were probably born in Caldwell County, North Carolina. The other four were born at home on a steep Tennessee hill not far from the North Carolina state line:

T326-1. WILLIAM FRANKLIN, *b. circa 1878* +

T326-2. NETTIE BELLE, *b. 22 December 1879, d. 1970. She m. Robert McCracken (he had four children by a previous marriage). Robert d. when Agnes was only age 4 and 'Pat' age 2. McCracken children: Charles, James, Agnes, and John Virgil ('Pat')*

T326-3. WALTER LENOIR, *b. 24 January 1883* +

T326-4. SAL (SARAH?), *b. circa 1885, m. Lee Suddreth from Caldwell County, b. March 1883, the son of Toliver and Laura (Harris) Suddreth. Their one known child, Mildred, was born in Sterling, Nebraska.*

T326-5. JOSEPH EDWARD, *b. 21 April 1887* +

T326-6. ELLA, *b. 10 June 1889, d. 8 September 1904, buried Harpers Chapel, Patterson NC*

T326-7. ROBERT LEWIS, *b. 24 March 1892* +

T326-8. JOHN HOUSTON, *b. 30 September 1893* +

T326-9. WHEELER MCKINLEY, *b. 5 April 1896* +

T326-A. FRED HILL, *b. 24 April 1899, d. 1974. He m. Estol Reily.*

T327. JOSEPH MILTON[4] AUSTIN (*Thomas J.,*[3] *Jesse,*[2] *Thomas*[1]) was born 21 October 1859, probably in Caldwell County, North Carolina. He was married circa 1885 to Margaret Matilda Greene, who was born on 14 June 1858/61. Margaret died on 24 February 1943, and is buried in Harpers Chapel, Patterson, Caldwell County. Joseph died on 25 March 1944. Their children were probably born in Caldwell County:

CHILDREN: T327-1. HORRIE, *b. August 1886, m. Annie Coffey*

T327-2. GWYN M., *b. September 1888, went to Seattle, Washington*

T327-3. OLLIE C., *b. June 1891, m. Lee Smith. In the 1910 Census Ollie was age 19, her husband Lee was age 29.*

T327-4. RUSSELL M./H.?, *b. 30 October 1897 (or November 1896), d. 13 January 1965, buried Harpers Chapel*

T327-5. BEULAH MAY, *b. 28 August 1899, m. Clyde Hall*

[CONTINUED ON PAGE 227]

★★★★★★★★★★★★★★★★★★★★★★★★★★★

Austins of America is intended to serve present and future genealogists researching Austin family lines. Readers are encouraged to submit queries, genealogical and historical articles for publication. Previously published books, pamphlets or articles containing Austin genealogical data are also sought for reprinting or review.

EDITOR

DR. MICHAEL EDWARD AUSTIN   CONCORD, MA

ASSOCIATE EDITORS

ANTHONY KENT AUSTIN   PROSPECT, KY

BERT ADDIS AUSTIN   QUEEN CREEK, AZ

PATRICIA BIEBUYCK AUSTIN   CONCORD, MA

PAULINE LUCILLE AUSTIN   MARION, IA

Austins of America is published each February and August by The Austin Print, 23 Allen Farm Lane, Concord, Massachusetts 01742. All correspondence, including subscriptions, articles and responses to queries, should be sent to this address. Subscriptions are $4.50 per year postpaid.

★★★★★★★★★★★★★★★★★★★★★★★★★★★

AUSTINS IN VOLUNTEER WISCONSIN REGIMENTS DURING THE CIVIL WAR

by Harris Monroe Austin

Note: The following data was found on Mormon Church microfilms in Salt Lake City, Utah. All the regiments were 'Infantry' unless otherwise designated.

Albert Austin, Pvt.	not listed
Alfred E. Austin, Cpl.	Company D, 38th Regiment
Alonzo J. Austin, Pvt.	Company B, 14th Regiment
Ambrose Austin, Pvt.	Co. A, 3rd & 46th Regiments
Anson L. Austin, Pvt.	Co. L, 2nd Cavalry Regiment
Arva O. Austin, Pvt.	Company D, 6th Regiment
Bradford Austin, Pvt.	12th Indep. Batt. Light Artillery
Chauncy J. Austin, Pvt.	Company K, 25th Regiment, Co. B, 42nd Regiment, Promoted to Lt., died in Andersonville
Charles Austin, Pvt.	Company I, 2th Regiment
Charles C. Austin, Pvt.	Company I, 36th Regiment
Charles P. Austin, Pvt.	Company G, 2nd Regiment
Clark Austin, Pvt.	Company C, 3rd Regiment
Daniel D. Austin, Pvt.	Company L, 3rd Regiment
David Austin, Pvt.	Company E, 16th Regiment
David Austin, Pvt.	Company H, 46th Regiment
Edgar A. Austin, Sgt.	Company G, 3rd Regiment
Edward A. Austin, Pvt.	Batt. I 1st Wisc. Heavy Artillery transferred to 7th Ind. Light Artillery
Edward Austin, Lt.	Company G, 14th Regiment
Edward Austin, Pvt.	Company I, 32nd Regiment
Edwin Austin, Pvt.	Company C, 1st Regiment
Edwin H. Austin, Pvt.	Company H, 5th Regiment
Edwin J. Austin, Pvt.	Co. K, 4th Cavalry Regiment
Eli Austin, Pvt.	Co. C & H, 3rd Cavalry Regiments
Eli Austin, Pvt.	Company G, 39th Regiment
Eli Austin, Pvt.	Company F, 46th Regiment
Elijah W. Austin, Pvt.	Company K, 22nd Regiment
Ezra B. Austin, Pvt.	Company E, 14th Regiment
Francis B. Austin, Pvt.	Company B?, 49th Regiment
Francis E. Austin, Pvt.	Company E, 50th Regiment
Frank M. Austin, Pvt.	Company A, 53rd Regiment, Company G, 51st Regiment
Franklin Austin Cpl.	Company D, 42nd Regiment
George Austin, Pvt.	Co. K, 36th Regiment, Musician
George B. Austin, Pvt.	Company H, 44th Regiment
George M. Austin, Pvt.	Company G, 25th Regiment
Harry Austin, Pvt.	Company B, 25th Regiment
Henry S. Austin, Pvt.	Company A, 21st Regiment
Henry S. Austin, Pvt.	Battery A 1st Heavy Artillery
Hezekiah Austin, Pvt.	Company H, 2nd Regiment
Hiram Austin, Pvt.	Co. L & D, 3rd Cavalry Regiments
Isaac Austin, Pvt.	Company G, 25th Regiment
Isaiah L. Austin, Pvt.	Co. D, 4th Cavalry Regiment, Co. H, 10th Cavalry Regiment
James Austin, Pvt.	Company D, 19th Regiment
James A. Austin, Pvt.	Battery A, 3rd Light Artillery, A Wagoner, he was transferred to 6th & 8th Light Artillery
James Monroe Austin, Pvt.	Company E, 10th Regiment, Died in field hospital #4 near Louisville in 1862.
James P. Austin, Substitute	Unassigned
James R. Austin, Pvt.	Company A, 39th Regiment
James W. Austin, Pvt.	Company H, 5th Regiment
John Austin, Pvt.	Battery C, 1st Heavy Artillery
John Austin, Pvt.	Company H, 1st Regiment
John Austin, Pvt.	Temporary Co. B, 23rd Regiment, Permanent Co. B, 11th Regiment
John Austin, Pvt.	Company G, 36th Regiment
John Austin, Pvt.	Company A, 42nd Regiment
John Austin, 1st Lt.	Company I, 51st Regiment
John B. Austin, Pvt.	Company G, 14th Regiment
John Edwin Austin, Pvt.	Battery G, 1st Light Artillery
John S. Austin, Pvt.	Company I, 24th Regiment
John T. Austin, Pvt.	Company A, 21st Regiment
Joseph P. Austin, Pvt.	Company D, 32nd Regiment
Julius H. Austin, Pvt.	Battery D, 1st Heavy Artillery
Jonathan Austin, Pvt.	Company K, 10th Regiment
Marshal Austin, Pvt.	Company H, 46nd Regiment
Martin Austin, Pvt.	Company H, 38th Regiment
Murcienus Austin, Pvt.	Company B & I, 19th Regiment
Nelson Austin, Pvt.	Battery H, 1st Heavy Artillery
Nelson P. Austin, Pvt.	Company C, 19th Regiment
Ole O. Austin, Pvt.	Company C, 22nd Regiment
Orlando A. Austin, Sgt.	Company I, 49th Regiment, Capt., Co. I, 17th Regiment
Orville Austin, Pvt.	Battery ? 7th Light Artillery
Palmer Austin, Pvt.	Company D, 18th Regiment
Pardon Austin, Pvt.	Company D, 49th Regiment
Richard H. Austin, Lt.	Company A, 24th Regiment, promoted to Captain
Robert B. Austin, Pvt.	Company G, 47th Regiment
Ruben Austin, Pvt.	Company C, 32nd Regiment
Samuel R. Austin, Pvt.	Company K, 44th Regiment
Seth Austin, Pvt.	Company K, 22nd Regiment
Shadrack Austin, Pvt.	Battery D, 1st Heavy Artillery
Silas F. Austin, Pvt.	Company 8 & 10 Light Artillery
Simeon P. Austin, Pvt.	Company G, 33rd Regiment
Smith Austin, Pvt.	Company G, 1st Regiment
Stephen Austin, Pvt.	Company A, 3rd Regiment
Stephen Austin, Pvt.	Company ?, 46nd Regiment
Welcom P. Austin, Pvt.	Company C, 19th Regiment
William Austin, Pvt.	Battery ? 12th Light Artillery
William Austin, Pvt.	Company O ?, 16th Regiment
William Austin, Pvt.	Company K, 37th Regiment
William G. Austin, Pvt.	Company C, 19th Regiment
William G. Austin, Sgt.	4th Light Artillery
William H. Austin, Pvt.	Company D, 3rd Regiment
William H. Austin, Pvt.	Company C, 23rd Regiment
William W. Austin, Corp.	Company K, 19th Regiment

SOME DESCENDANTS OF
BENJAMIN AUSTIN AND ELIZABETH WATSON
OF TENNESSEE AND ILLINOIS

by Becky Moyer Boone

B. BENJAMIN[1] AUSTIN was born 14 April 1791 in North Carolina or Tennessee. He was first married on January 1811 to Elizabeth Watson, who was born on 16 September 1793, also in North Carolina or Tennessee. Their first seven children were born in Sumner County, Tennessee. Sometime before the 1830 Census, Benjamin and Elizabeth moved their family to Clark County, Illinois. They and all but one of their children are accounted for (by age and gender) in the 1830 Census of Clark County. One of their two daughters age 10-15 does not appear: possibly Eliza had died young or was living elsewhere? The same census also lists one female slave age 10-24, and three free colored females (one age 24-36, one age 55-100, one over 100 years old) as part of Benjamin Austin's household. Elizabeth died on 9 October 1836 in Hutton, Coles County, Illinois. Benjamin married a second time on 5 January 1841 in Coles County to Elizabeth (—) Dyer, apparently a widow who had at least five sons and two daughters by her previous marriage. By the 1850 Census in Salisbury Precinct, Coles County, only Rhoda Austin and Elizabeth's two youngest boys were still living at home with Benjamin and Elizabeth. Benjamin died 30 November 1860 in Hutton. Mentioned in his Probate Record were his widow Elizabeth, Nathan Austin, heirs of Candice Parker, Emily Parker, Jane Austin, Rhoda Dorman, and Mary Chenowith heirs, together with personal property to the (probable) amount of $400. Mary was likely born in Illinois or Sumner, Tennessee. The youngest two children were born in Hutton:

CHILDREN: B1. NATHAN, *b. 10 December 1812* +
B2. WILLIAM, *b. 27 March 1815* +
B3. ELIZA, *b. 9 October 1817*
B4. MARTHA, *b. 14 Nov. 1819, d. 17 August 1836*
B5. BETTIE, *b. 28 March 1822, d. 2 April 1858*
B6. CANDICE, *b. 29 April 1824, m. 4 June 1844 to Felix R. Parker by Wm. Gilman, J.P. Known children: Prior, Benjamin, John, Lydia and Leander. Candice d. 12 July 1858-60*
B7. EMILY, *b. 15 December 1826, d. 22 July 1863, m. 21 February 1848 to James Parker. Known children: Jacob, Charlotte, Rufus and George.*
B8. MARY, *b. 22 April 1829, m.(1) 27 October 1851 to Robert Chenowith. Robert's Will was filed 26 January 1863. Mary m.(2) — Cutright, they had a son Austin Cutright.*
B9. ELLEN JANE, *b. 10 August 1831, unmarried, d. 16 April 1889*
BA. RHODA CATHERINE, *b. 26 April 1835, m. 16*

December 1852 to George Franklin Dorman, who was b. 18 December 1827 in Tiffen, Seneca County, Ohio, and d. 2 March 1884 in Fair Groves, Greene County, Missouri. Their son Simon Henry Dorman was b. 1869 in Coles County. Rhoda d. 27 December 1894 in Illinois.

SECOND GENERATION

B1. NATHAN[2] AUSTIN (*Benjamin*[1]) was born 10 December 1812 in Sumner County, Tennessee. He was first married on 2 August 1834 to Lucinda Parker in Coles County, Illinois. He married a second time in Coles County on 21 January 1844 to Harriet Parker by John Dougherty, M.G. The family is recorded in Salisbury Precinct of Coles County in 1850. Listed with the family in that census were five Walker children, all born in Illinois: Stanley B. 17, Sarah Q. 15, Perry 13, Merena 11, and Mary 9. Nathan died on 25 July 1871. His first two children were by his first wife, all are believed to have been born in Coles County:

CHILDREN: B11. WILLIAM H., *b. ca. 1838 (12 in 1850 Census)*
B12. BENJAMIN F., *b. ca. 1839 (11 in 1850)*
B13. CANDICE, *b. ca. 1846 (4 in 1850 Census)*
B14. ISABEL, *m. — Lee*
B15. HELEN, *m. — Wells*

B2. WILLIAM[2] AUSTIN (*Benjamin*[1]) was born 27 March 1815 in Sumner County, Tennessee. On 26 March 1839 a William Austin was married in Coles County, Illinois, to Mrs. Rebecca Woodall by Abram L. Hollis, M.G. William Austin Sr. and William D. Austin Jr. signed as Executors of the estate of John M. Austin on 14 November 1846 in Coles County. William D. Austin married on 4 March 1847 to Hester Ann Sousley by Robert Graham, L.D. M.G. According to Coles County Probate records, the final settlement of William Austin's estate paid 1851 taxes, so he probably died around then, leaving the following heirs: William D. Austin, Elizabeth Woodall, Jesse Meadows and wife, John and Susan Austin heirs, Robert Mitchel's heirs, M. Duties heirs, Aminadal? Austin, Samuel Austin, and Lucinda Prince. Coles County Probate Records show that on 1 July 1901, W. N. Austin swore on oath that on 28 June 1901 he served notice on Ester A. Austin, heir to the estate of William D. Austin.

References

Biography on Benjamin Austin by his grandson Simon Henry Dorman; 1850 Census for Coles County; *Early Marriages of Coles County 1830-1850*; *Early Coles County Marriage Records*; data from Naomi Hughes of Checotah, Oklahoma; Coles County Probate Records.

SOME AUSTIN MARRIAGE RECORDS
FOUND IN THE STATE OF OHIO

by Pauline Lucille Austin

Editor's Note: The following data was gleaned from the author's rather extensive genealogical notes relating to Austins in the state of Ohio. Mrs. Austin has undertaken considerable correspondence for many years in gathering data on Austin lines in Ohio and several other states. As an Associate Editor of Austins of America, she generously continues to share her research efforts with our present readers and with future generations.

A. Austin to Josiah Mclaughlin on 1 January 1862 in Brown County

Aaron Austin to Ann Harper on 6 May 1840 in Ashtabula County

Aaron Austin to Nancy Enos on 23 January 1862 by J. G. Schouller

Abel J. Austin to Deborah Cummings on 23 September 1836 in Meigs County

Albert Austin to Ann Norton on 19 May 1847 Portage County

Albert Austin to Emma Newton on 5 January 1842 in Portage County

Alexander Austin to Lois D. Foot 17 January 1862 by John Whitworth in Knox County

Alexander Austin to Matilda Mitchell 3 March 1853 by Burgess M.G. in Marion County

Alfred Andrew Austin to Miss Ann McGee on 11 August 1842 in Meigs County

Almira Austin to Wm. Reeves on 22 December 1835 in Portage County

Alonzo Austin to Alice Gaston on 4 September 1865 in Meigs County

Amos Austin to Rebecca J. Johnson 12 September 1857 in Lake County

Andrew G. Austin to Anna H. Freeman on 28 June 1853 in Clark County

Angeline Austin to Augustus Burr on 20 December 1841 of Ashtabula County in Ravenna, Portage County

Ann Austin to John Moon on 15 April 1857 in Portage County

Ann Eliza Austin to James Day on 18 September 1835 in Sheffield, Lorain County

Ann P. Austin to William L. Browning 8 January 1800 by John Kyle in Licking County

Anna Austin to Isaac Ewing on 1 January 1860 in Wayne County

Annette Abigail Austin to Arnold M. Cleveland on 1 January 1856 in Granville, Licking County

Benjah Austin, Jr. to Belinda Dean on 1 October 1840 in Trumbull County

Benjamin A. Austin to Mary Cowgill in 1838 in Clinton County

Benjamin Austin b.VT of Knox County to Rachel Kimble on 13 October 1853 by D. Grey M.G. 3rd m. in Hancock County

Benjamin Austin to Rebecca Durbin on 29 December 1829 by A. Goff in Knox County

Benjamin D. Austin to Sarah R. ? residents in 1839 in Medina County

Benjamin A. Austin to Mary Smith in 1853 in Clinton County

Benson Austin to Sall Ross on 22 July 1830 by Samuel Cabeen J.P. in Muskingum County

Bessie Austine to A. C. Moore in Lorain County

Betsie (Austin) Goodale to ? Parks from Orange County VA in Lawrence County

Betsy B. Austin to Ephriam Sackett on 24 December 1846 in Geauga County

Betsy B. Austin to Lysander Weed on 3 March 1833 of Ashtabula County in Columbus, Franklin County

Bushnell Austin to Sally Page on 14 December 1838 in Lake County or Geauga County

Cale Austin to Bessie Bell in 1897 in Allen County

Calvin Austin to Martha Murdock on 16 June 1805 in Jefferson County

Camilla Austin to Edmund Day on 2 September 1846 in Sheffield, Lorain County

Caroline Austin to Fredrick Herton on 17 March 1840 in Portage County

Caroline R. Austin to William Hubbard on 16 March 1840 in Portage County

Cassius Austin to Lydia Jeffers on 5 November 1880 by S.D. Cowden in Gallia County

Catherine M. Austin to David R. Clifton in 1917 in Allen County

Charles A. Austin to Samantha Clingensmith on 18 December 1861

Charles B. Austin m. Sarah Ann Burroughs? 19 December 1844 by Levi Purviance M.G. in Preble County

Charles G. Austin to Harriet Curtis on 21 September 1825 in Portage County

Charlotte Austin to Bondinott Seely on 22 August 1828 in Ashtabula County

Charlotte Austin to Hamilton Kearns on 1 April 1839 in Shelby County

Chloe Austin to John Henderson on 22 July 1806 in Geauga County

Clarinda Austin to Harvey Sadd on 23 February 1835 of Ashtabula County in Columbus, Franklin County

Clarissa Austin to Rufus Sweet on 29 January 1835 of Ashtabula in Columbus, Franklin County

Cornelius Austin to Amanda Jollife 9 March 1850 in Zanesville, Muskingum County

Cornelius Austin to Roxy Norton on 14 December 1846 in Portage County

Cyrenthia Austin to George W. William on 1 March 1841 in Paulding County

Daniel Austin to Martha Frisk on 11 January 1844 in Portage County

David Austin to Anna Kimes on 25 February ? in Portage County

David Austin to Mary Fleming on 5 February 1829 by Albert Coal J.P. in Muskingum Co.

David Austin to Sarah Wood on 13 May 1848 in Cleveland, Cuyahoga County

David B. Austin to Melisse Thompson on 27 October 1850 by Thos. M. Burman M.G. in Preble County

David B. Austin to Rachel Grove on 18 March 1849 by Zibs Brown M.G. in Preble County

David L. Austin to Maranda A. Todd on 11 March 1852 in Ashtabula County

David S. Austin to Angie Middleton in 1870 in Clinton County

David S. Austin to Lois Smith in 1850 in Clinton County

Delila C. Austin to Alexander Lynn on 29 March 1878 by Ha. Kent Probate Judge in Gallia County

Easter Austin to John Dale on 10 May 1838 in Union County

Edward C. Austin to Laura J. Mills on 27 October 1845 in Ashtabula County

Edward W. Austin to Sarah I. Mostelle on 4 October 1855 by George Leonard in Knox Co.

Electa Austin to Charles Snyder on 11 May 1841 in Portage County

Elijah R. Austin to Susan Davis on 7 June 1841 in Meigs County

Eliphalet Austin to Julia R. Hawley on 20 September 1835 in Ashtabula County

Eliphalet Austin to Sally B. Cowles on 20/30 August 1819 in Ashtabula County

Eliza Aston to John H. Haver on 9 August 1829 in Knox County by John Roberts J.P.

Eliza Hannah Austin to Isaac S. Cole on 19 June 1836 in Knox County by Daniel Conant M.G.

Eliza J. Austin to George Akin Racey on 4 July 1857 in Caldwell, Noble County

Eliza R. Aston to Isaac F. Lindsey on 25 January 1845 in Clermont County

Elizabeth Ashton to George Good on 11 June 1868 in Muskingum County

Elizabeth Ashton to John Perry on 1 October 1837 in Hamilton County

Elizabeth Axtell to Robert Thompson on 28 September 1846 in Knox County

Elisabeth Austin to Samuel Akins on 5 July 1838 in Knox County by John Cockran J.P.

Elizabeth Austin to Edmond S. Snow on 23 October 1851 in Ashtabula County

Elizabeth Austin to Fountian Dear on 20 April 1865 in Clark County

Elizabeth Austin to John G. Somers on 21 February 1848 in Geauga County

Elnor Austin to John Sherbondy on 31 December 1850 in Summit County

Elsa Austin to Ransam Moore 27 November 1826 in Lorain County

Emilie Austin to Samuel Forward Hickok on 1 January 1840 in Aurora, Portage County

Emily Austin to Richard Blade on 18 October 1849 in Franklin County, by Thomas Hughs M.G.

Ethel Cecelia Austin to Frank Parker Taylor on 5 August 1909 in Toledo, Lucus County

Eve Austin to Moses Madkins on 13 March 1853 in Gallia County

Even Ashton to Sarah Frame on 22 August 1839 in Muskingum County

Ezra Austin to Betsy English on 11 January 1835 in Portage County

Flora A. Austin to Almon Amphear on 24 December 1861 in Portage County

Florilla Austin (Mrs.) to Lemuel J. Chester on 4 March 1846 in Portage County

Frances Maria Austin to George Parsons on 10 Dec. 1807 in Warren, Trumbull County

Franklin Austin to Harriett Hively on 30 August 1847 in Defiance County

Freeman Austin to Elizabeth Johnson on 26 February 1818 in Trumbull County

George Austin to Florence Angdon on 14 May 1862 in Hancock County, 1st m.

George Austin to Helbur Beach on 25 September 1872 in Hancock County, 2nd m.

George Austin to Mary Wright on 19 June 1828 in Meigs County

George M. Austin to Eliza Mills on 2 April 1839 in Ashtabula County

George W. Austin to Betsy M. Bissell on 31 July 1834 in Portage County

George Washington Austin to Martha Rose on 20 November 1845 in Warren, Trumbull County

Gotfried Austin to Christine Snyder on 10 March 1844 in Marion Co. by G. Snyder J.P.

Hannah Ann Austin to John A. Gage on 24 September 1840 in Champaign/Franklin/Butler County by Rev. Wm. Graham.

Hannah Austin to Isaac B. Cole on 19 June 1836 by Daniel W. Conant

Hannah Austin to Joseph Rigby on 15 November 1827 in Knox Co. by Andrew Scoles, J.P.

Hannah M. Austin to Richard P. Loveland on 16 December 1841 in Ashland County by D. Robinson J.P.

Harmon Austin to Minerva Sackett on 11 January 1843 in Trumbull County

Harriet Austin to Edward Cooper on 25 August 1861 in Portage County

Harrison Austin to Mary Elbert on 18 November 1858 in Zanesville, Muskingum County

Henry Austin to Catherine Eaton on 3 August 1851 in Knox County by John Inacho J.P.

Henry H. Austin to Mary Waterbury on 31 March 1849 in Ashtabula County

Henry L. Austin to Jane D. Warner on 13 October 1837 in Ashtabula County

Henry M. Austin to Mary Ann Wood on 30 March 1854 in Berlin Township, Knox County by W. I. Close.

Henry S. Austin to Laura Leed on 1 October 1844 in Trumbull County

Hiram Austin to Eunice Tilden on 5 February 1831 in Portage County

Hiram Austin to Elizabeth Sears on 1 June 1841 in Portage County

Homer Austin to Lucretia Curtiss on 4 December 1823 in Portage County

Homer Austin to Margaret J. Anderson on 3 March 1841 in Trumbull County (see Isaac)

Honor Austin to Robert Elwood in 1823 in Highland County

Horace Austin to Nancy Alfred on 5 May 1827 in Jefferson, Ashtabula County

Isaac Austin to Calista Silvers on 13 October 1842 in Montgomery County

Isaac Austin to Deborah F. Thompson on 22 August 1861 in Warren County

Isaac Austin to Jane Wood on 13 September 1860 in Morgan County

Isaac Austin to Margaret J. Anderson on 3 March 1841 in Trumbull County (see Homer)

Isabella Austin to Marc Wheeler on 22 May 1850 in Chagrin Falls, Cuyahoga County

Jacob Austin to Martha Price in 1833 in Carroll County

James Austin to Elizabeth King on 12 February 1854 in Clark County

James Austin to Hannah Hicklin on 27 October 1831 in Marborough, Stark County at the Quaker Meeting House.

James Austin to Martha Ritter on 24 June 1849 in Trumbull County

James Austin to Mary Ann Pratt on 12 July 1829 in Stark County

James L. Austin to Nora McKee in 1904 in Holmes County

James O. Austin to Catherine Spangler on 13 August 1837 in Mushingum County by J. K. Parmelee

James S. Austin to Marietta Reed on 13 May 1834 in Portage County

James S. Austin to Abigail E. Mason on 9 September 1869 in Lancaster, Muskingum Co.

James Van Austin to Lydia Mann on 16 February 1832 in Montgomery County

James W. Austin to Charlotte Funk on 9 April 1840 in Jefferson Twp., Muskingum County by John Jacobs J.P.

Joab Austin to Emeline C. Davis on 7 April 1851 or 57 in Portage County

John A. Austin to Harriett Bacon on 9 August 1855 in Franklin County by Henry Floyd Roberts M.G.

John Austin to Anna Braddock on 6 April 1834 in Knox County by James Irwin J.P.

John Austin to Emily M. Blair on 12 February 1836 in Portage County

John Austin to Irene Halbert on 1 September 1859 in Washington County

John Austin to Miss Martha Cooper on 8 March 1841 in Knox Co. by W. E. Clark M.G.

John Austin to Sarah Taylor on 20 November 1828 in Portage County

John D. Austin to Lucretia Ellen Glaze on 12 January 1847 in Knox Co. by Emil Harris JP

John D. Austin to Mary Jane Thompson on 6 February 1849 in Knox County by J. W. Marvin, M.G.

John E. Auten to Sarah Winters on 10 August 1852 in Knox County by M. C. Furlong M.G.

John J. Austin to Rebecca Bowes on 15 February 1855 in Preble County by Abraham Moses M.G.

John M. Austin to Sarah Falling on 6 April 1831 in Fairfield Co. by Henry Mathews MG

Jonathan Austin to Permillia A. Kerr on 14 August 1872 in Highland County, by Truman S. Cowden.

Jonathan Austin to Rebecca Belsford on 14 September 1826 in Greene County, by Joshua Carman

Joseph Austin to Ann Brewster on 11 March 1830 in Greene County, by Wm. Dixon M.G.

Joseph Austin to Malinda Woodruff on 10 February 1828 in Butler County

Josiah Austin to Isabelle Barker on 3 August 1825 in Champaign County by John C. Peirson M.G.

Josie Austin to William O. Wilson on 21 November 1883 in Gallia County by S.D. Cowden.

Julia Ann Aston to George Washington Jessup on 28 December 1841 in Hamilton County

Julius Austin to Frances E. Freeman on 24 January 1833 in Trumbull County

Justin Austin to Catharine Harper on 19 May 1850 in Greene County

Laura Austin to Erastus Rosseter 15 December 1825 in Portage County

Linus Austin to Louisa Collins Avery on 21 January 1852 in Middleburg, Logan County

Lizzie M. Austin to Willard C. Hull on 18 September 1861 in Trumbull County

Louisa A. Austin to Alex McIntyre 16 June 1859 in Lake County

Lucinda Ashton to John Lane on 16 February 1849 in Brown County

L(ucius) D(unham) Austin to Harriett M. Barker on 27 October 1863 in Lake County

Lucius M. Austin to Melissa Whiting on 7 March 1825 in Jefferson, Ashtabula County

Lucretia L. Austin to Alva Hart on 29 October 1833 in Portage County

Lucy A. Austin to Henry Bedell on 1 February 1853 in Ashtabula County

Lucy A./F./L. Austin to Thomas B./O. Radcliff on 12 July 1863 in Lake County

Lydia Austin to William L. Smith on 24 February 1840 in Meigs County

Lyman H. Austin to Emeline Olin on 15 April 1855 in Hartsgrove, Ashtabula County

Maggie Austin to Centenial Shope 1897 in Allen County

Malinda Austin to Henry M. Heinery on 19 June 1853 in Meigs County

Malissa Austin to Daniel B. Scofield on 4 August 1834 in Henry County

Malvina Austin to Samuel McGibbony/Gibbony on 9 October 1840 in Licking County by Timothy Howe, M.G.

Margaret Ashton to Chuck Peaslee on 23 October 1834 in Columbus, Franklin County

Margaret Austin to Henry Neel 1845 in Knox County

Margaret Austin to Moses W. Hart on 27 March 1864 in Franklin County, by E.H. Heagles V.D.M.

Margaret Auton to Robert Thompson 13 July 1828 in Preble County

Maria Austin to Davis Montgomery on 9 February 1820 or 21 in Ashtabula County, Jefferson

Marinda Austin to Joseph L. Taylor on 24 May 1864 in Portage County

Martha Austin to Andrew W. Loomis 9 March 1826 in Jefferson County

Martha J. Austin to John Doverly on 16 November 1873 in Defiance County

Martha LuVurn Austin to Floyd Jacob Simons 1929 Allen County

Mary Aston to John McMichael on 2 June 1825 in Muskingum County by D. Prodjet?

Mary A. Austin to Chauncey D. Taylor on 8 January 1839 in Medina County

Mary Ann Austin to Thomas Long on 14 February 1833 in Greene County, by E. Williams.

Mary Austin to Andrew Hicks on 4 September 1860 in Knox County by T. F. Hildreth, JP

Mary Austin to Atkins Gains on 25 September 1861 in Franklin County, by Silas Johnson M.G. colored.

Mary Austin to Ben Stover on ??? in Champaign County

Mary Austin to Daniel Pratt on 8 November 1827 in Stark County

Mary Austin to Elson Tickner on 12 April 1835 in Portage County

Mary Austin to James Harris on 20 August 1854 in Muskingum Co. by S. M. Lane J.P.

Mary Austin to John Newman on 5 June 1819 in Fairfield County

Mary Austin to Joseph Stokes on 23 April 1829 in Union County

Mary Austin to Nehemiah Barnhard on 20 October 1835 in Knox County by J. W. Hildreth J.P.

Mary Austin to William Brown on 20 March 1834 in Stark County

Mary Austin to William F. Neal on 28 October 1852 in Champaign County

Mary Austin to William Walker on ??? in Gallia County

Mary Belle Austin on ??? to Leonard L. Potter.

Mary E. Aston to Ce Abbe on 16 February 1870

Mary E. Austin to Georger Karas in 1916 in Allen County

Mary Jane Austin to David Jennings on 21 November 1865 in Noble County

Malinda Austin to Henry M. Heinery on 19 June 1853 in Meigs County

Mercy Austin to Harlow B. Mills on 27 March 1844 in Ashtabula County

Minerva Austin to George B. Clark on 7 January 1853 in Henry County

Nancy C. Ashton to Josiah Angle on 9 March 1862 in Hocking County

Nelson Austin to Mary Yonker in 1850 poss. Beaver, Pike County

Olga Marie Austin to William Mumbower in 1915 in Allen County

Olive E. Austin to Caleb S. Ely on 1 March 1865 in Portage County

Oliver Austin to Amelia Redding on 29 May 1858 in Marion County by James King.

Olivia C. Austin to Cort J. Adams on 17 June 1860 in Portage County

Orson A. Austin to Mariam B. Harrison on 1 November 1846 of Holmes County in Waterville, Wood County

Patricia Austin to Matthew Macy between 1817 and 1830 in Kendall, Stark County

Polly Austin m. Cornelius Conklin on 19 August 1821 in Richland County

Phebe Ashton to Peter Smith on 12 December 1825 in Guernsey County

Philip Ashton to Cordelia Dewitt on 16 May 1861 in Knox County

Rachel Austin to James Cosart on 3 August 1834 in Knox County by James Blair J.P.

Rachel D. Austin to Job Haines on 23 January 1843 in Green County

Ralph L. Austin to Francis Doty in 1925 in Holmes County

Rebecca Austin to David W. James on 9 January 1832 in Greene County, by John Osborn.

Rebecca Mills Austin to Ransom Lyman Coe on 26 October 1824 in Ashtabula/Portage County

Rosina Austine to Clinton H. Moore on ??? in Lorain County

Ruth Austin to Amos Kettle 12 June 1851 in Knox County by Elnathan Raymond M.G.

Sally Austin to Cornelius Van Horn 1 December 1812 in Jefferson Co. by Stephen Ford.

Sally Austin to Labon Waterman on 25 December 1828 in Ashtabula County

Sally Austin to Reuben Noah on 13 February 1820 in Portage County

Samuel Aston to Hattie Bartlett on 12 November 1833 in Athens County

Samuel Austin to Anny Spofford in 1825 in Medina County

Samuel Austin to Elizabeth Remline in 1842 in Portage County

Samuel Austin to Nancy Babb on 15 January 1824 in Clinton County

Samuel Austin to Rebecca Therrard on 4 November 1855 in Zanesville, Muskingum County

Sarah Austin to Caleb Powell 23/28/29 June 1832 in Knox County, by F. Phpha? J.P.

Sarah Ashton to Charles Fox Aultman on 3 January 1866 in Clermont County

Sarah Austin to Edward Cowles on 16 December 1840 in Ashtabula County

Sarah Austin to Peter Dunn on May 25 1836

Sarah Austin to William Conner on 20 November 1830 in Greene County by Wm. Dixon.

Sarah Ashton to William Martin on 24 December 1926 in Knox County by Jacob Dixon J.P.

Sarah Elizabeth Austin to John Wesley Ruby on 3 March 1866 in Rural Dale, OH

Sarah J. Austin to Phillip Cobbler 25 July 1853 in Delaware County, by Samuel Lynch.

Sarah Jane Austin to Michael Warren Lane/Lain on 27 December 18?? in Knox County by Geo. LitZenberg.

Sarah Lucretia Austin to Obed Cullens/Cullins on 12 May 1855/58 in Zanesville, Muskingum County

Seymour Austin to Eunice Bissell on 8 January 1818 in Geauga County

Seymour Austin to Julia E. Parker on 3 March 1864 in Trumbull County

Silas Austin to Emily Buckland on 13 October/24 November 1819 in Licking County by Levan Randall

Silas P. Austin to Martha Jane McDaniel on 17 November 1831 in Brown County

Sirena G. Austin to Fredrick E. Skinner on 17 January 1849 in Lake/Geauga County

Sophia Austin to Charles Hawkins on 2 January 1848 in Knox Co. by William Hays

Sophia Austin to Chauncey Hawley on 12 December 1810 in Geauga County

Susan Aston to George Waxler on 18 November 1824 in Muskingum Co. by W. Thompson

Susan Ashton to John Korn on 9 January 1834 in Holmes County

Sybil Austin to Henry Webb on 14 November 1824 in Ashtabula County

Sylvester Austin to Elizabeth Culbertson on 25 November 1850 in Marion County by B. Wall

Thaddeus Austin to Drusilla Hatfield on 4 June 1851 in Portage County

Thomas Austin to Mahala Walikins on 2 September 1828 in Montgomery County

Thomas W. Austin to Lucy J. Lattimer on 28 October 1863 in Franklin County, by D.D. Mather M.G. O.S.J. both of Norwich Twp.

W. H. Austin to Silva McCahn on 22 October 1883 in Hancock County

Walter Henry Austin to Eunice Louise Herren in 1931 in Allen County

Walter Austin to Sarah Nurse/Nourse on 12 July 1827 in Portsmouth, Scioto County

Warren Austin to Melissa Hunt on 23 September 1873 in Defiance County

Washington Austin to Mary Dunlap on 15 July 1847 in Trumbull County

William Austin to Anna Conner 9 July 1854 in Delaware County, by M.C. Bean J.P.

William Austin to Anne Wood on 19 August 1819 in Licking County by J. Johnson J.P.

William Austin to Mary French on 26 January 1853 in Knox County

William Austin to Nancy Jane Dwiggens 31 August 1871.

William C. Austin to Elizabeth Duncanson on 2 March 1872 in Highland County

William Jeremiah Austin to Elizabeth Johnston on 30 November 1830 in Knox County

William M. Austin to Charlotte Briggs on 29 January 1848 in Morgan County

William Ulysses Austin to Kate Leach in 1903, res. Newark, OH.

QUERIES

206-1. Charles L. Austin m. Pheriba (Permila?) ? in Wake Co. North Carolina. Daughters (all born in Wake Co. NC) were Delaney b. 1786, married William Poe; Pheriba b. 1791, married Ambrose Manion Jr.; Edith b. 1795, m. Thomas Caruth. Probable sons were William A., John C., and Charles A. Family moved to Allen County, Kentucky. Seek to exchange any information on this family.

206-2. Oliver Austin - several members of his family were in Beekman Precinct, Dutchess County, New York after 1760. Oliver Austin was there circa 1774 to 1780, and Jonathan and Silas were next to each other in the 1790 census for Pawling, New York. Mary, a daughter of Silas and Sarah, 'late of Beekman' m. Abel Force 1807. Grinman and Daniel Austin were in the Pawling census for 1800. Joshua Austin was a schoolmaster in 1795. Aaron Austin had a son Archer b. 1754 in the area. Any help on this family would be appreciated.

206-3. Robert B. Austin married Mary Frances Hillard. Their son Harry Adalbert Austin was born 10 May 1884 in Greene County, Iowa. Harry married Martha Pearl Petry on 26 September 1909 in Denver, Colorado. Seek more information on Robert and Mary.

206-4. Aaron Austin was born in circa 1768, possibly in Concord, New Hampshire. He married on 25 November 1790 to Judith Eastman of Concord. They had at least three children: William Gage Austin b. 24 April 1792, Betsey Austin b. 10 October 1793, and Sarah Austin b. 12 March 1794. There was another Aaron Austin who died in Concord on 14 March 1793 - perhaps the father or a son of Aaron? Another unnamed child of Aaron Austin died in 1802 in Concord. Aaron himself died in 1815 in Concord, and his widow Judith was appointed administrator of his estate (from South Paris, Oxford County, Maine probate court records). Seek ancestry of Aaron Austin, and any additional information on his family and descendants.

THE DESCENDANTS OF
JOHN AUSTIN AND ANN BADEN
OF ALBEMARLE COUNTY, VIRGINIA

by Bert Addis Austin

[CONTINUED FROM PAGE 174]

SIXTH GENERATION

J332-31. THEODORE[6] AUSTIN (*George A.,[5] Isaac Bill,[4] John L.,[3] Jonas R.,[2] John[1]*) was born 19 June 1888 in Casey County, Kentucky. He was married in Casey County on 31 March 1910 to Ellen Toms, the daughter of John C. Toms and Elizabeth French. Theodore was known as 'Theo' and was a Casey County merchant all his life. He also worked as a blacksmith, and when the local blacksmith was behind in his work, Theo would shoe horses for him. His store still stands across the road from his home at Labascus, Casey County. Theodore went every year to clean the graves of his grandparents. This gravesite is on the Forrest Austin farm in the woods, Dunnville, Casey County. I went with him in the Spring of 1970. Theodore died 22 April 1973 age 84 in Somerset, Pulaski County, Kentucky and is buried in Thomastown Cemetery, located in Dunnville. Ellen was still living in 1985. They had one child, recorded in Casey County:

    J332-311.   ISAIAH LEWIS, *b. 28 March 1918* +

J332-36. FORREST EGBERT[6] AUSTIN (*George A.,[5] Isaac Bill,[4] John L.,[3] Jonas R.,[2] John[1]*) was born 30 January 1922 in Dunnville, Casey County, Kentucky. He was married in New Wilmington, Pennsylvania, on 31 July 1943 to Mary Ellen Williamson. Mary, the daughter of Archibald Clark Williamson and Hannah Elizabeth Ewers, was born on 3 May 1923 in Bremen, Ohio. When Forrest entered the Army in World War II, they misspelled 'Egbert' with an 'A' and he now goes by 'Forrest A. Austin'. Forrest owns and resides on the farm of his grandfather J332 Isaac Bill Austin, in Dunnville. Oil was discovered on this farm in 1980 and was still pumping in 1985. His sister J332-35 Mossie (Austin) Reckner lives across the road from Forrest. Forrest, a great coon hunter, is known country wide as 'Buck Austin the Coon Hunter'. Forrest and Mary were both still living in 1985. They have two children:

    J332-361.   HAROLD EUGENE, *b. 3 August 1944 in Sharon, Pennsylvania. He m. on 12 February 1967 to Judy Gale Hagy. Harold has a Country Band and is a Preacher in the Christian Church, lives on farm with parents.*

    J332-362.   SHIRLEY, *b. 24 July 1946 in Boyle County, Kentucky. She m. Charles Wayne Sims, resided in Lexington, Kentucky.*

Robert L. Austin in April 1978

J333-21. ROBERT L.[6] AUSTIN (*George Jefferson,[5] Nicodemus (Nicholas),[4] John L.,[3] Jonas R.,[2] John[1]*) was born 20 February 1902 in Mt. Salem, Lincoln County, Kentucky, in the house built by George Jefferson Austin on land given to him by his uncle and father-in-law, Joshua L. Bradshaw (husband of J335 Sarah Austin). He was first married in February 1930 to Zella Warren in Hammond, Indiana. Zella died in July 1931, and is buried in Bethany, Illinois. Robert married a second time, in New Salem, Lincoln County, on 21 April 1935 to Helen Short Baker. Helen, the daughter of Jesse and Edith F. (Short) Baker, was born on 29 June 1915 in Middleburg, Casey County, Kentucky. Robert was a brakeman on the railroad, and he lost a leg in a 1932 railroad accident in Chicago, Illinois. Robert and Helen were living in Union City, California, on 14 March 1984. Robert had one child by his first wife Zella, and two by his second wife Helen:

    J333-211.   ROBERT LYNN, *b. 5 April 1931, d. circa 1975 Illinois*

    J333-212.   DONNA S., *born on 17 November 1937 in Kentucky* +

    J333-213.   NONA L., *b. 15 December 1939 in Kentucky*

J333-22. BERTMAN (BERT)[6] AUSTIN (*George Jefferson,[5] Nicodemus (Nicholas),[4] John L.,[3] Jonas R.,[2] John[1]*) was born 23 March 1904 in Mt. Salem, Lincoln County, Kentucky. He was married in Covington, Kentucky on 1 December 1925 to Eursla McAninch. Eursla, the daughter of Evert and Roshia (Morgan) McAninch, was born on 24

Bertman Austin in 1973.

Mary Austin and husband Oscar J. Griffin

March 1909 in Poplar Hill, Casey County, Kentucky. 'Bert' was a member of the Baptist Church in Middleburg, Casey County, while Eursla belonged to the Christian Church in Rich Hill, Casey County. Eursla died on 11 December 1957, in Cincinnati, Ohio, and is buried in Memorial Gardens, Mt. Healthy, Ohio. Bertman is shown above in a 1973 photograph taken in Los Angeles, California. He died on 3 April 1978 in Los Angeles, and he is buried there. Bert and Eursla's first child was born in Casey County, the others were born in Cincinnati, Ohio. Their eldest son Bert Addis served in the Air Force, the youngest David Lee served in the Marines. Indeed, with the exception of Robert, all of the boys have served in the military.

     J333-221.   BERT ADDIS, *born 11 December 1926* +

     J333-222.   JUNIOR, *b. 11 April 1928, d. 27 April 1928*

     J333-223.   ELNORE, *b. 11 February 1929, d. 13 February 1929*

     J333-224.   RUSSELL C., *born 16 April 1931* +

     J333-225.   DOROTHY MAE, *b. 3 November 1935* +

     J333-226.   ROBERT EUGENE, *b. 4 June 1937* +

     J333-227.   DELORES ANN, *b. 12 September 1939* +

     J333-228.   HAROLD J., *b. 2 February 1942* +

     J333-229.   DAVID LEE, *b. 21 July 1949* +

J333-34. MARY[6] AUSTIN (*William Clarence,*[5] *Nichodemus,*[4] *John L.,*[3] *Jonas R.,*[2] *John*[1]) was born on 22 December 1909 in Lincoln County, Kentucky. She was married four days before her 14th birthday, in Lincoln County on 18 December 1923, to Oscar J. Griffin, age 19 (first marriage for both). Oscar, the son of James Marion and Lee (—) Griffin, was born on 30 March 1904 in Woodford County, Kentucky. Mary and Oscar are pictured above. Their family records were burned in a house fire. I spoke with Mary in 1978 in Hustonville, Lincoln County, but unfortunately her memory was not the best. Mary and Oscar had eleven GRIFFIN CHILDREN: CLARA B. b.1924, PATSY R. b.1926, JAMES CLARENCE b.1927, CHARLES LEE b.1928, CHESTER VERNON b.1929, EDWARD b.1930, LUCILLE E. b.1932, PAUL WILBURN b.1933, ALEENE MAE b.1939, BILLY REEDY b.1941, ARTHUR b.1944.

J333-35. MARTHA[6] AUSTIN (*William Clarence,*[5] *Nichodemus,*[4] *John L.,*[3] *Jonas R.,*[2] *John*[1]) was born on 4 July 1912 in Lincoln County, Kentucky. She was married at age 17, in Lincoln County on 23 August 1929, to Thelmer Coffman of Lincoln County, age 21 (first marriage for both). Thelmer, the son of Samuel Coffman and Bernida Yocumn, was born on 1908 in Lincoln County. I spoke with Martha Austin Coffman on 14 August 1979 in

Martha Austin and husband Thelmer Coffman

Luther C. Austin (1892-1976)

Hustonville, Kentucky. A photograph of Martha and Thelmer, taken on their 50th Wedding Anniversary in 1979, appears above. They had six children recorded in Lincoln County. COFFMAN CHILDREN: ELIZABETH b.1931, FREDDIE b.1932, ORVILLE KENNETH b.1933, JOHNNIE W. b.1936, EVELYN b.1937, CHARLOTTE b.1938.

J343-31. LUTHER C.[6] AUSTIN (*John Laban,*[5] *John William,*[4] *Isaac,*[3] *Jonas R.,*[2] *John*[1]) was born on 13 November 1892 in Casey County, Kentucky. He taught school in Casey County in 1915-1916, then served in the U.S. Army in World War I. After the war he went to Louisville, where he served as a postal clerk. Luther was married in 1921 to Irma Meek of Jeffersonville, Indiana, and is pictured above as a young man. Luther retired from the Post Office in 1958. He died on 10 June 1976 at age 83 in Jeffersonville. His wife, four children and eight grandchildren survived him. Anyone knowing any names of Luther's descendants, please write to *Austins of America*.

J343-33. ORPHIA LEARIE[6] AUSTIN (*John Laban,*[5] *John William,*[4] *Isaac,*[3] *Jonas R.,*[2] *John*[1]) was born in 1896 in Casey County, Kentucky. She was married in her father's house in Casey County on 4 January 1914 to George Chester Cain of Casey County. George, the son of George

W. Cain and Magnolia Terry, was born on 18 April 1894 in Casey County. Orphia died in November 1964 in Casey County, and is buried in Salem Methodist Church Cemetery in Rheber, Casey County. George lived at the junction of State Highways 70 and 206, Rheber - Salem District in Casey County. He was blind for many years before his death on 20 May 1978 at age 84. He died at the Friendship Nursing Home in Danville, Boyle County, Kentucky. CAIN CHILDREN: FLOSSIE, DOROTHY, ORTHIA, MAGGIE.

J365-33. CARL WILLIAM[6] AUSTIN (*Robert Thomas,*[5] *John H.,*[4] *Robert J.,*[3] *Jonas R.,*[2] *John*[1]) was born 3 March 1905, probably in Missouri. He married on 3 January 1931 to Mildred Miller, who was born 13 August 1910. Children:

J365-331. MAURICE LEON, *b. 25 May 1932, m. Delores Gray b. 1 January 1939. They had son Jeffrey Leon b. 1 August 1959, they divorced in 1966. Maurice m.(2) on 22 March 1968 to Jolene Warren b. 11 November —, adopting her daughter Michelle b. 13 July 1960.*

J365-332. LELA SUE, *b. 2 November 1934, unmarried before July 1971*

J365-333. JEAN, *b. 11 March 1936, m.(1) Dennis Burke. They divorced, she m.(2) on 3 August 1968 to John McIntosh, who adopted her son Scott Burke b.1965. Steven John McIntosh was b.1970.*

J3B3-41. GEORGE NICOLO[6] AUSTIN (*George Benjamin,[5] Henry Shelton,[4] Joseph Harrison,[3] Jonas R.,[2] John[1]*) was born on 2 June 1919 in Canton, Oklahoma. He was educated largely in Norman, Oklahoma, and was married there on 12 May 1941 to Mary Annyce Briscoe of Hollis, Oklahoma. He saw service in World War II, and received an M.D. degree in 1950. They owned property in Nashville TN, Columbia MO, Baltimore MD, Thermopolis WY, Cody WY, Lansing MI, East Lansing MI, Flint MI, and Montgomery AL. For more information on this family, see George's article which starts on page 187 of *Austins of America*. Their first child was born in Eagle Pass, Texas. The next two children were born in Oklahoma City, Oklahoma. Their last child was born in Baltimore, Maryland:

J3B3-411. GEORGE LYNN, *b. 19 August 1944* +
J3B3-412. JOHN ANTHONY, *b. 1 November 1946* +
J3B3-413. ROBERT ALAN, *b. 18 August 1949* +
J3B3-414. SHARON ANNYCE, *b. 17 March 1953* +

J3E5-23. CECIL JOSEPH[6] AUSTIN (*William Clarence,[5] Archibald,[4] George Washington,[3] Jonas R.,[2] John[1]*) was born 1 August 1912 in Lincoln County, Kentucky. He was first married to Essie —, who was born on 1918. Essie died in 1941, and is buried in McKinney Cemetery, Lincoln County. Cecil was age 35 when he married a second time, in Casey County on 4 October 1947, to Genevieve Estes age 24 of Lincoln County. It was the first marriage for Genevieve, who was born in Lincoln County, the daughter of Emmett Estes and Monie Tinsley. Cecil was a farmer, residing in Lincoln County at the time of his second marriage.

J3E5-31. ALMA[6] AUSTIN (*Henry Jason,[5] Archibald,[4] George Washington,[3] Jonas R.,[2] John[1]*) was born on 27 June 1914 in Lincoln County, Kentucky. She was married at age 16, on 24 September 1930, to Jettie Tellious McWhorter, age 19. Jettie, the son of Floyd O. McWhorter and Daisy Lyons, was born on 22 March 1911 in Lincoln County. Alma and Jettie had eight McWHORTER CHILDREN: RONALD HAROLD b.1931, ANNA LEE b.1933, BONNIE DARLENE b.1935, WILLIAM E. b.1936 JACKIE LLOYD b.1939, DONNA MAY b.1943, BARBARA ANN b.1944.

J3E5-32. ARNOLD[6] AUSTIN (*Henry Jason,[5] Archibald,[4] George Washington,[3] Jonas R.,[2] John[1]*) was born on 13 January 1916 in Lincoln County, Kentucky. He was first married to Hazel Sims, the daughter of Oliver Sims and Naomi Delk, who was born circa 1922 in Lincoln County. They divorced, and Hazel Austin, resident of Hustonville, remarried in Casey County on 7 July 1959 to Tommy Privatt of McKinney. Arnold also remarried, to Myrtle Tinsley. Only one child, by his first wife, is known to me:

J3E5-321. KAY NORA, *b. circa 1947, m. on 21 September 1963 in Rockcastle County, Kentucky to Bobby R. Means age 18. Bobby, the son of Julius Means and Stella Martin, was born in Lincoln County. It was the first marriage for both.*

J3E5-34. GLENN ROBERT[6] AUSTIN (*Henry Jason,[5] Archibald,[4] George Washington,[3] Jonas R.,[2] John[1]*) was born on 5 December 1920 in New Salem, Lincoln County, Kentucky. He was married on 5 December 1946 to Betty Butt. Betty, the daughter of N. E. Butt and Nanny Taylor, was born on 24 September 1919 in Highland, Lincoln County. According to his father's obituary, Glenn and his brother Eugene resided in Indianapolis in 1972. In 1975 Glenn resided on Lakeview Drive in Somerset, Pulaski County, Kentucky. Glenn and Betty had one child, born in Highland:

J3E5-341. GLENDA, *born 13 November 1947, died the same day.*

J3E5-35. EDITH[6] AUSTIN (*Henry Jason,[5] Archibald,[4] George Washington,[3] Jonas R.,[2] John[1]*) was born on 11 September 1923 in Lincoln County, Kentucky. She was married in Lincoln County on 23 December 1939 to Carlos Bastin of McKinney, Lincoln County. Carlos, the son of James Bastin and Lula Reed, was born on 6 August 1920 in Lincoln County. Their children were all born in Lincoln County. Edith and Carlos were still residing in McKinney in September 1974. BASTIN CHILDREN: NELLIE b.1941, PENNIE b.1944, VEDA b.1947, MICHAEL b.1950.

J3E5-36. ORVILLE[6] AUSTIN (*Henry Jason,[5] Archibald,[4] George Washington,[3] Jonas R.,[2] John[1]*) was born on 15 August 1925 in Lincoln County, Kentucky. He graduated from McKinney High School, and served with the U.S. Army in World War II, and was married to Dorothy Cooper. He was a member of Indian Hills Christian Church in which he served as an elder, a song leader, and a Sunday School teacher. He also served on the church board, of which he was a past chairman. Orville was also a member of the Masonic Lodge at McKinney, and a member of the new suburban Kiwanis Club of Danville, and of the Southern Lads Quartet. Orville appears in the photograph on page 211. A sub-station foreman for the Kentucky Utilities Company, Orville sustained severe burns above the waist on Monday, 23 October 1967, while working on an oil circuit-breaker in the Campbellsville sub-station. Orville died of his injuries the following day, on 24 October 1967 at age 42 at the University of Kentucky Medical Center in Lexington, Fayette County, Kentucky. He is buried in Buffalo Springs Cemetery, Lincoln County. One child is known to have survived Orville:

[CONTINUED NEXT ISSUE]

Orville Austin (1925-1967)

J3E5-361.   CLYDE COOPER, *still living at home at the time of his father's death.*

J3E5-37. ARCHIBALD KENNETH[6] AUSTIN (*Henry Jason,[5] Archibald,[4] George Washington,[3] Jonas R.,[2] John[1]*) was born 23 April 1931 in Lincoln County, Kentucky. He was married in Lincoln County on 14 November 1952 to Donna Jean Hacker. Donna, the daughter of Clarence and Marion (Roe) Hacker, was born on 12 July 1936 in Cass County, Illinois. In 1972 they were residing in Mount Salem, Lincoln County. Their children are recorded in Lincoln County:

J3E5-371.   MARILYN, *b. 23 December 1953, m. Merrill Smith*
J3E5-372.   SUSAN, *b. 8 July 1955, m. Rickey Elmore*
J3E5-373.   STEPHEN, *b. 1 August 1962*

J3E5-38. HENRY JASON[6] AUSTIN, JR. (*Henry Jason,[5] Archibald,[4] George Washington,[3] Jonas R.,[2] John[1]*) was born 12 January 1933 in New Salem, Lincoln County, Kentucky. He was first married to Betty Coffman, by whom he had two children. He married a second time on 20 January 1967 to Sandra Amon of Lancaster, Kentucky. Sandra, born 8 January 1945 the daughter of Robert and Rosella (Chadwell) Amon, was previously married to Ralph Thomas Ray. In 1972 the family lived in Stanford,

Lincoln County. On 14 March 1972, while working as a Combinationman for the General Telephone Company of Liberty, Kentucky, Jason was installing a telephone when a two-year-old child's mother ran from the house crying for help. Jason found the child had stopped breathing and immediately administered artificial respiration. After a short time, she began to breath and cough, causing a large amount of phlegm that had blocked her respiratory passage to become dislodged. In June 1974 "Emanuel" Jason Austin, Jr., by then promoted to switchman for the General Telephone, was presented the company's LaCroix Bronze Medal for having saved the child's life. Jason still resided in Stanford in 1975. His first two children were born in Lincoln County, the third in Garrard County, Kentucky:

J3E5-381.   CATHY, *b. 9 December 1952*
J3E5-382.   MARLON, *b. 17 January 1953*
J3E5-383.   AARON LEE, *b. 5 July 1969*

J3E5-3B. SHIRLEY[6] AUSTIN (*Henry Jason,[5] Archibald,[4] George Washington,[3] Jonas R.,[2] John[1]*) was born 24 April 1939 in Lincoln County, Kentucky. She was married in Jellico, Tennessee, on 27 December 1958 to Ralph Freeman Maples. Ralph, the son of James and Ella (Hall) Maples, was born on 5 July 1937 in Casey County, Kentucky. At least in 1972 and 1974, Shirley was residing on Route 1, Hustonville, Lincoln County. Her first two children are recorded in Boyle County, Kentucky, the third in Lincoln County. MAPLES CHILDREN: DANNY LYNN 1959, DEBORAH RENE 1963, FREEMAN WAYNE 1966.

J3E6-E1. ROBERT OWEN[6] AUSTIN (*Elmer,[5] George Washington,[4,3] Jonas R.,[2] John[1]*) was born 6 April 1943 in Greenwood, Indiana. He was married in Casey County, Kentucky on 22 June 1963 to Shirley Randolph. Shirley, the daughter of Henry Horace and Emogene (Chaffen) Randolph, was born on 27 August 1945 in Casey County. In 1976 Robert owned and operated a Garage in Grove Ridge, Casey County. They were residing in Kings Mountain in 1983. They had five children:

J3E6-E11.   MICHAEL WAYNE, *b. 10 October 1964 in Franklin, Indiana. He was in college in 1985.*
J3E6-E12.   ROBIN RENE, *b. 20 April 1967 in Franklin. She was active in the Casey Co. High School Band, and received United States Achievement Academy awards for mathematics in 1983 and for leadership service in 1984.*
J3E6-E13.   REBECCA ANN, *b. 23 September 1969 in Boyle County, Kentucky. Like her older sister, Becky was active in the Casey County High School Band, serving as both section and squad leaders for flutes.*
J3E6-E14.   MELISSA KAY, *b. in Boyle County. She was crowned Princess at the Middleburg Fall Festival in 1984.*
J3E6-E15.   DUSTIN DAVID, *b. 21 July 1985 in Danville*

J3E6-E2. RENITA GAIL[6] AUSTIN (*Elmer,[5] George Washington,[4,3] Jonas R.,[2] John[1]*) was born 15 October 1945 in Lincoln County, Kentucky. She was graduated from Casey County High School. Renita married in the Baptist Church in Grove Ridge, Casey County, Kentucky on 5 April 1975 to Stephen Ray Roach of Creston, Casey County, son of Richard and Gertrude Roach. In 1985 they had a boy and a girl, and lived next to Elmer.

SEVENTH GENERATION

J332-311. ISAIAH LEWIS[7] AUSTIN (*Theodore,[6] George A.,[5] Isaac Bill,[4] John L.,[3] Jonas R.,[2] John[1]*) was born 28 March 1918 in Casey County, Kentucky. He was married in Casey County on 25 March 1939 to Imogene Russell. Imogene, the daughter of John H. and Ella Beatrice (Dick) Russell, was born on 4 February 1920 in Casey County. Isaiah has owned a grocery store in Liberty or Casey County all his life. Their two children are recorded in Boyle County, Kentucky:

J332-3111. DONALD LEWIS, *b. 26 March 1949, m. Linda Lou Ellis. He worked for Weddle & LaFavers Chevrolet and was residing in Liberty, Casey County in 1985.*

J332-3112. ROGER LLOYD, *b. 25 April 1954, m. in June 1975 to Donna Sayers, daughter of Arthur and Ina Sayers of Mintonville. Donna completed a two-year course to become a Medical Laboratory Technician. A daughter Sarah Elizabeth was b. 22 June 1985.*

J333-212. DONNA SUE[7] AUSTIN (*Robert L.,[6] George Jefferson,[5] Nicodemus (Nicholas),[4] John L.,[3] Jonas R.,[2] John[1]*) was born 11 November 1937 in Cincinnati, Ohio. Her son Donald was born in San Francisco. She married on 17 January 1954 to James Allen Waggoner, son of Luther Waggoner, who was born on 24 January 1930 in Jonesville, North Carolina. Their first two children were born in North Carolina, the third in San Francisco. Donna married again on 23 August 1960 to Laban Lee Cox who was born on 24 September 1928. Their son Timothy was born in Bishop, California. Laban Cox adopted Donna's first four children in 1975 in Hayward, California. From Donna Cox on 5 March 1985 in Union City, California, I learned her first four children are now married, and Don Cox is a Minister. CHILDREN: DONALD ANTHONY BLANCHARD 1953, JOHN ALLEN WAGGONER 1954, THERESA LYNN WAGGONER 1955, SHERYLE ANN WAGGONER 1957, AND TIMOTHY EDWARD COX 1960.

J333-221. BERT ADDIS[7] AUSTIN (*Bertman,[6] George Jefferson,[5] Nicodemus (Nicholas),[4] John L.,[3] Jonas R.,[2] John[1]*) was born 11 December 1926 in Poplar Hill, Casey County, Kentucky. He was married in Richmond, Indiana on

5 February 1955 to Fern Joan Hagemeyer. Fern, the daughter of Louis and Doris (Landenwich) Hagemeyer, was born on 7 April 1929 in Cincinnati, Ohio. Bert retired from the Air Force, and later served as a policeman. Patrolman Bert Austin appears in the photograph on the next page in front of City Hall in Liberty, Casey County, in November 1974. Fern was a Registered Nurse, and played softball for the 'Dales Angels' team sponsored by the Casey County Hospital in 1979. Bert has been researching Austin genealogies for many years. In 1980 he took over the Casey County Bookmobile, and in 1984 he and Fern were living in Queen Creek, Arizona. Bert joined *Austins of America* as an Associate Editor in 1984 and has been sharing his wealth of Austin information since that time.

J333-2211. JEFFERY LOUIS, *b. 13 December 1955 Arizona; resides in Phoenix, Arizona; unmarried.*

J333-2212. REBECCA, *b. 11 July 1957 Arizona, m. Michael Ellison who was killed in a house fire on 3 February 1980 in Mt. Salem, Lincoln County, Kentucky; Rebecca resides in Mt. Salem with their only child, Amey Lynn Ellison.*

J333-2213. DANIEL J., *b. 13 June 1959 Bermuda; m. Sheila Compton. In 1984 he was a Sonar Operator on a nuclear submarine operating out of Charleston, South Carolina.*

J333-2214. BRADLEY, *b. 14 April 1961 California, m. Carolyn Shell; adopted child: Chris Austin; reside in Liberty, Casey County.*

J333-2215. JOEL, *b. 18 July 1963 California, m. Theresa Durham, daughter of Linville C. and Mildred I. Durham of Yosemite, Casey County; one child: Morgan Austin; Joel and Theresa were residing in Yosemite in May 1984 when Army Private Joel Austin completed basic training at Fort Knox.*

J333-224. RUSSELL C.[7] AUSTIN (*Bertman,[6] George Jefferson,[5] Nicodemus (Nicholas),[4] John L.,[3] Jonas R.,[2] John[1]*) was born 16 April 1931 in Cincinnati, Ohio. He was married in Baltimore, Maryland, to Margaret Louise Barabas, born 25 May 1933 in John Hopkins Hospital, Baltimore. Margaret is the daughter of Ida Shapiro and stepfather Jack Caroll. Their first child was born in Maryland, the next four were born in Cincinnati, and the last two were born in California:

J333-2241. RUSSELL EDWARD, *b. 20 June 1955*

J333-2242. PATRICIA ANN, *b. 29 December 1956*

J333-2243. PHYLLIS KAYE, *b. 1 March 1958*

J333-2244. MARK STEVEN, *b. 22 June 1959*

J333-2245. JEFFERSON BURT, *b. 8 September 1961*

J333-2246. WAYNE MORRIS, *b. 8 December 1962*

J333-2247. LINDA CATHLEEN, *b. 16 March 1967*

Patrolman Bert Austin, Sergeant David A. Price, Patrolman Danny V. Black, Lt. George W. Wethington, Col. Larry F. Bowmer, Dispatcher Perry Cranston, and Patrolman Larry West in front of City Hall, Liberty, Casey County, Kentucky in November 1974.
— *photograph by Fred Burkhard, Editor, Casey County News*

J333-225. DOROTHY MAE[7] AUSTIN (*Bertman,*[6] *George Jefferson,*[5] *Nicodemus (Nicholas),*[4] *John L.,*[3] *Jonas R.,*[2] *John*[1]) was born 3 December 1935 in Cincinnati, Ohio. She was married first to Charles A. Boker, and second to Donald Lee Nash. Donald, the son of Edward Arthur and Mary Kathleen (Meadows) Nash, was born on 25 September 1929 in New Port, Kentucky. Donald had one child by a previous marriage to Ora Wade. Children were born in Cincinnati, except Danielle b. in West Covina, California: RICHARD LEE NASH 1947, CARON SUE BOKER 1952, REDINA MARIA BOKER 1953, CHARLENE BOKER 1954, SHEILA FAITH BOKER 1955, RICHARD DALE BOKER 1958, DANIELLE RENE NASH 1968.

J333-226. ROBERT EUGENE[7] AUSTIN (*Bertman,*[6] *George Jefferson,*[5] *Nicodemus (Nicholas),*[4] *John L.,*[3] *Jonas R.,*[2] *John*[1]) was born 4 June 1937 in Cincinnati. He was married in Butler County, Ohio on 4 November 1960 to Freda May Johnson. Freda, the daughter of Lester and Rosa Lee (Phipps) Johnson, was born on 26 June 1940 in Gray, Kentucky. The family was living in Butler County, Ohio, in 1984.

    J333-2261. ROBERT EUGENE, *b. 1 July 1961*
    J333-2262. MARK ALLEN, *b. 16 February 1965*

J333-227. DOLORES ANN[7] AUSTIN (*Bertman,*[6] *George Jefferson,*[5] *Nicodemus (Nicholas),*[4] *John L.,*[3] *Jonas R.,*[2] *John*[1]) was born 12 September 1939 in Cincinnati, Ohio. She was married in Cincinnati on 18 April 1959 to Angelo Florimonte. Angelo, the son of Joseph Michael & Rose (Minilla) Florimonte, was born on 6 May 1930 in Cincinnati. All their children were born in Cincinnati, where Angelo & Dolores own a flower shop. FLORIMONTE CHILDREN: ANGELA JEAN 1961, JAMES ALAN 1963, JEFFERY MICHAEL 1969, KEITH RYAN & KEVIN GERARD 1971 [twins died crib deaths five days apart at age 7 weeks in 1972], JONATHAN JOSEPH 1973, JEREMY SCOT 1974, JOSHUA PHILIP 1977.

J333-228. HAROLD JEFFREY[7] AUSTIN (*Bertman,*[6] *George Jefferson,*[5] *Nicodemus (Nicholas),*[4] *John L.,*[3] *Jonas R.,*[2] *John*[1]) was born 2 February 1942 in Cincinnati, Ohio. Harold served in the U.S. Army from 1959 to 1962. He married in Loveland, Ohio on 22 July 1967 to Peggy Carpenter, the daughter of Ova B. and Ida Gertrude (Kemplin) Carpenter, born 25 October 1945 in Cincinnati. Their two children were born in Lawrenceburg, Indiana:

    J333-2281. STEPHEN JEFFREY, *b. 17 June 1970*
    J333-2282. MELANIE CASSANDRA, *b. 3 August 1972*

J333-229. DAVID LEE[7] AUSTIN (*Bertman,[6] George Jefferson,[5] Nicodemus (Nicholas),[4] John L.,[3] Jonas R.,[2] John[1]*) was born 21 July 1949 in Cincinnati, Ohio. He was married in Fontana, California on 20 September 1968 to Leslie Joan Sharp. Leslie, the daughter of Jack David and Beverly Jeanne (Johnson) Sharp, was born on 12 August 1949 in Riverside, California. David Lee Austin is a career Marine, who should retire in three or four years. Their children are recorded in California:

> J333-2291. MICHAEL DAVID, *b. 5 Sept. 1969*
> J333-2292. DIANA LEE, *b. 18 January 1971*
> J333-2293. CHRISTINA MARIE, *b. 23 April 1974*

J3B3-411. GEORGE LYNN[7] AUSTIN (*George Nicolo,[6] George Benjamin,[5] Henry Shelton,[4] Joseph Harrison,[3] Jonas R.,[2] John[1]*) was born during W. W. II on 19 August 1944 in Eagle Pass, Texas. A graduate of Johns Hopkins University and the University of Maryland School of Medicine, George in 1985 was engaged in the practice of General Surgery, in Jeanette and Greensburg, Pennsylvania. He married Linda Colette Gitlitz, in Thermopolis, Wyoming on 6 March 1971. They have two daughters:

> J3B3-4111. JULIANNE BETH, *b. 27 March 1976 in Durham, North Carolina*
> J3B3-4112. KRISTINE NICOLE, *b. 8 May 1980 in Richmond, Virginia*

J3B3-412. JOHN ANTHONY[7] AUSTIN (*George Nicolo,[6] George Benjamin,[5] Henry Shelton,[4] Joseph Harrison,[3] Jonas R.,[2] John[1]*) was born in Oklahoma City, Oklahoma on 1 November 1946. Educated in Nashville, Baltimore and Columbia, Missouri, he graduated from the John Hopkins University and from the George Washington University School of Law (*cum laude*). He married Janice Mary Truitt, of Salisbury, Maryland on 12 June 1971. In 1985 he practices Law in Towson and Baltimore, Maryland. They have two sons:

> J3B3-4121. JASON CHRISTOPHER, *b. 3 November 1975*
> J3B3-4122. JORDAN ADAM, *b. 14 November 1977*

J3B3-413. ROBERT ALAN[7] AUSTIN (*George Nicolo,[6] George Benjamin,[5] Henry Shelton,[4] Joseph Harrison,[3] Jonas R.,[2] John[1]*) was born in Oklahoma City, Oklahoma, on 18 August 1949. Educated in Columbia, Missouri and in Baltimore, Maryland he graduated from the University of Maryland in 1971. A career officer in the United States Air Force, he has lived many places including overseas in Thailand and England. In 1985 he lived in Burke, Virginia. He married Carol Diane Lynn, of Baltimore, Maryland on 19 June 1971. They have two children:

> J3B3-4131. CAROLYN ANNYCE, *b. 25 February 1979*
> J3B3-4132. ROBERT DANIEL, *b. 15 November 1981*

J3B3-413. SHARON ANNYCE[7] AUSTIN (*George Nicolo,[6] George Benjamin,[5] Henry Shelton,[4] Joseph Harrison,[3] Jonas R.,[2] John[1]*) was born on 17 March 1953 at the Johns Hopkins Hospital in Baltimore, Maryland. She graduated from the University of Wyoming, in Laramie, Wyoming and received a Masters Degree in Interior Design from the Michigan State University in East Lansing, Michigan. She married Thomas Rudolf Albert Kuester of East Lansing, Michigan on 22 December 1979. This couple lived and taught in the King Feisel University in Saudi Arabia for three years, and lived in 1985 in Alexandria, Virginia. No children.

Acknowledgments and References

The author wishes to express his appreciation to those mentioned below who provided much of the information included in this article. The efforts of Patricia Biebuyck Austin in correlating my raw data and formatting it for this article are also greatly appreciated. Locations are in Kentucky unless otherwise noted: J3, J33 John L. Austin Bible in possession of Robert L. Austin of Union City CA 1984. J3B J3B5 Mrs. Ann Beeler, El Paso TX 1977. J39 Edith Austin Moore, Maryland 1974. J3 Casey Co. Deeds, 1830 & 1840 Casey Co. Census, Wills Book 1 p.427,477 Casey Co. J5 Mrs. Mable V. Shanklin, Crawfordsville IN 1973. J3 Land Office Book 17 p.364 Secretary of State Office, Frankfort. J5 Deed Book G p.353 Garrard Co. J6 Deed Books of Garrard Co. J31 Mortality Schedules of Casey Co. J312 Vital Statistics Casey Co. J31 Deed Book B p.377, Russell Co. J31 1850 & 1860 Census Casey Co. J32 Court Order Book 1 Casey Co. J32 Miss Anna J. Foley, Greensburg IN 1976. J36 *History of Gentry Co. Missouri.* J38 Wills Book 2 p.601 Court House, Jamestown, Russell Co. J3B Deed Book H p.254 Wayne Co. J3B Mrs. R. A. Lewis's Bible record of Henry Austin of Albilene TX, 1850 Texas Census, 1880 Casey Co. Census. J3B J3B3 J3B3-4 George B. Austin of Oklahoma City OK 1972. J3E George Washington Austin Bible. J3E J3E5 J3E6 J3E5-1,2 William Clarence Austin 1970. J3E Archibald Austin Bible. J3E J3E3 J3E3-4 Mrs. Emma Austin Price, Oklahoma City 1974. J332 Mr. Alvin Owens, Mrs. Mollie Austin Owens, Mrs. Patrie Coffey Butcher, John L. Austin Bible, Mrs. Mossie Austin Reckner, Mr. Ernest Austin, 1860-1880 Census & Marriage Records Casey Co. J332 J332-3,7,9 J332-36 Forrest Austin 1974. J333 File No. SC623-711 National Archives, Washington. J343 U. S. Special Schedule 1890. J343 Elmer Hatfield, grandson of George W. Hatfield & John W. Austin's Gravestone. J34A letter from Randal R. Campbell 1985. J365-3 J36B J365-31 J365-32,33,34 John W. Austin of Vista CA 1973. J386 1880 Census Casey Co. J38 J387 Lewis M. Owens of Nashville, TN 1970. J387 Faubush Cem. east of Russell Springs on Hwy 80 Russell Co. 1973. J387 Font Hill Cem. on Goose Creek Hill, Hwy 80 Russell Co. 1979. J3B5 *Cross Plains Review* newspaper of Cross Plains, TX, 15 March 1912 and 8 December 1933. J3B6 J3B6-1 Robert E. Austin, Los Angeles 1972. J3E5 J3E5-2 Pina Fletcher Austin 1970. J3E5 Henry Jason Austin 1970. J3E5 Eugene Austin. J3E5 Estes Cem. next to William Clarence Austin farm on New Salem Road, Lincoln Co. 1970. J3E6 Elmer Austin, Naomi Napier Austin, Everett & Elcie Austin, Old issues of *Casey Co. News*, Sarah Bastin Morgan, *Carman and Bastin Histories* by Dr. Ragel. J332-1,9 Vital Stat. Casey Co. J315 J332-2,3 1880 Census Casey Co. J332-2 Thomastown Cem. south of Dunnville, Casey Co. 1969. J332-3 Theodore Austin 1970. J332-3,4,7,9 J332-37 J332-46 Mossie Austin 1975. J332-3 Ernest K. Austin 1975. J332-5 *Casey Co. News* 1980. J332-6 *Casey Co. News* 15 July 1966. J332-9 Mary Martha Austin Owens, Jerald Austin, Lager TN. J332-B Alvin Owens 1972, Bessie William Owens Utterback 1973, Fannie Belle Owens Jeffries 1966, Bernetta Owens Atwood 1974. J332-D J332-34 J343-31 Co. Court Clerks Office, Liberty. J333-3,4 Martha Austin Coffman 1980. J333-5 Old Church Cem. Mt. Salem, Lincoln Co. 1971. J343-3 Wm. Pierce 1980. J3E5-1 Edsil Fletcher, Crab Orchard 1970.

THE MEMOIRS AND FAMILY OF
HENRY SHELTON AUSTIN
OF KANSAS AND OKLAHOMA

by George Nicolo Austin

[CONTINUED FROM PAGE 195]

weekly newspaper that Marsh Murdock had started in Wichita. We used to sit and swap hopes and fears with Murdock. We remember him as a very pleasant gentleman of unbounding faith in the 'Nile of America' as he called the Arkansas River. Yes, Cottonwood is gone with very few of the old gang left to drop a tear, but he was one of the boys when we were on the stage of action. The notice says he was a buffalo hunter, but for all the actors on that stage, I say that he was much more. Davis, like most of us was not a success at gaining wealth or fame, but was always above alms, and never was known to show the white flag in any battle of life. Like all the others, he played the last act in a high and noble manner. May his soul rest in peace."

To my knowledge Henry did not suffer from any serious systemic diseases. I think that Dr. Eva took him to one of her colleagues for a check-up from time to time, but I cannot recall any period of illness, requiring confinement to bed. He wore glasses, his hearing was good, and he was always alert mentally. Henry Shelton Austin died in his sleep on 18 July 1935 at age 87 in Oklahoma City.

Grandma's health was good, except for the life-long skin problem of eczema. This took the form of red, itchy areas around the fingers and hands, and sometimes the forearms. Her son George Benjamin Austin had a similar problem most of his life. Many treatments were tried over the years, but there was never any cure. Dietary control of certain allergens, namely wheat, eggs, and milk seemed to be the most effective management. I cannot recall any period of illness requiring confinement to bed. Grandma died in her sleep at age 84 in May 1942 in Oklahoma City.

William Rose Austin

In his memoirs Henry Shelton Austin made only a brief reference to his younger brother J3B6 William Rose Austin [see page 167]. I recall a story about Bill Austin, however, that was told to me by Grandma (Sylvia) Austin and should be included here. Bill was born in Casey County, Kentucky in 1855 and was only thirteen years old when Henry and Emerson left home to go west. Circa 1881 Bill came west to live with Henry and Sylvia for a few months. He was desperately ill, and had come west for his health. He was described as being very pale, very weak and very thin, with no energy or stamina. As I reflect on the symptoms that Grandma described, Bill must have had

either tuberculosis, or a bad heart, possibly from rheumatic fever. He was 26 years old, and at the time of his arrival Henry and Sylvia must have been living in the three room house that Henry described as the house he prepared for his bride. In any case, they gave Bill one room in which he spent most of his time, in bed. He got up for meals, but did not do any work, and did not go anyplace with Henry. Sylvia got his meals and took care of him. I assume that everyone thought Bill would soon get better and would then be able to get a job and get out on his own. However, one morning when Grandma called him for breakfast, there was no response and they discovered that he passed away during the night. I presume that he is buried in the vicinity of Sylvia, Kansas. The exact date of his death is unrecorded, but it was probably in 1880 or 1881.

Louisa Eveline Austin

My Aunt 'Eva'' described in this article was the J3B3-1 Louisa Eveline Austin who was born in 1882 and who married Walter W. Wells [see pages 134, 194-195]. Eva and Walter were both M.D.'s and practiced medicine in Oklahoma City for many years. Eveline died in 1969.

Walter Henry Austin

During summer vacations while attending the University of Oklahoma, both Walter and his younger brother George would return to the Major County area and work in the broomcorn harvest. Walter courted and eventually married Myrtle Willis of Fairview [see page 172]. During the years the family ran the Drug Store in Fairview, Walter and George were active in local civic, and social affairs. Walter later bought a drug store in Canton, Blaine County.

Walter and Myrtle's son Blair contracted polio and was left with a curvature of the spine and a partial paralysis of one arm and shoulder. Dr. Wells and arranged for him to come to Oklahoma City for treatments at the McBride Orthopaedic Clinic, which consisted of applying severe traction to the entire body and then applying a plaster of paris cast. The cast included the entire trunk and the right shoulder and arm to the elbow. The immobilization was such that the elbow was higher than the shoulder. In 1917 or 1918, Walter himself developed serious complications of tuberculosis, from which he had been suffering for several years. He was advised to 'go west' so he sold his drug store in Canton to his younger brother George and by 1919 moved his family to Roswell, New Mexico.

Grace Elizabeth Austin

Grace Elizabeth Austin was born in 1886 in Sylvia, Kansas [see page 134]. She married Joseph Kinch of Depew, Oklahoma. They had no children of their own, but adopted a daughter named Almeda Grace, who married David L. Pfleeger and in 1985 lived in Los Angeles. Grace died in Oklahoma City in the late 1960's.

George Benjamin Austin

As a boy on the family farm near Cleo Springs, George Benjamin Austin got some cactus needles in his eyes when he and his sister Grace were playing in the farm yard. A serious infection developed and George became ill. He was taken to local physicians, but his eyes got worse, and his vision became impaired. There was drainage from his eyes, and they were very sensitive to light. Eventually he came to wear a hood most of the time. How long this lasted is not known, but it is a matter of family record that Henry Shelton was making arrangements to send George to Wichita, or Kansas City to a school for the blind, when he suddenly began to improve. He eventually recovered his sight, but carried scars (probably on the corneas) for the rest of his life, and always required rather thick glasses.

As a young adult, George was average-sized, approximately five foot ten and weighing about 140 pounds. In his old age, George weighed perhaps 160 pounds, but was never 'fat'. His posture was very straight, and he was lean and muscular, but not muscle-bound. His physique was that of a runner rather than a weight-lifter. His hair was firey red or a bright, strawberry-red hair. Despite his red hair, George's complexion was quite fair, somewhat ruddy in the face, but he was not freckled.

George Benjamin Austin (1889-1976)
Julia Leah Shoemaker (1888-1972)

George dated Julia Leah Shoemaker for nearly seven years before they married on 18 April 1915. George and Julia are shown on the next page [and their family is discussed on page 172]. Julia was a local school teacher, born and raised near Wichita, Kansas, and in Ames, Oklahoma. Circa 1918 George bought the drug store in Canton from his older brother Walter and moved from Longdale to Canton. George subsequently sold the Canton drug store and moved back to Longdale where he and his father Henry Shelton operated the Austin Drug Company for about eight years.

Canton and Longdale were in Blaine County. Longdale was prosperous community of 400-500 people surrounded by a diversified farming area. There were many Indians in the area. A Government Indian School was in operation at Cantonment, between Canton and Longdale. Many Indian families lived in houses and teepees on abandoned land in and around Longdale. There were Indian customers in the drug store every day and the local school had an Indian enrollment of about ten per cent. These Indians were Cheyennes.

George was not only the principle owner and operator of the drug store, he was the only Pharmacist in town. In addition, the Longdale Post Office was located in the back of the drug store and George was the Postmaster. The area was serviced by three rural mail carriers. Agricultural products grown locally, were shipped out of Longdale as

freight, on the Orient Railroad. These products were processed through the Post Office (Freight Office) and the railroad station. George was able to augment his income by encouraging farmers to ship their eggs, chickens, corn, fruit, vegetables, turkeys and milk on the railroad.

The years in Longdale were happy ones. George and Julia were active in local civic and social affairs. They were very active in the single local Christian church, teaching Sunday School, entertaining the minister for Sunday dinner, and participating in the annual summer revival meetings. Otherwise they socialized with young couples their own age in the fashion of the day. They entertained in each others homes, played Rook, flinch and Old Maid. They had picnics, made ice cream in the summertime, arranged and participated in box suppers at the high school, pie suppers at the church, and supported the high school basketball team by attending every game. Arranging and carrying out a 'shivaree' was an especially exciting event.

George had a good voice and sang tenor in the local Men's Quartet. He ordered a violin from a mail order house and taught himself to play it. He achieved some degree of skill on the violin, and in later years he and Julia, who played the piano and sang soprano, often performed together. They played the popular music of the day, as well as hymns and seasonal music.

George also acquired several drums, some second-hand and some from mail order houses, and played bass drum in the local marching band. He played both the bass drum and the snare drum (traps) when the band played in concert. For additional money and diversion, he and a local piano player provided 'sound effects' for the silent movies at the theater. After watching the movie two or three times, the piano player could provide suitable background music, and George could provide sound effects with cymbals, wood blocks and drums that added zest to the performance.

George and Julia both took correspondence courses from the University of Oklahoma and from Phillips University (Enid, Oklahoma) during these years in order to "improve themselves." In 1927 George and Julia moved their family to Norman, Oklahoma. The reasons for this move are somewhat nebulous, but seem to be in the realm of seeking a more cultured environment for themselves and their children. To finance the move, it was necessary to sell the Austin Drug Store in Longdale.

In his adult years, he was called simply 'George' or 'Doc' as was the fashion for Pharmacists in those days. George did not work as a Pharmacist in Norman. He sold real estate for a few months, and then purchased a restaurant near the college campus. The resturant was called *The Student Eat Shop* and was located at Asp Avenue. It catered almost entirely to college students. George was

gregarious, with an out-going personality. He had a fine sense of humor and was a great 'kidder,' enjoying a practical joke. He related well to the public at all levels and "never met a stranger." He had joined the Masonic Lodge in Fairview, remaining more or less active in the Masons all of his life. He received a 50-year pin sometime after the age of seventy.

In 1935, aided by some financial assistance from his brother-in-law Dr. W.W. Wells, George purchased The Classen Drug Company, in Oklahoma City. George and Julia operated this independent, privately-owned, suburban drug store, located at the corner of Northwest 27th Street and Classen Boulevard, from 1935 to 1948. During these years and beyond they lived near the store, principally at 1229 N.W. 28th Street, their last permanent address.

After selling the Classen Drug Store in 1948, George went to work as a full-time Pharmacist in 1949 for the Katz Drug Company in downtown Oklahoma City, working there almost ten years before being forced to take mandatory retirement at the age of 70 in 1959. George did vacation-relief work at various drug stores for several months, then went to work three days a week for the Gilliam Prescription Shop in the Medical Arts Building in downtown Oklahoma City. At about age 75, George retired altogether, and did not work at his profession after 1964.

In the 1960's and early 1970's George and Julia did some traveling. They visited Mexico, Cuba, many cities in the western United States, and took many short local trips to see things of interest to senior citizens. They preferred to travel by bus, and very much enjoyed the conversation and camaraderie of a charter bus trip.

Julia developed heart trouble in the late 1960's and after a few years of decreasing activity died in early July 1972 at the age of 84. After the death of his wife, George lived alone in Oklahoma City. In the 1970's he made some trips by air and by bus to Mexico, Michigan, and Wyoming to visit his children and grandchildren. During the 1970's he experienced recurring bouts of chest pain and sustained several mild heart attacks. He died of a heart attack on 8 January 1976, in Oklahoma City at the age of 87. He is buried in an 'Austin-Wells-Kinch' family cemetery plot, with his parents, his wife and his two sisters, in the Memorial Park Cemetery in Oklahoma City, Oklahoma.

FOOTNOTE

During the summer of 1933, I was invited to visit the Wells in Oklahoma City for a week or so to type Grandpa's penciled notes and put them in some sort of chronological order. I was 14 years old at the time, and had taken typing in the 9th grade at school. The typewriter was an old Oliver, which had been used in the family drug store many years before. We got started and it was slow going. I was unable to read much of Grandpa's

The author's family - back row: John Anthony Austin, Robert Alan Austin, Diane Lynn Austin, Sharon Austin Kuester, Thomas Rudolph Albert Kuester, George Lynn Austin. Center row: Janice Truitt Austin, the author's wife Annyce Briscoe Austin, George Nicolo Austin, Linda Gitlitz Austin, Kristine Nicole Austin. Front row: Jason Christopher Austin, Jordan Adam Austin, Robert Daniel Austin, Carolyn Annyce Austin, Juliane Beth Austin. Descendants of J3B3 Henry Shelton Austin and J3B3-4 George Benjamin Austin (see *Austins of America* pages 210, 214).

writing, and his notes were very poorly organized. There were countless interruptions, trying to identify dates, places, and sequences in the various stories, all of which had happened over 50 years before. At one point, the Oliver typewriter developed a disabling malfunction. The carriage would not move along as the keys were struck. My cousin Blair Austin and I solved this problem by driving a nail into the window frame, and fastening a piece of elastic tape, which Grandma supplied from her sewing basket, from the nail to the knob on the typewriter carriage. By placing the table and the typewriter at just the right position, we achieved the right amount of tension on the elastic, and the carriage moved along beautifully. Needless to say, Henry's daughter Dr. Eva took an extremely dim view of us

driving a nail into the window frame of her fine house, but in the interest of keeping the project going, we were permitted to continue. I typed twenty or thirty pages that week. It was pretty bad. There were countless strike-overs, hundreds of misspelled words, and a complete lack of punctuation and chronology. From the outset we had made a carbon copy of each sheet. At the end of the week, I believe I took one copy back to Norman with me and left the other with Grandpa. He never did much of anything with it, and after his death I wound up with both copies. These notes have been kept by me, in one place or another, from 1933 until the present, and now Henry Shelton Austin's stories will continue to be preserved for future generations in *Austins of America*.   —*G.N.A.*

QUERIES

219-1. **Rebecca Austin** was born on 18 August 1823 in Arcadia, Wayne Co. New York, married Isaac Farley Vanderbilt. Seek more information on Rebecca's ancestry, and contacts with her descendants.

219-2. **Sarah Austin** married Isaiah Grinnell. He served in the Revolutionary War, in a unit that included cousins of his wife. There is no definite proof that the Isaiah Grinwell of Hancock, Mass. is the same individual who married Sarah Austin, but it is considered correct by the Grinnell Family Association. Isaiah and Sarah Grinnell's children included Amos Grinnell, born circa 1763, who fathered my g-g-g-grandfather Daniel Grinols (1798-1864). Need information on Sarah Austin's ancestors.

219-3. **Rebecca Austin** was born circa 1740-45, and married on 8 August 1758 to William Rumery in Biddeford, York County, Maine. He was born 3 February 1737 in Biddeford and died 21 November 1764 in Biddeford. Children: Rachel bp. 1759, Elizabeth bp. 1761, Dominicus bp. 1763, and William bp. 1765. Rebecca married second William Clark 23 July 1769 in Biddeford. Need Rebecca's parents and siblings.

219-4. **Willis Russell Austin** married Eliza Ann (—). They were from Tennessee, but their Austins were more than likely originally from Virginia. They had a son Willis Russell Austin who resided in Allen and Barren Counties, Kentucky. He married Margaret Katherine 'Maggie' Holder, the daughter of Edward and Cynthian (Whitney) Holder. Need more information on this Austin line.

219-5. **Joseph Austin** born circa 1616, later lived near Doverneck, Strafford N.H. His second marriage was to Sarah Starbuck. They had six children: Thomas, Deborah, Joseph, Mary, Benjamin and Nathaniel. He may have had two brothers, Samuel and Matthew and that they came originally from England. Need the parentage of Joseph, his first marriage, his birthplace.

219-6. **Susanna Austin** and Wyatt Herring married 5 October 1794. This marriage is listed in the Roxbury, Mass Vital Records to 1850, v.2 p.16 & p.203. I have ancestors by the name of Harring/Herring in the Boston area between 1790-1850 and would like to know if this Susanna Austin and husband Wyatt might be relatives.

219-7. **Elizabeth Austin** born circa 1850's married on 4 July 1878 to Clarence Hall, born 4 December 1857. Elizabeth died in the 1890's. Their daughter Nina Elizabeth Hall was born 27 September 1882 in Boyton-ville, N.Y. They apparently had money, lived in very large house in N.Y. state around Troy and Saratoga. This information is from a family Bible. I would like to make connections with my ancestors.

219-8. **John P. Austin** was born in 1809 in New York, his wife Mary (—) was born in 1816 in Virginia. Children: Sarah, Julius, Henrietta (married Ezra Thomas), Orphus, and John. Resided in Kentucky, Meigs County Ohio, Athens County Ohio, and possibly Missouri. Is Caliph Austin the father of John P. Austin? Is Sarah (married Samuel Cullen) a sister?

219-9. **Martha Viannah Austin**, called 'Ann,' was born in Kentucky in 1801. She married Moses Rhea, son of Ezekiel Rhea of White County, Tennessee. They resided in Wayne County TN in 1820, and in the 1840's moved to Marion County, Arkansas. Martha and Moses Rhea reared their niece, after the death of her sister — Austin, my g-g-g-grandmother. She married before 1823 to Thomas J. Macon, probably in Wayne County TN. Court records state he moved from Maury County to Wayne County about 1820. Their daughter Sophronia was born in 1823. Who were their parents?

219-10. **John Austin** and wife Sarah (—) had a daughter Rebecca who married William Boyd on 3 February 1813 in Monongalia County, Virginia, now West Virginia. Seek more information about this family.

219-11. **Nathaniel Austin** and his wife Abigail are buried in Westfield Flats Cemetery, adjoining the Presbyterian Church in Roscoe, NY. Nathaniel's gravestone says he died 28 December 1807 ae. 73y 8m 29d, thus he was b. circa 30 March 1734. Abigail's gravestone says she died 3 March 1813 ae. 66 yrs., thus she was b. circa 1747. Family documents indicate that Nathaniel and Abigail moved from Connecticut, perhaps Montville, to live with their dau. Elizabeth, 1778-1866, wife of Israel Dodge, 1773-1855, at Rockland, NY, circa. 1799. Edith Austin Moore in her *Richard Austin* book attempts to place Nathaniel in the family of Capt. Nathaniel Austin between Gad b. 15 October 1733 and Pheonix b. 4 September 1735, which is obviously incorrect. Also, Capt. Nathaniel's will does not include a Nathaniel among his children. Seek ancestry of both Nathaniel and Abigail Austin.

219-12. **Stephen Austin**, born circa 1769, son of Joseph Austin of Pittsylvania County, Virginia, was possibly the father of Owen Ed Austin, born circa 1803 in Virginia. Need to prove this. They resided across the road from one another in 1840 in Rutherford County, Tennessee, but an Indenture between the two parties mentions no relation.

219-13. **Eliza Ann Austin** was born circa 1800-04, possibly the daughter of Stephen Austin and Rebecca Hankins formerly of Pittsylvania County, Virginia. Eliza married William Wilson Deering/Dearing and they are both buried in Lynch Cemetery in Bedford County, Tennessee. Does anyone have a Deering connection and is Eliza indeed the daughter of Stephen and Rebecca?

QUERIES

220-1. Fanny May Austin was born 19 December 1859 in Wellington, Lorain County, Ohio. In 1887 she married John Poage Evans as his second wife, probably in Fort Wayne, Indiana. She died in Fort Wayne on 28 June 1928. Her death certificate states names of parents unknown but the birthplace of her mother was Maryland. Obituary lists a brother Walter, and a half-brother James Austin of Manila in the Philippines. Need Fanny May's parents.

220-2. Mary Austin was probably born in the 1750's. She married my g-g-g-g-grandfather Asaph Mather about 1770, probably in Lyme, New Loudon County, Connecticut. I have this information from Horace E. Mather's *Lineage of Rev. Richard Mather*, published in 1890. I believe it was in a *Boston Transcript* query that I found reference to the death of Mary Austin Mather on 29 August 1808. I think she died in Schuyler, Herkimer Co., NY. Seek information on Mary Austin's family.

220-3. William Franklin Austin was born circa 1822 and his wife Rachel Madison Austin was born circa 1821, both in England. Their children: Joseph Edgar born 1 May 1857 in Middlesprite, Fulton County, New York; William Sherman born 6 July 1863 in New York and moved to Tomah, Wisconsin; Julia, Cecil; two half sisters Addie Austin, and Nell Austin born 23 October 1868 or 1869. Joseph Edgar Austin married Mary 'Mollie' Elizabeth Adams on 14 June 1903 in North Dakota. They had four children, all born in Wells County, North Dakota: Alice Edna born 15 July 1904, Ada Lee, Ethel Mae, and Robert Edgar. I would like to learn more about this Austin family.

220-4. William Young Austin is believed to have been born on 10 June 1818. I need proof of this date. Harold Steiner's *Some Southern Austins* has William's birthplace as Orange County, North Carolina. William's death date of 14 July 1864 in Pope County, Arkansas, appears on a group sheet from Oliver Austin, but where is this documented? Were there any probate proceedings?

220-5. Bathsheba Austin married to Stephen Allen, probably in New York state prior to 1806. Children: Hannah born 1806, Sarah born 1810 and possibly others. Seek parents and ancestry of Bathsheba.

220-6. Elizabeth Alzena Austin was born on 23 March 1843. I have verified her birthdate from William Jackson's Pension records. I need proof of her birthplace, believed to be Lawrence County, Tennessee. I have William Austin in 1840-50-60 census but I am not sure this is enough. Also seek proof that Elizabeth was the daughter of William and Frances A. (Pollock) Austin. Again she is shown in the census, but it does not show the relationship of the child to the head of the household.

220-7. Mary E. Austin born circa 1835 in Missouri, married Benjamin F. Myers on 10 November 1853. He was born June 1819. Both are buried at Fairview Cemetery, south of Calwood, Missouri. Their eight children were born in Calloway County, Missouri: Missouri Ann 1854, Emily, Lydia 1857, Henry Benjamin 1858, Albert Green 1863, John Morgan 1866, Lewis Logan 1869, Ada V. 1878. Seek parents and ancestry.

220-8. Charles Benjamin Austin was born in 1857, married Phebe V. Sterling in 1880, and died in 1911. Lived in Schuyler County, NY. Seek his ancestry.

220-9. Elihu Austin and Abigail (—) had a son Lyman L. born 1799 who married Pauline Reed in 1817 in Berkshire, Mass. Pauline was born 28 June 1799. Need more information on the ancestors and descendants of Elihu.

220-10. Alice Austin born 15 January 1858 in Alabama, married George Washington Stapp/Stepp 15 July 1877 in Marshall Prairie, Boone County, Arkansas. They had 10 children. George Stapp had a half-brother in Texas. In October 1903, George, Alice, and family started out from Fort Smith, Arkansa, where they were living to Texas. Near Talihina, LeFlore County, Oklahoma, Alice miscarried and died. This was before death registration. Seek parents and ancestry of Alice.

★★★★★★★★★★★★★★★★★★★★★★★★★★★★★★★★

Austins of America is intended to serve present and future genealogists researching Austin family lines. Readers are encouraged to submit queries, genealogical and historical articles for publication. Previously published books, pamphlets or articles containing Austin genealogical data are also sought for reprinting or review.

EDITOR

DR. MICHAEL EDWARD AUSTIN   CONCORD, MA

ASSOCIATE EDITORS

ANTHONY KENT AUSTIN   PROSPECT, KY

BERT ADDIS AUSTIN   QUEEN CREEK, AZ

PATRICIA BIEBUYCK AUSTIN   CONCORD, MA

PAULINE LUCILLE AUSTIN   SAVANNAH, GA

Austins of America is published each February and August by The Austin Print, 23 Allen Farm Lane, Concord, Massachusetts 01742. All correspondence, including subscriptions, articles and responses to queries, should be sent to this address. Subscriptions are $4.50 per year postpaid.

★★★★★★★★★★★★★★★★★★★★★★★★★★★★★★★★

Austins in the Federal Census of 1850

Tennessee

by Sally Austin Day

BEDFORD COUNTY, TN

.... p.467-119

Austin, Harris		46	1804	m	NC
"	, Emily	36	1814	f	"
"	, Eliza	9	1841	f	TN
"	, Emily	4	1846	f	"

.... p.218-15

Austin, Stephen		81	1769	m	VA
"	, Rebecca	70	1780	f	"

BENTON COUNTY, TN

.... p.576-135

Axford, Samuel		46	1804	m	TN
"	, Mary	24	1826	f	"
"	, Sarah	21	1829	f	"
"	, Caroline	18	1832	f	"
"	, Margarette	17	1833	f	"
"	, John	15	1835	m	"
"	, James	13	1837	m	"
"	, Ede	11	1839	f	"
"	, Susan	6	1844	f	"
"	, Jane	4	1846	f	"
"	, Samuel	3	1847	m	"
"	, Mary	1	1849	m	"
Austin, Charles		2	1848	m	"

.... p.311-437

Auston, Rebecca		40	1810	f	VA
"	, John	18	1832	m	TN
"	, Charles	15	1835	m	"
"	, Amanda	12	1838	f	"
"	, William	10	1840	m	"
"	, Mary	8	1842	f	"
"	, James	5	1845	m	"
"	, Sarah	2	1848	f	"

BLEDSOE COUNTY, TN

.... p.703-6

Austin, Bird		26	1824	m	VA
"	, Margaret	25	1825	f	"
"	, Samuel	4	1846	m	TN
"	, James	2	1848	m	"
"	, Nancy	1	1849	f	"

.... p.704-8

Austin, Elijah F.		36	1814	m	TN
"	, Phebe	29	1821	f	"
"	, Rebecca A.	9	1841	f	"
"	, Joseph B.	7	1843	m	"
"	, William J.	4	1846	m	"
"	, Thomas J.	1	1849	m	"
Minton, Catherine		60	1790	f	NC

.... p.718-110

Austin, James		36	1814	m	TN
"	, Susan	32	1818	f	"
"	, Louisa	9	1841	f	"
"	, Thomas	8	1842	m	"
"	, Margaret L.	6	1844	f	"
"	, Jonathan P.	4	1846	m	"
"	, Elvy J.	3	1847	f	"
"	, Orpha	4/12	1850	-	"

.... p.718-111

Austin, Joel B.		26	1824	m	TN
"	, Elvy	26	1824	f	"
"	, Catharine	5	1845	f	"
"	, Ailey	4	1846	f	"
"	, Lorenzey	2	1848	m	"

.... p.716-96

Austin, Joseph		49	1801	m	VA
"	, Elizabeth	36	1814	f	"
"	, Sarah	22	1828	f	"
"	, Elizabeth	22	1828	f	"
"	, Edward	15	1835	m	"
"	, Jonathan M.	13	1837	m	TN
"	, Eliza J.	11	1839	f	"
"	, Nancy E.	9	1841	f	"
"	, Ruth N.	6	1844	f	"
"	, Martha A.	4	1846	f	"
"	, Fanny L.	3/12	1850	f	"

.... p.723-145

Smith, Bird		44	1806	m	TN
"	, Lucinda	40	1810	f	"
"	, Mary	18	1832	f	"
"	, Elizabeth	15	1835	f	"
"	, Martha	12	1838	f	"
"	, Sarah A.	10	1840	f	"
"	, Margaret	8	1842	f	"
Austin, Letty		20	1830	f	"

BLOUNT COUNTY, TN

.... p.215-1593

Austin, William		21	1829	m	TN
"	, Louisa	20	1830	f	"
"	, Robt.	10/12	1849	m	"

COFFEE COUNTY, TN

.... p.54-378

Austen, Lawrence		30	1820	m	GA
"	, Nancy	26	1824	f	KY
"	, David	9	1841	m	"
"	, Green	6	1844	m	"
"	, Nancy	3	1847	f	"
"	, John	1	1849	m	"

.... p.24-159

Austin, John B.		26	1824	m	TN
"	, Mary	22	1828	f	"
"	, Martha	2	1848	f	"
"	, Sarah	6/12	1850	f	"

.... p.23-148

Austin, Samuel G.		32	1818	m	NC
"	, Elizabeth	30	1820	f	"
"	, Mary	8	1842	f	"
"	, James	4	1846	m	"
"	, Charles	11/12	1850	m	"
"	, Isabella	20	1830	f	"

.... p.55-384

Austin, Zachariah		66	1884	m	VA
"	, Martha	64	1886	f	"
"	, Mary	24	1826	f	"
Taylor, Zachariah		3	1847	m	"

DAVIDSON COUNTY, TN

.... p.370-199

Austin, Ephm. T.		27	1823	m	TN
"	, Thompson	20	1830	m	"

.... p.270-820

Austin, Mary A.		53	1797	f	MD
"	, Mary J.	17	1833	f	TN

.... p.184-198

Austin, N.C.		30	1820	m	TN
"	, Eliz. L.	25	1825	f	"
"	, Wm.	4	1846	m	"
"	, Robt.	1	1849	m	"
"	, Lucinda F.	12	1838	f	"
"	, Caroline N.	6	1844	f	"

.... p.362-144

Austin, W.		34	1816	m	TN
"	, Hannah M.	31	1819	f	"
"	, Sarah	10	1840	f	"
"	, Susan	8	1842	f	"
"	, John	7	1843	m	"
"	, Martha	5	1845	f	"
"	, James	3	1847	m	"
"	, Edwin	1	1849	m	"

.... p.341-1379

Austin, Wm.		29	1821	m	TN
"	, Charlotte	21	1829	f	"
"	, Susan	1	1849	f	"

.... p.173-10

Austin, William		26	1824	m	TN
"	, Mary	17	1833	f	"

.... p.371-206

Johnston, Jno.		80	1770	m	PA
"	, Gilford	39	1811	m	TN
"	, John	37	1813	m	"
Austin, Jason M.		35	1815	m	"
"	, Lucinda	32	1818	f	"
"	, William	13	1837	m	"
"	, Jos. C.	9	1841	m	"
"	, John	6	1844	m	"
"	, Baylie P.	1	1849	m	"

.... p.321-1162

Plumber, Theophelius		22	1828	m	TN
Brown, Duncan		20	1830	m	"
Robb, E.J.D.		20	1830	m	"
Austin, Edwin J.		20	1830	m	"

DECATUR COUNTY, TN

.... p.123-33

Austin, P.W.		26	1824	m	TN
"	, Mary H.	19	1831	f	NC
"	, Martha J.	5	1845	f	TN
"	, Lucinda E.	3	1847	f	"
"	, Daniel C.	1	1849	m	"
White, Evan		43	1807	m	NC

DICKSON COUNTY, TN

. . . . p.271-660				
Austin, Abram J.	45	1805	m	KY
" , Martha	35	1815	f	TN
" , Jacob	18	1832	m	"
. . . . p.225-350				
Austin, John	33	1817	m	TN
" , Penelope	26	1824	f	NC
" , Martha	9	1841	f	TN
" , Parallu	8	1842	f	"
" , William	6	1844	m	"
" , Mary	4	1846	f	"
" , Samuel	6/12	1850	m	"
. . . . p.251-532				
Austin, Jno. B.	29	1821	m	TN
" , Fredonia	21	1829	f	"
" , James B.	3	1847	m	"
" , William G.	9/12	1850	m	"
. . . . p.252-535				
Austin, S.D.	59	1791	m	NC
" , Mary	51	1799	f	GA
" , James D.	25	1825	m	TN
" , M.P.	30	1820	f	"
" , Benj. F.	15	1835	m	"
" , H.G.	13	1837	m	"
" , E.C.S.	10	1840	f	"
" , C.V.D.	5	1845	m	"
. . . . p.268-644				
Austin, Samuel	41	1809	m	TN
" , Sarah A.	50	1800	f	"
" , Mary A.	22	1828	f	"
" , William	13	1837	m	"
" , Jonathan	11	1839	m	"
" , Benjamin	10	1840	m	"
" , Angeline	6	1844	f	"
" , Lucinda	4	1846	f	"
. . . . p.307-893				
Austin, Wm.	60	1790	m	NC
" , Dicey	50	1800	f	"
" , Geo. W.	22	1828	m	TN
" , Elizabeth	21	1829	f	"
" , Emeline	19	1831	f	"
" , Jane	16	1834	f	"
" , Calvin F.	14	1836	m	"
" , Newton	11	1839	m	"
" , Paralee	8	1842	f	"
" , Mary Z.	6	1844	f	"
. . . . p.250-524				
Austin, Wm. G.	44	1806	m	NC
" , Mary	45	1805	f	"
" , Nancy	20	1830	f	TN
" , Martha	17	1833	f	"
" , Saml. J.	15	1835	m	"
" , John F.	12	1838	m	"
" , Mary A.	10	1840	f	"
" , Levi C.	7	1843	m	"
" , Wm. D.	5	1845	m	"
" , Lewis C.	1	1849	m	"
Goodwin, Peter	28	1822	m	"
. . . . p.249-577				
Stanfield, Wm. B.	38	1812	m	TN
Austin, Geo.	21	1829	m	"
. . . . p.289-788				
Patterson, Wm.	27	1823	m	TN
" , Chantilly	21	1829	f	"
" , Cournel	1	1849	m	TN
Mathis, Lucy	18	1832	f	"
Austin, Wm. J.	27	1823	m	"

GILES COUNTY, TN

. . . . p.899-627				
Austin, Andrew A.	30	1820	m	TN
" , Eliza	26	1824	f	"
" , Nathaniel S.	7	1843	m	TN
" , John W.	6	1844	m	"
" , Nancy	4	1846	f	"
" , Elizabeth	3/12	1850	f	"
" , Elizabeth	75	1775	f	NC
. . . . p.914-732				
Austin, Sarah H.	63	1787	f	VA
Pitman, Sarah	18	1832	f	SC
Austin, Sarah	8	1842	f	"
Mathews, John H.	59	1791	m	VA
. . . . p.920-769				
Philips, Elizabeth	80	1770	f	VA
Austin, Elizabeth	28	1822	f	TN
" , Mary E.	7	1843	f	"
" , Georgiana T.	4	1846	f	"

GRAINGER COUNTY, TN

. . . . p.58-420				
Auston, Archabald	83	1867	m	VA
" , Rebecca	79	1771	f	"
" , Rebecca	22	1828	f	TN
. . . . p.59-434				
Auston, Mary	42	1808	f	TN
" , Wm.	20	1830	m	"
" , Catherine	17	1833	f	"
" , Joseph	15	1835	m	"
" , Thos.	12	1838	m	"
" , Clarissa	10	1840	f	"
" , Archabald	7	1843	m	"

HAMILTON COUNTY, TN

. . . . p.922-1319				
Austin, James	39	1811	m	TN
" , Martha	32	1818	f	"
" , Thomas	12	1838	m	"
" , Isabel	11	1839	f	"
" , William	8	1842	m	"
" , Elizabeth	4	1846	f	"
" , John	2	1848	m	"
" , George	6/12	1849	m	"
Jones, Mary	65	1785	f	"
. . . . p.854-821				
Austin, Jos. M.	20	1830	m	TN
" , Rebecca	23	1827	f	"
" , Melvina	18	1832	f	"
" , William	15	1835	m	"

HANCOCK COUNTY, TN

. . . . p.59-48				
Auston, James	26	1924	m	VA
" , Loucinda	24	1826	f	NC
" , Mary Jane	5	1845	f	KY
" , Margarett	4	1846	f	TN
. . . . p.30				
Austin, Jessie	25	1825	m	TN
" , Sarah	21	1828	f	"
" , Mary Jane	5	1845	f	"
" , George W.	1	1849	m	"
. . . . p.28				
Austin, Enoc	52	1798	m	TN
" , Nancy	52	1798	f	"
" , Enoc	9	1841	m	"
" , Solomon	7	1843	m	"
" , Amanda	4	1846	f	"

HARDIN COUNTY, TN

. . . . p.599-44				
Austin, A.S.	25	1825	m	TN
" , Martha	21	1829	f	"
" , Vicey	11/12	1849	f	"
. . . . p.414-98				
Austin, Aaron	28	1822	m	NY
" , Dulcina	26	1824	f	KY
Jackson, Alexander	23	1827	m	"
Guthenir, Tennessee	25	1825	f	TN
Austin, Sandy	6	1844	f	"
Mitchell, Elijah	22	1828	m	"
. . . . p.473-58				
Austin, Benjamin	63	1787	m	NC
" , Sarah G.	55	1795	f	"
Brady, William	19	1831	m	PA
. . . . p.599-45				
Austin, David	33	1817	m	TN
" , Nancy	38	1812	f	?
" , White M.	11	1839	m	AL
" , Martha	10	1840	f	"
" , Polly	9	1841	f	"
" , Thomas C.	8	1842	m	"
" , Emily	6	1844	f	"
" , John	5	1845	m	TN
" , Elizabeth	3	1847	f	"
Milligan, James C.	21	1829	m	AL
. . . . p.411-83				
Austin, James J.	33	1817	m	AL
" , Dorcas	33	1817	f	"
" , Eliza Jane	13	1837	f	TN
" , Uriah J.	12	1838	m	"
" , Camely W.	10	1840	f	"
" , Daniel L.	8	1842	m	"
" , Robert W.	6	1844	m	"
" , Mary C.	4	1846	f	"
" , Milly C.	2	1848	f	"
. . . . p.600-50				
Austin, John	35	1815	m	TN
" , Jane	31	1819	f	"
" , Ann	12	1838	f	"
" , Judy	10	1840	f	"
" , Francis	8	1842	m	"
" , Sarah	4	1846	f	"
" , Zachary T.	2	1848	m	"
. . . . p.439-63				
Austin, Richard	58	1792	m	NC
" , Elizabeth	64	1786	f	GA
. . . . p.473-55				
Austin, Sam'l A.	35	1815	m	NC
" , Mary J.	29	1821	f	TN
" , Sarah A.	5	1845	f	"
" , Louisa J.	4	1846	f	"
" , David W.	3	1847	m	"
" , Samuel T.	1	1849	m	"
" , Martha L.	3/12	1850	f	"
. . . . p.599-47				
Austin, Sanders	66	1784	m	VA
" , Nancy	59	1791	f	"
" , Robert	19	1831	m	TN
. . . . p.599-46				
Austin, Stephen	40	1810	m	TN
" , Ann	35	1815	f	"
" , Rachel	20	1830	f	"
" , Saunders	18	1832	m	"
" , Polly A.	16	1832	f	"
" , Henry	14	1836	m	"
" , Benjamin	12	1838	m	"

Name	Age	Year	Sex	BP
" , John	10	1840	m	"
" , Nancy	9	1841	f	"
" , Martha J.	6	1844	f	"
" , Archibald	5	1845	m	"
" , Sarah E.	2	1848	f	"

. . . . p.599-48

Name	Age	Year	Sex	BP
Austin, William	30	1820	m	?
" , Sarah	25	1825	f	AL
" , Polly	8	1842	f	TN
" , John	5	1845	m	"
" , Augustus	3	1847	m	"

. . . . p.439-64

Name	Age	Year	Sex	BP
Auston, Richard	19	1831	m	TN
" , Sarah F.	16	1834	f	AL
O'Neill, Polly	25	1825	f	"
Auston, Edward G.	8	1842	m	"

HAYWOOD COUNTY, TN

. . . . p.31-193

Name	Age	Year	Sex	BP
Austin, Robert G.	54	1796	m	VA
" , Margaret	56	1794	f	"
" , Susan R.	17	1833	f	"
" , Edwin	15	1835	m	"
" , Algernon	11	1839	m	"
" , John A.	7	1843	m	"

. . . . p.07-44

Name	Age	Year	Sex	BP
Langly, R. Y.	24	1826	m	VA
Austin, A. M.	25	1825	m	"
				Clerk

HENDERSON COUNTY, TN

. . . . p.410-23

Name	Age	Year	Sex	BP
Austin, Alfred C.	24	1826	m	TN
" , Margaret	21	1829	f	"
" , William C.	3	1847	m	"
" , Preston	1	1849	m	"

. . . . p.410-20

Name	Age	Year	Sex	BP
Austin, Atlas	33	1817	m	NC
" , Nancy	30	1820	f	"
" , Logan	12	1838	f	TN
" , Bryant	10	1840	m	"
" , Minerva	9	1841	f	"
" , Lucinda	6	1844	f	"
" , Nancy	3	1847	f	"

. . . . p.421-91

Name	Age	Year	Sex	BP
Austin, Charles	56	1794	m	NC
" , Phoebe	52	1798	f	"
" , James M.	18	1832	m	"
" , Francis M.	16	1834	m	"
" , Benjamin	12	1838	m	"
" , Cynthia E.	10	1840	f	"

. . . . p.408-07

Name	Age	Year	Sex	BP
Austin, Drury	22	1828	m	TN
" , Mary	19	1831	f	"
Lamb, Elizabeth	17	1833	f	"

. . . . p.410-22

Name	Age	Year	Sex	BP
Austin, Ephraim	30	1820	m	NC
" , Lucy	26	1824	f	"
" , John L.	5	1845	m	TN
" , Cynthia E.	4	1846	f	"
" , Margaret M.	2	1848	f	"
Beauchamps, William	55	1795	m	NC
" , Cynthia	60	1790	f	"

. . . . p.386-60

Name	Age	Year	Sex	BP
Austin, J.G.	26	1824	m	TN
" , Mary	35	1815	f	AL
Wright, Elizabeth	18	1832	f	TN
Collet, James W.	16	1834	m	"
" , Pinkney	11	1839	m	"

. . . . p.409-17

Name	Age	Year	Sex	BP
Austin, James	43	1807	m	NC
" , Zylpha	43	1807	f	"
" , Simeon	19	1831	m	TN
" , Sarah	17	1833	f	"
" , Rhody	15	1835	f	"
" , Elijah	12	1838	m	"
" , Elisha	11	1839	m	"
" , Elizabeth	9	1841	f	"
" , Rebecca	6	1844	f	"
" , Timothy	4	1846	f	"
" , Mary	2	1848	f	"

. . . . p.412-31

Name	Age	Year	Sex	BP
Austin, Nancy	60	1790	f	NC
" , Nancy	20	1830	f	TN
Anglin, Elizabeth	9	1841	f	"
" , John	9	1841	m	"

. . . . p.408-10

Name	Age	Year	Sex	BP
Austin, Pleasant	52	1798	m	NC
" , Charlotte	55	1795	f	"
" , Lovedy L.	20	1830	f	TN
" , James	14	1836	m	"
Laciter, Emeline	12	1838	f	"
Newman, John	10	1840	m	"
Austin, William	2	1848	m	"

. . . . p.409-11

Name	Age	Year	Sex	BP
Austin, William	24	1826	m	NC
" , Nancy	25	1825	f	"
" , John R.	4	1846	m	"
" , Henry W.	2	1848	m	"

. . . . p.314-05

Name	Age	Year	Sex	BP
Austin, William	30	1820	m	VA
" , Catherine	30	1820	f	NC
" , Martha	2	1848	f	TN

JACKSON COUNTY, TN

. . . . p.509-267

Name	Age	Year	Sex	BP
Auston, Godfrey	36	1814	m	TN
" , Salley	31	1819	f	"
" , Elizabeth	12	1838	f	"
" , Sarah	11	1839	f	"
" , William	9	1841	m	"
" , Polley	8	1842	f	"
" , John	6	1844	m	"
" , Mariah	3	1847	f	"
McCullough, Anna	19	1831	f	"

. . . . p.490-137

Name	Age	Year	Sex	BP
Auston, William	57	1793	m	NC
" , Sarah	57	1793	f	SC
" , Enoch	30	1820	m	"
" , John	24	1826	m	"
" , Sarah	22	1828	f	"
" , Elizabeth	19	1831	f	"
" , William	18	1832	m	"

JEFFERSON COUNTY, TN

. . . . p.796-1004

Name	Age	Year	Sex	BP
Austin, Jane	72	1778	f	SC
" , Malissa	34	1816	f	TN

. . . . p.774-844

Name	Age	Year	Sex	BP
Austin, Benjamin	23	1827	m	CT
Oldham, John	47	1803	m	KY

KNOX COUNTY, TN

. . . . p.150-407

Name	Age	Year	Sex	BP
Austin, Archibald	26	1824	m	IN
" , Matilda	20	1830	f	TN
" , Sarah Ellen	10/12	1849	f	"
Potter, Robert	18	1832	m	"

Name	Age	Year	Sex	BP
Austin, Claria	19	1831	f	"
" , Sarah	16	1834	f	"
" , Matilda C.	15	1835	f	"
" , Adaline	13	1837	f	"
" , Eliza	11	1839	f	"

. . . . p.144-364

Name	Age	Year	Sex	BP
Austin, Samuel	22	1828	m	NC
" , Sarah	28	1822	f	TN
" , Joseph Strong	2/12	1850	m	"
Perry, Claibourn	17	1833	m	"

. . . . p.133-280

Name	Age	Year	Sex	BP
Austin, William	52	1798	m	NC
" , Saphronia	49	1801	f	"
" , Rebecca	21	1829	f	"
" , Susannah	17	1833	f	"
" , Catherine	15	1835	f	"
" , Rosanah	12	1838	f	"
" , Rutha	9	1841	f	"
" , Joseph	5	1845	m	"

LAUDERDALE COUNTY, TN

. . . . p.545-354

Name	Age	Year	Sex	BP
Austin, Nancy	40	1810	f	NC
" , John	16	1834	m	"
" , Hezehiah	15	1835	m	"
" , Martha A.	13	1837	f	"
" , Mary E.	11	1839	f	TN
" , Stephen	7	1843	m	"

LAWRENCE COUNTY, TN

. . . . p.580-13

Name	Age	Year	Sex	BP
Austin, John W.	35	1815	m	NC
" , Phillip W.	12	1838	m	KY
" , George Ann	10	1840	f	"
" , Charles H.	8	1842	m	TN
" , John W.	3	1847	m	"

. . . . p.580-15

Name	Age	Year	Sex	BP
Austin, Phillip G.	32	1818	m	NC
" , Mary F.	22	1828	f	TN
" , Wm. J.	3	1847	m	"
" , John H.	1	1849	m	"

. . . . p.740-177

Name	Age	Year	Sex	BP
Aulton, Easther	50	1800	f	TN
" , Wm.	25	1825	m	KY
" , David	20	1830	m	TN
" , John	17	1833	m	"
Austin, Sarah	23	1827	f	"
" , Martha	13	1837	f	"

. . . . p.580-12

Name	Age	Year	Sex	BP
Ramsey, Rufus	41	1809	m	SC
" , Saline	29	1821	f	TN
Lindsay, Alanzo	9	1841	m	"
Ramsey, Amanda	1	1849	f	"
Austin, Wm. E.	30	1820	m	VA
Ramey, Thos. C.	27	1823	m	TN
Austin, Sarah A.	8	1842	f	"

. . . . p.739-167

Name	Age	Year	Sex	BP
Hucherson, Jas.	25	1825	m	TN
" , Easther	25	1825	f	"
" , Mary	4	1846	f	"
" , Easther C.	3	1847	f	"
" , Sarah E.	1	1849	f	"
" , Jessie E.	1/12	1850	f	"
Austin, Martha J.	14	1836	f	"

. . . . p.743-197

Name	Age	Year	Sex	BP
Morris, John F.	38	1812	m	KY
" , Jane	40	1810	f	"
" , Aramenta E.	13	1837	f	TN
" , Sarah A. E.	10	1840	f	"

"	, Wm. H. A.	8	1842	m	"
"	, Mary P.	7	1843	f	"
"	, Elizabeth J.	5	1845	f	"
"	, Martha C.	3	1847	f	"
"	, Eliza Ann	7/12	1849	f	"
Austin, Sarah		18	1832	f	"

LEWIS COUNTY, TN

.... p.804-187

Austin, Charles		64	1786	m	NC
"	, Sylvia	57	1793	f	"
"	, James M.	22	1828	m	TN
"	, Carley P.	20	1830	m	"

LINCOLN COUNTY, TN

.... p.82-588

Austin, Eleanor		46	1804	f	TN
"	, Henry R.	23	1827	m	"
"	, Amzi	20	1830	f	"
"	, Elijah	17	1833	m	"
Fortinberry, Mahala J.		7	1843	f	"

.... p.82-589

Austin, Jesse		20	1830	m	TN
"	, Mahala	24	1826	f	"

.... p.83-594

Austin, John R.		24	1826	m	TN
"	, Nancy E.	20	1830	f	"
"	, Sarah E.	1	1849	f	"

.... p.79-569

Austin, William		24	1826	m	TN
"	, Nancy C.	18	1832	f	"
"	, John H.	2	1848	m	"

.... p.82-583

Austin, William		23	1827	m	TN
"	, Caroline	20	1830	f	"
"	, John H.	1	1849	m	"

.... p.83-593

Austin, William		23	1827	m	TN
"	, Angelina	17	1833	f	"
"	, Willis H.	1/12	1850	m	"

.... p.248-271

King, A. J.		37	1813	m	TN
"	, Eliza	31	1819	f	"
"	, Martha	10	1840	f	"
"	, Ephriam	8	1842	m	"
"	, Pamelia	7	1843	f	"
"	, Eliza	4	1846	f	"
"	, Mary Kay	2	1848	f	"
"	, Jones	8/12	1849	m	"
Austin, Henry		23	1827	m	"

MACON COUNTY, TN

.... p.385-755

Austin, Wilson		49	1801	m	NC
"	, Rhoda	29	1821	f	KY
"	, Luthenia H.	8	1842	f	"
"	, Luticen A.	6	1844	f	TN
"	, Angeline W.	5	1845	f	"
"	, Mary M.	3	1847	f	"
"	, Canzada	2	1848	f	"

MARION COUNTY, TN

.... p.787-243

Austin, Edward		35	1815	m	TN
"	, Sarah	28	1822	f	"
"	, Mary	3	1847	f	"

.... p.823-493

Austin, James		39	1811	m	TN
"	, Carroll	21	1829	f	"
"	, Elijah	19	1831	m	"
"	, Lucretia	17	1833	f	"
"	, Margaret	9	1841	f	"
"	, John	7	1843	m	"
"	, Sarah	6	1844	f	"
"	, James	4	1846	m	"

.... p.859-733

Austin, Thomas		29	1821	m	TN
"	, Bethany	27	1823	f	"
"	, James	7	1843	m	"
"	, Clarisa	3	1847	f	"
"	, Alexander S.	3/12	1850	m	"

MARSHALL COUNTY, TN

.... p.130-548

Minton, Zacharia		68	1782	m	NC
"	, Jane	43	1807	f	"
"	, John	10	1840	m	"
Austin, Margaret		9	1841	f	"
"	, John	5	1845	m	"

OVERTON COUNTY, TN

.... p.55-370

Austin, William		50	1800	m	NC
"	, Nancy	48	1802	f	?
"	, Elizabeth	15	1835	f	TN
"	, Nancy	12	1838	f	"
Phillips, Elizabeth		71	1779	f	NC

ROBERTSON COUNTY, TN

.... p.106-1306

Northington, Sam		58	1792	m	NC
"	, Sarah	44	1806	f	"
"	, Atlas	23	1827	m	TN
"	, Maria	16	1834	f	"
"	, Mary	10	1840	f	"
"	, Samuel	7	1843	m	"
"	, Sarah	5	1845	f	"
Allen, Sarah		42	1808	f	"
Austin, Mary		21	1829	f	NY

.... p.8-606

Barr, Wm. C.		44	1806	m	TN
"	, Elizabeth	56	1794	f	NC
"	, Sylas	23	1827	m	TN
"	, Elizabeth	16	1834	f	"
Austin, William		18	1832	m	"

RUTHERFORD COUNTY, TN

.... p.573-543

Austin, O. E.		47	1803	m	VA
"	, Tabitha	37	1813	f	"
"	, Tabitha G.	18	1832	f	TN
"	, Eliza	17	1833	f	"
"	, Lafayette	14	1836	m	"
"	, Lavina	11	1839	f	"
"	, John	10	1840	m	"
"	, James	7	1843	m	"
"	, Mary	2	1848	f	"

SHELBY COUNTY, TN

.... p.370-1547

Austin, E. K.		34	1816	m	MA
"	, Miriam	28	1822	f	NY

SMITH COUNTY, TN

.... p.538-797

Austin, Christian		41	1809	m	TN
"	, Sarah	39	1811	f	"
"	, Silas F.	20	1830	m	"
"	, Rebecca H.	18	1832	f	"
"	, Martha A.	16	1834	f	"
"	, Celia J.	14	1836	f	"
"	, Mary A.	10	1840	f	"
"	, Sarah	9	1841	f	"

.... p.547-865

Austin, Ephriam P.		36	1814	m	TN
"	, Mary I.	31	1819	f	VA
"	, Malissa A.	11	1839	f	TN
"	, Cynthia J.	10	1840	f	"
"	, Henry D.	8	1842	m	"
"	, Martha E.	6	1844	f	"
"	, Balana S.	4	1846	f	"

.... p.483-423

Austin, James		38	1812	m	TN
"	, Rebecca	38	1812	f	"
"	, Wm.	15	1835	m	"
"	, James	12	1838	m	"
"	, Enoch	10	1840	m	"
"	, Reuben	7	1843	m	"
"	, Amos	5	1845	m	"

.... p.537-791

Austin, John		24	1826	m	TN
"	, Martha	26	1824	f	"
"	, Sophia A.	4	1846	f	"
"	, Sarah A.	2	1848	f	"

.... p.465-295

Austin, John		54	1796	m	NC
"	, Mary	46	1804	f	VA
"	, Dosia	18	1832	f	TN
"	, Mary	16	1834	f	"
"	, Celia	12	1838	f	"
"	, Elijah	9	1841	m	"
"	, Elmina	6	1844	f	"

.... p.537-790

Austin, Levi		68	1782	m	NC
"	, Anna	59	1791	f	KY
"	, Polly	26	1824	f	TN
"	, Anna	22	1828	f	"
"	, Caroline	19	1831	f	"
"	, Levi	16	1834	m	"
"	, Booker W.	23	1827	m	"

.... p.541-821

Austin, Miles W.		27	1823	m	TN
"	, Sally	37	1813	f	"

.... p.537-789

Austin, Philip		42	1808	m	TN
"	, Phoebe	41	1809	f	"
"	, Maywood N.	17	1833	m	"
"	, Shelby	15	1835	m	"
"	, John	10	1840	m	"
"	, Thomas	8	1842	m	"
"	, Miles C.	6	1844	m	"
"	, Cynthia	33	1817	f	"
"	, Louisa J.	1	1849	f	"

. . . .				p.468-315
Austin, Solomon	34	1816	m	NC
", Susan	25	1825	f	TN
", John J.	3	1847	m	"
", Illinoy M.	11/12	1849	f	"
", William	8	1842	m	"
", Susan	77	1773	f	NC
Webster, Noel	17	1833	m	TN
. . . .				p.465-296
Merritt, John	45	1805	m	NC
", Nancy	40	1810	f	?
", Elizabeth	20	1830	f	TN
", Sarah	17	1833	f	"
", Eliza J.	14	1836	f	"
", William	10	1840	m	"
", Albert	8	1842	m	"
", Cymantha	6	1844	f	"
", Benj.	4	1846	m	"
", Nancy I.	1	1849	f	"
Austin, Nathaniel	23	1827	m	"
", John	21	1829	m	"
. . . .				p.467-311
Manor, Sarah	42	1808	f	NC
", Susan	11	1839	f	TN
Austin, Rhoda	25	1825	f	"
", Peggy	4	1846	f	"

SUMNER COUNTY, TN

. . . .				p.357-722
Austin, A. Gelson	47	1803	m	VA
", Amanda	41	1809	f	TN
", George	18	1832	m	"
", Henry	14	1836	m	"
", Emily	12	1838	f	"
", Marcus	8	1842	m	"
", Martha	5	1845	f	"
", Pamelia	2	1848	f	"
. . . .				p.471-163
Austin, Allen	27	1823	m	TN
", Jane	25	1825	f	"
", John	5	1845	m	"
", Rufus	2	1848	m	"
Henderson, Martha	26	1824	f	"
. . . .				p.467-133
Austin, Dickerson	52	1898	m	VA
", Emily	35	1815	f	"
", Lucy	14	1836	f	"
", Elizabeth	10	1840	f	"
. . . .				p.287-232
Austin, Mary	72	1778	f	VA
. . . .				p.287-233
Austin, Flemming	35	1815	m	TN
. . . .				p.467-131
Austin, James	42	1808	m	VA
", Nancy	42	1808	f	"
", William	17	1833	m	"
", Harrison	15	1835	m	"
Harper, Martha	20	1830	f	"
. . . .				p.467-132
Austin, John	43	1807	m	VA
", Rhoda	35	1815	f	"
", Isabella	14	1836	f	"
", James	12	1838	m	"
", Mary A.	8	1842	f	"
", John	3	1847	m	"
Henderson, Frances	30	1820	f	"

. . . .				p.382-896
Austin, Maiah	47	1803	f	VA
", Agleston	21	1829	m	"
", Elizabeth	18	1832	f	TN
", John	14	1836	m	"
", Henry	12	1838	m	"
", Christopher	10	1840	m	"
", Margaret	8	1842	f	"
. . . .				p.472-164
Austin, Samuel	32	1818	m	TN
", Angeline	24	1826	f	"
", Betsey Baker	4	1846	f	"
", Thomas	1	1849	m	"
. . . .				p.472-165
Austin, Thomas	36	1814	m	TN
", Elizabeth	24	1826	f	"
", James	6	1844	m	"
", Thomas	4	1846	m	"
", Isaac	2	1848	m	"
", Elizabeth	6/12	1849	f	"
. . . .				p.370-812
Austin, Wilkerson D.	44	1806	m	VA
", Amanda D.	43	1807	f	"
", Amandy M.	15	1835	f	TN
", John B.	12	1838	m	"
", Clarissa A.	10	1840	f	"
", Clarinda A.	7	1843	f	"
. . . .				p.368-797
Dickerson, William H.	24	1826	m	TN
", Susan	39	1811	f	VA
Austin, Lucy D.	15	1835	f	TN
", Mary	13	1837	f	"
", Elizabeth	10	1840	f	"
", Agnes	8	1842	f	"
Dickerson, Jane	1	1849	f	"
. . . .				p.302-347
Parker, Arabella	30	1820	f	TN
Austin, Lucy	32	1818	f	"

VAN BUREN COUNTY, TN

. . . .				p.748-109
Austin, Rolley	36	1814	m	VA
", Maryan	32	1818	f	SC
", Thomas	11	1839	m	TN
", Shelby	6	1844	m	"
", Nathaniel G.	4	1846	m	"
", Henry R.	4	1846	m	"
", John	1	1849	m	"
McDaniel, Elizabeth	16	1834	f	"

WARREN COUNTY, TN

. . . .				p.48-313
Austin, Granberry	50	1800	m	NC
", Elizabeth	40	1810	f	GA
", Staley N.	13	1837	m	TN
", Riley J.	11	1839	m	"
", Ruth J.	7	1843	f	"
", Mary C.	4	1846	f	"
", Sally A.	2	1848	f	"
", Elizabeth A.	1	1849	f	"
Adams, Emeline	12	1838	f	"

WEAKLEY COUNTY, TN

. . . .				p.768-134
Austin, A. W.	23	1827	m	TN
", Emily	32	1818	f	VA
", Elizabeth	13	1837	f	TN
", Joseph	10	1840	m	"
", Racina	8	1842	f	"
", Emily	6	1844	f	"
", George	4	1846	m	"
", Thomas	8/12	1849	m	"
Bynum, F. N.	22	1828	m	"
. . . .				p.895-40
Austin, J.	60	1790	m	NC
", Mary	60	1790	m	"
", Nancy	18	1832	f	TN
", Jasper	16	1834	m	"
", Newton	16	1834	m	"
", Cylvesta	13	1837	f	"
. . . .				p.769-1
Austin, M.	44	1806	m	NC
", Mahala	32	1818	f	KY
", Green	19	1831	m	TN
", Vincent	17	1833	m	"
", Mary	16	1834	f	"
", Emaline	15	1835	f	"
", Jane	14	1836	f	"
", Martha	12	1838	f	"
", Mildred	6	1844	f	"
", Allen	5	1845	m	"
", George	4	1846	m	"
", Jasen	2	1848	m	"
. . . .				p.768-135
Austin, P. A.	25	1825	m	TN
", Damina	24	1826	f	MO
. . . .				p.767-130
Austin, S. F.	47	1803	m	NC
", Amanda	31	1819	f	"
", Moses	18	1832	m	TN
", Frederick	16	1834	m	"
", John	14	1836	m	"
", Matilda	12	1838	f	"
", Vincent	10	1840	m	"
", Mary	8	1842	f	"
", Charity	6	1844	f	"
", Sarah	4	1846	f	"
. . . .				p.771-22
Austin, Vincent	50	1800	m	NC
", Sarah	45	1805	f	"
", Sarah	22	1828	f	TN
", Mary	20	1830	f	"
", Philip	18	1832	m	"
", Evelinea	16	1834	f	"
", Elizabeth	14	1836	f	"
", Samuel	6	1844	m	"
", Araminta	3	1847	f	"
Burnett, J. B.	19	1831	m	"
. . . .				p.774-36
Cook, E. R.	30	1820	m	IL
", Eliza	23	1827	f	GA
", John	4	1846	m	KY
", Taylor	2	1848	m	TN
", Mary	11/12	1849	f	"
Hawke, M.	17	1833	f	GA
Austin, T. J.	23	1827	m	?

WHITE COUNTY, TN

Editor's Corner...

COMPUTERIZING GENEALOGICAL RESEARCH - PART II

Part I of this article, on pages 86 to 90, discussed how the genealogist might benefit from personal computers in his research. In this part we recommend a class of computers to those considering the purchase of a computer for genealogy.

When we published Part I of this article in 1983, most home computers were using CP/M as their 'operating system,' for it had become the *de facto* standard for 8-bit microcomputers. The IBM Personal Computer was relatively new to the market – just another microcomputer among many – and making any personal computer recommendations was still difficult at that time.

Few of us realized in 1983 how strongly the IBM PC and its successors were to dominate the market in setting personal computer standards. IBM was selling 'PC-DOS' as the Disk Operating System for its PC. MicroSoft Corporation began selling the virtually identical product as 'MS-DOS.' Other manufacturers bought MS-DOS for use in their own microcomputers, which were then marketed as 'compatible' with the IBM PC. Hundreds of companies wrote thousands of programs (several of them useful for genealogy) which would work with the IBM PC and compatible computers.

Today the compatibles are generally less expensive than the equivalent IBM computer, but one must consider the reliability of the manufacturer's after-sales hardware and software support, so the choice is not always an easy one.

The successors to the original PC – the PC/XT and the PC/AT computers – support 'hard disks' in addition to 'floppy diskette' drives. With hard disks, the genealogist can store millions of characters in his computer, enabling him to access programs and data quickly, without having to insert and remove floppy disks frequently. The XT and the AT were designed to operate with later versions of PC-DOS, so most genealogical software written for the PC also runs on the later machines. With its greater speed and storage capabilities, the IBM PC/AT (or one of the 'AT-compatible' computers) makes an excellent choice for those doing genealogical research.

— Michael Edward Austin

THE DESCENDANTS OF
THOMAS AUSTIN AND REBECCA TURNER
OF AMHERST COUNTY, VIRGINIA

by Cornelia Bradshaw Austin

[CONTINUED FROM PAGE 181]

T328. MARGARET ELLA[4] AUSTIN (*Thomas J.,*[3] *Jesse,*[2] *Thomas*[1]) was born 24 May 1864 in Patterson, North Carolina. She was married in Caldwell County, North Carolina, on 4 January 1882 to John Daniel Bean. John, the son of Enoch and Elizabeth (Crump) Bean, was born on 8 May 1862 in Caldwell County. John was a farmer, logger, millwright, filer, and a sawyer. It has been said that he could move to a new sawmilling location, build a cabin, and be moved into it in the same day! They lived at Saw Mills, Caldwell County, and their children were all born in Caldwell County. In 1913 he decided to go to the big timber country, so they sold out and on 24 March 1913 he and Margaret, together with their daughter Alice and her husband Roby, Katherine, and Oscar, stepped off the train in Eureka, Lincoln County, Montana, into nearly knee-deep snow. In June Connie and husband Ed, Bob and Lula and their three children arrived to join them. Ella and husband Walter arrived 20 March 1914, returned to Lenoir for a year in September 1915, then returned to Eureka in 1916. They homesteaded in Tobacco Valley, where John built a neat white two-story home. Margaret and John appear in the photograph to the right. John died on 5 May 1941, and is buried in Eureka Cemetery. Margaret died on 3 April 1953, also in Eureka, and is buried with her husband. BEAN CHILDREN: MARY EDNA 1883, ROBERT AUSTIN 1885, ELLA JANE 1888, SARAH CONSTANCE 1890, FRANCES ALICE 1893, HATTIE MAE 1898 (died at age 8 months), KATHERINE LOUISE 1901, JOHN OSCAR 1904.

T329. RUFUS LENOIR[4] AUSTIN (*Thomas J.,*[3] *Jesse,*[2] *Thomas*[1]) was born in September 1866. He was married on 1 November 1884 to Mattie L. Curtis, perhaps the daughter of Samuel and Mary Curtis. Mattie was born in January 1864. They lived for a period of time across Yadkin River from Harpers Chapel Church at Fin Curtis' place, and worked on the Cilley Farm. 'Rufe' was listed as a farmer in the 1900 Census for Caldwell County. Later they lived on Pistail Road. Rufus is pictured with two of his brothers on page 199, taken while they were building a wall at the church. Mattie died 7 March 1907 at age 43y 1m 16d, and is buried in Harpers Chapel in Patterson, North Carolina. Rufus died on 20 February 1936 age 71 and is also buried in Harpers Chapel. Rufus and Mattie had six sons and four daughters:

John Daniel Bean (1862-1941)
Margaret Ella Austin Bean (1864-1953)

T329-1. THOMAS EDGAR, *b. August 1885, was in the Army, m. — Joseph. They had two boys and a girl. Thomas is buried in San Francisco.*

T329-2. LULA J., *b. April 1887, died as a child*

T329-3. JULIUS J. ('DUDE'), *born in December 1889, m. Frances Day ( ). They had a son Clifford and a daughter Margie who m. Marshall Money. Julius died on 3 March 1947.*

T329-4. WILLIAM W., *b. in August 1891, m. Pansi Brown. He died young, and Pansi remarried to — Norris. A daughter Lila was b. 28 January 1917.*

T329-5. LEWIS CLYDE, *b. December 1893, m. Mary Zelphia Harrison. They resided in Patterson, near Hollywood Ridge Road. Their son Hubert Ray was born 10 March 1923, died 31 October 1969, buried in the Victor Sterling Memorial Cemetery.*

T329-6. ALMA, *b. January 1895, d. 19 March 1948*

T329-7. JOHN CLAUDE, *b. 28 November 1898, m. Mattie Bean on 17 April 1917. John d. 26 September 1977, buried at Harpers Chapel.*

T329-8. ANNA MARY, *b. January 1900, d. 6 March 1902, buried at Harpers Chapel.*

T329-9. VIOLET, *b. 1902, m. Wes Welborn, res. Ronda, North Carolina.*

T329-A. EUGENE McKINLEY, *resided in San Francisco.*

T355. T. WALTER[4] AUSTIN (*Alfred Webb,[3] Jesse,[2] Thomas[1]*) was born circa 1859 in Tennessee, for he was age 42 when registering to vote in 1902. He was married to Sarah Emma Hartley, who was born circa 1863. In the 1910 Census they were in Lower Creek Township, Caldwell County, North Carolina. Walter died 15 November 1939 and is buried in the Harpers Chapel Methodist Church Cemetery in Patterson Township, near Lenoir, Caldwell County. His will dated 15 November 1937 mentions Ella, William, and Alice, and Gwyn Piercy (no kin). According to the somewhat uncertain memory of Jane C. Austin, Walter and Sarah had seven children who married as follows:

    T355-1. NELLIE MAE, *b. 27 October 1899, m. Charles Pearson*

    T355-2. DORA JOE ('DODE'), *m. — Greer*

    T355-3. MARY, *m. Will Hall*

    T355-4. ELLA, *m.(1) to John Suddreth, m.(2) to Claude Osler, although T. Walter Austin's Will mentions an 'Ella Walker.'*

    T355-5. HARVEY EDMUND, *m.(1) to Alice Porch?, m.(2) — Brown, he d. 18 June 1950. Ch: Gladys, Pearl, Grace, —, and Clarence.*

    T355-6. WILLIAM J., *d. 1938 in Hansen, Idaho, 'out West' according to Aunt Ruth.*

    T355-7. ALICE

T359. EDMUND JONES[4] AUSTIN (*Alfred Webb,[3] Jesse,[2] Thomas[1]*) was born 22 June 1870 in Tennessee. He was married on 4 October 1890 to Emma Thomas in Johnson County, Tennessee. Emma was born on 11 December 1871 in Tennessee. They resided in Johnson County in 1898 when May was born. He was age 32 when he registered to vote in Caldwell County, North Carolina, in 1902. In the 1910 Census they resided in Lower Creek Township, Caldwell County. They resided in 1920 in Lenoir, Caldwell County. Emma died 12 June 1940, Edmund died shortly thereafter on 8 February 1941, and is buried in Belleview Cemetery in Lenoir. They had three girls:

    T359-1. ALMA, *b. 1892, m. — Nelson*

    T359-2. MAUDE, *b. 1896, m. Cromwell Robbins*

    T359-3. MAE, *b. 25 January 1898 in Johnson County, m. Ernest Wayne Crews. She d. 22 March 1983 at age 85, is buried Bellview Cemetery, Lenoir. Her obituary mentions sons William Austin Crews and Eddie Crews, and daughters Mrs. Mary Emma Willard and Mrs. Janelle Brooks.*

T361. G. HARPER[4] AUSTIN (*William Thomas,[3] Jesse,[2] Thomas[1]*) was born circa 1856. He was married to Mary Josephine Fullwood. He became a methodist minister and following in the footsteps of his great grandfather, Rev. William Fullwood, spent most of his adult life preaching in

the community where he was born and serving the Obeth Methodist Church. His obituary, which appeared in *The News Herald*, stated that "he was a true Christian, happy in his religion and in the service of his church and fellow men." He was instrumental in establishing an annual homecoming at Obeth. Harper and Mary had no children.

T363. WILLIAM THOMAS[4] AUSTIN (*William Thomas,[3] Jesse,[2] Thomas[1]*) was born circa 1864. He was married to Mary Thomas, and was the Morgantown Jailer at one time. William and Mary had one son known to me:

    T363-1. FOREST B., *resided in Black Mountain*

T364. WALTER L.[4] AUSTIN (*William Thomas,[3] Jesse,[2] Thomas[1]*) was born circa 1866. He was married to Margaret L. Alexander, by whom he had seven children:

    T364-1. WINNIE, *died at age 21, buried in Obeth Church Cemetery.*

    T364-2. ESSIE, *m. Ernest Noles*

    T364-3. EARL, *m.(1) Virginia Snyder, m.(2) Lou A. Miller*

    T364-4. ELIZABETH, *m.(1) to Edgar Fish, m.(2) Charles Campbell*

    T364-5. BONNIE, *m.(1) Vance Buchanan, m.(2) Rev. Hobson Jaynes*

    T364-6. CARL, *m. Louise Dotson*

    T364-7. LOTTIE, *m. Hugh Bennett*

T365. SAMUEL EDWARD[4] AUSTIN (*William Thomas,[3] Jesse,[2] Thomas[1]*) was born circa 1869. He was first married to Sarah Elizabeth Carswell, and later he married to Emma Clarke. He served in the Spanish-American War. One son is known to me:

    T365-1. J. D., *killed in World War I.*

T366. VANCE ZEBULON[4] AUSTIN (*William Thomas,[3] Jesse,[2] Thomas[1]*) was born circa 1871. He was married to Margaret Chapman. He lived in Norman, Oklahoma. They had five children:

    T366-1. MYRTLE, *m. Arthur Anglemier*

    T366-2. WILLIE LEE, *never married*

    T366-3. RALPH, *d. while young*

    T366-4. PEARL, *m. John Fleming. Pearl remembered being reminded many times over the years that great-Aunt Sarah, sister of William T. Austin, delivered her at birth.*

    T366-5. ANNA

T367. JOHN FULLWOOD[4] AUSTIN (*William Thomas,[3] Jesse,[2] Thomas[1]*) was born circa 1875. He married Nora Alexander and lived in Akron, Ohio. No children.

T3B2. CARL BAGBY[4] AUSTIN (*Jesse Lafayette,*[3] *Jesse,*[2] *Thomas*[1]) was born 30 July 1888 in Iredell County, North Carolina. He was married to Annie Belle Eagle. Annie, the daughter of Robert and Myra (McHargue) Eagle, was born on 20 August 1897 in Iredell County. Children:

T3B2-1. JAMES CARL

T3B2-2. ALBERT

T3B2-3. FRANK

T3B2-4. ROBERT

T3B2-5. BLAKE

T3B2-6. CHARLES KENNETH, *b. 26 August 1927 in Iredell County, m. Louise Spicer Reeves 13 September 1950. Two sons: James Carl and Kenneth Lee. James was b. on 3 September 1952 in Iredell County, m. Jonna Evetta Whitley on 9 September 1972, has two sons Andrew Bryan and Matthew David. Kenneth m. in 1975 and has a daughter Noel Elizabeth.*

T3B2-7. LYNN

T3B2-8. ESTHER

FIFTH GENERATION

T322-2. WILLIAM JEFFERSON[5] AUSTIN (*Julius Jefferson,*[4] *Thomas J.,*[3] *Jesse,*[2] *Thomas*[1]) was born 4 April 1874. He was married on 9 July 1905 to Mary Lou Coffey, the daughter of Thomas and Rachel H. Coffey, who was born 13 February 1882. Mary is buried in Harpers Chapel, Lenoir, North Carolina. They had five children:

T322-21. THOMAS LESTER

T322-22. EARL JEFFERSON

T322-23. HERBERT WILLIAM

T322-24. NED

T322-25. VIOLA

T324-2. GEORGE THOMAS[5] AUSTIN (*George Thomas,*[4] *Thomas J.,*[3] *Jesse,*[2] *Thomas*[1]) was born 21 April 1881. He was married on 4 August 1906 to Nadie Perley of Globe. Nadie, the daughter of Larkin and Sarah Penley, was born on circa 1886. George died in 14 December 1939 and is buried in Harpers Chapel. They had eight children:

T324-21. MABEL *b. circa 1906, age 4 in 1910 Census.*

T324-22. HELEN PAULINE, *b. 10 September 1908, m. Benjamin O. Teague, d. 18 October 1940.*

T324-23. WILMA, *m. J. H. Bungarner, resided in 1981 in Hickory*

T324-24. HAZEL, *m. A. L. Clark, res. 1981 in Hickory*

T324-25. THOMAS EDWARD, *b. 30 October 1914, resided in 1981 in Hickory, North Carolina.*

T324-26. ALMA, *m. C. Q. Church, resided in 1981 in High Point.*

T324-27. HUGH, *m. Lonabelle (—), d. 23 November 1981 in Culver City, Calif. at age 62*

T324-28. IRIS, *b. Rob Bolick.*

T326-1. WILLIAM FRANKLIN[5] AUSTIN (*Charles David,*[4] *Thomas J.,*[3] *Jesse,*[2] *Thomas*[1]) was born circa 1878. He married in Kansas to Ella Suddreth from Caldwell County, North Carolina. Ella, the daughter of Toliver F. and Laura (Harris) Suddreth, was born on January 1878 in Caldwell County. William was the first of the family to go West. He sold Real Estate in Sterling and in Bayard, Nebraska, where he and Ella are buried in City Cemetery. Children:

T326-11. ZELLA, *b. in Sterling, Nebraska, m. — Ulmer. resided in 1982 in San Bernadino, California, about age 79. No children.*

T326-12. IRENE, *m. — Ballenger, adopted a daughter. Was in San Bernadino, California, nursing home in 1982.*

T326-13. GEORGE, *m. Mae (—) in California, resided in Denver in 1981. Only one with children.*

T326-14. ROBERT, *m. Birdie (—), no children. Maybe buried in Denver, Colorado.*

T326-3. WALTER LENOIR[5] AUSTIN (*Charles David,*[4] *Thomas J.,*[3] *Jesse,*[2] *Thomas*[1]) was born 24 January 1883 in Caldwell County, North Carolina. He married first on 13 July 1905 to Estol Reily in Johnson County, Tennessee, their children were born in Nebraska. He married second to Opal Smith, who was born on 24 December 1917. They lived for about three years in Nebraska, then moved to California where Walter worked in a shipyard during the War. In late life they returned to Tennessee, living about 29 miles from Boone. Walter died circa 1962, either in Banner Elk, North Carolina, or in Shouns, Tennessee, where he is buried in the Austin Family plot in a pasture near his home. He had three children by each wife:

T326-31. RAYMOND, *died of scarlet fever, buried in Bayard, Nebraska.*

T326-32. PAUL, *d. in car wreck, buried in Bayard.*

T326-33. NORMA, *m. Art Stroad, d. of cancer, probably in Bayard*

T326-34. LORRAINE, *b. 19 January 1942 in Nebraska, m.(1) — Hamby, m.(2) John Hess*

T326-35. WALTER MARK, *b. 1953, d. 1953, buried in family plot in Shouns.*

T326-36. MICHAEL LANE, *b. 27 November 1957*

T326-5. JOSEPH EDWARD[5] AUSTIN (*Charles David,*[4] *Thomas J.,*[3] *Jesse,*[2] *Thomas*[1]) was born 21 April 1887 in Shouns, Tennessee. He married on 11 October 1909 to Lula Jane Carlton in the Court House of Caldwell County, North Carolina. Jane, the daughter of Thomas C. and Millie Louise (Triplett) Carlton, was born on 4 July 1889 in Sampson, Watauga County, North Carolina. Joseph died 28 September 1955 in Morganton, North Carolina, and is buried in the Shiloh Methodist Church Cemetery, Lenoir, North Carolina. He and Jane had nine children:

Joseph Edward Austin (1888-1955) and his wife Lula Jane Carlton (1889-—)

T326-51. ALVA ESTER, *b. 13 August 1910 near Tecumseth, Nebraska, she m. John D. Beard in 1928*

T326-52. NORMAN CHARLES, *b. 28 November 1912 in Patterson Twp., Caldwell County, m. to Annie Holsclaw on 18 January 1936.*

T326-53. CLARENCE DONALD, *b. 4 November 1914, m. Willie Mae Jones on 25 January 1936.*

T326-54. STERLING RAY, *b. 18 March 1917, d. 8 January 1967, buried Shiloh Church Cemetery*

T326-55. VERNON ROBERT, *b. 17 March 1919, d. June 1919, is buried at Harpers Chapel*

T326-56. BENO CARLTON, *b. 24 January 1921, m. Reita Mae Hampton*

T326-57. EDWARD THOMAS, *b. 21 January 1923, m. Cornelia Bradshaw on 11 February 1949, they live in Lenoir, North Carolina 1987.*

T326-58. REUBEN GETTA, *b. 5 December 1924, d. 20 November 1947, buried Shiloh Church*

T326-59. BONNIE LOUISE, *b. 8 February 1930, m. James Coffey on 11 March 1946.*

T326-7. ROBERT LEWIS⁵ AUSTIN (*Charles David,⁴ Thomas J.,³ Jesse,² Thomas¹*) was born 24 March 1892 in Mountain City, Tennessee. He was married on 20 November 1915 to Josie Etta Chambers. They lived around Sterling and Bayard, Nebraska, about 20 miles from others. Robert d. 21 June 1978, buried in American Falls, Idaho. Children:

T327-71. HAZEL, *66 in 1982, m. Jim Shoopman, lived at American Falls & Pocatello, Idaho & Nappa*

T327-72. LEWIS, *m. Vera —*

T327-73. BERTHA, *d. in a car wreck at about age 16*

T327-74. CHARLES, *d. from blood poisoning due to a nail in his foot at about age 6, buried in Bayard*

T327-75. GLENDA, *m. twice*

T327-76. LEONARD, *b. in Bayard, Nebraska, m. Lavon Snyder from Bayard. He died in a car wreck in 1970 in American Falls.*

T326-8. JOHN HOUSTON⁵ AUSTIN (*Charles David,⁴ Thomas J.,³ Jesse,² Thomas¹*) was born 30 September 1893 in Caldwell County, North Carolina. He was married to Ruth Stevens in Bridgeport, Nebraska. Ruth, the daughter of Thomas Henry and Cora Mae (Vertrees) Stevens, was born on 18 December 1898 in Norcatar, Kansas. Her family went by covered wagon with cattle, settled near Camp Clark then Bridgeport. After marriage John and Ruth lived at Bayard, Nebraska, and later moved to Pendleton, Oregon and Boise, Idaho. John worked on an Air Base, Ruth worked at Yellowstone. John died in October 1942 in Boise, and is buried in City Cemetery, Bayard, Nebraska. Ruth still lived in Boise in 1982. John and Ruth had two children:

T326-81. JUNE ETTA, *b. 3 May 1917, m. Merlin Purcell of Eureka, California. He was born 30 August 1919, died in 1978, and is buried in Boise, Idaho.*

T326-82. CHADWICK LEROY, *b. 27 February 1919, died in September 1921, buried in Bayard.*

T326-9. WHEELER McKINLEY[5] AUSTIN (*Charles David,*[4] *Thomas J.,*[3] *Jesse,*[2] *Thomas*[1]) was born 5 April 1896 in Caldwell County, North Carolina. He was first married on 16 April 1919 to Okie Billings in Burke County, North Carolina. He married second to Ann (—). Wheeler was living in a rest home in Bayard, Nebraska, in 1985. He had three children:

T326-91. HELEN, *twin b. circa 1916, m. Dick Furr, lived in 1977 in Denver, Colorado, was age 66 in 1982.*

T326-92. HAROLD, *b. twin, born circa 1916, died at age seven months of pneumonia, buried Bayard, Nebraska.*

T326-93. LOUISE, *b. circa 1918, m. James Bassett, resided in Maryland in 1982.*

References

All locations are in Virginia unless otherwise noted. T: Mrs. Reba Bentley Montague of Baltimore MD 1950, *The Fullwood Family* Alexander Burke County Library in Lenoir NC, *Here Will I Dwell* by Nancy Alexander Caldwell County Library, *Tucker's Barn* a newsletter of West Caldwell High School of Spring and Summer 1982. T,T3: Amherst County Wills & Inventory Book 4 p. 387, Amherst marriage register, Tax list in *Virginia Genealogist* Vol. 5 No. 2 p. 80, Amherst County Inventory Book 4 p. 175, Nelson County Marriage Bonds 1808-1866, Nelson County 1850 Census house 66-66 & 1870 Census Rockfish Township p. 24 houses 184 & 186, 1830 & 1840 Census Burke County NC, *Index to North Carolina Wills* by Wm. Perry Johnson, Raleigh NC Archives file #14-103 (Will of Rebecca Turner Austin Jopling), Washington County TN Marriage Bonds, Mrs. Frances Townsend Miles of Bartlesville OK 1973. T3: Caldwell County NC Marriage Bonds. T3, T32,T322-2: "Jesse Austin" by Joan Rabb Austin in the *Caldwell County NC Heritage Book* 1983 referencing Family Bible & marriage certificates records. T3,T32,T34,T35: letters from Walter B. Davis and Janet Austin Curtis, 1870 1890 1900 Census for Patterson Township, Caldwell County, 1870 p. 9 houses 67 & 68, 1860 Census for Lenoir Township, Caldwell County NC Marriages, 1841-1872 several marriage records. T35: *The Story of Caldwell County.* T36: 1880 Linville Township Burke County Census p. 327 on microfilm in Burke Library. T36,T361,T363,T364,T365, T366,T367: Family bible, Obeth Cemetery & church records, *The News Herald*, Marriage and Death notices from Asheville NC, NC Census 1840-1870, *Burke: The History of a North Carolina County* by Edward W. Phifer

**Wheeler McKinley Austin (1896-)
and his first wife Okie Billings**

Jr., "William T. Austin" by Nell James Elmore in the *Burke County NC Heritage Book* 1983. T3B: "The Austin Family" by Margaret Payne Carter in the *Iredell County NC Heritage Book* 1983. T321,T322, T323,T325,T351: Caldwell County NC Marriages. T322: Lenoir News Topic & Hickory Daily Record June 1946, T323,T324, T325,T326,T327,T328,T329,T32A: Janet Austin Curtis. T328: "The John Daniel Bean Family" by Mrs. J. Percy (Lena Pipes) Bumgarner. T352: Mrs. Ada Allen's Bible records. T359,T326-3: Marriages of Johnson County TN 18?7 to 1905. T3B2,T3B2-6,T3B2-61,T3B2-62: "Carl Bagby Austin" by Charles Kenneth Austin in the *Iredell County NC Heritage Book* 1983, T324-7: Ann Austin Faw (personal knowledge). T326-3: Opal Smith Austin interview by E. T. & C. B. Austin 1982, delayed Caldwell birth records. T359-1: Lenoir Newspaper 23 March 1983.

THE AUSTIN FAMILY OF
STANLY AND UNION COUNTIES
IN NORTH CAROLINA

by D. Nance

Editor's Note: The following article was derived from the author's article *Genealogy of The Austin Family of Stanly and Union Counties*, 'Being a Most Complete and Accurate Tree From Which All The Austins And Those Related To The Austins May Trace Their Kinship.' The article appeared on pages 6 and 7 of *The Stanly News-Herald* newspaper of Albemarle, North Carolina, on 4 June 1929. The article was submitted by S. Randall Austin, who found it in the D.A.R. Library in Washington, D.C. Union County was formerly a part of Anson County.

U. UNKNOWN[1] AUSTIN was the father of at least two sons, as can be learned from the records in the Family Bible of his son Charles Austin. Nothing is known of this man, except that his son Charles immigrated from Ireland to North Carolina before the American Revolutionary War, and that Charles' nephews also settled in North Carolina.

    U1. CHARLES +
    U2. UNKNOWN +

SECOND GENERATION

U1. CHARLES[2] AUSTIN (*Unknown[1]*) was married to Mary (—). Prior to the Revolutionary War, Charles and Mary came to this section from Ireland. They brought with them their family Bible, which was still in the Austin family in 1929. After Charles died, his widow married a Mr. Hood, and they had one son named Charles Austin Hood. Seven children came with their parents from Ireland:

    U11. PEGGY, *born 9 June 1751*
    U12. WILLIAM, *born 11 April 1754*
    U13. CHARLES, *born 31 May 1756*
    U14. JOHN, *born 3 January 1759*
    U15. MARY, *born 10 June 1761*
    U16. JAMES, *born 10 March 1764* +
    U17. SARAH, *born 3 September 1766*

U2. UNKNOWN[2] AUSTIN (*Unknown[1]*) was a brother to Charles Austin, for Charles Austin's Family Bible lists the children below as being his nephews. Bryant, Richard, Michael and John are known to be brothers. We assume here that Jake and Jonathan were in this same family:

    U21. BRYANT +
    U22. RICHARD, *settled on Richardson Creek, below his cousin James Austin. He sold his land about 1820 and went West with his brother Michael.*
    U23. MICHAEL ('MIKE'), *also settled on Richardson Creek, in the same section as his brother Richard. He sold his land about 1820 and went West with his brother Richard.*
    U24. JACOB ('JAKE')
    U25. JOHN +
    U26. JONATHAN

THIRD GENERATION

U16. JAMES[3] AUSTIN (*Charles,[2] Unknown[1]*) was born 10 March 1764 in Ireland, and came to this country with his parents. He was married to Fanny Snipes, and they settled on Richardson Creek near the old Nance Mill. James is buried beside his wife and grandson Clement Nance near the old homestead. James and Fanny reared ten children:

    U161. EADY, *m. to Jesse Gurley*
    U162. BERRY, *b. 23 December 1795* +
    U163. BRYANT, *b. 16 May 1797, m. to Mariah Tarlton. They had a son Lawson Austin.*
    U164. JAMES, *b. 3 April 1799* +
    U165. CHARLES, *b. 16 May 1797 (sic)* +
    U166. MARY, *b. 12 September 1802, m. to Blackstone Mullis, went to Georgia.*
    U167. AARON, *b. 12 November 1804* +
    U168. DELANEY, *b. 29 September 1806, m. to Henry Baucom. Baucom children: James, Riley, William, Hiram, H. M., Ellis, Calvin, Sarah, and Mrs. George Tucker.*
    U169. FRANKY, *b. 17 November 1808, m. to Harbert Nance. Nance children: Clement, Henry, James, and Silas.*
    U16A. JOHN, *b. 21 April 1811, m. to Nicey Barber, they went West.*

U21. BRYANT[3] AUSTIN (*Unknown,[2] Unknown[1]*) was married to Miss — Osborn. They settled on Rocky River, in what is now Stanly County, North Carolina, just above the Coble Mill. He lived there during the Revolutionary War, and was among the Regulators who Governor Tryon refused to pardon. Bryant fled from Hillsboro and settled in the wilds of what is now Stanly County. Tryon's officers went to his home to arrest him, he offered them a barrel of brandy if they would go on and say nothing about him. They backed their cart up to his cellar door and he rolled the barrel of brandy into their cart and they went on their way rejoicing, and left him to be the ancestor of a large and influential family:

    U211. JACOB +
    U212. BRYANT +
    U213. JONATHAN +
    U214. AISLEY +
    U215. SARAH, *b. 23 December 1783, d. 14 April 1852, m. to John Griffin. Children: Hurley and Nancy.*
    U216. REBECCA, *m. to Enoch Griffin. Griffin children: McGuire, Thomas, Sidney, John, Mrs. Green Phifer, Mrs. Ervin Phifer, Mrs. Andrew Helms.*

U25. JOHN[3] AUSTIN (*Unknown,[2] Unknown[1]*) was married to Rebecca (—). Like his brother Bryant, John was also a member of the Regulators, and there was a warrant issued for him and the officers traced him from Hillsboro to Salisbury where he, with a Mr. Mills, was arrested and compelled to take the oath of allegiance. He then came to what is now Union County and settled between Rocky River and Richardson Creek. Only one child is known:

U251.   JOHN +

FOURTH GENERATION

U162. BERRY[4] AUSTIN (*James,[3] Charles,[2] Unknown[1]*) was born on 23 December 1795. He was married to Susanna Gurley, they had sons and six (sic) daughters:

U162-1. JACOB
U162-2. JOSEPH, *m. Lydia Holley. Children: Marcus C. Austin, William Austin, and Milton Austin.*
U162-3. JOHN J., *m. Miss Smith. Children: Rev. D. M. Austin and John Austin.*
U162-4. SOPHIA, *m. to Riley Griffin. Griffin children: J. Wilson, Milton, Cornelius and Hiram D.*
U162-5. MARY, *m. to Andy Moore. Moore children: Troy, Frank, James, Ellison, Henry & Thomas.*
U162-6. [daughter], *m. Wyatt Holmes. Holmes children: William and John.*
U162-7. FANNY, *m. Hugh Purser. Purser children: David, William and Hugh.*
U162-8. BETTIE, *m. Cass Hasty. Hasty children: John W., Ell(is?), and Brac.*

U164. JAMES[4] AUSTIN (*James,[3] Charles,[2] Unknown[1]*) was born on 3 April 1799 and was married to Winny Thomas. James and Winny had four sons:

U164-1. JOHN M.
U164-2. THOMAS
U164-3. JAMES
U164-4. ALPH, *father of lawyer R. E. Austin, Dr. Jim Austin, and Dave Austin.*

U165. CHARLES[4] AUSTIN (*James,[3] Charles,[2] Unknown[1]*) was born on 16 May 1797 (sic). He was married to first to Betsy Nance by whom he had six children, and second to Gilla Tyre by whom he had one child:

U165-1. WYATT
U165-2. JAMES
U165-3. JANE, *m. Sanders Brewer*
U165-4. POLLY, *m. William Stewart*
U165-5. LUCY, *m. Frazzier Carpenter*
U165-6. MARTHA, *m. John Brewer*
U165-7. ASHLEY

U167. AARON[4] AUSTIN (*James,[3] Charles,[2] Unknown[1]*) was born on 12 November 1804, and was married to Nicey Hinson. Aaron and Nancy had three sons and three daughters:

U167-1. JAMES
U167-2. WILLIAM
U167-3. PHILIP
U167-4. FRANKY, *m. James Walters*
U167-5. POLLY, *m. Emberry Walters*
U167-6. JANE, *m. J. Stanly Smith*

U211. JACOB[4] AUSTIN (*Bryant,[3] Unknown,[2] Unknown[1]*) was married to twice, although the name of his first wife is unknown. He married second to Miss — Marshall. Jacob had eleven children, six by his first wife, and five by his second wife:

U211-1. JACOB COLEMAN, *m. Elizabeth Griffin. Ch: Charles H. Austin who m. Frances Smith, Green D. Austin who m. Margaret Lewis, Jacob Austin, Cull Austin who was killed in Civil War, Marcus N. Austin, Robert Austin who m. Nellie Garrison, Elizabeth Austin who m. — Garrison, Emily Austin who m. Edward Garrison.*
U211-2. MARCUS, *m.(1) Miss — Polk. Children: Permelia Austin who m. — Redfern, William D. Austin, Henry Austin, and Mrs. James D. Gordon. Marcus m.(2) Gilly Grady. Children: Mrs. W. A. Lane, and Marcus Austin, Jr.*
U211-3. JOHN E., *m.(1) Levina Hamilton, by whom he had eight children: Esq. William A. Austin, James Austin who was killed in the battle of Petersburg, Mrs. William G. Long, John C. Austin, Thomas E. Austin, Mrs. Caldwell Helms, Culpepper Austin, and J. Ellis Austin. Levina was killed on a cliff by her slave, and John m.(2) widow — (Sikes) Griffin, by whom he had a son J. Lonnie Austin of Wingate, North Carolina. John m.(3) to Miss — Yandle, their descendants lived near Indian Trail in 1929.*
U211-4. CULPEPPER, *m.(1) Hester Curlee, and to this union was born a daughter Jane Austin who m. — Sikes. He m.(2) Martha B. Griffin and they had three sons: John Austin, E. W. Austin who m. Frances Houstin, and Vernon Austin.*
U211-5. CHARLOTTE, *m. to — Lingle.*
U211-6. BRYANT E., *the father of George P. Austin and Westley Austin.*
U211-7. DAVID, *m. to Miss — Marshall. Children: Malissa Austin who m. — McCorkle, Fanny Austin who m. — Howell, Sydney Austin, Percy Austin, Fred Austin, and Odell Austin.*
U211-8. WHIT, *m. Miss — Kirk. Children: John Austin, Fanny Austin, and Dotts Austin.*
U211-9. STANLY, *the father of Jacob Austin, Murph Austin, and Fred Austin, all went to Arkansas.*
U211-A. THOMAS, *the father of Dr. Austin and lawyer James Austin.*
U211-B. LAMSON, *moved to Arkansas.*

U212. BRYANT[4] AUSTIN (*Bryant,*[3] *Unknown,*[2,1]) was married to Temperance Williams. Temperance was born on Clark Creek in Montgomery County, the daughter of Alfred Williams and grand-daughter of Isham Williams. Bryant and Temperance are buried with his father on the old homestead above the Coble Mill in Stanly County. They had ten (sic) children:

U212-1.   RILLA, *m. T. Wilson Griffin. Griffin children: Dr. Brady, Crag, Jestice and Gertie.*

U212-2.   CALVIN S., *never married*

U212-3.   NICEY, *m. John Foil of Cabarrus County.*

U212-4.   REBECCA, *m. to Sherd Rowland. Rowland children: Minnie, Alice, Mrs. W. D. Mask.*

U212-5.   NANCY

U212-6.   LILLY, *m. John Exum Smith. Smith children: Calvin J., Stanly, W. Jasper, George W., Mrs. George Bryant, Mrs. Tempe Huneycutt*

U212-7.   SARAH M., *never married*

U212-8.   JANE, *m. — Holley, moved to Tennessee.*

U212-9.   LEAH N., *never married.*

U213. JONATHAN[4] AUSTIN (*Bryant,*[3] *Unknown,*[2,1]) was married to Miss — Williams, and they had seven children:

U213-1.   MILTON S., *moved to Texas.*

U213-2.   BRYANT DEBERRY, *m. Elizabeth Hamilton. Children: Johnathan L. Austin, William M. Austin, James K. P. Austin, Mrs. Sandy Gaddy, Mrs. R. N. Bivins, Mrs. D. M. Thomas, Mrs. A. J. Brooks, Mrs. Henry M. Brooks, Mrs. T. J. Perry, and Bryant D. Austin.*

U213-3.   WILLIAM M., *m. to Sarah Brooks. Children: Hampton D. Austin, William Columbus Austin, John C. Austin, Margaret Austin who m. — McCorkle, Caroline Austin who m. — Chaney, and James Austin.*

U213-4.   [daughter], *m. to Ervin Lotharp. Lotharp children: Neal, and Mrs. Cyrus Lemond.*

U213-5.   MARY, *m. to John W. Hoose.*

U213-6.   STANHOPE

U213-7.   PERMELIA, *m. to Daniel Palmer.*

U214. AISLEY[4] AUSTIN (*Bryant,*[3] *Unknown,*[2,1]) was married to Amos Griffin, and they had ten children: Riley Griffin who m. Sophia Austin (parents of Mrs. E. M., Milton, J. Wilson, ex-sheriff of Union County, Cornelius, Hyram D. and Mrs. Wm. D. Liles), Amos Hurley Griffin who m. Sarah L. Austin (parents of one child who died young), Kinley Griffin, Huberry Griffin, Thomas Jefferson Griffin who m. Mary (Polly) Austin (parents of Ashley Calvin and Mrs. Wm. R.), Enoch Griffin who m. Ann Ramsey, Jack Griffin who m. Susan Coley, Madison Griffin who m. Patsy Rowland, Betsy Griffin who never married, and Sally Griffin who m. John Curlee.

U251. JOHN[4] AUSTIN (*John,*[3] *Unknown,*[2,1]) was born on 25 October 1775. He was married to Lucretia Coburn,

who was born on 9 July 1779, the daughter of John and Mary Coburn. Information here was obtained from records in Jonathan Austin's papers, supposed to have been compiled at the time of the settlement of the estate of John Austin, Jr. Mary and John Austin had eight children:

U251-1.   JESSE, *born in 1803, m. Elizabeth Curlee. Children: Albert Austin, Sarah Austin who m. Hamp Little, the son of Labe Little.*

U251-2.   ELIZABETH, *b. 2 September 1803, m. John A. Nance. Nance children: Jesse Pinctney, James D., Alfred H., Ferington I., Wyatt D., Jane and Quintina.*

U251-3.   NANCY, *b. 11 April 1806, m. John Sasser*

U251-4.   JONATHAN (JOHNATHAN), *m. Miss Efird. Children: Riley Austin, John Austin, Jacob Austin, Lindsey Austin, James Austin, Mrs. B. Smith, Mrs. Thomas A. Fowler, Elvy who m. Reverend R. H. James.*

U251-5.   MARY (POLLY), *b. 9 July 1812, m. T. J. Griffin. Griffin children: Jane, Emeline, Deberry, Ashley and Calvin.*

U251-6.   RICHARD, *b. 27 January 1815, nothing else is known of him.*

U251-7.   SARAH L., *b. 21 September 1815, m. Amos Hurley, Jr.*

U251-8.   REBECCA, *b. 3 September 1818, m. J. W. Huneycutt*

★★★★★★★★★★★★★★★★★★★★★★★★★★★★

Austins of America is intended to serve present and future genealogists researching Austin family lines. Readers are encouraged to submit queries, genealogical and historical articles for publication. Previously published books, pamphlets or articles containing Austin genealogical data are also sought for reprinting or review.

EDITOR

DR. MICHAEL EDWARD AUSTIN   CONCORD, MA

ASSOCIATE EDITORS

ANTHONY KENT AUSTIN   PROSPECT, KY

BERT ADDIS AUSTIN   QUEEN CREEK, AZ

PATRICIA BIEBUYCK AUSTIN   CONCORD, MA

PAULINE LUCILLE AUSTIN   SAVANNAH, GA

Austins of America is published each February and August by The Austin Print, 23 Allen Farm Lane, Concord, Massachusetts 01742. All correspondence, including subscriptions, articles and responses to queries, should be sent to this address. Subscriptions are $4.50 per year postpaid.

★★★★★★★★★★★★★★★★★★★★★★★★★★★★

INDEX TO AUSTIN REAL ESTATE TRANSFERS
IN CALDWELL COUNTY, NORTH CAROLINA

by Cornelia Bradshaw Austin

Editor's Note: The real estate transfers indexed below are listed alphabetically by the Austin involved, whether Grantor or Grantee, and chronologically for the same Austin name. The last numbers in each transfer are the Deed Book number and page on which the transfer is recorded in the Caldwell County records. Transfers between two Austins are listed alphabetically under the Grantee's name. Many of these Austins are found in the author's article *The Descendants of Thomas Austin and Rebecca Turner of Amherst County, Virginia* (see page 178).

A. W. Austin sold land to Julius Conley in 1855.   4-132

A. W. Austin sold real estate to E. W. Jones in 1871.   6-112

A. W. Austin sold real estate to E. W. Jones in 1872.   6-335

A. W. Austin bought land from Henry M. & Laura A. Mood in 1872.   9-563

A. W. Austin bought land from E. P. Miller (by N. A. Miller) in 1872.   11-367

A. W. & Julia A. Austin sold land to J. Mason Spainhour in 1872.   11-369

A. W. Austin and others bought land from Nicholas & Robena Jenkins in 1876.   8-404

A. W. & Julia Austin sold land to John Hayes in 1877.   9-87

A. W. & Julia A. Austin sold land to Fanny Wiesenfeld in 1878.   9-558

A. W. & Julia A. Austin sold land to Mrs. M. L. Spainhour, Executrix, in 1883.   13-4

A. W. & Julia A. Austin, T. J. & M. J. Austin and others sold land to G. W. F. & S. F. Harper in 1888.   21-340

Addie L. Austin bought land from K. C. & M. E. Menzies in 1894.   27-255

Amanuel Austin sold land to Isaac Coffey in 1856.   4-671

Benjamin Austin sold land to Andrew Read Jr. in 1837.   1-38

Daniel Austin bought land from William Austin in 1842.   4-782

David H. & Margaret Austin sold land to Joseph Stearnes in 1861.   5-107

E. J. & Emma Austin bought land from William A. & Laura Fulwood in 1903.   36-543

Mrs. E. L. Austin bought land from William H. & Mary Cloer in 1895.   28-151

Elijah Austin, Jr. sold land to Merritt Austin in 1840.   4-265

Elijah Austin sold to Elijah Reed 1844. 1-326

Elijah Austin sold to Andrew Reid 1854. 4-269

Elhanan Austin bought land from David,

Juley J., Enoch, Lewis, Mattie & Phillip Austin, Jno. & Mary Clayton, Dora & J. W. McGuire in 1895.   27-548

G. H. & Harriet A. Austin sold land to W. A. Presnell in 1871.   16-535

G. H. Austin bought land from T. W. & Sarah Austin in 1887.   20-485

G. T. Austin sold land to Wilson Lumber & Milling Company in 1910.   26-469

George L. Austin bought land from H. H. & E. M. Messick in 1900.   39-298

George L. Austin bought land from Alice V. & Jno. A. Bush in 1904.   38-129

George L. & Alice G. Austin sold land to E. & Lance Carver in 1905.   39-588

Henrietta Austin bought land from Isaac S. & Sarah E. Austin in 1885.   19-167

Isaac S. Austin bought land from S. F. Patterson Chr CCPQS in 1863.   6-551

Isaac S. Austin bought land from James Harper in 1863.   7-134

Isaac S. Austin bought land from George W. Livingston in 1864.   7-135

Isaac Austin bought land from Ed W. Jones in 1865.   7-276

Isaac S. Austin bought land from Randy & Rebecca E. Taylor in 1868.   7-8

Isaac S. & Sarah E. Austin sold land to George W. F. Harper in 1869.   5-621

Isaac S. Austin bought land from North Carolina in 1872.   7-7

Isaac S. & Sarah E. Austin sold land to George W. F. Harper in 1873.   6-449

Isaac Austin bought land from William M. & Evaline Heffner in 1882.   13-104

Isaac S. & Sarah E. Austin sold land to William C. Newland in 1884.   14-56

Isaac S. & Sarah E. Austin sold land to L. L. Munday in 1898.   30-392

J. L. & Rebecca Austin bought land from Narsie & W. L. Hartley in 1904.   38-3

J. M. Austin bought land from A. C. & Lucy Gilbert in 1903.   39-214

J. W. Austin bought land from S. L. Icard in 1890.   33-428

J. W. & S. E. Austin bought land from L. L., J. E., N. J. & W. H. Austin, H. L. & Jones S. Crump in 1895.   33-412

J. W. Austin bought land from S. L. Icard (by E. G. Icard, Administrator) in 1901.   33-429

Jesse Austin sold land to Thomas Austin in 1849 (by Sheriff).   2-131

Joseph M. Austin bought land from Elizabeth & Louis Harris in 1883.   15-579

Joseph M. & Maggie M. Austin sold land to Elizabeth Harris in 1886.   20-107

Joseph M. Austin bought land from Thomas J. & Margaret J. Austin in 1887.   20-532

Joseph Austin bought land from Boon, Lewis, Dela & Minyard Harris, Annie & Monro Hutchings, J.M. & S.C. Hamlet 1899. 32-504

Joseph M. & Maggie M. Austin sold land to James H. Harris in 1901.   33-563

Joseph Austin sold land to J. L. Nelson in 1901.   34-221

Julius J. Austin bought land from Thomas J. & Margaret J. Austin in 1879.   15-144

Julius Jefferson & Celia Isabelle Austin sold land to Wilson Lumber & Milling Company in 1905.   39-534

J. J. Austin granted right of way to Wilson Lumber & Milling Company in 1905.   40-340

L. L. & N. J. Austin bought land from W. H. & J. E. & J. W. & S. E. Austin, Jones S. & H. L. Crump in 1895.   33-475

L. T. Austin bought land from Thomas J. & Margaret J. Austin in 1899.   32-142

Levi Austin sold to Moses Austin 1839. 1-110

Louis & Martha J. Austin sold land to Henry C. Coffey in 1892.   24-596

Manuel Austin bought land from Samuel Austin in 1850.   2-200

Martha H. Austin bought land from Isaac S. & Sarah E. Austin in 1885.   17-575

Mary E. Austin bought land from W. H. & J. E. Austin & Sarah Watson in 1888.   21-1

Mary E. Austin bought land from W. H. H. & M. S. Hartley and others in 1888.   21-1

Mary E. Austin bought land from W. J. & J. E. Watson and others in 1888.   21-1

Merritt Austin bought land from Elijah Austin Jr. in 1840.   4-265

Merret Austin sold land to G. W. Long in 1862.   18-193

Moses Austin bought land from Levi Austin in 1839.   1-110

Moses Austin bought land from Jesse Starnes in 1840.   1-109

N. J. & L. L. Austin bought land from W. H. & J. E. & J. W. & S. E. Austin, Jones S. & H. L. Crump in 1895.   33-475

Nancy M. Austin bought land from Joseph Corpening in 1884.   14-16

Nathan Austin sold land to Christian Baker in 1838.   1-136

Nathan T. Austin sold land to James F. Monday in 1840.   1-404

Nathan Austin bought land from North Carolina in 1843.   1-257

Noah Austin bought land from Samuel Austin in 1850.   19-108

Noah Austin sold land to Carmy McGowan in 1851.   19-109

Noah Austin bought land from Jesse Freeman in 1854.   13-504

R. I. Austin bought land from Calaway, Adah, Austin, Luetty, Marcus and Jennie Coffey in 1901.   34-543

R. T. & Emer (sic - Emma?) Austin sold land to J. T. Tolbert in 1903.   36-547

Rose Anna Austin bought land from Nathan & Mary Reed in 1873.   7-144

R. L. Austin bought land from C. L. & Emily Coffey in 1897.   32-266

Rufus L. Austin bought land from Henry H. & Elvira Messick in 1903.   37-393

Mrs. S. E. Austin bought from Isaac S. & Sarah E. Austin et al in 1897.   29-546

Mrs. S. E. Austin bought land from B. & M. H. Bellringer in 1897.   29-546

Mrs. S. E. Austin bought land from W. H. Bower in 1897.   29-546

Samuel Austin bought land from North Carolina in 1838.   1-386

Samuel Austin bought land from North Carolina in 1842.   1-285

Samuel Austin sold land to Elijah Reed in 1843.   1-330

Samuel Austin sold 50 acres of land to John Jackson in 1844.   1-410

Samuel Austin bought from Burton & Margaret Hollar in 1883.   13-14

Samuel & M. E. sold land to A. J. Hollar in 1886.   20-434

Samuel & M. E. sold land to S. H. Hollar in 1887.   20-432

Samuel & M. E. Austin sold land to G. F. E. Cline & wife in 1887.   41-375

Samuel & M. E. sold land to D. C. & H. S. Bolick in 1892.   24-346

Sarah Austin bought land from Joseph & Malinda Palmer in 1878.   14-510

Sarah E. Austin bought land from A. D. Lingle in 1901.   33-411

Sarah E. Austin sold land to Edgar A. Poe in 1905.   39-449

T. J. Austin bought homestead land from North Carolina in 1877.   9-170

T. J. & M. J. Austin, A. W. & Julia A. Austin et al sold land to G. W. F. & S. F. Harper 1888.   21-340

T. W. & S. E. Austin sold land to Mary E. Hartley in 1884.   14-72

T. W. Austin bought land from Henkel & Corpening in 1885.   14-512

T. W. Austin bought land from A. W. & Julia A. Austin in 1886.   20-483

T. W. Austin bought land from Caroline & Jno. R. Hartley in 1887.   22-276

T. W. & Sallie Austin sold land to Caldwell & Northern Railroad Company in 1894.   27-283

T. W. & Sarah E. Austin leased land to J. M. Bernhardt in 1905.   40-151

T. W. & Sarah E. Austin leased land to J. M. Bernhardt in 1907.   26-275

T. W. Austin leased land from Elgina, John & James Miller in 1910.   26-446

Thomas Austin bought land from Jesse Austin (by Sheriff) in 1849.   2-131

Thomas J. Austin sold land to Benjamin Jopling in 1849.   2-134

Thomas Austin sold land to Adelaide E. Largent in 1858.   16-316

Thomas Austin bought land from Smith H. Powell in 1859.   5-298

Thomas Austin sold land to Robert McCall in 1860.   5-147

Thomas Austin sold land to William A. Lenoir in 1860.   5-297

Thomas J. Austin bought land from John Catron in 1862.   3-316

Thomas J. Austin bought land from John Catron in 1862.   3-317

T. J. & M. T. (sic) Austin sold land to James Harper in 1873.   7-16

Thomas J. & Margaret J. Austin sold land to S. F. Harper in 1879.   10-273

Thomas & Clara G.(sic) Austin sold land to H. C. Mackie in 1902.   35-568

Thomas & C. J. Austin sold land to A. S. Hartley in 1902.   39-234

Thomas A. & Clara J. Austin sold to D. H. & M. I. Link in 1903.   37-276

Thomas & C. J. Austin sold land to D. H. & M. I. Link in 1904.   39-1

Thomas & Clara J. Austin sold to M. E. & V. E. Teague in 1904.   39-161

W. F. Austin bought land from A. W. & Julia A. Austin in 1884.   17-223

W. F. & Addie L. Austin sold land to D. P. Mast in 1893.   25-209

W. F. Austin bought land from G. H. & H. A. Austin in 1893.   25-267

W. H. & Julia E. Austin bought land from W. H. H. & M. S. Hartley et al in 1888.   19-474

W. H. & Julia E. Austin bought land from J. E. & W. J. Watson et al in 1888.   19-474

W. H. & Julia E. Austin bought land from M. E. Austin et al 1888.   19-474

W. H. & J. E. & M. E. Austin et al sold land to W. H. H. Hartley in 1888.   19-520

W. H. & J. E. & M. E. Austin et all sold land to Sarah A. Watson in 1888.   19-476

W. H. & Julia E. Austin bought land from Sarah A. Watson in 1892.   24-308

W. H. & J. E. Austin bought land from Jones S. & H. L. Crump et al in 1895.   28-210

W. H. & Julia E. Austin bought land from J. W. & S. E. and N. J. & L. L. Austin in 1895.   28-210

W. H. & J. E., J. W. & S. E., L. L. & M. J. (sic) Austin sold land to Jones L. & H. L. Crump in 1895.   33-520

W. W. & Cora D. & Etta Austin sold land to W. M. Earnhardt in 1886.   19-171

W. W. & Cora D. Austin sold land to L. L. Munday in 1891.   30-264

William Austin bought land from North Carolina in 1792 (sic).   32-320

William Austin bought land from Samuel Austin in 1842.   1-177

William Austin Jr. sold land to Andrew Reide Jr. in 1842.   4-230

William Austin sold land to William Reed in 1846.   16-315

William Austin (by Sheriff) sold land to Andrew Reid in 1857.   4-318

William H. & Julia C. Austin bought from Nicholas & Robena Jenkins in 1896.   35-384

William & Mary Austin sold land to B.F. Eaton in 1884.   14-118

William Wightman Austin bought land from Isaac S. & Sarah E. Austin in 1885.   17-235

William W. Austin bought land from Isaac S. & Sarah E. Austin in 1885.   19-169

GRAVE REGISTRATIONS OF MAINE AUSTINS IN THE REVOLUTIONARY, CIVIL AND SPANISH-AMERICAN WARS

by Patricia Biebuyck Austin

Editor's Note: The following data was obtained by the author at the Maine State Archives in Augusta, and at the Farmington Library.

Alfred H. Austin of Bath, Sagadahoc County: Civil War, born May 1836 and killed in action on 11 November 1864 at Petersburg, buried at Maple Grave Cemetery Lot 7, Range 9, Section 1.

Alonzo F. Austin of Berwick, York County: Civil War, buried at Evergreen Cemetery Lot 340.

Benjamin Austin of Rome, Kennebec County: Civil War, born Belgrade ME and buried at Rome ME, Cemetery Lot 4 Grave 1. Date of enlistment was 3 September 1861, date of discharge was 10 August 1865.

Carlton M. Austin of Lamoine, Hancock County: Civil War, born 1842 at Trenton ME, died 1 July 1882, buried at Forest Hill Cemetery, Section C, Lot 29. Date of enlistment was 28 July 1862 at Bangor ME, date of dischange 1 January 1865.

Charles Austin of Gardiner, Kennebec County: Civil War born 1838 at Vassalboro ME, died 16 September 1906 at Togus ME. George Austin, father, next of kin. Buried at Mount Hope Cemetery, Lot 185, Grave 1 Book 9 Page 98.

Charles Austin of Brooks, Waldo County: Civil War, born at Brooks, buried at Friends Cemetery Section 1. Date of enlistment was 10 September 1862 at Bangor ME, date of discharge was 17 August 1863.

Charles L. Austin of Chelsea, Kennebec County: Civil War, born 1840 at Hallowell ME; buried at Riverside Cemetery Section ? Lot 206 Date of enlistment 21 August 1861 at Vassalboro ME, date of discharge 28 June 1865.

Cyrus Austin of Lewiston, Androscoggin County: Civil War, born 1804, and died 14 November 1885. Buried at Riverside Cemetery, Old Section Lot 5.

Daniel Austin of St. Albans, Somerset County: Civil War born 1824 at Parkman ME, buried at Village Cemetery, Old Part, Section C, Lot 67. Date of discharge was 5 April 1865.

Daniel Austin of Turner, Androscoggin County: Civil War, born 17 April 1842 at Buckfield ME, died 7 June 1925 at Turner ME from Cron. Cystitis. Buried 10 June 1925 at Turner, Centre Cemetery, Section A, Lot 98. Book 5 Page 160. Next of kin: Daniel Austin of Buckfield.

David Austin of Dresden, Lincoln County: Revolutionary War, Private, saw service at Claverack. Date of enlistment was 14 October 1779, date of discharge was 22 November 1779.

E. Austin, Civil War, buried at National Point of Rocks Cemetery.

Edward S. Austin of Veazie, Penobscot County: Civil War, born 1837, died 1896, buried at Fairview Cemetery, Section 1, Lot N-44.

Edwin Austin of Togus, Kennebec County: Civil War, died 15 August 1911, buried at V.A.F. Togus Cemetery, Section A, Lot 5-18, Grave 2898.

Ezekiel Austin of Pittsfield, Somerset County: Civil War, born 1828 at York ME, buried at Pittsfield Section D, Range 9, Lot 19. Date of enlistment was 15 August 1862, date of discharge was 12 June 1865.

George E. Austin of Norway, Oxford County: Civil War, born June 1836 at Oxford ME, died 2 April 1901 at Norway ME from heart disease, buried 5 April 1901 at Pine Grove Cemetery, Old Section, Range 5, Lot 40, Book 2, Page 35. Next of kin was Thomas Austin.

H. M. Austin of Orrington Center, Penobscot County: Civil War, born 1843, died 1916, buried at Oak Hill Cemetery, Section 5, Lot 19.

Henry D. Austin of Hallowell, Kennebec County: Civil War, born 30 September 1842 at Hallowell ME, died 30 June 1911 at Auburn NH, buried 3 February 1911 at Hallowell Cemetery, Section 6, Lot 605 Grave 8, Book A, Page 43. Date of enlistment was 14 August 1862 at Augusta ME, date of discharge was 25 March 1865.

Hovey C. Austin of Hallowell, Kennebec County: Civil War, born at Belgrade ME, buried at Hallowell Cemetery, Section 7, Lot 738, Grave 1, Book 5, Page 153. Date of enlistment was 21 August 1861 at Presque Isle ME, date of discharge was 23 March 1863.

J. B. Austin of Pittston, Kennebec County: Civil War, born 1824, buried at North Pittston, Lot 18, Grave 1. Date of enlistment was 29 August 1864 at Wales ME, date of discharge was 27 May 1865.

James Austin of Togus, Kennebec County: Civil War, died 1 January 1913. Grave No. 3079 buried at V.A.F. Togus Cemetery, Section A., Lot 2-2. Date of enlistment was 29 February 1864 at Unity ME, date of discharge was 18 January 1866.

John Austin of Togus, Kennebec County: Civil War, died 8 July 1890 and buried at V.A.F. Togus Cemetery, Section E., Lot 2-11. Next of kin: Mrs. Phoebe A. Hines.

John Austin of Rumford, Oxford County: Civil War, born 1811, died 19 July 1890, buried at South Rumford, Wyman Cemetery. Date of enlistment was 2 January 1864 at Peru ME, Private, date of discharge was 28 March 1864.

John Austin, Jr. of Rumford, Oxford County: Civil War, born 3 May 1841, died 30 October 1904, buried at South Rumford, Wyman Cemetery, Grave 68. Date of enlistment 22 September 1861 at Rumford ME, date of discharge was 5 January 1863 for disability.

John Gorham Austin of Dresden, Lincoln County: Civil War, born 1846, died 1914, buried at Forest Hill Cemetery, Section 1, Lot 32.

John H. Austin of Brooksville, Hancock County: Civil War, born 24 September 1827, died 13 October 1890, buried at Condon Cemetery, A. Avenue 1, Lot 10 Grave 2. Date of enlistment was 11 August 1862 at Brooksville ME, date of discharge was 17 August 1863.

Jonah Austin of Windham, Cumberland County: Revolutionary War, Private, died 1834. Date of enlistment was 11 July 1775, date of discharge was 20 January 1780.

Jonah Austin of Windham, Cumberland County: Civil War, born 1819 at Windham ME, died 17 May 1894 at Windham of old age, buried at Scotland Cemetery. Next of kin was Jonah Austin.

Joseph Austin of New Portland, Somerset County: Civil War, born 28 November 1838 at Belgrade ME, died 13 November 1904 at New Portland from Acute Bright's disease, buried at Village Cemetery, Block E, Lot 32. Date of enlistment was 19 July 1862 at Portland ME, date of discharge was 4 June 1865. Next of kin was Cyrus Austin of Belgrade ME.

Joseph P. Austin of Auburn, Androscoggin County: Civil War, born 12 June 1843, died 25 October 1869, buried at Mount View Cemetery, Section B, Lot 128. Date of enlistment was 14 August 1862 at Skowhegan ME, date of discharge was 5 June 1865.

King Austin of Windham, Cumberland County: Revolutionary War, buried in Cemetery in field near Lucas Libby farm. Upright stone.

Merritt Austin of Thomaston, Knox County: Civil War, born 22 September 1813, died 10 February 1893, buried at Thomaston Cemetery, Section 5, Lot 2.

Nahum Austin, Jr. of Belgrade, Kennebec County: Civil War, born 1836, died 1901, buried at Woodside Cemetery, Lot 459, Grave 1.

Nathaniel Austin of North Berwick, York County: Spanish-America War, born 17 August 1858 at North Berwick ME, died 29 April 1927 at Portland ME of angina pectoris, buried at Mount Pleasant Cemetery, Grave 200, Book 1, Page 30. Next of kin was David Austin.

Otis Austin of Togus, Kennebec County: Civil War, died 23 February 1890, buried at V.A.F. Togus Cemetery, Section F, Lot 1-15, Grave 781. Next of kin was Elizabeth Austin.

Reuel Austin Civil War, died 12 November 1864, buried at National Cemetery at Barrancas, Florida.

Robert Albert Austin of Littleton, Aroostook County: Civil War, born 7 July 1841, died 26 October 1919, buried at Littleton Cemetery, Lot 68.

Samuel Austin of Portland, Cumberland County: Civil War, born 1826, died 27 October 1866 of dysentery, buried at Forest City Cemetery, Section E, Lot 25. Date of enlistment was 16 July 1861.

Samuel W. Austin of Dresden, Lincoln County: Civil War, born 1828 buried at Forest Hill Cemetery, Section 1, Lot 33. Date of enlistment was 21 September 1863 at Bath ME, date of discharge was 11 September 1865.

Samuel W. Austin of Perham, Aroostook County: Civil War, born 6 October 1835, died 28 December 1902, buried at Fairview Cemetery, Lot 53.

Sidney A. Austin of West Peru, Oxford County: Civil War, born 1848, died 22 September 1909 at Rumford ME of heart disease, buried at Demerritt Cemetery, Grave 236. Next of kin was Justus Austin (father).

William Alvah Austin of Vassalboro, Kennebec County: Civil War, born 18 February 1846 at Vassalboro ME, died 25 May 1916, buried at Cross Hill Cemetery, Lot 21, Grave 1. Date of enlistment was 10 September 1862 at Augusta ME, date of discharge was 23 June 1865.

William H. Austin of North Berwick, York County: Spanish-American War, born 5 January 1855 at North Berwick ME, died 21 June 1929 at North Berwick, of angina pectoris. Buried at Mount Pleasant Cemetery, Grave 225, Book 1, Page 32. Next of kin was David Austin (Family Monument).

William King Austin of Windham, Cumberland County: Civil War, born 21 October 1829, died 16 December 1902, buried at Austin Cemetery, Grave 7. Date of enlistment was 24 June 1861 at Windham ME, date of discharge was 17 December 1861.

A REVERENCE FOR WOOD

by Eric Sloane

Editor's Note: The following article first appeared as part of a chapter "The New World" on pages 92-98 of the author's book *A Reverence for Wood*, published in 1965 by Ballantine Books of New York.

The ship's master, Robert Carter, was dining at the estate of Ralph Austin, "an extraordinary practicer in ye art of planting." The dinner had been a bon voyage meeting, for Robert Carter was to leave on the next tide. The time for fruit and brandy had come.

"I envy you your journey," said the host, "and drink Godspeed to you. You will reach America at Goose Summer, and the harvesting will be at its peak; it will be an exciting and colorful spectacle."

"In America they call it Indian Summer," said Carter, "and indeed there is color such as we never see in England. They say the first frost sets the leaves afire, and from then on a man can look at the hills and tell by the colors what kind of trees are there. The browns and tans are hickory, the yellows are tulip and beech and ironwood; the black gum and oak and maple turn flaming red, while the purples are the leaves of the white and mountain ash."

"They say that the orange colors are so bright they hurt your eyes."

"Yes, they do — those are the leaves of sassafras and sugar maple."

"And when you arrive in America," said Ralph Austin, "I hope that you will remember to gather what information you can about the orchards there. The plague of ice that struck us here in England last year must surely have killed many orchard trees; only the most hardy can have survived. I shall want grafts and layers of them for England. And you must keep accounts for me, telling me of all the astounding trees of the New World."

"I shall do this indeed," said Robert, "but I am of the opinion that many of the American trees would not survive the temperate mildness of the air of Britain — they seem to need the intense atmospheric changes of America. Birch, for example, has been known to grow in England for centuries, yet nothing like the American birch has ever been seen here. The Indians choose one large birch tree and make two cuts down its trunk on opposite sides; then they make two encircling cuts at top and bottom. In the spring when the bark is peeling, the Indians lift away these two curled pieces of bark and sew them together to make a boat which they call a 'canoo.' "

"Remarkable!" said Ralph Austin. "And what do they use for sewing?"

"Again a tree! They use the roots of the white spruce, and to make the boat watertight they heat the wood of balsam fir until its resin oozes out and they mix it with the pitch of pine. But the biggest 'canoos' are the ones made of solid wood. There is tale of one made from a hollowed sycamore that is sixty-five feet long and carries nine thousand pounds. In American the old sycamore usually has a hollow trunk, and great barrels are made with the slightest effort. Even well-linings are made from these hollow sycamore trunks, and sometimes they are used as storage bins, as big around as an armspread and a perch in height."

"This very year," he continued, "a mast was felled in Maine which proved too big for any of our mast ships. Even after it was hewn and shaped, it had a useable length of one hundred and thirty feet and weighed over twenty-five tons. Why, there are pines in Massachusetts that have no extending limbs until a hundred feet from the ground!"

"But these wonders are not what I can write about in these times," said Austin. "England is badly in need of timber because of the waste of its resources; we must implant the value of the growing tree and inspire the farmer in a Godly way, so that he will plant and know the benefits of propagating timber trees and orchards."

"I have read your writings, good Ralph," said Robert, "and I can perhaps even quote you. 'The world is a great library, and fruit trees are some of the books wherein we may read and see plainly the attributes of God.' Perhaps America will need such a philosophy, too, before it wastes its trees, thinking of them as just so much material wealth. I shall take your book with me and show it to those who will read its wisdom."

Agriculture and husbandry during the 1600's and 1700's were not a business, but a way of life. This explains why writings about agriculture were so filled with Biblical quotations and moral philosophy. Austin, in speaking of pruning, for example, tells how fruit trees that spread widely and grow near the ground bear more and larger fruit than high trees, and the fruit is easier to reach. This might be forgotten by the reader, except for the typical religious application as he writes, "...and humble Christians, too, bring forth more and fairer fruit than lofty persons, while their acts are easier to reach."

A servant entered with a tray of nuts and fruits, and Austin passed them to his guest.

"England's orchards of forest trees are most depleted. Some of the boat builders are using fruitwoods, as are the joiners. Nothing is wasted now, but it is almost too late. The ship *Mayflower* is now the beams and rafters of a barn in Buckingham. Whatever new wood we need for our navy will come from the New World."

Robert Carter broke an apple in two, admired its meat, and sprinkled it with cinnamon spice. "It is time for me to leave," he said. "I should like to take one of these fine apples with me and plant the seed in America."

"What a fine idea! But the seed would not propagate the same apple, and a graft might not last the voyage. But wait! I shall get you a layering plant, and you shall be the first to bring my prize across the ocean. I have worked a long time to create this variety; I have not named it yet. I would be pleased for you to name it. Perhaps the 'Westfield,' after your farm in Massachusetts? Perhaps it might be named after your ship! What is the name of your ship?"

"It is called the *Seek-no-further.*"

References

A Treatise of Fruit-Trees, by R. A. Austin, Practiser in y Art of Planting; Oxford, printed for Tho: Robinson, 1657. Shewing the manner of Grafting, Setting, Pruning, and Ordering of them in all respects: According to divers new and easy Rules of experience; gathered in y space of Twenty yeares.

The Spirituall use of an Orchard, or Garden of Fruit-Trees. Set forth in divers Similitudes betweene Naturall and Spirituall fruit-trees, in their Natures, and Ordering, according to Scripture and Experience. The second Impression; with the addition of many Similitudes. By R. A. Austin, Author of the first part. OXFORD Printed by HEN: HALL, Printer to the University, for Tho: Robinson. M.DC.LVII Hos: 12.10; Jer: 17.8; Rom: 11.23; Joh: 15.1.2; Cant. 2.3; Cant. 4.12.13.

★★★★★★★★★★★★★★★★★★★★★★★★★★★★

Austins in the Federal Census of 1850

All current volunteers are requested to send in their state's information as soon as possible. Some additional volunteers are still needed, please write *Austins of America* for details.

★★★★★★★★★★★★★★★★★★★★★★★★★★★★

QUERIES

240-1. John Austin was born circa 1728, married Miss — Crenshaw or Miss — Grisby circa 1748. Their daughter Susan Austin was born circa 1749 in Hanover County, Virginia, she married John Anthony Jr. in 1771 in Evington, Campbell County, Virginia. John Anthony was born in 1746 in Evington, and died on 3 February 1817 in Evington. Anthony children: John b. 1773, William Banks b. 1775, Mary C. b. 1777, Sarah b. 1780, James Crenshaw b. 1782, Mark b. 1783, Abner b. 1789, Charles b. 1794. Need John Austin's wife and ancestry.

240-2. William Austin married Experience Dawson, daughter of Martin Dawson of Rutland, VT I believe. William and Experience lived in Franklin, Franklin Couny, Vermont from 1820-1840. The lived near David Brown Austin. David was the son of Jotham Austin a descendant of Robert Austin. Is there any connection between David and William.

240-3. Joseph Austin according to the *History of Dover, New Hampshire* by John Scales, probably resided in Hampton, NH in 1642, owned mill property at Cocheco Falls in 1649, married Sarah Starbuck in 1659 or 1660, and died between 6 June 1662 and 1 July 1663. His son, Thomas Austin, married Ann Otis, their daughter Rose was born 3 April 1678, she married Ephraim Tibbetts. I would appreciate any further information on this line.

240-4. Mary Austin was married on 17 May 1674 to Richard Gardner II (1653-1728). Her parents were Joseph Austin and Sarah Starbuck of Dover NH, as given in *The History of Nantucket* Massachusetts by Alexander Starbuck. Need the ancestors and descendants of Mary.

240-5. Elizabeth Austin married Henry Tebbets according to information from the book *History of Dover*. I would appreciate any further information on this line.

240-6. Matthew Austin married Mary Littlefield, their son Benjamin was born circa 1707, died circa 14 May 1787, he married Catherine —. Their son Nathaniel Austin married Lydia, daughter of Francis Brock? and Sarah Hodsdon? Nathaniel's Will was dated 1 May 1822. He and Lydia had a son, William Austin born 1781 and died 2 April 1837, int. of marriage 4 April 1808 to Susan (Ana) Brock who was b. 1784 and d. 1808. Their daughter, Susan Austin born 19 December 1808 and died 5 April 1831 married 10 October 1828 John James Wentworth born 23 September 1804. Need Matthew's ancestry and maiden names of Catherine and Lydia.

240-7. James Austin and his wife Eleanor (Brander) Austin who immigrated from Elgin, Scotland circa 1780 had a son, Alexander, born in 1792, died in 1887 in Philadelphia. Need James's ancestors and descendants.

241-1. **William Thompson Austin** was born in 1829, probably in Morristown, Tennessee, died circa 1903 in Newkirk, Oklahoma. He married on 28 March 1849 to Louisa Peck Easley, who was born in 1829 in Grainger County, Tennessee, and died in 1905 in Newkirk. William and Louisa's son Robert White Austin was born on 8 January 1849/50 in Eastern Tennessee, died on 3 or 30 March 1934 in Newkirk. Robert married on 28 July 1869 to Mary H. Jeffreys, who died 5 October 1889 in Grainger County. Robert and Mary's son James Franklin Austin was born 12 August 1878 in Morristown, died 4 June 1964 in Oklahoma City where he is buried. William, Robert and James settled in Oklahoma in the early 1900's. James married on 30 August 1905 in Perry, Oklahoma, to Jessie Beulah Peters. She was born on 22 September 1884 in Washington, Kansas, and died on 5 June 1954 in Sulphur, Oklahoma. According to family records, an Archibald Austin born on 3 February 1754 in Durham, Connecticut, was William's great-grandfather. William's father was perhaps either James C. Austin or Archibald Austin. William Austin's g-g-granddaughter thinks many of her Austin ancestors are buried in a family graveyard in Austin Springs, Tennessee, located near Johnson City, and seeks more information on William's ancestry.

241-2. **Ebenezer Austin** married Mehitable Forbes born circa 1769. Their children: Ebenezer born 21 March 1790, John born 17 December 1791, Susanna born 19 August 1793, Zadoc born 30 March 1796, Esther born 29 May 1798, and Daniel born 31 January 1801, and died 29 January 1868. Need more information on the ancestors and descendants of Ebenezer.

241-3. **John Sweet Austin** married Sally Maria Whitford. Their daughter, Laura born 10 June 1831, married Silas B. Wood. Their son John Austin Wood married Harriet Adaline Titus Harmon. According to records of Edwards, NY, Harriet had a brother Albert and a sister Mary. It is believed that this branch of both Woods and Austins came from NH. Any data on the Austin genealogy and any of the other branches would be greatly appreciated.

241-4. **Stillman Blanchard Austin Sr.** was born in Vermont, who had a son Stillman Blanchard Jr. born in New York who had a son Loran born 1899 in Northern Minnesota and died 12 March 1987. Husband of Grace C. Austin. Need the ancestors and descendants of this family.

241-5. **Daniel Austin** – on 10 September 1767 a warrant was issued for Daniel Austin and my ancestor Francis Douglass, accused of murdering, on 1 June 1767, an Indian family at Sebago Pond and stealing their beaver pelts. (See Documentary History of the State of Maine, 2nd Series, vol. 24, pp. 144-148, 153-156.) Who was Daniel Austin? Were they ever arrested and tried?

Candace Austin (1781-1869)

241-6. **Candace Austin** was born 3 February 1781 in Wilkes County, North Carolina. On 27 October 1801 she married William Parker, also born in Wilkes County, the son of John and Mary Ann Parker, who owned land on Beaver Creek between Ferguson and Wilkesburo. On 20 June 1824, William Parker received a land grant in Claiborne County, Tennessee, and Benjamin Austin and a Gideon Wright were "Sworn Chainers." Was Benjamin Austin Candace's brother? On 25 October 1829 William Parker wrote in his Bible he arrived in Indiana. Gideon Wright and his wife Martha had a land grant close by, they were younger than the Parkers. When Gideon and Martha died, Candace and William took their two teenage daughters into their home. Was Martha related to Candace? After they had been married 14 years, Candace and William Parker had one son William Henley. In an 1884 Putnam County, Indiana, history a son of William H. said his father was an only child. William Henley was about two years old when he came to Indiana with his parents. There was also a Nathaniel Parker in the same area in 1850. William died in 1851, Candace died in 1869, and they are buried in Mill Creek Cemetery, Putnam County, Indiana. Seek the ancestry of Candance Austin.

QUERIES

242-1. **Matthew Austin** was born in 1620 in York and died by 1686. He married Canney —. Their son, Captain Matthew was born in 1658 probably in York, ME. He married Mary Littlefield. Their son, Ichabod married in 1717 to Susannah Young. Ichabod died on 19 September 1718. Susannah and Ichabod had a son, Ichabod born on 29 March in 1717/18 in York and died possibly prior to 1748. He married on 5 September 1736 to Elizabeth Billings. Elizabeth died 26 October 1803 in York. Their daughter Susannah Austin was born 20 September 1736 in Saco, Maine, and she married Joshua Maddocks on 29 August 1754. Joshua was born on 1 April 1732 in Saco, and died after September 1790 in Ellisworth, Maine. Need the ancestors and descendants of Matthew.

242-2. **Solomon Austin** had ancestors who came from Wales and landed in Baltimore, Maryland. My great-great grandfather Caleb was born in North Carolina in 1777. His father moved to Canada after the Revolutionary War somewhere between Montreal and the U.S. border. Caleb married in Canada to Lydia Parker circa 1802, they moved to New York State, Lewis County circa 1803. When the Austins came from Maryland to North Carolina there were four sons. They moved to an area southwest of Hillsborough, Orange Co. N.C. on seven Mile Creek. The place was called "The Austin Settlement." I think that Absalom Austin was the father of Solomon. Absalom died in August of 1792, and Solomon put up bond and invested his estate and made a settlement. Then Solomon and his family left the following year 1793 for Canada. The brothers of Absolom may have been Samuel, Nathaniel and Caleb. I haven't been able to find out who lived in the "Settlement" in Orange County, North Carolina. Need all kinds of information on the family.

242-3. **Nathaniel Austin** of Wiscasset, Maine, was married on 8 August 1803 to Nancy Carleton, the daughter of Moses and Lois Hoyt Carleton. Any information on their ancestors and descendants greatly appreciated.

242-4. **Isaac Austin** bapt. 8 June 1823, married to Sarah —. They appear to have been from Franklin, Delaware County, New York, and attended a Congregational Church there according to the 1850 Census for Hamden, Delaware County. They had three children: Chester Mills Austin born 8 June 1823 married Maria E. — born 1825/6, had son John Cumming born 184?; Elijah Addision Austin born 7 October 1827; and Newell Welton Austin born 31 July 1831 born near Binghamton, New York, and died on 22 December 1913 in Riverside, California. Newell married Emeline Adelia Gardner on 22 December 1913 at Union, New York. Emeline was born 15 March 1834 in Union, died 19 April 1906 in Riverside. Newell and Emeline had five children: Lewis G. Austin born 24 December 1852, married Mary A. Simington; Lydia A. Austin born 17 February 1856 in Union, married at Monticello, Iowa, on 17 January 1874 to Herman H. Monroe, born 22 May 1852; Jennie L. Austin born on 15 July 1866, died 4 February 1873; Eva Austin adopted 17 May 1866; Nellie S. Austin born on 22 March 1875, married 1 June 1893 at Tacoma, Washington, to George Wesley Freeman who was born 20 April 1864 at Derbyshire, England. Nellie died in 1962 at Pasadena, CA and George Wesley died January 2 1906 at Riverside, CA. They had a daughter Patricia Joyce born in 1931. I need to know who Isaac and Sarah's ancestors were.

242-5. **Henry Austin** married Polly —. He died in 1842 in Sumner County, Tennessee. They possibly had a son Eggelston born in 1803 in Virginia, who married 12 October 1829 in Sumner County and died 12 August 1851. Eggelston had a son Henry Miers Austin born 1 May 1836, who married in Tennessee near Gallatin, Sumner County, to schoolteacher Mary Frances Gilliam, who was born in Sumner County. They lived near Bledsoe, Tennessee, and joined the Baptist Church in Siloam Springs, Tennessee. Henry died 8 March 1900 in Plainview, Texas, and Mary died at Hale Center, Texas. Their son Harry Austin born 24 July 1871, died at Hale Center, Texas, married on 12 October 1919 in Sweetwater, Texas, to Verda Mae Sherman born 21 November 1902 at Blackwell, Texas, and died 27 January 1970 at Andrews, Texas. They had a son Marvin Elwood Austin born on 5 October 1928 at Hale Center, married to — on 25 August 1956 in Denton, Texas. Marvin's children: Melwood Ray Austin born 30 August 1957 at Denton; Marshall Coir Austin born 31 August 1958 at Denton, married 25 July 1981 at Sinton, Texas, to Shana Lynn Goldman, who was born 16 February 1959, the daughter of Ronald K. and Jean Webb Goldman; Maxwell Tony Austin born 7 June 1960 at Arlington, Texas. I need proof that Henry was the son of one of Moses Austin's brothers – either Henry or Elijah – and that Eggelston Austin was a son of Henry Austin.

242-6. **Rebecca Austin** married on 10 September 1758 to William Rumery in Biddeford, Maine. Their children included: Rachel baptized 16 September 1759, Elizabeth bp. 1761, Dominicus bp. 1762, William bp. 1765, all in Biddeford. William was killed 21 November 1764 in Biddeford. She remarried 23 July 1769 to William Clark, no known children. Seek Rebecca's ancestry.

242-7. **John Heard Austin** married Minnie Bee Hightower. Their daughter Alice Valeria was born on 15 November 1894 in McDonald, Henry County, GA married John James Veal born on 17 January 1889 in Covington, Newton County, GA. John Heard died 12 September 1936 and Minnie died 12 September 1952. Alice was born, lived, and died in Georgia. Need information on this Austin family.

Austins in the Federal Census of 1850

California

by Rachel K. Laurgaard

Editor's Note: The following information was extracted from the book *Index to the 1850 Census of the State of California*, compiled by Alan P. Bowman, and published by the Genealogical Publishing Company, Baltimore 1972. Only 24 of the 27 California counties of 1850 appear in the Index, since the records for Contra Costa, San Francisco, and Santa Clara Counties no longer exist. California became a state on 9 September 1850, so this census was California's first Federal Census. It is available on microfilm from the National Archives, Washington D.C.

BUTTE COUNTY, CA

Austin, Jesse	30	1820	m	NC	028
" , William	52	1798	m	NH	023

CALAVERAS COUNTY, CA

Austin, Charles	34	1816	m	IL	204
" , J. M.	29	1821	m	IL	204
" , J. S.	32	1818	m	KY	127
" , James	22	1828	m	GB	157
" , James	19	1831	m	GB	216
" , Robert	20	1830	m	NY	079
" , Steven	37	1813	m	NY	078
" , William	30	1820	m	GB	157
" , Wllliam	38	1812	m	TN	204

COLUSA COUNTY, CA

ELDORADO COUNTY, CA

Austin, Edwin L.	30	1820	m	MA	274
" , Felix H.	14	1836	m	MO	363
" , Gabriel (blk)	34	1816	m	VA	363
" , Henry	41	1809	m	VA	363
" , Hezekiah R.	21	1829	m	IN	383
" , John F.	22	1828	m	MO	431
" , John H.	19	1831	m	MO	363
" , Joseph	40	1810	m	GB	366
" , Lewis	10	1840	m	MO	363
" , Peter	26	1824	m	MO	297
" , Simeon	27	1823	m	VA	380
" , Solon A.	29	1821	m	NY	425
" , Stores	30	1820	m	VT	382
" , Thos. H.	32	1818	m	TN	383
" , W. Haswill	17	1833	m	MO	363
" , Wm	20	1830	m	VA	363
" , Wm	53	1797	m	MA	403

LOS ANGELES COUNTY, CA

MARIN COUNTY, CA

MARIPOSA COUNTY, CA

Austin, Alexr	36	1814	m	GB	080
" , John	30	1820	m	KY	059
" , Wm W.	27	1823	m	MA	059

MENDOCINO COUNTY, CA

MONTEREY COUNTY, CA

NAPA COUNTY, CA

SACRAMENTO COUNTY, CA

Austin, Catharine	26	1824	f	OH	196
" , Chas H.	6	1844	m	IN	196
" , E.	30	1820	m	NY	205
" , E.	50	1800	m	RI	245
" , Edwd W.	28	1822	m	VT	153
" , Henry B.	3	1847	m	IN	196
" , Isaiah	23	1827	m	NY	196
" , Jas C.	41	1809	m	ME	196

SAN DIEGO COUNTY, CA

SAN JOAQUIN COUNTY, CA

Austin, Francis	25	1825	m	MX	286

SAN LUIS OBISPO COUNTY, CA

Austin, Alfred	33	1817	m	FR	328

SANTA BARBARA COUNTY, CA

SANTA CRUZ COUNTY, CA

SHASTA COUNTY, CA

SOLANO COUNTY, CA

SONOMA COUNTY, CA

Austin, Henry	40	1810	m	NY	011

SUTTER COUNTY, CA

TRINITY COUNTY, CA

TULUMNE COUNTY, CA

Austin, E.	25	1825	m	MA	177
" , H.	37	1813	m	KY	085
" , J. P.	32	1818	m	NY	135
" , Jas	23	1827	m	MA	177

YOLO COUNTY, CA

Austin, F.W.	22	1828	m	VT	185
" , S. B.	31	1819	m	VT	185

YUBA COUNTY, CA

Austin, David R.	21	1829	m	NJ	239
" , Edwd E.	37	1813	m	NY	296
" , H. S.	25	1825	m	ME	297
" , Henry	24	1826	m	PA	261
" , Jas F.	29	1821	m	MO	226
" , John	22	1828	m	RI	203

REFERENCES TO AUSTINS
IN THE NOVA SCOTIA ARCHIVES

by Michael Edward Austin
and Patricia Biebuyck Austin

Editor's Note: The information below was obtained by the authors in July 1984 from the Public Archives of Nova Scotia at Halifax. Numbers in brackets at the end of each item are reference sources, listed at the end of the article. The introductory material is abstracted from pages 237 & 238 of Ethel W. Williams book *Know Your Ancestors*, published in 1960 by Charles E. Tuttle of Rutland, Vermont. Painting of the frigate *Hancock* was done by noted marine artist C. G. Wales.

In studying Canadian sources one should not overlook the pre-Revolutionary migration from the New England Colonies to Nova Scotia, which occurred between 1755 and 1764. These people were not Tories, as they did not go there at the time of the conflict. Some of this migration returned to the colonies at the onset of the Revolution, or shortly afterward. Descendants of those who remained, in many instances, migrated to the United States between 1800 and 1838, and even later, from 1850 to 1860, and some even went to the west coast, so many families, throughout the country, will find missing links in Nova Scotia.

In 1749 after the exodus of the French Acadians, Halifax was settled by the English. Men from Massachusetts, Rhode Island, and Connecticut who had served at the Siege of Louisburg, together with some fishermen from Maine, located there. Then it was proposed that vacant French lands be offered New England settlers. The following were the terms of settlement announced by the Council of Nova Scotia, in 1759:

Townships were to be twelve square miles, or about 100,000 acres. 100 acres of wild woodland was to be allowed each settler, with 50 additional acres for each member of his family. Grantee agreed to cultivate or enclose one-third of the land within ten years, one-third more in twenty years, and the remainder in thirty years. No one could be granted more than 1000 acres, but on fulfillment of the terms, he could receive another grant under the same conditions, Quit rent of one shilling for each fifty acres was to begin ten years after date of grant. Each township of fifty or more families could send two representatives to the legislature. Courts of Justice were the same as in Massachusetts and Connecticut, and freedom of religion to all except Catholics.

The terms were so generous that the response was immediate. There was a Massachusetts migration to Annapolis Royal about 1760. Lists of these settlers are given in detail in Reference [7]. Granville, Annapolis County, was settled by people from Lunenburg, Massachusetts, and some from New Hampshire. Rhode Island sent many settlers to Nova Scotia, a list is given in Reference [8], and another account is found in Reference [9]. Connecticut settlers came as a colony, having secured the grant of two townships, Horton and Cornwallis.

From the Nova Scotia census of 1770 it is found that Amherst and Sackville were settled by people from Rhode Island, supplemented, in 1768, by the entire Baptist congregation from Swansea, Massachusetts, who, however, returned to Massachusetts, in 1776. Cumberland, Onslow, and Truro, were settled by Connecticut people.

Liverpool was settled by Massachusetts and Connecticut people. Barrington, Yarmouth, Annapolis and Granville were settled by Massachusetts people. Horton and Falmouth were settled by people from Londonderry, New Hampshire. In 1770 eighty-nine per cent of the population of Nova Scotia was either native born or American colonists. A good account by Rev. James Lyon of this migration is found in Reference [10].

Settlement began in 1760 and the bulk of the settlers were from New London, Lebanon, Norwich, Windham, Windsor, Killingsworth, Lyme, Colchester, Hebron, Saybrook, Stonington, and Tolland, Connecticut. There is a complete record of the names of those to whom grants of land were made in Reference [11].

Leota Austen died at her home in Central Economy on 3 March 1905. She was the beloved wife of Rev. J. M. Austen, leaving him and five small children to mourn the loss of a devoted wife and mother. *Liverpool Advance* 15 March 1905   [1]

A ship with **Captain Austin**, and a brig with Captain Smith, arrived at Medway to load with timber, etc. Mr. Mack loads the former, and Mr. Tinkham the latter. *Perkins*, 15 August 1776   [1]

Settle with my brother. Pay him... and a hhd. rum for **Capt. Austin**. *Perkins*, 11 September 1776   [1]

Ann Austin, born 12 June 1780 at 1 a.m., daughter of **Captain Austin Austin** and Mary Eades, and a sister of the Mary Austin who married John Letson, married John's brother, Robert Letson on 30 May 1803 at Halifax. Ann died in Halifax 4 August 1811. Robert Letson was born 11 March 1782, the son of Robert Letson and Elizabeth Norris. He was lost at sea in 1811.   [1]

Mary Eades Austin was the daughter of Captain Eades, who came to Halifax, N.S. from England with his wife and child and by chance remained in the Province. After the death of her first husband, **Captain Austin Austin**, Mary married John Howe. Mary and John had one daughter Sarah, who died, and one son, Joseph Howe, known as the Great Nova Scotian. Children: Ann Austin born 12 June 1780 at 1 a.m. at Halifax, died 4 August 1811 at Halifax, married 30 May 1803, Robert Letson Jr.; Mary Austin died and buried at Port Medway about 1848, married John Letson, no children; Henry Austin; Jesse Austin.   [1]

Henry Austin married Susan Letson born at Halifax 1783, daughter of Robert Letson and Elizabeth Norris. Children: Henry, Robert, Joseph, Mary, and Jesse. [1]

On 7 October 1874, James Austin of Liverpool and George M. Roberts of Yarmouth, while fishing out of Gloucester, lost their vessel in a heavy fog while tending their trawls. For eight days they drifted about with little or no food, but with drinking water which they caught in a trawl-tub during a heavy rain. They finally despaired, but were picked up by a steamer, the Captain of which said he was constrained "for some unknown reason" – some hours before to change his course half a point. Had he not done so, the men would have perished. Austin had to be carried on board. *Long*, page 1171. [1]

A typical sailor of the old school – preserved and pickled in salt water – was John (Jack) Austin. He and Jack Clint were types of the mariners of one hundred years ago. He lived when at home on the Upper part of Union Street, beyond "back" street – as it was then called. We recall but two of the name – James and William Austin, both sailors, but in 1857 we find recorded the marriage of Mrs Rachael Austin, and in 1866 (sic) the death of George Austin. *Long*, page 929. [1]

On 11 July 1857, George Austin, youngest son of John and Mary Austin, died in Liverpool at age 20 years. *Liverpool Transcript*, 16 July 1857 & *Long*, page 926. [1]

Mary Austin died and buried Port Medway about 1848, married John Letson – no children. John Letson was born 15 June 1780, son of Robert and Elizabeth (Norris). [1]

Thomas Austin married Elizabeth Letson, born in 1788, the daughter of Robert Letson by his second wife Elizabeth Brown. Children: Elizabeth, Susan, and Thomas. [1]

Gone out with the Tide: The solemn and pathetic truism, that the poor should always be with us, has had during many years, for the ratepayers of this District, an impressive illustration in the person of John Nostrum, commonly and familiarly known hereabouts as Johnny Austin, who died the other day, here, in the ninety-eighth year of his age. The deceased was born in London, England, and at an early age began to "Follow the Sea." In 1814 he left England in a vessel called the *Harrison* bound for Quebec with provisions for the British troops stationed there, and having on board a crew of 15 men. On nearing the coast the vessel was captured by an American vessel carrying eighteen guns and 100 men. The *Harrison* was taken into Boston Harbor, where her crew were kept as prisoners of war until early in the following year, when Nostrum with the rest of the crew were sent to Halifax, N.S., but adverse winds prevailing the vessel having them

Perhaps the finest early-American frigate, the *Hancock* sailed from Boston in May 1777 to raid off Nova Scotia.

on board ran into Lunenburg. There the subject of this notice, with three or four others, left the vessel and came on to Liverpool, where he has since made his home, and going to sea out of this port, at intervals, for some sixty years. *Liverpool Advance*, 20 February 1889. [1]

Mrs. James Austin was married when she was 16, her daughter married at 14. Several months ago the *Boston Post* offered a prize – a china tea set – to the youngest grandmother in New England. The youngest thus far heard from are Mrs. Hattie Gurthro, of Lowell, Mass., who is a grandmother at the age of 32 years, 4 months and 3 days, and Mrs. James Austin, of East Boston, formerly of this town, who has two grandchildren at the age of 34 years. We take the following from the *Post* of the 30th ult.:

"Another young grandmother. This one looks as if she were the daughter's sister, and is frequently taken for that. They say that more than one amusing episode has occurred from people's surprise at the relationship. It was Mrs. James Austin whom the *Post* woman saw yesterday, and she is already a grandmother at the age of 31 years and 5 months. It was a little blue-eyed, lively woman who opened the door for me at 141 Saratoga Street, East Boston, whom one would suppose to be hardly thirty yet. When she told me she was the 'grandmother' of whom I was in search, she laughed heartily at my amazement. "That's the way everyone looks," she said. They can't believe I have a daughter married, and they generally think my grandchildren are my own children.

"Mrs. Austin was born and brought up in Liverpool, N.S., and was married when she was only a little over 16. She is now a pretty woman, with blue eyes and dark hair and regular features. She is of middle height, and is plump enough to have no angles. Her daughter was married before she had reached the age of 15, and her first baby came before whe was 16. She is very pretty and is only 17 now, and one rather wonders if she wishes she "hadn't," but she declares she is much happier married. It must be a consolation, however, that her two girls are the little beauties they are.

"Mrs. Austin has only three children, this daughter and two sons, one of whom works in Jordan Marsh & Co's. She has had altogether, however, six children, and had four of them before she was 21. She thinks it is a mistake to marry so young, but agrees that it has its compensations, if you can get a nice tea set by it."

(It would be too much to expect of the *Advance* to enlighten one as to the name or parentage of Mrs. Austin. – T.B.S.) *Liverpool Advance*, 14 August 1895.   [1]

Mary Austen, widow, married to John Howe, widower, on 25 October 1798 by license (John was Joseph Howe's father).   [2]

Thomas Austin, a widower, was married to Anne Wenman, spinster, on 6 August 1799.   [2]

William Austin, bachelor, was married to Mary E. Mansfield on 7 March 1809.   [2]

Caroline Austen was married to John Page.   [2]

Henry Austen married to Susan Letson 24 May 1807.   [2]

Thomas Austin married to Elizabeth Letson on 17 December 1807.   [2]

Mary Austen married to John Letson on 24 June 1802 by license.   [2]

Ann Austen married to Robert Letson on 30 May 1805 by license.   [2]

William Austin married to Jane Howe 25 July 1816.   [2]

Henry Austin, bachelor, married to Elizabeth Marshman on 29 July 1794.   [2]

Henry & Mary Austen had their children recorded at St. Paul's Church: Mary 8 July 1781, Sarah 29 September 1782, Joseph 14 March 1784, Henry bp. 29 May 1786, William b. 26 October bp. 18 November 1787.   [2]

Baptisms of the children of **Thomas & Sarah Austin** and **Alexander & Mary Austin** are recorded in the Saint Matthew's Church Records at PANS.   [2]

Benjamin Austin had land transaction with Stephen Gouger and others in 1788 in Wilmot.   [3]

Caleb Austin had land transaction with Timothy Witmore and others in 1784 in Carlton (card 5).   [3]

James Austin had land transaction with Joseph Leonard and others in 1789 in Annapolis County (card 4).   [3]

James Austin had land transaction with Stephen Seaman and others in 1785 in Cumberland County (card 5).   [3]

John Austin had land transaction with Stephen Seaman and others in 1785 in Cumberland County (card 5).   [3]

Nicholas Austin had land transaction with Lt. Col. Allan Stewart in 1784 in Passamaquoddy.   [3]

Samuel Austin had land transaction with Samuel Dowling and others in 1784 in Grand Lake, Sunbury County, New Brunswick (card 2).   [3]

Warrant to Survey unto the disbanded Soldiers of the Royal Fusiliers American Regiment 10,100 acres of land within the County of Sunbury, New Brunswick: 100 acres to **John Austin** (no wife and no children). This is found in *Philip Bailey's Land Papers 1784-85*.   [3]

Notes on the Howe–Letson–Austen families relationships. MG 100 Vol. 19 #27 (manuscript).   [4]

Austen family - Some notes on the Austen family - half brothers and sisters of Joseph Howe. *James Spike*, No. 1 pages 2,3; MG 100 Vol. 231 #18 (manuscript).   [4]

For dates of marriages, deaths and other data on the Austen family see Miss Letson's notes on the Letson family in PANS *Family Records* MG 4 Vol. 128 also MG 100 Vol. 175 #17 (manuscript).   [4]

There are a number of baptisms and marriages of various members of the Austen family in St. Matthew's Church Records. PANS Manuscripts Room *Church Records* MG 4 Vol. 5 pages 46,47,47a (manuscript).   [4]

Notations referring to genealogy of **Henry Austen** (1741-1788) and **Thomas Austen** (1754-1821), Cork City, Ireland, emigrated to Halifax circa 1775. MG 1 Vol. 1487 #7 (manuscript).   [4]

Miss Catherine Austen died 27 January 1796, at age 17, daughter of Mr. Thomas Austen. *Royal Gazette*, 2 February 1796 (newspaper).   [4]

Request for pardon of **George Austen** confined in the Bridewell for horse stealing, 6 April 1832. RG 5, Series GP Vol.1, #56 (manuscript).   [4]

George Austen made another pardon request - has lost an eye and injured an arm since April. Dated 13 July 1832. RG 5, Series GP Vol.1, #58 (manuscript).   [4]

Notice dated Halifax, 10 July 1834, that **H. Austen** has assigned all his stock in trade, notes, books, debts, etc. to Joseph Tarratt & Sons. *The Novascotian*, 25 December 1834, page 416 col. 3 (newspaper).   [4]

Biography of **Henry Austen** – page 325 of *Nova Scotia Historical Quarterly*, Vol. 6, No. 3, September 1976. Library F5200 N93 H6 V.6 1976.   [4]

Nova Scotia

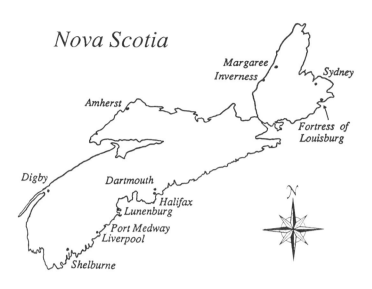

H. E. Austen of Dartmouth has a large collection of stuffed birds. *Halifax Herald,* 11 April 1893, page 2.　　[4]

Austens of Halifax – vital statistics and notes on over 700 Halifax families – Stayner Collection (manuscripts).　　[4]

Notes on Austen Family in Queens County, MG 1 Vol. 2393 #3 (manuscript).　　[4]

Henry Austen 1848 petition – Asks Lt. Gov. Sir John Harvey for an appointment. He is a maternal brother of Hon. Joseph Howe, Prov. Sec'y, a native of Halifax and been a merchant for over thirty years but am now reduced. "Your Excellency perhaps may think it strange that my application was not made through my brother – but I am aware that no interest of his with the Government would be exerted in favour of a relative – as I presume he might incur censure from the minority." Miss E. M. Letson provided some genealogical material on the Austens which is attached to the petition. Both Joseph Howe's mother and father had been married before. Captain Eades, an Englishman married Sarah —. Their daughter Mary married Henry Austen, a trader of Halifax and also a Captain. He left her some means including the Brig *Betty.* Their children were: Joseph who married Rebecca —, Henry who married Susanna Letson in 1802, William who married Jane Howe in 1816, Mary who married John Letson on 24 June 1802. Mary Eades Austen married second to John Howe, Sr. Recorded St. Paul's Church, Halifax by license. John Howe widower to Mary Austen widow 25 October 1790. Issue: Joseph Howe, Sarah – a daughter who died on a voyage from Lima, Peru. She was married; buried in Virginia. RG 5 GP, Vol. 10 #95.　　[4]

Mrs. Jane Austen letters from Joe Howe. Unpublished personal letters of Joseph Howe to his sister, Jane, Mrs. Austen of Digby. Appendix B on *Report of Public Archives of Nova Scotia* for the year 1953. F90 N85.　　[4]

Voucher from B. C. White to Joseph Austen for snuff, 1821. MG 100 Vol. 245 #18 White Family: Shelburne (manuscript).　　[4]

Joseph Austen informs his Friends and the Public, that his Snuff Mill (on Mr. Hosterman's Property, at the N.W.A.), has lately had a complete repair with new and approved Machinery, which has enabled him to manufacture a very superior quality of Snuff... *Novascotian,* 20 January 1831, page 22, col.3 (newspaper).　　[4]

Career of Joseph Austen, born at Halifax in 1782, died at Victoria, B.C. in July 1871. He was a half-brother of Joseph Howe. "Occasional's Letter" in *Acadian Recorder,* 7 May 1921, page 1 (newspaper).　　[4]

Joseph Austen 1782-1871. Death of Joseph Austen, Esquire (from the *Weekly British Colonist,* Victoria...) Born... Halifax... 1782... was an uncle to our much respected friend Joseph Austen of this city...*Halifax Reporter,* 29 July 1871, page 2, col.4 (newspaper).　　[4]

Joseph Austen, merchant, asks for drawback on cargo of tobacco, 1825. RG 5 Series P, Vol. 121 #13.　　[4]

Copartnership formed between Joseph Austen and George Wilson to be known as *Joseph Austen and Company,* Halifax Tobacco Manufactory No. 32 Bedford Row, on 1 January 1819. *Halifax Journal,* 4 January 1819, page 3 col.1 (newspaper).　　[4]

Dispute whether John Murphy should replace Richard C. Austen at Inverness, 1852. RG 5 Series GP Vol.10 #146 (manuscript).　　[4]

Joseph Austen petition in 1859. Warehousekeeper at the port of Halifax, health is impaired and wants an outdoor situation. Petition signed by a large number of merchants who endorse his request for appointment as landing waiter to carry out duties as weigher and gauger. *Assembly Petitions*: Trade and Commerce 1859. RG 5 Series P Vol. 126 #141 (manuscript).　　[4]

William Austin, son to Alexander and Mary Austin was baptized by Revd. Mr. John Seccombe on 24 September 1778 at St. Matthew's Church in Halifax. Page 11 of *St. Matthew's Church Records 1769-1857.* MG 4 Vol. 46 (manuscript).　　[4]

Sophia Minns Austen married on 22 September 1851 at Saint John, New Brunswick, by the Rev. William Donald, A.M., to R. S. Fitzrandloph, Esq., of Digby, N.S. Sophia is the eldest daughter of the late William Austen, Esq., of that city. *Novascotian,* 29 Sept. 1851, p. 310 col. 3.　　[4]

Henry Austen store. Long advertisement of Henry Austen, Water Street, Halifax, of goods he has for sale. *Nova Scotia Royal Gazette*, 5 January 1808, page 2 col.1 (newspaper on microfilm). [4]

James H. Austen, draftsman, worked in Crown Land Office, 1869. RG 5 Series P Vol. 49, #174. [4]

James A. Austen, Crown Lands Department official, asked for increased salary in 1871. RG 5 Series P Vol. 50 #7, 9 (manuscript). [4]

James H. Austen correspondence. Bound volume of carbon copies of all his correspondence is on file in Crown Lands Department in Halifax. Article by R. E. Dickie, "Surveyors Quest For Information," on page 18 of *The Nova Scotian Surveyor*, December 1960, Vol. 10 No. 25. TA N85 Vol. 10 #25. [4]

J. H. Austen, Deputy Commissioner of Crown Lands, retired in 1911 on superannuation after 43 years service... *Halifax Herald*, 9 December 1911, page 16, col.3. [4]

James Wakefield of Halifax, N.S. and Ann his wife sold land and house on Hollis Street in Halifax (Lot. No. 11) to **Thomas Auston** of Halifax, Trader, for £500 on 17 April 1780. Indenture, Vol. 16, page 273. [5]

Austin is found in the *T. B. Smith Collection*, Queens County Names: MG1 #818. [4]

Augustus Denneman of Halifax sold land on Grafton Street, Halifax, to John Mullowny, **Henry Austen** and John Stealing, merchants of Halifax, for £100 on 12 August 1786. — Witnessed by George Bayers and **Thomas Austen**. Indenture Vol. 23, page 264. [5]

Henry Austin was born 29 May 1786 and died 30 January 1859 at age 74 years at his son's residence in Dartmouth, N.S. Married Susan Letson - Marriage bond dated 22 May 1807. She died at son's residence in Sydney, N.S. in 1861. Information via Mr. C. St. C. Stayner, Halifax. [4]

Accounts and correspondence of **Henry Austin**, 1830. MG 100 Vol. 105 #31-31i (manuscript). [4]

Henry Austin's letter book, 1827-1833. Half brother of Joseph Howe, had hardware business in Halifax. *Business Papers* MG 3 Vol. 139 (manuscript). [4]

On Saturday 17 October 1852, **Emma H. Austin**, the daughter of Mr. **Robert Austin**, died at age 1 year and 3 months. *Novascotian*, 27 October 1852, page 349, col. 5 (newspaper). [4]

Short obituary of **Joseph Austin** - a nephew of Joseph Howe for whom he was named - appointed to Customs department 10 September 1842. *Acadian Recorder*, 11 August 1888, page 3 col. 4 (newspaper). [4]

Mary Austin died 19 January 1867 at her residence in Rue de Monceaux, Paris, France... Mary, Countess de Mac-Mahon de Thomond, widow of the late Count Alfred... daughter of Thomas Austin of Waterfall House, County Cork, sister of General Austin and aunt of Edward P. Archibold, Esquire, of this city. *Acadian Recorder*, 20 February 1867 page 3 col. 2. [4]

Pamphlet supporting Liberal candidate **Rae Austin** in 1980. MG 100 Vol. 23 #12 (manuscript). [4]

Thomas Cochran, James Cochran, and William Cochran of Halifax, merchants, sold land in Halifax, "late in the possession of Robert Gillespie, commonly called the Garden Lot," to **Henry Austin** of Halifax for £32 on 31 January 1784. Indenture Vol. 20, page 127. [5]

James Austin biography. RG 1 Vol. 128c page 413, 8 December 1902 (manuscript). [4]

Nova Scotia Greenbook - Families and Individuals - **Henry Austin** (1786-1859), Halifax, Halifax County. Merchant, stepbrother of Joseph Howe. Accounts, 1817-1832, originals, 9 items. Accounts and letters concerning hardware, including some letters concerning business transactions between Henry Austin, William Fairclough and Joseph Tarratt and Sons, Liverpool, England. (manuscripts file). [4]

Henry Austin of Halifax and Susan his wife sold land in Halifax to **William Austin** of Halifax for £500 on 4 July 1815. Indenture Vol. 43, page 12. [5]

William Austen, merchant of St John, N.B. and Jane his wife sold land in Halifax, N.S., to **Henry Austen**, merchant of Halifax, on 6 July 1827. Indenture Vol. 52, page 393. [5]

William Austen, merchant of St. John, N.B., and Jane his wife sold land in Halifax, N.S., to **Joseph Austin** of Halifax, Tabacconist, on 9 July 1827. Indenture Vol. 52, page 395. [5]

Joseph Austen of Halifax, Tabacconist, and Rebecca his wife agreed to pay to **Ann Austen** of Halifax £25 yearly on 4 August of each year during her life. Ann Austen widow of **Thomas Austin**. Indenture 4 August 1825, Vol. 48, page 429. [5]

Charles D. Austin, coppersmith of Halifax, and Eleanor his wife sold land in Halifax to Ann, Elisabeth, and Mary Miller, spinsters of Halifax, for £150 on 12 February 1829. Indenture Vol. 51, page 327. [5]

Robert Rashleigh, William Goodall, John Turner of Gaslick? Hill in the City of London, Merchants, sold land and house on Barrington Street, Halifax, to **Thomas Austen** of Halifax, Merchant, for £310 on 12 July 1787. Indenture Vol. 25, page 13. [5]

William Austen, bachelor, married on 1 March 1809 to Mary Ann Mansfield, spinster, at St. Matthew's Church. On July 25, 1816 William Austen, widower, married Jane Howe, Spinster, St. Matthew's Church. pp. 319,327 of St. Matthew's Church Records 1769-1857. Miss E. M. Letson said that William was the son of Henry Austen and his wife Mary Eades Austen who later married John Howe, Sr. and became the mother of Joseph Howe, and that Jane Howe was a half-sister of Joseph Howe. MG 4 Vol. 46 (manuscript).   [4]

Captain William Austen married yesterday morning, by Rev. Dr. Gray, to Jane, the daughter of John Howe, Esq. *Halifax Weekly Chronicle*, 26 July 1816, page 3 col. 3 (newspaper).   [4]

Jane Austen died at Pleasant Cottage, Digby, Tuesday 23rd inst. She was the widow of the late **William Austen**, Esq., and sister of Hon. Joseph Howe. *Acadian Recorder* 31 May 1865 (newspaper).   [4]

Notes on the Austin family in Queens County. MG 1 Vol. 2393 #4 (manuscript).   [4]

Brief sketch of the Austin family of Northeast Margaree. *History of Northeast Margaree*, by John F. Hart, pages 47-48, F107 M34 H26.   [4]

To all to whom it may concern, John Howe of Halifax... whereas Mary Howe the present wife of the said John Howe was formerly married to **Henry Austin**, late of Halifax, Merchant Deceased, who died leaving three sons and and a daughter: **Joseph Austin, Henry Austin, William Austin** and **Mary Austin** the issue of this marriage with... for 10 shillings John Howe gave up to **Thomas Austin**, coppersmith, his interest in Henry Austin's estate, in Trust for Mary (Austin) Howe and her children of Halifax. — Witnessed by **Thomas Austin, Jr.** 24 August 1804. Vol. 36, page 312.   [5]

The Austin family of Skye Glen, Inverness County, Cape Breton is discussed in *The Smiths of Cape Breton* by Perley W. Smith, pages 70-86 CS 90 S65.   [4]

Richard Austin family of North East Margaree, *Inverness County Genealogies*. Page 12. Notes by the Rev. C. H. Johnson. *Community Records*: Margaree, North East, MG 4 Vol. 110 (manuscript). See also Hart, pages 47-48 F5248 G99 H32.   [4]

On 1 June 1825, Sarah Jost of Halifax agreed to pay £7 10s annually to **Anne Austin** of Halifax, widow and relict of **Thomas Austin**, late of Halifax, coppersmith deceased. Will of Thomas gave 1/3 his real estate to Anne. Sarah Jost purchased from John Howe and John Merrick of Halifax (Executors of last will of Thomas Austen) land in Halifax bordered by end of **Charles Dickenson Austen** on Duke Street. Indenture Vol. 48, page 350.   [5]

Release of Heirs of **Thomas Austen** to Anne Letson and Thomas Austen on 15 October 1834: Joseph Jones Letson of Halifax, Trader, the son of Anne Letson deceased (wife of Robert Letson, gentleman deceased of Halifax) and daughter of Thomas Austin, coppersmith, of Halifax. Benjamin Stevens of Halifax, blacksmith, and Elizabeth his wife; Sarah Anne Austin of Halifax, spinster; James Maxwell of Halifax Yeoman and Susan his wife; Thomas Robert Austen of Halifax, Yeoman. **Elizabeth, Sarah, Susan** and **Thomas Robert Austen** were the "Only children of said Thomas Austin the younger, deceased, who was one of the sons of Thomas Austin coppersmith deceased." Vol. 61, page 88.   [5]

William Meaney of Halifax, Merchant, sold "Lot E in the late Mr. Luke Forman's Division," a corner lot on Dukes and Hollis Streets in Halifax "now occupied by Mr. William Slater," and another house "occupied by James Brown" to **Henry Austen**, Merchant of Halifax, for £880 on 29 July 1782. Indenture Vol. 18, page 266.   [5]

William Milward and wife Isabella of Halifax, blockmaker, sold land in Halifax to **Henry Auston** of Halifax, Trader, for £116 13s 4p on 24 November 1785. Indenture Vol. 22, page 267.   [5]

Henry Austin of Halifax, Trader, and Mary Austin his wife, sold 1500 acres in Amherst, Cumberland County, N.S. to **Thomas Austin**, Trader, for £36 on 22 August 1787. Indenture Vol. 25, page 236.   [5]

Sir Francis Austin presented a silver salver to the Halifax Club in 1943. MG 100 Vol. 35 #80 (manuscript).   [4]

References

1. *T. B. Smith Collection*, Public Archives of Nova Scotia, Halifax MG1 Vol. 818 #6.

2. Miss E. M. Letson's Notes, taken from marriage and baptismal records at St. Paul's Church.

3. Land Papers, Public Archives of Nova Scotia, Halifax.

4. Card Index to Biographies, Public Archives of Nova Scotia, Halifax.

5. Card Index to Nova Scotia Deeds, Public Archives of Nova Scotia, Halifax.

6. M. E. Austin, "Index to Austin Land Transactions in the Province of Nova Scotia," p. 265 *Austins of America*.

7. W. A. Calneck, *The History of the County of Annapolis*, and also in the Supplement to this work.

8. R. G. Huling, "The Rhode Island Emigration to Nova Scotia," pages 89-135 of *The Narragansett Historical Register*, Volume 7.

9. A. W. H. Eaton, "Rhode Island Settlers on the French Lands in Nova Scotia, in 1760 and 1761," pages 1, 83, 179 of *Americana*, Volume 10.

10. W. O. Sawtelle, "Acadia — The Pre-Loyalist Migration And the Philadelphia Plantation," page 244 of the *Pennsylvania Magazine of History and Biography*, Volume 51.

11. Eaton, *History of Kings County, Nova Scotia*.

250-1. Jacob Austin Jr. married first to Lucentia —, who died in 1821. He married second to Olive Grant on 2 April 1822 in Parkman, Maine. Seek additional information about this Austin family.

250-2. Pardon Austin married a girl from Massachusetts. I am looking for the origin of the patriachal Delaware County, New York, Austin. Seeking the parents and ancestry of Pardon Austin.

250-3. Caleb Austin born in Montreal, Canada or North Carolina according to an 1850 Ohio Census. Married Lydia Parker circa 1800 reportedly in Montreal, Canada. Children born in Whitestown/Whitesboro (perhaps Lewis County), New York were: Alfred Andrew b. 1804, George b. 1806, John P. 1808, Abel J. b. 1812, Elijah 1814, Sarah b. ?, Lydia b. 1820 in Meigs County, Ohio. She married William Smith of Allensville, Ohio in 1840. Caleb's family reportedly moved to Meigs County, Ohio in 1816. George and Abel moved to Randolph, Clay and St. Clair Counties, IL, John P. was one of the founding fathers of Minnesota (Anoka County) in 1856, and Alfred Andrew moved to Mason County, WV. Elijah Austin remained in Meigs County, Ohio. When the family moved from New York in 1816 a brother of Caleb's, probably Seth moved further west to the "Indian Territory of Texas" with cousins by the name of Huston. Seek ancestry of Caleb Austin and any additional information on his family and descendants.

250-4. Joseph N. Austin was born on 22 December 1867 in Robinson, Ottawa Co. MI, the son of Benjamin and Effie Post. Benjamin was 30 years old in the 1870 Census of Ottawa, Michigan, and both he and Effie were born in NY. Joseph had a cousin, George Austin born 23 March 1861 in Grand Haven, Ottawa, Michigan. Need more information on Joseph's parents and family.

250-5. Martha Veannah Austin born circa 1810, married Moses Ezekial Rhea. Moses might have been born in Virigina. Martha died in 1858 in Arkansas. A son John O. Rhea was born in 1842, there were possibly more children. Need the ancestry of Martha Austin.

250-6. Hiram Austin and his wife Phebe Cole were in the 1850 Census, Wyoming County, New York. Hiram was age 43, born in Vermont. Phebe was age 33, born in NY. Son James was age 15. Have descendants, need parents and ancestors of Hiram and Phebe Austin.

250-7. Aaron Austin born in 1804 in Anson (now Union) County, North Carolina, son of James b. 1764 in Anson County?, son of Charles who resided in North Carolina in the 1750's & 1760's and died after 1766?. I would like to correspond with anyone having information on this family.

250-8. Hiram/Homer Austin married Zenia Frigner of Copake, New York. Had a daughter Catherine born in 1829 in Ohio, a son William born in 1832 in Ohio. Need death date and place of Hiram/Homer and Catherine, also the names of other children.

250-9. William Wallace Austin born in 1832, married Julia Ann Miller, who was born in 1835, the daughter of James and Kate (Poucher) Miller in Martindale NY. They had two sons, Amon Austin and Morris Austin, and two daughters, Alice Austin and Mary Austin. They lived in New Marlborough, Clayton, & Sheffield, Massachusetts, and in Winsted & Waterbury Connecticut. Need data on Alice and Mary.

250-10. Richard 'Dicky' Austin and his wife Sarah Morgan's children: Charles Austin b. 26 March 1796 in Anson County, North Carolina; Morgan B. Austin, James Austin, Jeremiah Austin, and Isabella Austin who married John Stanfill. Pleasant Austin was a half-brother to Charles. Seek more information on Richard and Sarah.

250-11. Benjamin Austin was born 5 June 1770 in Pittsfield, Berkshire County, Massachusetts, and died 4 May 1854 in Houndsfield, New York. He married Jerusha Mather, who was born on 25 February in 1763 Lyme, Connecticut, the daughter of John and Mary (Higgins) Mather. Jerusha died in Sacketts Harbor, New York. Their son Benjamin Franklin Austin was born 30 May 1803 in Redfield, Oneida County, New York, and died on 25 May 1877 in Shenandoah, Iowa. Benjamin Franklin married on 8 November 1825 in NY to Lois Louise Baxter, who was born 8 May 1807 in Canada and died on 25 May 1895 in Independence, Missouri. Their daughter, Sophia Amelia was born on 30 June 1828 in Watertown, NY. Sophia married Eri James Moore. Need more information on the ancestors of Benjamin and his descendents.

250-12. Jerusha Austin was born on 25 February 1779, probably in New York state. She married on 1 January 1804 to Joseph Lawrence. He was born on 25 December 1782 and died on 17 March 1875. He was the son of Oliver and Patty Ann (Wait) Lawrence. Seek to learn the ancestry of Jerusha Austin and more on her family.

250-13. David Austin owned a house back in the 1900's in New Sharon, Maine, called the "Old Austin Place." I believe the house, which my grandmother lived in, was on Swan Road. My grandfather was Juinus Austin Taylor. Need to determine whether there is a connection between our Taylor family and the Austins.

250-14. Lemuel Austin was born in 1814. He married Clarissa Brown. Their son, James F. Austin, was born in 1847 in South Carolina. He married Sarah Jane Cody. James F. and Sarah are both buried at Beech Creek Cemetery in Rome, Georgia. Seeking Lemuel ancestry.

SOME DESCENDANTS OF
ARCHIBALD WILLIS AUSTIN
OF CASEY COUNTY, KENTUCKY

by Lillian Austin Hudson

Editor's Note: The following article is based on information submitted by the author to correct and add to the information on her father Archibald Willis Austin appearing on page 169 of *Austins of America*, as part of the article "The Descendants of John Austin and Ann Baden of Albemarle County, Virginia" by Associate Editor Bert Austin, which begins on page 114 of *Austins of America*.

J332-7. ARCHIBALD WILLIS[5] AUSTIN (*Issac Bill,*[4] *John L.,*[3] *Jonas R.,*[2] *John*[1]) was born 25 August 1870 in Casey County, Kentucky. He called himself 'Wilse,' and was a farmer and owned a blacksmith shop on the state highway in Dunnville, Kentucky, where he also served as the Town Marshall. Wilse was married five times, the first time in Casey County on 8 July 1894 to Patsey W. Stephens. Patsey was perhaps the daughter of 'Duck' Stephens, for they were married at his home. She was born on 9 May 1876, and died 6 July 1908. Wilse and Patsey had four children:

J332-71. WILLIE JEFF, *b. 4 April 1895 in Dunnville, m.(1) Dora Waddle/Weddle in 1914 in Pulaski County, Kentucky. They divorced, and Willie m.(2) Emma —. They divorced and married again in the 1930's. Willie worked on the railroad, and died in the 1950's or 1960's. One son, Cecil Austin, lived in Covington, Kentucky. Willie's last known address was St. James Street in Cincinnati, Ohio.*

J332-72. OBIE S., *b. — October 1898, m. in Dayton, Tennessee, to Sis Jones, they had two children, Wallace Austin and Eugene Austin. Obie Austin died and was buried in Cincinnati, Ohio.*

J332-73. LESLIE [male], *b. Dunnville, m. Ann —, he worked and retired from a railroad in Cincinnati, where he lived on St. James Street. Leslie and Ann had two children: Nancy b. circa 1935, and another daughter whose name is unknown. Leslie died in Cincinnati.*

J332-74. SAMMIE B. ['JOHNNIE'], *d. 15 April 1907 at the age of 6 years from Whooping Cough.*

Widower Wilse Austin was 'age 48' when he married for the second time in Casey County on 24 September 1918 to widow Hannah Calhoon of Casey County. Hannah, whose parents were listed only as 'Calhoon', was age 42 and also born in Casey County. Hannah had five children from her previous marriage – Nora, Albert, Pearl, Beatrice, Oscar – whom Wilse and Hannah reared, along with a son Haskel whom they had together:

J332-75. NORA, *m. Bert Thurman, d. 1986 in Dayton.*

Archibald Willis Austin (1870-1941) with his fifth wife Margie Garrett Austin holding his youngest child Anna Sue Austin, and his sister Elnora Austin McDonald.

J332-76. ALBERT ['DEE'], *m. Linnie Roberts (sister to Mary below). Albert drowned at New Castle, Kentucky.*

J332-77. PEARL, *b. — November 1903, m. Carl Patter, she was residing in 1986 in Dayton, Tennessee.*

J332-78. BEATRICE ['PATSEY'], *b. November 1908, m. Dave Brown. They divorced, and Beatrice was residing in Dayton, Tennessee in 1986, using the Austin surname.*

J332-79. OSCAR, *m. Mary Roberts (sister to Linnie above), d. 1984 in Chattanooga, Tennessee.*

J332-7A. HASKEL, *b. 10 December 1920 in Arkansas, m. in Dayton, Tennessee to Dorothy Morgan, he died on 4 April 1984 at the Erlanger Hospital in Chattanooga, Tennessee. Three children: Nadine Austin, Helen Austin, and a son whose name is unknown at this time. Helen died before 1986, and Nadine resided in Florida in 1986.*

Hannah and Wilse divorced, and Wilse was still 'age 48' when he married for the third time in Liberty, Kentucky on 16 June 1921 to widow Mary A. (Williams) Love of Casey County. Mary, the daughter of Haden and Willie Ann Williams, was age 48 born in Casey County, and was the widow of John A. Love. Wilse and Mary had no children before they divorced.

Wilse married for the fourth time on 10 July 1928 to Gladys Leona Bridges, daughter of William Monroe and Martha Birdie Lee (Wilson) Bridges, who was born 16 February 1910 in Rome, Floyd County, Georgia. Wilse and Gladys had two children, Lillian and Peggy, who were born in Dayton, Tennessee. In 1933 Wilse took Lillian and Peggy to Dunnville and his sister J332-5 Elnora S. McDonald (my 'Aunt Woatie') helped him to care for them until 1935 when he and Gladys divorced in Dayton, Tennessee, and Wilse remarried. Gladys remarried to George C. Willis, Lillian lived with them in Eloy, Arizona, and they operated a motel on E. Van Buron Street in Phoenix between 1946 and 1948. Gladys now resides in Portsmouth, Virginia. Wilse's children by Gladys:

J332-7B. LILLIAN VIOLA, *b. 29 June 1928 in Dayton, Tennessee, m.(1) on 9 June 1945 in Florence, Arizona to Orbie Lee McManis, son of Clinton J. and Tisha McManis. Orbie was b. 24 October 1921 in Joplin, Missouri, still living in 1988. They had three McManis children: James Lee b. 1946 Phoenix, Arizona; Georgia Leona b. 1948 Hopewell, Virginia; William Walton b. 1955 in Portsmouth, Virginia. Lillian and Orbie divorced in September 1956 in Portsmouth, Virginia, and Lillian m.(2) on 18 October 1958 in Elizabeth City, North Carolina to Willie Master Hudson, son of John Hudson, who was b. 4 June 1918 in Mecklenburg County, Virginia. Lillian and Willie had no children, they divorced in November 1969. Lillian now resides in Portsmouth, Virginia.*

J332-7C. MILDRED JO ['PEGGY'], *b. 20 June 1931 in Dayton, m. on 9 August 1947 in Hopewell, Virginia, to Thomas Edward McClenney, the son of Henry Edward and Stella Mae (McCoy) McClenney, who was b. 24 February 1925 in Edenton, North Carolina. They had three McClenney children: Suellen b. 1948 in Portsmouth; Thomas Edward Jr. b. 1950 in Portsmouth; George Henry b. 1957 Waukegan, Illinois. In 1987 Peggy and Thomas were living in Indiana.*

Wilse was only 'age 45' when he married for the fifth time in Casey County on 19 October 1935 to Margie Garrett of Casey County. It was the first marriage for Margie, the daughter of J. R. & Venie Garrett, who was age 19 and born in Casey County. Wilse and Margie had two children born in Dunnville, Kentucky:

J332-7D. W. J., *was b. and d. 23 April 1938 (stillborn).*

J332-7E. ANNA SUE, *b. 11 April 1939, m. on 14 June 1954 to Earl Thomas Gasper. Two Gasper children were born in Amo, Indiana: Earl Douglas b. 1955 and Deborah Sue b. 1957.*

Archibald Willis Austin died on 29 May 1941 in Dunnville, Casey County, and is buried there in Thomastown Cemetery. I was nearly thirteen years old when my father died. I never remembered or recall my father getting angry or upset. He was very soft spoken, and a hard worker. We had a very nice country home in Dunneville, about one-half mile before you reach Forest Austin's home. At times my father had lots of land, a large farm across the road from us was never paid for at his death. Also, two of my half brothers came from Cincinnati and took what money Daddy had and supposedly bought a farm in Indiana. They had got my father some type of pension, and he was not to work anymore, since he had had a couple of heart attacks. Wilse and his five wives raised fourteen children, but during the Depression years everyone got scattered. The author would like to correspond with any of her half brothers and sisters, or indeed with anyone having information on Wilse's descendants – please contact me through *Austins of America.*

★★★★★★★★★★★★★★★★★★★★★★★★★★★★★

Austins of America is intended to serve present and future genealogists researching Austin family lines. Readers are encouraged to submit queries, genealogical and historical articles for publication. Previously published books, pamphlets or articles containing Austin genealogical data are also sought for reprinting or review.

EDITOR

DR. MICHAEL EDWARD AUSTIN   CONCORD, MA

ASSOCIATE EDITORS

ANTHONY KENT AUSTIN   PROSPECT, KY

BERT ADDIS AUSTIN   QUEEN CREEK, AZ

PATRICIA BIEBUYCK AUSTIN   CONCORD, MA

PAULINE LUCILLE AUSTIN   CEDAR RAPIDS, IA

Austins of America is published each February and August by The Austin Print, 23 Allen Farm Lane, Concord, Massachusetts 01742. All correspondence, including subscriptions, articles and responses to queries, should be sent to this address. Subscriptions are $4.50 per year postpaid.

PAUL AUSTIN COMMEMORATES LANDING

WITH MACARTHUR IN THE PHILIPPINES

by William Branigin

Editor's Note: This article is abstracted from a Washington Post Service article entitled "Vets Again Heed Call 'I Shall Return' – 40 Years Later It's Back to Leyte," which appeared in the 20 October 1984 issue of the *Honolulu Advertiser.*

TACLOBAN, PHILIPPINES – To Vicente Sydiongco, the first shells sounded like thunder. It was 20 October 1944, and a typhoon had struck the central Philippines island of Leyte the night before. Then Sydiongco heard the secondary explosions, and he realized this was no typhoon. He knew then that true to the promise of General Douglas MacArthur, the Americans had returned.

Captain Paul Austin of Fort Worth, Texas, was one of those Americans who hit the beaches of Leyte Gulf 40 years ago today as part of MacArthur's drive to recapture the Japanese-occupied Philippines and split Tokyo's World War II empire in half. The operation, the General wrote later in his memoirs, would become a springboard "for the final assault on Japan itself."

Paul Austin's unit came under heavy Japanese artillery and machine-gun fire that day as the Americans established their beachhead, but the hardest fighting was yet to come. Austin, then a Company Commander, would later lead a bayonet charge and engage the Japanese in hand-to-hand combat.

Today, Paul Austin and about 400 other, veterans from the United States, Australia and Japan gather here with Sydiongco and thousands of Filipino veterans to mark the 40th anniversary of the Leyte landing. For the Americans it was "A-Day," a day of triumph for MacArthur and the culmination of a 1,500-mile seaborne jump by some 200,000 troops that has been described as one of the most daring amphibious operations ever conceived. It was also the prelude to what U.S. historian William Manchester has called "the greatest naval battle in history," the battle of Leyte Gulf in which an American armada routed the Japanese fleet a few days later.

By the time it was over, the Japanese had lost four aircraft carriers, three battleships, eight destroyers, six heavy cruisers and three light cruisers in an unsuccessful bid to trap and bombard the American landing force. By comparison, the U.S. naval forces under Admirals William Halsey and Thomas Kinkaid had lost one light carrier, two escort carriers and three destroyers in the battle, which had involved a total of 282 warships on both sides. For the Japanese, Manchester wrote, "Leyte had been a catastrophe." They lost 65,000 crack troops, the backbone of their fleet and virtually all of their air force except for kamikazis, who debuted during the Philippine campaign.

In commemoration of the events at Leyte, veterans of the U.S. 96th and 24th Divisions, Australia's Allied Land Forces and the Japanese 16th Division will tour battle sites, lay wreaths to honor their fallen comrades and watch a joint amphibious landing exercise by combined unite of the U.S. and Philippine armed forces.

MacArthur's landing, in which he waded to shore accompanied by Philippine President Sergio Osmena and top generals and aides, is to be re-enacted with an American officer playing the part of the U.S. commander in the Pacific, who died in 1964. Vice Admiral James Hogg, the Commander in Chief of the U.S. 7th fleet, has been chosen to represent the Pentagon at the ceremonies. According to James Hofrichter, 63, one of the organizers of the veterans trip here, more than 180 officers and men who fought in the Philippines are taking part in the ceremonies.

Many American veterans feel the Leyte landing anniversary has been overshadowed by the commemoration earlier this year of the 40th anniversary of the Allied invasion of France at Normandy beach that helped defeat Nazi Germany. But the memories of the U.S. Pacific theater veterans are no less vivid, and the suffering of many of them at Japanese hands was no less real. One of the returning veterans who suffered most was Richard Deuitch, 65, of Garrett, Indiana a former 2nd petty officer taken prisoner by the Japanese in 1942 after being wounded on Corregidor. A survivor of the infamous "Bataan death march" in which thousands of captured American and Filipino soldiers died. Deuitch spent a year in a prison camp in the Philippines and about two years in a labor camp in Japan until the war ended.

Out of 405 prisoners of war in his group in Japan, he said, "133 of us walked out." Thousands of American prisoners were starved, beaten or tortured to death, he said, and others suffered unspeakable cruelties at the hands of their captors. Filipinos also suffered severely, especially after MacArthur began his drive to recapture the Philippine islands and was welcomed by the populace as a returning hero. According to Manchester, nearly 100,000 Filipinos were murdered by rampaging Japanese troops in Manila after MacArthur's forces put the Philippine capital under siege. Hospitals were set on fire, women of all ages were raped, and even babies were mutilated or slaughtered by the Japanese, he wrote. When the siege ended, Manila lay in ruins. Of Allied cities during World War II, only Warsaw suffered greater devastation.

Conversations this week with 10 American veterans who fought under MacArthur also show that forgiveness does not come easy. Some want nothing to do with the Japanese veterans here and have never reconciled themselves to the postwar partnership between the United States and Japan. "When I'm over here and I think about the buddies I helped bury on Leyte, I can't help it." said James Frederick, 59, of Arlington, Texas. "It's still embedded in my mind."

EARLY AUSTINS FOUND IN ENGLAND

by Miss Elizabeth French

Editor's Note: The following article is part of the author's article entitled "Genealogical Research in England 1913," which appeared in the *New England Historical and Genealogical Register* in Volume LXVII pages 34-36 and 161-167, published in 1913.

The will of Henrye Austen of Byddenden in the County of Kent, 28 December 1570. To be buried in the churchyard of Byddenden. To Marye and Thomasyn Austen my daughters 40s. each, to be paid to either of them at marriage or age of twenty years. To Thomas Austen my son £4 in money or goods, he paying to Dorothe Austen and Rebecca Austen my daughters 40s. each at marriage or age of twenty years. The residue of all my moveable goods to my wife Anne and my son Walter, whom I make my executors. My will regarding my lands and tenements lying in Benenden. To my son Thomas Austen and his heirs my tenement and lands on the den of Mapestenstrow in the parish of Benenden, he paying 26s. 8d. a year to my wife for life, and after her death paying to my son Walter Austen £10. Witnesses: John Domeryghte, clerk, John Maye, Laurence Earell, and John Carpenter the younger. Proved 22 May 1572 by the executors named in the will. (Archdeaconry of Canterbury, vol. 41, fo. 146.)

The Will of Wacher Austen Senior of Bethersden, yeoman, 20 December 1600. To four poor men, Thomas Whittington, Richard Lappam, John Kinge, and Richard Longe, to carry me to church, a "tolvett" of wheat each. To John son of Thomas Gillam a heifer. To Alice Gillam my daughter two steers. To Catherine my daughter a lamb. To John Grinnell a lamb. Executors: my wife Elizabeth and my son William Asten. Josias Seiliard of Byddenden, gent, William Gylberd, Phillip Homewode of Biddenden, John Austen of Rolvinden, and John Carpenter of Bidden-den to divide my household goods equally between my said wife and son. Overseers: Thomas Stonestreet and Edward Wills, both of Bethersden. [Signed] Walter Asten senior. Witnesses: Richard Grezebrooke, Thomas Stone-street, and Edward Wills. Proved 27 January 1600/1 by the executors named. (Archdeaconry of Canterbury, vol. 52, fo. 219.)

Austen Entries in the Parish Registers and Transcripts of Biddenden, Co. Kent, 1538-1636

(records for 1558, 1562-1565 are defective)

1540 William son of Thomas Austen christened on 11 November.
1551 John Austen and Doryte Mount married 17 October.
1552 Jane daughter of — Austen christened 8 May. [1]
1552 Katherine dau. of — Austen christened 8 May. [1]
1552 Jane daughter of — Austen buried 9 May.
1552 Katherine daughter — Austen buried 9 May.

1557 Margaret daughter of Henry Austen christened 15 March [1557/8].
1559 Clement Downe and Elizabeth Austen married 23 October.
1560 Rebecca daughter of Henry Austen christened 18 November.
1561 Phillippe daughter of Henry Austen christened 13 April. [sic]
1561 John Buste and Jone Awsten married 1 July.
1566 John son of Henry Austen buried 21 May.
1566 Margaret daughter of Henry Austen buried 22 May.
1568 William Lyncke and Elizabeth Asten married 24 January [1568/9].
1570 John Mvnge and Mary Asten married 5 June.
1570 Henrye Asten householder buried 21 February [1570/1].
1571 Goddard Asten servant to Walter Asten buried 16 March [1571/2].
1572 Walter Austen and Julyan Cousheman married 12 January [1572/3].
1574 Anne daughter of Walter Asten christened 27 June.
1574 Julian wife of Walter Asten buried 17 November.
1576 Walter Austen and Alice Taylor married 2 July.
1577 Henry son of Walter Asten christened 11 August.
1579 John son of Walter Asten christened 6 September.
1580 Thomas Foster widower and Dority Austen mayden married 20 January [1580/1].
1581 George Parke and Hester Austen married 2 October.
1582 Peter son of Wacher Austen christened 17 June.
1582 Peter son of Wacher Austen buried 24 June.
1584 The son of Jeremy Austen buried 26 July.
1584 Thomas son of Wacher Austen christened 28 September.
1586 Steven Cooke and Rebecca Austen married 27 June.
1587 William son of Wacher Austen christened 18 February [1587/8].
1591 Thomas Gyllam and Alice Austen married 24 January [1591/2].
1592 John Winsett and Thomasine Austen married 19 June.
1596 A son of Jeremy Austen buried unchristened 28 December.
1597 Mary daughter of Michael Austen christened 12 March [1597/8].
1599 Alice wife of Wacher Austen buried 10 March [1599/1600].
1600 Richard son of Michael Austen christened 30 March.
1600 George Bourne and Mary Austen married 21 May.
1600 Wacher Austen and Mary Grinnell married 27 May.
1604 Hannah daughter of Wacher Austen christened 21 November.
1604 Hannah daughter of Wacher Austen buried 25 November.

1604 John Sloman and Marye Austen married 25 November.

1605 Mercy daughter of Michael Austen christened 27 December.

1605 Henry Austen a poor man being a drover of Tenterden buried 14 February [1605/6].

1608 William son of Michael Austen christened 24 April.

1612 Syluan Johnson of Sandwitch and Sarah Austen of Hawkhurst married by faculty 9 November.

1612 Elizabeth daughter of William Austen christened 27 December.

1612 A daughter of William Austen buried unchristened 29 December.

1612 Elizabeth daughter of William Austen buried 1 January [1612/3].

1612 Margaret wife of William Austen buried 7 January [1612/3].

1612 Mercy daughter of Michael Austen buried 11 February [1612/3].

1613 George Austen and Jone Kelsden married 31 May.

1613 William Austen and Agnes Tufnode married 28 November.

1614 Jane daughter of Michael Austen christened 29 May.

1616 John Austine buried 11 August.

1619 Henry son of Michael Austen christened 18 April.

1620 John Austen servant to Edward Aynscombe buried 18 May.

1621 Elizabeth daughter to Michael Austen christened 14 October.

1625 Francis son to Michael Austen christened 1 May.

1627 Margaret daughter of Michael Austin christened 23 March [1627/8].

1630 Margaret daughter of Michael Austin buried 24 February [1630/1].

1631 Margaret daughter of Michael Austin christened 2 April.

1636 Annis daughter of Michael Austin and wife Elizabeth christened 7 August.

Author's Note 1: Jane and Katherine were probably twins.

Thomas Besbeech was baptized at Biddenden 3 March 1589/90, the younger son of John Besbeech, the testator of 1609, married there on 14 January 1618/19 to Anne Baseden. They resided for a few years at Frittenden, where two daughters were born and his wife died. Later he lived at Headcorn and Sandwich. In the spring of 1635 he emigrated to New England, where he lived at Scituate and Sudbury, Massachusetts, and died 9 March 1673/4, leaving issue. His mother Dorothy, the testator of 1619, was the daughter of Henry Austen of Biddenden and sister of Wacher or Walter Austin of Bethersden, the testator of 1600. She was married first to Thomas Foster of Biddenden, by whom she had, besides other issue, a son Richard

Foster, who married Patience Bigg; the latter, with her son Hopestill Foster, went to New England in 1635 and settled at Dorchester, Mass. Hopestill Foster was thus nephew by the half-blood of Thomas Besbeech. The Besbeech (originally Byxpitch) family is of great antiquity in the Weald of Kent, and numerous early wills of the family are extant; but extensive search has failed to establish the identity of John Besbeech, the 1609 testator, among the numerous individuals of that name.

The Will of William Robinson of Tenterden in the County of Kent, husbandman, 26 June 1625. To my son William Robinson all my husbandry tools, a bed furnished, one acre of wheat next to the wood in a field containing four acres, and 20s. If he be not satisfied but claim £10 which I partly promised him, then he shall have but 10s. of the above bequest, the rest to be given to my wife Constance. To my daughter Eales Wilverden 6s. 8d., and to her two children John and Elizabeth Wilverden 4s. each. To my daughter Lidia Robinson £5 at her age of twenty-one or day of marriage, and if she die before said age, reversion to my son William and my wife Constance, equally divided. The residue of my goods and chattels to my wife Constance, whom I make my executrix. Witnesses: Nathaniel Tilden, William Glover, John Huckstepp, and Robert Haffinden. Proved 3 June 1626 by the relict and executrix named in the will. (Archdeaconry of Canterbury, vol. 65, fo. 163. Nathaniel Tilden was an emigrant to New England in March 1634/5.)

Some Austen Entries in the Parish Registers of Tenterden, County Kent

Between 1544 and 1640 there are over 200 Austen entries in the Tenterden registers, but none except those given here appear to apply to emigrant Jonas Austen's family:

Christenings

1628 Marie daughter of Jonas Austen 24 August.

1629 Jonas son of Jonas Austen 28 February [1629/30].

1632 Mary daughter of Jonas Austen 5 August.

Marriage

1626 Jonas Austen and Constance Robinson 22 January [1626/7] (Editor's note: see William Robinson Will above.)

Burial

1629 Mary daughter of Jonas Austen 18 December.

Austen Entries on the Parish Registers and Transcripts of Staplehurst, Co. Kent, 1538-1630

1538 Yden daughter of Ja[mes] Austen christened 18 November.

1539 Annes wife of Jamys Awsten buried 11 September.

1541 Poenall son of Jamis Austin christened 2 February [1541/2].

1543 John son of James Austen christened 19 August.

1543 John son of James Austen buried 19 August.

1543 William Asten and Jone Longle married 28 January [1543/4].

1544 Thomas Asten and Jone Pyckkynden virgin married 27 July.

1544 Percyvall son of Wyllyam Asten christened 1 November.

1544 Thomas son of Jamis Asten christened 12 November.

1544 stephen Asten and Margaret Wrigley "yong folkes" married 18 November.

1544 Willyam son of Stephen Asten christened 19 November.

1544 percyvall son of William Asten buried 21 November.

1544 Wyllyam son of Stephen Asten buried 1 January [1544/5].

1544 Wyllyam Asten and Margery Symon "yong folkes" married 26 January [1544/5].

1545 John son of Thomas Asten christened 15 July.

1545 Simon son of William Asten christened 13 October.

1545 Robert Asten servant buried 21 February [1545/6].

1546 Katherin daughter of Stephen Asten christened 16 May.

1546 Symon son of Williyam Asten "about ij yeres off age" buried 21 February [1546/7].

1547 Richard son of Stephen Asten christened 28 February [1547/8].

1548 Roberth son of Thomas Asten christened 28 May.

1548 Roberth son of Thomas Asten buried 31 May.

1549 Thomas son of Thomas Asten taylor christened 23 June.

1549 Richarde son of James Asten christened 1 January [1549/50].

1549 Edward son of Stephen Asten laborer christened 21 February [1549/50].

1549 Godlif wife of James Asten buried 21 February [1549/50].

1550 Margaret wife of Stephen Asten buried 2 May.

1550 Edward son of Stephen Asten laborer born 21 February last past buried 4 August.

1551 "Was Maried Stevyn Asten Widoer unto Elsabetht bassocke synglewoma" 16 November.

1552 Kateryn daughter of Thomas Awsten christened 3 June.

1552 Joanne daughter of Stevon Awsten christened 1 January [1552/3].

1553 Christoffer son of Thomas Awstin christened 20 March [1553/4].

1554 "The xvi day of July was Chrystened Gerves Austin the Sonne of Stepefane Austen."

1554 James son of James Austin [christened?] 16 July.

1556 John Reder child of James Asten christened 28 July.

1557 Margery daughter of stevyn Asten christened 26 March; godfather Robert Bassock, godmothers Elizabeth Carter and Tomsyn Borag.

1557 Agnes daughter of Alexander Berye christened 24 June; godfather John Austen, godmothers Agnes Vyny and Katherine Gararde.

1557 "Humatum corpus Stephani Asten" 17 November.

1559 James Asten widower and Agnes Merian born at Boughton quarrie married 12 February [1559/60].

1560 Laurence son of Laurence Asten christened 19 July.

1560 Laurence son of Laurence Asten christened 30 August.

1560 Augustyne supposed son of James Asten and Deonice Hughes singlewoman christened 1 December.

1561 Willm Eden and Elizabeth Asten widow married 14 January [1561/2].

1562 Rycharde Awsten a child buried 5 January [1562/3].

1564 Walter son of Thomas Austen christened 10 September.

1565 Henry son of James Austen christened 12 August.

1565 Myghell Draner and Agnes Austin widow of the parish of Louse [Looze] married 25 November.

1565 Margery Asten "a yong mayden" buried 13 January [1565/6].

1566 James Austen an householder buried 29 January [1566/7].

1570 Walter son of Thomas Austen buried 30 August.

1572 Persyvall Austyn and Bennytt Selve "yong folke" married 8 June.

1572 Mary daughter of Percyvall Asten christened 22 February [1572/3].

1572 mary daughter of Persyvall Asten buried 4 March [1572/3].

1573 elsebeth daughter of Persyvall Austin christened 20 December. [Note 2]

1574 James son of Persyvall Austen christened 4 September.

1577 Margery daughter of George Austen christened 1 September.

1577 Margaret daughter of Thomas Austen christened 15 September.

1579 Henry Harris and Johan Austin "yong ffolke" married 25 October.

1580 Thomas son of Thomas Austin christened 17 April.

1582 Thomas son of Thomas Austen "the yonger" buried 7 July.

1582 Judith daughter of Thomas Austin the younger christened 25 December.

1584 Joan daughter of George Austen christened 29 March.

1584 "Octobris 26 wear maryed Jeruas Austen & Mary Bassocke yong folke."

1584 William the son of Thomas Austen the elder buried 3

February [1584/5].

1584 Elizabeth the base-born child of Jone Austen buried 3 February [1584/5].

1585 Mary daughter Jeruis Austen christened 29 August.

1585 Rychard Austen and Mary Hawkes married 20 December.

1586 Jeames son of George Austine christened 8 May.

1586 William son of Richard Austin christened 3 July.

1586 Elisha son of Thomas Austein christened 25 September.

1586 Elisha son of Thomas Austen buried 13 October.

1586 Stephen son of Jeruas Austen christened 26 February [1586/7].

1587 A woman child of Rychard Austine buried unchristened 19 March [1587/8].

1588 Alysander Snode and Mary Awstyn "yonge folkes" married 10 July.

1589 Cateryn daughter of Jervys Awsten christened 6 April.

1589 Cateryn daughter of Jervys Awsten buried 9 April.

1589 Olde Thomas Awsten houscholder buried 12 April.

1589 Marye daughter of Rychard Awsten christened 27 April.

1589 Jone wife of George Awsten buried 22 March [1589/90].

1590 Marye daughter of Jervys Awsten christened 5 April.

1590 Benett wife of Thomas Awsten of Leedes buried 2 January [1590/1].

1591 George ye son of an harlot and ye mother saith ye son of Jervys Awsten christened 28 October.

1591 Thomas son of Richard Awsten christened 31 October.

1591 Marye wife of Rychard Awsten buried 27 January [1591/2].

1591 Tearsye and Denys daughter of Jervys Awsten christened 13 February [1591/2].

1591 Tearsye daughter of Jcrvis Awsten buried 16 February [1591/2].

1592 Jone Awsten an ancient widow buried 16 May.

1593 Thomas son of Rychard Awsten buryed 19 September.

1593 Isbell daughter of Jervys Awstin christened 17 November.

1596 John son of Jarvis Austyne christened 15 August.

1598 "Jonas the sonne of Gervis Austen" christened 3 December.

1599 Susanna daughter of James Austin christened 23 March [1599/1600].

1600 Buried a still-born child of Jarvis Austin 21 March [1600/1].

1602 Jonne daughter of James Austine christened 9 January [1602/3].

1605 Sewsan daughter of Jervis Austin christened 4 July.

1607 Mildred daughter of Jervis Austin christened 2 August.

1610 Marie wife of Jarvis Austine buried 12 May.

1610 Jarvis Austine buried 5 June.

1625 Gilles Cocket and Patience Austin widow married 15 July.

1626 Samuel son of George Austine christened on 2 November.

1626 Richard Austine and widow Aiherst married 28 November.

1627 Samuel son of George Austine buried 10 December.

1627 Stephen Austine housekeeper buried 14 January [1627/8].

Author's Note 2: The original old-paper register gives this surname as Garbytt, but the surname Austin is found in a parchment copy of the original register.

QUERIES

257-1. **Aaron Austin** was born circa 1778 in New Jersey. He died in Oxford Township, College Corners, Ohio circa 1860. Seeking Aaron Austin's parents and birthplace.

257-2. **Frances Austin** married Captain Richard Littlepage. Richard died in 1717 in New Kent County, Virginia, leaving Frances with a number of small children. Frances Austin Littlepage died in 1734. Seeking her ancestry.

257-3. **George William Austin** was born on 23 December 1804 in Tennessee, perhaps the son of Levi Austin of Rutherford County, Tennessee. George William married circa 1836 to Ann Rodgers, possibly in Tennessee. Ann was born on 7 August 1811 and died on 27 May 1891. George died on 15 December 1866 in Johnson County, Texas. Their children were: Mary, William, John, Margaret, and George William, Jr. Seeking the parents and ancestry of George William Austin and his wife Ann.

257-4. **Hannah Austin** descends from the Robert Austin line. She was born on 1 April 1739, and married on 11 June 1769 at Exeter, RI to Samuel Whaley Jr. of Kingstown. Seek the dates of death for Hannah and Samuel, and the names of their children.

257-5. **Nathaniel Austin** was born 31 March 1734, son of Captain Nathaniel and Agnes (Adams) Austin. He married Abigail (—), who was born in 1747 and died on 3 March 1803 in Sullivan County, New York. Nathaniel died on 28 February 1807 in the same county. Need all data on and ancestries of both Nathaniel and Abigail.

257-6. **Thomas J. Austin** appears in the 1880 Census for Calloway County, Kentucky, which lists: Thomas J. Austin age 54, born in Tennessee, father and mother born in North Carolina, Elizabeth C. Austin age 53, born in Kentucky, and James Manley Austin age 21, farm, born in Kentucky. Seeking the ancestry of Thomas J. Austin.

ACCOUNT OF A JOURNEY ACROSS
THE OHIO VALLEY TO THE MISSISSIPPI

by Moses Austin

Editor's Note: The following article is from the author's journal, signed by Moses on 25 March 1797 after he had returned to Virginia, although it was probably written earlier. It originally appeared in the *American Historical Review*, Volume V, pages 523-542. Moses Austin was the father of Stephen Fuller Austin of Texas – see page 288.

Departure from Virginia

On December 8, 1796, in the evening, I left Austinville, on horseback, taking Joseph Bell as an assistant, and a mule to pack my baggage; and that night went to Mr. James Campbell's, who, on the morning of the 9th, started with me for Kentucky. Nothing of note took place from Mr. Campbell's to Captain Cragg's, where we arrived on the 11th at evening, furnishing ourselves with blankets, etc., at Abington as we passed.

The morning of the 12th I left Captain Cragg, in company with a Mr. Wills from Richmond, bound to Nashville in the state of Tennessee. That night I arrived at the Block House, so called from being some years past used as such but at this time in the hands of Colonel Anderson, at whose house it was expected good accommodations could be had; more so in consequence of his being a friend of Mr. Campbell's. However, it was with great trouble that he admitted us under his roof or would allow us anything for our horses and mules. Colonel Anderson's is thirty-six miles from Captain Cragg's, which I left by daylight, taking the road through Powell's Valley.

At this place I parted with Mr. Wills, who took the road for Cumberland, which forked at this place. The road being bad and the weather uncommonly cold, I found it was with hard traveling that we reached the foot of Wallon's Ridge that night. From Anderson's to Benedict Yancy's is thirty-four miles and an uncommon mountainous road. Fifteen miles from the Block House is Clinch Mountain and the river of the same name. I, the same day, passed a number of mountains and ridges, the most considerable of which are Copper Creek, Powell's, and Wallon's, as also several large creeks and Powell's River.

Mr. Yancy's is the entrance into Powell's Valley. A wagon road has lately been opened into and down the valley, and notwithstanding great pains and expense, the passage is so bad that at many of the mountains the wagoners are obliged to lock all the wheels and make fast a trunk of tree forty feet long to the back of the wagon to prevent it from pressing on the horses. In this manner many wagons have passed on to Kentucky.

Moses Austin (1761-1821)

It was late in the evening of the 13th that I arrived at the house of this Mr. Yancy, and badness of the weather had made me determine not to go any farther, being then 8 o'clock and snowing fast. However, I found it was not so easy a matter to bring the old man and woman to think as I did; for when I demanded, or rather requested, leave to stay, they absolutely refused me, saying that we could go to a house six miles down the valley. Finding moderate words would not answer, I plainly told Mr. Yancy that I should not go any farther and that stay I would. Old Mrs. Yancy had much to say about the liberties some men take, and I replied by observing the humanity of others; and so ended our dispute. Our horse was stripped and some corn and fodder obtained. We soon found ways and means to make the rough ways smooth, and, taking out our provision bag, made a good supper; after which, placing our blankets on the floor with our feet to the fire, I slept well.

The 14th we started from Mr. Yancy's and, the day being bad with snow and rain, we stopped at Mr. Ewing's, five miles below Lee's Court House and ten from Mr. Yancy's. At Mr. Ewing's we received the welcome of Mr. and Mrs. Ewing, at whose house we stayed until the morning of the 15th, when, after being furnished with everything we wanted and a good piece of beef to take with us, we took leave of Mr. and Mrs. Ewing and family and that night about sundown arrived at Cumberland Mountain. About half a mile before you pass this mountain you come into the road from Hawkins' Court House and Knoxville, which is said to be the best road.

After passing the mountain, which we did this night, we stopped at Mrs. Davis', who keeps a tavern down the mountain, and met with very good accommodations. Powell's Valley has lately been made a county by the name of Lee, taking all the country from Washington County to the Kentucky line. The Court House is about thirty miles up the valley from the pass of Cumberland Mountain, at which place is a small town of six or ten houses and two stores. Powell's Valley is, I am informed, about six miles broad and sixty in length. It is good land but so enclosed with mountains that it will be always difficult to enter with wagons. When the valley becomes well improved, it will be an agreeable place, but at this time it is thinly settled and [has] small farms.

On the 16th, by daylight, our horses being ready, we took our leave of Mrs. Davis, who I must take the liberty to say may be justly called Captain Molly of Cumberland Mountain, for she fully commands this passage to the New World. She soon took the freedom to tell me she was a come-by-chance — her mother she knew little of and her father, less. As to herself, she said pleasure was the only thing she had in view and that she had her ideas of life and its enjoyments, etc.

A Mr. Hay from Knoxville joined us this day. The weather still continued cold and the road which had been much broken up was now hard frozen. However, we arrived by dark at Ballinger's Tavern, thirty-seven miles from Cumberland Mountain. At this place I met with a number of gentlemen from Kentucky and a Doctor Rosse from the Illinois, with whom I had much conversation respecting that country. Our horses suffered this night, being obliged to make them fast to a tree and feed them on cane; but the accommodations for ourselves were good, considering the newness of the place.

The 17th, leaving Ballinger's, we traveled that day over an unpleasant road, passing several large waters and Cumberland River. We came at night to a small hut on Little Rock Castle, thirty miles from Richland or Ballinger's. At this place our accommodations were abominably bad. The house was about twelve feet square, and the night, which was distressingly cold, obliged all that were stopped at the place to take shelter in the hut – in all, women and children included, seventeen in number – nor can a more filthy place be imagined.

This night our horses suffered much. A few oats was all that the place afforded. After taking a supper from our provision bag, we took some rest on our blankets; and at daylight started on our journey, and in the evening arrived at the Crab Orchard, and took up our quarters at a Mr. Davis', twenty-three miles from Rock Castle, making in all ninety miles from Cumberland Mountain to the Crab Orchard. . .

I cannot omit noticing the many distressed families I passed. . . traveling a wilderness through ice and snow; passing large rivers and creeks without shoe or stocking and barely as many rags as covers their nakedness; without money or provisions, except what the wilderness affords — the situation of such can better be imagined than described. To say they are poor is but faintly expressing their situation — Life, what is it, or what can it give, to make compensation for such accumulated misery? Ask these pilgrims what they expect when they get to Kentucky. The answer is land. "Have you any?" "No, but I expect I can git it." "Have you anything to pay for land?" "No." "Did you ever see the country?" "No, but everybody says it's good land."

Can anything be more absurd than the conduct of man? Here are hundreds, traveling hundreds of miles — they know not for what nor whither, except it's to Kentucky — passing land almost as good and easy obtained, the proprietors of which would gladly give on any terms. But it will not do. It's not Kentucky. It's not the Promised Land. It's not the goodly inheritance, the Land of Milk and Honey. And when arrived at this Heaven in Idea, what do they find? A goodly land, I will allow, but to them forbidden land. Exhausted and worn down with distress and disappointment, they are at last obliged to become hewers of wood and drawers of water. . .

Vincennes, Indiana

January 1, 1797, on Monday, I arrived at the town of St. Vincennes, which I found to be much larger than I had an idea of. The situation is quite charming, nor can fancy paint a more desirable spot.

From Harvies to Vincennes – five miles – is an open champaign country and extremely fertile, interspersed with islands of trees and plains or prairies quite to the banks of the Wabash. Two miles from the town are two mounds which overlook the country for some miles, as also the town and river. These mounds arise in the middle of a large plain and are said to be Indian burial grounds. However, I cannot suppose this to be true unless the world has been in being much longer than some pretend to say, and the destruction of the human family greater than we have any account of in this part of the world. However, I was told by a gentleman in Vincennes that he had taken human bones from out of the mounds and that he discovered many more in the ground. I suppose each of the mounds to be at least half a mile in circumference and from the common level of the plain to the summit, sixty feet. They are now well set with grass and have every appearance of the works of nature and not of art.

Vincennes may contain 200 houses in all, but they are small and generally one story and badly finished. The streets are narrow and very irregular. At this time not more than three-fourths of the houses are inhabited. The inhabitants, since the treaty made by General Wayne, are gone onto their farms. This place is said to have been settled in or about the year 1726 and has undergone many changes since that time, but was always a place of considerable trade and wealth until General Clark took possession of it in the year 1778 for the United States; from which time until within the last eighteen months it has been on the decline.

Vincennes is settled with French from the towns on the Mississippi and Canada. And after the town came into the hands of the United States, many of the most respectable and wealthy families left the place and either went to Detroit or the Spanish side of the Mississippi; but the natural advantage of the place and the beauty of the country will, if the Indians are peaceable, soon make Vincennes a place of consequence. The garrison at this place is commanded by Captain Parsters. It consists of fifty men. The fort or citadel commands the town and Wabash River, in which are four six-pounders.

The Wabash River

The Wabash may be numbered among the beauties of nature. It is about 350 yards wide at the town. The banks are not high and the prairies on each side extend as far as the eye can command, forming a landscape, when viewed from the mounds back of the town, equal to anything of the kind I have ever seen. The God of this comely land has been lavish in finishing His work, for notwithstanding that the sovereign hand of winter had extended its terrific influence over all the face of creation, yet inexpressible charms could be discovered which the severity of winter could not change.

The navigation from the Ohio to Vincennes is said to be 130 miles safe and easy, upward from Vincennes, 150 miles for canoes; and the waters of the river in the spring may be navigated within a few miles of the Miami. The lands on this river are said to be equal to any in the world, forming large and extensive plains and groves of timber, and must at some time not long distant form a settlement equal to any in the United States. The west bank of the Wabash is said to overflow every spring, but the east bank, on which the town stands, is something higher and is not subject to overflow.

The aborigines which are settled on the Wabash, near Vincennes, are much reduced and some nations entirely extinct. The Piankishas [Piankashaws] had a town within one mile of St. Vincennes, but it is now destroyed and their number reduced to about 120 men. They have not any town or fixed place of residence but wander about from place to place, always calling Vincennes their home. The Wyatonas [Weas] are said to be 150 men and are settled up the Wabash, 200 miles from Vincennes. The Shakis [Sacs] I could get no information about, nor is there such a nation now known. If any of them are in being, they are united with some other nation.

I was directed to go to Colonel Small's for quarters, to which place I went and found good accommodations. The colonel and his lady were from home on a party of pleasure. And being informed of a Mr. Henry who was in town on his way to Illinois, I got a gentleman to direct me where he could be found; and calling at the house of Monsieur Dubois, I found Mr. Henry at table with a number of French gentlemen. I was unfortunate in not having letters to any gentlemen in Vincennes; however, the embarrassment I felt on this account was soon removed by the politeness of Monsieur Dubois, who, without ceremony, took me to the table and placed me beside the Roman priest. At Monsieur Dubois', I met with a number of Americans, and, notwithstanding I was a stranger to all, yet I found myself very agreeably situated.

After spending an agreeable afternoon, I returned to Colonel Small's and that evening went to a ball, where I was introduced to several gentlemen. Major Vanderburg, a man of some note, requested Mr. Henry and myself to take breakfast with him, which we did the next morning. I received much politeness from Colonel Small, Doctor Tisdale, and Monsieur Dubois, to all of whom I am much

indebted, as well as Major Vanderburg. Colonel Small keeps the only tavern in Vincennes at which good accommodations can be had. There is a Catholic church at Vincennes, but the building is not of sufficient note to be known by strangers unless informed, but to whom this church is dedicated I did not learn.

Crossing the Mississippi River into Spanish Louisiana Territory

The morning of the 15th, Mr. Henry and myself crossed the Mississippi on the ice to St. Louis, and being told there was not any tavern in the town, I left Joseph Bell and the mule at Kahokia; nor was it without great trouble that I procured quarters for myself. And I believe I should have been obliged to have returned to Kahokia the same day had I not met with a man by the name of Drake, who spoke English and went with me to a Monsieur le Compt, who politely took Mr. Henry and myself into [his] house. After changing our dress, we immediately paid our respects to the commandant, Monsieur Zeno Trudeau, to whom we had letters. The commandant received us with much politeness and promised us all the assistance the nature of our business demanded. I had letters to a merchant, Monsieur Charles Gratiot, from whom I received much attention. Monsieur Gratiot spoke English well and was of great advantage to me as I could not speak French.

St. Louis is prettily situated on a rising spot of ground, and has a commanding prospect of the Mississippi for some distance up and down the river, and also the American side. The town of St. Louis is better built than any town on the Mississippi, and has a number of wealthy merchants and an extensive trade, from the Missouri, Illinois, and upper parts of the Mississippi. It is fast improving and will soon be a large place; the town at this time contains about 200 houses, most of which are of stone, and some of them large but not elegant. The exports of St. Louis are supposed to amount to £20,000 per annum. The trade of this place must increase, being within fifteen miles of the Missouri and thirty of the Illinois rivers.

The large settlements making on the Missouri by the Americans will be of great advantage to St. Louis, the wealth of which is so much greater than any other town on the Mississippi that it will take a long time to change the trade even from the American side to any other place. And the great advantages held out by the government of Spain will soon make the settlements on the Missouri formidable. Land has already been granted to 1,000 families, near 400 of which have arrived from different parts of the United States. Back of St. Louis is a small fort mounting four four-pounders. It is not of much strength, has a guard of twenty men only. The church is a frame building and makes but an indifferent appearance, has neither steeple nor bell.

The aborigines which trade to St. Louis are the Kakapoos [Kickapoos], Piankishas, Piorias [Peorias], Sioux, Shawanees [Shawnees] (west of the Mississippi), and Osages on the Missouri. There is none of the above Indians that confine their trade to St. Louis except the Osages. But St. Louis gets the best part of all as well as many other nations, both on the Mississippi and Missouri, which seldom or ever visit the town of St. Louis but have goods taken to them by traders employed by the merchants of St. Louis, who make their returns in the months of April and May.

The lands on the west side of the Mississippi are not equal to those on the American side, except on the Missouri River, which enters the Mississippi fifteen miles above St. Louis, and the Maramag [Meramec], ten miles below, and the Saline, six miles below St. Genevieve and sixty below St. Louis.

The River Maramag is navigable for batteaux thirty miles at all times in the year and in the spring much higher; it is about 100 yards wide at its mouth and keeps nearly its width until its forks, after which it loses its name and makes what is called the Grand River and the Mine Fork. Between the Mine Fork and Grand River are the lead mines known by the name of the Mines of Briton, which without doubt are richer than any in the known world. These mines are about forty miles from St. Louis, and thirty from St. Genevieve, and fifteen from the navigation of the Maramag. On the Maramag are several salt springs from which some salt is made, but the Saline will, it's most likely, furnish this country with salt, there being a great number of salt springs on its banks from which much salt is now made. And when the works are extended, it may furnish all the upper settlements on the Mississippi.

Back to the "Northwest Territory"

[On the] 16th I waited on the commandant and received letters from him to the commandant of St. Genevieve. Leaving St. Louis, I recrossed the Mississippi to Kahokia, and on the 18th arrived at the town of Kaskaskia. From Kahokia to Kaskaskia is about fifty miles and the best body of land in the world. The bottom, which extends from Kahokia to the mouth of the Kaskaskia, is in common five miles in width and, except immediately on the bank of the river and one-fourth of a mile out, is in order for any kind of farming use, being a natural meadow the whole way. Between the town of Kahokia and Kaskaskia you pass the village of Prairie Du Rocher, which has about sixty houses, as also the Little Village, which, I am told, when under the English, had fifty families and a good church, but at this time there are but three families in the town and the church is destroyed. The church at Prairie Du Rocher is a frame house and not large. It is much out of repair, has a small bell, [and] is dedicated to St. Joseph.

[CONTINUED ON PAGE 288]

SOME AUSTIN MARRIAGES, BIRTHS, WILLS AND LAND RECORDS FROM LAGRANGE COUNTY, INDIANA

by Pauline Lucille Austin

MARRIAGE RECORDS 1881-1870

Albert M./N. Austin to Margaret A. Strager 10 June 1877

Artemisia Austin to E. P. Spelman on 19 October 1875

Charles Austin to Oral Robbins on 1 January 1876

Charles W. Austin to Isabinda A. Magown 16 August 1863

Dora Austin to Fred Racine on 10 October 1878

Ellen Austin to Francis Gilbert on 13 August 1866

Emery E. Austin to Mary M. Dodge on 12 July 1883 by Joel H. Austin

Florance B. Austin to Alice A. Cochran 11 October 1881

Huldah M. Austin to George D. W. Stancliffe on 28 January 1851

John W. Austin to Louisa Fothergill on 4 June 1841

Lola Austin to Benjamin Winaus on 24 December 1883

Nelson M. Austin to Ellen Beals on 12 March 1874

Rebecca Austin to Philip Bower on 29 March 1866

Richard Austin to Charity J. Dunbar on 1 July 1849

Richard Austin to Rebecca Falkner on 29 January 1863

Sarah Austed (sic) to Frederick Filkie on 27 May 1851

Sarah Austin to Marcus Atwater taken out on 19 March 1867 and by this book was never returned

BIRTH RECORDS 1882-1919

— Austin b. 25 November 1882, daughter of Charles and Isabuda (Magown) Austin

— Austin b. 22 April 1883, daughter of John and Julia (Raum) Austin

— Austin b. 5 April 1885, daughter of Nelson and H. A. (Hand) Austin

— Austin b. 10 July 1886, son of Albert and — (Strayer) Austin

— Austin b. 1 December 1887, son of Albert and — (Hollum) Austin

— Austin b. 27 February 1890, son of Albert and — (Kellam) Austin

— Austin b. -- August 1892, son of Nelson Austin

— Austin b. 19 September 1895, son of Will and Emma (Holmes) Austin

— Austin b. 19 October 1899, daughter of Frank and Lulu (Elco) Austin

— Austin b. 2 November 1900, son of Claude and — (Scisson) Austin

— Austin b. 30 June 1901, son of Nelson and — (Tillston) Austin

— Austin b. 14 October 1902, daughter of Charles E. and Anna (Miller) Austin

— Austin b. 21 June 1903, daughter of Flora and — (Gunn) Austin

— Austin b. 14 October 1903, son of William and — (Fish) Austin

— Austin b. 13 February 1905, son of Charles and Anna (Miller) Austin

— Austin b. 10 May 1906, son of Welson and Hazel (Archer) Austin

— Austin b. 20 April 1910, daughter of Sabin and Ena (Esheleman) Austin

— Austin b. 20 July 1919, daughter of Hay A. and Maggie (Wilson) Austin

Beatrice Austin b. 9 November 1913, daughter of Emoral K. and Joy E. (Henry) Austin

Emma E. Austin b. 19 March 1917, daughter of Guy and Mable F. (Anderson) Austin

Eveline Austin b. 28 November 1917, daughter of Floyd and Maggie (Wilson) Austin

Frank O. Austin b. 9 November 1907, son of Charlie E. and Anna (Miller) Austin

Kenneth Austin b. 22 June 1910, son of William and Hattie (Fish) Austin

Kenneth E. Austin b. 7 October 1915, son of Frank and Lulu (Elco) Austin

Maxine B. Austin b. 24 September 1912, daughter of Sabin B. and Eva S. (Eshelman) Austin

WILL ABSTRACTS 1880-1929

Stephen H. Austin left all property to his wife Eleanor W. Austin. After death of wife, all property remaining in her possession shall be given to daughter Cornelia Pool and her heirs. Will dated 2 September 1880, names Nelson Slater executor, signed by Samuel Preston and E. A. Preston.

Isabinda Austin Will dated 11 February 1915 naming husband Charles W. Austin, executor, and children Fred Austin, Rose Gunn, Grace Sherman, Dora Vesey, Frank Austin, and Floyd Austin. Proof of Will 8 September 1928.

LAND RECORDS 1832-1865

Albert Austin sold land to Jeremiah Case on 5 October 1837 for $119.   3-459

Charles Austin and wife sold land to L. D. Magowan 6 October 1864 for $450.   16-462

Joshua Austin bought 60 acres from James McKenzie on 14 April 1848 for $320.   8-118

Justin Austin heirs sold land to Richard Austin on 11 August 1865.   17-430

Lorenzo D. Austin sold land to Nelson M. Austin on 18 June 1866 for $300.   18-276

Nelson M. Austin bought land from Lorenzo D. Austin on 18 June 1866 for $300.   18-276

Noah Austin and wife sold land to Harrison Harding on 3 March 1866 for $400.   18-115

Orin P. Austin bought land from Preston Bowman's heirs on 17 August 1853.   10-21

Rebecca Austin sold land to Edmund Shehan on 29 March 1848 for $300.   8-42

Reuben Austin, Jr. sold land to Hugh Compton on 4 August 1836 for $500.   2-483

Reuben Austin and his wife sold land to Hugh Compton on 1 September 1836 for $500. Reuben lived in Adrian Township, Lenawee County, Michigan. Witnessed by Asa Austin.   2-535

Reuben Austin and wife Angeline sold land to John Hutchins 9 January 1837 for $400. 3-73

Richard Austin bought 80 acres of land from Benjamin B. Waterhouse on 13 June 1844 for $212.   6-613

Richard Austin bought land from Justin Austin heirs on 11 August 1865.   17-430

Smith F. Austin bought 40 acres of land from Moses Young 31 March 1852 for $300. 9-291

Stephen H. Austin and wife sold land to Lorenzo D. Austin on 12 May 1865.   17-316

Wallace Austin sold land to John Tull on 11 October 1832 for $100.   8-37

LODRICK AUSTIN AND THE

DRIVERLESS STAGECOACH

by Donald A. Hutslar

Editor's Note: The following article was submitted by Barbara W. Austin. Mr. Hutslar is the Assistant Curator of Ohio History for the Ohio Historical Society. His article appeared in the Society's publication *ECHOES*, Volume 1, Number 10, in October 1962.

A tale my grandfather told. . . a suitable phrase to introduce the following short story, for such a tale led to the discovery of the headstone of Lodrick Austin. About the year 1885, when my grandfather was a young boy, he attended a funeral in the local cemetery at Clifton. After the brief service, the sextons were beginning to fill the grave when "sounds" were heard coming from the coffin.

Fear did not give way to curiosity and the grave was quickly filled. Thus the tale arose of the "haunted burial."

After hearing this tale from my grandfather, I visited the cemetery to look for the burial. The Austin headstone was found by chance during this visit. It is located in the north-central area of the cemetery on the brow of a hill. The stone is large, about two by five feet. What immediately attracted my attention was the carving. Surmounting the stone is a representation of an eagle grasping a fasces, the Roman symbol of authority.

> ERECTED
> *to the memory of*
> LODRICK AUSTIN
> *who departed this life*
> Sept 1st
> 1836
> *Aged 26 years, 7 months & 1 day*
>
> *Remember friends, as you pass by,*
> *As you are now, so once was I.*
> *As I am now: so must you be.*
> *Prepare you all to follow me.*
>
> *Saml F. Bunnel, Xenia, O. 1836.*

Below the eagle symbol is the graphic portrayal of a rather spirited coach-and-four. The horses are pictured as galloping; clouds of dust roll up behind them and the coach which carries one female passenger. The wheels have circular lines suggesting motion. The detail work is quite good, especially the harness. Of further interest, the reins have been drawn tightly to the floorboard of the driver's seat, and the horses' necks are arched. To gain leverage, the driver could cleat the reins to the floorboard with a half-hitch; when the slack was taken up, the horses could not pull loose. This was important if the horses for some reason were uncontrollable.

However, where is the driver in this scene? Either he is obscured by the weeping willow tree, a common funerary symbol of the mid-19th century, or he is simply not present. Certainly if the work were intended as a spirited coaching scene, the driver would have been shown for he would have been the center of the action. His obscurity or absence connotes a further meaning.

Several years went by without the discovery of any facts relating to Austin or the strange coaching scene. The first crack on the sometimes impregnable wall of time was found this year: In a small book entitled "The History of Glen Helen," by Dr. William A. Galloway, there is a paragraph history of the fate of Lodrick Austin. Austin was an expert "whip" for one of the stage lines that serviced the watercure area of the gorge, now known as Glen Helen, at Yellow Springs. (The gorge extends from Yellow Springs to Clifton and the old stage route followed the gorge closely.) On Thursday, September 1, 1836, while coming down the tanyard road hill directly in front of the Clifton cemetery, Austin lost control of his horses and was thrown off the coach by its wild gyrations. He struck a large boulder near the main gate of the cemetery and was fatally injured. His final resting place was a scant seventy-five yards away. Consequently, the rather confusing scene presented on his headstone is probably the sculptor's interpretation of the runaway coach after Austin had been thrown off.

Several questions still remain: Who was the feminine passenger in the coach and what happened to her (if she actually existed)? Why did the sculptor Bunnel take such pains in producing this stone which is so unlike the usual severe work of the period? Who financed the erection of the stone? No doubt such information does exist and is either known or will be found by historians who have access to local records.

QUERIES

263-1. **Charles Benjamin Austin** was born in 1857. He married Phebe V. Sterling in 1880, and they lived in Schuyler County, New York. Charles died in 1911. Seek information on parents & ancestry of Charles Benjamin.

263-2. **John Austin** born 1796 in North Carolina, wife Mary born 1804 in Tennessee or Virginia. Children born in Tennessee: Nathaniel born 1827, John born 1829/30, Theodocia born 1833, Mary born 1834, Celia born 1838, Elijah Harrison born 1841, and Elmina born 1843. John and Mary were listed in 1850 Census of Smith County, Tennessee and in the 1860 Census of Monroe County, Kentucky. Need ancestry of John and Mary.

263-3. **Solomon Austin** born on 28 February 1779 in Rhode Island. Married Delight (—) who was born on 11 October 1784 in Albany County, New York. Seeking the parents and ancestry of Solomon and Delight Austin.

263-4. **Mary Austin** married on 26 September 1799 to Joseph Hinkson in Belfast, Maine. There were five children from this union all born in Belfast. By 1850 they were in Roxbury, Maine. Seeking both the ancestry and the descendants of Mary Austin.

AUSTIN AND THE GALLIA COUNTY, OHIO
UNDERGROUND RAILWAY STOP

by James Sands

Editor's Note: This article is abstracted from one appearing in the Gallipolis *Sunday Times-Sentinel* on 14 February 1988. It was based upon the reminiscences of a 97-year-old man found at the Ohio Historical Society in Columbus, and was submitted by Arthur Wayne Austin.

In 1857 in Morgan Township of Gallia County a fugitive slave was captured by four slavehunters who resided in Morgan Township. The five people were moving along a ridge in Cheshire Township some 4 miles from Porter and were approaching a clearing where a man by the name of Austin (a veteran of the 1846-47 Mexican War) was at work with his son, a lad some eighteen years old.

When Austin saw that the fugitive slave was being led back to Virginia and slavery, he took off in a run to this group of five and asked the fugitive slave if he wanted to go back to slavery. Obviously the fugitive answered in the negative.

Shouted Austin: "Then I'll be danged if you shall!" Austin took out his knife and cut the rope which had bound the fugitive. The four men were not too pleased with this action and a disagreement ensued. Austin's son then brought to the fight a hand spike which tipped the odds a little more in the favor of the slave and his two rescuers.

Declared Austin to the four slavehunters: "Any soldier that could beat five Mexicans led by Santa Anna at Monterey could surely whip four lowly slave-hunters." After Austin had got the slavehunters into an attitude of submission he demanded that they give the fugitive slave a revolver. Whereupon the fugitive took the gun, thanked his rescuers and parted with advice from Austin: "If any man stops you, kill him!"

There were a couple of important stops on the Underground Railroad in Morgan Township, one was the home of Howell James who was a black and the other was a White Pine Grove Methodist Church. We picture today the present Pine Grove although now it is a Holiness Church. This particular building was erected in 1865 by the Pine Grove Methodist Episcopal congregation to replace a log church that stood near here on the farm of Thomas Lowden. The original church which was put up in 1844 and was set in a grove of pine trees and this setting offered good protection for runaway slaves.

In 1854 some seventeen fugitives passed along the Underground Railroad through Morgan Township. A company of slavehunters had pursued the fugitives and operators of the road to the home of Howell James. The slavehunters forced entry into the home and were surprised

to find the seventeen fugitives plus a number of operators. It was too late to admit the error of their judgement after they had already broken in and so the slavehunters received a surprise thrashing.

According to Dr. N. B. Sisson about 1848, a black woman who was very lightly complexioned came to Porter to George Payne's home. Mrs. Hogsett, the wife of the Presbyterian minister dressed the slave in Mrs. Hogsett's dress, shawl, and bonnet. A lady named Lucevia Blakley then walked the slave in Mrs. Hogsett's costume to the residence of Rev. H.R. Howe who was also a Presbyterian

minister and director of the Porter Academy. Rev. Howe then took the woman north with the excuse that he was taking "Mrs. Hogsett" to Wilkesville for a Presbyterian meeting there. By relating this story Sisson was making the point that many heroic deeds were done by men and women, black and white to lead people along the railroad to Canada and freedom.

Sisson reported as many as three hundred people in a gang coming in pursuit of runaway slaves. Often they forced entry into homes, sometimes they got a search warrant, but usually slaves were given up reluctantly. Slavehunters were driven off by Gallians with chairs, scalding water, ferocious dogs and often with some tall tales of misleading information, the masters of which were mostly women.

INDEX TO AUSTIN LAND TRANSACTIONS
IN THE PROVINCE OF NOVIA SCOTIA

by Michael Edward Austin

Editor's Note: The real estate transfers indexed below are listed alphabetically by the Austin involved, whether Grantor or Grantee, and chronologically for the same Austin name. The last numbers in each transfer are the Deed Book volume number and page on which the transfer is recorded at the Registry of Deeds in Halifax, Nova Scotia. Transfers between two Austins are listed alphabetically under both their names.

A. Austen was granted mortgage by Sarah Jost in 1825.   48-350

A. Austen was granted mortgage by Joseph Austen in 1826.   48-429

A. Austen granted release of mortgage to H. Hall in 1835.   61-119

Charles Austin was granted mortgage by John Jost in 1823.   47-479

Charles D. Austen granted mortgage to Ann Austen in 1825.   48-349

C. H. Austen sold land to Howe & Merrick in 1826.   48-471

C. D. Austen bought land from — Howe in 1827.   49-426

C. D. Austen granted mortgage to Ann Miller et al in 1829.   51-327

Charles Austin granted mortgage to Ann Miller in 1830.   52-435

Charles D. Austen granted mortgage to Ann Miller in 1831.   54-299

C. D. Austin granted mortgage to Miss Millers in 1833.   57-413

Charles D. Austen sold land to Thomas Austin in 1834.   60-329

Henry Austen bought land from William Meaney in 1782.   18-266

Henry Austin sold land to William Moth in 1783.   19-105

Henry Austin bought land from Thomas Cochran et al in 1784.   20-127

Henry Austin sold land to John Dilworth in 1784.   20-128

Henry Austen bought land from William Milward in 1785.   22-267

Henry J. Austin bought land from Augustus Deneman in 1786.   23-264

Henry Austin sold land to Thomas Austin in 1787.   25-236

Henry Austin sold land to Thomas Austen in 1804.   36-312

Henry Austin sold land to William Austin in 1816.   43-012

Henry Austin granted release of mortgage to Ann Marshall in 1823.   47-247

H. Austen granted mortgage to Alexander Keith in 1826.   49-119

Henry Austin bought land from William Austin in 1830.   52-393

Henry Austin sold land to Joseph Tarratt in 1834.   60-040

Henry Austin sold land to Joseph Tarratt in 1834.   60-042

J. Austin was granted release of mortgage by Howe & Merrick in 1835.   61-093

J. Austin bought land from Howe & Merrick in 1835.   61-099

J. Austin bought land from W. Stairs in 1835.   61-084

James Austin sold land to Joseph Miles in 1833.   57-303

Joseph Austen bought land from Mathias Richardson in 1817.   43-113

Joseph Austen granted mortgage M. Richardson in 1817.   43-116

Joseph Austen bought land from J. Sterns in 1818.   44-134

Joseph Austen granted mortgage to J. Sterns in 1818.   44-135

Joseph Austen granted mortgage to A. Austen in 1826.   48-429

Joseph Austin bought land from Samuel Cunard in 1826.   48-471

Joseph Austin granted mortgage to Howe & Merrick in 1826.   48-529

Joseph Austin bought land from William Austin in 1830.   52-395

Joseph Austin sold land to Mary Howe in 1830.   52-414

Joseph Austen granted mortgage to G. P. Lawson in 1830.   53-171

Joseph Austen granted mortgage to G. P. Lawson in 1830.   53-173

Joseph Austen bought land from Ann Miller in 1831.   54-025

Joseph Austin granted mortgage to Ann Miller in 1831.   54-029

Joseph Austen was granted release of mortgage by Garret Miller in 1831.   54-084

Joseph Austen sold land to Daniel Mullowney in 1832.   55-257

Joseph Austen was granted mortgage by Daniel Mullowney in 1832.   55-259

Joseph Austen bought land from Lewis Johnston in 1832.   55-494

Joseph Austin sold land to Thomas McKie in 1833.   58-123

Joseph Austin sold land to William Foster in 1833.   58-124

Joseph Austin sold land to John Clarke in 1833.   58-198

Joseph Austin sold land to John Slayter in 1833.   58-230

Joseph Austin sold land to John Roles in 1834.   59-153

N. Austen sold land to Enos Collins in 1835.   61-404

R. Austen granted release of mortgage to V. Bernardi in 1826.   49-140

R. Austen sold land to William Muncey in 1827.   49-462

R. Austen granted release of mortgage to Sarah Slayter in 1827.   49-497

R. Austin sold land to William Stairs in 1834.   60-185

R. Austin sold land to Charles D. Austin in 1834.   60-324

R. Austin sold land to Charles C. Austin in 1834.   60-327

Richard C. Austen sold land to George M. Jost in 1834.   60-319

Richard C. Austen sold land to George M. Jost in 1834.   60-322

Robert Austen bought land from John English in 1820.   46-013

Robert Austen granted mortgage to V. Bernardi in 1820.   46-014

Robert Austen granted mortgage to V. Bernardi in 1821.   46-453

Robert Austen granted release of mortgage to W. Strickland in 1827.   50-082

Robert Austin bought land from P. Lennergan in 1832.   55-269

Sarah Austin was granted mortgage by John Howe in 1822.   47-038

Sarah Austin bought land from John Howe in 1822.   47-040

Sarah Austin sold land to George Little in 1828.   50-462

T. Austen bought land from Thomas Austen in 1835.   61-088

Austins in the Federal Census of 1850

Help wanted. . . see page 240

Editor's Corner. . .

LOSING SIGHT OF THE PURPOSE OF YOUR GENEALOGICAL RESEARCH

Genealogy is so much fun that it's easy to forget that the purpose of our research is to preserve family records for our families and future generations. Publishing even incomplete research can help others while yielding surprising benefits.

Genealogy attracts people with widely varying interests. Those who enjoy jigsaw or crossword puzzles find genealogical problems equally fascinating, as their facts correlate to complete a picture. Those who enjoy travel find genealogy leads them to unexpected places, while those who like history find genealogy enhances their interest, as they discover their own ancestors participated in regional and national events and migrations.

It is not difficult to understand how we can become 'hooked' on genealogical research. Indeed, genealogy can be so much 'fun' that it is easy to forget why most of us begin researching our lines in the first place – to compile a record of our ancestry or the descendants of an ancestor. If we devote years to genealogical research and yet fail to publish it, we have lost sight of our purpose of providing a permanent record for posterity.

While many genealogists have created manuscripts or published their research, many more have not. Everyone intends to publish "someday, but not yet," for more research always remains to be done – another name, date or place is still unknown – their information is never quite complete enough. Besides the obvious danger of never publishing (recall poor Amos Sprague on page 68!), these procrastinators are missing the opportunity of furthering and expanding their research through publishing what they already know.

For an excellent example of the benefits of publishing even incomplete data, compare the rather sketchy writeup Bert Austin published on Archibald Willis Austin on page 169 with the writeup he inspired by Lillian Austin Hudson on page 251. By publishing what he knew, Bert learned many other facts on Archibald Austin, including another wife and thirteen children!

I would urge readers to consider submitting their genealogical research to *Austins of America* for publication, even if it is not 100% complete. It certainly will not mean the end of your genealogical enjoyment, and sharing your research with others may even lead you to new discoveries!

— *Michael Edward Austin*

REMINISCENCES OF ALBERT AUSTIN
OF PORTAGE COUNTY, OHIO

by Raymond H. Welch

Editor's Note: This article is abstracted from a column "Ohio Songs and Citizens," which appeared on 29 March 1942 in *The Cleveland Plain Dealer* newspaper in Cleveland, Ohio.

From today's picture of feverish activity in this part of Portage County I was whisked back to what had gone on here 100 years ago, for this was a place that got a lot of attention then as well as now. The 30-acre tract where the dormitories are built is not far from Augerburg, that lies to the east, on the way to the arsenal. Here was a shop that turned out tools of such fine craftmanship that they were in demand in all parts of United States, many of them being shipped by canal from Campbellsport, not far away, on Route 14.

I got the story of Augerburg from 85-year-old Albert Austin who has lived since 1916 at 356 N. Freedom Street in Ravenna, but who was born in Charlestown on a farm now across the road from the arsenal. His grandfather, Amos Austin had homesteaded there in 1817 having come from Torrington, Connecticut, home of John Brown, whose family he undoubtedly knew, as the Browns had come to Ohio only 13 years before.

Justin and Norris Wattrous, brothers also from Connecticut, had bought a tract of land in what came to be known as Augerburg, so Mr. Austin told me. They made carpenter's tools and these had a ready market in a land where men were building homes and barns and fashioning by hand nearly everything that went into them. The brothers were particularly clever with their augers, and eventually specialized in them. They even built a little factory, and in Mr. Austin's boyhood the tall chimney still stood, he remembers.

The Wattrouses did everything by hand, of course, and it seems remarkable that this little work shop could have turned out as many good products as it did. Long before the Civil War the business folded up, and the building, now no longer standing, was used for many years as a cheese factory and warehouse.

The corners, where the dormitories are, now Cotton Corners, were called Bean's Corners, from a landowner here. I have not been able to find a word of Augerburg's history in any book, though I have run upon three augers that were prized as having been made in "some Portage County town near Ravenna where my grandfather was a boy." Now this is the story of those old tools.

Mr. Austin talked to the accompaniment of a cheerful tick from a beautiful old clock that his grandfather had brought with him from Connecticut and which has been going, and going accurately, ever since. "I always say," he explained with a prideful chuckle, "that the Ravenna whistles can't blow until that old clock strikes."

Mr. Austin's wife, who died a little more than two years ago, was nationally known as a hybridizer of gladioli, having perfected several famous varieties "out at the old farm," where they lived for many years. Among them is the Evelyn Kirtland, named for their niece, daughter of Mr. and Mrs. Clyde Kirtland who now lives with Mr. Austin.

QUERIES

267-1. **Bill Austin** 'famous Indian Scout', had a son, William captured by the Indians. William allegedly married a daughter of Wamsutta, son of Massasoit and brother of King Philip. William's daughter, Mercy was born at Bath, Maine, 5 June 1762. Mercy married James LaBree. Seek ancestry of Bill Austin and that of his wife.

267-2. **David Austin** and Hannah (Buckley) Austin were of Mainesburg, Sullivan Township, Tioga County, Pennsylvania. There is a Revolutionary War Pension File Abstract on David Austin. Their son, Alvin Bolviar Austin who married Sarah Drinkwater Rumsey is our great-great-great-grandfather. Need to know more about David Austin's ancestry and descendants.

267-3. **Eva May Austin** was born on 13 April 1887 in Neosho, Newton County, Missouri, the daughter of William and Cora Dixon (Dickson) Austin. Eva May married on 5 September 1903 to Frederick Sollars. Eva May died on 26 October 1918 in Morris, Okmulgee County, Oklahoma and her husband Frederick died on 28 May 1956 in Norman, Oklahoma. Both are buried in Morris. I need to know the ancestors of Eva May.

267-4. **John N. Austin** and Lizea J. (Speakman) Austin had a daughter Celia Elizabeth Austin born on 28 May 1891-92 in Macon County, Tennessee. Celia married circa 1909 to William H. Brewington, who was born in March 1890 in Monroe County, Kentucky. Celia died on 19 May 1978 in Macon County, Illinois. Need to know more of John and Lizea's ancestry.

267-5. **Zephaniah Austin Jr.** was born on 12 March 1762/4 in Sheffield, Massachusetts, son of Zephaniah and the former Sarah Eggleston. Zephaniah Sr., his brothers, a son and cousins served in the Revolutionary War. By 1790 both the Zephaniahs, accompanied by Amos, Anthony, and Reuben Austin moved to Whitehall, New York. Zephaniah Austin Jr. married — Comstock, and had only one known child, Amasa Comstock Austin born 29 August 1796 in Whitehall, New York. I need any available information on Miss — Comstock and her ancestry.

SOME DESCENDANTS OF

DAVID AUSTIN OF WISCONSIN

by Sharon Austin Cutsforth

Editor's Note: The information below was derived from the references listed on page 270. David Austin is of the Robert Austin of Kingston, Rhode Island line, well documented by genealogist Edith Austin Moore [Reference 1, pages 55f]. For more on his son Cornelius Austin and his descendants, see pages 119-123 of *Austins of America*.

R123-19. DAVID[6] AUSTIN (*Gideon,*[5,4] *Pasko,*[3] *Jeremiah,*[2] *Robert*[1]) was born 12 March 1797 in Rhode Island. He moved to the state of New York, where he was employed as a pilot and lumberman on the Susquehanna River. David married on 5 October 1820 to Olcha Downing, the daughter of Cornelius and Polly (Lyon) Downing. Olcha was born on 22 May 1800 in County Cork, Ireland, daughter of Asel/Asiel/Aschel Downing [according to Reference 3, but "Cornelius Downing" according to Reference 1] and Polly (Lyons) Downing. Polly's father was a Revolutionary soldier who was killed on the field of battle.

David later took up farming in Otsego County, New York, and was thus engaged until 1844, in which year he removed to McHenry County, Illinois. David Austin was a man of broad understanding and liberal ideas, one who did his own thinking, but was not intolerant of the opinions of others.

On 21 November 1847 David Austin drowned when the steamship *Phoenix* caught fire in Lake Michigan off Waukegan, Illinois. Over 160 persons perished during that great tragedy, but according to Reference 2, very few were identified, and there was no Austin listed.

After David's death, his widow Olcha made the difficult overland journey to Portland, Oregon, where she subsequently resided for many years. She died at the home of her son Cornelius on 23 January 1888, and is buried with his family in the Lone Fir Cemetery in Portland. David and Olcha had fourteen children:

R123-191.   MARY ANN, *b. 24 February 1822, m. 25 April 1846 to Dexter Bartholomey. She d. on 1 May 1856 in Chicago, Illinois.*

R123-192.   CAROLINE MARIE, *b. 15 April 1823, m. George Washington Russell. See Ref. 1 p. 121*

R123-193.   ISAIAH CALEB, *b. 22 January 1825, m. Nancy I. Hitchcock. See Ref. 1 p. 122.*

R123-194.   RUSSELL DOWNING, *b. 12 February 1827, m. 3 October 1855 to Mary A. Collins. He d. 15 February 1887 in Portland, Oregon. See also page 119 of Austins of America.*

R123-195.   GEORGE ALBION, *b. 12 March 1829 +*

R123-196.   POLLY MALINDA, *b. 20 September 1830, m. Andrew B. Wightman. See Ref. 1 p. 123.*

R123-197.   WILLIAM BAINBRIDGE, *b. 23 September 1832; m. Harriet Bunker. See Ref. 1 pp. 123f.*

R123-198.   ASEL/ASCHEL ANDREW, *b. 15 September 1834, d. 5 February 1835.*

R123-199.   CORNELIUS, *b. on 12 September 1836, m. Effie Morgan. See also the article on page 119 of Austins of America.*

R123-19A.   ANDREW J., *b. 6 January 1838, d. 18 July 1861.*

R123-19B.   ANGELA ROSE, *b. 17 September 1840, m.(1) 25 December 1862 to Oscar Hildreth, m.(2) 23 August 1881 to Martin L. Canfield. Angela was the first woman mayor of Warren, Illinois. She d. 23 August 1925 in McMinnville, Oregon.*

R123-19C.   CHARLES, *b. on 8 February 1843, d. on 11 February 1843.*

R123-19D.   HELEN ADELAIDE, *b. 15 December 1843 in Waukegan, Illinois, m. 17 January 1866 to Oren F. Hutchinson in Harvard, Illinois. Oren was the son of Rodolphus and Lydia Hutchinson, b. 14 July 1840 in McHenry County. He d. 6 January 1916 in Denver, Colorado, while Helen d. 8 April 1925 in Ouray, Colorado. Hutchinson children: Mae Elsie b. 1967, Rose Blanche b. 1870.*

R123-19E.   HARRIET ADELIA, *b. 14 August 1847 in McHenry County, m. on 2 October 1873 to Frank Shelly Spafard in Warren, Illinois. Frank died on 30 March 1920 in Chicago, Harriet died 30 October 1929. Children: Dorothy Belle b. 1874, Florence S. b. 1878.*

R123-195. GEORGE ALBION[7] AUSTIN (*David,*[6] *Gideon,*[5,4] *Pasko,*[3] *Jeremiah,*[2] *Robert*[1]) was born 12 March 1829 in Unadilla, Otsego County, New York. He worked upon the family farm in McHenry County, Illinois and attended school until 1849. For a time he worked upon the Illinois and Michigan Canal, and in 1850-51 he taught school. George studied law, was admitted in 1853 to the bar and began his law practice at Woodstock, Illinois, where that same year he married Marinda Nancy Kimball. She was the daughter of Jonathan and Nancy J. (Gay) Kimball, and was born on 20 November 1835 in New Hampshire. Marinda was the granddaughter of General Gay, who had served in the Revolutionary War. Her father Jonathan moved to Illinois when she was twelve years old, he farmed and died near Woodstock. Jonathan had served as Company Sergeant in the War of 1812.

Reference 3 contains a biographical sketch published circa 1918 of George A. Austin which provides considerable information on his life: George Austin was not quite 32 years old when the Civil War broke out, and participating in that patriotic sentiment which animated most young of the North, he enlisted on 24 May 1861 in Company A, Fifteenth Illinois Infantry, being assigned the rank of Corporal. After three years of service George re-enlisted in a battalion, composed of the Fourteenth and

Fifteenth Illinois Regiments, being made Quartermaster in the latter regiment, with which rank he was subsequently mustered out. During his military career he saw much hard and dangerous service, taking part in the Missouri campaign, then going up the Tennessee river to participate in the Battle of Shiloh, called by the Confederates, Pittsburg Landing, and subsequently taking part in the seige of Vicksburg and other noted battles or military operations. Though he was never wounded, he had many very narrow escapes, as was evidenced by the fact that the overcoat he wore at the second battle of Champion Hill had twenty-two bullet holes through it. After rising to the rank of Company Lieutenant he was captured at Etawa and sent to the Confederate prison at Columbia, South Carolina. His rank saved him from being sent to Andersonville, the authorities of which prison were afraid of Northern officers who were prisoners organizing the men to effect escape.

At the end of the Civil War in the spring of 1865, George remained in the army, and was sent on the expedition organized to drive the French out of Mexico, but the death of Maximillian and the subsequent departure of the French army from that country caused the expedition to be halted before it ever reached Mexico.

George Austin was mustered out on 4 October 1865, after four and a half years of military service. He returned home to Woodstock, and for five years was engaged in stock buying. In 1870 he went to Neillsville, Wisconsin, where he decided to go into the milling business. He took over a flour mill that stood on the site of the mill that was later converted into a condensory, and he began business as the head of the firm of G. Austin & Co. He soon controlled the price of grain in this section of the state, it being hauled to him from as far away as the Mississippi River. He paid a good price to the farmers and his business flourished, so that it was no uncommon thing to see sixty or seventy teams standing in line at his mill. His flour was known as the 'Neillsville Mills' brand, and commanded a good sale on the market, being of a high quality. The flour mill was a wooden building, and connected with it by the same power was a shingle and planing mill. Across the creek also, where the electric plant now stands, George had a sawmill which cut about one million feet of lumber each year.

About 1877, Mr. Austin sold his mill properties and located on a farm on East Ridge, in Pine Valley Township. The farm contained eighty acres, and he devoted it to dairying, being the pioneer in that branch of industry in this county. On this farm he also built the first creamery in the county, and in addition to this he started a cheese factory on the farm, which was the second cheese factory erected in the county, but which he subsequently converted into a creamery. He kept some eighty or ninety cows, and continued farming and dairying until he sold out and retired in 1901 or 1902.

George Albion Austin retired in the city of Neillsville, and was one of Clark County's best known citizens. Though he never cared for public office, he served as chairman of the township board. While residing on his farm, Mr. Austin traveled for four or five years as a lecturer for the Farmers Institute, this being during the winter seasons, and while thus engaged he advocated the extension of dairying on the part of the farmers, and also the use of silos, he himself having built the first silo in the state. He was the first to advocate the use of native corn for stocking the silo, and also wrote excellent articles on silage in those days for the agricultural papers and journals. His reputation as an authority on dairying and silage spread all over the state, and his farm was often visited by Professor Babcock, the inventor of the butter test, besides other persons interested in these subjects. George thus took a prominent part in advancing the farming and dairying interests of the county, and played a large role in laying the foundations for much of the prosperity the farmers of Clark County now enjoy.

Mr. Austin was a member of the Christian Science Church, which he helped to organize in Neillsville. He also belonged to the local G.A.R. Post, to the Sons of Temperance and Temple of Honor, being active in the temperance movement. He had joined the Masonic order at Woodstock, and afterwards transferred his membership to the Neillsville lodge, and in that order he advanced to the K.T. degree.

George Albion Austin died on Wednesday night, 7 February 1917 in Neillsville. "He remained in full possession of his faculties to the last, taking an active interest in the affairs of the world, and enjoying in a wholesome way the best things of the community." His widow Marinda was still in Neillsville in 1918, she died in September 1921 in Beaver Dam, Wisconsin. Children:

R123-1951. CHARLES EUGENE, *b. 3 October 1853 +*

R123-1952. MARY ELLA ('MAMIE'), *b. July 1855, m. John H. Thayer in 1876. In April 1934 widow Mamie resided in Minneapolis.*

R123-1953. IDA MAY, *b. May 1857, m. 13 September 1877 to Merritt Clark Ring. Ida was a widow by 1918, she died before April 1934.*

R123-1951. CHARLES EUGENE[8] AUSTIN (*George Albion,*[7] *David,*[6] *Gideon,*[5,4] *Pasco,*[3] *Jeremiah,*[2] *Robert*[1]) was born on 3 November 1853 in Woodstock, McHenry County, Illinois. He came to Clark County, Wisconsin, in 1870 at the age of 17 years, where his father had a half interest in the saw and grist mill with Charlie Blakeslee. Charles, together with Henry Carleton, drove tote teams to and from Sparta with freight from the mill. It took them three days to make a trip. Later Charles' father George Austin took over the mill and carried it on for many years. The mill was then sold to the late James Hewett and Mr. Wood.

Mr. Austin then went to farming on Pleasant Ridge. On this farm was built the first silo to be erected in Clark County. They also operated the first creamery and cheese factory in Clark county and operated the first separator in the county. Later this farm was sold to an English syndicate and then to John Langreck.

Charles was married in Neillsville, Clark County, Wisconsin on 8 September 1887 to Miss Esther Ann (Essie) Ward. Esther was the daughter of Thomas Griffin and Katherine (McKercher) Ward, and was born on 1 June 1862 in Waterford, Ontario, Canada.

In 1892 Charles Austin moved to the farm on the Cunningham where he operated a creamery for six years. During this time he shipped butter to West Superior and out of this butter 16 pounds or one tub, was entered at the World's Fair in Chicago 40 years ago. This butter scored 99.5 points and won for Mr. Austin a diploma and a gold medal.

Later Charles and Essie operated a store in the city of Neillsville for two years and then moved to the farm at Days Corner south of Neillsville. Here Mr. Austin passed on 8 April 1934 at 6 p.m. The funeral was held at the Lowe Funeral Home on 11 April 1934 and he was laid to rest in the Neillsville Cemetery. Essie died 2 January 1944, and was buried with Charles. Their children were probably born in Neillsville Clark County:

R123-1951-1. MARINDA KATHERINE, *b. 7 February 1889. She was working for Congressman Baily of Texas in Washington, D.C., in April 1934. She d. on 6 April 1973, never married.*

R123-1951-2. BEATRICE S., *b. on 5 February 1893; d. 17 April 1912.*

R123-1951-3. KENNETH WARD, *b. on 10 November 1895 +*

R123-1951-4. CHARLES EUGENE, *b. on 25 February 1901 and d. on 18 May 1901.*

R123-1951-3. KENNETH WARD[9] AUSTIN (*Charles Eugene,[8] George Albion,[7] David,[6] Gideon,[5,4] Pasco,[3] Jeremiah,[2] Robert,[1]*) was born 10 November 1895 in Neillsville, Clark County, Wisconsin. He married first in Neillsville on – October 1921 to Ramona B. Short, born 22 May 1902 in Neillsville. They divorced, he married second in Barron, Barron County, Wisconsin on 20 November 1935 to Margaret Allison McKee the daughter of William Anthony and Millicent Irene (Doe) McKee. Margaret was born on 17 February 1910 in Barron. Kenneth was employed at Barron in April 1934. He died on 21 October 1952 in Arland Township, Barron County. Margaret died on 25 May 1972 in Rice Lake, Barron County, is buried with Kenneth at Wayside Cemetery in Barron. The four children by his second wife were born in Barron County, three in Maple Grove, the last in Prairie Farm village:

R123-1951-31. ANN, *b. on 25 July 1923, m. to Warren Mulligan, one child: Cathleen LaVerne b. 1945 in Milwaukee, Wisconsin.*

R123-1951-32. KAREN ALLISON, *b. on 27 November 1936, m.(1) 25 October 1956 to Lawrence M. Hogan, m.(2) on 30 March 1963 to Richard Dean Lewis.*

R123-1951-33. SHARON KATHERINE, *b. 28 September 1938, m. on 18 February 1959 to George William Cutsforth.*

R123-1951-34. WILLIAM CHARLES, *b. 23 Oct. 1942, m. on 12 June 1965 to Linda Ellen Hoit*

R123-1951-35. JON DWIGHT, *b. 6 September 1947, m. 11 June 1977 to Mary Margaret Antenna*

References

1. Edith Austin Moore, *A Genealogy of the Descendants of Robert Austin of Kingstown, Rhode Island*, privately published in 1951. Mrs. Moore references a bible record from R123-19E Mrs. Harriet A. Spafard of McMinnville, Oregon, and the Battey Genealogy, written by H. V. Battey of Council Bluffs, Iowa.

2. James T. Lloyd, *Lloyd's Steamboat Directory and Disasters on the Western Waters.*

3. *History of Clark County, Wisconsin*, published circa 1918.

FREEMAN AND PHOEBE AUSTIN OF LA SALLE COUNTY, ILLINOIS

Editor's Note: The following was based upon a writeup submitted by reader Duan Dingman on Freeman E. Austin appearing in the History of La Salle County, Illinois in the chapter on Mendota. See also Austins of America Queries 26-2, 26-3, and 186-7, and pages 184, 204.

Freeman Austin was born in Delaware County, New York on 26 May 1804. He moved to Niagara County with his father when a young man, where he married Phoebe Adair, a native of Canada. In 1850 he moved to La Salle County, Illinois, and settled on the southwest quarter of Section 26, Ophir Township, on an 1848 land warrant.

Freeman and Phoebe had three sons: Freeman E. Austin, John A. Austin, and Abraham H. Austin. John A. Austin was drowned near Starved Rock, 16 June 1860, aged twenty years. Abraham H. Austin was a member of Company D, 104th Illinois Infantry, and was killed in Hartsville, Tennessee, in 1862, aged nearly nineteen years. In 1871 Freeman and Phoebe sold their farm, and lived thereafter with their oldest son Freeman E. Austin. Phoebe died in 1879, Freeman was still living in 1883.

Freeman E. Austin was born 11 May 1838 in Niagara County, New York. In 1869 he located in Mendota and has since worked at the carpenter and bridge building trades. He married Louisa Austin a native of Yates County, New York, daughter of Orrin Austin. They have four children; Abram A. born September 1863, Ward L. born September 1864, Elmer E. born June 1866, and Ida H. born June 1868. Another child died in infancy.

SOME DESCENDANTS OF
WILLIAM HENRY AUSTIN
AND MARY ELIZABETH HILL
OF BUTLER COUNTY, KENTUCKY

*by John Marshall Ford
and James Findley Austin II*

Editor's Note: Earlier generations of this Austin line can be found in the article *The Descendants of John and Charity Kendrick Austin of Frederick County, Maryland*, which begins on page 34. J163 William Henry Austin appears with his parents and siblings on pages 40 and 42.

FOURTH GENERATION

J163. WILLIAM HENRY[4] AUSTIN (*Samuel*,[3] *Zachariah*,[2] *John*[1]) was born 2 March 1841 in Logansport, Butler County, Kentucky. He married Mary Elizabeth Hill, daughter of William 'Samuel' Hill & Martha (Wade) (Wilson) (Burks) Hill, who was born on 13 June 1843 in Morgantown, Butler County. William was a farmer, he died on 31 January 1911 of pulmonary tuberculosis in Morgantown, where he is buried in Riverview Cemetery. Mary Elizabeth died on 7 November 1919 of endocarditis and nephritis in Logansport, and is buried in Whalin Cemetery, Kentucky. Their ten children were born in Morgantown:

> J163-1. EMMA O.. *born 12 November 1865, married 28 February 1884 to John Q. Davenport. Emma died on 3 July 1889, and is buried in Whalin Cemetery, Kentucky.*

> J163-2. OLLIE H., *born circa 1867-68, she married Elbert Doolin. Ollie is buried in New Harmony Cemetery, Kentucky. Doolin child: Ethel.*

> J163-3. ALONDIE ZULA [female], *b. circa January 1870, she m. J. R. Moore, buried in Cooks Cemetery, 3 miles S.E. of Morgantown; Moore child: Temp.*

> J163-4. MARTHA ANN ['ANNIE'], *born 12 December 1871, married 1 November 1894 to Edward G. Austin, believed a double cousin. Annie died 9 August 1903, buried in Schultztown Community Cemetery in Prentice, Kentucky.*

> J163-5. MARY ZERELDA, *born circa 1873-74, she married John Clark. Mary is buried in Riverside Cemetery, Morgantown.*

> J163-6. JAMES FINDLEY, *born 12 February 1876 +*

> J163-7. HERBERT LEWIS ['HUB'], *born 15 September 1878, married Emma Phelps on 15 July 1903. Herbert died 3 November 1959, is buried in Riverview Cemetery, Morgantown.*

> J163-8. ESTILL W. [male, twin to Ethel], *born circa 1882, married Alice Hines Faught. Estill is buried in Riverview Cemetery.*

> J163-9. ETHEL [twin to Estill], *born circa 1882 died in infancy, buried in Whalin Cemetery.*

William Henry Austin (1841-1911) with his wife Mary Elizabeth Hill (1843-1919). *Photograph by R. B. Morehead, Jr.*

> J163-A. WILLIAM SANFORD, *born circa 1885, m. Minnie Mae Wilson. William died in July 1966 in Logansport, Kentucky. Their children are recorded in Kentucky: Jessie Mae who m. Luther Hudnall, Christine, James T., and Thelma.*

FIFTH GENERATION

J163-6. JAMES FINDLEY[5] AUSTIN (*William Henry*,[4] *Samuel*,[3] *Zachariah*,[2] *John*,[1]) was born 12 February 1876 in Morgantown, Kentucky. He was married on 25 July 1905 near Walters, Commanche County, Oklahoma, to Kittie Lee Martin, the daughter of James and Susan Emma

James Findley Austin (1876-1923)
Kittie Lee Martin (1885-1931)

(Maxey) Martin. Kittie Lee was born 30 June 1885 in Council Grove, Kansas. James died on 20 August 1923 in an auto-trolley car accident in Oklahoma City. He is buried in Rose Hill Cemetery, Oklahoma City, along with an infant son, William Roy, who was killed in the same accident. Kittie Lee died in Oklahoma City on 4 October 1931, and is also buried in Rose Hill Cemetery. Their first three children were born in Walters, the last three in Oklahoma City:

J163-61. OLIVIA ELIZABETH, *b. 8 May 1907, m.(1) circa 1927 to Ernest William Whitten, m.(2) circa 1941 to Arthur E. Simon b. 10 January 1889, d. 21 February 1974 Oklahoma City, buried in Rose Hill Cemetery with Olivia who d. 11 October 1984 Oklahoma City. Whitten ch: William Ernest b. 1932, Nancy Kidd b. 1933.*

J163-62. JULIA MARTIN ['JUDY'], *born 19 January 1909, m. 17 September 1932 James T. Edwards II, b. 15 May 1906 in Texas, d. 18 October 1978. Judy d. 20 September 1947 in Oklahoma City, buried with James in Rose Hill Cemetery. Edwards children: James T. b. 1933, Joan ('Jody') b. 1937.*

J163-63. MARY RUTH, *born 28 January 1912, she m. 2 February 1935 to Leonard Otis Ford, b. 21 April 1910 Oklahoma City, d. 20 June 1983 Oklahoma City, buried there in Memorial Park Cemetery. Mary Ruth d. 1 November 1985, Oklahoma City, buried Rose Hill Cemetery; Children: Charles Otis b. 1936 Pawhuska, Oklahoma, d. 1978; John Marshall b. 1941 Sulphur, Oklahoma.*

J163-64. JOSEPHINE FRANCES, *b. 16 June 1917, m. 30 June 1940 to William Reed Handshy b. 17 May 1915, d. 21 April 1978 in Duncan, Oklahoma. Handshy children: Carole Lynne b. 1943, Marilyn Deloris b. 1946, Susan b. 1951 d. 1951, William Austin b. 1952 in Duncan.*

J163-65. WILLIAM ROY, *b. 10 November 1920, d. 20 August 1923, buried in Rose Hill Cemetery.*

J163-66. JAMES FINDLEY II, *born 25 August 1923 +*

SIXTH GENERATION

J163-66. JAMES FINDLEY[6] AUSTIN II (*James Findley,[5] William Henry,[4] Samuel,[3] Zachariah,[2] John,[1]*) was born 25 August 1923 in Oklahoma City, Oklahoma. He married Mary Lee Williams on 30 May 1949 in Okmulgee, Oklahoma. Mary Lee was born on 31 July 1926, the daughter of Stanley Reuben and Mary Lois (Price) Williams. James and Mary have three children:

J163-661. JEFFREY WILLIAMS, *born 15 June 1951 in Oklahoma City, m. Leah Jo Greene, daughter of Charles Hope and Anna Mae (Jerome) Greene. Jeffrey and Leah's children were born in Oklahoma City: Jennifer Michelle born 5 August 1981, Jeri Ann born 18 September 1982, Mary Elizabeth born 2 March 1985.*

Photograph of William Henry Austin's wife Mary Elizabeth (Hill) Austin and relatives taken in 1916.

J163-662. JAMES FINDLEY III, *b. 12 February 1953 in Oklahoma City, m. Karen Ann Champlain, the daughter of Kenneth Walter and Jeannie S. (Lewis) Champlain. Children: Jade Shenah b. 21 April 1979 in Oklahoma City; Sarah Ann b. 22 July 1983 in Wichita Falls, Texas; Rebeka Lee, b. 21 March 1985 in Oklahoma City.*

J163-663. PETER MARTIN, *b. 8 February 1956 in Oklahoma City, m. Lisa Ann Horton. Their son Jeffrey Charles was b. 7 June 1980 in OK City.*

Further Information Needed

If anyone has further information on the individuals in the above photograph and their relationships to William Henry Austin or Mary Elizabeth (Hill) Austin, please share it with others by sending a copy of your information to:

Austins of America
23 Allen Farm Lane
Concord, MA 01742

The persons appearing in the above photograph were identified in 1950 by William Sanford Austin, and have been further clarified by the authors as far as possible:

Front row, left to right: Lyndon James, Theron James, Ethel Doolin, Marie Hill, Opal Austin, James T. Austin, Jessie Mae Austin, Erie Austin, Kenneth Austin, Thomas Austin, Ruth Austin, Christine Austin, Glen Austin.

Second row (seated): Elbert Doolin & wife Ollie (Austin) Doolin, Edward G. Austin [see J163-4], John W. Brown & wife Zerelda Brown [see J166 on page 42], Mary Elizabeth (Hill) Austin and her sister-in-law Mary E. (Davenport) Hill, Dona Miller.

Third row: Thelma Austin held by Minnie Mae (Wilson) Austin, Palma Hill held by Zella Goodall, Bell James, Clarence James, Herbert Lewis 'Hub' Austin, Dave Luke Goodall, William Sanford 'San' Austin, Temp Flowers, Fannie Flowers, Temp Moore, Estell Austin, Emma Austin, Alice Austin, Orville Wilson, Grace Wilson, Lonnie Moore.

Back row: Roy Moore, Frankie Doolin, Elbert Austin, Mary Shultz, Edith Austin, Sallie Shultz, Ben E. Doolin, Rose Austin, Irma Render, Duey Ward, Eunice Flowers, Harry Edmond (head only), Jeff Doolin, and Hazel Doolin holding Findley.

Austins in the Federal Census of 1850

Mississippi

by Linda Gladys Thomas

Editor's Notes: The numbers preceding each household are the page number, dwelling number, and family number. After the listing of household members are shown occupations, the dollar value of the head of household's real estate, and the date of the census.

CARROLL COUNTY, MS

```
....................................... 482-520
Austin, Elizabeth      19   1831   f   TN
Atwood, David          11   1839   m   MS
        David was a student - 28 September
....................................... 359-364
Austin, John           22   1828   m   MS
        Brickmoulder - 3 October
```

CHICKASAW COUNTY, MS

```
....................................... 261-261
Carter, Joel L.        32   1818   m   TN
  ''  , Martha          28   1822   f   NC
  ''  , James            6   1844   m   MS
  ''  , Susan            2   1848   f   ''
  ''  , Termelia?        1   1849   f   ''
Austin, Martha         20   1830   f   AL
        Joel was a farmer
....................................... 681-681
Austin, Gideon         63   1787   m   NC
  ''  , Elender?        50   1800   f   SC
  ''  , Samuel          21   1829   m   TN
  ''  , Michael         16   1834   m   ''
        Gideon was a farmer - $400
....................................... 772-772
Austin, Thomas         53   1797   m   GA
  ''  , Debbie          41   1809   f   SC
  ''  , Rachel          14   1836   f   GA
  ''  , Thomas J.       12   1838   m   AL
  ''  , Lucinda         10   1840   f   ''
  ''  , Louisa           8   1842   f   ''
  ''  , Jesse            6   1844   m   ''
  ''  , John             2   1848   f?  ''
        Thomas was a farmer - $280
```

CHOCTAW COUNTY, MS

```
....................................... 599-599
Austin, William        25   1825   m   SC
        Farmer with G. B. Nations - 5 November
....................................... 449-450
Austin, A.             38   1812   m   SC
  ''  , Martha          33   1817   f   ''
  ''  , John W.         15   1835   m   ''
  ''  , Mary I./T.      14   1836   f   ''
  ''  , Susan           12   1838   f   ''
  ''  , Elizabeth       10   1840   f   ''
```

```
  ''  , Sarah A.         8   1842   f   MS
  ''  , Berry A.         6   1844   m   ''
  ''  , William          4   1846   m   ''
  ''  , Virginia         2   1848   f   ''
A. Austin was a farmer - $400 - 12 December
```

FRANKLIN COUNTY, MS

```
................................. p.7——109
Austin, Ira F.         39   1811   m   NY
  ''  , Louisa A.       43?  1807   f   MS
  ''  , Ira A.           9   1841   m   LA
  ''  , Lucinda          7   1843   f   ''
  ''  , Jerusha?         3   1847   f   MS
Austin, Martha         20   1830   f   AL
        Ira was a millwright - 7 September
```

HINDS COUNTY, MS

```
............................. p.135——232
Austin, William        55   1795   m   NC
  ''  , Nancy           48   1802   f   ''
  ''  , Mary            20   1830   f   MS
  ''  , Martha          17   1833   f   ''
  ''  , Esperia         13   1837   f   ''
  ''  , William         10   1840   m   ''
        William a planter - $22,700 - 3 September
............................. p.147——414
Austin, H. D.          28   1822   m   TN
        Overseer - 14 September
............................. p.163——687
Austin, H. R.          39   1811   m   VA
  ''  , Eliza           30   1820   f   MS
  ''  , Liethia? J.     13   1837   f   ''
  ''  , Mary V.         11   1839   f   ''
H. R. was an attorney - $12,000 - 25 October
```

HOLMES COUNTY, MS

```
....................................... 274-274
Walton, Nancy          52   1798   f   GA
Austin, Eliza          31   1819   f   AL
  ''  , Mary            12   1838   f   MS
  ''  , Ann Eliza        8   1842   f   ''
Walton, Nancy          19   1831   f   ''
  ''  , Laura           14   1836   f   ''
White, Eliza A.        42   1808   f   NC
  ''  , Susan W.        17   1833   f   VA
        Census in Lexington city - $500 - 23 October
```

```
................................. 939-939
Austin, Wesley H.      37   1813   m   TN
  ''  , Adeline?        28   1822   f   MS
  ''  , William          9   1841   m   ''
  ''  , Robert           6   1844   m   ''
  ''  , Henry            5   1845   m   ''
  ''  , James            2   1848   m   ''
        Wesley was a farmer
```

JACKSON COUNTY, MS

```
................................. p.7——113
Austin, John           29   1821   m   MD
  ''  , Martha          26   1824   f   LA
  ''  , John             2   1848   m   MS
  ''  , Elizabeth        1   1849   f   ''
        John was a shingle-maker - 24 August
............................. p.27-406-406
Austin, Martha         50   1800   f   TN
  ''  , John E.         10   1840   m   MS
  ''  , Martha           8   1842   f   ''
  ''  , Louisa           4   1846   f   ''
  ''  , William M.       1   1849   m   ''
        Martha $2000 - 14 September
```

JASPER COUNTY, MS

```
............................. p.59-376-396
Austin, Richard        27   1823   m   GA
        Attorney in town of Paulding - 4 October
......................... p.64——472/672
Austin, Nathaniel      29   1821   m   MS
  ''  , Lucy            18   1832   f   ''
  ''  , Elizabeth        1   1849   f   ''
        Nathaniel was an overseer - 10 October
```

LAFAYETTE COUNTY, MS

```
....................................... 1294-1294
Austin, G. G.          30   1820   m   VA
  ''  , Miranda E.      28   1822   f   ''
  ''  , Thompson         9   1841   m   ''
  ''  , Adrin            5   1845   m   ''
  ''  , Randolph         3   1847   m   MS
  ''  , J. G./T.        25   1825   m   VA
G. farmer $2000, J. merchant $300 - 22 Nov.
```

LEAKE COUNTY, MS

```
....................................... 514-638
Austin, Pamela         43   1807   f   GA
  ''  , Andrew J.       22   1828   m   MS
  ''  , George A.       16   1834   m   ''
  ''  , Laura           14   1836   f   ''
  ''  , Johnson         11   1839   m   ''
  ''  , James            8   1842   m   ''
Andrew, George were farmers - 19 October
```

LOWNDES COUNTY, MS

```
....................................... 3-3
Thomas, Jesaly         62   1788   f   GA
Austin, Jane B.        37   1813   f   SC
Loftis, Martha H.      32   1818   f   ''
Thomas, Abraham D.     21   1829   m   AL
  ''  , Frank M.        18   1832   m   ''
  ''  , Margaret E.     16   1834   f   ''
Loftis, Virginia M.    13   1837   f   MS
Austin, Sarah F.       13   1837   f   ''
Jesaly $5000, Abraham a farmer - 26 August
```

.... 38-38

Austin, Zeriah	47	1803	f	MA
", George	25	1825	m	"
", Mary C.	23	1827	f	"
", Charlotte	16	1834	f	"
", Elizabeth W.	13	1837	f	"
", Sarah A.	12	1838	f	"

Census in Columbus city - 6 December

MADISON COUNTY, MS

.... 460-470

Battle, James M.	38	1812	m	NC
Austin, Darling	39	1811	m	TN

James planter, Darling overseer - 14 Nov.

.... 659-673

Austin, Leonidus	27	1823	m	MS

Leonidus a planter - $1200 - 13 December

MARSHALL COUNTY, MS

.... 684-684

Todd, John	33	1817	m	SC
", Nancy	35	1815	f	"
", William J.	9	1841	m	MS
", James L.	7	1843	m	"
", Benjamin F.	5	1845	m	"
", Amanda J.	2	1848	f	"
", Threadgill, Kirby	26	1824	f	NC
Austin, James	21	1829	m	"

John $600, Kirby, James A. farmers - 31 Oct.

.... 687-687

Hurt, John	24	1826	m	TN
", Sarah	21	1829	f	NC
", Charles	2	1848	m	MS
Austin, Wyatt	22	1828	m	NC
Rush, William	23	1827	m	"

John $600, Wyatt, William farmers - 31 Oct.

.... 878-878

Harris, Robert	30	1820	m	AL
", Ellen	27	1823	f	NC
Birmingham, Joshua	35	1815	m	"
Austin, Hugh	19	1831	m	TN
", James	18	1832	m	"
?????, Erasmus	19	1831	m	"

All men were farmers - 14 November

NESHOBA COUNTY, MS

.... 302-318

Germany, John	54	1796	m	GA
", Eliza	32	1818	f	SC
", Frances	18	1832	f	MS
", Thomas	16	1834	m	"
", Jane	13	1837	f	"
", Elanor	8	1842	f	"
", John	7	1843	m	"
", Virginia	5	1845	f	"
", Benjamin	3	1847	m	"
", Susan	1	1849	f	"
", Adalin	9	1841	f	"
Austin, T. C.	23	1827	m	NC

John farmer $100, T. C. teacher - 15 August

NEWTON COUNTY, MS

.... 26-26

Austin, Francis	30	1820	m	MS
", Mary	25	1825	f	NC
", William	3	1847	m	MS
", Francis	2	1848	m	"

Francis was a blacksmith - $100 - 5 August

RANKIN COUNTY, MS

.... 294-294

Austin, N.	35	1815	m	NY
", Eliza	26	1824	f	OH
", Frederick	6	1844	m	MS
", Martin	1	1849	m	"

N. was a farmer - $3000 - 14 September

SMITH COUNTY, MS

.... 58-58

Lutruck, Henry	50	1800	m	NC
", Susan	48	1802	f	"
", Nelees	23	1827	m	"
", Leah	18	1832	f	"
", Edward	15	1835	m	"
", John	11	1839	m	MS
", William	9	1841	m	"
", Jane	8	1842	f	"
", Emiline	6	1844	f	"
Austin, Charles	43	1807	m	SC

Henry $400, Nelees, Edward were farmers,
Charles a Lutheran Minister - 12 August

.... 67-67

Austin, William	61?	1789	m	SC
", Mary	62	1788	f	"
", Lucretia	40	1810	f	"
", Isaiah	26	1824	m	"
", Sarah	18	1832	f	"
", Absalom	16	1834	m	"
", James	14	1836	m	"
", Robert	12	1838	m	"
", Celia	7	1843	f	"
", Martin	10	1840	m	"
", George	5	1845	m	"
", Manuel	2	1848	m	"

Isaiah and Absalom farmers - 12 August

TALLAHATCHIE COUNTY, MS

.... 169-169

Hamlin, James	30	1820	m	KY
", Mary M.	29	1821	f	AL
", Robert B.	4	1846	m	MS
", Elizabeth J.	1	1849	f	"
Austin, John	28	1822	m	TN

James raftsman $200, John farmer - 10 Oct.

TIPPAH COUNTY, MS

.... 187-187

Austin, Leroy	35	1815	m	TN
", Naoma	30	1820	f	SC
", Jesse	12	1838	m	AL
", John	10	1840	m	"
", Martha	6	1844	f	MS
", Robert	4	1846	m	"
", Lucinda	6/12	1850	f	"

Leroy was a farmer - $100 - 9 September

.... 283-283

Austin, John	39	1811	m	TN
", Elizabeth	32	1818	f	"
", Carroll J.	16	1834	m	"
", Martha	14	1836	f	"
", Elizabeth A.	10	1840	f	MS
", Amanda	7	1843	f	"
", Eliza	5	1845	f	"
", Joseph	2	1848	m	"
Stern, Jesse O.	23	1827	m	TN
Sypert, T. J.	22	1828	m	"

John $600, Jesse, T. J. farmers - 17 Sept.

TISHOMINGO COUNTY, MS

.... 550-550

Austin, G. W.	45	1805	m	TN
", Ann	40	1810	f	"
", Mary	14	1836	f	AL
", James	12	1838	m	"
", William	10	1840	m	"
", John	6	1844	m	MS
", Margaret	4	1846	f	"
", George	2	1848	m	"

G. W. was a farmer - $350

TUNICA COUNTY, MS

.... 69-69

Chambers, John	38	1812	m	VA
", Sarah	25	1825	f	KY
", F. E.	9	1841	f	MA
", James M.	7	1843	m	"
", William S.	5	1845	m	"
Austin, Solomon T.	11	1839	m	AR

John was a laborer

WARREN COUNTY, MS

.... 56-56

Austin, John	22	1828	m	VA

John was a raftsman, living in a Vicksburg
tavern that rented rooms - 3 August

WILKINSON COUNTY, MS

.... 3-4

Dunbar, Alex	44	1806	m	MS
Austin, John Q.	28	1822	m	LA
", Amelia	18	1832	f	MS
", Charles B.	10	1840	m	"

Alex was a planter - 2 July

WINSTON COUNTY, MS

.... 670-677

Austin, J. S.	38	1812	m	NC
", Margaret	30	1820	f	SC
", Emma	6	1844	f	MS
", Mary	4	1846	f	"
", Sarah	1/2	1850	f	"
David, Mary	56	1794	f	TN
", Jane	31	1819	f	SC

J. S. was a mechanic - $186 - 8 October

YALOBUSHA COUNTY, MS

.... 1115-1115

Austin, Wade	30	1820	m	TN
", Elizabeth	27	1823	f	AL
", Maninva?	12	1838	f	MS
", Sarah	10	1840	f	"
", John	8	1842	m	"
", Thomas	5	1845	m	"
", Louisa	1	1849	f	"

Wade was an overseer - 28 September

SOME DESCENDANTS OF
RODERICK RANSOM AUSTIN
OF MUSKINGUM COUNTY, OHIO

by Pauline Lucille Austin

Editor's Note: The following article is largely based on a story told by Roderick's great-grandson Robert Briggs Austin II of Afton, Iowa, which was written down by his wife Mattie (Wilson) Austin in September 1960. Additional information was provided in November 1981 by Roderick's great-grandson Sam Doran Creasman of McCook, Iowa, and in February 1984 by Jerry Austin of St. Charles, Iowa.

R. RODERICK RANSOM[1] AUSTIN, is believed to have been the oldest of a large family, born 18 February 1797 in New York state, although possibly he was born in Connecticut. Roderick's ancestry has not been proven, but one theory is that he was the son of a James Austin (a son of R211-3 Seth Austin of the Richard Austin of Charlestown, Massachusetts, line), and that he was named after James' older brother Roderick R. Austin who was born in 1759 in Suffield, Connecticut, and died in 1841 in Otsego County, New York. In any case, our Roderick Austin came from Westchester County, New York, to Muskingum County, Ohio, where he resided for many years in Ruraldale, about 12 miles southeast of Zanesville. He married Nancy Wear/Weir on 14 September 1822 in Belmont County, Ohio. Nancy was born in Virginia in 1805. Roderick never wrote to his parents for 25 years, so he never heard any more from them. The Postmaster wrote and said they had all left. In 1876 Roderick and Nancy moved to Pontiac, Illinois, and in 1878 they moved on to Fairfield, Clay County, Nebraska. Nancy died in 1879 in Fairfield, and Roderick died there also, at about 98 years of age, outliving all of his sons. Roderick and Nancy are buried near Fairfield. They had nine children:

R1.   WILLIAM A., *born circa 1825.* +

R2.   DAVID E., *born circa 1827.*

R3.   THOMAS, *born circa 1829.*

R4.   JEPTHA, *born circa 1832.*

R5.   JONATHAN, *born circa 1835.*

R6.   JAMES, *born circa 1837.*

R7.   ELIZA, *born circa 1843, married Joseph Bird on 12 January 1869.*

R8.   SARAH ELIZABETH, *b. 3 May 1845 in Ruraldale, Ohio, m. John Wesley Ruby 3 March 1866. John was b. 11 July 1840 in Harrison County, Ohio. A Civil War veteran, John died 13 November 1895 in Danbury, Red Willow County, Nebraska. Sarah died on 29 December 1916 in Danbury. They probably had more, but only one child is known: Lucretia Garfield Ruby b. 1880 in Cass County, Nebraska.*

R9.   ANNA M., *born in 1849, married Hoshia Brown on 13 April 1869.*

SECOND GENERATION

R1. WILLIAM A.[2] AUSTIN (*Roderick Ransom*[1]) was born in 1825 in Morgan County, Ohio. His son William was known as 'Dell' and his grandson Harry had a middle name 'Adelbert,' which might also have been William's middle name. In any event, William married Charlotte Briggs on 29 January 1848 in Morgan County. Charlotte was born on 27 August 1832 in Ohio. Circa 1855 the family moved to Boscabel, Grant County, Wisconsin, where William built mills on rivers in Wisconsin. He died and was buried between 1863 and 1869 near Boscabel. Charlotte married a second time after William's death to William Miles, her deceased sister's husband, by whom she had two other children. Charlotte died 10 October 1900 in Fort Dodge Iowa, and is buried in the Otho Cemetery, Otho, Iowa. William and Charlotte had seven children:

R11.   ROBERT BRIGGS, *born in 1849.* +

R12.   JAMES, *born in 1851, buried at Fort Dodge.*

R13.   NANCY, *b. 5 December 1853 in Mushingham County, Ohio, m.(1) — Bedant, m.(2) George Barber in 1872, m.(3) Carl Rabine/Rehbein. She died in 1915 in Fort Dodge, Iowa, buried in Otho Cemetery. Nancy had three children by George Barber: Will, Joe, and Grant.*

R14.   DAVID FRANKLIN, *buried at Fort Dodge.*

R15.   WILLIAM A., *known as 'Dell,' perhaps his middle name was Adelbert like his nephew Harry?*

R16.   PERRY, *born circa 1863* +

R17.   SARAH JANE ['JANIE'], *died at 14 years of age, is buried at Fenamore Center, Wisconsin.*

THIRD GENERATION

R11. ROBERT BRIGGS[3] AUSTIN (*William A.,*[2] *Roderick Ransom*[1]) was born in 1849 in Zanesville, Muskingum County, Ohio. Robert enlisted at age 15 and served in the Union Army, Company G-47, Wisconsin Infantry. His experiences as remembered by his son Robert:

"The company started on foot the next morning to the front, without any drilling, they drilled on the road. They made up a company at Boscobel, Wisconsin. Robert saw Abraham Lincoln after he was assassinated in Chicago, Illinois, as he laid in state a couple of days there. They let the soldiers review him. I never heard him say how far South he got, but he got pneumonia and was sent back to Chicago to the hospital. He never was well afterwards as one lung was destroyed. When he first got to Chicago in the Hospital they had wired his folks and his father came to see him and he was going to give him some of his money. He said to get his clothes and when they couldn't find them, he said he had $500.00 in the pocket and they said the clothes were all burned up. But an orderly heard them talking and he said he saw some clothes in a room where

two men had come in by themselves so they went and looked and found it. It was the bonus he received the day he enlisted and he had never spent any of it. His father went on home. Robert had a long siege in the hospital, but as soon as he was able, he was discharged and sent home. He lacked a little of being gone from home a whole year."

Robert Briggs Austin was married to Mary Hilliard on 9 November 1870 in Manchester, Iowa. Mary was born on 3 December 1843 in Trafton County, New Hampshire, a daughter of John and Philena (Moulton) Hilliard. The family came to Hopkinton, Iowa, from New Hampshire in 1861 when Mary was 18 years old. She had two brothers, George and Henry, and a married sister Vesta Willoughby, who had come ahead and had settled earlier in Greene County, Iowa. Robert was a farmer and sawmill owner. They resided near Jefferson, Greene County, Iowa. Their son Robert further continues:

"In the fall of 1877 my father and mother and four children left from near Jefferson and headed to Republican City [Harlan County], Nebraska. They drove a team of cows, and milked them as they went. On the trip out there my father met up with quite an incident. They were camped for dinner out on the plains close to another wagon, and after they had eaten dinner he got to talking to two of the men from the other wagon. A fellow passed with a small team of horses – kind of ponies. One of these fellows said "that wouldn't be much of a team from where we came from!" My father said "Where did you come from?" The man replied "Zanesville, Ohio." Father said to him "Did you ever know anyone around there by the name of Roderick Austin?" One of them said "Yes, he's right in that wagon now!" Roderick was my father's grandpa, and the men he was talking to were his uncles! They traveled together a ways, but they were going to Red Willow County and my folks were going to Republican City, so they separated.

"Arriving in Republican City, Robert and Mary took a Homestead, where they lived in a sod house where a snake intruded occasionally. In Nebraska they put up with the grasshopper plague for a year or two, as well as the drought. One year my father sowed six bushels of wheat, but the wind and drought almost destroyed it. When he thrashed it he had 12 bushels and he and mother, driving the cows, took it to a mill which was 30 miles away, but the miller said it wouldn't be fit to eat unless he had it fanned out. So they went 30 miles farther to a fan mill and had it fanned out, after which he had six bushels left, exactly what he planted! Then they stopped at the mill and had it ground into flour. Meanwhile, the children at home became so uneasy that my two oldest brothers made a cart with cultivator wheels for the baby, and broke a calf to drive. They were going to start the next morning to see if they could find our folks, but fortunately the folks arrived home about 4 o'clock in the morning. . . I guess they were all pretty glad to see each other!

"They stayed in Nebraska until 1881, then they came back to Iowa driving the same cows and moving onto the same farm they had left for Nebraska! They had only 35 cents when they started back to Iowa, but they had raised a little corn and they had corn meal and they milked the cows, and when they got back into the edge of Iowa they got some work picking corn. They finally got back to Jefferson, Iowa, where mother's sister lived. They were not very prosperous, but had considerably more experience than they had before they went.

"Before father's grandpa Roderick Austin died, he came and lived with us in Iowa a while. He lived to be 98 years old. That was before my time, but the story has been rehearsed around the fireside on many a night from the time I remember till I grew into manhood." Robert and Mary also lived in Allendale, Missouri, Lehigh & Shannon City, Iowa, and Keller, Minnesota. Mary died on 1 April 1923, William on died 8 May 1929, both are buried in Evergreen Cemetery in Brainerd, Minnesota. Children:

R111. JAMES HENRY, *born 12 August 1871, m. Hanna Griffith. James died on 23 December 1952.*

R112. JOHN WILLIAM, *born 18 May 1874, m. Mary Melissa ('Lizzie') Petry. John died March 1950.*

R113. MATTIE JANE, *born 20 August 1875, m. Martin Swanson. Mattie died in 1947.*

R114. GEORGE FRANKLIN, *born 29 April 1877, m. Annie Swanson. George died in 1932.*

R115. HARRY ADELBERT, *born 10 May 1884, m. Martha Perl Petry. Harry died on 1 January 1951.*

R116. ROBERT BRIGGS II, *born 18 February 1886 weighing only 2 1/2 pounds. He married Martha (Mattie) Jane Wilson. Robert died in 1967.*

R16. PERRY A.[3] AUSTIN (*William A.,[2] Roderick Ransom[1]*) was born in October 1863 in Wisconsin. He married Alice Anne Walker on 23 December 1896 in Jewel County, Kansas. Alice was born on 19 March 1875, daughter of Hiram and Rebekah Walker. Perry operated a produce station near St. Joseph, Missouri, and died in 1941 in Burr Oak, Jewel County. Alice died on 22 March 1966 in Burr Oak, and is buried with Perry in Burr Oak. Perry and Alice had one son born in Burr Oak:

R161. ROY J., *b. 11 May 1901 +*

FOURTH GENERATION

R161. ROY J.[4] AUSTIN (*Perry A.,[3] William A.,[2] Roderick Ransom[1]*) was born on 11 May 1901 in Burr Oak, Jewel County, Kansas. He enlisted in the armed services in 1917, and was discharged in 1919. Roy returned to Burr Oak where he married Zelma Broden on 17 February 1922. Roy moved to California, but returned to Burr Oak in 1963. He died 20 July 1971. Children:

R161-1. PERRY B., *died in infancy in 1925.*

R161-2. DOROTHY ANN., *m. — Evens, in 1966 lived in Los Angeles with her son Randy.*

SOME DESCENDANTS OF
SOLOMON AUSTIN AND JOANNA THOMAS
OF NORFOLK COUNTY, ONTARIO, CANADA

by Marian J. Wiley

Editor's Note: In the following article the author corrects and adds to the information on Solomon Austin and his family which appeared on pages 83 and 102ff. She notes that only three of Solomon's sons served in the War of 1812, and that the husbands of S2. Solomon and Sarah's daughters were scrambled in the previous articles. We have supplemented the author's data with Solomon's birth, spouse, and death information found in the *Miscellaneous Records* of Austin genealogist Edith Austin Moore, who references Miss Emma May Austin residing in 1950 in Memorial Home Community, Penney Farms, Florida.

S. SOLOMON[1] AUSTIN was born in 1744, married Joanna Thomas who was born in 1752. He was a Tory who lived in North Carolina until 1794, when the family removed to Woodhouse, Ontario, Canada shortly thereafter. An 1812 census taken for part of Norfolk County, Ontario, Canada, shows that Solomon and Joanna had one child, Moses age 10, still at home. Since there are ample War of 1812 military records for Solomon and his sons Solomon, Jonathan and Philip, but not for Moses, it is unlikely Moses served in that war as stated in earlier articles. Solomon died in Lynn Valley, Norfolk County, on 18 February 1826, while Joanna died there on 24 April 1834. Solomon and Joanna had nine children:

S1. MARY, *b. —, m. Henry Walker, six children including James, Solomon, and Esther.*

S2. SOLOMON, *born circa 1782* +

S3. AMY, *born —, married Selah Styles, three children: Peter, Selah, and Lavinia.*

S4. JONATHAN, *born circa 1785* +

S5. ESTHER, *born —, married Reynard Potts. They have numerous descendents southeast of Simcoe.*

S6. PHILIP, *born 7 May 1790* +

S7. ELIZABETH, *born —, married John Pegg. They had two sons, Nathan, and Philip.*

S8. ANNA, *born —, she married David Marr, by whom she had ten children: Joseph, Edward, Solomon, Hiram, Duncan D., Esther, Jane, and three others who went to Iowa.*

S9. MOSES, *born circa 1802* +

SECOND GENERATION

S2. SOLOMON[2] AUSTIN (*Solomon[1]*) was born circa 1782. He married Sarah Slaght of Townsend, daughter of John and Elizabeth (Clouse) Slaght. Solomon died on 3 August 1850, while Sarah died on 29 January 1863. They are buried together in the Baptist churchyard at Vittoria, Ontario, where their gravestones are still clearly legible. Solomon and Sarah reared ten children together:

S21. PHILIP, *b. circa 1810, married his cousin S44. Mary Austin. Philip was a farmer in their native township. Philip and Mary had six children.*

S22. JOHN SLAGHT, *was born on 3 February 1817, m.(1) Phoebe Ann Walker, m.(2) in 1849 to Maria Ryerse. John and his brother Jonathan Austin were, for a quarter of a century, the leading carriage manufacturers in this County. They disposed of their carriage works, but remained in Simcoe, engaging in other business. John died 29 on March 1894. He and Maria had six children.*

S23. DAVID, *b. circa 1820, m. Sarah Sims. David was a farmer, he and Sarah had eleven children.*

S24. JONATHAN, *born circa 1822, m. Harriet Beemer. Jonathan was a carriage manufacturer with his brother John Slaght Austin. Jonathan and Harriet had five children.*

S25. ABRAHAM, *b. circa 1824, m. a widow, Hannah Potts. Abraham was a Baptist Minister in Woodhouse, he and Hannah had four children.*

S26. SAMUEL, *was born on 18 September 1826, m. Mary McLean, they had two sons. Samuel died on 20 April 1854.*

S27. SUSAN, *b. circa 1828, m. Alfred Farnum, they had two sons.*

S28. JULIA ANN, *b. circa 1830, m. Nathan Pegg, they had seven children.*

S29. MARY ANN, *b. circa 1831, m. William Shand, they had seven children.*

S2A. ELIZABETH, *b. circa 1832, m. Henry Paskins, they had seven children.*

S4. JONATHAN[2] AUSTIN (*Solomon[1]*) was born circa 1785. He married Hannah Potts, daughter of Jacob Potts, and a sister of the Raynard Potts who married Jonathan's sister Esther. He and his son John built Austin's Mills near the Lynn Valley station. Jonathan apparently died before the 1851 Census. Jonathan and Hannah had eight children:

S41. WILLIAM, *never married.*

S42. JOHN, *b. circa 1814, m. Catherine White.*

S43. CHARLOTTE, *b. circa 1808, m. (John?) Wheeler. They had five children.*

S44. MARY, *b. circa 1810, m. her cousin S21. Philip Austin, they had six children — see above.*

S45. JOANNA, *b. in June 1811, m. John Hinds/Hindes. They had four children.*

S46. CATHERINE, *b. circa 1818, never married.*

S47. ELIZABETH, *b. circa 1819, married Thomas M. England. They had five children.*

S48. REBECCA ANN, *b. circa 1822, m. Robert Laning. They had three children.*

S6. PHILIP[2] AUSTIN (*Solomon[1]*) was born on 7 May 1790 in Orange County, North Carolina. He married Mary Slaght (a sister of Solomon's wife) who was born in 1795 in Newton, New Jersey. Philip was a farmer. He died on 17 October 1876 in Lynn Valley, Norfork County, Ontario,

Canada. Philip lived to be 87 years old, a greater age than his father or any of his brothers or sisters. Philip and Mary had seventeen children:

S61. NANCY, *born 19 May 1812, m. Samuel Decou. Nancy died in Iowa.*

S62. AARON, *born 28 November 1813.* +

S63. ELIZABETH, *b. 20 August 1815, m. Samuel Decou. She died in Woodbine, Iowa.*

S64. JAMES, *b. 14 April 1817.*

S65. REBECCA, *b. 19 May 1818.*

S66. MARY, *b. 11 September 1819, m. Richard Smith.*

S67. ISAAC, *b. 18 October 1820, m.(1) Margery (Margaret) Waddle, m.(2) Margery Walker. Isaac served several terms as Reeve in the Township and is at present the leader of the Grangers in the Township. He had ten children.*

S68. SARAH, *b. 18 July 1822.*

S69. JACOB, *b. 10 March 1823.*

S6A. PHILIP BARBER, *born 23 April 1825, married to Mary Ann —.*

S6B. HANNAH, *b. 19 July 1826, never married.*

S6C. JOSHUA, *b. 9 October 1828, m. to Elizabeth Anderson, they had five children. Joshua was one of the most successful merchants of Simcoe, in partnership with Mr. George Werrett, who had married his sister S6G. Emily Jane Austin.*

S6D. ESTHER ANN, *b. 3 December 1831, m. James Dell. They had three children.*

S6E. JOSEPH, *b. 9 April 1833, m. Margaret Teller, was a 'progressive' Woodhouse farmer, six children.*

S6F. OLIVER, *b. 25 December 1834, m. Charity DeCou. Oliver resided on the old homestead, and took a very great interest in all matters pertaining to the development and public improvement of his native land. In agriculture, in education, in politics, in temperance and in religious movements, he was a zealous and energetic worker.*

S6G. EMILY JANE, *b. 19 April 1837, m. George Werrett. They had four children.*

S6H. PRISCILLA, *b. 10 July 1840, m. James Hatch, residence in Half Moon, California.*

S9. MOSES[2] AUSTIN (*Solomon*[1]) was born circa 1792. He married Mary Misner of Townsend, and they resided in Woodhouse and Townsend. They had eight children: LEWIS, EDWARD, NATHANIEL, WILLIAM, MARGARET, MARY, SARAH, JULIA, many descendants live near Tyrrel.

THIRD GENERATION

S62. AARON[3] AUSTIN (*Philip,*[2] *Solomon*[1]) was born on 28 November 1813 in Norfolk County, Ontario, Canada. He married Willimena Waddle, the daughter of Robert and Isabella (Rolph) Waddle, in July 1834. Aaron was a progressive farmer in Woodhouse, he died in 1890. He and Willimena had seven children together:

S62-1. PHILIP WADDLE, *was born on 25 January 1840, m. Emeline Eastman, daughter of Jonas. Philip died on 22 November 1926. They had ten children, but only two are known to me: Elliott Austin born 9 September 1875, settled in Oregon, and J. Charlton Austin born 8 April 1878, settled in Wyoming.*

S62-2. ISABELLA, *born circa 1835.*

S62-3. MARY, *born circa 1838.*

S62-4. ROBERT, *born circa 1841.*

S62-5. NANCY, *born circa 1845.*

S62-6. JAMES, *born circa 1846.*

S62-7. JANE, *born circa 1847.*

THE AUSTIN FAMILY from the 1887 Atlas of Norfolk County

At one of the minor engagements of the Revolutionary War called the Battle of the Horseshoe, in which the "Queen's Rangers," commanded by Colonel Simcoe, took an active part, the standard bearer was killed, and the flag fell to the ground, but was immediately picked up by Solomon Austin, a private in the company, and borne by him through the remainder of the engagement. At its close the Colonel enquired the name of the man who had so gallantly rescued the colors, and on receiving information, called him before him, highly commended him for his conduct, and intimated his desire to assist him in the future.

In the month of June, 1794, there arrived at the Niagara frontier nine families that had been expelled from their homes and property in North Carolina on account of their loyalty to the British Crown. At the head of one of those families was the before mentioned Solomon Austin, accompanied by his wife and nine children (four sons and five daughters). He was kindly received by his former Colonel, now Governor Simcoe, and was offered a home in the house he had lately occupied (before removing from Newark to York) until he could make a selection of land for himself. For his faithful defence of British connection he was rewarded by a grant of six hundred acres of land in any unselected part of the Province. He was directed to inspect the country, locate his lots, and the patents would be give him; accordingly, after traversing Western Canada on foot from Niagara to Detroit, the whole country being one vast unbroken forest no roads except the Indian trails – he finally chose a home on Patterson's Creek, now called the river Lynn, about three miles southeast of Simcoe, in the County of Norfolk, which proved to be a very pleasant, fertile valley, and which is now known as Lynn Valley, a station on the Port Dover and Lake Huron R.R.

Thither he moved with his family early in the spring of 1795, and, by hard labor, a portion of the forest was cleared away, a log cabin erected, and a pioneer home established. There was no mill nearer than Fort Erie, a distance of eighty miles, and the only way of procuring flour or meal was either to row in an open boat that distance to mill or else pound their corn with a rough pestle in a hollow stump. The latter was the common method.

The forests abounded with game, and streams with abundance of choice fish. Thus began the settlement in this part of the County. A few years had passed away when the war of 1812 broke out, and the peace of their new homes was again disturbed. The father with his three sons, named respectively, Solomon, Jonathan, and Philip shouldered their muskets and went forth again to defend their home and firesides. They did service under General Brock, and were engaged at Malden, Malcom's and Lundy's Lane. Colonel Nicol and Major Salmon had command of the Norfolk militia, and under them the three sons were promoted to the rank of Captain. And thus, from this one family sprang, as it were a whole colony of brave, sturdy and energetic men and women.

AUSTINS VIA BARBADOS

by Michael Edward Austin
and Anthony Kent Austin

Editor's Note: Barbados was, during the seventeenth century, a great port of entry to the Amercian colonies. Many Barbados settlers later emigrated to New England, Carolina, Virginia and New York. Thus genealogists unable to locate any record of their ancestors arriving in America from England should consider the possibility that they arrived via Barbados.

The English In Barbados

Barbados is a small island in the West Indies, about 166 square miles in area (see map on next page). Barbados was claimed for England in 1605 when it was visited by Leigh's Guiana expedition, and was first settled in 1626 under the auspices of Courteen. In 1627 Barbados was included in a grant to the Earl of Carlisle, whose settlers overcame those of Courteen in 1629 [1]. The island prospered initially from its trade in sugar, later exporting molasses and rum as well. The sugar industry was carried on by negro slaves brought from Africa. In 1652 Barbados submitted to the authority of the Commonwealth. The early inhabitants are said to have been those who retired there "to be quiet and to be free from noise and oppressions in England."

Quakers Ann Austin and Mary Fisher

Among the earliest Austins in Barbados was Ann Austin. Little is known of her history, except that she was the mother of five children, apparently a resident of London, and already "stricken in years" when she arrived in Barbados with Mary Fisher near the end of the year 1655. They spent about six months in Barbados publishing their message of "the truth," as early Quakers persistently called their Gospel.

In July 1656 Ann Austin and Mary Fisher departed from Barbados for Boston on the ship *Swallow*, sailing under the command of Master Simon Kempthorn. Massachusetts Governor Endicott was absent from Boston, and it was Deputy Governor Richard Bellingham who ordered that the women be kept on the ship while their boxes were searched for books containing "corrupt, heretical, and blasphemous doctrines." One hundred such books were found in their possession. These books were seized and burned in the market-place by the common hangman. This being done the women were brought to land and committed to prison on the sole charge of being "Quakers," deprived of light, and of all writing materials, though as yet no law had made it a punishable offense to be a Quaker. A fine of five pounds was laid upon anyone who should speak with them, and to make assurance doubly sure, their prison window was closely boarded up. They were furthermore "stripped stark naked," and searched for "tokens" of

witchcraft upon their bodies. One man (evidently Nicholas Upsall) came to the prison and offered gladly to pay the fine of five pounds if he might be allowed to have conversation with the prisoners.

After they had been kept five weeks in confinement under these extraordinary conditions, the master of the vessel which brought them was put under a bond of one hundred pounds, to see that they were transported back to Barbados, and he apparently was compelled to pay the costs of their transportation. Ann Austin and Mary Fisher sailed out of Boston harbor on 5 August 1656, the Boston jailer had kept their bedding and their Bibles for his prison fees. Governor Endicott, on his return, remarked that if *he* had been at home, they would not have got away without a whipping. Two days later another ship carrying eight Quakers arrived in Boston and they were put in the same prison cell that had held Ann Austin and Mary Fisher [1].

Hotten's Austins in Barbados

Following England's "Monmouth Rebellion" of 1685, hundreds of convicted "rebels" were sent to Barbados. The following Austins have been extracted from the many lists given by Hotten [2]:

John Austin, son of widow Ann Austin, was buried 28 June 1678 in the Parish of St. Michaels.

James and Angeletta Oistins had a son James baptised 2 July 1679 in the Parish of Christ Church.

John Austin's servant Katherine Davies was granted a ticket in the ship *Young William* for Virginia on 2 August 1679.

James Oistine had 67 acres of land, 1 white servant and 17 negroes in a 22 December 1679 list in the Parish of Christ Church.

John Austine had 30 acres of land and 16 negros in a 22 December 1679 list in the Parish of Christ Church.

Nicholas Oistine had 4 acres of land and 1 negro in a 22 December 1679 list in the Parish of Christ Church.

Thomas Austine had 5 acres of land in a 22 December 1679 list in the Parish of Christ Church.

Samuell Austen had 6 acres of land and 2 negros in a 3 June 1680 list in the Parish of St. Andrews.

Thomas Austin purchased rebel John Hitchcocke, out of the ship *Betty* from London, according to a certificate signed 1 February 1685.

Thomas Austin was among the rebels on the ship *Jamaica Marchant*, according to a list dated 12 March 1685.

Thomas Austin was among the one hundred Prisoners to be transported from Taunton (England) to Barbados by John

Rose, a London Merchant, who signed a receipt for the Prisoners on 12 October 1685. A list dated 9 December 1685 listed Thomas as being 27 years of age, and a "Mercer" by trade.

Omitted Austins from Hotten's

The following information was extracted by A. K. Austin from a book found in the Burton Historical Collection at the Detroit Public Library [3]:

PARISH AND MILITARY CENSUS RECORDS

Account of the Inhabitants in the Parish of St. Philips in 1680 lists Mr. Edward Austine, 80 acres, 1 servant, and 11 negroes.

A list of all children christened in the Parish of St. Peter's All-Saints since the 25th of March 1678 to the 29th of September 1679 included Susana Austin.

A list of all people buried in the Parish of St. Peter's All-Saints from the 25th of March 1678 to the 29th of September 1679 included Ester Auston.

A list of soldiers under the command of John Adams on 6 January 1679 included Nicholas Oistin and Thomas Oistin.

A list of soldiers under the command of Richard Elliott on 8 January 1679 included James Oistine.

A list of soldiers under the command of William Lewgar on 6 January 1679 included Samuell Austen.

A list of the officers and soldiers that did appear in Capt. Wm. Allemby's company on 6 January 1679 included Jno. Ostin.

Under the command of Capt. Thomas Morris was an Edward Oistine.

Capt. Francis Burton's company included Cornelius Austrian, himself, and land, 6 acres, one souldrs.

Colonel Newton's and Colonel Lombert's Regiments of Horse; Col. Samuell Newton's Troope of Horse included Mr. John Austine and Capt. James Austen.

A list of the troup belonging to Major Rouland Bulkeley included Mr. Tho. Austine, 1 horse.

The St. Ann's Garrison, St. Michael's, Christ Church, and other Records found at Bridgetown in Barbados dealing with the Austin/Oistin family, were furnished courtesy of Neville Connell, Esq., Director of the Barbados Museum and Historical Society, on 21 November 1956.

Among the early emigrants to Barbados in Capt. Powell's ship *Peter* in February 1627 occurs the name of Henry Austine.

Among those who owned more than 10 acres of land in Barbados in 1638 are Mrs. Oistine and Edward Oistine.

The 1715 Census of Barbados in Christ Church Parish included: John Austin age 14, Edward Austin age 13, Angelletta Oistin age 65, Elizabeth Emperour age 16, Mary Oistin age 33 with her son James age 8.5 and daughters Elizabeth age 7 and Angelletta age 2.5, Susanna Austin age 85, Thomas Austin age 53.

From *A True & Exact History of the Island of Barbados*, by Richard Ligon in 1657, pages 25-26 we find: "Three Bayes there are of note on this Island; one, to the eastward of this, is called Austin's Bay (Oistin's Bay), not in commemoration of any Saint, but of a wilde and drunken fellow, whose lewd and extravagant carriage made him infamous in the Island; and his Plantation standing neer this Bay, as it was called by his name. The other two. . ."

In Sir Robert H. Schomburgk's *A History of Barbados* published in 1848, on page 220, one finds: "At the infancy of the colony, the most easterly plantation in the parish belonged to a person named Oistin, from whom the large bay in the neighborhood received its name. Ligon does not speak in very flattering terms of the character of this man, whom he calls profligate; nevertheless, as the population increased, a number of houses were erected in the neighborhood, which received the name of Oistin's town. The bad repute of this person was probably the reason that an attempt was made to call it Charlestown; but this failed and its original name was retained."

Neville Connell notes "The plantation 'Oysten' is marked on Ligon's map of 1657 and on subsequent maps as being situate on the south east point of the island of Barbados."

INDEX TO SOME OISTIN MARRIAGES

Marriages from the Registration Office, Bridgetown, Barbados, British West Indies (indexed by volume-page):

1655	Joan Oistin in Parish of Christ Church	20-19
1659	Edward Oistin in Parish of Christ Church	20-25
1664	Elizabeth Oistin in Parish of Christ Church	20-37
1664	Huncks Oistin in Parish of Christ Church	20-39
1670	Sarah Oistin in Parish of St. Michael's	1-168
1679	Sarah Oistin in Parish of Christ Church	20-64
1681	Joanna Oistin in Parish of Christ Church	20-66
1681	Gollifrey Oistin in Parish of Christ Church	20-66
1681	Sarah Oistin in Parish of Christ Church	20-66
1681	Joan Oistin in Parish of Christ Church	20-66
1684	Maria Oistin in Parish of Christ Church	20-69
1695	Elizabeth Oistin in Parish of Christ Church	20-81
1697	James Oistin in Parish of Christ Church	20-83
1699	James Oistin in Parish of Christ Church	20-86
1703	Nicholas Oistin in Parish of St. Michael's	2-30
1711	Angelletta Oistin in Parish of Christ Church	20-99

INDEX TO OISTIN BAPTISMS IN CHRIST CHURCH PARISH

INDEX TO OISTIN BAPTISM IN ST. PHILIP'S CHURCH PARISH

INDEX TO OISTIN DEEDS

INDEX TO OISTINE WILLS

INDEX TO OISTIN BURIALS

References

1. Rufus M. Jones, "The Quakers in the American Colonies," published by MacMillan and Company, Ltd., London 1911.

2. John Camden Hotten, "The Original Lists of Persons of Quality; Emigrants; Religious Exiles; Political Rebels; Serving Men Sold For a Term of Years; Apprentices; Children Stolen; Maidens Pressed; and Others Who Went From Great Britain to the American Plantations 1600-1700."

3. James C. Brandow, "Omitted Chapters from Hotten's Original Lists of Persons of Quality," – Census returns, Parish registers, Militia Rolls from the Barbados Census of 1679-80. Genealogical Publishing Company, Baltimore, 1980.

QUERIES

282-1. Isaiah Austin was born on 24 August 1834 in Kentucky. He married to Nancy J. (Green) (Grubbe) on 9 October 1870. Nancy J. Green was born on 6 June 1843 in Charlestown, South Carolina, she died 16 April 1920 in Olathe, Colorado. They had a son, Jesse Francis born on 23 July 1873, who married six times. One of his wives was Mary Hanna Jones, born in June 1861 in Pennsylvania. They had four children: Arthur born in 1895 in Missouri, Bulah born in 1897, and Lawrence Jesse born in 1899 in Caldwell County, Missouri, Gladys Elizabeth born on 13 September 1902 in Cowgill, Caldwell, Missouri. Seek ancestry of Isaiah Austin and his descendants. Also need to know all about Lawrence, his six wives and children.

282-2. Lydia Austin married Reuben Frost on 23 February 1815 in Lebanon, Maine. They moved to Smithfield, near Belgrade, Maine. Austins, Berrys, Clements, Frosts, Mills and others moved from Rockingham County, New Hampshire and from Berwick and Lebanon, Maine to the Belgrade, Maine, area in a block. I believe Reuben and Lydia had a daughter Lydia born circa 1823, who possibly married George Locke, intention date 18 February 1849. In the 1860 Census of Smithfield, Lydia Locke age 37 years old and a Mary E. Locke age 8 years were living with the Reuben Frost household. George Locke died in May 1856 in a distant town, but recorded in Smithfield. Reuben died on 20 September 1880 aged 91y 5m 8d and Lydia, his wife died on 19 April 1866 at age 74 years, both died in Smithfield. Is Lydia related to the David Austin of nearby Belgrade who married Betsey Farnum on 5 October 1848? Seeking ancestry and descendants of Reuben and Lydia.

282-3. Rebecca Austin married William Boyd in 1815. He was born circa 1776, they had a son William born in 1819. They lived in the Morgantown, Monongalia (West) Virginia area. Seeking Rebecca Austin's ancestry.

282-4. Nancy Melvira Austin was born 8 January 1827 in Illinois, married Edward Reed on 7 January 1848, the son of Moses Reed. Nancy and Edward had a son, Moses born on 12 March 1858 in Shelby County, Illinois. Need all information on Nancy's ancestry.

282-5. Samuel Austin was one of six brothers who left England and settled in Virginia prior to the Revolution. Samuel was a Loyalist and moved to New Brunswick, Canada in 1783. He married an Eve —, two of their descendants were Grant Austin and Grace Austin. They lived in the Rochester, New York area around 1920. My uncle Walter Austin used to have a watch repair shop on Massachusetts Avenue in Massachusetts from 1915 to 1935. Around 1954 he was a guide at Faneuil Hall in Boston. I would like to know more about Samuel Austin, his brothers, his parents, and his descendants.

283-1. David H. Austin was born in 1792. He married Nancy Watson. They resided in Cayuga County, New York. David H. came to Howell Township, Livington County, Michigan in 1835. From Howell, David removed to Farmington, Oakland County. David died in July 1878 in Milford (or Farmington, Michigan. David and Nancy had a daughter, Jane Watson Austin born on 11 December 1823. She first married a Mr. Hitchcock, second to Townsend Drew in 1847 who was born in 1810 in New York and he died on 4 July 1882 in Howell, Michigan. Jane and Townsend had eight children: Fedilia, Townsend born 1850, Carol, Violetta, Delana, Martha, Lilly, Archibald Windsor born 1863. Jane died 18 October 1900 in Howell. Seeking ancestry of David H. Austin.

283-2. James Wilson Austin was born near LaGrange in Oldham County, Kentucky. He became an attorney and practiced law both in the Commonwealth of Kentucky and the State of Florida, having a partner in each state. He had a son, James Francis born in Brookeville, Florida, on 18 July 1883 and died 17 December 1962 in Louisville, Kentucky. Seeking the ancestry of James Wilson Austin.

283-3. Glorianna Austin born 18 December 1758 and died 9 September 1811. She married a Dr. Aaron Eliott and lived primarily in St. Genevieve, Missouri. They both died in 1811. They had four children, Henry b. 1782, Elias Austin b. 1784 d. 1822, Charles b. 1786 d. 1811, Anna Marie b. 1785. Any information Glorianna's ancestry or this family would be appreciated.

283-4. Nathaniel Austin born on 8 February in 1781 in Virginia or Tennessee and John Austin born 6 January 1779 in North Carolina were brothers and moved to White County, Tennessee sometime after 1800. Nathaniel married Mary — and John married first to Rachel Denny. All four are buried in Austin Cemetery, White County. Seeking all data and ancestry of these Austin brothers.

283-5. Catherine Austin born 23 April 1829, possibly in Elyria, Ohio, the daughter of of Homer and Sena Austin. Married David M. Dutcher, son of James and Christine Dutcher, born on 23 September 1823 in Copake, New York. Catherine died on 18 March 1897 in Winchester (Winsted) Connecticut. David died 22 February 1910 in Winchester. Need date of their marriage, also proof of parents of both Catherine and David.

283-6. Phineas H. Austin born 8 July 1790 in Vermont married Sabrina Miller on 14 February 1814 in Rutland, Vermont. Children were Sally L. b.1815; Polly L. b.1818 married Isaac Dolphin 1836; John B. b.1819; Stillman B. b.1821; Charlotte b.1823; Eucibies? b.1826; Eliza b.1827; Sally (Sarah) b.1832; and Stephen L. b.1835 in Canada. The 1820 Federal Census shows Phineas in Swanton, Vermont, and in 1860 he was shown in Winnebago County, Illinois. Need the ancestry of Phineas & Sabrina.

283-7. Isaac Austin was born on 19 December 1791 in Boston. He was married in New York State to Lucy Fish, born on 19 September 1794. They had one child, Job born in Boston then six more children in Canada, one by the name of Charles Starbuck Austin. Need the ancestry of Isaac Austin.

283-8. Anna S. Austin born on 22 April 1828 in Clyde, Michigan and died in 1869 in Benecia, CA. She married William D. Chilson in 1845. Need the ancestry of Anna Austin, and any information on her descendants.

283-9. James Henry Austin married Lena Cross, they had a son, Clyde Lee born on 22 November 1898 in Fort Worth, Texas. Clyde married Juanita Alice Smith, they had a son, Robert Lee born on 1 October 1925 in Provo, Utah. Need the ancestry of James Henry Austin.

283-10. Roswell Austin born early 1900's in England. Married to Elspeth Murison circa 1927 in New York. Seeking both the ancestry and descendants of Roswell.

283-11. William W. Austin born 15 September 1832 in Ohio, possibly the son of Hiram and Zenia (Frigner) Austin. He married Julia Ann, daughter of James and Katie (Poucher) Miller of Martindale, New York. William died 3 April 1911 in Waterbury, Connecticut. Need names of their children and proof of William's parents.

★★★★★★★★★★★★★★★★★★★★★★★★★★★★★★★

Austins of America is intended to serve present and future genealogists researching Austin family lines. Readers are encouraged to submit queries, genealogical and historical articles for publication. Previously published books, pamphlets or articles containing Austin genealogical data are also sought for reprinting or review.

EDITOR

DR. MICHAEL EDWARD AUSTIN   CONCORD, MA

ASSOCIATE EDITORS

ANTHONY KENT AUSTIN   PROSPECT, KY

BERT ADDIS AUSTIN   QUEEN CREEK, AZ

PATRICIA BIEBUYCK AUSTIN   CONCORD, MA

PAULINE LUCILLE AUSTIN   CEDAR RAPIDS, IA

Austins of America is published each February and August by The Austin Print, 23 Allen Farm Lane, Concord, Massachusetts 01742. All correspondence, including subscriptions, articles and responses to queries, should be sent to this address. Subscriptions are $4.50 per year postpaid.

SOME AUSTIN RECORDS FROM

WHITE COUNTY, TENNESSEE

by Anthony Kent Austin

Author's Note: Tax List and Land Grant information was copied from the Card Index by Terry McBroom of Cookeville, Tennessee. The Index to White County Tax Records was copied from the Card File in the Archives at Nashville. Other Tax records were obtained from the Court Clerk's Office in Sparta, White County, Tennessee.

Thomas Austin; see Thomas Maston, Private, a North Carolina Soldier.   Deeds Book 4, page 263

Thomas Austin, North Carolina soldier [rank not shown], sold 640 acres on Stone's River in Davidson County to Howell Tatum and Henry Wiggins on 6 December 1797.
Grant 3282, Warrent 4166, Deeds Book 4, page 264

Stephen Austin was deeded 309 acres of land by Thomas K. Harris, as acknowledged in Court on 11 May 1808

Nathaniel Austin bought 175 acres of land for $600 on 10 March 1818 from W. P. White. Registered by Elijah Chism, witnessed by Jacob A. Lane.   Deeds Book F, page 149

John Austin bought "one acre on the waters of Hickory Valley, on the Mountain" for $4.00 from George Tucker on 9 September 1818, witnesses were A. Dilwell and Moses Norman. This land was part of a 100-acre survey conveyed from William C. Brightwell to Tucker on 21 January 1818.   Deeds Book F, page 270

John Austin sold "8 acres more or less" for $100.00 to Thomas Wilson on 19 January 1822.   Deeds Book G, page 146

John Austin sold 50 acres of land "on the waters of Mine Lick Creek" for $200 to William Austin on 27 August 1829, witnesses were John Austin and Solomon Austin.
Deeds Book H, page 67

John Austin, sold land "for love and affection" to the heirs of William Austin on 14 October 1833. The heirs of William Austin, deceased, are the grandchildren of the above John Austin: Mary, John, Andrew and Madison Austin.   Deeds Book H, page 526

John Austin received a Brown Bay stud, one wagon, and one yoke of oxen from Archibald Conner on 26 August 1834, in payment of the $100 debt which Conner owed Austin.   Deeds Book I, page 75

WHITE COUNTY TENNESSEE LAND GRANTS

James Austin was granted 25.75 acres 24 poles in Mountain District on 23 March 1844.   Grant 8936, Book T, pgs 228-9

James Austin was granted 11 acres and 8 poles in Mountain district on 1 February 1854.   Grant 11179, Book X, page 237

John Austin was granted 18 acres in Mountain District on 1 February 1820.   Grant 15233, Book 9, page 8

John Austin received a General Grant for 18 acres on 1 February 1821.   Grant 15233, Book R, page 8

John Austin was granted 50 acres in Mountain District on 8 December 1824.   Grant 571, Book 1, page 50

John Austin was granted 50 acres in Middle Tennessee District on 8 December 1824.   Grant 571, Book 1, page 571

John Austin was granted 50 acres in Middle Tennessee District on 19 July 1827.   Grant 6395, Book 8, page 45

John Austin was granted 39 acres and 36 poles in Mountain District on 13 August 1827.   Grant 6486, Book 3, page 477

John Austin was granted 39 acres and 36 poles in Middle Tenn. District on 13 August 1827.   Grant 6486, Book 8, p. 136

John Austin was granted 50 acres in Mountain District on 19 July 1827.   Grant 6395, Book 2, page 724

John Austin was granted 50 acres in Mountain District on 27 September 1828,   Grant 946, Book B, pages 373-74

John Austin was granted 237 acres in Mountain District on 12 December 1835,   Grant 4229, Book F, page 268-9

John Austin was granted 47 acres, 3 rods, 80 poles in Mountain District on 10 March 1846.
Grant 9157, Book U, pages 96-98

John Austin was granted 93 acres in Mountain District on 1 March 1851.   Grant 10593, Book V, page 273

Nathaniel Austin was granted 54 acres in Mountain District on 7 December 1824.   Grant 565, Book 1, page 33

Nathaniel Austin was granted 54 acres in Middle Tenn. District on 7 December 1824.   Grant 565, Book 1, page 565

Nathaniel Austin was granted 25 acres in Mountain District on 24 May 1828.   Grant 7838, Book 3, page 230

Nathaniel Austin; was granted 25 acres in Middle Tenn. District on 4 May 1828.   Grant 7838, Book 9, page 680

Pleasant Austin was granted 856.25 acres in Mountain District on 30 June 1875.   Grant 12858, Book AA, pages 305-306

WHITE COUNTY TENNESSEE TAX RECORDS

1811 Tax List mentions Saunders Austin in Capt. William Ridge's company.

1812 Tax List mentions David Austin and John Austin.

1813 Tax List mentions John Austin of Hickory Valley.

1814 Tax List mentions John Austin of Hickory Valley.

1818 Tax List mentions in William Burden's company: John Austin of Hickory Valley and Nathaniel Austin of Lost Creek. (Hickory Valley and Lost Creek are both just south of Sparta.)

1825 John Austin, Sr. found in tax records index   page 99

1825 John Austin, Jr. found in tax records index   page 99

1825 Nathaniel Austin found in tax records index   page 99

1825 William Austin found in tax records index   page 99

1833 James Austin found in tax records index   page 141

1833 John Austin found in tax records index   pages 133,140

1833 Nathaniel Austin found in tax records index   page 140

1833 William Austin in tax records index   pages 133,137,140

WHITE COUNTY COURT CLERK'S OFFICE

1837 John Austin - 349 acres, value $1780   District 2

1837 Nathaniel Austin - 175 acres, value $1421   District 2

1837 Rolly [Raleigh] Austin   District 2

1837 William Austin   District 3

1837	John Austin	District 7
1838	James Austin	District 1
1838	John Austin - 349 acres, value $1780	District 2
1838	Nathaniel Austin - 175 acres, $1421	District 2
1838	Heirs of William Austin: Raleigh Austin and James M. Austin	District 2
1838	William Austin	District 3
1838	Nathaniel Austin - 149.75 acres, $700	District 6
1838	John Austin	District 7
1839	James Austin	District 1
1839	John Austin - 349 acres, value $1780	District 2
1839	Nathaniel Austin - 175 acres, $1421	District 2
1839	Rolly [Raleigh] Austin	District 2
1839	James M. Austin	District 2
1839	William Austin - 70 acres, value $400	District 3
1839	Rolley [Raleigh] Austin	District 3
1839	Nathaniel Austin - 149.75 acres, $700	District 6
1840	Nathaniel Austin - 175 acres, $1421	District 2
1840	John Austin - 349 acres value $1780	District 2
1840	James M. Austin	District 2
1840	John Austin, Jr.	District 2
1840	James Austin	District 2
1840	William Austin - 70 acres, value $400	District 3
1840	Raleigh Austin	District 3
1840	Nathaniel Austin - 149.5 acres, $700	District 6
1841	John Austin - 420 acres, value $2130	District 2
1841	Nathaniel Austin - 195 acres, value $1000	District 2
1841	James M. Austin	District 2
1841	John Austin, Jr.	District 2
1841	James Austin	District 2
1841	William Austin - 70 acres, value $400	District 3
1841	Raleigh Austin	District 3
1841	Nathaniel Austin	District 6
1848	James Austin - 24.75 acres, value $10	District 1
1848	William Austin - 205 acres, value $350	District 3
1848	James Austin - 40 acres, value $100	District 3
1849	John Austin, Sr. - 677 acres, value $1451	District 2
1849	Nathaniel Austin - 250 acres, $1000	District 2
1849	John Austin, Jr.	District 2
1849	James M. Austin	District 2
1849	Raleigh Austin	District 2
1849	Glenn Austin	District 2
1849	William Austin - 205 acres, value $350	District 3
1849	James Austin - 40 acres, value $100	District 3
1849	Lawrence Austin	District 4
1849	Nathaniel Austin - 150 acres, value $700	District 6
1850	John Austin, Sr. - 667 acres, value $1451	District 2
1850	Nathaniel Austin - 250 acres, value $1000	District 2
1850	John Austin, Jr.	District 2
1850	James M. Austin	District 2
1850	Pleasant Austin	District 2
1850	William Austin - 205 acres, value $350	District 3
1850	James Austin - 40 acres, value $100	District 3
1850	Nathaniel Austin - 150 acres, value $700	District 6

QUERIES

285-1. Andrew Austin was born in Missouri circa 1831, he was married to Margaret — before 1854, perhaps in Livingston County, MO. Their children were: Martha Jane, Sally Ann, Polly Ann, Julia Ann, Mary Ann, and possibly Jeff. Andrew was in DeKalb County in 1860 and 1870. I have papers of an 1855 land purchase from Joseph Shannon. Need the ancestry and descendants of Andrew.

285-2. Francis E. Austin was born in 1820 in New York, where his parents were also born. He married on 26 May 1844 to Mahala Osborn/Ausborn in Chautauqua County, New York. Mahala was born on 1825 in New York to parents who were born in New York. Francis was a carpenter and he fought in the Civil War for the Union. He died on 2 January 1895 in Lodi, Wisconsin, Mahala died on 13 December 1913 in Madison, Wisconsin. From this union 11 children were born in Wisconsin. Two who died in infancy were James and Nancy. The others: Phoebe born circa 1849, married to William Cleland, two children; Janet born circa 1851, married to ? Draves, three children; Anna Elizabeth born on 4 May 1853, married to Christoffer Odegaard on 22 May 1880 in Lodi, six children, Anna died on 9 July 1929 in Lodi; Alsina born circa 1855, married to ? Hall, at least two children; Emmett born circa 1857, three children; Jane born circa 1860; Francis H. born circa 1862; Thomas J. born circa 1864, Charles (Carl?) born circa 1869. Seeking the ancestry and the descendants of Francis Austin.

285-3. Phoebe Lockwood Austin resided in the McHenry or Kane County, Illinois in 1860-70-80. Seeking Phoebe Austin's husband, who would be my g-g-grandfather.

285-4. Bennett Austin was born on 10 April 1793, he married on 9 February 1817 to Margaret Colson/Carson in Rowan County, North Carolina. Margaret was born on 2 December 1794. They had a son, Thomas J. Austin b. in January 1827 in Tennessee who married widow Elizabeth Curd Utterback on 16 December 1852 in Calloway County, Kentucky. Bennett died on 8 January 1873 in Calloway County, Margaret died 22 April 1873. Need to prove the relationship between Bennett and Margaret, and would also like the ancestry of Bennett Austin.

285-5. William Tennant Austin was born on 30 January 1809 in Bridgeport, Connecticut. His parents were John Punderson and Susannah (Rogers) Austin. William married Johanna Thomas. Johanna was born ca. 1809 in New York City. Their daughter Caroline was born in 1828, probably in New York, she married Hudson Gaston. William died 25 February 1874 in Galveston, Texas and Johanna died in August 1833 in Washington, Texas. Need William and Johanna's marriage place and date, also the exact birthdates of Caroline and Hudson.

SOME DESCENDANTS OF
WILLIAM AND ELIZABETH AUSTIN
OF BARREN COUNTY, KENTUCKY

by Margaret Bullion Daniel

Author's Note: The close relationships mentioned below between the families of William Austin and Charles Austin – plus the proximity of a John Austin – leads me to speculate that these three Austins are somehow related. I am nearly positive that William Austin and Charles Austin are brothers, and John may also have been a brother, cousin or nephew of Charles. William's second child is known to have been born in North Carolina, and there were three brothers U12 William Austin, U13 Charles Austin, and U14 John Austin mentioned in the article *The Austin Family of Stanly and Union Counties in North Carolina*, which appears on page 232 of *Austins of America*. The following article is written as though these Williams are the same person and the numbering of generations and persons here corresponds to that used in the referenced article. Further proof or disproof of William's origins is certainly needed, but I publish this article now to encourage anyone who might have additional information on William's origins or descendants to contact me through *Austins of America*.

THIRD GENERATION

U12. WILLIAM[3] AUSTIN (*Charles,[2] Unknown[1]*) was perhaps the William Austin who was born on 11 April 1754 in Ireland, and who came to this country as a boy with his parents Charles and Mary Austin, who settled in North Carolina (see *Austins of America*, page 232). In any case, our William Austin was married to Elizabeth ——. They moved around some, as their second child was born in North Carolina (census record), their third child was born in Tennessee, and their fourth child was born in Kentucky. William Austin moved to Allen and Barren Counties, Kentucky, and there also were a Charles Austin and a John Austin in the area, whom I believe to be William's younger brothers. William and Elizabeth resided in Barren County in 1808, and William probably died in that county about 12 May 1808. He left some things in his Will to Elizabeth, apparently a widow left with their four small children. Charles Austin was appointed guardian of William's children. When Charles Austin himself later died in Smith County, Tennessee, Willis Austin was the Administrator of his estate. Children known to me:

>U121. ALICE, *b. 10 November 1798* +
>U122. WILSON, *b. circa 1801* +
>U123. WILLIS, *b. 1804* +
>U124. WILLIAMSON, *b. 1807* +

FOURTH GENERATION

U121. ALICE[4] AUSTIN (*William,[3] Charles,[2] Unknown[1]*) was born 10 November 1798 She married to Henry Brown, who was born 4 February 1794. Henry died on 14 October

1877. Alice died on 23 August 1880, and is buried with Henry in the Downing-Johnson Cemetery in Allen County, Kentucky. BROWN CHILDREN: HARRISON b.1819, OLIVER, ROBERSON, WILLIAM HENRY, and ADELINE.

U122. WILSON[4] AUSTIN (*William,[3] Charles,[2] Unknown[1]*) was born in North Carolina circa 1801 (age 49 in the 1850 Census) He married to Rhoda H. ——, who was born in Kentucky circa 1821 (age 29 in 1850). In the 1850 census the family resided in Macon County, Tennessee, where Wilson owned 180 acres of land on Lick Creek. Wilson was still living in Macon County when he sold 83.75 acres of land and a "parcel" of slaves in 1857. The land was sold to F. Brown for $125.00. Five daughters of Wilson and Rhoda are known from the 1850 Census, the first was born in Kentucky, the others in Tennessee:

>U122-1. LUTHENIA H., *b. circa 1842*
>U122-2. LUTICEN A., *b. circa 1844*
>U122-3. ANGELINE W., *b. circa 1845*
>U122-4. MARY M., *b. circa 1847*
>U122-5. CANZADA, *b. circa 1848*

U123. WILLIS[4] AUSTIN (*William,[3] Charles,[2] Unknown[1]*) was born in Tennessee circa 1804 (age 46 in the 1850 Census). He was married by Payton Welch on 10 October 1833 to Eliza Ann (—) Dixon, who was born in Kentucky circa 1808 (age 42 in 1850). Eliza's first marriage had been to Thomas F. W. Dixon. They resided near Holland, Allen County, Kentucky. Willis lived on Long Creek where he owned land and had a mill, known as Austin Mill. The family was recorded in Allen County in the 1850 Census. Willis died on 19 July 1858, and he and Eliza are probably buried in Allen County. They had five children at the time of the 1850 Census, all born in Allen County:

>U123-1. MARY ELIZABETH, *b. circa 1834, m. James T. High ("Bill"). One known child: Vada High.*
>U123-2. WILLIAM M. R., *b. circa 1836 in Allen County, m. Mary E. Pitchford. Two known daughters, M. W. Austin and M. E. Austin, were born on the Barren River.*
>U123-3. WILLIS RUSSELL, *b. 30 October 1838* +
>U123-4. JOHN B., *12 July 1841* +
>U123-5. NANCY JANE, *b. circa 1844, m. on 3 July 1865 to Schuyler Franklin by William Seamonds. Known Franklin children: Lela, Ed, Dick, and Ruby.*

U124. WILLIAMSON[4] AUSTIN (*William,[3] Charles,[2] Unknown[1]*) was born in Kentucky circa 1807 (he was age 43 in the 1850 Census). He married to Martha ——, who was born in Kentucky circa 1811 (she was age 39 in 1850). They resided in Allen County, Kentucky, in the 1850 Census, along with their children, all born in Kentucky:

U124-1.   W. T. [male], *b. circa 1836*
U124-2.   N. A. [female], *b. circa 1838*
U124-3.   T. W. [male], *b. 30 October 1841*
U124-4.   M. E. [female], *b. circa 1844*
U124-5.   J. P. [male], *b. circa 1847*

FIFTH GENERATION

U123-3. WILLIS RUSSELL[5] AUSTIN (*Willis,*[4] *William,*[3] *Charles,*[2] *Unknown*[1]) was born 30 October 1838 in Allen County, Kentucky. He married on 15 August 1860 to Margaret Katherine Holder near the town of Austin, Barren County, Kentucky, where her parents W. Edward and Cynthia (Whitney) Holder resided. Margaret, known as 'Maggie', was born 4 December 1840, probably in Allen or Barren County, Kentucky. The family moved to Texas in 1876, they settled in Mineral Wells, Texas, where Maggie died on 5 April 1907. Russ died on 15 December 1913 in Amarillo, Texas, and is buried with Maggie in Mineral Wells, Texas. Russ and Maggie had twelve children:

U123-31.   SEABORNE HART, *b. 26 July 1861, d. 3 June 1862, buried in William Holder Cemetery near Brownsford in Allen County.*

U123-32.   EMMA PORTER, *born 5 January 1863 in Barren County, d. 22 January 1953. She m. on 20 October 1884 to B. F. Smith, and is buried with him in Seymour, Texas. Smith Children: Ben, Margaret, and Burwell.*

U123-33.   ELIZA ANN, *b. 30 September 1864, d. 10 March 1957. She moved from Barren County with her parents to Texas in 1876, m. on 10 October 1881 to William Ludd Wade who was b. 26 May 1860 and d. 13 April 1939. Wade children: Mayme Katherine b.1882, Emma Douglas b.1884, Ludd Austin b.1886, Lela Florence b.1888, Joseph William b.1890, stillborn girl b.1893, Russell Frank b.1894, Seth Erwin b.1897, Sybil Lois b.1899, Cornelius Yeager b.1903, Maggie Bob b.1908.*

U123-34.   LELA FLORENCE, *b. 18 April 1866, d. 14 March 1945, buried in Abernathy, Texas. She moved from Barren County with her parents to Texas in 1876, m. on 8 January 1882 to Douglas Wade who was b. 26 June 1862, d. 26 July 1928 and buried in Rio Vista, Texas. Wade children: Bonnie, Willie b.1885, Anna Mae b.1887, Joel/Jodie (female) b.1902, twins Eunice and Bernice b.1893.*

U123-35.   CYNTHIA ALICE, *b. 9 April 1868, d. 19 March 1935, m. on 24 August 1894 to John Milton Durrett who was b. 29 October 1859, d. on 19 March 1935, buried with Cynthia in Amarillo, Texas. Durrett children: Sarah Margaret Austin, Catherine.*

U123-36.   MARY ELIZABETH, *b. 28 February 1870 in Barren County, d. 28 March 1894 in Oklahoma, buried in Mineral Wells, Texas. 'Lizzie' married in Mineral Wells on 3 September 1891 to Rufus P. ('Jim') Highnote. Highnote child: Mary Elizabeth b. 1894.*

U123-37.   KITTIE DORINDA, *b. 8 December 1871 in Barren County, d. 1 October 1954 in Mineral Wells, Texas. She m. on 30 May 1900 to William Thomas Sims who was b. 19 June 1867 near Greshamville, Georgia, d. 10 November 1947. 'Tom' is buried with 'Kit' in Mineral Wells. No children.*

U123-38.   EDWARD WILLIS [female], *b. 26 August 1873 in Barren County, d. 7 October 1957. She m. on 28 February 1892 to Dr. Cornelius Franklin Yeager who was b. 9 January 1848 in Johnson City, Tennessee, d. 19 January 1915. 'Eddie' and Cornelius are buried in Mineral Wells. Yeager children: Edward Franklin b.1893, Margaret Selina b.1895, Abraham Austin b.1898, Mary Alice b.1900, Cornelius Franklin b. 1902, Ruth b. 1904, Rebekah Frances b.1906, Elizabeth Lillian b.1910.*

U123-39.   RUSSELL BRIANT, *b. 23 August 1875, d. 3 November 1875, buried in the Edward Holder Cemetery in Austin, Barren County.*

U123-3A.   IRVIN AYERS, *b. 26 January 1878 in Staggs Prairie, Texas, d. 26 April 1944. He m. on 17 August 1905 to Ruth van Winkle who was b. 17 June 1879 in Morgan County, Georgia, d. 14 September 1963. Irvin and Ruth are buried in Greshamville, Georgia. Only two children are known: Helen Austin b. 7 September 1914 at Greshamville, m. Billie Edwards; Worth Russell Austin b. 17 June 1922, d. 11 June 1986, m. Ruby Nickerson Jones.*

U123-3B.   JAMES ROBERT, *b. 1 February 1880 at Staggs Prairie, Texas, d. 8 July 1950. 'Bob' m. on 4 December 1912 to Rose LaJenesse, they are both buried in the Mount Calvery Cemetery in Austin, Texas with their adopted daughter Rose Mary who never married.*

U123-3C.   CHARLES RAINES, *b. 24 January 1884 in Mineral Wells, d. 10 August 1957, m. in November 1913 to Margaret Saddler. They are both buried in Amarillo, Texas. Children: Sarah Margaret Austin and Jane Austin.*

U123-4. JOHN B.[5] AUSTIN (*Willis,*[4] *William,*[3] *Charles,*[2] *Unknown*[1]) was born 12 July 1841. He served as a 2nd Lieutenant in the 9th Kentucky Volunteers, Union Army, and he fought in the battle of Shiloh, Tennessee. He first married on 17 December 1860 to Mary E. Woodcock, who was born in Allen County, Kentucky. He married second on 28 March 1865 to Mary Elizabeth ("Mollie") Ferguson, who was born 24 April 1846, the daughter of Dougal G. Ferguson. John was a Baptist preacher. He died on 3 August 1901, while Mollie died on 22 March 1914. Both are buried in the Mount Olivet Cemetery in the town of Austin, Barren County, Kentucky. John had one child by his first wife, two by his second wife:

U123-41. EMMA, *b. 22 February 1861 in Allen County.*

U123-42. RUSSELL YETMAN, *b. 4 October 1876, d. 3 November 1918, buried in Mount Olivet Cemetery. He m. on 26 December 1900 to Fannie Jewell Harston who was b. 18 March 1874, d. 6 May 1915. Children: John Gillock, Anna Jewell, Herschell Bryan, Mary Lewis.*

U123-43. HERSCHELL B., *b. 22 September 1869, never married. He was a lawyer, lived at Scottsville, Kentucky. He died on 7 February 1901, and is buried in Mouth Olivet Cemetery in Austin, Kentucky.*

QUERIES

288-1. **Levi Austin** was born ca. 1782 in North Carolina, ca. 1805/7 to Anna — born circa 1791 in Kentucky. He was listed in the 1850 Census of Smith County Kentucky, but not in the 1860 census. They had ten children born in Tennessee: Philip b. ca. 1808 m. ca. 1832 to Phoebe; Christian b. ca. 1809 m. ca 1819 to Sarah —; James b. ca. 1812 m. ca. 1834 to Rebecca —; Ephraim b. ca. 1814, m. ca. 1838 to Mary —; Cynthia b. ca. 1817; — b. ca. 1818/21; Miles W. b. ca 1823 m. to Sally —; Polly (Mary) b. ca. 1824 m. 9 July 1853 to William Patterson; John b. circa 1825/6; Booker W. b. ca. 1827, m. 1 December 1853 to Nancy M. —. Seek ancestry and descendants of Levi.

288-2. **Elizabeth Austin** was born on 25 April 1852 in Russell County, Virginia to Thomas and Nancy (—) Austin. She married on 14 March 1866 to Samuel Worley Helton in Lebanon, Virginia. Elizabeth and Samuel had twelve children. Elizabeth died on 1 April 1930. I need help on this Austin line.

288-3. **Hannah Austin** married John Canfield, they were both born in New York. Their son, Charles was born on 28 June 1847 in New York and died in Michigan. Would appreciate anything pertaining to this family.

288-4. **Cain Austin** married Tabitha —, they had ten children: Samuel; Hannah, who m. William Fenimore Smith (William died in 1867); Hezekiah; Rebecca; Gertrude; Joseph; Seth; David; Charles; Esther. Need information on this family from the Burlington, New Jersey - Philadelphia, Pennsylvania area.

288-5. **Edward Austin** was born circa 1800, married ca. 1823 to Adaline Franklin, born in 1808 in Virginia. Adaline Austin married a second time to Edward Ferguson. Edward and Adaline Austin had one daughter, Nancy Jane Hinley Austin born on 12 March 1824 in Virginia. Nancy Jane married John E. Ferguson on 22 September 1841 in Butler County, Kentucky. Nancy died on 3 January 1903 in Woodbury, Butler County, and is buried in Cook Cemetery, Woodbury. Seek the ancestry of Edward Austin and the descendants of Nancy Jane.

ACCOUNT OF A JOURNEY ACROSS THE OHIO VALLEY TO THE MISSISSIPPI

by Moses Austin

[CONTINUED FROM PAGE 261]

About thirty miles from Kahokia stands Fort Chartres [Charters]. It is a notable work, and the manner in which it is neglected proves how much the country had been and still is neglected by government. Fort Charter, when built, I am told, was a mile from the Mississippi, but the river has so changed its channel that it has demolished the west side of the fort entirely and it has fallen into the river. Each angle of the fort is 140 paces, or steps. It is built of stone taken from the Mississippi cliff; and where the walls are unhurt, they are about twenty feet high. But the south walls are much injured; the east and north are more perfect; the ditch which surrounds the fort is almost filled up. The gate was finished with hewn stone, but it is much defaced.

Within the walls of the fort is a range of stone barracks, within which is the parade. At the southeast corner of the fort stands the magazine, which is also of stone and not in the least injured. The arch appears to be as good as when finished. At the southwest corner stands the guardhouse, a part of which has fallen with the west wall into the Mississippi; between the guardhouse and the west range of barracks is a deep well walled up with hewn stone and is as good as when made. The woodwork of the barracks was destroyed, I am told, by fire. The last English garrison had orders to demolish the fort and turned their cannon against the walls for some days; however, the pieces were not sufficiently large to effect the destruction, but the walls are much injured.

The French from the Spanish side of the Mississippi have pillaged the windows and doors of the barracks of many of the best hewn stones and taken them up to St. Louis for private use. Fort Charter is said to be the best work of the kind in America.

It is not easy to account why this country had been neglected by the government of the United States; and when it is considered that it is not only a frontier as to the Indians but also as to Spain, who are taking every step to make their country formidable in case of an attack, it is not unreasonable to suppose that the executive of the United States have not a just idea of the importance of the Mississippi country or the trade they are daily losing, and which will soon be so fixed on the Spanish shore as to be hard to withdraw. Some of the standing laws of Congress as they respect the Illinois country are distressing and unjust in their operation. The law, which makes the property of all the people forfeited to the United States who

have left the government of said States and do not return within five years, is cruel and severely unjust.

It ought to be remembered that in 1778 General Clark took the Illinois and left a small garrison at Kaskaskia only, who, instead of protecting the people, pillaged them at will; and when that garrison was withdrawn, which I believe was in the year '82, the whole settlement was unprotected. And notwithstanding, garrisons have been established from Georgia north for the protection of much smaller settlements, yet the Illinois have not received the least assistance from government from the time of Clark until the present moment; which obliged many families to take shelter under the Spanish government. And because they did not return and stand the scalping knife, they are to lose their property; for it is to be known that all the towns on the Mississippi have been at the mercy of the Indians until the treaty made by General Wayne. That government should take away the property of a people they could not or would not protect is something new, more especially a government like ours.

Kaskaskia, which is a place of the most consequence of any on the American side of the Mississippi and the county town of Randolph, is situated in about 38°48′ N and longitude 16° W from Philadelphia, on the banks of the River Kaskaskia, two miles from the Mississippi and five from the mouth of the Kaskaskia, in a level champaign country; and is overlooked by a hill on the opposite side of the Kaskaskia River, which commands an extensive prospect, as well of the country below as of the Mississippi and the Spanish villages of St. Genevieve and New Bourbon, forming all together a landscape beautiful and pleasing.

It is supposed to have been settled much about the same time as Philadelphia, or at least about a century ago; the oldest records in the office, which are dated in the year 1722, being marked with the number 1015, show that it was settled at an earlier period. It was formerly populous and in a flourishing condition. At present no more than from 500 to 600 souls are in the town, and it is much diminished in wealth as well as population. The many changes that have taken place in the government of this country have greatly contributed to this decay, and more especially the last when taken possession of by the Americans in the year 1778; from which time to the year 1790 it was in a manner left without any civil authority, which induced numbers of the most wealthy of the inhabitants to remove to the Spanish dominions. It is now the capital of the county of Randolph, having in the year 1795 been detached from the county of St. Clair.

The Illinois country is perhaps one of the most beautiful and fertile in America and has the peculiar advantage of being interspersed with large plains or prairies and

---

Moses Austin

Moses Austin, the author of this article, was born on 4 October 1761 in Durham, Connecticut. He was a descendant of immigrant Richard Austin of Charlestown, Massachusetts (see page 57 of Edith Austin Moore's *Richard Austin* book). In 1783 Moses became a member of a Philadelphia merchant firm, which he and his brother, Stephen Austin, expanded. Moses later went to Richmond, Virginia, and by 1789 he had bought lead mines in what is now Wythe County, Virginia. In 1796 he extended his interests to the lead fields in Missouri, where he received a grant from the Spanish governor near Potosi, Missouri, which he founded.

The panic of 1819, however, cost him his fortune, and he applied to the Spanish government for a permit to settle 300 families in Texas. This was granted on 17 January 1821, but Austins death in St. Francis City, Missouri, on 10 June 1821, prevented his completing the project. Moses had bequeathed his grant to his son Stephen Fuller Austin, born 3 November 1793, the famed founder and administrator of the principal Anglo-American colony in Texas.

---

woodlands, where a crop can be made the first year without the trouble and expense of felling the timber, which in every other part of American exhausts the strength and purse of a new settler. The Mississippi affords an easy and certain conveyance for his produce, at all seasons of the year, to New Orleans, which place or some other on the lower parts of the river bids fair to be one of the greatest marts in the world. Nature has undoubtedly intended this country to be not only the most agreeable and pleasing in the world but the richest also. Not that I suppose there are many, if any, silver mines or gold dust. Nor do I consider either of them sufficient to make a country rich.

But the Mississippi has what is better — she has a rich landed country. She has the richest lead mines in the world, not only on the Maramag and its waters but also on the banks of the Mississippi, about 700 miles up from St. Louis at a place called Prairie du Chien, or Dog Prairie, at which place, or near it, is also a copper mine of malleable-copper, the veins of which are more extensive than any of the kind heretofore found. She has salt springs on each side of the river and also iron ore in great quantities. These minerals are more useful in a country than gold or silver. A

country thus rich by nature cannot be otherwise than wealthy with a moderate share of industry. It is also to be remembered that all the wealth of this extensive world may be warfted [shipped] to a market, at any time of the year, down the Mississippi, at an easy expense.

The 19th I passed the Mississippi on ice to St. Genevieve, which is about two miles from the bank of the river, which at this place is about a mile over. I presented my letters from the commandant of St. Louis to Monsieur Valle, the commandant of St. Genevieve, who received me with much politeness and promised me all the assistance in his power. And on the 21st, being furnished with a carryall and two horses, I left St. Genevieve in company with a Mr. Jones of Kaskaskia for the Mines of Briton; and on the 23rd arrived at the place. I found the mines equal to my expectation in every respect. The weather turning warm, we were obliged to make a quicker return than I wished. However, I satisfied myself as to the object I had in view and returned to St. Genevieve on the 26th.

The Mines of Briton, so called in consequence of their being found by a man of that name, are about thirty miles from the town of St. Genevieve. There is a good wagon road to the place, and all the lead that has been made at them is by making a fire over the ore with large logs, which melts some of the ore, by which means about two-thirds of the lead is lost. Notwithstanding the imperfect manner in which they melt the ore, yet at the Mines of Briton last summer was made 400,000 pounds of lead; and from an experiment I made, the same quantity of ore that was made use of to make the 400,000 pounds would have made 1,200,000 pounds of lead, if I was rightly informed as to the quantity of ore they took to make 1,000 pounds of lead in the log fires. The ore at the Mines of Briton covers about forty acres of ground and is found within three feet of the surface of the earth in great plenty and better quality than any I have ever seen, either from the mines in England or America.

The town of St. Genevieve is about two miles from the Mississippi on the high land from which you have a commanding view of the country and river. The old town stood immediately on the bank of the river in an extensive plain. But it being sometimes overflowed by the Mississippi and many of the houses washed into the river by the falling of the bank, it was thought advisable to remove the town to the heights. The place is small, not over 100 houses, but has more inhabitants than Kaskaskia and the houses are in better repair and the citizens are more wealthy. It has some Indian trade; but what has made the town of St. Genevieve are the lead and salt that are made near the place, the whole of which is brought to town for sale, and from thence shipped up and down the Mississippi River, as well as up the Ohio to Cumberland and Kentucky. And when the lead mines are properly worked and the salt springs advantageously managed, St. Genevieve will be a place of as much wealth as any on the Mississippi.

One mile from St. Genevieve, down the river, is a small villiage called New Bourbon, of about twenty houses. At this place I was introduced to the Chevalier Pierre Charles de Hault de Lassus, a French nobleman, formerly of the Council of the late king of France. Chevalier de Lassus told me he had an estate in France of 30,000 crowns, but was obliged to make his escape to American and leave all, which has since been taken by the present government. Madame de Lassus had an estate of half that sum per annum, so that the yearly income of the family, besides the sums allowed him by the king, amounted to 45,000 crowns per annum. Madame de Lassus did not appear to support the change of situation so well as the chevalier. I was examining a large piece of painting, which was in Madame de Lassus' bedchamber, representing a grand festival given by the citizens of Paris to the queen on the birth of the dauphin and a parade of all the nobles on the same occasion. She came to me and putting her finger on the picture pointing out a couch: "There," said she, "was I on that happy day. My situation is now strangely changed."

After taking leave of Chevalier de Lassus, I recrossed the river to Kaskaskia; and on the 8th of February took my leave of the good people of Kaskaskia, taking a Frenchman by the name of Degar as a guide to Fort Massac, setting my face homeward. After rafting and swimming several rivers, I arrived at the Ohio about eighteen miles above Fort Massac, where a number of Frenchmen were camped for hunting. With much trouble and danger I swam my horses over the Ohio, getting another Frenchman as a guide.

I, on the 17th day of February, arrived at the town of Nashville, on [the] Cumberland River in the state of Tennessee. At this place I rested myself and horses six days. And then, in company with fourteen others, some women and some men, took the wilderness for Knoxville; and without meeting anything uncommon, arrived at Knoxville on the 4th day of March, where I stayed but a night; and on the 9th day of the month arrived at the village of Austinville after an absence of three months and nine days, making a journey of upward of 2,000 miles, 960 of which was a wilderness, and the snow most of the way two feet deep. Five days of the time I was without provisions.

I have made these few observations of my journey to the Mississippi for the use of my son, should he live to my age, not doubting but by that time the country I have passed in a state of nature will be overspread with towns and villages; for it is not possible a country which has within itself everything to make its settlers rich and happy can remain unnoticed by the American people. ☐

STEPHEN FULLER AUSTIN:

THE FATHER OF TEXAS

by Jean Ehly and
Robert Krause Austin

Editor's Note: The following is based upon Jean Ehly's article "Stephen Austin – Father of Texas," published circa 1970 and submitted by Keotah Fannin of Las Vegas, Nevada, and upon Robert Krause Austin's 1983 manuscript "Austin Family Portraits: From Richard to Stephen F." Stephen's ancestry can be found in Edith Austin Moore's 1969 book *The Descendants of Richard Austin of Charlestown, Massachusetts 1638.* His father Moses Austin was himself a most interesting individual, as can be seen in his *Account of a Journey Across the Ohio Valley to the Mississippi* which begins on page 258 of *Austins of America.* The reproductions of the Stephen Austin paintings are courtesy of the Archives Division of the Texas State Library in Austin.

Stephen Fuller Austin was a gentle, aristocratic, and cultured man, yet he also had the wiry toughness of the pioneer who began the transformation of the wilderness that Texas was, into an anglo-American community. He never sought fame or glory and worked only to promote the welfare of his Texas colonists. He devoted his life that others might have land holdings, homes, and family lives. While Stephen himself never found time to achieve family life, he is remembered by all as the "Father of Texas."

Today the capital of Texas is named for him. Two Texas colleges bear his name, as do two state schools and numerous local public schools in Texas. Some historians believe that had it not been for Stephen F. Austin there exists a possibility that Texas and the other Southwestern states would still belong to Mexico. He had a unique talent for dealing with Mexico as had no other; he was also a man endowed with long-range vision and common sense.

Few of his contemporaries recognized Austin's genius, and even today few realize the magnitude of his work. Why was his contribution to history so little publicized? Austin answered this question himself circa 1835 when he wrote "A successful military chieftain is hailed with admiration and applause and monuments perpetuate his fame. But the bloodless pioneer of the wilderness, like the corn and cotton he causes to spring where it never grew before, attracts no notice. . . no slaughtered thousands or smoking cities attest his devotion to the cause of human happiness, and he is regarded by the masses of the world as the humble instrument to pave the way for others. . ."

R219-73. STEPHEN FULLER[6] AUSTIN (*Moses,[5] Elias,[4] Richard,[3] Anthony,[2] Richard[1]*) was born on 3 November 1793 near the site of the old Cheswell Lead Mines, located on the New River in Austinville, Wythe County, Virginia. His parents were Moses and Maria (Brown) Austin. Stephen was the the first of their children to survive beyond infancy, as two previous children, Anna Maria and Eliza Fuller, had died before reaching the age of eight months.

Stephen Fuller Austin (1793-1836) in hunting costume, a stylized portrait painted in 1833.

Stephen had a sister Emily Margaret Brown Austin born on 22 June 1795 in Austinville, and a brother James Elijah Brown Austin born on 3 October 1803 in Potosi, Missouri.

In 1789 Moses and his brother Stephen rented a lead mine in southeastern Virginia, and in 1791 he moved there to manage the mining, much of it done with slave labor. That same year, at age thirty, Moses started the present town of Austinville, Virginia. The brothers had a contract to roof the Virginia capitol with lead, and Moses started a factory for molding lead buttons. The lure of lead caused Moses to explore the West in the winter of 1796-97 [see pages 258ff], and having received a grant of land rich in lead deposits, Moses and his family left Austinville on 8 June 1798, sailed the Mississippi and Missouri Rivers until reaching

an uninhabited area 40 miles west of St. Genevieve, Missouri Territory, on 8 September 1798. The territory into which they had moved had a population of mostly French and Spanish settlers, with only a sprinkling of adventurous Americans. At the spot near the lead mines, Moses established the town of Potosi, and he built there an improved furnace, a flour mill, saw mill, sheet-lead mill, and a shot tower. The family operated a mine and a general store. They prospered, and Moses built one of the finest houses on the frontier, a two-story home with fine furnishings. It was named Durham Hall in memory of the family home in Connecticut.

Stephen's Education

Moses sent young Stephen to the Bacon Academy in Colchester, Connecticut, when he was eleven years old. In New England, Stephen was associated with fine families and prosperous cultivated relatives, and it was here that he learned to appreciate the finer things of life. At age fourteen he was sent to Transylvania University in Lexington, Kentucky, where he studied until he was eighteen. As a young man he was quite handsome; he was nearly six feet tall, with curly hair, hazel eyes and a countenace that could be gay or serious, as the mood prompted. He was a graceful dancer, and loved good fellowship; he was generally gregarious.

Returning to Missouri, Stephen had varied experiences as a trader, land speculator, and lead miner & manufacturer with his father. He also served in the Territorial Legislature in 1814-1820, and as an adjutant in the militia. While he was in the Legislature, the slavery question was raised to a high pitch over the Talmadge proposal to exclude slavery upon the admission of Missouri as a state.

Family's Fortune Lost

Unfortunately, the years after the War of 1812 reduced the Austins to poverty as it did almost everyone else. Although their assets were more than $310,000, collections were slow and their own debts menaced the family. Stephen tried to help his father prosper in the mines and the store, but to no avail. Stephen was a director of the Bank of St. Louis, which his father had helped to establish in 1816. The bank's downfall eradicated the family estate. The panic of 1818-19 had made conditions impossible.

Thus Moses, downhearted and dejected after many fruitful years, looked for new horizons to alleviate the family's proverty. They followed the frontier movement to Arkansas and operated a farm at Long Prairie on the Red River. It was in 1820, in Little Rock, Arkansas, that Moses and Stephen talked about colonizing Texas, the great wilderness which was then part of Mexico. Mexico belonged then to Spain, as did all the land from west of the Mississippi River to the Pacific Ocean.

In June of 1820 the governor appointed Stephen Austin judge of the First Judicial Circuit in Arkansas. He probably never held any court sessions, as he moved almost immediately to New Orleans, where he began the study of Law. For six months, while reading law, he also did editorial work for the Louisiana *Advertiser*.

Debts Lead to Texas

Moses and Stephen were obsessed with the desire to pay off the family's debts – Stephen once said that he would only marry when all debts were paid – and colonizing Texas might solve their financial problems. Accordingly, Moses mounted a gray horse, and leading a mule, he set out with a Negro servant to travel a thousand miles to San Antonio to get permission to establish a colony, while Stephen in New Orleans prepared for the transportation of families – should the Mexicans grant the petition!

In 1820, after a long and tedious trip, Moses arrived in San Antonio and applied to Spanish Governor Martinez for permission to settle Texas, saying he would import three hundred colonists and cultivate cotton. On 17 January 1821, through the help of Land Commissioner Baron de Bastrop, Moses' application was approved by the Governor. In granting settlement privileges to Austin, the Mexicans hoped that the American colony would form a buffer between Mexico and the Plains Indians.

Colonization Task Passes to Stephen

Moses' trip back to New Orleans was one of hardship, cold and near-starvation. Moses was almost fifty years old when he died on 10 June 1821, shortly after his return to Hazel Run, St. Francis, Missouri. On his death bed he told his wife Maria to urge their son Stephen to carry on the colonization project.

At first, Stephen was not enthusiastic about pioneering the wilderness, but his loyalty to his father prompted him to set forth for Texas. He had not ridden far when he became excited over the rich land, the heavy timber of oak and pecan, the deer, the fish, the wild horses, turkeys, squirrels and rabbits. When he reached San Antonio, he found the streets crowded with joyous people – Mexico had won its independence from Spain!

Choosing Land in Texas

Stephen was welcomed warmly by Governor Martinez. Later he and his entourage went forth to look for the lands which would best lend themselves to colonization. Austin chose the land that lay between the Colorado and the Brazos Rivers. He was privileged to settle his families on two-hundred thousand acres, and the terms of the colonization agreement made with Mexico was that in return for subsistence and transportation until 1822 the settlers were to build houses, enclosures, stockades and a block house.

They were also to fence farms and start businesses in town. Austin had agreed to charge twelve and a half cents an acre for his work in securing the land for the settlers; he was also to survey this land and give legal deeds to the colonists for the same fee. The Mexican government also demanded that all colonists become Roman Catholic, and Stephen Austin became a Catholic.

Stephen was encouraged and felt a new dedication. Texas would be a refuge for people deeply in debt, who needed a fresh start in life – good, honest people in financial troubles through no fault of their own. Back in New Orleans, Austin borrowed needed funds to buy provisions for his colony from a Mr. Hawkins, who was to have a half interest in the lands and profits. All seemed like smooth sailing for Austin and his colonists.

Traveling to Mexico City

After separation from Spain, the new government of Mexico would not recognize Austin's rights as a colonizer, so he had to return to Mexico City to persuade the new government to recognize his contracts as legal. It was a 1200-mile trip on horseback through a wilderness inhabited by savage Indians, and the country swarmed with bandits. But Austin was not worried about the Indians, and one morning he got up from his pallet in the wilderness and said to his two companions, a Dr. Andrews and a Mr. Waters: "I feel so weak and dispirited, I believe I shall make a fire and brew some coffee." "But Mr. Austin, that might attract the Indians!" protested Mr. Waters.

Austin looked out over the tall prairie grasses waving in the morning breeze. He saw no forest or boulders for savages to hide behind. He said good-naturedly, "I'll just make a little fire," and soon the smoke spiraled upward in the fresh morning air and the smell of coffee was heartening. Austin was pouring some from the old coffee pot when he heard a thundering of hoofs and looking up, saw a group of Comanches riding madly toward them, their spears glittering in the early light.

A Man of Great Persuasion

Austin grabbed his saddlebags that held his important papers and money and waited. Even his gun would be of no use against so many heavily armed savages in their grotesque war paint. The warriors encircled the men. They jumped from their horses and began plundering the camp, stealing food and houses and clothing. They grabbed Austin's saddlebags but did not attempt to kill their white prisoners. Suddenly one of Austin's companions called out loudly: "Don't harm us! We are Americans and we are your friends, we are not Mexicans." Austin remembered that the Indians were friendly to Americans but were at odds with Mexicans. Austin approached the chief. "We are not at war with you now! We are your friends," he repeated emphatically. The chief nodded, relenting. "The Americans are your friends – they give you blankets and guns and trade for your horses – so why do you rob us? We would not rob you, our Indian friends!" The chief thought this over and conceded, "You are right." Then he ordered his warriors to return the stolen goods and his Comanches reluctantly did so, then mounted their horses and rode off. Austin felt lucky to have escaped and knew that he should never have started the telltale fire, as it could have resulted in tragedy.

The men rode on toward Monterey where Austin left two of his companions, while he continued on toward Mexico City with one other man. The threat now was bandits who plundered rich travelers, and for this reason Austin and his companion donned raggedy clothes and threw a dirty blanket or serape over themselves. Austin hid his money and important papers about his person, and thus they arrived unmolested in Mexico City.

A Man of Great Patience

The first thing he did then was go to the government officials and seek the validation of the contracts for colonization made with him under the Spanish rule of Mexico. He was on the verge of achieving this when the Mexicans overthrew the government again! Now General Agustin de Iturbide was the Emperor, and Austin had to wait eight months longer to get his colonization contract validated in Mexico.

Finally the Emperor signed the decree, but just as Austin was leaving for Texas with the good news, the Mexican government was overthrown again, and the New Congress declared all previous acts and decrees null and void. Austin had to exert great patience again. However, he used his head and employed his time profitably.

A Man of Great Diplomacy

Austin made friends with the Mexican officials and was entertained lavishly in the new regime's official homes; furthermore, he studied the language to perfect it, so that he might commmunicate fluently in Spanish. Finally his contracts were validated by the New Congress and this time he really scored a victory. He was so diplomatic, so understanding and so truly respectful of the Mexicans that he won their confidence and respect as few others ever have. Instead of 300 families for colonists, he was now permitted to settle 600, and instead of 640 acres per man, he could offer 4600 acres per man!

Problems in the Texas Colony

Austin returned to Texas, happy with his phenomenal success. He had been gone 15 months from his colonies while getting affairs straightened out in Mexico. He returned physically weary from much tedious traveling

and privation, but he persevered as always. But while he had been in Mexico all had not been running smoothly with the colonists. A number of them had returned to their original homes because of drought and the consequent scarcity of crops and game, but there were some new settlers who in spite of adversity did not lose faith.

Expedition Against Indians

Indian troubles also gave the first settlers considerable concern. The Karankawas along the coast were said to be cannibals who frequently feasted on the bodies of their victims. They were physically large men, and strong; they usually went barefooted and were ferocious, mean hunters. The Karankawas were hated and feared by the colonists. Austin, though a gentle and peaceable man by nature, was fully responsive when action was indicated. He led an expedition against the Karankawas in 1824, and eventually came to terms with them by negotiations, taming them down considerably.

Dipolomacy with Indians

Another menacing tribe, the Tonkawas, also gave Austin trouble. He led an expedition against them, when their braves stole a string of horses. Austin convinced their chief, Carita, that the horses should be returned and the thieves publicly whipped! This was shameful to the Tonkawas, and they ceased to be so bothersome to the colonists after this disgrace.

In fact, Austin had great success in dealing diplomatically with the Indians to secure peace. They seemed to trust him, and he was eventually successful in concluding peace treaties with the Tonkawas, the Karankawas, the Wacos and the Tahuacanos on the Brazos. He made it plain to them that if his settlers violated the treaties they would be punished, as would the offending treaty-breaking Indians. Oddly, the tribes kept their bargain with Austin reasonably well. To Austin's credit, he would and did definitely punish colonists who did not treat the Indians fairly.

Besides subduing the Indians, Austin surveyed land, walking miles over rough prairies and through wildernesses, measuring the "good earth." Austin is responsible for the first map of Texas because of these excursions. The establishment of the first town San Felipe de Austin, on the Brazos, furnished a capital for Austin's colony. It was built around a plaza.

Sacrifices Great and Small

Austin's home in San Felipe was a humble two-room log cabin. One room was his bedroom, the other his office. In keeping with his station, he could have built a fine, pretentious home, but as he wrote in his papers; "We are all poor in this country, and therefore all on an equality, and so long as this continues, we shall get on well and

Stephen Fuller Austin (1793-1836)

harmoniously." Stephen and his brother James lived in the humble dwelling. James was a great help to his brother and gave him a feeling of belonging to a family, as he was often lonely. He would have enjoyed making friends with certain of his colonists, but he realized this would provoke jealousies and disharmony. Always Austin took the long-range view and made sacrifices, great and small, for the good of the whole.

When it was possible, he sent for his mother, his sister Emily who was a widow, and her four children. He wanted to make a home for them all and warm his own heart with family joys and love. Just thinking about having his mother and sister near him gave him renewed vigor. But alas, his mother died and his sister remarried and decided to stay in Missouri, so, for the time being, he was still without much family life, and very lonely.

However, Austin's work engrossed him considerably. Colonists were flocking to Texas by the hundreds now and he wrote, in explaining his duties: "I have to receive in my household most of those who come to see the country preparatory to moving – entertaining them, spending days

and weeks, going over the land with them; to furnish them translations of the laws and explain them. After all this, when the colonist arrives with his family to settle, the law requires him to present a certificate of character. All these documents are in English or French and I have the labor of translating them into Spanish."

High Standards for His Colony

Austin was extremely particular about the character of his colonists. They were not the usual frontiersmen larded with roughnecks, gamblers, thieves or whoremongers. Here Austin showed much wisdom, realizing that colonists in Texas must be substantial, home-loving, industrious people of high character if the colonies were to become a success. He did not encourage war-like people in any respect. Too often, before, the warlike had tried to colonize and failed. Austin, as chief, had to maintain law and order. Upon his shoulders fell all this responsibility. The offenses among the colonists were mostly stealing, disturbing the peace and mistreating the Indians. These offenses were punished by fines, public whippings or banishment from the colony. Austin imported good people, but if some erred, they could not get by with it without retribution.

Protection Against Creditors

One of Austin's early problems was protecting his colonists from their creditors. Most of them were deeply in debt and had migrated to Texas for a new start. Austin knew that if the creditors were allowed to move in and claim the colonists' land, his small herd and few possessions, the colonies would fail. Thus this astute governor was instrumental in passing a law in 1829 that protected the debtor for 12 years; his home, land and equipment could not be seized during those years for the satisfaction of his debts. This gave the colonists time to accumulate enough to eventually pay what they owed. This law has been regarded as the foundation of the successive homestead exemption laws that are operative in Texas today, and set an example for laws of this kind in other states. Austin, however, never claimed the privilege of the debt exemption for himself, continuing to pay his family's creditors as and when he was able to do so.

The Slavery Issue

Another of Austin's early problems was the question of slavery. Mexico proscribed slavery, but the colonists from the South brought their slaves to work the fields and pick the cotton, and it is doubtful if they could have survived without their slave labor, or so they believed. Austin was never in any sense a dictator. He governed the colonies as justly and wisely as he knew how, but he was usually of the opinion that he knew what was best for his colonists. However, if he could not convince the greater number of colonists of his views, he usually accepted the decision of the majority, and it was thus in the question of slavery. He worked with the Mexican authorities to change the decree that forbade slavery in the colonies, and as a result of his efforts some compromises were made. The Texans were permitted by the Mexicans to keep the slaves they brought with them as lifetime "indentured servants," but their children were to be freed at 14 years of age.

Mexico Closes the Door

But Mexico lowered the boom in another area. There were so many Americans migrating to the new colonies that Mexico feared Texas would become a part of the United States – so they passed the Colonization Law of 6 April 1830, forbidding any further American immigration to Texas. This was a dreadful blow to Austin – he feared his colonization project would be lost. He started, again, to maneuver diplomatically. And again his tact and diplomacy won out, and the Law of 1830 was considerably shorn of its barbs. What Austin did was convince the Mexican government that the law should be applied only to colonies that were yet to be established. Realistically, this meant Americans could continue to migrate to the established colonies of which Austin was so proud. And his strategy proved correct. Other colonies struggling to establish themselves under the severely inhibiting Law of 1830 died, while Austin's established colonies flourished. Again the wisdom of Austin had saved his Texas colonies at a crucial time.

Stephen Close to Marriage?

During these years Austin worked without ever sparing himself, always mindful of his obligations. He was always lonely at heart, however. He was considerably devoted to his cousin, a widow named Molley Holley, to whom he wrote many of his most personal, heart-felt letters. Some surmised that he might marry the beautiful widow who visited his colonies, but destiny did not decree that he ever marry, nor have the happy rural life he so desired – farmland where he would work happily and feast his eyes on uncluttered horizons.

Sister Emily Comes to Texas

Austin's younger sister Emily finally came with her new second husband and children to live in the colonies near Austin, but she was not happy. The privations were too much for her and she complained bitterly, often blaming Austin for this state of affairs. Once Austin mildly reprimanded his sister, saying, "You let trifles too much influence you. A puncheon hut or an Indian camp is nothing, a mere trifle, when it is to be only a stepping place to get into a comfortable home and farm for life. Your removal to Texas will make you all independent, which would never have been in Missouri."

Austin's younger brother, James Elijah Brown Austin, born 3 October 1803 in the Missouri Territory, had gone to New Orleans on business and died while there of yellow fever on 24 August 1829. At the same time, in the colonies, Austin, too, nearly died and was unconscious for days. His friends feared for his life also, but he finally recovered to continue his wearying, strenuous activities. Twice in but a few years he nearly died.

Stephen's Splendid Uniform

It is written that Austin was an unassuming man, seldom seeking publicity or acclaim, preferring to colonize quietly without a blowing of trumpets. But a very human part of his personality was revealed in a letter he wrote to his sister's husband who was, at that time, coming out to Texas. He asked for materials for a new uniform for himself! "Uniform that of Colonel of Infantry in the Mexican Army, with gold epaulets and gold or yellow mounted sword. I must have a sword, a sash, and belt – yellow mounted. I also want a military surtout [a long, close-fitting overcoat – Editor] with a standing collar, handsomely though plainly trimmed with a black silk cord and pantaloons trimmed in the same manner – all of navy blue cloth. Also a scarlet westcott with gold round cord on the edges, a pair of boots, and yellow spurs. As I am the highest militia officer in Texas, it is expected I provide myself with these things."

The Texas Colonies Prosper

In 1829 the colony was seven years old and Austin realized it had really taken root. There were about 30,000 Americans in Texas then. There were almost a dozen towns and trade was prospering by land and sea; the ports were busy with migrating pioneers and roads had been built so supplies could be taken from the colony to ships for export. Most settlers farmed and the land proved fruitful. Stock raising was also an important industry and Austin started the first stock farm of the colony in San Felipe. There was little this man could not do. He had established the colonies, made land grants, surveyed the land, protected debtors, maintained a modified slavery for some of his colonists, subdued the hostile Indians, handed down decrees for law and order, kept down religious differences and persecutions, kept out undesirable colonists, worked as none other had ever been able to work with the Mexican government in such matters.

Independent Mexican State Sought

But new problems arose! The colonists, ultimately, did not like living under Mexican rule. They wanted their own laws, their own judges. They had been part of the State of Coahuila since 1824. Coahuila was across the Rio Grande and was like a "foreign" country, different from the Texas colonies. The colonists sought their own independent

Mexican state. The Mexicans had promised the colonists such freedom as soon as they were strong enough and able to rule themselves. The colonists felt the time had come. They even called a convention in 1832 and another in 1833 to air their grievances. Austin feared that Mexico would not approve of these conventions and he was right! Even the Mexicans from San Antonio were fearful lest the Mexican government consider these conventions held for Texas Statehood an insult. San Antonio at this time was the capital of Texas and the oldest, most populated town in the country.

Reluctant Trip to Mexico City

Finally, after much dickering on the part of the colonists, Austin was more or less drafted to go to Mexico City to acquaint the government there with the new constitution the colonists had adopted for their proposed Mexican State. Austin did not want to go. He yearned to devote some time to his private business affairs and improve a farm for himself, but as always, he put himself last and his duty to his colonists first. Thus it was that Austin, after ten years, was on his way again to Mexico City. He traveled partly by mule and partly by boat. It was a long, tiresome trip that exacted much of Austin's already failing strength.

Caught in Cholera Epidemic

He arrived in Mexico City three months later on 18 July 1833, only to find a terrible epidemic of cholera taking lives by the hundreds. When he arrived in the city, Austin was already ill from a mild attack of the terrible disease. Luckily, he had taken a remedy that probably saved his life. Of the epidemic in Mexico City Austin wrote, "I never witnessed such a horrible scene of distress and death." When the cholera epidemic died down Austin took his petition for Texas Statehood to Congress; he also tried to obtain the repeal of the 1830 Colonization Law. For a while it looked as if he would fail. Fortunately, Santa Anna, the President of Mexico at that time, returning from a victorious battle just then, supported many of Austin's demands. Thus Congress repealed the hated Colonization Law, but they would not yet grant Texas Statehood.

Thrown into Prison

Austin set out for his colonies, happy, at least, over the repeal of the hated law. Maybe at last he could settle down and improve his own little farm and have some restful home life. En route to his beloved colonies, however, Austin was arrested at Saltillo because of a letter he had written in the past to the San Antonians, requesting them to assume the lead in forming a Mexican State government. The Mexicans considered this an attempt to instigate a revolt. Ironically, Austin had written it really to squelch a revolt, not to start one. His intention was not considered, now, and he was escorted back to Mexico City to be

imprisoned in the worst prison in Mexico City, the old stone prison of the dreaded Spanish Inquisition. He was confined in a small stone cell not knowing if he were to be shot or imprisoned for life. He had nothing to read, nothing with which to write, and his health was seriously impaired by the dampness.

The Texans did not come to his aid. In fact, in his absence the rumor was spread that he was enormously wealthy from his colonization efforts. In actuality, he was very poor and could not even have bought his freedom from prison. Austin was imprisoned nine months by the Mexican government, with not a word from his colonists. One can easily imagine his despair and heartache.

Released On Bail After Nine Months

Then out of the blue, one day, two Texas lawyers, Peter Grayson and Spencer Jack, came with a petition from Texas stating that Austin was acting as their representative with no intention of starting a rebellion in San Antonio. The petition urged his immediate release and eventually, as a result of these lawyers' pleading on his behalf, he was released on bail.

His trial never came to pass. Instead he was freed on 22 June 1835 under a law the Congress passed pardoning all political prisoners in Mexico. While out on bail had been permitted to enjoy the gala events of Mexico. Many prominent citizens, feeling sorry about his imprisonment, tried to make it up to him by inviting him to their luxurious homes. Moreover, Austin was now in ill health and had aged beyond his years. He still yearned for home life and peace, without the responsibility of so many colonists.

Mexican Dictator Seizes Power

But Santa Anna now became a menace to Austin's colonies, so there would be no rest. In the Spring of 1834 Santa Anna overthrew the Mexican Republic and set himself up as a dictator. He was a cruel ruler, having punished one of the resisting Mexican states by burning its cities, looting the homes and shooting the leaders. Austin realized what the Texans would have to endure if they objected to Santa Anna's leadership. Obviously Texas would be punished next. Texans would not submit to Santa Anna's tyranny without war.

Texans Seek Austin's Leadership

Austin had always sought peace for his colonies and encouraged friendship with Mexico. Sam Houston, a newcomer to Texas, and William B. Travis, a young lawyer, thought Austin too conservative in dealing with the Mexicans. Now, after his imprisonment, Austin knew that the Mexicans under Santa Anna could not be trusted. So he returned to Texas realizing the decision for war or peace rested upon him. His welcome home was over-whelming. As one patriot wrote, "Your coming would always have been hailed by the people as the coming of a father, but your coming at this time is doubly dear to the people of Texas." William B. Travis wrote in a letter to Austin "All eyes are turned to you. Texas can be wielded by you and you alone and her destiny is now in your hands."

Declaration of War with Mexico

Austin accordingly made a speech upon his homecoming – and it was a declaration of war with Mexico. He went to Gonzales and was made Commander-in-Chief of about 400 men gathered to organize a Texas army. He did not want this position; he was a man of peace and he felt he could do more for Texas in getting money for food and equipment. The army had no uniforms and most men wore western gear – buckskin pants, moccasins and coonskin caps. They did not even have regular ammunition, and traveled on foot or rode mules and mustangs. It was a raw, undisciplined army, but it grew to nearly a thousand, unafraid to face Santa Anna's multitudes. Austin led them to San Antonio and had several skirmishes en route. But outside San Antonio, Austin's brief military career ended.

Seeking United States Support

The Convention had selected him as a member of the commission to go to the United States to raise money for the war and he was happy to do so. He was so weak and sick he could not mount his horse alone to set out for his journey. His nephew, Moses, helped him mount. When he was in the saddle Austin smiled. "When you think about it," he sad, half sad, half joking, "it's a pretty sorry thing that the Commander-in-Chief of the Texas Army is so weak... that he can't mount his horse by himself." Moses reached up and took his uncle's hand. "When you think about it," he said, "it's a pretty magnificent thing."

Speeches Pursuade Bankers

Austin and other Texans set out to raise money in the United States for the war. It was the year 1834 and this was a life-or-death matter, money had to be raised to support the Texas armies. It would not be easy – bankers would not be anxious to loan money on the uncertain future of Texas. Austin and his supporters went to Washington and New York bankers, made speeches at dinners for the Texans in their struggle. The mission was more successful than anticipated. Thousands of dollars were borrowed for the supplies and equipment for the Texans.

Goliad and Alamo Massacres

During this time the tragic fall of the Alamo occurred where every Texas defender died fighting rather than surrender. There was also the terrible massacre at Goliad and the retreat of Sam Houston's army before the soldiers

of Santa Anna. Sometimes bankers doubted the future of Texas in the face of such tragic losses, but Austin was so confident of victory that he pledged all his own land as security for the money he borrowed.

After the fall of the Alamo he wrote; "My heart and soul are sick, but my spirit is unbroken. Santa Anna has raised the bloody flag of a pirate – the fate of pirates will sooner or later be his fate. Texas will rise again!"

Texas Independence Won

And true to Austin's prediction Texas did rise again. Santa Anna surrendered to Sam Houston at San Jacinto. Texas Independence was won, but Texas needed more money to carry on its affairs and business men wondered whether Mexico would rise up against Texas again.

Gaining Texas Recognition

Austin was instrumental in using Santa Anna to gain Texas recognition by the United States. While Santa Anna was a prisoner, Austin persuaded him to write a letter to President Jackson stating that Mexico could not conquer Texas – and the U.S. should recognize her as independent. Santa Anna was actually sent to the United States to convince the President that Mexico had no further claim on Texas. After that Santa Anna was given his freedom and permitted to return to Mexico. This strategy of Austin's, at first criticized by many, staved off another Mexican invasion and made it possible for the United States to recognize the independence of Texas.

Defeated for Texas Presidency

Austin ran for the job of first President of the Republic of Texas, though he was ill and did not seek the job on his own. All he wanted was peace on a little farm. However, he was convinced that it was his duty. History tells us he was defeated by General Sam Houston, military hero at San Jacinto, who ran against him.

Appointed Secretary of State

General Houston asked Austin to be his Secretary of State, the most difficult position in the new Republic. Austin at first refused, but then assumed it as a duty. Once again he put aside his personal hopes and dreams, to serve as the first Secretary of State of the Republic of Texas.

Austin was happy in this work, but remained exhausted and ill. As he wrote: "I have no house, not a roof in all Texas I can call my own. I make my home where the business of the country calls me; I have spent the prime of my life and worn out my constitution in trying to colonize this country. What I have been able to realize in actual means has gone – where my health and strength and time have gone, which is in the service of Texas – I am therefore not ashamed of my poverty."

Stephen Dies Awaiting Statehood

Austin developed pneumonia on a Christmas in his 43rd year. Because his bedroom was so cold, he lay on a pallet before the fireplace in his office. Before he died, he spoke deliriously saying happily: "Texas Recognized." However, it was still some months before the United States would recognize Texas. Stephen Fuller Austin died on 27 December 1836 and was buried in Peach Point, Brazoria County, Texas.

Truly the "Father of Texas"

Stephen Austin's work was done quietly, without fanfare and big talk. So much so that he scarcely attracted even the attention of his contemporaries. Yet the great work of Austin – and his father, Moses – is responsible for the first American colonization of Texas, and from this resulted the Texan revolution, the annexation of Texas, the Mexican War and the acquisition of the Southwest below the 42nd parallel from the Rio Grande to the Pacific.

Texans will not forget Stephen Fuller Austin. On the banks of the Colorado, where he yearned to build a home but never did, is the city of Austin. This capital of Texas is named for Stephen, and where he hoped to found an academy is the University of Texas.

On 18 October 1910 Stephen F. Austin's body was disinterred from Peach Point. His remains lay in state for two days in the Capitol rotunda before they were moved with great fanfare to the highest point in the Texas State Cemetery in Austin. His tomb is surmounted by a handsome bronze statue of "The Father of Texas."

REFERENCE MATERIALS

Stephen F. Austin's Legacies, by W. E. Long of Austin, Texas.

Stephen F. Austin, Father of Texas, by C. Beals, published by McGraw-Hill, 1953.

The Descendants of Richard Austin of Charlestown, Massachusetts, by Edith Austin Moore and William Allen Day. Privately published in 1969.

The Encyclopedia Americana, Americana Corporation, Danbury, Connecticut.

The Encyclopedia Britannica, William Benton, Publisher, 1973.

Compton's Encyclopedia, published by the F. E. Compton Company.

Dictionary of American Biography, published by Charles Scribner & Sons, New York.

Encyclopedia of American Biographies, published by Harper and Rowe, New York, 1974.

Story of the Great American West, published by the Reader's Digest Association, Inc., 1977

AUSTIN BAPTISMS FROM 1836 TO 1875

IN THE PROTESTANT CHURCHES OF

MONTREAL, QUEBEC, CANADA

by Michael Edward Austin

Editor's Note: The following records were copied from microfilms of the original Montreal church records at the Provincial Archives in Trois Rivieres, in the Province of Quebec, Canada. A capital 'X' indicates the person could not write, but instead made his or her 'mark.' The numbers in brackets following each record indicate the church (the churches are listed on page 301) and page number on which the record appears. A few death and marriage records were also discovered, and these have been included here as well.

Thomas Son of Thomas Austin and Mary his Wife was born at St. Helens 8th April & Baptized 24th April 1842. Sponsors: John X Hannah, Margaret X Hannah, William X Hannah. By Me (sic). [1-3]

Arthur Henry James Son of Thomas Austin a Private Soldier in the fourth Battalion of the Sixtieth Royal Rifles and of Emily Rogers his wife was born on the fifteenth day of October in the year One thousand eight hundred and Sixty four and was baptized on the Eleventh day of December immediately following by me F H W Bartlett Chaplain to the Forces. Sponsors: James Dempster, James Pette?, Elizabeth Dempster. [1-39]

Sidney Kate daughter of Henry H. Austin, Bookkeeper, & of Anna E. Dougherty his wife was born on the twenty-first day of November Eighteen Hundred & Fifty Nine & was Baptized on the fifth day of June Eighteen Hundred & Sixty-two. By me, Wm. Bond. Sponsors: Sidney F. Austin, Elizabeth Morris [7-11]

Maud Elizabeth daughter of Henry H. Austin, Book keeper, & of Anna E. Dougherty his wife was born on the twenty fourth day of April, Eighteen Hundred & Sixty-two & was baptized on the fifth day of June of the same year by me, Wm. Bond. Sponsors: F. I.(J.?) Austin, S. S. Austin [7-11]

Mary Violett daughter of Henry H. Austin, Book keeper, & of Eliza Anna Dougherty his wife was born on [the] Eighteenth day of December One Thousand Eight-Hundred and Sixty-three & was Baptized on the nineteenth day of January One thousand Eight Hundred and Sixty-four. By me, Wm. Bond. Sponsors: S. S. Austin, W. Austin [7-3]

Thomas, son of Thomas Austin, Labourer, died on the twenty first and was Buried on the twenty third day of March One Thousand Eight Hundred and Sixty Eight, aged four months and twenty two days. By me, E. Sullivan. Witnesses: Wells? Parker, Thos. Austin [7-?]

Augusta Margurite daughter of Henry Hamilton Austin Accountant & of Anna Eliza Dougherty his wife, was born on the first day of July One Thousand Eight Hundred and Sixty-Seven and was Baptized on the twenty-third day of July One Thousand Eight Hundred and Sixty Eight. By me, Wm Bond. Sponsors: E. B. M. Austin, Emily Darraerth?, A. E. Austin (proxy for Lillian Weilland) [7-20]

On the thirty first day of October one thousand eight hundred & sixty I baptized Ada Maud, daughter of Capt [torn] Austin & Ada his wife, residing in the Parish of Chambly, born on the first day of August this same year. [Signed by] J. P. White, Rector. Sponsors: Hugh Austin (proxy for Hon. Mr. J. J. Bery and Sir Fred Abbott), Ada Austin, (proxy for Hon Mrs. Bery and Lady Abbott). Parents: Hugh Austin, Ada Austin [8-11]

On the eighteenth day of December one thousand Eight Hundred and Sixty I baptized privately Augustus Frederick son of Augustus Bruce Austin Esqr. residing in the Parish of Chambly, & of Ellen his wife, born on the twenty-first day of September this same year. [By] J. P. White, Rector. Witnesses to Baptism: Wyndham B. Austin, Ellen L. B. Austin [8-13]

On the tenth day of March one thousand Eight hundred & sixty three I baptised privately Wyndham Bruce, son of Wyndham B. Austin Esqr. & of Ellen his wife, residing in the Parish, born on the 9th day of January this same year. [By] J. P. White, Rector, Witnesses to Baptism: Bisdfehm? Bencrdy? X, Wyndham Bruce Austin [8-7]

Constance May, daughter of Hugh Austin, and of his wife, Ada, by her maiden name Cox, both of the Parish of Chambly, was born on the fifteenth day of April, and was baptized on the twenty ninth day of June, in the year of Our Lord, One thousand eight hundred and sixty three, by me, Henry James Petry, Rector. Sponsors: Harriet Cox for Mary Jane Korlau?, Wyndham B. Austin, Charlotte Austin for Ellen Austin [8-6]

William Winchester, son of Wyndham Bruce Austin, and of his Wife Ellen by her maiden name Winchester was born [blank space] and privately baptized on the fifteenth day of June in the year of our Lord, one thousand, eight hundred and sixty four, by me, Henry James Petry, B. A., Rector. [Present:] Wyndham Bruce Austin, Ellen L. B. Austin [8-5]

Charlotte DeClare daughter of Capt Austin and Ada his wife by her maiden name Cox was born on the fifteenth day of June One thousand eight hundred and sixty eight and was baptized on the twenty-third day of May One thousand eight hundred and sixty nine by me, F. Thorndike, Rector. Parents: Hugh H. Austin, Ada Austin Sponsors: F. Thorndike, Eliza M. Yrele?, Emily Thorndike proxy for Harriet Cox. [8-8]

James Alexander Austin, son of James Austin of Montreal, Shoemaker, and of Sophia Lorangen his wife, was born on the fourth day of January, in the year of our Lord One thousand eight hundred and fifty and baptized this eleventh day of February One thousand eight hundred and fifty one. [Signed by] W. Taylor, Min., James Austin. Witness: Carter, Pears. [5-4]

Samuel Taylor Austin, son of James Austin of Montreal, Shoemaker, and of Sophia Larougie his wife, was born on the fourth day of January, in the year of Our Lord One thousand eight hundred and fifty two, and was baptised on this eighteeth day of July of the same year. [Signed] James Austin. Witnesses: John L. Becket, James Poet. W. Taylor, D. D. Min. [5-15]

Benjamin Francis Austin, son of James Austin of Montreal, Shoemaker, and of Sophia Larougie his wife, was born on the seventh day of January in the year of Our Lord One thousand eight hundred and fifty four, and baptised on the twelfth day of March of the same year. [Signed] James Austin, [and witnesses] James Poet, John C. Becket. [5-5]

Charles Austin son of James Austin of Montreal, Shoemaker, and of Sophia Loranger his wife, born on the twelfth day of February in the year of Our Lord One thousand and eight hundred and fifty six, was baptised on the first day of June of the same year. [Signed by] James Austin. Witnesses: John C. Becket, R. S. Oliver, W. Taylor, D. D. Min. [5-18]

Charles Andrew Austin, son of James Austin of Montreal, Shoemaker, died on the twenty-third day of December in the year of Our Lord One thousand eight hundred and fifty eight, aged two years and ten months, and was buried this twenty fourth day of the same month, in presence of these witnesses. [Signed by] W. Taylor, D. D. Min., James Austin Witnesses: John Harold, George Danyels [5-25]

Matilda Sophia Austin, daughter of James Austin of Montreal, Shoemaker, and of Sophia Larronge his wife, born on the twenty second day of May, in the year of Our Lord One thousand eight hundred and fifty eight was baptised this eighth day of August of the same year. [Signed by] W. Taylor, D. D. Min., James Austin. Witnesses: George Ragers, Warden King [5-16]

John, son of Private John Austin Co. No 10 Royal Canadian Rifles, & of Julia his wife by her maiden name Cowan, born at Niagara C. W. June 3rd 1847 privately baptized at Toronto C. W. June 12th 1847, was received into the Congregation of Christ's flock June 27th in the year of our Lord one thousand eight hundred and forty seven by me, Fredk Robinson, Deacon. Sponsors: William Calais, Daniel Jone?, Ellen Geirney?, In the presence of John Austin the father. [See also next record] [4-4]

John, infant son of Private John Austin, Company Number Ten, Royal Canadian Rifles, having died July twenty seventh in the year of our Lord one thousand eight hundred and forty seven, was buried on the following day. By me, Fredk Robinson, In the presence of John Scott, John Sutherland Le Seyient [Seyiant?], John Austin father [4-8]

James Austin, son of John Austin, private in the detachment of the Ms Royal Canadian Rifles, stationed at Coteau Du Lac, & of Julia, his wife, by her maiden name Cowan, born on the twenty eighth day of July in the year of our Lord One thousand eight hundred & forty eight, was baptised on the sixth day of the month following by me, Jacob J. S. Mountain, Mipy at Coteau du Lac. Sponsors: John Austin father, Julia X Austin mother, Deh? Jones [4-9]

Margaret Jane, daughter of James Austin, Cordwainer of the village of St. Georges in the parish of Montreal, and Sophia Laronger his wife, was born on the nineteenth day of January, and was baptised on the Seventh day of December, one thousand eight hundred and forty three. [Signed by] Caleb Strong, Min., James Austin, Sophia X Laronger, David Dobie, Wm Clark [2-21]

John Alexander Son of James Austin of the city of Montreal, shoemaker, and Sophia Lorange his wife was born on the eighteenth day of April One thousand eight hundred and forty seven and was baptized on the twenty sixth day of January One thousand eight hundred and forty eight by me, John McLoud Minr. [Signed by] James Austin, [and witnesses] Sophia X Lorange, Elizabeth X Kennedy. [See also next record] [2-2]

John Alexander son of James Austin of the city of Montreal, shoemaker, died on the twenty ninth, and was buried at Montreal on the thirty-first day of January One thousand eight hundred and forty eight by me, John McLoud, Min. [Signed by] James Austin, [and witnesses] Sophia X Lorange, Elizabeth X Kennedy. [See also the previous record] [2-2]

This Certifies That William Austin, of the City of Montreal, widower, and Minnie Bradshaw of the City of Montreal, Spinster, were married by the authority of Special License, on the seventeenth day of February, Eighteen hundred and Sixty four, in the presence of the subscibing witnesses, & me. [Signed by] N. F. Bland, Minister. [Witnesses] William Riley, John Stern [9-19]

This Certifies That Eva Jane Bradshaw, daughter of William Austin and Minnie Gertrude Bradshaw, his wife, born in Montreal on the fourth day of June, Eighteen hundred and sixty five, was baptized by me, on the third day of October for the same year. [Signed by] N. F. Bland, Minister. Witnesses: Wm Austin, B. G. Austin. [9-19]

Susan Margaret Moore Austin daughter of John Austin and Mary Ann Griffin his wife, was born on the Tenth day of February A. D. One Thousand Eight hundred and Fifty seven and was baptized on the Tenth of April in the same year. By me, G. Young, Minister, in presence of Mary Ann Austin, George Anderson.　　　　　　　　　　　　[6-13]

On the twenty eighth day August one thousand eight hundred and sixty Riley C. Austin of St. Albans, Vermont, Bachelor, and Alisia Sarshorm? of Richmond C. E. parish were united in Matrimony by authority of License in presence of subscribing Witnesses. [signed by] E. H. Dewart, Minister [and witness] Matilda Dewart　　　[6-?]

William Henry Austin file de James Austin originaire de Rilkeel conte de Dowv an Grlande (Europe) et de Zephyie Loranger son espose est nee a 1st Henry district de Montreal le six Mars mil huit cent guarante cinq (1845) ct a ete baptise le vingt Janvier ml huit cent guarante six (1846) [signed] J. E. Farmer [present:] James Austin, Marque de Z. Austin nee Loranger, Louis Maris　　[3-2]

Margaret Jane, daughter of John Austin private in Her Majesty's 93 Regiment of Highlanders and Julia Cowan His wife was born on the thirteenth and Baptized on the fifteenth day of April One Thousand Eight Hundred and Forty five by me. [signed by] Alex Mathieson D. D. Min. [in presence of] John Austin, R. Pollock　　　[10-32]

Caroline daughter of John Austin and of his wife Mary C. Connon was born in the fourteenth day of April Eighteen hundred and sixty nine and was privately baptized on the [blank] day of May and was admitted in to the Church on [blank]. By me Millrefoun? Caulfield? Parents: John Austin, Mary Austin. Sponsors: Baroline English, Alise Grey, James Austin　　　　　　　　[11-9]

1954 June 12 John Ritchie ([son of] Colin W. & Rachel Pinsonneault) mj. [major (vs. minor)] in the Cathederal Gwendolyn-Marie Austin, caissiere [cashier], mj. ([dau. of] J.-Alphonse & Ada- Marie Schoupp).　　　　　　[12]

1956 August 18 Stanley Crinall, mj. ([son of] x Stanley & June Blackburn) married Veronica Austin, mj ([dau. of] x Andrew & Catherine Durbin) of Liverpool, England [the x's here mean deceased]　　　　　　　[12]

MONTREAL CHURCH REFERENCES

[1] Garrison Anglican Church　　　[7] St. George Anglican Church

[2] American Presbyterian Church　　[8] Chambly Anglican Church

[3] Evangelical French Congr. Ch.　　[9] East End Methodist Church

[4] Coteau du Lac Church　　　　[10] St. Andrew Presbyterian Church

[5] Erskine Presbyterian Church　　[11] St. Stephens Anglican Church

[6] Methodist Mountain Church　　[12] St. Cecile Parish, Trois-Rivieres

QUERIES

301-1. Caleb Austin was born circa 1777 in New Hampshire. He is neither the Caleb Austin who married Molly McColley nor the Caleb Austin who married Clarissa Peterson Brooks, although both were born about the same time as my Caleb. He is believed to have migrated with his parents to Canada at an early age. He was in the New York 1810 Census with three little boys and a wife Lydia (Parker). She was born in Connecticut circa 1784. They had two more boys and two girls, the last one born in Meigs County, Ohio in 1820. Lydia died in 1850 and Caleb married a second time to Elizabeth Ryon in 1852. Seeking both the ancestry and descendants of Caleb Austin.

301-2. Elihu Austin married Catherine —. Their son Lyman L. Austin was born in Connecticut in 1799. They moved to Oswego County, New York in the early 1800's. Lyman married Pauline Reed circa 1820. Seeking the ancestry of Elihu and all his descendants.

301-3. Elizabeth Austin born 5 September 1810 in Virginia, Tennessee, or Kentucky and buried in Smith Cemetery, White County, Illinois, near New Haven. She married circa 1826 to James Davis, possibly born in Virginia circa 1800-10, he was killed by a horse. The 1880 Census of Evansville, Vanderburgh County, Indiana, lists Elizabeth as 69 born in Tennessee, her father and mother both born in Virginia living in the home of her son Thompson having been widowed for the second time. On 24 May 1856 Elizabeth signed a relinquishment of her "right of dower" in Butler County when she and husband sold a property there. The land adjoined that of G. Austin. Was it property she had inherited from her first husband, or was in a dowry from her first marriage? Was she of the Butler County Austins? Seeking all information on Elizabeth's ancestry.

301-4. Malinda/Melinda/Matilda Austin was probably born circa 1839, somewhere in Canada. She lived in Franklin and Boscawen, New Hampshire, and possibly in Wilmot, Springfield or Andover, New Hampshire. She married Louis A. Bassett. They had at least three childen: Albert A., Charles A., & Edward Louis. I need to know her correct full name, the places and dates of her birth, marriage and death, and any information available on her ancestry or her descendants.

301-5. Pardon Austin married Rhoda Stanton in 1793. Their daughter Jane A. Austin was born in 1810 in Middletown, Delaware Co., New York. She married Adoniram Sanford. Pardon Austin was listed in the 1800 Census of Middletown along with his wife and four children. They were not named. Also listed were the George Sherman family, Samuel Hull family and the Aaron Hull family. I need to know the ancestry of Pardon and his descendants.

SOME DESCENDANTS OF
JOHN AND JOAN AUSTEN OF
HORSMONDEN IN COUNTY KENT

by William Austen Leigh
and Montagu George Knight

Editor's Note: This article is taken from Chapter VII of the authors' book, *Chawton Manor and Its Owners, A Family History*, published in 1911 by Smith, Elder & Company, 15 Waterloo Place, London. It was contributed to *Austins of America* by Associate Editor Sally Austin Day.

The family of Austen had been long settled in Kent; and the particular branch of it with which we are concerned emerges into notice early in the seventeenth century at Horsmonden in that county. There are brasses in the church of that parish to John Austen, who died in 1620, and to Joan his wife. Joan had died in 1604, after giving birth to twins who came at the end of a long family. She met her death, says the inscription, 'often utteringe these speeches, Let neither husband nor children, nor lands nor goods, separate me from my God.'

As to 'lands' we can say nothing more definite than that in the course of the seventeenth century the Austens became possessed of the two small manor houses of Broadford and Grovehurst in Horsmonden parish, both of which their descendants still own. Broadford is a picturesque Elizabethan residence of very moderate size, standing just above the valley. A large room on the first floor is completely panelled with oak (now whitewashed), and contains over the fireplace and elsewhere the alternate rose and carnation which are supposed to mark the Tudor age. Over the fireplace in the entrance-hall are the Austen arms, with the date 1587. When they were placed there is not known, but the date given must be anterior to the Austens' possession of Broadford. Grovehurst is about three-quarters of a mile from Broadford, and at the top of the hill. The north front of the house exhibits a charming assemblage of gables, with rough-cast below.

The Austens, no doubt, made their money as clothiers, and the rollers used in the exercise of that trade may still be seen attached to the ceiling of one of the upper rooms at Broadford. The John Austens (they were nearly always christened 'John') of that century evidently desired to take their place as squires of the county, and with the one who died, after a long reign, in 1705 this must have been a dominating motive of action. He contented himself, however, with occupying the smaller of his two houses, viz. Grovehurst; while his son, another John, on his marriage with Elizabeth Weller in 1693, was installed at Broadford.

The elder John seems to have been something of a Tartar, or at all events to have liked ruling his family as well as upholding his position; John the younger must have been easy-going and careless, and possibly pleasure-loving. He died of consumption in 1704, and his poor wife was left in a position the difficulties of which she afterwards unfolded to her children in a memorandum still extant.

She had one daughter and six sons to maintain, and it transpired that her husband had left behind him considerable debts, of some of which she had been ignorant. She cast around for the means of paying them, and naturally appealed in the first instance to her 'father Austen.' He began by refusing her petition so positively that it seemed as if no expedient would be left her but a sale of her furniture. Later on, however, he said he would give her £200; not enough to pay the debts, but leaving (after taking credit for certain assets) only a small sum to make up. John the elder had just arranged to do this, when he fell ill and died. It might have been thought that Elizabeth's position would be improved by this event; but it appeared that the old man had tied up the estate tightly in favour of her eldest little boy; while the executors held that they had no right to pay her the promised £200, as to which no legally binding arrangement had been concluded before the father's death.

She did, however, eventually manage to pay off the debts by the sale of a leasehold house (which seems to have been in her own power), and a few valuables, and she lived on four more years at Broadford with the children: Betty, Jack, Frank, Tom, Will, Robin, and Stephen. Then the question of education began to be urgent; there was none to be got at Horsmonden. So she decided to move to Sevenoaks ('Sennocks,' she called it) and to take a roomy house within reach of its grammar school. There she was to board the schoolmaster and some of his pupils. Her accounts go down to the time when her boys were beginning to go out into the world; but she died in 1720, too soon to see the success which, on the whole, attended them.

Jack, the Squire, had been taken off her hands when she moved to Sevenoaks. Frank was a solicitor at Tonbridge and Sevenoaks who eventually amassed a considerable fortune. While his two next brothers, Tom and Will (both of whom had adopted the medical profession) were marrying young, and on small incomes, he remained single, and acted as a good uncle to his nephews. In later life he married twice; one of his grandsons by his first marriage was Colonel Thomas Austen M.P. for Kent, whose second wife was a sister of Cardinal Manning; a grandson of the second family, Rev. John Thomas Austen, was Senior Wrangler in 1817. Soon after the beginning of the nineteenth century the line of John Austen of Broadford came to an end, and the Horsmonden estate came into the possession of Frank's descendants, who still hold it. Of Frank's brothers, Tom the doctor, married, and has left descendants in the female line, and Stephen became a

well-known bookseller and publisher in London. Concerning Robin, history is silent; he probably died young.

William (the fourth brother), whose fortunes particularly concern us, was a surgeon. His profession seems to have given him an introduction into medical circles, for his wife was daughter of one M.D. and widow of another. Born in 1701, William must have married when he was twenty-seven or twenty-eight, and he seems to have chosen discreetly. Rebecca Walter was the daughter of Sir George Hampson, a doctor who had succeeded to a baronetcy, which his descendants still hold. By her first husband, Dr. Walter, she had a son, who remained on intimate terms with his half-brother and half-brother's family.

Judging from the character of her son, George Austen, we may guess that Rebecca was a woman of force and intellect, but unfortunately she died in giving birth to her fourth child and third daughter in 1732-3. The eldest daughter died in infancy, the youngest unmarried. The father only lived till 1737. How the children – George, Philadelphia and Leonora – were brought up we do not exactly know; but, at any rate, George was befriended by his uncle Frank and sent to Tonbridge School, whence he got a scholarship at St. John's College, Oxford. He became a Fellow of his College, and from his striking appearance was well known in the University as the 'Handsome Proctor.' It is a curious coincidence that by his marriage his descendants became entitled to hold – and more than one of them did hold – Fellowships at St. John's College, as Founder's kin.

His sister Philadelphia went out to India in the adventurous manner often adopted by portionless girls in the early days of the English occupation, and married a friend of Warren Hastings.

We must now return to Elizabeth Weller and her brothers-in-law. One of them, the husband of a Jane Austen, was Stephen Stringer of Triggs in the parish of Goudhurst. The Wellers and the Stringers, like the Austens, seem to have been familes who were stepping from trade into the ownership of land; Stephen Stringer was High Sheriff of Kent in 1708. Of the five daughters of Stephen and Jane Stringer, one, Mary, married her cousin John Austen, another, Hannah, married William Monke. The Monkes were people of property near Shoreham, distantly related to George, Duke of Albemarle, and descended from the ancient family of Le Moine, of Powdridge in Devonshire. It was therefore quite in the natural order of things that their daughter, Jane, should become the wife of the owner of Godmersham, Thomas Brodnax, afterwards Knight. Mr. Knight was thus second cousin by marriage to George Austen, and he acknowledged his cousinship by presenting him to the rectory of Steventon in Hants, which he had inherited, as part of the Lewkenor property, from Mrs.

Reverend George Austen (1731-1805). He was the Rector of Steventon, near Basingstoke, from 1761.

Elizabeth Knight. His son was destined to be a still greater benefactor to one of his Steventon cousins.

George Austen, to whom we have now returned, was evidently a fine specimen of the parson of the eighteenth century, a class of whom hard things have often been said. Striking and refined in appearance, cultured in his tastes, beneficent, and attentive to is clerical duties, he must have attracted regard and affection wherever he was known. Like many of the family, he married with discretion. Cassandra Leigh, daughter of the Rector of Harpsden near Henley, and granddaughter of Theophilus Leigh of Adlestrop, was vigorous, lively, and shrewd. She had a large family and lived to an advanced age. Her husband not only educated his own sons at home, but also took pupils; and with these to care for, and not infrequent guests, Cassandra's time must have been fully occupied.

Hers, as we have seen, was the deciding voice which sent their son Edward to pay that visit to the last Mr. and Mrs. Thomas Knight (the Mr. Thomas Knight whose father had settled the Austens at Steventon) which had such important results to the boy. But his adoption by his patrons must have been a gradual affair. They can only have been married a very short time when he first attracted their notice, and the idea of adopting a distant cousin as their heir would not arise till some time afterwards.

Many years later Edward Austen's niece, Caroline Austen, wrote down her reminiscences of what her uncle Henry had told her in 1848 concerning his brother Edward's early life. Henry Austen could not remember the exact date of the invitation to his brother to go to Godmersham. Indeed, he evidently ante-dated it considerably in his own mind. But, his niece adds, 'he was very clear as to the purport of the discourse which he heard between his Father and Mother on the morning when they received a letter from Godmersham, begging that little Edward might spend his Holidays there.

There was a pleasant exchange of letters and presents between Prince Maximilian of Saxony and 'Edward Knight, *ci-devant* Austen.' After his return from an educational tour which included Rome, Edward was no doubt more completely under the protection of his kind friends at Godmersham, and accepted as their eventual heir; and it was under their auspices that he married in 1791 Elizabeth, daughter of Sir Brook Bridges and was settled in a house called Rowling, belonging to the Bridges family and situated near Goodnestone. The lovely features of Mrs. Edward Austen have been preserved to the family in a beautiful miniature by Cosway, along with a miniature of her husband, taken in his old age.

The death of Mr. Thomas Knight in 1794 put Edward Austen at once in a more prominent position and opened the prospect of a further advancement. The whole of the estates, both in Kent and Hants, subject to the life interest of Mrs. Knight, were devised to him. In 1799 Mrs. Knight, in a spirit of rare generosity, resigned everything to him, reserving only to herself an annuity of £2000, and retired to a house in Canterbury. She continued to bestow on him the interest and affection of a mother. She survived his own wife, who died at the birth of her eleventh child in 1808. Mrs. Knight lived on till 1812, and it was not till after her death that Edward Austen took the name of Knight.

In 1801 Edward had served as High Sheriff of Kent, and he continued for nearly half a century to take an active part in local county business, though he shrank from entering on a political career, and consistently declined any suggestion that he should offer himself as a candidate for Parliament; nor did he encourage any political ambitions that his sons may have entertained.

The other members of George Austen's family must now occupy our attention. His eldest son James, Rector of Steventon after his father, was of a more literary and less practical cast than Edward. Their mother thus describes them in a letter written to her sister-in-law, Mrs. Leigh Perrot of Scarlets, Berks., in 1820, after the death of James. Edward, she says, 'has a most active mind, a clear head, and a sound judgement; he is a man of business. That my dear James was not. Classical knowledge, literary

taste, and the power of elegant composition he possessed in the highest degree; to these Mr. Knight makes no pretensions. Both equally good, amiable and sweet-tempered.' We may add that James's only son, James Edward (who became James Edward Austen Leigh on succeeding to the property of his great-uncle, Mr. Leigh Perrot) inherited his father's literary tastes, and had a long and honourable career in the service of the church, besides being the biographer of his Aunt Jane.

Henry, successively soldier, banker, and clergyman, was apparently the most brilliant, though the least successful of the brothers. Frank and Charles were sailors – Frank self-contained, self-respecting, dignified, and devout; Charles expansive, affectionate, and eminently loveable; 'our own particular little brother' as his sister Jane calls him. They both rose to be Admirals – the former to be Admiral of the Fleet; though he lost his best chance of fame from the accident of his ship having put in for water at Gibraltar at the actual time when Trafalgar was being fought.

Cassandra, the elder sister, was both clever and sensible, and became a real power in the family. She lived to be an old lady, and, living at Chawton, was thrown principally with her brother Edward's children, on whom she bestowed the most constant affection. Cassandra was called after her mother, who had an only sister, Jane. Nearly three years after Cassandra's birth, Mrs. Austen gave the name of Jane to her second daughter. She can little have imagined how familiar the name 'Jane Austen' was to become in the course of the next century. Her father in a letter to a relation announces the arrival of another girl, who is to be called 'Jennie,' and who will be, he thinks, 'a present plaything for her sister Cassey and a future companion.' This prophecy was fully borne out in the life-long attachment of the two sisters: but Cassandra is by no means the only one to whom the author of *Pride and Prejudice* has proved to be a loved and honoured companion.

Jane Austen never married, but resided and worked in her family's home. Her novels were written with a spare, witty style and satiric insight, along with values reflecting the sensitivity of the romantic poets. Her early pieces, written in the 1790's, deal with a comparatively affluent society, and caricature the incongruities of contemporary fiction. Her comic heroines faint or issue dire warnings against fainting. Sir Walter Scott, her contemporary, Macaulay in the mid-1800's, and Kipling in later years were ardent admirers, but her work was not widely known until its reappraisal in the 1900's, when Virginia Woolf and others initiated serious criticism of her fiction.

"Of all great writers," Virginia Woolf remarked, "she is the most difficult to catch in the act of greatness." No successor has been able to assimilate her methods. As a result, her fiction has been, from the first, in fact, inimitable. □

TENNESSEE AUSTINS IN THE CIVIL WAR

by Sally Austin Day

Editor's Note: The following names were obtained from *Civil War Pension Records* at the Tennessee State Archives and from a volume *Tennesseans in the Civil War - Part 2*. The "Cld" found in these records was an abbreviation used to denote "colored" soldiers.

Civil War Pensions

Austin, C. V.	14841, Dickson, 11th Infantry
Austin, Ed	2618, White, 25th Infantry
Austin, George W.	3482, Henderson, 2nd Infantry
Austin, H. G.	9951, Dickson, Napier's Bn. Cavalry
Austin, Jacob	6441, McNairy, 14th N.C. Infantry
Austin, James	6592, Washington, 29th Infantry
Austin, J. J.	14219, Decatur, 19th Biffle's
Austin, John	1952, White, 16th Infantry
Austin, John	2511, Hawkins, 4th Virginia Infantry
Austin, Johnathan	13172, Sequatchie, 35th
Austin, J. T.	3898, Sumner, 7th Bn, Benn--- Cavalry
Austin, Nathaniel Glenn	1806, White, 28th Infantry
Austin, Robert	2498, White, 8th Dibrell's
Austin, Robin	5181, White, 8th Dibrell's
Austin, Thomas	11466, White, 28th Infantry
Austin, William H.	10724, White, 25th Infantry

Serving in the Federal Army

Austin, Abram	Private, K Company, 40th U.S. Cld. Infantry
Austin, Albert A.	2nd Lieut., C Company, 15th U.S. Cld. Infantry
Austin, Anthony	Private, C Company, 44th U.S. Cld. Infantry
Auston, Augustus	Private, D Company, 2nd MI
Austin, Bird M.	Private, D Company, 6th MI
Austin, Bob	Private, C Company, 3rd U.S. Cld. H-Arty.
Austin, Caswell	Corporal, F Company, 3rd U.S. Cld. H-Arty.
Austin, Charles	Private, C Company, 14th U.S. Cld. Infantry
Austin, Charles	Private, 16th U.S. Cld. Infantry
Austin, Charles	Private, B Company, 44th U.S. Cld. Infantry
Austin, Cornelius	Private, C Company, 9th U.S. Cld. H-Arty.
Austin, Frank	Private, F Company, 1st U.S. Cld. H-Arty.
Austin, George	Private, I Company, 3rd U.S. Cld. H-Arty.
Austin, Goodman H.	Tptr, B Company, 10th Cavalry
Austin, Henry	Private, B Company, 1st U.S. Cld. H-Arty.
Austin, Henry	Corporal, I Company, 14th U.S. Cld. Infantry
Austin, Henry M.	Captain, L Company, 4th U.S. Cld. H-Arty.
Austin, Henry R.	1st Lieut., B Company, 14th U.S. Cld. Inf.
Austin, Isaac	Private, C Company, 4th U.S. Cld. H-Arty.
Austin, Isaac	Private, F Company, 12th U.S. Cld. Infantry
Austin, Isom	Corporal, B Company, 3rd U.S. Cld. H-Arty.
Austin, James	Private, C Company 8th MI
Austin, James	Corporal, E Company, 3rd U.S. Cld. H-Arty.
Austin, James	Private, I Company, 88th U.S. Cld. Infantry
Austin, James M.	Private, C Company, 4th MI
Austin, Jasper	Private, B Company, 4th MI
Austin, John	Private, A Company, 44th U.S. Cld. Infantry
Austin, John	Private, F Company, 1st MI
Austin, John	Private, F Company, 6th Cavalry
Auston, John	Private, D Company, 2nd MI
Austin, John E.	Sergeant, C Company, 4th MI
Austin, Joseph	11th U.S. Cld. Infantry
Austin, Joseph	Corporal, A Company, 1st U.S. Cld. Infantry
Austin, Lewis	Mus., K Company, 61st U.S. Cld. Infantry
Austin, Mason B.	Lieut., G Company, 1st L-Arty. Bn.
Austin, Nathan	Private, C Company, 44th U.S. Cld. Infantry
Austin, Nathan	Private, K Company, 59th U.S. Cld. Infantry
Austin, Phillip	Private, A Company, 61st U.S. Cld. Infantry
Austin, Reuben	Private, B Company, 11th U.S. Cld. Infantry
Austin, Thomas	Private, E Company, 16th U.S. Cld. Infantry
Austin, Thomas C.	Private, F Company, 10th Infantry
Austin, Wake	Private, A Company, 4th U.S. Cld. H-Arty.
Austin, William	Corporal, A Company, 1st L-Arty. Bn.
Austin, William	Private, A Company, 3rd U.S. Cld. H-Arty.
Austin, William	Private, C Company, 1st MI
Austin, William	Private, G Company, 11th U.S. Cld. Infantry
Austin, William	Private, H Company, 1st MI
Austin, William	Private, B Company, 59th U.S. Cld. Infantry
Austin, William	Private, C Company, 6th Cavalry
Austin, William N.	Sergeant, C Company, 4th MI
Auston, William P.	Private, H Company, 6th Cavalry

Serving in the Confederate Army

Austin, A.	Private, I Company, 1st Field's Infantry
Austin, A.	Private, I Company, 27th Infantry
Austin, A. A.	Private, B Company 27th Infantry
Austin, Albert N.	Private, D Company 49th Infantry
Austin, Allen	Private, D Company, 27th Infantry
Austin, A. N.	Sergeant, L Company, Bailey's Infantry
Austin, Archibald	Private, K Company, 37th Infantry
Austin, A. S.	Private, 7th Cavalry
Austin, A. S.	Second Lieutenant, K Company, 7th Cavalry
Austin, Calvin F.	Private, K Company, 11th Infantry
Austin, Calvin W.	Private, D Company, 37th Infantry
Austin, C. D. V.	Sergeant, K Company, 11th Infantry
Austin, C. B.	Sergeant, K Company, 2nd Infantry
Auston, Daniel	Private, G Company, 30th Infantry
Austin, Daniel S.	Private, Newsom's Cavalry
Austin, David	Private, C Company, 43rd Infantry
Austin, D. S.	Private, I Company, 33rd Infantry
Austin, E. K.	Sergeant, D Company, 20th Infantry
Austin, Ed	Private, D Company, 7th Cavalry
Austin, Ed	25th Infantry
Austin, E. D.	Private, G Company, 28th Infantry
Austin, Edward	Private, C Company, 84th Infantry
Austin, E. H.	Private, H Company, 21st Wilson's Cavalry
Austin, E. T.	Private, C Company, 2nd Ashby's Cavalry
Austin, Francis M.	Private, K Company, 4th McLemore's Cavalry
Austin, G. B.	Private, F Company, 22nd Infantry Bn.
Austin, G. G.	Sergeant, D Company, 18th Infantry
Austen, G. G.	Private, D Company 18th Infantry
Austin, Green B.	Private, K Company, 4th Murray's Cavalry
Austin, G. W.	Private, K Company, 11th Infantry
Austin, G. W.	Cpl., H Company, 49th Infantry
Austin, H. C.	Cpl., D Company, 18th Infantry
Austin, Henry	Private, B Company, 21st Wilson's Cavalry
Austin, Henry	Private, F Company, 20th Infantry
Austin, Henry	Private, K Company, 20th Infantry
Austin, Henry M.	Captain, E Company, 24th Infantry
Austin, H. G.	1st Cavalry Bn.
Austin, Irvin	Cpl., C Company, 52nd Infantry
Austin, J.	Private, B Company, 51st Infantry
Austin, J. A.	Private, 2nd D Company, 5th Infantry
Austin, J. Alex	Sergeant, F&S, 31st Infantry
Austin, James	Private, B Company, 5th Cavalry Bn.
Austin, James	29th Infantry
Austin, James T.	1st Lieutenant, F Company, 22nd Cavalry
Austin, J. B.	Private, G Company, 4th Murray's Cavalry
Austin, J. B.	Private, G Company, 22nd Infantry Bn.
Austin, J. C.	Private, D Company, 14th Cavalry
Austin, J. C.	Private, C Company, 20th Infantry

Austin, J. H.	Private, G Company, 30th Infantry
Austin, J. H.	Private, G Company, 31st Infantry
Austin, J. M.	2nd Lieutenant, F Company, 22nd Infantry Bn.
Austin, John	Private, F Company, 19th Cavalry
Austin, John	Private, D Company, Cox's Cavalry Bn.
Austin, John	Private, K Company, 16th Infantry
Austin, John	Private, K Company, 34th Infantry
Auston, John	1st Lieutenant, D Company, 18th Infantry
Austin, John A.	Private, C Company, 1st Cavalry Bn.
Austin, John B.	Captain, K Company, 20th Infantry
Austin, John B.	1st Lieutenant, D Company, 49th Infantry
Austin, John J.	Private, Cox's Cavalry Bn.
Austin, John W.	Private, I Company, 55th McKoin's Infantry
Austin, Jonathan	Private, F Company, 2nd Ashby's Cavalry
Austin, Jonathan	Private, H Company, 35th Infantry
Austin, Jonathan M.	2nd Lieut., K Co., 4th Murray's Cavalry
Austin, Jonathan P.	Private, K Company, 4th Murray's Cavalry
Austin, Joseph	Private, D Company, 37th Infantry
Austin, J. P.	Private, F Company, 22nd Infantry Bn.
Austin, J. R.	Private, H Company, 8th Cavalry
Austin, J. R.	Private, K Company, 11th Cavalry
Austin, J. R.	Private, D Company, 14th Cavalry
Austin, J. R.	Private, G Company, 4th Infantry
Austin, J. R.	Private, G Company, 31st Infantry
Auston, J. R.	Private, D Company, Holman's Cavalry Bn.
Austin, J. T.	Private, D Company, 7th Cavalry Bn.
Austin, J. W.	2nd Lieut., L Company, 11th Cavalry
Austin, J. W.	2nd Lieut., Bruster's Co., Douglas' Cavalry Bn.
Austin, L. C.	Private, H Company, 49th Infantry
Austin, Levy	Private, B Company, 5th Cavalry Bn.
Austin, Lewis	Private, I Company, 3rd Cavalry
Austin, Marcous	Private, Day's Co., 55th McKoin's Infantry
Austin, Mark S.	Private, H Company, 44th Infantry
Austin, Michael	Corporal, D Company, 3rd Lillard's MI
Austin, M. L.	Private, D Company, 14th Cavalry
Austin, M. V.	Private, K Company, 11th Infantry
Austin, M. V.	Private, H Company, 33rd Infantry
Austin, N. G.	Private, C Company, 84th Infantry
Austin, N. G.	Private, G Company, 28th Infantry
Auston, R. H.	Private, I Company, 19th Cavalry
Auston, R. J.	Private, B Company, 19th Cavalry
Austin, Riley	Private, D Company, 9th Cavalry
Austin, Robert	13th Cavalry
Austin, Robin	Private, D Company, 13th Cavalry
Austin, S.	Private, B Company, 51st Infantry
Auston, S. H.	Private, A Co., 15th Stewart's Cavalry
Austin, S. W.	Private, G Company, 4th Infantry
Austin, S. W.	Private, Cons. Cp. Instr
Austin, Sam V.	Private, E Company, 6th Infantry
Austin, Samuel	Private, B Company, 30th Infantry
Auston, Sanders	Private, Tackitt's Company Infantry
Austin, T. G.	Private, D Company, 27th Infantry
Austin, Thomas	Private, A Company, 28th Infantry
Austin, Thomas	Private, K Company, 37th Infantry
Austin, Thomas M.	Private, K Co., 4th Murray's Cavalry
Austin, T. M.	Private, F Company, 22nd Cavalry Bn.
Austin, W. J.	Private, G Company, 31st Infantry
Auston, Walter	Private, C Co., 15th Stewart's Cavalry
Austin, Walter A.	Sergeant, E Company, 47th Infantry
Austin, William	Private, K Company, 13th Cavalry
Austin, William	Private, F Company, 25th Infantry
Austin, William	Private, K Company, 33rd Infantry
Austin, William	Private, G Company, 61st MI
Auston, William	Private, F Company, 11th Cavalry Bn.
Austin, William E.	Private, G Company, 28th Infantry
Austin, William H.	Sergeant, C Company, 25th Infantry
Austin, William T.	Private, M Company, 10th Cavalry
Austen, Willis	Private, E Company 22nd Cavalry

THE FAMILY OF LYMAN L. AUSTIN AND PAULINA REED OF NEW YORK, PENNSYLVANIA AND WISCONSIN

by David C. Dewsnap

Editor's Notes: Lyman's father Elihu moved to Mexico, New York in 1815. It is interesting to note that in 1825 twin brothers Henry and Daniel Austin, formerly from Cambridge, New York, also moved to Mexico, and that Daniel married a daughter of Annah Reed. The relationships, if any, between Elihu and these Austin brothers or between Paulina and Annah is unknown. The author of this article is a great-great-grandson of Minerva Austin and Peleg L. Peckham.

E1. LYMAN L.[2] AUSTIN (*Elihu,*[1]) was born on 26 May 1799 in Connecticut, the son of Elihu Austin and his first wife Abigail Austin (Elihu married second to Catherine —). Shortly after Lyman's birth the family moved to Pompey, Onondaga County, New York. They settled down as farmers, but they did not remain in this area for long. In 1814 Elihu Austin sold land (Lot 39) at Pompey, New York, and by 1815 he had purchased Lot 143 in Mexico, Oswego County, New York, separated from Lot 142 to the west by "French Street."

In 1819 Lyman married in Oswego County to a local girl of Mexico, Paulina Reed, who was born 25 June 1799 in Lee, Massachusetts, the daughter of John and Elizabeth (Crocker) Reed. The Reed family had moved to Mexico shortly after Paulina's birth. Lyman and Paulina settled in a subdivision of Lot 19 of Oswego County. This area became part of Parish, New York, in 1828 when Township boundaries were changed.

In the fall of 1836, Lyman sold out his farm and moved his family to Springfield, Erie County, Pennsylvania, where they farmed for nine years. In 1845, with the pioneering spirit, Lyman and family moved to Mackford (District #16), Greenlake County, Wisconsin. This was part of the Lake Maria Settlement. Lyman spent his remaining years at this farm. He was a Methodist and supported the Republican Party.

Paulina died on 8 September 1854 at age 55 years, and was laid to rest in the Lake Maria Cemetery in Mackford. Lyman married secondly on 31 March 1855 to Cornelia (Cooper) Smith. Cornelia had children from an earlier marriage, and Lyman and Cornelia had two sons together. With the death of each succeeding wife, Lyman married a third time on 12 February 1866 to Eliza Brikford, and for a fourth time on 18 February 1869 to Lucinda Peterson. Lyman himself died on 28 October 1871, and was buried with his first wife Paulina in the Lake Maria Cemetery. Lyman had experienced a very full life. He was a true pioneer, and raised a large family that proved their responsibilities as good citizens. Children:

E11. ANGELINE, *b. 1820, m. in Mexico, New York, to Henry Crouch b. 1817. They went to Wisconsin in 1845, were in Dodge County, Minnesota in 1890.*

E12. LYMAN, JR., *b. 26 October 1821 +*

E13. AMANDA M., *b. circa 1824, d. 24 Sept. 1904, m. Alanson/Landsing Martin b. 1818 d. 10 August 1891. They resided in Ripon, Fond du Lac County, Wisconsin, in 1890. Martin children: Martha, Ester A., Ellen M., Amanda.*

E14. MINERVA, *b. 4 October 1825, d. 22 November 1894, on 19 April 1846 she m. Peleg L. Peckham of Columbia County, Wisconsin, b. 24 May 1819, d. 26 November 1886 in Columbia County. Peckham children: John E., Lucretia, Elizabeth A., Charles W., William H.*

E15. THERON S., *born — March 1828, m.(1) Lorilla Mashom, who was b. 21 December 1829, d. 25 February 1854. Theron m.(2) —— in Pennsylvania. He enlisted in one of the Keystone Regiments in the Civil War, and was killed near Petersburg, Virginia, on 14 August 1863. He is buried with Lorilla in the Lake Maria Cemetery in Mackford, Wisconsin.*

E16. ANDREW J., *b. — February 1830, m. Edna Brown b. 1836. They lived near Sparta, Monroe County, Wisconsin in 1890. Children: Edson L., Anna J., Alice M., Allen M.*

E17. MELINDA, *born in 1832, m. Benjamin Baker of Winona, Minnesota. Benjamin was b. in 1825.*

E18. ELIZABETH, *b. August 1836, d. 9 October 1889, m. on 26 November 1856 to Edward Ames, b. 1832. Resided in Mackford, Greenlake Co., Wisconsin. Ch: Rosa R., Mary, Elizabeth, Edward M.*

E19. MATILDA, *b. 1838, m. Thomas Phillips b.1832. Phillips children: Addison L., Malinda, Sarilla, Nelson R. Matilda d. in Dodge County, Minnesota.*

E1A. WILLIAM H., *b. 1840, m. Miss Hannah Courier, they resided in Missouri in 1890.*

E1B. MERRITT D. ['EMMIT'], *b. 3 June 1854, d. 10 May 1920. He m. Elsie A. —, b. in November 1866. They resided in Portage, Columbia County, WI. Children: Harry E., Bert V., Myrtle.*

E1C. NELSON, *b. 19 June 1860, d. 17 March 1931, m. Eliza —, b. March 1872. He was a resident of Wyocena, Columbia County, WI. In 1900 Census (inmates in asylum), one child died.*

E12. LYMAN[3] AUSTIN JR. (*Lyman,[2] Elihu,[1]*) was born on 26 October 1821 in Oswego County, New York. At age 14 he moved with his parents to a farm in Springfield, Erie County, Pennsylvania. Nine years later he moved to Mackford, Wisconsin, where he obtained 160 acres of land on section 12. A year later he returned to Pennsylvania where on 18 September 1845 he married Miss Lou Emma Church, born in 1821, the daughter of Joshua and Sophronia (Shertleff) Church. With his young bride, Lyman returned to the home which he had prepared in the Wisconsin. In 1854 they sold out and the following year in 1855 Lyman purchased a farm on Section 9 in Mackford. From time to time Lyman added to his landed possessions which at one time totaled more than 1,200 acres being situated in Eau Claire, Buffalo and Green Lake Counties, Wisconsin, and 165-acres tract in Faribault County, Minnesota. Lyman and Lou had one adopted daughter, Emma L. Austin.

REFERENCE SOURCES

Portrait and Bibliography of Green Lake, Marquette, and Waushara Counties, Wisconsin, Acme Publishing Company, Chicago 1890.

Vital Statistics of Marquette, Green Lake and Columbia Counties, Wisconsin.

United States Census for 1790 through 1880 for Oswego and Onondago Counties, New York, Berkshire County, Massachusetts, Erie County, Pennsylvania, Marquette and Green Lake Counties, Wisconsin.

Family records of genealogy.

Cemetery Records, Lake Maria Cemetery, Green Lake, Wisconsin.

Land Abstracts for Oswego and Onondago Counties, New York, and Green Lake County, Wisconsin.

★★★★★★★★★★★★★★★★★★★★★★★★★★★★

Austins of America is intended to serve present and future genealogists researching Austin family lines. Readers are encouraged to submit queries, genealogical and historical articles for publication. Previously published books, pamphlets or articles containing Austin genealogical data are also sought for reprinting or review.

EDITOR

DR. MICHAEL EDWARD AUSTIN   CONCORD, MA

ASSOCIATE EDITORS

ANTHONY KENT AUSTIN   PROSPECT, KY
BERT ADDIS AUSTIN   QUEEN CREEK, AZ
PATRICIA BIEBUYCK AUSTIN   CONCORD, MA
PAULINE LUCILLE AUSTIN   CEDAR RAPIDS, IA
SALLY AUSTIN DAY   LIVONIA, MI

Austins of America is published each February and August by The Austin Print, 23 Allen Farm Lane, Concord, Massachusetts 01742. All correspondence, including subscriptions, articles and responses to queries, should be sent to this address. Subscriptions are $4.50 per year postpaid.

★★★★★★★★★★★★★★★★★★★★★★★★★★★★

Austins in the Federal Census of 1850

Wisconsin

by Russell Ambrose Williams

Editor's Notes: The numbers preceding each household are the page number, dwelling number, and family number. After the listing of household members are shown occupations, the dollar value of the head of household's real estate, and the date of the census.

BROWN COUNTY, WI

GRAND CHUTE - District 12....... p.98
Austin, Calvin   20 1830 m NY
    Clerk living with hotel-keeper
    B. P. Edgarton - 10 September

HORTONIA - District 44... p.166-142-142
Austin, John   35 1815 m NY
  " , Catherine   29 1821 f   "
  " , Pardon   7 1843 m   "
  " , Edward   5 1845 m   "
  " , Janette   3 1847 f   "
    John a farmer - $150 - 3 September

MARINETTE - District 44...... p.134-7-7
Austin, George   21 1829 m IRE
    laborer - 16 August

.... p.135-9-9
Austin, Richard   25 1825 m IRE
    laborer - 16 August

COLUMBIA COUNTY, WI

OTSEGO................. p.58-475-475
Austin, Ephriam   32 1818 m NY
    farmer - 7 August

LOWVILLE.............. p.63-520-520
Austin, James   39 1811 m OH
  " , Martha   31 1819 f PA
  " , Manerva   7 1843 f   "
  " , Rachel D.   5 1845 f OH
  " , George   3 1847 m   "
  " , May   1 1849 f   "
    James was a farmer - 8 August

.... p.63-521-521
Austin, Washington   24 1826 m OH
  " , Mary   21 1829 f   "
  " , James   1 1849 m   "
    Washington was a farmer - $150 - 8 August

MARCELLON......... p.182-1446-1446
Austin, Horace   33 1817 m NY
  " , Maria   34 1816 f   "
  " , Anna   10 1840 f   "
  " , Orlando   9 1841 m   "
  " , Lebbins   1 1849 m WI
    Horace was a farmer - $300 - 19 September

.... p.182-1447-1448
Austin, Freeman   40 1810 m NY
  " , Sally (Polly?) 43 1807 f   "

  " , W. H.   15 1835 m   "
  " , Emily   11 1839 f   "
    19 September

RANDOLPH...... p.195 & 196-1161-1161
Austin, Powel   53 1797 m VT
  " , Maria   38 1812 f   "
  " , Catherine   15 1835 f   "
  " , Amelia   10 1840 f   "
  " , Adelia   7 1843 f WI
  " , Nancy   5 1845 f   "
    Powel was a farmer - $1500 - 4 October

DANE COUNTY, WI

District 44.............. p.129-289-295
Austin, Ira   49 1801 m VT
  " , Elmira N.   38 1812 f   "
  " , Ann E.   10 1840 f NY
Howe, Samuel   70 1780 m VT
    Ira a blacksmith, Samuel a farmer - 20 Sept.

.... p.157
Austin, William   32 1818 m NY
  " , Malinda   31 1819 f MA
  " , Lydia A.   11 1839 f NY
  " , Garnelia   2 1848 f WI
    William was a farmer - 21 September

District 144.............. p.278-784-786
Austin, Chas. D.   54 1796 m NY
  " , Charlotte   47 1803 f   "
  " , Ovilia   13 1837 f OH
  " , R. N.   17 1833 m NY
  " , S. M.   11 1839 f   "
Shears, Chas.   9 1841 m   "
Austin, Mary G.   8 1842 f MI
    Chas. D. & R. N. were farmers - 11 Sept.

..........................p.31-981-986
Austin, E.   33 1817 m OH
  " , P. J.   33 1817 f NY
  " , M. S.   2 1848 f †
    E. Austin was a hotel-keeper - $1000
    † M. S. was b. in NY or WI - 11 Sept.

WILLIAMSTOWN.......... p.?-161-169
Austin, J.   63 1787 m CT
    farmer - $400 by lot sample - 3 August

DODGE COUNTY, WI

ELBA................. p.484-105-113
Austin, Samuel   56 1794 m MA

  " , Mercy   52 1798 f NH
  " , Samuel   21 1829 m   "
  " , Hiram   17 1833 m PA
  " , William   13 1837 m OH
  " , Sarah   12 1838 f   "
  " , Abigail   9 1841 f   "
  " , Edward   7 1843 m   "
    Samuel a farmer - $1200 - 21 August

EMMETT................ p.460-166-172
Austin, Buel   32 1818 m CT
  " , Lucinda   23 1827 f NY
  " , Charles   2 1848 m WI
    Buel a farmer - $2000 - 7 October

LeROY.................... p.407-5-5
Austin, Hiram   26 1824 m VT
    carpenter - $300 - 14 September

PORTLAND................ p.319-2-2
Austin, Moses F.   28 1822 m NY
  " , Catherine   29 1821 f WI
  " , Albert G.   3 1837 m   "
  " , Zecary T.   4/12 1850 m   "
    23 August

GRANT COUNTY, WI

District 24..........................
Austin, Elizabeth   40 1810 f TN
    with William Salmer family - 14 August

PARIS................. p.245-528-532
Austin, A. E.   36 1814 m TN
  " , Eliza A.   34 1816 f IN
  " , James R.   13 1837 m IL
  " , William   10 1840 m IN
  " , Margaret   7 1843 f   "
    A. E. Austin was a laborer - 6 September

SMELSER.............. p.259-618-624
Austin, Potter   23 1827 m NY
    miner - 11 September

HAZEL GREEN.......... p.306-985-995
Austin, Charles   12 1838 m WI
    with miner J. M. Chander - 28 September

LIMA............... p.377-25-45
Austin, Samuel R.   25 1825 m IL
  " , Minerva   24 1826 f   "
  " , William T. (?)   5 1845 m   "
  " , Jane   4 1846 f WI
  " , Thomas   2 1848 m   "
  " , Un-named   1/12 1850 f   "
    Samuel was a farmer - 31 October

GREEN COUNTY, WI

CLARNO................ p.22-13-13
Austin, Elija   38 1812 m OH
  " , Ruanna   31 1819 f NY
  " , Miron   13 1837 m WI
  " , Newel S.   11 1839 m   "
  " , Elija R.   9 1841 m   "
  " , James A.   7 1843 m   "
  " , Hariet   5 1845 f   "
  " , Cyrus N.   6/12 1850 m   "
    Elija was a farmer - $1200 - 18 July

MONROE.............. p.92-114-119
Austin, Julius   41 1809 m OH
  " , Ann   35 1815 f   "
  " , John M.   10 1840 m WI
  " , Wm. J. (?)   7 1843 m   "
  " , Julius H.   5 1845 m   "
  " , Seth B.   2 1848 m   "
    Julius was a farmer - $5000 - 9 August

EXETER. p.213-83-83
Austin, William   25   1825   m   ENG
           miner - 9 August

LAFAYETTE COUNTY, WI

BENTON. p.251-293-293
Austin, Nathan   40?   1810?   m   NY
        miner - $1000 - 3 October

MANITOWOC COUNTY, WI

MANITOWOC RAPIDS. p.60-274-285
Austin, James   32   1818   m   ME
  "   , Cordelia   24   1826   f   "
  "   , Ira   3   1847   m   WI
  "   , Miron   2/12   1850   m   "
  "   , Mary   59   1791   f   ME
  "   , Sarah   24   1826   f   "
  "   , Martha   22   1828   f   "
        James - $300 - 6 August

MARQUETTE COUNTY, WI

BUFFALO. p.49-384-384
Austin, Marvin S.   29   1821   m   NY
  "   , Lydia S.   28   1822   f   "
  "   , Elias W.   8   1842   m   "
  "   , Ellen   3   1847   f   WI
     Marvin a farmer - $200 - 14 August

MACKFORD. p.3-19-19
Austin, Lyman   28   1822   m   NY
  "   , Suemura (?)   32   1818   f   "
     Lyman a farmer - $1400 - 22 July

. . . . p.5-37-37
Austin, Lyman S.   51   1849   m   CT
  "   , Palina   51   1849   f   MA
  "   , Theron   22   1828   m   NY
  "   , Andrew J.   20   1830   m   "
  "   , Malinda   18   1832   f   "
  "   , Elizabeth   14   1836   f   "
  "   , Matilda   12   1838   f   PA
  "   , William H.   10   1840   m   "
     Lyman a farmer - $1200 - 22 July

. . . . p.10-75-75
Austin, Julius   28   1822   m   CT
         clerk - 22 July

. . . . p.58-458-458
Austin, Hiram   25   1825   m   NY
  "   , Betsey   21   1829   f   "
           22 July

. . . . p.58
Austin, William H.   27   1823   m   NY
  "   , Esther   28   1822   f   "
  "   , Celestia J.   6   1844   f   IN
           22 July

. . . . p.63-506-506
Austin, Harvey   55   1795   m   NY
  "   , John   22   1828   m   "
  "   , William   16   1834   m   "
  "   , George   12   1838   m   "
  "   , Rachel   22   1828   f   "
  "   , Sarah   18   1832   f   "
     Harvey a farmer - $100 - 17 August

GREEN LAKE. p.18-140-140
Austin, Jane   14   1836   f   IRE
    in household of John M. Milligan
       from Ireland - 26 July

BERLIN. p.127-1024-1024
Austin, U. T. (I.?)   23   1827   m   NH
       laborer - 7 August

. . . . p.142-1136-1136
Austin, Susan   18   1832   f   ?
           7 August

MILWAUKEE COUNTY, WI

MILWAUKEE - 3rd Ward.   p.154-1224-1289
Austin, Geo. F.   42   1808   m   CT
  "   , Maria   35   1815   f   NY
  "   , Edward A.   7   1843   m   OH
  "   , James R.   3   1847   m   "
MILWAUKEE 1st Ward. .   p.221-1788-1935
Austin, R. N.   27   1823   m   NY
  "   , Sarah   22   1828   f   "
    R. N. was a sawyer - $1200 - 22 August

. . . . p.236-1897-2048
Austin, Mary   58   1792   f   NY
   in Silas Chapman household - 22 August

LAKE. p.483-9-11
Austin, Samuel   50   1800   m   VT
  "   , Sarah   38   1812   f   NH
  "   , John C.   18   1832   m   VT
  "   , James D.   14   1836   m   "
  "   , Martha E.   11   1839   f   "
  "   , John   63   1787   m   "
Samuel & John both farmers - $4000 - 11 July

. . . . p.500 128-140
Austin, Isaac   28   1822   m   NY
  "   , Sarah   21   1829   f   "
  "   , Henry J. (?)   3   1847   m   WI
   Isaac was a farmer - $3000 - 11 July

ROCK COUNTY, WI

BRADFORD. p.502-1090-1223
Austin, Ruben   41   1809   m   NY
  "   , Jenett   35   1815   f   "
  "   , Oral   12   1838   m   "
  "   , Harriet   10   1840   f   "
  "   , Francis   1   1849   m   WI
   Ruben was a farmer - $1200 - 5 September

BELOIT - District 21. . . . . . . p.378-308-326
Austin, Ira B.   33   1817   m   NY
  "   , Louisa   25   1825   f   "
  "   , Charles C.   3   1847   m   WI
    Ira was a cooper - $2000 - 30 July

UNION. p.320-1137-1197
Austin, Elijah   50   1800   m   VT
  "   , Cathrine   47   1803   f   NY
  "   , Cornelia (?)   17   1833   m?   "
  "   , Clark   11   1839   m   "
  "   , James   9   1841   m   "
  "   , Edwin   6   1844   m   "
       $400 - 15 August

CENTER. p.243-634-634
Austin, Daniel   55   1795   m   NH
  "   , Lucretia   43   1807   f   "
  "   , Gillman   23   1827   m   VT
  "   , Henry (?)   19   1831   m   "
  "   , Lucretia   12   1838   f   OH
  "   , Arcinath   ?   ?   f   "
  "   , Harvey   1   1849   m   WI
    Daniel was a farmer - $720

JANESVILLE. p.196-306-306
Austin, Gillman B.   24   1826   m   VT
farmer living with William Blount - 20 July

JANESVILLE, East of river. . .   p.19-133-133
Austin, Ann E.   16   1834   f   NY
   in Philo E. Doby household - 15 August

. . . . p.16-112-112
Austin, Ellen   6   1844   f   OH
  "   , Eva   3   1847   f   WI
  in home of lawyer L. F. Kimball - 15 August

. . . . p.8-69-69
Austin, James   59   1791   m   VT
  "   , Belny   57   1793   f   NY
  "   , Bradford   22   1828   m   "
  "   , Chas.   14   1836   m   "
  James a harness-maker - $1000 - 15 August

. . . . p.174-130-130
Austin, Charles   14   1836   m   NY
    living W. of Rock River - 17 July

LIMA. p.137-6-6
Austin, John   59   1791   m   NY
  "   , Rebecca   52   1798   f   "
  "   , John   30   1820   m   "
  "   , Thos.   21   1829   m   "
  "   , Eben   17   1833   m   "
  "   , Mary   24?   1826?   f   "
  "   , Sarah   14   1836   f   "
  "   , John   11   1839   m   "
  "   , Ann E.   6   1844   f   "
  "   , Catherine   5   1845   f   "
    John was a farmer - 15 August

. . . . p.145-68-68
Austin, David W.   26   1824   m   WI
  "   , Jane   23   1827   f   "
  "   , Mary   1   1849   f   "
    David was a farmer - 15 August

. . . . p.144-61-61
Austin, Ruth   40   1810   f   NY
  in Nathan Pierce household - 15 August

SHEBOYGAN COUNTY, WI

PLYMOUTH. p.182-1596-1596
Austin, William   30   1820   m   OH
  "   , Maria   22   1828   f   "
  William a farmer - $2000 - 16 September

WALWORTH COUNTY, WI

DELEVAN. p.61-444-454
Austin, Daniel   61   1789   m   MA
  "   , Elma   50   1800   f   CT
   Daniel a farmer - $200 - 21 August

. . . . p.67-486-496
Austin, Erastus   55   1795   m   NY
  "   , Anna   48   1802   f   "
  "   , William S.   23   1827   m   "
  "   , Andrew I.   22   1828   m   "
  "   , Thomas   18   1832   m   "
  "   , Harriet   18   1832   f   "
  "   , Phebe A.   13   1837   f   "
Erastus a farmer, William & Thomas wagon-
makers, Andrew a shoemaker - 23 August

SUGAR CREEK. p.146-691-717
Austin, Palmer   20   1830   m   NY
  laborer in Elinor Fisher household

. . . . p.436-420-427
Austin, Thomas   32   1818   m   NY
  "   , Schyler   25   1825   m   "
Thomas a farmer, Schyler a wagon-maker,
     in boarding-house - 13 August

TROY - Dist. 36. . . . . p.?-177-186

Austin, John	51	1799	m	CT
" , Jane	46	1804	f	NY
" , Julius	20	1830	m	CT
" , Josephus	16	1834	m	NY
" , Philander	14	1836	m	"
" , Adelaide	10	1840	f	"
" , John	9	1841	m	"
" , Daniel	1	1849	m	CT
Reed, Thomas	25	1825	m	MA
" , Ann Eliza	23	1827	f	NY
Van Patten, Samuel	25	1825	m	CT
" , Susan	19	1831	f	NY
" , Orlando S.	7/12	1849	m	"

John a cooper - $400, Thomas a paper-
maker, Samuel a cooper - 9 August

DELEVAN - District 33. . . . . p.?-?-?

Austin, Daniel	51	1799	m	MA
" , Elma	50	1800	f	CT
Sweet, Ellen	14	1836	f	OH
" , Giles	12	1838	m	"
Hamblin, Clarissa	70	1780	f	CT

Daniel was a farmer - $200 - 21 August

. . . . p.?-582-597

Austin, Elizabeth	35	1815	f	NY

she had real estate $1000 - living
with Rockwell family - 29 August

WAUKESHA COUNTY, WI

OCONOMOWOC. . . . . p.?-346-357

Austin, A.	51	1799	m	NY
" , Lucinda	44	1806	f	"
" , Edwin	16	1834	m	"
" , Orlando	14	1836	m	"
" , H.	12	1838	m	PA
" , Chauncey	10	1840	m	"
" , Susan	9	1841	f	"
" , Mary	18	1832	f	NY
" , Caroline	7	1843	f	"
" , Ann	4	1846	f	WI

A. Austin a farmer - $1000 - 27 July

DELAFIELD. p.53-372-385

Austin, Caroline	14	1836	f	NOR

29 July

OTTAWA. . . . . p.250-?-?

Austin, Jerome	31	1719	m	OH
" , Electa	29	1821	f	NY
" , Chas. G.	4	1846	m	OH
" , E.	2	1848	m	"
" , Emma	2/12	1850	f	"
" , Alba (Alva?)	40	1810	m	NY

Jerome & Alva farmers - $800 - 24 August

Austins in the
Federal Census of 1850

Write to us if you can help!

Editor's Corner. . .

TEN YEARS OF PUBLISHING. . . TIME TO
PUBLISH A COMPREHENSIVE INDEX!

After ten years, this issue completes Volume I of
the newsletter. Below we respond to two common
reader questions: "Why don't you publish names
and addresses with the Queries?" and "When are
you going to publish an Index to the newsletter?"

As we wrap up our 10th year of publishing *Austins of America*, we want to thank you, the hundreds of readers and researchers who have contributed your Austin families research to *Austins of America*. By generously sharing your information through the newsletter, you have helped many others – now and in the future – in searching for their Austin roots. Thanks to your support and "passing the word" to others, in just ten years we have grown to become the largest national organization serving Austin family researchers, and your research contributions have made the *Austins of America* files the largest Austin genealogical database available anywhere!

With a high-speed computerized retrieval system for finding information in the *Austins of America* files, we are able to answer many reader queries. We publish the rest, and other readers may respond to them through *Austins of America*. We forward responses to querists, and send querists' names and addresses to respondants. Publishing these names and addresses with the queries would take up additional newsletter space, and we would not learn of others interested in those Austin lines. Also, several querists have died though the years, and dozens of others have moved. By responding to the queries through *Austins of America*, you are sure of getting a querist's most current address available. . . we recently forwarded a response to a querist who had moved three times in the last four years!

This fall we plan to publish an Index to these first 310 pages. The Index will be available to readers, and included in the bound Volume I of *Austins of America*. It will comprehensively include all person and place names, plus some time and geographic information. Frustrated looking up 'John Austin' and finding dozens of them? The Index will enable you to narrow down your candidates, to sort them out both in time and geographically!

We welcome Sally Austin Day of Livonia, Michigan, as a new Associate Editor. Sally has frequently contributed articles and information – her efforts have benefited many. She joins the *Austins of America* Staff at a bright time, just as we begin a second decade of service to Austin family researchers!

— Michael Edward Austin

INDEX TO PERSONS

——— A ———

ABBE, Ce 205
  Mary E. (Aston) 205
ABBOT, Peter 47
ABBOTT, Charity 101
  Harriet 62
  Lady 299
  Nathaniel 8
  Sir Fred 299
ABDELLIA, Julia 49
ABNER, Milton 61

Orval 61
ABSHER, Jacob W. 117
  Nancy J. (Austin) 117
ADAIR, Phebe 26
  Phoebe 186, 270
ADAMS, Abigail ( ) 73
  Agnes 257
  Anna 157
  Charles F. 73
  Colonel 65
  Cora Lee (Austin) 199
  Cort J. 205
  Emeline 225
  Finn 199
  James 178
  Jasper 157
  John 66, 73, 281
  John Quincy 66
  Lois 82
  Martin 157
  Mary Elizabeth 220
  Mary Elizabeth (Austin) 175
  Olivia C. (Austin) 205
  Samuel Milton 175
  William 108
ADKINS, Mollie (Astin) 124
  W. H. 124
AIHERST, widow 257
AINSLIE,
  Joan Elizabeth (Austin) 139
  Terrance Andrew 139
AISTON, Robert 11
  Sarah (Leete) 11
AKINS, Elisabeth (Austin) 204
  Samuel 204
ALBEE, Elias O. 54
  Isaac 54
  Jennie (Austin) 54
  Sophia (Lincoln) 54
ALBRO, John 266
ALEXANDER, Hubert L. 60
  James D. 60
  John 107
  Margaret L. 228
  Nancy 178, 231
  Nora 228
  Sophia C. (Austin) 107, 109
ALFORD,
  Jenny 6, 10, 26, 110, 155
  Thomas 10
  William 10, 26, 155
ALFRED, Nancy 204
ALLEMBY, Capt. William 281
ALLEN, — 158
  Ada ( ) 231
  Bathsheba (Austin) 220
  Charles Channing 7
  David 19
  Ellen 171
  Eunice 50
  George 11
  Hannah 146, 220
  John Warren 181
  Margaret Caroline (Austin) 181
  Mary S. 100
  Nathaniel 45
  Noah 10
  Sarah 220, 224
  Sarah (Leete) 11
  Stephen 220
  Thomas 107
  Virginia R. 82
  W. G. 181
  Warren 178
ALLING, Eunice 50
ALLSTON, Washington 18
ALSOP, John 37
ALSTON, — 159
AMBLER, — 158, 159
AMBROSE,
  Caroline (Austin) 43
  Hiram William 43
AMES, Agnes 141
  Edward 307
  Edward M. 307

Elizabeth 307
Elizabeth (Austin) 67, 307
Mary 307
Rosa R. 307
AMON, Robert 211
  Rosella (Chadwell) 211
  Sandra 211
AMOS, Hazel Marie 82
  Julia May (Austin) 82
  Paul 82
AMPHEAR, Almon 204
  Flora A. (Austin) 204
AMPLEMENT, Fr. 56
ANDERSON, Colonel 258
  Elizabeth 279
  Emily 182
  George 301
  Kate 20
  Mable F. 262
  Margaret J. 204
  Rachael 182
ANDREWS, Aaron 147
  Adelaide Hannah (Austin) 62-64
  Betsey 147
  Dr. 293
  Fanny R. 62
  Frances (Townsend) 178
  Gertrude 64
  Herbert 64
  John Whiteside 63, 64
ANDRUS, — 16, 36
  Arvilla (Austin) 16, 36
ANGDON, Florence 204
ANGLE, Eunice 124
  Josiah 205
  Nancy C. (Ashton) 205
ANGLEMIER, Arthur 228
  Myrtle (Austin) 228
ANGLIN, Elizabeth 223
  John 223
ANTENNA,
  Mary Margaret 270
ANTHONY, Abner 240
  Charles 240
  James Crenshaw 240
  John 240
  John Jr. 240
  Mark 240
  Mary C. 240
  Sarah 240
  Susan (Austin) 240
  William Banks 240
APPLEBEE,
  Hannah Rosetta 98
APPLETON, Frank 32
ARBUCKLE, Lizzie 42
ARCHER, Hazel 262
  Thomas 182
ARCHIBALD, Edward P. 248
ARMSTRONG, Don 19
  L. 124
  Sarah A. 60
ARNOLD, Benedict 72, 73, 83
  Ellen E. 153
  Elsie Myrtle 133
  John William 133
  Katherine 42
  Myrtle Ann (Austin) 133
  William Elvis 133
ARVIN, — 174
ASBERRY, George 157
ASHBURN, Susan C. 31
ASHBY, — 305, 306
ASHE, Marguerite (Loudon) 164
  Maude L. 160
ASHENHURST,
  Catherine Ann (Austin) 115
  John B. 115
ASHFORD, Laura 51
ASHLEY, Tommie 124
ASHTON,
  Cordelia (Dewitt) 205
  Elizabeth m.1837 OH 204
  Elizabeth m.1868 OH 204
  Even m.1839 OH 204

Lucinda m.1849 OH 205
Margaret m.1834 OH 205
Nancy C. m.1862 OH 205
Phebe m.1825 OH 205
Philip m.1861 OH 205
Sarah (Frame) 204
Sarah m.1866 OH 206
Sarah m.1926 OH 206
Susan m.1834 OH 206

ASTEN,
  Andrew r.1771 MA 24
  Benjamin r.1771 MA 24
  Caleb r.1771 MA 24
  David r.1771 MA 24
  Hannah r.1771 MA 24
  Isaac r.1771 MA 24
  James r.1812 TN 158
  Jerusha d.1804 ME 5
  John Jr. r.1771 MA 24
  John r.1771 MA 24
  Moses r.1771 MA 24
  Nathan r.1771 MA 24
  Nathaniel L. r.1817 IL 185
  Peter r.1771 MA 24
  Reuben r.1771 MA 24
  Samuel b.1669 MA 8
  Thomas r.1771 MA 24

ASTENS,
  Joseph r.1771 MA 24
  Lydia m.1789 MA 36

ASTIN, Alma L. (Hodges) 124
  Benoni r.1771 MA 24
  Clarence E. m.1921 AR 124
  Florence E. (Hawkins) 124
  James W. m.1883 AR 124
  Mary b.1686 ME 56
  Mollie m.1881 AR 124
  Moses b.1742 17
  Nora (Moulder) 124
  S. L. m.1903 124
  Samuel C. m.1876 AR 124
  Samuel H. m.1884 AR 124
  Walter r.1839 IL 186
  Wilson r.1812 VA 159

ASTON,
  Aetabe m.1928 AR 124
  Alice Elizabeth b.1869 QU 151
  Altabe m.1937 124
  Anna b.1874 r.OH 12
  Annie (Hill) 124
  Archibald r.1812 SC 158
  Beaulee (Finley) 124
  Betsy b.1878 28
  Charlie m.1941 AR 125
  E. C. (Molder) 124
  Earl m.1906 AR 124
  Earline (Whittingham) 125
  Edith m.1940 AR 125
  Edward m.1867 QU 151
  Eliza R. m.1845 OH 204
  Eliza b.1878 r.OH 12
  Eliza m.1829 OH 204
  Elizabeth (Hazel/Heazle) 151
  Ellen ( ) d.1853 CA 38
  Emanuel b.1875 r.OH 12
  Emma b.1876 r.OH 12
  Emma (Bradsher) 124
  Emma (Whitlock) 124
  Era m.1945 AR 125
  Etnea m.1932 AR 124
  Eunice (Angle) 124
  Fannie (Moulder) 124
  Garnett (Qualls) 125
  George b.1880 OH 12
  Gertrude m.1930 AR 124
  Gilbert b.1845 ENG 12
  Harry Lewis m.1941 AR 125
  Hattie (Bartlett) 206
  Herman m.1933 AR 124
  Hulbert b.1873 r.OH 12
  J. C. m.1906 AR 124

J. E. m.1907 AR 124
J. W. m.1901 AR 124
James r.1853 CA 38
James b.1876 WI 28
Jeanette (Williams) 124
John b.1859 WAL 12
Juanita (Highland) 125
Julia Ann m.1841 OH 205
Lois b.1878 OH 12
Louise (Goodman) 125
Mabel (Williams) 124
Margaret ( ) b.1842 WAL 12
Margaret b.1867 WAL 12
Mary m.1825 OH 205
Mary b.1874 OH 12
Mary ( ) b.1848 ENG 28
Mary ( ) b.1850 ENG 12
Mary (Davis) 124
Mary E. m.1870 OH 205
Ollie m.1932 AR 124
R. (Bell) 124
Ray m.1944 AR 125
Richard b.1868 WAL 12
Roy m.1938 AR 124
S. L. m.1914 AR 124
Sam m.1918 AR 124
Samuel m.1833 OH 206
Samuel m 1906 AR 124
Sarah b.1865 WAL 12
Susan m.1824 OH 206
Thomas b.1853 ENG 28
Thomas b.1908 AR 124
Ure r.1844 IL 186
William 159
William b.1870 OH 12
William b.1871 OH 12
Willie (Davis) 124
Winetta (Robertson) 125
Winston m.1942 AR 125

ASTOR, — 67
ATHERTON, Clarissa (Austin) 105
  Joshua 105
ATKINSON, James H. 60
  Osha (Austin) 60
  Rose Ann 60
ATWATER, Marcus 262
  Mercy 6, 186
  Sarah (Austin) 262
ATWOOD, Bernetta (Owens) 214
  David 274
AUTLIN, — 147
  John 147
  Lodatha 147
  Minerva 147
AULD, — 159
  Jennie Mae (Austin) 156
AULTMAN, Charles Fox 206
  Sarah (Ashton) 206
AULTON, David 223
  Easther 223
  John 223
  William 223
AUSBORN, Mahala 285
AUSDON, Murray m.1928 AR 124
  Tommie (Ashley) 124

AUSTAIN, Anthony 147
  Armina 147
  Charlotte 147
  Daniel B. b.1863 PA 107
  George 147
  Henry 147
  Joel H. b.1857 107
  Jonas r.1812 LA 159
  Joseph 147
  Julia 147
  Justus P. b.1879 107
  L. B. b.1835 PA 107
  Mary 147
  Mary E. ( ) b.1838 PA 107
  Melvina b.1868 PA 107
  Paul 147
  Rozetta ( ) b.1861 107
  Seviah 147

AUSTIN,
Addison (Capt.) b.1825 ME 4
Addison b.1830 KY 42, 126
Addison b.1837 VT 147
Addison A. b.181– MA 7
Addison M. b.1850 KY 42
Adelaide b.1840 NY 310
Adelaide Hannah b.1851 NY 62, 64
Adelia b.1843 WI 308
Adelia A. b.1834 VT 146
Adeline b.1812 PA 105, 106, 109
Adeline b.1836 NY 54
Adeline b.1840 VT 147
Adeline b.1848 VT 145
Adeline b.1853 PA 107
Adeline ( ) b.1818 CAN 145
Adeline ( ) b.1822 MS 274
Adeline M. (Harris) 197
Adell m.1818 AR 125
Adin b.1823 VT 144
Adoline F. b.1840 KY 126
Adoph K. b.1876 28
Adrin b.1845 VA 274
Agitty (Lewis) 154, 175
Agleston b.1829 VA 225
Agnes b.1813 ME 196
Agnes b.1839 KY 175
Agnes b.1842 TN 225
Agnes b.1886 MS 130
Agnes ( ) m2.1565 ENG 256
Agnes (Adams) 257
Agnes (Richardson) 10
Agnes (Tyckowski) 79
Agrippa r.1858 NY 148
Ailey b.1846 TN 221
Ailsey (Curry) 155
Aincy (Morton) (Dear) 37
Aisley b.178– NC 232, 234
Alba b.1810 OH 310
Albert b.1775 VT 145
Albert b.1812 NY 54
Albert b.1821 26, 36
Albert b.18— NC 234
Albert b.1832 AL 157
Albert r.1837 IN 262
Albert b.1839 AL 156
Albert m.1842 OH 203
Albert b.1846 VT 144
Albert m.1847 OH 203
Albert b.1848 VT 143
Albert b.1857 OH 267
Albert r.1863 WI 201
Albert b.1874 IL 55
Albert r.1886 IN 262
Albert r.1890 IN 262
Albert b.1901 KY 169, 251
Albert b.191– NC 229
Albert m.194– TN 60
Albert A. r.1861 TN 305
Albert B. r.1852 IL 183
Albert B. b.1878 OH 12
Albert E. b.1835 VT 146
Albert G. b.1834 AL 157
Albert G. b.1847 WI 308
Albert M./N. m.1877 IN 262
Albert N. b.1832 VT 146
Albert N. r.1861 TN 305
Albert O. m.1946 AR 125
Alberta P. b.1878 106
Alcephus L. b.1867 IL 96
Alden b.1799 ME 4
Aleada Helen (Hammond) 30
Alenda b.1867 28
Alene (Skidmore) 167
Alex b.18— SCO? 73
Alex r.1921 OK 27
Alexander r.1776 MD 34
Alexander r.1778 NS 247
Alexander b.1792 240
Alexander b.1796 SC 156
Alexander r.1812 PA 158, 182
Alexander r.1812 VA 158, 182
Alexander b.1814 ENG 243
Alexander b.1832 KY 127
Alexander r.1849 IL 183
Alexander m.1853 OH 203
Alexander m.1862 OH 203
Alexander r.1866 ENG 12
Alexander r.NS 246
Alexander H. r.1884 AZ 116
Alexander S. b.1850 TN 224
Alfred b.1817 FR 243

Alfred b.1828 VT 146
Alfred Andrew b.1804 NY 39, 203, 250
Alfred B. b.1809 MA 7
Alfred C. b.1826 TN 223
Alfred E. r.1863 WI 201
Alfred H. b.1836 ME 237
Alfred John m.1841 QU 151
Alfred Kelly b.1839 KY 42
Alfred Knight b.1859 QU 151
Alfred Lyman b.1856 VT 26
Alfred Webb b.1829 NC 180, 181, 228, 236
Alfred Webb Jr. b.1860 NC 181
Algernon b.1811 ME 4
Algernon b.1839 VA 223
Algernon Jr. r.1870 IL 183
Alice b.1783 MA 109
Alice b.1798 NC 286
Alice b.18— MA/CT 250
Alice b.18— 199
Alice b.1822 VT 147
Alice b.1846 VT 143
Alice b.1848 VT 145
Alice b.1849 KY 129
Alice b.1849 VT 145
Alice b.184– KY 51
Alice b.1857 KY 85
Alice b.1858 AL 220
Alice b.1862 28
Alice b.1863 NC 181
Alice b.1864 ENG 12
Alice b.1867 28
Alice d.1868 PA 99
Alice b.1880 OH 12
Alice b.19— NC 228
Alice b.KY 169
Alice (Gaston) 39, 203
Alice (Holcomb) 97
Alice (Moss) 97
Alice (Porch?) 228
Alice (Ramo) 26
Alice A. (Cochran) 262
Alice Alvira 111
Alice Anne (Walker) 277
Alice Charity b.1892 NY 101
Alice Edna b.1904 ND 220
Alice G. ( ) 235
Alice Hines (Faught) 271, 273
Alice M. b.18— WI 307
Alice Valeria b.1894 GA 242
Alicia Alice b.1888 WV 39
Alina A. b.1843 VT 146
Alinisia b.1850 KY 128
Alisia (Sarshorm?) 301
Alison b.1812 NY? 50
Alison r.1921 OK 27
Allbrina b.1847 VT 144
Allen b.1805 TN 156
Allen b.1823 TN 225
Allen b.1826 144
Allen r.1833–53 IL 183
Allen b.1845 TN 225
Allen b.1845 VT 145
Allen r.1861 TN 305
Allen Duane b.1933 MO 172
Allen M. b.18— WI 307
Allie (George) 124
Allie M. b.1901 TN? 60
Allison b.1964 OH 82
Alma (Setzer) 199
Alma b.1844 VT 143
Alma b.1892 NC 228
Alma b.1895 227
Alma b.1914 KY 173, 210
Alma r.1981 NC 229
Almer m.1937 AR 124
Almira b.1836 KY 127
Almira m.1835 OH 203
Almira b.1854 MO 131
Almira b.1860 NE,IA? 84
Almira r.1921 OK 27
Almira ( ) b.1816 VT 145
Almira ( ) b.1823 VT 146
Almira (Haywood) 6, 26
Almira L. ( ) b.1818 VT 148
Almon b.1828 VT 146
Almon A. b.1830 17
Almond b.1827 VT 146
Almond H. b.1853 IA 84
Almyra b.1834 NY? 50
Alondie Zula b.1870 KY 271
Alonzo b.1825 VT 145
Alonzo b.1836 VT 143

Alonzo m.1865 OH 203
Alonzo b.KY 167
Alonzo 130
Alonzo D. m.1865 OH? 39
Alonzo F. r.1861 ME 237
Alonzo J. r.1863 WI 201
Alph 233
Alpha b.1820 VT 144
Alpheus M. b.1828 16
Alphonse b.1847 NC 156
Alsina b.1855 WI 285
Alta 130
Alta (White) 124
Alva b.1799 PA 108
Alva b.1810 NY 310
Alva Ester b.1910 NE 230
Alvin b.1810 VT 145
Alvin b.1845 PA 107
Alvin m.1887 PA 108
Alvin 108
Alvin B. b.1800 NY 105
Alvin B. b.1801 PA 107
Alvin B. b.1864 106
Alvin B. d.1882 PA 109
Alvin Bolviar 267
Alvina b.1817 NY? 50
Aly b.1827 NC 129
Alzada (Haynes) 16
Amanda b.1824 NY 67
Amanda b.1828 KY 128
Amanda b.1828?? KY 42
Amanda b.1832 KY 126
Amanda b.1838 TN 221
Amanda b.1838 VT 143
Amanda b.1843 MS 275
Amanda b.1846 TN 222
Amanda b.1861 PA 108
Amanda r.1921 KS 27
Amanda ( ) b.1809 TN 225
Amanda ( ) b.1819 NC 225
Amanda ( ) b.1811 CT 144
Amanda (Harris) 7
Amanda (Hurlburt) 78
Amanda (Jollife) 203
Amanda (Thomas) 51, 85
Amanda A. b.1866 KY? 41
Amanda D. ( ) b.1807 VA 225
Amanda Jane b.MO 118
Amanda M. b.1824 NY 307
Amanda Y. b.1858 116
Amandy M. b.1835 TN 225
Amanuel b.1832 MEX 157
Amanuel r.1856 NC 235
Amasa Comstock b.1796 NY 267
Ambrose b.1757 ENG 67
Ambrose b.1802 KY 127
Ambrose b.1804 11, 20
Ambrose r.1863 WI 201
Ambrose 175
Ameda b.182– NY 105, 109
Ameda b.1864 PA 107
Amelia b.1768 NY 11, 34
Amelia b.1811 KY 128
Amelia b.1840 VT 308
Amelia b.185– NY 175
Amelia b.1866 28
Amelia r.1882 PA 105, 109
Amelia ( ) b.1832 MS 275
Amelia (Barnes) 42
Amelia (Dunbar) 275
Amelia (Redding) 205
Amelia C. b.1844 KY 128
Amelia H. b.1833 KY 128
Amelia R. b.1849 VT 148
Aminadah b.1814 TN 202
Amon b.18— MA/CT 250
Amon r.1812 SC 158
Amond b.1837 NY 175
Amorette b.1849 VT 143
Amos b.1758 NY 6
Amos b.1775 MD 11, 34
Amos r.1790 NY 267
Amos r.1817 OH 267
Amos r.1830 OH 155
Amos b.1845 TN 224
Amos m.1857 OH 203
Amos r.1896 NY 109
Amos E. b.1818 VT 146
Amos E. b.1844 VT 143
Amy b.1784 NC 103, 104, 278
Amy b.1821 NY 109
Amy b.1822 NY 107
Amy b.1870 28
Amy d.1902 PA 106

Amy 107
Amy (Qualls) 60
Amy (Ria) 2
Amy Bridget b.1963 NY 139
Amy Jean b.1972 CT 101
Amzi b.1830 TN 224
Andee 196
Andrew b.1800 VT 143
Andrew b.181– SCO 73
Andrew b.1816 KY 128
Andrew b.1831 MO 285
Andrew r.1833 TN 284
Andrew b.1834 VT 145
Andrew b.1838 VT 144
Andrew b.1891 KY 169
Andrew r.19— ENG 301
Andrew A. b.1820 TN 222
Andrew Bryan 229
Andrew G. m.1853 OH 203
Andrew I. b.1828 NY 309
Andrew J. b.1826 KY 127
Andrew J. b.1828 MS 274
Andrew J. b.1830 NY 67, 307, 309
Andrew J. b.1838 NY 268
Andrew J. b.1839 AL 157
Andrew Jackson b.1816 KY 35, 51, 85
Andrew Mellison b.1865 OR 119, 120
Andrew Miles b.1904 OR 120, 123
Anetta b.1831 VT 145
Angela Rose b.1840 NY 268
Angela Rose 119
Angelina b.1822 148
Angelina ( ) b.1833 TN 224
Angeline b.1818 PA 105, 106, 107, 109
Angelline b.1820 NY 67, 307
Angeline b.1825 TN 61
Angeline m.1841 OH 203
Angeline b.1844 TN 222
Angeline b.1847 TN 226
Angeline 110
Angeline ( ) b.1826 TN 225
Angeline ( ) r.1837 MI 262
Angeline (Austin) 118
Angeline W. b.1845 TN 224, 286
Angie (Middleton) 203
Anie Gene (Highland) 125
Ann b.1756 NJ 196
Ann b.1758 VA 175
Ann b.1780 NS 244
Ann b.1780 VA 127
Ann b.1790 NY 107
Ann b.1801 KY 219
Ann b.1807 QU 151
Ann m.1808 TN 31
Ann b.1815 TN 222
Ann b.1817 KY 127
Ann b.1838 TN 222
Ann b.1846 IL 55
Ann b.1846 WI 310
Ann b.1849 KY 127
Ann m.1857 OH 203
Ann b.1891 NC 199, 231
Ann b.1923 WI 270
Ann ( ) r.1654 ENG 280
Ann ( ) r.1655 BAR 280
Ann ( ) r.1678 BAR 280
Ann ( ) b.1786 CT 6
Ann ( ) b.1793 VT 146
Ann ( ) b.1805 KY 126
Ann ( ) r.1802 MD 35
Ann ( ) b.1810 TN 275
Ann ( ) b.1815 OH 308
Ann ( ) b.190– KY 251
Ann ( ) r.NE 231
Ann ( ) (Quarles) 182
Ann (Baden) b.1757 11, 114, 131, 167, 171, 187, 207, 251
Ann (Belden) 79
Ann (Brewster) 205
Ann (Harper) 203
Ann (Howard) 11, 20, 22, 175
Ann (Lamb) 61
Ann (McConnell) 125
Ann (McGee) 39, 203
Ann (Norton) 203
Ann (Otis) 240
Ann (Rappleye) b.1823 101
Ann (Rodgers) 257
Ann (Sherwood) 116, 117

Ann C. b.1848 KY 128
Ann Celeste b.1960 NY 139
Ann E. b.1834 NY 309
Ann E. b.1840 NY 308
Ann E. b.1844 NY 309
Ann E. r.TN 155
Ann E. ( ) b.1855 31
Ann E. O. b.1848 KY 128
Ann Eliza b.1827 NY 310
Ann Eliza m.1835 OH 203
Ann Eliza b.1842 MS 274
Ann Elizabeth b.1848 KY 42
Ann Frances (Evans) 117, 131
Ann Jennine (Sumbler) 139
Ann Lou (Tate) 168
Ann Modesta b.1849 20
Ann Nancy (Howard) 34
Ann P. m.1800 OH 203
Ann R. (Rappleye) 100
Ann Richard (Wade) 42
Anna m.1731 RI 175
Anna b.1791 CT 146
Anna b.1794 NC 103, 104, 278
Anna b.1806 VT 143
Anna b.1828 TN 224
Anna b.1829 PA 107
Anna b.1840 NY 308
Anna b.1841 VT 145
Anna b.1842 AL 157
Anna m.1860 OH 203
Anna b.1867 28
Anna b.1869 r.OH 12
Anna b.1888 MS 130
Anna b.190– r.OK 228
Anna ( ) b.1784 VT 147
Anna ( ) b.1791 KY 224, 288
Anna ( ) b.1794 MD 128
Anna ( ) b.1802 NY 309
Anna ( ) b.189–/190– OK 12
Anna ( ) 186
Anna (Braddock) 204
Anna (Conner) 206
Anna (Kimes) 203
Anna (McConnell) 17
Anna (Miller) 262
Anna (Nash) 79
Anna (Penley) 197
Anna (Redman) 35
Anna (Reed) 306
Anna A. m.1865 PA 99
Anna C. (Hall) 17
Anna Edine b.1881 MO 79
Anna Eliza (Dougherty) 299
Anna Elizabeth b.1853 WI 285
Anna Elvira (Nash) 78
Anna H. (Freeman) 203
Anna J. b.18— NY 307
Anna Jewell b.19— KY 288
Anna L. b.1875 PA 108
Anna M. b.1849 OH 276
Anna M. (Yolman/Yeoman) 38
Anna Mable (Hogue) 96
Anna Maria b.d.1789 VA 291
Anna Mary b.1900 227
Anna Pearl b.KY 168
Anna S. b.1828 MI 283
Anna Sue b.1939 KY 251,252
Anne b.17— VA/NC 10
Anne b.1806 QU 151
Anne (Stouffer) 98
Anne (Wenman) 246
Anne (Wood) 206
Anne McKenzie (Vance) 151
Annette Abigail m.1856 OH 203
Annette C. b.1838 VT 145
Annie b.18— IL? 97
Annie ( ) b.1845 28
Annie (Coffey) 200
Annie (Frazier) (Parks) 171
Annie (Holsclaw) 230
Annie (Kirkpatrick) 155
Annie (Milton) 125
Annie (Swanson) 277
Annie Belle (Eagle) 229
Annie Carrie b.1876 21
Annie Frances (Brown) 39
Annie H. b.1880? 28
Annis b.1596 ENG 175
Annis b.1636 ENG 255
Annis Agnes r.1596 ENG 175
Anny ( ) b.1806 TN 156
Anny (Spofford) 206
Ansel Piette b.1846 100
Anson L. r.1863 WI 201

AUSTIN,
Carrie m.1878 PA 107
Carrie b.1883 MS 130
Carrie b.1894 106
Carrie b.KY 167
Carrie (Snow) 63
Carrie B. m.1878 PA 108
Carrie May b.1876 28
Carroll b.1829 TN 224
Carroll J. b.1834 TN 275
Cassandra b.1844 KY 42
Cassandra (Odle) 34, 35
Cassandra West b.1802 MD 35
Cassie Catherine 196
Cassie Lola b.1884 TN? 61
Cassius m.1880 OH 203
Cassius Columbus b.1850 39
Caswell r.1861 TN 305
Catharine b.1842 TN 226
Catharine b.1845 TN 221
Catharine (Harper) 205
Catherine b.1780 VA 114
Catherine b.1797 KY 129
Catherine b.1797 11, 20
Catherine b.1818 ON 103, 278
Catherine b.1824 OH 243
Catherine b.1829 OH 130, 250, 283
Catherine b.1831 NC 156
Catherine b.1831 OH? 110
Catherine b.1833 TN 222
Catherine b.1834 VT 145
Catherine b.1835 NC 223
Catherine b.1835 VT 145, 308
Catherine b.1839 VT 147
Catherine r.1844 IL 183
Catherine b.1845 NY 309
Catherine b.1848 144
Catherine b.1849 KY 51, 128
Catherine b.1883 MS 130
Catherine ( ) r.17— ME 240
Catherine ( ) r.18— CT/NY 306
Catherine ( ) b.1803 NY 309
Catherine ( ) b.1820 NC 223
Catherine ( ) b.1821 NY 308
Catherine ( ) b.1821 WI 308
Catherine ( ) r.1799 CT 301
Catherine ( ) b.1854 BAV 12
Catherine (Durbin) 301
Catherine (Eaton) 204
Catherine (Huffman) 115
Catherine (Inyard/Inyart) 118
Catherine (Spangler) 204
Catherine (Van Wagenen) 26, 186
Catherine (Waters) 82
Catherine (White) 278
Catherine A. b.1846 143
Catherine Ann b.1821 KY 115
Catherine Clare (Manning) 21
Catherine Epha (Morgan) 119
Catherine M. m.1917 OH 203
Cathy b.1952 KY 211
Cecil b.186– NY 220
Cecil Joseph b.1912 KY 173, 210, 251
Cedenia Elvira (Pierson) 50
Celestia J. b.1844 IN 309
Celia b.1838 TN 224, 263
Celia b.1843 SC 275
Celia A. 96
Celia Angeline 196
Celia Elizabeth b.1891 TN 267
Celia Isabelle (Harris) 197, 198, 199, 235
Celia J. b.1836 TN 224
Celia Melissa b.1867 NH 48
Chadwick Leroy b.1919 231
Chalista b.1830 VT 145
Champness b.1769 VA 37
Chancy b.1846 VT 144
Chandler b.1832 VT 146
Chapman r.1812 VA 158
Charity b.1838 AL 157
Charity b.1844 TN 225
Charity (DeCou) 279
Charity (Kendrick) 11, 34, 40, 85, 271
Charity J. (Dunbar) 262
Charlene Theresa (Flynn) 139
Charles r.17— NC 232
Charles r.1750 NC 250
Charles b.1756 IRE 232, 286
Charles b.1786 NC 224
Charles b.1788 151

Charles b.1788 MA 13, 15
Charles r.1789 KY? 155
Charles b.1794 NC 223
Charles b.1796 NC 250
Charles b.1797 233
Charles b.1797 NC 126, 232
Charles b.18— 288
Charles d.18— TN 286
Charles b.1805 VT 148
Charles b.1807 SC 275
Charles r.1808 KY 286
Charles b.1808 VT 145
Charles d.181– 182
Charles r.1812 GA 158, 182
Charles r.1812 VA 158
Charles d.1813 QU 151
Charles b.1815 PA 105, 106, 107, 109
Charles b.1816 IL 243
Charles r.1818 IL 183
Charles r.1823 NS 265
Charles b.1827 TN 156
Charles b.1835 TN 221
Charles b.1836 NY 309
Charles b.1837 VT 144
Charles b.1838 ME 237
Charles b.1838 VT 145
Charles b.1838 WI 308
Charles b.1839 KY 127
Charles m.1843 PA 107
Charles b.d.1843 NY 268
Charles b.1843 VT 145
Charles b.1844 MI 38
Charles b.1844 PA 107
Charles b.1848 TN 221
Charles b.1848 WI 308
Charles b.1849 AL 130
Charles b.1850 NC 221
Charles r.1861 ME 237
Charles r.1861 TN 305
Charles r.1863 WI 201
Charles r.1864 IN 262
Charles r.1865 28
Charles b.1869 WI 285
Charles b.1871 NY 196
Charles m.1876 IN 262
Charles b.1876 28
Charles b.189– IA 85
Charles d.1897 PA 108
Charles b.1914 OH 82
Charles r.1921 OK 27
Charles b.192– NE 230
Charles r.KS 160, 162, 164
Charles A. r.18— KY 206
Charles A. r.1812 LA 158
Charles A. m.1861 OH 203
Charles A. r.ME 2
Charles Andrew b.1856 QU 300
Charles B. b.1840 MS 275
Charles B. m.1844 OH 203
Charles B. S. b.186– 97
Charles Benjamin b.1857 220, 263
Charles C. b.1813 VA 128
Charles C. r.1834 NS 265
Charles C. b.1847 WI 309
Charles C. r.1863 WI 201
Charles D. b.1796 NY 308
Charles D. r.1829 NS 248
Charles David b.1856 NC 181, 200
Charles E. b.1839 ENG 12
Charles E. b.1842 VT 147
Charles E. b.1849 VT 143
Charles E. r.1902 IN 262
Charles Edward b.1810 MA 7
Charles Edwin r.1986 AL 31, 58
Charles Eugene b.1853 IL 269, 270
Charles Eugene b.d.1901 WI 270
Charles F. b.1848 CT 75
Charles G. m.1825 OH 203
Charles G. b.1846 OH 310
Charles Gordon 11
Charles H. b.1842 KY 126
Charles H. b.1842 TN 223
Charles H. b.1844 IN 243
Charles H. d.1901 PA 99
Charles H. b.NC 233
Charles Henry r.1798 ME 2, 85
Charles Kenneth b.1927 NC 229
Charles Kenneth 231
Charles L. b.1807 VT 147
Charles L. b.1840 ME 237

Charles L. b.1848 VT 144
Charles L. b.1872 17
Charles L. m.NC 206
Charles M. b.1875 r.OH 12
Charles Martin b.1869 21
Charles Maxwell r.1980 ME 7
Charles P. b.184– PA 107
Charles P. r.1863 WI 201
Charles R. d.1873 PA 106
Charles R. b.1892 TX 167
Charles Raines b.1884 TX 287
Charles S. b.1858 PA 99
Charles S. b.1892 OR 123
Charles Starbuck b.CAN 283
Charles W. b.1843 PA 99
Charles W. b.185– 96
Charles W. m.1863 IN 262
Charles William b.1884 AR 50
Charley Albert b.1886 31
Charlie m.1919 AR 124
Charlie E. b.1880 IL 55
Charlotta b.1835 AL 157
Charlotte b.1776 NH 146
Charlotte b.1784 MA 109
Charlotte r.1806 PA 43
Charlotte b.1808 ON 103, 278
Charlotte b.1820 VT 143
Charlotte b.1823 VT 283
Charlotte m.1828 OH 203
Charlotte b.1830 NY 143
Charlotte b.1834 MA 275
Charlotte m.1839 OH 203
Charlotte b.1843 KY 128
Charlotte r.1863 QU 299
Charlotte b.1876 106
Charlotte b.NC 233
Charlotte ( ) b.1795 NC 223
Charlotte ( ) b.1803 NY 308
Charlotte ( ) b.1829 TN 221
Charlotte ( ) b.1812 VT 147
Charlotte (Briggs) 206, 276
Charlotte (Ewing) 196
Charlotte (Funk) 204
Charlotte Ann b.1842 KY 42
Charlotte B. ( ) b.1827 54
Charlotte C. 109
Charlotte DeClare b.1868 QU 299
Charlotte Emma b.1882 OH 81,82
Charlotte L. b.1832 VT 147
Charlotte Loduska b.1868 MI 80, 81, 82
Charlotte R. (Moore) 16
Charlotte S. b.1823 ME 140
Charlotte Sophia (Ewing) 80, 81
Chauncey b.1795 NY r.PA 106, 107, 109
Chauncey b.1840 PA r.WI 310
Chauncey J. r.1863 WI 201
Chester James b.1885 OH 81, 82
Chester Mills b.1823 NY 242
Chester b.1826 VT 147
China A. ( ) b.1830 KY 126
Chloe m.1806 OH 203
Chloe (Joyce) 95
Chloe E. m.1849 VT 146
Chris r.KY 212
Christian b.1809 TN 224, 288
Christian b.1873 r.WI 28
Christina ( ) b.1831 VA 129
Christina Marie b.1974 CA 214
Christine r.1916 273
Christine b.KY 271
Christine (Davis) 125
Christine (Snyder) 204
Christopher b.1840 TN 225
Christopher r.1853 IL 183
Christopher b.1854 KY 51
Christopher B. r.1817 IL 183
Christopher Mark b.1972 CT 101
Christopher P. b.1854/5 85
Cintha (Martin) 40
Clair (male) 196
Clara b.1849 VT 146
Clara d.1868 PA 99
Clara ( ) d.1853 PA 108
Clara ( ) d.1874 PA 108
Clara (Hook) 88
Clara A. (Mooney) 98, 104
Clara Bell (Meek) 82
Clara Belle 99
Clara Catherine (Simpson) 139
Clara E. b.18— IL 95
Clara E. b.1870 97
Clara E. b.1898 NY 100, 101

Clara Edith b.1877 ME 4
Clara J. ( ) 236
Clara M. (Dartt) 107
Clara M. r.1868 PA 99
Clara N. d.1871 PA 106
Clarence b.186– IL 95
Clarence b.188– IA 85
Clarence b.1891 OH 81
Clarence b.19— 228
Clarence Donald b.1914 230
Clarence E. b.d.1878 PA 108
Claria b.1831 TN 223
Clarinda b.1833 VT 143
Clarinda m.1835 OH 203
Clarinda A. b.1843 TN 225
Clarissa b.1785 106
Clarissa m.1835 OH 203
Clarissa b.1822 TN 222
Clarissa b.1844 PA 107
Clarissa b.1847 TN 224
Clarissa ( ) b.1792 VT 144
Clarissa ( ) b.1802 VT 143, 147
Clarissa (Brown) 250
Clarissa (Peterson) (Brooks) 105, 106, 107, 109, 301
Clarissa A. b.1840 TN 225
Clarissa M. ( ) b.1826 VT 148
Clarissa M. (Harris) 98
Clarissa H. d.1905 PA 99
Clark b.1839 NY 309
Clark b.1840 VT 145
Clark r.1863 WI 201
Clark D. b.1873 97
Clarsitta b.1843 GA 157
Clary b.1823 155
Claude b.1877 21
Claude r.1900 IN 262
Claudia Morton (Ely) 21
Clay b.KY? 38
Clement Reid b.1871 KY? 41
Clemenza Josephine b.1845 OH 155
Cleo (Edwards) 124
Cleo (Lawler) 167
Cliffe r.1812 VA 158
Clifford b.19— 227
Clifford m.1934 AR 124
Clyde Cooper r.1967 KY 211
Clyde Edward 111
Clyde Lee b.1898 TX 283
Clyde R. b.18— MI 196
Collins b.1834 NY 43, 155
Columbus b.183– KY 42
Columbus b.1847 AL 157
Columbus m.1943 AR 125
Constance b.1850 VT 145
Constance ( ) b.1830 VT 145
Constance May b.1863 QU 299
Cora 95
Cora (Penley) 197
Cora Alice (Tate) 21
Cora Ann b.MO 118
Cora B. (Leonard) 6, 26
Cora Belle b.1861 OH 80, 81
Cora D. ( ) 236
Cora Dixon (Dickson) 267
Cora Lee b.1894 NC 199
Cordelia b.1826 VT 144
Cordelia b.1830 VT 143
Cordelia b.1831 VT 143
Cordelia b.1835 VT 145
Cordelia ( ) b.1826 ME 309
Cordelia ( ) b.1823 VT 143
Cordelia Angeline b.MO 118
Cordelia E. b.1840 54
Corinna ( ) b.1827 KY 128
Corinna (Thomas) 40
Cornelia b.1833 NY 309
Cornelia b.1833 VT 144
Cornelia b.1849 CT 310
Cornelia r.1880 IN 262
Cornelia (Bradshaw) 178, 197, 227, 230, 231, 235
Cornelia (Cooper) (Smith) 306
Cornelia A. (Smith) 95
Cornelia Jane b.1902 22
Cornelius b.1797 MD? 85
Cornelius r.1812 NC 158
Cornelius b.1836 NY 119, 123, 268
Cornelius m.1846 OH 203
Cornelius m.1850 OH 203
Cornelius r.1861 TN 305

Cornelius 120
Corrah b.1888 OH 81
Cull 233
Culpepper 233
Curtis b.1834 VT 145
Curtis L. b.1853 VT 26
Cylvesta b.1837 TN 225
Cyntha N. b.1839 AL 157
Cynthia b.1785 SC 156
Cynthia b.1817 TN 224, 288
Cynthia ( ) b.1823 GA 157
Cynthia Alice b.1868 KY 287
Cynthia E. b.1840 NC 223
Cynthia E. b.1846 TN 223
Cynthia J. b.1840 TN 224
Cynthia Jane b.1822 NY? 50
Cyrenthia m.1841 OH 203
Cyrus b.1804 ME 237
Cyrus b.1827 NY? 50
Cyrus r.1837 IL 183
Cyrus b.1845 ENG 12
Cyrus r.1904 ME 238
Cyrus N. b.1850 WI 308

AUSTIN, D
D. b.1844 KY 126
D. A. b.1849 KY 126
D. C. b.1840 KY 127
D. M. 233
D. P. b.1849 KY 127
D. S. r.1861 TN (male) 305
D. W. b.1821 (male) 157
Daisy b.1871 OR 119
Dallas b.1844?? KY 51
Dallas D. b.1852 KY 85
Dalton Willard m.1944 AR 125
Damina ( ) b.1826 MO 225
Daniel b.1698 MA 8, 14
Daniel b.1711 MA 8, 9, 10, 29
Daniel b.1724 MA 14
Daniel b.1727 MA 14
Daniel r.1767 ME 241
Daniel b.1771 MA/ME 109, 186, 196
Daniel b.1773 ME/MA 148
Daniel b.1773 MA 62
Daniel b.1782 MA 6, 148
Daniel b.1783 NH 44
Daniel b.1788 ME 2
Daniel b.1789 MA 309
Daniel b.1793 KY 31
Daniel b.1793 TN 58
Daniel b.1795 NH 309
Daniel b.1797 KY 129
Daniel b.1799 MA 310
Daniel m.1800 CT 67
Daniel r.1800 NY 206
Daniel b.1801 241
Daniel b.1805 MA 29
Daniel b.1806 NY 78
Daniel b.1806 VT 143
Daniel r.1812 KY 158
Daniel r.1812 TN 182
Daniel r.1815 TN 59
Daniel b.1817 NY 107
Daniel b.1824 ME 237
Daniel r.1825 NY 306
Daniel b.1827 KY 129
Daniel b.1829 ENG 12
Daniel b.1832 AL 31
Daniel b.1833 VT 143
Daniel b.1835 PA 107
Daniel b.1838 VT 145
Daniel r.1842 ME 237
Daniel r.1842 NC 235
Daniel b.1842 KY 129
Daniel b.1842 ME 237
Daniel b.1842 MO 75, 85
Daniel m.1844 OH 203
Daniel b.1848 KY 129
Daniel b.1849 CT 310
Daniel r.1861 TN 305
Daniel r.1893 CA 108
Daniel B. b.182– PA 105, 109
Daniel B. b.1863 PA 107
Daniel Brackett b.1800 ME 148
Daniel C. b.1849 TN 221
Daniel D. r.1863 WI 201
Daniel D. m.1871 PA 108
Daniel H. b.1821 VT 146
Daniel Henry b.1834 3
Daniel J. b.1959 BER 212
Daniel L. b.1823 96
Daniel L. b.1842 TN 222

AUSTIN,

Daniel Milton b.1876 MO 79
Daniel S. r.1861 TN 305
Daniel Webster b.1844 NY 148
Daniel Wesley b.1832 AL 26
Darkis b.1779 NH 44
Darling b.1811 TN (male) 275
Dave b.18— 233
David b.17— r.TX 175
David b.17— VA? 196
David b.17— 106
David b.1740 MA 15
David b.1754 r.NY/PA
David b.177– CT 79, 100
David b.1776 VA 37
David r.1779 ME 237
David b.1780 AL 156
David b.178– VA 177
David b.1788 VT 143
David b.1792 CT 144
David b.1797 RI 119, 268
David b.18— NY 43
David b.18— 288
David b.1808 VT 145
David b.1811 NY 6
David r.1812 IN 158
David r.1812 MD 158
David r.1812 TN 158, 182, 284
David r.1812 VA 158
David b.1813?? 60
David b.1814 WALES 28
David b.1816 TN 61
David b.1817 TN 222
David r.1820 OH 25
David b.1820 ON 103, 278
David m.1829 OH 203
David b.1829 NJ 243
David b.1833 AL 156
David r.1834 IL 183
David b.1836 VT 146
David b.1839 AL 156
David r.1839 IL 183
David b.1839 NY 175
David b.1845 ENG 12
David b.1846 VT 145
David b. 1846 111
David b.1847 AL 156
David m.1848 ME 282
David b.1848 OH 203
David b.1849 KY 129
David b.1860 107
David b.1860 28
David r.1861 TN 305
David b.1862 QU 151
David r.1863 WI 201
David r.1895 NC 235
David r.1900 ME 250
David r.1927 ME 238
David r.1929 ME 238
David r.NC 233
David m.OH 203
David r.PA 267
David B. b.1797 NY 145
David B. m.1849 OH 203
David B. m.1850 OH 203
David Brown 240
David Don b.1955 OH 82
David E. b.1827 OH 276
David Franklin d.IA 276
David H. b.1792 283
David H. r.1861 235
David Hamilton b.1836 KY 42
David Jr. b.1826 VT 144
David L. m.1852 OH 203
David L. b.1870 ENG 12
David Lee b.1949 OH 208, 214
David P. r.1846 IL 183
David P. Trigg b.1823 TN 129
David Paul b.1950 NY 139
David S. b.1805 VT 145
David S. r.1812 VA 158
David S. r.1814 VA 158
David S. m.1850 OH 203
David S. m.1870 OH 203
David W. b.1824 WI 309
David W. r.1846 IL 183
David W. b.1847 TN 222
Davidella b.1848 KY 127
Davis r.1768 SC 129
Debbie ( ) b.1809 SC 274
Deborah b.1737 MA 15
Deborah b.1780 VT 6
Deborah ( ) r.1809 IN/WI 155
Deborah ( ) r.1820 OH/MI 129

Deborah b.NH 219
Deborah (Cummings) 203
Deborah (Hall) 4
Deborah (Reynolds) 96
Deborah F. (Thompson) 204
Dee Clayton 196
Deedie May b.1889 MO 79
Dehlia (Smith) 124
Delaney b.1786 NC 206
Delaney b.1806 NC 232
Delia b.1823 VT 146
Delia b.1834 VT 144
Delia b.1838 AL 26, 31
Delight ( ) b.1784 NY 263
Delila b.1838 AL 26, 31
Delila C. m.1878 OH 203
Della ( ) 172
Della (Pharr) 197
Della (Wells) 74
Della B. (Wilham) 169
Dellie b.KY 169
Dellie 131
Delores (Gray) 209
Delores Ann b.1939 OH 208
Delia b.1820 VT 144
Dennis b.1825 IN 96, 97
Dennis b.1855 MI 166
Dennis Bradford b.1855 MI 165
Densy d.VT 55
Dewey 97
Dexter b.1806?? MA 7
Diadama 36
Diadama ( ) b.1827 VT 144
Diana b.1850 VT 145
Diana Lee b.1971 CA 214
Dianna b.1823 VT 148
Diantha 106
Dicey ( ) b.1800 NC 222
Dicey (Horner) 182
Dickerson r.1812 TN 182
Dickerson b.1898 VA 225
Dilla (Pace) 175
Dinah ( ) b.1840 ENG 12
Docia Mae m.1938 AR 124
Dollie b.1890 KY 168
Dolly b.1740 NH 15
Dolores Ann b.1939 OH 213
Donald b.1935 KY 173
Donald Lewis b.1949 KY 212
Donna (Currier) 139
Donna (Sayers) 212
Donna G. (Brown) 174
Donna Jean (Hacker) 211
Donna S. b.1937 KY 207
Donna Sue b.1937 OH 212
Dora m.1878 IN 262
Dora r.1915 IN 262
Dora (Hawkins) 124
Dora (Waddle/Weddle) 251
Dora (Wakely) 98
Dora Joe 228
Dorcas b.1771 NH 148
Dorcas b.1779 MA 109
Dorcas ( ) b.1817 AL 222
Dorcas ( ) d.1836 TN 61
Dorcas (Carlton) 29
Dorcas Carolina b.1838 KY 42, 128
Dorna A. b.1867 106
Dorothea ( ) b.1822 128
Dorothy ( ) 89, 90
Dorothy (Cooper) 210
Dorothy (Morgan) 251
Dorothy Ann b.1925 KS 277
Dorothy Ann (Bean) 30
Dorothy B. (Chinn) 51, 85
Dorothy Jane b.1832 ME 140, 141
Dorothy Jean (Mitchusson) 125
Dorothy Mae b.1935 OH 208, 213
Dorothy May (Pulver) 101
Dory b. 1825 TN 126
Dosia b.1832 TN 224
Dotts 233
Drewry r.1768 SC 129
Drury r.1768 SC 129
Drury b.1828 TN 223
Drury Jane 196
Drusilla (Hatfield) 206
Dulcina b.1824 KY 222
Duley b.1852 IL 183
Dustin David b.1985 KY 211
Dwight 105
Dyer b.1829 VT 143

AUSTIN, E

E. b.1800 RI 243
E. b.1817 OH (male) 308
E. b.1820 NY 243
E. b.1825 MA 243
E. b.1848 OH (male) 310
E. r.1861 ME 237
E. ( ) b.1792 KY 126
E. A. ( ) b.1808 KY 126
E. B. M. r.1867 QU 299
E. C. S. b.1840 TN 222
E. D. r.1861 TN (male) 305
E. D. m.1892 98
E. F. b.1850 TN 126
E. H. r.1861 TN (male) 305
E. J. r.1903 NC 235
E. K. r.1861 TN (male) 305
E. K. b.1816 MA 224
E. T. r.1861 TN (male) 305
E. W. 233
Eady b.1793 NC 232
Earl b.18— MO? 118
Earl b.189– NC 228
Earl Jefferson 229
Earnest G. 12
Easter m.1838 OH 203
Easter m.1920 AR 124
Easter (James) 11
Eben b.1833 NY 309
Eben H. r.1843 IL 183
Ebenezer r.1771 MA 24
Ebenezer m.1789 241
Ebenezer r.1790 VT 25
Ebenezer b.1790 ME 241
Ed r.1861 TN 305
Edgar b.1822 VT 144
Edgar m.1935 AR 124
Edgar A. b.1834 NY 63
Edgar A. r.1863 WI 201
Edgar F. r.1849 PA 106
Edgar F. b.1823 PA 107
Edgar H. r.1862 PA 99
Edgar S. Y. 109
Edith b.1795 NC 206
Edith b.1842 96
Edith r.1916 273
Edith b.1923 KY 173, 210
Edith ( ) b.1855 CAN 28
Edith (Boyd) 172
Edith Allen (Rand) 172
Edith M. 97
Edith Mae d.1973 MO 111
Edith May b.1882 NY 3, 5, 11, 25, 38, 57, 109, 111, 112, 119, 125, 150, 214, 219, 289, 298
Edith P. 104
Edith Pauline (Smith) 125
Edith Virginia b.1906 96
Edmond b.1819 VT 144
Edmund b.1835 QU 151
Edmund b.1835 PA 109
Edmund b.1838 PA 107
Edmund b.1868 OR 123
Edmund b.1901 OR 123
Edmund A. b.1868 OR 119, 120
Edmund Hale b.1867 QU 151
Edmund Jones b.1870 NC 181
Edmund Jones b.1870 TN 228
Edmund St. C. 153
Edna b.187– IL 97
Edna b.1887 OH 81
Edna b.188– IL 95
Edna (Barker) 39
Edna (Brown) 307
Edna (McGahan) 169
Edna Christine b.1895 22
Edna M. b.1887 OH 83
Edson L. b.18— WI 307
Edson Norman b.1857 NY 135
Edward r.1680 BAR 281
Edward b.1702 BAR 281
Edward m.1737 98
Edward m.1748 98
Edward b.1773 RI 3
Edward b.1778 VT 143
Edward b.1800 288
Edward b.18— ON 104
Edward r.1812 VA 158
Edward b.1815 TN 224
Edward b.1832 KY 20
Edward b.1833 TN 226
Edward b.1835 VA 221
Edward b.1837 QU 151

Edward b.1842 VT 145
Edward b.1843 OH 308
Edward b.1845 NY 308
Edward b.1845 TN 226
Edward r.1851 IL 183
Edward r.1861 TN 305
Edward b.1862 28
Edward r.1863 WI 201
Edward b.1864 r.OH 12
Edward b.1866 r.OH 12
Edward b.1872 IA 84
Edward b.1879 NC 199
Edward r.1880 MA 76, 77
Edward m.1902 79
Edward b.1917 KY 174
Edward b.KY 168
Edward d.MO 43
Edward b.ON 279
Edward A. b.1843 OH 309
Edward A. b.1853 NY 63
Edward A. r.1863 WI 201
Edward C. m.1845 OH 203
Edward E. b.1813 NY 243
Edward E. b.1816 NY 111
Edward Ferris b.1917 OH 83
Edward G. b.1842 AL 223
Edward G. m.1894 KY 271, 273
Edward H. b.1856 MA 6, 26
Edward L. b.1817?? MA 7
Edward Nash b.1897 MO 79
Edward P. b.1830 VT 145
Edward S. b.1837 ME 237
Edward Thomas b.1923 NC 230, 231
Edward W. b.1822 VT 243
Edward W. r.1840–42 IL 183
Edward W. m.1855 OH 203
Edward Willis b.1873 KY (female) 287
Edwin b.1818 TN 128
Edwin b.1820 MA 243
Edwin b.1834 NY 310
Edwin b.1835 VA 223
Edwin b.1835 VT 143
Edwin b.1844 NY 309
Edwin b.1845 VT 147
Edwin b.1849 TN 221
Edwin r.1861 ME 237
Edwin b.1862 r.OH 12
Edwin r.1863 WI 201
Edwin b.1870 28
Edwin b.1879 28
Edwin d.TX 133
Edwin H. r.1863 WI 201
Edwin J. b.1830 TN 221
Edwin J. r.1863 WI 201
Edwin L. b.1817?? MA 7
Edwin Zenas 6
Effie b.187– IL 95
Effie (Morgan) 120, 268
Effie (Post) 250
Eggelston b.1803 VA 225, 242
Eggleston b.1829 VA 225
Elan b.1813 VT 145
Elanson B. 99
Elbert r.1916 273
Elcie ( ) 214
Eleanor b.1826 KY 127
Eleanor r.1837 IL 183
Eleanor m.1850 OH 204
Eleanor r.1851 IL 183
Eleanor ( ) b.1804 TN 224
Eleanor ( ) r.1829 NS 248
Eleanor ( ) 115
Eleanor (Brander) 240
Eleanor (Fittock) 73
Eleanor (Warnick) 110
Eleanor L. (Whitten) 74
Eleanor T. b.1848 KY 128
Eleanor W. ( ) r.1880 IN 262
Eleazer b.1786 RI 144
Eleazer r.1818 IL 183
Eleazer b.1840 VT 145
Eleazer Hazen r.1842 IL 183
Electa b.1801 VT 146
Electa m.1841 OH 203
Electa b.1843 VT 145
Electa b.1845 VT 145
Electa b.1850 VT 144
Electa ( ) b.1821 NY 310
Electa (Lyman) 44
Electa A. b.1847 VT 146
Elen b.1844 KY 126
Elender ( ) b.1800 SC 274

Elener T. b.1848 KY 128
Elenor b.1826 KY 127
Elhanan b.1825 VT 145
Elhanan r.1895 NC 235
Elhanan 181
Eli r.1773 VT 57
Eli b.1779 VT 146
Eli b.1824 CAN 145
Eli b.1827 VT 143
Eli b.1835 IL 183
Eli b.1846 VT 145
Eli r.1863 WI 201
Eli r.NY/PA 110
Elias b.1780 RI 6
Elias b.1803 VT 144
Elias G.r.NY/PA 110
Elias W. b.1842 NY 309
Elihu r.1779 CT 301, 306
Elihu r.1799 220
Elihu r.180– NY 306
Elijah b.1751 CT 242
Elijah b.1774 NC 6
Elijah b.1777 MA 44
Elijah b.1790 VT 144
Elijah b.1794 VT 146, 196
Elijah b.1800 VT 309
Elijah b.1812 NC 75
Elijah b.1812 OH 308
Elijah b.1814 NY 250
Elijah b.1825 VT 143
Elijah b.1831 TN 224
Elijah b.1833 TN 224
Elijah b.1835 NC 75, 85
Elijah b.1838 TN 223
Elijah r.1839 IL 183
Elijah b.1841 TN 224
Elijah b.1844 NC 235
Elijah Addison b.1827 NY 242
Elijah F. b.1814 TN 221
Elijah Harrison b.1841 TN 263
Elijah Jr. r.1840 NC 235
Elijah R. m.1841 OH 203
Elijah R. b.1841 WI 308
Elijah R. r.OH 39
Elijah Sopher b.1799 r.VT 196
Elijah W. r.1863 WI 201
Eliphalet r.1799 OH 19
Eliphalet b.1819 OH 203
Eliphalet m.1835 OH 203
Eliphalet 22
Elisa b.1853 ENG 28
Elisabeth b.1573 ENG 256
Elisabeth m.1838 OH 204
Elise (Weaver) 98
Elisha r.1834–50 IL 183
Elisha r.1837–53 IL 183
Elisha b.1839 TN 223
Elisha r.1854 IL 184
Eliza b.1811 VT 143
Eliza b.1817 TN 202
Eliza b.1822 NY 54
Eliza b.1823 SC 156
Eliza b.1827 VT 283
Eliza b.1829 KY 127
Eliza b.1830 KY 42
Eliza b.1830 VT 143
Eliza b.1830 AL 26
Eliza b.1833 TN 224
Eliza b.1839 TN 223
Eliza b.1839 VT 143
Eliza b.1841 TN 221
Eliza b.1842 AL 156
Eliza b.184– TN 38
Eliza b.1843 OH 276
Eliza b.1845 MS 275
Eliza b.1854 AL 130
Eliza b.MD d.1839 35
Eliza ( ) b.1794 VT 144
Eliza ( ) b.1803 KY 128
Eliza ( ) b.1805 VT 147
Eliza ( ) b.1813 KY 129
Eliza ( ) b.1814 VT 148
Eliza ( ) b.1819 AL 274
Eliza ( ) b.1820 MS 274
Eliza ( ) b.1821 VT 143
Eliza ( ) b.1823 AL 157
Eliza ( ) b.1824 OH 275
Eliza ( ) b.1824 TN 222
Eliza ( ) b.1872 r.WI 307
Eliza (Brikford) 306
Eliza (Harrington) 144
Eliza (Harris) 97
Eliza (Hobart) 74, 75
Eliza (Huyck) 54

AUSTIN,

Eliza (Mason) 40
Eliza (Mills) 204
Eliza (Walton) 274
Eliza A. ( ) b.1813 VT 146
Eliza A. ( ) b.1816 IN 308
Eliza A. ( ) b.1816 VT 145
Eliza Ann 196
Eliza Ann ( ) (Dixon) 286
Eliza Ann ( ) 219
Eliza Ann b.1802 219
Eliza Ann b.1825 ME 125
Eliza Ann m.1842 ME 125
Eliza Ann b.1864 KY 287
Eliza Anna (Dougherty) 299
Eliza B. b.1828 MA 7
Eliza C. b.1833 AL 156
Eliza E. b.1851 KY 118
Eliza Fuller b.d.1790 VA 291
Eliza Hannah m.1836 OH 204
Eliza J. b.1836 TN 128
Eliza J. b.1839 TN 221
Eliza J. b.1843 CAN 145
Eliza J. m.1857 OH 204
Eliza J. b.1859 KY 85
Eliza Jane b.1824 MA 7
Eliza Jane b.1837 TN 222
Eliza Jane b.1850 QU 152
Eliza P. b.1825 ME 140
Eliza P. b.1836 VT 147
Elizabeth r.1660 RI 73
Elizabeth r.16—/17— NH 240
Elizabeth m.1713 RI 175
Elizabeth b.1726 MA 14
Elizabeth b.176– RI 148
Elizabeth b.1762 MD 79
Elizabeth b.1773 MA 44
Elizabeth b.177– VA 177
Elizabeth b.1775 NC 222
Elizabeth b.1778 148
Elizabeth b.1778 CT 219
Elizabeth b.1783 TN 58
Elizabeth b.1785 VA 114, 156
Elizabeth b.1786 GA 222
Elizabeth b.1786 VA/TN 31
Elizabeth b.1788 129
Elizabeth b.1790 KY 127
Elizabeth b.1792 NC 103, 104, 278
Elizabeth b.1796 NY/CAN 11
Elizabeth b.1798 GA 127
Elizabeth b.1800 KY 129
Elizabeth b.1803 NC 234
Elizabeth b.1806 TN 127
Elizabeth b.1807 MD 35, 42
Elizabeth b.1808 TN 226
Elizabeth b.1810 TN 301, 308
Elizabeth b.1810 ENG 28
Elizabeth b.1812 KY 127
Elizabeth b.1814 KY 128
Elizabeth b.1815 NY 310
Elizabeth b.1815 ON 103, 279
Elizabeth b.18— NS 245
Elizabeth b.1819 ON 278
Elizabeth b.1820 155
Elizabeth b.1820 NC 221
Elizabeth b.1822 SC 157
Elizabeth b.1822 TN 222
Elizabeth b.1822 d.NY 54
Elizabeth b.1823 OH 40
Elizabeth b.1825 KY 127
Elizabeth b.1825 NY? 50
Elizabeth b.1827 KY 128
Elizabeth b.1828 GA 156
Elizabeth b.1828 VA 221
Elizabeth b.1829 TN 156, 222
Elizabeth b.1831 NY 148
Elizabeth b.1831 SC 223
Elizabeth b.1831 TN 274
Elizabeth b.1832 ON 278
Elizabeth b.1832 QU 84
Elizabeth b.1832 TN 225
Elizabeth b.1833 VT 145
Elizabeth b.1835 OH 128
Elizabeth b.1835 TN 224
Elizabeth b.1836 NY 307, 309
Elizabeth b.1836 PA 67
Elizabeth b.1836 TN 225
Elizabeth b.1837 TN 225
Elizabeth b.1838 TN 223
Elizabeth b.1840 KY 126
Elizabeth b.1840 SC 274
Elizabeth b.1840 TN 128, 225
Elizabeth b.1840 VA 225

Elizabeth b.1840 VT 144
Elizabeth b.18— NC 233
Elizabeth b.1841 KY 117
Elizabeth b.1841 TN 223, 226
Elizabeth b.1842 KY 127
Elizabeth b.1845 KY 126, 127
Elizabeth b.1846 IL 38
Elizabeth b.1846 KY 51, 85
Elizabeth b.1846 TN 222
Elizabeth b.1847 TN 222
Elizabeth m.1848 OH 204
Elizabeth b.1848 NY 54
Elizabeth b.1848 VA 148
Elizabeth b.1848 MS 274
Elizabeth b.1849 TN 225
Elizabeth b.1850 219
Elizabeth b.1850 TN 222
Elizabeth m.1851 OH 204
Elizabeth b.1852 VA 288
Elizabeth b.1862 KY 51, 85
Elizabeth m.1865 OH 204
Elizabeth b.1865 KY 51, 85
Elizabeth b.1866 NY 155
Elizabeth r.1874 NY 54
Elizabeth b.1875 ENG 12
Elizabeth b.1880 28
Elizabeth r.1890 ME 238
Elizabeth b.189–/190– NC 228
Elizabeth b.1922 NY 139
Elizabeth ( ) r.1636 ENG 255
Elizabeth ( ) r.17— 129
Elizabeth ( ) b.1792 MA r.NY 148
Elizabeth ( ) r.1800 MD 35
Elizabeth ( ) r.1807 KY 286
Elizabeth ( ) r.1808 QU 151
Elizabeth ( ) r.1809 QU 154
Elizabeth ( ) b.1810 GA 225
Elizabeth ( ) b.1814 NY 127
Elizabeth ( ) b.1814 VA 221
Elizabeth ( ) b.1818 TN 275
Elizabeth ( ) b.1823 AL 275
Elizabeth ( ) r.1825 ME 125
Elizabeth ( ) b.1826 AL 156
Elizabeth ( ) b.1826 TN 225
Elizabeth ( ) r.1829 PA 98
Elizabeth ( ) b.1832 31
Elizabeth ( ) b.1847 r.OH 12
Elizabeth ( ) b.1848 r.MN 28
Elizabeth ( ) b.1850 r.WI 28
Elizabeth ( ) b.1857 r.WI 28
Elizabeth ( ) r.1902 IL 111
Elizabeth ( ) (Dyer) 202
Elizabeth (Anderson) 279
Elizabeth (Barnard) 152
Elizabeth (Billings) 242
Elizabeth (Boyer) 98
Elizabeth (Brown) 171
Elizabeth (Burgess) 182
Elizabeth (Clark) 17, 67
Elizabeth (Culbertson) 206
Elizabeth (Curd) (Utterback) 285
Elizabeth (Curlee) 234
Elizabeth (Deal) 182
Elizabeth (Duncanson) 206
Elizabeth (Fletcher) 116, 117, 133
Elizabeth (Gordon) 6, 10, 43
Elizabeth (Gover) b.1796 37
Elizabeth (Griffin) 233
Elizabeth (Hamilton) 234
Elizabeth (Howard) 26, 36
Elizabeth (Johnson) 204
Elizabeth (Johnston) 206
Elizabeth (King) 204
Elizabeth (Letson) 245, 246
Elizabeth (Lindsey) 69
Elizabeth (Marshall) 175
Elizabeth (Marshman) 246
Elizabeth (Metcalf) 84
Elizabeth (Nest) 20
Elizabeth (Odle) 35
Elizabeth (Oliver) b.1778 37
Elizabeth (Osborne) 99, 104
Elizabeth (Pettengill) 44
Elizabeth (Rasmus) 74
Elizabeth (Remline) 206
Elizabeth (Ryon) 301
Elizabeth (Sears) 204
Elizabeth (Stevenson) 11
Elizabeth (Strawn) 182
Elizabeth (Tatum) b.1842 31
Elizabeth (Urbansky) 139
Elizabeth (Watson) 202
Elizabeth (Webster) 31
Elizabeth (Williams) 186

Elizabeth A. b.1840 MS 275
Elizabeth A. b.1849 TN 225
Elizabeth Alice (Bullard) 139
Elizabeth Alzena b.1843 220
Elizabeth Ann 114
Elizabeth Ann b.1846 KY 118
Elizabeth Ann b.1956 NY 139
Elizabeth C. ( ) b.1827 KY 257
Elizabeth C. (Jensen) 30
Elizabeth C. (Julian) 197
Elizabeth D. (Filkins) 196
Elizabeth E. (Reynolds) 98
Elizabeth F. b.1847 KY 118, 129
Elizabeth J. b.1845 KY 127
Elizabeth Ketura (Lord) b.NH 144
Elizabeth L. ( ) b.1825 TN 221
Elizabeth M. b.1831 KY 128
Elizabeth Melvina b.1831 KY 42
Elizabeth P. b.1807 KY 114, 116
Elizabeth P. b.1842 KY 116, 126
Elizabeth Pauline b.1838 20
Elizabeth Pearl (Wall) 173
Elizabeth W. b.1837 MA 275
Elizabeth W. r.1854 IL 184
Ella b.1889 TN 200
Ella b.1903 NE 229
Ella b.NC 228
Ella (Birdsall) 81
Ella (Suddreth) 229
Ella (Wilson) 124
Ella A. b.1841 VT 145
Ella Annette, b.1841 16
Ella Bertha b.1857 NY 63–64
Ella H. b.1861 VT 16
Ella H. d.1868 PA 106
Ella L. b.1846 VT 144
Ella V. b.1850 KY 42
Ella W. b.1876 NC 197
Ellen b.1837 VA 127
Ellen b.1840 IRE 28
Ellen b.1844 KY 118, 126
Ellen b.1844 OH 309
Ellen b.1846 AL 157
Ellen b.1847 WI 309
Ellen b.1849 MO 131
Ellen b.1855 KY 85
Ellen b.1862 ENG 12
Ellen r.1863 QU 299
Ellen m.1866 IN 262
Ellen ( ) r.1860 QU 299
Ellen (Allen) 171
Ellen (Beals) 262
Ellen (Toms) 207
Ellen Eliza (Collins) 98
Ellen H. b.1847 VT 146
Ellen J. b.1858 NC 181
Ellen Jane b.1831 IL 202
Ellen L. b.VT 144
Ellen L. B. (Winchester) 299
Ellike r.1833 IL 184
Elliot b.1824 VT 146
Elliot b.1834 VT 144
Elliot b.1875 279
Elliot Charles b.1982 NY 139
Ellsworth Allan r.1982 NH 30
Ellwin b.1823 VT 147
Elly Ann (Lee) 40
Elma ( ) b.1800 CT 309, 310
Elmer b.1921 KY 168, 174, 212, 214
Elmer E. b.1866 IL 270
Elmina b.1843 TN 224, 263
Elmira b.1845 NC 157
Elmira Elsie 186
Elmira N. ( ) b.1812 VT 308
Elnathan b.1800 VT 144
Elnor m.1850 OH 204
Elnora b.1870 r.WI 28
Elnora b.1929 OH 208
Elnora S. b.1866 KY 131, 251
Elnora (Gruff) 125
Elsa m.1826 OH 204
Elsie (Boyer) 125
Elsie (Calevro) 82
Elsie (Tapscott) 168, 173, 174
Elsie A. ( ) b.1866 307
Elsie Mae b.1906 OH 82
Elspeth (Murison) 283
Elva b.1891 OR 120
Elvira (Marsh) 10
Elvira J. b.1851 IA 84
Elvira (Birdsall) 81
Elvis b.185– KY 42

Elvy b.1824 TN 221
Elvy r.NC 234
Elvy J. b.1847 TN 221
Elwin b.1823 VT 147
Emeline b.1807 MA 7
Emeline b.1831 TN 222
Emeline b.1832 AL 156
Emeline b.1835 TN 225
Emeline b.183– PA 99
Emeline m.1847 PA 107
Emeline r.1853 PA 109
Emeline (Clark) 7
Emeline (Eastman) 279
Emeline (Olin) 205
Emeline (Seeley) 106
Emeline A. b.18— 186
Emeline Adelia (Gardner) 242
Emeline C. (Davis) 204
Emer ( ) r.1903 NC 236
Emerilla b.1834 KY 129
Emerson b.1832 VT 146
Emerson b.1847 VT 144
Emerson Cooper b.1852 KY 118, 134, 189, 190, 215
Emery b.1829 VT 145
Emery d.1889 97
Emery E. m.1883 IN 262
Emily b.18— 233
Emily b.1813 PA 105, 109
Emily b.1825 AL 26, 31
Emily b.1826 TN 202
Emily b.183– KY 40
Emily b.1838 TN 225
Emily b.1839 NY 308
Emily m.1840 OH 204
Emily b.1844 AL 222
Emily b.1844 TN 225
Emily b.1846 TN 221
Emily m.1849 OH 204
Emily b.1850 VT 143
Emily b.1864 12
Emily b.OH 99
Emily ( ) b.1794 VT 143
Emily ( ) b.1814 NC 221
Emily ( ) b.1815 VA 225
Emily ( ) b.1818 VA 225
Emily ( ) b.1844 107
Emily ( ) b.1850 IL 17
Emily (Anderson) 182
Emily (Buckland) 206
Emily (Rogers) 154, 299
Emily (Turner) 196
Emily F. 152
Emily Jane b.1837 ON 103, 104, 279
Emily Kathleen b.1977 NY 139
Emily M. (Blair) 204
Emily Margaret Brown b.1795 VA 291, 294, 295
Emily Roxanna (Nash) 48
Emma b.1841 NY 175
Emma b.1844 MS 275
Emma b.1844 OH 80
Emma b.1850 OH 310
Emma b.1861 KY 288
Emma b.1866 NC 181
Emma b.187– IL/SD 97
Emma b.1876 IL 55
Emma b.1879 28
Emma b.1893 MO 167
Emma r.1916 273
Emma r.1921 OK 27
Emma r.OK 214
Emma ( ) b.1814 VT 143
Emma ( ) r.1903 NC 235, 236
Emma ( ) r.1930 KY 251
Emma (Chapman) m.1878 PA 108
Emma (Clarke) 228
Emma (Holmes) 262
Emma (Newton) 203
Emma (Phelps) 271
Emma (Thomas) 228
Emma E. b.1917 IN 262
Emma H. b.d.1851 NS 248
Emma L. r.WI 307
Emma Lewis b.1891 22
Emma May r.1950 FL 278
Emma N. d.1879 107
Emma O. b.1865 KY 271
Emma Porter b.1863 KY 287
Emma R. (Follansbee) 97
Emmett b.1857 WI 285
Emmie m.1939 AR 125

Emoral K. r.1913 IN 262
Emory W. b.1848 97
Enoch b.1798 TN 222
Enoch b.1799 MD 34, 40
Enoch b.1804 MA 146
Enoch b.1820 SC 223
Enoch b.1834 KY 128
Enoch b.1840 TN 224
Enoch b.1841 TN 222
Enoch b.1856 106
Enoch r.1895 NC 235
Ephraim b.1814 TN 288
Ephraim b.1818 NY 308
Ephraim b.1820 NC 223
Ephraim P. b.1814 TN 224
Ephraim T. b.1823 TN 221
Erasmus b.1823 VT 146
Erasmus b.1831 TN 275
Erastus b.1795 NY 309
Erastus b.1840 VT 148
Ercy (Rogers) 106, 107
Erie r.1916 273
Ermie b.187– IL 97
Ernest b.1872 28
Ernest H. b.1864 r.OH 12
Ernest K. b.1894 KY 168, 214
Ernie D. b.1893 OH 81
Erwin b.1862 r.OH 12
Esperia b.1837 MS 274
Essie b.189– NC 228
Essie ( ) b.1918 210
Essie (Cox) 82
Essie (Ward) 270
Estella Virginia b.1883 NC 199
Estelle b.1878 MS 130
Ester b.1678 BAR 281
Ester A. 202
Ester Mary b.1907 172
Esther b.1763 CT 146
Esther b.1788 NC 103, 104, 278
Esther b.1798 241
Esther b.18— 288
Esther b.1822 NY 309
Esther b.1827 NC 156
Esther b.1831 NY 148
Esther b.1873 28
Esther b.193– NC 229
Esther ( ) b.1792 MA r.NY 148
Esther (Easton) 123
Esther (Garland) 67
Esther (Huggins) 79
Esther (James) 11, 66
Esther A. b.1838 VT 148
Esther Ann (Ward) 270
Esther Ann b.1831 ON 103, 279
Esther W. b.1857 m.1876 97
Estill W. b.1882 KY (male) 271, 273
Estol (Reily) 200, 229
Ethan b.1789 VT 144
Ethel b.18— KY 21
Ethel b.187– r.KS 97
Ethel b.1877 r.OH 12
Ethel b.1882 KY 271
Ethel (Scott) 60
Ethel Cecelia m.1909 OH 204
Ethel Grace b.1890 NY 135, 137
Ethel L. b.1892 PA 105
Ethel Mae b.ND 220
Etta b.18— PA 95
Etta r.1886 NC 236
Eucibies b.1826 VT 283
Eugene b.1860 KY 51, 85
Eugene McKinley r.CA 227
Eugene b.1899 KY 167, 173, 214
Eugene b.1918 KY 173
Eugene b.KY 168
Eugene r.1972 IN 210
Eunice (Bissell) 206
Eunice (Kimball) 9
Eunice (Tilden) 204
Eunice Louise (Herren) 206
Eursla (McAninch) 207, 208
Eva b.1847 WI 309
Eva b.1866 NY 242
Eva 215
Eva (Stockoff) 39
Eva Ann b.1852 OH 39
Eva Belle (Dupies) 49
Eva Clare b.1898 22
Eva Jane Bradshaw b.1865 QU 300
Eva May b.1887 MO 267

AUSTIN,
Eva P. b.1879 r.OH 12
Eva Rhoda (Loomis) 172
Eva S. (Eshelman) 262
Evaline d.1874 PA 99
Evan r.1812 MS 158
Eve m.1853 OH 204
Eve ( ) 282
Eveline b.1891? IA 85
Eveline b.1917 IN 262
Eveline (Hurd) 96
Evelinea b.1834 TN 225
Evelyn r.1921 KS 27
Evelyn b.KY 169
Evelyn (Echols) 27
Everett b.1909 KY 168, 173, 174, 214
Ewen b.1838 TN 128
Exona J. b.1847 KY 118, 129
Experience (Dawson) 240
Ezekiel b.1774 VT 6
Ezekiel b.1782 RI 147
Ezekiel b.1828 ME 237
Ezra b.1849 16, 17
Ezra m.1835 OH 204
Ezra m.1861 PA 98
Ezra b.181– NY/IL 96
Ezra B. r.1863 WI 201
Ezra M. b.1849 VT 145
Ezra Merrill b.1824 16

AUSTIN, F,
F. b.1843 KY 126
F. !./J. r.1862 QU 299
F. J. b.1832 KY 126
F. W. b.1828 VT 243
Fannie (Lester) 7
Fannie (Wilson) 109
Fannie E. (Dartt) m.1875 PA 108
Fannie Jewell (Harston) 288
Fanny b.1847 VT 145
Fanny 233
Fanny (Herrington) m.1887 PA 10
Fanny (McGee) 96
Fanny (Snipes) 232
Fanny L. b.1850 TN 221
Fanny May b.1859 OH 220
Fanny Park (Newton) 17
Farris 167
Fay E. 97
Faye Ann Smith (Kirchner) 139
Felix H. b.1836 MO 243
Fern Joan (Hagemeyer) 212
Flavius Odle b.1851 KY 42
Fleming r.1812 VA 158
Flemming b.1815 TN 225
Flora r.1903 IN 262
Flora A. m.1861 OH 204
Florance B. m.1881 IN 262
Florence b.1876 r.OH 12
Florence 107
Florence (Angdon) 204
Florence B. (Moore) 49
Florence E. m.1879 PA 108
Florence Genevieve 21
Florence L. d.1850 PA 106
Florence Leighton 2
Florence Lucille b.1888 CO 165, 166
Florence M. b.1883 100
Florence P. (Turner) 169
Florence Picolla b.1887 MO 79
Florilla m.1846 OH 204
Floyd b.187– IL 95
Floyd b.189– MO 167
Floyd r.1915 IN 262
Floye C. b.1889 106
Forest r.KY 252
Forest B. 228
Forrest A. 131
Forrest A. b.1922 KY 207
Forrest Egbert b.1922 KY 168, 207, 214
Foster b.1839 KY 126
Foster Tuck b.1838?? KY 42
Fountain P. b.1831 TN 128
Frances d.1734 VA 257
Frances b.1788 QU 152
Frances m.1807 QU 152
Frances b.1827 KY 129
Frances b.1839 VT 143
Frances b.1842 AL 156
Frances b.1845 VT 143
Frances b.1846 KY 127

Frances b.18— 175
Frances m.1932 AR 124
Frances ( ) b.1833 KY 129
Frances (Carpenter) 98
Frances (Doty) 205
Frances (French) 51
Frances (Houstin) 233
Frances (Robertson) 42
Frances (Smith) 233
Frances A. (Pollock) 220
Frances A. b.1834 MA? 7
Frances Cornelia b.1854 100, 101
Frances Day ( ) 227
Frances E. 17
Frances E. (Freeman) 205
Frances Elizabeth (Casey) 21
Frances Frederika b.1859 CAN 152
Frances Mabel b.1898 106
Frances Maria m.1807 OH 204
Frances Rosalia b.1860 OH 80, 81
Frances Virginia b.1876 OH 81,82
Francis b.1696 NJ 155
Francis b.1799 NY 165
Francis b.18— CT 148
Francis r.1812 VA 158
Francis r.1818 QU 152
Francis r.1820 QU 153
Francis b.1820 MS 275
Francis r.1821 KY 66
Francis r.1825 MX 243
Francis r.1829 QU 154
Francis b.1830 KY 127
Francis b.1830 VT 147
Francis r.1835 QU 151
Francis b.1836 VT 143
Francis b.1838 AL 156
Francis b.1842 KY 129
Francis b.1842 TN 222
Francis b.1845 TN 226
Francis b.1845 VT 144
Francis b.1848 MS 275
Francis b.1849 WI 309
Francis r.1943 NS ('Sir') 249
Francis r.NJ 17
Francis B. r.1863 WI 201
Francis Brown 74
Francis Charles Gowen b.1861 QU 152
Francis E. b.1820 NY 285
Francis E. r.1863 WI 201
Francis H. b.1841 106
Francis H. b.1842 VT 144
Francis H. b.1862 WI 285
Francis Lewis Christian b.1864 QU 152
Francis M. b.1834 NC 223
Francis M. b.1837 KY 127
Francis M. b.1898 PA 108
Francis M. r.1861 TN 305
Francis Marion b.1845 AL 157
Francis O. b.1844 KY 127
Francis R. b.1828 KY 127
Francis Rosemond b.1828 20
Francis T. d.1853 QU 152
Francis William Gowen b.1818 QU 152, 153, 154
Francis Xavier b.1842 20, 21
Frank r.1861 TN 305
Frank m.1873 PA 98, 104
Frank b.1873 r.WI 28
Frank b.1874 r.OH 12
Frank b.1877 r.MN 28
Frank r.1898 PA 106
Frank r.1899 IN 262
Frank b.1904 OR 123
Frank r.1915 IN 262
Frank b.192– NC 229
Frank A. b.1898 PA 104
Frank Allen b.1881 NH 30
Frank B. b.185– NY 109
Frank B. b.1877 28
Frank Guy 99
Frank M. r.1863 WI 201
Frank O. b.1907 IN 262
Frank P. b.1853 r.SD 97
Frank W. b.1873 r.OH 12
Frankie (King) 26, 31
Franklin b.1813 VT 147
Franklin b.1824 VT 144
Franklin b.1825 VT 146
Franklin r.1841 PA 43

Franklin b.1841 VT 145
Franklin m.1847 OH 204
Franklin r.1863 WI 201
Franklin r.1929 NE 7
Franklin Dexter b.1819 MA 7
Franklin G. b.1915 106
Franklin Julius b.1849 NY 175
Franklin W. b.183– NY 43, 155
Franky b.17— VA/SC 10
Franky b.1808 NC 232
Franky b.18— NC 233
Franky (King) 26, 31
Fred b.1807 GER 127
Fred b.1893 NC 197
Fred b.1909 MO 172
Fred r.1915 IN 262
Fred r.1921 KS 27
Fred r.AR 233
Fred Elias b.1889 OH 81, 83
Fred H. b.1879 KY 134
Fred Hill b.1899 NC 200
Fred Marshall b.1899 NH 49
Fred Merrill b.1858 NH 48
Fred Winfield b.1912 NY 100,101
Freda May (Johnson) 213
Freddie b.1891 106
Freddie H. b.1885 IL 55
Frederick b.1780 VT 145
Frederick b.1834 TN 225
Frederick b.1844 MS 275
Frederick L. b.1846 VT 143
Frederick St. Clair b.1861 QU 152
Frederick T. b.1835 MA 147
Fredonia ( ) b.1829 TN 222
Fredye George b.1933 TN? 60
Freeman b.1770 MA 186
Freeman b.1770 RI/MA 26
Freeman b.1804 NY 270
Freeman b.1810 NY 308
Freeman m.1818 OH 204
Freeman r.1848 IL 184
Freeman E. b.1838 NY 270
Freeman Jr. m.1835 NY 186
Freeman, Jr. m.NY 26
Friend M. b.1792 VT 147

AUSTIN, G
G. b.1789 NC 126
G. r.1856 KY 301
G. B. r.1861 TN (male) 299
G. G. b.1820 VA (male) 274
G. G. r.1861 TN (male) 305
G. H. r.1871 NC 235
G. Harper b.1856 228 G????
G. T. r.1910 NC 235
G. W. b.1805 TN (male) 275
G. W. r.1861 TN (male) 305
Gabriel b.1816 VA 243
Gad b.1733 MA 219
Gad r.1771 MA 24, 36
Ganetta b.1828?? OH? 40
Gardner b.1780 MA 145
Garland b.1914 KY 173
Garnelia b.1848 WI 308
General b.18— 248
Genevieve (Estes) 210
George r.1586 ENG 257
George r.1626 ENG 257
George b.1761 RI 11
George b.1806 NY 250
George r.1812 KY 158
George b.1819 NY 107
George b.1820 VT 143
George b.1824 VT 144
George b.1825 MA 275
George m.1828 OH 204
George b.1828 KY 115, 127
George b.1829 AL 157
George b.1829 IRE 308
George b.1829 TN 222
George b.1831 AL 156
George b.1832 KY 128
George b.1832 TN 225
George b.1832 VT 147
George b.1832 VT/NY 26, 36
George b.1837 NS 245
George r.1838 ME 237
George b.1838 NY 309
George b.1840 VT 147
George b.1841 AL 157
George b.1841 VT 145
George b.1844 VT 146
George b.1845 SC 275
George b.1845 NY 175

George b.1845 VT 145, 196
George b.1846 PA 107
George b.1846 TN 205
George b.1847 OH 308
George r.1848 IL 184
George b.1848 MS 275
George b.1848 VT 146
George b.1849 NY 111
George b.1849 TN 222
George b.18— CT/NY 11
George r.1853 IL 184
George b.1855 CAN 38
George b.1855 IL 38
George b.d.185– OH 80
George b.1861 MI 250
George b.1861 TN 305
George m.1862 OH 204
George r.1863 WI 201
George r.1864 IL 184
George b.1865 r.MN 28
George b.1870 r.WI 28
George b.1871 IL 184
George m.1872 OH 204
George b.1872 r.OH 12
George b.1878 r.MN 28
George b.18— r.CA 133
George b.1919 KY 168
George m.1922 AR 124
George b.19— NE 229
George A. b.1834 MS 274
George A. b.1838 NH 146
George A. b.1863 KY 131, 132, 168
George A/E? C. b.1834 KY 117
George Aison b.1796 CAN 79
George Albion b.1829 NY 268, 269
George Ann b.1840 KY 223
George B. r.1863 WI 201
George Benjamin b.1889 KS 114, 134, 172, 194, 195, 214, 215, 216, 217, 218
George Dwight d.1843 PA 106
George E. b.1835 VT 146
George E. b.1836 ME 237
George E. b.1845 VT 148
George Earl b.1891 21
George Earl m.1946 AR 125
George Earlin b.1911 TN? 61
George Edward b.1866 21
George Edward b.1940 KY 174
George Erwin b.1886 PA 98
George F. b.1808 CT 309
George F. r.1861 QU 152
George Franklin b.1877 IA 277
George G. r.1884 KY 116
George H. b.1821 GA 156
George H. b.1840 KY 127
George H. b.1842 VT 143
George H. b.1845 PA 107
George H. b.1846 VT 143
George H. b.1849 VT 146
George H. r.IL 155
George Harvey b.1849 NC 181, 235, 236
George Herbert 2
George Hiram r.1886 PA 98
George Jefferson b.1864 KY 132, 133, 170, 171, 173, 207
George Jefferson b.1900 KY 171
George L. r.1900 NC 235
George Leroy b.1911 OH 82
George Lewis b.1880 NC 197
George Lynn b.1944 TX 210, 214, 218
George M. m.1839 OH 204
George M. r.1863 WI 201
George Morris b.1887 IL 55
George Nicolo b.1919 OK 172, 187, 191, 210, 215, 218
George P. 233
George Riley b.1879 TX 134
George T. b.1844 TN 128
George Thomas b.1854 NC 181, 199, 229
George Thomas Jr. b.1881 NC 199, 229
George W b.179– . 186
George W. r.1812 VA 158
George W. b.1812 TN 128
George W. b.1823 KY 35, 51, 85, 128

George W. b.1828 TN 222
George W. b.1831 VT 145
George W. m.1834 OH 204
George W. b.1849 TN 222
George W. b.185– r.IA 96
George W. r.1861 TN 305
George W. r.1869 IL 184
George Washington b.1832 KY 114, 118, 167, 214
George Washington m.1845 OH 204
George Washington b.1862 KY 118, 167, 168
George William Jr. 257
George William b.1804 TN 257
George William m.1836 TN 257
George William b.1918 IA 25, 142
Georgia Evelyn b.1940 KY 174
Georgia Homans 1, 2, 4, 5
Georgiana b.1837 97
Georgiana T. b.1846 TN 222
Georgie ( ) b.1859 Norway 28
Georgine ( ) b.1835 r.OH 12
Gerald b.KY 169
Gerald r.TN 214
German b.1845 NOR 28
Gerome b.1843 AL 156
Gertie (Cobleigh) 96
Gertrude b.18— 288
Gertrude (Clark) 21
Gertrude A. b.1879 WV 39
Gideon b.1787 NC 274
Gideon r.1812 SC 158
Gideon 155
Gideon H. b.1840 VT 146
Gilbert b.1876 r.OH 12
Gilbert 152
Gilbert Henry b.d.1804 QU 152
Gilbert Stevenson 11
Gilbert T. b.1857 Norway 28
Gilla (Tyre) 233
Gillman b.1827 VT 309
Gillman B. b.1826 VT 309
Gilly (Grady) 233
Gilman b.1808 VT 148
Gladys m.1938 AR 125
Gladys 228
Gladys Elizabeth b.1902 MO 282
Gladys Joan b.1930 IN 173
Gladys Leona (Bridges) 252
Glen r.1916 273
Glen D. 97
Glen Edbert m.1945 AR 125
Glen H. 97
Glenda b.1947 KY 210
Glenda 230
Glenn Matthew b.1965 MA 91
Glenn Robert b.1920 KY 173, 210
Glenn r.1849 TN 285
Glorianna b.1758 283
Godfrey b.1814 TN 223
Goodman H. r.1861 TN 305
Gotfried m.1844 OH 204
Gould b.18— CT/NY 11
Grace b.1890 OR 123
Grace b.1893 IL 55
Grace r.1915 IN 262
Grace b.1920 NY 282
Grace b.19— NC 228
Grace (Greene) 49
Grace (Wernett) 167
Grace C. ( ) 241
Grace Elizabeth b.1886 KS 134, 215, 216
Grace Elizabeth b.KS 194
Grafton b.1821 KY 127
Granberry b.1800 NC 225
Grant r.1920 NY 282
Grant Lincoln b.1853 NE 26
Granville b.1826 VT 147
Green b.1831 TN 225
Green B. b.1861 TN 305
Green D. 233
Grinman r.1800 NY 206
Grover C. b.1887 TN? 60
Grundy m.1945 AR 125
Grundy m.1947 AR 125
Guenn b.KY 169
Gurnell ( ) b.1833 NOR 28
Gustavus b.1812 VT 143
Gustie b.1907 TN? 61
Guy r.1917 IN 262

AUSTIN,
Ira A. b.1841 LA 274
Ira B. b.1817 NY 309
Ira B. b.1842 VT 143
Ira F. b.1811 NY 274
Irene b.NE 229
Irene (Halbert) 204
Irene (Thompson) 173
Iris b.192– NC 229
Irma b.1906 OR 120, 123
Irma m.1935 AR 124
Irma ( ) b.180– VT r.NY, MI 36
Irma (Meek) 209
Irvin r.1861 TN 305
Irvin Ayers b.1878 TX 287
Irving Powell b.1853 16, 17
Isaac b.17— 96
Isaac b.1723 MA 14, 79
Isaac b.1787 NY 107
Isaac b.1789 NH 44
Isaac b.1791 MA 283
Isaac r.1794 NY 79
Isaac r.1812 GA 158
Isaac b.1812 KY 128
Isaac b.1818 GA 157
Isaac b.1820 ON 103, 279
Isaac b.1822 NY 309
Isaac b.1823 NY 242
Isaac b.1830 VA 128
Isaac r.1831 KY 116
Isaac b.1832 KY 126
Isaac b.1833 PA 95
Isaac b.1837 VT 147
Isaac b.1848 TN 225
Isaac m.1841 OH 204
Isaac m.1842 OH 204
Isaac m.1860 OH 204
Isaac r.1861 TN 305
Isaac m.1861 OH 204
Isaac r.1863 WI 201
Isaac r.1865 NC 235
Isaac B. b.1810 KY 114, 117
Isaac Bill b.1831 KY 117, 131, 169, 207
Isaac F. b.1814 VT 148
Isaac N. b.1822 VT 144
Isaac R. r.1849 IL 184
Isaac S. b.1805 VT? 36
Isaiah r.1812 VA 158
Isaac S. r.1848 IL 184
Isaac S. r.1863 NC 235
Isaac S. r.1885 NC 236
Isabel b.1839 TN 222
Isabel b.1840 OH 155
Isabel b.IL 202
Isabell V. (Qualls) 61
Isabella b.1830 NC 221
Isabella b.1835 ON 279
Isabella b.1836 VA 225
Isabella b.1841 20
Isabella m.1850 OH 204
Isabella b.1858 NY 283
Isabella b.180–/1– NC 250
Isabella (Williams) 98
Isabelle (Barker) 205
Isabinda A. (Magown) 262
Isaiah b.1798 VT 146
Isaiah r.1820 VT 25
Isaiah b.1824 SC 275
Isaiah b.1827 NY 243
Isaiah b.1834 AR 282
Isaiah Caleb b.1825 NY 268
Isaiah L. r.1863 WI 201
Isaiah Lewis b.1918 KY 207, 212
Isaiah W. b.1831 VT 146
Isibelle b.1869 28
Isom r.1861 TN 305
Ivan b.1911 OR 123

AUSTIN, J
J. b.1787 CT (male) 308
J. b.1790 NC 225
J. r.1835 NS 265
J. b.1842 KY 126
J. r.1861 TN (male) 305
J. A. r.1861 TN (male) 305
J. A. m.1861 PA 98
J. Alex r.1861 TN 305
J. Alphonse r.1954 QU 301
J. B. b.1824 ME 237
J. B. b.1838 KY 129
J. B. b.1841 KY 126
J. B. r.1861 TN (male) 305
J. Brooks b.OH? 40
J. C. b.1837 KY 126
J. C. r.1861 TN (male) 305
J. Charlton b.1878 279
J. D. d.1918 228
J. E. b.1830 DE 129
J. E. r.1888 NC 235
J. E. r.1895 NC 236
J. Ellis 233
J. Enooks b.OH? 40
J. F. b.1852 31
J. G. b.1820 NC (male) 157
J. G. b.1824 TN 223
J. G. b.1825 VA (male) 274
J. H. r.1861 TN (male) 306
J. J. r.1861 TN (male) 305
J. L. r.1904 NC 235
J. Lonnie r.NC 233
J. M. b.1821 IL 243
J. M. r.1861 TN (male) 306
J. M. b.1892 OH 81
J. M. r.1903 NC 235
J. P. b.1847 KY (male) 287
J. P. b.1818 NY 243
J. P. b.1847 KY 126
J. P. r.1861 TN (male) 306
J. R. r.1861 TN (male) 306
J. S. b.1812 NC (male) 275
J. S. b.1818 KY 243
J. S. b.1832 d.TX 31
J. T. b.1825 VA (male) 274
J. T. r.1861 TN (male) 305, 306
J. W. r.1861 TN (male) 306
J. W. r.1890 NC 235
J. W. r.1895 NC 236
Jacob m.1771 MA 24
Jacob b.1823 ON 279
Jacob b.1832 TN 222
Jacob m.1833 OH 204
Jacob b.1842 KY 128
Jacob r.1861 TN 305
Jacob b.NC 232, 233
Jacob r.NC 232, 234
Jacob 233
Jacob Coleman 233
Jacob Jr. m.1822 ME 250
Jacob Louis b.1978 OH 82
Jade Shenah b.1979 OK 273
Jake r.NC 232
James r.1541 ENG 255
James r.1554 ENG 256
James b.1554 ENG 256
James b.1586 ENG 257
James r.1600 ENG 257
James b.1603 ENG 257
James b.1760 VA 175
James r.1762 MA 79
James b.1764 IRE 232
James b.1764 NC 250
James b.1765 MD 34
James m.1767 VA? 175
James b.17— SCO r.PA 240
James b.1770 VA 11, 20, 22, 175
James b.1771 MA 24
James b.1776 17
James b.1776 CT 36, 276
James r.1777 VA 37
James r.1777 ME 23
James r.1785 NS 246
James b.1790 IRE 147
James b.1790 NH 125, 140
James b.1790 NY 141
James b.1790 VA 129
James b.1791 VT 309
James r.1792 MD 35
James b.1799 233
James b.1800 VT 147
James r.1801 NY 79
James r.1802 MD 35
James r.1803 NY 54
James m.1804 PA 98
James b.1805 NY 54
James b.1806 NY/CAN 11
James b.1807 NC 223
James b.1807 TN 226
James b.1808 VA 225
James b.1809 QU 154
James b.1811 OH 308
James b.1811 TN 222
James b.1811 TN 224
James r.1812 KY 158, 182
James r.1812 SC 158
James r.1812 TN 158
James b.1812 TN 224, 288
James r.1812 VA 158
James m.1812 RI 17
James r.1814 VA 158
James b.1814 TN 221
James b.1817 ON 279
James b.1818 KY 128
James b.1818 ME 309
James b.1820 KY 115, 127
James b.1820 NY? 50
James b.1824 VA 222
James b.1826 AL 156
James b.1826 VT 148
James b.1827 MA 243
James b.1828 ENG 243
James m.1829 OH 204
James b.1829 GA 157
James b.1829 NC 275
James b.1830 AL 156
James m.1831 OH 204
James b.1831 ENG 243
James b.1832 TN 275
James r.1833 NS 265
James r.1833 TN 284
James b.1834 VT 146
James b.1835 AL 157
James b.1835 ENG 12
James b.1835 NY 250
James b.1835 VT 143
James b.1836 KY 127
James b.1836 SC 275
James b.1836 TN 223
James b.1837 OH 276
James b.1837 VT 145
James r.1838 IL 184
James r.1838 TN 285
James b.1838 AL 275
James b.1838 NY 26
James b.1838 TN 224
James b.1838 VA 225
James b.1838 VT 145
James b.1840 26, 36
James b.1841 NY 309
James b.1842 NY 111
James b.1842 MS 274
James r.1843 QU 300
James r.1843 KY 127, 128
James b.1843 NH 147
James b.1843 TN 224
James b.1843 KY 20
James r.1844 TN 284
James b.1844 TN 225
James b.1845 QU 301
James b.1845 KY 128
James b.1845 TN 221
James r.1846 KY 127, 129
James b.1846 NC 221
James b.1846 ON 279
James b.1846 TN 224
James b.1846 VT 144
James r.1847 IL 184
James r.1847 KY 127
James b.1847 TN 156, 221
James b.1847 VT 144
James b.1848 MS 274
James b.1848 QU 300
James b.1848 TN 221
James r.1849 IL 184
James m.1849 OH 204
James b.1849 ENG 12
James b.1849 OH 308
James r.1850 IL 184
James b.1850 KY 127
James b.1851 OH 276
James m.1854 OH 204
James r.1854 IL 184
James r.1854 TN 284
James b.1858 r.OH 12
James r.1861 ME 237
James r.1861 TN 305
James r.1863 WI 201
James b.1868 ME 140
James b.1869 QU 301
James r.1874 NS 245
James m.1895 MA 245
James m.1917 AR 124
James r.PA r.Philippines 220
James r.NC 233, 234
James b.NS 245, 248
James d.young WI 285
James A. b.1829 OH 155
James A. b.1843 WI 308
James A. b.1862 TN? 60
James A. r.1863 WI 201
James Alexander b.1850 QU 300
James Andrew b.1959 NY 139
James B. b.1817 MA 85
James B. b.1835 NY 250
James B. b.1847 TN 222
James B. r.1852 IL 184
James B. r.1853 IL 184
James Basil b.1837 20, 21
James C. b.1790 ME/MA 66
James C. b.1809 ME 243
James C. b.1845 KY 117
James C. b.1846 KY 128
James C. r.CT? 241
James C. G. b.1849 AL 156
James Carl b.191– NC 229
James Carl b.1952 NC 229
James D. b.1825 TN 222
James D. b.1836 VT 309
James D. b.1899 OH 81
James Earl b.1939 OH 82
James Elijah Brown b.1803 MO 291, 294, 296
James Elmer b.1863 NE 84, 85
James F. b.1821 KY 40
James F. b.1841 MD 243
James F. b.1847 SC 250
James Findley b.1876 KY 271, 272
James Findley II b.1923 OK 271, 272
James Findley III b.1953 OK 273
James Francis b.1883 FL 283
James Franklin b.1878 TN 241
James G. 196
James Gideon 196
James H. b.1840 KY 177
James H. b.1842 TN 156
James H. b.1843 VT 144
James H. b.1849 KY 128
James Henry b.1871 IA 277
James Henry r.1898 TX 283
James Herman b.1871 21
James Hill Bradshaw b.1858 QU 153
James J. b.1817 AL 222
James J. b.1889 TX 134
James Jackson b.1865 KY 118
James K. P. r.NC 234
James K. m.1871 PA 106, 107, 108
James L. m.1878 PA 108
James L. m.1904 OH 204
James M. b.1807 MD 177
James M. r.1812 TN 158, 182
James M. b.1814 TN 226
James M. b.1822 KY 127
James M. b.1828 TN 224
James M. b.1829 AL 157
James M. b.1832 NC 223
James M. b.1837 96
James M. r.1838 TN 285
James M. r.1861 TN 305
James M. E. b.1845 TN 226
Jason M. b.1815 TN 221
James Madison b.1834 AL 26
James Madison b.1852 OH 80, 81
James Manley b.1859 KY 257
James Monroe r.1863 WI 201
James Noble b.1871 IL? 74, 75
James O. m.1837 OH 204
James P. b.1827 TN 128
James P. b.1836 AL 157
James P. r.1863 WI 201
James R. b.1837 IL 308
James R. b.1846 PA 107
James R. b.1847 OH 309
James R. r.1863 WI 201
James Robert b.1880 TX 287
James Rolly b.1842 KY 85
James S. m.1834 OH 204
James S. r.1852 IL 184
James S. m.1869 OH 204
James S. b.1886 NC 199
James Scruggs b.1832 IL 59
James T. b.1819 ME 140, 141
James T. b.1839 VT 148
James T. r.1861 TN 305
James T. r.1916 273
James T. b.KY 271
James Trecothick b.1784 MA 18
James Van m.1832 OH 204
James W. b.1816 VT 143
James W. b.1830 KY 114
James W. m.1840 OH 204
James W. b.1849 KY 127
James W. r.1863 WI 201
James Wilson b.KY 283
James b.KY? 38
Jamis r.1541 ENG 255
Jane m.1771 PA 98
Jane b.1775 SC 127
Jane b.1778 SC 223
Jane b.1795 KY 156
Jane b.1801 MD 35
Jane b.1819 TN 222
Jane b.1834 TN 222
Jane b.1836 IRE 309
Jane b.1836 TN 225
Jane b.1838 VT 143
Jane b.1839 KY 131
Jane b.1840 VT 143, 145
Jane b.1840 OH 84
Jane b.1841 AL 157
Jane b.1846 WI 308
Jane b.1847 ON 279
Jane b.1854 NC 181
Jane b.1858 IL 38
Jane b.1860 WI 285
Jane b.1858 IL 55
Jane b.1866 ENG 12
Jane b.1872 NC 197
Jane b.19— TX 287
Jane r.NC 233, 234
Jane r.NY 54
Jane ( ) b.1804 NY 310
Jane ( ) b.1819 TN 226
Jane ( ) b.1825 NY 143
Jane ( ) b.1825 TN 225
Jane ( ) b.1827 WI 309
Jane ( ) b.1830 TN 126
Jane ( ) b.1845 ENG 12
Jane (Farnham) 17
Jane (Fitzpatrick) 175
Jane (Howe) 246
Jane (Lamb) 61
Jane (Wood) 204
Jane A. b.1810 NY 301
Jane B. b.1813 SC 274
Jane C. 228
Jane D. (Warner) 204
Jane E. b.1825 PA 107
Jane E. b.1825 TN 156
Jane L. b.1837 VT 145
Jane O. b.1855 OH 39
Jane Staton b.1850 KY 118
Jane Victoria b.1840 20, 21
Jane Watson b.1823 MI 283
Janet b.1851 WI 285
Janet Virginia b.1920 VA 10, 12, 28, 31, 37, 38, 94, 109, 111, 124, 150, 166, 231
Janetta b.1832 KY 128
Janette b.1847 NY 308
Janice Mary (Truitt) 214, 218
Jason b.1848 TN 225
Jason b.1888 KY 173
Jason Christopher b.1975 214, 218
Jasper b.1834 TN 225
Jasper r.1861 TN 305
Jasper W. b.1837 AL 157
Jauvier J. r.1853 IL 184
Jean r.1812 LA 158
Jean b.1936 MO? 209
Jean Marie (Carey) 82
Jeanette b.1820 VT 144
Jeanette (Sword) 168
Jeff b.1844 SC? 66
Jeff b.18— MO 285
Jefferson b.1810 KY 129
Jefferson b.1843 AL 156
Jefferson Bert b.1961 OH 212
Jefferson C. b.1830 WI 27
Jefferson M. b.1836 VT 148
Jefferson W. b.1827 GA 157
Jeffrey Charles b.1980 OK 273
Jeffrey Leon b.1959 209
Jeffrey Louis b.1955 AZ 212
Jeffrey Williams b.1951 OK 272
Jehial b.1814 NY 79, 100
Jehiel b.1835 VT 143
Jemima B. b.1828 OH? 40
Jenett ( ) b.1815 NY 309
Jennie b.189–/190– MO? 118
Jennie b.1848 NH 30
Jennie Arabella b.1846 SCO/NY 73

AUSTIN,

John W. b.1844 TN 222
John W. b.1846 AL 157
John W. b.1847 TN 223
John W. b.1850 VT 143
John W. b.1853 KY 85
John W. r.1861 TN 306
John W. 131, 214
John Wesley b.1901 MO 133, 172
John William b.1832 KY 117, 133, 172
John William b.1874 IA 277
John William b.1927 NY 137, 138, 139
John Williams Bradley b.1830 ME 140, 141
Johnnie b.1901 KY 169
Johnnie m.1929 AR 124
Johnny b.1791 ENG 245
Johnny W. b.1864 TN? 61
Johnson b.1839 MS 274
Joiner r.1838 IL 184
Jolene (Warren) 209
Jon Dwight b.1947 WI 270
Jonah b.1598 ENG r.MA 3, 11
Jonah r.1775 ME 238
Jonah b.1783 r.ME 2, 85
Jonah b.1819 ME 238
Jonah r.1894 ME 238
Jonas b.1778 MD 11, 34
Jonas b.1782 VA 187
Jonas b.1801 VA 128
Jonas b.1818 KY 129
Jonas b.1819 KY 116, 117
Jonas H. b.1824 KY 126
Jonas Jr. b.1819 KY 114
Jonas P. b.1840 KY 128
Jonas R. b.1782 VA 114, 116, 167,133
Jonas W. b.1842 KY 117, 171
Jonathan b.1742 MA 15, 109, 186
Jonathan b.1747 RI 6
Jonathan b.1770 MA 109
Jonathan b.1785 NC 278, 279
Jonathan r.1790 NY 206
Jonathan b.1796 VT 11
Jonathan b.1798 VT 147
Jonathan b.1822 ON 278
Jonathan m.1826 OH 205
Jonathan b.1828 96
Jonathan b.1833 KY 128
Jonathan, b.1835 OH 276
Jonathan b.1839 TN 222
Jonathan b.1847 KY 129
Jonathan r.1861 TN 305, 306
Jonathan r.1863 WI 201
Jonathan m.1872 OH 205
Jonathan r.1890 CT 11
Jonathan b.NC 232, 234
Jonathan 103, 105, 107
Jonathan Asbury b.1823 TN/AL 59
Jonathan B. b.1821 TN 222
Jonathan C. b.1815 GA 157
Jonathan L. b.1825 KY 129
Jonathan L. r.NC 234
Jonathan Loring b.1747 MA 18
Jonathan M. b.1837 TN 221
Jonathan M. r.1861 TN 306
Jonathan P. b.1846 TN 221
Jonathan P. r.1861 TN 306
Jonna Evetta (Whitley) 229
Jonne b.1603 ENG (female) 257
Jordan Adam b.1977 214, 218
Jordan W. b.1874 OH 81
Jordan Wilson b.1818 NY 80, 196
Joseph b.1616 ENG 219
Joseph r.1642 NH 3, 240
Joseph b.173– VA 37, 38, 196
Joseph r.1769 VA 219
Joseph b.1769 MA 44–47
Joseph r.1771 MA 24
Joseph b.1771 MA 146
Joseph b.1780 31
Joseph b.1782 TN 58
Joseph b.1792 MD? 85
Joseph m.1800 VA 6, 10, 26, 110, 155
Joseph b.18— 288
Joseph b.1801 VA 221
Joseph b.1809 VT 88
Joseph b.1810 ENG 243
Joseph r.1812 GA 159

Joseph r.1812 MO 159
Joseph r.1812 TN 159
Joseph r.1812 VA 182
Joseph d.1813 NY 54
Joseph b.1815 VT 145
Joseph d.1823 155
Joseph r.1827 NS 248
Joseph b.1827 26, 36
Joseph b.1827 QU 85
Joseph m.1828 OH 205
Joseph r.1830 IL 26, 184
Joseph r.1830 NS 266
Joseph m.1830 OH 205
Joseph b.1833 ON 103, 279
Joseph b.1835 TN 222
Joseph r.1836 IL 184
Joseph r.1838 IL 185
Joseph b.1838 ME 238
Joseph b.1838 OH r.1850 VT 144
Joseph b.1838 VT 147
Joseph r.1839 IL 185
Joseph b.1840 TN 225
Joseph b.1842 NS 248
Joseph b.1843 KY 126
Joseph b.1844 IL 185
Joseph b.1845 NC 223
Joseph b.1848 MS 275
Joseph r.1861 TN 305, 306
Joseph b.1867 r.MN 28
Joseph b.1871 r.WI 28
Joseph r.1899 NC 235
Joseph b.NC 233
Joseph b.NH 219
Joseph r.NY 110
Joseph b.NS 245, 249
Joseph r.1818 IN? 155
Joseph b.180– 177
Joseph B. b.1817 NY 62
Joseph B. b.1837 PA 105, 107, 109
Joseph B. b.1843 TN 221
Joseph B. r.1845 IL 185
Joseph B. r.1859 IL 185
Joseph C. b.1809 155
Joseph C. b.1841 TN 221
Joseph E. b.1882 TX 134
Joseph Edgar b.1857 NY 220
Joseph Edgar m.1903 ND 220
Joseph Edward b.1874 21
Joseph Edward b.1887 TN 200, 229
Joseph Edward b.1888 230
Joseph G. b.1855 IA 84
Joseph Garland b.1843 KY 42
Joseph H. b.1802 VT 84
Joseph H. b.1827 QU 84
Joseph Harrison b.1822 KY 187
Joseph Harrison b.1824 KY 114, 118, 167, 188
Joseph Henry 98
Joseph John b.1955 NY 139
Joseph Johnson b.1880 21
Joseph Jr. r.1771 MA 24
Joseph Jr. b.180– r.TN 110
Joseph Jr. r.1830 IL 26
Joseph L. b.1809 VT 148
Joseph M. b.1830 TN 222
Joseph M. b.1883 NC 235
Joseph Milton b.1859 NC 181, 200
Joseph N. b.1867 MI 250
Joseph P. b.183– MI 26
Joseph P. b.1843 ME 238
Joseph P. r.1863 WI 201
Joseph Pendleton b.1840 KY 42
Joseph Strong b.1850 TN 223
Joseph W. b.1845 KY 117
Josephine b.1832 OH? 40
Josephine b.1838 AL 157
Josephine b.1850 KY 128
Josephine 97
Josephine 155
Josephine (Brown) 51
Josephine Frances b.1917 OK 272
Josephine M. d.1849 PA 106
Josephus b.1834 NY 310
Joshua b.1740 MA 14
Joshua r.1771 MA 24
Joshua r.1795 NY 206
Joshua b.1828 ON 103, 104, 279
Joshua r.1836 IL 185
Joshua b.1839 KY 128
Joshua r.1848 IN 262

Joshua D. r.1823 IL 185
Joshua L. b.1834 KY 128
Joshua Louis b.1833 KY 42
Joshua N. r.1839 IL 185
Josiah r.1771 MA 24
Josiah b.1775 MA 44
Josiah b.1800 VT 143
Josiah r.1812 VA 158, 159
Josiah m.1825 OH 205
Josiah r.1836 IL 185
Josiah r.1846 IL 185
Josiah (Mclaughlin) 203
Josiah Jr. r.1771 MA 24
Josie b.1860 KY 133
Josie m.1883 OH 205
Josie Etta (Chambers) 230
Jotham 240
Joy E. (Henry) 262
Joyce Faye b.1937 TN 61
Joyce Faye b.1943 OH 82
Juanita (Frederick) 168
Juanita Alice (Smith) 283
Judah r.1771 MA 24
Judia b.1858 TN? 60
Judith b.1582 ENG 256
Judith b.1775 23
Judith (Chick) 42
Judith (Eastman) 206
Judith (Lyon) 88
Judson W. b.1838 VT 147
Judy b.1840 TN 222
Judy Gale (Hagy) 207
Judy Martin b.1909 OK 272
Juley J. r.1895 NC 235
Julia b.1835 VT 144
Julia b.1836 VT 145
Julia b.1838 NY 63–64
Julia b.1841 VT 147
Julia b.1842 VT 143
Julia b.1872 12
Julia b.ON 279
Julia 104, 220
Julia (Abdellia) 49
Julia (Church) 98
Julia (Cowan) 300, 301
Julia (Estes) 168
Julia (Goddard) 7
Julia (Raum) 262
Julia A. b.1838 VT 146
Julia A. (Bean) 181, 235, 236
Julia Ann 103
Julia Ann (Bowers) 81
Julia Ann (Miller) 250, 283
Julia Ann b.18— MO 285
Julia Ann b.1830 ON 278
Julia Ann b.KY 116
Julia C. ( ) 236
Julia E. ( ) 236
Julia E. (Parker) 206
Julia Emma b.1861 NH 48
Julia H. b.1835 AL 156
Julia Helena (Elder) 130
Julia Leah (Shoemaker) 172, 216, 217
Julia Martin b.1909 OK 272
Julia May b.1927 OH 82
Julia R. (Hawley) 203
Julia V. b.1855 16
Julianna b.1850 VT 146
Julianne Beth b.1976 NC 214, 218
Julie Ann b.1831?? OH 40
Juliette b.1842 VT 143
Julius b.1809 OH 308
Julius b.1812 NY 175,
Julius b.1822 CT 309
Julius b.1830 CT 310
Julius m.1833 OH 205
Julius b.1833 VT 143
Julius b.183–/4– r.KY/OH 219
Julius H. b.1845 WI 308
Julius H. r.1863 WI 201
Julius J. b.1889 NC 227
Julius Jefferson b.1850 NC 180, 181, 197, 198, 199, 235
Julius R. b.1835 VT 146
July Ann b.1831?? OH 40
June Etta b.1917 231
June Julian b.1896 NC 197
Junior b.1928 OH 208
Justin b.1819 NY? 50
Justin m.1850 OH 205
Justin r.IN 262
Justus r.1909 ME 238
Justus P. b.1879 107

AUSTIN, K

Karen Allison b.1936 WI 270
Karen Ann (Champlain) 273
Kate b.1847 VT 143
Kate ( ) b.1847 CAN r.OH 12
Kate (Anderson) 20
Kate (Leach) 206
Kate Douglas b.1892 MO 79
Kate Emily (Smith) 96
Katherine (Arnold) 42
Katherine (Lee) 165, 166
Katherine (Merideth) 125
Katherine (Tierney) 138
Katheryn (Childress) 27
Kathryn L. b.1877 WV 39
Katie b.1873 r.OH 12
Katie A. b.1884 TN? 61
Kay Nora b.1947 KY 210
Kendall Frederick b.1837 NH 48, 49
Kenneth b.19— NC? 199
Kenneth b.1910 IN 262
Kenneth r.1916 273
Kenneth m.1975 229
Kenneth b.1979 KY 132
Kenneth E. b.1915 IN 262
Kenneth Lee 229
Kenneth Ward b.1895 WI 270
Kennie C. b.1888 TN? 60
Kesiah r.1776 MD 34
Keyes r.1832 VT 147
Keziah b.1826 KY 116
Keziah r.1776 ME 238
King r.1776 ME 238
Kisiah b.1852 IL 185
Kit b.1854 KY 51
Kittie Dorinda b.1871 KY 287
Kittie Lee (Martin) 271, 272
Kittura b.1826 KY 116
Kitty Ann b.1809 MD 35, 51
Kristine Nicole b.1980 VA 214, 218

AUSTIN, L

L. b.1834 KY 126
L. (Church) 98
L. A. (Duncan) 98
L. B. b.1835 PA 107
L. B. 22
L. C. r.1861 TN (male) 306
L. C. 106
L. E. 109
L. Emory b.1868 106
L. Emory 105
L. L. r.1895 NC 235, 236
L. R. r.1876 PA (male) 108
L. R. m.1878 PA (male) 108
L. T. r.1899 NC 235
Laban Stewart b.1860 KY 118
Lacke (Gordon) 42
Lafayette b.1836 TN 224
Lafayette b.183–/4– 38
Lafayette Marcus b.1838 OH 39
Lamson r.AR 233
Langamire b.1852 Norway 28
Lannie b.1860? 12
Lanson b.1810 NY 129
Larkin R. r.1855 IL 185
Laura b.1831 241
Laura b.1836 MS 274
Laura b.1843 VT 144
Laura b.1865 WI 43
Laura b.1896 MA 130
Laura m.1825 OH 205
Laura ( ) b.1786 NY? 54
Laura (Leed) 204
Laura (Morse) 95
Laura A. ( ) b.1814 VT 144
Laura Ann (Baker) 42
Laura J. (Mills) 203
Laurel b.1836 VT 147
Lavanda (Jarrett) 55
Lavina b.1839 TN 224
Lavisa b.18— VT 147
Lavislana ( ) b.1808 AL 157
Lavon (Snyder) 230
Lawless r.1812 MD 159
Lawless r.1817 IL 185
Lawrence r.1849 TN 285
Lawrence b.1859 WI 43
Lawrence A. b.1898 NH 49
Lawrence G. 109
Lawrence Jesse b.1899 MO 282
Lawrence L. b.1906 106

Lawson b.1836 NC 157
Lawson b.18— NC 232
Leah Graice b.1895 PA 105
Leah Jo (Greene) 272
Leah N. r.NC 234
Leanden M. b.1834 NC 157
Leander R. b.1831 PA 105, 106, 107, 108, 109
Leanna G. b.1894 106
Lebbins b.1849 WI 308
Lebius H. b.1818 NY 148
Lee m.1944 AR 125
Lee m.1948 AR 125
Lee T. b.1887 21
Leila (Deloach) 125
Leila 97
Lela Florence b.1866 KY 287
Lela Sue b.1934 209
Lelia Ruth b.1921 MO 172
Lemuel b.1814 250
Lemuell r.1771 MA 24
Lena b.1852 KY 51, 85
Lena (Cross) 283
Lena (Crow) (Pancake) 39
Lenora b.1836 VT 144
Lenore 95
Leon b.1886 106
Leon m.1939 AR 125
Leona b.1852 KY 85
Leona (Stapleton) 133
Leona Bell b.1915 82
Leonard b.1803 QU 84
Leonard b.1810 NH 144
Leonard b.1889?? IA 85
Leonard b.189–/0– NE 85
Leonard b.191–/2– NE 230
Leonard r.NY 110
Leonard Demick 6
Leonard S. b.1849 IA 84
Leonidas B. b.1842 KY 127
Leonidus b.1823 MS 275
Leroy G. b.1876 106
Leroy b.1815 TN 275
Leroy b.1846 AL 156
Leslie b.KY 251
Leslie Joan (Sharp) 214
Lester b.1836 VT 145
Lester 95
Lester Moss b.1867 IL 129
Lettie 97
Letty b.1830 TN 221
Levi b.1782 NC 186, 224, 288
Levi r.1804 TN 257
Levi b.1811 VT 145
Levi r.1812 TN 159
Levi b.1824 VT 143
Levi b.1831 VT 143
Levi b.1834 TN 224
Levi r.1839 NC 235, 236
Levi Brown b.1867 IL? 74
Levi C. b.1843 TN 222
Levi W. 110
Levina (Hamilton) 233
Levina (Williams) 44
Levinia Margaret b.1830?? 38
Levisa ( ) b.1800 KY 126
Levy r.1861 TN 306
Lewis b.181– ON 104, 279
Lewis r.1812 PA 159
Lewis m.1815 PA 196
Lewis r.1817 IL 185
Lewis b.1835 OH 155
Lewis b.1840 MO 243
Lewis r.1843 IL 185
Lewis r.1844 IL 185
Lewis r.1861 TN 305, 306
Lewis b.1867 r.WI 28
Lewis r.1895 NC 235
Lewis b.191–/2– NE 230
Lewis r.1983 OH 89, 90
Lewis A. b.1834 VT 147
Lewis C. b.1849 222
Lewis Clyde b.1893 227
Lewis G. b.1852 NY 242
Lewis L. m.1813 PA 98
Lewis Thomas b.1870 NC 197
Lidle (Roberts) 124
Liethia? J. b.1837 MS 274
Lila b.1917 227
Lillian b.1859 IL? 74, 75
Lillian b.188–/9– IL/KS 97
Lillian Viola b.1928 TN 251, 252, 266
Lillie m.1932 AR 124

AUSTIN,

Lillie r.1921 OK 27
Lillie (Hatter) 171
Lillie Augusta (Wells) 120
Lillie E. (Lard) 61
Lillie Frances b.1874 MO 133
Lillie M. b.1914 134
Lillie Roberts (Gann) 125
Lilly r.NC 234
Lina (Tune) 61
Lincoln m.1920 AR 124
Lincoln A. b.1864 97
Linda r.1982 CA 27
Linda Cathleen b.1967 CA 212
Linda Colette (Gitlitz) 214, 218
Linda Ellen (Hoit) 270
Linda Lou (Ellis) 212
Lindsey r.NC 234
Linis b.1835 OH 155
Linnie (Roberts) 251
Linus m.1852 OH 205
Lisa Ann (Horton) 273
Liza (Barnes) 51
Lizea J. (Speakman) 267
Lizze (Herring) 51
Lizzie b.1882 TN? 60
Lizzie (Arbuckle) 42
Lizzie (Combest) (Vitatoe) 168, 169
Lizzie M. m.1861 OH 205
Lizzy b.1867 28
Lloyd b.189– IA 85
Lloyd Emerson b.1901 106
Locksed r.1812 NY 175
Lockwood r.1776 175
Lockwood b.1797 NY 154, 175
Lodatha b.1828 VT 147
Lodema b.1847 VT 144
Lodemia (Daniels) 7
Lodica b.1812 VT 62
Lodica (Washburn) 62
Lodrick b.1810 OH 263
Logan b.1838 TN 223
Lois d.1860 PA 106, 107
Lois (Adams) 82
Lois (Smith) 203
Lois D. (Foot) 203
Lois J. b.1931 106
Lois Louise (Baxter) 250
Lola m.1883 IN 262
Lona (Long) 74
Lonabelle ( ) 229
Loran b.1899 MN 241
Lorena ( ) 3, 30, 38
Lorenzey b.1848 TN 221
Lorenzo A. b.1805 VT 143
Lorenzo D. r.1865 IN 262
Lorenzo b.1842 VT 146
Lorilla (Mashom) 307
Lorin L. b.1848 VT 147
Lorine m.1941 AR 125
Lorraine b.1942 NE 229
Lorraine S. r.1981 WI 17
Lottie b.1880 OH 12
Lottie b.18– NC/TN 228
Lottie I. b.1888 MA 6
Lou A (Miller) 220
Lou Emma (Church) 307
Louella b.1859 NE 26
Louetta b.1854 KY 85
Louette b.1848?? KY 51
Louis r.1892 NC 235
Louis m.1939 AR 125
Louisa b.1810 KY 127
Louisa b.1815 NC 156
Louisa b.1818 VT 148
Louisa b.1820 GA 156
Louisa b.1826 VT 143
Louisa b.1830 TN 221
Louisa b.1837 NC 156
Louisa b.1839 AL 157
Louisa b.1839 KY 127
Louisa b.1841 PA 107
Louisa b.1841 TN 221
Louisa b.1842 AL 274
Louisa b.1842 KY 127
Louisa b.1845 KY 127
Louisa b.1846 MS 274
Louisa b.1849 MS 275
Louisa b.1849 VT 143
Louisa b.1850 KY 126
Louisa b.1851 KY 85
Louisa b.1879 OH? 12
Louisa d.1896 PA 106

Louisa b.NY 270
Louisa 186
Louisa ( ) 36
Louisa ( ) b.1825 NY 309
Louisa ( ) b.1826 KY 126
Louisa (Austin) 186
Louisa (Austin) b.NY 270
Louisa (Fothergill) 262
Louisa (Nichols) 11
Louisa (Reynolds) 95
Louisa A. b.1833 VT 145
Louisa A. m.1859 OH 205
Louisa A. ( ) b.1807 MS 274
Louisa C. b.1815 VT 146
Louisa Collins (Avery) 205
Louisa Eveline b.1882 KS 134, 194, 215
Louisa J. b.1846 TN 222
Louisa J. b.1849 TN 224
Louisa Jane b.1901 NH 49
Louisa Jane 186
Louisa Jane (Cooper) 118, 187
Louisa Peck (Easley) 241
Louise b.1918 231
Louise m.1937 AR 124
Louise ( ) r.WA 57
Louise (Dotson) 228
Louise Eveline b.1882 KS 218
Louise Spicer (Reeves) 229
Lovedy L. b.1830 TN 223
Lovina A. r.1849 PA 106
Loviza ( ) b.1797 VT 146
Loviza Ann b.1821 NH 146
Luanna b.1837 NY 144
Lubbonn b.1802 AL 157
Lucenon C. b.1850 PA 107
Lucentia ( ) 250
Lucia ( ) b.1808 VT 145
Lucia A. b.1822 VT 143
Lucian b.1833 VT 144
Lucian b.1844 KY 127
Lucian W. b.1889 KY 168
Lucile 22
Lucina b.1784 17
Lucind E. b.1831 VT 145
Lucinda b.1800 GA 156
Lucinda b.1800 VA 178
Lucinda b.182– OH? 40
Lucinda b.1832 TN 128
Lucinda b.1833 VT 145
Lucinda b.1840 AL 274
Lucinda b.1841 TN 226
Lucinda b.1843 LA 274
Lucinda b.1844 TN 223
Lucinda b.1846 TN 222
Lucinda b.1850 MS 275
Lucinda ( ) b.1805 VT 147
Lucinda ( ) b.1806 NY 310
Lucinda ( ) b.1818 TN 221
Lucinda ( ) b.1826 NC 222
Lucinda ( ) b.1827 NY 308
Lucinda ( ) b.1829 KY 127
Lucinda (Henry) 42
Lucinda (Parker) 202
Lucinda (Peterson) 306
Lucinda (Polk) 38, 55
Lucinda (Vaughn) 178
Lucinda E. b.1847 TN 221
Lucinda F. b.1838 TN 221
Lucinda J. ( ) b.1820 TN 128
Lucinda M. b.1894 OK 167
Lucinda Marcile (Thomason) 134
Lucinda W. (Thomas) 131
Lucius Dunham m.1863 OH 205
Lucius M. m.1825 OH 205
Lucius Monroe b.1826 VT? 74, 75
Lucretia b.1810 SC 275
Lucretia b.1824 VT 147
Lucretia b.1833 TN 224
Lucretia b.1838 OH 309
Lucretia ( ) b.1807 NH 309
Lucretia ( ) r.1818 QU 152
Lucretia ( ) r.1820 QU 153
Lucretia ( ) 154
Lucretia (Coburn) 234
Lucretia (Curtiss) 204
Lucretia (Hall) r.1837 QU 151
Lucretia Ann b.1840 PA 107
Lucretia C. b.1820 ME 140, 141
Lucretia Ellen (Glaze) 204
Lucretia L. m.1833 OH 205

Lucy b.1762 MA 10
Lucy b.1769 MA 10
Lucy b.1778 NH 148
Lucy b.1781 VT 144
Lucy b.1801 CAN 145
Lucy b.18– VA 177
Lucy b.1805 VT 62
Lucy b.1807 QU 153
Lucy r.1810 TN 37
Lucy d.1810 QU 153
Lucy b.1818 TN 225
Lucy b.1831 NY? 54
Lucy b.1834 KY 127
Lucy b.1834 NY 165
Lucy b.1836 VA 225
Lucy b.1838 VT 144
Lucy b.1845 128
Lucy r.1846 IL 185
Lucy b.1850 VT 148
Lucy m.1863 OH 205
Lucy b.1873 MS 130
Lucy b.1890 KY 168
Lucy b.1893 KY 169
Lucy r.NC 233
Lucy ( ) b.1824 NC 223
Lucy ( ) b.1832 MS 274
Lucy (Barnard) 50
Lucy (Fish) 283
Lucy (French) 26
Lucy (Kendrick) 48
Lucy (Poor) 8
Lucy (Thomas) 131
Lucy Ann A. m.1853 OH 205
Lucy Ann r.PA? 106, 108
Lucy C. ( ) b.1809 VT 148
Lucy Clementine (Lay) 168
Lucy D. b.1835 TN 225
Lucy E. b.1843 VT 148
Lucy Earl (Sandefur) 21
Lucy J. (Lattimer) 206
Lucy Louise b.1883 106
Lucy Maria b.1860 NY 54
Lue b.1912 TN? 60
Luisa D. J. b.1840 KY 128
Luke b.1803 NH 147
Lula J. b.1887 NC 227
Lula Jane (Carlton) 229, 230
Lulu b.1862 KY? 41
Lulu (Elco) 262
Lusynthia (Horton) 125
Luthenia H. b.1842 KY 224, 286
Luther b.1782 CT 107
Luther b.1829 PA 107
Luther d.1854 PA 106
Luther b.1868 28
Luther B. b.1828 PA 105, 106, 108, 109
Luther C. b.1892 KY 172, 209
Luticen A. b.1844 TN 224, 286
Lycidias b.1838 KY 127
Lydia b.1729 MA 14
Lydia b.1749 NH 15
Lydia b.1767 VT 147
Lydia b.1770 VT 147
Lydia b.1792 ME 282
Lydia b.1820 OH 250
Lydia b.1823 ME 282
Lydia b.1824 PA 107
Lydia b.1838 VT 66
Lydia b.1839 NC 129
Lydia m.1840 OH 205
Lydia b.1842 OH 84
Lydia b.1851 IA 84
Lydia b.1882 IL 55
Lydia ( ) b.1785 NY 143
Lydia ( ) b.1803 NY 165
Lydia ( ) b.1814 VT 147
Lydia ( ) r.1820 OH 39
Lydia (Brock) 240
Lydia (Gilbert) 84
Lydia (Holley) 233
Lydia (Jeffers) 203
Lydia (Mann) 204
Lydia (Parker) 242, 250, 301
Lydia (Thompson) 107, 109
Lydia A. b.1839 NY 308
Lydia A. b.1856 NY 242
Lydia Ellen (Gillespie) 39
Lydia I. b.1837 VT 148
Lydia Jennie ( ) b.1848 CAN 196
Lydia Margaret b.1838 KY 117
Lydia Minerva b.1811 MA 7
Lydia S. b.1822 NY 309
Lyle b.NY 135

Lyman b.1796 NH 44
Lyman b.1800 NY 55
Lyman b.1808 VT 148
Lyman b.1821 NY 67
Lyman b.1822 NY 309
Lyman b.1823 VT 146
Lyman b.1824 VT 26
Lyman m.1845 PA 98
Lyman b.18– PA r.IL 95
Lyman B. m.1885 PA 98
Lyman H. m.1855 OH 205
Lyman Jr. b.1821 NY 307
Lyman L. b.1799 CT 67, 220, 301, 306
Lyman L. r.1835 NY 306
Lyman L. r.1836 PA 306
Lyman L. r.1845 WI 306
Lyman M. b.1848 NY 111
Lyman S. b.1849 CT 309
Lyman Worth b.1848 OH 155
Lynn b.1929 NC 229

AUSTIN, M

M. b.1806 NC 225
M. b.1832 KY 126
M. r.1839 KY 175
M. b.1850 KY 126
M. ( ) b.1796 NC 126
M. ( ) b.1805 KY 126
M. ( ) r.1909 TN? 61
M. A. b.1812 KY 129
M. C. b.1821 SC 128
M. D. ( ) 134
M. E. b.1834 KY (female) 126
M. E. b.1839 KY 129
M. E. b.1844 KY (female) 126, 287
M. E. b.1846 TN 126
M. E. r.1888 NC 236
M. E. ( ) 236
M. Emily b.1842 106
M. J. r.1888 NC 235
M. J. ( ) r.1879 PA 108
M. J. ( ) r.1884 TN? 61
M. L. r.1861 TN (male) 306
M. M. b.1849 31
M. P. b.1820 TN 222
M. S. ( ) b.1848 NY/WI 308
M. V. r.1861 TN (male) 306
M. W. b.18– KY (female) 286
Mabel b.188– 97
Mabel b.1906 229
Mabel r.CT,NY 54
Mabel ( ) b.1859 r.OH 12
Mabel ( ) r.1898 PA 106
Mabel ( ) r.1899 PA 108
Mabel ( ) m.1905 KY? 21
Mable F. (Anderson) 262
Mabel G. b.1877 106
Mabel Marcelene b.1892 100
Mack b.1885 TN? 60
Madeline (Pack) 173
Madison r.1833 TN 284
Mae b.1898 TN 228
Mae ( ) 229
Mae Alda 199
Maggie b.1878 28
Maggie m.1897 OH 205
Maggie (Wilson) 262
Maggie L. 109
Maggie M. ( ) 235
Mahala b.1827 177
Mahala b.1846 AL 157
Mahala b.1853 IL 38, 55
Mahala ( ) b.1818 KY 225
Mahala ( ) b.1826 TN 224
Mahala (Ausborn) 285
Mahala (Osborn) 285
Mahala (Walikins) 206
Mahala Ann b.1834 20
Mahala C. ( ) b.1829 VT 146
Mahalia b.1825 26, 36
Mahallen b.1850 KY 128
Maiah b.1803 VA 225
Malinda b.1821 16
Malinda b.1829 AL 156
Malinda b.1832 NY 309
Malinda b.1839 CAN 301
Malinda m.1853 OH 205
Malinda ( ) b.1819 MA 308
Malinda (Woodruff) 205
Malinda Belle b.1821 TN/AL 59
Malissa b.1816 TN 223

Malissa m.1834 OH 205
Malissa b.1847 VT 145
Malissa 233
Malissa A. b.1839 TN 224
Malvina A. b.1846 KY 85
Malvina b.1816 16
Malvina m.1840 OH 205
Mamie (Vandyke) 169
Mammie (Watkins) 124
Manerva b.1813 VT 146
Maninva b.1838 MS 275
Manuel b.1848 SC 275
Manuel r.1850 NC 235
Manuel Elias b.1891 MS 130
Maple b.1877 28
Maranda A. (Todd) 203
Marcella b.1849 KY 51, 128
Marcia (Baine) 49
Marcous r.1861 TN 306
Marcus r.NC 233
Marcus C. r.NC 233
Marcus Henry b.1864 KY 131, 169
Marcus Jr. r.NC 233
Marcus N. r.NC 233
Marcus b.1842 TN 225
Marelda (Stevens) 51, 85
Marett (Haggarty) 99
Margaret b.1627 ENG 255
Margaret b.1631 ENG 255
Margaret b.1792 NY/CAN 11
Margaret b.1795 VA 114
Margaret b.1799 MD 35
Margaret b.18– ON 104, 279
Margaret b.18– TN/TX 257
Margaret b.1812 MD 35, 51
Margaret b.1820 SCO 28
Margaret b.182– OH? 40
Margaret b.1836 KY 128
Margaret r.1837 IL 185
Margaret b.1839 KY 128
Margaret b.1840 KY 127
Margaret b.1841 NC 224
Margaret b.1841 TN 224
Margaret b.1842 TN 225
Margaret b.1843 IN 308
Margaret b.1843 KY 129
Margaret b.1844 TN 221
Margaret m.1845 OH 205
Margaret b.1846 KY 128
Margaret b.1846 MS 275
Margaret b.1846 TN 222
Margaret b.1849 AL 156
Margaret b.1849 KY 129
Margaret b.1853 IA 84
Margaret m.1864 OH 205
Margaret b.191– NY 135, 136
Margaret b.NY 135
Margaret r.NC 234
Margaret ( ) b.1794 VA 223
Margaret ( ) h 1800 IRE 147
Margaret ( ) b.1808 VT 147
Margaret ( ) h 1812 KY 120
Margaret ( ) m.1815 PA 196
Margaret ( ) b.1820 SC 275
Margaret ( ) b.1825 VA 221
Margaret ( ) b.1829 TN 223
Margaret ( ) b.1846 31
Margaret ( ) b.1847 28
Margaret ( ) m.185– MO 285
Margaret ( ) b.1853 ENG 12
Margaret ( ) r.1861 NC 235
Margaret (Carson) 285
Margaret (Chapman) 228
Margaret (Colson) 285
Margaret (Damon) (Rand) 18
Margaret (David) 275
Margaret (Lewis) 233
Margaret (Livings) 96
Margaret (Morrison) 104
Margaret (Offutt) 34, 35, 65, 66
Margaret (Saddler) 287
Margaret (Smith) 74
Margaret (Sunderland) 6
Margaret (Teller) 279
Margaret (Waddle) 279
Margaret (Warnick) 110
Margaret (Yates) 20
Margaret A. (Strager) 262
Margaret A. b.1853 KY 118
Margaret Allison (McKee) 270
Margaret Ann b.1837 NY 66
Margaret Ann b.1843 20, 21
Margaret Bellona (Lundy) 197

AUSTIN,

Margaret Caroline b.1851 181
Margaret E. b.1844 AL 157
Margaret E. b.1855 IA 84
Margaret Edelia b.1850 20
Margaret Elizabeth b.1846 KY 85
Margaret Elizabeth (Hill) 118
Margaret Ella b.1864 NC 181,227
Margaret Ellen b.1835 KY 42
Margaret Fern (Ferris) 83
Margaret J. ( ) 235
Margaret J. (Anderson) 204
Margaret Jane (Bean) 180, 197, 236
Margaret Jane b.1840 20
Margaret Jane b.1843 QU 300
Margaret Jane b.1845 QU 301
Margaret Katherine (Holder) 219, 287
Margaret L. (Alexander) 228
Margaret Louise (Barabas) 212
Margaret Lynn b.1953 NY 139
Margaret M. b.1848 TN 223
Margaret Matilda (Greene) 200
Margaret R. b.1822 106
Margaret Rutherford McKee 73
Margery (Simon) 256
Margery (Waddle) 279
Margery (Walker) 279
Margie 227
Margie (Garrett) 169, 251, 252
Margie E. b.1878 r.OH 12
Marguerite E. 97
Marguerite Laura (Hempy) 111
Marguerite Mary b.1899 22
Maria b.1795 NY 6
Maria b.1804 VT 144
Maria b.1819 VT 147
Maria m.1820 OH 205
Maria b.1820 NY 96
Maria b.1824 NY 107
Maria b.1828 OH 109
Maria b.1828 VT 147
Maria b.1834 VT 143
Maria b.1860 NY 54
Maria d.1868 PA 106
Maria ( ) b.1812 NC 181
Maria ( ) b.1815 NY 309
Maria ( ) b.1816 NY 308
Maria ( ) b.1820 VT 148
Maria ( ) b.1842 Baden 28
Maria ( ) (Hoit) 39
Maria (Brown) 291, 292
Maria (Dockstader) 107, 109
Maria (Ryerse) 278
Maria (Sutton) 111
Maria A. ( ) b.1794 VT 146
Maria A. b.1813 NY? 54
Maria E. ( ) 242
Maria Ellen r.1860 QU 151
Maria L. d.1905 PA 99
Mariah b.1809 MA 7
Mariah b.1847 TN 223
Mariah b.1849 KY 85
Mariah ( ) (Hoit) 39
Mariah (Griffin) 124
Mariah (Tarlton) 232
Mariah C. ( ) b.1818 MA 145
Mariah Jane b.1812 KY 114
Mariam B. (Harrison) 205
Marian b.1847 KY 127
Marian ( ) b.1823 VT 144
Marian (Dockstader) 98
Marian F. (Hoskins) 172
Marian L. b.1835 VT 146
Marida b.1825 VA (male) 156
Marie b.1899 OR 123
Marie b.1911 KY 169
Marie ( ) d.1610 ENG 257
Marie Acton m.1938 AR 125
Marietta (Reed) 204
Marilda b.1847 KY 51, 85
Marilda ( ) b.1827 KY 128
Marilyn b.1953 KY 211
Marilyn Arlene b.1932 172
Marilyn Kay (Henry) 82
Marinda m.1864 OH 205
Marinda Katherine b.1889 WI 270
Marinda Nancy (Kimball) 268, 269
Marion b.1849 NH 148
Marion 96
Marion Pearl (Dickey) 74

Marjorie d.1984 WV 39
Mark Allen b.1965 OH 213
Mark Anthony b.1821 OH 38
Mark Paul b.1957 GER 139
Mark S. r.1861 TN 306
Mark Steven b.1959 OH 212
Marlon b.1953 KY 211
Marsella b.1849 KY 85
Marshal r.1863 WI 201
Marshall m.1868 WI 43
Marshall Coit b.1958 TX 242
Martha b.1725 MA 14
Martha b.1829 OH 40
Martha b.1742 MA 14
Martha b.1779 MA 146
Martha b.1793 SC 157
Martha b.1800 106
Martha b.1801 VA 114
Martha b.1805 NC 156
Martha b.1807 VT 143
Martha b.1819 TN 202
Martha b.1824 ME 2
Martha m.1826 OH 205
Martha b.1828 ME 309
Martha b.1829 KY 127
Martha b.1830 AL 274
Martha b.1832 AL 157
Martha b.1832 KY 129
Martha b.1832 VT 147
Martha b.1833 KY 127
Martha b.1833 MS 274
Martha b.1833 TN 222
Martha b.1836 TN 275
Martha b.1836 VT 147
Martha b.1837 TN 223
Martha b.1838 TN 225
Martha b.1840 AL 222
Martha b.1841 TN 222
Martha b.1842 MS 274
Martha b.1843 OH 155
Martha b.1844 MO 75
Martha b.1844 MS 275
Martha b.1845 TN 221, 225
Martha b.1846 KY 126
Martha b.1848 TN 221, 223
Martha b.1848 VT 144
Martha b.1850 KY 129
Martha b.1852 NC 181
Martha b.1886 VA 221
Martha b.1912 KY 171, 208, 209, 214
Martha r.NC 233
Martha ( ) r.1753 MD 35
Martha ( ) b.1796 IRE 107
Martha ( ) b.1797 VT 147
Martha ( ) b.1800 TN 274
Martha ( ) b.1803 VT 147
Martha ( ) b.1811 KY 126, 286
Martha ( ) b.1815 TN 222
Martha ( ) b.1817 SC 274
Martha ( ) b.1818 TN 222
Martha ( ) b.1819 PA 308
Martha ( ) b.1824 LA 274
Martha ( ) b.1824 TN 224
Martha ( ) b.1827 130
Martha ( ) b.1829 TN 222
Martha ( ) b.1855 28
Martha ( ) b.1758 MA 6
Martha (Benson) 60
Martha (Cooper) 204
Martha (Frisk) 203
Martha (Hill) 42
Martha (Jeffery) 152
Martha (Morgan) 98
Martha (Murdock) 203
Martha (Price) 204
Martha (Ritter) 204
Martha (Rose) 204
Martha (Searles) 54
Martha (Thompson) 11
Martha (Thomson) 31
Martha A. b.1834 TN 224
Martha A. b.1837 NC 223
Martha A. b.1840 VT 143
Martha A. b.1846 TN 221
Martha A. b.1860 AL 130
Martha A. ( ) 177
Martha A. E. b.1838 KY 128
Martha Adeline (Snow) 114
Martha Ann b.1815 115
Martha Ann b.1830 KY 117
Martha Ann b.1842 AL 157
Martha Ann b.1871 KY 271
Martha Ann (Austin) b.KY 271
Martha B. b.1836 KY 126

Martha B. (Griffin) 233
Martha C. b.184– MO 85
Martha C. b.184– NY? 6
Martha C. b.1856 KY 85
Martha C. m.1881 PA 108
Martha E. b.1839 VT 309
Martha E. b.1844 TN 224
Martha E. b.1846 KY 127
Martha Ellen b.1830 20
Martha Gifford b.1848 106
Martha H. r.1885 NC 235
Martha J. b.1829 OH 40
Martha J. b.1836 TN 223
Martha J. b.1844 TN 223
Martha J. b.1845 TN 221
Martha J. b.1846 KY 127
Martha J. m.1873 OH 205
Martha J. ( ) 235
Martha J. (Qualls) 61
Martha J. (Vaught) 117
Martha Jane b.18– MO 285
Martha Jane b.1824 TN 226
Martha Jane b.1835 VT 146
Martha Jane b.1849 TN 226
Martha Jane ( ) b.1821 KY 127
Martha Jane (McDaniel) 206
Martha Jane (Wilson) 277
Martha L. b.1843 KY 128
Martha L. b.1850 TN 222
Martha L. (Brown) 21
Martha LuVurn m.1929 OH 205
Martha Parke b.1821 MA 7
Martha Pearl (Petry) 206, 277
Martha Peely b.1869 28
Martha Prety b.MO 118
Martha T. b.1897 TN? 60
Martha Veannah b.1810 250
Martha Viannah b.1801 KY 219
Martin b.1838 IRE 147
Martin b.1840 SC 275
Martin b.1849 MS 275
Martin r.1863 WI 201
Martin b.1906 KY 168
Martin V. b.1833 97
Marvin Elwood b.1928 TX 242
Marvin Emmett b.1905 172
Marvin b.1879 61
Marvin S. b.1821 NY 309
Mary b.d.1573 ENG 256
Mary m.1588 ENG 257
Mary b.16– MA 11
Mary m.1674 240
Mary b.1687 ME 56
Mary b.1701 MA 8, 9
Mary b.1719 MA 14
Mary b.1734 MA 129
Mary b.1735 MA 15
Mary b.1750 220
Mary m.1754 MA 129
Mary b.1761 IRE 232
Mary b.1764 MA 147
Mary b.17– NC/SC 10
Mary r.1771 MA 24
Mary b.1771 MA 10
Mary b.1778 VA 225
Mary b.1780 CT 144
Mary b.1780 NC 103, 104, 278
Mary b.1781 NS 246
Mary b.1784 CT 295
Mary b.1787 NH 44
Mary b.1790 VT 146
Mary b.1792 NY 309
Mary m.1795 NH 110
Mary b.1796 ME 5
Mary m.1796 VA 37
Mary b.1798 VA 114
Mary m.1799 ME 263
Mary b.18– IL 95
Mary b.18– MA/CT 250
Mary b.1800 VA 127
Mary m.1802 NS 246
Mary b.1802 NC 232
Mary b.1804 NY/CAN 11
Mary r.1806 PA? 43
Mary b.1807 NY 206
Mary b.1808 KY 127
Mary b.1808 TN 222
Mary b.1810 KY 128
Mary b.1810 ON 278
Mary b.1812 NC 234
Mary m.1813 16
Mary b.1815 AL 223
Mary b.1815 GA 157
Mary b.1817 26

Mary b.1817 VT 147
Mary m.1819 OH 205
Mary b.1819 ON 103, 279
Mary r.1820 OH 25
Mary b.1820 KY 128, 129
Mary b.1821 NY 107
Mary b.1822 NC 157
Mary b.1824 TN 288
Mary b.1824 VT 143
Mary b.1825 IRE 147
Mary b.1825 TN 156
Mary b.1826 VA 221
Mary m.1827 OH 205
Mary b.1828 TN 221
Mary m.1829 OH 205
Mary b.1829 IL 202
Mary b.1829 NY 224
Mary b.183– TN 257
Mary b.1830 MS 274
Mary b.1830 TN 225
Mary b.1831 TN 127, 223
Mary b.1831 VT 143
Mary b.1832 147
Mary b.1832 NY 310
Mary b.1832 OH 127
Mary r.1833 TN 284
Mary b.1833 NY 107
Mary b.1833 VT 148
Mary b.1833 155
Mary m.1834 OH 205
Mary b.1834 TN 224, 225, 263
Mary m.1835 OH 205
Mary b.1835 VT 145
Mary b.1836 AL 26, 275
Mary b.1836 KY 129
Mary b.1836 NY 309
Mary b.1837 TN 225
Mary b.1837 VT 145
Mary b.1838 111
Mary b.1838 KY 129
Mary b.1838 MS 274
Mary b.1838 ON 279
Mary b.1839 TN 226
Mary b.1840 AL 156
Mary b.1840 NC/MO 75
Mary b.1841 VT 145
Mary b.1842 26, 36
Mary b.1842 AL 31
Mary b.1842 NC 221
Mary b.1842 TN 221, 225
Mary b.1843 KY 126
Mary b.1843 VT 145, 148
Mary b.1844 KY 117, 127, 129
Mary b.1845 KY 128
Mary b.1845 VT 147
Mary b.1846 106
Mary b.1846 MS 275
Mary b.1846 TN 222
Mary b.1846 VT 144
Mary b.1847 TN 224, 226
Mary b.1848 TN 223, 224
Mary b.1848 VT 147
Mary b.1849 KY 126
Mary b.1849 MA 144
Mary b.1849 VT 144
Mary b.1849 WI 309
Mary b.1850 AL 157
Mary b.1850 KY 127
Mary b.1850 VT 146
Mary m.1852 OH 205
Mary b.1852 PA 50
Mary m.1854 OH 205
Mary m.1855 PA 104
Mary b.1858 KY 51, 85
Mary m.1860 OH 205
Mary m.1861 OH 205
Mary b.1866 r.WI 28
Mary b.1871 r.OH 12
Mary b.1873 r.OH 12
Mary b.1875 MS 130
Mary m.1879 PA 108
Mary b.1909 KY 171, 208
Mary b.KY? 38
Mary r.NC 234
Mary b.NC 228
Mary b.NH 219
Mary b.NS 244, 245, 249
Mary m.OH 205
Mary b.ON 279
Mary b.PA 99
Mary r.NC 233
Mary ( ) b.1696 34

Mary ( ) r.17– NC 286
Mary ( ) r.1750 50
Mary ( ) r.1771 QU 154
Mary ( ) r.1778 NS 247
Mary ( ) b.1784 TN 226
Mary ( ) b.1788 SC 275
Mary ( ) b.1790 NC 225
Mary ( ) b.1791 ME 309
Mary ( ) b.1793 VA 127
Mary ( ) b.1797 TN 31
Mary ( ) b.1799 GA 222
Mary ( ) b.1799 KY 157
Mary ( ) b.1800 KY 128
Mary ( ) r.1800 TN 283
Mary ( ) b.1804 TN/VA 263
Mary ( ) b.1804 VA 224
Mary ( ) b.1805 NC 222
Mary ( ) b.181– QU 245
Mary ( ) b.1816 VA 219
Mary ( ) b.1817 KY 126
Mary ( ) b.1819 TN 226
Mary ( ) b.1825 NC 275
Mary ( ) b.1829 OH 308
Mary ( ) b.1829 TN 127
Mary ( ) b.1830 107
Mary ( ) b.1831 SC 157
Mary ( ) b.1833 TN 221
Mary ( ) b.1833 28
Mary ( ) m.1838 TN 288
Mary ( ) b.1839 IRE 12
Mary ( ) r.1842 QU 299
Mary ( ) b.1842 ENG 28
Mary ( ) d.1849 IN 175
Mary ( ) r.1850 TN 263
Mary ( ) r.1860 KY 263
Mary ( ) b.1860 IL 196
Mary ( ) d.1863 PA 99
Mary ( ) r.1884 NC 236
Mary ( ) r.NC 232
Mary ( ) r.TN 182
Mary (Austin) b.1810 ON 278
Mary (Baker) 182
Mary (Barton) 129
Mary (Bayley) 129
Mary (Borton) 155
Mary (Bracket) b.1780 148
Mary (Bradford) 181
Mary (Briggs) 36
Mary (Brown) 98
Mary (Calerman) 124
Mary (Cathey) 26
Mary (Chapman) 99
Mary (Countess) d.1867 FRA 248
Mary (Cowgill) 203
Mary (Dunlap) 206
Mary (Eades) 244, 246, 249
Mary (Elbert) 204
Mary (Fitzgerald) 98
Mary (Fleming) 203
Mary (French) 206
Mary (Gardiner) 75
Mary (Green) 148
Mary (Hilliard) 277
Mary (Johnson) 7
Mary (Kirksey) 177
Mary (Littlefield) 56, 240, 242
Mary (Lloyd) 187
Mary (Loyd) 114
Mary (Marshman) 74
Mary (McLean) 278
Mary (Minar) 26
Mary (Misner) 104, 279
Mary (Render) 42
Mary (Roberts) 251
Mary (Rowe) 26
Mary (Sanderfur) 40
Mary (Seymour) 17, 36
Mary (Sims) 129
Mary (Slaght) 103, 278, 279
Mary (Smith) 203
Mary (Stevens) 14
Mary (Teague) 6
Mary (Thomas) 22, 98, 228
Mary (Thompson?) 25
Mary (Waterbury) 204
Mary (Wright) 204
Mary (Yonker) 155, 205
Mary A. b.1797 MD 221
Mary A. b.1828 TN 222
Mary A. b.1829 AL 157
Mary A. b.1838 VT 145
Mary A. m.1839 OH 205
Mary A. b.1840 NC 85
Mary A. b.1840 TN 222, 224

AUSTIN,
Mary A. b.1842 VA 225
Mary A. b.1845 NY 107
Mary A. b.1847 KY 127
Mary A. b.1866 TN? 61
Mary A. 105
Mary A. ( ) b.1796 MD 226
Mary A. ( ) b.1835 ENG 28
Mary A. (Collins) 268
Mary A. (Simington) 242
Mary A. (Sousley) 96
Mary A. (Williams) 169
Mary A. (Williams) (Love) 252
Mary A. C. b.1873 ENG 12
Mary A. M. b.1842 AL 157
Mary Ann b.18— MO 285
Mary Ann b.1813 MA 7
Mary Ann b.1822 NY 268
Mary Ann b.1824 VT 145
Mary Ann b.1829 20
Mary Ann b.1830 VT 146
Mary Ann b.1831 ON 103, 278
Mary Ann m.1833 OH 205
Mary Ann b.1833 VT 145
Mary Ann b.1844 AL 156
Mary Ann b.1852 IL? 74
Mary Ann b.MD 35
Mary Ann ( ) 279
Mary Ann (Butt) 116
Mary Ann (Griffin) 301
Mary Ann (Herbert) 20
Mary Ann (Pratt) 204
Mary Ann (Railey) 20
Mary Ann (Wheeler) 16
Mary Ann (Wood) 204
Mary Ann Elizabeth b.1839 20, 21
Mary Annyce (Briscoe) 210, 218
Mary Arlene (Mercer) 172
Mary B. b.1817 KY 115
Mary Belle m.OH 205
Mary C. b.182– MA 7
Mary C. b.1827 MA 275
Mary C. b.1838 96
Mary C. b.1846 TN 222, 225
Mary C. (Bradley) 196
Mary C. (Connon) 301
Mary Cassandra b.1845 42
Mary Catharine (Frety) 98
Mary Clarke (McKee) 73
Mary Crawford (Knox) 160, 161, 164
Mary E. b.1812 AL 157
Mary E. b.1812 IN 156
Mary E. b.1822 AL 157
Mary E. b.182– MA 7
Mary E. b.1828 VT 147
Mary E. b.1835 KY 117
Mary E. b.1835 MO 220
Mary E. b.1839 AL 157
Mary E. b.1839 TN 223
Mary E. b.1843 TN 222, 226
Mary E. b.1848 TN 226
Mary E. b.1849 KY 129
Mary E. r.1888 NC 235
Mary E. m.1916 OH 205
Mary E. ( ) b.1838 PA 107
Mary E. (Hill) 42
Mary E. (Leonard) 21
Mary E. (Mansfield) 246
Mary E. (Pierce) 171, 172
Mary E. (Pitchford) 286
Mary E. (Rumsey) b.1828 106
Mary E. (Woodcock) 287
Mary E. M. b.1840 NC 157
Mary Elizabeth b.1834 KY 286
Mary Elizabeth b.1834 ME 140, 141
Mary Elizabeth b.1835 VA/KY 175
Mary Elizabeth b.1836 AL 157
Mary Elizabeth b.1854 KY 133
Mary Elizabeth b.1870 KY 287
Mary Elizabeth b.1985 OK 272
Mary Elizabeth b.MO 118
Mary Elizabeth (Adams) 220
Mary Elizabeth (Ferguson) 287
Mary Elizabeth (Hill) 271, 273
Mary Elizabeth (Wright) 26
Mary Ella b.1855 IL 269
Mary Ellen (Williamson) 207
Mary Ellen (Yates) 21
Mary Emeline (Sitler) 155
Mary Emma (Hardin) 21

Mary Emma (Wathen) 21
Mary F. b.1837 KY 126
Mary F. b.1837 116
Mary F. ( ) b.1828 TN 223
Mary Frances (Cooper) 51
Mary Frances (Gilliam) 242
Mary Frances (Hillard) 206
Mary G. b.1842 MI 308
Mary Geraldine b.1868 21
Mary H. b.1831 NC 221
Mary H. b.1856 16
Mary H. (Jeffreys) 241
Mary H. A. ( ) b.1839 ENG 12
Mary Hanna (Jones) 282
Mary I. ( ) b.1819 VA 224
Mary I./T. b.1836 SC 274
Mary J. b.1821 TN 222
Mary J. b.1833 TN 221
Mary J. b.1838 KY 131
Mary J. b.1840 KY 127
Mary J. b.1840 IL 38, 55
Mary J. b.1842 KY 127
Mary J. b.1846 PA 107
Mary J. b.1849 VT 144
Mary J. b.1849 106
Mary J. m 1871 PA 108
Mary J. ( ) (Bradley) 140
Mary J. (Wilkinson) m. 1872 PA
Mary Jane b.1842 OH 80
Mary Jane b.1845 KY 222
Mary Jane b.1845 TN 222
Mary Jane b.1855 NC 181
Mary Jane b.1856 NC 200
Mary Jane m.1865 OH 205
Mary Jane (Bender) 43
Mary Jane (Thompson) 204
Mary Jane (Wilson) 66
Mary Jennie b.1878 NC 197
Mary Jo ( ) b.1822 AL 157
Mary Johnson b.1819 155
Mary Johnson b.1820 OH/MI 129
Mary Joseph b.1883 22
Mary Josephine b.1923 IN 173
Mary Josephine 105
Mary Josephine (Fullwood) 228
Mary Katherine b.1954 NY 139
Mary L. b.1835 VT 147
Mary L. b.1845 KY 128
Mary L. b.1850 GA 157
Mary L. b.1877 TX 134
Mary L. 97
Mary Lee (Williams) 272
Mary Lee m.1943 AR 125
Mary Lewis b.19— KY 288
Mary Lois (Rodgers) 125
Mary Lou (Coffey) 229
Mary Louella b.1862 KY? 41
Mary M. b.1839 KY 127
Mary M. b.1842 PA 107
Mary M. b.1847 TN 224, 286
Mary M. b.1898 PA 98
Mary M. (Dodge) 262
Mary Magdeline b.1878 21
Mary Margaret (Antenna) 270
Mary Martha b.1882 KY 131, 169
Mary Martha 214
Mary Melissa b.1847 AR 160, 161, 162, 164
Mary Melissa (Petry) 277
Mary P. b.1844 KY 129
Mary Patience b.1844 KY 118
Mary Rosilena b.1832?? KY 42
Mary Ruth b.1912 OK 272
Mary S. (Allen) 100
Mary Smith (Hankins) 37
Mary T. (Martin) 42
Mary Teresa b.1876 PA 98
Mary Teresa (Loftus) 98
Mary V. b.1839 MS 274
Mary Violett b.1863 QU 299
Mary Weild 1
Mary Z. b.1844 TN 222
Mary Zelphia (Harrison) 227
Mary Zerelda b.1873 KY 271
Maryan b.1818 SC 225
Maryan b.1836?? NY 43
Maryon ( ) b.1823 VT 144
Mason B. r.1861 TN 305
Mathew J. b.1845 GA 157
Mathilda Ann b.1853 OH 80, 81
Matilda b.1830 TN 223
Matilda b.1838 PA 67, 307, 309
Matilda b.1838 TN 225
Matilda b.1839 CAN 301

Matilda b.1847 128
Matilda b.1850 KY 128
Matilda b.1850 OH 80
Matilda b.1852 IL 38, 55
Matilda ( ) b.1830 VT 144
Matilda (Mitchell) 203
Matilda (Swearingen) 118
Matilda C. b.1835 TN 223
Matilda E. b.1869 KY 131
Matilda P. b.1845 AL 156
Matilda Sophia b.1858 QU 300
Matt b.1891 MS 130
Matthew b.1620 ENG 242
Matthew b.1658 ME 3, 242
Matthew r.1707 ME 240
Matthew r.1771 MA 24
Matthew b.ENG 219
Matthew David 229
Mattie b.18— NY/WI 26
Mattie b.1871 TN 60, 61
Mattie r.1895 NC 235
Mattie (Bean) 227
Mattie (Lowe) 124
Mattie (Wilson) 276
Mattie Jane b.1875 IA 277
Mattie L. (Curtis) 227
Mattie Lue b.1907 31
Maude b.1896 NC 228
Maude Ann (Rhoades) 39
Maude Elizabeth b.1862 QU 299
Maude L. b.1889 KY 170
Maudie (Kellett) 125
Maurice b.1794 NY/CAN 11
Maurice Leon b.1932 209
Maxine B. b.1912 TN 228
Maxwell Tony b.1960 TX 242
May b.1844 KY 128
May b.1849 OH 308
May b.1898 TN 228
Maybelle (Harrison) 124
Maywood N. b.1833 TN 224
McKinzie Burton b.MO 118
Mehitabel b.1804 VT 147
Mehitabel b.1832 VT 147
Mehitable b.1772 26
Mehitable (Campbell) 75
Mehitable (Forbes) 241
Mehitable (Frye) 9
Mehitable (Harris) 79
Melanie Cassandra b.1972 IN 213
Melinda b.1830 VT 143
Melinda b.1832 NY 67, 307
Melinda b.1839 CAN 301
Melinda M. b.1830 VT 146
Melissa b.1815 VT 62, 63
Melissa b.1845 KY 51, 128
Melissa (Hunt) 206
Melissa (Whiting) 205
Melissa Elizabeth b.1978 MA 149
Melissa J. 133
Melissa Jane b.1831 KY 117
Melissa Kay b.KY 211
Melissa Samantha 111
Melisse (Thompson) 203
Melvin b.1826 NY 147
Melvin b.1899 OR 123
Melvina b.1832 TN 222
Melvina b.1868 PA 107
Melwood Ray b.1957 TX 242
Mercy b.1762 ME 267
Mercy b.1837 VT 144
Mercy m.1844 OH 205
Mercy ( ) b.1798 NH 308
Mercy ( ) b.1825 NH 146
Mercy (Atwater) 6, 186
Merill b.1832 VT 147
Merilla S. 186
Merritt b.1813 ME 238
Merritt r.1840 NC 235
Merritt D. b.1854 WI 307
Merritt F. b.1826 17
Merritt Leon, b.1870 17
Merwin b.1814 CT/MA r.NY 6, 26, 148
Michael r.1627 ENG 255
Michael r.1636 ENG 255
Michael b.1780 VT 145
Michael r.1820 NC 232
Michael b.1834 TN 274
Michael r.1861 TN 306
Michael b.1862 IRE 12
Michael David b.1969 CA 214

Michael Edward b.1940 MA 1, 3, 8, 11, 14, 18, 24, 29, 30, 38, 44, 49, 56, 62, 63, 68, 74, 86, 90, 94, 110, 111, 149, 150, 151, 166, 190, 200, 220, 226, 234, 244, 249, 252, 265, 266, 280, 283, 299, 307, 310
Michael John b.1957 NY 139
Michael Lane b.1957 229
Michael Wayne b.1964 IN 211
Michelle b.1960 209
Middy b.1856 CAN 26
Mikey (Gentry) 114
Milan P. b.1872 MI 196
Mildred b.1607 ENG 257
Mildred b.1844 TN 225
Mildred (Miller) 209
Mildred Estella m.1897 PA 98
Mildred Estella (Austin) 98
Mildred J. b.1850 MO 75
Mildred Jane b.1851?? MO 85
Mildred Jo b.1931 TN 252
Mildred Mabel (Hanson) 172
Miles r.1812 VA 159
Miles C. b.1844 TN 224
Miles W. b.1823 TN 224, 288
Milla (Larabee) 16, 36
Millard F. b.1850 97
Millard b.1907 TN? 61
Milley d.1802 TN 58
Milly ( ) b.1792 VT 145
Milly ( ) r.1801 TN 31
Milly (Bland) 115, 116
Milly C. b.1848 TN 222
Milo m.1887 PA 108
Milo D. b.1841 VT 148
Milton 233
Milton S. r.NC r.TX 234
Minerva b.1797 VT 144
Minerva b.1813 VT 146
Minerva b.1825 NY 67, 306, 307
Minerva b.1826 VT 146
Minerva b.1829 26, 36
Minerva b.1833 VT 148
Minerva b.1841 TN 223
Minerva b.1843 PA 308
Minerva b.1847 IL 38, 55
Minerva m.1853 OH 205
Minerva b.1857 OH 80
Minerva ( ) b.1815 VT 147
Minerva ( ) b.1816 KY 129
Minerva ( ) b.1826 IL 308
Minerva (Sackett) 204
Minerva (Stevens) 40
Minerva H. b.1833 VT 148
Minerva J. b.1847 KY 127
Minnie b.1854 ME 4
Minnie b.1863 r.OH 12
Minnie (Breeding) 132
Minnie (Chesebro) 3
Minnie (Pauley) 74
Minnie (Rumsey) 105
Minnie Beatrice 55
Minnie Bee (Hightower) 243
Minnie Bell m.1933 AR 124
Minnie E. (Rumsey) b.1869 106
Minnie Gertrude (Bradshaw) 300
Minnie Leland (Cox) 96
Minnie Mae (Wilson) 271, 273
Mintha I. ( ) b.1820 KY 127
Mirabelle Lavaun (Greer) 83
Miranda b.1822 96
Miranda b.1835 VT 146
Miranda E. ( ) b.1822 VA 274
Miriam b.1822 NY 224
Miron b.1837 WI 308
Miron b.1850 WI 309
Mitchel b.1812 KY 127
Mitchel b.1840 KY 127
Mittie E. (Smith) 105, 108, 109
Mollie b.1882 KY 169
Mollie 214
Mollie (Collins) 167
Molly b.1750 50
Molly b.183– OH? 40
Molly (Bennett) 37
Molly (McColley) 301
Mona Lee b.1942 OH 83
Monroe 6
Morgan r.KY 212
Morgan B. 250
Moroni b.1834 VT 144
Morris b.1790 MA 111

Morris b.1830 IRE 147
Morris b.18— MA/CT 250
Morris b.1873 d.CT 130
Morton r.1812 VA 159
Morton r.1817 IL 185
Moses b.17— 10
Moses b.1734 NH 110
Moses b.1742 ME 17
Moses b.1761 CT 242, 258, 288, 289, 290, 291, 292, 298
Moses m.1767 ME 67
Moses b.1778 153
Moses m.1785 PA 98
Moses b.1792 NC 279
Moses b.1802 ON 103, 104, 278
Moses r.1806 PA 43
Moses r.1806 QU 151, 153
Moses b.1817 MO 297
Moses b.1832 TN 225
Moses r.1839 NC 235, 236
Moses r.1841 PA 43
Moses b.OH 99
Moses F. b.1822 NY 308
Moses G. b.181– NY 6, 10, 43
Moses G. b.NY 133
Moses T. b.1845 VT 148
Mossie b.1912 KY 131, 168, 207, 214
Mrs. M. A. b.1819 31
Murcienus r.1863 WI 201
Murph r.NC 233
Myra A. (Gary) 96
Myra Elizabeth 59
Myra J. 96
Myrrha Charlotte b.1864 QU 153
Myrrha Harriet (Bradshaw) 152, 153, 154
Myrtle b.18— WI 307
Myrtle b.1913 OH 83
Myrtle 228
Myrtle (Tinsley) 210
Myrtle (Willis) 134, 172, 215
Myrtle (Wills) 167
Myrtle Ann b.1870 MO 133
Myrtle Dell (Kintz) 43

AUSTIN, N
N. b.1815 NY (male) 275
N. A. b.1838 KY (female) 126, 287
N. C. b.1820 TN 221
N. E. b.1834 KY 126
N. G. (male) r.1861 TN 306
N. J. b.1844 KY 126
N. J. r.1895 NC 236
N. J. ( ) r.1895 NC 236
N. J. ( ) 235
Nadie (Perley) 229
Nadine r.1986 FL 251
Nahum Jr. b.1836 ME 238
Nahum b.1789 17
Nancy b.1784 VT 144
Nancy m.1790 VA 175
Nancy b.1790 126
Nancy b.1791 TN 58
Nancy b.1795 VA 114
Nancy b.18— NC 234
Nancy b.1801 NY? 55
Nancy b.1806 NC 234
Nancy b.1808 NC 157
Nancy b.1812 ON 103, 279
Nancy b.1821 177
Nancy b.1825 KY 115
Nancy b.1830 TN 126, 222, 223
Nancy b.1832 TN 225
Nancy b.1838 TN 224
Nancy b.1841 TN 223
Nancy b.1844 KY 128
Nancy b.1845 ON 279
Nancy b.1845 WI 308
Nancy b.1846 TN 222, 226
Nancy b.1847 TN 223
Nancy b.1849 TN 221
Nancy b.1851 MO 131
Nancy b.1853 OH 276
Nancy b.1875 d.1876 31
Nancy b.1935 251
Nancy b.d.young WI 285
Nancy ( ) b.1785 CT 147
Nancy ( ) b.1790 NC 223
Nancy ( ) b.1791 VA 222
Nancy ( ) r.1792 MD 35
Nancy ( ) b.1794 VT 146
Nancy ( ) b.1798 TN 222

AUSTIN,

Nancy ( ) b.1802 NC 274
Nancy ( ) b.1802 224
Nancy ( ) b.1805 CAN 146
Nancy ( ) b.1808 VA 225
Nancy ( ) b.1809 KY 128
Nancy ( ) b.1810 NC 223
Nancy ( ) b.1812 222
Nancy ( ) b.1813 KY 126
Nancy ( ) b.1813 VA 128
Nancy ( ) b.1815 KY 128
Nancy ( ) b.1820 NC 223
Nancy ( ) b.1825 GA 156
Nancy ( ) b.1825 NC 223
Nancy ( ) b.1826 IRE 128
Nancy ( ) b.1828 KY 128
Nancy ( ) r.1848 VA 148
Nancy ( ) r.1852 VA 288
Nancy ( ) b.186– 43
Nancy (Alfred) 204
Nancy (Babb) 206
Nancy (Bener) 118
Nancy (Carleton) 242
Nancy (Edwards) 31, 182
Nancy (Enos) 203
Nancy (Fletcher) 117
Nancy (Gass) 75
Nancy (Hopper) 61
Nancy (Howard) 34
Nancy (Lard) 61
Nancy (Moore) 36, 60
Nancy (Morris) 134
Nancy (Presnell) 75
Nancy (Preston) 85
Nancy (Qualls) b.1791 VA 61
Nancy (VanHook) 115
Nancy (Watson) 283
Nancy (Wear/Weir) 36, 276
Nancy A. (Lewis) 99
Nancy C. ( ) b.1832 TN 224
Nancy C. b.1850 KY 128
Nancy E. b.1835 d.1900 PA 108
Nancy E. b.1841 TN 221
Nancy E. b.1843 KY 117
Nancy E. b.1868 TN? 60
Nancy E. ( ) b.1830 TN 224
Nancy E. ( ) b.1817 NY 129
Nancy E. (Carter) 117
Nancy E. (Cooper) 117, 118
Nancy E. (Gibson) 109
Nancy E. (Qualls) 61
Nancy Elizabeth b.1864 KY? 41
Nancy Ellen b.1843 KY 133
Nancy I. (Hitchcock) 268
Nancy J. b.1841 NC 129
Nancy J. b.1846 MO 75
Nancy J. b.1854 KY 118
Nancy J. m.1871 KY 117
Nancy J. (Green) (Grubbe) 282
Nancy J. (Richards) 118
Nancy Jane b.1844 KY 286
Nancy Jane b.1856 KY 133
Nancy Jane (Blevins) 31, 59
Nancy Jane (Dwiggens) 206
Nancy Jane (Fox) 131
Nancy Jane (Staton) 132
Nancy Jane Hinley b.1824 VA 288
Nancy Judy b.1848?? MO 85
Nancy M. r.1884 NC 236
Nancy M. m.1853 TN 288
Nancy May b.1937 96
Nancy Melvira b.1827 IL 282
Nancy Montgomery b.1853 KY 118, 133
Nancy Patience b.1863 KY 118
Nancy Patience b.1900 TX 167
Nancy S. b.1847 VA 129
Nancy Wand (James) 40
Nannie ( ) 171
Nannie (Chambers) 197
Nannie Bell m.1933 AR 124
Nannie Frances (McClelland) 129
Nanny (Rhoads) 42
Naoma ( ) b.1820 SC 275
Naomi (Napier) 174, 214
Naomi J. b.1833 KY 117, 133
Naomi J. (Austin) 117, 133
Nathan m.1725 MA 6
Nathan b.1725 MA 14, 135
Nathan b.1732 MA 15
Nathan b.1748 MA 62
Nathan b.1800 VT 146

Nathan b.1810 NY 309
Nathan b.1812 TN 202
Nathan b.1820 PA 105, 106, 107, 108, 109
Nathan r.1834 IL 185
Nathan r.1838 NC 236
Nathan m.1842 PA 98
Nathan r.1851 IL 185
Nathan r.1861 TN 305
Nathan T. r.1840 NC 236
Nathaniel b.1660 NH 219
Nathaniel b.17— 10
Nathaniel (Capt.) b.1703 CT 219
Nathaniel r.1734 257
Nathaniel r.1734 219, 257
Nathaniel r.1771 MA 24
Nathaniel b.1774 NH 22
Nathaniel b.1775 RI 50
Nathaniel b.1781 TN 226
Nathaniel b.1781 VA 177
Nathaniel b.1781 VA/TN 283
Nathaniel b.1786 ME 242
Nathaniel b.1789 VT 143
Nathaniel r.1790 VT 25
Nathaniel r.1802 TN 31, 58
Nathaniel m.1803 ME 242
Nathaniel b.1803 ME 4
Nathaniel b.1804 VT 144
Nathaniel b.1806 ME 186
Nathaniel d.1807 NY 155
Nathaniel b.181– PA/NY 36
Nathaniel r.1812 KY 159
Nathaniel r.1818 IL 185
Nathaniel r.1818 TN 284
Nathaniel b.1821 MS 274
Nathaniel r.1825 TN 284
Nathaniel b.1827 TN 225, 263
Nathaniel r.1831 VT 147
Nathaniel r.1833 VT 147
Nathaniel r.1837 TN 284
Nathaniel b.1838 TN 285
Nathaniel b.1838 NC? 75
Nathaniel b.1838 NC 85
Nathaniel b.1858 ME 238
Nathaniel r.1921 KS 27
Nathaniel r.MA 18
Nathaniel r.ME 240
Nathaniel r.ON 104, 279
Nathaniel C. b.1806 148
Nathaniel C. b.1811 m.1835 99
Nathaniel C. b.1845 NY 196
Nathaniel G. b.1827 TN 226
Nathaniel G. b.1846 TN 225
Nathaniel Glenn r.1861 TN 305
Nathaniel H. b.1829 VT 146
Nathaniel II r.1771 MA 24
Nathaniel James N. b.1837 KY 117
Nathaniel Jr. b.1745 ENG 10
Nathaniel S. b.1843 TN 222
Nathaniel Sr. b.1720 ENG 10
Nathaniel T. r.1841 IL 185
Ned 229
Nell b.1868 220
Nellie b.1865 106
Nellie b.1868 28
Nellie b.1874 28
Nellie 97
Nellie (Garrison) 233
Nellie (McNeese) 118
Nellie Beulah b.1891 NC 199
Nellie F. (Cleveland) 30
Nellie M. (Nichols) 84
Nellie Mae b.1899 NC 228
Nellie McComb (Stultz) 82
Nellie S. b.1875 NY 242
Nelson b.1817 PA 105, 106, 107, 110
Nelson b.1818 VT 145
Nelson b.1827 Norway 28
Nelson b.1828 OH 155
Nelson m.1850 OH 205
Nelson b.1860 WI 307
Nelson r.1863 WI 201
Nelson d.1865 PA 106
Nelson r.1869 PA 109
Nelson r.1885 IN 262
Nelson r.1906 IN 262
Nelson r.1980 ME 5
Nelson M. m.1874 IN 262
Nelson M. r.1866 IN 262
Nelson P. r.1863 WI 201
Nettie d.1887 PA 107
Nettie m.1920 AR 124

Nettie b.KY 171
Nettie b.186– IL 97
Nettie (Smith) m.1878 PA 108
Nettie (Thomas) 168
Nettie Belle b.1879 NC 200
Nettie May (Smith) 82
Nettie V. (Johnson) 21
Newel S. b.1839 WI 308
Newell Welton b.1831 NY 242
Newman b.1797 VT 144
Newton b.1834 TN 225
Newton b.1839 TN 222
Nicey r.NC 234
Nicey (Barber) 232
Nicey (Hinson) 233
Nichodemus b.1834 KY 126
Nicholas b.1774 NH 22
Nicholas r.1784 NS 246
Nicholas r.1793 QU 22
Nicholas b.1809 RI? 26
Nicholas b.1832 KY 117, 132, 133, 171
Nicholas b.1842 OH 128
Nicholas b.KY 171
Nicholas r.VT/CAN 38
Nicodemus b.1832 KY 117, 132
Noah r.1850 NC 236
Noah r.1866 IN 262
Noah b.1875 TN? 61
Noel Elizabeth 229
Nona L. b.1939 KY 207
Nora b.18— IRE 99
Nora b.1876 r.OH 12
Nora b.19— KY 251
Nora (Alexander) 228
Nora (Durant) 135, 136
Nora (McKee) 204
Nora Celeste b.1881 MS 130
Nora L. b.1885 KY 168
Norma d.NE 229
Norma 97
Normal Paul b.1960 NY 139
Norman b.1822 VT 145
Norman b.1895 NY 135, 137, 138
Norman Charles b.1912 NC 230
Norman Hobart b.1856 IL 74, 75
Norris C. b.1847 NY 196
Novice b.KY 168

AUSTIN, O

O. E. b.1803 VA 224
O. W. b.1895 KY 169
Obadiah r.1812 VA 159
Obie S. b.1898 251
Oda Clara b.1886 NY 135, 136
Odell 233
Oden Cassius b.1884 WV 39
Okie (Billings) 231
Ola b.18— KY 51
Ola b.1866 KY 85
Ola (Carter) 167
Ola Ethel b.1903 TN? 61
Olcha (Downing) 119, 268
Ole O. r.1863 WI 201
Olena b.1870? 28
Olga Marie m.1815 OH 205
Olison b.1838 Norway 28
Olive b.1774 MA 109
Olive b.1791 VT 146
Olive b.1803 VT 62
Olive r.1820 OH 25
Olive b.1824 VT 143
Olive b.1840 VT 143
Olive 196
Olive ( ) b.1802 VT 146
Olive ( ) b.1803 VT 147
Olive (Grant) 250
Olive (Hall) 25
Olive B. b.1860 97
Olive E. m.1865 OH 205
Olive Emily b.1844 OH 80
Olive M. 97
Oliver b.1760 r.VT 2
Oliver b.1761 16
Oliver b.1788 16
Oliver b.1788 VT 145
Oliver b.1801 VT 62
Oliver b.1809 VT 62–63
Oliver b.1834 ON 103, 104, 279
Oliver b.1848 IL 38, 55
Oliver m.1858 OH 205
Oliver r.1776 NY 206
Oliver r.1823 VT 36
Oliver r.1979 TX 220

Oliver Elhanon b.1826 16
Oliver Ezra Abijah b.1851 16
Olivia b.1844 AL 157
Olivia C. m.1860 OH 205
Olivia Elizabeth b.1907 OK 272
Ollie (Swafford) 134
Ollie C. b.1891 NC 200
Ollie H. b.1867 KY (female) 271, 273
Opal r.1916 273
Opal (Smith) 229
Opal Smith 231
Opie (Baker) 125
Oral b.1838 NY 309
Oral (Robbins) 262
Oratio b.1849 PA 107
Oren b.1809 RI? 26
Orin b.1800 186
Orin b.1809 NY? 26
Orin P. r.1853 IN 262
Orin S. b.1840 VT 146
Orlando b.1836 NY 310
Orlando b.1836 OH 143
Orlando b.1841 NY 308
Orlando A. r.1863 WI 201
Orlo H. b.1838 VT 146
Ormal b.1790 155, 186
Orpha b.1850 TN 221
Orphia Learie b.1896 KY 172,209
Orphus 219
Orrin b.1792 VT 146
Orrin b.1800 186
Orrin r.NY 270
Orrin Jr. b.1821 VT 146
Orrin Wilmer Nash b.1884 MO 79
Orson A. m.1846 OH 205
Orson David b.1818 NY 67
Orville r.1812 VA 159
Orville r.1863 WI 201
Orville b.1925 KY 173, 210, 211
Oscar b.1827 VT 147
Oscar b.1850 KY 127
Oscar b.KY 169
Oscar r.TN 251
Oscar Phelps 26
Osha b.1889 TN? 60
Otis r.1861 ME 238
Otis Lee b.1924 TN? 60
Ovilia b.1837 OH 308
Owen Ed b.1803 VA 38, 219
Ozias r.1812 MS 159

AUSTIN, P

P. b.1843 KY 126
P. A. b.1825 TN 225
P. J. ( ) b.1817 NY 308
P. W. b.1824 TN 221
Palmer b.1830 NY 309
Palmer r.1863 WI 201
Palmer r.NY 110
Pamela ( ) b.1807 GA 274
Pamelia b.1843 KY 128
Pamelia b.1848 TN 225
Pamelia ( ) b.1792 VT 144
Pansi (Brown) 227
Paralee b.1842 TN 222
Parallu b.1842 TN 222
Pardon b.1787 VT 143
Pardon m.1793 301
Pardon r.1800 NY 301
Pardon b.1843 NY 308
Pardon r.1863 WI 201
Pardon r.NY 250
Pardon 109
Parilee b.1839 AL 157
Parker b.1877 28
Pasco r.1775 RI 73
Pasco r.RI 110
Pasco b.17— RI/VT 6
Patience ( ) 257
Patricia m.1823 OH 205
Patricia Ann b.1956 OH 212
Patricia Ann (Biebuyck) 8, 10, 14, 30, 32, 38, 49, 56, 63, 74, 94, 111, 150, 166, 190, 200, 214, 220, 234, 237, 244, 252, 283, 307
Patricia Catherine b.1965 NY 138, 139
Patrick r.1812 VA 159
Patrick James b.1983 PA 139
Patsey W. (Stephens) 169, 251
Patsy m.1801 VA 37
Patsy b.1801 VA 114

Patsy Isabella b.1880 KY 131
Patty Jean b.1946 OH 82
Paul r.1768 SC 129
Paul b.1798 CAN 147
Paul b.1848 VT 147
Paul r.1944 TX 253
Paul d.NE 229
Paul Reginald b.1920 NY 137, 138, 139
Paul William b.1944 OH 82
Paulina b.1838 KY 127
Paulina ( ) b.1849 MA 309
Pauline (Reed) 55, 67, 220, 301, 306
Pauline Lucille (Plattner) 25, 44, 56, 57, 62, 68, 74, 84, 94, 98, 111, 142, 150, 166, 190, 200, 203, 220, 234, 252, 262, 276, 283, 307
Pauline b.1838 26, 36
Pauline b.KY 168
Pauline r.1921 TX 27
Peaceable b.1830 OH 155
Peamy b.1833 KY 126
Pearl b.1903 251
Pearl b.KY 167
Pearl 228
Pearl M. b.1890 WV 39
Pearl M. (Chausett) 17
Peggy b.1751 IRE 232
Peggy b.1846 TN 225
Peggy b.1931 TN 252
Peggy (Carpenter) 213
Pekn r.1812 VA 159
Penelope b.1841 NC 156
Penelope ( ) b.1824 NC 222
Penelope (Creach) 177
Percival m.1572 ENG 256
Percy 233
Percy Leroy b.1878 OH 81, 82
Permelia b.1879 31
Permelia r.NC 234
Permelia 233
Permelia E. (Brown) 171
Permila ( ) m.NC 206
Permillia A. (Kerr) 205
Perrigo 10
Perry b.1863 WI 276
Perry A. b.1863 WI 277
Perry B. d.1925 277
Persis b.1781 MA 109
Peter b.1730 MA 14
Peter b.1738 MA 14
Peter b.1746 MA 87, 88
Peter b.18— r.NY 10
Peter r.1812 KY 159
Peter r.1812 VA 182
Peter b.1815 NY? 50
Peter b.1824 MO 243
Peter r.1843 IL 185
Peter Amos b.1805 ME 17
Peter Martin b.1956 OH 273
Phebe b.1730 MA 15
Phebe b.1736 MA 14
Phebe b.1767 CT 186
Phebe b.1790 CT 148
Phebe b.1821 TN 221
Phebe b.1822 VT 144
Phebe ( ) b.18— r.IL 17
Phebe (Adair) b.CAN 26
Phebe (Barker) 62
Phebe (Cole) 250
Phebe A. b.1837 NY 309
Phebe Ann b.1844 VT 143
Phebe J. b.1834 VT 148
Phebe V. (Sterling) 220, 263
Phenix m.1783 MA 129
Pheobe b.17— TN 58
Pheobe b.1855 NY? 54
Pheonix b.1735 MA 219
Pheriba b.1789 155
Pheriba b.1791 NC 206
Pheriba ( ) m.NC 206
Philander b.1836 NY 310
Philena (Cunningham) 155
Philip b.1790 NC 278, 279
Philip b.1790 103, 104
Philip b.1808 TN 186, 224, 288
Philip b.1810 ON 103, 278
Philip b.1832 TN 225
Philip b.1847 KY 127
Philip r.NC 233
Philip Barber b.1825 ON 103, 279

AUSTIN,
Philip Waddle b.1840 ON 279
Phillip b.1798 NC 127
Phillip r.1861 TN 305
Phillip r.1895 NC 235
Phillip m.1925 AR 124
Phillip b.KY 169
Phillip G. b.1818 NC 223
Phillip W. b.1838 KY 223
Philo b.1824 VT 55
Philtus b.NY 36
Phineas b.1774 NH 6, 62
Phineas b.1790 VT 196
Phineas b.1798 VT 62-63
Phineas r.1847 IL 185
Phineas r.1851 IL 185
Phineas H. b.1790 VT 283
Phinehas b.1737 MA 14
Phinehas b.1774 NH 6, 62
Phoebe b.1760 67
Phoebe b.1795 31
Phoebe b.1809 TN 224
Phoebe b.1838 NY 165
Phoebe b.1849 WI 285
Phoebe b.18— IL 95
Phoebe ( ) b.1798 NC 223
Phoebe ( ) m.1832 TN 288
Phoebe ( ) b.1851 WI 196
Phoebe ( ) 186
Phoebe (Adair) 186, 270
Phoebe (Hussey) 110
Phoebe Ann (Walker) 278
Phoebe Lockwood r.1860 IL 285
Phoebe Orilla b.1863 IL? 74, 75
Phyllis Kaye b.1958 OH 212
Pierce m.1948 AR 125
Pina Belle (Fletcher) 172, 173, 214
Pleasant b.1798 NC 223
Pleasant r.1812 TN 159
Pleasant b.1823 TN 226
Pleasant b.1844 AL 157
Pleasant r.1850 TN 285
Pleasant r.1875 TN 284
Pleasant 250
Poenall b.1541 ENG 255
Polly b.1784 RI 145
Polly b.1798 VA 114
Polly b.180–/1– 186
Polly b.1818 155
Polly b.1824 TN 224
Polly b.1827 KY 127
Polly b.1841 AL 222
Polly b.1842 TN 223
Polly r.NC 233
Polly ( ) b.1807 NY 308
Polly ( ) r.1830 TN 242
Polly ( ) b.1795 VT 144
Polly (Bennett) 37
Polly (James) 182
Polly (Redman) 35
Polly (Render) 40, 42
Polly A. b.1832 TN 222
Polly Ann b.18— MO 285
Polly L. b.1818 VT 283
Polly Malinda b.1830 NY 268
Polly O. b.1822 KY 114
Potter b.1827 NY 308
Powel b.1797 VT 308
Powell b.1800 16
Presley b.1815 VA 127
Preston b.1849 TN 223
Priscilla b.1723 MA 14
Priscilla b.1726 MA 14
Priscilla b.17— KY? 175
Priscilla b.1840 ON 103, 279
Priscilla (Stevens) 14
Proctor Allen b.1874 NH 48–50
Prudence b.1800 KY 127
Prudence b.1843 VA 129
Prudence d.VT 55
Prudence (Bland) 115
Prudence E. b.1832 AL 157
Pruit b.1767 VA 37

AUSTIN, Q
Quint C. S. b.OH 40
Quintella Smith b.1859 KY 118
Quintin b.1837 KY 128

AUSTIN, R
R. b.1821 KY 126

R. b.1827 KY 126
R. b.1831 KY 126
R. r.1834 NS 265
R. b.1847 KY 126
R. E. 233
R. G. b.1839 KY 126
R. G. 108
R. G. (Coles) 108
R. H. r.1861 TN (male) 306
R. I. r.1901 NC 236
R. J. r.1861 TN (male) 306
R. L. b.1835 KY 127
R. L. r.1897 NC 236
R. N. b.1823 NY (male) 309
R. N. b.1833 NY (male) 308
R. P. b.1825 KY 127
R. T. r.1903 NC 236
Rachael r.1868 IL 185
Rachael ( ) m.1857 NS 245
Rachael (Anderson) 182
Rachael W. b.1848 GA 157
Rachel b.1746 NH 15
Rachel b.1828 NY 309
Rachel b.1830 TN 61, 222
Rachel b.183– OH? 40
Rachel b.1836 GA 274
Rachel m.1834 OH 205
Rachel b.1836 NY 175
Rachel ( ) b.1795 NY 50
Rachel ( ) b.1796 MD 128
Rachel (Benton) 40
Rachel (Denny) 283
Rachel (Grove) 203
Rachel (Hale) 38
Rachel (Kimble) 203
Rachel (Madison) 220
Rachel (Smith) 7
Rachel C. b.184–/5– NY 6
Rachel D. m.1843 OH 205
Rachel D. b.1845 OH 308
Rachel H. b.1833 TN 226
Rachel Matilda b.1829 PA 98
Rachel S. (Everett) 99
Racina b.1842 TN 225
Rae r.1980 NS 248
Raleigh r.1837 TN 284, 285
Ralph r.1657 ENG 237
Ralph r.1804–13 OH 155
Ralph b.189–/1– VA/OK 228
Ralph L. m.1925 OH 205
Ralph N. b.1877 TN? 61
Ramona B. (Short) 270
Randall b.1778 NY 10
Randolph b.1847 MS 274
Ransom b.1841 VT 145
Ransom r.1812 VA 159
Ransom L. b.1839 VT 148
Ray b.18— PA/IL 95
Ray b.187– IL/KS 97
Raymond b.1794 16
Raymond b.1795 VT 145
Raymond b.KY 168
Raymond b.NE 229
Rebakah b.1836 107
Rebecca b.1740 219
Rebecca b.1758 ME 242
Rebecca b.1778 VA 114
Rebecca b.1780 VA 221
Rebecca b.1786 VT 147
Rebecca b.1796 VA 129
Rebecca b.1796 MD? 85
Rebecca b.18— 288
Rebecca b.1810 VA 221
Rebecca b.1813 VA 219
Rebecca m.1815 282
Rebecca b.1818 NC 234
Rebecca b.1818 ON 103, 279
Rebecca b.1821 155
Rebecca b.1823 NY 219
Rebecca b.1828 TN 222
Rebecca b.1829 NC 223
Rebecca m.1832 OH 205
Rebecca b.1836 107
Rebecca b.1844 TN 223
Rebecca r.1848 IN 262
Rebecca b.1848 AL 156
Rebecca m.1866 IN 262
Rebecca b.1957 AZ 212
Rebecca r.NC 234
Rebecca b.NC 232
Rebecca ( ) b.1835 SCO 141

Rebecca ( ) b.1771 VA 222
Rebecca ( ) b.1796 NH 145
Rebecca ( ) b.1798 NY 309
Rebecca ( ) b.1799 CAN 145
Rebecca ( ) b.1812 TN 224
Rebecca ( ) b.1819 AL 226
Rebecca ( ) b.1827 TN 222
Rebecca ( ) m.1834 TN 288
Rebecca ( ) d.1876 PA 108
Rebecca ( ) r.1904 NC 235
Rebecca ( ) r.NC 233
Rebecca ( ) r.TN 196
Rebecca ( ) (Woodall) 202
Rebecca (Belsford) 205
Rebecca (Blankenship) 196
Rebecca (Bowes) 204
Rebecca (Brown) 105
Rebecca (Durbin) 203
Rebecca (Falkner) 262
Rebecca (Hankins) 37, 219
Rebecca (Main) 200
Rebecca (Moses) 58
Rebecca (Therrard) 206
Rebecca (Turner) 178, 179, 197, 227, 231, 235
Rebecca A. b.1841 TN 221
Rebecca Ann b.1822 ON 103, 278
Rebecca Ann b.1969 KY 211
Rebecca H. b.1832 TN 224
Rebecca J. (Johnson) 203
Rebecca June b.1942 OH 82
Rebecca Lee b.1985 OK 273
Rebecca Mills m.1824 OH 205
Recca (Runyon) 118
Redda b.1804 NC 156
Reeder C. m.1942 AR 125
Regina b.1894 21
Reita Mae (Hampton) 230
Rena (Hillard) 42
Renita Gail b.1945 KY 174, 212
Retha b.1902 TN? 60
Retha Fern b.1912 MO 172
Reuben r.1790 NY 267
Reuben r.1812 VA 159
Reuben b.1843 IL 185
Reuben b.1843 TN 224
Reuben b.1849 VT 145
Reuben r.1861 TN 305
Reuben b.1865 28
Reuben Jr. r.1836 IN 262
Reuben Jr. r.1836 MI 262
Reuel r.1861 ME 238
Rex 95
Rhoda b.1811 MA 147
Rhoda b.1825 TN 225
Rhoda b.1857 106
Rhoda b.1895 KY 131
Rhoda ( ) b.1802 VT 146
Rhoda ( ) b.1815 VA 225
Rhoda ( ) b.1821 KY 224
Rhoda (Stanton) 301
Rhoda A. ( ) 62
Rhoda Ann (McGuire) 109
Rhoda Catherine b.1835 IL 202
Rhoda Ellen b.MO 118
Rhoda H. ( ) b.1821 KY 286
Rhoda I. b.1845 VT 147
Rhody b.1835 TN 223
Rhuben b.1849 VT 145
Richard r.1586 ENG 257
Richard r.1596 ENG 175
Richard b.1598 ENG 3, 25, 38, 55, 57, 111, 112, 177, 219, 276, 289, 291, 298
Richard m.1626 257
Richard b.1632 ENG 177
Richard r.1651 MA 18
Richard r.1724 VA 196
Richard r.1771 MA 24
Richard b.1783 NY?? 54
Richard b.1792 NC 222
Richard b.1796 NC 250
Richard b.1815 NC 224
Richard r.1820 NC 232
Richard b.1822 KY 126
Richard b.1823 GA 274
Richard b.1825 IRE 308
Richard b.1831 TN 223
Richard b.1833 KY 126
Richard b.1841 KY 129
Richard r.1844 IN 262
Richard b.1847 KY 128
Richard m.1849 IN 262

Richard b.1854 QU 153
Richard m.1863 IN 262
Richard r.1865 IN 262
Richard b.1878 ENG 12
Richard r.ENG 18
Richard b.191– NY 135, 136
Richard r.ENG 18
Richard b.ENG 125
Richard b.KY? 38
Richard r.NS 249
Richard Elliott b.1833 KY 40, 41
Richard H. r.1863 WI 201
Richard Henry b.1847 KY 85
Richard L. r.1818 IL 185
Richard Logan b.1834 20
Riley b.1825 VT 147
Riley r.1861 TN 306
Riley r.NC 234
Riley C. b.1832 VT 146
Riley C. m.1860 QU 301
Riley J. b.1839 TN 225
Rilla r.NC 234
Rita (Danforth) 171
Riuben b.1841 VT 144
Robbie Marie (Benson) 60
Roberson b.1827 TN 226
Robert b.1634 196
Robert r.1661 RI 3, 78, 119, 257, 268, 270
Robert r.1776 PA 109
Robert r.1784 NH 148
Robert b.1785 VA 31, 156
Robert b.1788 VA 156
Robert b.1790 VA 114, 115
Robert b.1793 VA 127
Robert b.1804 MD 35, 42
Robert b.1805 MD 128
Robert r.1808 QU 151
Robert r.1809 QU 154
Robert b.180– 186
Robert b.1812 NC 129
Robert b.18— SCO? 73
Robert b.1820 AL 157
Robert b.1828 KY 116
Robert b.1830 NY 243
Robert b.1831 TN 222
Robert b.1838 SC 275
Robert r.1840 AL 31
Robert b.1841 ON 279
Robert b.1842 AL 156
Robert b.1843 AL 157
Robert b.1844 MS 274
Robert b.1846 MS 275
Robert b.1849 TN 221
Robert r.1850 CA 38
Robert b.1851 NS 248
Robert b.1851 SCO 28
Robert b.1860 IA 84
Robert r.1861 TN 305, 306
Robert b.1865 KY 117
Robert b.192– NC 229
Robert b.1964 OH 82
Robert b.19— KS/NE 229
Robert r.1983 KY 174
Robert r.NC 233
Robert r.NS 245
Robert r.NY 54
Robert A. r.1657 ENG 240
Robert Aaron b.1873 21
Robert Alan b.1949 OK 210, 214, 218
Robert Albert b.1841 ME 238
Robert B. r.1863 WI 201
Robert B. b.1884 IA 206
Robert Baldwin b.1962 NY 139
Robert Briggs b.1849 OH 276, 277
Robert Briggs II b.1886 IA 276, 277
Robert C. b.1815 TN 156
Robert Daniel b.1981 214, 218
Robert E. b.1894 PA 98
Robert E. r.1972 CA 214
Robert Edgar b.ND 220
Robert Edson b.1930 NY 137, 138, 139
Robert Emmett b.1884 KS 167, 172, 194
Robert Emmett Jr. b.1934 172
Robert Eugene b.1937 OH 208, 213
Robert Eugene r.1961 OH 213
Robert G. b.1796 VA 223
Robert G. m.1880 PA 108

Robert Glenn b.1941 OH 82
Robert H. b.1848 AL 156
Robert J. b.1814 KY 114, 117, 131
Robert J. b.1859 MO 133
Robert J. 118
Robert J. Jr. b.1859 MO 131
Robert J. L. r.1817 185
Robert Krause b.1922 PA 291
Robert L. b.1902 KY 170, 207, 214
Robert Lee b.1925 UT 283
Robert Lewis b.1851 AR 162
Robert Lewis b.1857 AR 160, 164
Robert Lewis b.1892 TN 200, 230
Robert Lynn b.1931 207
Robert Moffet 11
Robert Owen b.1943 IN 174, 211
Robert R. b.1833 NY 109
Robert Riley b.1833 106
Robert S. r.1814 VA 159
Robert Thomas b.1878 MO 133, 172
Robert W. b.1844 TN 222
Robert White b.1849 TN 241
Robert Wilson, b.191– OH 82
Roberta Catherine b.1892 22
Robeson b.1826 TN 226
Robin r.1861 TN 305, 306
Robin 177
Robin Lee b.1967 FL 101
Robin Rene b.1967 IN 211
Roderick R. b.1759 CT 276
Roderick Ransom b.1797 NY 36, 276, 277
Rodney b.1845 VT 145
Rodney N. b.1812 VT 145
Roe b.1877 TN? 61
Roger Lee b.1938 NY 101
Roger Lloyd b.1954 KY 212
Rolan b.1883 NH 30
Rolley b.1814 VA 225
Rolly r.1837 TN 284, 285
Ronald Jay b.1962 FL 101
Ronald L. b.1940 OH 82
Rosa (Hobbs) 124
Rosa (Leamed) 167, 194
Rosa (Smith) 134
Rosa Anna b.1884 NC 199
Rosalett b.1792 CAN 145
Rosalinda b.1843 VT 145
Rosaline b.1836 KY 126
Rosana ( ) b.1795 VA 127
Rosanah b.1838 NC 223
Rose b.1678 ME 240
Rose r.1915 IN 262
Rose r.1916 273
Rose (LaJenesse) 287
Rose Ann (Austin) 117
Rose Ann b.1807 11, 20
Rose Ann b.1839 KY 117, 126
Rose Ann b.1860 KY 133
Rose Anna b.1873 22
Rose Anna r.1873 NC 236
Rose Caroline b.1861 IL? 74, 75
Rose Mary b.19— TX 287
Rosea Ann b.1838 KY 127, 171
Rosella (Wilkinson) 105
Rosette b.1833 VT 147
Rosilena b.1832?? KY 42
Rosilla b.1892 106
Roswell r.1801 OH 19
Roswell b.190– ENG 283
Rosy Etta b.1875 TN? 60
Roxana b.1842 VT 143
Roxy (Norton) 203
Roy Arnold b.1946 KY 174
Roy Hobson b.1899 197
Roy J., b.1901 KS 277
Royal b.1831 VT 147
Royce b.KY 169
Rozetta b.1861 107
Ruanna ( ) b.1819 NY 308
Ruben b.1735 MA 15
Ruben b.1809 NY 309
Ruben b.1841 VT 144
Ruben b.1849 VT 145
Ruben r.1863 WI 201
Ruben m.1933 AR 124
Ruben Taylor b.1847 KY 117
Rubie E. b.1902 TN? 61
Rubin b.1848 KY 128
Ruby b.1876 OR 119
Ruby ( ) b.1807 VT 143

AUSTIN,

Ruby (Bruffee) 143
Ruby (Dauster) 82
Ruby E. b.1844 VT 143
Ruby Gene m.1944 AR 125
Ruby Nickerson (Jones) 287
Ruey (Meredith) 125
Rufus b.1792 VT 73
Rufus b.1848 TN 225
Rufus Lenoir b.1866 NC 181, 199, 227, 236
Russell b.1814 NY? 50
Russell r.1836 IL 185
Russell Briant b.d.1875 KY 287
Russell C. b.1931 OH 208, 212
Russell Downing b.1827 NY 119, 268
Russell Edward b.1955 MD 212
Russell M/H b.1897 NC 200
Russell Yetman b.1876 KY 288
Ruth b.1721 MA 14
Ruth b.1733 MA 14
Ruth r.1771 MA 24
Ruth b.1810 NY 309
Ruth b.1822 109
Ruth b.1822 PA 105, 106, 107
Ruth b.1830 VT 144
Ruth b.1839 VT 147
Ruth m.1851 OH 205
Ruth r.1916 273
Ruth ( ) b.1784 CT 2
Ruth ( ) b.1784 MA 145
Ruth ( ) b.1827 VT 144
Ruth ( ) b.1844 r.OH 12
Ruth ( ) b.1864 31
Ruth (Burleson) 110
Ruth (Hardesty) 25
Ruth (Stevens) 230
Ruth (VanWinkle) 287
Ruth A. b.1897 OR
Ruth A. d.1843 PA 106
Ruth Ann b.1831 VT 143
Ruth Arabelle, b.1847 16
Ruth Ellen (Carman) 167
Ruth I. m.1912 NY? 54
Ruth J. b.1843 TN 225
Ruth N. b.1844 TN 221
Rutha b.1841 NC 223

AUSTIN, S

S. b.1834 KY 126
S. b.1845 KY 126
S. r.1861 TN (male) 306
S. 106
S. Artemus b.1920 TN? 61
S. B. b.1819 VT 243
S. C. b.1852 106
S. C. 105
S. D. b.1791 NC 222
S. E. b.1839 KY 126
S. E. r.1895 NC 235, 236
S. E. 236
S. E. ( ) 31
S. F. b.1803 NC 225
S. F. b.1849 KY 126
S. H. r.1861 TN 306
S. M. ( ) b.1839 NY 308
S. P. b.1833 NC 126
S. S. r.1862 QU 299
S. Shelton b.1875 31
S. W. r.1861 TN 306
Sabin B. r.1910 IN 262
Sabrina (Miller) 283
Sadie 12
Sadie Ethel b.1897 197
Sal b.1885 NC 200
Saline T. b.1826 146
Sall (Ross) 203
Sallie (Bracken) b.1877 31
Sallie (Halbert) 182
Sallie (Porter) 42
Sallie C. b.1848 KY 85
Sallie C. (Bradshaw) 170, 171
Sally b.1767 NH 144
Sally b.1776 VT 143
Sally b.1786 VT 16
Sally m.1812 OH 205
Sally b.1813 TN 224
Sally m.1820 OH 206
Sally m.1828 OH 206
Sally b.1832 VT 283
Sally b.183– OH 40
Sally b.1835 KY 126

Sally b.1843 VT 144
Sally b.1847 KY 85
Sally b.1848 KY 128
Sally r.1989 MI 158, 182, 305, 307, 310
Sally ( ) b.1781 CT 146
Sally ( ) b.1800 VT 145
Sally ( ) b.1801 VT 107
Sally ( ) b.1807 NY 308
Sally ( ) b.1809 TN 127
Sally ( ) b.1814 KY 126
Sally ( ) b.1819 TN 223
Sally ( ) m.18— TN 288
Sally (Grant) 39
Sally (Hall) 182
Sally (Jopling) 178
Sally (Leftwich) 182
Sally (Page) 203
Sally A. b.1848 TN 225
Sally Ann b.18— MO 285
Sally B. (Cowles) 203
Sally D. (Rumsey) 105, 106
Sally Douglas b.1862 KY 133
Sally J. ( ) b.1820 NY 144
Sally L. b.1815 VT 283
Sally Maria (Whitford) 241
Sally Mary b.1843 KY 42, 128
Sally T. b.1844 KY 127
Saloma b.1847 VT 145
Sam V. r.1861 TN 306
Samantha b.1838 VT 144
Samantha (Clingensmith) 203
Sammie B. b.1901 251
Sammie B. b.1901 KY 169
Samuel b.1626 ENG 257
Samuel d.1627 ENG 257
Samuel b.164– r.MA 8, 14, 17, 29, 32, 33, 44, 49, 62, 63, 74, 91, 105, 135
Samuel b.1669 MA 8, 9, 32, 33, 91
Samuel b.17— 11, 242
Samuel b.1703 MA 129
Samuel r.1740 MD 175
Samuel r.1744 MD 148
Samuel b.1746 CT 57
Samuel r.1750 50
Samuel b.1765 MA 10
Samuel r.1771 MA 24
Samuel b.1773 CT 57
Samuel b.1773 VT 146
Samuel b.1774 ME 1, 4
Samuel b.1775 VA 282
Samuel r.1783 NB 282
Samuel b.1794 MA 308
Samuel b.18— 288
Samuel b.1800 KY 127
Samuel b.1800 VT 309
Samuel b.1801 MD 34, 40, 66
Samuel b.1802 MD 126
Samuel b.1806 VT 143
Samuel b.1809 TN 222
Samuel r.1812 MD 159
Samuel r.1812 TN 159
Samuel b.1818 TN 225
Samuel r.1820 NY 66
Samuel m.1824 OH 206
Samuel m.1825 OH 206
Samuel b.1825 TN 202
Samuel b.1826 ME 238
Samuel b.1826 ON 103, 278
Samuel b.1828 NC 223
Samuel b.1828 VT 147
Samuel b.1829 NH 308
Samuel b.1829 TN 274
Samuel b.1829 VT 143, 144
Samuel b.1830 KY 128
Samuel b.1831 OH 155
Samuel b.1831 ENG 12
Samuel b.1831 SCO 12
Samuel b.1833 KY 127
Samuel r.1837 IL 185
Samuel r.1838 NC 236
Samuel r.1839 IL 185
Samuel b.1839 VT 146
Samuel m.1842 OH 206
Samuel b.1842 NY 107
Samuel b.1844 26, 36
Samuel b.1844 TN 225
Samuel b.1846 KY 126, 128
Samuel b.1846 TN 221
Samuel b.1849 KY 127
Samuel r.1850 NC 235

Samuel b.1850 TN 222
Samuel b.1851 ENG 12
Samuel m.1855 OH 206
Samuel r.1861 TN 306
Samuel r.1883 NC 236
Samuel r.1888 IL 185
Samuel b.ENG 219
Samuel r.CT 186
Samuel A. b.1815 NC 222
Samuel A. b.1845 VT 145
Samuel A. d.1863 PA 106
Samuel B. b.1842 MO 177
Samuel D. b.1822 VT 143
Samuel D. r.1812 TN 182
Samuel Edward b.1869 ?? 228
Samuel Edward b.1869 NC 181
Samuel Elvis b.1869 KY? 41
Samuel G. b.1818 NC 221
Samuel G. r.1812 TN 159
Samuel Hamilton b.1845 KY 42
Samuel J. b.1835 TN 222
Samuel John b.1826 MA 7
Samuel McConnell b.1794 17
Samuel P. b.1864 MO 75
Samuel R. b.1825 IL 308
Samuel R. r.1863 WI 201
Samuel T. b.1849 TN 222
Samuel Taylor b.1852 QU 300
Samuel W. b.1824 NC 129
Samuel W. b.1828 ME 238
Samuel W. r.1835 VA/KY 175
Samuel W. b.1858 ME 238
Samuel Wilson b.1818 KY 115, 118
Sanders b.1782 VA 61
Sanders b.1784 VA 222
Sanders r.1861 TN 306
Sandra (Amon) (Ray) 211
Sandy b.1844 TN 222
Saphronia b.1840 VT 144
Saphronia b.1843 VT 145
Saphronia ( ) b.1801 NC 223
Sarah b.1692 MA 8, 9
Sarah b.17— MA 219
Sarah b.17— VA/NC 10
Sarah b.1717 MA 14
Sarah b.1731 MA 14
Sarah b.1735 MA 14
Sarah b.1737 MA 15
Sarah m.176– MA 219
Sarah b.1766 IRE 232
Sarah b.1767 MA 10, 109
Sarah b.1780 175
Sarah b.1781 NH 44
Sarah b.1782 NS 246
Sarah b.1783 NC 232
Sarah b.1784 NH 146
Sarah m.1786 PA 98
Sarah b.1787 NH 107
Sarah b.1788 NC 156
Sarah b.1793 CT/VT 55
Sarah b.1793 NY 96
Sarah b.1794 NH 206
Sarah b.1800 NH 157
Sarah b.18— ON 104
Sarah b.1801 VA 178
Sarah b.1806 NC 156
Sarah b.1806 KY 11, 20, 129
Sarah r.1822 NS 265
Sarah b.1822 ON 279
Sarah b.1825 KY 275
Sarah b.1827 TN 223
Sarah b.1828 SC 223
Sarah b.1828 KY 225
Sarah b.1828 VA 221
Sarah b.1828 VT 144
Sarah m.1830 OH 206
Sarah m.1832 OH 206
Sarah b.1832 KY 128
Sarah b.1832 NY 309
Sarah b.1832 SC 275
Sarah b.1832 TN 224
Sarah b.1833 KY 128
Sarah b.1833 TN 223
Sarah b.1834 AL 157
Sarah b.1834 TN 223
Sarah b.1835 KY 117, 132, 133, 170, 207
Sarah m.1836 OH 206
Sarah b.1836 NY 309
Sarah b.1836 VT 143
Sarah b.1837 KY 128
Sarah b.1837 VT 143

Sarah b.1838 OH 308
Sarah b.1839 TN 223
Sarah m.1840 OH 206
Sarah b.1840 MS 275
Sarah b.1840 TN 221
Sarah b.184– PA 99
Sarah b.1841 TN 224
Sarah b.1842 SC 222
Sarah b.1844 KY 128
Sarah b.1844 TN 224
Sarah b.1846 TN 222, 225
Sarah b.1848 KY 128
Sarah b.1848 TN 221
Sarah b.1848 VT 146
Sarah b.1850 MS 275
Sarah b.1850 OH 155
Sarah b.1850 TN 221
Sarah b.1851 KY 51
Sarah b.1854 IL 38, 55
Sarah b.1858 QU 153
Sarah b.1862 106
Sarah m.1867 IN 262
Sarah b.1869 r.OH 12
Sarah r.1878 NC 236
Sarah b.1885 NC 200
Sarah r.NC 234
Sarah r.OH 250
Sarah b.ON 279
Sarah ( ) b.1779 153
Sarah ( ) b.179– 44
Sarah ( ) b.1793 SC 223
Sarah ( ) b.1798 VT 148
Sarah ( ) b.1805 NC 225
Sarah ( ) r.1806 PA 43
Sarah ( ) b.1811 MA 144
Sarah ( ) b.1811 NC 224
Sarah ( ) b.1812 NH 309
Sarah ( ) b.1813 VT 145
Sarah ( ) b.1817 PA 107, 108
Sarah ( ) m.1819 TN 288
Sarah ( ) b.1820 KY 128
Sarah ( ) b.1822 TN 223, 224
Sarah ( ) b.1825 AL 223
Sarah ( ) b.1828 NY 309
Sarah ( ) b.1828 TN 222
Sarah ( ) b.1829 NY 309
Sarah ( ) b.1831 VT 145
Sarah ( ) b.1835 ENG 12
Sarah ( ) b.1836 r.OH 12
Sarah ( ) b.1837 MI 196
Sarah ( ) r.1850 NY 242
Sarah ( ) r.1852 QU 154
Sarah ( ) r.1887 NC 235
Sarah ( ) r.NY 206
Sarah ( ) r.NS 246
Sarah ( ) r.VA 219
Sarah ( ) (Dinninton) 153
Sarah (Bailey) 151-154
Sarah (Bradley) 66, 125, 140, 141
Sarah (Brooks) 234
Sarah (Eggleston) 11, 267
Sarah (Falling) 205
Sarah (Faucett) 182
Sarah (Fish) 36, 186
Sarah (Fletcher) 116, 117
Sarah (Fraley) 85
Sarah (Greenleaf) 106
Sarah (Gutterson) 14, 44
Sarah (Hardesty) 175
Sarah (Harrison) 175
Sarah (Jones) 175
Sarah (Losinger) 105
Sarah (Lovejoy) 14
Sarah (Morgan) 250
Sarah (Moulton) 15
Sarah (Nurse/Nourse) 155, 206
Sarah (Palmer) 175
Sarah (Powell) 16
Sarah (Purple) 155, 186
Sarah (Qualls) 61
Sarah (Sims) 278
Sarah (Slaght) 103, 278
Sarah (Starbuck) 219, 240
Sarah (Sutton) 84
Sarah (Taylor) 204
Sarah (Walker) 175
Sarah (Wetherby) 98
Sarah (Wood) 203
Sarah A. b.1818 106
Sarah A. b.1822 VT 144
Sarah A. b.1824 AL 157
Sarah A. b.18— MA 7

Sarah A. b.1838 MA 275
Sarah A. b.1842 MS 274
Sarah A. b.1842 TN 223
Sarah A. b.1845 TN 222
Sarah A. b.1847 PA 107
Sarah A. b.1848 TN 224
Sarah A. ( ) b.1800 TN 222
Sarah A. (Armstrong) 60
Sarah Angeline 105
Sarah Ann b.1834 TN 128
Sarah Ann b.1983 TX 273
Sarah Ann (Burroughs) 203
Sarah Ann (Green) 182
Sarah Ann (Lossinger) 107
Sarah Ann (Newman) 196
Sarah Ann (Sosinger) 109
Sarah Ann (Taylor) 51
Sarah Anne r.1834 NS 249
Sarah B. b.1841 100
Sarah C. b.1848 KY 85
Sarah C. (Rumsey) PA 108
Sarah Catherine b.1837 KY 117
Sarah Drinkwater (Rumsey) 267
Sarah E. b.1814 16
Sarah E. b.1840 GA 157
Sarah E. b.1843 KY 127
Sarah E. b.1848 TN 223
Sarah E. b.1849 TN 224
Sarah E. r.1901 NC 236
Sarah E. b.VT 147
Sarah E. ( ) m.1875 MO? 177
Sarah E. ( ) r.1885 NC 235
Sarah E. ( ) r.1901 NC 236
Sarah E. (Fullwood) 181, 197
Sarah Eliza b.1836 NC 180, 181, 197, 228
Sarah Elizabeth b.1845 OH 276
Sarah Elizabeth m.1866 OH 206
Sarah Elizabeth b.1887 TX 134
Sarah Elizabeth b.1985 212
Sarah Elizabeth (Carswell) 228
Sarah Elizabeth (Jones) 196
Sarah Ellen b.1839 20
Sarah Ellen b.1849 TN 223
Sarah Ellen b.1872 31
Sarah Ellen (Holt) 134
Sarah Emily b.1819?? OH? 40
Sarah Emma (Hartley) b.1863 228
Sarah Etta b.1869 NC 181
Sarah F. b.1834 AL 223
Sarah F. b.1837 MS 274
Sarah F. b.1842 KY 128
Sarah F. b.1846 KY 131
Sarah Frances b.1844 20
Sarah Frances b.1853 31
Sarah G. b.1795 NC 222
Sarah H. b.1787 VA 222
Sarah I. (Mostelle) 203
Sarah Isabell (Simmons) 199
Sarah J. b.1833 KY 126
Sarah J. m.1853 OH 206
Sarah J. b.187– r.PA 109
Sarah J. ( ) b.1852 ENG 12
Sarah J. (Phillips) 165
Sarah Jane b.1843 AR 160, 161, 162, 163
Sarah Jane m.OH 206
Sarah Jane d.WI 276
Sarah Jane (Cody) 250
Sarah Jane (Ryan) 167
Sarah Jane (Webb) 115
Sarah Jean (Washburn) 139
Sarah Jones m.1811 175
Sarah L. b.1815 NC 234
Sarah Lucretia m.1856 OH 206
Sarah Lucy b.1860 QU 154
Sarah M. b.1819 d.1899 PA 108
Sarah M. b.1842 VT 146
Sarah M. r.NC 234
Sarah M. ( ) b.1841 28
Sarah Margaret b.19— TX 287
Sarah Melinda 196
Sarah Naoma b.1889 31
Sarah Odle b.1802 MD 35
Sarah R. ( ) 203
Sasshia ( ) b.1775 VA 127
Saul C. b.1805 KY 129
Saunders r.1811 TN 284
Saunders b.1832 TN 222
Schyler b.1825 NY 309
Sciota b.1870 KY 132
Seaborne Hart b.1861 KY 287
Sean 110

Austins of America

INDEX TO PLACES

Census 1850

p 126 - Kentucky
156 - Alabama
221 - Tennessee
243 - California
274 - Mississippi
308 - Wisconsin